abnormal psychology
perspectives
fifth edition

david j.a. dozois
University of Western Ontario

PEARSON
Toronto

Vice-President, Editorial Director: Gary Bennett
Editor-in-Chief: Michelle Sartor
Acquisitions Editor: Matthew Christian
Marketing Manager: Lisa Gillis
Senior Developmental Editor: Patti Altridge
Project Manager: Ashley Patterson
Production Editor: Nidhi Chopra (Cenveo Publisher Services)
Copy Editor: Marcia Gallego
Proofreaders: Karen Alliston, Sharon Kirsch
Compositor: Cenveo Publisher Services
Photo and Permissions Researcher: Dominic Farrell
Manufacturing Specialist: Karen Bradley
Art Director: Julia Hall
Cover and Interior Designer: Miguel Angel Acevedo
Cover Image: Getty Images/Alfonse Pagano

Credits and acknowledgments for material borrowed from other sources and reproduced, with permission, in this textbook appear on the appropriate page within text, or on page 619.

10 9 8 7 6 5 4 3 2 [CKV]

Library and Archives Canada Cataloguing in Publication

Abnormal psychology : perspectives / edited by David J.A. Dozois. -- 5th ed.

Includes bibliographical references and index.
ISBN 978-0-13-281069-2

1. Psychology, Pathological--Textbooks.
I. Dozois, David J. A.

RC454.A26 2013 616.89 C2012-901630-6

PEARSON

ISBN 978-0-13-281069-2

Dedicated to my loving parents,
John and Judy Dozois

Brief Contents

Preface xv

Acknowledgments xxi

About the Editor xxiii

About the Contributors xxiv

CHAPTER 1

Concepts of Abnormality Throughout History 1

DAVID J. A. DOZOIS • FRANCOIS BOTHA

CHAPTER 2

Theoretical Perspectives on Abnormal Behaviour 23

DAVID J. A. DOZOIS • LYNDSAY E. EVRAIRE

CHAPTER 3

Classification and Diagnosis 48

UZMA S. REHMAN • DAVID J. A. DOZOIS

CHAPTER 4

Psychological Assessment and Research Methods 65

DAVID J. A. DOZOIS • PAMELA M. SEEDS

CHAPTER 5

Anxiety Disorders 96

DAVID J. A. DOZOIS • REBECCA MCDERMOTT • PAUL A. FREWEN

CHAPTER 6

Dissociative and Somatoform Disorders 128

ROD A. MARTIN 127

CHAPTER 7

Psychophysiological Disorders 146

KENNETH M. PRKACHIN • GLENDA C. PRKACHIN

CHAPTER 8

Mood Disorders and Suicide 173

KATE HARKNESS

CHAPTER 9

Schizophrenia 205

R. WALTER HEINRICHS • ASHLEY MILES • NARMEEN AMMARI • EVA MUHARIB

CHAPTER 10

Eating Disorders 233

JENNIFER COELHO • KATHRYN TROTTIER • JANET POLIVY

CHAPTER 11

Substance-Related Disorders 259

DAVID HODGINS • TERRI-LYNN MACKAY

CHAPTER 12

The Personality Disorders 293

STEPHEN PORTER • PAMELA BLACK • NATASHA KORVA

CHAPTER 13

Sexual and Gender Identity Disorders 324

CAROLINE F. PUKALL • PHILIP FIRESTONE

CHAPTER 14

Developmental Disorders 358

PATRICIA M. MINNES • MARJORY L. PHILLIPS

CHAPTER 15

Behaviour and Emotional Disorders of Childhood and Adolescence 391

TRACY VAILLANCOURT • KHRISTA BOYLAN

CHAPTER 16

Aging and Mental Health 416

COREY S. MACKENZIE • KRISTIN A. REYNOLDS

CHAPTER 17

Therapies 442

JOHN HUNSLEY • CATHERINE M. LEE

CHAPTER 18

Prevention and Mental Health Promotion in the Community 467

GEOFFREY NELSON • ISAAC PRILLELTENSKY • JULIAN HASFORD

CHAPTER 19

Mental Disorder and the Law 486

STEPHEN D. HART • RONALD ROESCH

Glossary 509

References 524

Name Index 585

Subject Index 600

Credits 619

Contents

Preface xv

Acknowledgments xxi

About the Editor xxiii

About the Contributors xxiv

CHAPTER 1

Concepts of Abnormality Throughout History 1

DAVID J. A. DOZOIS • FRANCOIS BOTHA

Attempts at Defining Abnormality **4**

Statistical Concept 4

Personal Distress 4

Personal Dysfunction 5

Violation of Norms 6

Diagnosis by an Expert 6

Summary of Definitions 7

Historical Concepts of Abnormality **7**

Evidence from Prehistory 8

Greek and Roman Thought 9

The Arab World 10

Europe in the Middle Ages 11

The Beginnings of a Scientific Approach 12

Development of Modern Views **15**

Biological Approaches 15

Psychological Approaches 18

The Growth of Mental Health Services in Canada **19**

Recent Developments 20

Summary 21

Key Terms 22

CHAPTER 2

Theoretical Perspectives on Abnormal Behaviour 23

DAVID J. A. DOZOIS • LYNDSAY E. EVRAIRE

The General Nature of Theories **24**

Levels of Theories 25

Testing Theories: The Null Hypothesis 25

The Search for Causes **26**

Biological Models **27**

The Role of the Central Nervous System 28

The Role of the Peripheral Nervous System 30

The Role of the Endocrine System 31

Genetics and Behaviour 32

Psychosocial Theories **33**

Psychodynamic Theories 34

Behavioural Theories 36

Cognitive Theories 39

Humanistic and Existential Theories 41

Socio-Cultural Influences 43

Integrative Theories **45**

Systems Theory 45

The Diathesis-Stress Perspective 45

The Biopsychosocial Model 46

Summary 46

Key Terms 47

CHAPTER 3

Classification and Diagnosis 48

UZMA S. REHMAN • DAVID J. A. DOZOIS

Why Do We Need a Classification System for Mental Disorders? **50**

The Perfect Diagnostic System **50**

Characteristics of Strong Diagnostic Systems **51**

The History of Classification of Mental Disorders **51**

DSM-IV-TR: A Multiaxial Approach **52**

Axis I Clinical Disorders 53

Axis II Personality Disorders 53

Axis III General Medical Conditions 53

Axis IV Psychosocial and Environmental Problems 53

Axis V Global Assessment of Functioning 53

Categories of Disorder in DSM-IV-TR **53**

Disorders Usually First Diagnosed in Infancy, Childhood, or Adolescence 54

Delirium, Dementia, Amnesia, and other Cognitive Disorders 55

Substance-Related Disorders 55

Schizophrenia and other Psychotic Disorders 55

Mood Disorders 55

Anxiety Disorders 56

Somatoform Disorders 56

Factitious Disorders 56

Dissociative Disorders 56

Sexual and Gender Identity Disorders 57

Eating Disorders 57

Sleep Disorders 57

Impulse Control Disorders 57

Adjustment Disorders 57

Personality Disorders 57

Other Conditions That May Be a Focus of Clinical Attention 57

Toward DSM-5 58

Issues in the Diagnosis and Classification of Abnormal Behaviour 59
Against Classification 59
Criticisms Specific to the DSM Diagnostic System 60
The Prevalence of Mental Disorders 62
Summary 63
Key Terms 64

CHAPTER 4

Psychological Assessment and Research Methods 65

DAVID J. A. DOZOIS • PAMELA M. SEEDS

Assessment 67
Assessment Tools: Striving for the Whole Picture 67
Reliability and Validity 67
Clinical Versus Actuarial Prediction 68
Biological Assessment 68
Brain Imaging Techniques 69
Neuropsychological Testing 71
Psychological Assessment 72
Clinical Interviews 72
Assessment of Intelligence 75
Personality Assessment 76
Behavioural and Cognitive Assessment 82
Research Methods 85
Experimental Methods 85
Controlled Experimental Research 85
Quasi-Experimental Methods 86
Non-experimental Methods 87
Correlational Research 87
The Case Study 88
Single-Subject Research 88
Epidemiological Research 89
Studies of Inheritance 90
Statistical Versus Clinical Significance 93
Summary 94
Key Terms 95

CHAPTER 5

Anxiety Disorders 96

DAVID J. A. DOZOIS • REBECCA MCDERMOTT • PAUL A. FREWEN

The Characteristics of Anxiety 97
Historical Perspective 97
Etiology 98
Biological Factors 98
Psychological Factors 99
Interpersonal Factors 99
Comment on Etiology 100
The Anxiety Disorders 100
Panic Disorder and Agoraphobia 100
Specific Phobia 103
Social Phobia/Social Anxiety Disorder 106
Obsessive-Compulsive Disorder 109
Post-traumatic Stress Disorder 113
Generalized Anxiety Disorder 117
Changes in DSM-5 119
Treatment of Anxiety Disorders 119
Pharmacotherapy 120
Cognitive Restructuring 120
Exposure Techniques 122
Problem Solving 123
Relaxation 123
Other Techniques 123
Treatment Efficacy 124
Treatment of Panic Disorder 124
Treatment of Specific Phobias 124
Treatment of Social Phobia 124
Treatment of Obsessive-Compulsive Disorder 124
Treatment of Post-traumatic Stress Disorder 125
Treatment of Generalized Anxiety Disorder 126
Comment on Treatments That Work 126
Summary 126
Key Terms 127

CHAPTER 6

Dissociative and Somatoform Disorders 128

ROD A. MARTIN

Historical Perspective 130
Dissociative Disorders 131
Prevalence 132
Dissociative Amnesia 133
Dissociative Fugue 133
Depersonalization Disorder 133
Dissociative Identity Disorder 134
Etiology 135
Treatment 136
Psychotherapy 136
Hypnosis 137
Medication 137
Somatoform Disorders 137
Prevalence 138
Conversion Disorder 138
Somatization Disorder 140
Pain Disorder 140
Hypochondriasis 141
Body Dysmorphic Disorder 141

Etiology 142
Treatment 143
Summary 144
Key Terms 145

CHAPTER 7
Psychophysiological Disorders 146
KENNETH M. PRKACHIN • GLENDA C. PRKACHIN
Historical Perspective 147
Diagnostic Issues 148
Psychosocial Mechanisms of Disease 149
The Endocrine System 150
The Autonomic Nervous System 151
The Immune System 152
The Psychology of Stress 153
Psychosocial Factors That Influence Disease 156
Social Status 156
Controllability 157
Social Support 158
Disease States and Psychosocial Factors 159
Infectious Disease 159
Ulcer 160
Cardiovascular Disease 164
Treatment 170
Summary 172
Key Terms 172

CHAPTER 8
Mood Disorders and Suicide 173
KATE HARKNESS
Historical Perspective 175
Diagnostic Issues 176
Unipolar Mood Disorders 176
Major Depressive Disorder 176
Prevalence and Course 177
Dysthymic Disorder 178
Bipolar Mood Disorders 178
Bipolar I and Bipolar II 180
Cyclothymia 181
Rapid Cycling Bipolar Disorder 181
Mood Disorder with Seasonal Pattern 182
Mood Disorder with Postpartum Onset 182
Etiology 183
Psychological and Environmental Causal Factors 183
Psychodynamic Theories 183
Cognitive Theories 183
Interpersonal Models 184
Life Stress Perspective 185
Biological Causal Factors 186
Genetics 186
Neurotransmitters 187
Stress and the Hypothalamic-Pituitary-Adrenal Axis 187
Sleep Neurophysiology 188
Neuroimaging 188
Treatment 189
Psychotherapy for Unipolar Depression 189
Pharmacotherapy 192
Medications to Treat Bipolar Disorder 193
Combinations of Psychological and Pharmacological Treatments 194
Phototherapy for Seasonal Affective Disorder 195
Neurostimulation and Neurosurgical Treatments 196
Suicide 197
Definition 198
Epidemiology and Risk Factors 198
What Causes Suicide? 199
Prevention 200
Treatment 200
Summary 202
Key Terms 204

CHAPTER 9
Schizophrenia 205
R. WALTER HEINRICHS • ASHLEY MILES • NARMEEN AMMARI • EVA MUHARIB
Introduction and Historical Perspective 207
Prevalence, and Demographic and Socio-Economic Features 208
Historical Perspective: The Missing Illness 208
Typical Characteristics 210
Positive (Psychotic) and Negative Symptoms 210
Diagnosis and Assessment 212
DSM-IV-TR Diagnostic Criteria 212
Symptom-Based Subtypes 213
Critique of DSM-IV-TR and Symptom-Based Diagnosis 214
proposed changes in DSM-5 214
Markers and Endophenotypes for Schizophrenia 214
Cognitive Subtypes of Schizophrenia 215
Etiology 216
Theories of Schizophrenia 217
Biological Factors 219
Treatment 227
Antipsychotic Medication 227
Psychotherapy and Skills Training 228
Summary 230
Key Terms 231

CHAPTER 10

Eating Disorders 233

JENNIFER COELHO • KATHRYN TROTTIER • JANET POLIVY

Introduction and Historical Perspective 234

Typical Characteristics 234
Anorexia Nervosa 234
Bulimia Nervosa 236

Incidence and Prevalence 237
Prognosis 237

Diagnosis and Assessment 238
Diagnostic Criteria 238
Diagnostic Issues 242
Assessment 243

Physical and Psychological Complications 243

Etiology 244
Genetic and Biological Theories 244
Psychological Theories 245
Integrative Models 250

Eating Disorders in Males 250

Treatment 251
Biological Treatments 251
Psychological Treatments 252
Prevention 255

Summary 257
Key Terms 258

CHAPTER 11

Substance-Related Disorders 259

DAVID HODGINS • TERRI-LYNN MACKAY

Historical Perspective 260

Diagnosis and Assessment 261
Defining Substance-Related Concepts 261
Polysubstance Abuse 263

Alcohol 265
History of Use 265
Canadian Consumption Patterns 265
Effects 268
Etiology 270
Treatment 275

Barbiturates and Benzodiazepines 278
Prevalence 278
Effects 278
Dependency 278
Treatment 278

Stimulants 279
Tobacco 279
Amphetamines and Designer Drugs 281
Cocaine 282
Caffeine 283

Opioids 284
Prevalence 284
Effects 285
Dependency 286
Treatment 286

Cannabis 286
Prevalence 287
Effects 287
Dependency 288

Hallucinogens 288
Prevalence 288
Effects 288
Dependency 290

Summary 291
Key Terms 292

CHAPTER 12

The Personality Disorders 293

STEPHEN PORTER • PAMELA BLACK • NATASHA KORVA

The Concept of Personality Disorder 294

Diagnostic Issues 299
Gender and Cultural Issues 300
Reliability of Diagnosis 301
Comorbidity and Diagnostic Overlap 301

Historical Perspective 302

Etiology 303
Psychodynamic Views 303
Attachment Theory 303
Cognitive-Behavioural Perspectives 304
Biological Factors 304
Summary of Etiology 305

The Specific Disorders 305

Cluster A: Odd and Eccentric Disorders 305
Paranoid Personality Disorder 305
Schizoid Personality Disorder 306
Schizotypal Personality Disorder 306

Cluster B: Dramatic, Emotional, or Erratic Disorders 307
Antisocial Personality Disorder and Psychopathy: A Confusion of Diagnoses 307
Borderline Personality Disorder 315
Histrionic Personality Disorder 317
Narcissistic Personality Disorder 317

Cluster C: Anxious and Fearful Disorders 318
Avoidant Personality Disorder 318
Dependent Personality Disorder 319
Obsessive-Compulsive Personality Disorder 319

Treatment 320
Object-Relations Therapy 320
Cognitive-Behavioural Approaches 320
Pharmacological Interventions 322

Summary 322
Key Terms 323

CHAPTER 13

Sexual and Gender Identity Disorders 324

CAROLINE F. PUKALL • PHILIP FIRESTONE

Historical Perspective 325

Diagnostic Issues 326

Sexual Response 327

Sexual Dysfunctions 331
Sexual Desire Disorders 332
Sexual Arousal Disorders 333
Orgasmic Disorders 334
Sexual Pain Disorders 334
Hypersexual disorder 335
Etiology of Sexual Dysfunctions 336
Treatment of Sexual Dysfunctions 338

Gender Identity 340
Gender Identity Disorders 341
Etiology of Gender Identity Disorders 342
Treatment of Gender Identity Disorders 343

The Paraphilias 344
Paraphilic Disorders That Involve Consenting Adults 345
Paraphilic Disorders That Involve Nonconsenting Persons 347

Summary 356
Key Terms 356

CHAPTER 14

Developmental Disorders 358

PATRICIA M. MINNES • MARJORY L. PHILLIPS

Historical Perspective 359

A Note About Terminology 360

Intellectual Disability 361
Prevalence 361

Diagnostic Issues 361
The Challenges of Assessing Intelligence 362
Measuring Adaptive Behaviour 362
Proposed Changes to Diagnostic Criteria in the DSM-5 363
Interviewing Strategies 363

Etiology 363
Genetic Causes 363
Environmental Causes 367
Postnatal Environmental Factors: Psychosocial Disadvantage 368

Two Specific Disorders 369
Down Syndrome 369
Fragile X Syndrome 370

The Effect of Developmental Disorders on the Family 372

Deinstitutionalization and Community Integration or Inclusion 373
Mainstreaming and Inclusion of Students with Disabilities in Educational Settings 374
Preparation for Community Living 374
Evaluating Quality of Life 374
The Issue of Sex Education 375

Challenging Behaviours and Dual Diagnosis 375

Pervasive Developmental Disorders: Autism 377
Prevalence 377

Description 378
Social Interaction 378
Verbal and Nonverbal Communication 379
Behaviour and Interests 379

Diagnostic Issues 379
Asperger Disorder 379
Child Disintegrative Disorder 380
Rett Syndrome 380
Assessment 380

Etiology 381

Treatment and Intervention 382
Medications and Nutritional Supplements 382
Behavioural Interventions 382

Learning Disorders 384
Historical Perspective 385
Diagnostic Criteria 385
Controversy in Diagnosis 386
Proposed Changes for the DSM-5 386
Reading Disorder 386
Mathematics Disorder 386
Disorder of Written Expression 386
Nonverbal Learning Disabilities 387
Prevalence 387
Etiology 387
Social and Emotional Well-Being of Children with Learning Disorders 387
Intervention 388

Summary 389
Key Terms 390

CHAPTER 15

Behaviour and Emotional Disorders of Childhood and Adolescence 391

TRACY VAILLANCOURT • KHRISTA BOYLAN

Historical Perspective of Child and Adolescent Mental Health 392
Current Issues in Assessing and Treating Children and Adolescents 393

Prevalence of Childhood Disorders 394

Attention Deficit/Hyperactivity Disorder 396
Clinical Description 396
Etiology 398
Assessment and Treatment 399

Oppositional Defiant Disorder and Conduct Disorder 401
Clinical Description 401
Etiology 405
Treatment 406

Anxiety Disorders 407
Clinical Description 408
Etiology 411
Treatment 412
Summary 413
Key Terms 415

CHAPTER 16
Aging and Mental Health 416
COREY S. MACKENZIE • KRISTIN A. REYNOLDS
Changing Demography 417
Vulnerability Versus Resilience in Old Age 418
Prevalence of Mental Disorders in Older Adults 419
Historical Perspective 420
Misconceptions About Treating Older Adults 420
Age-Specific Issues of Diagnosis and Treatment 422
Theoretical Frameworks of Aging 422
Selective Optimization with Compensation 423
Socio-Emotional Selectivity Theory 423
Strength and Vulnerability Integration Theory 423
Mood Disorders 424
Suicide 425
Etiology 425
Depressive Disorders 426
Sleep Disorders 427
Diagnostic Issues 427
Normal Changes in Sleeping Patterns 428
Primary Insomnia 429
Restless Legs Syndrome 430
Sleep Apnea 430
Anxiety Disorders 431
Diagnostic Issues 431
Treatment 431
Schizophrenia 432
Diagnostic Issues 432
Treatment 432
Delirium 433
Etiology 433
Diagnostic Issues 433
Treatment 434
Dementia 434
Mild Cognitive Impairment (MCI) 435
Alzheimer's Disease 436
Vascular Dementia 438
Other Forms of Dementia 439
Caregiver Stress 440
Summary 441
Key Terms 441

CHAPTER 17
Therapies 442
JOHN HUNSLEY • CATHERINE M. LEE
Biological Treatments 444
Electroconvulsive Therapy 444
Psychopharmacology 444
Psychotherapy: A Definition 448
Theoretical Orientations 448
Psychodynamic Approaches 448
Humanistic-Experiential Approaches 450
Cognitive-Behavioural Approaches 451
Eclectic and Integrative Approaches 453
Psychotherapy: Treatment Modalities 454
Individual Therapy 454
Couples Therapy 454
Family Therapy 454
Group Therapy 454
The Context of Psychotherapy 455
Who Provides Psychotherapy? 455
Who Seeks Psychotherapy? 455
The Duration of Treatment 456
Evaluating the Effects of Psychotherapy 456
Historical Context 456
Meta-Analysis 457
A Brief Review of Meta-Analytic Evidence 457
Effects of Psychotherapy for Specific Disorders 458
Couple Distress 460
Generalizing to Clinical Settings 461
EVIDENCE-BASED PRACTICE 462
Summary 465
Key Terms 466

CHAPTER 18
Prevention and Mental Health Promotion in the Community 467
GEOFFREY NELSON • ISAAC PRILLELTENSKY • JULIAN HASFORD
Community Psychology 468
Prevention and Mental Health Promotion: Some Definitions 469
Primary, Secondary, and Tertiary Prevention 469
Universal, Selective, and Indicated Prevention 469
Mental Health Promotion 469
Historical Perspective 471
Pre–germ Theory Era 471
Public Health Approach 471
Educational Approach 471
Resilience, Risk, and Protection 472
Resilience, Risk, and Protective Factors 472

Cumulative Risk 472
Mechanisms of Risk and Protection 473
Implications of Resilience, Risk, and Protection for Prevention 473

A Conceptual Framework for Prevention and Promotion **474**
The Contextual Field 474
The Affirmation Field 475

Research and Practice in Prevention and Promotion **475**
High-Risk (Selective) Prevention Programs 477
Universal Prevention and Promotion Programs 478

Prevention and Promotion Policy in Canada **481**
The Federal Role 481
The Provincial Role 482
Return on Investment 482

Implementation, Dissemination, and Social Justice **483**
Implementation 483
Dissemination 483
Social Justice 484

Summary 484
Key Terms 485

CHAPTER 19

Mental Disorder and the Law 486

STEPHEN D. HART • RONALD ROESCH

Mental Disorder in Canadian Law **489**

The Canadian Legal System **490**
Constitutional Law 490
Statutory Law 491
Common Law 491

A Closer Look at Civil Mental Health Law **492**
Involuntary Hospitalization 492
Involuntary Treatment 494
Reviews and Appeals 495
Some Examples of Research on Mental Health Law in Canada 495

A Closer Look at Mentally Disordered Offenders **498**
Criminal Responsibility: Mental State at the Time of the Offence 499
Competency to Make Legal Decisions: Mental State at the Time of Trial 500
Some Examples of Research on Mentally Disordered Offenders in Canada **501**

Psychology in the Legal System **503**

Psychological Ethics **503**
General Ethical Principles of Psychology 503
Specialized Ethical Guidelines 504

The Status of Psychology in the Legal System **505**
Summary 507
Key Terms 508

Glossary 509
References 524
Name Index 585
Subject Index 600
Credits 619

Focus and Clinical Research

Focus Boxes

Defining Mental Disorders: The Case of Pedophilia 5
Treatment and Mistreatment: The Depiction of Mental Asylums in the Movies 14
Neurotransmission 29
Comorbidity 56
Test Security: Posting of the Rorschach Inkblot Test 77
The MMPI–2: A Sample Profile 81
Cultural Differences in Anxiety 106
Repressed Memory or False Memory? 132
Putting It All Together: Stress, Marriage, Physiological Changes, and Health 154
Inferring Causality in Health Psychology 162
Sex Differences in Depression 189
An Eighteenth-Century Sculptor with Schizophrenia 209
How Different Are Patients with Schizophrenia from Healthy People? 222
Thin Ideal Media Images Make Women Feel Bad, Right? 246
Back to the Future: Addiction in the DSM-5 262
Aboriginal Canadians 264
Non-abstinence Drinking Goals in Treatment 274
Needle Exchange Programs: An Effective Harm Reduction Strategy 285
Gambling: An Addiction? 289
Paul Bernardo and Karla Homolka 308
A Hot Topic: Measuring Sexual Arousal in Men and Women 329
Nonspecificity of Sexual Response in Women 330
The Dangers of Hope: Lessons from Facilitated Communication and Other Miracle Cures 384
Youth at Risk 388
Famous People with Learning Disabilities 388
A New Childhood Disorder in DSM-5? Disruptive Mood Dysregulation Disorder 404
Suicidal Thoughts and Self-Harm in Youth 410
Older Adults: The Missing Clients 421
Should Psychologists Prescribe Medication? 449
Technological Advances in the Provision of Psychological Treatments 461
Preventing Substance Abuse and Dependence Among Canadian Children and Youth: Policy and Programs 480
Reports Documenting Return on Investment in Prevention 482
A Sample Item from the FIT-R Manual 502

Canadian Research Centre Boxes

Dr. Adam Radomsky 125
Dr. Laurence J. Kirmayer 144
Dr. Jane Irvine 171
Dr. Zindel Segal 202
Dr. Christopher Bowie 230
Eating Disorders Program, Douglas Mental Health University Institute (Montreal, Quebec) 256
Promoting Self-Recovery from Gambling Problems 290
Dr. Robert Hare 321
Dr. Elke Reissing, Human Sexuality Research Laboratory 355
Jean Vanier, Founder of L'Arche 389
Selective Mutism Service, McMaster Children's Hospital 413
Baycrest Centre for Geriatric Care 440
Dr. Keith S. Dobson 465
Better Beginnings, Better Futures 479
Dr.Christopher Webster 506

Applied Clinical Cases

An Olympian Speaks Out About Mental Health 44
David Helfgott 59
Hoarders 109
Dissociative Fugue 137
John Candy 164
Charlie Sheen 181
John Nash's Beautiful Mind: When Schizophrenia and Genius Coexist 218
Sheena Carpenter 251
Robert Downey Jr. 273
Diane 314
Dr. Richard Raskin 343
Actors with Disabilities 360
Bullying and Children's Mental Health 395
Ronald Reagan 439

Preface

The subtitle *Perspectives* was chosen for this text because it expresses the essence of its approach. First, since it is a contributed volume, a number of individual perspectives are discussed. Second, we have taken care to present a balance of the psychological perspectives by discussing various relevant paradigms. Although different perspectives are highlighted, we place greater emphasis on the conceptual approaches and therapeutic interventions that have garnered the most empirical support in the research literature. Finally, this text is written by Canadian experts. While it does pay tribute to the best of international research, it does not ignore the world-class scholarship happening in our own country, and this gives the book its uniquely Canadian perspective.

Why publish another introductory abnormal psychology text when there are many fine ones out there already? We feel that *Abnormal Psychology: Perspectives* offers a different approach:

1. *Canadian content, from the ground up.* Not just an adaptation of an American text, *Abnormal Psychology: Perspectives* was written entirely by Canadian authors with Canadian students in mind. Our universal health care system and relatively high level of secondary education in Canada have resulted in mental health issues that are unique in North America, and they are reflected in this text. As well, a large number of important issues—legal cases, laws governing therapists, ethical issues, prevention programs, ground-breaking research, even the history of abnormal psychology in this country—are considered from the perspective of people who will be studying, living, and working in Canada. Chapter 19 (Mental Disorder and the Law), for example, covers the topic most requested by Canadian instructors tired of having to supplement texts that discuss only the American situation. Each chapter also highlights many of the important contributions that Canadian researchers have made to the understanding and treatment of psychopathology.
2. *Expert contributors.* One of the advantages of a contributed abnormal psychology text is that each disorder chapter can be written by experts in that field, ensuring that the research discussed and the approach taken in each chapter are as accurate and up to date as possible. The panoply of well-known and highly respected contributors to this volume speaks for itself.
3. *A different approach.* The organization of the text has been fine-tuned to reflect the emerging importance of several areas of abnormal psychology. For example, an entire chapter is devoted to prevention and mental health promotion in the community because no matter how adept we become at diagnosing and treating mental disorders, their *incidence* will never decrease without programs designed to prevent them from occurring in the first place. As the familiar adage states, "An ounce of prevention is worth a pound of cure."
4. *Chapter organization.* The chapters in this text provide an excellent flow that we believe progresses well, from general historical and conceptual issues, to an overview of issues related to diagnosis and assessment, to a detailed review of specific disorders, to important issues in the field—such as mental disorders and aging, the efficacy of psychological interventions, prevention of disorders and promotion of mental health, and legal and ethical issues in mental health.

Although the book is multi-authored, we have striven at all times for consistency of level, depth, and format across the chapters. Where applicable, each chapter follows this pattern:

- ***NEW*** Learning objectives
- Opening case
- Overview/introduction of the disorder
- Discussion of diagnostic issues (with DSM-IV-TR criteria and proposed DSM-5 changes)
- Historical perspective
- Full description of the disorder
- Etiology (from various theoretical perspectives)
- Treatment (from various theoretical perspectives)
- ***NEW*** Within-chapter critical thinking questions ("Before Moving On")
- Within-chapter Applied Clinical Case
- Within-chapter Canadian Research Centre
- Summary
- Key words

We hope that students and instructors alike will benefit from this collaboration of many individuals who, no doubt like them, will always find the study of abnormal psychology endlessly challenging and utterly absorbing.

Changes to the Fifth Edition

Our new edition has been heavily revised with updated references and statistics, more Canadian research and studies, proposed changes to DSM-5, and three new senior authors (Chapters 3, 10, and 13). To provide you with a brief overview of these changes, we offer some chapter-by-chapter highlights:

CHAPTER 1

- Provides an overview of the strategies used to define abnormality over the course of history, with updated Canadian content
- Covers the developments of the Mental Health Commission of Canada
- Highlights the Canadian Psychological Association's recent task force on evidence-based practice of psychological treatments
- Uses the proposed changes to the definition of pedophilia in DSM-5 to illustrate in a new Focus box how views of abnormality change over time
- Features new Focus box on Treatment and Mistreatment and how Hollywood films depict mental asylums

CHAPTER 2

- Provides an updated overview of the different theoretical perspectives on abnormal behaviour
- Illustrates how theorists from biological, psychodynamic, behavioural, cognitive, humanistic/existential, and socio-cultural perspectives would view a particular case of abnormal behaviour
- Discusses new research on gene–environment interactions
- Highlights research on self-schemas
- Discusses new "third wave" approaches, including Mindfulness-Based Cognitive Therapy and Acceptance and Commitment Therapy
- Addresses the impact of public stigma and self-stigma and recent anti-stigma campaigns

CHAPTER 3—NEW

- New senior author describes why we need a classification system, outlines the criteria used to define abnormal behaviour, and provides a history of the classification of mental disorders
- Describes the main proposed changes with DSM-5
- Includes an updated Focus box on comorbidity
- Discusses the prevalence of mental disorders in Canada

CHAPTER 4

- Examines the issue of test security in a Focus box on the posting of the Rorschach Inkblot Test on Wikipedia
- Updates information on psychological assessment and testing
- Discusses new self-monitoring applications for smart phones and tablets
- Highlights new Canadian epidemiological research

CHAPTER 5

- Updates findings on etiology and describes proposed changes to DSM-5
- New Applied Clinical Case describes the reality TV show *Hoarders* and discusses the consequences of this debilitating problem, including recent fires in Vancouver and Toronto
- New Canadian Research Centre features the work of Dr. Adam Radomsky, Concordia University professor and OCD expert
- Discusses the latest treatment and epidemiological research on anxiety disorders

CHAPTER 6

- Highlights proposed changes to dissociative and somatoform disorders in DSM-5
- Covers updated research on the etiology and treatment of dissociative fugue, depersonalization disorder, and dissociative identity disorder
- Discusses new treatment research for somatization disorders

CHAPTER 7

- Provides an updated historical review of psychological factors involved in physical illness
- Highlights possible changes to the classification of psychophysiological disorders in DSM-5
- Describes research on the link between stress, abdominal obesity, and risk for cardiovascular disease

CHAPTER 8

- Provides additional information on historical views of depression
- Highlights proposed changes to the mood disorder diagnoses in DSM-5
- Features work by Dr. Daniel Klein on chronic depression
- New Applied Clinical Case focuses on the difficulties experienced by actor Charlie Sheen
- Provides additional information on the role of personality in depression and stress
- Examines Mindfulness-Based Cognitive Therapy, developed by Canadian psychologist Dr. Zindel Segal and his colleagues
- Reviews recent data on neurostimulation and neuro surgical treatments
- Highlights the National Suicide Prevention Strategy recently approved by the federal government

CHAPTER 9

- Showcases common delusions experienced by individuals with schizophrenia
- Highlights changes to the diagnostic criteria for schizophrenia proposed in DSM-5
- Provides updated information on cognitive subtypes and genetic markers of schizophrenia
- Reviews findings from functional imaging studies
- Clinical Research Centre focuses on the work of Queen's University researcher Dr. Christopher Bowie
- Provides new information on CBT, social skills training, and cognitive remediation programs for schizophrenia
- Features new section on early intervention

CHAPTER 10—NEW

- New senior author provides updated statistics on the prognosis of eating disorders
- New clinical case illustrates the phenomenological experience of anorexia nervosa
- Highlights proposed changes in DSM-5, including the merging of feeding disorders with the eating disorders section
- Provides additional information on socio-cultural factors influencing the development of eating disorders and Health Canada data on body size changes over the years
- Features updated information on "enhanced CBT" and on nutritional therapy and meal support
- Contains new information on preventative approaches
- New Canadian Research Centre focuses on the Eating Disorders Program at Douglas Mental Health University Institute in Montreal

CHAPTER 11

- Contains updates on a number of significant changes proposed for DSM-5 in how we conceptualize substance use disorders
- Provides updated information on Canadian alcohol consumption patterns and Canada's low-risk drinking guidelines
- Supplies new prevalence data on marijuana use

CHAPTER 12

- Contains information on the fundamentally different diagnostic model being proposed for personality disorders in DSM-5
- Discusses "The Dark Triad"—a constellation of personality traits deemed to be socially aversive
- Highlights new research on psychopathy, including the "selective impulsivity theory"
- Discusses social media and narcissism

CHAPTER 13—NEW

- New senior author discusses the history, classification, epidemiology, etiology, and treatment of sexual and gender identity disorders
- New Focus box features a hot topic—measuring sexual arousal
- Highlights the proposed changes in DSM-5
- New Focus box reviews the research of Dr. Meredith Chivers on nonspecificity of sexual response in women
- Discusses hypersexuality
- Describes new work on gender identity
- New Canadian Research Centre features the work of University of Ottawa professor Dr. Elke Reissing

CHAPTER 14

- Discusses the new terminology proposed for intellectual difficulties
- Highlights changes proposed in DSM-5
- Examines maternal serum screening and issues related to genetic testing
- Highlights a recent national survey on the impact of Fragile X syndrome for individuals and their families
- Discusses issues related to community integration or inclusion
- Provides new information on dual diagnoses
- Discusses famous people believed to have had Asperger syndrome
- Discusses controversies in the diagnosis of intellectual disability
- Provides new data on behavioural interventions and other treatment approaches

CHAPTER 15

- Provides new information on the prevalence of childhood mental disorders
- Discusses the impact of bullying on the brain and on children's mental health
- Details proposed changes for DSM-5
- Provides new discussion of the developmental trajectories of various childhood problems
- Discusses a new childhood disorder in DSM-5—disruptive mood dysregulation disorder

CHAPTER 16

- Focuses on the impact of Canada's aging population
- Presents new data on the prevalence of mental disorders in older adults
- Reviews commonly held myths about mental disorders in older adults
- Highlights proposed changes in DSM-5

CHAPTER 17

- Reviews evidence-based guidelines for the pharmacological treatment of schizophrenia and depression
- Identifies key issues in the development of evidence-based psychological practice
- Highlights the recommendations of the Canadian Psychological Association's Task Force on Prescriptive Authority for Psychologists in Canada
- Discusses recent trends in cognitive-behavioural therapy
- New Focus box features technological advances in the provision of psychological treatments
- Provides new information on clinical practice guidelines

CHAPTER 18

- Discusses new data and strategies from the Canadian Population Health Initiative
- Describes an educational approach to public health, prevention, and mental health
- Provides new Focus box on preventing substance abuse and dependence among Canadian children and youth
- Highlights issues related to the implementation and dissemination of prevention programs
- Describes the problems associated with social injustice

CHAPTER 19

- Opens with a new, more vivid and dramatic vignette
- Updates information regarding provincial civil mental health laws
- Discusses specialty guidelines for forensic psychology

Features

NEW Learning Objectives. New to this edition, each chapter opens with a set of learning objectives. These learning objectives focus on student performance. Each chapter begins with a statement about what the student should be able to learn. Critical thinking questions (titled "Before Moving On") that correspond to the learning objectives are positioned at appropriate locations within the chapter to allow the student to pause and reflect on the material. We believe that this new feature will better allow students to absorb, reflect on, and integrate the course material.

NEW "Before Moving On" Critical Thinking Questions. Throughout each chapter are a series of critical thinking questions positioned within the text so that students can stop and think about the content of the chapter before moving on. Each of these critical thinking questions links to one of the learning objectives identified at the beginning of the chapter, providing students with an excellent way to absorb, integrate, and apply the material. Answers to critical thinking questions are provided on MySearchLab for students to refer to. The questions and answers help promote in-class discussions and small group work.

Cases. Cases are, without a doubt, what students find most fascinating about abnormal psychology. Each chapter of this text opens with a case or cases designed to engage student interest. Subsequent cases or clinical examples appear throughout the remainder of the chapter, highlighted in the design by a box, to illustrate nuances between related disorders. Clinical examples are used to illustrate the discussion wherever possible.

Applied Clinical Cases. In addition to the cases that open each chapter, Applied Clinical Cases focus on celebrities or other well-known people. These interesting case examples serve to bring to life some of the concepts outlined in the text. Examples of Applied Clinical Cases are

- Chapter 2: Olympian Clara Hughes, who speaks out about mental health
- Chapter 5: The popular reality TV show *Hoarders* and the reality of this condition
- Chapter 8: Charlie Sheen's battle with bipolar disorder
- Chapter 9: John Nash's "beautiful mind"
- Chapter 11: Robert Downey, Jr.'s problems with substance abuse
- Chapter 14: Chris Burke, who was one of the first people with Down syndrome to work as a professional actor

Focus boxes. These feature boxes present interesting topical subjects, such as:

- Chapter 1: Treatment and Mistreatment: The Depiction of Mental Asylums in the Movies
- Chapter 6: Repressed Memory or False Memory?
- Chapter 8: Sex Differences in Depression
- Chapter 12: Paul Bernardo and Karla Homolka

- Chapter 13: A Hot Topic: Measuring Sexual Arousal in Men and Women
- Chapter 17: Should Psychologists Prescribe Medication?
- Chapter 19: A Sample Item from the FIT-R Manual

Canadian Research Centre. These insightful boxes highlight Canadian facilities and Canadian psychologists who have made major contributions in their fields as related to each chapter. Examples of people and programs featured in the Canadian Research Centre boxes in the text are:

- Chapter 5: Dr. Adam Radomsky, founding president of the Canadian Association of Cognitive and Behavioural Therapies and associate professor of psychology at Concordia University
- Chapter 8: Dr. Zindel Segal, professor in the Departments of Psychology and Psychiatry at the University of Toronto, and the director of the Cognitive Behaviour Therapy Unit at the Centre for Addiction and Mental Health in Toronto
- Chapter 12: Dr. Robert Hare, emeritus professor of psychology, University of British Columbia
- Chapter 13: Dr. Elke Reissing, Human Sexuality Research Laboratory, University of Ottawa
- Chapter 14: Jean Vanier, Founder of L'Arche
- Chapter 15: Selective Mutism Service, McMaster Children's Hospital, Hamilton, Ontario
- Chapter 17: Dr. Keith S. Dobson, professor of clinical psychology and head of psychology at the University of Calgary

Coverage of DSM-IV-TR and DSM-5. A discussion of the DSM-IV-TR, its strengths and its limitations, first appears in Chapter 3, Classification and Diagnosis. Thereafter, explanations of the various disorders are always accompanied by tables listing DSM-IV-TR criteria for the disorder. For this edition, the authors have addressed the upcoming DSM-5 by discussing small proposed changes in a summary statement or two. In other instances, a paragraph outlining the overarching changes proposed for DSM-5 is included.

Key Terms. These are bolded and clearly defined where they are first discussed in the chapter. These definitions also appear in the Glossary at the end of the book.

Summary and Key Terms lists. Each chapter ends with a concise bulleted summary of the important points of the chapter. A list of the key terms for that chapter, with page references, follows.

Weblinks. We recognize the growing presence of the Internet in almost every aspect of our lives and welcome the chance to use it as an additional learning and research resource. Relevant sites are listed on MySearchLab.

Student Supplements

MYSEARCHLAB WITH ETEXT

MySearchLab with eText provides access to an online interactive version of the text and contains writing, grammar, and research tools; access to a variety of academic journals; census data; Associated Press news feeds; and discipline-specific readings to help you hone your writing and research skills. It also features the *Speaking Out: The DSM in Context* video series and interactive chapter quizzes that students can take for practice. For more information and to redeem or purchase an access code, please visit **www.mysearchlab.com**.

PEARSON eTEXT

Pearson eText gives students access to the text whenever and wherever they have access to the Internet. eText pages look exactly like the printed text, offering powerful new functionality for students and instructors. Users can create notes, highlight text in different colours, create bookmarks, zoom, click hyperlinked words and phrases to view definitions, and view in single-page or two-page view.

COURSESMART FOR STUDENTS

CourseSmart goes beyond traditional expectations—providing instant, online access to the textbooks and course materials you need at an average savings of 60 percent. With instant access from any computer and the ability to search your text, you'll find the content you need quickly, no matter where you are. And with online tools like highlighting and note-taking, you can save time and study efficiently. See all the benefits at **www.coursesmart.com/students**.

Instructor Supplements

MyTest from Pearson Canada is a powerful assessment generation program that helps instructors easily create and print quizzes, tests, and exams, as well as homework or practice handouts. Questions and tests can all be authored online, allowing instructors ultimate flexibility and the ability to efficiently manage assessments at any time, from anywhere. MyTest for *Abnormal Psychology: Perspectives*, Fifth Edition, includes over 1900 fully referenced multiple-choice, true/false, and essay questions. Each question is accompanied by a difficulty level, type designation, topic, and answer justification. You may access MyTest at **www.pearsonmytest.com**.

Test Item File. The MyTest questions in multiple-choice, true/false, and essay formats are also provided in a Word document.

Instructor's Manual. The Instructor's Manual contains chapter summaries, key points, key terms, important names, supplementary lecture material, and questions to provoke class discussion.

The above instructor supplements are available for download from a password-protected section of Pearson Canada's online catalogue (vig.pearsoned.ca). Navigate to your book's catalogue page to view a list of those supplements that are available. See your local sales representative for details and access.

PEERSCHOLAR

Firmly grounded in published research, **peerScholar** is a powerful online pedagogical tool that helps develop students' critical and creative thinking skills through creation, evaluation, and reflection. Working in stages, students begin by submitting written assignments. peerScholar then circulates their work for others to review, a process that can be anonymous or not, depending on instructors' preferences. Students immediately receive peer feedback and evaluations, reinforcing their learning and driving development of higher-order thinking skills. Students can then resubmit revised work, again depending on instructors' preferences.

Contact your Pearson representative to learn more about peerScholar and the research behind it.

COURSESMART

CourseSmart goes beyond traditional expectations—providing instant, online access to the textbooks and course materials you need at a lower cost for students. And even as students save money, you can save time and hassle with a digital eTextbook that allows you to search for the most relevant content at the very moment you need it. Whether it's evaluating textbooks or creating lecture notes to help students with difficult concepts, CourseSmart can make life a little easier. See how when you visit **www.coursesmart.com/instructors**.

TECHNOLOGY SPECIALISTS

Pearson's Technology Specialists work with faculty and campus course designers to ensure that Pearson technology products, assessment tools, and online course materials are tailored to meet your specific needs. This highly qualified team is dedicated to helping schools take full advantage of a wide range of educational resources, by assisting in the integration of a variety of instructional materials and media formats. Your local Pearson Education sales representative can provide you with more details on this service program.

SPEAKING OUT DVD FOR ABNORMAL PSYCHOLOGY VOLUME 1 AND 2.

These two DVDs of full-length video segments allow students to see firsthand accounts of patients with various disorders. The interviews were conducted by licensed clinicians and range in length from 8 to 25 minutes. Disorders include major depressive disorder, obsessive-compulsive disorder, anorexia nervosa, PTSD, alcoholism, schizophrenia, autism, ADHD, bipolar disorder, social phobia, hypochondriasis, borderline personality disorder, and adjustment to physical illness. See your local sales representative for details.

Acknowledgments

I would like to thank the team at Pearson Canada who provided the initial encouragement to undertake this project and who helped so much in the process of generating the final result. In particular, I would like to thank our Acquisitions Editor, Carolin Sweig, and our Developmental Editor, Patti Altridge, for their hard work on this volume.

In addition, I would like to thank my family (Michelle, Rachel, and Joshua) for their love, support, and encouragement throughout this task, and for always reminding me what is really important in life. I am also extremely grateful to the chapter authors for their excellent contributions to this text.

Finally, I gratefully acknowledge the comments and suggestions of the many knowledgeable colleagues who reviewed the manuscript at various stages:

Richard Day,
McMaster University

Kathy Foxall,
Wilfrid Laurier University

Mary Manson,
University of Guelph

Melody Sorenson,
Memorial University

Beth Visser,
Trent University

Angela Weaver,
St. Francis Xavier University

About the Editor

David J. A. Dozois, Ph.D., is professor of psychology at the University of Western Ontario in London, Ontario. He completed his undergraduate and graduate studies at the University of Calgary. He is a fellow of the Canadian Psychological Association (CPA) Section on Clinical Psychology and the Academy of Cognitive Therapy and a former Beck Institute Scholar at the Beck Institute for Cognitive Therapy and Research. Dr. Dozois' research focuses on cognitive vulnerability to depression and cognitive-behavioral theories/therapy. He is editor of *Cognitive-Behavioral Therapy: General Strategies* (in press, Wiley) and co-editor of *Prevention of Anxiety and Depression: Theory Research and Practice* (2004, American Psychological Association) and *Risk Factors in Depression* (2008, Elsevier/Academic Press). Dr. Dozois has published over 120 scientific papers, book chapters and books and has presented over 250 research posters and papers at national and international conferences. Dr. Dozois has received career awards from the Canadian Psychological Association, the Canadian Institutes of Health Research, the National Alliance for Research on Schizophrenia and Depression, and the Ontario Mental Health Foundation. Dr. Dozois teaches Adult Psychopathology at the undergraduate level and courses in systems of psychotherapy and cognitive-behavioural therapy at the graduate level. He has been on the Board of Directors for the Canadian Psychological Association since 2005, serving a term as President (2011–2012). Dr. Dozois is a licensed psychologist, and practises cognitive therapy in London, Ontario.

http://psychology.uwo.ca/faculty/dozois_res.htm

About the Contributors

Concepts of Abnormality Throughout History

Francois B. Botha is currently completing his Ph.D. in the clinical psychology program at the University of Western Ontario. His research interests focus on mechanisms of change in therapy for depression and reducing stigma and increasing help-seeking for mental disorders.

Theoretical Perspectives on Abnormal Behaviour

Lyndsay E. Evraire received her B.Sc. (Hons.) in psychology from Queen's University and her M.Sc. in clinical psychology from the University of Western Ontario. She is currently completing her doctoral degree in clinical psychology at the University of Western Ontario. Her research interests lie in the area of relationship dynamics and cognitive vulnerability to depression. Specifically, her program of research has examined how the interpersonal cognitive schemas of individuals with depression influence the extent to which they engage in the interpersonally aversive behaviour of excessive reassurance seeking with close others.

Classification and Diagnosis

Uzma S. Rehman, Ph.D., C. Psych., obtained her doctorate in clinical psychology from Indiana University and completed her predoctoral internship at the University of Chicago. She is an associate professor in the Psychology Department at the University of Waterloo. Her research focuses on intimate relationships. In past studies, she has examined the role of specific stressors, such as depression, on the course and quality of romantic relationships. Dr. Rehman's research is funded by the Canadian Institutes of Health Research, the Ontario Mental Health Foundation, and the Social Sciences and Humanities Research Council.

Psychological Assessment and Research Methods

Pamela M. Seeds received her B.Sc. (Hons.) in psychology from Queen's University and her M.Sc. in clinical psychology from the University of Western Ontario. She is currently completing her Ph.D. in clinical psychology at the University of Western Ontario. Her research interests focus on the role of cognitive processes and life stress in the development of mood disorders in adolescence and young adulthood.

Anxiety Disorders

Rebecca McDermott is currently completing her Ph.D. in clinical psychology at Western University in London, Ontario. Her research focuses on the allocation of attention in affective disorders and how these patterns relate to disorder onset, symptoms, and outcomes.

Paul A. Frewen completed his Ph.D. in clinical psychology from Western University in London, Ontario, where he is now assistant professor in the Department of Psychiatry. Dr. Frewen completed his clinical psychology residency with the Royal Ottawa Health Care Group. His research interests include psychological assessment, and functional magnetic resonance imaging of emotional processing and sense of self in people with mood and anxiety disorders. He received the President's New Researcher Award from the Canadian Psychological Association in 2010.

Dissociative and Somatoform Disorders

Rod A. Martin completed his Ph.D. in clinical psychology at the University of Waterloo in 1984. Since then, he has been a professor in the Department of Psychology at the University of Western Ontario, where he served as director of the clinical psychology program for 12 years. He has taught courses in abnormal psychology at both the graduate and undergraduate levels for more than 20 years. In general, his research focuses on personality variables associated with resiliency and effective coping. A major focus of his research is the psychology of humour, particularly as it relates to psychological health and well-being. He has authored numerous journal articles and book chapters on this topic, and has recently published a book entitled *The Psychology of Humor: An Integrative Approach*, which provides a comprehensive review of humour research in all areas of psychology. He has also conducted research on depression, Type A personality, and the effects of stress on immunity.

Psychophysiological Disorders

Kenneth M. Prkachin received his Ph.D. in clinical psychology from the University of British Columbia in 1978. Subsequently, he taught in the Department of Psychology at the University of British Columbia and the Department of Health Studies at the University of Waterloo. He is currently professor of psychology and health sciences at the University of Northern British Columbia. His research is in the area of measurement of emotion, psychological determinants of cardiovascular reactivity, and psychological risk factors for heart disease.

Glenda C. Prkachin received her Ph.D. in biopsychology from the University of British Columbia in 1978. Subsequently, she was a Killam Postdoctoral Fellow in the Department of Neuroanatomy at the University of Washington and a Natural Sciences and Engineering Council of Canada University Research Fellow. She has taught at the University of Western Ontario, Mt. Allison University, Wilfrid Laurier University, and the Universities of Guelph and Waterloo. She is currently associate professor of psychology at the University of Northern British Columbia. Her current research is in the perception and neuroscience of emotion.

Mood Disorders and Suicide

Kate Harkness, Ph.D., received her B.Sc. in psychology from the University of Toronto and her M.Sc. and Ph.D. from the University of Oregon. She then completed a residency and post-doctoral fellowship at the Western Psychiatric Institute and Clinic in Pittsburgh. She is currently the director of clinical training in the Psychology Department at Queen's University. Her research has focused on the role of stress in the onset and recurrence of major depression in adolescents and adults, and she is currently conducting studies examining the specific genes that increase individuals' neurobiological and psychological sensitivity to stress. Dr. Harkness's research has been funded by the Canadian Institutes for Health Research, the Canadian Foundation for Innovation, the Ontario Mental Health Foundation, and the Hospital for Sick Children Foundation.

Schizophrenia

R.Walter Heinrichs is a professor in the Department of Psychology at York University in Toronto. He became interested in schizophrenia as a student at the Ontario College of Art when he was exposed to the Prinzhorn Collection of art produced by people with serious mental illness. After an undergraduate degree in psychology, he studied aesthetic perception and neuropsychology, obtaining his Ph.D. from the University of Toronto. Dr. Heinrichs then spent several years in hospital practice as a clinical neuropsychologist before embarking on a career in teaching and research. His interests range from the history of schizophrenia to meta-analysis of neuroscience evidence and the use of cognitive measures to improve understanding of the disorder.

Ashley Miles is a Ph.D. student in the clinical psychology program at York University in Toronto. She received her B.A. (Hons.) from McMaster University in Hamilton, Ontario. Her research interests are in schizophrenia, specifically examining the relationship between neurocognitive ability and community independence. She plans to utilize knowledge gained from this research to develop cognitive rehabilitation strategies that will help improve cognitive and independent living skills.

Narmeen Ammari is a Ph.D. student in clinical psychology at York University. She received her B.Sc (Hons.) degree from the University of Toronto and her master's degree from York University. Her interest in schizophrenia has been fostered through her graduate education, clinical placements, and research experience. Her research is focused on neurocognitive subtyping as an approach to enhancing the validity of the schizophrenia diagnosis and reducing the heterogeneity of the illness. Her ultimate objective is to translate research findings into applications in prevention, treatment, and other interventions that will lead to a higher quality of life for those diagnosed with schizophrenia.

Eva Muharib is a graduate student in the clinical psychology program at York University, Toronto. Throughout her undergraduate career and after completing her B.Sc. (Hons.), Eva has worked with diverse clinical populations in both research and treatment settings. Currently, her research interests focus on understanding varying levels of cognitive abilities in individuals with schizophrenia.

Eating Disorders

Jennifer Coelho is a researcher in the Eating Disorders Program at the Douglas University Institute for Mental Health, and an assistant professor in the Psychiatry Department at McGill University. Her research focuses on cognitions and beliefs that may play a role in the development and maintenance of eating disorders.

Kathryn Trottier is a staff psychologist at Toronto General Hospital's Eating Disorder Program and lecturer at the University of Toronto, Department of Psychiatry. Her research has examined socio-cultural influences on eating and body image, the overvaluation of weight and shape in eating disorders, and treatment efficacy and effectiveness in eating disorders.

Janet Polivy has been a full professor of psychology and psychiatry at the University of Toronto since 1985. Her research has focused on self-change; the influences of personality, emotion, and socio-cultural influences on eating; and the influences of chronic dieting on cognition, emotion, and behaviour. Her research has been funded by the Ontario Mental Health Foundation, the Natural Sciences and Engineering Research Council, and the Social Sciences and Humanities Research Council of Canada. Her clinical work mainly involves individual therapy with eating- or affective-disordered patients. In 1994 she was first elected to the Council of the College of Psychologists of Ontario and was chair of the Registration Committee, Fitness to Practice Committee, and Government Relations Committee; a member of the Executive Committee; and vice-president of the college during her years there. She was elected a fellow of the Royal Society of Canada in 2006.

Substance-Related Disorders

David Hodgins, Ph.D., is a professor in the clinical psychology program in the Department of Psychology, University of Calgary, and is also the head of the Department of Psychology. Dr. Hodgins is a coordinator with the Alberta Gaming Research Institute. He received his B.A. from Carleton University, and his M.A. and Ph.D. from Queen's University. His research interests focus on various aspects of addictive behaviours, including relapse and recovery from substance abuse and gambling disorders. He has a particular interest in concurrent mental health disorders. He has developed a brief treatment for gambling problems that uses a motivational enhancement model, and research examining its efficacy is funded by the Canadian Institutes of Health Research. Dr. Hodgins teaches in the clinical psychology program and has an active cadre of graduate students. He maintains a private practice in Calgary in addition to providing consultation to a number of organizations internationally.

Terri-Lynn MacKay, M.A., is a doctoral candidate in the Addictive Behaviours Laboratory in the clinical psychology program at the University of Calgary. Terri-Lynn received her master's degree in behavioural neuroscience from the University of Manitoba in 2003. She spent two years as a research analyst with the Addictions Foundation of Manitoba, where she conducted research with the Canadian Centre on Substance Abuse, the Ontario Problem Gambling Research Centre, and Manitoba Justice. Terri-Lynn's doctoral research has focused on psychological processes that influence Internet gambling behaviour. Her research has been funded by the Social Sciences and Humanities Research Council, the Alberta Heritage Foundation for Medical Research, and the Alberta Gaming Research Institute.

The Personality Disorders

Dr. Stephen Porter, Ph.D. (UBC), is a professor of psychology at the University of British Columbia–Okanagan, working as an educator, researcher, and consultant in the area of psychology and law. He is the founding director of the Centre for the Advancement of Psychological Science and Law (CAPSL). He has published numerous research and theoretical articles on forensic issues ranging from personality disorders, credibility assessment, and deception detection to psychopathy, violent crime, and memory for trauma. As a registered forensic psychologist, Dr. Porter has conducted nearly 200 assessments on offenders or accused persons, and has been called as an expert witness in several Canadian legal cases. He has also been consulted by police to aid in detecting deception and strategic interviewing during criminal investigations. In addition, he has provided training to professional groups, including parole officers, private investigators, police, psychologists, psychiatrists, numerous groups of Canadian judges, and other adjudicators. His current research is supported by SSHRC, NSERC, and CFI. Visit the Porter Forensic Psychology Lab website at **https://people.ok.ubc.ca/stporter/Welcome.html.**

Pamela Black received her B.A. (Hons.) in psychology from Memorial University of Newfoundland–Sir Wilfred Grenfell College campus. She is currently completing her master's degree at the University of British Colombia–Okanagan under the supervision of Drs. Stephen Porter and Michael Woodworth and is thrilled to have the opportunity to conduct research in the recently opened Centre for the Advancement of Psychological Science and Law (CAPSL). Pamela is currently conducting research on the Dark Triad personality traits and vulnerability. Her other research interests include predatory behaviour on the Internet, computer-mediated communication, sexual offending, and trauma.

Natasha Korva is in her final year of her psychology honours degree (forensic specialization) at the University of British Columbia–Okanagan. She currently conducts research in the areas of legal decision making, psychopathy, and deception detection, but is fascinated with all areas of forensic psychology. Upon completing her degree, she plans to pursue graduate school and continue research in this field. She also volunteers with forensic-related organizations, and works as a part-time auxiliary probation officer.

Sexual and Gender Identity Disorders

Caroline F. Pukall completed her undergraduate degree in psychology at McGill University, and she received her Ph.D. in clinical psychology from McGill University in 2003. She is an associate professor in the Department of Psychology at Queen's University and the director of the Sex Therapy Service at the Psychology Clinic at Queen's. Her research focuses on vulvodynia (i.e., chronic genital pain in women), sexual difficulties (e.g., sexual arousal issues, vaginismus), women's health issues, and same-sex relationships. Her work is funded by several organizations, including the Canadian Institutes of Health Research and the National Vulvodynia Association. Dr. Pukall is an associate editor of *The Journal of Sexual Medicine* and is on the editorial board of several journals, including *The Archives of Sexual Behavior*.

Philip Firestone is a professor in the School of Psychology and the Department of Psychiatry, University of Ottawa. Dr. Firestone received his B.A. and M.A. at Carleton University and his Ph.D. in clinical psychology at McGill University. Dr. Firestone has published extensively in behavioural medicine, as well as in behaviour disorders of childhood and adolescence. Since the early 1990s his research and publication interests have been focused solely on sexual offenders. He has a clinical practice in which he provides assessment and treatment for men convicted of sexual offences and has provided expert evidence in a wide variety of legal cases related to violent and and/or sexual offences. In addition, he is an active member of the Ontario Review Board.

Developmental Disorders

Patricia M. Minnes received a B.A. (Hons.) degree in psychology from Queen's University in Kingston, Ontario, and a master's degree in clinical psychology from the University of Edinburgh, Scotland. She completed her doctorate in psychology at York University, Toronto. Dr. Minnes is a professor in the Department of Psychology at Queen's University and is cross-appointed in the Department of Psychiatry and the School of Rehabilitation Therapy at Queen's. Dr. Minnes is a consulting psychologist at Ongwanada, an agency serving individuals with developmental disabilities, their families, and caregivers, and she is a member of the Developmental Disabilities Consulting

Program in the Department of Psychiatry at Queen's, serving individuals with dual diagnoses and their families. As part of her clinical responsibilities, Dr. Minnes contributes to the supervision of psychology practicum students at the Psychology Clinic at Queen's and psychology interns through the Kingston Internship Consortium.

Dr. Minnes's research focuses on three major areas relating to individuals with disabilities: stress and coping in families and caregivers, community inclusion and quality of life, and attitudes toward persons with disabilities. Within these areas, she has focused primarily on two disability groups: developmental disability and acquired brain injury, as well as issues related to aging and disability. Throughout her career, Dr. Minnes has worked as a scientist practitioner.

Marjory L. Phillips received a doctoral degree in clinical psychology from the University of Waterloo in 1992. Dr. Phillips is the director of clinical services and community education at Integra, the only accredited children's mental health agency in Canada to specialize in providing mental health services to children, youth, and families with learning disabilities. Previously, Dr. Phillips worked with children with disabilities in a children's treatment rehabilitation centre. She joined the Queen's University Psychology Department on a full-time basis in 2004 to establish a psychology training clinic for graduate students. Dr. Phillips also has held cross-appointments as an adjunct assistant professor at Queen's University and York University, and is a clinical supervisor with the University of Toronto.

Behaviour and Emotional Disorders of Childhood and Adolescence

Tracy Vaillancourt is a Canada Research Chair in Children's Mental Health and Violence Prevention at the University of Ottawa, where she is cross-appointed as a full professor in the Faculty of Education (counselling program) and in the School of Psychology, Faculty of Social Sciences. Dr. Vaillancourt is also an adjunct professor in the Department of Psychology, Neuroscience, and Behaviour at McMaster University and a core member of the Offord Centre for Child Studies. She received her B.A., M.A., and Ph.D. from the University of British Columbia (human development), her post-doctoral diploma from the University of Montreal and Laval University (developmental psychology), and post-doctoral re-specialization in applied child psychology (clinical) from McGill University. Dr. Vaillancourt's research examines the links between aggression and children's mental health functioning, with a particular focus on social neuroscience. She is currently funded by the Canadian Institutes for Health Research.

Khrista Boylan received a B.A. (Hons.) in biology and psychology and a doctorate in medicine from Dalhousie University, in Halifax. She completed a residency in general psychiatry followed by a two-year fellowship in child and adolescent psychiatry at McMaster University in Hamilton, where she practises as a child psychiatrist. She is currently completing a Ph.D. in health research methodology at McMaster University. She is particularly interested in the developmental significance of comorbidity and its mechanisms, and effect of diagnostic comorbidity on clinical psychiatric practice.

Aging and Mental Health

Corey S. Mackenzie, Ph.D., C. Psych., is a clinical psychologist, an associate professor and director of clinical training in the Department of Psychology at the University of Manitoba, and a research affiliate with the University of Manitoba's Centre on Aging. His research, clinical, and teaching interests focus on older adults' mental health. Three lines of research that are being explored in his Mental Health and Aging laboratory are investigating ways of improving the mental health of older individuals. Using both primary data collection and secondary analyses of national population surveys, research in his lab aims to (1) understand how age affects mental health, (2) enhance older adults' access to mental health services, and (3) help individuals cope with stress when caring for older adults with dementia. The University of Manitoba, the National Initiative for the Care of the Elderly, and the Manitoba Health Research Council fund his research.

Kristin A. Reynolds, M.A., is currently completing her Ph.D. in clinical psychology at the University of Manitoba. Her research interests are centred upon four main areas: older adults' help-seeking for mental health problems; knowledge translation of mental health information among young and older adults; the relationship between mental health, physical health, and quality of life among older adults; and the effects of community program participation on the mental health and well-being of older adults.

Therapies

John Hunsley is a professor of psychology in the School of Psychology at the University of Ottawa, and is director of the clinical psychology program. He is a registered psychologist who provides psychological services for the treatment of anxiety and mood disorders. He conducts research on evidence-based psychological assessment and the impact of psychological services. Dr. Hunsley has served as editor of the journal *Canadian Psychology* and is a recipient of the Canadian Psychological Association Award for Distinguished Contributions to Education and Training in Psychology. He is a fellow of the Canadian Psychological Association and of the Section on Clinical Psychology.

Catherine M. Lee is a professor of psychology in the School of Psychology at the University of Ottawa. She is a registered psychologist who provides psychological services to children and families. Her research interests focus on parent–child interaction and evidence-based services for children. She teaches courses on psychology of the family and psychological assessment. She has served as president of the Canadian Psychological Association and as chair of the Canadian Psychological Association Section on Clinical Psychology, as well as founding chair of the Section on Family Psychology.

Prevention and Mental Health Promotion in the Community

Geoffrey Nelson is a professor of psychology and a faculty member in the graduate program in community psychology at Wilfrid Laurier University. He has served as senior editor of the *Canadian Journal of Community Mental Health* and chair of the Community Psychology Section of the Canadian Psychological Association. Professor Nelson has held a senior research fellowship from the Ontario Mental Health Foundation, and in 1999 he was the recipient (with the Canadian Mental Health Association/ Waterloo Region Branch) of the Harry McNeill Award for Innovation in Community Mental Health from the American Psychological Foundation and the Society for Community Research and Action. From 2004 to 2005, he was university research professor at Laurier. His research and practice have focused on community mental health programs and supports for people with serious mental illness, and community-based prevention programs for children and families.

Isaac Prilleltensky is dean of the School of Education at the University of Miami in Coral Gables, Florida, where he is also a professor of educational and psychological studies and a professor of psychology. Isaac was born in Argentina and has studied and worked in Israel, Canada, Australia, and the United States. He has lectured widely in South America, Europe, North America, Israel, Australia, and New Zealand. Isaac is concerned with value-based ways of promoting child, family, and community well-being. He is the author, co-author, or co-editor of seven books dealing with psychological and community well-being. He has been involved in community research and action in various countries and is a fellow of the American Psychological Association and of the Society for Community Research and Action. In 2002 he was visiting fellow of the British Psychological Society.

Julian Hasford is a Ph.D. candidate in the community psychology program at Wilfrid Laurier University. He has a B.A. in environmental studies from York University and a master's degree in health promotion from the University of Toronto. Julian's scholarly interests are in community-based approaches to promoting environmental sustainability, health, and well-being with diverse populations and vulnerable youth. He is also interested in qualitative research and evaluation methodologies. Julian's professional experience includes work in child welfare and community gardening settings. He was a recipient of the Donald T. Fraser Award for Academic Excellence at the University of Toronto (2005) and the Council of Canadian Departments of Psychology Teaching Assistantship Award (2007).

Mental Disorder and the Law

Stephen D. Hart obtained his Ph.D. in clinical forensic psychology from the University of British Columbia. He holds appointments as a professor in the Department of Psychology at Simon Fraser University and the Faculty of Psychology at the University of Bergen. His work focuses on clinical forensic assessment in criminal and civil settings, and in particular on the assessment of psychopathic personality disorder and violence risk. For his work, he received the Saleem Shah Award for Early Career Contributions to Psychology and Law from the American Academy of Forensic Psychology and the American Psychology Law Society, and the Career Contributions Award, from the Society of Clinical Psychology (Division 12 of the American Psychological Association). He has served as President of the American Psychology Law Society (Div. 41 of the American Psychological Association) and editor of the *International Journal of Forensic Mental Health*.

Ronald Roesch obtained his Ph.D. in clinical psychology from the University of Illinois at Urbana-Champaign. He is a professor in the Department of Psychology at Simon Fraser University. He is director of the Mental Health, Law, and Policy Institute at SFU, and prior to that served for many years as director of clinical training. His research focuses on improving the delivery of mental health services in forensic settings. Outside SFU, he has served as president of the American Psychology Law Society (APLS, Div. 41 of the American Psychological Association), and editor of the journals *Law and Human Behavior*; *Psychology, Public Policy, and Law*; and the *International Journal of Forensic Mental Health*. In 2010 he received the Outstanding Contributions to Psychology and Law Award from APLS.

DAVID J. A. DOZOIS • FRANCOIS BOTHA

Chapter 1

Concepts of Abnormality Throughout History

LEARNING OBJECTIVES

AFTER READING THIS CHAPTER, STUDENTS WILL BE ABLE TO:

1. Describe the principles that have been used to define abnormality and apply them to determine whether a particular behaviour may meet the definition of abnormal behaviour.
2. Understand how the conceptualization of psychological disorders changed from antiquity to the 1800s.
3. Describe at least two treatments that are associated with the biological approach and outline the current status of these treatments.
4. Describe the contributions of at least two influential Canadian individuals in the field of mental health care.
5. Describe two recent significant developments associated with mental health in Canada.

Lisa appeared at a clinic saying that her husband and two teenage children had persuaded her to seek treatment for what they saw as dysfunctional behaviour. She told the clinician that after she took a shower (which she did at least three times a day), she felt she had to wash the floor and walls of the bathroom in order to ensure that no dirt or bacteria had splashed off her body and contaminated the room. Lisa also insisted that her family not touch the faucets in the bathroom with their bare hands because she was sure that they would leave germs. The family members agreed to use a tissue to turn the taps on and off. Visits to the house by friends and relatives were not allowed because Lisa felt she could not ask them to follow these instructions and, even if she could bring herself to ask them, she did not believe they would go along with her request. This, of course, meant that her husband and children could never invite friends to their house. This restriction, and various other limits that Lisa imposed upon them, led the family to send her for treatment. Lisa did not consider her problems to be quite as bad as her family saw them.

***

Since childhood, Paul had been sexually aroused by the sight of women's underwear. This caused him considerable distress as a teenager and young adult. The fact that he could become sexually aroused only in the presence of women's underwear made him feel different from others, and he was afraid that people would find out about his secret desires and ridicule him. When Paul was 26 years old, after years of secrecy, he decided to consult a therapist in an attempt to deal with his unusual desires.

***

Arnold had begun to develop odd ways of perceiving the world and had begun to have unusual thoughts shortly after he entered university. After he graduated from high school, his parents put pressure on him to enrol in an engineering degree program at university so he could earn a large salary. Arnold resisted this pressure for some time, but finally gave in and took up the program. However, he was afraid he would fail and let everyone down. He was afraid they would find out he was really not competent. The pressures from his family, the threat of failure, and the heavy workload of his studies soon became too much for Arnold, and he began to break down. He began to develop odd interpretations of world events and of his role in them, and he began to perceive personally relevant messages on the nightly television newscasts. These unusual thoughts and perceptions quickly escalated until finally Arnold went to the local police station requesting a meeting with Canada's prime minister and the American president so he could give them directions to solve the world's problems. Not surprisingly, Arnold's grades dropped and he had to leave school. He was placed in hospital.

Clearly, Lisa, Paul, and Arnold all have abnormalities of behaviour and thought, but they are also very different from one another. There is no doubt, however, that most people would agree that each of them displayed very unusual, if not bizarre, behaviour. Arnold's problems seriously interfered with his life and his ambitions. Lisa was not as concerned about her problems as her family was, but they nevertheless markedly restricted her social life and interfered with other aspects of her functioning. Paul's case, on the other hand, turned out well. A few months after receiving treatment, he found a partner who could share in his unusual sexual activities, and his life was happy and apparently fulfilled.

What these three cases have in common is that each meets the criteria outlined in current diagnostic manuals for one or another psychological disorder. The current edition of the *Diagnostic and Statistical Manual of Mental Disorders* (DSM-IV-TR) of the American Psychiatric Association (2000) is the most broadly accepted system for identifying particular types of disorders (the next edition, the DSM-5, is expected to be published in 2013), although the *International Classification of Mental and Behavioral Disorders* (ICD-10), issued by the World Health Organization (1992), is also used by practitioners, primarily outside North America (for details of these diagnostic systems, see Chapter 3). Both of these diagnostic manuals would classify the three cases described above as disordered: Lisa would be classified as manifesting obsessive-compulsive disorder, Paul as having a paraphilia (in this case, a fetish), and Arnold as suffering from schizophrenia.

However, there are many people who engage in behaviours or express thoughts that most of us would consider to be strange or deviant, and who may cause distress to others, yet who are not identified in diagnostic systems as disordered. Consider the cases in the following box.

Case Notes

Eileen is a 19-year-old female whose religious beliefs forbid her to wear makeup or colourful clothes, or to listen to the radio or watch television. She will only go out with potential boyfriends in the company of her parents, and she will not attend dances or parties. Along with the rest of the people who attend her church, Eileen believes that the end of the world is imminent, and she has been peacefully preparing herself for that day. In addition, and somewhat contrary to her religious teachings, Eileen believes that the planets and stars control our destiny, and she subscribes to a monthly astrology magazine and consults daily astrological forecasts. Eileen also believes that she can communicate with the spirits of the dead and occasionally participates in seances with her family and their friends.

***

Roger is a professor at a large university. At age 46, he has never married and lives alone in a house whose windows he has painted black to shut out, as he says, "the views of his nosy neighbours." Roger has worn the same tattered suit for years and he wears a rather dirty baseball cap that he says is a family heirloom. He often wears heavy coats in the summer and sandals in the winter. His office is cluttered and he never seems able to find things; in fact, on several occasions he has lost students' essays. In the classroom, Roger wanders about among the desks as he lectures, and his lessons are rambling and difficult for the students to follow. He often introduces odd ideas that seem to have little to do with the topic on which he is lecturing. However, his research is greatly admired, and his colleagues do their best to make up for his teaching inadequacies.

***

James has been a career criminal since he was an early teenager. He has broken into many homes and stolen property; he has been convicted of selling marijuana on several occasions; and he has stolen and then sold numerous bicycles and cars. Not surprisingly, James has spent some of his 42 years in prison. Recently, he was living with a woman whom he had met at a bar one week prior to moving in with her and her three children. This was the most recent in a series of relatively short-lived common-law relationships that James had been involved in throughout his adult life. He did not have a job and, despite his promises to his partner, he made little effort to get one. Instead, he stayed home watching television and drinking beer. This led to numerous arguments with his partner and, over time, these arguments became more physical, with each partner hitting the other. Finally, during one of these clashes, James lost his temper and beat his partner with his fists so severely that she lapsed into a coma and died.

Eileen and Roger would both be considered eccentric by most people and, indeed, some students found Roger scary, although he never did anything that would suggest he was dangerous. However, neither Roger nor Eileen has ever been diagnosed as having a psychological disorder. Many people think that anyone who murders is insane, at least temporarily. However, careful examination of James by three independent psychiatrists led them to conclude that, although he had a personality disorder, James was otherwise normal, and the killing resulted from the persistent antagonistic relationship he had with the victim. Therefore, James was held to be responsible for his actions and duly convicted and imprisoned.

These cases illustrate two problems with defining abnormality. First, eccentric and unusual behaviour or beliefs are not necessarily abnormal according to diagnostic criteria, although the boundary between eccentricity and abnormality is not always clear. Arnold was clearly eccentric but also obviously disturbed. Both Eileen and Roger were eccentric but not so obviously disturbed. Second, behaviours that are repugnant and threatening to others, such as aggression and murder, are not always signs of an underlying psychological disorder. James has acted very badly and in a damaging way to others throughout his life, yet he is not considered to be seriously psychologically disordered. Neither Paul nor Lisa caused distress to other people, but they are judged to be suffering from a disorder.

This book describes our present understanding of the nature of psychological abnormality, the different forms such abnormality takes, how people become abnormal, and what, if anything, can be done to make their functioning normal. A fundamental issue we will have to consider from the outset, then, is just what it is we mean when we say that someone (or a particular behaviour of that person) is psychologically abnormal.

Our notions about abnormality have a long history. From the time of the earliest written records, and no doubt long before that, humans have identified some of their fellow humans as abnormal and offered various explanations and treatments for their behaviours. It is also clear that, over time, definitions of what constitutes abnormal functioning have changed, as have the explanations and treatments for abnormal behaviour. In this chapter, we first consider the various ways in which abnormality has been defined, and then examine the historical developments in the explanations and treatment of abnormality.

First, let us clarify some terms. **Psychological abnormality** refers to behaviour, speech, or thought that impairs the ability of a person to function in a way that is generally expected of him or her, in the context where the unusual functioning occurs. **Mental illness** is a term often used to convey the same meaning as psychological abnormality, but it implies a medical rather than psychological cause. A **psychological disorder** is a specific manifestation of this impairment of functioning, as described by some set of criteria that have been established by a panel of experts. In this book, we will use the term **psychopathology** to mean both the scientific study of psychological abnormality and the problems faced by people who suffer from such disorders. Psychological disorders occur in all societies and have been apparent at all times in history. However, what is considered a disorder varies across time and place.

Attempts at Defining Abnormality

Why is there such confusion about normality and abnormality, and is it possible to resolve the issue? Perhaps the answer to the last part of the question is no, because the concept of abnormality changes with time and differs across cultures and subcultures. However, it is also possible that we cannot easily resolve these problems because the concepts of normality and abnormality are so vague, despite the attempts of many writers to provide clear criteria.

Several principles are commonly considered in attempts to establish criteria for abnormality. As will become evident, however, no one principle can be considered sufficient to define this elusive concept. Rather, depending on circumstances, the contribution of several criteria may be necessary. The following principles, either alone or in combination, have at one time or another been used to define abnormality.

STATISTICAL CONCEPT

According to this view, behaviour is judged as abnormal if it occurs infrequently in the population. It would, of course, make little sense to describe as abnormal ways of functioning that characterize the majority of people. Relative infrequency, then, ought to be one defining feature of abnormality. However, not all infrequent behaviours or thoughts should be judged abnormal. For instance, innovative ideas are necessarily scarce or they would hardly be original, but most people would not consider the person who had such ideas as displaying abnormality, at least not in its usual pejorative sense. The same is true of athletic prowess. We admire people like professional hockey player Sidney Crosby, who grew up in Cole Harbour, Nova Scotia, and is currently the captain of the Pittsburgh Penguins (the youngest captain in NHL history). In 2006–07 Crosby became the youngest player in NHL history to win the scoring title and the only teenager in major North American sports leagues to have ever done so. In 2009 he became the youngest captain in NHL history to win the Stanley Cup. Although it is true that individuals like "Sid the Kid" are abnormal in the sense that their athletic skills are rare, we would usually describe such people as exceptional, a term that has no derogatory overtones.

An additional problem with the statistical criterion is that it is not clear how unusual a given behaviour has to be in order to be considered abnormal. For example, a study of Canadian undergraduate students from a small university found that 7 percent of males and 14 percent of females met diagnostic criteria for clinical depression in the preceding year. Thirteen percent of men and 19 percent of women also met criteria for one or more anxiety disorders (Price, McLeod, Gleish, & Hand, 2006). Although the depression rates reported in this study are higher than other one-year Canadian prevalence figures (e.g., Patten & Juby, 2008; Patten et al., 2006), neither depression nor anxiety can be considered that statistically infrequent—yet both are thought to reflect a disorder in need of treatment. Similarly, the common cold is considered an illness and yet it has a lifetime prevalence of 100 percent (Lilienfeld & Landfield, 2008).

PERSONAL DISTRESS

Many people who are considered to have a psychological disorder report being distressed. Someone who has an anxiety disorder, for example, will report feeling afraid or apprehensive most of the time. Depressed patients are obviously distressed. Yet distress is not present for all people identified as abnormal. An elderly manic patient who was evaluated at a local hospital would persistently pace rapidly around the ward, frequently bumping into people in his rush, despite having no obvious destination. While striding about quickly, he would keep up a constant conversation with no one in particular, and he would leap from topic to unrelated topic. He seemed to be in exuberant spirits, and he described himself as being extremely happy. Obviously, he was not personally distressed and yet, just as obviously, he was suffering from a mental disorder. An individual with antisocial personality disorder, who violates the rights of others, breaks numerous laws, and lacks empathy and remorse is not distressed by his or her behaviour; instead, it is the individuals in society who are distressed by this behaviour.

Some people who outwardly appear happy and successful may reveal to intimate friends that they feel a vague sense of dissatisfaction. They may complain that, despite their apparent success, they feel unfulfilled. There may even be an associated sense of despair at not having achieved something significant, and such people may seek professional help. It is unlikely, however, that they would be labelled abnormal.

In fact, all of us are distressed, or even depressed, at times. When someone we love dies, it is normal to be distressed; indeed, if we do not mourn, our response might be judged to be abnormal. If this distress passes within a reasonable amount of time, our response would be considered normal.

However, if our grief did not abate with time, and our depression deepened and persisted for several years, our suffering would be described as abnormal. Distress, then, appears to be a frequent, but not essential, feature of abnormality.

PERSONAL DYSFUNCTION

When behaviour is clearly maladaptive (that is, it interferes with appropriate functioning), it is typically said to be abnormal. Yet the definition of dysfunction itself is not clear-cut. What is appropriate functioning? What is appropriate functioning in a given context? Many of us responded with feelings of vulnerability, anxiety, anger, and sadness following the terrorist attacks on the World Trade Center and Pentagon on September 11, 2001. Some of us have become increasingly vigilant about possible threats when going through airport security or attending large gatherings such as Canada Day celebrations. Students and faculty have also become more vigilant at universities and colleges following the Dawson College shootings in Montreal (September 2006) that claimed 1 life and injured 19 people, and the Virginia Tech massacre (April 2007) that killed 32. Within reason, such vigilance and anxiety, although distressing, are not abnormal given the circumstances. In fact, scanning the environment for such threats is, to some extent, adaptive as it serves a survival function.

Wakefield (1992, 1997, 1999) has concluded that harmful dysfunction is the key notion—where dysfunctions refer to "failures of internal mechanisms to perform naturally selected functions." To conclude that a given behaviour is disordered "requires both a scientific judgment that there exists a failure of designed function and a value judgment that the design failure harms the individual" (Wakefield, 1999, p. 374). By their functions, Wakefield is referring to what an artifact or behaviour was originally designed to do. For example, the function of a pen is to write—that is the purpose of a pen's design. The fact that we can also use a pen as something to chew on when we are nervous or as a weapon for self-defence does not explain why pens were designed the way they were. Thus, the failure of a pen to help protect an individual would not entail a failure of its function (Wakefield, 1997). Wakefield (1997, 1999) argues that unless there are dysfunctional consequences to the individual, in that he or she is unable to perform a natural function, it makes little sense to call behaviour abnormal.

Using harmful dysfunction as a potential criterion for abnormal behaviour also creates an interesting link between abnormal and evolutionary psychology (see Focus box 1.1). In terms of evolutionary theory, a trait may be dysfunctional if it harms an organism's capacity to reproduce successfully. Antisocial behaviour, for example, may result in being excluded from everyday society, thereby hurting such a person's capacity to reproduce. If the underlying reason for the antisocial behaviour is a lack of inhibition, this may be seen as abnormal. Certain forms of antisocial behaviour, such as unethical business practices, may, however, actually increase an individual's wealth and therefore increase his or her capacity to reproduce (Murphy, 2005).

The boundaries between normal and abnormal and what specifically constitutes "harmful dysfunction" are therefore not clear and are a matter of considerable controversy (e.g., Fabrega, 2007; Houts, 2001a, 2001b; Lilienfeld & Landfield, 2008; Lilienfeld & Marino, 1995). These fuzzy boundaries notwithstanding, categorical distinctions between normal and abnormal can be useful. We discuss this issue further in Chapter 3.

FOCUS 1.1

Defining Mental Disorders: The Case of Pedophilia

The proposed changes to the definition of pedophilia in the DSM-5 allow the opportunity to explore how views of abnormality may change over time. In the current DSM-IV, pedophilia is defined as sexual attraction or sexual behaviour toward prepubescent children. This definition is closely related to the idea of harmful dysfunction. Sexual attraction in general is an adaptive function that promotes the continuation of a person's genes across time. Attraction to prepubescent children does not allow for sexual reproduction and can therefore be seen as dysfunctional. In addition, such attraction may lead to the individual being censured socially, further reducing the individual's capacity to reproduce.

In contrast, the proposed criteria for pedophilia (now termed *pedohebephilic disorder*) in the DSM-5 also refer to sexual attraction or sexual behaviour toward early pubescent children as abnormal. Behaviour that may increase an individual's capacity to reproduce has, therefore, now been included in the definition. Such behaviour may in fact have been highly adaptive earlier in human history when life expectancy was much lower. Part of the rationale for this decision is that many people are being given the diagnosis of *paraphilia not otherwise specified* when they show sexual attraction or sexual behaviour toward early pubescent children. Arguably, the new definition takes certain social norms and the opinion of experts into account, although it does stop short of using the legal definition for pedophilia, which would capture a wider range of people.

Although the practice of marrying child brides is now outlawed in most countries, it was still common in certain areas in the recent past. This practice raises the question of cultural norms and whether men who marry child brides in these cultures should receive diagnoses of pedophilia. It can be further be noted that personal distress may be not be a suitable part of diagnostic criteria in that people receiving a diagnosis of pedophilia may not be disturbed by their behaviour. The need to protect those who cannot defend themselves therefore becomes an important criterion for including this behaviour as a mental disorder. Finally, sexual interest in prepubescent children fortunately appears to be rare and may therefore be seen as abnormal in the context of statistical occurrence.

VIOLATION OF NORMS

The behaviour and thoughts of many psychologically disordered individuals run counter to what we might consider appropriate. The thoughts expressed by individuals with paranoid schizophrenia, for example, are often so bizarre that observers do not hesitate to declare the ideas irrational and as reflecting an extreme departure from what would be expected in the context. Similarly, a man who dresses in women's clothing in order to generate sexual arousal would be judged by most people to be displaying behaviours that are contrary to socially acceptable ideas. On the other hand, criminals clearly engage in behaviours that violate social norms, but few of them meet the criteria for any disorder. No doubt their criminal acts upset others, but discomfort in an observer alone cannot count as the basis for judging someone's behaviour to be disordered. For example, the lyrics of some songs make many people uncomfortable. In October 2000, some politicians attempted to stop rapper Eminem from performing at the SkyDome in Toronto because of lyrics that promoted violence against women ("Confronting Eminem," 2000). An attempt was also made by MP Dan McTeague to ban 50 Cent from performing in Ontario based on the concern that the rapper may promote gun violence in the province ("MP Wants Rapper," 2005). More recently, Canadian radio stations were banned from playing the song "Money for Nothing" (performed by Dire Straits) for nine months in 2011 because the song included a word that was deemed offensive to homosexual men ("Dire Straits' Song," 2011). The fact that offensive content is contained within their songs would not justify classifying these lyricists as psychologically abnormal, although that is a characteristic response that people often make to ideas and behaviours they find personally repulsive.

Related to the notion of violating norms is the idea that psychologically abnormal people are unpredictable and somehow dangerous. In fact, very few people suffering from a psychiatric disorder are dangerous to others. Even psychotic patients, who are the most bizarre of all disordered people, rarely attempt to hurt anyone. Most psychologically disordered people are no more dangerous, and no more unpredictable, than are the rest of the population. Conversely, while television and movies like to portray all killers and rapists as mad, most are not. Apparently, it comforts us to think that someone who would do something as repugnant as killing or maiming another person must be insane.

Perhaps the most serious flaw in this criterion is that social norms vary over time and place. In fact, few disorders are truly universal across different cultures. Depression, for example, has a much higher prevalence rate in Canada and the United States (approximately 17 percent lifetime prevalence; Kessler, Berglund, et al., 2005) than in some other parts of the world, such as Taiwan or Korea (4 percent lifetime prevalence; e.g., Chang et al., 2008). Different cultural and ethnic groups also manifest psychopathology differently and exhibit their own strategies for dealing with psychological distress. For example, the lower prevalence of depression in Asian cultures may be due to the emphasis placed on physical symptoms and the avoidance of the stigma of mental disorders. Neurasthenia is a condition that includes many of the physical symptoms of depression and it is still frequently diagnosed in Asia, but this diagnosis has largely been abandoned in the West. It is important to bear in mind that how we define abnormality is **culturally relative**. The norms of a particular culture determine what is considered to be normal behaviour, and abnormality can be defined only in reference to these norms. Fortunately, the most recent versions of the DSM (DSM-IV and DSM-IV-TR) have been far more explicit than previous editions were in encouraging clinicians and researchers to consider cultural diversity.

Society's criteria for defining behaviour as acceptable or unacceptable are also not temporally universal; rather, they reflect the predominant view in society, which changes over time. Thirty-five years ago, when homosexuality was classified as abnormal, it was also considered to be a violation of social norms. Is it a reflection of changing norms that psychologists no longer consider homosexuality to be abnormal? Much earlier, in the late 1800s, masturbation was considered to be a manifestation of a mental disorder without any consideration of the base rate of this behaviour in the general population (see Mash & Dozois, 2003). To take a more extreme example, in Germany in the 1930s, Jews, homosexuals, gypsies, mentally retarded people, and others were persecuted, tortured, or killed on the basis that they represented inferior specimens of human beings. These views, which are repugnant to our society, were apparently sufficiently acceptable to the German populace at the time to allow the Nazis to carry out their so-called ethnic cleansing. Do we conclude that 1930s Germany was an abnormal society—and if so, what does it mean to say that a whole population is abnormal?

DIAGNOSIS BY AN EXPERT

Before we consider this issue, it is an opportune time to identify the professionals involved in the mental health field. **Clinical psychologists** are initially trained in general psychology and then receive graduate training in the application of this knowledge to the understanding, diagnosis, and amelioration of disorders of thinking and behaviour. Psychologists have a thorough grounding in research methods, and some of them spend their careers doing research on abnormal functioning, although many also provide treatment. The treatment methods of clinical psychologists primarily involve psychological interventions of one kind or another. **Psychiatrists** are trained in medicine prior to doing specialized training in dealing with mental disorders. This specialized training focuses on diagnosis and medical treatment that emphasize the use of pharmacological agents in managing mental disorders. Not surprisingly, most psychiatrists attend to the medical aspects and biological foundations of these disorders, although they usually also consider psychological and environmental influences. **Psychiatric nurses** have received formal training in nursing before completing a specialization in psychiatric problems. These professionals typically work in hospital settings where they manage the day-to-day care of mentally disordered patients. In addition to these professionals, **psychiatric social workers** attend to the influence of the social environment on disordered clients. Psychiatric social workers usually have a graduate degree in social work, and they provide assistance to clients in adjusting to life within their families and the community. **Occupational therapists (OTs)** may practise in Canada with a baccalaureate degree along with field-training experience. OTs are sometimes involved in providing mental health care. These individuals may provide a broad range of services on rehabilitation teams and typically focus on helping clients to improve their functional performance (e.g., training in community living skills).

The fact is that the identification of a psychological disorder in any specific individual is ultimately left to a professional to judge. In the final analysis, the opinions of particular mental health workers (usually psychologists and psychiatrists) determine whether a person is said to suffer from a psychological abnormality. In this sense, the DSM-IV-TR (or ICD-10) provides the operational criteria for the various disorders and thereby defines abnormality. This, of course, does not clarify the criteria by which such judgments are made, and an examination of the various criteria for the different disorders suggests that different aspects of the notions outlined above serve to define different disorders. It is hard to discern any clear common thread in the different criteria.

Thomas Szasz (1961), in a book entitled *The Myth of Mental Illness*, suggested that the idea of mental disorders was invented by psychiatry to give control to its practitioners to the exclusion of other people, such as clergymen, who in the past had greater power over the psychologically disordered (see also Schaler, 2004). In addition, Szasz (1970) contended that the institution of the church and the person identified as, for example, a "witch" were replaced by the institution of psychiatry and the patient being treated, respectively. Such criticisms, while perhaps overstating the case (Lilienfeld & Landfield, 2008), do serve a valuable function by encouraging the generation of evidence to support the existence of mental disorders. There seems to be little doubt today that there is overwhelming evidence of the reality of various disorders. Nevertheless, the power held by mental health professionals remains an issue.

SUMMARY OF DEFINITIONS

As we have seen, not one of the various criteria that have been offered for defining abnormality seems satisfactory on its own. There are many ways to approach defining a person's functioning as normal or abnormal, and the criteria discussed above do not exhaust all possible approaches. Nevertheless, together they represent the core defining features of abnormality. To identify a person or a behaviour as abnormal, no single criterion is either necessary (that is, must be present) or sufficient (enough on its own). Typically, some combination of these criteria is used, with one or more features having greater relevance depending upon the specific circumstances or features of the client. Our purpose in discussing various criteria for abnormal psychological functioning has been to alert the reader to the rather elusive nature of the concept and to suggest that, while such a notion may have some general value, it has little practical application. In practice, most diagnosticians avoid the use of the term *abnormality* and simply prefer to match their clients' symptoms to a set of criteria appearing in the latest edition of the diagnostic manual. While this approach does not clarify the nature of abnormality, it works effectively in practice. Defining specific behaviours, thoughts, and feelings as representing particular disorders, as does the fourth edition of the *Diagnostic and Statistical Manual of Mental Disorders* (DSM-IV-TR), is useful because then we can plan the management and treatment of the person displaying such problems. Searching for criteria that will define any and all instances of disordered functioning (or abnormality), however, may be pointless. Nevertheless, throughout the ages people have held quite different views, not only about what abnormality is, but also about its causes.

1 BEFORE MOVING ON

How do you determine when someone's behaviour is abnormal? What are the strengths and weaknesses of the four general attempts at defining abnormality?

Historical Concepts of Abnormality

We now turn to an examination of the different notions that have, over time, guided approaches to dealing with abnormality. Looking at changes in the conceptualization of abnormal psychological functioning can provide a basis for understanding how we arrived at our current formulations and responses to abnormality. We will see how societal concepts are shaped by the prevailing views of the time concerning all manner of phenomena. Indeed, as Erwin Ackerknecht, a historian of psychiatry, has suggested, "The criterion by which a person in any society is judged to be mentally ill is not primarily the presence of certain unvarying and universally occurring symptoms. It depends rather on whether the affected individual is capable of some minimum of adaptation and social functioning within his [or her] society" (Ackerknecht, 1968, p. 3).

Revolutions in philosophy and science, such as the Renaissance and the era of Enlightenment, generally had profound effects on all aspects of society, including a change in the way that mad people were seen. For example, Darwin's radical conceptualization of the mechanism of evolution, which he called natural selection, had an immediate influence not only on all the biological sciences but also on psychology, politics, and economics. Modern evolutionary biologists have since rejected the implications that were drawn from Darwin's theory by eugenicists (Gould, 1985). Proponents of this view, who included Darwin's cousin Sir Francis Galton (1822–1911), interpreted Darwin's work to mean that those whose intellectual, social, or economic functioning was seen as inferior were defective, or maladaptive. Many further argued that because society and the advancement of medicine now protected these deficiencies from the forces of natural selection, they ought to be selected by society for sterilization in order to eliminate their defective genes. In the hands of the Nazis, eugenics led to the extermination of millions of people. Our own Canadian history was also affected by this type of thinking. In 1928, Alberta passed a Sexual Sterilization Act under which individuals who were deemed "feebleminded," "mentally deficient," or "mentally ill" were to be involuntarily sterilized to prevent deterioration of the intellectual level of the general population. A total of 2832 individuals were sterilized in Alberta alone (British Columbia also passed a similar act in 1933). One case involved a 17-year-old woman from Edmonton who was diagnosed as a "moron." The rationale for her sterilization was that she was "rather bossy and bad tempered" and had a tendency to go "out alone a lot" and "pick up with anyone and talk and chat with them" (Park & Radford, 1998, p. 327). In 1999, the government of Alberta publicly apologized for the suffering experienced by those who were sterilized under this Act and negotiated a financial settlement with victims (Government of Alberta, 1999).

An examination of the historical development of our ideas about abnormality, then, will reveal that such ideas are simply one aspect of the general views of the time. This is important for another reason. When we consider some past notions about abnormality, we might tend to scoff and treat them as absurd, and so they may be from the perspective of the present day. However, they must have seemed correct at the time because they matched the general ideas of the day. Reflecting on this may help us to recognize that perhaps our own conceptualization of abnormality seems so right to us only because it fits with our current world views and beliefs (see Mash & Dozois, 2003). Remember that earlier ideas about abnormality were accepted not only by those who made decisions about the insane, but also by many of the sufferers and their families. Treatments that seem bizarre or even cruel to us today may have helped sufferers because they believed that the procedures would be effective. Perhaps the same is true to some degree of our current ideas and treatments (Kirsh et al., 2008). We encourage the student of psychopathology to be a critical consumer of research—it is possible, after all, that at some point in the future we will view our current ideas as archaic and ill-founded.

Throughout recorded history, and no doubt long before that, people have been concerned with identifying and treating psychological dysfunction. What has been seen as evidence of madness or of other disturbed thinking or behaving, however, has changed over the course of evolving societies. For many years, people who claimed to be able to foretell the future were revered and frequently given jobs in royal courts to assist kings and queens in their decision making. Today, most people regard with skepticism the claims of soothsayers and may even doubt the sanity of people who repeatedly say that they can foresee future events. Not only have the notions about what constitutes abnormality changed over time, so too have explanations for the causes of such behaviour. Likewise, treatments have also differed across time. They have ranged from compassionate care to brutal torture, depending upon the type of abnormality and the accepted account of its origin.

All these changes in the acceptability, treatment, and theories of etiology of abnormal behaviour have reflected, and continue to reflect, the values of society at a particular time. A society that explains everyday events (weather, seasons, war, etc.) as a result of **supernatural causes**—causes beyond the understanding of ordinary mortals, such as the influence of gods, demons, or magic—will view madness similarly. Psychological dysfunction in various historical periods was thought to result from either possession by demons or the witchcraft of evil people. Treatment involved ridding the mad person of these influences by exorcism or other magical or spiritual means. When worldly events are seen to have **natural causes** (that is, causes that can be observed and examined), so too are mental afflictions, and they are treated in a way that addresses these presumed natural causes.

EVIDENCE FROM PREHISTORY

Paleoanthropologists have discovered human remains from the Stone Age that were originally interpreted as providing evidence of supernatural beliefs as early as half a million years ago. Skulls have been found with circular sections cut out of them. Since there are clear signs of bone regeneration around these holes, it was concluded that the operations (called **trephination**) were done while the person was still alive. Apparently a stone tool was used to cut the holes, and it was originally presumed that this was done to let out evil spirits that were causing the victim to engage in severely abnormal behaviour. There may, however, be simpler explanations. Maher and Maher (1985), for example, suggest that trephination may have been intended to remove bone splinters or blood clots caused by blows to the head during warfare. Piek, Lidke, and Terberger (2008) recently presented evidence consistent with this medical explanation. Whatever the reason for these neat circular holes in the skulls of Stone Age people, we know from early written records that demonic possession was popularly accepted in early human societies as the cause of madness. Egyptian papyri from almost 4000 years ago describe supernatural explanations for various disorders and the use of magic and incantations as treatment procedures. These early Egyptians recognized that the brain was the site of mental activities, although they believed that its functioning was disrupted in mad people by demonic possession. Thus, their belief was something of a mixture of natural and supernatural assumptions.

Hunter-gatherer societies that have been examined over the past 100 years may provide clues to how our own prehistoric ancestors viewed madness. These societies characteristically do not distinguish mental from physical disorders; both are seen as having supernatural causes. Sadly, the belief in a demonological view of abnormality

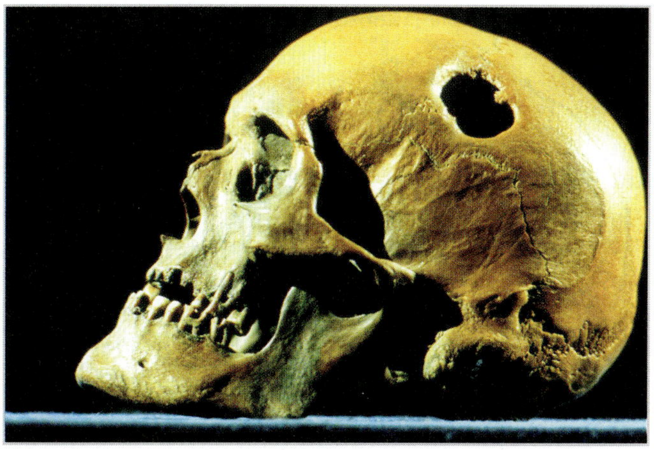

Trephination, the prehistoric practice of chipping a hole into a person's skull, was an early form of surgery, possibly intended to let out evil spirits.

still exists even today. In February 2001, the CBC program *The National* broadcast a documentary entitled "The Mentally Ill of Africa's Ivory Coast." This documentary featured a man named Koffi and his struggle with schizophrenia. The people in Koffi's community believed that he was possessed by demons and chained him to a tree outside of the village for more than 10 years. Many more people are incarcerated in a similar way in this area of the continent. Food and water are provided on occasion, but often such individuals go for days without eating anything.

GREEK AND ROMAN THOUGHT

With the rise of Pericles (495–429 BC) to the leadership of Athens, the Golden Age of Greece began. Temples of healing were soon established that emphasized natural causes for mental disorders and that developed a greater understanding of the causes and treatment of these problems. The great physician Hippocrates (460–377 BC), who has been called the father of modern medicine, denied the popular belief of the time that psychological problems were caused by the intervention of gods or demons. This represented the first recorded instance of a rejection of supernatural causes for mental illness. Hippocrates did not distinguish mental diseases from physical diseases. Instead, he thought that all disorders had natural causes. Although he emphasized the primacy of brain dysfunctions, Hippocrates argued that stress could influence mental functioning. He also thought that dreams were important in understanding why a person was suffering from a mental disorder, and in this he predated Freud and the psychoanalysts of the twentieth century. As for treatment, Hippocrates advocated a quiet life, a vegetarian diet, healthful exercise, and abstinence from alcohol. If these procedures did not work, and sometimes as a supplement to them, Hippocrates considered induced bleeding or vomiting to be of value.

This latter claim for the value of vomiting or bleeding arose primarily as a result of Hippocrates' idea that psychological functioning resulted from disturbances of bodily fluids or **humours**, as they were then called. Both vomiting and bleeding were thought to reduce excesses of one or another of the humours. Cheerfulness, so Hippocrates thought, was caused by an excess of blood; ill-temper by an excess of yellow bile; gloom by an excess of black bile; and listlessness by an excess of phlegm. Hippocrates was the first to describe what he called *hysteria*, which is now known as *conversion disorder:* psychologically induced blindness, deafness, or other apparent defects in perceptual or bodily processes (see Chapter 6). Hippocrates claimed that hysteria occurred only in women and was due to a "wandering" uterus. While Hippocrates' ideas seem absurd to us now, at the time they represented a significant advance because they pointed to natural causes rather than demonic possession and other supernatural events. As a consequence, Hippocrates' theories encouraged the beginnings of a scientific understanding of disordered behaviour and thought.

Many of Hippocrates' ideas were taken up by the Greek philosophers Plato (427–347 BC) and Aristotle (384–322 BC). However, Plato placed more emphasis on socio-cultural influences on thought and behaviour. Elaborating on Hippocrates' notions about dreams, Plato suggested that they served to satisfy desires because the inhibiting influences of the higher faculties were not present during sleep. This view foreshadows Freud's theory of dreams. Plato declared that mentally disturbed

Hippocrates (460–377 BC).

people who commit crimes should not be held responsible, since they could not be said to understand what they had done. In this respect, he anticipated modern notions of legal insanity, which exempt afflicted people from responsibility for their crimes (see Chapter 19). Plato also suggested treatment responses that presaged current approaches. For example, he said that in most cases, the mentally ill should be cared for at the homes of relatives, anticipating the present trend toward community care. For those who must be hospitalized, Plato said their thinking must be rationally challenged in a conversational style of therapy that was remarkably like some forms of present-day psychotherapy.

Aristotle wrote extensively on mental disorders and on other aspects of psychological functioning. He accepted Hippocrates' bodily fluids theory and denied the influence of psychological factors in the etiology of dysfunctional thinking and behaving. In keeping with Greek tradition, Aristotle advocated the humane treatment of mental patients.

After Alexander the Great founded Alexandria, Egypt, in 332 BC, the Egyptians adopted and expanded the medical and psychological ideas of the Greeks. They established temples to Saturn, which came to be sanatoriums for people who were psychologically unwell. These temples provided pleasant and peaceful surroundings, the opportunity for interesting and calming activities, healthful diets, soothing massages, and education. The priests who attended these disturbed clients also employed bleeding, purges, and restraints, but only when all other attempts had failed.

After 300 BC, there emerged in ancient Greece various schools of thought that rejected Hippocrates' theories of mental illness. The most important and best known of these was Methodism, its principal advocate being Soranus of Ephesus (circa AD 100). Methodism regarded mental illness as a disorder that resulted either from a constriction of body tissue or from a relaxation of those tissues due to exhaustion. The head was seen as the primary site of this affliction. Mania, Soranus said, resulted from overexertion, licentiousness, or alcoholism. Ordinarily, so Soranus thought, natural bloodletting (for example, by hemorrhoids or menstruation) would provide an avoidance of the disorder, but in cases where this did not happen, mania or some other mental illness would result. Soranus rejected the mind–body distinction so common among Greek thinkers and maintained instead that there was no difference between mental and physical disorders; they all arose from problems in the body. The Greek physician Aretaeus (AD 50–130), however, considered emotional factors to be primary in causing disturbances of mental functioning and advocated using psychological, rather than strictly medical, methods.

The Greeks were first and foremost empirical. They provided the first clinical observations of disorders and made the first attempts at classification. Treatment, for the Greeks, was primarily physical, but some psychological and social components were typically included. Even though their theories were rarely accurate, and their treatments were sometimes unsuccessful, the Greeks remained devoted to naturalistic explanations and responsive to the world as they saw it.

After the Romans assumed control of the ancient world, their physicians carried on the work of the Greeks. Galen (AD 129–198), a Greek physician living in Rome, continued the work of Hippocrates. He thought there were two sources of mental disorder: physical and mental. Physical causes included head injuries, alcohol abuse, and menstrual disturbances, whereas psychological factors included stress, loss of love, and fear. The Romans thought it was necessary for effective treatment to provide comfortable surroundings for patients; even when they employed physical treatments, Romans did not use any stressful procedures, preferring things like warm baths. Galen suggested that having people talk about their problems to a sympathetic listener had value in treating the mentally disordered. Apparently, this was an early form of what we now call psychotherapy.

THE ARAB WORLD

With Galen's death in AD 198, the enlightened period of mental health research and treatment that began with Hippocrates in the fifth century BC came to an end in Europe, but it was carried on by the Arab world. While the Dark Ages descended on Europe, the Arabs continued the Greco-Roman traditions of investigation and humane treatment of the mentally ill. In Egypt, the gentle methods used in the temples of Saturn persisted into the Mohammedan period. These generally supportive and kindly approaches to the mentally ill continued to characterize the Arab world's approach throughout the period, during which the writings of the Greek scholars were lost to Europeans. The Quran itself reflects compassionate attitudes toward the mentally ill, and it is interesting that, despite Western assumptions to the contrary, Arab societies in general continue to hold to these admirable views and practices. Today, the mentally disordered are treated with sympathy in the Arab world, as they were in the period beginning in the eighth century AD. Units for the mentally ill within the great Arab hospitals were established in Baghdad in AD 800, and asylums were created in other Arab cities in the years thereafter—some 500 years before Europeans built their first asylums. In these Arab **asylums** (a word meaning place of refuge and protection), treatment followed the tradition of care, support, and compassion (Polvan, 1969).

The Islamic physician Avicenna (AD 980–1037) developed an astonishing understanding of medicine and psychological functioning, which he described in his remarkable volume *The Canon of Medicine*. This book is considered to be one of the most widely read and authoritative medical texts in the history of medicine (see Dols, 2006). Avicenna's analyses of mental disorders reflect a practical approach characterized by an emphasis on natural causes, particularly environmental and psychological factors. His treatment recommendations followed the Greco-Roman emphasis on care and compassion, but he also employed procedures not unlike early behaviour therapy methods of the twentieth century. For example, Browne (1921) describes Avicenna's way of dealing with a prince who believed himself to be a cow and repeatedly asked to be killed and made into a stew. When Avicenna first examined the case, the young man had stopped eating altogether, a cause for great concern. Avicenna began by sending a message to the prince telling him that a butcher would arrive soon to slaughter him. Shortly thereafter, Avicenna appeared brandishing a knife, saying, "Where is this cow that I may kill it?" He then felt the patient's body all over and declared, "He is too lean, and not ready to be killed; he must be fattened." The attendants then offered the prince food, which he enthusiastically ate. As he gradually regained his strength, the prince's delusion disappeared.

This picture illustrates the practice of exorcism, which was used to expel evil spirits that had possessed people.

EUROPE IN THE MIDDLE AGES

After the fall of the Roman Empire at the end of the fifth century, Europe entered a period, approximately AD 500–1500, when the teachings of the Greeks and Romans were either lost or suppressed. It is often claimed that the natural theories of Greco-Roman times were entirely replaced during this period by supernatural explanations, while the compassionate and practical treatment of the mentally disturbed was supplanted by quite unpleasant procedures meant to free the afflicted person of possession by the devil or his minions. However, this is not entirely true and, in fact, some of Galen's theories survived and were expressed in naturalistic approaches to treatment (Schoenman, 1984). Whereas demonological theories of insanity attributed disorders to sin on the part of the sufferer, Kroll and Bachrach (1984), in an examination of cases recorded in the fifteenth and sixteenth centuries, note that in very few cases was sin considered to be an etiological factor. Kroll and Bachrach point out that the notion of "possession," so popular in the writings of authors during the Middle Ages, may have meant much the same as our own current expression "nervous breakdown." It may simply have been a colloquial descriptor applied to a vague and general set of problems without necessarily implying, in all cases, that the afflicted person had been taken over by the devil or some other supernatural force.

Perhaps the issue to which earlier historians most frequently misapplied these demonological ideas was witchcraft (Zilboorg & Henry, 1941). Until the 1980s, it was generally held that people identified as witches during the late Middle Ages were mad and that their madness was considered to result from possession by the devil. There was some truth to this notion. For example, some of the most eminent physicians of the early sixteenth century firmly believed that mad people were possessed and in need of exorcism. Furthermore, Martin Luther (1483–1546) claimed that when people sinned in particularly bad ways, God would deliver them over to Satan, who could possess them either corporally (that is, bodily) or spiritually. According to Luther, if the devil possessed them corporally, they would become mad, but if he possessed them spiritually, they should be considered witches. Luther, then, made a clear distinction between madness and witchcraft. Despite earlier historical interpretations that the many thousands of so-called witches who were tortured or killed during the fifteenth and sixteenth centuries were insane, it appears that most were not, nor were they considered to be insane at the time. The majority of these unfortunate victims were accused of exercising evil powers over others by people who simply wanted to be rid of them, and the accusations were all too often eagerly accepted by those who were appointed to seek out witches for punishment.

Throughout the Middle Ages in Europe, people suffering from psychological disorders for the most part received treatment and care from the clergy, as they were the only ones with sufficient concern and resources to provide assistance. For a long time, the insane were provided refuge from the world in monasteries and pilgrimages. The treatment they were given was typically mild, and emphasized prayer and a generally caring approach. As the idea of possession by the devil became more popular, exorcism replaced these gentle approaches. Exorcism, meant to drive out the evil forces that possessed the afflicted, was itself initially mild, but over time became more and more vigorous. To rid the person of the possession, exorcists would curse and insult the devil. If this did not succeed, they would attempt to make the body uncomfortable for him by subjecting the disordered individual to all manner of bodily insults. In some cases, these bodily insults amounted to torture, becoming progressively more severe until the person was either cured or died—which was also considered a cure.

Such approaches to mental illness were not without critics, who also opposed the idea of witchcraft and vehemently protested the torture and killing of those identified as witches. This opposition grew with the onset of the Renaissance, when Greco-Roman thought was rediscovered and passed into the hands of secular scholars. Paracelsus (1493–1541), a famous Swiss alchemist and physician, was one of the first to attack the beliefs about supernatural possession. He was determined to develop a new approach to mental disorders and attempted to create a new system of classification. Paracelsus rejected the four-humours theory of the Greeks and Romans and instead claimed that all mental illness resulted from disturbances of

This fifteenth-century engraving shows peasant women overcome by St. Vitus' dance.

the *spiritus vitae* (breath of life). In some cases, the *spiritus vitae* was upset by the stars, in others it was disturbed by vapours arising in various parts of the body. Although we would today consider these ideas false, they do represent an attempt to offer naturalistic rather than magical or demonic origins to madness.

During the waning years of the Middle Ages, there arose in Europe what came to be known as **St. Vitus' dance**. This was an epidemic of mass hysteria, where groups of people would suddenly be seized by an irresistible urge to leap about, jumping and dancing, and sometimes convulsing. Some of these dancers claimed to have been bitten by tarantula spiders, apparently in order to excuse their behaviour so it would not be attributed to possession by evil spirits. Thus the behaviour was originally called the Tarantella, which subsequently became the name of a dance. However, the more general explanation at the time was that these people were possessed. Paracelsus denied this assertion and instead declared the problem to be a disease; in fact, he was among the first to suggest that psychic conflicts might cause mental illness, and he treated disordered people with what appears to have been an early version of hypnotism.

The efforts of Paracelsus were followed by Johannes Weyer (1515–1588), who, despite still accepting that the devil was the cause of some cases of mental illness, advocated natural and physical treatments while rejecting exorcism. Weyer also observed that mental illness could arise from natural causes. For instance, he claimed that "fantasies" (he probably meant delusions or hallucinations) could be traced in some patients to their use of belladonna ointments. He based this claim on both clinical observation and experiments carried out by two earlier physicians, Cardona and Della Porta. Weyer's views are quite interesting because they reflect a characteristic of Renaissance thought—that is, the mixture of traditional ideas (such as possession by the devil), theological concerns, and original observations. His views represented a significant move toward a more scientific and naturalistic attitude about the insane.

This new humane attitude was most apparent in Spain due to the influence of the Moors. The Moors, Muslims from North Africa, had conquered the Iberian peninsula in the eighth century and had brought with them the knowledge and attitudes of the Arab world. Although the Moors were finally expelled from Spain in 1502, their influence remained. During the Renaissance, Spain enjoyed a golden era of medicine. Mental institutions were established in Valencia in 1409, in Seville in 1436, and in Toledo in 1430. In fact, the first mental institution in North America was built by the Spaniards at San Hippolyto in Mexico.

THE BEGINNINGS OF A SCIENTIFIC APPROACH

While Paracelsus's analysis of St. Vitus' dance represents a far more scientific view of mental disorders than had existed in Europe for centuries, he also enthusiastically held that the moon influenced emotional and mental processes (the term *lunatic* stems from the Latin for moon). Accordingly, Paracelsus did not have the influence on scientific thinking he might otherwise have had. This was left to others, the most significant of whom was Teresa of Avila in Spain, the head of a group of nuns at the time of the Spanish Inquisition (sixteenth century). When her charges began to display hysterical behaviours and were in danger of being accused of possession by the devil, St. Teresa (she was later canonized) defended them by claiming that they were sick (actually, "as if sick," *comas enfermas*); her argument was so convincing that she saved them from the Inquisition (Radden, 2004). Another eminent religious teacher, St. Vincent de Paul (1576–1660), who is today widely recognized for his compassion, also challenged heterodoxy by claiming that mental disease and bodily disease are not different. He advocated the protection of people suffering from mental disorders and declared that it was society's responsibility to develop means to relieve such individuals of their suffering. St. Vincent was, therefore, arguing for the development of a scientific and humane approach to dealing with the problems of the insane.

As a result of this movement toward a more caring and naturalistic way of construing psychological dysfunctions, asylums began to be established in Europe.

Teresa of Avila (1515–1582).

While the intentions of those who created these institutions may have been compassionate, the reality was that most asylums were places where the residents were treated cruelly and lived in appalling conditions. Perhaps the most famous of these early European asylums was the one established by Henry VIII in 1547 when he had the monastery of St. Mary of Bethlehem in London converted to a place where mentally disordered individuals could be housed. Although it has been moved to several locations since then, the Bethlem Royal Hospital (as it is now known) still exists, although it is now an exemplary mental hospital in the pleasant countryside south of London. While Henry VIII provided an institutional setting, he did not satisfactorily fund the asylum. Those in charge had to raise funds by whatever means they could. One procedure was to invite the public to visit the asylum and charge them a small sum. The entrance fee provided the tourists with the opportunity to tease and poke with sticks the hapless residents who, not surprisingly, screamed and moaned, much to the visitors' pleasure. This noise and disruption among the residents prompted the use of the word **bedlam** (the local corruption of "Bethlem") to describe any form of rowdy, chaotic behaviour.

Other asylums in Europe followed a form similar to that of Bethlem, with the treatment of the insane being much the same. La Bicêtre in Paris was one of the most notorious. There, patients were shackled to the walls in unlit cells, unable to lie down even to sleep. Their food was inadequate, they were not permitted to wash regularly, and they were essentially treated like animals. In North America, the conditions of mental asylums were no better, and the treatments offered were harsh, including electric shocks, bleeding, and plunging the patients into ice-cold water (see Focus box 1.2). Bennett (1947) examined historical records from these institutions in the United States dating from the early 1800s. These records revealed that patients were placed in unlit cells, had their heads shaved, and were given a restricted diet, often accompanied by purgatives. They were often isolated from all other patients, apparently to "cure" their frenzied behaviour. Not surprisingly, success rates of these procedures were quite low.

In the midst of these otherwise dreadful approaches, there was at least one shining example of a distinctly humanitarian attempt to deal more effectively with these unfortunate people. A legendary tale, dating from the thirteenth century, tells of the flight of a young princess who had escaped from her incestuous father and fled to Belgium. Her father caught up with her just outside the town of Gheel, whereupon he killed her. She was said to have attended to the insane prior to her escape from her father. Some years after her death, five lunatics slept one night under the tree where she was slain. When they awoke in the morning, their insanity had disappeared; thereafter, the place became a shrine visited by the mentally ill seeking a cure. These pilgrims frequently stayed on in Gheel, where the townsfolk took them into their houses and allowed them to live comfortably, which seems to have produced remarkably beneficial results (Karnesh & Zucker, 1945). In fact, the tradition lives on today, with as many as 1000 patients living with families in Gheel and working in local community centres. Although this unusual program is effective, it receives little recognition and has had little influence on the general approach to dealing with the mentally ill.

While there was significant progress toward a more humane and rational approach to understanding and managing the mentally ill during the sixteenth century, the trend did not continue in the following century. The large number of poor was seen as a serious social problem that the absolutist governments of the day wanted to get rid of. Their solution was to establish what the English called "workhouses," where the poor, the old, orphans, and others, including the insane, were incarcerated in dreadful conditions. Mad people were chained to the walls, flogged regularly, and given only the bare minimum of care; physicians were rarely, if ever, consulted. In Paris, men were sent to the Bicêtre and women to the Saltpêtrière.

As a result of the European philosophical movement known as the Enlightenment, the eighteenth century saw radical changes in the way in which abnormal behaviour was conceptualized. The basic ideas of the Enlightenment concerned the superiority of reason in the analysis of problems, the idea that progress was an inevitable and desirable feature of human society, and the belief that it was both appropriate and necessary to challenge traditional ideas,

FOCUS 1.2

Treatment and Mistreatment: The Depiction of Mental Asylums in the Movies

The conditions that existed in asylums and reports of maltreatment made mental health treatment during the asylum era a popular subject for Hollywood films. In the 2010 movie *Shutter Island* (Scorsese, 2010), U.S. Marshal Teddy Daniels (played by Leonardo DiCaprio) is sent to investigate the escape of a patient from an asylum for criminally insane patients. Teddy is soon confronted by rumours of people being drugged against their will, lobotomies being performed, patients being experimented on, and torture. It is eventually revealed that Teddy is actually an inpatient who murdered his wife and is now suffering from delusions and hallucinations. His psychiatrist and other staff members play along with his delusion in the hope of being able to confront him with the reality of what he had done. Although most of the rumours Teddy hears about turn out to be false, the treatment he receives is still conducted without his approval, which would raise ethical concerns in a modern treatment environment.

The rumour that Teddy Daniels hears about patients being experimented upon is, however, not without any foundation in historical reality. Perhaps the worst instance of abuse of psychiatric power in Canada is the well-documented story of Dr. Ewen Cameron's brainwashing experiments at Montreal's Allen Memorial Hospital during the late 1950s and early 1960s (Collins, 1988). Cameron's work was funded, at least in part, by the American Central Intelligence Agency (CIA), which apparently hoped to discover ways both to overcome the effects of brainwashing by its enemies and to brainwash captured enemies. None of the unfortunate participants in these studies, most of whom were mental patients seeking Cameron's help, were ever informed that they were part of a research project, let alone that such research was funded by the CIA. Under the guise of therapy, Cameron subjected his patients to massive and repeated doses of electroconvulsive therapy (ECT), prolonged sensory deprivation, and chemically induced sleep. This last procedure was employed for days on end, during which time audiotapes telling the patients how awful they were and how they must change were played under their pillows. Patients were also repeatedly injected with lysergic acid diethylamide (LSD), a hallucinogenic drug, without ever being told what it was or how it would affect them. Of course, most of them experienced terror.

The abuse of psychiatric power is also vividly portrayed in the Oscar-winning movie *One Flew over the Cuckoo's Nest* (Forman, 1975). In the movie, Randle McMurphy (portrayed by Jack Nicholson) fakes a mental disorder in order to obtain a transfer from prison to an asylum. He soon incurs the wrath of the head nurse, Nurse Ratched, who runs the ward with an iron fist. After a series of confrontations that culminate in an attack upon Nurse Ratched, she uses her psychiatric power to force McMurphy to receive drug treatment and ECT as punishment, and eventually suggests that he should be lobotomized. These forms of biological intervention were usually used as an attempt to cure or reduce harm rather than to punish, but, as we discuss later, these interventions may have been overused.

A more benign and more modern portrayal of mental health institutions can be found in the 2001 movie *K-Pax* (Softley, 2001). A man (portrayed by Kevin Spacey) who claims to be an alien called Prot from the planet K-Pax is being treated in a mental health facility by Dr. Mark Powell (portrayed by Jeff Bridges). The facility has many windows, adequate lighting, a garden that is open to patients, and meaningful daily activities for patients. Client consent is obtained for all procedures that are performed, and institutional personnel are reserved in their use of force to control patients. The movie is guilty of overdramatizing the process of hypnosis and suggesting that trauma is the primary cause of psychotic behaviour, but overall it is a fairly realistic portrayal of current institutionalized care.

Mental asylums were established throughout the world in the nineteenth century in response to the deplorable conditions in which the mentally disordered were kept (Porter & Wright, 2003). Mentally disordered individuals were often forced to wander from town to town or to fend for themselves in the countryside. Turned out of their homes, they became part of the cavalcade of beggars across Europe. Conditions were no better for those allowed to stay at home.

The conditions in which the mentally disordered were forced to exist led many reformers to demand that proper hospitals be established to care for the mentally disordered. Dorothea Dix (1802–1887), a Boston schoolteacher who taught at the local prison, was shocked by what she saw there and became a crusader for better conditions for offenders. Her concern quickly spread to mental patients, and she launched an effective nationwide campaign to improve the lot of the mentally ill. Her campaign resulted directly in the opening of 32 state hospitals, including two in Canada, and many more indirectly.

In *The Shame of the States*, journalist Albert Deutsch (1948) reported on a 1946 tour of U.S. mental institutions. He described "hundreds of patients sleeping in damp, bug-ridden basements." One doctor complained to Deutsch, "I know I should see many more patients individually. But how can I when I have five hundred patients under my care?" The furor that resulted from this book along with the advent of antipsychotic drugs in 1954 led to a massive deinstitutionalization of mental patients.

including religious doctrine. One of the many consequences of such thinking was a re-examination of the ways in which society dealt with the insane. One of the leaders of this movement was Philippe Pinel (1745–1826), who was appointed by the French revolutionary government as director of the Bicêtre in 1792.

In response to seeing the appalling conditions at Bicêtre, Pinel ordered that the inmates' chains be removed. He had the institution cleaned and the windows replaced to let in full sunlight, encouraged healthful exercise on the grounds, and instructed staff to treat the patients with kindness rather than giving them regular beatings. Although evidence (Weiner, 1979) indicates that it was the institution's manager, Jean-Baptiste Pussin, who had in fact begun these reforms, Pinel carried on these dramatic changes at a time when it was clear that, had the experiment failed, he would likely have been led off to the guillotine along with other failed revolutionaries. Pinel's actions were those of a courageous and compassionate human being, and he is properly remembered as one of the leaders of the humanitarian reforms that swept through Europe in the late eighteenth and early nineteenth centuries. What brought an end to this approach was not its failure (for it was in fact quite effective) but the remarkable increase in mental patients, primarily as a result of the proliferation of patients suffering from general paresis of the insane and those affected by alcoholism. This overcrowding of mental institutions made it all but impossible to treat every patient in the way that Pinel recommended.

Pinel should be remembered for his humanity but also for the influence he exerted on psychiatry as a whole. He developed a systematic and statistically based approach to the classification, management, and treatment of disorders. Pinel emphasized the role of psychological and social factors in the development of mental illness, and he elaborated clear descriptions of the symptomatology of the various disorders. He saw the asylum as therapeutic, a place where patients could be separated from their families and from the stresses of their everyday lives. Patients were to be treated respectfully so as to inspire their confidence, and they were given activities to stimulate them. Pinel did not discard physical approaches to treatment, but rather saw the humane management of patients as the basis on which physical treatments could have their effects. Pinel was thoroughly scientific and looked only to natural explanations for the origins of mental disorders. In Britain, William Tuke (1732–1822) followed Pinel's example by establishing similar approaches in psychiatric hospitals, and Benjamin Rush (1745–1813) brought **moral therapy** to North America.

These efforts came to be known as the **mental hygiene movement**, which was characterized by a desire to protect and to provide humane treatment for the mentally ill. Despite noble aims to alleviate human suffering, the movement of enormous numbers of individuals with mental disorders into large asylums did not, in fact, improve their lot. The asylums were overcrowded, custodial, and countertherapeutic and the staff had no time to do more than warehouse patients (Sussman, 1998). Restraints such as straitjackets were more refined than the old fetters but no less cruel (Bockoven, 1963). In addition, the average population within asylums in North America increased dramatically over the years, resulting in the construction of even more institutions. Hunter, Shannon, and Sambrook (1986) argued that one reason for the increase in patient numbers was that the responsibility for the care of the insane shifted from the family and local community to the states and provinces.

2 BEFORE MOVING ON

In what way does our world view today influence the understanding and treatment of mental health problems? When you look back through history you may view the so-called treatments for mental health problems as barbaric. Indeed, many of these interventions were inhumane by our standards. How do you think we will view our current treatments in 50 or 100 years?

Development of Modern Views

BIOLOGICAL APPROACHES

Toward the end of the eighteenth century, theorists had abandoned the notions of Hippocrates and Galen that stated that disruptions in the four humours cause people to become mentally ill. As a result of anatomical examinations of the cadavers of mad patients, and the concurrent discoveries regarding the functioning of the nervous system, mental disorders came to be viewed as disruptions in nervous system functioning. The culmination of this line of thought was expressed most clearly by Cabanis (1757–1808), who combined psychological and somatic factors in his account of mental disorders. His theories were particularly influential and encouraged the development of psychological approaches to treatment. Cabanis provided the first clear theoretical basis for moral therapy. The eighteenth century can be seen as the first flowering of what later became known as psychotherapy, and it more generally set the stage for a move toward a thoroughly rational and scientific approach to abnormal behaviour.

HEREDITY Benedict Augustin Morel (1809–1873), a Viennese physician, was the first to introduce "degeneration" theory. This idea proposed that deviations from normal functioning are transmitted by hereditary processes and that these deviations progressively degenerate over generations. Morel's final version of this theory appeared in 1857, just one year before the publication of Charles Darwin's remarkable *The Origin of Species*. Darwin's notion of the inheritance of advantageous features and the disappearance of disadvantageous features by natural selection lent support to theories like Morel's that proposed an inherited basis for human functioning. The possibility that human behaviour (both normal and abnormal) could be seen as being passed on genetically from generation to generation inspired many theorists to suggest that it might be possible to identify people as potential madmen or criminals before they developed such problems. Cesare Lombroso (1836–1909) concluded from his observations that criminality was inherited and could be identified by the shape of a person's skull. While phrenology (as this study was called) enjoyed a good deal of popularity for a time, it did not withstand more careful scrutiny. However, the idea that disorders of functioning could be passed on genetically not only survived, but now enjoys widespread acceptance in psychiatry and psychology.

SYNDROMES AND THE BEGINNING OF CLASSIFICATION

Perhaps the most influential person in the latter part of the nineteenth century, however, was Emil Kraepelin. In 1883, he published a very important textbook, *Clinical Psychiatry*, which attempted to classify mental illness. Classification is, as we will see in Chapter 3, the fundamental basis on which research is generated. It also attempts to guide the selection of treatment and to indicate the likely course and outcome of the disorder. In any case, without some form of classification, research would be markedly restricted, since it would be impossible to group people according to their common disorder. Kraepelin, however, was not interested in treatment, because he believed that all mental disorders were the result of biological problems for which, at that time, there were no treatments available. Accordingly, he focused on diagnosis and classification as ends in themselves. Kraepelin noted that certain groups of symptoms tended to occur together, and he called these groupings **syndromes**. These different syndromes, Kraepelin observed, could serve as a way of grouping patients who shared certain features into categories that identified specific disorders. He was the first to recognize that the different disorders not only had distinct features, but also differed in terms of the age of onset and their typical course over time. As a result, Kraepelin suggested that the different disorders probably had different causes, although he thought that these different causes were all biological in one way or another.

Kraepelin's efforts led to an interest in classification that lives on in the current versions of DSM-IV-TR and ICD-10. Although these more recent classification systems owe much to Kraepelin's innovative work, they have evolved into a considerably different, far more detailed and research-driven system of classifying mental disorders.

INFECTION AS A CAUSE OF MENTAL DISORDER

Following Kraepelin's view that mental disorders were the result of biological processes, Richard von Krafft-Ebing (1840–1902) became interested in the possibility that patients with **general paresis of the insane (GPI)** might have acquired this disorder by an infection. GPI (or neurosyphilis) is now known to result from untreated infections by the syphilis spirochete (a coil-shaped bacterium). Initial infection results in a sore on the genitals and sometimes swollen lymph glands of the groin. Untreated, the spirochete does not disappear but remains in the bloodstream; after about one year, it enters the meningeal lining of the brain and spinal cord, although it does not affect functioning at this stage. The immune system sometimes overcomes the infection at this point, but if it does not, then a decade or so later the affected person becomes symptomatic. Mania, euphoria, and grandiosity are the first marked features of this delayed response, followed by a progressive deterioration of brain functioning (called *dementia*) and paralysis. In the latter part of the nineteenth and early part of the twentieth century, patients with GPI filled most of the beds in psychiatric hospitals (Shorter, 1997).

Louis Pasteur had established the germ theory of disease in the 1860s, and Krafft-Ebing noted that it had been observed that some patients with GPI had previously had syphilis. His guess was that GPI was a long-term consequence of syphilis. To test this theory, Krafft-Ebing infected GPI patients with syphilitic material (Valenstein, 1986). If his theory was correct, then his injected patients would not develop syphilis since they had already been infected. Although the ethics of his procedures are repugnant to modern readers, Krafft-Ebing's guess turned out to be correct. Subsequently, the spirochete that causes syphilis was discovered, and it was shown that there was a link between infection and later destruction of particular areas of the brain that produced the mental and physical deterioration shown by patients with GPI.

This confirmation of the idea that such a widespread and serious mental disorder as GPI was the result of an infectious agent encouraged confidence in the view that all mental disorders would soon be found to be caused either by infections or by some other biological factor. **Somatogenesis** (the idea that psychopathology is caused by biological factors—*soma* meaning "body" in Latin) not only gained prominence as a result of the success in identifying the cause of general paresis, but also followed quite logically from the remarkable successes that occurred in the middle and latter half of the nineteenth century in science in general and in medicine more specifically. It seemed at the time that all disorders (physical as well as psychological) would be solved quite soon as a result of applying biological science. While such optimism proved unfounded, these views did encourage a scientific approach to abnormal functioning that became progressively more sophisticated.

The discovery that GPI had an organic cause not only led to a search for the somatic bases of other mental illnesses, but also encouraged trials of various physical approaches to treatment (see Valenstein, 1986). Because GPI was now known to result from an infection, it was thought that deliberately inducing a fever in such patients would cause the increased body temperature to kill the infectious agent. In 1890, Julius von Wagner-Jauregg injected GPI patients with a vaccine in order to induce a fever. Shorter (1997) says it was tuberculin, a vaccine for tuberculosis, whereas Ackerknect (1968) says it was typhus vaccine. Whichever it was, Wagner-Jauregg got reasonably good results, but the unreliability of the approach encouraged him to try infecting these patients with malaria to induce a fever more reliably. This actually worked to kill off the syphilitic spirochete and prevent further progress of the disease. In fact, it proved so successful that Wagner-Jauregg was awarded the Nobel Prize in 1927.

SHOCK THERAPY Since antiquity, it has been known that shocks could produce recovery from mental illness. For example, sudden submersion in water had been shown to alleviate the symptoms of some people suffering from disturbances of mental functioning (Ackerknect, 1968). It occurred to Manfred Sakel, a German physician, that shock treatments might, therefore, be effective in treating the insane (Valenstein, 1986). He had used insulin in the late 1920s to manage the withdrawal symptoms of morphine addicts. When insulin was occasionally given in an accidentally high dose, it induced a coma in the patient. Sakel observed that after the coma passed, the patient's desire for morphine disappeared and patients who were previously agitated became tranquil. Soon after these observations, Sakel began examining the value of insulin-induced comas for individuals with schizophrenia. He reported that 70 percent of these patients fully recovered and a further 18 percent were able to at least function well. Sakel's procedure was taken up enthusiastically by others and, by 1944, Eliot Slater and William Sargent's influential English psychiatric textbook listed insulin-coma as the first choice in treating the mentally ill. This physical procedure was appealing not only for its effectiveness, but also because it allowed asylum psychiatrists to become more than just custodians and it aligned them with medicine (Shorter, 1997).

Insulin administrations not only induced a coma, but also occasionally produced convulsions, and some theorists thought these might be the main active feature of the treatment. In 1934, Ladislas von Meduna suggested that deliberately provoking convulsions, by the administration of Metrazol (a drug similar to camphor), might ameliorate the symptoms of schizophrenia. Meduna noted that the brains of epileptic patients (that is, patients who suffered from chronic convulsions or seizures) were quite different (or so he thought) from those of individuals with schizophrenia, and it was also reported about the same time that epileptics who developed schizophrenia thereafter experienced fewer seizures. Meduna deduced from this that producing seizures in people with schizophrenia might eliminate their disorder. He tried his procedure with 110 patients and 50 percent completely recovered from their illness. As a result, a series of Metrazol-induced convulsions became reasonably popular in the treatment of psychotic patients. However, there were undesirable side effects, including a terror of dying, such that many patients refused a second injection. With the discovery that electricity applied to the head could induce convulsions, other forms of coma or convulsive therapy disappeared.

The first individual to employ electricity to induce a seizure in mental patients was Ugo Cerletti in 1938. After a series of animal studies established the difference between convulsive and lethal shock intensity, and the optimal placement of electrodes on the skull, Cerletti and his assistants began to use the procedure on human patients. The device they developed delivered a shock of 80 to 100 volts to the temples for a fraction of a second. After 11 treatments, Cerletti's first patient, an individual with severe schizophrenia, was able to be discharged, although he did return one year later. **Electroconvulsive therapy (ECT)**, as this treatment was called, was enthusiastically welcomed by psychiatry throughout the world and very soon replaced most other physical treatments. Although ECT was initially used only for the treatment of schizophrenia, it was found to be most effective with patients suffering from major depression, on whom it is still used to this day (see Chapter 8).

One problem with the initial uses of ECT was that during the bodily convulsion produced by the brain seizure, some patients suffered broken limbs or cracked vertebrae. These were obviously very undesirable side effects. However, the finding that curare (a poison extracted from the South American vine *Strychnos toxifera* and applied by natives to the tip of their arrows), in very small doses, produced relaxation of the limbs of spastic children suggested that it could be useful in preventing the bodily reactions to ECT. It proved effective, but was risky, so it was replaced by the less dangerous drug succinylcholine which, when combined with a fast-acting barbiturate, allowed patients undergoing ECT to avoid pretreatment anxiety and within-treatment risks of fractures.

THE BEGINNINGS OF PSYCHOPHARMACOLOGY In the 1950s, pharmacological agents for the treatment of psychiatric disorders became widely available and began what the Canadian psychiatric historian Edward Shorter (1997) calls "the second biological psychiatry." The view of this period, which continues to the present, was that mental illness results from disordered brain chemistry. The widespread acceptance of this view led to the rejection by much of psychiatry of psychological perspectives, including psychoanalysis. Interestingly, this point in time corresponds to the revival, among psychologists, of the application of behaviourism to the amelioration of psychological disorders.

The first neurotransmitter was isolated in 1926 by Otto Loewi at the University of Graz in Austria. He identified the action of acetylcholine (a neurotransmitter) as mediating the transmission of nerve impulses within the brain (see Chapter 2 for a discussion of neurotransmission). Although this might have suggested a possible way to change brain functioning in mental patients by introducing an *agonist* (something that facilitates the production of acetylcholine) or an *antagonist* (something that inhibits its production), such approaches did not develop until the 1950s. Some of the early work on the effects of drugs derived from these ideas was done by Heinz Lehmann at Montreal's Verdun Protestant Hospital. His experiments, while unsuccessful, nevertheless paved the way for further research.

In an attempt to calm soldiers before surgery, Henri Laborit in 1949 examined the value of some recently developed antihistamines of the phenothiazine group of drugs. He found these drugs to be very effective in inducing a calm and relaxed state in his patients. Following this, Laborit obtained the latest drug in this series, called chlorpromazine, and persuaded some psychiatrist friends to try it with their patients. It virtually eliminated one manic patient's problems. Subsequently, it was evaluated in more systematic trials and chlorpromazine soon enjoyed widespread popularity. In her book on the history of psychopharmacology, Anne Caldwell (1978) provides a dramatic description of the benefits and changes resulting from the adoption of this drug as a treatment for patients with mental disorders:

> The atmosphere in the disturbed wards of mental hospitals in Paris was transformed: straitjackets, psychohydraulic packs, and noise were a thing of the past! Once more Paris psychiatrists, who long ago unchained the chained, became pioneers in liberating their patients, this time from inner torments, and with a drug: chlorpromazine. It accomplished the pharmacological revolution of psychiatry. (Caldwell, 1978, p. 30)

Due to the success of antipsychotic medications (and the advent of tricyclic antidepressants in the 1960s), the patients' rights movement (which suggested that patients can better recover if they are integrated into the community), and U.S. President Kennedy's community mental health movement, a process of **deinstitutionalization** was set in motion. Beginning in the 1950s, hundreds of thousands of institutionalized patients were discharged. However, because the closure of psychiatric institutions had not been balanced by a strengthening of community resources, many mentally disordered individuals were homeless and lacked adequate support (Sussman, 1998). In 1988, the government of Canada published *Mental Health for Canadians: Striking a Balance*, which was intended to promote mental health and improve community care.

Chlorpromazine had remarkable advantages over other forms of treatment and management at the time. Not only did it do away with physical restraints and make psychiatric management an easier task, it was less dangerous than ECT and more easily tolerated by patients.

Thereafter, the pharmaceutical industry began to produce a plethora of neurotransmitter-affecting drugs to treat patients with schizophrenia, mania, and depression. The era of psychopharmacology had arrived. However, psychological or environmental explanations of mental disorders did not simply disappear throughout the twentieth century. Indeed, it was one of the strongest periods for such theorizing. Somatic and psychological explanations and treatments of psychiatric patients, often seen by their proponents as antithetical to one another, proceeded to develop somewhat independently. It has only been in recent years that they have been seen by many as complementary and interactive.

3 BEFORE MOVING ON

There was great hope for biological therapies in the early 1900s, and a recent revival in the application of these interventions, particularly drug treatments, has occurred. Is this because the evidence about their effectiveness is convincing, or is it because they offer an easy, but limited, solution to problems?

PSYCHOLOGICAL APPROACHES

Psychological accounts of the etiology of mental disorders had been popular throughout history and obtained some eminence in the latter part of the eighteenth century. An increased interest in psychological explanations was sparked by the work of Anton Mesmer (1734–1815) with hysteria (see Chapter 6 for a description of this disorder, now called *conversion disorder*), although Mesmer's explanation was physiological. Mesmer thought that hysteria was the result of a disturbed distribution of the magnetic fluid present in all bodies. His procedure involved a good deal of mystery and required that the patients be touched by Mesmer with various rods that were said to transmit, from Mesmer directly to the patients, a magnetic force he called "animal magnetism" that would rearrange their fluids and cure the disorder. These procedures obviously required Mesmer to present his treatment very convincingly, using various tactics to suggest strongly to his patients that they would recover. In fact, a subsequent study, conducted by Benjamin Franklin, indicated that mesmerism was essentially due to the "power of suggestion." Mesmer's approach was a predecessor of hypnotism and, in fact, it was called this by James Braid, a British surgeon in the mid-1800s, who saw great promise in the technique.

HYPNOTISM AND THE BIRTH OF PSYCHOANALYSIS

Although Mesmer was generally viewed by his contemporaries as a charlatan, the popularity of his procedure and his numerous apparent successes prompted an interest in the powers of suggestion. The Parisian neurologist Jean Charcot (1825–1893), in particular, came to believe that hypnotism might have value in treating hysterics and, accordingly, he revised his earlier somatogenic view to suggest that psychological factors caused hysteria. One of his students, Pierre Janet (1859–1947), elaborated this view into an account that claimed hysteria resulted from a break in the organized system of thought and emotion. Hysteria, in fact, became a focus of interest in itself, particularly among Viennese physicians. Josef Breuer (1842–1925) and his younger colleague Sigmund Freud (1856–1939) not only elaborated complex psychological conceptualizations of mental disorders (see Chapter 2 for an account of Freud's approach), but also developed specific treatment methods. Breuer's approach employed hypnosis in order to have the patient talk freely about, and relive, unpleasant past events that he believed caused the hysteria. He thought that vividly reliving these past experiences would somehow exhaust the emotional problems that resulted from them. Breuer called this treatment the *cathartic method*. Freud's approach was similar, although he also used procedures other than hypnosis, and his treatment came to be called *psychoanalysis*.

BEHAVIOURISM Another psychological approach to understanding abnormal behaviour emerged in the early part of the twentieth century. John B. Watson (1878–1958) produced a revolution in psychological thought (and, for that matter, in philosophical thought) with the publication in 1913 of a provocative article entitled "Psychology as the Behaviorist Views It." This, and subsequent work by Watson, established what became known as **behaviourism.** This viewpoint declared that if psychology were to become a science, it must be restricted to the study of observable features: namely, the behaviour of organisms. From this perspective, Watson considered abnormal functioning to be learned and, consequently, he believed it could be unlearned. His model for learning was derived from Ivan Pavlov's (1849–1936) studies of classical conditioning. All problematic functioning, Watson claimed, was the result of unfortunate conditioning experiences. Although this theory had a profound impact on thinking about mental disorders, it has not quite lived up to Watson's rather grand expectations. Nevertheless, behavioural approaches to the understanding and treatment of psychological disorders were reintroduced in the late 1950s and early 1960s and enjoyed considerable success and acceptance. In various forms, they have become established and empirically supported parts of the overall approach to dealing with mental disorders.

Throughout the twentieth century, conceptualizing and theorizing about abnormal behaviour have followed one of the paths initiated by the earlier thinkers outlined above. Somatogenic theories remain very popular and have enjoyed better success in the analysis of some problems than others, although it is fair to say that the research generated by such views has contributed to a better understanding of all mental disorders. Similarly, psychogenic theories (Freudian, behavioural, and numerous others) and the research their advocates have produced have expanded our knowledge and treatment of all disorders—although, again, psychological approaches have proven to be more valuable with some disorders than with others. The various models derived from these two views are the subject of the next chapter.

The Growth of Mental Health Services in Canada

The history of the development of proper places of care for individuals with mental disorders in Canada is well documented in a very detailed account by Hurd and colleagues (1916). It reveals a reluctance on the part of the various provinces (except for Quebec) to deal with the issue during the early days of settlement. The early British, and then provincial, leaders were content to place the insane in prisons along with criminals (Bartlett, 2000). Of course, they offered little or no treatment to these unfortunate citizens.

The Hôtel Dieu in Quebec was the first asylum anywhere in what would become Canada to house the mentally ill. This institution was founded by the Duchess d'Aiguillon, niece of the powerful Cardinal Richelieu, who was at that time First Minister of France and the effective ruler of the country. The Hôtel Dieu housed not only so-called idiots, who included patients suffering from all types of mental disabilities and dysfunctions, but also indigents and cripples. Similar hospitals were built in Quebec throughout the latter part of the seventeenth century. However, asylums were not established in other parts of Canada until the nineteenth century (Sussman, 1998).

The delay in establishing proper housing for the insane in places outside Quebec was not due simply to the fact that Quebec was the first area to be extensively settled. After all, the British were well entrenched in North America in the seventeenth century. The area that became known as Ontario was a British territory by the middle of the eighteenth century, and Upper Canada was officially constituted in 1791. Yet it was not until 1841 that a mental asylum in Toronto first took in patients (Wright, Moran, & Gouglas, 2003). This was followed shortly thereafter by the opening of the Rockwood asylum in Kingston, which was directed by Dr. J. P. Litchfield, an Australian who had at best minimal experience with the mentally ill. A tardy and rather careless approach, with little real concern for how these institutions were operated, characterized the early efforts of various provincial governments to provide care for the insane. In the latter part of the nineteenth century, the Dominion government began to pressure provinces to remove lunatics from their prisons; this became an order in 1884. Some provinces had already done so and others followed suit. Asylums were first established in the various provinces in the following years: New Brunswick, 1835; Prince Edward Island, 1847; Newfoundland, 1853; Nova Scotia, 1858; Manitoba, 1871; British Columbia, 1872; Alberta, 1907; and Saskatchewan, 1913. The first textbook printed in Canada dealing with the care and housing of the mentally ill was published in 1840 under the authorship of J. F. Lehman. Lehman's views were harsh and certainly did not reflect the approach referred to as moral therapy in other countries. He strongly advocated a regimen of severe discipline to rid the afflicted of their disorder, and he suggested that recalcitrant individuals should be flogged. Lehman deplored indulgence toward the insane, believing that it simply worsened their problems. Fortunately, his views did not receive popular support, although later treatments employed in Canada were equally harsh.

For example, psychosurgery was widely used in Canada from the mid-1940s until the mid- to late 1960s. During this time, tens of thousands of Canadians had **lobotomies** (surgical removal, or disconnection, of the frontal lobes of the brain) intended to relieve all manner of mental and emotional disorders (Simmons, 1987; Valenstein, 1986). Fortunately, in the early 1970s, legislation was enacted requiring review boards to be established in all mental hospitals with the responsibility to decide in each individual case whether psychosurgery was justified. Thereafter, psychosurgery was rarely done. According to Simmons (1987), archival evidence reveals that, prior to 1970, most of the early lobotomies were performed primarily to alleviate hospital management problems or to advance research rather than out of a concern to benefit the patient. It is also interesting to note (Simmons, 1987) that in Ontario during this period, the majority of lobotomies were performed on women (well over 60 percent of all psychosurgery patients were women). The same was true of mandatory sterilization in Alberta (Park & Radford, 1998).

By no means has all mental health care in Canada been reprehensible. As the reader will discern in subsequent chapters of this text, Canada has had its share of dedicated, helping professionals, including many on the cutting edge of research. For example, Dr. Ruth Kajander, who now practises in Thunder Bay, Ontario, was one of the first psychiatrists in North America to recognize the potential value of a major tranquilizer in the treatment of schizophrenia (Schuck, 1999). Dr. Kajander came to Canada from her native Finland in 1953 to train at Oshawa General Hospital. During her time there, she observed an anaesthesiologist using a recently introduced drug to prepare patients for surgery, and she recognized it as the same drug (chlorpromazine) that was used in Europe to reduce anxiety in patients prior to surgery. Later in the same year, when Kajander moved to the London Psychiatric Hospital as a resident psychiatrist, it occurred to her that chlorpromazine might be useful in the treatment of overactive schizophrenics in her care. Her ideas, apparently formed quite independently and without knowledge of the developments occurring in Europe at the same time, matched Laborit's similar steps in discovering the value of chlorpromazine. Kajander obtained permission from the hospital superintendent to run a trial with the drug on 25 patients over a period of several months. The results were very encouraging: the drug calmed the patients' restlessness, reduced their activity, allowed them to discuss their problems, and made them able to eat and sleep without the difficulties they had previously shown. Kajander's subsequent presentation of the results at the Ontario Neuropsychiatric Association's conference in late 1953 represents what appears to be the first scientific report of the use of chlorpromazine with psychiatric patients in North America. At about the same time, Heinz Lehmann began using it with his patients in Montreal. Kajander received an Order of Canada for her work in mental health care on May 26, 2011. Interestingly, she recently spoke out against an overreliance on psychopharmacological treatment, noting that many alternative therapies are being ignored in favour of drug treatment (Miner, 2009).

Over the years, many other Canadians have made significant contributions, in terms of both theory and new treatment approaches. Albert Bandura, who now lives and works in the United States but was raised in Canada, developed one of the most influential theories of human functioning to emerge in recent times. Social learning theory (see Chapter 2) was originally developed by Bandura and Richard Walters (who taught at the University of Waterloo in Ontario) to explain how aggressive behaviour is acquired as part of the learning process that occurs mostly in childhood (Bandura, 1973; Bandura & Walters, 1963). Bandura's analysis of aggression was so successful that he subsequently extended it to human behaviour in general (Bandura, 1973, 1977, 2000a, 2000b) and generated a variety of very effective treatment techniques for numerous disorders.

One of the most significant treatment developments of the 1970s was the extension of behavioural approaches to include the modification of cognitions (for example, thoughts, feelings, beliefs, and attitudes). This approach, which came to be called *cognitive-behaviour therapy* (CBT; see Chapter 17), was led by a handful of researchers; prominent among them was Canadian psychologist Donald Meichenbaum (2003). Meichenbaum's early work provided a significant impetus to the growth of cognitive-behaviour therapy (Meichenbaum, 1974), and his subsequent efforts have led to the development of very effective treatments for various problems, including impulsivity (Meichenbaum & Goodman, 1971); pain, anxiety, and anger (Meichenbaum, 2002; Meichenbaum & Turk, 1976); stress (Meichenbaum, 1985, 2007); and post-traumatic stress disorder (Meichenbaum, 1997). An important extension of CBT has involved mindfulness training, which was developed by Zindel Segal (Centre for Addiction and Mental Health, Toronto; see Chapter 8) and his colleagues as a strategy for preventing relapse in depression (Segal, Williams, & Teasdale, 2002; Williams, Teasdale, Segal, & Kabat-Zinn, 2007).

A number of other Canadian researchers who have made significant contributions will be mentioned throughout this book. Canadian scientists are at the forefront of developments in the mental health field and will remain so for the foreseeable future.

RECENT DEVELOPMENTS

Before proceeding to the next chapter, it is important to point out two additional developments pertaining to mental health services in Canada. In August 2007, Prime Minister Stephen Harper announced the establishment of the **Mental Health Commission of Canada (MHCC)**. This commission grew out of a report on the status of mental health in Canada called *Out of the Shadows at Last* (Kirby & Leon, 2006). The goal of the MHCC is to develop an integrated mental health system that encourages better co-operation among governments, mental health providers, employers, the scientific community, and Canadians who live with or care for those with mental disorders. Some specific goals of the MHCC are to

- be a catalyst for the reform of mental health policies and improvements in service delivery;
- act as a facilitator, enabler, and supporter of a national approach to mental health issues;
- work to diminish the stigma and discrimination faced by Canadians living with mental disorders; and
- disseminate evidence-based information on all aspects of mental health and mental illness to governments, stakeholders, and the public. (MHCC, 2011)

At a Collaboration for Change forum in Vancouver in April 2008, the Honourable Michael Kirby (chair of the

MHCC) spoke about the stigma associated with mental health problems:

> Half a century ago, a report on mental illness in Canada began with these words: "In no other field, except perhaps leprosy, has there been as much confusion, misdirection and discrimination against a patient as in mental illness . . . Down through the ages, they have been estranged by society and cast out to wander in the wilderness. Mental illness, even today, is all too often considered a crime to be punished, a sin to be expiated, a possessing demon to be exorcised, a disgrace to be hushed up, a personality weakness to be deplored or a welfare problem to be handled as cheaply as possible." Those words were written 50 years ago. In many ways they are still true today (Kirby, 2008).

The MHCC has announced that it will shift away from emphasizing the biological basis of mental disorders (i.e., the disease model) as a means of reducing mental disorder stigma. Although the disease model has shown some success in reducing stigmatization of mental disorders, it also has been shown to reduce the effort patients make toward their own recovery and to reduce patients' sense of efficacy in dealing with the symptoms of their disorder. The focus of the MHCC is now on promoting the ability of people with mental disorders to either recover from their symptoms or to live meaningful lives despite ongoing vulnerability or persisting symptoms (MHCC, 2009). Hopefully, the MHCC will be able to foster reduced stigma and better access to care for those individuals with mental health problems.

4 BEFORE MOVING ON

What stigma reduction programs have you been exposed to? Has the portrayal of people with mental disorders in these programs increased your expectations of their ability to recover from their disorders? How has the portrayal of mental health in the media affected your beliefs regarding people with mental disorders?

A second major development pertaining to mental health services in Canada is an increased focus on encouraging evidence-based practice (EBP) for psychologists, which was partly motivated by the introduction of evidence-based care in medicine. **Evidence-based practice (EBP)** refers to the integration of scientific evidence with individual expertise in order to inform optimum client care (American Psychological Association [APA] Presidential Task Force on Evidence-Based Practice, 2006). The purpose of EBP is to bolster the efficacious treatment of mental disorders, to maintain the competitiveness of psychologists in the mental health market, and to increase accountability and reduce liability. In practising EBP, psychologists could be expected to consider the use of treatments that research has shown to be effective. The promotion of EBP would therefore preclude psychologists from prescribing and administering treatments that are without a sound scientific basis and ensure that research findings are relevant to real-world environments.

In 2011 the Canadian Psychological Association initiated a task force on the evidence-based practice of psychological treatments. The purpose of this task force will be to operationalize what constitutes evidence-based practice in psychology, to make recommendations about how psychologists can best integrate evidence into practice, and to suggest strategies for dissemination. A significant gap exists between scientists and practitioners: we need more evidence-based practice and more practice-based evidence. Practitioners need to be competent consumers of research, and researchers need to ensure that their findings apply to real-world environments (Dozois, 2011).

5 BEFORE MOVING ON

Do you think it is important for psychologists to be trained in both research and practice?

SUMMARY

- According to the statistical view, abnormal behaviour can be determined by how frequently it occurs in the population.
- Personal distress can indicate the presence of abnormal behaviour.
- The personal dysfunction viewpoint emphasizes that abnormal behaviour interferes with appropriate functioning in a particular situation or environment.
- Abnormal behaviour could be defined in terms of whether it violates societal norms and values.
- Experts may determine what qualifies as abnormal behaviour.
- None of these principles is necessary or sufficient in defining abnormal behaviour; therefore, our definition of psychological disorders includes elements of all these principles.
- Evidence from prehistoric times suggests that supernatural explanations for psychological disorders may have been dominant.
- Greek and Roman philosophers and physicians held surprisingly modern views and emphasized biological and psychological causes and treatments of disorders.

- In the Arab world, treatment was humane and environmental and psychological factors were emphasized.
- During the Middle Ages, attributing supernatural causes to psychological disorders became more common again, although some individuals continued to explore other potential causes. Asylums were established around the 1500s, but treatment was often harsh and ineffective.
- During the Enlightenment, social and psychological factors became increasingly emphasized and treatments became more humane, although resources for caring for the mentally ill were still scarce.
- Abnormal behaviour may be caused by medical problems such as syphilis. These problems are normally treated pharmacologically and potential medical causes are often ruled out before diagnosing a mental disorder.
- Surgical procedures such as lobotomies were used to remove areas of the brain that were implicated in mental disorders.
- Electroconvulsive therapy employs electricity in order to induce a seizure in patients. This treatment has become much safer over the years and is still used for severe depression.
- Pharmacological treatments for psychological disorders usually target neurotransmitters and are currently a popular treatment method.
- Dr. Ruth Kajander was one of the first psychiatrists to use major tranquilizers to treat schizophrenia.
- Albert Bandura developed a theory of learning of aggressive behaviour in childhood and generated a number of treatment approaches emphasizing learning theory.
- Donald Meichenbaum played a key role in the development of cognitive-behavioural therapy, which is now used as a treatment for a variety of psychological disorders.
- The Mental Health Commission of Canada was established to improve access to mental health care and to reduce the stigma of mental illness. An emphasis on the potential for recovery is characteristic of the MHCC's approach to reducing stigma.
- Practitioners are now being encouraged to engage in evidence-based practice, i.e., to consider and integrate research evidence into their decisions regarding the best treatment for their clients.

MySearchLab offers you extensive help with your writing and research projects and provides round-the-clock access to credible and reliable source material. Chapter quizzes and a full electronic version of the text are also provided. Answers to the Before Moving On feature are provided on the MySearchLab. Take a tour at www.mysearchlab.com.

KEY TERMS

psychological abnormality (p. 4)
mental illness (p. 4)
psychological disorder (p. 4)
psychopathology (p. 4)
culturally relative (p. 6)
clinical psychologists (p. 6)
psychiatrists (p. 6)
psychiatric nurses (p. 6)
psychiatric social workers (p. 7)
occupational therapists (OTs) (p. 7)
supernatural causes (p. 8)
natural causes (p. 8)
trephination (p. 8)
humours (p. 9)
asylums (p. 10)
St. Vitus' dance (p. 12)
bedlam (p. 13)
moral therapy (p. 15)
mental hygiene movement (p. 15)
syndromes (p. 16)
general paresis of the insane (GPI) (p. 16)
somatogenesis (p. 16)
electroconvulsive therapy (ECT) (p. 17)
deinstitutionalization (p. 18)
behaviourism (p. 19)
lobotomies (p. 19)
Mental Health Commission of Canada (MHCC) (p. 20)
evidence-based practice (EBP) (p. 21)

DAVID J. A. DOZOIS • LYNDSAY E. EVRAIRE

Chapter 2

Theoretical Perspectives on Abnormal Behaviour

LEARNING OBJECTIVES

AFTER READING THIS CHAPTER, STUDENTS WILL BE ABLE TO:

1. View behaviour and thinking (disordered or not) as arising from the interaction between biological and environmental experiences.
2. Define neurotransmitters and describe the four ways in which they can influence abnormal behaviour, using examples.
3. Describe the role of the id, ego, and superego as personality structures and explain how they influence an individual's defence mechanisms.
4. Explain how classical and operant conditioning can influence an individual's behaviour and provide examples.
5. Define schemas and describe how they come to influence an individual's thoughts, beliefs, information processing, and behaviours.
6. Understand how close others (e.g., partners, friends, family) can influence the development and maintenance of mental health disorders through stigma or social support.
7. Identify how gender, race, and poverty influence mental health disorders.

Hailey suffered from major depressive disorder. Shortly after Hailey's birth, her mother experienced an episode of postpartum depression, and was often physically or psychologically unavailable to her daughter. As a result, Hailey learned that caregivers were often inconsistent when responding to her needs and feared that she would be abandoned. Her parents noted that, from a young age, Hailey was very reactive to stressful situations and overly responsive to changes in her environment.

When Hailey was 16, she began dating her first boyfriend. Although her boyfriend was supportive and would often tell her that he loved her, Hailey found herself constantly asking for reassurance of his affection because she feared that he would abandon her. Frustrated by her behaviour, Hailey's boyfriend eventually broke up with her.

Following the breakup Hailey began to experience low mood and started to withdraw from her friends, family, and participation in school. As a result, she lacked the necessary support from others to overcome her disorder and her low mood worsened. By the time she sought treatment a few months later, Hailey was having difficulty sleeping, had no appetite, had lost interest in things she used to enjoy doing, and lacked energy.

The General Nature of Theories

Chapter 1 traced the development of ideas about abnormal behaviour from the ancient Greeks to the present. Beginning in the early twentieth century, there have been two main streams of thought concerning mental disorders: one focusing on the biological aspects of disorders and the other focusing on environmental influences, roughly following the nature/nurture distinction that is made in so many areas of human functioning. Although a number of variations exist within each stream, biological approaches tend to dismiss or downplay the influence of experience, whereas psychological or environmental approaches tend to emphasize external factors (e.g., poverty, parenting style) in the development of disorders. Indeed, some behavioural theories (e.g., Skinner, 1953) attribute no effects at all to biology, assuming that, as British philosopher John Locke (1632–1704) put it, humans are born *tabula rasa* (a blank slate upon which experience writes all that is meaningful in thought and behaviour).

As we discuss in this chapter, biological and psychodynamic formulations view dysfunctional behaviour as the product of forces beyond the individual's control, whereas humanistic and existential approaches lay the responsibility for action and choices squarely on the shoulders of the individual. In contrast, behavioural and cognitive theories imply that a mixture of external and internal factors produce dysfunctions.

The perspective taken when examining the cause of psychopathology determines many things. It directs research, guides diagnostic decisions, and defines treatment responses. The acceptance of the biological model, for example, encourages researchers to seek a physical basis for disorders, leads to the formulation of a diagnostic system that classifies people as disordered, and implies that physical interventions should be the treatments of choice. The behavioural perspective, on the other hand, leads researchers to seek environmental events that shape specific dysfunctional responses and emphasizes the classification of behaviours rather than of people. From the behavioural perspective, treatment involves either manipulating the environment or (for those who adopt a cognitive-behavioural perspective) modifying the perceptions people have regarding their experiences and themselves.

As an example of how different perspectives would shed light on a disorder, let's look at what might have caused Hailey's depression. Biological and psychodynamic formulations view dysfunctional behaviour as the product of forces beyond the individual's control. In Hailey's case, a biologically oriented theorist would point out the fact that Hailey's mother also suffered from depression, supporting a genetic basis for Hailey's problem. Hailey was also very reactive to her environment as a child, suggesting an innate predisposition to higher stress reactivity, which is often associated with a risk for developing depression. A Freudian, or psychodynamic theorist, would want to examine Hailey's childhood relationships with her mother. Behavioural and cognitive theories, on the other hand, suggest that a mixture of internal and external factors produce dysfunction. For example, in Hailey's case, a behaviourist would examine Hailey's reassurance seeking and her withdrawal behaviours resulting from her depression. A cognitive theorist would examine how Hailey's schemas or beliefs (her fear of abandonment), automatic thoughts, and the way she processes information influence her disorder. Humanistic and existential approaches lay the responsibility for action and choices on the individual suffering from the disorder. These two approaches would focus on Hailey's personal decisions, level of acceptance, and perceptions of her experience with depression. A socio-cultural formulation would examine factors such as whether or not Hailey has good social supports to help her handle her disorder, how being female influences her depression, or how being labelled as being depressed affects her life. Someone who took an integrative perspective would look at the dynamic and reciprocal relationships among all these factors.

In the rest of this chapter, we will look more closely at these various theoretical approaches. In fact, throughout this book we will see confirmation of the theme illustrated by Hailey's case: that the origins of psychological disorders are complex, with no one factor providing a complete explanation.

Interestingly, the adoption of a perspective is influenced far less by the weight of evidence than by the prevailing social belief system and by an individual's disposition to see human behaviour as determined by factors beyond or within the control of the individual. Indeed, theorists often stubbornly hold on to a view in spite of evidence to the contrary. This tenacious clinging to a specific theory is not necessarily a bad thing, since it allows that theory to be fully explored. A theory is useful not so much because it is true, but because it generates research that leads to an increase in knowledge. A theory should be abandoned only when there is a better one available (that is, one that does a better job of integrating current knowledge and that generates more research). Thus, the scientific theories of the past should be judged not by how well they match current information, but rather by how much new information they generated.

LEVELS OF THEORIES

To state that a genetic defect or a single traumatic experience causes a mental disorder is to accept a **single-factor explanation**, which attempts to trace the origins of a particular disorder to one factor. For example, a single-factor explanation of social anxiety may be that it runs in families. It is important to point out that most single-factor models reflect the primary focus of the researcher, theorist, or clinician rather than the belief that there really is a single cause. For instance, a cognitive therapist would emphasize the modification of negative automatic thoughts and core beliefs in the treatment of depression. However, this therapist would not ignore or discount other contributing causes and might, in fact, suggest that a patient receive a trial of antidepressant medications as a useful complement to cognitive therapy. However, human behaviour, in all its complexity, is unlikely to be the product of a single defect or experience. **Interactionist explanations**, which view behaviour as the product of the interaction of a variety of factors, generally make more satisfactory theories in describing mental disorders. As knowledge of any single disorder increases, so, characteristically, does the complexity of theories offered to account for its development and maintenance. Single-factor theories, then, often simply reflect the lack of current comprehensive knowledge of disorders. Interactionist explanations take into account the biology and behaviour of the individual, as well as the cognitive, social, and cultural environment, given that any one component inevitably affects the other components.

Theories may also be classified according to their level of explanation (Marshall, 1982; Mash & Dozois, 2003). Some theories try to explain all human behaviour (for example, Maslow's [1954] theory of self-actualization), some try to explain all abnormal behaviour (for example, Freud, 1917/1971), and others try to account for all disorders within a particular category, such as all types of personality disorders (e.g., Millon & Davis, 2000). Even more specifically, there are theories that endeavour to reveal the causes of a particular problem such as panic disorder (for example, McNally, 2002). Finally, there are theories that attempt to elucidate the influence of a single factor within a more general theory. For example, our own work has tested the organization of the self-schema within the broader context of cognitive vulnerability to depression (Dozois, 2007; Dozois & Dobson, 2001a, 2001b; Evraire & Dozois, 2012; Seeds & Dozois, 2010).

Single-factor theories, however, should not be considered valueless simply because they may later be discarded for more complex explanations. The history of science is replete with the rejection of theories that at one time were broadly accepted and seemed to explain phenomena. To expand on an earlier point, scientific theories are judged to be valuable not because they describe the enduring truth about an issue, but rather because they embody three essential features:

1. they integrate most of what is currently known about the phenomena in the simplest way possible (parsimony);
2. they make testable predictions about aspects of the phenomena that were not previously thought of; and
3. they make it possible to specify what evidence would deny the theory.

TESTING THEORIES: THE NULL HYPOTHESIS

Theories are replaced in science not because the evidence against them is significant (although that is a good reason to search for alternatives), but rather because another theory comes along that is open to being disproved and that does a better job of integrating knowledge and generating novel predictions.

This latter notion often puzzles students; however, it is the cornerstone of science. Experiments are *not set up to prove the worth of a theory* but rather *to reject (or fail to reject)* what is called the null hypothesis. The **null hypothesis** essentially proposes that the prediction made from the theory is false. Let us look at a simple example. Suppose we claim that low self-esteem causes and maintains depression. A prediction from this claim would be that patients suffering from depression should have lower self-esteem than do non-depressed patients. If we compare these two groups of patients and find that the depressed group scores significantly lower than does the non-depressed group, we may have offered some support for the theory, but we have not proved it to be true: some other, as yet unknown, factor may produce both depression and low self-esteem. However, these results allow us to reject the null hypothesis, which, in this case, says there are no differences in self-esteem between the depressed and non-depressed groups. This at least eliminates an alternative possible theory; namely, that low self-esteem is characteristic of all people regardless of whether or not they are suffering from depression.

Theories gain strength not just because the evidence supports their predictions, but primarily because alternative explanations are rejected. Despite popular belief to the contrary, scientists do not set out to prove their theories to be true and, in fact, no amount of evidence can ever prove the truth of a theory. Theories are not facts, they are simply the best approximation we have at any moment, so that current theories are almost inevitably going to be replaced as knowledge accumulates. It is the very process of trying to prove our theories wrong that generates the new knowledge that will one day lead to their rejection.

Some accounts of abnormal behaviour, or indeed of psychological functioning more generally, do not in fact meet the criteria of scientific theories because they are essentially immune to disproof. For example, many critics have maintained that the theories of Sigmund Freud are not open to disproof.

The Search for Causes

The general aims of theories about mental disorders are to: (1) explain the **etiology** (that is, the causes or origins) of the problem behaviour; (2) identify the factors that maintain the behaviour; (3) predict the course of the disorder; and (4) design effective treatments. Of course, theories of abnormal behaviour are chosen presumably because they fit with theorists' more general sentiments about human nature. Some people feel uncomfortable attributing causes of behaviour to factors over which a person has little or no control (for example, biological causes or unconscious processes). Such theorists are likely to be attracted to accounts of human dysfunction that attribute causation to environmental influences. These theorists are, therefore, optimistic about the potential for environmental manipulations to produce behaviour change. Other people are more attracted to biological explanations because they hold similar hopes for effective medical treatment.

It is important to note that factors involved in the etiology of a problem may not be relevant to its maintenance. For example, as was the case with Hailey, an individual may become depressed as a result of the termination of a significant relationship (e.g., the end of an intimate relationship or death of a family member). However, once depressed, the individual may withdraw from others or frustrate close others by continuously trying to gain acceptance and approval, leading to an environment of social isolation in which the individual with depression cannot receive the necessary support to overcome his or her disorder (Evraire & Dozois, 2011). Similarly, the factors that determine the course of a disorder may have more to do with the lifestyle of the sufferer than with the factors that caused the disorder in the first place. For example, a frightening experience with a dog may cause a person to become phobic. However, subsequent careful avoidance of all dogs will maintain the disorder in some individuals, whereas others may force themselves to interact with the animals and thereby overcome their irrational fears.

Even in disorders where there is a clear biological cause, environmental manipulations may alleviate or even prevent the development of the most serious symptoms. For example, phenylketonuria (PKU) is an inborn metabolic defect that causes the body to be unable to metabolize phenylalanine, a substance present in many foods. This metabolic problem is genetically transmitted as a recessive autosomal trait, meaning that both parents must have the gene that carries the disorder for the child to develop PKU. Untreated PKU will markedly raise blood levels of phenylalanine, resulting in a decrease in various neurotransmitters in the brain, thereby producing severe mental retardation, microencephalopathy, seizures, and other behavioural disturbances (Hellekson, 2001). However, when PKU is detected in newborns (screening tests for PKU are now routine) the infant is given a diet low in phenylalanine, and most of the disastrous consequences are avoided, allowing the child to live a relatively normal life.

Along these lines, a modified version of Aaron T. Beck's cognitive formulation of depression and anxiety (discussed later in this chapter) has been proposed to describe how cognitive therapy (CT) can not only alter an individual's cognitive processes in order to reduce symptoms of depression or anxiety, but also affect his or her neurobiology (Clark & Beck, 2010a). In this model, depressive and anxious symptoms result from the activation of negative schemas, or core beliefs, and negative emotions, which are associated with increased activation in the amygdalohippocampal subcortical region of the brain. Depression and anxiety are also associated with restricted access to reflective processes or cognitive control (e.g., the control of negative emotion) associated with the anterior cingulated cortex (ACC), medial and lateral prefrontal cortex (PFC), and orbitofrontal cortex. Cognitive therapy directly seeks to reduce symptoms by modifying maladaptive thoughts, attitudes, and beliefs, as well as information processing biases. However, the literature has recently demonstrated that CT is also associated with reduced activation of the amygdalohippocampal subcortical region along with increased activation of the brain regions listed above involved in the cognitive control of negative emotion (Gotlib & Joormann, 2010). Thus, the proposed model of Clark and Beck (2010a) is evidence that external factors such as CT can affect biological functioning quite dramatically (see also Frewen, Dozois, & Lanius, 2008); no doubt the converse is also true.

Many different theories have been advanced regarding the etiology of mental disorders. We limit ourselves here to a description of the most popular, grouped by the primary proposed cause: (1) biological; (2) psychodynamic (derived from the theories of Freud or his followers); (3) behavioural or cognitive-behavioural theories; (4) cognitive theories examining dysfunctional thoughts or beliefs; (5) humanistic or existential theories that examine interpersonal processes; and (6) socio-cultural influences. Of course, it is reasonable to assume that these various influences interact to produce mental disorders. Even within each of these models, various causes are seen as primary by one or another theorist. For example, within the biological category, some theories emphasize abnormal brain functioning, whereas others place the site of the problem in the autonomic nervous system, in genetic endowment, or in a dysfunctional endocrine system.

Strict biological determinism all too often leads to the dismal conclusion that psychological or environmental interventions will do no good. When it comes to criminal behaviour, such arguments appeal to many people who wish simply to punish offenders while ignoring the possible social factors related to a higher incidence of crime (for example, unemployment, poverty, and overcrowding). Similarly, well-intentioned clinicians may assume that disorders that are difficult to treat are completely biological. For instance, schizophrenia has traditionally been viewed as predominantly biologically based. However, recent studies suggest that cognitive therapy and other psychosocial interventions are effective supplements to antipsychotic medication (e.g., Beck, Rector, Stolar, & Grant, 2009; Grant, Huh, Perivoliotis, Stolar, & Beck, 2011; Turkington & Morrison, in press) and are now recommended aspects of routine care.

Frequently, cultural or environmental determinists feel obliged to deny the influence of biological disadvantages. However, no amount of devoted training, expert guidance, or determination would ever make a person who is 1.5 metres tall into a world-class high jumper. Lifestyle and education may ease the life of someone who inherits the defective gene that causes Huntington's disease but will not prevent the development of dementia, jerky body movements, depression, and psychosis.

In fact, all of these systems (that is, biological, behavioural, etc.) work in concert and it is almost impossible (if not meaningless) to disentangle their influence. Dividing this interrelated system of theories into its presumed components all too often has the effect of convincing some theorists that one or another aspect is causally more important than all other features. This type of thinking, which may attribute primary causation to biological problems (biological determinism), or to socio-cultural or environmental influences (cultural or environmental determinism), is a form of reductionism, in that the actions of the whole are said to be caused by (that is, reduced to the influence of) one or other of the component parts. This is akin to saying that body temperature is entirely determined by our internal thermal regulatory system, or alternatively by our external environment, when, of course, it is a product of the dynamic interaction of the two, each of which is complexly determined. Reductionist thinking ignores the rather obvious possibility that human behaviour in all its forms is a product of an array of features (biological, developmental, environmental, personal choice, cultural, etc.) interacting. Being able to run a marathon in world-record time requires not only a biologically appropriate body, but also a devoted training schedule and the right footwear (environmental features), and a culture that allows or encourages such long-distance running (cultural or social influences). Why, for example, is there a seemingly endless supply of great marathon athletes from Kenya and Ethiopia? Is it because of the genetic constitution of people from these countries, or because they live at high elevations that promote maximum oxygen use by their bodies, or simply because they grow up in a culture that requires them to run many miles from a young age? More likely, it is the interaction of all these factors, and perhaps others as well.

To understand the various theoretical approaches to abnormal behaviour, we will have to consider them separately, as that is the way they have always been described. This separation, however, should not be taken to mean that we agree with any one model that assumes the prior causal control of behaviour. We view behaviour and thinking (whether normal or disordered) as arising from the integrated dynamic and essentially inseparable interactions between multiple biological and environmental experiences.

1 BEFORE MOVING ON

Pharmaceutical advertisements and other media often portray the message that psychological problems are caused by chemical imbalances. How convinced are you that this is true? What are the advantages and disadvantages of adopting this belief?

Biological Models

Biological theorists of human behaviour typically not only borrow their model from medicine, but also co-opt the language of medicine, calling clients "patients" and their problems "symptoms" or "syndromes," and describing the response to these problems as "treatment." Thus, adopting a biological model has implications for the way in which people with problems are treated. The same, of course, is true for all theoretical perspectives, and it is necessary to consider the ramifications of these, often unnoticed, implications when deciding on a particular point of view about abnormal behaviour. A model may be appealing because it fits with current thinking, but it also may have less obvious features that are not so attractive.

To appreciate the meaning of the various biological explanations of disordered behaviour or thinking, it is necessary to have some understanding of relevant aspects of bodily functioning. Biological theories have primarily implicated dysfunctions in or damage to the brain (the central nervous system, or CNS), problems of control of one or another aspect of the peripheral nervous system (that is, the autonomic nervous system or the somatic nervous system), or malfunctioning of the endocrine system.

For purposes of exposition, the nervous system is divided into the CNS and the peripheral nervous system, although in normal functioning the activities of these two complex systems are integrated, and their actions are further coordinated with activity in the endocrine system.

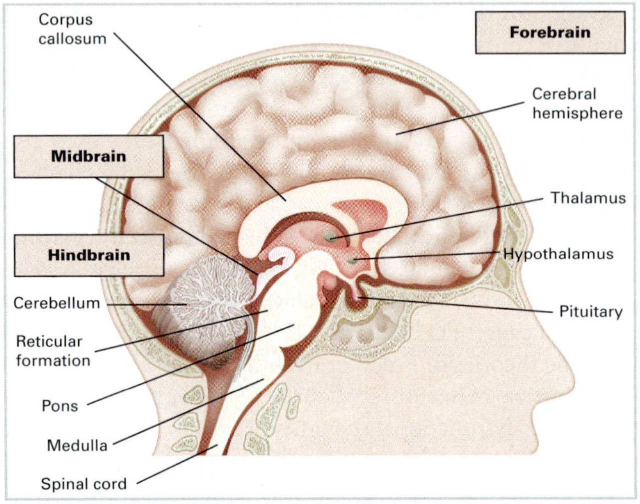

FIGURE 2.1 The Human Brain (Side View)

Source: Baron, *PSYCHOLOGY*, © 1992. Reproduced by permission of Pearson Education, Inc.

THE ROLE OF THE CENTRAL NERVOUS SYSTEM

The brain is estimated (Kolb, Gibb, & Robinson, 2003) to have some 100 billion neurons (that is, nerve cells) and thousands of billions of glia cells (presumed to be support cells, although recent evidence suggests that they exert a more active role in neuronal functioning). These cells group together into anatomically distinct areas, which appear to have somewhat distinctive functions, although active interconnections throughout the brain indicate that no one area exclusively performs any one function. It is perhaps better to think of brain activity related to particular functions or actions not as *located* in a single area of the brain but as *concentrated* in one or more areas.

Figure 2.1 depicts the anatomical areas of the brain. The hindbrain primarily directs the functioning of the autonomic nervous system, which in turn controls primarily internal activities such as digestion, cardiovascular functioning, and breathing. The midbrain is the centre of the reticular activating system, which controls arousal levels (often called the sleep–wake centre) and thereby attentional processes.

The forebrain controls thought, speech, perception, memory, learning, and planning—indeed, all the processes that make us sentient, self-conscious beings. Obviously, damage to any of these parts of the brain will cause proportionate dysfunction in many areas, including psychological functioning.

Some disorders have been shown to be directly linked to brain damage. Dementia (a deterioration in all cognitive processes, particularly memory and learning) that occurs in disorders such as Parkinson's or Alzheimer's is linked to the loss or ineffective functioning of brain cells. These losses of brain cell functioning can be transitory, but in many cases they are irreversible and may result from various sources such as direct head injuries, diseases, or toxins. Sophisticated methods are now available for detecting even quite small areas of damage or dysfunction in the brain. Various imaging techniques, such as computerized axial tomography (CAT scans), magnetic resonance imaging (MRI), and positron emission tomography (PET scans), have all enabled the detailed, although expensive, examination of brain functioning. However, current theories about the brain bases of abnormal behaviour have given more weight to the role of neurotransmitters than to actual neuronal damage.

Neurotransmitters are the chemical substances that carry the messages from one neuron to the next in the complex pathways of nervous activity within the brain. Nerve cells are not connected to one another, so activity in one neuron does not directly stimulate activity in other neurons. There is a gap (called a synapse or synaptic cleft) between the axons (which carry the nerve impulse to the synapse) of one neuron and the dendrites (which pick up the activity from the first neuron) of neighbouring neurons. The transmission of the electrical activity in the axon to the neighbouring dendrites occurs as a result of the release of chemicals called neurotransmitters (see Focus box 2.1). There are numerous neurotransmitters, but to date the majority of research attention has been given to the role of dopamine, serotonin, norepinephrine, and, more recently, gamma aminobutyric acid (or GABA). These neurotransmitters act either on their own, or more likely in concert with others, in the spread of nerve impulses throughout the brain. Different types seem to be concentrated in different areas of the brain and, therefore, are thought to play a role in different functions. For example, pleasure-seeking and exploratory behaviours seem to be associated with dopamine activity, whereas serotonin activity appears to be related to the constraint or inhibition of behaviour; these two neurotransmitters, then, seem to act to create a balance in behaviour (Depue, 1999).

FOCUS 2.1

Neurotransmission

Nerve impulses are electrochemical discharges that are received by the dendrites of one neuron, thereby activating (or inhibiting) that neuron, and then travel down the axons of that neuron to activate (or inhibit) the electrochemical activity in the dendrites of another neuron. At the point of contact between the axon of the neuron propagating the nerve impulse (called the presynaptic neuron) and the dendrite of the receiving neuron (called the post-synaptic neuron) is the synapse. This is a minute space through which strictly chemical messengers (neurotransmitters) pass from the axon terminals to the receiving dendrites, where they either activate or inhibit electrochemically generated impulses.

The neurotransmitters (of which there are several kinds, all serving apparently different activating or inhibiting functions) are held in vesicles within the axon terminals. When these vesicles are stimulated by the neural impulse, which travels down the axon, they move to the releasing site and emit the neurotransmitters into the synapse. Some of the released transmitters are reabsorbed (a process called reuptake) by the axon, some are deactivated by substances in the synapse, and the remainder are taken up at receptor sites on the dendrites of the post-synaptic neuron. These receptor sites are highly specialized and can take up only transmitters whose structure exactly fits into the structure of the receptor so that each receptor can absorb only particular neurotransmitters. This makes it possible to create drugs whose chemical structure is an exact match for particular transmitters, so that when they are released into the synapse these drugs block the action of the transmitters by taking their place in the receptors. Other drugs can be made to accelerate or inhibit the action of the deactivators, again specifically affecting particular neurotransmitters, or they can stimulate or reduce the release of particular neurotransmitters.

Anatomy of a Neuron

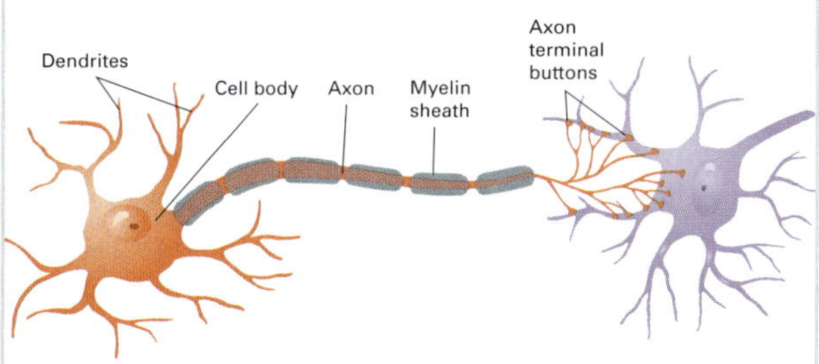

Transmission of Neural Impulses across the Synapse

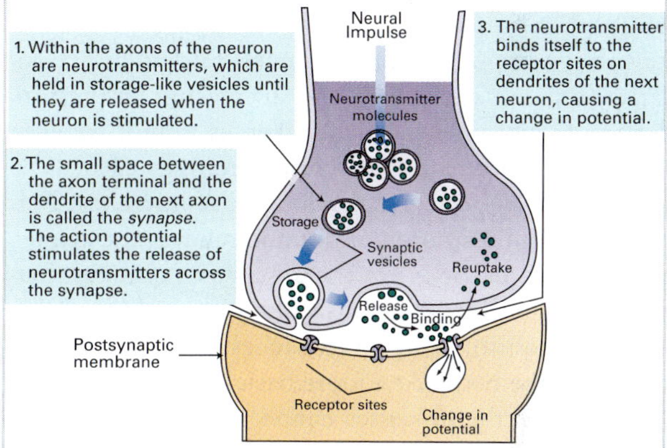

Source: Baron, *PSYCHOLOGY*, © 1992. Reproduced by permission of Pearson Education, Inc.

Certain neurons seem to be more sensitive to one or another type of neurotransmitter, and these neurons seem to cluster together, forming particular brain circuits. There appear to be as many as tens of thousands of such pathways or brain circuits that overlap one another, although they may finally separate into specific pathways (Dean, Kelsey, Heller, & Ciaranello, 1993).

When neurotransmitters are released into the synapse, some will be taken up at the receptor sites on the dendrites and thereby activate or inhibit (depending upon the action of the transmitter) an impulse in the post-synaptic neuron. However, within the synaptic cleft are substances that deactivate neurotransmitters, so some of the released transmitters will be destroyed before they can act on the dendrites. Furthermore, many of the released neurotransmitters are quickly drawn back into the releasing axon by a process called reuptake. Thus, abnormal behaviour can result from disturbances in neurotransmitter systems in various ways: (1) there may be too much or too little of the neurotransmitter produced or released into the synapse; (2) there may be too few or too many receptors on the dendrites; (3) there may be an excess or a deficit in the amount of the transmitter-deactivating substance in the synapse; or (4) the reuptake process may be too rapid or too slow. Any or all of these problems can cause either too much excitation or too much inhibition in the particular brain circuits, and this excessive or reduced activity may result in abnormal functioning. Schizophrenia, for example, is thought by some theorists to result from too much activity in the brain circuits (the dopamine system) that mediate the importance we attach to stimuli in our environment so that the patient experiences his or her world as overwhelming; everything seems important and relevant. However, most researchers now believe that brain functioning is much more complex than this. Disturbances in neurotransmitter systems are currently thought more likely to have general rather than specific effects, and it is the interaction of various neurotransmitters and their subtypes that is related to behaviour (Cummings & Mega, 2003; LeDoux, 2003). Even within particular neurotransmitters the picture is more complex than previously supposed. Researchers have now determined, for instance, that there are at least 14 distinct subtypes of serotonin receptors and 5 different dopamine receptors (Kaplan & Sadock, 1998). This diversity has triggered new research that examines the relationships between these receptor subtypes and psychopathology and the design of subtype-specific medications. At present, research seems more concentrated on detecting the role that neurotransmitter pathways play in specific disorders, particularly in the interaction between various pathways.

The logic involved in inferring a causal relationship between disturbances in neurotransmitter functioning and abnormal behaviour depends to some extent on the methods used in examining this claim. For example, it is now known (with reasonable certainty) that drugs that ameliorate the symptoms of schizophrenia exert their action primarily (but not exclusively) by decreasing activity in the dopaminergic system. This is taken as supportive evidence for the hypothesis that schizophrenia is caused by excessive dopamine, but this may be a false inference. For example, the administration of quinine relieves the symptoms of malaria, but it is not the absence of quinine that causes malaria; rather, malaria is caused by the bite of the *Anopheles* mosquito, which introduces the *Plasmodium* protozoa into the body. At a more basic level, it is important to note that the processes connecting behaviour and the neurochemical bases of brain activity do not represent a one-way street. No doubt neurotransmitter activity affects behaviour, but behaviour also affects neurotransmitter activity. Dr. Bryan Kolb, a distinguished neurophysiologist at the University of Lethbridge in Alberta, reviewed the incredible capacity of the brain to reorganize its circuitry—what is called **brain plasticity**. Brain plasticity can be influenced by a number of experiences that occur pre- and postnatally through hormones, diet, aging, stress, disease, and maturation (for a review see Kolb & Teskey, 2011). In one experiment, the offspring of rats that were raised in a complex environment exhibited increased synaptic space on the neurons in their cerebral cortex. Kolb, Gibb, and Robinson (2003) argue that "virtually any manipulation that produces an enduring change in behavior leaves an anatomical footprint in the brain" (p. 3). At present, it remains a possibility, although not one supported by many theorists, that environmental events cause schizophrenia and that the behavioural response to these events results in increased activity in neurotransmitter systems. Much more likely is the possibility that environmental events, the person's response to them, and biological substrates all play a part in causing abnormal functioning.

2 BEFORE MOVING ON

> Antidepressants take several weeks to take effect and decrease symptoms of depression. Explain why this might be the case considering what you know about how neurotransmitters influence abnormal behaviour.

THE ROLE OF THE PERIPHERAL NERVOUS SYSTEM

The peripheral nervous system includes the *somatic nervous system*, which controls the muscles, and the *autonomic nervous system (ANS)*. The ANS has two parts: the sympathetic nervous system and the parasympathetic nervous system (see Figure 2.2). These two systems typically function co-operatively to produce homeostatic (that is, balanced) activity in a variety of bodily functions such as heart rate, digestive and eliminatory processes, sexual arousal, breathing, perspiration, et cetera. In times of stress, however, they function antagonistically. During stress, or when a person feels threatened, the sympathetic nervous system readies the body for action (fight or flight) by, for example, increasing heart rate, pupil size (making vision more acute), and breathing (which becomes faster and deeper to take in more oxygen). At the same time, the parasympathetic nervous system shuts down digestive processes, since energy given to this function would be wasted in a time of emergency.

Since humans display variability in all other response systems, it would not be surprising to find that, in some people, the ANS response to stress or threat is either exaggeratedly strong or remarkably weak. Canadian physician Hans Selye studied responses to stress, beginning in 1936 and continuing until his death in 1983. Selye's work established the area of study now known as *stress physiology*. It has become clear that individuals differ in both the strength and the duration of their response to threat, and this variability has been related to the person's propensity to develop psychophysiological disorders (Friedman & Booth-Kewley, 1987). The ANS (more particularly, the sympathetic nervous system) is involved in fear and anxiety reactions. Thus, an overreactive ANS may increase readiness to acquire phobias or other anxiety disorders. For example, it is assumed by some behavioural therapists that conditioning processes are the basis for acquiring anxiety disorders. The strength of an individual's ANS response to a "frightening experience" may determine whether he or she acquires a conditioned phobic reaction, and it has been found that there is a heritable component to the level of emotionality (Barlow, 2002). Such differences in responsivity may explain why one person exposed to a traumatic experience develops a severe and enduring conditioned emotional response while another person exposed to exactly the same experience does not.

Individual differences in the *regulation* of various ANS and somatic nervous system functions may also play a part in disordered behaviour. For example, patients

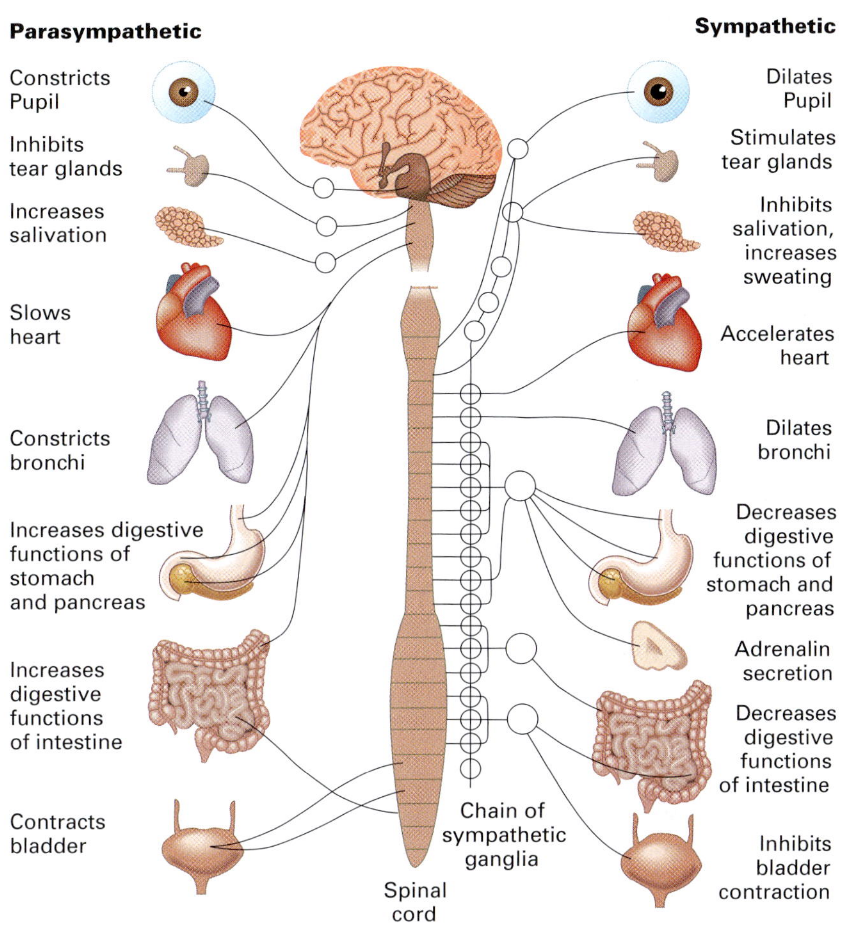

FIGURE 2.2 The Sympathetic and Parasympathetic Divisions of the Autonomic Nervous System

Source: Baron, *PSYCHOLOGY*, © 1992. Reproduced by permission of Pearson Education, Inc.

diagnosed with generalized anxiety disorder (GAD) tend to show decreased parasympathetic regulation of changes in heart rate and respiration when compared to non-anxious individuals. Moreover, worry, the hallmark feature of GAD, is also associated with decreased parasympathetic regulation (Thayer, Friedman, & Borkovec, 1996). These same patients display chronic muscle tension, which is under the control of the somatic nervous system (Barlow, 2002). In other words, it appears that autonomic and somatic *inflexibility* may be particularly important to GAD. Behaviourally, this inflexibility is seen in the chronic worry exhibited by individuals with GAD: they display cognitive inflexibility in that they are unable to stop or control their worries (Thayer & Friedman, 2002). Furthermore, this type of repetitive thought, or rumination, has been demonstrated to specifically predict later symptoms of GAD, but not depression, in male and female undergraduate students (Calmes & Roberts, 2007).

THE ROLE OF THE ENDOCRINE SYSTEM

Aspects of the CNS interact with the endocrine system in a feedback loop that maintains appropriate levels of hormones circulating in the bloodstream. Hormones are chemical messengers that are secreted by various glands. These secretions maintain adequate bodily functioning and play an important role in the development of the organism; they also appear to be involved in the activation of some behaviours.

The relationship of the endocrine glands both to each other and to the CNS is complex. For example, in response to feedback indicating that the circulating levels of sex hormones (or sex steroids) are low, the CNS activates the hypothalamus (a small CNS structure located in the lower central part of the forebrain), which secretes what are called "releasing" hormones that, in turn, activate the pituitary gland. Increased levels of circulating sex steroids alert the hypothalamus and pituitary to shut down this activity. The hormones secreted by the pituitary influence hormonal production in the adrenal gland and the testes (in males) and the ovaries (in females). The pituitary (which is often called the "master gland" because it plays such a controlling role in activating the other endocrine glands) releases many different hormones, some of which, as we have seen, activate other glands while others have a more direct action. Growth hormone promotes and regulates muscle, bone, and other tissue growth; prolactin stimulates milk production in women; and adrenocorticotrophic hormone helps the body handle stress. Obviously, the endocrine system has many and complex effects on behaviour.

Two disorders are known to be related to malfunctioning endocrine glands. Cretinism, a disorder involving a dwarflike appearance and mental retardation, is a result of a defective thyroid gland. Hypoglycemia, which results from the pancreas failing to produce balanced levels of insulin or glycogen, produces experiences that mimic anxiety, and some patients who report to anxiety disorder clinics are in fact suffering from hypoglycemia. Similarly, thyroid dysregulation has been associated with a variety of psychiatric symptoms including anxiety and depression (Beckwith, 2001).

One system that has also been studied extensively with regard to depression and anxiety is the hypothalamic-pituitary-adrenal (HPA) axis (see Chapter 7). The HPA axis is activated in response to stressors and involves an intricate system of communication between the hypothalamus, the pituitary gland, and the adrenal cortex. An important action of the HPA axis involves the release of the stress hormone cortisol into the bloodstream by the adrenal cortex. This hormone facilitates an individual's response to short-term threat by producing a number of changes in the body. For example, it causes an increase in intracellular glucocorticoid receptors, which leads to anti-inflammatory effects and other survival benefits. Sensitivity to stress (as in the case of Hailey at the beginning of the chapter) has been strongly implicated in the etiology of major depression and anxiety disorders (Heim & Nemeroff, 2001; McFarlane, Bellissimo, Norman, & Lange, 2005). Consistent with this idea, the HPA axis is chronically activated in many individuals diagnosed with major depression, as well as in some individuals with anxiety disorders (Barden, 2004; Risbrough & Stein, 2006; Shea, Walsh, MacMillan, & Steiner, 2005).

GENETICS AND BEHAVIOUR

The idea that human behaviour is inherited has a long history. This idea is part of the more general concept of biological determinism: that what a person is is determined largely by inherited characteristics. Thomas Hobbes, a seventeenth-century English philosopher, thought that aggression and self-interest were inborn features of all humans and that it was the business of political systems to restrain and usefully channel these impulses. By the nineteenth century, it was widely believed that all people took their biologically allotted place in society (that is, the destitute were condemned by their inherited characteristics to be poor, whereas the wealthy and the aristocracy were simply displaying their hereditary advantages). Cesare Lombroso (1836–1909) declared that criminals could be identified by the physiological features they had inherited from their degenerate parents. The eminent neuroanatomist Paul Broca (1824–1880) claimed that males were born with brains superior to those of females. Similar claims were made with respect to racial differences—with Europeans being seen as the supreme race. Some of these hereditary arguments about the superiority of one race (that is, whites) over another (that is, blacks) live on in the writings of Herrnstein and Murray (1994), Arthur Jensen (1997), and Philippe Rushton (2002) about presumed IQ differences.

It is good to keep in mind that claims about the inheritance of defective features can easily be used by those who would treat these individuals in a prejudicial manner. Those students who wish to read further on the controversies surrounding inherited differences between races in IQ may consult Fish (2002).

While these criticisms should make us cautious, they should not blind us to the possibility of genetic contributions to psychological disorders. Rejecting the idea that genes completely determine behaviour does not require us to accept that society, culture, or personal experience wholly account for human thought and action. It seems more reasonable to expect that most, if not all, behaviours are the product of an interaction between these sources of influence. **Behavioural genetics** offer us an insight into the biological bases of abnormal functioning. In the case of psychopathology, however, "genes confer a liability not a certainty" (Wallace, Schneider, & McGuffin, 2002, p. 179). Unfortunately, most researchers make little more than a token effort to spell out the way in which inherited features interact with the environment to produce behaviour. More recent research, however, has emphasized the **genotype–environment interaction** (Kendler & Prescott, 2006). It appears as though genes may influence behaviours that contribute to environmental stressors, which, in turn, increase the risk of psychopathology. This type of reciprocal relationship between genetic predisposition and environmental risk factors has been found in both animal models and human studies (Lesch, 2004). In one study, Caspi and colleagues (2003) examined the interactive effects of a genotype associated with depression and stressful life events (SLEs). The genotype of interest in their study was a gene that influences the transmission of serotonin (a neurotransmitter implicated in depression and other disorders) in the brain. This gene that Caspi et al. were studying comes in two different versions or alleles: the long allele (L) and the short allele (S). Prior work with animals suggested that individuals with at least two copies of the long allele (LL) would better cope. All participants in the study reported experiencing SLEs, but the relationship between SLEs and depression was much stronger among adults who also had two S alleles. For example, people with two copies of the S allele were twice as likely to experience a major depressive episode if they had at least four SLEs, compared with people who experienced the same amount of stress but had two L alleles. Importantly, there was no direct link between the genotype and depression. In other words, adults with two S alleles developed depression only if they also experienced SLEs. Similarly, recent research has demonstrated that adolescents who use cannabis are more likely to develop schizophreniform disorder as adults if they also have a particular variant of a gene associated with schizophrenia (COMT; Caspi et al., 2005). Importantly, whereas some studies have replicated such genotype–environment interactions, others have failed to do so (Zammit & Owen, 2006). The studies discussed above demonstrate very clearly that neither genes nor environmental events can explain the onset of a disorder such as depression. Rather, a complex interaction of the two factors is required.

Behavioural research into the genetic bases of psychiatric disorders typically takes one of three forms: family (or pedigree) studies, twin studies, and adoption studies. In all such studies, a person with a disorder is identified (called the index case or proband) and other people (family or non-family members) are examined to see if there is a match for the disorder. When the problem that characterizes the index case also occurs in the comparison person, the two are said to be *concordant* (or to display **concordance** for the problem). The degree of concordance is thought to reveal the influence of genetics. However, this assumption is not altogether accurate, since concordance can reveal environmental influences, depending on the circumstances.

More recent techniques for studying genetic influences include **genetic linkage studies** and research methods in **molecular biology**. In genetic linkage studies, researchers examine families that have a high incidence of a particular psychiatric disorder. Within these extended families, researchers look for the presence of particular traits (called genetic markers) that can be linked to the occurrence of the disorder. Common among these genetic markers are features like hair or eye colour, colour blindness, and the presence of medical disorders that have a known genetic basis. If all members of the family who have the mental disorder also have the genetic marker, but the unaffected family members do not, then the conclusion is that the mental disorder has a genetic origin. These sorts of genetic linkage studies have provided strong evidence of a genetic basis for bipolar disorder and schizophrenia, although a number of studies have failed to replicate these findings and particular chromosomal regions have not been confirmed (Charney et al., 2002; Sullivan, 2008).

Researchers in molecular biology have been able to compare specific DNA segments and identify the genes that determine individual characteristics. These are the methods underlying the attempt to map the entire human genome, and researchers have been able to pinpoint the defective genes that cause various medical and psychological disorders (Glausiusz, 1997; Sullivan, 2008). In most of these cases, multiple gene defects appear to interact with environmental factors to produce the disorder.

A detailed description of the research strategies involved in attempting to determine genetic influences in psychopathology, and the potential interpretations of the data derived from these studies, is provided in Chapter 4.

Psychosocial Theories

Case Notes

"Little Hans" was a five-year-old boy whose father brought him to the attention of Sigmund Freud (1905). The boy was so fearful of being bitten by a horse that he would not leave the house. The father told Freud that one day he and Hans had boarded a streetcar (pulled, in those days, by horses). At some point during the trip, the horses, frightened by a loud noise, reared up, pushing the streetcar backwards, and then bolted, dragging the careening car after them. When they finally stopped, the boy was very frightened and distressed, and his father took him home. Freud apparently analyzed this case without ever seeing Hans. He dismissed the experience with the bolting horses as a cause, considering the fear to have hidden, unconscious origins.

Many theorists have ignored, or relegated to a lesser role, the influence of biological processes on behaviour and thought. Psychodynamic theorists, like Freud, have suggested that behaviour is motivated by unconscious processes acquired during the formative years of life. In the case above, Hans's phobia was seen as a symbol of underlying psychic conflict. Hans's apparent fear of being bitten by a horse, Freud said, was a symbolic representation of his dread of being castrated by his father. Freud cast the story in terms of his famous Oedipus complex (explained later in this chapter). Other theorists believe that behaviours are learned responses to environmental stimuli. This belief characterizes behavioural, cognitive-behavioural, and social learning theorists. For example, Little Hans's case has been seen as clear evidence of a behavioural or conditioning explanation for phobias. Strictly cognitive theorists claim that it is the way people think about or perceive their world that causes them to develop disorders. (No doubt they would argue that it was the way in which Little Hans viewed and remembered the experience that caused him to become fearful.) Humanists and existentialists suggest that personal experience provides the basis for the development of self-directed behaviour. Finally, socio-cultural theorists suggest that the surrounding society or culture exerts powerful influences on people; that such influences may cause a disorder to occur; and, moreover, that a particular society may define a person as abnormal because it suits the ends of that society. What all of these different theories have in common is that they stress experience.

PSYCHODYNAMIC THEORIES

Sigmund Freud (1856–1939), a Viennese neurologist, was the founder of the **psychodynamic** school of thought. Psychodynamic theories claim that behaviour is controlled by unconscious forces of which the person is unaware. In this sense, psychodynamic theories, like biological theories, see the person as having little control over his or her actions. However, psychodynamic theorists consider the origins of unconscious controls to reside in the individual's personal experience (albeit during the very early formative years).

Freud's analysis of a patient known as "Anna O" provided the insights he needed to develop his theory. Anna O had quite complex symptoms, including paralysis, deafness, and disturbances of vision, which apparently were psychologically induced rather than a result of physical damage. During hypnosis, Anna O revealed traumatic past experiences associated with deep emotional responses. Memories of these experiences were apparently repressed, since the patient could not recall them during her waking state, but after she had expressed them during hypnosis, Freud and his mentor, Josef Breuer (1842–1925), judged Anna O to have improved. This led Freud to conclude that traumatic experiences early in life become repressed (that is, inaccessible to awareness) because they are too distressing to contemplate. Freud further assumed that these repressed or unconscious memories influence current functioning. Discharging the emotional responses attached to these unconscious memories, by identifying the original traumatic experiences during hypnosis, was called *catharsis* by Breuer and Freud, and they saw this as the effective element in treating such problems.

Interestingly, Anna O (whose real name was Bertha Pappenheim) continued to suffer from intermittent recurrence of her problems for some years after being discharged as effectively treated, and she subsequently became quite hostile toward what she called "the talking cure" (what Freud came to call *psychoanalysis*). Pappenheim finally recovered completely and became not only Germany's first social worker, but also a leading feminist. She would not allow any of the girls in the home she ran to be psychoanalyzed despite their often considerable problems.

In Freud's theory, four features together determine current behaviour and thinking, both normal and abnormal. The different levels of consciousness determine the accessibility of thoughts and desires; the structures of personality represent the embodiment of the various controlling forces; the stages of psychosexual development indicate the points in experience where problems can arise; and, finally, defence mechanisms are the means by which people channel their psychic energy in functional or dysfunctional ways.

LEVELS OF CONSCIOUSNESS Freud distinguished what he believed to be three levels of awareness:

- the **conscious**, which contains information of which we are currently aware;

Sigmund Freud (1856–1939), founder of the psychoanalytic movement.

- the **preconscious**, which holds information not presently within our awareness but that can readily be brought into awareness; and
- the **unconscious**, which, according to Freud, contains the majority of our memories and drives that, unfortunately, can only be raised to awareness with great difficulty and typically only in response to particular techniques (that is, by psychoanalytic procedures).

For Freud, the unconscious was the most important level of the mind. All of our biological drives, particularly sexual and aggressive drives, reside at this level, as do our traumatic memories. Freud thought that sexual and aggressive drives, which he considered to be instinctual, upset people so much that they could not face the fact that they had such urges. These unacceptable drives and the traumatic memories were kept out of awareness by what Freud called *defence mechanisms*.

STRUCTURES OF PERSONALITY According to Freud, three structures of personality (see Figure 2.3) are in constant conflict. Whether Freud really meant these to be understood as actual structures or as metaphors for different psychic forces is not altogether clear, but there is no doubt that he thought they represented the sources that determined personality.

The **id** is the structure present at birth and it contains, or represents, the biological or instinctual drives. These drives demand instant gratification without concern for the consequences either to the self or to others. In this sense, the id acts according to what Freud called the *pleasure principle*.

In the first year of life, the ego begins to develop. The **ego** develops to curb the desires of the id so that the individual does not suffer any unpleasant consequences. There is no concern here for what is right or wrong, but only for the avoidance of pain or discomfort and the

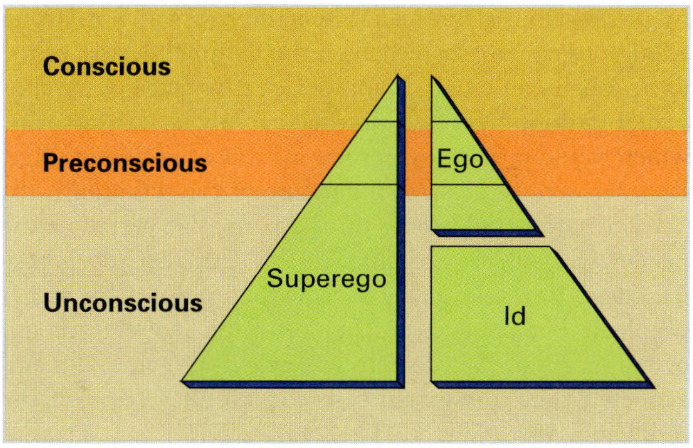

FIGURE 2.3 Levels of Awareness and Structures of Personality, According to Sigmund Freud

TABLE 2.1 SUMMARY OF PSYCHOSEXUAL STAGES OF DEVELOPMENT

Stage	Duration	Manifestations
Oral	Birth–18 months	Focus on oral activities (for example, eating and sucking)
Anal	18 months–3 years	Toilet training—child may co-operate or resist by soiling or withholding
Phallic	3–6 years	Oedipal or Electra complex
Latency	6–12 years	Consolidation of behavioural skills and attitudes—relatively quiescent stage
Genital	Adolescence–death	Achievement of personal and sexual maturity

maximization of unpunished pleasure. As the individual learns what expressions of desires are practical and possible, the ego comes to be governed by the *reality principle*. Early in life, then, there is a constant clash between the id and the ego, which is reduced over time so long as the ego develops normally.

As the child gets older, the **superego** begins to develop. The superego is the internalization of the moral standards of society inculcated by the child's parents. The operating guide of the superego is the *moral principle*, and it serves as the person's conscience by monitoring the ego. The ego, therefore, attempts to satisfy the id while not offending the principles of the superego. The more strongly developed the ego, the better able it is to handle these often opposing pressures.

PSYCHOSEXUAL STAGES OF DEVELOPMENT Freud thought that sexual drives were the most important determinants of behaviour, and that even the most innocent actions might be driven by sexual desires. Sexual drives were seen as the major life instinct, which Freud called *eros*, the energy for which was libido. Sexual pleasure, or the expression of libidinal energy, was focused on different body parts, which Freud called *erogenous zones*, and the focus of these zones differed at different stages of psychosexual development (see Table 2.1). Failure to resolve a stage would result in a fixation on the erogenous zone associated with that stage. For example, individuals fixated at the oral stage (that is, those who failed to have their oral desires fully satisfied) were thought to produce later behaviours that are either directly oral (for example, smoking, alcoholism, or overeating) or symbolically so (for example, constantly talking).

The **phallic stage** has received the greatest attention from psychoanalysts. In this stage, boys are presumed to develop sexual desires for their mother and to see their father as a competitor for their mother's love. This is described as the **Oedipal complex**, in reference to the character of Oedipus in the play by the Greek tragedian Sophocles. In Sophocles' play, Oedipus unwittingly kills his father and marries his mother, Jocasta. At the same time that a boy recognizes his father as a threat to the fulfillment of his desire for his mother, he also fears reprisal from his father. In Freud's view, the boy fears that his father will mutilate the boy's genitals to prevent any union with the mother. This fear is called *castration anxiety*—an odd choice of term, since castration denotes removal of the testicles, not the penis, and would not prevent intercourse. Because this fear is not consciously recognized, it can manifest itself as fear of something apparently unrelated, as in the case of Little Hans.

Similarly, girls are thought to desire their father—not to win their father's love, but rather, by seducing him, to gain what they truly desire: a penis. In girls, this desire for the father is called the **Electra complex**, again by analogy to a character who appears in several Greek tragedies. (Electra, in fact, did not desire her father, but rather helped her brother, Orestes, to kill their mother, who had murdered their father.)

DEFENCE MECHANISMS Remember that the function of the ego is to restrain the direct expression of the libidinal desires of the id. It does so by employing, at an unconscious level, a kind of censoring system. The ego uses **defence mechanisms** to allow the expression of libidinal desires in a distorted or symbolic form. The id, however, does its best to break through these defences, so that psychic energy is used up in this almost constant conflict between the ego and the id. The weaker the ego (that is, the less resolved the individual's psychosexual stages), the greater the conflict and, thereby, the greater the exhaustion of psychic energy. This exhaustion of psychic energy leads to a breakdown of psychological functioning, with the particular symptoms of this breakdown reflecting the unresolved stage of psychosexual development. Table 2.2 describes some of the more commonly identified defence mechanisms. Among clinicians, this aspect of Freud's theory has witnessed the greatest acceptance of any of his ideas.

TABLE 2.2 SOME TYPICAL DEFENCE MECHANISMS

Defence Mechanism	Description	Example
Repression	Burying in the unconscious the unacceptable impulses of the id	Inability to recall being sexually abused as a child
Regression	Employing behaviours typical of an earlier stage of development	Petulance or tantrums in response to frustration
Projection	Attributing one's own desires to others	Someone who cheats on an exam, or is tempted to cheat, claiming everyone cheats
Intellect-ualization	Hiding the real issues behind a screen of abstract analyses	A criminal appealing his conviction, despite admitting guilt, on the grounds of improper trial procedures
Denial	Refusal to acknowledge an unpleasant reality	A person, told she has two months to live, planning a holiday in a year's time
Displacement	The transfer of feelings from one person to another, less threatening person	A person humiliated by her employer directing her anger toward her spouse
Reaction formation	Repressing unacceptable desires by expressing the opposite viewpoint	A man who has strong sexual desires toward most women berating people who are promiscuous
Sublimation	Transformation of sexual or aggressive energy into some more acceptable activity	Freud thought that artists who painted nudes were sublimating their sexual desires

3 BEFORE MOVING ON

Do you use defence mechanisms? How accurate do you think Freud was in his conceptualization of defence mechanisms?

Freud thought that sexual desires were often unwelcome to the ego or superego and, accordingly, were repressed or channelled into other activities. This repression, however, frequently led to problems for the person, although these problems would not be manifestly sexual and would be disguised from the person's own awareness by unconscious defences. When the ego was not strong enough to contain or rechannel the libidinal desires of the id, it was because one or another of the stages of psychosexual development had not been resolved satisfactorily, which would produce symptoms associated with that stage. By interpreting the symbolic nature of the symptoms, the psychoanalyst could focus on the particular period of the person's formative years (that is, the particular psychosexual stage) to reveal to the patient the origin of his or her problem. The patient's acceptance of the analyst's account of the origin of the problem was called *insight*, and it was expected that this would result in an alleviation of the problem.

FREUD'S INFLUENCE Freudian theory is largely speculative and has little empirical support. Attempts to test Freud's ideas experimentally have run into the problem that no matter what the results are, they can be explained within the theory. Yet some aspects of Freud's thinking have been valuable to psychology. He legitimized discussion and research on sexual matters; he encouraged a concern with processes beyond our awareness; and he recognized that the motives for human behaviour were not always the obvious ones. In short, no single psychological theorist has been more influential than Freud, even though psychoanalysis is much less popular today than it was in the early and middle parts of the twentieth century. Some of Freud's followers (e.g., Carl Jung, Alfred Adler, Melanie Klein) have developed or modified Freud's theories and treatment approach. These modified theories have enjoyed greater acceptance in recent years. Unlike Freud's original theory, these newer perspectives in psychodynamic thought generate testable hypotheses and have led to novel and apparently effective treatments.

BEHAVIOURAL THEORIES

CONDITIONING ACCOUNTS As noted in Chapter 1, behaviourism was first introduced as a perspective on human behaviour by John B. Watson. Early behaviourists such as Watson were environmentalists in that they assumed that all (or almost all) human behaviour, including abnormal behaviour, was learned. Watson (1913) took the view that **classical conditioning**, as described by the Russian physiologist Ivan Pavlov (1849–1936), was the basis for this learning. Pavlov demonstrated classical conditioning in his famous experiment with dogs (see Figure 2.4). Every time the dogs were fed, a bell was rung. At first, the dogs salivated when they saw and smelled the meat. After a number of conditioning trials, they would salivate at the sound of the bell alone. To put it in Pavlov's terms, initially, a bell (that is, the conditioned stimulus, or CS) elicited an orienting response; that is, the dog looked toward the sound and listened. The meat (the unconditioned stimulus, or UCS) elicited an unconditioned response, salivation. Repeated pairings of the CS and UCS result in the CS eliciting some degree of salivation (the conditioned

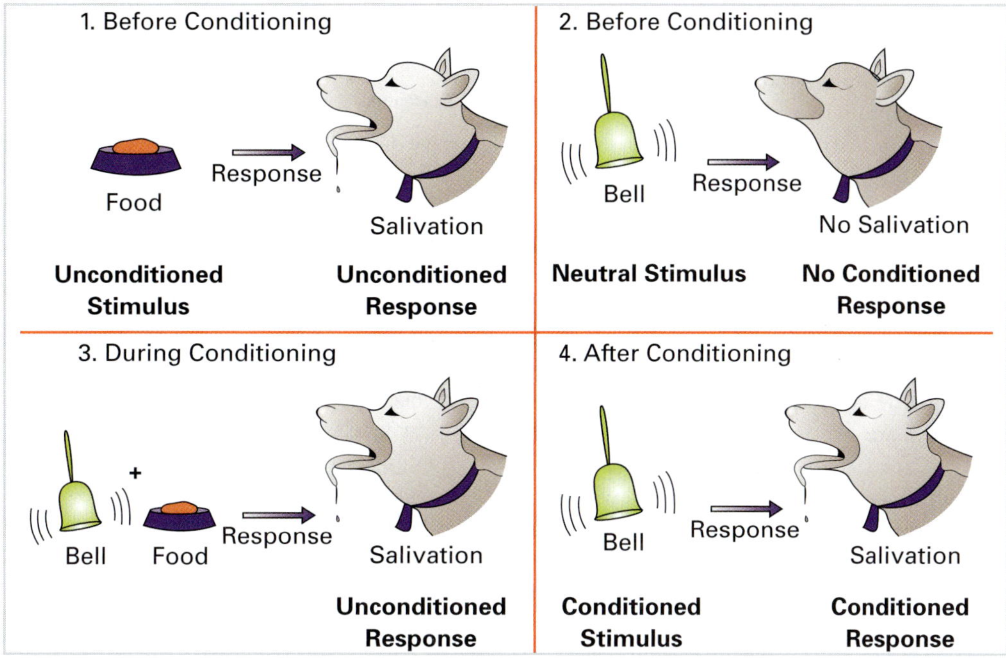

FIGURE 2.4 Pavlov's Experiment: The Process of Classical Conditioning

response, or CR). What is learned in classical conditioning, then, is the transfer of a response (that is, the UCR or its practical replication, the CR) from one stimulus (UCS) to another (CS). This process is called *stimulus–stimulus learning*.

Watson's most famous application of this type of analysis was to the acquisition of phobias: unrealistic fears of usually harmless things, such as cats or dogs. According to Watson, people with a phobia of dogs must have had a frightening experience with a dog at one time. The case of Little Hans's horse phobia, described at the beginning of this section, has been interpreted as an example of classical conditioning (Wolpe & Rachman, 1960). Prior to the frightening experience, a horse was a neutral stimulus (that is, a CS) in that it did not elicit fear. The bolting horses and careening streetcar represent the UCS, and automatically elicited a fear response (the UCR). Watson believed that an unconditioned response to pain or threat was inborn, and served, along with other similar inborn UCS–UCR connections, as the basis for all subsequently acquired responses (CRs). The frightening experience with the horses invoked the conditioning processes that would instill a fear response (CR) to the sight, or even the thought, of a horse (CS).

Watson and Rayner (1920) demonstrated that classical conditioning could instill a fear of a white rat in an 11-month-old boy identified as Little Albert. This boy was first shown a white rat, to which he displayed no fear; in fact, he appeared to enjoy trying to play with it. After several presentations like this to ensure that Little Albert was not fearful of the rat, Watson and Rayner followed the rat's appearance by making a sudden loud noise close behind the boy. This loud noise startled and upset Little Albert. After seven presentations of the rat (the CS) paired with the sudden loud noise (the UCS), Little Albert displayed a conditioned fear response to the rat. Watson and Rayner had indeed demonstrated that conditioning procedures could instill a phobic response to a harmless animal. On the basis of this single demonstration, Watson concluded that all phobias resulted from classical conditioning experiences. This, of course, was an overgeneralization.

4 BEFORE MOVING ON

Ever since Phil was bitten by a dog at a young age he has been afraid of all dogs. Describe how classical conditioning could have played a role in the development of Phil's phobia of dogs.

However, this study has served as a model for demonstrating conditioning possibilities in humans, and was for a long time taken as the basis for a conditioning account of human fears. As we will see in Chapter 5, classical conditioning alone cannot explain many facets of phobias, most particularly their persistence. For instance, when the UCS is removed from classical conditioning studies, extinction (that is, the loss of response to the CS) occurs quite rapidly. In Pavlov's study, for example, withdrawal of the meat followed by repeated presentations of the bell causes the bell to cease eliciting salivation. Most people with phobias repeatedly encounter their phobic stimulus without any dreadful consequences occurring. Under these conditions (that is, the CS occurs repeatedly in the absence of the UCS), they should lose their fears (that is, CRs should cease to occur when the CS is presented). Yet, in fact, phobias display remarkable persistence.

Faced with this problem, Mowrer (1947) developed what came to be known as the **two-factor theory** of conditioning. He suggested that two types of learning take place in the acquisition and maintenance of phobias: (1) classical conditioning establishes the aversive response to a previously neutral stimulus (the CS); and (2) thereafter, the organism avoids the CS in order to prevent feeling afraid. Avoiding the CS, of course, effectively prevents extinction from occurring. This latter component of Mowrer's theory is derived from the work of Burrhus F. Skinner (1904–1990), who developed the ideas involved in **operant conditioning**. In Skinner's operant conditioning, the consequences of behaviour are important. All actions are followed by consequences of one kind or another. Some consequences encourage the repetition of the behaviour that produces them, whereas other consequences result in the opposite effect. When behaviour increases in frequency as a result of consistent consequences, **reinforcement** is said to occur; when a behaviour decreases in frequency as a result of its consequences, this is described as **punishment**. Some behaviours (for example, opening a refrigerator door) lead to pleasant consequences or rewards (for example, eating ice cream), and the behaviour of going to the refrigerator increases; this is called *positive reinforcement*. Other behaviours (for example, taking an aspirin) result in a reduction of distress (that is, the headache goes away); this is called *negative reinforcement*. When a behaviour is reduced by the consequent occurrence of an unpleasant experience, it is called *positive punishment*, and when the behaviour is reduced following the removal of something desirable, *negative punishment* is said to have occurred. (Note that "positive" and "negative" are not used to mean good and bad; rather, positive refers simply to the presence of something and negative to the absence of something.) Table 2.3 summarizes these consequences and their effects.

TABLE 2.3 OPERANT CONDITIONING: CONSEQUENCES AND THEIR EFFECTS

Examples	Condition	Effects
Reinforcement		
(a) Rat presses lever and gets food	Positive	Lever pressing increases
(b) Child imitates mother's speech and mother smiles		Imitation increases
(a) Rat escapes from white side of box to black side and shock terminates	Negative	Escape behaviour increases
(b) Student quits seminar course and feels relief from speech anxiety		Avoidance of seminar courses increases
Punishment		
(a) Rat gets shocked for exploratory behaviour	Positive	Exploratory behaviour decreases
(b) Bully starts a fight and is badly beaten		Attempts to start fights decrease
(a) Food tray is removed when a pigeon pecks a red key	Negative	Pecking red key decreases
(b) Child is rude and is not allowed to have ice cream		Rudeness decreases

Burrhus F. Skinner (1904–1990) developed the ideas involved in operant conditioning.

Two-factor theory explains the persistence of phobias, in a way that simple classical conditioning cannot, by adding a negative reinforcement component to the process. Once a person has acquired a classically conditioned fear of a harmless stimulus, he or she begins to escape from the stimulus whenever it appears. Escape behaviour is negatively reinforced by the consequent reduction in fear, and the person soon learns that avoiding the stimulus altogether eliminates the distress. Thus, the person never experiences the CS (that is, phobic stimulus) in the absence of the UCS (for example, an attack by a dog), and therefore extinction cannot occur.

Various other elaborations on basic learning paradigms have been developed to explain a variety of pathological behaviours, and behaviour therapists have had significant successes in treating numerous problems with procedures derived from learning principles. Perhaps the most influential of these more recent learning-based approaches is

social learning theory, which was initially developed in Canada by Albert Bandura and Richard Walters.

SOCIAL LEARNING THEORY As originally outlined by Bandura and Walters (1959), social learning theory suggested that, although classical and operant conditioning experiences are important, the majority of these experiences occur within a social context and are primarily acquired vicariously—that is, by observation of others rather than by direct personal experience. Accordingly, it was shown that children could learn to be aggressive by observing others being rewarded for aggression (Bandura, Ross, & Ross, 1961, 1963), or they could learn to be fearful by watching their phobic parents (Bandura & Menlove, 1968). Subsequently, this theory has been extended to include not only direct observation of others but also information derived from books, movies, and television.

Because Bandura's theory (1976) emphasized the importance of cognitive processes, such as perceiving the behaviour of others and storing such information in memory, it gave rise to the notion that other mediational processes play a part in learning. The idea underlying mediation is that a simple stimulus-response model does not account for the acquisition of all human behaviour. Rather, a number of individual characteristics (expectations, abilities, appraisals, feelings, and so on) appear to influence different responses to stimuli. The loss of a job, for example, does not invariably trigger depression; an individual's appraisal of the situation also contributes to his or her feelings and responses. Some individuals might view this unemployment with excitement as they see it as a new opportunity to do something different. Others might be relieved because they have detested the work that they do. Still others may be saddened because they believe that their sense of achievement is an important defining feature of self. Eventually, this idea of mediation led to the development of what became known as cognitive-behavioural theory (Dobson & Dozois, 2010).

Cognitive-behavioural theory reflects the view that both thinking and behaviour are learned and, therefore, can be changed. This approach assumes that the way in which people view the world, including their beliefs and attitudes toward the world, themselves, and others, arises out of their experience and that these patterns of thinking and perceiving are maintained by consequences in the same way that overt behaviour is maintained.

COGNITIVE THEORIES

There are many different clinically oriented cognitive theories, each of which shares three principles: (1) that thinking affects emotion and behaviour; (2) that thoughts can be monitored and changed; and (3) that by altering one's thoughts, one will experience desired behavioural and emotional change (Dobson & Dozois, 2010). Two preeminent cognitive theorists have offered accounts of the etiology and treatment of abnormal behaviours: Albert Ellis and Aaron Beck.

RATIONAL-EMOTIVE BEHAVIOUR THERAPY Albert Ellis developed **rational-emotive behaviour therapy** more than four decades ago (Ellis, 1962, 2004). Ellis (1962) has argued that, when faced with unfavourable life circumstances, human beings tend to make themselves feel frustrated, disappointed, and miserable, and behave in self-defeating ways, mainly because they construct irrational beliefs about themselves and their situations. Ellis (1999) argued that adaptive feelings and behaviours stem from rational and functional thoughts. At the crux of this conceptualization is the ABC model of human disturbance, which states that the consequences (C) of life events (e.g., symptomatology, negative affect) are not contingent upon the activating event (A) per se, but are mediated by one's beliefs (B) about these experiences (Dryden, David, & Ellis, 2010).

Ellis (1991) identified a number of distinctive irrational beliefs that may contribute to emotional disturbance (e.g., things must always go right; I must be loved and have approval at all times). These beliefs are considered maladaptive because they are expressed in absolutist terms and held on to rigidly as needs, demands, and evaluative statements rather than as more flexible preferences, wishes, or desires (Dryden et al., 2010; Walen, DiGiuseppe, & Dryden, 1992).

Since his original proposal (Ellis, 1962), Ellis has made some modifications to his theory. For example, he now acknowledges that it is not simply the irrational propositions (e.g., words, phrases) that people use that contribute to feelings of dysphoria and negative affect, but the "basic meaning" and "core philosophy" that underlie each of these statements that are the prime denigrator of their sense of self-worth (Ellis, 1999).

COGNITIVE THEORY AND THERAPY Aaron Beck's cognitive model (Beck, 1963; Beck & Dozois, 2011, in press; Beck, Rush, Shaw, & Emery, 1979; Clark, Beck, & Alford, 1999) states that emotions and behaviours are heavily influenced by individual perceptions or cognitive appraisals of events. Three main levels of cognition are emphasized in this theory: (1) schemas; (2) information processing and intermediate beliefs (including dysfunctional rules, assumptions, and attitudes); and (3) automatic thoughts (Dozois & Beck, 2008; Dozois, Frewen, & Covin, 2006).

Schemas refer to internal representations of stored information and experiences. They are used to organize new information in a meaningful way and help to determine how we perceive and understand what goes on around us (Clark & Beck, 1999). Many of the core beliefs that are indicative of psychopathology (e.g., "I am incompetent," "I am bad," "I am unlovable," "I am defective") stem from an individual's self-schema. Young (1999) described a set of core beliefs, which he has labelled Early Maladaptive Schemas (EMS), that originate from repetitious, aversive experiences in childhood. These EMSs are broad, pervasive themes or patterns that are composed of memories, emotions, cognitions, and bodily sensations regarding self and one's relationships with others (Young, Klosko, &

TABLE 2.4 EARLY MALADAPTIVE SCHEMAS

1. Disconnection and rejection
   a. Abandonment/instability
   b. Mistrust/abuse
   c. Emotional deprivation
   d. Defectiveness/shame
   e. Social isolation/alienation
2. Impaired autonomy and performance
   a. Dependence/incompetence
   b. Vulnerability to harm or illness
   c. Enmeshment/underdeveloped self
   d. Failure
3. Impaired limits
   a. Entitlement/grandiosity
   b. Insufficient self-control/self-discipline
4. Other directedness
   a. Subjugation
   b. Self-sacrifice
   c. Approval seeking/recognition seeking
5. Overvigilance and inhibition
   a. Negativity/pessimism
   b. Emotional inhibition
   c. Unrelenting standards/hypercriticalness
   d. Punitiveness

Source: Young, J. E., Klosko, J. S., & Weishaar, M. E. (2003). Schema therapy: Conceptual model. In *Schema therapy: A practitioner's guide* (p. 7). New York: Guilford Press.

Dr. Aaron T. Beck, the founder of cognitive therapy.

Weishaar, 2003). EMSs act as a priori truths and influence how an individual processes later experiences, and thinks, acts, feels, and relates to others throughout life. The five sets of EMS and their constituents are listed in Table 2.4.

According to Beck, the development and organization of a maladaptive self-schema occurs during early childhood, but the schema does not become active until it is triggered by negative life events. For example, an individual who is vulnerable to depression may fundamentally believe that he or she is worthless and unlovable. This belief, however, may not affect this individual until he or she experiences rejection from a peer or partner. Once this belief is active in an individual's mind, he or she may start to selectively attend to and recall information that is consistent with this negative view of self. For instance, this person might start to pay attention to cues that are suggestive of unlovability and disqualify information that does not fit that expectation and belief. For example, Hailey's core belief that close others are inconsistent and may abandon her caused her to doubt the reassurance that her boyfriend provided. Different types of beliefs are considered to be related to different kinds of abnormal behaviour—what Beck referred to as **content-specificity** (Dozois & Beck, 2008; Dozois et al., 2006). Individuals who are depressed are theorized to have negative automatic thoughts that focus on themes of personal loss, deprivation, and failure (Beck et al., 1979). Anxiety tends to be related to thoughts about the world being dangerous, the future uncertain, and the self inadequate (Beck & Emery, 1985). Paranoia is associated with cognitions that people cannot be trusted and that others are malevolent, abusive, and deceitful, whereas excessive dependency is related to a view of self as weak, helpless, and incompetent (Beck & Dozois, in press).

Information processing biases and intermediate beliefs compose the next level of cognition (Clark et al., 1999; Ingram, Miranda, & Segal, 1998). These biases often take the form of selective attention or enhanced memory for information that is schema-consistent. For example, compared to low-anxious individuals, people with high levels of anxiety have been shown to pay more attention to threatening stimuli (see Bar-Haim, Lamy, Pergamin, Bakermans-Kranenburg, & van Ijzendoorn, 2007, for a meta-analysis), to negatively interpret ambiguous stimuli (Amir, Beard, & Bower, 2005), and to show enhanced memory for stimuli related to their fears (Radomsky & Rachman, 2004). This pattern of information processing is consistent with an anxious individual's schema, in that he or she tends to view the world as dangerous and the self as vulnerable.

Information processing biases are also represented as "if–then" statements and inaccurate causal attributions. For example, a person may engage in "all-or-nothing thinking" in which he or she evaluates personal qualities or situations in absolutist terms (e.g., an "A" student receiving a lower-than-expected grade may regard him- or herself as a complete failure). Recent research has demonstrated that these types of "cognitive errors" are associated with anxious and depressive symptoms in children (Weems, Costa, Watts, Taylor, & Cannon, 2007), psychological distress and parenting stress in mothers of toddlers (Mazur, 2006), and increased depressed mood in undergraduate students following negative social feedback (Henriques & Leitenberg, 2002).

Finally, *automatic thoughts* refer to the frequent thoughts that pop into our minds and that are not accompanied by conscious appraisal. An analogy is that of learning how to drive a car. When an individual first learns to drive, he or she is acutely aware of how much pressure is being placed on the gas or the brakes, whether the radio is on or off, whether the window is open or closed, and what is happening on the other side of the windshield. Every skill involved in driving becomes a conscious and sometimes frightening task for the young driver. As people become more adept at driving, however, these skills become easier to carry out and the processes become increasingly automated such that individuals are able to sing along to music, carry on a conversation, and enjoy the landscape as they perform the multiple tasks involved with manipulating their vehicle. Every day, each of us experiences hundreds of automatic thoughts, but people who experience psychopathology have a greater number of negative and threat-related automatic thoughts.

Automatic thoughts are considered to be cognitive by-products because they stem directly from an individual's core beliefs, or schemas, in interaction with the environment. For example, an individual who is passed in the corridor at work without a colleague's salutation may have the automatic thought "She doesn't like me," perhaps stemming from a core belief of being unlovable or undesirable. Similarly, someone with a self-schema focused on incompetence may have the thought "I will never be able to do this" when faced with a novel task.

Cognition is the primary focus of Beck's theory; however, the model does not simply state that cognitions *cause* emotions and behaviours. Instead, it is acknowledged that these variables are interrelated and that many other factors (e.g., biological predispositions) are involved (Alford & Beck, 1997; Beck & Dozois, 2011).

Consistent with the major tenets of this cognitive theory of psychological functioning, cognitive therapy aims to help clients shift from unhealthy appraisals to more realistic and adaptive ones. Treatment is highly collaborative and involves designing specific learning experiences to teach clients how to monitor automatic thoughts; understand the relationships among cognition, affect, and behaviour; examine the validity of automatic thoughts; develop more realistic and adaptive cognitions; and alter underlying beliefs, assumptions, and schemas (Dozois et al., 2006). The primary assumptions of Beck's theory have been well supported by the research literature (Beck & Dozois, 2011; Dozois & Beck, 2008). As we will see in later chapters, cognitive therapy has also enjoyed success in the treatment of many disorders, most particularly anxiety and mood disorders.

5 BEFORE MOVING ON

In what ways do you think your early childhood experiences have influenced your schemas? How do your schemas influence your thoughts, beliefs, information processing, and behaviour?

HUMANISTIC AND EXISTENTIAL THEORIES

Humanistic and existential theories can be considered to be variants on the phenomenological approach to understanding human behaviour. Phenomenology as a philosophical position had many antecedents, but Edmund Husserl (1859–1938) is generally considered the first to clearly formulate this viewpoint. Husserl's account was subsequently elaborated by French philosopher Maurice Merleau-Ponty (1908–1961). According to this view, it is through experience that people form their sense of themselves and of the world. However, experience is not the objective observation of external events, but rather the accumulation of perceptions of the world. The way in which the world is perceived by an individual is a product of the personal experiences that have produced his or her sense of self. This sense of self guides, and is formed by, the person's perception of his or her experiences. Life is said to involve a continuous synthesis of experience that progressively refines our sense of self and develops our values. This sense of self, along with our values and our accumulated experience, provides the basis for our choices of action. Behaviour is not determined by experience alone, since experience simply provides the basis for choice. These choices represent the expression of our free will.

From this perspective of human experience, phenomenologists developed theories about all manner of psychological functioning, including, of course, perception, but also the development of human values, and, most importantly, they generated accounts of personal development.

HUMANISTIC VIEWS The two most eminent advocates of humanistic psychology were Carl Rogers (1902–1987) and Abraham Maslow (1908–1970). Both emphasized the dignity and potential of humans and saw experience (as perceived by the individual) as providing the basis for improving oneself. Rogers's position has been called a *person-centred* theory of personality because he considered the person to be of central importance in understanding behaviour. According to Rogers, self-fulfillment is achieved by accepting oneself, being honest in all interactions, trusting experience (which he said is the highest authority), and relying on oneself for personal evaluations. People who can do so will be able to accept others for who they are, thus encouraging both themselves and others to be more honest, and such honesty will help accumulate experiences that will lead them to realize their potential.

According to Rogers (1961), abnormal behaviour results from a person's distorted view of himself or herself, which in turn arises from an inability to trust experience. Such lack of trust is said to result from distressing life events (or the perception of these events as distressing), which distort the person's perception of all subsequent experience. Thus, distorted perceptions misshape the person's sense of self, which provides the basis for choices of action. These choices will, accordingly, be detrimental to personal development and further entrench the distorted views of self and experience, thereby perpetuating dysfunctional behaviour.

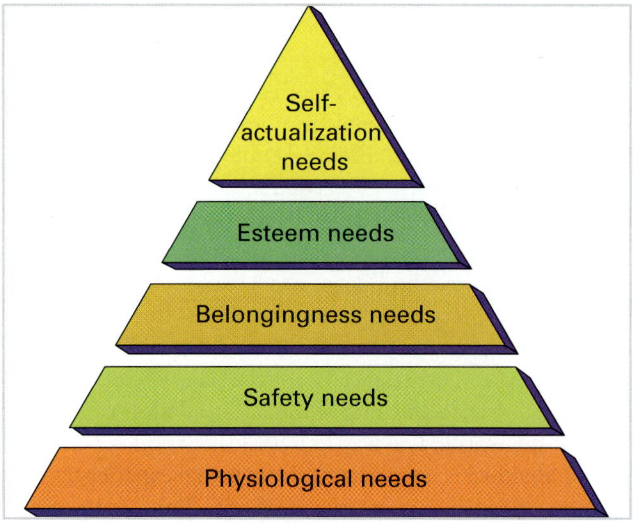

FIGURE 2.5 Maslow's Hierarchy of Needs

Source: Motivation and Personality, 2/e, by Maslow. © Reprinted by permission of Pearson Education, Inc., Upper Saddle River, NJ.

Abraham Maslow (1908–1970), who developed the theory of self-actualization.

Maslow (1954) essentially believed that people are good and that they only behave dysfunctionally or nastily as a result of experience (or their interpretation of it) that has diverted them from the path of **self-actualization**. He described a hierarchy of needs that, when fully satisfied, result in the actualization of the person's potential. It is toward this realization of personal potential that all persons should strive. Maslow's hierarchy of needs can be visualized as a pyramid (see Figure 2.5). At the base of the pyramid are biological or survival needs, including food, water, and shelter; safety occupies the next level. Unless these are met, the person will not survive, and if they are unsatisfactorily met, the person will not be able to move up the hierarchy toward self-actualization. The need to belong represents the next step up in the hierarchy and refers to needs for friendship and affiliation. When these are met, the individual seeks an assurance of self-worth, which comes from giving and receiving love and from an internalized sense of self-esteem derived from experience. From this base of self-confidence, self-actualization becomes possible. In Maslow's view, abnormal or dysfunctional behaviour results from a failure to attain the self-esteem necessary to achieve self-actualization.

Both of these humanists have an optimistic view of people and consider human behaviour to result from personal decisions and perceptions of their experience and of themselves. Thus, they hold the individual to be responsible, rather than forces beyond the individual's control (for example, biological determinants, unconscious processes, or actual external events). Obviously, then, if dysfunctional behaviour is derived from people's view of themselves and their experiences, they can be helped to change their perspective and, thereby, overcome their problems.

EXISTENTIAL VIEWS Existentialists see the individual's awareness of his or her own existence as a critical feature of human functioning. This awareness brings with it the realization that we could, and obviously eventually will, cease to exist. However, it is not just the possibility of death that existentialists consider to be a threat, but also the loss of direction and meaning in our lives. Existentialists also stress our responsibility for our choices and, therefore, for our actions. We make free choices and must necessarily take responsibility for them.

According to the existentialist point of view, this awareness of the possibility of nonbeing (whether death or the emptiness of no meaning) and the acceptance of responsibility for our actions makes us anxious. It is this existential *angst* (a German word that means something more than the English "anxiety" and conveys a sense of more severe distress) that causes people problems, so life becomes a search for meaning. Making the effort to seek meaning is said to reflect the "courage to be" (Tillich, 1952), whereas the alternative is to give up the struggle and become full of despair. This is a somewhat gloomier view of the human condition than the humanistic view, since the struggle to "be" is very difficult and few actually display the necessary courage. However, like humanistic psychology, existentialism sees the individual as responsible and as potentially capable of dealing effectively with life.

The leading exponents of the existential view, as applied to human problem behaviour, have been Rollo May (1961) and Viktor Frankl (1962). Both of these theorists see the struggle to find meaning in our lives and our acceptance of responsibility for our choices as critical in understanding human behaviour. Treatment, therefore, is directed at confronting clients with their responsibility for their actions and assisting them in finding meaning in their lives. Until recently, very little research has evaluated either this interesting approach or the humanistic approach to understanding and treating human problems.

Over the past few decades, research has focused on the investigation of mindfulness as a form of clinical intervention. Mindfulness is defined as the awareness that arises through "paying attention in a particular way: on purpose, in the present moment, and nonjudgmental" (Kabat-Zinn, 1994, p. 4). The components of mindfulness, particularly awareness and acceptance of one's experiences in the moment, have been shown to be effective against worry, fear, anxiety, anger, and other forms of psychological distress (for a review see Keng, Smoski, & Robins, 2011). There are four major forms of mindfulness-based interventions: Mindfulness-Based Stress Reduction (MBSR), Mindfulness-Based Cognitive Therapy (MBCT), Dialectical Behaviour Therapy (DBT), and Acceptance and Commitment Therapy (ACT). A growing body of research supports the effectiveness of these mindfulness-based interventions in treating a number of disorders, including depression, substance abuse, borderline personality disorder, and anxiety disorders (Keng et al., 2011). Mindfulness-based interventions have a positive impact on an individual's psychological health through various mechanisms. For example, mindfulness training causes individuals to view their thoughts and emotions as passing mental events rather than identifying with them or believing thoughts to be an accurate representation of reality (Segal et al., 2002; Shapiro, Carlson, Astin, & Freedman, 2006). Furthermore, as a result of attending to all experiences in a nonjudgmental manner, mindfulness training desensitizes individuals such that distressing situations that may otherwise have been avoided, along with accompanying thoughts and emotions, become less distressing (Carmody, Baer, Lykins, & Olendzki, 2009).

SOCIO-CULTURAL INFLUENCES

Various theorists and researchers have considered the role that society or close others (e.g., friends, parents, partners) play in the etiology and maintenance of mental health disorders.

STIGMA Stigma surrounding mental health issues plays an important role in the maintenance of a number of mental health disorders, since it is one of the largest barriers to individuals seeking treatment (Corrigan, 2004; Komiya, Good, & Sherrod, 2000; Vogel, Wade, & Haake, 2006). Despite the fact that one in five Canadians will experience a mental health illness in their lifetime, only about one-third of those who need mental health services in Canada actually receive them (Health Canada, 2002; Statistics Canada, 2003a). Stigma causes people to avoid treatment so that they are not labelled publicly as being "mentally ill" and so that they don't have to accept the label of "someone who needs psychological help," both of which lead to decreases in self-esteem (Corrigan, 2004).

Mental health labels serve the important function of communicating to health professionals which disorder an individual is suffering from and assisting the individual in receiving supports (e.g., financial assistance, medication, or therapy). However, **labelling theory** (Rosenhan, 1973) suggests that a person being identified as having a disorder results in other people perceiving that person as dysfunctional and different. This perception, which can persist even after recovery, results in the person being treated disadvantageously and even disrespectfully. For example, if an individual is labelled with a mental health disorder, the public may apply stereotypes associated with mental illness, such as having social skills deficits, being unkempt in appearance, and displaying psychiatric symptoms (Corrigan, 2000; Penn & Martin, 1998). Thus, even though labelling does not produce mental disorders, it may have a number of negative outcomes, such as discrimination, devaluation, and a corresponding loss of self-esteem (Link, Struening, Neese-Todd, Asmussen, & Phelan, 2001).

A recent study examined the influence of both **public stigma** (the typical societal response that people have to stigmatizing attributes) and **self-stigma** (the internalized psychological impact of public stigma) on undergraduates' perceptions of seeking mental health services (Bathje & Pryor, 2011). The authors discovered that simply being aware that mental health issues are stigmatized by the public did not directly influence attitudes toward help-seeking. Rather, it was the internalization of stigmatizing beliefs (self-stigma) that caused a decrease in self-esteem and led individuals to have negative attitudes toward help-seeking. Furthermore, greater sympathy for individuals suffering from a mental disorder (in this case depression) and less blame directed toward them were both related to more positive attitudes toward help-seeking.

The importance of reducing mental health stigma and increasing the use of mental health services in Canada is just beginning to be realized. A number of anti-stigma campaigns have recently been launched throughout the country (see the Applied Clinical Case on the next page). If you are interested in reading more about initiatives and projects being run throughout Canada, visit the Mental Health Commission of Canada website at www.mentalhealthcomission.ca.

6 BEFORE MOVING ON

What are the advantages and disadvantages of being labelled with a mental health disorder?

SOCIAL SUPPORT There is clear evidence that **social support** from close others is a significant factor in preventing or reducing the intensity of psychological problems, and that the absence of such support is a factor in the causal chain leading to dysfunction (Cohen & Wills, 1985). For example, people who experience a severe trauma (e.g., a terrorist attack or a natural disaster) may subsequently suffer from post-traumatic stress disorder (PTSD), a debilitating problem that is discussed in more detail in Chapter 5. However, not all people who are exposed to such traumas develop PTSD. Among the factors that reduce the probability of suffering from PTSD after a traumatic experience is support from friends and family (see Charavustra & Cloitre, 2008). Similarly, adolescents at high risk for psychopathology, because their parents exhibit an affective or personality

APPLIED CLINICAL CASE

An Olympian Speaks Out About Mental Health

Clara Hughes, a Canadian Olympian, is the only athlete in the world to have won multiple medals in both the summer (cycling) and winter (speed skating) games. In the Vancouver 2010 Olympics she was given the honour of carrying the country's flag, and she went on to win a bronze medal for long-track speed skating. Clara also plans on cycling in the 2012 Olympic Games in London. Among her numerous accomplishments, Clara is an Officer of the Order of Canada, has received several honorary doctorates, and was inducted into the Canadian Walk of Fame in November 2010.

What fewer Canadians might know about this accomplished and inspiring woman is that Clara, like countless other Canadians, has struggled with depression. Following her Olympic debut in 1996, she began to notice that something was wrong, even though she didn't know what it was at the time. When Clara's depression first began she was living alone in Hamilton; she slept 17 hours a day, cried uncontrollably, gained weight, and wished sometimes that she wasn't on the earth so she wouldn't have to deal with things. Most of all, she felt embarrassed by how she felt and looked. Like many other people, because of this embarrassment, Clara initially found it difficult to seek help and talk about her struggles with depression.

Clara battled her depression for two years by relying on the support system of her husband, family, friends, and coaches; talking to a counsellor; changing her diet; and exercising. Having seen the importance of seeking help from others to overcome her depression, Clara recently acted as national spokesperson for Bell Let's Talk Day. This campaign is about increasing awareness, reducing stigma, and helping to change people's attitudes and behaviours about mental health issues.

Clara's story emphasizes the importance of reducing stigma so that individuals suffering with mental health issues can feel comfortable in reaching out to others to receive the support they need to overcome their disorders.

disorder, are less likely to develop psychiatric symptoms if they have greater perceived social support (Hoefnagels, Meesters, & Simenon, 2007).

A recent longitudinal study examined the effects of social networks (size and frequency of contact with close others) and social support (perceived quality of support) on common mental health disorders following specific life events (Maulik, Eaton, & Bradshaw, 2010). Across all life events, more social support from a spouse, friend, or relative was associated with a significant reduction in the odds of suffering from psychological distress; social networks and social support had almost no direct or buffering effect on major depressive disorder, general anxiety disorder, and alcohol abuse or dependence disorder. The results emphasize the importance of the quality of support, rather than frequency of contact or the number of close others an individual has, particularly for milder forms of mental health issues such as psychological distress. That is, it is critically important for individuals to involve their social networks and social support at earlier stages of their illness to reduce the risk of developing a mental health disorder.

GENDER The influence of societies' stereotypes and people's consequent reaction to specific groups also seems to play a role in the development of disorders, as do poverty and social class. There are very obvious differences in male and female rates for several disorders (Ingram & Price, 2010), and it may be that gender-specific socialization processes render males and females differentially likely to acquire one or another disorder. For example, 90 to 95 percent of individuals diagnosed with eating disorders are women (American Psychiatric Association, 2000). In Western cultures, including Canada and the United States, being thin is associated with fitness, health, and attractiveness, whereas being overweight is associated with poor health, a lack of willpower, and unattractiveness (for a review, see Walcott, Pratt, & Patel, 2003). Female adolescents in particular are at risk for being influenced by other individuals' views of attractiveness, including those portrayed by the media. The more women internalize the Western view of attractiveness (that female beauty is synonymous with a lean body) portrayed by the media, the more likely they are to be unhappy with their own body type and the more likely they are to engage in disordered eating patterns to obtain the "thin ideal" (Stice, Schupak-Neubert, Shaw, & Stein 1994; Tiggemann & Pickering, 1996).

In addition, Canadian psychologists Pantony and Caplan (1991) point out that certain personality disorders appear to reflect exaggerated features of either female or male stereotyped behaviours. For example, dependent personality disorder is characterized by dependency and submissiveness, whereas antisocial personality disorder involves aggressiveness and self-interest. Very few men are diagnosed with dependent personality disorder and very few women are considered to have antisocial personality disorder. Is this sharp difference due to bias in the diagnostic criteria or related to which clinicians are doing the diagnosis, or is it simply the case that men and women are diagnosed with personality disorders as a result of displaying exaggerated features of their gender roles that have been reinforced since childhood? Clearly, gender roles have an influence on the identification of disorders, but it is not clear yet exactly what form this influence takes.

7 BEFORE MOVING ON

To what extent do you think altering gender stereotypes might change the prevalence rates of mental health problems for males and females?

RACE AND POVERTY Race and poverty have also been linked to the prevalence of psychiatric disorders. However, because ethnic minorities tend to be concentrated in poorer areas, it is difficult to disentangle these two influences. Members of ethnic minorities are the victims of various forms of prejudice that exclude them from many opportunities available to the dominant group, and they are often treated as inferior and subjected to denigrating jokes. These prejudices, and lack of opportunities, create stress in the lives of minorities in the same way that poverty does. When minority ethnicity and poverty go together, as they so often do, we can expect a number of psychological and social problems.

Poverty is a significant risk factor for mental disorder (Bruce, Takeuchi, & Leaf, 1991; Samaan, 2000; Wang, Schmitz, & Dewa, 2010). Severe psychological problems are three times higher among the lowest income groups (Dohrenwend et al., 1992). These findings may reflect similar effects noted for racial prejudice. The resentment at being poor, in an otherwise reasonably wealthy society, may generate behaviours that are viewed by others as antisocial or dysfunctional. Of course, it may be that because being poor produces such high levels of stress (Adler et al., 1994), higher rates of psychological dysfunction are to be expected. However, it might also be that dysfunctional people gravitate to the lower end of the socio-economic spectrum. Finally, it may be that professionals from the privileged classes are more apt to apply denigrating diagnoses (for example, antisocial personality disorder or schizophrenia) to patients from the lower classes, while reserving more acceptable diagnoses (for example, chronic fatigue syndrome) for the upper classes.

Integrative Theories

Throughout this book, we will see evidence for the influence of various biological factors in the onset of many psychological disorders. We will also find that environmental influences (psychological as well as socio-cultural) have an important role to play. In fact, it is only through the interaction of all of these various influences that disorders emerge. Three models have been proposed that attempt to integrate these diverse influences.

SYSTEMS THEORY

Systems theory proposes that the whole is more than the sum of its parts, whereas reductionism says that the whole is the sum of its parts. A systems theory approach has had profound influences on many areas of science, including biology, engineering, and computer science (Davidson, 1982). This view of the way things behave sees causation as the combined effect of multiple factors that are likely to be bidirectional. For example, persistent misbehaviour of a child appears to influence parental behaviour such that the parents' actions worsen the child's behaviour (Hinshaw & Lee, 2003). This is an example of bidirectional causation unlike the unidirectional causation so dear to the hearts of reductionists.

Not only does systems theory suggest that causation is the result of multiple factors interacting, and that causation is a bidirectional process, it also points out that the same end result can arise from one of many possible causes. In medicine it is clear that the same disease can have different causes in different people. As will be shown in Chapter 7, heart disease can result from stress, a particular behavioural style, smoking, poor diet, lack of exercise, and constitutional factors. Systems theory, therefore, would seem to have something significant to offer theorists and researchers who study abnormal human behaviour.

THE DIATHESIS-STRESS PERSPECTIVE

According to the **diathesis-stress perspective**, a predisposition to developing a disorder (the diathesis) interacting with the experience of stress causes mental disorders. According to this view, this interaction underlies the onset of all disorders, although either the predisposition or the stress may be more important in a particular disorder, or in a particular person.

Note that this perspective cannot be categorized as either a biological or a psychological model. A diathesis may be either biological or psychological—as may a stressor. One example of a biological diathesis is the role played by genetics in schizophrenia, mood disorders, and alcoholism. Dysfunctions of the central or peripheral nervous system or of the endocrine system may have a genetic basis or may be caused by events such as problems of gestation or birth, but in either case would be seen as a biological diathesis.

Psychological diatheses may arise as a result of temperament, childhood abuse, inappropriate parenting, or social and cultural pressures. For example, a readiness to acquire dissociative identity disorder appears to come from childhood sexual abuse. A series of unpredictable and unpleasant events may produce a sense of resignation that predisposes a person to depression (Dozois, Dobson, & Westra, 2004). Socio-cultural standards of an attractive body shape seem to create a diathesis for eating disorders (Brownell & Fairburn, 1995).

However, a predisposition will not produce a disorder without the trigger of some stress, whether biological (such as physical illness), psychological (such as breakdown of a relationship), or social (such as perceived pressure from others to meet certain standards). In the case of Hailey, described at the beginning of the chapter, her high reactivity to stress, along with the fact that depression runs in her family, could be considered the diathesis; her breakup with her boyfriend was likely the stressor that triggered her disorder.

The advantage of this perspective is that it encourages us to look at a range of possible influences rather than fixing on a single factor. This perspective also allows the possibility that different individuals may develop disorders through the influence of different diatheses and different stressors.

THE BIOPSYCHOSOCIAL MODEL

Like the diathesis-stress perspective, the **biopsychosocial model** declares that disorders cannot be understood as resulting from the influence of one factor, be it biological, psychological, or social. Each of these factors must be taken into account, again with differing emphases depending on the disorder in question.

Several lines of research indicate the significance for human functioning of the interaction among multiple biological and environmental processes (Ingram & Price, 2001). For example, Plomin and Neiderhiser (1992) have integrated research findings to strongly suggest that genetics and environment interact to determine human behaviour. Brain functions have been shown both to influence and to be influenced by psychological and social processes; the relationship is reciprocal (Cacioppo & Berntson, 1992).

There is increased recognition of the need to integrate existing models to provide a more comprehensive understanding of abnormality. Such integration often requires interdisciplinary research and a general openness to relating concepts from diverse theoretical perspectives. In recent years, such integration has become more commonplace. For example, research by Elizabeth Hayden, currently at the University of Western Ontario, and her colleagues has investigated the relationships between genotype, personality, cognition, and behaviour in childhood vulnerability to mood and anxiety disorders (Hayden et al., 2010a, 2010b; Hayden et al., 2008a, 2008b). Attachment theory has also been integrated with cognitive models (Ingram et al., 1998; Ingram & Price, 2001). Another related shift that has occurred over the years has been the movement away from conceptualizing psychopathology as "within the individual" to examining contextual factors that operate "outside of the individual" (Mash & Dozois, 2003).

SUMMARY

- There has been a consistent move toward viewing the etiology of mental health problems from an integrative perspective.
- Biological, psychological, and socio-cultural factors interact in complex ways to produce psychiatric disorders.
- Single-factor theories are unlikely to explain the etiology of any disorder, and are gradually falling into disuse.
- Theories gain strength not because the evidence supports their predictions but rather because alternative explanations are rejected.
- Biological views propose that brain dysfunction, neurotransmitters, hormonal or peripheral nervous system problems, or genetic errors cause psychological problems.
- Neurotransmitters are chemical substances that carry messages from one neuron to the next. Disturbances in neurotransmitter systems can often result in abnormal behaviour.
- Recent research emphasizes the importance of the genotype–environment interaction, which describes how features that are inherited interact with the environment to produce behaviour.
- Freud and other psychodynamic theorists suggested that behaviour is controlled by unconscious forces.
- Freud discussed three levels of consciousness that determine the accessibility of thoughts and desires: the conscious, which contains information of which we are currently aware; the preconscious, which holds information that is not presently in awareness but can be brought into awareness; and the unconscious, which contains the majority of an individual's memories and drives that can be raised into awareness only with difficulty or particular techniques.
- The three personality structures of psychodynamic theories include the id, which represents biological or instinctual drives; the ego, which develops to control the desires of the id; and the superego, which is the internalization of the moral standards of society.
- The ego develops defence mechanisms in an attempt to control the desires of the id.
- Freud also described stages of psychosexual development, which indicate points in experience where problems can arise.
- Behavioural theorists argue that all or almost all human behaviour, including abnormal behaviour, is learned.
- In classical conditioning, a neutral stimulus (the CS) comes to elicit a conditioned response (CR) through its

being paired with another stimulus (UCS) that already elicits that reflexive response (UCR).

- In operant conditioning, when a behaviour increases in frequency in response to consistent consequences, reinforcement is said to occur; when the behaviour decreases in frequency as a result of its consequences, this is described as punishment.
- Cognitive theorists believe that mental health problems stem from dysfunctional beliefs, attitudes, or ways of thinking.
- Three main levels of cognition are emphasized in cognitive theory: schemas, information processing and intermediate beliefs, and automatic thoughts.
- Schemas, or internal representations of stored information and experiences, influence an individual's thoughts, beliefs, information processing, feelings, and behaviour.
- Identifying an individual as having a disorder often results in other people perceiving that person as dysfunctional and different.
- Being stigmatized for having a mental health disorder can cause an individual to experience a decrease in self-esteem and fail to seek treatment for the disorder or the support of close others.
- Reducing mental health stigma is essential so that individuals suffering with mental health issues can feel comfortable reaching out to others and receive the necessary support to overcome their disorders.
- Having high-quality relationships with close others (e.g., partner, friends, family) prevents or reduces the intensity of psychological distress following stressful events, while the absence of such support is a factor in the causal chain leading to dysfunction.
- There are clear differences between male and female rates for several disorders.
- Race and poverty have also been linked to the prevalence of psychiatric disorders.

MySearchLab offers you extensive help with your writing and research projects and provides round-the-clock access to credible and reliable source material. Chapter quizzes and a full electronic version of the text are also provided. Answers to the Before Moving On feature are provided on the MySearchLab. Take a tour at www.mysearchlab.com.

KEY TERMS

single-factor explanation (p. 25)
interactionist explanation (p. 25)
null hypothesis (p. 26)
etiology (p. 26)
neurotransmitters (p. 28)
brain plasticity (p. 30)
behavioural genetics (p. 32)
genotype–environment interaction (p. 32)
concordance (p. 33)
genetic linkage studies (p. 33)
molecular biology (p. 33)
psychodynamic (p. 34)
conscious (p. 34)
preconscious (p. 34)
unconscious (p. 34)
id (p. 34)
ego (p. 34)
superego (p. 35)
phallic stage (p. 35)
Oedipal complex (p. 35)
Electra complex (p. 35)
defence mechanisms (p. 35)
classical conditioning (p. 36)
two-factor theory (p. 38)
operant conditioning (p. 38)
reinforcement (p. 38)
punishment (p. 38)
social learning theory (p. 39)
cognitive-behavioural theory (p. 39)
rational-emotive behaviour therapy (p. 39)
schemas (p. 39)
content-specificity (p. 40)
self-actualization (p. 42)
labelling theory (p. 43)
public stigma (p. 43)
self-stigma (p. 43)
social support (p. 43)
systems theory (p. 45)
diathesis-stress perspective (p. 45)
biopsychosocial model (p. 46)

UZMA S. REHMAN • DAVID J. A. DOZOIS

Chapter 3

Classification and Diagnosis

LEARNING OBJECTIVES

AFTER READING THIS CHAPTER, STUDENTS WILL BE ABLE TO:

1. Describe why we need a classification system for mental disorders.
2. Outline what criteria can be used to evaluate a system of classification.
3. Describe the history of classification of mental disorders.
4. Describe the multiaxial system of classification of mental disorders.
5. Identify the key reasons why the current system of classification (DSM-IV-TR) is being revised.
6. Outline the major criticisms of the current and past systems of classification of mental disorders.

Nick is a 30-year-old single man who lives with his widowed mother. Although his mother has repeatedly encouraged him to move out in order to gain his independence, Nick is comfortable residing with his mother and very resistant to these suggestions. Every time he thinks about living on his own, Nick becomes overwhelmed by feelings of anxiety and uncertainty regarding the possibility of having to take care of himself. He has suffered from diabetes and high blood pressure for the past five years, at least partially as a result of weight issues. Given that his medical conditions require strict and regimented medical care, Nick is convinced that he requires his mother's assistance to ensure that he is properly medicated.

In addition to his medical conditions, Nick has had a lifelong history of anxiety. His panic attacks have increased in frequency over the past year, often occurring twice a day. Nick's first panic attack occurred when he was 22 years of age. He recalls being in a movie theatre with a friend, and suddenly becoming paralyzed by an intense feeling of terror. He began to tremble and sweat while feeling helpless in gaining control over the anxiety. Following this incident, Nick became afraid of social situations or places where he might experience another attack and be unable to leave.

Although Nick began to limit his time spent in social settings with friends, he was still able to work full time as a computer technician for a small business located close to his home. His job entailed minimal contact with others, and allowed Nick to work from home most of the time. He found this job appealing not only because he could avoid having to work among others, but also because he could work in the comfort of his own home with his mother present to prepare him meals and keep him on task. However, just over a year ago, Nick was laid off from his job as a result of company cutbacks. Since this setback, he has rarely worked up the nerve to leave the house. At the urging of his mother, Nick went to a psychologist for an assessment and received the following diagnoses:

- *Axis I:* Panic Disorder with Agoraphobia
- *Axis II:* Dependent Personality Disorder
- *Axis III:* Obesity and Diabetes
- *Axis IV:* Unemployed (loss of job)
- *Axis V:* Level of Functioning: 55

In the realm of medicine and abnormal psychology, a **diagnosis** consists of a determination or identification of the nature of a person's disease or condition, or a statement of that finding. In Nick's case, the psychologist who assessed him determined, based on information that he gathered, that Nick's symptoms were consistent with a diagnosis of panic disorder with agoraphobia. In Chapter 5, we will review the specific symptoms that have to be present for such a diagnosis to be made. Later in this chapter, we will also discuss why the psychologist diagnosed Nick on five different axes. In order to make Nick's diagnosis, the psychologist relied on a **diagnostic** (or classification) **system**, a system of rules for recognizing and grouping various types of abnormalities (Glanze, Anderson, & Anderson, 1985).

Why Do We Need a Classification System for Mental Disorders?

Classification is a fundamental activity of all humans. From a very early age we learn to classify objects by their colours, shapes, and sizes. As we get older, our understanding of these objects becomes more sophisticated and we refine our taxonomy. The term *bird* may have been used initially to refer to "all things that fly." As we develop, however, we start to make more specific distinctions among these objects, identifying them as robins, crows, sparrows, airplanes, and so on. Classification is also of vital importance to science. The ability to categorize information allows scientists to better identify and understand various phenomena, from molecular structures, to personality, to galaxies.

A diagnostic system for mental disorders serves a number of important functions, including providing a description of different mental disorders. For example, what are the features of a panic disorder, and how does this disorder differ from depression or schizophrenia? By describing and organizing different mental disorders, a diagnostic system gives us a vocabulary for communicating about mental disorders with others. Let's say that the psychologist who worked with Nick had to refer him to someone else for treatment; in his referral he would note "panic disorder," and this diagnosis would provide the other mental health professional with information about what type of symptoms Nick is experiencing. In research, too, diagnostic systems serve a critical function. For example, psychopathology researchers rely on diagnostic systems to identify individuals who meet criteria for a particular disorder and to exclude individuals who do not meet criteria for that disorder. Research findings, in turn, help us to refine and improve our diagnostic systems. This feedback loop is vital for the continued improvement of our diagnostic systems. Accurate diagnosis also provides important information for effective clinical intervention. Nick's diagnosis of "panic disorder" should inform the type of treatment he receives. Diagnostic systems are also needed for surveying population health and for understanding the prevalence and etiology (i.e., causes) of particular mental health problems (Hyman, 2010).

To gather all the information required for a proper diagnosis, a thorough assessment is required. Students often confuse assessment and diagnosis. An **assessment** is a procedure through which information is gathered systematically in the evaluation of a condition; this assessment procedure yields information that serves as the basis for a diagnosis. A mental health assessment may include interviews with the patient or the patient's family, medical testing, psychophysiological or psychological testing, and the completion of self-report scales or other report rating scales (see Chapter 4). A diagnostic system provides a number of criteria for a disorder; if a certain number of these criteria or indications are present, the person is diagnosed as having that particular disorder. Therefore, information from each of the assessment procedures contributes to the formulation of a diagnosis.

1 BEFORE MOVING ON

In psychology, who are some of the stakeholders in having a useful and effective system of classification of mental disorders?

The Perfect Diagnostic System

The perfect diagnostic system would classify disorders on the basis of a study of presenting symptoms (pattern of behaviours), etiology (history of the development of the symptoms and underlying causes), prognosis (future development of this pattern of behaviours), and response to treatment. In the development of this diagnostic system, a large number of people would have been thoroughly assessed psychologically and physically, in terms of feelings, thoughts, behaviours, and various other important features (e.g., laboratory tests and physical examination findings; see Widiger & Clark, 2000). A thorough history would have been taken in order to understand how various features developed. These people would then have been observed over a long period of time to assess the natural progression of their problems. In addition, various treatments would have been tried on groups of these patients, in a controlled fashion, to assess their effectiveness. Diagnostic categories would then be established by determining exactly which patterns of presenting problems, with what kind of history, developed in which particular manner and responded differentially to various treatments. Presumably, different symptom clusters, with dissimilar histories and differing normal progression, would signal different syndromes. In the resulting perfect system, each sign or symptom would be found in only one diagnostic category; there would be no overlap in the symptom profiles presented by patients. Furthermore, treatment modalities would be so thoroughly developed that we would have at our disposal a perfect cure for each diagnostic category, which would alleviate suffering for people who fit that category with pinpoint accuracy.

Unfortunately, scientific research is not so neat; nor are human beings. Practicalities preclude us from being able to systematically observe and measure many aspects of functioning in large numbers of people, in a controlled way, over long periods of time. Even if we knew which symptoms were important to note, human beings are incredibly complex, rapidly changing, and socially embedded organisms, and multiple interacting events and processes contribute to both adaptive and maladaptive behaviour (Mash & Dozois, 2003). The history of therapeutic interventions has also revealed how difficult it is to implement procedures following strict scientific principles.

Characteristics of Strong Diagnostic Systems

Most researchers and clinicians believe that a good diagnostic system is very useful, if not essential (see Table 3.1). What criteria are used to determine whether a diagnostic system is useful or not? The first criterion is **reliability**. To be useful, a diagnostic system must give the same measurement for a given thing every time. For example, let's say that when you get home tonight, you decide to weigh yourself. You are surprised by the reading and you decide that you want to check again, just to be sure. This time, when you weigh yourself, your scale reading suggests that you are five pounds heavier! A little annoyed, you stand on the scale again, and this time you are back to the original reading. You might think to yourself, "Time to throw out the scale." It is difficult to trust the reading on the scale because it's not reliable. You certainly wouldn't use it any longer if accurate measurement of weight was important to you. A type of reliability that is particularly relevant when evaluating the value of a diagnostic system is inter-rater reliability. **Inter-rater reliability** refers to the extent to which two clinicians agree on the diagnosis of a particular patient. For example, if a system does not allow clinicians to agree on the signs and symptoms that constitute a specific disorder, inter-rater reliability will remain low. A classic study on the reliability of the diagnostic process was carried out many years ago (Beck et al., 1962). In this investigation, four highly experienced psychiatrists interviewed 153 new inpatients in a psychiatric hospital. Each patient was interviewed first by one psychiatrist and then a few hours later by a second psychiatrist. The psychiatrists were asked to formulate a diagnosis based on the interviews. The overall percentage agreement between pairs of raters was rather low, at 54 percent. That is, just over half of the time, the two psychiatrists agreed on a given patient's diagnosis.

One might speculate that this disagreement arose because the patient did not give the same report to both psychiatrists. A patient might, for example, mention domestic violence during one interview and not the other. Indeed, such discrepancies did occur, but when the authors of the study analyzed the data, they found this to be the least important contributor to poor reliability. A more significant cause was differences between the interviewers, such as different interview techniques or differences in interpretation and in the importance given to certain symptoms. However, the factor most responsible by far for poor inter-rater reliability was the inadequacy of the diagnostic system itself.

The second criterion is **validity**. In a diagnostic system, validity is determined by whether a diagnostic category is able to predict behavioural and psychiatric disorders accurately. The two most important types of validity for diagnostic systems are concurrent validity and predictive validity. **Concurrent validity** refers to the ability of a diagnostic category to estimate an individual's present standing on factors related to the disorder but not themselves part of the diagnostic criteria. For example, although significant academic underachievement and a downward drift in socio-economic status are not diagnostic items for schizophrenia, they are clearly found in most people with schizophrenia. If an assessment of the non-schizophrenic siblings of people diagnosed with schizophrenia revealed that they had better education and higher income, this would be an indication of concurrent validity. A major criticism of the DSM is that it sheds little light on the non-symptom attributes of people with a given diagnosis. Another essential requirement of a good diagnostic system is **predictive validity**, the ability of a test to predict the future course of an individual's development. The key to a clear understanding of a disorder is its progression. As we will see in Chapter 15, a diagnosis of conduct disorder in early adolescence has been found to be highly related to a diagnosis of antisocial personality disorder as an adult. If all children with conduct disorder were reassessed at 20 years of age, and achieved a diagnosis of antisocial personality disorder, the predictive validity of conduct disorder would be perfect. As we shall see later, this is certainly not the case.

TABLE 3.1 FUNCTIONS OF A GOOD CLASSIFICATION SYSTEM

Function	Description
1. Organization of clinical information	It provides the essentials of a patient's condition coherently and concisely.
2. Shorthand communication	It enhances the effective interchange of information, by clearly transmitting important features of a disorder and ignoring unimportant features.
3. Prediction of natural development	It allows accurate short-term and long-term prediction of an individual's development.
4. Treatment recommendations	It allows accurate predictions of the most effective interventions.
5. Heuristic value	It allows the investigation and clarification of issues related to a problem area. It also enhances theory-building.
6. Guidelines for financial support	It provides guidelines to services needed, including payment of caregivers.

2 BEFORE MOVING ON

Why is it important to have a classification system that helps us understand the prognosis of disorders?

The History of Classification of Mental Disorders

As we learned in Chapter 1, an interest in the classification of psychopathology dates back at least to the Middle Ages. Modern efforts at classification owe much to Kraepelin's work in the nineteenth century, but even his categories and descriptors bear little resemblance to contemporary systems.

A milestone in the modern development of a comprehensive diagnostic scheme was the World Health Organization's decision to add mental health disorders to the International List of the Causes of Death. In 1948, the list was expanded to become the International Statistical Classification of Diseases, Injuries, and Causes of Death (ICD), a comprehensive listing of all diseases, including abnormal behaviour. In response to perceived inadequacies of the ICD system, the American Psychiatric Association published its own classification system, the *Diagnostic and Statistical Manual* (DSM), in 1952. However, the original DSM, and its second edition (DSM-II; American Psychiatric Association [APA], 1968), proved highly unsatisfactory. These two volumes were very brief and contained only vague descriptions of the diagnostic categories. For example, DSM-I contained 106 categories of disorders that fell under the rubric of 3 major categories (organic brain syndromes, functional disorder, and mental deficiency). The current system contains 407 separate categories (Cantwell, 1996). DSM-I and DSM-II were also greatly influenced by psychoanalytic theory, focused on internal unobservable processes, were not empirically based, and contained few objective criteria. Such influences are illustrated by an excerpt from the preamble to the specific diagnostic categories in DSM-II (APA, 1968, p. 39), describing "Neuroses":

> Anxiety is the chief characteristic of the neuroses. It may be felt and expressed directly, or it may be controlled unconsciously and automatically by conversion, displacement and various other psychological mechanisms. Generally, these mechanisms produce symptoms experienced as subjective distress from which the patient desires relief.

Not surprisingly, the system proved wholly unreliable, and as a result it was not unusual for clinicians to come up with widely differing diagnoses for the same person.

In 1980, the American Psychiatric Association published a newly revised and transformed diagnostic manual, DSM-III, which was followed by a more modest revision in 1987, DSM-III-R. DSM-III introduced several significant differences. In an attempt to improve reliability, field trials were conducted, substantiating the content of the manual by placing greater emphasis on empirical research. Some 12 500 patients and 550 clinicians were involved in these trials (Widiger & Trull, 1991). Furthermore, these versions of the manual became **atheoretical**; that is, they moved away from endorsing any one theory of abnormal psychology, becoming more pragmatic as they moved to more precise behavioural descriptions. To increase precision, they operationally defined the required number of symptoms and specified how long the symptoms had to last in order to meet diagnostic criteria. DSM-III-R was developed to be **polythetic**, meaning that an individual could be diagnosed with a certain subset of symptoms without having to meet all criteria. Perhaps the greatest innovation was the development of a **multiaxial** requirement. For the first time, in addition to a primary diagnosis, diagnosticians were required to provide substantial patient information, evaluating and rating patients on five different axes, or areas of functioning (this is more fully explained in the next section of this chapter).

Against this background, the American Psychiatric Association charged a task force to begin work on DSM-IV, to improve on its previous work. Thirteen work groups were established to cover each major diagnostic category. Professionals from all fields related to mental health were consulted. In addition to comprehensive literature reviews, old data sets were reanalyzed and an additional 12 multisite field trials were conducted to collect new data (Widiger & Clark, 2000). These field trials were constituted to ensure that participants represented diverse socio-economic, cultural, and ethnic backgrounds. The field trials included 70 sites, and evaluated some 6000 patients. In addition to reliability of the diagnoses, these field trials assessed the validity of the diagnoses, and set out to establish improved criteria. Clinicians used several draft versions of proposed diagnostic categories in their work and reported back to the work groups on their findings. Representatives from all over the world, including 27 Canadian psychiatrists and psychologists, sat on the committees or consulted with them. The result of this mammoth undertaking was DSM-IV (APA, 1994). A minor text revision of the manual was released in 2000 (DSM-IV-TR), and substantial work has been conducted on the next major edition, the DSM-5.

Currently, DSM-IV-TR is widely used in Canada and the United States; it is also the most used classification system worldwide for research in psychopathology. Clinicians in the European Union more commonly use the tenth edition of the World Health Organization's (1992) *International Classification of Diseases* (ICD). Like the DSM, the ICD is also undergoing revision (Millon, Krueger, & Simonsen, 2010). It is important to appreciate, however, that due to the considerable consultation among mental health researchers around the world, these latest revisions reflect increasing similarities between two modern classification systems for mental disorders (Andrews et al., 2009; Bernstein, 2011). For instance, to facilitate the use of DSM-IV-TR internationally, its appendix contains diagnostic criteria with ICD-10 codes.

3 BEFORE MOVING ON

One of the major limitations of DSM-I and DSM-II is that these systems were based on psychoanalytic conceptualizations of psychopathology. Why is this a problem?

DSM-IV-TR: A Multiaxial Approach

One of the major innovations introduced in the DSM-III and retained in all future editions was the use of a multiaxial system for classification. Previously, clinicians typically rated patients on the most conspicuous aspect of their abnormal behaviour. Beginning with DSM-III, the system acknowledged that a person's life circumstances as a whole need to be considered; diagnosticians were required to evaluate an individual on a broad array of information that might be of concern. With DSM-IV-TR, clinicians assess patients under five different axes, or aspects, of the person's condition. Each of the five axes addresses a different type of information.

AXIS I CLINICAL DISORDERS

Axis I records the most obvious disorders. Included in Axis I are the psychological disorders that have been recognized for centuries because of their bizarre nature (e.g., schizophrenia) or the difficulty they pose in the everyday life of individuals (e.g., mood disorders).

AXIS II PERSONALITY DISORDERS

Axis II focuses on the presence of generally less severe long-term disturbances, which nevertheless may interfere with a person's life. Lilienfeld and Landfield (2008) suggest that the authors of DSM-IV-TR wanted Axis I to reflect what the patient *has* and Axis II to describe who the patient *is*. Usually, individuals with these problems can function in jobs and relationships, albeit with significant difficulty. In our opening case, Nick was found to have a dependent personality disorder; this diagnosis is not his most obvious problem, but it is still significant. Previously, these less dramatic behaviour patterns were often missed in the presence of more prominent Axis I symptoms. Suppose that a psychologist is assessing someone with an alcohol use disorder. The psychological and medical problems associated with alcohol abuse may be so severe that the psychologist overlooks a subtler lifelong behaviour pattern of pervasive social inhibition and feelings of inadequacy. This pattern may indicate an Axis II disorder called avoidant personality disorder. Did the personality disorder lead to the alcohol use disorder? Will it affect the required treatment? Maybe or maybe not, but without being directed by Axis II the psychologist might not have seen the whole range of the person's problems.

AXIS III GENERAL MEDICAL CONDITIONS

Axis III covers any medical disorder that might be relevant to understanding or managing the case. This axis recognizes that medical disorders may cause psychological disorders, or they may affect future development or treatment. Suppose that a previously well-functioning individual is left partially paralyzed by a car accident and then develops depression. The paralysis has to be considered not only in terms of how it contributes to the depression but also in terms of what treatments are possible and what outcomes can be expected.

AXIS IV PSYCHOSOCIAL AND ENVIRONMENTAL PROBLEMS

Axis IV and Axis V are significant additions to the DSM classification system. *Axis IV* collects information on the patient's life circumstances, recognizing that individuals live within a social milieu and that stressful social circumstances might contribute to symptom onset. Suppose that two women have anxiety disorder; one is single, and the other has an abusive husband and three children. Although their primary diagnosis is the same, their course of the illness and response to treatment might be quite different.

AXIS V GLOBAL ASSESSMENT OF FUNCTIONING

Axis V (see Table 3.2) measures how well a person is able to cope with the circumstances related to his or her problems. This information can be indicative of the need for treatment and of the person's coping mechanisms and can assist in planning intervention. Suppose that two people both saw children die in a terrible school bus accident, and both are suffering acute stress disorder. One finds himself unable to work and is having suicidal thoughts (Axis V: Level of current functioning: 50). The other is somewhat depressed and experiencing mild insomnia, but generally functioning satisfactorily (Axis V: Level of current functioning: 70). The first person may be given a fast-acting psychotropic medication to ensure that he does not deteriorate or attempt suicide. The other may need only short-term psychological counselling.

Although the multiaxial system was first introduced to encourage a multi-faceted understanding of individuals suffering from psychopathology, some critics contend that DSM-IV-TR does not really facilitate a comprehensive evaluation of patients, and further suggest that the coding of all the axes is rarely implemented in practice. It is quite probable that DSM-5 will include additional information under the five axes to facilitate a more well-rounded diagnostic evaluation and to assist with the formulation of a patient's vulnerabilities and sources of resilience (Gruenberg & Goldstein, 2003). For example, Axis II may encourage clinicians to gather information on an individual's temperament and dimensions of personality. In addition to current stressors, Axis IV may cover early traumatic experiences that may be related to the eventual onset of the main clinical syndrome.

Categories of Disorder in DSM-IV-TR

Although the organizational structure will change in DSM-5 (APA, 2010), DSM-IV-TR groups all the disorders listed on either Axis I or Axis II into 15 categories, on the basis of broad similarities in how they affect people, or how the people suffering from them may appear to the clinician.

TABLE 3.2 DSM-IV-TR MULTIAXIAL CLASSIFICATION SYSTEM, FIFTH AXIS

Axis V

Global Assessment of Functioning Scale (GAF Scale)

Consider psychological, social, and occupational functioning on a hypothetical continuum of mental health-illness. Do not include impairment in functioning due to physical (or environmental) limitations.

Code	Description
100–91	Superior functioning in a wide range of activities, life's problems never seem to get out of hand, is sought out by others because of his or her many positive qualities. No symptoms.
90–81	Absent or minimal symptoms (e.g., mild anxiety before an exam), good functioning in all areas, interested and involved in a wide range of activities, socially effective, generally satisfied with life, no more than everyday problems or concerns (e.g., an occasional argument with family members).
80–71	If symptoms are present, they are transient and expectable reactions to psychosocial stressors (e.g., difficulty concentrating after family argument); no more than slight impairment in social, occupational, or school functioning (e.g., temporarily falling behind in school work).
70–61	Some mild symptoms (e.g., depressed mood and mild insomnia) OR some difficulty in social, occupational, or school functioning (e.g., occasional truancy, or theft within the household), but generally functioning pretty well, with some meaningful interpersonal relationships.
60–51	Moderate symptoms (e.g., flat affect and circumstantial speech, occasional panic attacks) OR moderate difficulty in social, occupational, or school functioning (e.g., few friends, conflicts with peers or co-workers).
50–41	Serious symptoms (e.g., suicidal ideation, severe obsessional rituals, frequent shoplifting) OR any serious impairment in social, occupational, or school functioning (e.g., no friends, unable to keep a job).
40–31	Some impairment in reality testing or communication (e.g., speech is at times illogical, obscure, or irrelevant) OR major impairment in several areas, such as work or school, family relations, judgment, thinking, or mood (e.g., depressed man avoids friends, neglects family, and is unable to work; child frequently beats up younger children, is defiant at home, and is failing at school).
30–21	Behavior is considerably influenced by delusions or hallucinations OR serious impairment in communication or judgment (e.g., sometimes incoherent, acts grossly inappropriately, suicidal preoccupation) OR inability to function in almost all areas (e.g., stays in bed all day; no job, home, or friends).
20–11	Some danger of hurting self or others (e.g., suicide attempts without clear expectation of death, frequently violent, manic excitement) OR occasionally fails to maintain minimal personal hygiene (e.g., smears feces) OR gross impairment in communication (e.g., largely incoherent or mute).
10–1	Persistent danger of severely hurting self or others (e.g., recurrent violence) OR persistent inability to maintain minimal personal hygiene OR serious suicidal act with clear expectation of death.
0	Inadequate information.

Source: Reprinted with permission from the *Diagnostic and Statistical Manual of Mental Disorders, Fourth Edition, Text Revision.* (Copyright © 2000). American Psychiatric Association.

DISORDERS USUALLY FIRST DIAGNOSED IN INFANCY, CHILDHOOD, OR ADOLESCENCE

Included in this broad-ranging category are the intellectual, emotional, and physical disorders that typically begin before maturity (discussed in Chapter 15). Under the general classification of "Attention Deficit and Disruptive Behaviour Disorders" are *attention deficit/hyperactivity disorder*, in which the individual displays maladaptive levels of inattention, hyperactivity, or impulsivity, or a combination of these; *oppositional defiant disorder*, in which there is a recurrent pattern of negativistic, defiant, disobedient, and hostile behaviour toward authority figures; and *conduct disorder*, in which children persistently violate societal norms, rules, or the basic rights of others. Other diagnostic categories include *separation anxiety disorder*, in which the child becomes excessively anxious over the possibility of separation from parents or significant others; *mental retardation* (which will be called *intellectual developmental disorder* in DSM-5; APA, 2010), below-average intelligence with impairments in social adjustment, identified at an early age; *autistic disorder*, in which the child shows severe impediments in several areas of development, including social interactions and communication; *learning disorders*, in which the person's functioning in particular academic skill areas is significantly below average; *motor skills or communication disorders*, in which the individual experiences significant developmental problems with coordination or has difficulty with the reception or expression of language; *feeding and eating disorders* (for example, Pica's disorder involves eating substances that have no nutritional value, such as sand and feces, on a persistent basis); *tic disorders*, in which the body moves repeatedly, quickly, suddenly, and/or uncontrollably (tics can occur in any body part, or can be vocal); and *elimination disorders*, which refer to the repeated passage of urine (enuresis) or feces (encopresis) at inappropriate times and in inappropriate places.

DELIRIUM, DEMENTIA, AMNESIA, AND OTHER COGNITIVE DISORDERS

This broad category will be referred to as "Neurocognitive Disorders" in DSM-5 (APA, 2010). *Delirium* is a clouding of consciousness, wandering attention, and an incoherent stream of thought. It may be caused by several medical conditions as well as by poor diet and substance abuse. *Dementia*, a deterioration of mental capacities, is typically irreversible, and is usually associated with Alzheimer's disease, stroke, several other medical conditions, and substance abuse. *Amnestic syndrome* involves impairment in memory when there is no delirium or dementia, and is frequently linked to alcohol abuse. Some clinicians have argued that mild cognitive impairment, an early form of dementia, should be considered for inclusion in DSM-5 (Petersen & O'Brien, 2006), and it appears as though this will be the case (APA, 2010).

SUBSTANCE-RELATED DISORDERS

These disorders are brought about by the excessive use of a substance, which can be defined as anything that is ingested in order to produce a high, alter one's senses, or otherwise affect functioning. When the use of these substances results in social, occupational, psychological, or physical problems, it is considered a mental disorder. Individuals with such diagnoses may be unable to control or stop their use of substances and may have become physically addicted to them. Included in the group of substance abuse disorders are *alcohol use disorders*, *opioid use disorders*, *amphetamine use disorders*, *cocaine use disorders*, and *hallucinogen use disorders*, among others; however, there is early evidence that this section of the DSM will be significantly amended in the forthcoming DSM-5. For example, one of the recommendations put forward by the Substance-Related Disorders Work Group of the DSM-5 is that the diagnostic category include both substance use disorders as well as behavioural additions (e.g., gambling addiction) (APA, 2010). These disorders are discussed in Chapter 11.

SCHIZOPHRENIA AND OTHER PSYCHOTIC DISORDERS

The disorder known as *schizophrenia* is marked by severe debilitation in thinking and perception. People with schizophrenia suffer from a state of *psychosis*, often characterized by *delusions* (false beliefs, such as believing that people are trying to hurt them when there is no evidence of this) and *hallucinations* (false perceptions, such as hearing voices that comment on ongoing activity). People suffering from schizophrenia often lose the ability to care for themselves, relate to others, and function at work. Thought disorder is often prominent, demonstrated by *incoherent speech*, *loose associations* (unconnected pieces of thought), *inappropriate affect* (such as laughing while at a funeral), and *disorganized behaviour* (such as public masturbation). Essentially, people in a psychotic state have lost contact with the world and with others. Schizophrenia is discussed in Chapter 9.

MOOD DISORDERS

The most prominent and prevalent mood disorder is **major depressive disorder**, in which a person is extremely sad and discouraged, and displays a marked loss of pleasure in usual activities (see Chapter 8). Clinically depressed people often have severe problems sleeping, experience weight loss or gain, lack energy to do things, have difficulty concentrating, and feel worthless, hopeless, and

Children may develop disorders most commonly seen in adults, such as depression or schizophrenia. These are diagnosed according to the same basic criteria as those used for adults.

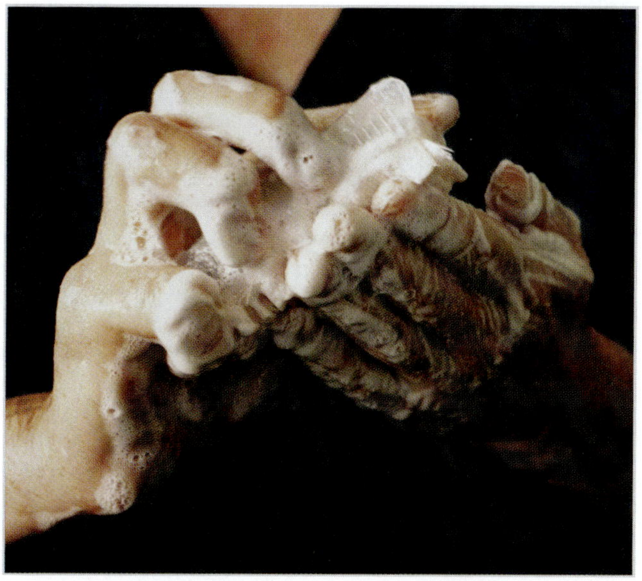

Compulsive handwashing is one possible manifestation of an anxiety disorder.

sometimes suicidal. Another mood disorder is **mania**, a condition in which a person seems extremely elated, more active, and in less need of sleep, and displays flights of somewhat disconnected ideas, grandiosity (an illusion of personal importance), and impairment in functioning. Severity of mood disorders can vary. In **bipolar disorders**, both depression and mania are exhibited. Less severe variants of these mood disorders include *dysthymia*, which is a more chronic low-grade depression, and *cyclothymia*, in which the person fluctuates between more mild bouts of mania and less severe depressive symptoms. Students may be surprised by the heterogeneity of depressive disorders; one proposal (Klein, 2008) is to classify the depressive disorders along two dimensions, one reflecting severity and the other reflecting chronicity.

ANXIETY DISORDERS

Anxiety is the predominant disturbance in this group of disorders (discussed in Chapter 5). Individuals who suffer from an anxiety disorder experience excessive fear, worry, or apprehension; the excessive fear usually produces a maladaptive pattern of avoidance. A person can have an intense fear of a specific object or situation, which is referred to as a *phobia*. Another anxiety disorder is characterized by *obsessions* (recurrent, unwanted, and intrusive thoughts) and *compulsions* (strongly repetitive behaviours), which, when not performed, cause overwhelming distress. Individuals may also experience long-standing anxiety subsequent to extraordinarily traumatic events (*acute stress disorder* and *post-traumatic stress disorder*). Some individuals have an extreme fear of social situations (*social phobia*); experience panic attacks and fear that they will go crazy, have a heart attack, or die (*panic disorder*); or have difficulty controlling excessive worry (*generalized anxiety disorder*). Anxiety disorders and mood disorders are often diagnosed in the same individuals at the same time (see Focus box 3.1 for a discussion of comorbidity).

SOMATOFORM DISORDERS

The physical symptoms of somatoform disorders have no known physiological cause, but seem to serve a psychological purpose. *Somatization disorder* is characterized by a long history of bodily problems, including symptoms of pain, gastrointestinal function, sexual function, and pseudoneurological symptoms. However, medical investigations reveal no physiological basis for the symptoms, and this discrepancy suggests a psychological basis for them. In *conversion disorder*, the person reports the loss of motor or sensory function, for example, a paralysis or blindness. Individuals with *pain disorder* experience severe, prolonged, and unexplained pain believed to stem in part from psychological factors. *Hypochondriasis* involves the misinterpretation of minor physical sensations as abnormal; individuals become preoccupied with the fear that they have a serious illness. Finally, people with *body dysmorphic disorder* are overly preoccupied with an imagined defect in their appearance. These disorders are discussed in Chapter 6.

FACTITIOUS DISORDERS

This diagnosis is given to individuals who intentionally produce or complain of either physical or psychological symptoms, due to a psychological need to assume the role of a sick person.

DISSOCIATIVE DISORDERS

Dissociation is characterized by a sudden and profound disruption in consciousness, identity, memory, and perception. People with *dissociative amnesia* may forget their entire past or, more selectively, lose their memory for a

FOCUS 3.1

Comorbidity

One of the limitations of the DSM-IV-TR is that it is characterized by high levels of comorbidity. In broad terms, **comorbidity** is defined as the presence of more than one disorder in the same individual (Watson, 2005). We know that rates of comorbidity for certain psychological disorders tend to be very high (Watson, Wakiza, & Simms, 2005). One concrete illustration of comorbidity is that approximately 50 percent of people suffering from anxiety disorders also have mood disorders (see Hunsley & Lee, 2010).

One of the principles that form the basis of a categorical system of classification is the idea that any one specific disorder is distinct from another disorder. However, when disorders co-occur at a much greater frequency than would be expected by chance, it suggests that the lines between disorders may be fuzzy, and in some cases, artificial and arbitrary. Yet the architects of the current classification system argue that it is a rationally based system that groups disorders based on their shared phenomenological features (DSM–IV; APA, 1994, p. 10).

A phenomenological approach to classification is one that places emphasis on observed similarities and differences rather than the underlying structure or nature of mental disorders. Watson (2005) argues that "we now have sufficient knowledge to eliminate this rationally based system and replace it with an empirically based structure that reflects the actual—not the apparent—similarities among different disorders" (p. 524). Watson views comorbidity not necessarily as a liability, but rather as an empirical basis on which to improve the existing system of classification. As an example, given the high comorbidity of anxiety and depression disorders, Watson and colleagues recommend that we have one category representing both depression and anxiety rather than two distinct categories. Although this change will not be incorporated in DSM-5, we are optimistic that each iteration of the DSM will do a better job of incorporating empirical evidence so that we are able to develop a classification system that represents an empirically based structure of psychopathology.

particular time period. With *dissociative fugue*, individuals suddenly and unexpectedly leave their home and travel to a new locale, start a new life, and forget their previous identity. Individuals with *dissociative identity disorder* possess two or more distinct personality states, each with unique memories, behaviour patterns, preferences, and social relationships. *Depersonalization disorder* involves a severe and disruptive feeling of self-estrangement or unreality (see Chapter 6).

SEXUAL AND GENDER IDENTITY DISORDERS

The sexual disorders section of the DSM-IV-TR includes three main categories. Individuals who suffer from a *sexual dysfunction* are characterized by disturbance in sexual desire or in the psychophysiological changes that accompany the sexual response cycle. Inability to maintain an erection, premature ejaculation, and inhibitions of orgasm are some examples of their problems. Individuals with *paraphilias* are characterized by sexual urges, fantasies, or behaviours that involve unusual objects or activities, such as exhibitionism, voyeurism, sadism, and masochism. People with *gender identity disorder* feel extreme and overwhelming discomfort with their anatomical sex and identify themselves as members of the opposite sex (see Chapter 13).

EATING DISORDERS

Eating disorders (discussed in Chapter 10) are characterized by disturbances in eating behaviour. This can mean eating too much, not eating enough, or eating in an extremely unhealthy manner (such as repetitively bingeing and purging). In *anorexia nervosa*, the individual refuses to maintain a minimally normal weight for her or his age and height. Such people avoid eating and become emaciated, often due to an intense fear of becoming fat. In *bulimia nervosa*, there are frequent episodes of binge eating coupled with compensatory activities such as self-induced vomiting or the use of laxatives.

SLEEP DISORDERS

Sleep disorders will be referred to as sleep-wake disorders in DSM-5 (APA, 2010). Primary sleep disorders are divided into two subcategories. *Dyssomnias* are those disorders relating to the amount, quality, and timing of sleep (for example, not being able to maintain sleep, not feeling adequately rested after sleep, or being unable to sleep during conventional sleep times). *Parasomnias* relate to abnormal behaviour or physiological events that occur during the process of sleep or sleep–wake transitions (for example, *sleep terror disorder* or *sleepwalking disorder*).

IMPULSE CONTROL DISORDERS

This category involves disorders characterized by failure or extreme difficulty in controlling impulses, despite the negative consequences. For example, in *intermittent explosive disorder*, the person has episodes of violent behaviour that result in the destruction of property or injury to others. In *pathological gambling*, the individual is preoccupied with gambling, is unable to stop, and gambles as a way to escape from problems. Persons suffering from *trichotillomania* experience intense urges to pull out their own hair.

ADJUSTMENT DISORDERS

This diagnosis refers to the development of emotional or behavioural symptoms within three months after a major stressful event, such as a divorce or business difficulties. The reaction usually involves distress and impairment in social or occupational functioning, or other symptoms that exceed the reaction one would normally expect to such a stressor. However, the symptoms are not severe enough to meet the criteria for any Axis I diagnosis.

PERSONALITY DISORDERS

These disorders (discussed in Chapter 12) are characterized by an enduring, pervasive, inflexible, and maladaptive pattern of behaviour that has existed since adolescence or early adulthood, markedly impairs functioning, and/or causes subjective stress. One common example of personality disorder is *antisocial personality disorder*, in which the person displays a history of continuous and chronic disregard for and violation of the rights of others. In *dependent personality disorder*, a person manifests a pattern of submissive and clinging behaviour and fear of separation. The DSM-IV-TR includes 10 distinct personality disorders, listed separately from the other clinical disorders, on Axis II. However, this may be changed in the DSM-5; Krueger (2005) concluded that the personality disorders do not differ reliably from the other clinical disorders in terms of temporal stability, age of onset, treatment response, insight, diagnostic co-occurrence, or etiology. Similarly, Flanagan, Keeley, and Blashfield (2008) found that, when asked, clinicians do not perceive Axis II disorders as being substantively different from those on Axis I.

OTHER CONDITIONS THAT MAY BE A FOCUS OF CLINICAL ATTENTION

This broad category is used for conditions that are not considered to be mental disorders but may still be a focus of attention or treatment. For example, if a person's medical illness appears to be in part psychological, or exacerbated by a psychological condition, the diagnosis is *psychological factors affecting physical condition* (referred to in previous editions of the DSM as psychophysiological or psychosomatic disorders). The other conditions in this category include academic problems, marital problems, occupational problems, and physical or sexual abuse. For example, a student's academic performance may decrease for a significant period of time, even though the student is not suffering from an anxiety disorder, clinical depression, a learning disability, or any other mental disorder that would account for the underachievement.

4 BEFORE MOVING ON

"The multiaxial system sufficiently takes into account the social and interpersonal context of mental disorders." Provide one argument supporting this position and one argument against this position.

TOWARD DSM-5

As noted earlier, a minor text revision of the manual was released in 2000 (DSM-IV-TR), and substantial work has already been conducted on the next major edition, the DSM-5. Again, 13 work groups have been established and, while these groups reflect the diagnostic categories of psychiatric disorders in the DSM-IV, it is expected that those categories will evolve to better reflect changes in scientific understanding. The DSM-5 is expected to be published in May 2013.

There are a number of reasons why this latest revision of the DSM has been undertaken. As researchers gather new empirical evidence about mental disorders (e.g., how different disorders are related to and distinct from each other), it becomes necessary to revise and update our classification system to reflect the new knowledge and understanding. This is consistent with the principle of evidence-based practice, which means that the assessment and treatment of psychological disorders should be based on the most current and valid research findings (Smith & Oltmanns, 2009).

An example of changes that are being introduced in DSM-5 to reflect new scientific evidence is the revised diagnostic criteria for reading disorder. The DSM-IV-TR cites the following as one of the criteria for this diagnosis: "reading achievement, as measured by individually administered standardized tests of reading accuracy or comprehension, is substantially below that expected given the person's chronological age, measured intelligence, and age-appropriate education" (APA, 2000). The proposal is to change this criterion to "difficulties in accuracy or fluency of reading that are not consistent with the person's chronological age, educational opportunities, or intellectual abilities." The rationale for this change is that "there is little evidence to support the DSM-IV-TR criterion of a substantial discrepancy between achievement and intellectual ability" (APA, 2010). The name of the disorder has also been changed to *dyslexia* to correspond with the terminology that is used to describe this disorder internationally and in scientific work.

In each of the chapters that covers particular mental disorders, the authors have focused on the diagnostic criteria that are established and accepted to date (i.e., DSM-IV-TR). Proposed changes to DSM-5 are also discussed. In some instances (e.g., mood disorders), the changes are modest. For other disorders (e.g., personality disorders), the anticipated changes are substantial. It is important for students to bear in mind, however, that these revisions to the DSM are only *proposed* at this time. It will be interesting to see what the final organization and criteria will be (for updates, visit the DSM-5 website at www.dsm5.org).

A major criticism that has been levelled against DSM-IV-TR (as well as earlier versions of the DSM) is its **categorical approach** to the classification of mental disorders. That is, an individual is deemed to either have a disorder or not have a disorder, with no in-between. One reason for this approach is historical. It is psychiatrists who have developed mental health classification systems for the most part, and, being physicians, they have used the same approach taken in medicine. For example, if a person reports pain in the lower right abdomen, vomiting, and fever, and if a blood sample reveals an elevated white blood cell count, the physician makes a categorical decision: Does this person need surgery for appendicitis or not? There is no in-between. But is this a reasonable model for assessing mental function? After all, a categorical system does not recognize the continuum between normal and abnormal.

Consider the case of a teenager who engages in significant bullying and cruelty to animals. Would one conclude that because he falls short of the required criteria for conduct disorder, he has *no* problems? Does this mean that the large body of research on children with conduct disorder is completely irrelevant to this youngster? It is troubling, but undeniably true, that people are denied help because they fall just short of diagnostic criteria. Several investigations have demonstrated that these subthreshold syndromes are not only highly prevalent but also result in substantial impairment. Ezpeleta, Keeler, Erkanli, Costello, and Angold (2001), for instance, found that 27 percent of children in a community sample experienced significant disability (peer, school, or family) related to psychological problems, yet only 30 percent of these children met full diagnostic criteria for a psychiatric disorder. Furthermore, critics allege, a categorical approach does not provide a meaningful description of an individual's psychological problems. For these reasons, some researchers (e.g., Brown & Barlow, 2009) have advocated a **dimensional** approach to diagnosis, based on a continuum for mental disorders from non-existent or mild to severe.

In light of these criticisms, one of the principles guiding the current revisions of the DSM is to incorporate a dimensional approach to diagnosis, where appropriate. Accordingly, the Personality and Personality Disorders Work Group, appointed by the American Psychiatric Association to revise this category for the DSM-5, has stated that they will be introducing a hybrid dimensional-categorical model for the assessment and diagnosis of personality disorders. A hybrid approach means that they will be combining aspects of both dimensional and categorical systems of classification. Another major advantage of incorporating dimensional ratings to diagnostic evaluations of mental disorders is that such assessments allow clinicians to evaluate the severity of symptoms and take into account symptoms that cut across multiple diagnoses.

Enhancing the clinical utility of DSM-5 represents another important revision being considered. *Clinical utility* refers to the extent to which a diagnostic system assists clinicians in performing functions such as communicating clinical information to patients, their families, and other health care providers; selecting effective interventions; and predicting the course of a disorder (First et al., 2007). Consistent with this goal, the DSM-5 introduces new scales for assessing suicide risk, designed to help clinicians identify patients who are at highest risk.

5 BEFORE MOVING ON

One set of proposed changes for DSM-5 is to lower the threshold for certain disorders. There is a lot of controversy about this, with one vocal group arguing against any proposed changes that would reduce the threshold for any diagnosis and others vociferously backing such changes. Identify two to three problems with reducing the diagnostic threshold for certain disorders and two to three reasons why reducing diagnostic thresholds is necessary and important.

Issues in the Diagnosis and Classification of Abnormal Behaviour

Despite the long history and widespread use of the DSM and other diagnostic systems for mental health, considerable controversy still surrounds them (Frances, 2009). There are two main arenas of controversy. One body of opinion objects to classification per se, and suggests that any classification system for mental disorders is irrelevant at best and inappropriate at worst. The second type of opposition targets the DSM in particular.

AGAINST CLASSIFICATION

MEDICAL MODEL A substantial number of professionals argue that the whole diagnostic endeavour is flawed because of its adherence to the medical model. Medical disorders are legitimate, they argue, because they have a clear indication, such as a lesion, which serves as a recognizable deviation in anatomical structure, whereas most mental disorders involve no such anatomical deviations. Diagnosis of "mental illness," these critics suggest, is simply a de facto means of social control (Szasz, 1961). In a succinct rejection of this position, Wakefield (1992) pointed out that there are many medical disorders for which there are no known lesions or anatomical abnormalities. Trigeminal neuralgia, for example, is classified on the basis of associated dysfunction alone; furthermore, it is possible that at some future point we may discover anatomical anomalies associated with some mental health disorders.

STIGMATIZATION Another argument against diagnosis is that it unfairly stigmatizes individuals. A person diagnosed with schizophrenia, for instance, is often seen simply as a "schizophrenic," rather than as a complex individual with skills and interests. Such a label might have a major impact both socially and occupationally because the individual may not fit in or may have difficulty seeking employment; he or she may also come to identify with the label, leading to further deterioration or impeding rehabilitation (i.e., a self-fulfilling prophecy). Wakefield (1992) argues that the flaw lies not

APPLIED CLINICAL CASE

David Helfgott

The problems associated with labelling someone mentally ill are brought into focus in the widely acclaimed 1996 movie *Shine*, which depicts the life of David Helfgott. David, a teenage piano prodigy, moved from Australia to London, England, to accept a music scholarship. He suffered a major mental collapse in the mid-1970s and spent more than a decade in psychiatric hospitals before emerging in the mid-1980s to perform at a Perth piano bar. Although no official diagnosis has been disclosed, the fact that he was on the antipsychotic medication Serenac for many years is suggestive of schizophrenia or some other psychotic disorder. His wife reveals that he is still on medication, and that when he stops taking it he deteriorates. David travels under protective circumstances to prevent him from wandering off and cannot perform on consecutive nights. Nevertheless, he is a loving husband, a charming individual, an engaging entertainer, and a prodigiously skilled pianist. Any diagnosis such as schizophrenia would fall far short of describing the many attributes that have helped him to overcome the problems often ascribed to people with schizophrenia. One also wonders how he would have fared had his wife, Gillian, not been attracted to his many qualities and made a special effort with him.

David Helfgott, whose extraordinary life was documented in the 1996 film *Shine*.

in the classification system but in people's reactions to mental disorders. Professionals must guard against discouraging or belittling people with mental disorders, and must help to educate the public appropriately. As mentioned in Chapter 1, reduction of stigmatization and discrimination is a primary mandate of the Mental Health Commission of Canada.

LOSS OF INFORMATION A frequent charge against diagnosis is that inherent in any label is a loss of information. You have probably already learned in your statistics courses what happens when you dichotomize a continuous variable: there is a loss of statistical power and a resultant loss of information. How can anyone's uniqueness be summarized in a word or two, whether the label is favourable (e.g., "beautiful" or "smart") or unfavourable (e.g., "lazy" or "aloof")? Similarly, an individual with depression is characterized by many other qualities, not just her or his depression. The label alone can give us a false sense of confidence in understanding the person and making assumptions about his or her personhood and life that are not valid. How can we reconcile this drawback with the need to be able to discuss a patient's symptoms in an efficient and clear manner? As discussed earlier, such information is often needed for mental health professionals to speak to each other and to provide health care in a coordinated fashion. Also, patients often report that knowing the name of a disorder helps them understand their experiences and may even provide some relief. Perhaps the take-home message from this is not that diagnostic labels should be abandoned but that they should be used in an educated, informed, and nuanced manner. As the study by the psychologist Rosenhan, discussed below, illustrates, our diagnostic system is fallible.

Rosenhan (1973) conducted an influential study that highlighted many of the problems associated with diagnosis of mental disorders and raised important questions about the validity of psychiatric diagnoses. Rosenhan recruited pseudo-patients (individuals instructed to fake the symptoms of a mental illness), who faked auditory hallucinations in order to gain admission to psychiatric hospitals. After admission, the pseudo-patients stopped displaying any psychotic symptoms and informed hospital staff that they were no longer experiencing hallucinations. Despite this, many of the pseudo-patients were confined as inpatients for significant periods of time and all were discharged with the diagnosis of a psychiatric disorder. One of the important lessons of this study is that it demonstrates how powerful the process of labelling can be. Once the pseudo-patients were seen as having the label of a psychiatric disorder, all their subsequent behaviour was seen through the prism of this diagnosis. Thus, if the pseudo-patients did not display symptoms, the mental health professionals working with them interpreted this to mean that their symptoms were being managed well, not that there might have been a mistake in the original diagnosis or that the diagnosis may no longer apply.

Few would argue that all forms of classification of mental disorders should be abandoned. However, what the critics of the current classification system state, and studies such as the one conducted by Rosenhan highlight, is that mental health professionals need to be aware of the biases and fallibility in our systems of diagnosis and classification. Similarly, mental health professionals need to be aware of the power differential that is inherent in clinician–patient relationships and that a system of classification can be used incorrectly to perpetuate and establish that power differential. Furthermore, there have to be parallel efforts to bring about changes in the public's perception of mental disorders and to reduce the stigma of having a mental health problem.

CRITICISMS SPECIFIC TO THE DSM DIAGNOSTIC SYSTEM

GENDER BIAS IN THE DSM The late 1960s saw poignant criticisms of gender bias and sexism in the mental health system (Chesler, 1972). DSM-I and DSM-II were strongly influenced by psychoanalytic theory, which has been charged with sexism (Kaschak, 1992). In 1974, the American Psychological Association set up a task force to investigate gender bias and sex-role stereotyping in mental health assessment and therapy. The first step was to survey female clinicians to determine what practices indicate gender bias or sexism. Four categories were developed: fostering traditional gender roles, bias in expectations and devaluation of women, sexist use of psychoanalytic concepts, and treating women as sex objects, including the seduction of a female patient (which was not specifically labelled unethical by a professional body until 1978). Nonetheless, DSM-III was in no way free of gender bias.

Some writers have claimed that the DSM describes many psychiatric disorders in a fashion that makes a diagnosis more probable for women, even when no pathology is involved (Kaplan, 1983a, 1983b; Tavris, 1992). They contend that diagnostic categories in the DSM are based on professional assumptions regarding the nature of psychopathology, which are in turn influenced by societal norms that value stereotypical masculine behaviour, such as assertiveness and goal-directed behaviour, over stereotypical feminine behaviour, such as co-operation and nurturing others. These feminine behaviours are considered secondary to mental health and may even be seen as signs of emotional immaturity and psychopathology (Cook, Warnke, & Dupuy, 1993; Hartung & Widiger, 1998).

Another criticism of the DSM is that it does not take life circumstances sufficiently into account, assuming that psychological problems can be attributed largely to the individual. Although recent years have seen increased acknowledgment of the extent to which women may be oppressed in Western society, there is still insufficient recognition of these factors in the diagnostic assessment (Cook et al., 1993).

The personality disorders of Axis II have also come under fire because some seem to correspond to exaggerated female stereotypes (for example, histrionic personality disorder and dependent personality disorder), and thus may be diagnosed more frequently in women than in men. Investigations suggest that gender bias in diagnoses is not merely an artifact of the experimental procedure employed. For example, Adler, Drake, and Teague (1990) presented clinicians with case summaries of patients who met the criteria for several different personality disorders. They found that clinicians tended to diagnose these patients in accordance with gender stereotypes. Furthermore, even when males and females were diagnosed with the same personality disorder (histrionic personality disorder and antisocial personality disorder, in this particular experiment), women were judged to be more pathological (Hamilton, Rothbart, & Dawes, 1986). Sampling bias represents another problem that has confounded this issue. Hartung and Widiger (1998) argued that many clinical studies fail to obtain a representative sample of individuals with a given disorder. For example, much of the research on conduct disorder is confined to boys. Such an unrepresentative sample not only will affect our understanding of prevalence differences but also might inadvertently contribute to further biases (e.g., in this case, researchers may develop a male-biased description of the disorder).

CULTURAL BIAS IN THE DSM Just as mental health professionals have learned to recognize gender bias, they have been led by recent developments to grapple with similar concerns related to culture. More than 220 000 immigrants from all over the world have moved to Canada annually over the past 10 years. The North American milieu now includes a greater variety of religions and languages, and a tremendous increase in the diversity of cultural practices. More than ever, clinicians must be aware of cultural factors that might influence the diagnostic process.

DSM-IV-TR has striven to be atheoretical and to take cultural differences into account. It stresses that an individual's primary social and cultural reference group, as well as his or her unique personal experience, must be taken into account during an assessment (Mezzich et al., 1993). Despite these improvements to the DSM-IV-TR, the designation of behaviour as normal or abnormal is fraught with cultural and professional assumptions, especially considering that disorders in the DSM are determined largely by the consensus of English-speaking scientists trained primarily in the United States and, to a lesser extent, in Canada.

It is important to note that some behaviours considered abnormal in white North American culture may not be considered abnormal in other cultures. For example, hallucinations should not necessarily be considered abnormal during North American Aboriginal religious ceremonies (Rogler & Hollingshead, 1985). In addition, since the belief that evil spirits can possess an individual is held by many in Hispanic nations such as Puerto Rico, such reports should not always be considered a sign of schizophrenia in individuals from this culture.

A related area of controversy has to do with cultural bias in intelligence testing. In reviewing the literature on intelligence test scores and later outcomes, such as school achievement, Baydala and colleagues (2009) note that the link between intelligence scores and subsequent academic and career outcomes tends to be weaker for indigenous children in the United States and Canada, calling into question the validity of these tests for these individuals. Similarly, it has been noted that Aboriginal culture instills a sense of co-operation, valuing the group more than the individual. The same has been reported with African-Americans (Helms, 1992). Furthermore, North American Aboriginals are overrepresented in the lower socio-economic strata, and several studies have shown that IQ tests underestimate the intelligence of people in these strata (Dauphinais & King, 1992; National Commission on Testing and Public Policy, 1990).

During the past decade, there has been a particularly large influx of immigrants from the Pacific Rim to the west coast of Canada. Research has suggested that diagnostic procedures used with people of Japanese and Chinese origin need to be sensitive to cultural and attitudinal factors. For example, the widely used Minnesota Multiphasic Personality Inventory (MMPI) contains an F (for frequency) subscale. It is often assumed that people who score high on this subscale are unable to understand the questions, answering carelessly, or faking an illness. Yet Cheung and Okazaki (1991) found that people in Hong Kong and the People's Republic of China tend to score higher than North Americans on this subscale. Thus, a relatively high score for a Chinese respondent on this scale may not indicate this type of responding or faking, but merely a different cultural background.

Certain syndromes appear only within a particular culture. The DSM-IV-TR lists 25 different syndromes that appear to be culture-bound. *Taijin kyofusho*, a syndrome found only in Japan, is characterized by an excessive fear that one will embarrass or offend others. This syndrome afflicts 7 to 36 percent of people treated by psychiatrists in Japan and primarily affects young Japanese men. Interestingly, *taijin kyofusho* differs from social phobia in that the fear is not for oneself but for others (Essau et al., in press), although researchers have recently contested this point. According to Suzuki, Takei, Kawai, Minabe, and Mori (2003), this syndrome is categorized in the Japanese diagnostic system into four subtypes, based on the content of the patient's fear. One subtype, *sekimen-kyofu* (fear of blushing), is consistent with the category of social phobia. *Shubo-kyofu* (fear of a deformed body) appears to meet the criteria for body dysmorphic disorder in DSM-IV-TR (see Chapter 6). The remaining two subtypes (*jikoshisen-kyofu*, the fear of eye-to-eye contact, and *jikoshu-kyofu*, the fear of one's own foul body odour) do not fit neatly within the DSM system but are diagnosed in other countries as specific phobias. Thus, it is not entirely clear whether *taijin kyofusho* is truly a culture-bound syndrome.

Research in the United States has suggested that emotional difficulties may be diagnosed differently in

African-American and Hispanic populations than in white populations. Several studies found that clinicians shown a case summary were more likely to diagnose the patient with schizophrenia if told the patient was black. Hospital-based studies have also suggested that blacks were overdiagnosed with schizophrenia and underdiagnosed with mood disorders (Garb, 1997). Alternatively, there is also some evidence to suggest that psychopathology has been underestimated in Hispanics as a result of a reluctance to disclose information to non-Hispanics (Levine & Padilla, 1980; Lopez, 1989; Lopez & Hernandez, 1986).

The developers of the DSM-IV-TR attempted to address some of the concerns about cultural bias that were voiced about earlier versions of the DSM. For example, the DSM-IV-TR has encouraged clinicians to be culturally sensitive in their assessments and diagnoses of persons from diverse ethnic backgrounds. Within the description of each disorder is included a list of cultural and ethnic factors to consider. In addition, the appendix of DSM-IV-TR contains important information related to conducting a systematic review of an individual's culture and determining the influence of a patient's culture on the expression and evaluation of symptoms. As previously mentioned, a list of culture-bound syndromes is also provided.

POLITICS AND THE DSM Another criticism of the DSM is that the decisions about diagnostic criteria are too often influenced by factors other than pure empiricism. For example, students might be surprised to learn that homosexuality was included as a diagnostic category in the DSM until the release of DSM-III in 1980; it was removed not due to accumulated empirical evidence, but because the members of the American Psychiatric Association were asked to vote on the matter. Furthermore, some authors have suggested that post-traumatic stress disorder was included at the behest of groups representing Vietnam veterans, not because of compelling evidence that it was demonstrably different from existing anxiety diagnostic categories (Kutchins & Kirk, 1997). Concerns have also been voiced about the individuals selected for the panels responsible for revising the existing edition of the DSM. One study investigated the extent to which each of the 170 panel members who contributed to the diagnostic criteria for DSM-IV and DSM-IV-TR had financial ties to the pharmaceutical industry. This study revealed that more than half (56 percent) of the panel members did have such ties; perhaps more troubling, however, was the fact that 100 percent of the panel members responsible for "Mood Disorders" and "Schizophrenia and Other Psychotic Disorders" had such ties (Cosgrove, Krimsky, Vijayaraghavan, & Schneider, 2006). Lastly, concern has recently been articulated about the secrecy that surrounds the DSM revision process. Ironically, Robert Spitzer, chair of the task force for DSM-III and a major architect of the modern classification of mental disorders, has been most vocal about these concerns. In 2008, Spitzer revealed that he was being denied the minutes of the DSM-5 task force meetings, and that the APA was continuing to assert the importance of confidentiality. Spitzer also revealed that task force and work group members had been forced to sign "confidentiality agreements." At the time of this writing, this contentious issue has not been resolved.

6 BEFORE MOVING ON

Why should we be concerned about possible pharmaceutical influences on the development and evolution of the DSM?

THE PREVALENCE OF MENTAL DISORDERS

In 2002 Health Canada published *A Report on Mental Illnesses in Canada*. The purpose of this report was to collate existing data on prevalence rates of mental disorders in Canada in an effort to start building a more complete picture of the mental health needs of Canadians. The report concluded that one out of five Canadians will experience a mental illness in their lifetime (Health Canada, 2002). An updated report, which incorporated new data on mental health from the 2002 Statistics Canada survey, the Canadian Community Health Survey Cycle, the 2002–2003 Hospital Mental Health Database, and the 2004 Health Behaviours of School Children Survey (Government of Canada, 2006), also reported a 20 percent lifetime prevalence of mental disorders. Mental disorders represent the second leading cause of disability and premature death in Canada (Canadian Medical Association, 2008). Global data on prevalence rates of mental disorders are even more sobering. Globally, it is estimated that one-third of the world's population has some form of mental disorder and, of those individuals, about two-thirds receive no treatment, even in high-income countries (World Health Organization, 2000).

SUMMARY

- A diagnostic system for mental disorders serves a number of important functions, such as providing a description of mental disorders, distinguishing between different types of mental disorders, providing a vocabulary for communicating about mental disorders, and facilitating research in psychopathology. Furthermore, accurate assessment and diagnosis, as well as effective treatment of mental disorders, rely on a system of classification. Diagnostic systems are also needed for surveying population health and for understanding the prevalence and etiology of particular mental health problems.
- Every science includes a system for categorizing information. In abnormal psychology, the perfect diagnostic system would be based on etiology, presenting symptoms, prognosis, and response to treatment. This diagnostic system would also enhance the organization of clinical factors and provide a shorthand to help professionals communicate easily.
- Although attempts to classify mental disorders date back to at least the Middle Ages, modern efforts at classification owe much to Kraepelin's work in the nineteenth century. A milestone in the modern development of a comprehensive diagnostic scheme was the World Health Organization's decision to add mental health disorders to the International List of the Causes of Death. In 1948 the list was expanded to become the International Statistical Classification of Diseases, Injuries, and Causes of Death (ICD), a comprehensive listing of all diseases, including abnormal behaviour. In response to limitations of the ICD system, the American Psychiatric Association published its own classification system, the Diagnostic and Statistical Manual (DSM), in 1952. Both of these systems of classification (ICD and DSM) have undergone numerous revisions, in efforts to address inadequacies of previous editions (e.g., poor reliability) and to ensure that research evidence informs our classification of mental disorders. Currently, the system of classification used most commonly in North America is the DSM-IV-TR, soon to be replaced by DSM-5.
- The editions of the DSM have progressed considerably in arriving at DSM-IV-TR. The use of a multiaxial classification system has been adopted in recognition of the importance of psychosocial features in the development and maintenance of psychological problems.
- To address some of the limitations of the current diagnostic system, the DSM-IV-TR is being revised and DSM-5 is scheduled to be published in 2013. The guiding principles behind the current set of revisions are to update the diagnostic system, based on the most current available scientific evidence, and to enhance the clinical utility of the diagnostic system.
- Many professionals feel that current and past versions of the DSM remain too closely aligned with the medical model, and that this leads to excessive stigmatization and loss of information about individuals. The whole enterprise of diagnosis of mental disorders is also criticized for using categories that do not do justice to the complexity of human behaviour and for displaying gender and cultural biases.
- As we have seen, the DSM-IV-TR is far from perfect. However, as the history of classification in the natural sciences has demonstrated, the development of a diagnostic classification system is an ongoing process that requires continual refinement. Classification is an accepted procedure in all sciences, and it is very likely that the field of mental health will continue to use it. It is encouraging to note that the field of mental health is continually looking to efforts to improve and validate the diagnostic system using empirical evidence, as illustrated by the revisions that are currently under way. This scientific attitude should allow the detection of flaws in the present system and lead to an improved, albeit imperfect, diagnostic system. Gradually, the diagnostic categories should be refined as we fill in the present gaps in our knowledge and come to recognize how culture, politics, and social norms have influenced professional concepts of mental health. This refinement process is well under way.

MySearchLab offers you extensive help with your writing and research projects and provides round-the-clock access to credible and reliable source material. Chapter quizzes and a full electronic version of the text are also provided. Answers to the Before Moving On feature are provided on the MySearchLab. Take a tour at www.mysearchlab.com.

KEY TERMS

diagnosis (p. 49)
diagnostic system (p. 49)
assessment (p. 50)
reliability (p. 51)
inter-rater reliability (p. 51)
validity (p. 51)
concurrent validity (p. 51)
predictive validity (p. 51)
atheoretical (p. 52)
polythetic (p. 52)
multiaxial (p. 52)
major depressive disorder (p. 55)
mania (p. 56)
bipolar mood disorders (p. 56)
comorbidity (p. 56)
categorical approach (p. 58)
dimensional (p. 58)

DAVID J. A. DOZOIS • PAMELA M. SEEDS

Chapter 4

Psychological Assessment and Research Methods

LEARNING OBJECTIVES

AFTER READING THIS CHAPTER, STUDENTS WILL BE ABLE TO:

1. Differentiate between psychological testing and psychological assessment and describe the importance of this distinction.
2. Explain the importance of reliability and validity in clinical assessment.
3. Describe the strengths and weaknesses of clinical versus actuarial prediction.
4. Compare and contrast structured versus unstructured interviews and describe circumstances in which you might want to favour one format over the other.
5. Define what an "experiment" is and explain what differentiates it from non-experimental research methods.
6. Explain why it is important to consider clinical significance in addition to statistical significance.

Aidan was a boy, aged 5 years and 10 months, whose parents had requested a psychological assessment because his teachers had reported him as being disruptive in class and as performing below his potential in Grade 1. Aidan's teachers and parents viewed him in a similar way. Aidan was a talkative, happy-go-lucky child, well liked by the other children. He was sometimes a little aggressive, but with no evidence of meanness. He had difficulty following instructions and frequently did not comply with classroom rules. His teachers wondered whether Aidan's mediocre academic achievement and disruptive behaviour might be caused by family or emotional problems.

The psychologist addressed this assessment on three fronts. First, he interviewed Aidan's family, starting with the whole family together: Aidan, his parents, and his brother, who was three years older. Then he spoke to the parents alone, to each of the boys alone, and to the two boys together. The psychologist also asked the teachers to complete a checklist widely used to assess classroom behaviour. Finally, Aidan's IQ was assessed using the Wechsler Intelligence Scale for Children, and he was given a projective test (Children's Apperception Test) that is widely used in assessing children's personalities.

The psychologist rated Aidan's home environment as fairly good. There was no evidence of marital problems or family issues beyond the normal strains of raising two young boys. The behaviour checklist showed a problem only on the scales that measure attention/impulsivity, on which Aidan scored at approximately the twenty-first percentile for his age group. Aidan scored within normal limits on scales that measure anxiety, depression, and antisocial behaviour. The projective test revealed that Aidan had a rich emotional life. He felt involved and loved in his world. His comments suggested that he had difficulty accepting general rules of play and was reluctant to share toys. He regarded himself too highly, and did not want to admit that other children might be better than he was at games, sports, or other activities. Aidan's IQ was very high. His overall score placed him in the ninety-eighth percentile, with good performance in all areas.

The psychologist's report, which was provided to both the parents and the school, included the following interpretations:

- There was no evidence of family issues leading to Aidan's problem behaviour.
- Aidan's problem behaviour in class was largely a result of difficulty with concentration and impulsivity.
- Aidan's personality assessment suggested that he was a bit immature.
- Aidan's IQ was in the gifted range. His academic performance was indeed below his potential.

The report noted that because Aidan was born in the fall, just before the school's January cutoff for registration, he was the youngest boy, and one of the youngest children, in his class. Some of his impulsive actions and failure to pay attention might simply reflect his youth, and might cease to be a problem in another year or so. His intellectual abilities may have allowed him to function as well as he did despite this immaturity. Emotionally, Aidan was all right, but may have had a somewhat overinflated self-image—perhaps because he was excessively praised for the precociousness achieved through high intelligence and an older brother's influence. The report suggested that since Aidan was only in Grade 1 and his problems were not severe, the school should simply monitor his behaviour for another year. The only action recommended was that both the parents and the school be firm in response to Aidan's aggressive behaviour to ensure that no one was hurt and that Aidan received a clear message as to what is considered acceptable.

In the following school year, Aidan was placed in an accelerated class containing only 12 children. Due to the Increased structure and supervision of a smaller class, Aidan did very well academically and his classroom behaviour improved dramatically. However, during free play or recess he still displayed more disruptive and aggressive behaviour than was acceptable.

Assessment

As mentioned in Chapter 3, an accurate diagnosis provides a shorthand description of many important attributes of a patient and allows some predictions about the individual's development. This diagnosis usually results from a **psychological assessment**, a systematic gathering and evaluation of information pertaining to an individual with suspected abnormal behaviour. This assessment can be carried out with a wide variety of techniques to appraise social, psychological, and/or biological factors.

A diagnosis is only as good as the assessment on which it is based, and the assessment, in turn, is only as good as the tools used to carry it out. Therefore, good diagnosis hinges on the development of accurate assessment tools. Think of your car, for example. If the gas gauge is faulty, you cannot easily tell when you come to a sudden grinding halt whether your engine is shot or you are simply out of gas.

Psychological assessment is not a single score but a series of scores placed *within the context* of the history, referral information, behavioural observations, and life of an individual in order to provide a comprehensive understanding of that individual (Meyer et al., 2001). It is important to remember that a test is only a sample of behaviour—a tool to be used in this process of assessment (Groth-Marnat, 2009). A good medical analogy is that of a blood sample; the medical assessment takes the blood work information from the lab and integrates it with other information (e.g., symptoms, age, history) so as to arrive at a comprehensive understanding of the client's presenting complaints and problem. Unfortunately, many individuals fail to appreciate the differences between testing and assessment and, particularly with the advent of computerized testing, the process of comprehensive assessment may be overlooked.

Although assessments are usually thought of in relation to diagnosis, they may also have other specific purposes. An IQ test may be used to guide school placement, a neuropsychological test to assess the natural progression of a disorder, or a symptom checklist to facilitate case formulation or gauge the success of treatment.

A good assessment tool depends on two things: an accurate ability to measure some aspect of the person being assessed, and knowledge of how people in general fare on such a measure, for the purposes of comparison. Because this knowledge is derived from research, in the second half of this chapter we turn our attention to research methods. You will also notice that assessment and research often use similar methods—sometimes even the same tools—and must deal with similar issues of reliability and validity.

1 BEFORE MOVING ON

What is the difference between psychological testing and psychological assessment? Why is it important to distinguish between them?

ASSESSMENT TOOLS: STRIVING FOR THE WHOLE PICTURE

A diagnostician trying to understand someone is attempting to piece together a puzzle. The patient may be able to present a partial description of issues related to the suspected psychological abnormality, from his or her unique perspective. This report gives one piece of the puzzle, but the clinician needs a more objective perspective. Glimpses of the past, revealing the patient's behaviour and experiences at various ages and in various settings, will provide a few more pieces, but the puzzle remains incomplete. Missing at this point from the overall picture are accounts of the patient's emotional, cognitive, and physiological states. Sometimes patients cannot report on their own internal states, even when they can accurately describe their observable behaviour. Fortunately, psychological methods are available to fill in many of the missing pieces. The most useful understanding of a patient draws on a combination of procedures that shed light on a range of different aspects of an individual's functioning.

RELIABILITY AND VALIDITY

Of course, to be useful, any test must be both reliable and valid, as discussed in Chapter 3. Several types of reliability are particularly important for psychological tests.

Test-retest reliability refers to the degree to which a test yields the same results when it is given more than once to the same person. For example, if your score on an IQ test is dramatically different from one day to the next, the test does not provide a good measure of intelligence. Test-retest reliability can be evaluated by correlating a person's score on a given test with the same person's score on the same test taken at a later time. The higher the relationship between the two scores (expressed as a correlation coefficient), the greater the reliability. One obvious problem is that a person may improve on a test the second time around because of practice with the procedures or familiarity with the questions. To circumvent this problem, behavioural scientists often attempt to ascertain a test's **alternate-form reliability**. To do this, the test designers prepare two forms of the same test—that is, they decide what construct they want their test to measure, think up questions (or items) that would test that construct, and then word those questions in a slightly different way to create a second test that measures the same construct as the first one. A high correlation between scores on the first and second tests demonstrates alternate-form reliability.

Internal consistency refers to the degree of reliability within a test. That is, to what extent do different parts of the same test yield the same results? One measure of internal consistency is **split-half reliability**, which is often evaluated by comparing responses on odd-numbered test items with responses on even-numbered test items. If the scores for these responses are highly correlated, then the test has high split-half reliability. Another method for evaluating internal consistency, **coefficient alpha**, is calculated by averaging the intercorrelations of all items on a given test.

The higher the coefficient alpha, the higher the internal consistency of the test.

Clearly an unreliable measure is useless. However, as discussed in Chapter 3, a reliable measure may be of little value if it is not *valid*. As we shall see later in this chapter, there are several measures of intelligence that have excellent reliability quotients. However, their usefulness is still hotly debated. What exactly do they measure? How well do they predict future functioning? In addition to concurrent validity and predictive validity, discussed in Chapter 3, there are several other types of validities related to psychological tests.

Face validity means that the user of a test believes that the items on that test resemble the characteristics associated with the concept being tested for. For example, suppose that a test for assertiveness asks questions like "How do you react when you are overcharged in a store? When someone cuts in front of you in a line?" Because such behaviours seemingly relate to the general concept of assertiveness, the test would have face validity.

Content validity goes one step further and requires that a test's content include a representative sample of all behaviours thought to be related to the construct (that is, the concept or entity) that the test is designed to measure. For example, the construct of depression includes features such as lack of energy, sadness, and negative self-perception. To have content validity, an instrument designed to assess depression should address such features. A test that focused only on sadness without considering other features would not have good content validity.

The concept of **criterion validity** arises because some qualities are easier to recognize than to define completely. Suppose you wanted to know whether a calculator was working properly; one way to test it would be to work out a problem to which you already know the answer: say, "6 times 5." If the calculator gives an answer of 368, you know it is not a valid instrument. Now suppose you wanted to develop a test for artistic ability. You design an instrument that asks many questions about creative behaviour and activities. You then give the test to a large group of well-known and highly regarded artists and to a control group of people not identified as artistic. If the artists' test scores are much higher than the non-artists' scores, your test has good criterion validity. Note that this large survey is not an assessment of the people involved; you started with the assumption that the artists are artistic. It is the test instrument that is being evaluated.

Construct validity refers to the importance of a test within a specific theoretical framework and can only be understood in the context of that framework. This type of validity is especially useful when the construct to be measured is rather abstract. As an example, self-esteem is considered important for success in many endeavours. To evaluate how well a measure assesses self-esteem, we would look to a theory for a prediction and see whether the measure correlates well with that prediction. Developmental psychologists suggest that children who are given a great deal of emotional support and unconditional positive regard should develop more self-esteem than those who are not supported or who are raised in abusive homes. One might compare the scores on the measure of self-esteem in two groups of teenagers, one from intact and nurturing families and the other from homes where there has been documented neglect or abuse. One would judge the construct validity of the self-esteem measure in terms of how closely it was related to the backgrounds of these teenagers.

❷ BEFORE MOVING ON

Issues of reliability and validity are obviously important in the context of research. Why do you think they are important for clinical assessment?

CLINICAL VERSUS ACTUARIAL PREDICTION

How can one best take all the information available about a patient and put it together? How does one evaluate and interpret a collection of data—interviews, case histories, responses to tests—to describe the patient, make predictions, and come to decisions? These broad questions have been debated for years within the mental health professions. Two very different approaches have been developed. People who endorse the **clinical approach** argue that there is no substitute for the clinician's experience and personal judgment. They prefer to draw on all available data in their own manner; they are guided by intuition honed with professional experience rather than by formal rules. Those who endorse the **actuarial approach** argue that a more objective standard is needed—something more unbiased and scientifically validated. They rely exclusively on statistical procedures, empirical methods, and formal rules in evaluating data.

Which method is superior? It has been suggested that the actuarial approach tends to be much more efficient in terms of making predictions in a variety of situations (e.g., relapse, dangerousness, improvement in therapy, success in university), especially when many predictions must be made and the base of data is large (Meehl, 1954, 1959).

In spite of the research evidence (which has favoured actuarial methods unequivocally), clinicians still tend to rely on the clinical method (Grove & Lloyd, 2006). Statistical rules (e.g., regression equations) do outperform clinical hunches, but there are two basic problems with them. First, many of the equations and algorithms found in the literature do not generalize to practice settings. Second, there are no prediction rules for the bulk of our decisions.

❸ BEFORE MOVING ON

What are the strengths and weaknesses of clinical versus actuarial prediction?

Biological Assessment

In trying to determine the cause of abnormal behaviour, it is important to be aware of any medical conditions that may be causing or contributing to such behaviour. For example, it has been well established that one form of psychosis may be caused by syphilis (see Chapter 1), which is readily diagnosed with a simple blood test. We also know that disruptions in the functioning of the thyroid may mimic anxiety and depression in previously psychologically stable individuals. When medication stabilizes the thyroid functions, their psychological symptoms abate. Many other medical conditions can also affect behaviour. Therefore, it is important that a general physical examination be conducted as part of an assessment for psychological disorders.

BRAIN IMAGING TECHNIQUES

The central nervous system has been the focus of considerable research in the attempt to understand the causes of psychopathology. One of the oldest and most well-established techniques is the electroencephalogram (EEG). The EEG uses electrodes placed on various parts of the scalp to measure the brain's electrical activity. These electrical impulses are carried to special electronic equipment that is able to amplify and record the activity in many parts of the brain. On occasion, patients may be asked to carry out a variety of visual or auditory tasks to see how various brain parts respond. Since we know so much about normal brain patterns, deviations in a particular part of the brain might be considered an indication of a problem for further investigation. It has been established that many seizure disorders, brain lesions, and tumours can be detected through EEG examinations.

Neuroimaging techniques can provide both structural and functional information concerning the physiological health of the central nervous system. Prior to the 1970s, brain imaging was done through radiography; it could identify problems with the cerebral vasculature, but could not identify differences in tissue density.

COMPUTED TOMOGRAPHY (CT) At the beginning of the 1970s, rapid developments in computer technology made possible a revolutionary brain imaging technique known as **computerized axial tomography (CAT)**, or CT scan. In this procedure, a narrow band of X-rays is projected through the head and onto scintillation crystals, which are much more sensitive than X-ray film. The X-ray source and detector then rotate very slightly and project another image; to complete the scan, the source rotates a total of 180 degrees, producing a number of images at predetermined angles. Each separate exposure produces a matrix of dark and light areas, which are later combined by a computer to produce a highly detailed *tomography*, a two-dimensional image or cross-section of the brain. The resolution of this image can be further improved by injecting an iodinitic radiopaque substance to enhance the contrast between different sorts of tissue. The resolutional capability of a CT scan is in the range of about 1 millimetre in soft tissue, and it can resolve structures such as cerebral vasculature, ventricles, grey and white matter, and some subcortical structures such as the thalamus and basal ganglia. This provides a wealth of information about an individual living brain.

Case Notes

Several years ago, a physician referred Michael, a seven-year-old boy, to one of this book's authors. Michael's mother, a registered nurse, told the psychologist that Michael had experienced eight short, unpredictable seizures over a period of three months. Michael's parents were very frightened and upset, but Michael remarked that he could not remember having the seizures, which had occurred only when his mother was around. On one occasion, Michael had a seizure while in the car with his mother, only 10 minutes from a hospital. By the time they reached the hospital, Michael was fine, and there was no medical evidence of any seizure activity. Michael had been given a full medical and neurological examination and declared perfectly healthy. The referring physician suspected that Michael may have been faking or holding his breath until he passed out, in order to get attention or sympathy from his parents. The psychologist spent several sessions with the family together and with each family member alone. Once, while the parents were in the psychologist's office at the hospital, Michael fell and had what appeared to be a very short seizure while in the neurology waiting area. This was the first time that someone other than his mother had been present. Once again, there were no medical signs of a seizure. In the opinion of the psychologist, Michael and his parents were a happy, well-adjusted family with no emotional problems, so, although no cause for the seizures had been identified, the psychologist stopped seeing the family. About six months later, the psychologist saw Michael being pushed in a wheelchair by his mother. By a few weeks after that, Michael had deteriorated rapidly. He started having many more seizures. Only at that point were physicians able to diagnose a very rare and progressive brain disorder that would lead to death within a year. The disorder could not be diagnosed in its early stages with the technology available at that time.

This is not the only case we have seen—though it was certainly the most dramatic—in which what appeared to be a psychological disorder was the first sign of some medical problem.

CT scans have confirmed a number of ideas about how the brain works in abnormal psychology. For example, scientists have long suspected that schizophrenia and degenerative neurological disorders such as Alzheimer's disease involve cortical atrophy—that is, shrinkage of the number of brain cells or the size of individual brain cells. CT scans have shown that these scientists were right (Das, Lagopoulos, Sæther, & Malhi, 2008). Individuals with schizophrenia have smaller frontal lobes than do non-psychiatric controls (Charney et al., 2002). Moreover, autistic children show evidence of atrophy in the cerebellum, and people suffering from bipolar disorder show some tissue loss throughout the brain (Black & Andreasen, 2010). The findings, although replicated, often lacked specificity and were noted in a number of different disorders. Fortunately, significant advances in brain imaging technology have permitted a clearer understanding of anatomically relevant regions of the brain.

MAGNETIC RESONANCE IMAGING (MRI) Nuclear magnetic resonance imaging, or simply **magnetic resonance imaging (MRI)**, is a non-invasive technique, developed in the early 1980s, that reveals both the structure and the functioning of the brain. A strong homogeneous magnetic field is produced around the patient's head. This field causes atoms with odd atomic weights (especially hydrogen) to align their electrons parallel to the direction of the field. Brief pulses of radio waves are subsequently introduced, causing these electrons to move in a characteristic gyroscopic manner. When the radio waves are turned off, the electrons return to their original configuration and, in doing so, emit radio waves of their own at a characteristic frequency, which can then be detected outside a patient's head. By adding a small magnetic gradient to the field, the frequency of radio wave transmission by atoms within the brain is altered to correlate with the gradient, allowing scientists to determine the location of the radio source. The information gathered is then integrated into a computer-generated image of the brain (see Figure 4.1). MRI techniques are capable of discriminating extremely small differences in water concentration. MRI is also a safe technology: because it uses neither high-energy radiation (X-rays) nor injections, it avoids the risks of overexposure and neurological complications. Studies using MRI have now corroborated results found in previous imaging studies, including the decreased grey matter volume and cortical thinning seen in schizophrenia (Takayanagi et al., 2011).

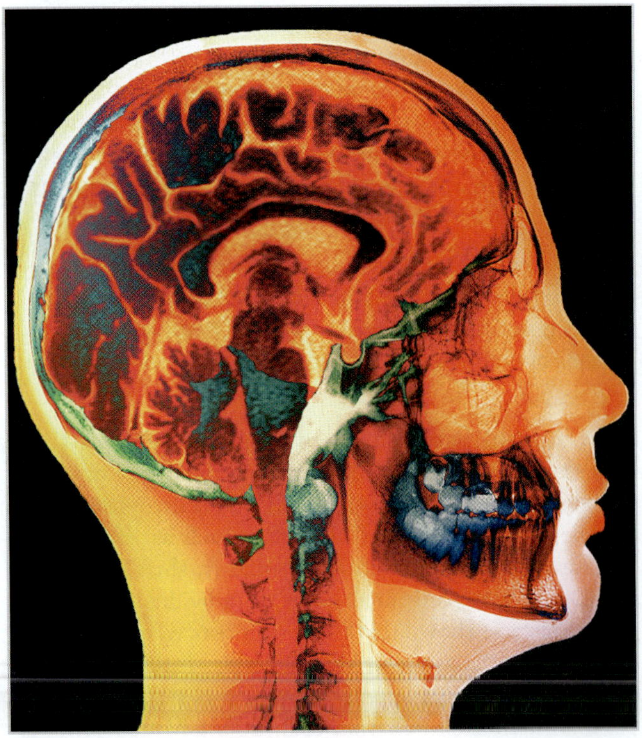

FIGURE 4.1 An Image of the Brain Produced Through Magnetic Resonance Imaging

Functional magnetic resonance imaging (fMRI) is a recent modification (early 1990s) of MRI. fMRI provides a dynamic view of metabolic changes occurring in the active brain (Seibyl, Scanley, Krystal, & Innis, 2004). A recent study conducted by researchers in Montreal helps to illustrate what kinds of information can be gleaned from fMRI investigations (Mendrek, Jiménez, Mancini-Marïe, Fahim, & Stip, 2011). This research focused on brain activity during the processing of emotions in patients with schizophrenia and the types of symptoms these patients had. Negative symptoms of schizophrenia (i.e., blunted affect, poverty of speech, anhedonia, lack of desire to form relationships, lack of motivation) were associated with significantly less activation in the right prefrontal cortex during the processing of sad versus neutral emotional stimuli. The researchers hypothesized that this pattern of brain activity may represent the neural basis of negative symptoms of schizophrenia, because of impairments in the brain's emotional processing circuitry located in those regions.

MRI research is also being enhanced by scalp recordings of electrical activity (event-related potentials, or ERPs) and magnetic fields (e.g., magnetoencephalography, or MEG). The ERP methodology has been widely used but, because the brain is not electrically homogeneous, finding the source of the electrical potential is difficult and the spatial resolution is low. MEG, in contrast, allows for a more precise determination of the source of activation because the brain is magnetically homogeneous (Charney et al., 2002).

POSITRON EMISSION TOMOGRAPHY (PET) **Positron emission tomography (PET)** is a combination of computerized tomography and radioisotope imaging. As in MRI, radiation is detected outside the head. In the case of PET, the radiation is generated by injected or inhaled *radioisotopes*—that is, common elements or substances that have had the atom altered to be radioactive. Isotopes with half-lives of minutes to hours are required for a PET scan. As the substance is used in brain activity, radiation is given off and detected by the PET equipment. This process allows the scientist to measure a variety of biological activities as the processes occur in the living brain. Recall from Chapter 2 the importance of neurotransmitters in brain activity. Providing a radioactive version of a *ligand*—a common molecule present in the chemical bonding that characterizes neurotransmission—allows the PET scan to show the distribution of various neurotransmitters within the brain. Similarly, glucose with a radioactive "label" (so called because it makes the glucose show up for the equipment) allows the rate of metabolic activity to be measured. Thus, while CT scans and MRIs can produce a static image of the brain's anatomy, PET scans and fMRIs produce a dynamic image of the functioning brain (see Figure 4.2).

Clinicians often use CT or MRI in addition to PET scans to determine the cause of structural abnormalities,

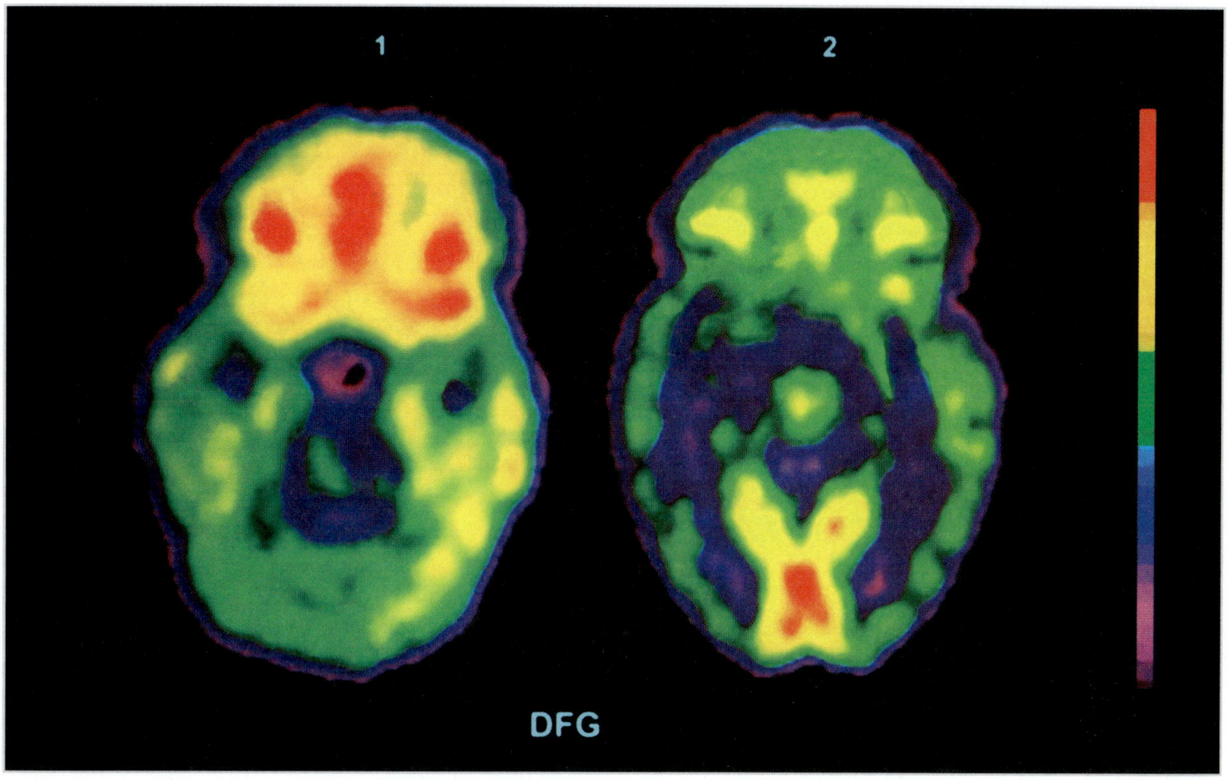

FIGURE 4.2 PET Scan Images of a Schizophrenic Brain and a Normal Brain

such as reduced blood flow. PET scans have confirmed that there are abnormal patterns of metabolic activity in people with seizures, tumours, stroke, Alzheimer's disease, schizophrenia, bipolar disorder, and obsessive-compulsive disorder; they also show atypical patterns of cortical blood flow as they perform cognitive tasks (Fischbach, 1992). A group of Canadian researchers from the Rotman Research Institute at Baycrest Centre and the Centre for Addiction and Mental Health in Toronto used PET to study brain changes in individuals who were receiving cognitive-behaviour therapy (CBT) for depression (Goldapple et al., 2004). The findings from these patients were compared to an independent sample of individuals who had responded to a serotonin-based antidepressant (paroxetine). These researchers found a distinct pattern of metabolic changes (in limbic and cortical regions) in patients who received CBT compared to those who received antidepressants (also see Frewen, Dozois, & Lanius, 2008).

The future of neuroimaging rests in the integration of various techniques to provide a comprehensive understanding of both normal and abnormal brain functioning (Charney et al., 2002).

NEUROPSYCHOLOGICAL TESTING

Neuropsychological assessments are used to determine relationships between behaviour and brain function. The **Bender Visual-Motor Gestalt Test** (Bender, 1938) is the oldest and most commonly used of these tests (Camara, Nathan, & Puente, 2000; Rabin, Barr, & Burton, 2005). It is easily administered and is often used to screen for neuropsychological impairment. The test consists of a series of nine cards containing lines and shapes drawn in black on a piece of white cardboard (see Figure 4.3). Respondents are asked first to copy the images on another card and then to draw them from memory. Errors in reproducing these lines and shapes may indicate neurological problems, but may also be caused by a tremor in the hand or by simple nervousness. However, certain types of errors are characteristic of neurological impairment: rotation of figures, perseveration (e.g., continuing to copy a line past the scale of the original pattern), fragmentation, oversimplification, inability to copy angles, and reversals (Groth-Marnat, 2009).

The main problem with this test is that it produces many false negatives; that is, some people with neurological impairment can complete the test with few errors. Moreover, many typically developing young children make more errors than older children with brain damage as a result of developmental differences. The Bender is age-normed to help compensate for this shortcoming; that is, results are compared to the results expected at a given age. While some clinicians prefer to interpret this test subjectively, others use a standardized scoring system. The test-retest reliability coefficient is 0.70 with the scoring system, and clinicians can discriminate between unimpaired participants and those with neurological impairment approximately 77 percent of the time (Groth-Marnat, 2009).

Newer tests are available. Neuropsychological assessments now usually employ a battery of tests to identify not

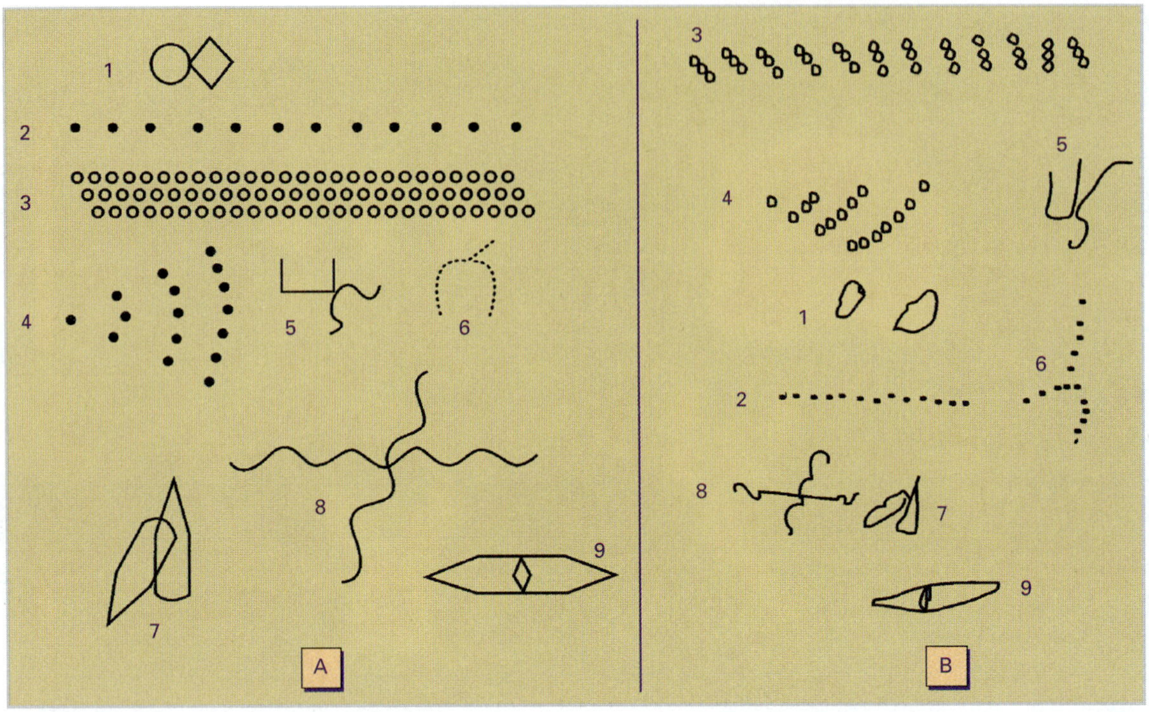

FIGURE 4.3 The Bender Visual-Motor Gestalt Test

Note: Part A shows the nine images that respondents are asked to reproduce. Part B shows the drawings of a person known to have brain damage.

Source: Patricia Lacks, The Bender Visual-Motor Gestalt Test, from *Bender-Gestalt Screening for Brain Dysfunction*, p. 34. © 1984 by John Wiley & Sons. Reprinted with permission of John Wiley & Sons, Inc.

only the presence of cognitive and motor impairment but also the nature and area of neurological impairment. By examining the pattern of results and deficits in performance, it is possible to discriminate between various forms of organic damage. The most popular neuropsychological battery is the Halstead-Reitan (Camara et al., 2000; Reitan & Wolfson, 2004); the Luria-Nebraska is also widely used (Golden, 2004). The former was developed by psychologist Ralph Reitan, who adapted tests created by his mentor, Ward Halstead, an experimental psychologist who studied patients with organic brain damage. The Halstead-Reitan consists of the following six subtests, with five more optional tests available:

1. *Category test.* This test measures abstract thinking. The examinee is called on to determine the principles that relate images varying in shape, size, location, colour, and other characteristics. Several images are shown on a screen, and the examinee is asked to choose, by pressing a button, which ones represent the given category. Performance on this test is believed to reflect frontal lobe functioning.
2. *Rhythm test.* In this test of concentration and attention, the examinee listens to 30 pairs of tape-recorded rhythmic beats, and is asked to identify which pairs are the same and which are different. Performance on this test is associated with right temporal lobe functioning.
3. *Tactual performance test.* The examinee is required to fit blocks of various shapes into their corresponding spaces on a board while blindfolded. He or she later draws the board from memory in order to test visual memory.
4. *Tapping test.* The examinee taps rapidly on a lever.
5. *Grip strength test.* The examinee grasps a dynamometer, which measures grip strength; this test can help to identify the location of brain damage.
6. *Auditory test.* The examinee is asked to identify aurally transmitted nonsense words.

The tests described above are meant for adults; versions are also available for children aged five and older (Nussbaum & Bunner, 2009). The Halstead-Reitan is quite time-consuming, requiring six hours or more to administer it and additional time to score it.

Psychological Assessment

CLINICAL INTERVIEWS

Interviews occur in every realm of life. Chances are you were interviewed before you got your first job, and will have more interviews as you begin your career. Mental health professionals, too, use the interview. The clinical interview is the most common assessment tool, used by almost every clinician. It is an important and comfortable way to collect information about an individual during a psychological evaluation. As mentioned earlier in this chapter, a psychological test is meaningless unless it is placed within the context of an individual's life. The clinical interview provides this valuable contextual information. Practitioners ask about many aspects of the individual's life: medical history, psychiatric history, age, marital status, family, education, and lifestyle, as well as the reason the person is seeking consultation.

Not all interviews are the same. Different types of interviews are often used to provide different kinds of information.

UNSTRUCTURED INTERVIEWS As the name implies, unstructured interviews tend to be open-ended affairs that allow interviewers to concentrate on a person's unique style or on certain aspects of the presenting problem. Having no script, the interviewer can pursue a line of questioning to see where it leads. One advantage of the free-flowing interview is that the clinician can follow the patient's lead. Patients are often under considerable stress, and are being asked to reveal very private, personal, and sometimes embarrassing information that they may find difficult or impossible to discuss with a stranger. In an unstructured interview, it is relatively easy to avoid a sensitive topic until a patient is more at ease. Thus, the main advantage of unstructured interviews is that they facilitate **rapport**, mutual trust, and respect between clinician and patient.

Although all interviews depend partly on the training, insight, personality, and skills of the interviewer, these factors are essential in the unstructured interview. The major criticism of this type of interview is its poor reliability and validity. The clinician's own theoretical orientation greatly influences the type of information sought. A psychodynamically oriented interviewer is more likely to ask individuals about their childhood, memories of their parents, sexual history, and dream content. A clinician working from a behavioural perspective may well concentrate on the immediate circumstances surrounding an individual's presenting problem and the contingencies reinforcing maladaptive behaviours. Thus, clinicians may tend to uncover only information that fits their theoretical orientation and confirms their hypotheses.

STRUCTURED INTERVIEWS How can an interview get away from the subjectivity of the interviewer and become a reliable procedure? A number of *structured interviews* have been developed that are very specific in the order and wording of questions and in the rules governing the evaluation of responses. The Diagnostic Interview Schedule, Version IV (DIS-IV; Robins et al., 2000), is a highly structured interview that may be administered by both mental health professionals and trained lay interviewers. The DIS-IV was developed for large-scale epidemiological research. Because of the large number of participants required for epidemiological studies, the cost of paying for professional diagnosticians is often prohibitive. By increasing the standardization of a diagnostic interview, and requiring that each question be read aloud verbatim, researchers are able to obtain the information they need without having to rely on the judgments of individual lay interviewers (Compton & Cottler, 2004). Although highly structured interviews may increase reliability, they tend to jeopardize rapport.

4 BEFORE MOVING ON

What are the advantages and disadvantages of structured and unstructured interviews? In what circumstances might you want to favour one format over another?

SEMI-STRUCTURED INTERVIEWS To reap the benefits of unstructured and highly structured approaches while simultaneously avoiding their pitfalls, *semi-structured interviews* have been developed. As in the unstructured interview, the clinician has considerable leeway about what questions to ask, in what order, and with what wording. The questions are guided, however, by an outline that lists certain dimensions of the patient's functioning that need to be covered. The most frequently used semi-structured interview in psychiatric settings is the **mental status examination** (see Table 4.1), which screens for patients' emotional,

TABLE 4.1 DIMENSIONS ASSESSED BY THE MENTAL STATUS EXAMINATION

1. *Appearance.* Is the patient clean and well groomed?
2. *Behaviour.* Are there any peculiar aspects to the patient's behaviour, such as atypical speech patterns (speed or cadence), odd mannerisms or tics, strange posture or gait?
3. *Sensorium* (sensory apparatus). Do the five senses appear to be intact?
4. *Affect* (expressed emotional responses). Has the patient expressed anger, anxiety, or any other general state during the interview? Has the patient's affect been inappropriate to the topic (for example, laughing or smiling when sad things were being discussed)?
5. *Orientation.* Is the patient aware of who he or she is, where he or she is, the time, date, and year?
6. *Thought content.* Does the patient describe hearing or seeing things whose existence is questionable? Does the patient seem to have delusions of persecution, grandeur, or the like?
7. *Memory.* How intact is the patient's memory for long-past events and recent events?
8. *Intelligence.* How sophisticated is the patient's vocabulary? How well does the patient express thoughts and ideas, use and understand abstractions and metaphors? Is the patient able to express and understand sophisticated concepts?
9. *Thought processes.* Is thought logical and coherent, or is there evidence of a loosening of associations, apparently unconnected ideas that are joined together?
10. *Insight.* Is the patient aware of his or her situation, and able to appreciate its severity and the necessity for clinical assistance?
11. *Judgment.* Has the patient shown ability to make sound and well-thought-out decisions, in the past and presently?

During an assessment interview, a clinician obtains information about various aspects of a patient's situation, behaviour, and personality makeup. The interview is usually conducted face-to-face and may have a relatively open structure or be more tightly controlled depending on the goals and style of the clinician.

Rating Scales As in the case of interviews, the use of rating scales in clinical observation and in self-reports helps both to organize information and to encourage reliability and objectivity (McDowell, 2006). That is, the formal structure of a scale is likely to keep observer inferences to a minimum. The most useful rating scales are those that enable a rater to indicate not only the presence or absence of a trait or behaviour but also its prominence or degree. The following item is an example from such a rating scale; the observer would check the most appropriate description.

Sexual Behaviour

_______1. Sexually assaultive: aggressively approaches males or females with sexual intent.

_______2. Sexually soliciting: exposes genitals with sexual intent, makes overt sexual advances to other patients or staff, masturbates openly.

_______3. No overt sexual behaviour: not preoccupied with discussion of sexual matters.

_______4. Avoids sex topics: made uneasy by discussion of sex, becomes disturbed if approached sexually by others.

_______5. Excessive prudishness about sex: considers sex filthy, condemns sexual behaviour in others, becomes panic-stricken if approached sexually.

Ratings like these may be made not only as part of an initial evaluation but also to check on the course or outcome of treatment.

intellectual, and neurological functioning. It is used in formal diagnosis or to plan treatment.

Many semi-structured interviews are designed to look for specific problems, such as behaviour problems of childhood (Mash & Barkley, 2007), depression (Dozois & Dobson, 2010), anxiety disorders (Summerfeldt, Kloosterman, & Antony, 2010), and personality disorders (Widiger & Lowe, 2010). The most used semi-structured interview to assess psychopathology is the Structured Clinical Interview for DSM-IV (SCID; First, Spitzer, Gibbon, & Williams, 1996, 2007). The SCID follows the same approach as the decision trees for differential diagnoses found originally in DSM-III and now in DSM-IV-TR. At each point, the interviewer is instructed to ask a specific question. Patient responses are rated, and the interviewer is instructed to carry on with another set of questions depending on the patient's response. A "yes" response from the patient leads to a very different set of questions than a "no" response. The SCID is also available both as a booklet and as DTREE software, a computerized structured interview (First, Williams, & Spitzer, 1996). The developers of the SCID have also created a SCID-II to assess for Axis II personality disorders according to the criteria in the DSM-IV (First, Gibbon, Spitzer, & Williams, 1997).

ASSESSMENT OF INTELLIGENCE

Intelligence tests were the first assessment tools developed by psychologists to win widespread acceptance; by now, virtually everyone in our society has heard of them. The first scientific study of intellectual functioning was conducted by the biologist Sir Francis Galton (1822–1911) in 1883, to test the hypothesis that intelligence has a hereditary aspect, a concept still being explored today. Galton believed that pure intelligence could best be measured by studying physiological cues—for example, the speed of response to a flash of light—an attribute later known as *sensory intelligence.* This was the first attempt to demonstrate the biological correlates of intelligence.

The first widely accepted and successful test of intelligence was designed to predict academic performance. The French psychologist Alfred Binet (1857–1911) was commissioned by the Paris school board to develop a means of determining which children should receive a public school education and which required special education. He did so by developing separate tests of judgment, comprehension, and reasoning. Binet was the first to use a large sample of participants to establish norms for the purpose of describing intelligence. His approach was to take a child's mental age, which was determined by the child's successful performance on age-grouped tests that had been normed, divide it by the child's chronological age, and multiply the quotient by 100. This would result in an **intelligence quotient**, or **IQ**. Theoretically, at least, an individual's IQ was always a reflection of that person's performance compared with the population of others of the same age. Therefore, a person aged 14.8 years who received a mental age score of 15.6 would achieve an IQ of $(15.6/14.8) \times 100 = 105$. Binet's work developed into the **Stanford-Binet Intelligence Scales**, which have been revised over the years and are now in their fifth edition (Roid, 2003). The most recent Stanford-Binet assesses five general kinds of ability: fluid reasoning, knowledge, visual-spatial processing, quantitative reasoning, and working memory (Becker, 2003; Kamphaus & Kroncke, 2004). It produces separate scores for each of these functions as well as a global IQ score that summarizes the child's ability.

Virtually all contemporary standardized tests of intelligence, as well as other types of psychological tests, share Binet's basic principle of comparison. A person's IQ is a function of how his or her score compares to others of the same age. Convention has dictated that the average be set at 100: those who perform more poorly have lower IQs; those who perform better have higher IQs (see Chapter 1).

The most popular IQ tests were developed by David Wechsler (1896–1981). In 1939, he published the first widely used intelligence tests for adults. The most recent version of the **Wechsler Adult Intelligence Scale**, or WAIS, was published in 2008 and is called the **WAIS-IV**. This test was designed to measure diverse aspects of intelligence and consists of 10 core subtests and 5 supplementary subtests: 4 verbal comprehension tests (general information, abstract thinking, the capacity to recognize and act on well-learned societal rules and expectations, and vocabulary), 3 working memory tests (short-term memory, arithmetic ability, and mental manipulation of symbols and numbers), 5 perceptual reasoning tests (puzzles, reproduction of designs, manipulation of objects and symbols), and 3 processing speed tests (searching for visual items, copying patterns). Figure 4.4 shows examples of two of the perceptual reasoning tasks. Average intelligence on this scale is an IQ of 100. The standard deviation (a measure of how far from the mean an average score will fall) on this instrument is 15, so scores below 70 fall in the lower extreme (called mental retardation in previous editions of the WAIS) and scores above 130 indicate exceptional intelligence. In 1974, the Wechsler Intelligence Test for Children (WISC) was published. The most recent version is the WISC-IV, published in 2003. The Wechsler Preschool and Primary Scale of Intelligence (WPPSI) was originally published in 1967 and the WPPSI-III was released in 2003. These Wechsler scales are the epitome of well-designed and well-researched assessment tools. They have very good test-retest and split-half reliability and concurrent validity, and readily distinguish between the intellectually gifted, those with learning disabilities, and individuals with intellectual disabilities (Gordon, 2004; Groth-Marnat, 2009; Sattler, 2008).

Of all psychological traits, IQ shows the most stability. As demonstrated in Table 4.2, the correlation diminishes with time, but a correlation of 0.78 from 8 to 15 years of age is quite remarkable. It should be noted, however, that more than half of all children show a variation of 10 points or more between early school years and adolescence. Some children have shown as much as a 40-point change in IQ within the same time period (Bukatko & Daehler, 2012).

But what does IQ really predict? The typical correlation between IQ scores and academic performance is in the range of 0.50 to 0.70, depending on the IQ tests being studied, the age of the individuals assessed, and how academic performance is measured (Brody, 1992). A strong correlation would be expected, because many of the same skills are required for intelligence tests and for academic success: skills such as verbal ability, rote memory, and reasoning. In fact, one might wonder why the correlation is not even stronger. The explanation seems to be that academic performance is also critically influenced by such factors as family, personality, and community. Some research has demonstrated a weak correlation (correlation coefficients of 0.20 to 0.30) with job trainability and performance. However, there is no evidence that IQ is significantly related to other measures of success in life, such as income earned, physical or mental health, or general life satisfaction (Bukatko & Daehler, 2012).

The use of IQ tests has become quite controversial. Do they really measure innate capacities or do they simply measure achievement? The issue of fairness is perhaps the most sensitive. Critics have argued that the IQ differences that have been found in North America between whites, blacks, and people of Asian background are actually a function of poor test construction; others argue that these differences are a function of respondents' socio-economic

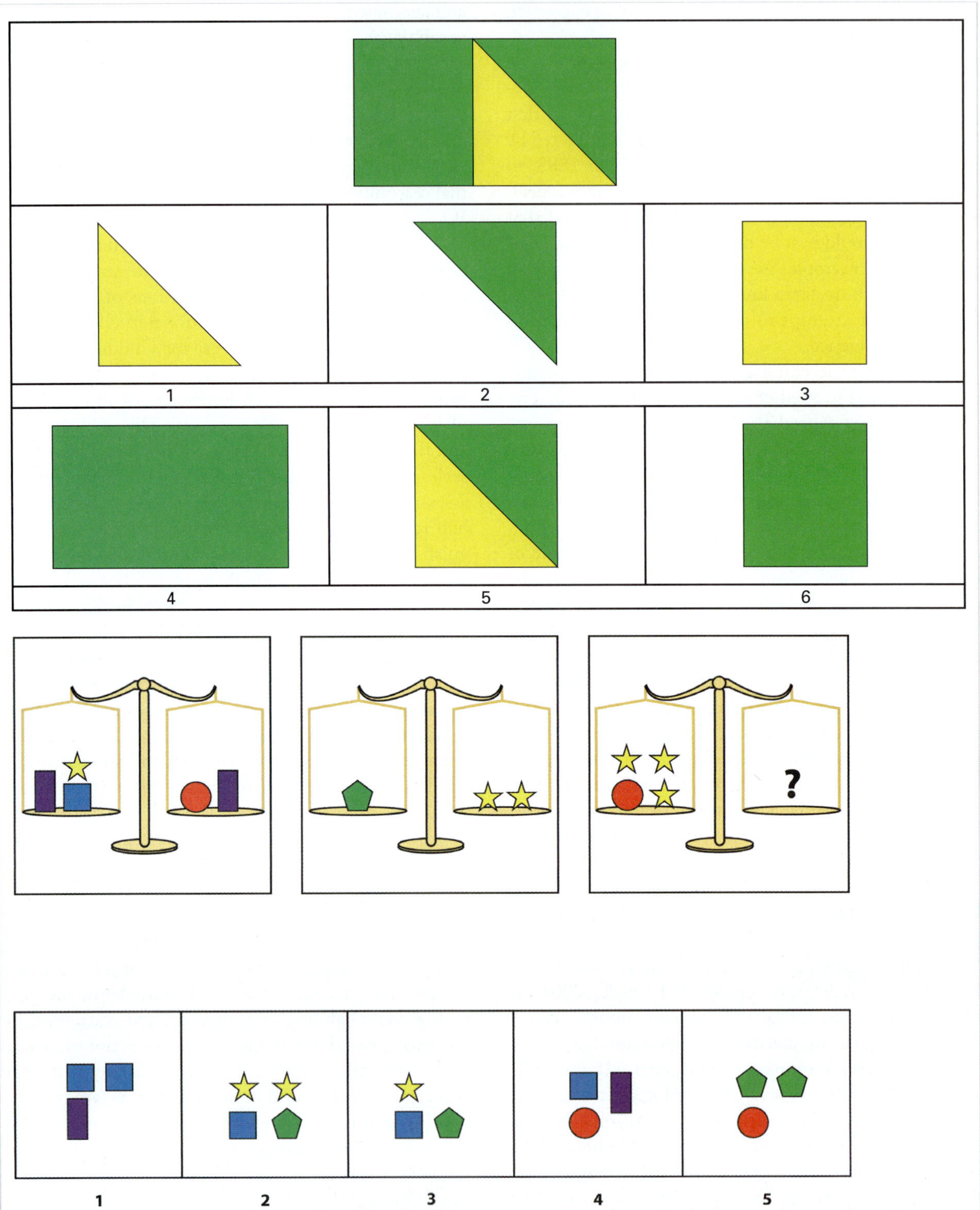

FIGURE 4.4 Items Similar to Those on the Performance Subtests of the Wechsler Adult Intelligence Scale IV

Source: Wechsler Adult Intelligence Scale—Fourth Edition (WAIS-IV). "Wechsler Adult Intelligence Scale" and "WAIS" are trademarks, in the US and/or other countries, of Pearson Education, Inc., or its affiliates.

environments (Groth-Marnat, 2009). See Chapter 3 for a discussion of cultural bias. Certainly, IQ scores have to be evaluated within the context of ethnic, age, gender, and culturally appropriate norms. Dr. Donald Saklofske at the University of Western Ontario has been instrumental in developing Canadian norms for the Wechsler intelligence scales (e.g., Bowden, Saklofske, & Weiss, 2011; Weiss, Saklofske, Coalson, & Raiford, 2010).

PERSONALITY ASSESSMENT

The early success of intelligence tests in predicting academic performance stimulated research and study of the

TABLE 4.2 CORRELATIONS OF INTELLIGENCE FROM 3 TO 15 YEARS OF AGE

Age	3	4	5	6	7	8	9	15
2	.74	.68	.63	.61	.54	.58	.56	.47
3		.76	.72	.73	.68	.67	.65	.58
4			.80	.79	.72	.72	.71	.60
5				.87	.81	.79	.79	.67
6					.86	.84	.84	.69
7						.87	.87	.69
8							.90	.78
9								.80

Source: This adapted table was published in *Intelligence*, vol. 2, 1992, by Nathan Brody, page 232, copyright 1992, Copyright Elsevier 1992.

measure of personality. While intelligence tests tend to produce total scores, personality assessments usually describe various characteristics that make up an individual's unique personality. A wealth of tests, questionnaires, and rating scales are available that offer shortcuts to understanding an individual and to predicting behaviour. These formal personality tests, and other assessment methods, are widely used for a variety of tasks including research, personnel selection, and diagnosis in clinical settings.

PROJECTIVE TEST Projective tests have the longest history in modern personality assessment, and generally have their roots in psychoanalytic principles. The theory behind a **projective test** is that a person presented with an ambiguous stimulus will project onto that stimulus his or her unconscious motives, needs, drives, feelings, defences, and personality characteristics. Thus, the test reveals information that the person cannot or will not report directly. Projective tests are used to help clinicians form hypotheses about an individual's personality. Although the use of these tests remains controversial, they are still frequently adopted by clinicians (Camara et al., 2000; Frick, Barry, & Kamphaus, 2010).

Rorschach Inkblot Test. The oldest and probably best known projective test is the **Rorschach inkblot test**. Hermann Rorschach (1884–1922), a Swiss psychologist, was intrigued as a child by the game of dripping ink on paper and folding the paper to make symmetrical figures. He noticed that people saw different things in the same inkblot, and he believed that their "percepts" reflected their personality. In high school, his friends gave him the nickname "Klecks," meaning "inkblot" in German. As a professional, he continued to experiment with hundreds of inkblots to identify those that could help in the diagnosis of psychological problems. The year following the publication of these

FOCUS 4.1

Test Security: Posting of the Rorschach Inkblot Test

The Rorschach inkblot test made headlines in 2009 when an emergency room physician from Moose Jaw, Saskatchewan, posted the entire set of 10 inkblots along with a listing of possible responses to the test on the Wikipedia website (http://en.wikipedia.org/wiki/Rorschach_test). The doctor believed that such information should be available to anyone interested and not held in secrecy by psychologists and psychiatrists (Cohen, 2009). At the same time, information about the Rorschach test is already available in books at your neighbourhood library or bookstore (Exner, 2002; Exner & Erdberg, 2005).

In some ways, the Wikipedia posting is a "cheat sheet" for those wishing to beat the test (Cohen, 2009; White, 2009). In response to the Wikipedia posting, both professional psychologists/psychiatrists and Hogrefe & Huber Publishing, the German company that owned the rights to Hermann Rorschach's seminal book, were outraged. They pleaded for Wikipedia to remove the diagrams and answers, stating that the public posting would jeopardize one of the oldest continually used psychological tests. Despite these efforts to have the pictures of the blots removed from the website, the pictures have not been taken down because copyright for the test has expired and the pictures are in the public domain. There are growing fears that the images will be distributed widely through other Internet sources, like YouTube, Facebook, MySpace, Twitter, Google+, and LinkedIn. Dr. Karen Cohen, chief operating officer of the Canadian Psychological Association, has stated that "the test becomes meaningless. If someone has all the questions and the answers, you can't administer the test. That compromises its usefulness" (Canadian Psychological Association, 2009; White, 2009). Essentially, people could study the answers they should give before receiving the test to purposely portray a particular disorder or condition, or a healthy state of mind.

At the same time, the problem could be overcome by using new inkblots, but they would lack the years of normative data and empirical research that the current set have. More fundamentally, there are ethical concerns whenever a protected diagnostic test falls into the hands of amateurs who have not been trained to administer, score, and interpret it properly. Access to such tests generally requires graduate-level training and state/provincial licensing. This protects the public by allowing only those individuals who can ethically and competently administer such tests to use them. Otherwise, who is to say that the test will be used properly? At the same time, the public release of the Rorschach could set a dangerous precedent. What might happen if intelligence tests or personality tests became readily available to the public?

It is unclear what the impact of the Wikipedia exposure will be. Some psychologists consider the exposure to be of little importance in the context of their practice. Only time will tell if the Rorschach's utility in clinical settings and research will diminish (Butcher, 2010). More empirical research is required to evaluate the impact of this exposure on the test's norms and interpretations. Will an update to the Exner system ensue? Or will the Rorschach become extinct?

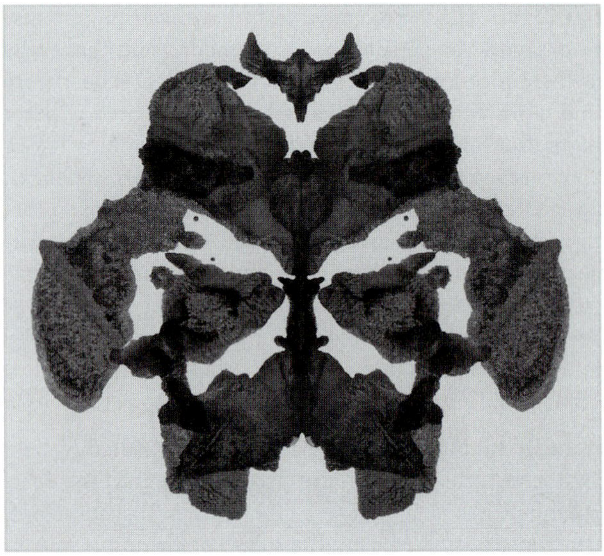

FIGURE 4.5 Inkblots Like Those on the Rorschach Test

inkblots, at the age of 38, he died of complications from a ruptured appendix. Figure 4.5 shows inkblots like those on the Rorschach test. Each inkblot is presented on a separate card and is handed to the respondent in a particular sequence. Initially, most clinicians used their own clinical approach to interpreting the results of a Rorschach examination. They would generally use the content of a patient's responses to the inkblots (for example, "I see two people fighting"), as well as colour, shading, texture, and movement in the interpretation of results. The **Exner system** developed in an attempt to increase reliability and validity by standardizing the scoring of responses (Exner, 1993). Evidence suggests that the Exner system may have greater clinical validity for testing schizophrenia than for depression or personality disorders (Vincent & Harman, 1991). Dr. John Hunsley at the University of Ottawa has closely reviewed the scientific literature about the Rorschach and suggests that its weak psychometric properties make its clinical utility questionable (Hunsley & Bailey, 1999, 2001; Hunsley, Lee, & Wood, 2003). Unfortunately, the Rorschach test, as well as other projective instruments, tends to be used in ways that extend beyond what is warranted based on the empirical literature and remains highly popular with some clinicians (Butcher, 2010; Widiger & Boyd, 2009; Wood & Lilienfeld, 1999).

Thematic Apperception Test (TAT) **The thematic apperception test (TAT)** was developed by psychologists Henry Murray (1893–1988) and Christiana Morgan (1897–1967) at Harvard University. *Apperception* is a French word that can be translated as "interpreting (new ideas or impressions) on the basis of existing ideas (cognitive structures and past experience)." The TAT consists of drawings on cards depicting ambiguous social interactions (see Figure 4.6). Individuals are asked to construct stories about the cards. Respondents are asked what they believe is happening in the scenes, what led up to these actions, what thoughts and feelings the character is experiencing, what happens next, and so on. Psychodynamically oriented clinicians assume that respondents identify with the protagonist or victims in their stories, and project their psychological needs and conflicts into the events they apperceive. On a more superficial level, the stories also suggest how respondents might interpret or behave in similar situations in their own lives. Validity and reliability of scoring techniques are open to the same criticisms as the Rorschach inkblot test.

In general, advocates of projective tests argue that they may yield meaningful material not easily obtained by self-report questionnaires or interviews. Because people want to be judged favourably, many people will give socially desirable responses to questionnaires; that is, consciously or unconsciously, they try to answer according to what they think they ought to be rather than what they are. Projective tests avoid this problem by presenting an ambiguous picture and by not asking directly about the subject. Because they allow freedom of expression, they may also shed light on areas that a questionnaire might not cover. However, research has not been very supportive of the reliability and validity of many of the projective techniques (Groth-Marnat, 2009; Hunsley et al., 2003). Rather, it appears that clinicians tend to interpret responses in a way that confirms their own clinical assumptions, without empirical validation of their accuracy. It appears that the degree of comfort professionals have with projective methods depends more on their acceptance of the underlying theories than on the reliability and validity of the techniques.

PERSONALITY INVENTORIES A range of instruments have also been developed that use scientifically accepted procedures such as standardization, establishment of norms,

FIGURE 4.6 A Drawing Similar to Those on the Thematic Apperception Test

TABLE 4.3 THE MMPI-2 SCALES

The list below is a sample of the Validity and Supplementary Scales.		
Validity Scales		
Cannot say scale (?)		Measures the total number of unanswered items
Lie scale (L)		Measures the tendency to claim excessive virtue or to try to present an overall favourable image
Infrequency scale (F)		Measures the tendency to falsely claim or exaggerate psychological problems in the first part of the booklet; alternatively, detects random responding
Infrequency scale (Fb)		Measures the tendency to falsely claim or exaggerate psychological problems on items toward the end of the booklet
Defensive scale (K)		Measures the tendency to see oneself in an unrealistically positive way
Response inconsistency scale (VRIN)		Measures the tendency to endorse items in an inconsistent or random manner
Response inconsistency scale (TRIN)		Measures the tendency to endorse items in an inconsistent or false manner
Superlative Self-Presentation (S)		Measures the tendency to appear excessively good. Improves upon the K scale
Clinical Scales		
Scale 1	Hypochondriasis (Hs)	Measures excessive somatic concern and physical complaints
Scale 2	Depression (D)	Measures symptomatic depression
Scale 3	Hysteria (Hy)	Measures hysteroid personality features such as "rose-coloured glasses" view of the world and the tendency to develop physical problems under stress
Scale 4	Psychopathic deviate (Pd)	Measures antisocial tendencies
Scale 5	Masculinity-femininity (Mf)	Measures gender-role reversal
Scale 6	Paranoia (Pa)	Measures suspicious, paranoid ideation
Scale 7	Psychasthenia (Pt)	Measures anxiety and obsessive, worrying behaviour
Scale 8	Schizophrenia (Sc)	Measures peculiarities in thinking, feeling, and social behaviour
Scale 9	Hypomania (Ma)	Measures elated mood state and tendencies to yield to impulses
Scale 0	Social introversion (Si)	Measures social anxiety, withdrawal, and overcontrol
Special Scales		
Scale A	Anxiety	A factor-analytic scale measuring general maladjustment and anxiety
Scale R	Repression	A factor-analytic scale measuring overcontrol and neurotic defensiveness
Scale Es	Ego strength	An empirical scale measuring potential response to short-term psychotherapy
Scale Mac	MacAndrew Revised Addiction Scale (MAC-R)	An empirical scale measuring proneness to become addicted to various substances

Source: Excerpted from the MMPI®-2(Minnesota Multiphasic Personality Inventory®-2). Manual for Administration, Scoring and Interpretation, Revised Edition.

clinical and control groups, and statistically validated methods of interpretation.

Minnesota Multiphasic Personality Inventory (MMPI). The most widely used objective test of personality is probably the **Minnesota Multiphasic Personality Inventory**, or **MMPI**. It was originally published in 1943 by Hathaway and McKinley. The revised and updated versions, the MMPI-2 for adults and the MMPI-A for adolescents, were published by Butcher, Dahlstrom, Graham, Tellegen, and Kaemmer (1989), and Butcher, Williams, Graham, Archer, Tellegen, Ben-Porath, and Kaemmer (1992), respectively. It is multiphasic because it assesses many aspects of personality. The MMPI contains 567 questions grouped to form 10 content scales plus additional scales to detect sources of invalidity such as carelessness, defensiveness, or evasiveness (see Table 4.3). Each item is a statement; the respondent is asked to check "True," "False," or "Cannot Say." Many items appear to have little face validity—it is difficult to infer what the question is supposed to measure.

To establish the categories and items, the creators of the test compared the responses of a large number of patients with well-diagnosed disorders like depression, anxiety, antisocial disorders, paranoia, schizophrenia, and mania to each other and to the responses of normal, non-diagnosed individuals.

The MMPI is based on the *contrasted-groups* method of ascertaining validity: items were chosen only if people known to have the characteristic the scale is intended to measure responded differently to the item than did people who did not have that characteristic. For example, a question would appear on the depression scale only if there was a clear difference between the responses of a group of depressed people and a group of people who were not depressed. This technique establishes concurrent validity, with group membership as the criterion by which the validity of the test is gauged.

As is common with the new breed of actuarially based personality assessments, raw scores are converted into standard scores with a mean of 50 and a standard deviation of 10. An individual's personality profile is depicted as elevation on a graph, which facilitates interpretation. Results of an MMPI-2 assessment do not constitute a diagnosis, but rather a profile of personality characteristics compared to psychiatric and non-psychiatric groups that may assist in forming a diagnosis. As an example, a standard score of 65 or higher on a particular scale places an individual at approximately the ninety-second percentile or higher of the revised normative sample, and is considered to be clinically significant. The higher a score, the more likely is the presence of a disorder. Although a single scale may be informative, MMPI experts typically interpret the pattern of relative scores from the entire profile. However, in the hands of a trained clinician, this profile can provide considerable insight into the functioning of an individual. Focus box 4.2 gives an example of how an individual's scores can be analyzed.

Many items on objective tests like the MMPI are clearly indicative of disturbed thoughts and feelings. The transparency of these items opens the opportunity for faking. MMPI validity scales include the L (lie) scale, the F (infrequency) scale, and the K (defensive) scale, among others. The L scale contains items that refer to minor foibles or flaws in character that nearly all of us possess and admit to readily. People who disavow these foibles may also deny items with more serious clinical implications. The lie scale identifies individuals who are trying to "fake good." The F scale contains items that were endorsed by fewer than 10 percent of the normal sample. A high F score may suggest random or careless responding, difficulty in reading or comprehending the test items, or an effort to "fake bad" to exaggerate complaints. An irony that clouds interpretation of the MMPI is that abnormal validity scale scores do not necessarily invalidate the test for highly disturbed respondents such as individuals with schizophrenia. The K scale measures a more subtle form of distortion, called psychological defensiveness or guardedness—respondents' tendency to conceal genuine feelings about sensitive issues to create a favourable impression. The K scale is used as a correction factor; scores on clinical scales that may be biased by defensive tendencies are augmented (corrected) by a fraction of the K scale score.

A concern about the original edition of the test (MMPI) was the narrowness of the group of participants on whom it was standardized. All were white, and most were young married people living in small towns or rural areas near Minneapolis. With the revision (MMPI-2), the test was standardized on a much more representative sample based on census information and modernized in other ways as well. Sexist language was removed, as were test items that seemed aimed at identifying people's religious beliefs. The MMPI-2 and MMPI-A have been validated in a wide number of studies (Archer, Krishnamurthy, & Stredny, 2007; Butcher, Atlis, & Hahn, 2004; Greene & Clopton, 2004).

Millon Clinical Multiaxial Inventory (MCMI). Whereas the MMPI-2 focuses primarily on Axis I disorders (see Chapter 3), the **Millon Clinical Multiaxial Inventory (MCMI)** was developed to help clinicians make diagnostic judgments about Axis II personality disorders and other clinical syndromes found on Axis I in the DSM. The most recent version of this instrument is the MCMI-III (Millon, 1994). The MCMI-III consists of 175 self-reported true-false items that yield scores for 24 clinical scales, associated with DSM-IV categories, and 4 validity indices. The normative sample used to validate the instrument consisted of 1000 people, including males and females and representing a wide variety of diagnoses. The clinical groups included patients seen in private practice, clinics, mental health centres, residential settings, and hospitals. The MCMI has been criticized because it consistently underestimates the severity of depressive syndromes (Piersma, 1987a) and over-diagnoses personality disorders (Piersma, 1987b). However, the diagnostic efficiency of this test seems to have improved with the third edition (Millon & Meagher, 2004).

Personality Assessment Inventory (PAI). The Personality Assessment Inventory (PAI; Morey, 1991) is a self-administered, objective inventory of adult personality. This instrument provides information relevant for clinical diagnosis, treatment planning, and screening for psychopathology. It is a fairly sophisticated instrument that uses the most recent techniques in test construction and psychometrics and shares many of the positive features of the MMPI-2 and MCMI-III and arguably fewer of their limitations.

In contrast to the MMPI-2 and MCMI-III, which use true-false response options, the 344 PAI items are each scored using a 4-point Likert scale. This continuum in scoring is intentional and reflects the purpose of the PAI to assess symptoms that range from mild to severe. There are 4 validity scales, 11 clinical scales (much like the previous personality tests we have discussed), 5 treatment consideration scales (e.g., suicidality, aggressiveness), and 2 interpersonal scales. The reliability and validity of this instrument appear to be well supported (Blais, Baity, & Hopwood, 2010; Kurtz & Blais, 2007; Morey, 1991).

A major limiting factor in any self-report test is that many people do not give accurate reports about themselves. Some will lie, and others will fall into what are called *response sets*, or test-taking attitudes that lead them to shade their responses in one way or another, on the basis of their own personal traits (for example, some people like to say "yes"), cognitive traits, or *demand characteristics* (that is, answering as one thinks the tester would desire). A common response set is *social desirability*—answering to make oneself look good (Jackson & Messick, 1961). Despite control

FOCUS 4.2

The MMPI-2: A Sample Profile

MMPI Form

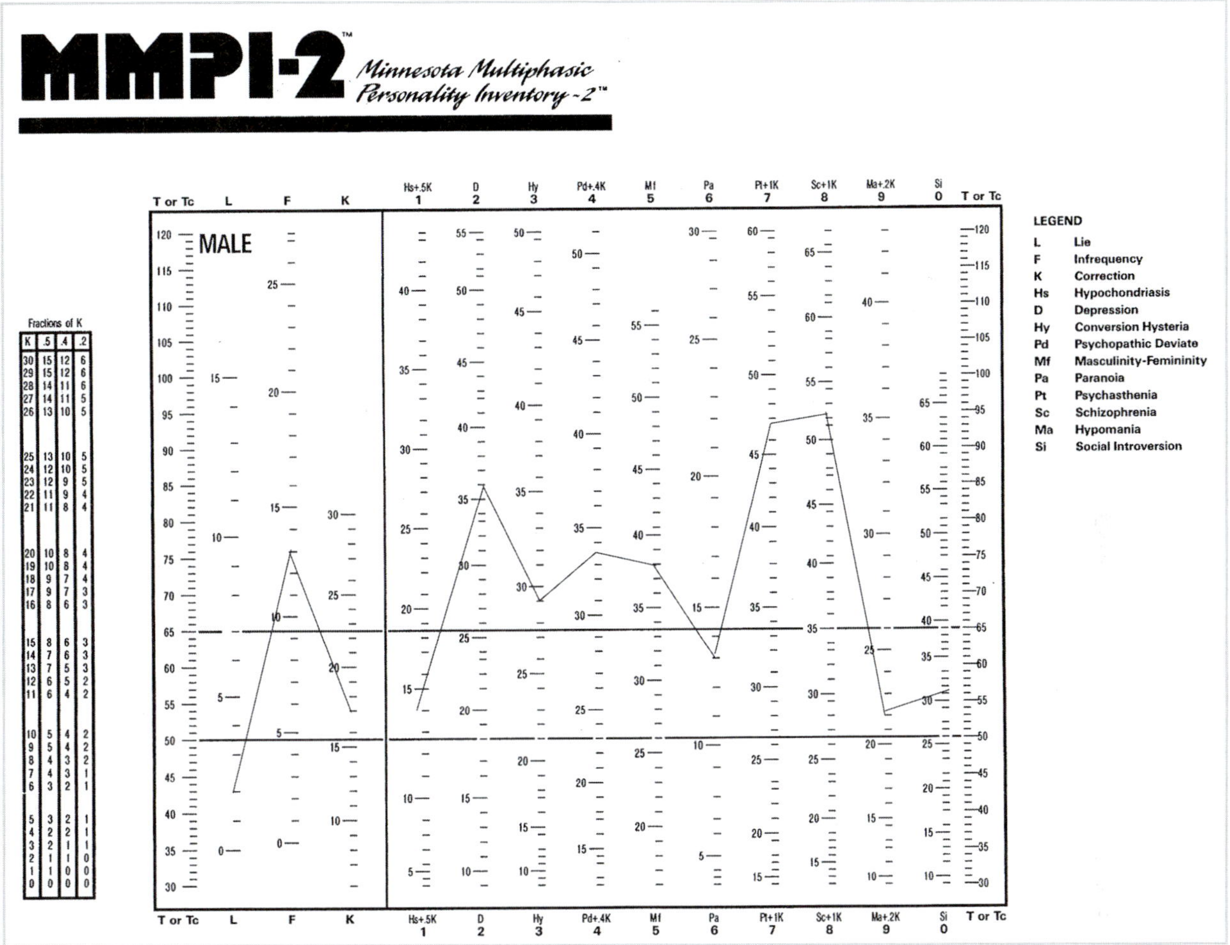

The above is a profile of a patient referred to our clinic by a physician. The physician was concerned about possible schizophrenic ideations, level of depression, and possible suicidal tendencies. It was interpreted by a senior psychologist who specializes in the MMPI, and who knew only the patient's sex, age, level of education, and marital status. This is called a *blind interpretation*.

REPORT

This is a blind analysis of an MMPI profile completed by Mr. Smith. This profile is valid. The MMPI profile completed by Mr. Smith suggests that he is currently experiencing a considerable amount of psychological distress in the form of tension, worry, and anxiety. He is a passive, dependent man who is having considerable difficulty coming to grips with his underlying dependency needs. It would not be unusual for such an individual to form very strong passive relationships. He is an angry man, whose anger is modified somewhat by his own self-image as a soft, esthetically inclined individual who has rejected the traditionally masculine role.

However, he pays for this role rejection with a high level of anxiety and tension, and also experiences a moderate level of depression.

Although the level of anxiety may produce some interference in his thinking, it is unclear from the profile whether a thought disorder exists. It would be necessary to definitively ascertain this from other data sources.

However, he is a ruminative and obsessive man who tends to externalize sources of anger. He is subtly suspicious of the motives of others but feels uncomfortable in stating this directly. Again, this is reflective of his own difficulty in dealing with anger in a direct, but still very controlled, way.

Individuals with profiles such as this often do engage in self-destructive behaviour. However, I would suspect Mr. Smith would give some warning about any such acts. It should be noted that he is highly vulnerable to loss and does have the potential to become seriously disorganized around such issues. Should he sustain the loss of a significant other person, or significant function, he may become acutely suicidal.

scales designed to detect such distortions, no professional assumes that the problem is eliminated.

Walter Mischel (1968) eloquently argued, with considerable empirical support, that personality tests are flawed by an inherent basic assumption common to all of them: that an individual's personality, or behavioural characteristics, are stable traits, generalizable across situations and over time. Many researchers supported Mischel's view, arguing that predicting a person's behaviour requires knowledge of both the person's typical behaviour patterns and the characteristics of the setting, sometimes called the **person by situation interaction** (Endler & Magnusson, 1976).

In addition to general psychopathology- and personality-based instruments are myriad symptom-specific self-report measures that are useful for diagnostic assessment, case formulation, treatment planning, and outcome assessment (Dozois & Dobson, 2010). For example, when assessing an individual with panic disorder, a clinician may decide to administer a measure of panic symptoms, an index that taps into fear of bodily sensations, and a questionnaire that asks patients questions about what situations they avoid. There are literally several hundred measures that may be used to assess anxiety (Antony, Orsillo, & Roemer, 2001) and depression (Nezu, Ronan, Meadows, & McClure, 2000) alone.

BEHAVIOURAL AND COGNITIVE ASSESSMENT

The development of the DSM from DSM-I to DSM-IV-TR has been marked by an increased reliance on behaviour that is readily observable and quantifiable. This has been a response, in part, to the rejection of older theories of personality that stressed the importance of underlying traits in predicting behaviour. Led by social learning theorists (Mischel, 1968), many working in the field of psychopathology have concluded that the underlying personality structures and traits assessed by more traditional psychological tests (such as hostility, rigidity, paranoia, or obsessiveness), while interesting, are of limited usefulness in predicting behaviour. They have suggested that the best predictor of behaviour in the future is past behaviour. As a result, a number of techniques arose to assess behaviour itself.

OBSERVATIONAL TECHNIQUES Behavioural clinicians try, whenever possible, to observe their patients' troubled behaviours directly. Techniques have been developed for observing the behaviours of a wide range of clinical populations. One form of behavioural observation employs behaviour rating scales—a preprinted sheet on which the observer notes the presence and/or intensity of targeted behaviours, usually by checking boxes or by filling in coded terms. This form of assessment is particularly popular when working with children and adolescents, because they all attend school. Consequently, parents and teachers can rate a child's behaviour independently and in different environments. One such rating scale, the Child Behaviour Checklist (Achenbach & Rescorla, 2001), is considered an excellent tool that can detect a broad array of problems in children, including aggressive behaviour, delinquent behaviour, attention problems, social problems, anxiety, and somatic complaints. It has undergone rigorous and sophisticated research for more than a decade, with parents, teachers, and the youths themselves using various versions of the rating scales. The development of these scales has included boys, girls, men, and women from all over the world, resulting in excellent norms based on age and sex. This test also has a computerized version to assist in scoring and interpretation.

However, often behaviour therapists are interested in more focused rating scales developed for particular populations, in which it is quite clear that behaviour problems exist. Raters are required to respond only to a small number of items, most of which are present in all individuals with this problem. These types of rating scales are particularly useful as before-and-after assessments in treatment programs.

Behaviourally oriented therapists often observe children's problem behaviours in relation to the *antecedents* (what happens before the behaviour) and *consequences* (what happens after the behaviour). To determine why particular behaviours are maintained, clinicians may gather observational data about sequences of behaviours to determine the function of the behaviour. For example, Table 4.4 presents an illustration of a child who misbehaves at school. The antecedent-behaviour-consequence (ABC) chart helps the clinician to determine why the child behaves in the way he does—in this case, to escape or avoid the situation or demand being placed on him.

How do environmental variables—perhaps the actions of parents, siblings, and friends—affect a behaviour of concern? When this is an important question, a clinician may go into a person's everyday environment to record a running narrative of events, using pencil and paper, video, or still camera. This is called **in vivo observation** (literally, "in the living being"). More commonly, observations are made by *participant* observers—key people in the client's environment—and reported to the clinician. However, observation in the natural environment is often impractical because of time constraints and the unpredictability of modern family life. Therefore, clinicians sometimes create an **analogue observational setting**, an artificial setting in an office or laboratory constructed to elicit specific classes of behaviour in individuals. For example, practitioners might want to observe the interaction between a mother and her defiant school-aged child. The clinician may have both parties play in a clinic playroom for 30 minutes, during which time the clinician is able to view the interaction pattern between mother and child (e.g., how the mother issues instructions, how the child complies with instructions, and how the mother reacts to defiance). This information can then be used to formulate a conceptualization of the child's behaviour problems and to develop a treatment plan.

Although useful, such observational methods are fraught with difficulty. Validity may be undermined by **reactivity**, the change in behaviour often seen when people know they are being observed or filmed. Moreover, because behaviour is often specific to particular situations, observations

TABLE 4.4 ANTECEDENT-BEHAVIOUR-CONSEQUENCE (ABC) CHART

Time	Activity	Antecedent	Behaviour	Consequence	Response	Function
9:03a	Circle Time/ Letter Activity	Sitting on rug pointing to letters	Nicky laid down	Teacher verbally redirected, "sit up and point to your letters, please"	Nicky continued to lay on the rug	Escape from letter activity
9:25a	Transition to Playground	Peer swinging on swing	Nicky began to follow peer and demand the swing	Teacher verbal redirection to "Go play with your friends for a little bit and then you can have a turn on the swing"	Continued to stand behind peer and demand swing	Access to preferred item (swing)
10:20a	Centers	Ms. Jane helping other students	Nicky laid down on empty chairs at table	Verbal redirection, "Sit up please"	Nicky verbalized "Oh, sorry" and sat up	Ms. Jane's attention
11:15a	Waiting for snack	Verbal direction "Wash your hands please"	Ran around into the closet and slammed door	Ignored	Nicky remained in the closet until hand washing time elapsed, before returning to his seat	Avoidance of hand washing
1:30p	Vocabulary Worksheet	Working independently at desk	Nicky clapped his hands in a quick repetitive fashion	Ignored	Nicky clapped his hands in a quick repetitive fashion	Automatic reinforcement

Note: Actual data but the names of those mentioned have been changed for the purposes of confidentiality.

in one setting cannot always be applied to other settings (Sattler, 2008). Methodological issues include inconsistency between observers, which may be avoided by training them properly. Frequent monitoring of observers is also important to avoid *observer drift*, a steady deterioration in accuracy as a result of fatigue or of a gradual, inadvertent change in the criteria over a long period of observation (Sattler, 2008). Finally, any assessment requiring observation of individuals, in natural or analogue situations, is fraught with logistical concerns, and is often expensive in terms of time, equipment, and scoring procedures, making it very difficult to implement in clinical practice.

Partly in response to such difficulty, clinicians or researchers may use challenge tests tailored to an individual's problem. This technique is particularly popular when dealing with phobias. We have brought real cats to our office, for example, to gauge the severity of a patient's cat phobia: How close to the cat can the patient stand to be while it walks around? While it is held by someone? Of course, this technique would hardly be possible with a phobia of thunder.

COGNITIVE-BEHAVIOURAL ASSESSMENT The thoughts that precede, accompany, and follow maladaptive behaviour are sometimes very important to a clinician's understanding of an individual (Beck & Dozois, 2011). But how can they be determined? Cognitive assessment tools are a relatively recent development used to address this question through tests and questionnaires carefully constructed to provide reliable, valid information. Kanfer and Phillips (1970) described four sets of variables that behavioural and cognitively oriented clinicians are concerned with, sometimes referred to by the acronym **SORC**:

- The S stands for *stimuli*. In this model, a clinician would attempt to establish the particular environmental situations that frequently precede the problem, or in which the problem often arose.
- The O stands for *organismic*, referring to physiological or psychological factors within the individual that might increase the probability of a behaviour, such as alcohol use, a tendency to low blood sugar, or poor self-esteem.
- The R refers to the overt *responses*, or the problem behaviour itself; the intensity, frequency, and duration of the behaviour would be important.
- The C refers to *consequences* of the behaviour, particularly those that might reinforce or punish the behaviour.

Researchers have also advocated for the use of theoretically appropriate measures to assess treatment outcome. Because cognitive-behavioural therapy (CBT) emphasizes the modification of unhelpful automatic thoughts and dysfunctional attitudes, the measurement of cognition is an important component of outcome assessment in this modality of treatment. A number of self-report measures are available to assess cognitive change in treatment (e.g., Dozois, Covin, & Brinker, 2003). Researchers have also tested changes in information processing (e.g., attention and memory biases) that are associated with clinical improvement (e.g., Andrés et al., 2008; Dozois, 2007; Dozois & Dobson, 2001b). Perhaps one day such methodologies will be employed in clinical practice to determine when treatment may be terminated or to assess a patient's risk of relapse.

SELF-MONITORING As its name implies, self-monitoring converts a patient into an assessor. Patients are usually asked to note the frequency with which they perform various acts, and sometimes the circumstances surrounding these occurrences and their response to them. Self-monitoring–type tasks have also been used with other, less overt "behaviour" such as thoughts and feelings (Piasecki, Richardson, & Smith, 2007; Simpson, Kivlahan, Bush, & McFall, 2005). For example, behaviour therapists treating people who are depressed may ask them to monitor their own thoughts and feelings to help them become aware of the sequence of events leading to their self-defeating or self-damaging cognitions. Obviously, this technique depends on a competent, diligent, and motivated self-monitor. It is not an appropriate technique for children or people with schizophrenia, for example. Self-monitoring has proved to be useful and cost-effective in many different types of behavioural intervention programs (Kratochwill, Sheridan, Carlson, & Lasecki, 1999).

Behaviour rating scales and systems may be categorized as ranging from direct to indirect, depending on how closely the observational setting approximates the setting in which the behaviour naturally occurs. Time, resources, and privacy should be considered in choosing an assessment technique. Another distinction is between *broad band* instruments, which seek to measure a wide variety of behaviours, and *narrow band* instruments, which focus on behaviours related to single, specific constructs such as hyperactivity, shyness, or depression (Skinner, Freeland, & Shapiro, 2003). Narrow band tests are appropriate when the psychological problems of a patient are fairly well known.

Behaviourally oriented therapists will often require patients to keep a diary, in which they record factors related to their problems. For example, clinicians may have clients keep track of their panic attacks, along with the associated bodily sensations, thoughts, and behaviours. As shown in Figure 4.7, a panic attack record can provide the clinician and the client with information about events that occurred outside the therapy session. By recording such data as soon as possible after a panic attack, more accurate information about the frequency, duration, and context of the panic attacks may be gleaned (Craske & Barlow, 2008). Applications for smart phones and tablet computers now make self-monitoring much easier. For example, eCBT Mood, T2 Mood Tracker, Mood Journal Plus, Thought Diary Pro, and Mood & Anxiety Diary allow people to track their symptoms and thoughts on their electronic personal devices without needing to write things down. This can make it much easier for people to comply with their therapists' requests for gathering information for an assessment.

We often think of psychological assessment as falling under the rubric of "soft sciences" as opposed to being able to examine a piece of tissue under a microscope, as is

Date: ________________ Time Began: ________________

Triggers: ________________________________

Expected: ______________ Unexpected: ________________

Maximum Fear: 0____1____2____3____4____5____6____7____8____9____10

None (0), Mild (2), Moderate (5), Strong (7), Extreme (10)

Check all symptoms present to at least a mild degree:

Chest pain or discomfort	________	Sweating	________
Heart racing/palpitations/pounding	________	Nausea/upset stomach	________
Short of breath	________	Dizzy/unsteady/lightheaded/faint	________
Shaking/trembling	________	Chills/hot flushes	________
Numbness/tingling	________	Feelings of unreality	________
Feelings of choking	________	Fear of dying	________
Fear of losing control/going crazy	________		

Thoughts: ____

Behaviours: ____

FIGURE 4.7 A Panic Attack Record

Source: Craske, M. G., & Barlow, D. H. (2008). Panic disorder and agoraphobia [Figure 1.2, p. 21]. In D. H. Barlow (Ed.), *Clinical handbook of psychological disorders: A step-by-step treatment manual* (pp. 1–64). New York: Guilford Press. Adapted with permission.

the case in the harder sciences. Interestingly, however, a meta-analytic review indicated not only that the validity of many psychological tests is compelling, but also that these tests yield validity coefficients similar to many medical tests (Meyer et al., 2001). Of course, these tests must be supplemented with other information about patients to provide a thorough understanding of their difficulties, their context, and the appropriate targets for intervention.

Research Methods

Psychological assessment and diagnosis are inextricably entwined with research. It is research that validates the tools used in assessment. Conversely, psychological assessment and diagnosis provide the descriptive and measurement tools used by researchers in examining the attributes of clinical populations. To the extent that diagnostic criteria are impaired or the tests are undependable, research results are doomed to be erroneous.

One of the primary goals of clinical research is the **description** (defined as the specification and classification of an event) of clinical phenomena. The other is the prediction of behaviour. The two are linked; without some descriptive strategies and subsequent classification scheme it would be difficult to predict the likelihood of future events.

In this section, we will review some of the science required in the study of abnormal behaviour. The word **science** comes from the Latin *scientia* ("knowledge") and is defined as "knowledge ascertained by observation and experimentation, critically tested, systematized, and brought under general principles." Behavioural investigators strive to explore human behaviour in the same manner as scientists explore physical phenomena. The assumption is that the scientific method and principles are immutable, whether one is studying the path of the sun, why water turns to ice, or why some people become depressed and others do not. Those studying human behaviour have obstacles different from the ones faced by material scientists, while clinical researchers, those who study abnormal psychological behaviour, have their own unique challenges.

All scientific research can be divided into two broad categories: experimental methods and non-experimental methods.

Experimental Methods

CONTROLLED EXPERIMENTAL RESEARCH

One of the distinguishing features of all science is that questions must be posed in a manner that allows clear and precise answers. To allow this clarity, investigators must have as much control as possible over all aspects of the research, but this proves most difficult in clinical studies. The flagship of research into psychopathology is the **experiment**.

In an experiment, variables are manipulated and the effects of these manipulations on other variables are gauged. Large groups of participants are generally used, and the results are analyzed with proven statistical techniques. In a true experiment, participants are randomly assigned to experimental and control groups. **Random assignment** is a procedure that ensures that each participant has an equal probability of being in either the experimental or the control group, guaranteeing the equivalence of these groups. Both groups are then assessed on traits of interest. The **experimental group** is the one that is exposed to a variable that is manipulated, the **independent variable**. Then, the groups are given an assessment on measures the researchers hypothesized would be affected by the manipulation. These behavioural responses constitute the **dependent variables**. The **control group** experiences all aspects of the experiment, including assessments, in a manner identical to the experimental group, except for the manipulation of the independent variable. An **experimental effect** is obtained when differences in a dependent variable are found to occur as a function of manipulation of the independent variable. Acceptable statistical methods are employed to determine the probability that differences in the dependent variable reflect an experimental effect rather than the influence of chance. The results are then interpreted and discussed.

A common question in psychopathology is which treatment is most effective for a certain type of patient. An experiment can address this question. Some of the issues associated with this type of research can be seen in a clinical experiment with adolescents with depression (Kennedy et al., 2009; Treatment for Adolescents with Depression Study [TADS] Team, 2003).

The Treatment for Adolescents with Depression Study (TADS) was designed to compare the relative effectiveness and combined effectiveness of two common treatment procedures for depression: medication (in this case, fluoxetine) and cognitive-behavioural therapy. One of the most important requirements of a good experiment is participant selection. To ensure that others can replicate the study, participants should meet well-defined criteria and be well described in terms of any features that may be important. In the TADS experiment, the results would have been meaningless if the adolescents did not actually have depression. Therefore, the TADS research team used only adolescents who met the criteria for a DSM-IV diagnosis of a current major depressive disorder. In addition, the adolescents were required to score above cut-offs on both a well-known clinician rating scale completed by clinicians after they interviewed the adolescents and a test of intellectual ability. As well, adolescents were required to be free of other significant psychological or medical disorders, concurrent treatment with another psychotropic medication, or psychoses (see TADS Team, 2003, for the full list of inclusion and exclusion criteria).

Once a suitable sample was obtained, participants were randomly assigned to treatment groups. Why not let parents or the adolescents themselves choose which intervention they wanted? If they had been allowed to choose, it might have turned out that the families who chose one treatment over another were those with a higher (or lower) education level, a higher (or lower) income, a bias against medication, or some other factor that could influence the outcome. It would then be impossible to say whether any difference in outcome between the groups was caused by the different treatments or by the differences among the families. To prevent this type of bias, adolescents were randomly assigned to treatment groups. Adolescents were put into one of four groups: (1) fluoxetine (Prozac) alone (F); (2) cognitive-behavioural therapy alone (CBT); (3) placebo medication (P); or (4) combination of fluoxetine and cognitive-behavioural therapy (F+CBT).

In this experiment, the types of treatment being compared (F, CBT, P, and F+CBT) were the independent variables. For descriptive purposes, participants were assessed on many measures prior to treatment. This is often referred to as a **pretest**. To get a comprehensive picture of the effects of manipulating the independent variable, adolescents were assessed on several dependent variables judged to be important to their functioning (rating scales filled out by parents and adolescents). This is often called a **post-test**.

Research experience has revealed that individuals in treatment programs expect to get better, or report improvement to please the experimenter (Kazdin, 2003b). This has been called the **placebo effect**. To avoid having results reflect this effect, all participants should have, as nearly as possible, the same expectations. Thus, in TADS, adolescents who were not receiving fluoxetine were given placebo medication. A **placebo** is a substance that looks and feels like the substance being tested, but does not contain the active ingredient. Although originally used in medication research, this approach has also been adopted to include placebo psychological treatments, such as spending time talking generally with the individual, or asking the participant to draw and discuss pictures that do not relate closely to the study topic. It is also known that experimenters can unwittingly influence the results. If the experimenter expects that participants receiving the treatment will show more improvement than the controls, this expectation can be subtly communicated to the participants. Therefore, to further ensure that expectations would not influence the outcome of the study, a **double-blind** procedure was used; that is, neither the participants nor the experimenters knew who was getting medication and who was getting a placebo. In a perfect experiment, one would have provided a placebo to match the cognitive-behavioural therapy in the CBT condition. However, resources and ethics precluded this.

A key issue in any experiment is validity. The first type of validity to consider is **internal validity**, the degree to which the changes in the dependent variables are a result of the manipulation of the independent variable; this reflects the internal integrity of the study. If no alternative explanations are possible, one has strong internal validity. The other is **external validity**, the generalizability of the findings, or the degree to which the findings in the investigation apply to other individuals in other settings. How well do you think TADS controlled for internal and external validity? Are there any problems that you can think of?

Pros and Cons. The strength of the controlled experiment is that it allows inference concerning causes and effects, the prime goal in all research. However, the controlled experiment is arguably the most difficult research strategy to implement, because of the need to control for so many factors. If strict control cannot be achieved, the internal validity of any experiment is threatened. Profound ethical dilemmas can arise relating to random assignment. For example, early in the development of a treatment for AIDS, research required that some participants be provided with active medication, which was withheld from the control group of patients. Is it ethical to withhold treatment, no matter how speculative, from a seriously ill population, and if so, for how long is it reasonable to do so? A similar question arose in the TADS experiment. Adolescents had agreed to stay in their assigned treatment condition for 12 weeks before being informed of their medication status (placebo versus fluoxetine). It would have been ethically unacceptable to keep adolescents who were doing poorly on placebo for longer than that given that there are two empirically supported treatments available in the study (medication and CBT). On the other hand, to keep on placebo only those adolescents who showed an improvement would compromise the validity of the experiment. Finally, the rigorous requirements of participant selection and the intervention procedures required in many controlled experiments limit the generalizability of findings.

QUASI-EXPERIMENTAL METHODS

Many important questions in abnormal psychology cannot be addressed in a pure experiment, since it is impossible—or, where possible, highly unethical—to create psychological disturbance in individuals in order to carry out investigations. Quasi-experimental studies, which do not face some of the challenges of controlled experiments, have therefore been essential in the development of various classification systems, including the DSM. A **quasi-experimental study** is one in which the participants in the experimental group are not randomly assigned but selected on the basis of certain characteristics, and in which there is no manipulation of independent variables.

Some of the issues arising in quasi-experimental investigations can be seen in an investigation of teenagers with migraine headaches led by Dr. Pat McGrath of Dalhousie University, a well-known specialist in the study of pain (Cunningham et al., 1987). The study grew out of a notion that people with certain types of personalities—those who were anxious, depressed, and had a poor self-concept—were prone to headaches. A group of adolescents who met accepted medical criteria for significant migraine headaches was selected. In a quasi-experimental design, this group is designated the experimental group. The control group in a quasi-experimental study is selected not through random assignment but through matching; that is, attempting to ensure that the participants in all conditions are comparable on all variables that might be important to the research except for the key variable: in this case, the presence of migraine headaches.

Selecting the control group in this project presented a particularly intriguing problem. The normal control group was constituted by finding other children attending the same hospital who were the same age and sex as the migraineurs, with similar social and medical histories, except that they did not suffer from disorders that involved prolonged pain. However, if the study had proceeded with only these two groups, the results would have been *confounded*. A **confound** occurs when two or more variables exert their influence at the same time, making it impossible to accurately establish the causal role of either variable. In the migraine study, if psychological differences emerged between the experimental and control groups, two interpretations would be possible: it could be that these psychological differences *led* to the migraines; however, it could also be that the psychological differences *resulted* from the pain endured by the migraineurs. To control for this problem in interpretation, the researchers included a *clinical control group* as well: a group similar to the control group but possessing some pathology similar to that of the experimental group. In this study, the clinical control group was made up of teenagers who suffered from chronic musculoskeletal pain such as rheumatoid arthritis.

The results revealed that the migraineurs did in fact demonstrate more psychological problems than the normal controls. However, when the three groups were compared, it was clear that it was the level of pain, not the source of pain, that was associated with personality and behavioural differences. In the end, the results did not support the hypothesis that personality and behavioural styles put one at risk for developing migraines. Rather, it seemed that people who suffer pronounced and prolonged pain respond by becoming anxious and depressed.

Pros and Cons. The quasi-experimental study allows for meaningful analysis of many aspects of psychological disorders that cannot be studied by experiment. In fact, the development of DSM-IV was based largely on such quasi-experimental procedures. Nevertheless, the assignment of participants on the basis of their personal characteristics limits the cause-and-effect inferences that are possible. In addition, experience has demonstrated that it is difficult to match participants on all factors but the one in question.

Non-experimental Methods

CORRELATIONAL RESEARCH

The **correlational method** measures the degree of relationship between two variables and generally requires a large number of participants. It is not invasive; behaviour is not manipulated, just measured quantitatively and then analyzed statistically. The resulting correlation coefficient statistic describing the relationship between two variables is analyzed by a test of statistical significance to determine whether it is likely that the observed relationship could have occurred simply by chance. *Correlation coefficients* are represented by the symbol r and range in value from −1.00 to 1.00. A *positive correlation*, such as $r = 0.68$, indicates that an increase in one variable is associated with an increase in the other. A *negative correlation*, such as $r = -20.63$, indicates that an increase in one variable is associated with a decrease in the other. When the correlation coefficient is close to zero, there is no significant relationship between the two variables. Generally, psychologists are interested in correlation coefficients greater than or equal to 0.30.

Correlational research is frequently carried out where experimental manipulation is impossible or unethical. For example, in studying the effects of maternal smoking on a developing fetus, it would be unacceptable to randomly assign expectant mothers to groups and force some of them to smoke. However, a common misconception is that if two variables are reliably correlated, a causal relationship must exist. Actually, a significant correlation may have one of three interpretations. First, it is possible that variable A caused variable B. Second, it is possible that variable B caused variable A. Finally, a third variable may be responsible for the occurrence of both A and B.

For example, suppose that it is found that children who take piano lessons get higher grades than children who do not. It may be that studying the piano improves academic performance. It may be that only children with high grades are allowed to take piano lessons. Or it may be that a third factor—perhaps parents with an interest in cultural pursuits—leads to both high grades and an interest in the piano. (Can you think of further studies that would clarify the relationship?) Thus, correlational research methods possess no internal validity and cannot establish that a causal relationship exists. Nonetheless, the correlational method has played a major role in the study of abnormal behaviour and still occupies a deserved place as a research method.

One way to reduce the ambiguity regarding the direction of correlational relationships is to conduct longitudinal studies. **Longitudinal studies** permit an examination of early factors that precede the onset of a disorder. However, longitudinal studies are generally extremely demanding in terms of resources (i.e., money, time, sample size, etc.), especially when the disorder or outcome of interest has a low base rate in the general population. Thousands of people would have to be studied and followed up over several years just to have an acceptable sample size of people who actually develop the disorder of interest. One variation on the longitudinal approach considers only people who have an elevated likelihood of developing the disorder of interest. This is referred to as the *high-risk method*. In this longitudinal design, a sample of people who will more likely experience the desired outcome compared to the more general population (e.g., children of depressed mothers who are at greater risk for developing depression themselves) is selected.

Pros and Cons. Correlational research is a relatively inexpensive method of studying the relationship between naturally occurring phenomena. It can indicate whether a meaningful relationship exists between two variables. This knowledge may be of value even if the reasons for the relationship are not evident. Furthermore, it can also be used to illuminate areas that might benefit from more rigorous research strategies. Nevertheless, it is impossible to make cause-and-effect inferences with this design.

THE CASE STUDY

The case study method is undoubtedly the oldest approach to the study of abnormal behaviour and has been used extensively by clinicians to describe patients they have treated. The **case study** is a description of the past and current functioning of a single individual. Variables such as family history, education, employment history, medical history, social relationships, and the patient's level of psychological adjustment are described within the case study. This information is collected primarily by interview, but may be supplemented by test scores, archival records, consultations with family members, and actual observation during the clinical interview (for example, behavioural tics, emotional state, posture). The goal of the case study is a description of an individual's current problem, and its relation to his or her past. Ultimately, it seeks to provide a theory concerning the etiology of a patient's problem or psychological makeup, and/or a course of treatment and outcome.

Pros and Cons. As a method of investigating abnormal psychology, the case study possesses definite, albeit limited, advantages. Its approach is classified as *idiographic* in that it offers rich detail and vividness concerning a particular individual that is frequently lost in large studies. In contrast, the *nomothetic* approach, more favoured by scientists, studies large groups of participants to uncover the basic principles governing behaviour. The case study can be an excellent source for the generation of new hypotheses concerning the etiology and treatment of psychological disorders, which may later be tested under more rigorous statistical controls. In addition, the case study is useful in the description of particularly rare disorders and in their treatment. Finally, the case study can be used to supply a counter-example to universally accepted principles, since the existence of only one exception can render a proposition false. As an example, it has often been asserted that all sex offenders have themselves been victimized as children. If one is able to find any sex offender who has not been victimized, this assertion is incorrect. The exception to the rule does not, however, preclude the suggestion that there may be a higher incidence of sexual victimization in the history of sex offenders than in that of normal controls.

These advantages notwithstanding, the case study has limited use in the study of psychopathology. It does not employ the scientific method or control for rival hypotheses, and so cannot demonstrate cause and effect. Thus, the case study cannot prove a theory. In addition, one cannot be certain of the generalizability of the findings. Finally, the clinician's theoretical background has been shown to influence the questions asked and therefore skew the information gleaned. A Freudian, for instance, might focus on childhood conflicts, and a social learning theorist on the antecedents and consequences of behaviour. Thus, although the case study method has an assured position within the field of abnormal psychology, its usefulness will always be limited.

Case Notes

Peter was a four-year-old with attention deficit/hyperactivity disorder (ADHD), enrolled in a regular preschool program, who was often both physically and verbally aggressive toward other children, using commands, threats, teasing, and verbal conflicts. Children and parents complained regularly about his conduct. He had been told by staff and parents many times not to act in this fashion, to no avail. It was decided to target his physical aggression first. The teachers and researchers first agreed on what constituted physical aggression. For the next five days, all adults working in the school, including the researchers, were asked to surreptitiously record every aggressive incident on a prepared chart and to deal with it as they had previously. This generally consisted of separating Peter from the other child, reprimanding him verbally, and sending him to play in another part of the room. At the end of each day, all adults gave their charts to the researcher. As expected, and as demonstrated in Figure 4.8, the talk with Peter did little to change his physical or verbal aggression. This constituted the A1 phase of the intervention.

Peter was then told that every time he was aggressive toward another child, he would be placed in "timeout": that is, he would have to sit in a chair facing the corner in an unused part of the room until he was quiet for two minutes. As the figure demonstrates, Peter's aggressive behaviour rapidly diminished. This constituted the B1 phase of intervention.

After five days in phase B1, it was decided to stop putting Peter into timeout and return to the approach used before the study started (A2). Within three days, his aggressive behaviour returned to nearly pre-intervention levels. At the request of the parents and teachers, it was decided to reinstate the timeout after day 3 of this condition (B2). This time, Peter's aggressive behaviour appeared to decrease even more rapidly than it had the first time. Interestingly, his activity level did not change.

SINGLE-SUBJECT RESEARCH

Like the case study, **single-subject designs** are based on the intense investigation of an individual participant. However, this approach avoids many of the criticisms of

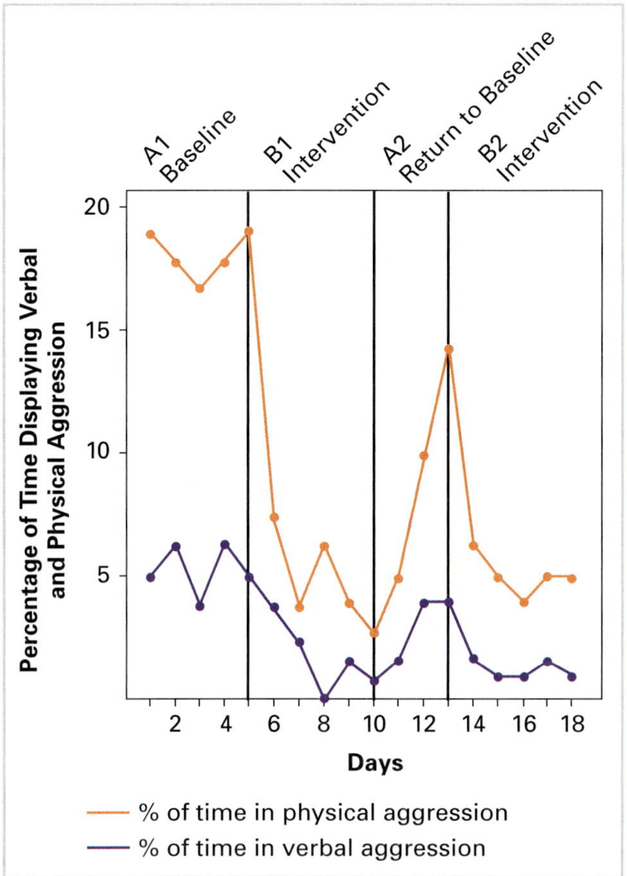

FIGURE 4.8 The Effect of Timeouts on Aggressive Behaviour: A Single-Subject Design

the case study by using experimentally accepted procedures. The variations of this design have several common elements: they use observable behaviours that are quantifiable; they quantify the presence of the behaviour prior to any intervention; they systematically apply readily observable and quantifiable interventions; and they measure the effects of the intervention on the behaviours of the participant. The **ABAB** design, also called the **reversal design**, requires the quantification of behaviour in its naturally occurring environment prior to any intervention. This constitutes the *A* phase or the baseline of the procedure. Next, in the *B* phase, the treatment is introduced in a controlled manner for a period of time. The next *A* phase constitutes the reversal, during which time the treatment is not provided, and the participant is exposed to the original baseline conditions. Finally, the treatment is provided once again and represents the final *B* (Firestone, 1976).

Pros and Cons. Peter's case (see above) demonstrates how a single-subject design differs from a case study. The single-subject design has the advantage of being relatively inexpensive. Moreover, the variables in question are clearly defined, observable, and quite accurately measured, removing the element of personal bias from the observations. An individual's performance can be judged more accurately than in even a well-executed group design, where performance is based on group means.

One problem inherent in this research strategy was demonstrated in Peter's case. While his undesirable behaviour improved dramatically in response to the first intervention, the behaviour did not immediately return to pre-study levels when the intervention was withdrawn. Peter's initial state was not recoverable within the time constraints of the present study. We assume that this was a result of some permanence in the change of Peter's behaviour pattern—which is the goal of most treatment. The other, perhaps more important, problem with the ABAB design is an ethical one: Can one justify reinstating contingencies that don't work in order to demonstrate that others do? More practically, participants are often unwilling to give up treatment that works just to preserve the integrity of the research design. This problem appeared in Peter's case, where the adults refused to continue with the second baseline. Finally, results are not generalizable; there is clear support that timeouts are effective with Peter, but we cannot say that they will be effective for all children with similar behaviour. Single-subject design reports are thus usually treated as demonstrations of interventions that warrant further study.

EPIDEMIOLOGICAL RESEARCH

Epidemiology is the study of the incidence and prevalence of disorders in a population. **Incidence** refers to the number of new cases of a disorder in a particular population over a specified time period, usually a year. **Prevalence** is the frequency of a disorder in a population at a given point or period of time. Epidemiological research also identifies risk factors that, if present, increase the probability of developing the disorder. In psychopathology, epidemiological research can help to identify the frequency of disorders in various populations and assist in the understanding of their development and maintenance or in the design of intervention strategies.

Perhaps the most famous epidemiological study occurred during a cholera outbreak in London, England, in the nineteenth century. At that time, John Snow noted that most people coming down with cholera congregated at or drank water from one source, the Broad Street Pump. He also noted that rates of cholera were lower upstream from London, where the water was less contaminated. He was thus able to demonstrate that the cholera was being spread by contaminated water.

We have no example in psychopathology of an epidemiological study that was able to prevent a disorder. However, Statistics Canada recently conducted an epidemiological survey of seven mental health disorders affecting Canadians (major depression, mania, panic disorder, social phobia, agoraphobia, alcohol dependence, and illicit drug dependence). In 2002 the Canadian Community Health Survey: Mental Health and Well-being collected data from 36 984 respondents aged 15 years and older from households in every province of Canada (Statistics Canada, 2003a). According to that survey, the 12-month prevalence for any mood disorder was 4.9 percent, for any anxiety disorder was 4.7 percent, and for any substance dependence was 3.0 percent. In total, approximately 1 in 10 Canadians reported symptoms consistent with a substance dependence problem or one of five mental disorders covered by the survey in the 12 months prior to the interview. This study shows the huge impact that mental health problems have on the Canadian public and provides a starting place for determining the allocation of mental health resources. Furthermore, this large data set allows researchers to examine more specific questions related to the particular mental health samples (e.g., Cairney et al., 2007; Schaffer, Cairney, Cheung, Veldhuizen, & Levitt, 2006). The Canadian government is currently collecting information in a number of prospective epidemiological studies, including the National Longitudinal Survey of Children and Youth (NLSCY), following Canadian children's development and well-being from birth to early adulthood; Survey of Youth Canadians (SYC), assessing cognitive, emotional, and behavioural development of Canadian children; National Population Health Survey—Household Component—Longitudinal (NPHS), following the health of the Canadian population and related socio-demographic characteristics; and Canadian Community Health Survey (CCHS), following health status, health care utilization, and health determinants for the Canadian population.

Pros and Cons. The advent of epidemiological research strategies allowed for the detailed collection of information concerning the incidence and prevalence of disorders in large populations. Such information is essential to the understanding of factors that contribute to the health of a population and the design of intervention strategies. However, this research strategy does not easily allow inferences concerning cause and effect. The final hindrance to epidemiological research is that it requires very large numbers of participants in order for relationships between factors to be recognized. This means that these types of studies can be very time-consuming and financially costly to conduct.

STUDIES OF INHERITANCE

Is a person born with a disorder, or a tendency to a disorder, or is it developed through environmental influences? As a general question, this may be termed the nature/nurture debate, and, as discussed in Chapter 1, the short answer is that there is no simple answer: both factors are important. However, the question still remains for particular disorders and particular cases: Is the source of a problem genetic or environmental? (In this discussion, *genetic* refers to inherited traits. In fact, some genetic disorders are not inherited but caused by mutation; for example, in Down syndrome, genetic damage occurs to the cells produced by parents whose own cells are normal. Such disorders are not, of course, tracked through family studies.)

FAMILY STUDIES Researchers often examine the incidence of a disorder among family members, frequently including distant as well as close relatives. Genetic similarity between family members is greater than between non-family members. Furthermore, genetic similarity is greater

TABLE 4.5 GENETIC RELATIONSHIPS

Relationship to Proband	Genes Shared
Non-family member	0%
Spouse	0%
Cousin	12.5%
Grandparent	25%
Grandchild	25%
Aunt or uncle	25%
Niece or nephew	25%
Parent	50%
Child	50%
Non-twin sibling (brother or sister)	50%
Non-identical twin (dizygotic twin)	50%
Identical twin (monozygotic twin)	100%

between parents and their children, and between siblings, than it is between cousins, aunts/uncles, or grandparents. Table 4.5 shows the genetic relationships between family members and non-family members. (Note that the genetic relationship between a parent and child is not exactly the same as between siblings. A child gets half of his or her genes from each parent; therefore, parent and child always have 50 percent of their genes in common. Siblings each get half of their genes from the mother and half from the father, but it is not known which of a parent's genes each child will get. Therefore, two siblings could in theory have anywhere from 0 to 100 percent of genes in common; the average genetic similarity between siblings is 50 percent.)

In family studies, the patient, or the person who has come to the attention of the clinician or researcher, is called the index case or **proband**. If the proband and a comparison person are alike on the characteristic of interest (if, for example, they show the same abnormal behaviour), the two are said to be *concordant* (or to display **concordance**). If the concordance rate for the disorder increases with increasing genetic similarity, this will offer support for, but will not confirm, a genetic basis for the problem. After all, families typically live in, and create, far more similar environments than are found between people from different families. Heredity and environment are thus confounded in family studies. For these reasons, behavioural geneticists have turned to other methods of studying these influences.

ADOPTION STUDIES Adoption studies offer researchers an opportunity to determine the separate effects of genetics and environment on the development of psychological disorders (Charney et al., 2002). In the prototypical investigation, a group of individuals who were adopted away from their biological parents at an early age and who demonstrate a psychological disorder are studied. The rates of disorder in the biological and adoptive parents are then compared. This allows researchers to control for environmental effects, assuming that the children were adopted at birth. Presumably, if there is greater agreement between adoptees and biological parents than there is between adoptees and adoptive parents, then a genetic link likely exists. Unfortunately, this type of research has demonstrated how difficult it is to match parent groups. For example, groups of parents who adopt children tend not to be a random representation of the community at large, and this may unduly influence the results. They tend to come from higher socio-economic strata and tend to have fewer problems such as alcoholism or substance abuse. This is not surprising, since in most jurisdictions parents wanting to adopt children are screened by agencies for suitability.

Cross-fostering is a great improvement on the traditional adoption study. In this case, one group comprises adopted children whose biological parents have a disorder and whose adoptive parents demonstrate no psychopathology. The other group comprises adopted children whose biological parents have no disorder but whose adoptive parents develop psychopathology. The comparisons available in this design allow statements concerning the relative impact of genes and environment.

There are several limitations to adoption studies as a research tool. It is very difficult to obtain full, accurate information concerning the biological parents of adoptees. Frequently, only the mothers are considered in this research, since it is not possible to verify who the fathers are. It is also difficult to control for the contact adoptees have had with their biological parents. Researchers may have difficulty in acquiring samples large enough to permit inferences. Furthermore, adoption studies do not control for the effects of prenatal exposure to toxins, maternal illness, or perinatal trauma; such factors can have significant physiological effects on the fetus, but are not transmitted genetically (Bohman, Sigvardsson, & Cloninger, 1981).

TWIN STUDIES Examination of the concordance rates among twins has been seen as a more accurate basis from which to infer genetic contributions to disorders, because the genetic similarity between twins is known. For example, identical twins share exactly the same genotype (they have inherited exactly the same genes from their parents), whereas non-identical twins share only half of their genotype. Identical twins, also known as **monozygotic (MZ) twins** (from *mono* meaning "one," and *zygote* meaning "fertilized egg"), result from the fertilization by a single sperm of a single ovum. This is followed by an unusual extra division into exactly matched zygotes, which subsequently develop into genetically identical fetuses. Thus, MZ twins have 100 percent of their genes in common. Non-identical (or *fraternal*) twins, also known as **dizygotic (DZ) twins** (from *di* meaning "two"), result when two independent sperm separately fertilize two independent ova at approximately the same time. Thus, DZ twins, like non-twin siblings, have, on average, just 50 percent of their genes in common. If there is greater concordance for a disorder among MZ twins than among DZ twins, so the argument goes, we can infer a genetic basis for the disorder.

It is not easy, however, to amass a large number of participants for such studies, because only a little more than 1 percent of all children are twins, and only one in three of these are monozygotic. For any particular disorder, there will be even fewer twins to select from, since most disorders occur in only a very small percentage of the population. For example, schizophrenia, a disorder that has been persistently examined for a genetic basis, occurs in only 1 percent of the population. Researchers are going to have to search far and wide to find enough monozygotic twins where at least one has schizophrenia. Typically, this has forced researchers to examine hospital records spanning many years. The difficulty is that, since diagnostic procedures have changed over the years, it is hard to be sure what the sample truly includes.

Other important criticisms attack the basic assumption of twin studies. For example, it is assumed that environmental influences are held constant in these comparisons between MZ and DZ twins and that, therefore, only genotypic differences can account for differential concordance rates. Lewontin, Rose, and Kamin (1984) point out that the environment of MZ twins is remarkably more similar than that of DZ twins. After all, MZ twins look alike, they are almost invariably dressed the same by their parents, and most everyone, including their parents, has great difficulty telling them apart. Lewontin and colleagues argue that these facts suggest that MZ twins will be treated almost identically; that is, the environmental responses to them will be the same. For DZ twins, however, who do not look the same (or at least no more alike than non-twin siblings), environmental responses can be expected to differ from one twin to the other. Therefore, according to Lewontin and colleagues, different concordance rates between MZ and DZ twins could readily be accounted for in terms of environmental rather than genetic influences. Moreover, identical twins have been found to exert greater influence over each other than do fraternal twins (Carey, 1992).

It is interesting to examine the differences in concordance rates between DZ twins and non-twin siblings. Since fraternal twins and non-twin siblings are equally similar genetically, what is one to make of differences in concordance rates between these two groups? Studies of schizophrenia consistently show that DZ twins have higher concordance rates than do non-twin siblings. Given that DZ twins are born at the same time, go through the same temporal changes, attend the same school, and often share the same friends, it is likely that environmental similarities play a significant role. Even more to the point, same-sex fraternal twins can be assumed to share far more environmental experiences in common than opposite-sex fraternal twins, although these two different sorts of fraternal twins have exactly the same genetic relationships. Six studies (Lewontin et al., 1984) have shown greater concordance among same-sex DZ twins than among opposite-sex DZ twins, a further indication of environmental influence. Recent research has demonstrated that the mother's health, perinatal trauma, viral infections, and environmental toxins, all interacting with the sex of the fetus, may be implicated in the long-term development of children through non-genetic, physiological processes. These elements may contribute, at least in part, to the higher concordance rates reported in DZ, same-sex twins than in DZ, opposite-sex twins (Bohman et al., 1981).

Obviously, it would be ideal to combine twin and adoption strategies by studying large numbers of MZ and DZ twins who suffer from the disorders of interest and were adopted early in life. However, finding sufficient numbers of such individuals who are willing to participate is a demanding task. Nevertheless, there has been a great deal of converging research, using a wide variety of research strategies, with several pathological groups, including individuals with schizophrenia, those with bipolar disorders, and substance abusers. Such studies have generally revealed higher concordance rates for disorders in MZ than in DZ twins. Some scientists have developed statistical procedures to calculate the degree to which genetics, as opposed to environmental factors, is responsible for psychological characteristics, using correlational data obtained with the twin study method. In one procedure, the correlation coefficient for DZ twins is subtracted from the correlation coefficient for MZ twins, and the result is then multiplied by 2 (Falconer, 1960). Using this formula, Plomin (1990) has suggested that height is correlated 0.90 among MZ twins and 0.45 among DZ twins. One could therefore conclude that height is 90 percent inherited, and by subtraction determine that 10 percent may be due to environmental factors. However, this simple calculation must be viewed with caution. It is only an estimate of the average contribution of genetics to the development of disorders, and, under extreme circumstances, the environment can exert a greater influence than is suggested by this simple computation. For example, factors such as extreme malnutrition or prenatal exposure to toxins may result in the genetic propensity of a trait not manifesting itself.

We have examined a number of different research designs in this chapter, each with particular strengths and weaknesses. Table 4.6 summarizes the pros and cons of all of these methods.

TABLE 4.6 PROS AND CONS OF DIFFERENT RESEARCH DESIGNS

Research Design	Pros	Cons
Controlled experiment	1. Cause and effect can be established	1. Difficult to implement because of control required (internal validity) 2. Ethical problems due to required manipulation of variables 3. External validity problematic
Quasi-experimental	1. Allows research when manipulation of variables is not possible 2. Provides information on pathological groups	1. Cause-and-effect statements compromised by lack of random assignment 2. Difficult to match participants in different groups
Correlational study	1. Relatively easy and inexpensive to implement 2. Allows study of relationships and between common phenomena variables	1. Cause and effect cannot be established
Case study	1. Very easy to implement 2. Idiographic approach provides rich detail 3. Allows some insight into infrequently occurring disorders 4. Provides for generation of new hypotheses	1. Cause and effect cannot be established 2. Highly biased by clinician's perspective 3. Cannot generalize to other patients or populations
Single-subject design	1. Relatively easy and inexpensive to implement 2. Allows cause-and-effect statements 3. Allows some insight into infrequently occurring disorders	1. Ethically and practically difficult to implement some reversals 2. Impossible to generalize results to other settings or participants
Twin and adoption study	1. Allows insight into genetic and environmental contributions to pathology	1. Generally cause and effect cannot be established (some diseases such as Tay-Sachs are the exception)
Epidemiological study	1. Provides information on the incidence and prevalence of problems 2. Provides information on factors related to the occurrence of problems	1. Impossible to make cause and effect statements 2. Large numbers of participants required

GENE–ENVIRONMENT INTERACTIONS Genes guide individuals to their maturation, but do not fully determine their development. Each person's **phenotype**, or the observable expression of his or her genetic contribution, is more accurately determined by the interaction of one's genes and the environment. That is to say that genetic factors influence one's sensitivity to environmental effects, or that environmental exposure to situations moderates the effect of genetic risk factors. Studies examining these **gene–environment interactions** (G × E) have become plentiful in the literature, as researchers search to discover why only certain individuals react to environmental circumstances in particular ways (Caspi et al., 2003; Gunter, Vaughn, & Philibert, 2010). Since gaining popularity in the early 2000s, hundreds of studies have now examined gene–environment interactions in various psychological disorders.

Unfortunately, we cannot consider genes and environment to be two independently functioning influences on developmental outcomes. Instead, there is a correlation between individuals' genotypes and the properties of their environmental experience. In general, there are three different ways that genotypes and environments are related and can influence development (Scarr & McCartney, 1983). They are not mutually exclusive, but rather all three can influence one's development.

1. *Passive gene–environment correlation.* In this situation, one's biological parents determine not only one's genotype, but also the quality of one's early experiences created by those biological parents. For example, parents with higher intelligence may pass this genetic predisposition to their offspring. As well, because of their higher intelligence and potentially higher-than-average salaries, these parents may have better access to more nutritious meals, have access to better child care and schools, and provide a more stimulating environment for their children. Children in these situations passively receive genotypes and early environmental experiences contributing to high intelligence.
2. *Evocative (reactive) gene–environment correlation.* In this situation, individuals' heritable behaviours evoke an environmental response. Continuing with the example used above, children who, like their parents, begin to show signs of above-average intelligence may behave in particular ways. They may show better verbal skills, learn more quickly, or work more independently in class. All of these behaviours will elicit certain responses from others, such as school personnel labelling them as "gifted," schools providing them with a more enriched educational experience, and prestigious universities offering them academic scholarships.
3. *Active gene–environment correlation.* In this situation, individuals possessing particular heritable propensities by virtue of their genotype will be more likely to actively select certain environments. For example, highly intelligent children may be more likely to develop friendships with other bright children with similar interests, join clubs or associations that satisfy their curiosity in a particular subject field, or choose demanding majors in university. This tendency to select environmental experiences based on genotype is sometimes referred to as "niche-picking."

Beyond this, research now examines **epigenetics**, or the study of modifications of gene expressions that are caused by mechanisms other than changes in the underlying DNA sequence. There is now evidence to suggest that environmental and psychosocial factors can change one's underlying genes to some degree (Masterpasqua, 2009).

5 BEFORE MOVING ON

What is an experiment, and how is it different from non-experimental methods of research?

Statistical Versus Clinical Significance

In experimental research, the concept of **statistical significance** is crucial, since it is the standard by which most research is judged as valuable or worthy of being published. Basically, experimental results are deemed statistically significant if it is extremely unlikely that the obtained results could have occurred purely by chance. The convention in psychological research is to set a significance level of 0.05 (often written as $p = 0.05$, where p stands for "probability"), meaning that if the independent variable exerted no effect whatsoever, the obtained findings would be observed no more than 5 percent of the time, solely by chance. Thus, if $p = 0.05$, it seems reasonable to assume that the independent variable is exerting an effect. However, there is a big difference between demonstrating statistical significance and finding a treatment that works in real life.

Suppose that a psychologist has developed a treatment for depression and has found, through careful quantitative research using large groups of participants, that the intervention significantly decreases symptoms of depression. As a result, she offers this new treatment to a few patients outside the study. Some show no symptom relief. Others score somewhat lower on a scale of depression, or report that some symptoms have decreased but their lives have not improved in any meaningful way; they still feel depressed. Assuming that the clinician correctly administered the treatment, why did a seemingly promising therapy fail to ameliorate the patients' quality of life?

At issue is the concept of **clinical significance**, which refers to a treatment's practical utility, and which does not follow automatically from statistical significance (Kazdin, 2003a). In a study with a large number of participants, statistically significant results may demonstrate that small changes are not due to chance. However, it is possible that only a minority of participants in the group experienced improvement, or that the improvement was measurable but small. Unless change is sufficient to be of value to a patient, the treatment has little merit. In fact, the cost in terms of time and money, and possible side effects, may render the treatment worse than useless. Moreover, some interventions work better in controlled circumstances than in the everyday world. Suppose, for example, that a medication worked only if administered eight times a day at precisely the same time. It might work fine when administered by a nurse in a hospital, but once home, the patient would be unable to stick to the schedule, and the treatment would become ineffective.

To control for the potential irrelevance of statistical significance in research, it has been suggested that it is equally important to evaluate the social validity of a treatment and attend to the qualitative changes in patients' functioning. This might be accomplished by collecting subjective input on therapy results from patients and significant others in their lives. Another meaningful approach, called **normative comparison**, compares treatment results to non-disturbed samples (Dozois et al., 2003; Ingram, Nelson, Steidtmann, & Bistricky, 2007; Jacobson & Truax, 1991; Kendall, Marrs-Garcia, Nath, & Sheldrick, 1999). Concern with clinical significance has now grown to the point that many journals will not accept articles (especially those dealing with interventions that have already been well studied) unless the authors can provide data showing meaningful, practical outcomes.

6 BEFORE MOVING ON

Why do you think it is important to consider clinical significance in addition to statistical significance?

SUMMARY

- Psychological testing involves gathering a sample of behaviour to determine a set of scores on a given measure. Psychometrically strong (i.e., reliable and valid) psychological tests contribute to a well-rounded psychological assessment. Psychological assessment plays an important role in abnormal psychology, providing a comprehensive system for describing an individual's psychological profile. A psychological test provides a piece of information that must be integrated and evaluated *within the context* of other information to create a thorough psychological assessment.
- Reliability and validity are important for both research and clinical assessment. Having measurement tools that are reliable and valid helps ensure that clinicians can consistently measure what they are hoping to, and are measuring what they think they are measuring.
- The debate between clinical and actuarial prediction has continued for years. It involves the contrast between clinicians' professional experience and intuition versus statistical procedures and empirical methods in clinical decision making. Both clinical and actuarial prediction have benefits and limitations.
- Biologically based procedures used in the study of psychological problems include EEG, CT scan, MRI, and PET. Although the results of most brain imaging assessments cannot be used to help in diagnoses, aside from circumstances in which there is obvious neurological impairment, they have contributed greatly to research.
- A number of neuropsychological tests are used to study brain–behaviour relationships, including the Bender Visual-Motor Gestalt Test, the Halstead-Reitan battery, and Luria-Nebraska battery.
- Clinical interviews have always been an integral part of any psychological assessment, and more structured components have been recently developed to reduce bias. Both structured and unstructured interviews have advantages and disadvantages. Semi-structured interviews provide a nice balance between facilitating rapport with clients while affording standardization and reliability.
- IQ tests were the first psychological tests to gain wide acceptance, and they do a fairly good job of predicting school performance. IQ tests with good psychometric properties also readily distinguish between individuals who are intellectually gifted, individuals who have learning disabilities, and individuals with intellectual disabilities.
- Projective tests, initially based on psychoanalytic theory, were the first personality tests. The Rorschach inkblot test and Thematic Apperception Test are two examples of projective tests. However, actuarial personality tests like the MMPI-2, MCMI-III, and PAI, based on more psychometrically sound procedures, have become more favoured among clinicians. Behavioural and cognitive-behavioural assessment techniques have become widely accepted. Most of these tests focus on specific behaviour problems (e.g., risk of suicide, level of depression, ability to concentrate) rather than on the whole range of personality functioning.
- The controlled experiment is not always possible in human research for ethical and logistical reasons. However, quasi-experimental and correlational research can provide a great deal of insight into human behaviour. Although not as scientifically rigorous, case studies and single-subject research designs may raise important questions and may point the way to more controlled

research. Family, adoption, twin, and gene–environment interaction studies offer valuable insight into the relative contribution of heredity and the environment. Experiments differ from these other forms of non-experimental research in that they manipulate variables, randomly assign participants to experimental and control groups, and can draw clear inferences about cause and effect.

- Recently, researchers have stressed that it is not enough to simply demonstrate statistically significant results of an intervention. The more important question is whether the treatment offers meaningful relief of the distress or difficulty of people with psychopathology. Research now recognizes the importance of examining *both* statistical and clinical significance when determining if a treatment is effective and will be useful in the real world.

MySearchLab offers you extensive help with your writing and research projects and provides round-the-clock access to credible and reliable source material. Chapter quizzes and a full electronic version of the text are also provided. Answers to the Before Moving On feature are provided on the MySearchLab. Take a tour at www.mysearchlab.com.

KEY TERMS

psychological assessment (p. 67)
test-retest reliability (p. 67)
alternate-form reliability (p. 67)
internal consistency (p. 67)
split-half reliability (p. 67)
coefficient alpha (p. 67)
face validity (p. 68)
content validity (p. 68)
criterion validity (p. 68)
construct validity (p. 68)
clinical approach (p. 68)
actuarial approach (p. 68)
computerized axial tomography (CAT) (p. 69)
magnetic resonance imaging (MRI) (p. 70)
positron emission tomography (PET) (p. 70)
Bender Visual-Motor Gestalt Test (p. 71)
rapport (p. 73)
mental status examination (p. 73)
intelligence quotient (IQ) (p. 75)
Stanford-Binet Intelligence Scales (p. 75)
Wechsler Adult Intelligence Scale (p. 75)
WAIS-IV (p. 75)
projective test (p. 77)
Rorschach inkblot test (p. 77)
Exner system (p. 78)
thematic apperception test (TAT) (p. 78)
Minnesota Multiphasic Personality Inventory (MMPI) (p. 79)
Millon Clinical Multiaxial Inventory (MCMI) (p. 80)
person by situation interaction (p. 82)
in vivo observation (p. 82)
analogue observational setting (p. 82)
reactivity (p. 82)
SORC (p. 83)
description (p. 85)
science (p. 85)
experiment (p. 85)
random assignment (p. 85)
experimental group (p. 85)
independent variable (p. 85)
dependent variable (p. 85)
control group (p. 85)
experimental effect (p. 85)
pretest (p. 86)
post-test (p. 86)
placebo effect (p. 86)
placebo (p. 86)
double-blind (p. 86)
internal validity (p. 86)
external validity (p. 86)
quasi-experimental study (p. 86)
confound (p. 87)
correlational method (p. 87)
longitudinal studies (p. 87)
case study (p. 88)
single-subject designs (p. 88)
ABAB (p. 89)
reversal design (p. 89)
epidemiology (p. 89)
incidence (p. 89)
prevalence (p. 89)
proband (p. 90)
concordance (p. 90)
cross-fostering (p. 91)
monozygotic (MZ) twins (p. 91)
dizygotic (DZ) twins (p. 91)
phenotype (p. 93)
gene–environment interactions (p. 93)
epigenetics (p. 93)
statistical significance (p. 93)
clinical significance (p. 93)
normative comparison (p. 94)

DAVID J. A. DOZOIS • REBECCA MCDERMOTT • PAUL A. FREWEN

Chapter 5

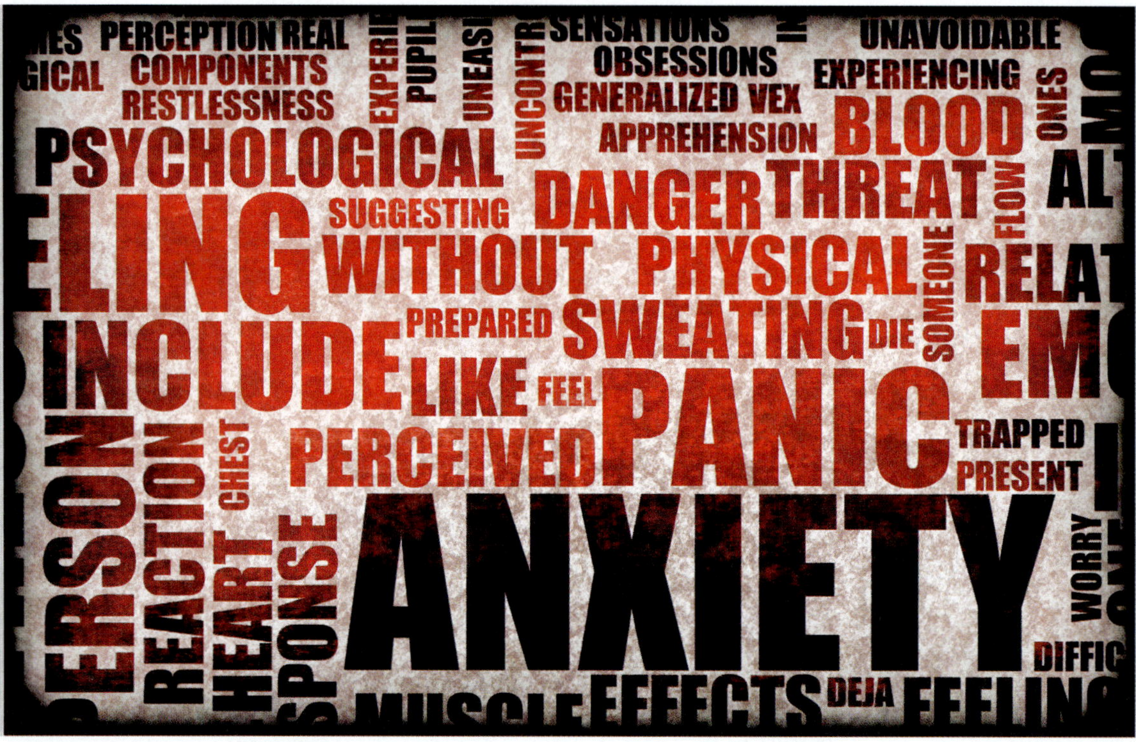

Anxiety Disorders

LEARNING OBJECTIVES

AFTER READING THIS CHAPTER, STUDENTS WILL BE ABLE TO:

1. Describe the characteristics of anxiety.
2. Discuss various etiological factors involved in anxiety disorders.
3. Identify and describe the methods involved in the assessment of anxiety disorders.
4. Differentiate the anxiety disorders from one another.
5. Summarize and discuss common treatments for anxiety disorders.

On the morning of her Abnormal Psychology exam, Crystal is experiencing a number of noticeable but mild symptoms of anxiety. Her body is tense, her heart is beating a little faster than usual, and she has a few worried thoughts coursing through her mind (e.g., "Did I study enough to do well on this exam?"). Sitting next to Crystal is Greg, whose symptoms are more severe. Greg's heart is pounding in his chest, his breathing is quick and shallow, and he too has a number of worried thoughts, although they are different in content and more distressing than Crystal's. Greg is worried that he is going to have a panic attack during the exam, and he is frantically scanning the examination room to mark all the exits should he feel the need to escape. Furthermore, he is very worried that others will notice his anxiety symptoms and that this will be embarrassing. To top it all off, he also has the exam to worry about!

Both Crystal and Greg are experiencing symptoms of anxiety. Crystal's anxiety is fairly typical of what many undergraduates experience before an important exam. However, Greg's symptoms are much more severe, cause him extreme discomfort, and impair his ability to concentrate. Greg may even get up and leave the exam before it begins.

The Characteristics of Anxiety

Before we discuss anxiety and two other related emotional states (panic and fear), we must distinguish among three distinctive components of emotion: physiological, cognitive, and behavioural. The physiological component involves changes in the autonomic nervous system that result in respiratory, cardiovascular, and muscular changes in the body (e.g., changes in breathing rate, heart rate, and muscle tone). The cognitive component includes alterations in consciousness (e.g., in attention levels) and specific thoughts a person may have while experiencing a particular emotion. For example, it is common for individuals experiencing a panic attack to think "I'm going to die," or for someone with social phobia to think "I'm going to embarrass myself in front of everyone." Finally, specific behavioural responses tend to be consequences of certain emotions. For example, if Greg experiences a panic attack during his exam, he may feel compelled to leave the situation. It is important to remember that the three components of emotional states are highly interrelated, and that each affects the other two.

There are also important theoretical distinctions between anxiety, fear, and panic (Barlow, 2002; Clark & Beck, 2010b). **Anxiety** is an affective state whereby an individual feels threatened by the potential occurrence of a future negative event. In the examples above, both Crystal and Greg are concerned about the possibility of something "bad" happening in the immediate future. Thus, anxiety in general is "future oriented." In contrast, **fear** is a more "primitive" emotion and occurs in response to a real or perceived current threat. Therefore, fear is "present oriented" in the sense that this emotion involves a reaction to something that is believed to be threatening at the present moment. From an evolutionary perspective, fear is a very important emotion because of the behavioural response that it elicits. This behavioural response is popularly known as the **"fight or flight" response**, so named because fear prompts a person (or organism) to either flee from a dangerous situation or stand and fight. When one considers the physiological symptoms involved in the emotion of fear, which include increased heart rate, muscle tension, and breathing rate, it is easy to see that this reaction is the body's method of preparing to respond to danger. **Panic** is very similar to fear, making these two emotional states difficult to distinguish in terms of their physiological and behavioural components. However, whereas fear is an emotional response to an objective, current, and identifiable threat, panic is an extreme fear reaction that is triggered even though there is nothing to be afraid of (it is essentially a "false alarm"; Barlow, 2002).

Historical Perspective

References to anxiety or fear have been made since the beginning of recorded history. Fear, for instance, is mentioned in ancient Greek writings and in biblical accounts. One of the earliest examples is from Hippocrates (see Chapter 1), who described a man who was terrified of flute music (Moehle & Levitt, 1991).

Until 1980, anxiety disorders were classified together with the somatoform and dissociative disorders (see Chapter 6) under the heading of **neurosis**. In the eighteenth century, people who were not psychotic but who still had emotional problems were labelled "neurotic." This term implied that the cause was presumed to be due to a disturbance in the central nervous system. Freud was one of the earliest theorists to focus on anxiety. His theories of anxiety can be traced to several of his works, including his 1895 paper "Obsessions and Phobias," his 1895 book *Studies in Hysteria,* and his 1926 text *Inhibitions, Symptoms and Anxiety.* Freud theorized that there was an important difference between objective fears and neurotic anxiety. He proposed that neurotic anxiety is a signal to the ego that an unacceptable drive (mainly sexual in nature) is pressing for conscious representation. Anxiety was viewed as a signal to ensure that the ego takes defensive action against these internal pressures. If anxiety rose above a certain level of intensity (e.g., beyond what the psychological defences can handle), symptoms ensued. In other words, anxiety was thought to occur because defence mechanisms failed to repress painful memories, impulses, or thoughts.

Research conducted over the past few decades has greatly expanded our understanding of the nature of anxiety and its treatment. The major models of anxiety today are behavioural and cognitive behavioural, although it is recognized that the causes of anxiety are complex and require an integrative understanding of biological, psychological, and interpersonal processes.

1 BEFORE MOVING ON

What are the primary differences between anxiety, fear, and panic? Give an example of how each can be adaptive and maladaptive.

Etiology

BIOLOGICAL FACTORS

GENETICS Evidence of a genetic influence in the etiology of anxiety disorders comes from epidemiological studies of families and twins, which demonstrate that virtually all of the anxiety disorders show at least a moderate level of concordance within family members. Individuals who have a family member who is diagnosed with an anxiety disorder are four to six times more likely to have an anxiety disorder than are those without a family history. The estimated heritabilities range from 23 to 40 percent, depending on the specific anxiety disorder studied (Hettema, Neale, & Kendler, 2001; Leonardo & Hen, 2006; Tambs et al., 2009). In addition, studies reveal that environmental factors particular to specific individuals account for a greater degree of the non-genetic variation in risk for anxiety disorders than do shared family factors (e.g., place of living; Hettema et al., 2001).

The genetic risk associated with anxiety disorders, however, appears to be fairly nonspecific. Rather than inheriting a risk for a specific type of anxiety disorder, the genetic risk for anxiety disorders is more likely passed on in terms of broader temperamental and/or dispositional traits, such as behavioural inhibition and neuroticism (Bienvenu, Hettema, Neale, Prescott, & Kendler, 2007; Rogers, Shelton, Shelledy, Garcia, & Kalin, 2008). Individual differences in these dimensions in turn likely serve as early risk factors for the later development of full-scale anxiety disorders when co-occurring with particular types of stress.

Although family and twin studies clearly demonstrate that genetic factors are involved in the etiology of anxiety disorders, the specific genetic basis of this risk remains to be understood. A number of preliminary studies have provided evidence of specific genetic abnormalities, but none of the findings have been sufficiently replicated to allow any firm conclusions.

NEUROANATOMY AND NEUROTRANSMITTERS The majority of what is known about the neurobiology of fear, anxiety, and panic comes from research with animals, although recent neuroimaging studies are rapidly increasing our knowledge concerning the neural underpinnings of anxiety disorders in humans (Dunsmoor, Prince, Murty, Kragel, & LaBar, 2011).

The neural fear circuit as studied in animals is thought to begin with the registry of sensory information at the thalamus; this information is then sent to the amygdala. From the amygdala, information is sent to areas in the hypothalamus, and then through a midbrain area (the periaquaductal grey) to the brain stem and spinal cord. The brain stem and spinal cord connect with the various autonomic (e.g., increased heart rate, blood pressure, body temperature) and behavioural (e.g., freezing or flight) output components that are involved in the expression of fear. Direct electrical stimulation of this circuit at low levels causes subjective anxiety in humans and freezing in rats, whereas stimulation at high levels provokes feelings of terror and flight behaviour (Panskepp, 1998). Human neuroimaging studies also suggest a role for the insular cortex, which may represent some of the somatic manifestations of anxiety (Etkin & Wager, 2007).

It is therefore important to note that higher cortical areas are not directly involved in the fear circuit. Instead, the fear system principally involves a subcortical network that can be aroused without the influence of complex cortical input. For example, the amygdala can effectively process external stimuli and determine its survival relevance without the influence of higher brain functioning (Kim et al., 2011; LeDoux, 2000). However, cortical and subcortical areas of the brain interact. These higher cortical areas are necessary for extinguishing conditioned fears (i.e., for learning that something that was previously feared no longer need be; Kim et al., 2011).

Information transfer between the neuroanatomical structures involved in fear, anxiety, and panic is mediated by a complex and interacting number of neurotransmitter systems. However, no neurotransmitter system has been found to be solely dedicated to the expression of fear, anxiety, or panic. Rather, each of the neurotransmitters involved in fear, anxiety, and panic is also involved in an assortment of general cognitive, affective, and behavioural functions. For example, gamma-aminobutyric acid (GABA) is the most pervasive inhibitory neurotransmitter in the brain, and receptors for this transmitter are well distributed along the neural fear circuit described above. Benzodiazepines are a class of anti-anxiety medications that operate primarily on GABA-mediated inhibition of the fear system. Other neurotransmitter systems are also involved, the most studied of which are the serotonin and norepinephrine systems. These systems serve general arousal regulatory functions in the central nervous system, and many of the medications used in the management of anxiety disorders have serotonin- and/or norepinephrine-based modes of action.

PSYCHOLOGICAL FACTORS

BEHAVIOURAL FACTORS The idea that anxiety and fear are acquired through learning has a long history. The origins of this proposal stem from Pavlov's discovery of classical conditioning, an idea that was expanded upon by Watson and Rayner (1920) and the case of Little Albert (see Chapter 2). In 1947, Mowrer proposed his **two-factor theory** that attempted to account for the acquisition of fears and the maintenance of anxiety. Mowrer suggested that fears develop through the process of classical conditioning and are maintained through operant conditioning. In the first phase, a neutral stimulus (the conditioned stimulus, or CS) becomes paired with an inherently negative stimulus (e.g., a frightening event, the unconditioned stimulus, or UCS). The individual later learns to lessen this anxiety by avoiding the CS, a behaviour that is negatively reinforced through operant conditioning. In the case of Little Albert, for example, Watson and Rayner (1920) showed how the fear of a rat (the CS) became conditioned through pairings with a sudden loud noise (the UCS). If Albert subsequently avoided rats, he would probably feel less anxious (at least in the short term), which would increase the probability that he would continue this avoidance behaviour. As we discuss later in this chapter, avoidance can be effective in reducing one's anxiety in the short term, but can serve to increase anxiety over the long haul. Imagine what would happen if you had a fear of dogs and tried to avoid them altogether. As long as you are able to avoid them, your anxiety would be fairly low; however, you would inevitably have to confront a dog at some point in the future and, during these moments, your anxiety would increase. Moreover, by avoiding dogs you would miss many opportunities for learning that they are usually not harmful. In other words, avoidance feeds the belief that there is something to fear.

Although there is support for Mowrer's two-factor theory, it does not do an adequate job of explaining the development of all phobias. Subsequent research has demonstrated, for instance, that not all fears develop through classical conditioning. For example, it is possible to develop fears by observing the reactions of other people (**vicarious learning** or modelling). Some people also develop fears by hearing fear-relevant information. For example, one of the authors heard a mother calling her son. This little boy was standing in some tall grass paying little attention to his mother's increasing demands to "come when he is called." Exasperated, the mother resorted to scaring her son, stating, "Come over here quickly, there are snakes in there and you will be bitten." There is also evidence that we are biologically prepared to fear certain types of stimuli (Seligman, 1971), a topic that is discussed in the section on the etiology of specific phobias.

COGNITIVE FACTORS Although there are many specific cognitive theories that pertain to each of the anxiety disorders, the main cognitive model for anxiety stems from the work of Dr. Aaron T. Beck (Beck & Emery, 1985; Clark & Beck, 2010b). Beck proposed that people are afraid because of the biased perceptions that they have about the world, the future, and themselves. Anxious individuals often see the world as dangerous, the future as uncertain, and themselves as ill-equipped to cope with life's threats (Beck & Emery, 1985). Individuals who are susceptible to anxiety often have core beliefs that they are helpless and vulnerable. These individuals also selectively attend to and recall information that is consistent with this threatening view of self (e.g., paying special attention to information suggestive of uncontrollability while ignoring information that does not fit with that expectation).

Numerous studies have demonstrated that anxious individuals tend to focus on information that is relevant to their fears (Clark & Beck, 2010b). For example, individuals who are phobic of spiders tend to orient toward words like *crawl* or *hairy* relative to positive or neutral words, whereas individuals with social phobia show this effect for words such as *boring* or *foolish* (Williams, Mathews, & MacLeod, 1996). Individuals who are highly anxious may also filter out or ignore information that contradicts the presence of an objective danger. For example, individuals with recurrent panic attacks often have fears that focus on bodily (e.g., "I am going to have a heart attack"), mental ("I am going to go crazy"), or interpersonal ("I am going to be embarrassed") danger when less threatening interpretations of their symptoms are far more likely.

Although cognitive models are considerably more complex than what we describe (e.g., Beck, 1996; Beck & Dozois, in press; Dozois & Beck, 2008), schemas, information processing biases, and automatic thoughts (see Chapter 2) are believed to be relevant to the development and maintenance of anxiety.

INTERPERSONAL FACTORS

Parents who are anxious themselves tend to interact with their children in ways that are less warm and positive, more critical and catastrophic, and less granting of autonomy when compared to non-anxious parents. Such parenting styles may foster beliefs of helplessness and uncontrollability in children that contribute to a general psychological vulnerability to anxiety.

The early attachment relationship may be important in the development of anxiety. Attachment theorists have postulated that early parent–child interactions can lead to the development of general belief systems (or "internal working models") for how relationships operate in general (Bowlby, 1973; Thompson, 2008). Children who develop an "anxious-ambivalent" attachment style learn to fear being abandoned by loved ones. This attachment style may develop from interactions with parents who are inconsistent in their emotional caregiving toward the infant. Later in life, these individuals may be wary of the availability of significant others and become chronically worried about negative interpersonal events. Although anxious-ambivalent attachment is presumed to predict anxiety problems in adulthood, few longitudinal studies have tested this hypothesis (Bar-Haim, Dan, Eshel, & Sagi-Schwartz, 2007). The available research offers some support. Warren, Huston, Egeland, and Sroufe (1997) found that an anxious-ambivalent attachment style in infancy predicted anxiety problems when the children were 17.5 years old.

COMMENT ON ETIOLOGY

Clearly, no single factor causes anxiety. Instead, there is a complex and dynamic interplay among biological, psychological, and interpersonal factors. Barlow (2002) advanced a "triple vulnerability" etiological model of anxiety in which generalized biological (e.g., a genetic predisposition to being high-strung, behaviourally inhibited, nervous), nonspecific psychological (e.g., diminished sense of control, low self-esteem), and specific psychological (i.e., experiencing a real danger, false alarm, or vicarious exposure) vulnerabilities interact to increase risk (see Allen, McHugh, & Barlow, 2008; Suárez, Bennett, Goldstein, & Barlow, 2009). While it is likely that some individuals have a generalized biological tendency to be high-strung or nervous (Barlow, 2002), a generalized psychological vulnerability to anxiety can also develop as a result of learning experiences and interactions with parents and peers. Over time, individuals may come to believe that the world is dangerous and threatening and that they have few resources to deal with it. Therefore, various combinations of biological, psychological, and interpersonal vulnerabilities contribute to anxiety.

The Scream was painted by Edvard Munch, a Norwegian expressionist. Munch suffered from a number of psychological problems, including panic disorder. In 2012, this painting sold for $119.9 million at a New York auction.

2 BEFORE MOVING ON

Briefly describe three factors that are involved in the etiology of anxiety disorders and describe an experiment that might test the role of each of these factors.

The Anxiety Disorders

Anxiety disorders represent the most common of all mental disorders (Kessler et al., 2009; Kessler, Chiu, Demler, & Walters, 2005). For example, epidemiological studies conducted in the United States suggest that this rate may be as high as 31 percent (Kessler et al., 2009).

Without treatment, anxiety disorders tend to be chronic and recurrent, and are associated with significant distress and suffering (Dozois & Westra, 2004; Konnopka, Leichsenring, Leibing, & König, 2009). Individuals with anxiety disorders are often impaired across multiple domains of functioning. The reduced quality of life reported among individuals with anxiety disorders is comparable to and in some instances worse than other major medical illnesses (Norberg, Diefenbach, & Tolin, 2008; Rapaport, Clary, Fayyad, & Endicott, 2005). Anxiety disorders are also costly both in terms of treatment and lost productivity. In Europe, anxiety disorders have been estimated to cost approximately $548 million for every million people (Konnopka, et al., 2009). Although comparable data in Canada are not currently available, the cost per capita is estimated to be similar (Koerner et al., 2004).

PANIC DISORDER AND AGORAPHOBIA

DESCRIPTION Individuals with panic disorder experience recurrent and unexpected panic attacks. **Panic attacks** involve a sudden rush of intense fear or discomfort during which an individual experiences a number of physiological and psychological symptoms. To be considered a true panic attack, at least 4 of the 13 symptoms outlined in Table 5.1 must be present. According to DSM IV-TR, the attack must also develop suddenly, reaching a peak within 10 minutes (American Psychiatric Association [APA], 2000). Individuals with panic disorder usually experience

TABLE 5.1	DSM-IV-TR DIAGNOSTIC CRITERIA FOR A PANIC ATTACK

Note: A Panic Attack is not a codable disorder. Code the specific diagnosis in which the Panic Attack occurs (e.g., 300.21 Panic Disorder With Agoraphobia).

A discrete period of intense fear or discomfort, in which four (or more) of the following symptoms developed abruptly and reached a peak within 10 minutes:

1. palpitations, pounding heart, or accelerated heart rate
2. sweating
3. trembling or shaking
4. sensations of shortness of breath or smothering
5. feeling of choking
6. chest pain or discomfort
7. nausea or abdominal distress
8. feeling dizzy, unsteady, lightheaded, or faint
9. derealization (feeling of unreality) or depersonalization (being detached from oneself)
10. fear of losing control or going crazy
11. fear of dying
12. paresthesias (numbness or tingling sensations)
13. chills or hot flashes

Source: Reprinted with permission from the *Diagnostic and Statistical Manual of Mental Disorders, Fourth Edition, Text Revision.* (Copyright © 2000). American Psychiatric Association.

numerous bouts of panic, but at least two unexpected attacks are required for this diagnosis.

Panic attacks themselves are not atypical. Twenty-one percent of Canadians aged 15 years or older (roughly 7.5 million people) experience at least one panic attack in their lifetime (Ramage-Morin, 2004). In contrast, only about 1.5 percent of the Canadian population meets criteria for panic disorder (Caron & Liu, 2010). Panic attacks are a common feature of other anxiety disorders. For example, it is not uncommon for an individual with social anxiety disorder to experience a panic attack when initiating social contact or for an individual with arachnophobia to have a panic attack when he or she confronts a spider. In panic disorder, however, the attacks occur (at least initially) "out of the blue" and are not cued by obvious triggers.

Diagnostically, at least one of the panic attacks must be followed by persistent concerns (lasting at least one month) about having additional attacks or by worry about the ramifications of the attack (e.g., worry that one will lose control, go "crazy," have a heart attack, or die). Alternatively, panic disorder is diagnosed when at least one panic attack results in a significant alteration in behaviour. Panic disorder is not an appropriate diagnosis, however, if the onset of an individual's panic attacks is judged to be due to a general medical condition or to the ingestion of a substance (APA, 2000).

In DSM-IV-TR, an individual is classified as having *panic disorder with or without agoraphobia*. **Agoraphobia** (literally meaning "fear of the marketplace") pertains to anxiety about being in places or situations where an individual might find it difficult to escape (e.g., being in crowds, standing in lineups, going to a movie theatre, being on a bridge, travelling in a car) or in which he or she would not have help readily available should a panic attack occur (e.g., being outside of his or her home alone, travelling). Individuals with panic disorder often avoid these types of situations or endure them with marked distress or anxiety. When this avoidance is persistent and pervasive, the diagnosis is panic disorder with agoraphobia. If agoraphobic avoidance is not present, a person is diagnosed with panic disorder without agoraphobia. In rare instances, agoraphobia can occur without a history of panic disorder. One proposal for the DSM-5 is that panic and agoraphobia be considered separate disorders (APA, 2010).

Most people who develop panic disorder do so in the late teenage years or early adulthood (Kessler, Berglund, et al., 2005), although treatment is usually sought much later, around 34 years of age (Craske & Barlow, 2008). Women are twice as likely as men to be affected by panic disorder, a finding that has been replicated across countries (Weissman et al., 1997). As illustrated in the case of Judy (see Case Notes on the next page), panic disorder is often comorbid with other mental disorders, most notably depression, substance abuse problems, and other anxiety conditions.

Panic disorder with or without agoraphobia tends to be chronic and results in serious financial and interpersonal costs. These financial costs are due, in part, to the overuse of medical resources such as emergency room visits and medical tests (Arch & Craske, 2008).

DIAGNOSIS AND ASSESSMENT A number of additional issues are relevant to diagnostic practice. Conducting a differential diagnosis can be tricky at times because panic attacks themselves are not unique to panic disorder and occur in other anxiety disorders. The cardinal feature of panic disorder is that individuals initially experience uncued panic attacks and have marked apprehension and worry over the possibility of having additional panic attacks. In contrast, panic attacks associated with other anxiety disorders are usually cued by specific situations or feared objects. To illustrate, although an individual with social phobia may experience a panic attack during a social function, it would be brought on by the fear of being humiliated or embarrassed. People with a phobia of flying may be concerned that their plane will crash, but those with panic disorder may fear getting on a plane because they might have a panic attack and not be able to escape. There are also a number of medical conditions that create symptoms that mimic panic disorder (e.g., hypoglycemia, hyperthyroidism). Therefore, it is important for clinicians to ensure that a patient has received a proper medical examination before diagnosing panic disorder (Baker-Morrissette, Bitran, & Barlow, 2010).

Case Notes

Judy was a 29-year-old from Burnaby, British Columbia, who began to experience uncued panic attacks five months ago. These panic attacks persisted for approximately three weeks, at which time she sought treatment and was prescribed a benzodiazepine. Secondary to her anxiety, Judy also experienced a number of symptoms of depression. She had moved to Canada a few years ago and had difficulty adjusting to this change. She became increasingly isolated and lonely. Judy described her upbringing as psychologically abusive. While growing up, she worked hard at the family-owned store and achieved good grades at school. She thought that by working hard enough she might gain the approval of her father, but this approval never materialized and she was instead humiliated publicly and criticized. After completing university, Judy worked in a government job in her country of origin. She married shortly thereafter and terminated her employment to devote time to raising her children. When Judy first met her psychologist, she continued to experience a significant number of panic attacks, although the severity of these episodes had decreased somewhat subsequent to taking anti-anxiety medication. Initially, these panic attacks came "out of the blue" and occurred frequently. During these panic attacks she experienced tachycardia (increased heart rate), perspiration, hyperventilation, facial flushing, feelings of dizziness and unsteadiness, shaking, chest pressure and pain, nausea, and peripheral numbness and tingling sensations. She also worried that she was doing to die, have a heart attack, or go crazy.

As is the case for all the anxiety disorders, a multimethod assessment that includes a clinical interview, behavioural measurement, psychophysiological tests, and self-report indices is the ideal assessment strategy (Baker-Morrissette et al., 2010). The Structured Clinical Interview for DSM-IV (First, Gibbon, Spitzer, & Williams, 1996) is a semi-structured interview that covers the Axis I disorders, including panic disorder (see Chapter 4). Another popular semi-structured interview is the Anxiety Disorders Interview Schedule (ADIS-IV; DiNardo, Brown, & Barlow, 1994), which is used to establish differential diagnosis among the anxiety disorders.

Behavioural assessment is also frequently used to assess avoidance and severity. For example, a clinician may decide to observe individuals in their naturalistic environments to assess their degree of agoraphobic avoidance. One strategy is the **behavioural avoidance test (BAT)**. In this test, patients are asked to enter situations that they would typically avoid. They provide a rating of their degree of anticipatory anxiety and the actual level of anxiety that they experience. Another behavioural assessment strategy for panic disorder is the symptom induction test. For example, a patient may be asked to hyperventilate, to shake his or her head from side to side, or to spin in a chair in order to bring on symptoms of panic. Such exercises can be useful both as a way of assessing symptom severity and as a strategy for exposure treatment.

Psychophysiological assessment strategies can include the monitoring of heart rate, breathing, blood pressure, and galvanic skin response while a patient is approaching a feared situation or experiencing a panic attack (see Baker, Patterson, & Barlow, 2002). Finally, at least 30 empirically supported self-report questionnaires are available that specifically assess panic-related thoughts, behaviours, and symptoms (Antony et al., 2001; Baker et al., 2002). One popular instrument is the Anxiety Sensitivity Index (Peterson & Reiss, 1993), which measures an individual's fear of anxiety-related symptoms. Drs. Steve Taylor (University of British Columbia) and Brian Cox (University of Winnipeg) developed expanded versions of this instrument (Taylor & Cox, 1998; Taylor et al., 2007).

ETIOLOGY Panic disorder is rooted in both biological and psychological factors. First, panic disorder tends to run in families. The biological relatives of individuals with panic disorder are about five times more likely to develop panic disorder than are individuals who do not have panic-prone relatives (Hettema et al., 2001). Attempts to find specific genetic markers, however, remain inconsistent (Arch & Craske, 2008). Second, there is evidence that biological challenges induce panic attacks in individuals with panic disorder more frequently than they do in non-psychiatric controls (Barlow, 2002; McNally, 1994). A biological challenge refers to the presentation of a stimulus (e.g., breathing in certain levels of CO_2, hyperventilating) intended to induce physiological changes associated with anxiety. However, as Barlow (2002) pointed out, there does not appear to be an underlying biological mechanism that can account for the fact that the same basic physiological and psychological responses are displayed across these many diverse types of challenge procedures. In addition, between 44 and 71 percent of individuals with panic disorder report **nocturnal panic** (Craske & Barlow, 2008)—attacks that occur while sleeping (most often during the lighter stages of sleep, between one and three hours of falling asleep)—and some people experience panic when they are attempting to relax. A sense of losing control elicited by a somatic response may underlie the panic-inducing properties of many biological challenge procedures. In the case of nocturnal or relaxation-induced panic attacks, the cognitive experience may be similar—a fear of letting go. These findings have led to the development of cognitive theories of panic.

Cognitive theories focus on the idea that individuals with panic disorder **catastrophically misinterpret** bodily sensations (Clark, 1986, 1996). Most of us experience variability in our bodily sensations throughout the day. For example, we may get up too quickly and feel dizzy or our heart may beat fast or we may feel shortness of breath. For those of us who do not have panic disorder, these sensations are often ignored or attributed to something benign. An individual with panic disorder, on the other hand, may quickly misinterpret these symptoms as a sign that something must be wrong (e.g., "I am going to have a heart attack"). This reaction may then cause even more apprehension such that the person worries about additional symptoms. Although the intention is to reduce these sensations, they paradoxically increase because of the response of the autonomic nervous system (the fight or flight response) to real or perceived threat. This process continues until the person feels out of control and experiences another panic attack (see Figure 5.1). People may then begin to avoid situations or bodily sensations that become associated with having panic attacks. A related theory contends that there is a trait-like tendency to be anxiety sensitive. **Anxiety sensitivity** has to do with the belief that the somatic symptoms related to anxiety will have negative consequences that extend beyond the panic episode itself (McNally, 1994).

Barlow and his colleagues (Barlow, 2002; Bouton, Mineka, & Barlow, 2001) have proposed an "**alarm theory**" of panic. As mentioned earlier, uncued panic attacks are not uncommon in the general population. When a real danger is present, a "true alarm" occurs and our bodies kick in an incredibly adaptive physiological response that allows us to face the feared object or flee from the situation. If you were just about to be hit by a bus, you would be grateful for this alarm system—it means that your blood is circulating to the main muscle groups to help you escape, your breathing is increasing in anticipation that you will be burning off the carbon dioxide, and so on. In some instances, however, this system can be activated by emotional cues (e.g., the perception of threat rather than objective threat). The same response occurs but in this instance it is a "false alarm." The panic attack, or the situation that triggered it, then becomes associated with neutral cues through classical conditioning and the person may begin to fear internal sensations or external stimuli. Individuals with panic disorder develop apprehension about experiencing further panic attacks and they associate weak bodily sensations with the experience of a full-blown panic attack. Because of this anxiety, they focus intensely on their bodily sensations (and on other environmental cues that may have been present during the attack) to prepare for and prevent future panic attacks. However, these individuals also perceive these experiences as uncontrollable and unpredictable. Bouton et al. (2001) argue that most people who experience panic attacks do not go on to develop panic disorder and that numerous biological, cognitive, and experiential factors come into play.

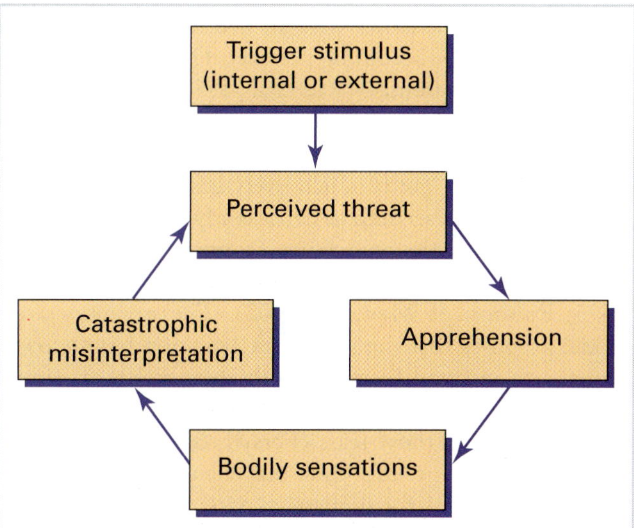

FIGURE 5.1 Cognitive Model of Panic

Source: Reprinted from *Behaviour Research and Therapy, 24.* D. M. Clark, A cognitive approach to panic, 461–470. © 1992. With permission from Elsevier Science, The Boulevard, Langford Lane, Kidlington, U.K. OX5 1GB.

3 BEFORE MOVING ON

List and describe four methods that are integral to a multimethod assessment of anxiety disorders.

SPECIFIC PHOBIA

DESCRIPTION Many of us have specific fears, such as a fear of spiders, snakes, or lightning. However, these fears tend not to be significant enough to interfere with our day-to-day activities. Many people may momentarily cringe and become scared upon seeing a spider, but most of us do not go about our day worrying about spiders. However, for some people like Donna in the case below, such fears cause marked distress and significantly disrupt their daily lives. When an individual's fears are this extreme, we refer to them as specific *phobias*. Fears are adaptive reactions to threats in the environment, but phobias are excessive and unreasonable fear reactions.

Kessler and his colleagues found that 8.7 percent of the population had a diagnosable specific phobia in a given year (Kessler, Chiu, et al., 2005), and that 12.5 percent of the population could expect to develop a specific phobia at some point in their lives (Kessler, Berglund, et al., 2005). The prevalence rates are higher among females, with a lifetime prevalence rate of 15.7 percent compared to 6.7 percent for men.

The frequency of normal fears varies dramatically, with some fears more common than others (Depla, ten Have, van Balkom, & de Graaf, 2008). The prevalence of fears also varies across gender. Women typically report a greater number of animal (e.g., snakes and spiders) and situational (e.g., closed spaces, lightning, flying) fears than do men. However, men and women report an equal number of fears related to injections and dental procedures. When asked to rate *how much* they fear various stimuli, women report experiencing a greater degree of fear than do men across all types of fear stimuli. In terms of specific phobias, fear of animals appears to be the most prevalent (Becker et al., 2007).

DIAGNOSIS AND ASSESSMENT For the diagnosis of specific phobia, there must be marked and persistent fear of an object or situation. Furthermore, exposure to the feared object or situation must invariably produce an anxiety reaction that is excessive and unreasonable. As with all of the anxiety disorders, a diagnosis is given when the symptoms interfere with everyday functioning (e.g., spending excessive amounts of time avoiding or worrying about encountering the feared object or situation) or cause considerable distress.

The DSM-IV-TR outlines five subtypes of specific phobia:

Animal Type: The phobic object is an animal or insect.

Natural Environment Type: The phobic object is part of the natural environment (e.g., thunderstorms, water, heights).

Blood Injection–Injury Type: The person fears seeing blood or an injury, or fears an injection or other type of invasive medical procedure.

Situational Type: The person fears specific situations, such as bridges, public transportation, and enclosed spaces.

Other Type: Used for all other phobias not covered in the other categories, such as extreme fears of choking, vomiting, and clowns. This category also includes what is known as **illness phobia**, which involves an intense fear of developing a disease that the person currently does not have. Illness phobia is different from hypochondriasis, where people believe that they *currently have* a disease or medical condition (see Chapter 6).

Having a phobia from one of these subtypes increases the probability of developing another phobia within the same category (APA, 2000; Hofmann, Lehman, & Barlow, 1997; LeBeau et al., 2010). For example, if someone has a phobia of spiders, he or she is also more likely to be afraid of snakes, and more likely to be afraid of other animals than of thunderstorms.

Individuals with a natural environment phobia fear such things as heights, storms, and water.

ETIOLOGY The classical conditioning theory of fear, based on the work of Watson and Rayner (1920), was described earlier in this chapter. One of the main criticisms of this model is that it assumes that all neutral stimuli have an equal potential for becoming phobias. This is known as the **equipotentiality premise** (Rachman, 1977). In other words, the chances of being afraid of a lamp and a snake are presumed to be equal. However, it is not the case that people have phobias for pretty much everything; rather, a select number of stimuli seem to be consistently related to phobias.

Contrary to the associative (conditioning) model of phobias is the **nonassociative model** (Menzies & Clarke, 1995; Poulton & Menzies, 2002). The nonassociative model proposes that the process of evolution has endowed humans to respond fearfully to a select group of stimuli (e.g., water, heights, spiders), and thus no learning is necessary to develop these fears (Forsyth & Chorpita, 1997). Essentially, the types of stimuli that elicit fear do so because it is too dangerous for humans *to have to learn* to fear the stimuli with personal experience. For example, a biological predisposition to fear heights is very useful when you consider that one bad experience with falling could be deadly (Menzies & Clarke, 1995).

Evidence for nonassociative theories also comes from the finding that babies seem to be born with certain kinds of "prewired" anxiety that is elicited at various developmental stages. For example, between the ages of four and nine months, infants develop stranger anxiety, whereby they appear to instinctively fear strangers. This type of anxiety has been found across numerous countries regardless of rearing practices (Skuse, Bruce, Dowdney, & Mrazek, 2011).

Based on the underpinnings of this theory, why don't all adult humans have phobias? If we are biologically prepared to fear snakes, then shouldn't we fear snakes for the rest of our lives once we've encountered one? Menzies and Clarke (1995) argue that most of us eventually habituate to the feared stimulus over time. For instance, even though most of us may have initially feared heights as an infant, our fear likely dissipated over time after repeated exposure to heights. However, some people may fail to habituate to certain stimuli. This failure to habituate may occur because they did not have appropriate opportunities for exposure during development, or because of individual differences in the rate of habituation (Poulton & Menzies, 2002).

Case Notes

Donna is a 42-year-old woman who lives in southwestern Ontario. She has an intense fear of thunderstorms. Although she was always warned about the dangers of thunderstorms during childhood, this fear did not fully develop until she was pregnant with her first daughter at the age of 21. She recalled falling asleep on the couch and being awakened abruptly by a loud crash of thunder; she was frightened for her daughter's safety and could only think of protecting her. Since that time, she has been extremely frightened of thunderstorms and worries that they will turn into tornados and result in utter catastrophe. For large parts of the day, Donna pays close attention to any alterations in the weather and she regularly monitors the weather channel, even when the forecast is good. Her fear has increased drastically over the years, causing considerable distress and interfering with her daily functioning. For example, she avoids booking any appointments during the summer months because she is afraid to leave her house due to the possibility of a storm. When a thunderstorm does occur, Donna experiences panic attacks.

Support for nonassociative theories includes the fact that researchers have identified a genetic contribution to fears (Distel et al., 2008). A study of 5465 twins and their siblings found that the heritability of select specific phobias was between 35 and 51 percent. However, there are also problems with nonassociative theories. For example, not all fears entail major threats to the species. For instance, of the 35 000 varieties of spiders in the world, only 0.1 percent of them are dangerous, yet spider phobias constitute a large proportion of phobias (Diaz, 2004). In contrast, mushrooms are rarely the focus of specific phobias but can be fatally poisonous; indeed, vastly more people die of mushroom poisoning in North America than die from spider bites (Langley, 2005; Trestrail, 1991).

Another theory of etiology combines elements of both the associative and the nonassociative models. In 1971, when learning was the primary etiological model of phobias, Seligman (1971) argued that there has to be more to their etiology than classical conditioning. He suggested that people are more likely to fear certain types of stimuli because of **biological preparedness**. Similar to the nonassociative model, it is believed that the process of natural selection has equipped humans with the predisposition to fear objects and situations that represented threats to our species over the course of our evolutionary heritage. However, unlike the nonassociative model, associative learning is still necessary to develop a phobia. This helps to obviate problems with the equipotentiality premise discussed earlier, as associative learning experiences will produce phobias for those stimuli that represent threats in an evolutionary sense. Hence, this explains why learning to fear snakes is easier than learning to fear lamps.

Recent research has focused on the role not only of fear but also of disgust sensitivity in the formation and maintenance of phobias. **Disgust sensitivity** refers to the degree to which people are susceptible to being disgusted by a variety of stimuli such as certain bugs, types of food, and small animals (Woody & Tolin, 2002). The main hypothesis is that people develop some phobias because the phobic object is disgusting and possibly contaminated. For example, in a classic study on phobias, Mulkens, de Jong, and Merckelbach (1996) asked two groups of women (a group with a spider phobia and a control group) to do something pretty simple—choose a cookie they would like to eat and then eat it. However, there was one catch; before they ate the cookie, they had to watch an actual spider walk across it. Few of the women with a spider phobia (25 percent) were willing to eat at least some of the tasty cookie, unlike a majority of women not afraid of spiders (70 percent). Women tend to have a higher degree of disgust sensitivity than do men, and recent evidence suggests that this gender difference might partly explain the higher prevalence of specific phobias for women (Connolly, Olatunji, & Lohr, 2008). Overall, there appears to be growing support for the role of disgust sensitivity in phobias, including findings that individuals with spider and blood injection–injury phobias have higher levels of disgust sensitivity and fears of contamination than individuals without these phobias (de Jong & Merckelbach, 1998; Sawchuk, Lohr, Tolin, Lee, & Kleinknecht, 2000). These studies support the notion that the cause of phobias may not always involve only fear of danger, but other emotions, such as disgust and possibly fear of contamination.

FOCUS 5.1

Cultural Differences in Anxiety

Cross-national epidemiological research confirms that anxiety disorders occur worldwide, but the experience and prevalence of anxiety may vary across different cultures (APA, 2000). The prevalence of social anxiety disorder, for example, is lower in Asian countries (0.5 percent) than in countries such as France and Switzerland, where the rate is closer to 4 percent (Lépine, 2001). A recent study revealed that the prevalence rate of anxiety disorders is lower in Japan than in Western cultures (Tsuchiya et al., 2009).

Even the interpretation of anxiety symptoms may vary widely. Culture provides the rules and the context for how we interact and express complex emotions such as anxiety (Norasakkunkit & Kalick, 2009). The culturally bound syndrome of *taijin kyofusho* in Japan, for example, shares many symptoms of social anxiety disorder. However, this syndrome is related to concerns about embarrassing or offending others rather than just being personally embarrassed or humiliated. This focus on others is consistent with the Japanese emphasis on showing deference and attentiveness to where one fits in the social hierarchy (Norasakkunkit & Kalick, 2009).

The DSM-IV-TR includes an appendix that outlines various "culture-bound syndromes" related to anxiety disorders. The following are some examples:

Ataque de nervios—this expression refers to a sense of being out of control and is recognized among many Latinos from the Caribbean. The symptoms include uncontrollable shouting, bouts of crying, trembling, heat in the chest, and verbal or physical aggression.

Dhat—this term is used in India to refer to extreme anxiety and fears related to the discharge of semen, discoloration of the urine, and exhaustion.

Koro—this syndrome involves intense anxiety that the penis (or, in females, the vulva and nipples) will retract into the body. It is reported in South and East Asia.

Shen-k'uei (Taiwan) or *shenkui* (China) refers to panic symptoms that are attributed to excessive semen loss. This is feared because of the belief that semen loss can be life threatening.

Taijin kyofusho—this is a culturally distinctive phobia that resembles DSM-IV-TR social phobia. This syndrome is included in the Japanese diagnostic system and refers to an intense fear that one's body (appearance, odour, facial expressions) will displease, embarrass, or offend others.

Kirmayer (2001), a scientist at the Culture and Mental Health Research Unit in Montreal, reports that in many areas of the world people do not view symptoms of anxiety as problematic and may even reject psychological explanations and treatments. He argues that a clinician's objective should be to understand, from the patient's point of view, how his or her symptoms are experienced and to derive a treatment strategy that will be acceptable to that patient. ●

SOCIAL PHOBIA/SOCIAL ANXIETY DISORDER

Case Notes

Tony found it extremely difficult to open up or relate to others and claimed that he was constantly anxious, particularly in social situations. He stated that his problems with anxiety dated back to when he was a young child. Tony claimed that he felt extremely uncomfortable in most social situations, especially when he was around unfamiliar people. His anxiety was not restricted to speaking in front of others but also extended to eating and writing in the presence of others and using public washrooms. Tony feared that others were looking at him and that he might do something that would be embarrassing or humiliating. Because of this nervousness, he avoided most interpersonal interactions. As a child, Tony avoided school and felt extremely anxious when he did attend class. His anxiety and avoidance increased over the years, to the point where he was only able to go to five locations (the homes of close friends and relatives). As a result of his anxiety, Tony "self-medicated" with alcohol. He reported that he drank an average of 36 beers per week. "It's not the drinking that's the problem," he said, "but dealing with people when I'm not drunk."

Steve: Social Phobia

Watch this Speaking Out video at www.mysearchlab.com

DESCRIPTION People like Tony suffer from *social phobia*, a marked and persistent fear of social or performance-related situations. Often their anxiety focuses on the fear of acting in a way that will be humiliating or embarrassing. People with social phobia have an underlying fear of being evaluated negatively and frequently worry about what others might be thinking about them. This may include fears that they will expose their inner-felt anxiety to others by not making eye contact, by blushing, or by being awkward in their speech or posture during social interactions. One of the most prototypical fears is being the "centre of attention." Table 5.2 lists the DSM-IV-TR diagnostic criteria for social phobia.

Individuals with *non-generalized social phobia* fear specific social situations or activities. Diagnostically, these situations may include casual speaking, eating or writing in public, or giving formal public speeches. *Generalized social phobia*, in contrast, involves the fear of most social settings and interactions. As one would predict, the latter condition tends to be more disabling. Although probably everyone has experienced social or performance anxiety at one time or another, social phobia is not merely synonymous

Individuals with social anxiety disorder find most social gatherings terrifying.

with shyness or the "social butterflies." Exposing socially phobic individuals to their feared situation almost invariably provokes intense anxiety, which may take the form of situationally predisposed panic attacks. This description still characterizes social phobia as described by the DSM-5 criteria. Although a number of modifications to the wording have been proposed, the general criteria will likely remain similar (APA, 2010).

Individuals with social phobia are generally well aware of the fact that their fears are excessive and unreasonable. Thus, one of the keys to understanding their condition is that their fears persist despite this knowledge (Hirsch & Clark, 2004). Outside the anxious situation they may be fully cognizant of the extreme nature of their fears, although somehow this adaptive and logical perspective holds less force relative to the overwhelming anxiety they experience during actual social encounters. Consequently, these individuals frequently avoid social situations; those situations they cannot avoid are otherwise endured with intense anxiety and distress. In these latter situations, they may manage their anxiety by taking refuge in the periphery of the situation, where their anxiety may be less prominent. For example, at a large social gathering, they might converse only with long-familiar friends, as opposed to acquainting themselves with other people. Alternatively, in a large group discussion, they may listen quietly but contribute nothing to the dialogue themselves. Even more subtle methods of avoidance may be present as well. For example, when needing to entertain company at their home, individuals with social phobia may busy themselves with preparations (e.g., cooking, cleaning) so as to covertly avoid having to engage in conversation with guests.

Over time, these patterns of *overt* and *covert avoidance* may result in socially phobic individuals becoming considerably lonely and isolated (Alden & Taylor, 2004). Added to this are frequent self-critical thoughts about their social performance and hopelessness that they will ever overcome their social inhibition. Accordingly, individuals with social phobia often have low self-esteem, and are at increased risk for mood problems such as depression (Ohayon & Schatzberg, 2010).

Based on the Canadian Community Health Survey (Health Canada, 2002), the one-year prevalence of social

TABLE 5.2 DSM-IV-TR DIAGNOSTIC CRITERIA FOR SOCIAL PHOBIA

A. A marked and persistent fear of one or more social or performance situations in which the person is exposed to unfamiliar people or to possible scrutiny by others. The individual fears that he or she will act in a way (or show anxiety symptoms) that will be humiliating or embarrassing. **Note:** In children, there must be evidence of the capacity for age-appropriate social relationships with familiar people and the anxiety must occur in peer settings, not just in interactions with adults.

B. Exposure to the feared social situation almost invariably provokes anxiety, which may take the form of a situationally bound or situationally predisposed panic attack. **Note:** In children, the anxiety may be expressed by crying, tantrums, freezing, or shrinking from social situations with unfamiliar people.

C. The person recognizes that the fear is excessive or unreasonable. **Note:** In children, this feature may be absent.

D. The feared social or performance situations are avoided or else endured with intense anxiety or distress.

E. The avoidance, anxious anticipation, or distress in the feared social or performance situation(s) interferes significantly with the person's normal routine, occupational (academic) functioning, or social activities or relationships, or there is marked distress about having the phobia.

F. In individuals under age 18 years, the duration is at least 6 months.

G. The fear or avoidance is not due to the direct physiological effects of a substance (e.g., a drug of abuse, a medication) or a general medical condition and is not better accounted for by another mental disorder (e.g., Panic Disorder With or Without Agoraphobia, Separation Anxiety Disorder, Body Dysmorphic Disorder, a Pervasive Developmental Disorder, or Schizoid Personality Disorder).

H. If a general medical condition or another mental disorder is present, the fear in Criterion A is unrelated to it, e.g., the fear is not of Stuttering, trembling in Parkinson's disease, or exhibiting abnormal eating behavior in Anorexia Nervosa or Bulimia Nervosa.

Source: Reprinted with permission from the *Diagnostic and Statistical Manual of Mental Disorders, Fourth Edition, Text Revision.* (Copyright © 2000). American Psychiatric Association.

phobia in Canada is approximately 3 percent, with rates almost identical in females (3.4 percent) and males (2.6 percent). Higher rates (7 percent, across both sexes) have been observed in epidemiological studies in the United States (Kessler, Chiu, et al., 2005). As such, social phobia is one of the most prevalent psychiatric disorders, with a prevalence rate comparable to unipolar depression. The majority of individuals with social phobia have one or more additional psychiatric diagnoses. In the National Comorbidity Survey, 63 percent of individuals were diagnosed with comorbid conditions, with the most common co-occurring disorders involving anxiety, mood, and substance disorders (Ruscio et al., 2008). For most individuals with comorbid social phobia, the onset of their social phobia predates the onset of the comorbid disorder (Kessler, Berglund, et al., 2005).

DIAGNOSIS AND ASSESSMENT Assessment of social phobia usually takes the form of a structured or semi-structured interview combined with completion of various self-report measures. Interviews provide clinicians with an opportunity to assess social phobia and other psychiatric problems, which is important for individual treatment planning. Self-report measures are also used to quantify an individual's thoughts, feelings, and behaviours associated with social anxiety and to allow an individual's personal score to be compared to normative values. Considering these scores can assist clinicians in conceptualizing a particular individual's unique problems with social anxiety (see Antony et al., 2001).

Certain diagnostic considerations are particularly relevant to social phobia. One of these is distinguishing between social phobia and agoraphobia. Although individuals with both social phobia and agoraphobia may experience anxiety in public places, the reason for this fear is fundamentally different in the two disorders. The anxiety that characterizes social phobia involves a fear of being negatively evaluated or embarrassed in social situations.

ETIOLOGY The etiology of social phobia includes genetic-biological, environmental, and cognitive factors (Rapee & Spence, 2004). Genetic factors appear to account for approximately one-half or more of the variance in risk for social phobia (Beatty, Heisel, Hall, Levine, & La France, 2002). What seems largely to be inherited, however, is a predisposition to develop social anxiety rather than the disorder itself, and whether or not this genetic vulnerability is determined by environmental factors. Behavioural inhibition (a temperamental characteristic of some children to respond to new situations with heightened arousal) is an early marker of risk for social phobia. Toddlers who are behaviourally inhibited are approximately twice as likely to develop social phobia by the end of adolescence when compared with non-inhibited toddlers (Schwartz, Sidman, & Kagan, 1999).

Research is beginning to identify the neurocircuitry involved in social phobia, although most studies have investigated social anxiety in general rather than ensuring that participants met diagnostic criteria for social phobia specifically. Studies reveal similarities in the neuroanatomy and physiology involved in socially submissive behaviour and the fear of novelty in animals, on the one hand, and socially phobic behaviour in humans on the other (Freitas-Ferrari, Hallak, & Trzesniak, 2010). Reduced synaptic reuptake and receptor binding of dopamine-2, and dysregulation of the interplay between serotonin, norepinephrine, and corticotropin releasing factors during stress responses are associated with socially phobic behaviour. Whether or not a primary dysfunction in gamma-aminobutyric acid (GABA) is also involved in social anxiety is not yet clear. Knowledge of the neuroanatomy involved in social phobia behaviour patterns necessitates an understanding of the interactions among structures involved in fear recognition and conditioning (e.g., amygdala), arousal, and stress (e.g., hypothalamic-pituitary-adrenal axis), and the regulation and areas of the brain that monitor negative affect (e.g., anterior cingulate cortex, prefrontal and orbitofrontal cortex).

Early psychosocial experiences play a large role in shaping an individual's risk for social phobia. A Hamilton, Ontario, study revealed that 92 percent of an adult sample of individuals with social phobia reported that they were bullied or severely teased during childhood; this was at least twice as frequent in social phobia as it was in obsessive-compulsive disorder or panic disorder (McCabe, Antony, Summerfeldt, Liss, & Swinson, 2003). In addition, individuals with social phobia report being exposed to a greater level of parental criticism, overprotection, and control as a child (Alden & Taylor, 2004; Boelen & Reijntjes, 2009). As a result of these negative peer and family influences, individuals may develop a lack of confidence and a negative self-focus that creates and reinforces the anxiety they experience in social situations (Alden & Taylor, 2004; Rapee & Spence, 2004).

Cognitive factors associated with social phobia involve both negative beliefs and judgments about self and others, as well as abnormal processing of social information (Hirsch & Clark, 2004). For example, people with social phobia exhibit greater concern about making mistakes in general, and are more doubtful about the accuracy of their decision making and behaviour than non-psychiatric controls (Antony, Purdon, Huta, & Swinson, 1998). In addition, individuals with social phobia tend to judge themselves as inferior to others and to engage in negative self-referential thinking (Antony, Rowa, Liss, Swallow, & Swinson, 2005). As a result of their perfectionistic and self-critical tendencies, individuals with social phobia may develop a negative view of self that is similar to individuals with depression (Dozois & Frewen, 2006).

Individuals with social phobia also display elements of abnormal social information processing (Bögels & Mansell, 2004). For example, individuals with social phobia tend to avoid looking directly at other people's faces, although they exhibit vigilance for signs of social threat (e.g., angry expressions of others) in their environment (Bar-Haim, Lamy, Pergamin, Bakermans-Kranenburg, & van IJzendoorn, 2007). Consistent with these attentional biases, individuals with social phobia show increased brain activity in the amygdala when viewing others' facial expressions, suggesting increased threat monitoring (Birbaumer et al., 1998; Stein, Goldin, Sareen, Zorrilla, & Brown, 2002).

Additionally, these individuals are high in *public self-consciousness*, which refers to the awareness of oneself as an object of attention, or the tendency to see one's actions from the perspective of an outside observer rather than through one's own eyes (Bögels & Mansell, 2004).

University of British Columbia researchers Lynn Alden and Charles Taylor (2004) make the important point that social phobia entails more than simply the presence of anxiety symptoms. Instead, they characterize social phobia as an *interpersonal disorder*—a condition that is commonly associated with marked disruption in the ability to relate with other people. These theorists call attention to the importance of "self-perpetuating interpersonal cycles" in the onset and maintenance of social phobia, whereby excessive social anxiety leads to avoidance and eventual peer rejection, with further social anxiety and possible depression as a consequence. Although it remains unclear whether or not people with social phobia actually exhibit social skill deficits, the most likely explanation is that their excessive anxiety during interpersonal interactions interferes with their ability to effectively communicate with others. Research also shows that individuals with social phobia not only report experiencing elevated anxiety but also report difficulties in experiencing positive emotions similar to what is found in depression (Kashdan, 2007).

OBSESSIVE-COMPULSIVE DISORDER

Case Notes

Scott experienced a number of bizarre and disturbing thoughts that he would be contaminated by germs. He responded to these fears by engaging in a number of cleaning rituals. For instance, he washed his hands two to three times before eating. He reported that the extent to which he washed varied depending on the situation. When he was at a friend's house, he washed an average of two to three times; at a public washroom, this increased to six or more times. Scott worked in the shipping and receiving department at The Bay in downtown Montreal. At work, he wore gloves during the day and kept his own bars of soap in his desk drawer. He washed

APPLIED CLINICAL CASE

Hoarders

Hoarders is a popular reality TV show that depicts the life and trials of individuals who exhibit hoarding behaviour. During an average episode, two individuals are featured along with their loved ones and members of the cast who help them dispose of their excessive possessions. Often the hoarding behaviour is so severe that it causes a serious safety or health risk. One featured individual, Augustine, allowed 8000 pounds (3628 kg) of garbage to accumulate in her house. However, garbage is not the worst thing to accumulate in these houses—rodents, animals, and fecal matter have all been found. The show illustrates not only the unsanitary aspect of this behaviour but also the detrimental effect it can have on the afflicted individuals and their friends and family.

The problems associated with hoarding have been featured in the Canadian news a lot over the past few years. In September 2010 the 24th floor of a Toronto high-rise apartment caught on fire, displacing 1100 people for more than a week. The speed at which the fire spread was directly associated with the excessive amount of combustible material that was jam-packed on the balcony and in the suite of a person who hoarded. In October 2011 a Vancouver home was completely engulfed by flames, taking the life of a male victim. The place was loaded with so much stuff that firefighters were unable to enter the house—in this case, the disorder was not only life-limiting but also life-ending (see video clip at www.ctv.ca/CTVNews/Canada/20111010/bc_hoarder_fire_111010). As these examples illustrate, hoarding behaviour does not just provide interesting material for so-called reality shows—the problems associated with hoarding are very real and very debilitating.

The problems associated with hoarding are very debilitating.

Currently in DSM-IV-TR, hoarding is a subtype of obsessive-compulsive disorder (OCD). However, according to the proposed changes in DSM-5 (APA, 2010), hoarding will constitute its own diagnostic category, placed within a new chapter called "Obsessive-Compulsive and Related Disorders." Some of the core clinical features of hoarding involve persistent difficulty discarding or parting with a possession (regardless of the value that others may attribute to these possessions), strong urges to save these items, or distress associated with discarding them. Another criterion is that the individual accumulates a large number of items that clutter active living areas. There has been some debate about whether hoarding is a subtype of OCD or its own distinct disorder. Recent evidence has suggested that there may be a specific genetic locus associated with hoarding behaviour (Samuels et al., 2007). In addition, although the other OCD subtypes are intercorrelated, hoarding seems to be somewhat distinct from these constructs (Wu & Watson, 2005). However, this debate has yet to be resolved, and we may see continued revisions of these diagnoses.

his hands at every occasion possible. At home, Scott scrubbed his walls with bleach, going through eight litres per week. He thoroughly washed the walls in his house three times a week and spot cleaned twice a day. He also vacuumed his home a few times a day. His dishes and the countertop were washed numerous times every day. These washing and cleaning rituals would consume several hours of each day. Scott was also unsure as to whether he had locked the doors or turned off the stove; consequently, he checked these multiple times before leaving his house. These symptoms interfered greatly with his work performance and he received a number of verbal and written warnings from his employer that he was wasting too much time at work.

DESCRIPTION The primary features of obsessive-compulsive disorder (OCD) are recurrent obsessions and compulsions that cause marked distress for the individual. Kessler, Chiu, and colleagues (2005) have estimated that the one-year prevalence rate for OCD in the general population is about 1 percent, with a lifetime prevalence rate of 1.6 percent (Kessler, Berglund, et al., 2005). The typical age of onset occurs during adolescence and early adulthood, although childhood OCD is not uncommon (APA, 2000).

OCD: Dave

Watch this Speaking Out video at www.mysearchlab.com

Obsessions are defined as recurrent and uncontrollable thoughts, impulses, or ideas that the individual finds disturbing and anxiety-provoking. Common obsessions include thoughts related to uncertainty (e.g., doubting if one has locked the door or turned off the stove), sexuality (e.g., homosexual imagery), violence (e.g., harming a child), and contamination (e.g., believing one is dirty and covered with germs). Individuals with OCD often consider their obsessions to be so disturbing that they try to conceal them from others (Newth & Rachman, 2001), fearing that others will react negatively to their thoughts. Because their obsessions are a source of personal shame and embarrassment, patients with OCD may be reluctant to reveal the exact nature of these obsessions even to their therapists. Yet a recent Canadian study revealed that intrusive thoughts are common. Clark and Purdon (2009) found that 80 percent of students reported intrusive worry thoughts. Hence, some therapists attempt to reduce distress about these cognitive symptoms by sharing this information with their patients and "normalizing" the occurrence of obsessional thinking.

As demonstrated in the case of Scott, individuals with OCD often attempt to cope with their feelings of discomfort by engaging in compulsions. **Compulsions** are repetitive behaviours or cognitive acts that are intended to reduce anxiety. Examples of repetitive behaviours include handwashing, checking, and rigidly maintaining order and organization (e.g., placing ornaments around the house in a particular order). Cognitive acts include things like counting numbers, praying, and repeating words or phrases over and over. Thus, compulsions involve observable behaviour or mental acts that are used to reduce anxiety. Approximately 80 percent of patients exhibit both behavioural and mental compulsions (Foa & Kozak, 1995).

A related way that patients deal with anxiety is through neutralizations. **Neutralizations** are behavioural or mental acts that are used by individuals to try to prevent, cancel, or "undo" the feared consequences and distress caused by an obsession (Rachman, 1997; Salkovskis, 1985). Rachman, Shafran, Mitchell, Trant, and Teachman (1996) tested undergraduates' use of neutralization in an experiment. The researchers induced a discomforting and intrusive thought by having participants complete the following sentence: "I hope ______ is in a car accident" by inserting a friend's name in the blank space, and imagining that the situation had actually happened. Following this manipulation, the research participants were told that they could do whatever they wanted to do to cancel the effects of writing the sentence. All the students engaged in some neutralizing activity. For example, some students inserted the word *not* in the sentence, others crossed out the sentence, and some students scrunched up the paper and threw it away. One participant even asked to take the paper home to burn it! Two important things are noteworthy with regard to this experiment. First, the participants tended to feel better after engaging in a neutralizing act. Second, the participants were undergraduate students and not OCD patients. This shows that neutralizing is a normal and common activity.

One of the more striking aspects of individuals with OCD is their excessive beliefs about personal responsibility and feelings of guilt (Lawrence & Williams, 2011; Rachman, 1993). Individuals with OCD are often quite concerned with making sure their behaviour will not lead to negative consequences, particularly to others. In addition to an excessive sense of responsibility for their behaviours, there can be an inflated sense of responsibility for their thoughts. Having an unwanted thought such as hitting a child can make people feel immoral—and the more responsible they feel for the content of their thoughts, the worse they feel (Rachman, 1993). In fact, one of the more interesting findings with OCD patients is their tendency to fuse thoughts and behaviours together (Shafran & Rachman, 2004).

Thought-action fusion (TAF) refers to two types of irrational thinking: (1) the belief that having a particular thought increases the probability that the thought will come true; and (2) the belief that having a particular thought is the moral equivalent of a particular action. The first type of thinking is referred to as Likelihood TAF, and includes thoughts about the self, also known as Likelihood-Self (e.g., "If I think about getting hit by a car, I'm more likely to get hit by a car"), and thoughts about others, also known as Likelihood-Others (e.g., "If I think about my mother drowning, she's more likely to drown"). The second type of irrational thinking is referred to as Moral TAF. One example of Moral TAF is the belief that having a thought about harming someone is the moral equivalent of actually doing it. Research shows that this

TABLE 5.3 DSM-IV-TR DIAGNOSTIC CRITERIA FOR OBSESSIVE-COMPULSIVE DISORDER

A. The presence of *either* obsessions *or* compulsions:

Obsessions as defined by (1), (2), (3), *and* (4):

(1) recurrent and persistent thoughts, impulses, or images that are experienced, at some time during the disturbance, as intrusive and inappropriate and that cause marked anxiety or distress

(2) the thoughts, impulses, or images are not simply excessive worries about real-life problems

(3) the person attempts to ignore or suppress such thoughts, impulses, or images, or to neutralize them with some other thought or action

(4) the person recognizes that the obsessional thoughts, impulses, or images are a product of his or her own mind (not imposed from without as in thought insertion)

Compulsions as defined by (1) *and* (2):

(1) repetitive behaviors (e.g., hand washing, ordering, checking) or mental acts (e.g., praying, counting, repeating words silently) that the person feels driven to perform in response to an obsession, or according to rules that must be applied rigidly

(2) the behaviors or mental acts are aimed at preventing or reducing distress or preventing some dreaded event or situation; however, these behaviors or mental acts either are not connected in a realistic way with what they are designed to neutralize or prevent, or are clearly excessive

B. At some point during the course of the disorder, the person has recognized that the obsessions or compulsions are excessive or unreasonable. **Note:** This does not apply to children.

C. The obsessions or compulsions cause marked distress, are time consuming (take more than 1 hour a day), or significantly interfere with the person's normal routine, occupational (or academic) functioning, or usual social activities or relationships.

D. If another Axis I disorder is present, the content of the obsessions or compulsions is not restricted to it (e.g., preoccupation with food in the presence of an Eating Disorder; hair pulling in the presence of Trichotillomania; concern with appearance in the presence of Body Dysmorphic Disorder; preoccupation with drugs in the presence of a Substance Use Disorder; preoccupation with having a serious illness in the presence of Hypochondriasis; preoccupation with sexual urges or fantasies in the presence of a Paraphilia; or guilty ruminations in the presence of Major Depressive Disorder).

E. The disturbance is not due to the direct physiological effects of a substance (e.g., a drug of abuse, a medication) or a general medical condition.

Source: Reprinted with permission from the *Diagnostic and Statistical Manual of Mental Disorders, Fourth Edition, Text Revision.* (Copyright © 2000). American Psychiatric Association.

latter type of irrational thinking is highly related to religiosity (Rassin & Koster, 2003).

All three forms of TAF are related to OCD symptoms (Einstein & Menzies, 2004), but only the Likelihood-Other form is considered to be a *pathological OCD belief.* Moral TAF and Likelihood-Self TAF are often just as prevalent among students as among patients with OCD (Rassin, Merckelbach, Muris, & Schmidt, 2001; Shafran & Rachman, 2004). Similar to neutralizations, we all tend to engage in some form of TAF from time to time. Have you ever felt so superstitious about something that you didn't want to think about it just in case you might jinx the outcome?

DIAGNOSIS AND ASSESSMENT The diagnostic criteria for OCD are presented in Table 5.3. The first criterion for a diagnosis of OCD is the presence of either obsessions or compulsions. Although they may occur in isolation, obsessions co-occur with compulsions most of the time (96 percent; Foa & Kozak, 1995). When assessing for the presence of obsessions, it is important to distinguish obsessions from excessive worries about everyday problems. This may be difficult given that obsessions and pathological worry have a number of similarities (e.g., intrusiveness and uncontrollability of thoughts). However, there are characteristics that distinguish obsessions from worries, including the fact that obsessions tend to be more bizarre and involve more imagery than do worries (Comer, Kendall, Franklin, Hudson, & Pimental, 2004). An additional diagnostic criterion is that individuals recognize that their obsessions or compulsions are excessive and irrational; however, this will likely be excluded from DSM-5 (APA, 2010). As with most disorders, the diagnostic criteria also require that the symptoms cause marked distress or significantly interfere with the person's life.

It is also often useful to distinguish between certain OCD subtypes. Given the fact that OCD is a relatively heterogeneous disorder, subtyping may provide a greater understanding of the condition and lead to more effective treatments. McKay and colleagues (2004) identified several subtypes found consistently across studies (see Table 5.4).

ETIOLOGY There is no fully accepted model of what causes OCD, and over 20 different theories exist (Jenike, 1998; Taylor, Afifi, Stein, Asmundson, & Jang, 2010). We review two of the more prominent models of OCD: the neurobiological model and the cognitive-behavioural model.

There has been limited conclusive research on the role of genetics and OCD, although over 30 potential genes have been investigated (Stewart & Pauls, 2010). However, based on the available evidence, there does appear to be a mild genetic risk factor for the disorder. For example, Taylor and colleagues (2010) found that heritability accounted for 32 to 40 percent of the variance in dysfunctional beliefs that give rise to OCD. Heritability of OCD symptoms has been found to be between 13 and 54 percent in teenagers (van Grootheest et al., 2008).

TABLE 5.4 SUBTYPES OF OBSESSIVE-COMPULSIVE DISORDER

Subtype	Description
Contamination and Washing/Cleaning	According to Feinstein, Fallon, Petkova, and Liebowitz (2003), there appear to be two types of patients in this subgroup: (1) Individuals who experience discomfort and distress because they "feel" contaminated or dirty. They wash excessively in order to rid themselves of this dirty feeling. (2) Individuals who are primarily concerned that being contaminated will lead to harm. They wash excessively in order to avoid harming themselves, and especially to avoid spreading contamination to others.
Checking	Individuals in this subtype have a strong tendency to repeatedly use checking behaviour. Quite often, the checking behaviour is preceded by aggressive obsessions (e.g., thoughts of hitting someone with their car or the house burning down). Checking rituals are then used to relieve anxiety caused by the harming obsessions (e.g., repeatedly checking to make sure the stove is off).
Hoarding*	These individuals tend to have a very difficult time discarding possessions. They overestimate the importance of objects, and have the irrational belief that they will need the object for some purpose in the future.
Ordering/Symmetry	These individuals have a pathological need for exactness and for organizing objects in a particular manner. For example, they might organize household ornaments in a particular way, because it "feels" right.

Source: McKay, D., Abramowitz, J. S., Calamari, J. E., Kyrios, M., Radomsky, A., Sookman, D., Taylor, S., & Wilhelm, S. (2004). A critical evaluation of obsessive-compulsive disorder subtypes: Symptoms versus mechanisms. *Clinical Psychology Review, 24,* 283–313.

* Hoarding will likely be a new diagnostic category in DSM-5.

Most neuropsychology models of OCD implicate the basal ganglia and frontal cortex (Baxter et al., 1987; Rauch, Whalen, Dougherty, & Jenike, 1998; Rosenberg & Keshavan, 1998). One of the primary functions of the basal ganglia is to control motor behaviours, whereas the frontal cortex is responsible for a wide range of higher cognitive functions such as abstract reasoning, inhibition, planning, and decision making. These two areas of the brain are connected and form a looped system through which information travels back and forth. Structural and/or functional abnormalities in this brain system may be responsible for compulsions and obsessions. For example, Pujol and his colleagues (2004) found that patients with OCD have less brain volume in parts of the frontal cortex and more brain volume in parts of the basal ganglia than do individuals without OCD.

Savage (1998) postulated that dysfunction in the frontal cortex of OCD patients may prevent them from processing and organizing relevant information when thinking. As a consequence, they may become too focused on irrelevant details, poor at self-monitoring behaviour, and unable to initiate appropriate behaviour change. Furthermore, the inability to effectively organize information can lead to memory deficits (Greisberg & McKay, 2003; Savage et al., 1999). However, the hypothesis that memory problems (e.g., compulsive checkers actually cannot remember if they locked the door) are a causal factor in OCD has been examined by Dr. Adam Radomsky of Concordia University. He and his colleagues have found that people with OCD are more likely to be affected by poor memory confidence, as opposed to poor memory accuracy (Coles, Radomsky, & Horng, 2006; Radomsky & Alcolado, 2010; Radomsky, Gilchrist, & Dussault, 2006). In other words, people with OCD are more likely to recheck the door because they do not have much confidence in their memory of having locked it the first time.

Neurochemical theories of OCD have also been proposed. The leading neurochemical theory is the serotonin hypothesis, which is based on the notion that abnormalities in the serotonin system are responsible for OCD symptoms (Abramowitz, 2008). For example, the success of selective serotonin reuptake inhibitors (SSRIs) in alleviating OCD symptoms has led many researchers to implicate abnormalities in serotonin neurotransmission in the pathophysiology of OCD (Denys, van Nieuwerburgh, Deforce, & Westenberg, 2007). However, this kind of logic has been criticized by researchers as flawed; in fact, evidence that serotonin is causally related to OCD has been inconclusive (Abramowitz, 2008; Rauch et al., 1998).

The cognitive-behavioural conceptualization of OCD posits that problematic obsessions are caused by the person's *reaction* to intrusive thoughts (Salkovskis, 1985). Many people have intrusive thoughts but most do not go on to develop abnormal obsessions. Rachman (1998) argued that abnormal obsessions arise from "catastrophic" misinterpretations of these intrusive thoughts. Individuals with OCD have high levels of personal responsibility and believe that their thoughts can influence the probability that others will be harmed. When they have thoughts of harming another, for example, people with OCD tend to conclude: "This must mean I'm actually a dangerous person" or "There's a greater chance I might actually harm someone."

Obsessions are believed to persist because of the person's maladaptive attempts to cope with them. Because misinterpretations often involve serious consequences (e.g.,

"I could contaminate or hurt another person"), the person feels compelled to take action. These actions include suppression of thoughts, avoidance behaviours, and neutralizations. Unfortunately, each of these responses can unintentionally serve to perpetuate obsessional thinking. For example, trying to suppress obsessional thoughts can have the paradoxical effect of increasing their frequency—known as the *rebound effect* (Wenzlaff & Wegner, 2000). Also, if people use avoidance behaviour (e.g., avoiding children for fear of harming them) or neutralizations to combat their obsessions, they may never learn that their assumptions and beliefs are incorrect. In fact, engaging in compulsive behaviours may serve to strengthen irrational beliefs. Consider individuals who have obsessive fears about germ contamination. Each time they wash their hands they momentarily feel less anxious, their obsessive concerns about germs temporarily settle, and they fail to develop any serious physical illness. These consequences are rewarding and serve to maintain the use of compulsions in the long term. Compulsions are believed to persist because they tend to (1) lower the severity of anxiety, (2) lower the frequency of obsessions, and (3) "prevent" obsessions from coming true. However, this short-term relief comes at the expense of failing to learn that the feared illness likely would not occur anyway and that their anxiety would have eventually decreased on its own.

POST-TRAUMATIC STRESS DISORDER

Case Notes

Raúl was born in Cuba. His parents separated when he was a young child and he lived with his grandparents for a number of years. At the age of 12, he enrolled in military school. He later became a paratrooper in the Cuban army and was posted in various locations around the world. While engaged in military combat, he saw several of his friends shot to death or killed from shrapnel. He was later "grounded" because of high blood pressure and assigned to work on naval ships. After hearing rumours that the authorities were after him due to suspected anti-government activities, he fled from Cuba on a ship that was headed to Germany. He jumped ship while the vessel was docked in Nova Scotia, and showed up at one of the city's hospitals a few months later, complaining of flashbacks, recurrent nightmares, and feeling easily startled and always on edge.

DESCRIPTION Raúl suffers from post-traumatic stress disorder (PTSD), a psychological condition that may ensue following exposure to a traumatic life event. Such events may include serious accidents, natural disasters, physical or sexual assault, or, as in Raúl's case, military combat. Diagnostically, the event must have involved actual or threatened death or serious injury, or a threat to the physical integrity of self or others, and have been experienced with intense fear, helplessness, or horror. The diagnosis of PTSD is defined by a profile of psychological symptoms that are experienced following the traumatic incident (see Table 5.5). Substantial revisions have been proposed for DSM-5 (see Friedman, 2009), but these remain consistent with the previous diagnostic criteria. A number of additional symptoms and behaviours are being proposed to better incorporate the variety of emotional, cognitive, and behavioural reactions that individuals experience after a traumatic event. Many of these symptoms represent a natural human response immediately following a traumatic event. To qualify for a diagnosis of PTSD, the individual must display the symptoms for longer than one month after the event. Individuals experiencing symptoms directly after an event but for less than one month may be diagnosed with acute stress disorder.

PTSD (Bonnie)

Watch this Speaking Out video at www.mysearchlab.com

Sep 11, 2001

Aug 4, 2011

Survivors of traumatic events, such as the terrorist attack on the World Trade Center, may experience symptoms of PTSD.

TABLE 5.5 DSM-IV-TR DIAGNOSTIC CRITERIA FOR POST-TRAUMATIC STRESS DISORDER

A. The person has been exposed to a traumatic event in which *both* of the following were present:
(1) the person experienced, witnessed, or was confronted with an event or events that involved actual or threatened death or serious injury, or a threat to the physical integrity of self or others
(2) the person's response involved intense fear, helplessness, or horror **Note:** In children, this may be expressed instead by disorganized or agitated behavior

B. The traumatic event is persistently reexperienced in one (or more) of the following ways:
(1) recurrent and intrusive distressing recollections of the event, including images, thoughts, or perceptions **Note:** In young children, repetitive play may occur in which themes or aspects of the trauma are expressed
(2) recurrent distressing dreams of the event **Note:** In children, there may be frightening dreams without recognizable content
(3) acting or feeling as if the traumatic event were recurring (includes a sense of reliving the experience, illusions, hallucinations, and dissociative flashback episodes, including those that occur on awakening or when intoxicated). **Note:** In young children, trauma-specific reenactment may occur
(4) intense psychological distress at exposure to internal or external cues that symbolize or resemble an aspect of the traumatic event
(5) physiological reactivity on exposure to internal or external cues that symbolize or resemble an aspect of the traumatic event

C. Persistent avoidance of stimuli associated with the trauma and numbing of general responsiveness (not present before the trauma), as indicated by three (or more) of the following:
(1) efforts to avoid thoughts, feeling, or conversations associated with the trauma
(2) efforts to avoid activities, places, or people that arouse recollections of the trauma
(3) inability to recall an important aspect of the trauma
(4) markedly diminished interest or participation in significant activities
(5) feeling of detachment or estrangement from others
(6) restricted range of affect (e.g., unable to have loving feelings)
(7) sense of foreshortened future (e.g., does not expect to have a career, marriage, children, or a normal lifespan)

D. Persistent symptoms of increased arousal (not present before the trauma), as indicated by two (or more) of the following:
(1) difficulty falling or staying asleep
(2) irritability or outbursts of anger
(3) difficulty concentrating
(4) hypervigilance
(5) exaggerated startle response

E. Duration of the disturbance (symptoms in Criteria B, C, and D) is more than 1 month.

F. The disturbance causes clinically significant distress or impairment in social, occupational, or other important areas of functioning.

Source: Reprinted with permission from the *Diagnostic and Statistical Manual of Mental Disorders, Fourth Edition, Text Revision.* (Copyright © 2000). American Psychiatric Association.

Living with PTSD

Watch this Speaking Out video at www.mysearchlab.com

A central diagnostic feature of PTSD that distinguishes it from other anxiety disorders is that the individual re-experiences the event in some way upon being reminded of the traumatic event. This may include recurrent, intrusive, and distressing recollections of the event (e.g., in the form of images, thoughts, perceptions, and dreams) or psychological and physiological distress upon exposure to internal (i.e., bodily) or external cues that symbolize or resemble some aspect of the trauma. These cues may assume virtually any sensory form, such as certain sights, sounds, or smells that by association resemble stimuli that were present during the trauma. The situational cues may have a fairly direct relation to the trauma, such as when a female rape victim encounters a male co-worker who looks, talks, or acts like her rapist. Alternatively, the cues may be relatively indirect, such as when she smells a fragrance of cologne resembling the scent of her perpetrator on a paper card given to her by a friendly department store clerk. Individuals with PTSD are generally aware of a number of their triggers, particularly those that exhibit a fairly direct and logical relation to remembered features of their traumatic event. However, they may be less conscious of the potential of other cues to prompt their re-experiencing episodes, especially those that are more subtly associated with their trauma. Consequently, the onset of certain re-experiencing episodes may seem to arise at random.

For some individuals, re-experiencing phenomena may involve them in acting or feeling as if the traumatic event is recurring in the present, such that they actually feel as if they are *reliving* the event. This experience is very different from simply remembering what happened to them with a felt sense of the past tense; reliving episodes are often referred to as *flashbacks* and involve transient breaks from reality, including visual and auditory hallucinations that "replay" the traumatic event for the individual in the here and now, as if it is actually happening (Brewin, 2011). Not surprisingly, the majority of individuals experience these episodes with intense fear. However, some individuals dissociate when they are reminded of their trauma. Individuals who dissociate display a relative absence of physiological reactivity, appear to be "spaced out," and seem momentarily non-responsive to their environment. Research increasingly suggests that the neurobiological basis of flashbacks versus dissociative reactions may be different (Lanius et al., 2010). Symptoms of dissociation are central to the diagnosis of acute stress disorder.

Partly as a result of their susceptibility to re-experiencing episodes, individuals with PTSD display a hallmark symptom of anxiety disorders: avoidance. Specifically, they commonly attempt to avoid thinking or talking about their traumatic event, as well as avoid places, people, or activities that may remind them of the trauma. These symptoms can be classified as *cognitive avoidance* and *behavioural avoidance*, respectively, and they often co-occur as prototypical features of anxiety-spectrum behaviour.

DSM-IV-TR classifies a number of additional symptoms under the rubric of avoidance criteria (see Table 5.5), although research suggests that these other symptoms are distinct and probably best considered separate from cognitive and behavioural avoidance (King, Leskin, King, & Weathers, 1998). For instance, some of the "avoidance" symptoms correlate more with symptoms of depression than they do with other anxiety disorders. Specifically, these additional PTSD symptoms include a markedly diminished interest or participation in pre-trauma daily-living activities, feeling detached or estranged from others, being unable to experience certain feelings (especially positive affect), and feeling that one's future is significantly foreshortened (e.g., that one won't live long, or experience any future quality of life). Rather than anxiously avoiding feelings or situations, this set of symptoms more distinctively represents an inability to experience emotions, and has been referred to as **emotional numbing** (Frewen et al., 2008; Orsillo, Theodore-Oklota, Luterek, & Plumb, 2007). Accordingly, the DSM-5 is likely to distinguish between symptoms of avoidance, on the one hand, and negative alterations in cognition and mood, on the other (APA, 2010). Another symptom that has been harder to classify is the difficulty some individuals with PTSD demonstrate when attempting to recall certain important aspects of what transpired during their trauma. Individuals with PTSD also experience sleep difficulties, concentration problems, irritability, and other symptoms of elevated arousal. These individuals are frequently *hypervigilant* to threatening stimuli and exhibit an exaggerated startle response to unexpected stimuli.

Lieutenant-General Roméo Dallaire was the commander of the UN peacekeeping forces in Rwanda until he retired as a result of PTSD. In 2008, he received the Humanitarian Award from the Canadian Psychological Association.

Although not included in the diagnostic criteria, people with PTSD often experience a tremendous amount of guilt and shame, which complicates the clinical picture of this disorder. An individual may experience guilt for *acts of commission* (things he or she did) or *omission* (things he or she did not do) during or after the trauma. *Survivor guilt* may also be experienced. To illustrate, survivors of the tsunami and earthquake in Japan that killed more than 18 000 in March 2011 may not only feel the painful loss of loved ones but may also feel guilty for surviving.

DIAGNOSIS AND ASSESSMENT The diagnosis and assessment of PTSD generally involves the combination of a semi-structured clinical interview and the results of psychometric scales. One of the most well-used and validated interview measures of PTSD is the *Clinician Administered PTSD Scale* (CAPS; Blake et al., 1990). This interview can be used to quantify both the frequency and the intensity of an individual's PTSD symptoms. Several questionnaire measures of PTSD symptoms and associated problems are also available. Additionally, although used relatively infrequently in actual clinical practice, physiological (e.g., cardiac and respiratory) measures can be useful in determining PTSD severity (Pole, 2007).

An essential component of PTSD diagnosis and assessment involves determining whether comorbid disorders are present. As a rule, individuals with non-comorbid PTSD are infrequently found. A Manitoba study found that in PTSD sufferers 37 percent had comorbid depression, 34 percent had panic disorder, and 19 percent had social phobia (Sareen et al., 2007). Personality disorders (e.g., borderline personality disorder) are also frequently present in more complex and severe cases of PTSD.

Another important consideration in the assessment of PTSD involves determining whether the disturbance involves a reaction to a single event or to multiple events. In general, individuals who develop PTSD following a single event (e.g., a car accident) that constitutes a disruption in an otherwise psychologically healthy lifestyle have a much better treatment prognosis than do individuals who develop the symptoms over the course of long-standing and recurrent traumatic experiences (e.g., spousal or child abuse). Many clinicians refer to the former type of scenario as *uncomplicated PTSD*, and to the latter as *complex PTSD*.

ETIOLOGY By definition, exposure of an individual to a traumatic life event plays a role in the development of PTSD. However, clearly not every individual who has experienced a traumatic event develops PTSD. Indeed, traumatic events are unfortunately not uncommon human experiences. A study with undergraduate students found that 85 percent reported experiencing a traumatic event in their lifetime and 21 percent reported experiencing such an event in the last two months (Frazier et al., 2009). Women are approximately two times as likely to develop PTSD following exposure to a traumatic event than are men (risk rates are 20 percent and 8 percent, respectively; Kessler et al., 1995).

There are also gender differences in the types of traumatic experiences to which men and women are exposed. Men more often reported witnessing someone badly injured or killed; being exposed to fires, floods, and/or natural disasters; being involved in life-threatening accidents, physical attacks, or war-related combat; being threatened with weapons; or being held captive or kidnapped. In contrast, women more often reported being raped, sexually molested, neglected by their parents as children, and physically abused as a child. Although men are exposed to a greater number of traumatic events on average than are women, women are exposed to more events particularly likely to be associated with the development of PTSD, such as rape (Tolin & Foa, 2006). This at least partly explains the increased risk of PTSD that is associated with being female (Olff, Langeland, Draijer, & Gersons, 2007).

A number of risk factors for the development of PTSD have been identified, including both *pre-event* and *post-event* factors (Cougle, Resnick, & Kilpatrick, 2009). Pre-event risk factors for adult PTSD include being low in socioeconomic status, education, and tested intelligence; having a previous psychiatric history; and experiencing childhood adversity, including being abused as a child. Post-event risk factors are somewhat more powerful predictors of PTSD than are pre-event factors, and include the severity of the traumatic event, lack of social support, and whether or not additional stressful experiences occur after the traumatic event. Also, exposure to *interpersonal traumas* (e.g., related to physical violence or sexual abuse) is generally more likely to provoke PTSD than exposure to *non-interpersonal traumas* (e.g., natural disaster, car accident). Certain genetic factors may also predispose individuals to be more likely both to be exposed to traumatic events and to develop PTSD in response to these events (Broekman, Olff, & Boer, 2007).

Neuroimaging and endocrinology studies are beginning to uncover physiological markers of PTSD. An important biological component of the stress response is the functioning of the hypothalamic-pituitary-adrenal (HPA) axis (see Chapter 7, p. 150). In major depressive disorder, studies have found abnormal HPA-axis function, including increased secretion of corticotropin releasing factor (with corresponding increased release of adrenocorticotropin hormone and cortisol), in addition to reduced negative feedback of adrenal cortisol secretion. In contrast, several studies with male combat veterans and Holocaust survivors have found *decreased* cortisol and/or *enhanced* negative feedback of adrenal function, even in the context of PTSD comorbid with depression (Metzger et al., 2008; Yehuda, Golier, Halligan, Meaney, & Bierer, 2004; Yehuda, Halligan, Golier, Grossman, & Bierer, 2004).

Another consistent finding is that the volume of the hippocampus is less in individuals with PTSD than in individuals without PTSD (Karl et al., 2006). Although reduced hippocampal volume may be a pathological consequence of hypercortisolism in some cases of PTSD, one study found that it was significantly correlated in trauma-exposed and non-trauma-exposed twins, and significantly predicted vulnerability to PTSD in the context of exposure to trauma (Gilbertson et al., 2002). Therefore, small hippocampus volume may, in some cases, be a hereditary risk factor for PTSD that overlaps with findings that low intelligence is also a risk factor for PTSD.

A movement in cognitive psychological theorizing about the nature of PTSD is to emphasize the multiple levels upon which traumatic experiences can affect the mind (Dalgleish, 2004). For example, Dual Representation Theory details differences in the way that traumatic memories and non-traumatic memories may be stored and retrieved (Brewin, 2011; Brewin, Dalgleish, & Stephen, 1996). Traumatic memories may be initially stored and retrieved in a non-verbal sensory-based form, whereas a verbal element typically permeates memory encoding and retrieval of non-traumatic memories. Therefore, effective resolution of the trauma may involve transferring loosely connected sensory-based memories into a more verbal form. This theory is consistent with the results of much of the brain-based evidence reviewed above (Brewin, 2011) and with the beneficial effects of therapies that involve repeated writing or talking about one's traumatic experiences (e.g., Pennebaker, 1995; Resick & Schnicke, 1993).

Additional cognitive theories focus on how individuals appraise traumatic events in terms of their meaning for themselves, others, and their environment, and how these trauma appraisals may drastically alter previously held beliefs. Ehlers and Clark (2000) articulated a comprehensive appraisal-based model of PTSD, in which they argue that thoughts that lead to feelings of *current and generalized* threat, despite the fact that the event is in the past and may be relatively circumscribed in its effect, are cognitive factors that partly cause and maintain PTSD. To illustrate, following a rape a woman may begin to believe that "all men are dangerous." She will constantly feel threatened so long as she is in a place where men are present. Similarly, an individual who is robbed in a back alley late in the evening who comes to believe that "the world is dangerous" as opposed to "back alleys are dangerous places especially at night" is much more likely to experience chronic arousal, distress, and hypervigilance for threat.

GENERALIZED ANXIETY DISORDER

Case Notes

Elizabeth was a "worrier" for as long as she could remember. Her worry became worse, however, when she experienced a work-related injury that bruised her chest wall. Following this injury, she began to experience health-related anxiety and presented at the emergency room on two occasions complaining of chest pain. Elizabeth reported that she experiences far more than just health anxiety. She worries constantly about the safety and well-being of her loved ones. For example, when her daughter is ill, she cannot bring herself to provide medicine because she fears that the dose she gives will be too much or too little and that harm will come to her daughter. She also worries about family members who live out of town and phones them regularly to ensure their safety. Elizabeth worries, as well, about finances, about getting into an accident whenever she drives, and about the safety of gas appliances. She even avoids pumping gas at a service station for fear that an explosion may result. She recognizes that her worry is excessive but finds it difficult to control, and she experiences symptoms of fatigue, muscle tension, restlessness, and sleep difficulties.

Living with GAD (Philip)

Watch this Speaking Out video at www.mysearchlab.com

GAD (Philip)

Watch this Speaking Out video at www.mysearchlab.com

DESCRIPTION Elizabeth's symptoms are characteristic of generalized anxiety disorder (GAD), in which the central difficulty involves uncontrollable and excessive worry (also called *pathological worry*). We all worry to some degree, but it becomes pathological when it is chronic, excessive, uncontrollable, and essentially takes the joy out of life (Borkovec, Ray, & Stober, 1998). Although significant negative life events have the capacity to create feelings of distress and anxiety even in the most resilient of individuals, the anxiety experienced by people with GAD is far in excess of what would be naturally elicited by a given set of life stressors. For individuals with GAD it is often not the amount of stress in their lives that is the clinical problem, but rather the amount of anxiety and worry they experience as a result of a relatively normal level of life stress. An estimated 3 percent of the population has GAD in any 12-month period (Kessler, Chiu, et al., 2005), while almost 6 percent of the general population can be expected to develop this disorder at some point in their lives (Kessler, Berglund, et al., 2005). As with many of the other anxiety disorders, women make up the majority of those diagnosed with GAD. About two-thirds of individuals with GAD are female (APA, 2000).

DIAGNOSIS AND ASSESSMENT Historically, GAD has been a disorder whose diagnostic criteria have been transitory and under construction. Two decades ago, a diagnosis of GAD was given only if the client did not meet the diagnostic criteria of another Axis I disorder, and was therefore considered to be a residual category (Brown, O'Leary, & Barlow, 2001). It was not until the publication of the DSM-III-R that worry was acknowledged to be the main symptom. The criteria were also revised again with the publication of DSM-IV to emphasize the process of worry (Brown et al., 2001). Further alterations to the criteria for GAD have been proposed for DSM-5 (APA, 2010). These changes are in some respects more inclusive (e.g., shorter length of illness, less symptoms necessary), which may allow a greater number of individuals with diagnostically similar features to meet criteria for GAD (Andrews et al., 2010).

The primary criterion for GAD, in DSM-IV-TR, is the presence of excessive worry, which must be present for more days than not for a period of at least six months (see Table 5.6). Three or more other symptoms of anxiety must also be present, such as restlessness, muscle tension, and sleep problems. In addition, changes to DSM-5 may require one or more behaviours instigated in reaction to excessive worry, such as avoidance, excessive preparation, or procrastination. One of the challenges in making the diagnosis of GAD involves determining that the source of a person's anxiety and worry is not confined to another Axis I disorder. This sometimes makes diagnosis difficult because worry is a prominent feature in many of the anxiety disorders. For example, individuals with panic disorder often worry about future panic attacks, and those with social anxiety disorder tend to worry about upcoming social interactions. Worry can also be a prominent symptom in other "non-anxiety" disorders. For example, individuals with hypochondriasis (see Chapter 6) often spend a lot of time worrying about the possibility that they might have a disease or medical condition. Therefore, it is important for the clinician to make sure that worry is fairly ubiquitous in the sense that it is not specific to one content area. In contrast to the worries of individuals with other anxiety disorders, which tend to be restricted to a single domain or theme, individuals with GAD "worry about everything." They often worry about several things at once and report a long history of worrying.

Living with Generalized Anxiety Disorder with Insomnia

Watch this Speaking Out video at www.mysearchlab.com

Christy: Living with GAD with Insomnia

Watch this Speaking Out video at www.mysearchlab.com

ETIOLOGY Given that worry is the central symptom in GAD, it is not surprising that many of the etiological models

TABLE 5.6 DSM-IV-TR DIAGNOSTIC CRITERIA FOR GENERALIZED ANXIETY DISORDER

A. Excessive anxiety and worry (apprehensive expectation), occurring more days than not for at least 6 months, about a number of events or activities (e.g., work, school performance).

B. The person finds it difficult to control the worry.

C. The anxiety and worry are associated with three (or more) of the following six symptoms (with at least some symptoms present for more days than not for the past 6 months). **Note:** Only one item is required in children.

(1) restlessness or feeling keyed up or on edge

(2) being easily fatigued

(3) difficulty concentrating or mind going blank

(4) irritability

(5) muscle tension

(6) sleep disturbance (difficulty falling or staying asleep, or restless unsatisfying sleep)

D. The focus of the anxiety and worry is not confined to features of an Axis I disorder, e.g., the anxiety or worry is not about having a Panic Attack (as in Panic Disorder), being embarrassed in public (as in Social Phobia), being contaminated (as in Obsessive-Compulsive Disorder), being away from home or close relatives (as in Separation Anxiety Disorder), gaining weight (as in Anorexia Nervosa), having multiple physical complaints (as in Somatization Disorder), or having a serious illness (as in Hypochondriasis), and the anxiety and worry do not occur exclusively during Posttraumatic Stress Disorder.

E. The anxiety, worry, or physical symptoms cause clinically significant distress or impairment in social, occupational, or other important areas of functioning.

F. The disturbance is not due to the direct physiological effects of a substance (e.g., a drug of abuse, a medication) or a general medical condition (e.g., hyperthyroidism) and does not occur exclusively during a Mood Disorder, a Psychotic Disorder, or a Pervasive Developmental Disorder.

Source: Reprinted with permission from the *Diagnostic and Statistical Manual of Mental Disorders, Fourth Edition, Text Revision.* (Copyright © 2000). American Psychiatric Association.

are primarily cognitive in nature. Tom Borkovec and his colleagues have proposed that individuals with GAD use worry primarily as an avoidance strategy. One thing that individuals with GAD appear to "avoid" by worrying is physiological arousal. The physical feeling of anxiety can be quite discomforting and bothersome, and therefore avoidance of arousal is reinforcing to the individual. Interestingly, then, the process of worry tends to *decrease* somatic arousal (Borkovec & Hu, 1990; Borkovec, Lyonsfields, Wiser, & Deihl, 1993; Thayer, Friedman, & Borkovec, 1996). For example, Borkovec and Hu (1990) had participants worry before exposing them to a phobic image. Results showed that worrying decreased their physiological reaction to the phobic stimulus by inhibiting cardiovascular activity.

How does worry decrease physiological arousal? The answer seems to relate to the fact that worrying is primarily accompanied by verbal thought and very little imagery. When the majority of people are asked to report the content of their thoughts while in a relaxed state, they tend to report a preponderance of imagery over verbal thoughts. In contrast, those with GAD report an equal balance of imagery and verbal thoughts. However, when both groups are induced to worry, imagery soon disappears and verbal statements dominate thinking (Borkovec & Inz, 1990). It appears that anxious images elicit arousal, whereas verbal thoughts decrease arousal. Hence, worrying is negatively reinforced because it can lead to a reduction in anxiety symptoms.

Another purpose of worry is to avoid future threat. For many people with and without GAD, worry is considered to be a very useful way of preparing for the future. Indeed, there are a number of reasons why people report worrying, some of which are listed in Table 5.7. As illustrated in this table, many people believe that worry is an effective way of preventing or preparing for future threat (Borkovec & Roemer,

TABLE 5.7 REASONS FOR WORRYING AND SAMPLE ITEMS FROM THE REASONS TO WORRY SCALE

Reason	Example (sample items)
Motivation	"Worry helps to motivate me to get things done that I need to get done."
Problem Solving	"Worrying is an effective way to problem solve."
Preparation	"If I worry about something, when something bad does happen, I'll be better prepared for it."
Avoidance	"If I worry about something, I am more likely to actually figure out how to avoid or prevent something bad from happening."
Distraction	"Worrying is a way to distract myself from worrying about even more emotional things, things that I don't want to think about."
Superstition	"Although it may not actually be true, it feels like if I worry about something, the worrying makes it less likely that something bad will happen."

Source: Borkovec & Roemer (1995).

1995; Freeston, Rheaume, Letarte, Dugas, & Ladouceur, 1994). Worry becomes quite reinforcing because the worst-case situation rarely comes true. This might have been due to the fact that the feared outcome may never have come true anyway, but it might also be due to the actual behaviour of the person. At certain times during the semester, when your work piles up, you may start to worry. This process may lead you to work hard and to do well. But getting a good grade may reinforce the habit of worry—you may not, for example, want to take a chance and see how you would do with hard work alone (i.e., without worry). Individuals with GAD tend to worry so much that it significantly disrupts their life and causes more problems than benefits.

People with GAD also worry about multiple extraneous issues as a way to avoid thinking about issues of more central emotional significance in their lives (Borkovec & Roemer, 1995). For example, rather than thinking about a friend's serious illness, you may busy your mind worrying about schoolwork and the minor problems you have with your significant other. Unfortunately, this strategy can backfire in the long run, because attempts to distract oneself from something stressful often increase the number of thought intrusions (Wells & Papageorgiou, 1995).

Drs. Michel Dugas and Robert Ladouceur are two Canadian researchers who have had a tremendous impact on the field of GAD research. Together with their colleagues, they have proposed their own theory of GAD, which primarily focuses on a cognitive vulnerability factor they call intolerance of uncertainty (Dugas, Gagnon, Ladouceur, & Freeston, 1998; Gentes & Ruscio, 2011). **Intolerance of uncertainty (IU)** refers to an individual's discomfort with ambiguity and uncertainty. Everyone has a different threshold for accepting and dealing with life's uncertainties; individuals with GAD tend to have lower thresholds for these uncertainties, leading to anxiety and distress. IU is responsible for creating and exacerbating "what if . . . " questions, which are questions we all ask ourselves at some point in time. The following is a list of "what if . . . " questions asked by many undergraduate students:

- "What if I don't do well on my next exam?"
- "What if I don't get a good job after I graduate?"
- "What if my boyfriend (or girlfriend) is cheating on me?"

Notice that each of these questions addresses uncertainty about the future. Fortunately, many of us are forced to deal with only a limited number of such questions. However, individuals with GAD are constantly grappling with these questions because they have a selective bias for uncertainty. For example, Dugas and his colleagues (2005) found that individuals with high levels of IU tend to interpret ambiguous information as more threatening than do those with low IU. Therefore, not only does IU lead to the identification of more uncertainty in both daily life and the future, but this uncertainty is also considered to be more threatening.

Several studies have supported IU as an etiological risk factor for GAD (Dugas et al., 1998; Dugas, Marchand, & Ladouceur, 2005; Gentes & Ruscio, 2011). This construct consistently correlates with pathological worry and anxiety (Gentes & Ruscio, 2011) and distinguishes between individuals with GAD and those without the disorder (Dugas et al., 1998).

4 BEFORE MOVING ON

Sara is constantly worried that she is going to die in a car accident. When she was a child, her father died in a car accident on his way to pick her up from school. However, her fear of dying in a car accident didn't occur until she went away to university at the age of 18. Sara reports that she often has intrusive thoughts of being involved in a motor vehicle accident and that these thoughts persist no matter how much she tries to ignore them. Sara avoids driving or being in a car whenever possible. If she has to ride in a car, Sara spends more than an hour checking it over before she gets in. Sara understands that these thoughts and her avoidance are negatively affecting her life. Based on this information, which anxiety disorder do you think Sara most likely has?

Changes in DSM-5

Throughout this chapter, we have highlighted proposed changes for the upcoming version of the DSM (also see McKay, Abramowitz, Taylor, & Asmundson, 2009). As with all science, it is important to ensure that changes are consistent with the latest empirical evidence. In order to update the diagnostic criteria for mental disorders, a number of important questions must be asked. Some of these questions refer to the specific diagnostic criteria: Are the criteria broad enough to encompass the majority of similar cases? Are the criteria specific enough to exclude dissimilar cases? In response to such inquiries, criteria are added, removed, or modified, as was the case with the GAD criteria. Other types of scientific questions focus on how the disorders are related, and how they should be organized so that they are clearest to clinicians and the population at large.

In response to these concerns, some reorganization has been proposed. For example, both hoarding and agoraphobia may be reorganized as distinct disorders with their own diagnostic criteria in DSM-5. In addition, the disorders currently listed in the anxiety chapter have been divided into anxiety disorders, obsessive- and compulsive-related disorders, and trauma- and stressor-related disorders. The development of the last two new general categories and the reorganization of disorders are intended to group disorders into clusters that share etiological, symptomatic, and biological similarities. The current revisions to the DSM are, however, only *proposed* at this stage, and discussion continues as to what the final organization and criteria will be.

Treatment of Anxiety Disorders

Although the management of anxiety disorders often includes medication, psychological interventions have received tremendous empirical support. When considering both short- and long-term outcomes, exposure-based behavioural interventions and cognitive-behavioural therapy are the most effective treatments for anxiety disorders. In fact, various treatment guidelines now recommend that the cognitive-behavioural interventions be administered as first-line treatments (Anxiety Review Panel, 2000; Department of Health, 2001; National Institute for Health and Clinical Excellence, 2011; Norton & Price, 2007). The main components of these psychological treatments are highlighted after a description of pharmacotherapy. We then briefly summarize the literature on treatment effectiveness.

PHARMACOTHERAPY

Canadian researchers Hoffman and Mathew (2008) reviewed the effectiveness of various medicinal treatments for different anxiety disorders. Before the development of antidepressants, benzodiazepines were the most widely prescribed psychiatric medication. These drugs are appropriately referred to as *minor tranquilizers*; they provide rapid, short-term relief from physiological symptoms of acute anxiety such as heart palpitations, muscle tension, and gastrointestinal distress. Benzodiazepines bind to receptor sites for the neurotransmitter gamma-aminobutyric acid (GABA), which functions to temporally inhibit activity broadly across neural sites, including brain systems that are involved in generating fear and anxiety.

However, being the brain's primary inhibitory neurotransmitter, GABA is involved at least to some extent in virtually all cognitive, affective, and behavioural functions (i.e., including those that are not particular to fear and anxiety). Thus benzodiazepines have many side effects, which include psychomotor (e.g., dizziness and drowsiness) and cognitive (e.g., attention and memory) impairments, depending on the dosage and type of benzodiazepine used. Accordingly, these drugs are most appropriately used for temporary relief of subjective distress associated with infrequently encountered anxiety-provoking situations. They are less suitable as a long-term treatment for anxiety disorders, especially because they have a significant addictive potential and are associated with withdrawal symptoms in long-term users who try to discontinue the drug. In fact, patients typically find that their anxiety symptoms return, often in a worsened form, upon discontinuing benzodiazepines after long-term use.

Drs. Henny Westra (York University) and Sherry Stuart (Dalhousie University) have made a strong case against the use of benzodiazepines as a long-term treatment for anxiety. These researchers argue that exposure therapies seek to increase clients' self-efficacy by demonstrating to them that physiological symptoms of anxiety are not harmful in themselves, and that anxiety-provoking situations can be managed despite anxious feelings. In contrast, pharmacological therapies may teach patients that their anxiety symptoms themselves are "pathological" and can be controlled only by medication. This may focus patients' attention even more on their anxiety symptoms rather than on finding solutions to the life problems that give rise to them (Westra & Stewart, 1998). Indeed Westra, Stewart, and their colleagues have shown that use of benzodiazepines on an as-needed basis is associated with increased hypervigilance for signals of threat (Stewart, Westra, Thompson, & Conrad, 2000) and decreased memory for psychoeducational material presented during cognitive-behavioural therapy (Westra et al., 2004).

Antidepressant drugs are currently the most well-used and effective medications for the treatment of anxiety disorders. As the name implies, these medications were first used in treating depression, and their efficacy in the treatment of both anxiety and depression suggests that there may be some level of overlap in how these two conditions are neurologically expressed. The monoamine oxidase inhibitors are so called because they interfere with the action of monoamine oxidase, an enzyme that degrades certain neurotransmitters (including norepinephrine and serotonin) after being released by neurons, thus increasing the number of these transmitters in the brain generally. Although once widely used in the treatment of anxiety disorders, research has revealed that these drugs can have significant adverse effects on the digestive and cardiovascular systems, especially when taken in combination with foods prepared by fermentation (e.g., alcohol), and their use has decreased accordingly. However, this medication type is effective in the treatment of social phobia (Schneier, 2011). In contrast, the tricyclic antidepressants (TCAs) are in more widespread use, and function to block the reuptake of the neurotransmitters norepinephrine and serotonin. These drugs have been found to be particularly effective in the treatment of OCD (especially clomipramine), although they too are associated with significant side effects, which include possible weight gain, blurred vision, dry mouth, and constipation. The selective serotonin reuptake inhibitors (SSRIs) are the most well-prescribed anxiolytic medications. As their name implies, these drugs have a particular affinity for serotonin receptors. Patients usually find the side effects of SSRIs to be more tolerable.

Two categories of medications have been introduced more recently. One of these, azapirones, appears also to elicit its anxiolytic effects primarily through serotonergic effects, but as well it alters dopamine levels in the brain. Venlafaxine hydrochloride is a newer antidepressant medication that is particularly effective in the treatment of GAD. This medication acts not only to increase serotonin but also to increase both norepinephrine and dopamine levels in the brain, and is generally associated with fewer side effects than traditional SSRI medications. With increasing research, the pharmacology of different existing anxiolytic medications is becoming better understood.

COGNITIVE RESTRUCTURING

Cognitive restructuring is based on the idea that anxiety and other emotional disorders are, at least in part, due to faulty, maladaptive, or unhelpful thinking patterns (Beck

& Dozois, 2011; Dozois & Beck, 2008; Dozois, Seeds, & Collins, 2009). In the case of anxiety, these thoughts are future-oriented and involve themes of imminent or looming threat. Individuals with anxiety problems often overestimate the probability and severity of various threats (risk) and underestimate their ability to cope with them (resources). The goal of cognitive restructuring is to help patients develop healthier and more evidence-based thoughts—to help them adjust the imbalance between perceived risk and resource (Beck & Emery, 1985; Clark & Beck, 2010b). Patients learn to become better scientists of their own thoughts by monitoring and identifying automatic thoughts and underlying beliefs, examining the validity of these cognitions, and developing more balanced appraisals.

A number of strategies are used to help facilitate this process. One commonly used technique involves the thought record. An example of a thought record is shown in Table 5.8. The thought record serves many purposes. Early on in therapy, it is used to help patients understand the important relationship between what they are thinking and how they are feeling. Whenever their anxiety increases, patients learn to ask themselves, "What was I thinking just before I started to feel this way?" Patients also learn to monitor and "catch" their automatic thoughts and beliefs systematically, so that they can examine the utility and validity of them. With the help of a therapist, patients examine the evidence for or against various beliefs and are taught strategies for developing more balanced thinking styles. Throughout this process, therapists use a style of Socratic questioning to elicit and test a patient's beliefs. The Socratic approach involves asking a number of questions to query and evaluate the beliefs and behaviours that contribute to anxiety. Therapists also engage in collaborative empiricism, meaning that the therapist and patient operate as a team to conceptualize a patient's difficulties and modify his or her beliefs (e.g., "What is the evidence for and against this belief?"; "Are there different ways of looking at this situation?"; "Are you confusing a low probability event with a high probability one?"; see Beck & Emery, 1985). Patients are also encouraged to conduct "behavioural experiments" to test certain beliefs and assumptions. For example, the belief that one will be

TABLE 5.8 EXAMPLE OF A THOUGHT RECORD

Situation	Moods (intensity in %)	Automatic Thoughts	Supporting Evidence	Contradictory Evidence	Alternative Thoughts	Re-rate Emotion (intensity in %)
Starting to relax while watching my favourite TV show and my heart started to pound for no apparent reason	Panic (98%)	My heart is beating faster than normal. I am shaking and sweating. I am going to have a heart attack.	My heart is beginning to race. I am shaky and sweaty.	I do not have any family history of heart disease. I take care of myself physically. As my therapist warned, I may be experiencing anxiety because I am relaxing and I fear letting go. The heart is supposed to beat fast at times and it can handle the strain—it is a muscle after all. A quick heartbeat does not mean that I am having a heart attack; there could be other explanations.	Although I am experiencing physical sensations, the odds are good that I am not having a heart attack.	Panic reduced to 30%
Driving from London to Toronto on Highway 401	Worry (80%)	There are so many trucks on this highway. I am getting nervous. I am going to get into an accident and die.	The 401 is a more dangerous highway than many others.	Just because I fear getting into an accident doesn't mean I am going to. Even if I do get into an accident, it doesn't mean I will die (many, even serious, accidents are non-fatal). I am doing what I can to protect myself—I wear my seatbelt, I drive carefully, I am not tired.	Although accidents do occur, the chance is not as high as I feel it is. Besides, most accidents are not fatal. I am a careful driver, which improves my odds of being safe.	Worry reduced to 25%

Note: The patient circled the thought that he or she recognizes contributes most to the negative emotion.

rejected if one initiates a social interaction can be tested behaviourally.

Usually, deeper cognitive change occurs when the elicited cognitions are also connected to significant emotionally charged responses. Greenberger and Padesky (1995) refer to these thoughts as "hot cognitions." Thus, an important component of cognitive restructuring involves probing the patient to find out what deeper beliefs and schemas are triggering his or her automatic thoughts.

EXPOSURE TECHNIQUES

Few researchers would disagree that exposure is the main therapeutic ingredient across all psychological interventions for anxiety. Although the specific focus of exposure differs depending on the disorder being treated, the principle is the same: by facing anxiety-provoking stimuli, one's fears become extinguished (through the process of habituation), new coping skills are developed, and significant cognitive change occurs. The change in threat-related cognitions occurs as new evidence is accumulated that is discrepant from one's beliefs, thereby providing an opportunity for new learning to take place.

One of the earliest forms of exposure was **systematic desensitization**, initially developed by Joseph Wolpe (1958). With the assistance of a therapist, the patient develops a **fear hierarchy**. A fear hierarchy is a list of feared situations or objects that are arranged in descending order according to how much they evoke anxiety. Often therapists use the term *subjective units of distress*, or SUDS, which is a rating that patients provide from 0 (meaning that there is no anxiety at all) to 100 (meaning that the anxiety is the worst the individual has ever experienced). Systematic desensitization starts by having patients imagine the lowest feared stimulus and combining this image with a relaxation response. Patients gradually work their way up the fear hierarchy so that they can learn to handle increasingly distressing stimuli.

The rationale underlying this approach is that anxiety is a learned or conditioned response. By pairing a relaxation response with the feared stimulus, counter-conditioning or extinction is believed to occur. That is, because relaxation is an incompatible response to anxiety, the patient learns to be less anxious in the presence of the feared object or situation. Systematic desensitization has frequently been used to treat specific phobias. However, this approach is used less frequently now because research has indicated that **in vivo** (meaning real life) **exposure** itself is more effective than imaginal exposure and that the inclusion of relaxation provides no better response than exposure alone (Antony & Barlow, 2002). One area where imagery tends to be useful is in the treatment of GAD. Because many of the worries in GAD are not amenable to exposure, coupled with the fact that pathological worry is used as a means of avoiding intense negative emotions and arousal, patients are sometimes encouraged to engage in **worry imagery exposure** (Waters & Craske, 2005). This involves systematic exposure to feared images that are related to an individual's worries. After holding a worry image in their minds for 25 to 30 minutes (which helps individuals with GAD to tolerate and habituate to their fearful images), patients may be encouraged to think about a number of possible outcomes other than the worst-case scenario that was initially envisioned.

Exposure that is in vivo is effective for a wide range of anxiety problems. In gradual exposure, the patient approaches the items in his or her fear hierarchy beginning at a lower level of intensity and working up, over time, to face higher-intensity stimuli. We often tell our patients that exposure works optimally when they try to increase its frequency, duration, and intensity. In other words, they should do it as often as they can and for as long as they can handle it, and move up their hierarchy in increments of increased intensity. Imagine, for instance, that you have a fear of elevators. You could overcome this fear much faster by going into an elevator numerous times a day than by facing this fear only once a week. Another variation of exposure is called **flooding** or **intense exposure**. This involves starting at a very high level of intensity rather than working gradually through the fear hierarchy. Graduated and intense exposure are both effective; which approach is taken sometimes simply depends on what the patient is willing to tolerate.

There are many variants of exposure. Individuals who suffer from social phobia, for example, are asked to engage in social interactions like initiating a conversation, going to a party, and asking for directions. People with PTSD are instructed to write about, describe, and recall the details of the traumatic event (imaginal exposure) so that they can learn that the event, although horrific, is a memory rather than an ongoing occurrence. In the treatment of panic disorder, individuals are often exposed to both external feared situations and internal sensations. For example, they may be encouraged to go into a grocery store or a movie theatre. Exposure to internal cues (i.e., bodily sensations) is called **interoceptive exposure** and is also effective for panic disorder. Interoceptive exposure involves the induction of physical sensations (e.g., dizziness) by means of hyperventilating, spinning in a chair, exercising, and so on (Craske & Barlow, 2008).

The main treatment for OCD involves exposure and **ritual prevention** (also called response prevention). Ritual prevention involves promoting abstinence from rituals that, while reducing anxiety in the short term, only serve to reinforce the obsessions in the long run (Franklin & Foa, 2008). Scott, the individual with obsessions and compulsions described earlier, was treated with exposure exercises, response prevention, and cognitive restructuring. After identifying a specific hierarchy of fears, he engaged in gradual exposure. Exposure began within the hospital by having him eat off of cafeteria plates that he did not wash personally. Several sessions were also spent in the hospital washroom, because that is where his main fears of contamination were triggered. Exposure eventually moved to outside the hospital setting in order to generalize therapy to other settings. Following each of these exposure exercises,

Scott was encouraged to refrain from washing his hands or engaging in other cleaning rituals.

An important component of exposure also involves helping individuals to reduce their **subtle avoidance** (Abramowitz, Deacon, & Whiteside, 2011). An individual with agoraphobia might be willing to go to a movie theatre as part of an exposure exercise. However, this individual would not get the full benefit of exposure if he or she used distraction strategies or engaged in other "safety behaviours," which are covert avoidance strategies that only serve to reinforce anxiety in the long run (e.g., sitting on the aisle, checking where the emergency exits are, or going to the movie with a "safe" person). Similarly, exposure would not be very effective if, during the course of facing his or her fears, an individual engaged in distraction. Canadian researchers Stanley (Jack) Rachman (University of British Columbia) and Adam Radomsky (Concordia University) have argued that whereas the *judicious* use of safety behaviours may be helpful early in treatment by making exposure less threatening and fostering a sense of control, as treatment continues, these safety behaviours should be reduced or eliminated (Rachman, Radomsky, & Shafran, 2008).

PROBLEM SOLVING

Problem solving is based on the assumption that by generating and implementing effective solutions to problems, patients will experience less anxiety (Epp & Dobson, 2010). This approach begins with a problem-orientation phase, in which individuals are encouraged to approach and deal with their problems constructively rather than worry about, avoid, or deny them. This phase involves teaching an individual to accept that the occurrence of problems is an inevitable part of life rather than being due to personal deficiency, to view problems as challenges rather than as sources of threat or harm, and to view anxiety as a signal of a problem that needs to be dealt with rather than as a feeling to get rid of. The basic problem-solving strategy involves defining a specific problem, generating a wide range of alternative solutions, deciding on and implementing one or more of the solution-focused strategies, and evaluating the outcome.

RELAXATION

Relaxation strategies aim to reduce anxious arousal directly, and can be classified into two general types: mental relaxation and physical relaxation. Training in mental relaxation often takes the form of guided imagery exercises. During guided imagery, the client and therapist work together to develop a personalized description of positive thoughts and images that promote a calm and peaceful state. The scripted scenes may involve images of walking along the shore of a warm sandy beach or climbing a majestic mountain range.

Progressive muscle relaxation involves tensing and then releasing various muscle groups and noting the difference in sensations between the two. Muscle groups where the client particularly experiences tension (e.g., neck, shoulders, back) are especially targeted, although the full body is relaxed, including the facial muscles. Given that the sensations involved in tension and relaxation are incompatible, the individual learns how to reduce his or her anxiety by deliberately relaxing the tension in his or her muscles. In addition, focusing on the body often distracts from the influence of negative thinking (e.g., worry and rumination), at least temporarily.

Another common relaxation method is breathing retraining, which involves teaching patients how to breathe using their diaphragm as opposed to their thoracic (chest) muscles. Research shows that different breathing patterns are associated with different emotional states, and that a pronounced thoracic breathing style can produce hyperventilation symptoms that eventually lead to panic attacks in some individuals. In contrast, diaphragmatic breathing is a more relaxing natural respiration pattern. Although training in relaxation strategies often produces some immediate benefit, research generally shows that exposure is the more important treatment component (Craske & Barlow, 2001).

OTHER TECHNIQUES

The majority of the therapeutic strategies previously discussed have a long history and strong empirical basis in the effective treatment of anxiety disorders. However, a number of additional strategies are also beginning to be applied in anxiety treatment. Mindfulness-based strategies combine the practice of sitting and moving (e.g., yoga, walking) meditation with a number of principles intended to promote psychological well-being, physical health, and stress management (Baer, 2003; Kabat-Zinn, 2003). Mindfulness-based strategies seek to cultivate a state of present-focused "being," often contrasted with various forms of "thinking" (e.g., worrying) and "doing." Research suggests that mindfulness-based approaches are effective therapies for anxiety disorders (Hofmann, Sawyer, Witt, & Oh, 2010).

An additional emerging trend in the treatment of anxiety involves the use of virtual reality technology (Wiederhold & Wiederhold, 2004). These strategies use virtual environments to expose individuals to the objects they fear. These technologies are able to create vivid environments for use in exposure therapies that are otherwise too difficult to conjure in real life (e.g., battlefields in the treatment of combat-related PTSD) or too expensive for repetitive in vivo exposure (e.g., riding airplanes during flight disturbance). A somewhat controversial treatment is Eye Movement Desensitization and Reprocessing (EMDR; Shapiro, 2001), which is primarily used for the treatment of post-traumatic stress disorder. In EMDR, an individual remembers an actual or imagined negative life event while simultaneously focusing his or her attention on a stimulus that oscillates from left to right. Although EMDR is an effective method for treating PTSD, it has no clear advantage over traditional exposure or CBT (Cloitre, 2009).

5 BEFORE MOVING ON

Select three exposure treatments that you might use in treating an anxiety disorder. Describe each treatment and explain how you would employ it.

Treatment Efficacy

In the absence of treatment, anxiety disorders are chronic and recurrent. Fortunately, a number of effective treatments have been developed over the years. In this final section of the chapter, we summarize the main approaches to treatment that have been supported in the research literature.

TREATMENT OF PANIC DISORDER

Many of the techniques described in the previous section are key elements of cognitive-behavioural therapy (CBT) for panic disorder (Sánchez-Meca, Rosa-Alcázar, Marín-Martínez, & Gómez-Conesa, 2010). Barlow's panic control treatment, for example, involves psychoeducation (i.e., education about the nature and physiology of anxiety), cognitive restructuring, breathing retraining, applied relaxation, interoceptive exposure, and in vivo exposure (Craske & Barlow, 2008; White & Barlow, 2002). CBT is the most well-studied and empirically supported treatment for panic disorder. A number of studies have shown that CBT is as effective as benzodiazepines and antidepressants in the short term. CBT also produces more powerful long-term results (e.g., Barlow, Gorman, Shear, & Woods, 2000). Whereas patients receiving pharmacotherapy have to continue to take drugs in order to maintain therapeutic gains, 70 to 80 percent of CBT patients are panic-free at the end of treatment, and these gains tend to be maintained (Arch & Craske, 2008; Craske & Barlow, 2008). As such, CBT is a cost-effective treatment option (Kar, 2011), particularly when administered in a group setting. In a meta-analysis of 43 controlled studies, CBT showed the largest effect sizes and the smallest drop-out rates compared to medication or the combination of drug and psychological treatments (Gould, Otto, & Pollack, 1995).

TREATMENT OF SPECIFIC PHOBIAS

Pharmacological interventions offer little benefit for the treatment of specific phobias and in fact can interfere with exposure-based treatments by dampening anxiety during these exercises (Antony & Barlow, 2002). The main form of treatment for specific phobias is in vivo exposure. The results have been encouraging: approximately 80 to 90 percent of individuals are effectively treated with exposure (Choy, Fyer, & Lipsitz, 2007). More short-term (e.g., one-day) but intensive treatment approaches have also been successful (Antony & Barlow, 2002). Martin Antony and his colleagues from Hamilton, Ontario, for example, administered a two-hour session of exposure to a group of individuals with a specific phobia of spiders. Patients improved significantly, as indicated by physiological, self-report, and behavioural measures (Antony, McCabe, Leeuw, Sano, & Swinson, 2001). Exposure via virtual reality seems to be effective for a number of specific phobias, including fear of heights, public speaking, and flying (Parson & Rizzo, 2008; Wallach, Safir, & Bar-Zvi, 2009).

TREATMENT OF SOCIAL PHOBIA

The most popular treatment for social anxiety disorder, cognitive-behavioural group therapy (CBGT), integrates both cognitive restructuring and exposure (Turk, Heimberg, & Magee, 2008). In some cases, social skills training and relaxation training are incorporated into the treatment package as well. The group setting itself provides ample opportunities for exposure. After working together as a group on various cognitive restructuring exercises, participants practise social interactions and role-play situations that are associated with social anxiety. CBGT is effective for the treatment of social phobia, although the research is presently unclear about whether adding cognitive interventions improves treatment efficacy over and above exposure alone (Hofmann & Barlow, 2002).

CBGT has also been compared to medications in several studies. Overall, few differences exist between CBGT and medication in terms of treatment response (Ledley & Heimberg, 2005). However, individuals in CBGT appear to be better protected against relapse than are individuals in pharmacotherapy alone (Hofmann & Barlow, 2002). At present, the data are not conclusive as to whether combined CBGT and medication is superior to either treatment alone (Ledley & Heimberg, 2005). Researchers have recently demonstrated that D-Cycloserine (an antibiotic drug used to treat tuberculosis) can enhance the learning that takes place in exposure treatment for social anxiety by working on glutamatergic receptors (N-methyl-D-aspartate, or NMDA) in the amygdala (Hofmann, Pollack & Otto, 2006). Future research will determine whether this pharmacological agent reliably augments exposure treatment; however, preliminary research has been promising (Morissette, Spiegel, & Barlow, 2008).

TREATMENT OF OBSESSIVE-COMPULSIVE DISORDER

The main psychological treatment approach for obsessive-compulsive disorder has involved exposure and ritual prevention (ERP). Recently, there has been a growing interest in more cognitively oriented strategies that also appear to be effective for this population (Whittal, Thordarson, & McLean, 2005; Wilhelm & Steketee, 2006). Without question, ERP alters the faulty appraisals and beliefs of individuals with OCD. In fact, cognitive change may be an important mechanism of improvement in these behavioural interventions. Not surprisingly, then, cognitive therapy and ERP have both yielded impressive results in therapy outcome trials. Considerable research has also tested the efficacy of medications (especially serotonin-based medications like clomipramine, fluvoxamine, and fluoxetine) for the treatment of OCD, with supportive results. Studies

CANADIAN RESEARCH CENTRE

Dr. Adam Radomsky

Dr. Adam Radomsky is the founding president of the Canadian Association of Cognitive and Behavioural Therapies and an associate professor of psychology at Concordia University. He joined Concordia in 2001 after completing his Ph.D. in clinical psychology under the supervision of Jack Rachman at the University of British Columbia and a subsequent fellowship at Harvard Medical School/Massachusetts General Hospital. At Concordia, he directs the Anxiety and Obsessive-Compulsive Disorders Laboratory. His research investigates obsessive-compulsive disorder and a number of other anxiety disorders from a cognitive-behavioural perspective. He has received several national and international awards for his work, including the Canadian Psychological Association President's New Researcher Award and Canadian Institutes of Health Research (CIHR) New Investigator Award, and was named a Beck Institute Scholar.

Dr. Radomsky has published a number of peer-reviewed articles and book chapters related to his work on cognition, behaviour, and anxiety disorders, and is a frequent speaker at national and international conferences. His research is funded by CIHR and by the Natural Sciences and Engineering Research Council of Canada. Dr. Radomsky is a scientific advisor to the Québec OCD Foundation, and was a co-chair of the Scientific Advisory Committee of the Anxiety Disorders Association of Canada. He is a member of l'Ordre des psychologues du Québec and is a diplomate in cognitive therapy with the Academy of Cognitive Therapy. In his clinical practice he specializes in cognitive-behavioural therapy for anxiety and obsessive-compulsive disorders.

How did you become interested in the study of anxiety disorders?

I first became interested in the study of anxiety disorders during my undergraduate introductory psychology class on classical conditioning at the University of Toronto. The class was attended by more than 1800 students (a very large class indeed) and the instructor fired a starter's pistol each time he said "CS" (for conditioned stimulus), very quickly conditioning all of us to experience a startle response upon hearing the letters "CS." I was fascinated by how quickly, commonly, and easily fear/startle conditioning took place that day, and wanted to know more about how these factors played a role in the etiology and treatment of anxiety disorders.

What do you think of the proposed changes to the DSM-5 classification of anxiety disorders?

There are always pros and cons to proposed changes to the DSM. What's most relevant for me is that psychologists used to use the DSM only reluctantly, preferring to generate specific formulations of our clients' problems based on their individual experiences and our knowledge about the science of anxious psychopathology. I fear that we have lost this emphasis in our work. There are problems inherent to any classification system and, although the DSM is a necessary document, too much importance is placed on its use, and not enough is placed on arriving at a detailed understanding of the nuances underlying each individual's specific anxiety problem.

What is your general approach to the treatment of anxiety disorders?

My approach to the treatment of anxiety disorders is cognitive-behavioural, but with an emphasis on developing a cognitive formulation of the problem, followed by collaboratively implementing a cognitively based solution. Although exposure is a powerful and effective strategy, its importance in the treatment of anxiety disorders has been overplayed and dramatically overemphasized. I prefer an evidence-based emphasis on behavioural experiments designed to test hypotheses stemming from the case formulation. This approach allows for close collaboration with the client and for immense flexibility and creativity on the part of the therapist.

What do you see as the hot topics in the area of anxiety disorders?

Hot topics in the area of anxiety disorders include finding ways to make existing (primarily behavioural) treatments more acceptable to those struggling with the full range of anxiety disorders, finding effective and efficient ways to train CBT therapists, and developing novel evdence-based cognitive-behavioural techniques, which will hopefully provide an increasing number of alternatives to traditional exposure. Many of these newer interventions appear to result from advances in cognitive science and information processing research. A current and controversial interest of mine relates to a re-examination of the role of safety behaviour in the cognitive-behavioural treatment of anxiety disorders.

that have investigated the combination of medication and ERP, although not conclusive, indicate that it is no better than ERP alone (Barlow, 2002; Franklin, Abramowitz, Bux, Zoellner, & Feeny, 2002). In a report developed for Health Canada, Antony and Swinson (1996) suggested that, all things considered, cognitive-behavioural interventions are the treatment of choice for OCD.

TREATMENT OF POST-TRAUMATIC STRESS DISORDER

The treatment of PTSD typically involves facing the trauma (using imaginal exposure) and discussing it in detail. By doing so, patients begin to realize that these are indeed memories rather than ongoing events and can make sense of them and integrate them with other aspects of their lives.

Ehlers and Clark (2000, pp. 336, 337) suggest that a useful analogy is to "compare the trauma memory to a cupboard in which many things have been thrown in quickly and in a disorganised fashion, so it is impossible to fully close the door and things fall out at unpredictable times. Organising the cupboard will mean looking at each of the things and putting them into their place. Once this is done, the door can be closed and remains shut." An underlying assumption of cognitive processing theories is that a traumatic event creates a discrepancy between new information (e.g., witnessing a homicide) and one's prior schemas (e.g., that the world is a safe place). Overall, imaginal exposure and cognitive reprocessing strategies are effective for the treatment of PTSD.

Another approach that has been used for a considerable period of time is psychological debriefing. Often a critical incident stress debriefing team will meet with individuals shortly after a traumatic event (for example, after the Dawson College shootings in Montreal on September 13, 2006). This brief intervention is intended to help survivors of trauma express their feelings related to the trauma and normalize their reactions. Although the purpose of psychological debriefing is to prevent PTSD, Ehlers and Clark (2003) have found that intervening too early (i.e., within one month of the trauma) is not effective and can in fact make matters worse, increasing rather than decreasing the likelihood that individuals will develop PTSD.

TREATMENT OF GENERALIZED ANXIETY DISORDER

Benzodiazepines are commonly used to treat GAD. Studies have shown that this class of medications is effective in reducing 65 to 70 percent of symptoms in the short term (Roemer, Orsillo, & Barlow, 2002). The long-term outcome data are not encouraging, though. Many patients experience an increase in symptoms while on these medications, and relapse following treatment is common. In addition, the long-term use of benzodiazepines can result in the development of tolerance and physical dependence (Ashton, 2005). Other pharmacological treatments (e.g., antidepressants and azapirones) are also used with some positive results. CBT is the most highly recommended psychological therapy for GAD (Ouimet, Covin, & Dozois, in press), and a number of variants of CBT have been developed for treating this disorder. Michel Dugas (Concordia University), for example, has been instrumental in developing the notion of intolerance of uncertainty (IU) and in testing new approaches aimed at reducing it in treatment (e.g., Dugas & Robichaud, 2007). A meta-analysis conducted by researchers at the University of Western Ontario found that CBT results in a significant reduction of pathological worry (the core symptom of GAD), with the largest effects stemming from the intervention developed by Dugas and his colleagues (Covin, Ouimet, Seeds, & Dozois, 2008).

COMMENT ON TREATMENTS THAT WORK

CBT is regarded as the treatment of choice for anxiety disorders. Yet the majority of individuals who suffer from anxiety do not seek psychological treatment, and those that do often do not receive referrals for the most effective treatments (Collins, Westra, Dozois, & Burns, 2004). The national mental health survey (Health Canada, 2002) reported that only 32 percent of individuals with mental health problems had contact with a health care professional in the past year. A Toronto study found that only 12 percent of individuals who sought help for an anxiety disorder received treatment (Ohayon, Shapiro, & Kennedy, 2000). It is imperative that we enhance awareness among the public, physicians, and other mental health providers that psychologists have a number of effective evidence-based treatments for anxiety disorders (see Collins et al., 2004).

SUMMARY

- There are three distinctive components of emotion: physiology, cognition, and behaviour. When anxiety occurs, we might expect to see increased heart rate and breathing (physiology). The individual may also experience thoughts such as "Something terrible will happen" (cognition), and avoid the anxiety-provoking trigger (behaviour). Anxiety is distinct from panic and fear. Although these are all emotional states, in anxiety the individual feels threatened by a potential future event. In fear, the individual responds to a present or perceived threat. Panic is similar to fear but, in contrast to fear, which is often in response to an objective threat, panic is extreme and can be triggered in the absence of an actual threat.
- Three main etiological factors are known to be involved in anxiety disorders: biological, psychological, and interpersonal. Biological factors encompass genetic heritability and the role of brain systems, including the amygdala and neurochemicals such as GABA. Learning (a psychological factor) and attachment influences (interpersonal factors) are also contributing factors.
- Methods of assessment include the use of structured and semi-structured interviews to establish if the individual meets diagnostic criteria for a particular disorder. Behavioural and psychophysiological indices are sometimes used to measure severity and to determine how the disorder is manifested. For example, the clinician could measure heart and breathing rates in an individual who describes

having panic attacks or behavioural avoidance in an individual with social phobia. Self-report measures are also an invaluable part of assessment. These reports can measure each individual's self-reported behaviour, symptoms, and emotions.

- Etiological models of anxiety disorders include the two-factor theory, the equipotentiality premise, and the nonassociative model. Concepts important to understanding anxiety disorders include panic attacks, compulsions, and obsessions.
- This chapter highlighted descriptions of the major anxiety disorders listed in DSM-IV: panic disorder with and without agoraphobia, specific phobia, social phobia, OCD, GAD, and PTSD.
- Interventions include pharmacotherapy, cognitive restructuring, exposure techniques, problem solving, relaxation, and other techniques such as exercise and mindfulness strategies.

MySearchLab offers you extensive help with your writing and research projects and provides round-the-clock access to credible and reliable source material. Chapter quizzes and a full electronic version of the text are also provided. Answers to the Before Moving On feature are provided on the MySearchLab. Take a tour at www.mysearchlab.com.

KEY TERMS

anxiety (p. 97)
fear (p. 97)
"fight or flight" response (p. 97)
panic (p. 97)
neurosis (p. 97)
two-factor theory (p. 99)
vicarious learning (p. 99)
panic attack (p. 100)
agoraphobia (p. 101)
behavioural avoidance test (BAT) (p. 102)
nocturnal panic (p. 103)
catastrophic misinterpretation (p. 103)
anxiety sensitivity (p. 103)
alarm theory (p. 103)
illness phobia (p. 104)
equipotentiality premise (p. 104)
nonassociative model (p. 104)
biological preparedness (p. 105)
disgust sensitivity (p. 105)
obsessions (p. 110)
compulsions (p. 110)
neutralizations (p. 110)
thought-action fusion (TAF) (p. 110)
emotional numbing (p. 115)
intolerance of uncertainty (IU) (p. 119)
systematic desensitization (p. 122)
fear hierarchy (p. 122)
in vivo exposure (p. 122)
worry imagery exposure (p. 122)
flooding (intense exposure) (p. 122)
interoceptive exposure (p. 122)
ritual prevention (p. 122)
subtle avoidance (p. 123)

ROD A. MARTIN

Chapter 6

Dissociative and Somatoform Disorders

LEARNING OBJECTIVES

AFTER READING THIS CHAPTER, STUDENTS WILL BE ABLE TO:

1. Describe the symptoms and clinical features of the major dissociative disorders.
2. Compare and contrast two competing theories of the etiology of dissociative identity disorder.
3. Describe the symptoms and clinical features of the major somatoform disorders.
4. Explain how biological, psychological, and social-environmental factors can work together to cause somatoform disorders.
5. Discuss the goals and methods of contemporary psychological treatments for somatoform disorders.

Kathy is 35 years old and has been in and out of the mental health system for approximately 15 years. Her previous therapists have given her a number of diagnoses, including generalized anxiety disorder and borderline personality disorder. During an initial assessment, her current psychotherapist learned that Kathy had an extensive history of sexual abuse perpetrated by her father and grandfather. Kathy told the therapist that when she was a child she often felt like a robot, and described herself as feeling "dead from the neck down" when she was repeatedly raped by these family members. The psychologist noted that there were sizable gaps in Kathy's memory of her psychosocial history and that she was better able to recount her history on some days compared to others. Her therapist also began to notice dramatic changes in Kathy's appearance from one day to the next. For example, on one day she would be dressed provocatively, wearing a great deal of makeup, and on other days she would be dressed conservatively, with little makeup and her hair pulled into a bun. The psychologist decided to work with Kathy to help her cope with her history of sexual abuse, beginning very slowly by helping her build her trust until she felt comfortable in the therapy sessions. After a year of working together, Kathy feels comfortable enough with her psychologist to tell her about the other personalities she experiences, something she has not been able to do previously.

***

Casey is a 30-year-old man who is very afraid that he might die of cancer, as his mother did several years ago. He has made frequent visits to different doctors, complaining of a pain in his left leg. He began checking for lumps in his leg several times a day and reading about cancer on the Internet. He went to the emergency room complaining of pain in his leg, thinking this a sure sign that a tumour was growing. After conducting several tests, the doctors found nothing wrong with his leg, and reported that he was in excellent physical condition. After a year without a diagnosis, Casey found that he was experiencing chest pain in addition to the pains in his leg. He went to the emergency room three times, certain that he was dying of a vicious cancer that had now spread to his lungs. Each time, the doctors assured him that, although his pains might be real, they could find no physical cause. Casey decided that the doctors were simply not competent enough to find his disease. He became increasingly frustrated and began to stay at home as much as he could to learn more about his perceived condition and to chat with cancer patients on Facebook and MSN. His relationships with family and friends have become strained, and he is becoming increasingly socially isolated.

Kathy's and Casey's cases are clinical examples of two fascinating groups of disorders known as the dissociative and somatoform disorders. Kathy has one of the most severe types of dissociative disorders, dissociative identity disorder, in which an individual has two or more distinct identities that alternate control of his or her behaviour. As a group, the dissociative disorders include a wide range of different symptoms that involve severe disruptions in consciousness, memory, and identity (Kihlstrom, 2005). Casey has hypochondriasis, a somatoform disorder in which people have long-standing beliefs that they have a serious illness despite medical reassurance to the contrary. As a group, the somatoform disorders include conditions in which individuals complain about a physical defect or dysfunction for which no medical explanation can be found.

Many clinicians and researchers believe that these disorders result from maladaptive ways of coping with extreme stress. However, as we will see, there is a great deal of debate among experts concerning the nature and causes of these disorders. Although a large clinical literature of case studies and observational reports has accumulated over more than a century, more systematic research has only begun in recent years, and our knowledge about these two groups of disorders is still quite limited.

Although the dissociative and somatoform disorders are classified as two separate diagnostic categories in DSM-IV-TR, they are strongly linked historically and share common features. In early versions of the DSM, these groups of disorders were classified together with the anxiety disorders under the general category of neuroses. It was assumed that anxiety was the predominant underlying feature in the etiology of these disorders, whether or not anxiety could be observed overtly. With DSM-III, however, the classification of psychological disorders shifted in emphasis from etiology to observable behaviour, a trend even more evident in DSM-IV. This shift resulted in the dissociative and somatoform disorders being separated into two groupings independent of the anxiety disorders, due to their different symptom presentations.

Historical Perspective

The dissociative disorders and some of the somatoform disorders were once viewed as expressions of **hysteria**. Dating back to ancient Greece, *hysteria* was a term used to describe a symptom pattern characterized by emotional excitability and physical symptoms (e.g., convulsions, paralyses, numbness, loss of vision) in the absence of any evident organic cause. Plato believed that these symptoms were caused in women by a wandering womb (*hysteros*). He thought the womb was like an animal that desired to reproduce; if it remained inactive for too long, it became angry and wandered around the body, blocking the channels of respiration and causing illness (Merskey, 1995).

With the rise of Christianity, organic theories of hysteria were replaced by supernatural explanations: dissociation and related complaints were now seen as the result of demonic possession, and exorcism was the favoured treatment (Ross, 1989). Only after the decline in acceptance of possession as an explanation for abnormal behaviour did more psychologically based theories develop. Over time, the components of hysteria were examined as separate processes, and many of the pioneers of modern psychological theories, such as Alfred Binet, Jean-Martin Charcot, and Carl Jung, wrote about dissociative and somatizing processes. Pierre Janet, a French philosophy professor who trained with Charcot, was the first to systematically study the concept of dissociation, which he viewed as a pathological breakdown in the normal integration of mental processes, occurring as a result of exposure to traumatic experiences (van der Kolk & van der Hart, 1989).

Around the same time, Josef Breuer and Sigmund Freud, in their classic 1895 publication *Studies in Hysteria*, posited that trauma, often of a sexual nature, was a predisposing factor for hysteria and established a relationship between dissociation and hypnotic-like states. They described in some detail the usefulness of hypnosis in the treatment of such patients. The book consisted primarily of case studies of female patients suffering from dissociation, most of whom had been sexually abused.

"Anna O." (Bertha Pappenheim; 1859–1936) developed a bizarre range of physical and psychological symptoms. Her case was influential in the development of Freud's ideas.

Several of these patients also suffered from somatoform disorders. For example, the first case described "Anna O.," a 21-year-old woman treated by Breuer who developed visual and hearing problems, total paralysis of both legs and her right arm, partial paralysis of her left arm, a nervous cough, and periods of disturbed consciousness in which she seemed to be quite a different person. The classic Freudian view of somatoform and dissociative disorders began with such cases and was modified over several years. Freud eventually began to doubt the accuracy of his patients' retrospective reports of traumatic sexual abuse and decided instead that their memories of trauma were fantasized and not real. He believed that dissociation and other intrapsychic defences developed in order to protect individuals from their unacceptable sexual impulses, not from real traumatic memories.

Freud also viewed conversion symptoms as expressions of unconscious psychological conflicts. He suggested that "conversion" of anxiety to more acceptable physical symptoms relieved the pressure of having to deal directly with the conflict. This avoidance of conflict was termed *primary gain*, and was viewed as the primary reinforcement maintaining the somatoform symptoms. Freud also recognized that hysterical symptoms could help a patient avoid responsibility and gain attention and sympathy, referring to these reinforcements as *secondary gains* of the symptoms. The term *secondary gain* is still commonly used today to refer to the benefits a patient may either unknowingly or knowingly seek by adopting the sick role.

The study of dissociation has followed a particularly interesting course through history. After a peak of interest in the last two decades of the nineteenth century, interest in dissociative processes dropped off exponentially during the early part of the twentieth century (Goettman, Greaves, & Coons, 1994). This decrease in interest has been attributed to many factors, including the rise of behaviourism and biological approaches within psychology, which did not allow for the study of internal states such as consciousness (Ross, 1996). However, a resurgence of interest in dissociative processes took place from the 1970s to the 1990s. This renewal of interest was shaped by several events, including the publication of popular accounts of cases of multiple personality, the inclusion of dissociative identity disorder in the DSM-III (published in 1980), and new research into consciousness and hypnosis (Hilgard, 1986). More recently, though, interest in dissociative disorders appears to have waned once again, with the annual number of scientific publications on this topic dropping in the first few years of the twenty-first century to only about 25 percent of its peak level in the 1990s (Pope, Barry, Bodkin, & Hudson, 2006). Many researchers now believe that dissociative disorders were overdiagnosed in recent decades when they enjoyed a brief "bubble" of fashion that has now declined.

1 BEFORE MOVING ON

Why were dissociative and somatoform disorders traditionally grouped together in early diagnostic systems, and why were they divided into separate diagnostic groups with the publication of DSM-III?

Dissociative Disorders

Dissociative disorders are characterized by severe maladaptive disruptions or alterations of identity, memory, and consciousness that are experienced as being beyond one's control. The defining symptom of these disorders is **dissociation**, the lack of normal integration of thoughts, feelings, and experiences in consciousness and memory (Bernstein & Putnam, 1986). Normally, there is a unity in our consciousness that gives rise to our sense of self. We know who we are. We know our names, where we live, and what we do for a living. But for individuals with dissociative disorders, these simple aspects of daily living are bizarrely disturbed and remain unintegrated, so that a coherent sense of self does not always exist.

Dissociation itself is not necessarily a pathological process. In fact, a certain degree of dissociation can be harmless and, in some cases, even adaptive (Barlow & Freyd, 2009). If you have ever become lost in a daydream or become so absorbed in a book or movie that you forgot about your surroundings and the passage of time, you have had a mild dissociative experience. Dissociative experiences of this sort are commonly reported in the general population (Gershuny & Thayer, 1999; Ross, 1996). If normal functioning is not impaired by these occasional lapses and if the person can "snap out of it," there is no concern about pathological dissociation. However, a problem exists when one is unable to control these drifts of consciousness or behaviour and they affect one's ability to function in everyday life.

There are also fairly stable individual differences in the degree to which individuals tend to have dissociative experiences: some people dissociate more frequently than others (Carlson, Yates, & Sroufe, 2009). Dissociative tendency is related to other personality traits such as hypnotizability. Research by Waller, Putnam, and Carlson (1996) indicates that dissociative experiences fall into two groups. The first group involves mild, non-pathological forms of dissociation, such as absorption and imaginative involvement, that are normally distributed on a continuum across the general population. The second group involves more severe, pathological types of experiences, such as amnesia, derealization, depersonalization, and identity alteration, that do not normally occur in the general population and that form a discrete category or *taxon*. Psychological trauma and emotional distress are commonly viewed as causal factors in such pathological forms of dissociation.

Four types of dissociative disorders will be discussed in this chapter: dissociative amnesia, dissociative fugue, depersonalization disorder, and dissociative identity disorder, which, prior to the publication of DSM-IV, was commonly referred to as multiple personality disorder. Table 6.1 outlines the characteristics of these four disorders.

TABLE 6.1 TYPES OF DISSOCIATIVE DISORDERS

Disorder	Description	Comments
Dissociative amnesia	Inability to recall important personal information	Can be used as a legal defence. Suppressed memories of sexual abuse would fit into this category.
Dissociative fugue	Sudden, unexpected flight from home; inability to remember past and who one is	Typically, someone turns up in another province or country wandering about, unaware of his or her identity.
Dissociative identity disorder	Presence of two or more personalities	Formerly known as multiple personality disorder. The classic case is *The Three Faces of Eve* (Thigpen & Cleckley, 1957).
Depersonalization disorder	Feeling of being detached from oneself	Depersonalization experienced for a short period of time is very common and not pathological.

FOCUS 6.1 Repressed Memory or False Memory?

At the age of 23, Alana sought help from a therapist because of feelings of depression and difficulty establishing meaningful relationships. After several sessions of therapy involving the use of hypnosis to help her recall her early relationship with her father, Alana remembered, in a vague way at first but subsequently in increasing detail, that her father had sexually abused her during her childhood. She was shocked but learned from her therapist that these traumatic memories had been **repressed** so that she could survive in her family for all these years. Although Alana had been somewhat distant from her father, she had not remembered this abuse for 17 years. She confronted her parents, and both her father and her mother vehemently denied any sexual abuse. With support from her therapist, Alana took her accusation to the police, who, after some investigation, charged her father with sexual abuse.

Alana's father claimed total innocence. After he was charged, he consulted a lawyer and learned about **false memory syndrome** (Loftus & Davis, 2006), a proposed condition in which people are induced by therapists to remember events that never occurred. Loftus and other researchers posit that some therapists unwittingly implant these memories by using leading questions and repeated suggestion while patients are under hypnosis. Several experiments have been conducted to demonstrate the existence of illusory or distorted memories and the idea that false memories can successfully be produced. For example, a study by Loftus and Pickrell (1995) showed that adults could be convinced that they had been lost for an extended period of time when they were about five years old, after a trusted companion was recruited to "plant" this memory.

On the other side of this debate, proponents of recovered memory therapy point to research evidence indicating that early traumatic experiences can cause selective dissociative amnesia (Gleaves, 1996; Kluft, 1999), although critics have noted methodological weaknesses in these studies (Kihlstrom, 2005). The concept of repressed memory derives from Freudian theory, which suggests that very traumatic events can be entirely forgotten in order to protect the child from the severe anxiety associated with the event. Research examining the effects of stress on the neurobiology of memory supports a link between trauma and amnesia. Studies have shown that extreme stress can have long-term effects on memory, by altering brain regions and neurochemicals responsible for memory functions (Bremner, 2001).

However, critics of the trauma–repression hypothesis have noted that it is based on the faulty assumption that the mind records memories of childhood accurately, and that these recorded memories can be repressed and then recovered at a later time through psychotherapy or hypnosis. These assumptions are contradicted by a considerable amount of memory research indicating that most experiences are not recorded as with a video camera, but are distorted by various life events (Paris, 1996). Furthermore, most memories are far from factually correct. In fact, as Loftus (1993) has pointed out, experimentally implanted false memories, once they are accepted as true by participants, are reported as fact with enormous conviction and are often embellished over time.

A further complicating factor is that it is generally not possible to establish the accuracy of a recovered traumatic memory. Recent functional magnetic resonance imaging (fMRI) studies have attempted to determine whether differences between true and false memories can be detected by means of brain scans, but little progress has been made in this area to date (e.g., Baym & Gonsalves, 2010). At present, there is no objective way to determine whether a memory elicited in psychotherapy is true or false, aside from corroborating evidence, which is often not available. On the other hand, there is considerable evidence that hypnosis can implant highly detailed but untrue memories.

The highly controversial issue of repressed memory is not likely to be resolved soon. Because false memories can be created through strong repeated suggestions, therapists need to be very careful about making suggestions of early abuse when patients do not raise the topic themselves. On the other hand, it is also possible that people who have experienced extreme abuse or trauma could have dissociated these memories from awareness. Advocates on both sides of this issue agree that clinical research needs to focus on identifying the conditions under which the implantation of false memories is likely and to define markers that indicate real traumatic amnesia. In the meantime, mental health professionals must be extremely careful not to cause unnecessary suffering to either victims of actual trauma or victims falsely accused as abusers. ●

PREVALENCE

Not surprisingly, dissociation is more common among psychiatric patients than the general population. Studies of the prevalence of dissociative disorders in adult psychiatric inpatient populations suggest that as many as 15 to 21 percent of inpatients in Canada have some kind of dissociative disorder (Horen, Leichner, & Lawson, 1995; Ross, Anderson, Fleisher, & Norton, 1991). A study of adult outpatients at an inner-city psychiatric facility found that as many as 29 percent met the criteria for diagnosis of a dissociative disorder (Foote, Smolin, Kaplan, Legatt, & Lipschitz, 2006). To determine the prevalence of dissociative disorders in the general population, Johnson and colleagues (2006) conducted structured clinical interviews with a representative sample of 658 adults from New York State. They found that 9.1 percent of these individuals could be diagnosed with dissociative disorders, including 0.8 percent with depersonalization disorder, 1.8 percent with dissociative amnesia, 1.5 percent with dissociative identity disorder, and 5.5 percent with dissociative disorder not otherwise specified. No cases of dissociative fugue were found in this sample. There were no differences between men and women in the prevalence of these disorders, and they were slightly more common in younger than in older adults. This study also found high rates of comorbidity with other psychological disorders, including anxiety disorders, mood disorders, and personality disorders.

Dissociative Amnesia

The primary symptom of **dissociative amnesia** is the inability to recall significant personal information in the absence of organic impairment. Typically, this amnesia occurs following a traumatic event, such as an automobile accident or battlefield experiences during wartime. Afflicted individuals usually have no memory of the precipitating traumatic event, and may be unable to recall their own name, occupation, and other autobiographical information, even though they may still retain general knowledge of world events, such as the name of the current prime minister of Canada. In many cases, the amnesia remits spontaneously within a few days after the person is in a safe environment. In other cases, amnesia can be more chronic or recurrent. Five patterns of memory loss characteristic of dissociative amnesia are described in DSM-IV-TR, including (1) *localized amnesia,* wherein the person fails to recall information from a very specific time period (e.g., the events immediately surrounding a trauma); (2) *selective amnesia,* wherein only parts of the trauma are forgotten while other parts are remembered; (3) *generalized amnesia,* wherein the person forgets all personal information from his or her past; (4) *continuous amnesia,* wherein the individual forgets information from a specific date until the present; and (5) *systematized amnesia,* wherein the individual only forgets certain categories of information, such as certain people or places. The latter three patterns of memory loss are less common, usually associated with more significant psychopathology, and are more commonly associated with a diagnosis of dissociative identity disorder. For the proposed revision of DSM-5, the diagnostic criteria for dissociative amnesia remain largely unchanged from DSM-IV-TR (APA, 2010).

2 BEFORE MOVING ON

Amnesia can also result from brain damage due to various causes (e.g., car accident, Alzheimer's disease). How might clinicians distinguish between these types of organic amnesia and dissociative amnesia?

Dissociative Fugue

Dissociative fugue is an extremely rare and unusual condition in which an individual travels suddenly and unexpectedly away from home, accompanied by a loss of memory for one's past and personal identity. Some individuals travel thousands of miles from their home before they recall their personal history. Frequently, the individual has left behind an intolerable situation. The disorder is usually brief in duration, lasting from a few days to a few weeks, but there are rare cases where the individual disappears for a prolonged period of time. The behaviour of individuals presenting with dissociative fugue is not all that unusual; they are able to function reasonably well and may even successfully adopt a new identity and occupation if the disorder is prolonged. Disturbance or confusion will only be noted if the individual is questioned about his or her personal history. Dissociative fugue may end either abruptly or gradually with persistent confusion or amnesia about identity. Often, those who have recovered from the disorder report no memory of what occurred during the fugue state.

Dissociative fugue is probably the least understood dissociative disorder, due in part to the fact that most of these patients do not present for treatment. If they do seek treatment, patients often present themselves to emergency rooms complaining of memory loss that resolves after a relatively short period of time (Coons, 1998). The incidence of dissociative fugue has been reported to increase during times of greater stress, such as during war or following a natural disaster. Child abuse, severe marital or financial distress, and/or sexual indiscretions are events thought to be precipitating factors in this condition. Comorbid diagnoses of mood disorders and substance abuse are frequently found (Coons, 1999).

In the proposed revision of DSM-5, dissociative fugue will no longer be a separate diagnosis, but instead will be subsumed as a subtype of dissociative amnesia (APA, 2010). This change reflects a view of fugue as a particular type of amnesia involving an inability to recall one's identity along with sudden, unexpected travel away from home (Ross, 2009).

Depersonalization Disorder

Depersonalization is an experience in which individuals feel a sense of unreality and detachment from themselves. Fleeting experiences of depersonalization are relatively common, with approximately half of the general population reporting such symptoms, often during times of stress (Reutens, Nielsen, & Sachdev, 2010). As a symptom, depersonalization can also occur in several different disorders. In fact, it is the third most commonly reported clinical symptom among psychiatric patients, after depression and anxiety. **Depersonalization disorder** is diagnosed only when severe depersonalization is the primary problem, and when the symptoms are persistent and cause clinically significant impairment or distress. Individuals with this disorder experience recurrent episodes of depersonalization, in which they feel as though they are living in a dream, observing their own mental processes or body from the outside, or as if time is moving slowly. They commonly describe feeling like a robot that is able to respond to their environment, but without feeling connected to their actions (Simeon, 2009). This disorder is often also accompanied by episodes of **derealization**, an experience of detachment and altered relationship to the surrounding world, in which the person perceives people and objects in the environment as unreal, dreamlike, distant, or distorted. In the proposed revision of DSM-5, the name of this disorder will be changed to *depersonalization/derealization disorder*, with the diagnostic criteria requiring symptoms of either depersonalization or derealization or both (APA, 2010).

Unlike the other dissociative disorders, depersonalization disorder does not tend to be characterized by memory impairment or identity confusion. This disorder typically begins in adolescence and tends to be chronic in nature. Studies by Simeon and colleagues (1997, 2001) suggest that this disorder is highly related to a history of trauma, particularly emotional abuse. High rates of comorbidity with anxiety, depression, personality disorders, and other dissociative disorders have been found (Simeon, Knutelska, Nelson, & Guralnik, 2003). Laboratory research suggests that individuals with depersonalization disorder have reduced emotional reactivity to stressful or emotionally arousing stimuli (Sierra et al., 2002; Simeon, Guralnik, Knutelska, Yehuda, & Schmeidler, 2003; Stanton et al., 2001), as well as cognitive disruptions in perceptual and attentional processes (Guralnik, Giesbrecht, Knutelska, Sirroff, & Simeon, 2007). The mechanisms for these emotional and cognitive deficits are still not clear, although medical imaging research by Simeon and colleagues (2000) suggests that brain abnormalities in perceptual pathways may play a role.

Dissociative Identity Disorder

We all wear many hats or play different roles. For example, many of us could describe ourselves as students, siblings, Canadians, employees, partners, or spouses. In addition, it is not unusual to behave quite differently depending on the role we are playing. For example, you might appear to be a more patient person when dealing with difficult customers at your job than you are at home when your partner fails to take out the trash. For most of us, it is not difficult to juggle these multiple roles or identities and adopt the behaviour most appropriate to a particular setting. We remain conscious of these shifts and, no matter how many different roles we must play within a particular day, we continue to have the experience of being a single person with one consciousness.

Dissociative identity disorder (DID) (formerly known as *multiple personality disorder*) is one of the most controversial and fascinating disorders recognized in clinical psychology. This unusual disorder is diagnosed when the patient presents with two or more distinct personality states that regularly take control of the patient's behaviour. The DSM-IV-TR diagnostic criteria for DID are listed in Table 6.2. Typically, in DID, one of the personalities is identified as the "host," whereas subsequent personalities are identified as **alters**. Each of the personalities is distinct and presents with different memories, personal histories, and mannerisms. Different personalities may identify themselves as men or women, as adults or children, or more rarely as animals. Some researchers have reported differences between alters in terms of eyeglass prescriptions, EEG patterns, allergies, and other physical parameters (Nijenhuis & den Boer, 2009). Some personalities may be less evolved and only represent certain emotional states such as rage or despair. The host personality may or may not be aware of the presence of one or more of the alters and may report strange occurrences, such as strangers claiming to know them and calling them by another name, or new articles of clothing appearing in their wardrobe that they do not recall purchasing. Although the number of alters can range from 1 additional personality to more than 100, the average number appears to be somewhere between 13 and 16 (Coons, 1998; Ross et al., 1989).

The process of changing from one personality to another is referred to as **switching**. Switching often occurs in response to a stressful situation, such as an argument with a spouse, or physical or sexual abuse, and may also occur if the therapist makes a request while the individual is hypnotized. The switch may or may not be dramatic enough to grab the attention of others, and may involve eye blinking or eye rolling (Coons, 1998). The presence of a new alter may also lead to a change in the tone of voice, demeanour, or posture of the individual.

The average age at diagnosis of DID is 29 to 35 years and this disorder is diagnosed three to nine times more frequently in women than in men (APA, 2000). Self-destructive behaviour is common among people with DID, including self-inflicted burns, wrist slashing, and overdosing. About 75 percent of patients with DID have a history of suicide attempts and more than 90 percent report recurrent suicidal thoughts (Ross, 1997). DID is chronic by nature and patients often spend six to seven years seeking help from a variety of therapists for other problems, such as depression or anxiety, before they are diagnosed with the disorder. Not surprisingly, given the severity of this

TABLE 6.2 DSM-IV-TR DIAGNOSTIC CRITERIA FOR DISSOCIATIVE IDENTITY DISORDER

A. The presence of two or more distinct identities or personality states (each with its own relatively enduring pattern of perceiving, relating to, and thinking about the environment and self).

B. At least two of these identities or personality states recurrently take control of the person's behavior.

C. Inability to recall important personal information that is too extensive to be explained by ordinary forgetfulness.

D. The disturbance is not due to the direct physiological effects of a substance (e.g., blackouts or chaotic behavior during Alcohol Intoxication) or a general medical condition (e.g., complex partial seizures). **Note:** In children, the symptoms are not attributable to imaginary playmates or other fantasy play.

Source: Reprinted with permission from the *Diagnostic and Statistical Manual of Mental Disorders, Fourth Edition, Text Revision.* (Copyright © 2000). American Psychiatric Association.

condition, patients with DID often have multiple diagnoses, including depression, post-traumatic stress disorder, borderline personality disorder, substance abuse disorders, eating disorders, and various anxiety disorders (Rodewald, Wilhelm-Gossling, Emrich, Reddemann, & Gast, 2011). The clinical picture is complex, and these patients have developed a reputation for being notoriously difficult to treat. Once diagnosed, most specialists in the area agree that several years of therapy are required before there is the possibility of integration of the host and alter personalities (Kluft, 1999).

There is a great deal of debate among mental health professionals about the prevalence of DID, and even about the legitimacy of this diagnosis. Only about 200 cases of dissociative identity disorder were reported in the entire world literature prior to 1980 (Greaves, 1980). Over the next two decades, however, diagnoses of this disorder increased exponentially. By 1986, it was estimated that 6000 cases had been diagnosed in North America (Coons, 1986), and many thousands more appeared in subsequent years. In recent years, however, the number of diagnoses has dropped precipitously (Pope et al., 2006). This dramatic rise and fall in prevalence has led some practitioners to believe that the disorder was overdiagnosed in highly suggestible people by well-intentioned but overly zealous clinicians. This view will be explored further in the next section.

Etiology

Our knowledge of the causes of the dissociative disorders is minimal compared to many other Axis I disorders, such as the mood and anxiety disorders. As noted previously, this issue has generated a great deal of debate, particularly with regard to the etiology of DID. Two competing explanatory models have been proposed: the trauma model and the socio-cognitive model. The **trauma model**, which is a diathesis-stress formulation, has a long history and continues to be widely accepted by many clinicians and researchers. According to this model, dissociative disorders are a result of severe childhood trauma, including sexual, physical, and emotional abuse, accompanied by personality traits that predispose the individual to employ dissociation as a defence mechanism or coping strategy. Initially, dissociation may be an adaptive response to traumatic events that helps individuals cope with their trauma. For a chronically abused child, for example, dissociation offers a means of escape when no other means is possible. If the child can escape into a fantasy world and become somebody else, and if this escape blunts the physical and emotional pain temporarily, he or she will likely do it again. However, this defence mechanism is no longer adaptive when it is maintained as a habitual way of coping throughout adulthood.

Not all people who are abused as children or who experience other types of trauma develop dissociative disorders. According to the trauma model, certain personality traits, such as high hypnotizability, fantasy proneness, and openness to altered states of consciousness, may represent a diathesis, predisposing some individuals to develop dissociative experiences in the face of trauma. These personality traits themselves do not lead to dissociative disorders (Rauschenberger & Lynn, 1995). However, they may increase the risk that people who undergo severe trauma will develop dissociative processes to cope with this trauma. In contrast, people who are low in dissociative tendencies may develop anxious, intrusive thoughts rather than a dissociative reaction (Kirmayer, Robbins, & Paris, 1994).

There may also be a genetic heritability component to these personality traits that makes some individuals more vulnerable to dissociative disorders. Some studies comparing identical and fraternal twins have found that genetic factors account for approximately 50 percent of the variance in dissociative symptoms (Becker-Blease et al., 2004; Jang, Paris, Zweig-Frank, & Livesley, 1998). There is also evidence for heritability of the related traits of hypnotizability, absorption, and fantasy proneness (Morgan, 1973; Tellegen et al., 1988). However, at least one study has failed to find evidence for heritability of pathological dissociative tendencies (Waller & Ross, 1997).

Some researchers have advanced the notion that attachment theory can also help to explain why some people are more vulnerable to dissociative disorders (Harari, Bakermans-Kranenburg, & van Ijzendoorn, 2007; Liotti, 2009). According to attachment theory, sensitive responding by the parent to an infant's needs results in a child who demonstrates secure attachment, developing the skills and confidence necessary to relate to others later in adult life. The lack of such sensitive responding by the caregiver results in insecure attachment, wherein children lack confidence in relations with others. One type of insecure attachment style observed in infants has been labelled the "disorganized pattern," which is characterized by inconsistent, contradictory behaviours when faced with stress, including stereotypical and anomalous movements or postures, freezing, and trance-like states. Attachment researchers have noted similarities between these behaviours and dissociative states, and have proposed that disorganized attachment may be a risk factor for the development of pathological dissociation in adult life (Liotti, 2009; Main & Morgan, 1996). Several studies suggest that disorganized attachment is most likely to occur in infants whose parents have experienced unresolved losses and other traumatic events and who relate to the child in ways that are frightening and unpredictable (Hesse, Main, Abrams, & Rifkin, 2003). Disorganized attachment by itself does not necessarily lead to the development of dissociative disorders, but when individuals with this attachment style also experience overwhelming trauma, they may be particularly vulnerable to developing a dissociative disorder (Lieberman, Chu, van Horn, & Harris, 2011). Research evidence in support of this theory includes a longitudinal study by Carlson (1998), which found that individuals who had a disorganized attachment style in infancy were more likely to develop dissociative symptoms in adolescence, particularly if they had experienced childhood trauma. In addition, West and colleagues (2001) investigated a sample of Canadian adolescents receiving psychiatric treatment and found a significant association between disorganized attachment and dissociative symptomatology.

In contrast to the trauma model, the **socio-cognitive model** represents a very different etiological position that is taken by many mental health professionals who do not accept DID as a legitimate disorder. The late psychologist Nick Spanos, who was a professor at Carleton University in Ottawa, was a leading proponent of this model of DID. According to this perspective, multiple personality is a form of role-playing in which individuals come to construe themselves as possessing multiple selves and then begin to act in ways consistent with their own or their therapist's conception of the disorder. Spanos (1996) did not suggest that these individuals were faking or malingering their illness, but did assert that it is entirely possible to alter one's personal history so that it is consistent with the belief that one has DID. Spanos believed that therapists' leading questions, cues, and other demand characteristics play an important role in the generation and maintenance of this disorder.

This view has also been championed by Harold Merskey, a psychiatrist and professor emeritus at the University of Western Ontario (Merskey, 1992; Piper & Merskey, 2004a, 2004b). Merskey (1992) argued that DID is an **iatrogenic** (literally meaning "caused by treatment") condition, which means that it is largely caused by therapists themselves during the course of therapy. While treating emotionally troubled individuals by means of hypnosis, therapists may plant suggestions in their patients that they have multiple personalities. Highly hypnotizable patients, who have grown up in a culture in which stories of DID are widely reported in the media, may then develop the symptoms of DID as a learned social role. In support of this view, Merskey (1992) pointed to the sharp increase in diagnosed cases of DID following the release of films that portrayed this disorder, such as *The Three Faces of Eve* and *Sybil.* Furthermore, the vast majority of cases have appeared in North America, whereas the diagnosis is quite rare in many other parts of the world, such as Europe and Japan. In addition, most cases have been reported by a relatively small number of clinicians who are strong believers in the legitimacy of this diagnosis, whereas many other clinicians who work with severely disturbed and abused patients never encounter it. These arguments have led to a considerable amount of skepticism about the trauma model of DID among many mental health professionals. Surveys of psychiatrists in Canada and the United States show that less than one quarter of these clinicians believe that DID has strong scientific validity (Lalonde, Hudson, Gigante, & Pope, 2001; Pope, Oliva, Hudson, Bodkin, & Gruber, 1999).

A critical issue dividing these two theories is whether or not DID actually develops in childhood as a result of abuse. Proponents of the socio-cognitive model point out that DID is usually diagnosed in adults and almost never observed during childhood, when it is supposed to begin (Piper & Merskey, 2004a).

Proponents of the trauma model point to a considerable amount of research evidence linking dissociative disorders with a history of trauma. For example, published research on DID indicates that more than 90 percent of diagnosed patients report severe childhood physical and/or sexual abuse (Ross, 1997). Childhood trauma or abuse is also often reported in cases of dissociative amnesia and depersonalization disorder (Coons, Bowman, Pellow, & Schneider, 1989; Simeon et al., 2001). However, critics of this view have noted that most of this research is based on adult patients' retrospective reports, which are very difficult to corroborate (Kihlstrom, 2005). Although some studies have attempted to validate patients' accounts of early abuse through the reports of close family members and court records (Coons, 1994; Yeager & Lewis, 1996), critics have pointed out many methodological weaknesses in these studies (Piper & Merskey, 2004a).

3 BEFORE MOVING ON

The trauma model and the socio-cognitive model represent two very different ways of explaining DID. What types of evidence have been used to support each of these explanations?

Treatment

PSYCHOTHERAPY

Most psychotherapies for dissociative disorders focus on helping patients resolve emotional distress associated with past traumas and learn more effective ways of coping with stress in their lives (Harper, 2011). Treatment of DID tends to be a quite prolonged and arduous process, going through a series of stages leading to the eventual integration of the various personalities (Kluft, 1999). The first stage of therapy involves the establishment of a trusting, safe environment for the patient to discuss emotionally charged memories of past trauma. The next stage begins by helping patients develop new coping skills that will be required when discussions of past history of abuse take place. Agreements for open communication between alters may be necessary to establish these new patterns of responding to stress. Therapy can then focus on remembering and grieving the abuse that the patient experienced at the hands of those who should have protected him or her. Once the patient develops more effective coping strategies and has reached a certain level of acceptance of his or her past history of abuse, therapy can move on to the final stage: integration of the personalities. Here the goal is for the alters to merge into a single personality or at least a group of alters that are working together and are aware of each other.

APPLIED CLINICAL CASE

Dissociative Fugue

On September 10, 2006, a man appeared in the emergency room of a hospital in Denver, Colorado, in obvious distress. He said he did not know his name or where he came from. Since waking up on the sidewalk with no memory of his previous life, he had been wandering the streets in confusion. Doctors at the hospital diagnosed him with dissociative fugue, and over the following weeks they tried unsuccessfully to recover his memory by means of hypnosis and sodium amytal (truth serum) treatments. After more than six weeks with no improvement, he appeared on national television, pleading for someone to recognize him. Within hours, a woman telephoned from Olympia, Washington, saying that he was her fiancé, Jeff Ingram, a 40-year-old man originally from Canada. He had disappeared after leaving on a trip to visit his parents in northern Alberta, and his family and friends had been searching frantically for him for nearly two months. When he was reunited with his fiancée and family, Jeff did not recognize them, and six months later he still had no memory of his past, although he and his fiancée were making plans for their wedding. The mystery of how he ended up in Denver was never solved.

A recent review of research on the effectiveness of several types of psychotherapy for dissociative disorders concluded that there is promising evidence of treatment effectiveness (Brand, Classen, McNary, & Zaveri, 2009). For example, approximately two-thirds of patients with DID showed substantial improvement following therapy, although fewer than one-third showed full integration of their personalities. However, the authors also noted that very little systematic research has been conducted, and most of the existing studies have methodological flaws.

HYPNOSIS

The use of hypnosis has been a popular treatment method for many clinicians working with patients with DID to confirm the diagnosis, to contact alters, and to uncover memories of traumatic childhood abuse (Kluft, 1999). However, others have criticized the use of hypnosis in this patient population because of the potential of retrieving confabulated memories and personalities.

MEDICATION

Medication is generally not useful in the direct treatment of the dissociative disorders. However, psychopharmacology may be helpful in treating comorbid disorders, such as depression and anxiety. "Truth serum" or sodium amytal, a barbiturate causing drowsiness, has sometimes been used to help the individual recall previously forgotten memories or identify additional alters. However, other psychotherapies are typically used at the same time because the chemical does not always work or the individual does not remember what was reported while under the influence of this drug.

Somatoform Disorders

The word *somatoform* derives from the Greek *soma*, meaning "body." The **somatoform disorders** are a group of disorders in which individuals have physical symptoms suggestive of medical illnesses, but no organic basis can be found to account for them, and there is reason to believe they reflect psychological factors. People with somatoform disorders do not consciously produce or control the symptoms. Instead, they truly experience them, and these symptoms typically resolve only when the psychological factors that led to them are addressed. The physical symptoms can take a number of different forms. In dramatic cases, they involve substantial impairment of a sensory or muscular system, such as reporting paralysis in one arm. In other types of somatoform disorders, the individual has numerous, constantly evolving complaints about chronic pain, upset stomach, sexual dysfunction, and symptoms suggestive of a neurological condition (e.g., double vision or seizures). Still other individuals become unduly preoccupied with the belief that they have a serious disease over a long period of time, despite negative medical tests and clear reassurance by a physician. In the proposed revision of DSM-5, this group of disorders is to be renamed *somatic symptom disorders* (APA, 2010).

Assessment of the somatoform disorders is a difficult process. Diagnosis requires that several other possibilities be ruled out. First, it must be shown that there is no physiological cause for the individual's symptoms. Sometimes such a cause can be ruled out quite easily, although most often medical diagnostic tests cannot provide definitive proof that the individual's symptoms do not have physical causes. Over the years, a number of studies have suggested that many people diagnosed with somatoform disorders were actually suffering from a physical disorder that diagnostic tests could not identify. For example, early studies found that one-quarter to one-half of all patients thought to have conversion disorders were ultimately diagnosed with medical conditions (Slater & Glithero, 1965). However, a recent review of the research found that rates of misdiagnosis have averaged only about 4 percent in recent decades, likely due to improved knowledge and diagnostic techniques (Stone et al., 2005). Clinicians must also ensure that the primary problem is not the result of direct effects of prescribed medications or illicit drugs, or another psychological disorder such as panic disorder or schizophrenia.

Another very important diagnostic consideration is whether the symptoms are a product of purposeful faking.

TABLE 6.3 SOMATOFORM DISORDERS

Disorder	Description	Comment
Somatization disorder	Multiple symptoms including pain, gastrointestinal problems, sexual problems, and pseudo-neurological symptoms.	Best described as having multiple symptoms without known cause.
Conversion disorder	Symptoms affecting voluntary motor or sensory functions, for example, hysterical blindness, paralysis, or lack of feeling (anaesthesia).	Conversion disorders are now quite unusual and are seen primarily in very poorly educated individuals or in primitive societies.
Hypochondriasis	Excessive preoccupation with the fear of having a serious illness based on misinterpretations of bodily systems when no underlying illness exists.	The most common diseases people worry about are cancer and heart disease. Often leads to "doctor shopping."
Pain disorder	Pain without sufficient known physical cause.	Pain disorder is very common and a leading cause of lost days of work.
Body dysmorphic disorder	Severe preoccupation with an imagined defect in appearance in any part of the body.	Also known as dysmorphophobia. There may be ideas of reference ("Everyone is looking at my ugly nose").

Somatoform disorders are not to be diagnosed if this is the case. DSM-IV-TR describes two conditions in which the individual intentionally pretends to be ill. In **malingering**, the individual deliberately adopts the sick role and complains of symptoms to achieve some specific objective, such as receiving insurance money, evading military service, or avoiding an exam. In the **factitious disorders** (also called ***Munchausen syndrome***), people deliberately fake or generate the symptoms of illness to gain medical attention. For example, they might take excessive amounts of laxatives, contaminate urine samples, or inject cleaning fluids into their skin to make it appear that they have a serious illness. Besides physical symptoms, factitious disorders can involve faking psychiatric symptoms, such as hallucinations or delusions. The motivation of these individuals is to gain the sympathy, care, and attention that accompany the sick role.

Several different somatoform disorders are identified in DSM-IV-TR (APA, 2000). The major categories are *conversion disorder*, *somatization disorder*, *pain disorder*, *hypochondriasis*, and *body dysmorphic disorder* (see Table 6.3).

PREVALENCE

Many patients visit their family physicians complaining of bodily symptoms for which no clear medical cause can be found. Indeed, it has been estimated that between 25 and 60 percent of visits to general medical practitioners involve such medically unexplained symptoms (Kirmayer & Looper, 2007). Medical specialists are also familiar with numerous "functional" or "idiopathic" (unexplained) physical syndromes, involving vague complaints of pain, weakness, fatigue, or gastrointestinal problems (e.g., fibromyalgia, chronic fatigue syndrome, irritable bowel syndrome). However, most of these patients do not receive a diagnosis of somatoform disorder, unless psychological factors are perceived to play an important role and the patient is therefore referred to a psychiatrist or psychologist. Consequently, although medically unexplained symptoms are very common, somatoform disorders are diagnosed relatively rarely.

A review of epidemiological studies assessing the prevalence of somatization disorder found an average prevalence of 0.4 percent in the general population (Creed & Barsky, 2004). Conversion disorders are also quite rare in the general population. One investigation found a 0.4 percent prevalence of conversion symptoms in an urban community sample (Weissman, Myers, & Harding, 1978). However, this disorder appears to be more common in neurological treatment settings, with one study estimating that 10 to 20 percent of all patients referred to epilepsy centres have non-epileptic seizures with no identifiable organic basis (Benbadis & Allen-Hauser, 2000). A review of several studies assessing the prevalence of hypochondriasis in the general population showed this to be about 5 percent (Creed & Barsky, 2004). The prevalence of body dysmorphic disorder is hard to estimate because, by its very nature, it tends to be kept secret. However, a survey of American university students found that 4 percent could be diagnosed with this disorder (Bohne, Keuthen, Wilhelm, Deckersbach, & Jenike, 2002).

Conversion Disorder

Conversion disorder is the most dramatic somatoform disorder. Individuals with this disorder have a loss of functioning in a part of their body that appears to be due to a neurological or other medical cause, but without any underlying medical abnormality to explain it. They may have motor deficits such as paralysis or localized weakness, impaired coordination or balance, inability to speak, difficulty swallowing or the sensation of a lump in the throat, and urinary retention. Behaviour resembling seizures or convulsions may also occur. In other cases, individuals have sensory deficits such as loss of touch or pain sensation, double vision, blindness, or deafness. Psychological factors, such as conflict or stress, are presumed to be associated with the onset or exacerbation of the condition. Patients with conversion disorder often have other diagnosable psychological disorders, such as depression and anxiety disorders (Aybek, Kanaan, & David, 2008; Stone, Warlow, & Sharpe, 2010).

Careful medical evaluation of these patients is always essential to ensure that a genuine medical condition is not misdiagnosed as a conversion disorder. In making a diagnosis of conversion disorder, clinicians often look for particular signs that help to distinguish these symptoms from those with an organic origin (Aybek et al., 2008). For example, electroencephalographic recordings might show that a patient's seizures are not accompanied by the distinctive brainwave activity seen in epilepsy (Marchetti, Kurcgant, Neto, Von Bismark, & Fiore, 2009). Patients may also show inconsistencies over time (e.g., inadvertently moving a "paralyzed" limb when attention is directed elsewhere) or unusual symptom patterns (e.g., unusual head movements during seizures). A careful physical exam may indicate substantial strength in muscles that have supposedly been immobilized for a long time. Another indicator that symptoms are likely due to conversion disorder is when they are clearly inconsistent with known physiological mechanisms. A classic example is **glove anaesthesia**. This involves a loss of all sensation (e.g., touch, temperature, and pain) throughout the hand, with the loss sharply demarcated at the wrist, rather than following a pattern consistent with the sensory innervation of the hand and forearm (see Figure 6.1). Another classic sign that was previously thought to identify conversion symptoms was **la belle indifférence**, a nonchalant lack of concern about the nature and implications of one's symptoms. However, recent research indicates that this is found in only a minority of cases and it does not reliably distinguish between conversion symptoms and symptoms of organic disease (Stone, Smyth, Carson, Warlow, & Sharpe, 2006).

Several recent studies have employed brain imaging techniques such as fMRI to examine the brain regions involved in conversion disorders (Aybek et al., 2008; Bryant & Das, 2011). These studies suggest that conversion symptoms result from a dynamic reorganization of the brain circuits that link volition, movement, and perception, leading to an inhibition of normal cortical activity (Black, Seritan, Taber, & Hurley, 2004). Interestingly, these mechanisms are not observed in individuals who are instructed to feign conversion symptoms, suggesting that individuals with conversion disorders are not simply faking their symptoms.

As discussed earlier, prior to the publication of DSM-III, conversion and dissociative disorders were grouped together under the concept of hysteria. Recently, a number of experts have suggested that conversion disorder might best be viewed as a form of dissociative disorder and should be moved back into that category in future versions of the DSM (Brown, Cardena, Nijenhuis, Sar, & van der Hart, 2007). According to this view, conversion disorders involve a process of dissociation in which there is a lack of integration between conscious awareness and sensory processes or voluntary control over physical symptoms. This argument is supported by findings that individuals with conversion disorders also frequently meet the criteria for diagnoses of dissociative disorders, tend to have high scores on measures of dissociative experiences and hypnotizability, and frequently have a history of childhood abuse and trauma (Roelofs et al., 2002). Nevertheless, in the proposed revision of DSM-5, conversion disorder, under the new diagnostic name of *functional neurological disorder*, will continue to be grouped with the traditional somatoform disorders (APA, 2010). The argument against grouping this diagnosis with the dissociative disorders is that the assumed dissociative mechanism is still an unproven hypothesis that may turn out to be incorrect, and that it is more practical, from a clinical perspective, to group together all the conditions that present with somatic symptoms. Proposed changes to the diagnostic criteria for this disorder in DSM-5 include removing the requirements that the clinician establish that the patient is not feigning and that there are associated psychological factors, and adding a requirement of neurological testing to ensure that the symptoms are incompatible with a recognized neurological disorder.

4 BEFORE MOVING ON

When diagnosing a conversion disorder, what steps should be taken by a clinician to rule out possible physiological causes for the symptoms?

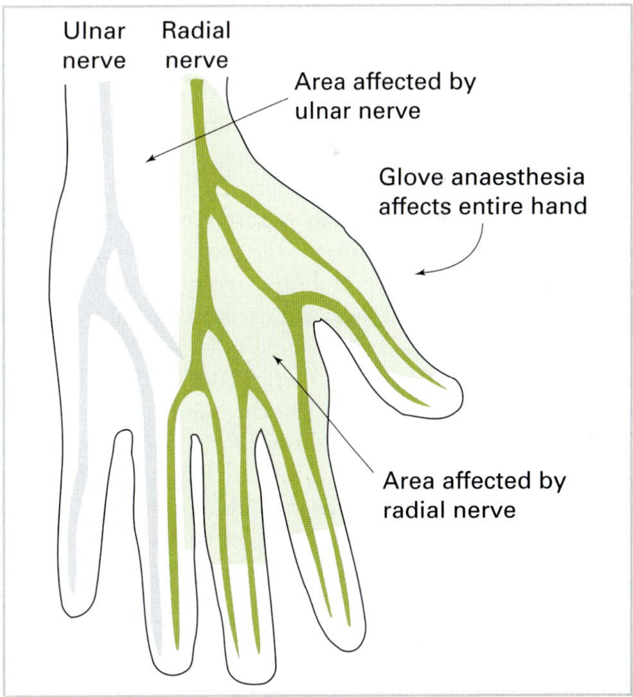

FIGURE 6.1 Glove Anaesthesia

The non-coloured area represents the area affected by the ulnar nerve and the coloured area represents the area affected by the radial nerve. It would be expected that a person with nerve damage would have loss of sensation in one of these areas. However, people with glove anaesthesia lose sensation in the entire hand and part of the arm.

Source: From *Abnormal Psychology*, 4e, by Ronald J. Comer. © 2004 by Worth Publishers. Used with permission.

Somatization Disorder

The essential feature of **somatization disorder** is a pattern of multiple, recurring somatic complaints that change over time and have no diagnosable basis, leading the individual to seek medical treatment and impairing social, occupational, or other important areas of life activity. Patients usually attribute their symptoms to serious medical problems, but physicians find themselves unable to verify the conditions suggested by the patient. Patients also tend to be quite resistant to suggestions that psychological or social factors might contribute to their illness or disability.

To be diagnosed with somatization disorder, the individual must have a history of changing somatic complaints occurring over a period of several years and beginning before age 30. A key feature in the diagnosis is involvement of multiple organ systems. There must be a history of pain in at least four different sites (e.g., head, abdomen, back, joints, extremities, chest, rectum) or during bodily functions (e.g., menstruation, sexual intercourse, urination). As well, there must be at least two gastrointestinal symptoms other than pain (e.g., nausea, vomiting, diarrhea, or food intolerance). There must also be a history of at least one sexual or reproductive symptom other than pain. In women, this might involve irregular menses or vomiting throughout pregnancy. In men, the complaints may concern erectile or ejaculatory dysfunction. Finally, there must also be a history of at least one symptom other than pain that suggests a neurological condition (e.g., impaired balance, paralysis, loss of touch, double vision, or deafness).

Patients with somatization disorder often describe their problems in a colourful or exaggerated manner, but without specific factual information. Their accounts can be very persuasive and potentially expose them to danger as a result of invasive or risky diagnostic procedures (e.g., X-ray examinations or invasive probes), surgery, hospitalization, side effects from potent medications, or treatment by several physicians at once, perhaps leading to complicated or even hazardous care (Woolfolk & Allen, 2010). Multidisciplinary assessment is often required. On the one hand, physicians need to rule out medical conditions for which there can be vague, multiple, and confusing somatic symptoms (e.g., systemic lupus, multiple sclerosis, or chronic parasitic disease). On the other hand, psychologists need to assess emotional, cognitive, behavioural, and social issues.

These patients are often prone to periods of anxiety and depression that they cannot express or cope with adaptively. One large study of patients with somatization disorder found that 76 percent had lifetime histories of episodes of major depression (Rief, Hiller, & Margraf, 1998), whereas another study found that these patients often had histories of anxiety disorders, personality disorders, and substance abuse (Noyes et al., 2001).

Cultural variations in somatic complaints are evident in somatization disorder, with the type and frequency of symptoms differing across cultures. For example, burning hands and feet or the non-delusional experience of worms in the head or ants crawling under the skin represent pseudo-neurological symptoms that are more common in Africa and South Asia than in North America. The *dhat syndrome* in India concerns a strong conviction of the loss of semen. In North America, somatization disorder is diagnosed much more frequently in women than in men, whereas it has a higher frequency among men than women in Greece and Puerto Rico, suggesting that the sex ratio of this disorder is affected by cultural factors. Understanding the socialization of the individual in a specific family and culture is an important feature in the diagnosis of this disorder (Kirmayer & Sartorius, 2007).

Pain Disorder

Pain as a consequence of injury or disease is a very common experience. Fortunately, it is usually self-limiting, and most sources of pain can be identified and eliminated. However, pain can also be extraordinarily severe and distressing, or it can persist long beyond the span of time one would expect necessary for damaged tissue to heal. These experiences of pain are not infrequent. Using a community-based sample, von Korff, Dworkin, and LeResche (1990) found that 45 percent of the general population suffered recurrent or persistent pain of varying severity. When pain persists beyond its expected time span, and a specific physical pathology cannot be identified, a patient can often benefit from a consideration of the role of psychosocial factors. Pain is an individual and subjective experience, and both its onset and its course are known to be affected by a number of psychological factors, including anxiety, depression, and degree of perceived control over the situation. These psychological dimensions of pain establish an important role for psychologists in understanding and controlling pain (Wall & Melzack, 1999).

According to the DSM-IV-TR diagnostic criteria, to diagnose **pain disorder**, there must be complaints of pain in one or more body sites sufficiently serious to warrant clinical attention. The pain must be severe enough to cause significant distress or to disrupt the individual's daily life, possibly leading to an inability to work, attend school, or socialize with others. Moreover, psychological factors must be judged to have an important role in the onset, exacerbation, severity, or maintenance of the pain, irrespective of whether the patient also suffers from some medical condition. If the pain appears to be explained adequately by a medical condition and psychological issues are not related to the onset or severity of the problem, then no psychiatric diagnosis would be made. However, even when a medical condition is present, attention to psychological features of pain may reduce pain severity.

Patients with pain disorder run the risk of becoming dependent on prescription medications such as painkillers or tranquilizers, or may develop complications due to overuse of over-the-counter treatments. Chronic pain is also often associated with comorbid depression, anxiety disorders, and

People with somatization disorder, hypochondriasis, or pain disorder often become frustrated with physicians and embark on an intense search for the drug or device that will solve their problems.

sleep disturbances. Based on psychoanalytic theory, it was once thought that "psychogenic pain" was caused by unconscious conflicts in individuals with certain dysfunctional personality traits. However, these views are now considered pejorative, because they imply that the pain does not have a real foundation and exists only in the patient's imagination (Gagliese & Katz, 2000). Contemporary clinicians recognize that the experience of pain is a complex synthesis of thoughts and feelings, as well as sensory input.

In the proposed revision of DSM-5, somatization disorder and pain disorder will no longer be separate diagnoses, but instead will be combined into a new diagnosis called *complex somatic symptom disorder* (APA, 2010). Two main diagnostic criteria are proposed for this new diagnosis: (1) one or more somatic symptoms that are distressing and/or cause disruption of daily life; and (2) excessive thoughts, feelings, and behaviours related to these somatic symptoms (e.g., high levels of health-related anxiety; excessive time and energy devoted to the symptoms or health concerns). In addition, these symptoms must be chronic, with a duration lasting more than six months.

Hypochondriasis

Hypochondriasis: Henry

Watch this Speaking Out video at www.mysearchlab.com

People with **hypochondriasis** have long-standing fears, suspicions, or convictions about having a serious disease, despite medical reassurance that the disease is not present. This preoccupation with fears of having an illness reflects misinterpretation of bodily symptoms or bodily functions. This fear leads to clinically significant distress or impairment in social, occupational, or other important areas of functioning. The morbid fear of physical illness such as cancer, heart disease, or AIDS is not of delusional proportion, so that patients are able to recognize the possibility that they may be exaggerating the extent of the feared disease or that it might not exist at all.

Hypochondriacal preoccupation often arises out of excessive sensitivity to relatively minor symptoms. The patient may be alarmed by his or her heartbeat, breathing, or sweating; become apprehensive about a small sore; worry about a minor cough; or have very vague and ambiguous physical sensations, such as "a tired heart" or "aching veins." These symptoms are attributed to some serious disease and serve to confirm the patient's fears that an illness is indeed present, resulting in a great deal of time spent thinking about the meaning, authenticity, or etiology of the somatic experiences. If you have read Chapter 5 on anxiety disorders, you may have noticed a similarity between hypochondriasis and panic disorder, in that both disorders involve excessive concern with and misinterpretation of bodily symptoms (Deacon & Abramowitz, 2008). A difference, however, is that those with panic disorder typically fear *immediate* symptom-related disasters that may occur during the panic attack itself, whereas individuals with hypochondriasis focus on the *long-term* process of illness and disease.

In the proposed DSM-5 revision, hypochondriasis will be divided into two different diagnoses. Approximately 80 percent of patients currently diagnosed with hypochondriasis have significant somatic symptoms, and these individuals would receive the proposed diagnosis of complex somatic symptom disorder, described above. The remainder of these patients, who do not have any actual bodily symptoms, but who nevertheless have excessive, chronic preoccupation and anxiety about becoming ill, would receive a new proposed diagnosis called *illness anxiety disorder*.

5 BEFORE MOVING ON

If you were suffering from a somatoform disorder (e.g., pain disorder), how might you identify any secondary gains that might be reinforcing the disorder?

Body Dysmorphic Disorder

Many people express some dissatisfaction with certain aspects of their physical appearance. In **body dysmorphic disorder (BDD)**, however, there is excessive preoccupation with an imagined or exaggerated body disfigurement, sometimes to the point of a delusion. For example, individuals may become preoccupied with a perceived defect in their face, the shape or size of their nose, or other parts of their body. If a slight physical anomaly is actually present, the diagnosis is made only if the individual's concern is markedly excessive. When considering this diagnosis, clinicians look not only for this preoccupation, but also for significant distress or impairment in social, occupational, or another important aspect of life. The excessive preoccupations are described as being difficult to control, and sufferers typically spend many hours of each day dwelling on their "defect," to the detriment of work, family, or other social situations (APA, 2000). Patients with BDD often face intense suffering and they tend to describe their

TABLE 6.4 LOCATION OF IMAGINED DEFECTS IN 30 PATIENTS WITH BODY DYSMORPHIC DISORDER*

Location	*n*	%
Hair[a]	19	63
Nose	15	50
Skin[b]	15	50
Eyes	8	27
Head/face[c]	6	20
Overall body build/bone structure	6	20
Lips	5	17
Chin	5	17
Stomach/waist	5	17
Teeth	4	13
Legs/knees	4	13
Breasts/pectoral muscles	3	10
Ugly face (general)	3	10
Ears	2	7
Cheeks	2	7
Buttocks	2	7
Penis	2	7
Arms/wrists	2	7
Neck	1	3
Forehead	1	3
Facial muscles	1	3
Shoulders	1	3
Hips	1	3

Source: Reprinted with permission from Phillips, McElroy, Keck, Pope, & Hudson (1993). Body dysmorphic order: 30 cases of imagined ugliness. *American Journal of Psychiatry*, 150(2): 302–308.

* Total is greater than 100% because most patients had "defects" in more than one location.
[a] Involved head hair in 15 cases, beard growth in 2 cases, and other body hair in 3 cases.
[b] Involved acne in 7 cases, facial lines in 3 cases, and other skin concerns in 7cases.
[c] Involved concerns with shape in 5 cases and size in 1 case.

preoccupations as "tormenting" or "devastating." In fact, approximately 25 percent of these patients attempt suicide (Phillips & Diaz, 1997). Table 6.4 provides a list of imagined defects of patients with body dysmorphic disorder. BDD usually begins in adolescence, reflecting the concern for body image that often emerges at that age, and usually persists throughout the lifespan.

Many experts have pointed out similarities between BDD and obsessive-compulsive disorder (OCD), one of the anxiety disorders discussed in Chapter 5 (Phillips et al., 2007). Individuals with BDD have prominent obsessions and compulsive behaviours, similar to patients with OCD. Recent research comparing individuals with the two disorders has found many similarities, including a tendency for the two to occur together in families. However, there are also some differences between the two disorders. Notably, individuals with BDD tend to be more severely disturbed than those with OCD, with higher rates of suicidal ideation, delusions, major depression, substance abuse, and social phobia. Phillips and colleagues (2007) concluded that, although the two disorders have many common features, BDD should not be viewed simply as a subtype of OCD. Another disorder that seems quite similar to BDD is anorexia nervosa, an eating disorder (discussed in Chapter 10) that also involves strong dissatisfaction with and misperception of one's body size and shape. However, Grant and Phillips (2004) reviewed the relevant research and concluded that, despite their similarities, these two disorders are quite distinct. In particular, they do not show the same gender distribution, familial patterns, or response to treatments. Nonetheless, some experts have suggested that BDD and anorexia nervosa should be conceptualized "OCD-spectrum disorders," forming a continuum of disorders that share many characteristics of OCD (Castle & Rossell, 2006). Members of the working group involved in the revision of DSM-5 are still undecided about whether body dysmorphic disorder should continue to be classified as a somatoform disorder (perhaps as a type of complex somatic symptom disorder) or as an anxiety disorder.

Etiology

Although the category of somatoform disorders was introduced with the publication of DSM-III in 1980, there continues to be a considerable amount of debate among mental health professionals about the appropriateness and usefulness of this category (Mayou, Kirmayer, Simon, Kroenke, & Sharpe, 2005; Wise & Birket-Smith, 2002). The somatoform disorders form a rather disparate cluster of conditions that have little in common except for the fact that they all involve bodily symptoms without an identified medical explanation. Some experts have suggested that the somatoform disorder category should be eliminated in future versions of the DSM, and that the individual disorders should be grouped with other disorders with which they seem to have more in common. For example, as we have discussed, some researchers have suggested that body dysmorphic disorder should be grouped with obsessive-compulsive disorder, and others have argued that conversion disorder belongs in the category of dissociative disorders. In addition, it has been noted that somatization disorder has more in common with personality disorders, whereas hypochondriasis may be best classified as a type of anxiety disorder (Collimore, Asmundson, Taylor, & Abramowitz, 2009). However, the working group involved in the revision of these disorders for DSM-5 favours continuing to group them together as a separate category involving somatic symptoms (to be renamed *somatic symptom disorders*). The main argument for retaining this category is that patients with all of these conditions tend to be seen primarily in general medical settings, and therefore it is clinically useful to group them together.

In view of the heterogeneity of the somatoform disorders, it is likely that somewhat different etiological processes are involved in each of them. Traditional psychoanalytic explanations proposed that these disorders resulted from conversion of the anxiety associated with unconscious conflicts and unacceptable sexual drives into somatic symptomatology and distress. However, this view is not widely held today. Kirmayer and Looper (2007) have proposed an integrative biopsychosocial model to explain the development of somatoform disorders. According to this theory, a number of physiological, psychological, and social factors may interact in a series of vicious cycles, with different somatoform disorders resulting from different patterns of interaction.

Although there is no consistent evidence for a genetic basis in the development of somatoform disorders, various *physiological* factors likely play a role. For example, chronic stress produces activation of the hypothalamic-pituitary-adrenal (HPA) axis, producing high levels of cortisol, which can adversely affect the immune system and also produce feelings of fatigue, pain, and general malaise (Kirmayer & Looper, 2007). These feelings in turn can cause individuals to perceive themselves as having a physical illness when they are actually experiencing stress.

Cognitive factors also seem to play an important role in the development of somatoform disorders, particularly interpretations of the meaning and significance of somatic events, uncontrollable preoccupation with somatic experiences, and excessive bodily concerns and worry (Kirmayer & Looper, 2007). Barsky and Klerman (1983) introduced the concept of somatic amplification, a hypothesized tendency for individuals to experience bodily sensations as intense, noxious, and disturbing. We all experience many bodily sensations arising from various aches and pains, common viral infections, and feelings of apprehension or dysphoria arising from stressful life experiences. Individuals who develop somatoform disorders seem to attend to these sensations selectively, magnifying their seriousness or importance and attributing them to serious illnesses, leading to increased distress and further physiological arousal.

Individual differences in various *personality traits*, such as negative affectivity and a tendency to suppress emotional expression, have also been proposed as contributors to the development of somatoform disorders (Kirmayer et al., 1994). As we have seen, recent research also suggests that many people with conversion disorders, like people with dissociative disorders, are highly hypnotizable (Roelofs et al., 2002), and that conversion symptoms result from spontaneous self-hypnosis, in which sensory or motor functions are split off from consciousness in reaction to extreme stress. The cognitive-behavioural concept of health anxiety (Salkovskis, 1996; Salkovskis & Warwick, 1986) is particularly relevant for the etiology of hypochondriasis. According to this view, we all develop beliefs and attitudes about our physical well-being through personal experiences with illness and information from others about their experiences. However, some individuals develop health anxiety, becoming attentionally biased to misinterpret information in a self-alarming and personally threatening manner. Behavioural patterns then emerge, leading to avoidance of illness-related information, tendencies to seek reassurances about health, repetitive symptom checking, and persistent demands for health care (Hadjistavropoulos, Craig, & Hadjistavropoulos, 1998).

Early life experiences and social learning also likely play a role in the etiology of somatoform disorders. A good deal of evidence has been offered for a relationship between trauma and these disorders. A significant degree of childhood physical or sexual abuse or other severe childhood adversity has been reported in many patients with somatization disorder (Salmon & Calderbank, 1996) as well as in patients with pain disorder (Imbierowicz & Egle, 2003). From a social learning perspective, illness-related behaviours and the "sick role" can be positively reinforced by the care, concern, and attention received from others, and negatively reinforced by allowing the individual to avoid burdensome work activities or uncomfortable social situations. This does not mean that individuals with these disorders are consciously faking their symptoms to obtain rewards, but rather that people learn to adopt roles as a result of their reinforcement history.

Treatment

Generally, treatment of the somatoform disorders has shifted away from traditional psychodynamic therapy, which viewed somatic symptoms as masked expressions of psychological conflict and focused on helping individuals acquire insight into the origins of their difficulties. Current treatments focus on the cognitive, affective, and social processes that maintain excessive or inappropriate behaviour (Woolfolk & Allen, 2007). Because patients with somatoform disorders are usually very reluctant to view their symptoms as having a psychological cause, establishing a co-operative therapeutic environment is crucial when treating these disorders. Simon (2002) notes the important features of developing such an environment, including identifying the patient's primary concerns, establishing the position that all symptoms are "real" and distressing, negotiating a mutually acceptable treatment goal (e.g., tolerance of reasonable uncertainty about health or improved functioning despite some pain), shifting attention from somatic symptoms to life stresses or affective states that may provoke or exacerbate symptoms, and focusing on symptom management and rehabilitation rather than medical diagnosis and cure. Identification and treatment of comorbid anxiety and depressive disorders is also vital, and pharmacotherapeutic interventions are often prescribed when these conditions are comorbid. In particular, patients with the obsessional cluster somatoform disorders (i.e., hypochondriasis and body dysmorphic disorder) appear to respond well to antidepressant medications, whereas less is known about the responsiveness of the primarily somatic cluster of somatoform disorders (i.e., somatization disorder and pain disorder) (Fallon, 2004).

The cognitive-behavioural approach to treating somatoform disorders involves restructuring morbid thoughts and preoccupations, and works to bring dysfunctional behaviour patterns under control. A critical review of controlled studies by Kroenke and Swindle (2000) showed that cognitive-behavioural therapy is an effective method for treating patients with somatoform disorders. For example, Woolfolk and Allen (2010) described a treatment for somatization disorder that has been shown to be effective in several randomized controlled trials. The therapy makes use of cognitive restructuring techniques for modifying dysfunctional thoughts, interpretations, and preoccupations relating to bodily symptoms and illness, as well as methods for helping patients to identify, understand, and regulate their emotions. In addition, the therapy employs self-monitoring and relaxation techniques for reducing emotional arousal, and behavioural management methods for increasing enjoyable activities and social interaction, and for reducing inappropriate illness behaviour and the "sick role." Unfortunately, despite the fact that effective cognitive-behavioural treatments have been developed for each of the somatoform disorders, many patients do not seek psychological treatment, insisting that their problems are physical, even after extensive medical testing indicates otherwise.

6 BEFORE MOVING ON

In recent years, clinicians and researchers have begun to conceptualize hypochondriasis as a form of anxiety disorder. How might cognitive-behavioural methods for treating anxiety disorders be applied to the treatment of hypochondriasis?

CANADIAN RESEARCH CENTRE

Dr. Laurence J. Kirmayer

Dr. Kirmayer is a professor of psychiatry at McGill University, where he is the director of the Division of Social and Transcultural Psychiatry and editor-in-chief of the journal *Transcultural Psychiatry*. Following undergraduate studies in physiological psychology, he obtained a doctorate in medicine at McGill and completed a residency in psychiatry at the University of California, Davis. Since childhood, he has had a strong interest in cultural diversity and identity, and this has profoundly influenced his approach to understanding and treating psychological disorders. He is now an internationally renowned clinician and researcher in cultural psychiatry, a field that cuts across anthropology, sociology, and other social sciences. He has authored numerous research articles and co-edited several books on this topic. Dr. Kirmayer is particularly interested in the way that cultural factors influence the symptomatology and treatment of psychological disorders. A major focus of his research is on mental health, healing, and resilience among Aboriginal peoples in Canada and other countries.

Dr. Kirmayer's research has made particular contributions to our understanding of somatization and dissociation, both of which are key issues in cultural psychiatry. His studies of somatization in primary health care have led to the development of an influential theoretical model of somatization as illness behaviour triggered by psychosocial stress and emotional distress, emphasizing the role of causal attributions and interpersonal processes. His interest in dissociation stems from his earlier work with clinical hypnosis in behavioural medicine, and dissociation continues to be a topic of interest in his more recent cross-cultural research on trauma and healing processes.

SUMMARY

- Dissociative disorders are characterized by severe disturbances or alterations of identity, memory, and consciousness.
- The primary symptom of dissociative amnesia is the inability to recall significant personal information, usually of a traumatic or stressful nature, in the absence of organic impairment.
- Dissociative fugue is an extremely rare condition in which individuals forget who they are and suddenly and unexpectedly travel away from their home.
- The key feature of depersonalization disorder is a persistent feeling of unreality and detachment from one's self or surroundings, often described as feeling like one is in a dream.
- Dissociative identity disorder (DID) is diagnosed when the patient presents with two or more distinct identities or personality states that regularly take control of the patient's behaviour.
- According to the trauma model, DID results from a combination of (1) severe childhood trauma, including sexual, physical, and emotional abuse, and (2) particular personality traits that predispose the individual to employ dissociation as way of coping with that trauma.

Although dissociation may initially be an adaptive way of coping with traumatic events, it becomes maladaptive when it is maintained as a habitual way of coping throughout adulthood.

- In contrast, proponents of the socio-cognitive model argue that DID is an iatrogenic condition that results from well-intentioned but misguided therapists inadvertently planting suggestions in the minds of their patients that they have multiple personalities. Highly hypnotizable patients may then develop the symptoms of DID as a learned social role.
- Individuals with somatoform disorders complain about bodily symptoms suggestive of medical illnesses, but no organic basis can be found to account for them, and there is reason to believe they reflect psychological issues.
- In conversion disorder, symptoms are observed in voluntary motor or sensory functions (e.g., paralysis or seizures) that suggest neurological or other medical etiologies, but these cannot be confirmed by medical tests.
- Somatization disorder is a pattern of multiple, recurring somatic complaints that change over time and have no diagnosable basis, leading the individual to seek medical treatment and impairing social, occupational, or other important areas of life.
- Pain disorder is diagnosed when psychological factors are important in the onset, exacerbation, severity, or maintenance of the patient's pain complaints or disability, irrespective of whether the patient also suffers from some medical condition.
- People with hypochondriasis have long-standing fears, suspicions, or convictions about a serious disease, despite medical reassurance that the disease is not present, apparently reflecting misinterpretation of bodily symptoms.
- Body dysmorphic disorder (BDD) is characterized by an excessive preoccupation with an imagined or exaggerated body disfigurement, sometimes to the point of a delusion.
- According to the integrative biopsychosocial model (Kirmayer & Looper, 2007), somatoform disorders result from a series of vicious cycles involving physiological, psychological, and social factors.
- Physiological factors include stress-related increases in cortisol, which can adversely affect immunity and produce feelings of fatigue, pain, and general malaise, causing individuals under stress to perceive themselves as having a physical illness.
- Psychological factors include excessive attention to and misattribution of bodily symptoms, somatic amplification, and high levels of health anxiety.
- Social factors include early childhood abuse and social learning comprising both positive and negative reinforcement of illness behaviours and the "sick role."
- Establishing a co-operative therapeutic relationship between therapist and patient is a particular challenge and a vital first step in psychotherapy for somatoform disorders.
- Identification and treatment of comorbid anxiety and depressive disorders is also important.
- Cognitive interventions for somatoform disorders involve restructuring dysfunctional thoughts, interpretations, and preoccupations relating to bodily symptoms and illness.

MySearchLab offers you extensive help with your writing and research projects and provides round-the-clock access to credible and reliable source material. Chapter quizzes and a full electronic version of the text are also provided. Answers to the Before Moving On feature are provided on the MySearchLab. Take a tour at www.mysearchlab.com.

KEY TERMS

hysteria (p. 130)
dissociative disorders (p. 131)
dissociation (p. 131)
repressed (p. 132)
false memory syndrome (p. 132)
dissociative amnesia (p. 133)
dissociative fugue (p. 133)
depersonalization (p. 133)
depersonalization disorder (p. 133)
derealization (p. 133)
dissociative identity disorder (DID) (p. 134)
alters (p. 134)
switching (p. 134)
trauma model (p. 135)
socio-cognitive model (p. 136)
iatrogenic (p. 136)
somatoform disorders (p. 137)
malingering (p. 138)
factitious disorders (p. 138)
conversion disorder (p. 138)
glove anaesthesia (p. 139)
la belle indifférence (p. 139)
somatization disorder (p. 140)
pain disorder (p. 140)
hypochondriasis (p. 141)
body dysmorphic disorder (BDD) (p. 141)

KENNETH M. PRKACHIN • GLENDA C. PRKACHIN[1]

Chapter 7

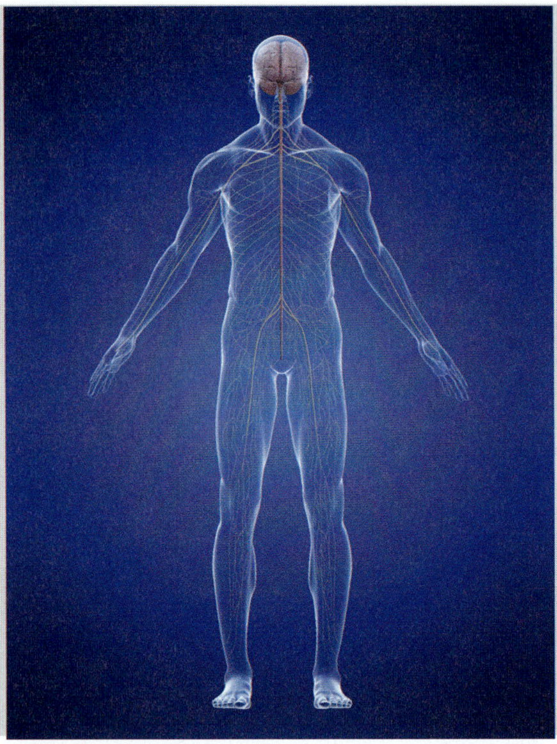

Psychophysiological Disorders

LEARNING OBJECTIVES

AFTER READING THIS CHAPTER, STUDENTS WILL BE ABLE TO:

1. Describe the history of the study of psychophysiological disorders and differentiate the fields contributing to it.
2. Explain the unique features of the approach to diagnosis for the disorders within this field.
3. Articulate the concept of a "mechanism" and describe four biologically plausible ways in which psychological factors or behaviours can contribute to physical disease.
4. Explain what is meant by "psychological stress," distinguish three different approaches to conceptualizing it, and describe how it is measured and studied.
5. Describe the disease processes resulting in gastric ulcer and coronary heart diseases.
6. Explain the psychosocial processes thought to contribute to infectious, ulcer, and coronary disease, using evidence from empirical studies.
7. Characterize psychological treatment techniques used with people suffering from psychophysiological disorders and explain how they relate to the psychosocial etiological mechanisms identified in this chapter.

[1]The authors' research reported in this chapter was supported by grants from the Heart and Stroke Foundation of Canada. We would like to express our thanks for the assistance of Julie Orlando and for the helpful commentary on earlier drafts of this article by Dana Edge and Cindy Hardy.

George, a 32-year-old high school music teacher, was referred for psychological evaluation by his family physician. For 16 months, George had been consulting his doctor about chest pains that had caused him great anxiety. He was convinced he was having a heart attack. Within the last year, George had consulted his doctor 37 times and had undergone extensive medical tests, none of which had provided an explanation for his symptoms. Although there was no unusual history of heart problems in his family and he was normal weight for his height, George was a smoker and lived a sedentary lifestyle.

Psychological evaluation revealed a man who was obviously distressed over his physical condition, but whose agitation extended beyond that. George readily expressed grievances with other people in his life: his principal for being demanding and incompetent, his wife for her sexual aloofness, his father for his coolness, and numerous other individuals or classes of individuals for a litany of reasons. He described his daily life as "going all out." He was up at 5:00 a.m., at work for early band practice, and usually finished at 6:30 each night. On his way home, he would pick up a six-pack of beer and a sandwich to eat on the fly. Once at home, he would prepare his lessons for the next day, finish the six-pack, and go to sleep.

George was an effective music teacher. His bands were always competitive in provincial championships and for the preceding two years had been judged the best in the province. Yet these achievements gave George no pleasure; he was always preoccupied with the deficiencies in his students' performances.

George's case is representative of many people who are referred for psychological or psychiatric evaluation yet do not readily fit into the diagnostic framework provided by the DSM-IV-TR. The presenting problem (recurrent chest pain) is ordinarily dealt with in clinical medicine, yet there are behavioural (drinking, smoking), psychological (inability to experience pleasure, hard-driven, hostile, and agitated), and social (isolation) characteristics that seem relevant to the symptoms he is experiencing. Moreover, a substantial scientific literature suggests that George's symptoms may be explained, at least in part, by psychological and behavioural variables that were identified in his psychological evaluation. Perhaps even more importantly, there is reason to believe that psychological therapies that target the psychological and behavioural characteristics George has displayed may alleviate his distress and enhance his physical health.

Historical Perspective

This chapter focuses on the role of psychological factors in physical illness. The idea that psychological processes can affect bodily states, even to the extent of producing physical disease, has a long history in Western intellectual tradition and may be even more deeply embedded in other cultures (Harrington, 2008). Cannon (1942) discussed the phenomenon of voodoo death. A member of a culture in which voodoo is practised may die as a consequence of learning that he or she has been cursed. Cannon took this phenomenon seriously, and attributed it to physiological processes elicited by threat and fear. As Western medicine evolved during the first half of the twentieth century, diminishing attention was paid to these ideas. However, advances in scientific methods, combined with the emergence of interdisciplinary approaches, often involving the simultaneous examination of psychological and physiological variables, led to a powerful rebirth of the field toward the end of the twentieth century.

In the early years of psychopathology, this field of study came to be referred to as *psychosomatic medicine* and the health problems as *psychosomatic disorders*. People often use this term to describe imaginary illnesses, or the experience of symptoms (headaches, for example) with no known pathophysiological cause. Yet the disorders in question usually involve identifiable disturbances (lesions) in bodily structures and functions and are in no way feigned. The term also implies a **dualistic** view of mind and body as separate entities, subject to different laws. To avoid such implications, in DSM-II (American Psychiatric Association [APA], 1968) the terminology was changed to *psychophysiological disorders*.

For many years, there was a set of "classic psychosomatic disorders," such as gastrointestinal ulcers, ulcerative colitis, hypertension (high blood pressure), asthma, and arthritis. These disorders were probably considered together for a number of reasons. First, because evidence available at the time could not identify a specific pathophysiological cause, dualistic thinking suggested that the roots of the disorders must be psychological. Second, there was evidence suggesting distinct psychological features in patients suffering from these disorders. Such thinking could be seen in early work of psychodynamically oriented theorists who posited specific psychological etiologies for each of the classic psychosomatic disorders. For example, Helen Flanders Dunbar (1935) theorized that specific disorders were the natural consequence of specific emotions and personality traits. The psychoanalyst Franz Alexander (1950) argued that the causes of classic psychosomatic disorders lay in characteristic intrapersonal conflicts. According to this theory, people who were prone to high blood pressure had a chronic sense of rage, but inhibited its expression. Consequently, they appeared unassertive and overly compliant. This conflict was thought to have physiological consequences that led to clinical disease. The specific symptomatology was seen as symbolic of the underlying conflict.

Such ideas are of more than historical interest, since elements persist to this day. For example, reminiscent of Alexander's theory, there is considerable evidence that the experience or expression of anger plays a role in heart disease (Chida & Steptoe, 2009; Myrtek, 2007; Smith et al., 2008).

In the late 1970s, a new perspective emerged from the realization that many, perhaps all, disease states are influenced directly or indirectly by social and psychological factors. The psychiatrist George Engel (1977) argued that the biomedical model of disease should be expanded to a "biopsychosocial" model (see Chapter 2). Engel's argument was based on evidence that psychological characteristics and societal forces must be invoked to explain the origins of many diseases and the nature of health.

At about the same time, psychologists uncovered increasing evidence of the important role that psychological factors and behaviour play in health and illness. For example, health care around the world began to incorporate the idea that pain could be influenced by psychological factors (Melzack & Wall, 1982) and treated using psychological techniques (Fordyce, 1976). A number of behaviours, for example, smoking and the use of other drugs, had already been identified as increasing risk of disease. Interest intensified as it became understood that such risk factors were determinants of the leading causes of death in Western societies. Behavioural therapy techniques offered apparently successful methods for controlling such behaviours. Increasing evidence justified the belief that other psychological variables, such as stress and characteristic styles of behaviour, were also associated with physical disease.

All of these developments converged in a new branch of psychology called behavioural medicine, or health psychology. **Behavioural medicine** usually refers to application of the methods of behaviour modification to the treatment or prevention of disease—for example, the use of psychological techniques to control pain in patients undergoing medical procedures, or interventions to improve diabetics' ability to control their blood glucose. The broader term, **health psychology**, refers to any application of psychological methods and theories to understand the origins of disease, individual responses to disease, and the determinants of good health. In this chapter, we shall highlight a number of key concepts, findings, and issues that health psychology has contributed to the study of psychopathology, focusing on those disorders that reflect the impact of psychophysiological variables.

1 BEFORE MOVING ON

The Greeks and their descendants in the Western intellectual tradition viewed disease as a consequence of the imbalance of four bodily fluids (blood, phlegm, and yellow and black bile), excesses in any of which were thought to be correlated with particular temperaments. Traditional Chinese medicine attributes certain diseases to imbalance of the life forces Yin and Yang. In thinking about contemporary views of psychophysiological disorders, people sometimes see parallels with these and similar conceptions. How do you think current conceptualizations are likely to differ from these earlier ideas?

Diagnostic Issues

Recall from Chapter 3 the multiaxial system of classification in DSM-IV-TR. When a major element of a disorder is a diagnosable medical condition, that condition will be noted on Axis III; the particular medical condition can be coded according to the *International Classification of Diseases* (ICD). On Axis I, under the category "other conditions that may be a focus of clinical attention," a specific code means "psychological factor affecting medical condition." Criteria for this diagnosis state that the designated psychological factor must (1) be correlated with the development of, exacerbation of, or delayed recovery from the medical condition; (2) interfere with treatment; (3) place the individual at additional risk to his or her health; or (4) precipitate the symptoms of the condition. The particular psychological factor involved should then be specified; it may be an identifiable Axis I (e.g., major depressive disorder) or Axis II disorder (e.g., borderline personality disorder), or it may be psychological symptoms that do not meet the threshold for diagnosis of a disorder, such as anger or anxiety, personality traits or coping styles (e.g., excessive job involvement or hostility), maladaptive health behaviours (e.g., smoking), or stress-related physiological response. Imagine a 55-year-old woman, Cindy, who has recently suffered a myocardial infarction (heart attack) resulting from underlying atherosclerosis. She is a partner in a law firm and has a recent history of uncontrollable and ruminative worry, sleep loss, fatigue, and restlessness, meeting the criteria for generalized anxiety disorder. In the past year, these symptoms have diminished her job performance, leading to considerable conflict with her firm's other partners. Table 7.1 depicts how her symptoms would be characterized using the DSM-IV-TR system.

TABLE 7.1	DSM-IV-TR DIAGNOSIS OF CINDY
Axis I: Generalized anxiety disorder	
Axis II: Not applicable	
Axis III: Myocardial infarction resulting from coronary atherosclerosis	
Axis IV: Occupational problems: stressful work schedule, discord with partners	
Axis V: Global assessment of functioning: 55	

At present, it is not clear how proposed changes to psychiatric diagnosis under DSM-5 (APA, 2011) are likely to affect a case like Cindy's. In preparation for revisions, the American Psychiatric Association struck a working group to look into the utility of Axis III. This group has recommended that the Axis I–III distinctions be abandoned in favour of one overall axis combining all medical and psychiatric conditions similar to the system used in the World Health Organization's current *International Classification of Diseases* system. Presumably, a patient like Cindy then would carry comorbid diagnoses of generalized anxiety disorder and myocardial infarction. It is not clear, however, how such a revision would deal with conditions in which a medical disorder is contributed to by psychological factors, but the medical disorder is not accompanied by a frank psychiatric disorder.

2 BEFORE MOVING ON

Imagine Mark, an adolescent boy with asthma, which is a chronic and occasionally fatal respiratory illness that causes the airways to constrict, leading to the inability to breathe. Now consider the DSM-IV-TR criteria that must be met in order to justify use of this axis. What might be some of the psychological factors that contribute to Mark's asthmatic condition?

Psychosocial Mechanisms of Disease

The idea that psychological processes may affect disease is widely held in our culture. People are said to have "died of a broken heart" or "worked themselves to death." Such notions may be oversimplified, yet they do have some basis in reality.

If there is a relationship between psychological factors and disease states, how does this connection work? A scientifically oriented person will not be convinced in the absence of a *biologically plausible mechanism* through which those factors may influence disease. A **mechanism** is an activity of a living system that mediates the influence of an antecedent factor on disease. For example, a person with acquired immune deficiency syndrome (AIDS) may die of pneumonia or sarcoma. The ultimate cause of those diseases is infection by the human immunodeficiency virus (HIV), but the mechanism of disease is the effect of that virus in decreasing the competence of the immune system.

What, then, are the mechanisms through which psychological factors may be responsible for illness and disease? Before answering this question we must first specify what we mean by illness and disease. Although we often think of the two terms as synonyms, there is a distinction. Illness is defined by *symptoms*, which are subjective reports of internal states. When you have the flu, you may complain of feeling hot and tired and of having aches and pains in various parts of your body. An interested observer, such as a physician or a concerned family member, cannot see, hear, or feel the heat, fatigue, and pain that you experience.

By contrast, disease is marked by *signs*, objective indications of an underlying disease process, observable either directly by a person with appropriate training or indirectly through the administration of a specific test. Although the feeling of feverishness that you report when you have the flu is a symptom, the high temperature that your doctor measures with a thermometer is a sign. When a sign involves the specific disturbance of bodily tissue, as in a gastric ulcer, or the normal functioning of a bodily system, as in high blood pressure, those disturbances are called **lesions.**

The distinction between illness and disease, and between symptom and sign, is important because it alerts us to the various mechanisms by which psychological factors may contribute to ill health. Certainly, one of the principal determinants of illness is disease. Ordinarily, the throbbing pain of a headache or the ache of arthritis would not be there, and would not be reported, without some underlying dysfunction. On the other hand, because symptoms are reports of subjective experiences, they may also be influenced by other factors that influence perception, independent of disease processes (Melzack & Katz, 2004). Examples are abundant. Have you ever endured a headache in silence because you did not wish to draw attention to yourself? Or, have you ever missed a day of school or work because you were feeling "sick," even though you may not have had aches, pains, or a temperature? If so, then your subjective report of your symptoms of distress was being affected by more than an underlying disease state. Psychological factors may influence illness by affecting our perception of, attention to, or tolerance of bodily signals.

But what about lesions, pathological changes in the structure or functioning of body systems? What are the mechanisms by which psychological factors might influence body systems? To answer this, we must understand the ways in which body tissues may be affected by behaviours and psychological processes. For the purposes of this discussion, *behaviour* is a discrete and potentially observable act, such as eating, exercising, smoking cigarettes, and so on. A *psychological process* is not observable directly, but may be inferred reasonably on the basis of other phenomena that are. For example, we cannot see another's depression, but we can see evidence—in facial expression, in the way the individual speaks, in changes in sleeping and sexual habits, and even in the individual's responses to a questionnaire—that allows us to infer with some confidence that depression is present.

Psychological influences on body tissues can be the effects of behaviours, particularly if those behaviours are repeated frequently over weeks, months, or years. For example, there is no longer any reasonable doubt that the effects of smoking are deadly. This is not because the act of smoking is inherently pathogenic, but because it repeatedly exposes body tissues to tar and nicotine, which are known causes of disease. There are many other examples of behaviours that promote disease by exposing body tissue to pathogenic substances. Conversely, there are also behaviours that have beneficial effects, for example, exercise.

Pathological influences on body tissues can also be a consequence of psychological processes. A host of such influences have been postulated, ranging from perceptual schemata (the ways in which people characteristically interpret experience) to emotions. (Hereafter, we will use the term *psychosocial variables* to refer to this broad class of influences.) How could such influences affect body tissue?

Three body systems are responsive to psychosocial variables: the endocrine system, the autonomic nervous system, and the immune system. Although we will discuss them separately, all three interact with the brain and with each other.

THE ENDOCRINE SYSTEM

The endocrine system consists of organs that manufacture hormones and, when the occasion is right, secrete them into the bloodstream. Hormones are biologically active substances that circulate in the blood until they reach a "target" organ such as the heart, the liver, or the bones, where they will cause certain changes. Figure 7.1 displays some of the endocrine organs in the human body.

Several endocrine organs are known to be highly responsive to psychosocial variables. Perhaps the best known is the system called the hypothalamic-pituitary-adrenal (HPA) axis (an axis is a system of different organs that act together

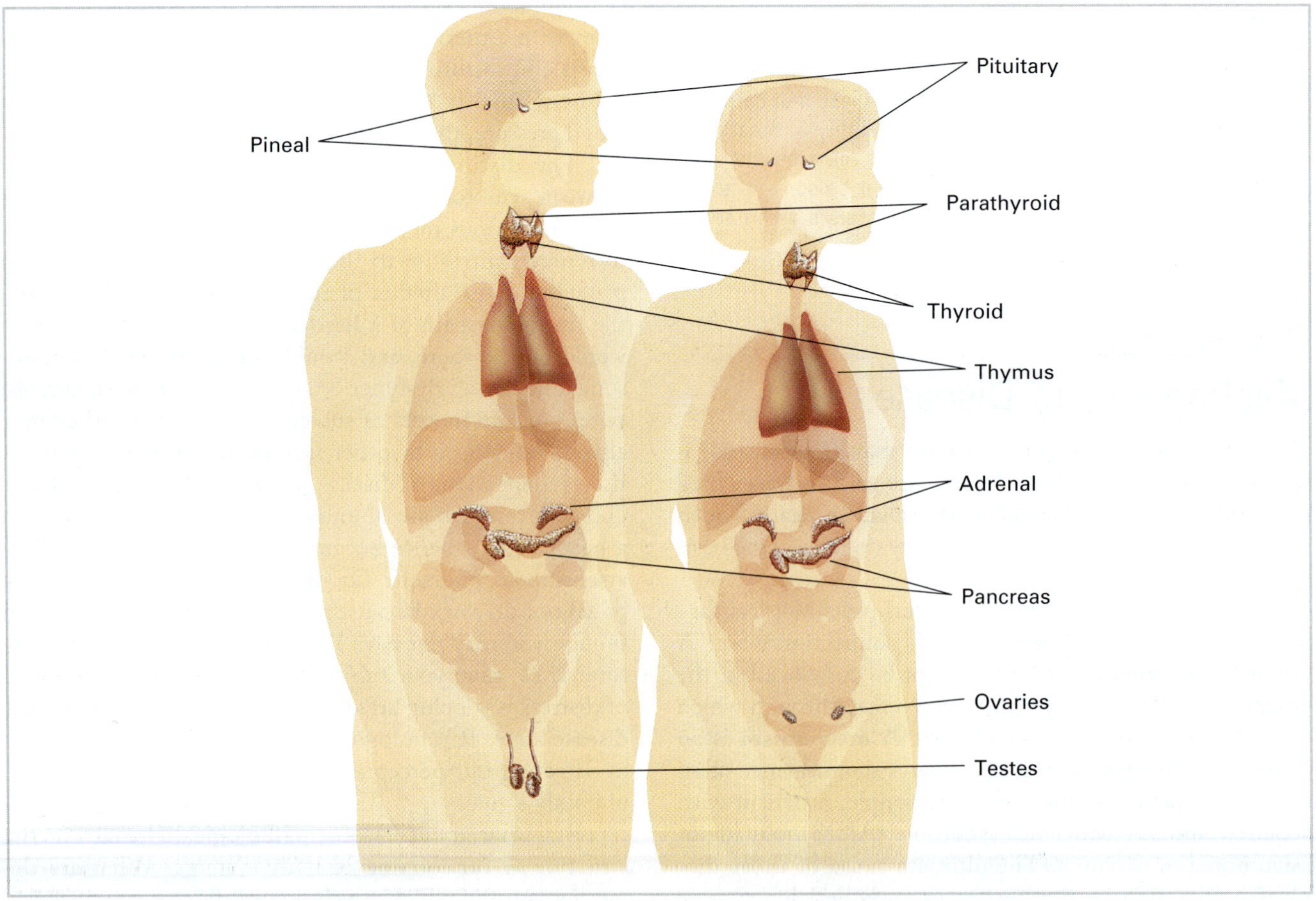

FIGURE 7.1 The Endocrine System

Source: Baron, PSYCHOLOGY, © 1992. Reproduced by permission of Pearson Education, Inc.

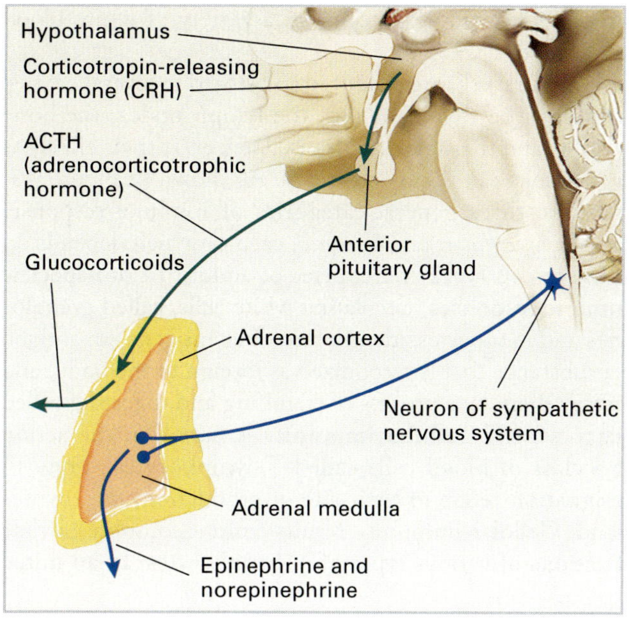

FIGURE 7.2 The HPA Axis

Source: Baron, PSYCHOLOGY, © 1992. Reproduced by permission of Pearson Education, Inc.

in a cascade of effects). This system, depicted in Figure 7.2, begins with the hypothalamus, a brain structure that controls a large number of body functions. The hypothalamus is responsive to psychosocial influences. When activated it can cause the pituitary gland, with which it is connected by nerve fibres, to secrete a substance called adrenocorticotrophic hormone (ACTH) into the circulation. The targets for ACTH are the cells in the adrenal cortex, the outer layer of the adrenal glands, located above the kidneys. When these tissues are stimulated, they in turn secrete a substance called cortisol (sometimes referred to as a glucocorticoid) into the circulation. Cortisol is a highly active hormone that produces a variety of effects. It suppresses inflammation, mobilizes glucose from the liver, increases cardiovascular tone, produces immune system changes, and inhibits other endocrine structures (Herman, Prewitt, & Cullinan, 1996). These features of glucocorticoid response are a defence mechanism. In the short term they promote immediate survival and inhibit unnecessary activity. However, they are maladaptive when prolonged or exaggerated. In particular, there is evidence that glucocorticoids suppress immune system function, enhance the development of atherosclerosis (discussed later in this chapter), and contribute to neuronal damage in the brain (Becker, Breedlove, Crews, & McCarthy, 2002; Chrousos & Kino, 2007; Miller, Chen, & Zhou, 2007) in a way that may contribute to the intellectual decline associated with dementia. It is also increasingly recognized that cortisol released during stress plays an important role in the development of abdominal obesity, a major risk factor for cardiovascular disease (see below). Fat cells in the abdominal region have a high concentration of receptors for glucocorticoids. When activated by glucocorticoid release this has the effect, among other things, of activating enzymes that increase the storage of fat within these cells (Bjorntorp, 2001). Complicating the matter, cortisol also plays a role in increasing the production of fat cells (Warne & Dallman, 2007). These and other known effects of cortisol release implicate the HPA axis in a wide variety of disease states.

THE AUTONOMIC NERVOUS SYSTEM

The second major body system that is responsive to psychosocial influences is the autonomic nervous system (see Chapter 2). Most people have found themselves perspiring before some important event like an examination, or blushing after doing something embarrassing. Most people are also aware of body changes that take place during other emotional states: the heart pounding, butterflies in the stomach, dryness in the mouth, and so on. Many of these changes result from the activity of the autonomic nervous system (ANS). The term *autonomic* comes from the same root as "autonomous," and reflects the belief that this system operates outside of consciousness and control. Although this is not totally correct, ordinarily it is true that we have little awareness or direct control of the ANS. Refer back to Figure 2.2 on page 31 for a diagram of the main structures in this system. As described in Chapter 2, the ANS consists of two anatomically distinct parts. The *sympathetic branch* consists of nerve fibres that emanate from the thoracic and lumbar (or middle) regions of the spinal cord and make contact with several organs: the heart, the stomach, blood vessels, et cetera. Notice, however, that most (but not all) organs that are innervated by the sympathetic system are also innervated by the *parasympathetic branch*, whose fibres emanate from the cranial and sacral (or end) regions of the spinal cord.

For many of the organs that are innervated by both, the sympathetic and parasympathetic systems tend to act as accelerator and brakes. When the sympathetic system is aroused, it tends to produce changes that prepare the body for vigorous action, such as increased blood pressure, heart rate, and perspiration and decreased digestive activity. Many of the effects of the sympathetic system would be dangerous if they were prolonged. For example, sustained increases in blood pressure could damage brain or vascular tissues. The parasympathetic branch "applies the brakes" to such changes to return the body to a more quiescent state that is within the body's tolerance. The level of activity of such systems is determined by the relative balance of input from the sympathetic and parasympathetic systems.

In comparison to endocrine effects, which rely on the bloodstream to convey hormones to target organs, ANS effects are rapid because they are based on the speed of nervous conduction. The sympathetic system itself, however, is part of a second endocrine subsystem whose effects involve release of hormones into the bloodstream: the *sympathetic-adrenal medullary* (SAM) axis. Nerve fibres from the sympathetic system stimulate the cells of the inner region of the adrenal gland, the adrenal medulla, to secrete the hormones epinephrine and norepinephrine (also known as adrenalin and noradrenalin). These belong to a broader class of hormones known as catecholamines. When they are released into the bloodstream, epinephrine and norepinephrine circulate to a variety of target organs where they can have powerful effects. Most of us are aware of these: we refer to exciting events as producing an "adrenalin rush" and describe risk-takers as "adrenalin junkies." Such descriptions convey the idea that catecholamines increase energy and activate the body. Notice that the effects are complementary to the direct effects of the sympathetic system.

THE IMMUNE SYSTEM

A third mechanism that is responsive to psychosocial factors is the immune system. The immune system comprises a network of cells and organs that defends the body against external, disease-causing forces (e.g., bacteria, viruses, fungi) or internal pathogens (e.g., cancerous cells) known as antigens. The immune system performs this function through the complex actions of a variety of white blood cells (Guyton, 1991).

Immune cells are produced and stored in several organs, including the thymus gland, the lymph nodes, the bone marrow, and the small intestines. They exert their effects as they circulate in the bloodstream. As shown in Figure 7.3, there are three general categories of immune response, *nonspecific*, *cellular*, and *humoral*, each of which depends on different cell types and courses of action. In **nonspecific immune responses**, circulating white cells, called granulocytes and monocytes, identify invading antigens (an antigen is a substance that is recognized as foreign to the body) and destroy them by a process of engulfing and digesting called phagocytosis. **Cellular immunity** is based on the action of a class of blood cells called T-lymphocytes. The "T" designation refers to their site of production, the thymus gland. Cellular immunity results from a complex cascade of actions of various types of T-lymphocytes. In an initial

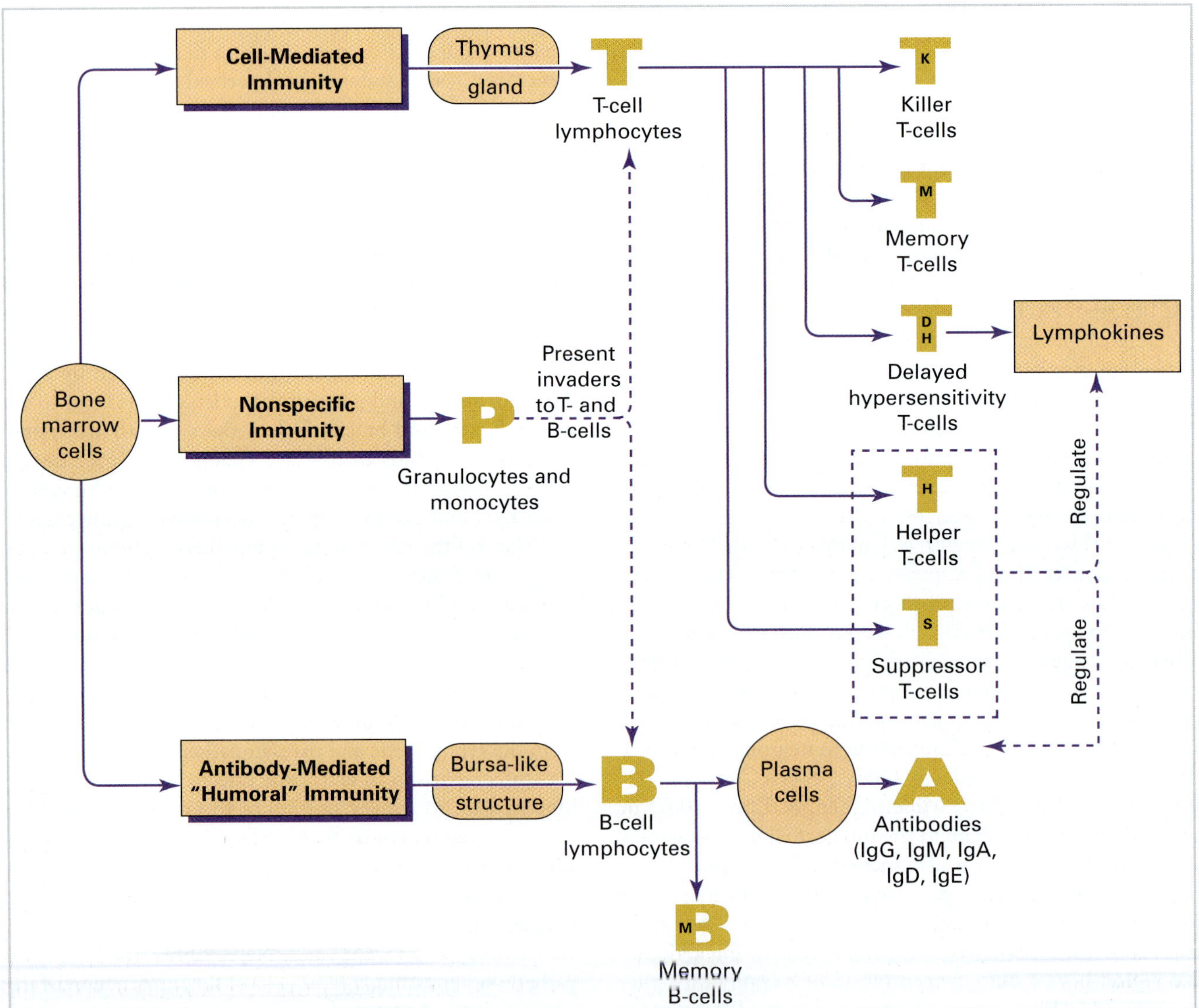

FIGURE 7.3 The Immune System

Source: Sarafino, E. P. (1997). Reprinted with permission of John Wiley & Sons, Inc.

episode of invasion by a foreign substance, an antigen is presented to T-lymphocytes by other cells, called macrophages (the antigen is recognized as such by biochemical markers on its cell surface). This causes the T-cells to proliferate (reproduce) and then circulate in the body. Several other types of T-cells participate in an immune episode. *Helper T-cells* secrete substances called *lymphokines* (e.g., the interleukins, interferon) that control the responses of other types of T-cells. One group of these, the so-called *killer (K) T-cells*, attack foreign or mutated cells directly. *Suppressor T-cells* inhibit the actions of both the helper cells and the natural killer cells, thereby providing a negative feedback mechanism to control the immune episode and prevent it from continuing indefinitely. In the course of an immune episode, certain T-cells become permanently altered and are transformed into *memory T-cells*, which are stored in the body in anticipation of the next time it needs to counter the same threat. This process is responsible for our "building up immunity" to certain kinds of microbes. In this way, we may become sick with a particular disease, such as chicken pox, only once. And, of course, it is this process that is taken advantage of when people are vaccinated against infectious diseases.

In **humoral immunity**, invading antigens are also presented by macrophages to *B-lymphocytes* ("B" stands for bursa, an organ in which such cells are produced in birds; in humans they come from the liver and bone marrow; Guyton, 1991). This causes the B-cells to reproduce, a process that is reinforced by lymphokine secretion from the helper T-cells. Some of the activated B-cells remain as *memory B-cells*. Others go on to be plasma cells, secreting antibodies called immunoglobulins that neutralize antigens by clumping, rupturing, or presenting them to phagocytic cells.

In the 1980s, scientists became aware that the immune system responds to psychosocial influences, giving rise to the new field of **psychoneuroimmunology**, the study of mind–brain–immunesystem interactions (Ader, Felten, & Cohen, 2001; Kendall-Tackett, 2010). For example, exposure of people to acute stressors, such as making them perform an extemporaneous speech, consistently produces changes such as increased numbers of natural killer and suppressor T-cells and reduced T-cell proliferation (Cohen & Herbert, 1996). Cohen and colleagues (1992) studied immune function in Cynomolgus (macaque) monkeys exposed to stable or unstable social conditions. Blood samples taken from animals exposed to social disruption by changing the monkeys in the experimental colony every month showed impairment of the ability of T-cells to proliferate, indicating a suppression of immune system functioning. Interestingly, impaired immune functioning was most pronounced in animals that showed less affiliative behaviour, such as contacting or grooming other animals, suggesting that such social behaviours have important stress-modifying effects.

There have been many demonstrations of similar effects of psychological conditions in humans (Herbert & Cohen, 1993). For example, Zakowski, McAllister, Deal, and Baum (1992) exposed healthy people to either an emotionally neutral film (of African landscapes) or a film depicting unpleasant surgical procedures like amputation. They collected blood samples periodically during exposure to and recovery from the stressor. The ability of lymphocytes taken from the blood samples to proliferate in response to an immune challenge was measured. The results indicated a decrease in proliferation of the lymphocytes taken from participants shown the gruesome film, compared with an increase among participants shown the neutral film (see Focus box 7.1 for a discussion of the effects of marital conflict on immunity).

Cohen and Herbert (1996) have described three pathways through which psychosocial variables can influence immune activity: (1) by the direct action of the central nervous system on organs and structures of the immune system; (2) as a secondary consequence of the hormonal changes discussed above; and (3) by changes in behaviour (e.g., poor dietary habits) that reflect personal characteristics or adaptations to changing life conditions.

3 BEFORE MOVING ON

The bodily changes mediated by the endocrine, autonomic, and immune systems are the products of evolution. Evolved characteristics are generally adaptive—they contribute to survival of the individual and reproductive advantage. But a process that contributes to the development of early disease and death could hardly support either advantage. How could the responses produced by neuroendocrine, autonomic, or immune systems be both adaptive *and* pathogenic?

The Psychology of Stress

The mechanisms identified thus far help us to understand some of the physiological processes that can mediate disease. But how might they be activated by psychological influences? The study of psychological stress has provided answers.

Stress has become one of the most pervasive ideas in psychology. Most of us implicitly understand the term. As you are reading this text, you may be cramming for final exams, the outcome of which may have an important influence on the rest of your life. If so, you know something about stress. As discussed in Chapter 5, post-traumatic stress disorder can result from extreme stress; depression may also sometimes be caused or exacerbated by events that most of us would call stressful (see Chapters 8 and 16). In the case that opened this chapter, one of the salient features of George's life was that he was constantly "on edge," largely because of his own attributes.

How can we understand the impact of stress on health? The term has been used (1) to refer to a *stimulus*, or a property of the external world; (2) to refer to a *response*; or (3) to refer to a *transaction* that mediates stimulus and response.

FOCUS 7.1

Putting It All Together: Stress, Marriage, Physiological Changes, and Health

Advances in research and technology have made it possible to study the effects of stress in realistic human contexts. One of the most interesting examples is the study of stress and physiology in the context of marital relationships. Marriage is obviously one of the most important of human relationships. It is entered into by a majority of people, it is a source of great pleasure for many, but it can also be a source of profound emotional distress. Virtually all marriages have points of tension, and issues of dominance, control, and social status. This has led investigators to study what happens psychologically and physiologically to couples during difficult marital situations. To do this kind of research, investigators identify couples who are willing to participate in controlled observations in a laboratory. Typically, they are asked to discuss specific topics for a designated period of time. Of greatest interest is what happens during conflict, so the researchers must find a way of inducing it. To do so, the couple may be interviewed or given questionnaires to identify areas of disagreement (e.g., finances, friendships). These points of disagreement then become the focus of discussion during the experiments. To evaluate the emotional tone of the discussions, participants are videotaped and the tapes are coded for different types of emotional behaviour.

Malarkey, Kiecolt-Glaser, Pearl, and Glaser (1994) studied 90 newlywed couples in this manner. Participants were admitted to a hospital research unit for a 24-hour period. Husband and wife had catheters implanted in their arms. The catheters were connected to plastic tubing that allowed nurses to draw samples of blood periodically without the participants' knowledge. The samples were stored and then tested for a variety of pituitary and adrenal hormones. The findings revealed interesting changes associated with the behaviours displayed by the participants during the conflict interviews. Some couples engaged in high levels of hostile behaviour during the interviews, such as criticizing, interrupting, and disapproving; others did not. Among couples who displayed these high rates of hostile behaviour, epinephrine, norepinephrine, and ACTH levels tended to be elevated during conflict or to remain high after conflict; in contrast, changes indicative of less arousal or enhanced recovery characterized the couples who displayed lower levels of hostility. The researchers suggested that this profile of changes is consistent with *downregulation*, or reduced effectiveness, of the immune system, which may play a role in long-term health consequences.

University of British Columbia psychologist Greg Miller and his colleagues (1999) investigated autonomic, neuroendocrine, and immune responses to marital conflict in 41 couples who had been married, on average, for almost four years. They found that behavioural predispositions played a significant role in influencing responses during conflict. Men who were high on a measure of cynical hostility (see the discussion of cardiovascular disease later in this chapter) showed anger during the discussion that was related to higher blood pressure levels, cortisol release, and natural killer cell activity. More recently, Kiecolt-Glaser and colleagues (2005) showed that the expression of hostility in marital interactions was associated with slower wound healing and a profile of inflammatory cytokine release that is known to promote a variety of age-related chronic conditions, including cardiovascular disease, diabetes, and some cancers.

These studies demonstrate the value of investigating meaningful interpersonal relationships using rigorous observational and biological methods. Clearly, specific behavioural processes that occur during marital conflict are associated with a range of biological consequences. Although the studies by themselves do not establish etiology, they do add detailed knowledge that advances our understanding of disease mechanisms.

The earliest views of stress emphasized its role as a response, particularly as a set of physiological changes. Eminent McGill University physiologist Hans Selye (1956) was the father of the stress concept. His theory emerged from early studies of the effects of an ovarian extract in rats. He noticed, at first, that animals treated with regular injections of this extract showed characteristic changes: enlarged adrenal glands, degenerated immune system organs, and ulcers in their stomach linings. To his surprise, however, rats injected with a simple saline solution showed the same changes! Rumour has it that Selye was a bit of a klutz at injecting rats, and his clumsiness caused the observed reactions. To his credit, he realized that the critical determinant of the effects he observed must have been something common to both conditions, namely change, unpleasantness, and a need to adapt. Later experiments confirmed that physiological changes could be produced by a wide variety of conditions involving both physical and psychological challenges. Integrating the results of many experiments and observations, Selye proposed that they all reflected the same underlying process, which he called stress.

Selye proposed that stress was a consequence of adaptation to demands placed on the body and argued that it followed a natural trajectory. In the first phase, **alarm**, the body mobilizes its defences. If the challenge persists, the body then enters the **resistance** phase, during which it actively copes with the challenge through immune and neuroendocrine changes. In the short term, these adaptive responses enhance the body's ability to ward off threats. If the challenge persists, however, **exhaustion** follows: energy is depleted and resistance can no longer be maintained. At this point, the characteristic tissue changes described above occur and the organism may succumb to a disease of adaptation, such as an ulcer. This **general adaptation syndrome (GAS)** was the first formal description and definition of stress. Note that, according to this model, stress is inferred from a set of bodily changes; that is, it is defined by a response. Note, as well, that by this definition any event that can bring about the characteristic set of changes is a *stressor*. This implication of the "stress as response" perspective has been controversial.

Others have taken the position that stress may be viewed as a kind of stimulus. Even in the GAS model, it is implicit that some event must take place to set off adaptation effects. Perhaps it would be helpful to characterize those events, or their psychological consequences, as stress. In another well-known line of research, investigators have attempted to characterize the stimuli that elicit stress through identifying more or less universally challenging events. The earliest and most famous of these attempts was the Social Readjustment Rating Scale by Holmes and Rahe (1967). These investigators developed a list of life events that required change. These events, such as divorce, marriage, trouble with the law, and taking out a mortgage, were rated according to the relative degree of change they entailed and assigned points through a process of psychophysical scaling (marriage served as the standard against which all other changes were assessed and was assigned an arbitrary change value of 50). Implicit in this approach is the idea that stress is a property of the environment—that is, a stimulus.

Scores of studies have shown that experiencing such events increases the likelihood of psychological disorders and physical diseases (Holmes & Masuda, 1974). Nevertheless, the approach has also been sharply criticized. One criticism is that major events are not representative of the common sources of stress in our lives. Kanner, Coyne, Schaefer, and Lazarus (1981) suggested that people's day-to-day lives are more affected by smaller events, or "hassles," such as troubling thoughts about the future, too many responsibilities, or fear of rejection. They developed a scale to assess the frequency of such events and how upsetting people found them. There is some evidence that a measure of the intensity of hassles predicts symptoms of physical illness (Weinberger, Hiner, & Tierney, 1987).

Neither the stress-as-response nor the stress-as-stimulus approach has been embraced by contemporary students. Defining stress by its physiological dimension forces us to consider very different processes as identical. For example, your heart rate will increase if you are frightened or if you walk up a flight of stairs. If we view stress only as a set of physiological responses, we are at risk of glossing over fundamental distinctions and of paying insufficient attention to other determinants of physiological responses. Defining stress as a stimulus is equally inadequate because people vary dramatically in what stimuli or events provoke physiological arousal or subjective distress. For example, divorce is probably a disturbing event for most people; yet for some it may be liberating. It is essential to take into account the individual's perspective when accounting for stress and its effects.

This view, which has been articulated forcefully by Richard Lazarus and his colleagues (e.g., Lazarus & Folkman, 1984), is called the **transactional model** of stress. It conceives of stress as a property of neither stimulus nor response, but rather as an ongoing series of transactions between an individual and his or her environment. Central to this formulation is the idea that people constantly evaluate what is happening to them. The eminent stress researcher Robert Sapolsky (1994, pp. 1–2) provides the following example:

> It's two o'clock in the morning and you're lying in bed. You have something immensely important and challenging to do the next day . . . You have to get a decent night's rest, but you're still wide awake. [S]omewhere around two-thirty, when you're lying there clammy and hyperventilating, an entirely new, disruptive chain of thoughts will no doubt intrude. Suddenly, . . . you begin to contemplate that nonspecific pain you've been having in your side, that sense of exhaustion lately, that frequent headache. The realization hits you—I'm sick, fatally sick! . . . When it's two-thirty on those mornings, I always have a brain tumor. They're very useful for that sort of terror, because you can attribute every conceivable nonspecific symptom to a brain tumor and convince yourself it's time to panic.

In the transactional model, such evaluations are called **appraisals**. Appraisals can take different forms, but one of the most critical is the appraisal of threat (see Chapter 5 for a discussion of appraisal as an element in the development of anxiety). When faced with an event that may have adaptational significance, such as the experience of symptoms of illness or a final examination worth half of one's grade, it is *as if* the individual poses the following question: "Is this a threat to me?" (Note the italics. Lazarus's view is that such appraisals may occur quite unconsciously so that they can only be described metaphorically.) This evaluative process is called **primary appraisal**, and it sets the stage for further events that may or may not lead to stress. If the individual concludes that the event poses no threat, the process comes to an end and the person continues to evaluate subsequent events. If the individual concludes that there is an element of threat, **secondary appraisals** then take place, characterized by the question: "Can I do anything?" The individual may have a number of options available, such as seeking the advice of a physician or trying to find out more about what will be on the final examination. Such approaches have been termed *problem-focused coping* because they attempt to identify and rectify the threat. Alternatively, the individual may focus on mollifying the bad feelings associated with the perception of threat. Such *emotion-focused coping* might involve engaging in diverting thoughts or activities or taking drugs to induce a different-feeling state. The individual will then evaluate the effectiveness of such coping activities. If the individual concludes that his or her coping is effective, stress will be minimized. If not, the appraisal of threat will be reconfirmed. Thus, the transactional model views stress as emanating from the balance between primary and secondary appraisals of threat and coping, respectively.

The transactional model is popular and has intuitive appeal. However, we must ask how it helps account for the relation between psychosocial factors and bodily processes that contribute to disease states. The first answer to this question is empirical. The transactional model grew out of evidence that the way a person perceives a potentially threatening event plays an important role in the physiological response to it. In a series of classic studies, Lazarus and colleagues demonstrated this by measuring autonomic reactions to films that many people would find gruesome or uncomfortable to watch. In one study, people watched a film depicting a coming-of-age rite among Australian Aborigines (Speisman, Lazarus, Mordkoff, & Davidson, 1964). In this film, young males undergo a procedure called subincision, in which the underside of the penis is cut open in public and without pain relief. Needless to say, people who view this film often show substantial autonomic arousal. However, people shown this film after instructions based on an "intellectualization" (emphasizing the importance of the ritual in its cultural context and minimizing the discomfort of the ceremony) or a "denial" strategy (downplaying the pain) showed less arousal than people whose instructions accentuated the discomfort and risks of the ritual. Thus, the way that one appraises events can modify the physiological response to them. Such findings have a direct implication for intervention: if one can manipulate the way people make stress-related appraisals, then presumably one can alter physiological responses to treat or prevent stress-related disease.

A second answer to the practical utility of the transactional model is that it can help us organize the way we think about psychosocial influences on disease. Shortly, we will review evidence that social conditions, personality characteristics, emotions, and perceptions are associated with disease states. Many of these variables are thought to exert their effects through the processes proposed within the transactional model. The model, then, encourages us to ask such questions as "How would having a supportive social network affect appraisal or coping processes?" or "What are the likely consequences of a particular coping process to a depressed person?" An organizing model that guides thinking about the processes elicited by potentially threatening conditions can be very valuable.

Psychosocial Factors That Influence Disease

Beginning with Selye's work, hundreds of studies of the effects of stress on bodily responses and health outcomes have been done. For example, Boscarino (1997) studied approximately 1400 Vietnam War–era United States Army veterans approximately 17 years after their service. Respondents were divided into those who had high and those who had low levels of combat exposure. Veterans with high combat exposure had higher rates of circulatory, digestive, musculoskeletal, nervous system, respiratory, and infectious diseases over the follow-up interval than those with low combat exposure. These differences remained even after the influence of potentially confounding variables was taken into account. In a more recent analysis of these veterans, Boscarino (2008) showed that those who met the criteria for post-traumatic stress disorder were more than twice as likely to have died from heart disease some three decades after their wartime experience. Exposure to combat is one of the most stressful experiences humans can undergo; consequently, these findings provide strong evidence for long-term effects of stress on a variety of health outcomes. The effects can be quite complex, however, and other variables can play mediating roles. Of the mediating variables studied to date, social status, controllability, and social support are three of the most important.

SOCIAL STATUS

Social status refers to an individual's relative position in a social hierarchy. Many human systems are organized hierarchically—some people occupy high positions that accord them status and power, others occupy low positions, and most fall somewhere in between. Social status may be represented by economic status, occupational prestige, dominance within a social group, or comparable variables. Differences in social status are also observed in other species, where they may be studied with respect to their implications for human differences. Sapolsky (1990), for example, has studied stress responses among baboons, a species organized in distinct dominance hierarchies.

The influence of social status on health should come as no surprise. It has been summarized by the University of British Columbia health economist Robert Evans (1994) as follows: top people live longer. Marmot and colleagues (Marmot, 1986; Marmot, Kogevinas, & Elston, 1987; Marmot & Theorell, 1988) have reported on one of the most extensive studies to address this issue. The Whitehall study collected information on the habits and health of 10 000 British civil servants over approximately 20 years (Whitehall is the district in London that houses the British government's main offices). Participants in the Whitehall study could be ordered along a gradient of occupational and income status from clerical workers at the bottom end to administrators at the top. The study established the importance of social status as an influence on health and suggested that its effects are more subtle, but more pervasive than one might imagine. For one thing, 40- to 64-year-old men in the lowest-status positions were between three and four times more likely to die in a 10-year period than men in the highest positions. This was not just a difference between the highest- and the lowest-status individuals; there was a *gradient* to this effect that applied across the range of social status (see Figure 7.4). This observation is extremely important. It implies that whatever is responsible for the differences varies quantitatively; there is no "threshold" below which one observes high mortality and above which one observes low mortality. Moreover, as Evans (1994) has pointed out, none of the people in the Whitehall study would be considered to be impoverished. Thus, something other than material deprivation must be responsible for the differences. One suggestion as to what that might be comes from Sapolsky's (1995) studies of baboons.

In baboons, social status can be assessed by observing such things as which animals will defer to others when competing for food, avoid eye contact, or make submissive gestures. The physiological correlates of social status can be studied by analyzing blood samples. Dominant and submissive baboons differ on a number of measures (Sapolsky, 1989). Dominant males show reduced concentrations of cortisol, higher levels of high-density lipoprotein cholesterol (the so-called good cholesterol that is associated with reduced risk of heart disease in humans), lower blood pressure, and higher levels of circulating lymphocytes than submissive baboons under resting conditions. In other words, dominance is associated with changed neuroendocrine, autonomic, and immune profiles. When stressed, for example in a fight, dominant baboons show a larger response on many of these parameters, but a faster return to resting conditions, suggesting that they are better at recovering from provocation. There is a parallel between these findings and further observations that have been made of the Whitehall civil servants. Marmot and Theorell (1988)

The big adult male is demonstrating his dominance. Baboons make good subjects for the effects of status because their hierarchies are clearly marked and fairly consistent. In this way, these animals resemble members of highly structured human hierarchies, such as feudal systems and the civil service.

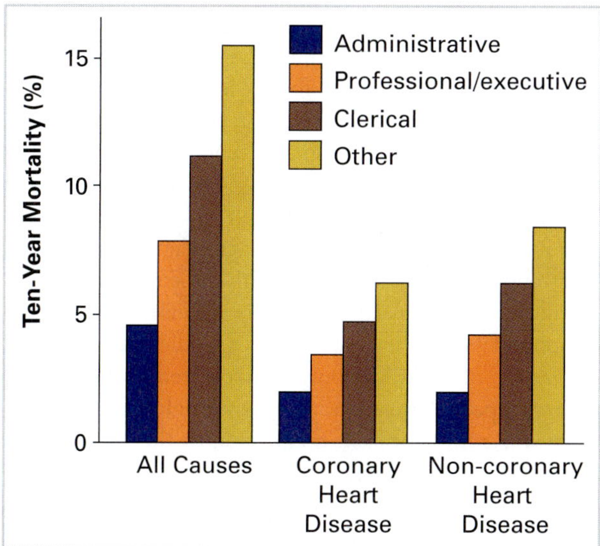

FIGURE 7.4 Mortality in Whitehall

Source: Marmot & Mustard (1994, p. 206).

found that although all grades of civil servants showed elevated blood pressure during the workday, the blood pressures of administrators dropped significantly more than that of lower-grade workers when they went home.

Thus, social status may have an effect on longevity through some of the stress-related physiological effects with which it correlates. These effects, in turn, probably depend on other psychosocial factors.

CONTROLLABILITY

A person's ability to control potentially stressful events often reduces their harmful effects (Seligman, 1975). Interestingly, there is evidence that people do not even need to truly *have* control over events to experience these benefits; they need only *believe* that they have control. In one study (Geer, Davison, & Gatchel, 1970), participants were shocked while performing a reaction time task. After the first part of the study, half of the participants were led to believe that they could reduce the shocks by reacting more quickly. Individuals who were led to believe that their behaviour could influence the shocks showed lower skin conductance arousal (a sympathetic nervous system response) than those who did not believe that they had control, even though all experienced the same shocks.

There is also a sizable literature indicating that people differ with respect to how much control they believe they exert in their daily lives. People who have an **internal locus of control** see themselves as the masters of their own destiny, whereas those with an **external locus of control** see themselves as being buffeted by the random events of the world. There is evidence that an internal locus of control protects against the harmful effects of stress on health.

Ideas about psychological control have influenced explanations of the effects of job stress on disease. Karasek, Theorell, Schwartz, Pieper, and Alfredsson (1982)

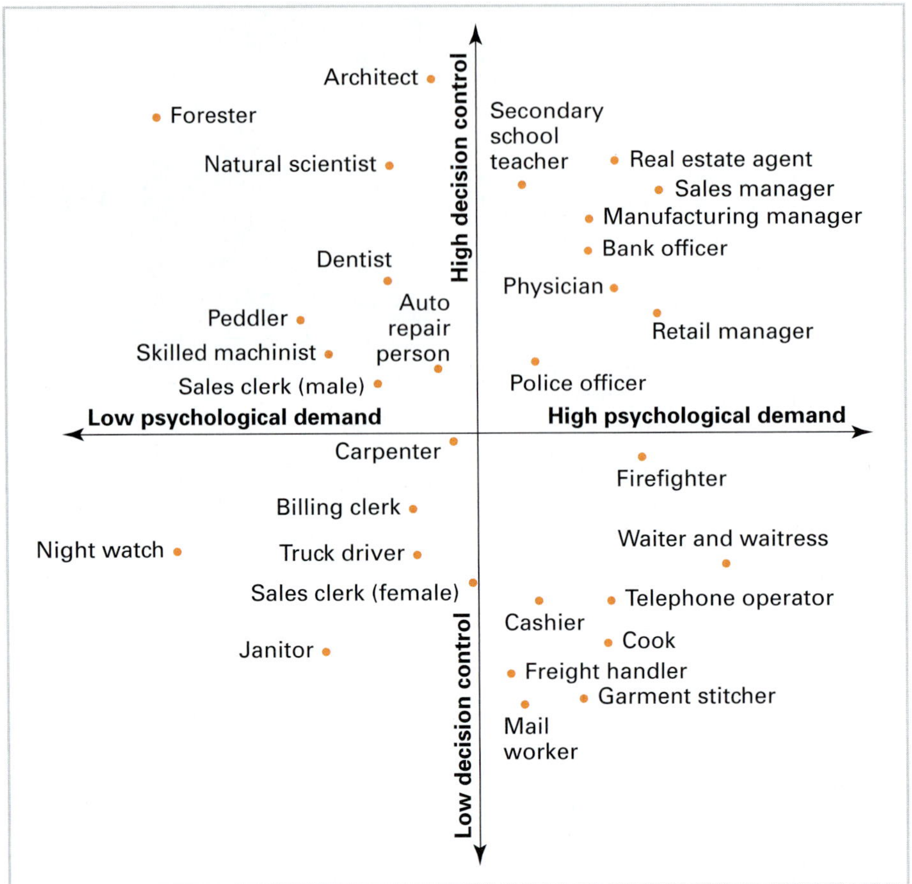

FIGURE 7.5 Karasek Job Strain Model

Source: Krantz et al. (1988, p. 334). Copyright © by The New York Times Co., 1995. Reprinted by permission.

characterized occupations on two dimensions: the degree of psychological demand involved in job activities and the amount of control that an individual can exert over decisions in the job (see Figure 7.5). Jobs that combine high demands with low control, such as waiter or postal worker, are said to be *high-strain* occupations and differ from *low-strain* occupations like forester or night security guard. High strain has been shown to be associated with increased risk of morbidity and mortality due to cardiovascular disease (Karasek, Baker, Marxer, Ahlborn, & Theorell, 1981) in prospective studies (see also Kivimaki et al., 2006; Kuper & Marmot, 2003; and Marmot, Siegrist, Theorell, & Feeney, 1999). LaCroix and Haynes (1987) found that men and women in high-strain positions were anywhere from one and a half to five times more likely to develop coronary heart disease over a 10-year period as those in low-strain positions.

SOCIAL SUPPORT

One psychosocial variable that has been consistently related to health status is social support: the extent to which an individual feels connected to other people in meaningful ways. It is usually assessed by asking people about the number of others with whom they have frequent contact, whether there is anyone they feel comfortable confiding in, and so on. The classic study of social support was performed in Alameda County, California. Berkman and Syme (1979) investigated the health outcomes of some 7000 residents, followed for nine years. At the beginning of the study, participants responded to a questionnaire that assessed their social ties with other people by asking questions about marital status, interpersonal relationships, and involvement in community organizations. At follow-up, through an intensive process of investigating health records and death certificates, researchers discovered that there were significantly fewer deaths among people with many social affiliations—people who were highly "connected" with others—than among people with few connections (see Figure 7.6). Social support appears to be associated with effects on a remarkably wide range of health indicators. House, Landis, and Umberson (1988) reviewed a series of studies showing that the presence of social support is associated with reduced mortality, especially in men. The beneficial effect of social support was comparable in magnitude to the well-known harmful effect of smoking.

The absence of social support also appears to make existing disease worse. Williams and colleagues (1992) and Case and colleagues (1992) both found that, among patients with diagnosed coronary heart disease, those with minimal social support were less likely to survive than those with adequate social support.

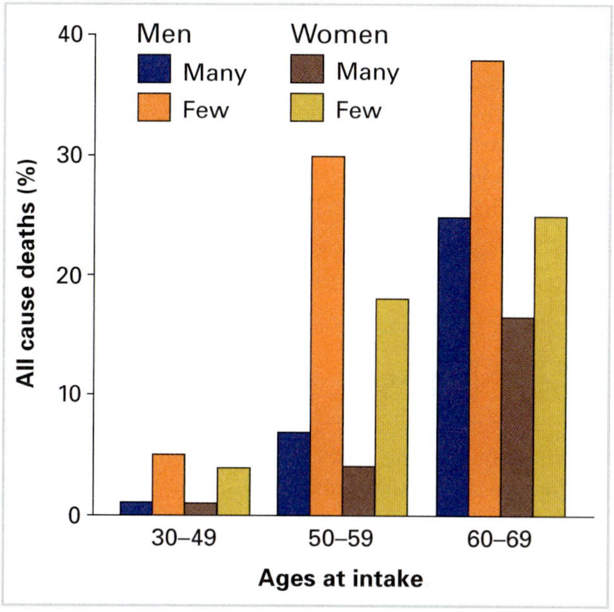

FIGURE 7.6 Deaths from All Causes Among Residents of Alameda County over Nine Years

Participants who had many social connections were more likely to be alive at follow-up than participants who had few social connections.

Source: Adapted from Berkman & Syme (1979), 109(2): 186.

Employees with high-demand jobs and unpredictable, berating bosses are prone to missing work due to illness.

Social support may even play a role in the impact of stressful events on non-human primates. Sapolsky (1995) observed that socially unskilful baboons (e.g., those who had difficulty determining whether or not a rival was threatening) and baboons that did not play or groom with others had elevated basal blood cortisol concentrations.

Although the effects of social support have been well documented, the reasons for these effects are unclear. Certainly, one possibility is that social support may be associated with material support in times of stress. Social support may also provide a means of discovering or testing coping strategies or a way of altering stress appraisals, as suggested by the transactional model.

We will return to some of these issues elsewhere in this chapter. For now it is time to turn to some specific disease states.

4 BEFORE MOVING ON

It is almost impossible to follow health stories in the media without coming upon an article or report of a study that suggests that stress is a causal factor for some disorder or other. Reports of this nature seem to surface almost monthly. This raises the question of whether the role of stress in health and illness may be oversold. When a concept becomes so pervasive and all-encompassing, many scientists become skeptical about whether it has any meaning at all. Do you think the stress concept has been oversold? In what areas do you think it has value, and in what areas might it be useless? What kinds of evidence do you think it is important to be able to see before we conclude that stress plays a role in the onset or development of a disorder?

Disease States and Psychosocial Factors

Psychosocial factors have been considered as possible contributors to many diseases. To illustrate the range of such contributions and the nature of thinking in this field, we will focus on three disease states: infectious disease, gastric ulcers, and cardiovascular disease.

INFECTIOUS DISEASE

Case Notes

Sarah is a student in her first year of medical school. It is her fifth year at university. She is a competitive athlete, in very good health, and careful to watch her diet. She had just finished a gruelling set of exams and was on an airplane flying home for Christmas break when she noticed the first symptoms of what she recognized as the flu. By the start of the next day, she was experiencing full-blown symptoms: high temperature, aches and pains, a deep cough, and a runny nose. Sarah, who is not used to being sick, was amazed by the intensity of her bout with the flu. She totally lacked energy and was barely able to make it out of bed on Christmas morning. Eventually, her symptoms improved, but there were residual effects when she returned to university after the break.

Although we all know that they are caused by infection, many people attribute infectious diseases like colds or the flu to the stresses and strains of daily life. Furthermore, the symptoms of some infectious diseases, like genital herpes, often seem to be exacerbated (made worse or made to flare up) during periods of emotional turmoil. What is the evidence that such casual observations may be valid?

Several studies have examined whether stressful life conditions predict or increase the likelihood of infectious diseases (Cohen & Herbert, 1996). In one of the most intriguing, Cohen, Tyrrell, and Smith (1993) exposed healthy individuals to nasal drops containing respiratory viruses or uninfected saline. Participants were quarantined for seven days after experimental exposure, and during this time indicators of infection were measured, including severity of cold symptoms, immune system markers of infection taken from nasal fluids, and measurements of mucous nasal tissue. Prior to the study, participants were assessed with respect to the number of stressful life events that had occurred to them in the previous 12 months, the perceived stressfulness of their lives, and current negative emotions. Those with higher perceived stress and negative affect (the tendency to experience unpleasant emotions) were indeed more likely to have clinical evidence of a cold and to show "hard" immune system changes indicative of infection than were subjects with lower stress. The underlying mechanism by which psychological stress might increase susceptibility to infection is unknown, but may reflect the functioning of the HPA axis.

In a more detailed study of the contribution of stress to infectious diseases (Cohen et al., 1998), volunteers were infected with rhinovirus ("common cold") drops and then followed to determine whether they became symptomatic. In addition, they underwent an extensive interview about their experience with life stressors in the last year. Participants who had experienced distinct stressors lasting one month or more had a higher likelihood of developing a cold than those whose stressors lasted less than a month. Long-standing difficulties associated with work (particularly unemployment or underemployment) and with interpersonal relationships (such as marital difficulties or grudges) were the main stressors that predicted cold symptoms.

There have been several studies of psychological influences on diseases mediated by the herpes viruses, such as genital herpes, cold sores, and mononucleosis (Chida & Mao, 2009). Once introduced, herpes infections remain in the body in a latent state, manifesting clinical disease only occasionally. Hoon and colleagues (1991) studied herpes symptoms in college students and reported that symptom recurrence was associated with variations in psychological stress.

It is natural to suspect that such stress effects on infectious diseases must be mediated by influences of stress on the immune system. For example, Glaser and colleagues (1994) measured the presence of antibodies to Epstein-Barr virus during a baseline period and during fall and spring examinations among medical students known to be infected. Both examination periods were associated with increases in antibodies to the virus, indicating its reactivation. However, we still lack clear understanding of the immune mechanisms responsible.

ULCER

Case Notes

One Sunday morning, Jack awakened with a peculiar burning sensation in his stomach. He didn't think much of it and attributed it to having overdone things the night before. He skipped breakfast, as he was inclined to do, and spent a typical Sunday morning watching football. The aching increased to such a point that the normally stoic Jack began complaining to his family. After a late lunch, it got better. Throughout the next two weeks, the burning pain returned periodically, but not every day, so Jack really did not think much was amiss. If he had, it would not have made much difference, because Jack was getting married that month and did not have time to think about it anyway. A few weeks later the wedding took place, and Jack and his wife departed on their honeymoon.

Over the next two weeks, however, the stomach pains grew worse, and Jack promised himself that he would see a doctor as soon as he got home. As it turned out, Jack did not get that option. The morning before they were due back, Jack and his wife set out to drive home, but had to pull the car over after about an hour because Jack was experiencing extreme pain and vomiting blood. He was taken to the nearest hospital, diagnosed with a perforated ulcer, and told he was lucky to be alive. Although he recovered well following hospitalization and changes to his diet, Jack's marriage did not thrive. He and his wife divorced after a few years. He would later confide that the months and weeks leading up to the wedding were full of conflict for him due to, among other things, his ambivalence about getting married. He directly attributed the cause of his ulcer to his psychological condition at the time.

If you were asked to name a disease-state affected by emotion, there is a good chance that ulcers would come to mind. The association has been long established in public consciousness, perhaps because we are very aware of the influence of emotional states on the gut. Most of us have experienced discomfort in the stomach during emotionally charged times, so it is not difficult to believe that emotional distress may lead to disease of the gut. Good-quality statistics on ulcers are difficult to obtain; however, a survey of a broadly representative sample of 1036 Canadian adults suggested that approximately 1 percent of the population experienced ulcer-like symptoms in the preceding year (Tougas, Chen, Hwang, Liu, & Eggleston, 1999). Indeed, the ulcer was one of Franz Alexander's "classic" psychosomatic disorders. As we shall see, there is some truth to these preconceptions. However, ulcers also illustrate the complexity of disease processes, because it is now generally accepted that they have a bacteriological cause. We are left with the need to sort out the implications for understanding the role of psychosocial determinants of ulcer disease.

First of all, what is an ulcer? A gastric ulcer is an erosion of the lining of the stomach or duodenum. Ulcers can be life-threatening when they perforate, but even when they do not they can produce excruciating pain. The events leading to an ulcer are thought to involve an interaction between the stomach's own digestive juices and its natural defence mechanisms. The digestive juices, one of which is hydrochloric acid, are produced and secreted in the stomach in order to digest food. They are highly corrosive to living tissue, including the stomach itself, which is normally protected by a mucosal lining. Ulcers occur when the digestive fluids penetrate the lining, thus leaving the stomach, or duodenal wall, defenceless against their corrosive action.

What role might psychosocial factors play in such lesions? Here we are left to piece together lines of information from clinical observations, epidemiological studies, and experiments in animals and humans. Clinicians have long observed that stressful life circumstances are associated with the development of ulcers in their patients. Alexander (1950) argued that a very specific, though unconscious, psychological conflict involving an unsatisfied desire for love was the main cause. This desire, symbolized by food, was thought to produce a state of chronic readiness to eat, which would lead to breakdown of the stomach lining and consequent disease by continually stimulating the physiological accompaniments of digestion. Appropriate treatment involved psychoanalysis geared toward uncovering the underlying conflict. There is little empirical support for this theory, and its influence is mostly of historical interest. However, other observations suggest psychological processes that may be more clearly involved.

Several studies have reported associations between profoundly stressful life conditions and ulcers (Levenstein, 2000). For example, during the German bombardment of London in the Second World War, rates of hospitalization for perforated ulcers were observed to increase significantly (Spicer, Stewart, & Winser, 1944). Prospective epidemiological investigations have shown that there is a significant increase in risk of development of peptic ulcer associated with measures of life stress (Levenstein, 2000; Levenstein, Kaplan, & Smith, 1995).

There have also been advances in our understanding of psychological aspects of ulcers, which follow from the understanding that the brain is an important regulator of the stomach and gut through autonomic and neuroendocrine mechanisms described earlier. We know, for example, that during stress-induced sympathetic arousal, blood flow is diverted away from the stomach lining to the skeletal muscles. It has been suggested that this may decrease the effectiveness of the mucosal lining of the stomach in protecting it against digestive juices, since blood vessels within that lining are thought to play a role in the deactivation of gastric fluids (Pinel, 1997).

Hypersecretion of digestive acid appears to be an important factor contributing to the development of ulcers. Studies have shown that psychological distress is associated with increased secretion of gastric acids, and that patients with duodenal ulcers respond to laboratory stressors with greater quantities of acid secretion than healthy controls (Levenstein, 2000). Another factor is slow, rhythmic contractions of the stomach that are different from the more frequent rhythmic contractions associated with the feeding cycle (Weiner, 1996). When such contractions occur in rats, gastric erosions develop (Garrick et al., 1989). Although this association has not been observed in humans, the animal observations make the argument for stress as a factor in ulcer disease more plausible (see Focus box 7.2 for a discussion of causal inference).

What is the evidence that stress can cause ulcers in animals? Since Selye's original observations, several methods have been used to demonstrate that manipulations of stress can produce ulcers. One common method is to restrain experimental animals by wrapping them tightly in a tube or some other device. Restrained animals reliably show more gastric ulceration than do controls (Brodie, 1971). Although this procedure does not provide a very realistic model of human stressors, it has the advantage of reliability and gives investigators the opportunity to investigate some of the mechanisms that are responsible for ulcers.

Such research has indicated that various brain regions involved in the regulation of emotional states are crucial for the development of restraint-induced ulcers. Peter Henke of St. Francis Xavier University, for example, showed that direct manipulation of the central nucleus of the amygdala by electrical stimulation increases gastric ulceration (Henke, 1988, 1992), whereas other manipulations, such as electrical stimulation of areas of the hippocampus that, in turn, affect the amygdala, are associated with reductions in ulceration due to restraint stress (Henke, 1990). Such findings establish the importance of brain regions in determining whether or not ulceration will occur during stress. Moreover, the particular brain regions implicated are known to be key structures involved in emotional states. For example, LeDoux (2000) has shown that the amygdala plays a critical role in the emotion of fear. The amygdala is known to influence bodily responses to stress by activating neurosecretory cells of the

FOCUS 7.2

Inferring Causality in Health Psychology

Is there a will to live? Does stress cause cancer? Does a particular kind of personality make one likely to become arthritic? While there is increasing acceptance of the contribution of psychological factors to illness and disease, many people, including health psychologists, continue to be skeptical. How do we begin to sort out reasonable answers to such questions?

As explained in Chapter 4, the gold standard for establishing causality is the experimental study in which an investigator manipulates one possible causal variable while holding all other variables constant, and observes the effects on an outcome. In the health sciences it is often difficult, for practical or ethical reasons, to meet the strictures of the experimental method. The development of a disease like rheumatoid arthritis, for example, may occur over many years, and this is difficult to study in a laboratory. Similarly, it would obviously be unethical to conduct a study in which people were exposed to severe stress in order to establish the role of stress in disease.

Epidemiological and correlational research (discussed in Chapter 4) can fill in some of the gaps. Hill (1965; see also Young, 1998) has outlined a number of criteria that may be applied to evaluate whether a psychological variable plays a causal role. A basic criterion is *association*; the psychological variable is more likely to be present when the disease is present than when the disease is not present. The case that there is a meaningful relationship is further supported by *consistency* across numerous studies and *strength* of association; that is, the variability in a psychological variable accounts for a great deal of the variability in an outcome. Yet none of these criteria show that the relationship is one of cause and effect. The fourth criterion, *precedence*, requires evidence that the alleged cause existed *before* the outcome developed. A common but expensive means of establishing precedence is the **longitudinal study**, in which a large group of people are evaluated for psychological or behavioural features and are then followed up, years or decades later, to determine whether they have developed a disease.

Several influential longitudinal studies have helped to establish precedence for psychological variables. For example, in the Harvard Mastery of Stress Study (Funkenstein, King, & Drolette, 1957), students enrolled at Harvard University in 1952, 1953, and 1954 underwent an extensive battery of interviews, questionnaires, and psychological stress tests. Later investigations of the health status of these individuals indicated that participants who experienced high anxiety during psychological stress testing and participants who perceived their parents to be uncaring were at substantially higher risk of a variety of illnesses 35 years later (Russek & Schwartz, 1997).

The final criterion relates to the logic of explanation. There must be both a biologically and a psychologically plausible mechanism linking a characteristic to the disease or illness outcome. Animal models or analogue studies are often used to investigate possible mechanisms (American Psychosomatic Society, 1996). For example, Anisman and his colleagues (Sklar & Anisman, 1979) at Carleton University have conducted studies to clarify the processes by which stress might affect cancer. To do this, they manipulated stressful experiences and observed their effects on growth of malignant tumours that they had experimentally implanted in mice. Of course, the variables manipulated in mice are not much like the stresses that humans experience, and mice are not humans. We must be very careful when generalizing from one species to another. However, it may be possible through such studies to illuminate the forces that affect human disease.

hypothalamus, thereby eliciting neuroendocrine and autonomic responses. For these reasons, it seems very unlikely that the association of threat appraisal, gastric ulceration, and the amygdala is coincidental.

Perhaps the most elegant studies implicating psychological factors in the development of ulcers were reported in the late 1960s and early 1970s by Jay Weiss of Rockefeller University. Weiss was interested in separating the physical and psychological aspects of stress. The stressor he employed was electric shock delivered to rats' tails by an electrode. In one study (Weiss, 1970), the shock was predicted by a warning signal (a beeping tone). Another group was exposed to both shocks and tones, but the events occurred at random so that the tones did not reliably predict the shocks. Yet another group was exposed to identical environmental conditions, but no tones or shocks. Examinations of the stomachs of these animals indicated that the unshocked rats had very little stomach ulceration; rats that were exposed to shocks without warning showed extensive stomach ulceration. The interesting finding was that rats that were shocked after a warning tone showed degrees of ulceration only slightly higher than the unshocked rats. Note that rats in the two shock conditions received the *identical* number and intensity of shocks; the only factor that could have explained why one group had more lesions than the other was the *predictability* of the stressor.

In a later study, Weiss (1971) investigated the effects of controllability: the ability to escape from or avoid a stressor. In these studies, rats were placed in cages with a wheel (see Figure 7.7). For two of the groups, shock was administered through an electrode attached to the tail, while the third group received no shocks. In one of the shocked groups, turning the wheel would delay the shock, or stop it if it had started. In the other group, turning the wheel had no influence. However, because they were wired in series, these two groups of rats received *exactly* the same number and intensity of shocks. The difference was that one group was able to control the stress, while the other was not. The results paralleled those found in the predictability study: the unshocked rats showed little ulceration; the animals that received shocks they could not control showed substantial degrees of ulceration. The rats that could control their shock stress showed only

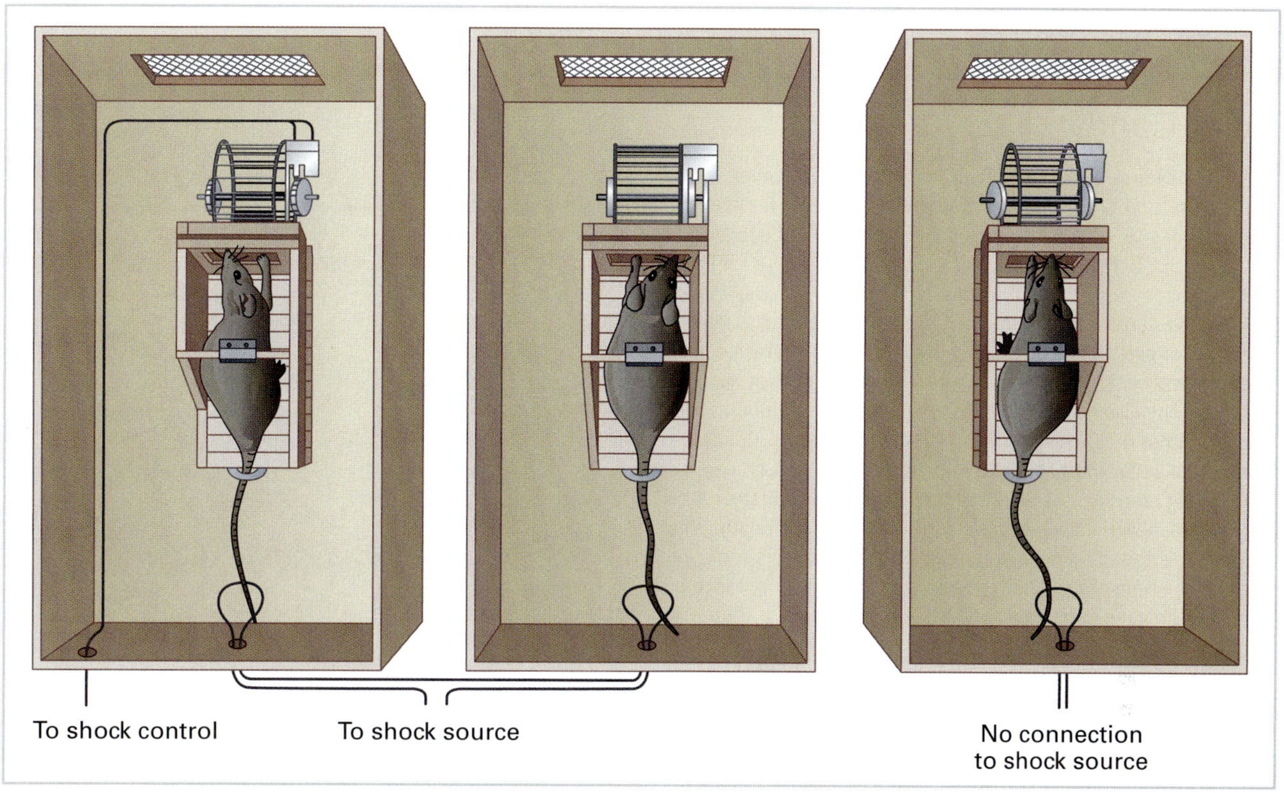

FIGURE 7.7 Weiss's Apparatus for Investigating the Effects of Controllability

Rats in Weiss's shock-stress experiment. The rat on the left receives a shock through its tail, but can control the shocks by turning the wheel; the rat in the middle receives the same shocks, but wheel activity in the middle cage has no effect on shocks; the rat on the right receives no shocks.

Source: From Weiss (1972).

about one-third as much ulceration as the rats that could not. These studies provide very strong evidence that manipulation of psychological variables can affect gastric ulceration. Moreover, they are consistent with evidence that lack of control mediates the effects of stressful events.

While studies of restraint and other forms of stress have helped to map the neural pathways that may be implicated in stress effects, there has been relatively little research in recent years extending these concepts to ulcer disease in humans. So far, our knowledge of stress and its psychosocial determinants has had little effect on the treatment or prevention of ulcers.

Considerable excitement was aroused in the medical community by the discovery of a bacterium, *Helicobacter pylori*, now believed to play the primary role in the genesis of ulcers (Rathbone & Healey, 1989). The bacterium is present in the stomachs of large proportions of individuals with ulcer disease and antibodies to it are present in their serum. Moreover, treatment with drugs to eliminate *H. pylori* produces improvement in affected patients (Graham et al., 1992). Does this discovery mean that stress is no longer relevant to ulcer disease? Not at all. Although *H. pylori* plays an important role in the genesis of ulcer disease, it cannot be said that that role is exclusive. As Weiner (1996) has pointed out, antibodies to the bacterium have also been found in the serum of healthy controls. According to Levenstein (2000), only 20 percent of people who test positive for the bacterium show evidence of ulcer. Therefore, the mere presence of *H. pylori* is not sufficient to produce disease. The bacterium also appears in association with a number of other diseases, calling into question its specificity of action. Finally, patients have been shown to improve even though the infection has not been eliminated.

The discovery of a bacterial agent is in no way inconsistent with the findings that implicate psychological conditions. As the diathesis-stress model emphasizes, psychological factors, such as stress, may lead a person to be more vulnerable to the influence of a physical agent. Bosch and colleagues (2000) have provided evidence that psychological stress may play an important role in the effects of *H. pylori* itself. Saliva was collected from healthy young men before, during, and after they watched a video depicting bloody dental procedures. The saliva samples were then purified in a laboratory dish and exposed to *H. pylori*. In this way, the researchers were able to determine the adhesion of *H. pylori*; that is, the effectiveness with which the bacterium establishes the first stage in the process of infection. Adhesion of *H. pylori* more than doubled in the saliva samples taken during stress exposure, thus suggesting that stressful conditions may play a role in the effectiveness of

APPLIED CLINICAL CASE

John Candy

John Candy was a Canadian success story. A member of the famous Second City comedy troupe, he was popular for his characterizations of public and imaginary figures on the television program *SCTV*. He parlayed his early successes into a career in movies, appearing in such successful films as *Stripes*; *Planes, Trains and Automobiles*; and *Uncle Buck*. On March 4, 1994, at 43 years of age, Candy died suddenly from a heart attack caused by a coronary embolism. He was well known for being overweight. A smoker, he also had a strong history of heart disease in his family (his father died in his thirties from heart disease). Candy was aware of his risk and had made attempts both to lower his weight and to quit smoking. We will never know for certain whether other psychological variables may have played a role in his death. What is certain is that he lived a pressured lifestyle, and it is rumoured that, at the time of his death, he was working hard to advance his career after some critical disappointments.

the microbe. More recently, Guo and colleagues (2009) have shown in mice that the stress of observing another mouse in distress enhances the ability of *H. pylori* to colonize gastric tissue, probably through the influence of glucocorticoid receptors.

Based on the proportion of participants in well-controlled studies who provided no evidence of psychosocial vulnerability factors and evidence of the excess of stressors among ulcer patients relative to controls, Levenstein (2000) has estimated that psychosocial variables are probably involved in 30 to 65 percent of cases. As discussed in this and earlier chapters, interactions between mind and body are complex, and there is rarely one single factor that accounts for any condition. Thus, ulcer disease represents, in Levenstein's (2000, p. 176) terms, "[t]he very model of a modern etiology."

CARDIOVASCULAR DISEASE

Diseases of the cardiovascular system—the heart and the blood vessels—are the leading causes of death and disability in Western societies. The two disease states that account for most of these deaths are **ischemic heart disease**, in which blood supply to the heart becomes compromised, leading to **myocardial infarction** (heart attack), and **stroke**, in which the blood supply to the brain is interrupted, leading to death of neural tissue. The disease processes underlying both end points are sufficiently similar that they are considered two sides of the same coin. Statistics for 2004 indicate that, in Canada, 72 338 people died of heart disease or stroke, accounting for 32 percent of deaths that year (Statistics Canada, 2004). Raw mortality, however, does not tell the whole story. Cardiovascular diseases are responsible for more **potential years of life lost (PYLL)**—a measure calculated by subtracting age of death from an individual's life expectancy—than any other cause except cancer and accidents. Cardiovascular disease also causes significant suffering and disability among survivors. Techniques for early identification and treatment have increased the chances of survival, and advances in rehabilitation have also improved the prospects for recovery. Nevertheless, many people who live with cardiovascular disease face diminished abilities, anxiety, and suffering, and their families must also adjust to the consequences of the disease.

Because of this pre-eminence, cardiovascular disease has been the focus of intensive research, and a great deal has been learned about it. This knowledge has paid off in a dramatic decline in death rates, which have dropped by almost 50 percent since the 1950s. As part of this research, the behavioural and psychological processes related to developing, triggering, and recovering from cardiovascular disease have been well studied.

CARDIOVASCULAR DISEASE PROCESSES To understand how psychosocial variables may contribute to cardiovascular disease, you need a basic understanding of the disease process. The cardiovascular system provides nutrients and oxygen, the basic requirements for life, to all tissues of the body and serves as a highway for the elimination of waste products. To do this, the heart acts as a pump, delivering blood, with its various constituents—platelets, plasma, etc.—through an extensive branching network of arteries, arterioles, capillaries, venules, and veins called the **vasculature**. The blood vessels consist of an opening, or *lumen*, and layers of cells that serve as the "tubing." The control of blood supply within this closed system is intricate. It is helpful to think of a water pumping system, wherein the heart is the pump and the vasculature is a hose. As the heart pumps, the blood constituents are distributed through the tubing in cycles that correspond to the pumping action. The peak of the wave of blood flow corresponds to the contraction of the left ventricle of the heart. This is the main chamber that pumps blood into the major arteries of the body at a point during the cardiac cycle that is called *systole*. However, when the pump is at rest, at a point in the cardiac cycle termed *diastole*, blood will still be flowing, albeit at a much reduced pressure. The pressure of the blood flowing through the vasculature is commonly measured in your doctor's office with the use of a *sphygmomanometer* (blood pressure cuff) and expressed in two numbers: **systolic blood pressure/diastolic blood pressure**, in terms of the number of millimetres of mercury (mm Hg) displaced by the measurement device (e.g., 120/70 mm Hg).

Persisting with the pump and hose analogy, we can see that the pressure within the hose will be influenced by two factors. The first is simply the amount of liquid being pushed into the hose with each beat of the pump; the more liquid, the greater the pressure, everything else being equal. Think of what happens with a garden hose when you turn the faucet up to "full blast." The more you open the faucet, the greater the pressure and the farther the water will spray. The second is the diameter of the tubing. What happens if you squeeze a garden hose (see Figure 7.8)? The pressure of the fluid within increases and the spray will be longer. Much the same thing happens when the diameter of the blood vessels is narrowed. Thus, blood pressure is a consequence of two major variables: **cardiac output** (the amount of blood pumped by the heart) and **total peripheral resistance** (the diameter of the blood vessels). Cardiac output is itself determined by two other variables: the rate at which the heart beats (commonly measured in beats per minute) and the amount of blood ejected on each beat (stroke volume).

This excursion into the physiology of the cardiovascular system is important because it allows us to begin to explain the mechanisms through which psychological factors can affect disease processes. Recall from our discussion of the autonomic nervous system that one of its targets is the cardiovascular system. Sympathetic and parasympathetic fibres can affect both cardiac output and peripheral resistance. Activation of the sympathetic system affecting beta-adrenergic receptors on the heart will speed up its rate, producing an increase in cardiac output and, consequently, in blood pressure. Activation of other components of the sympathetic system affecting alpha-adrenergic receptors can cause constriction of the blood vessels, again yielding an increase in blood pressure. Activity of the parasympathetic system opposes these effects. Complex

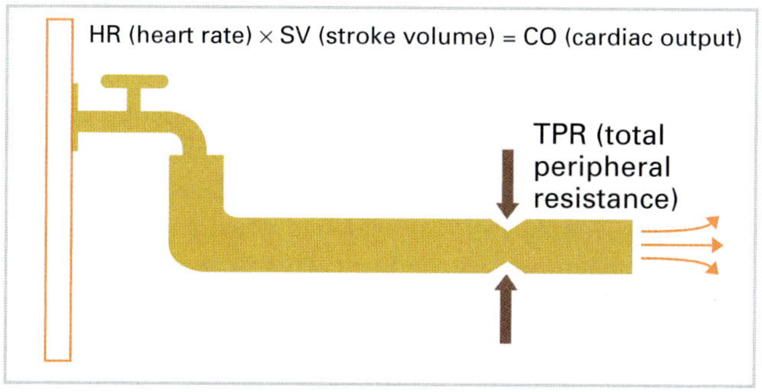

FIGURE 7.8 Plumbing Analogy for the Human Cardiovascular System

feedback mechanisms, involving blood pressure receptors located in the carotid artery, allow the hypothalamus to regulate blood pressure. In this way, the brain is always adjusting output and resistance to maintain blood pressure within certain limits.

Recall, as well, that the neuroendocrine system also influences the cardiovascular system. In particular, release of the catecholamines, epinephrine and norepinephrine, from the adrenal medulla reinforces the changes produced by sympathetic nervous system arousal, producing increased heart rate, peripheral resistance, and blood pressure. In addition to these effects, however, note that the catecholamines are distributed to the heart and vasculature by circulating *through* the bloodstream. Catecholamines can thereby not only affect the ongoing activity of the heart and vasculature, but also interact with blood constituents, such as the blood cells, and the cells lining vessel walls. Thus, these two physiological systems, both of which are regulated by the brain and consequently responsive to psychological influences, are ideally located to exert an ongoing influence on the system in which cardiovascular disease takes place.

CARDIOVASCULAR RISK FACTORS Deaths due to myocardial infarction can result from disturbances in the normal pumping rhythm of the heart (**arrhythmias**) or from compromised supply of blood to the heart itself. These proximal causes of death, as well as stroke, are influenced primarily by an underlying disease state called **atherosclerosis**, a buildup of deposits, known as *plaques*, on the walls of the blood vessels (see Figure 7.9). The growth of atherosclerotic plaques can ultimately narrow the openings of arteries enough to compromise the blood supply to the heart or the brain, leading to myocardial infarction or stroke.

Atherosclerotic plaques are complex structures built up from matter deposited on arterial linings over the course of a lifetime: primarily lipids (blood fats, especially cholesterol), but also blood platelets and cell fibres. Autopsy studies have shown the development of atherosclerosis (**atherogenesis**) as early as two years of age. Most people show signs of atherosclerosis by their thirties. These observations emphasize the long time frame over which the disease develops. Over decades, subtle influences on the disease process can play an important role. On the other hand, the slow development of the disease process gives plenty of opportunity for prevention.

But what do atherosclerotic plaques have to do with behavioural or psychosocial variables? For one thing, individual health-related behaviours may contribute directly to atherogenesis. Dietary factors, such as frequent consumption of fat and cholesterol, make lipids available for plaque formation. Smoking, too, is thought to play a role in atherogenesis. High blood cholesterol and cigarette smoking are considered major **controllable risk factors** for cardiovascular disease. Exercise is a **protective factor** that is thought to reduce risk of cardiovascular disease, at least in part by preventing atherosclerotic buildup. Another potential source of atherogenesis lies in the effects of the ANS and endocrine regulatory mechanisms discussed above.

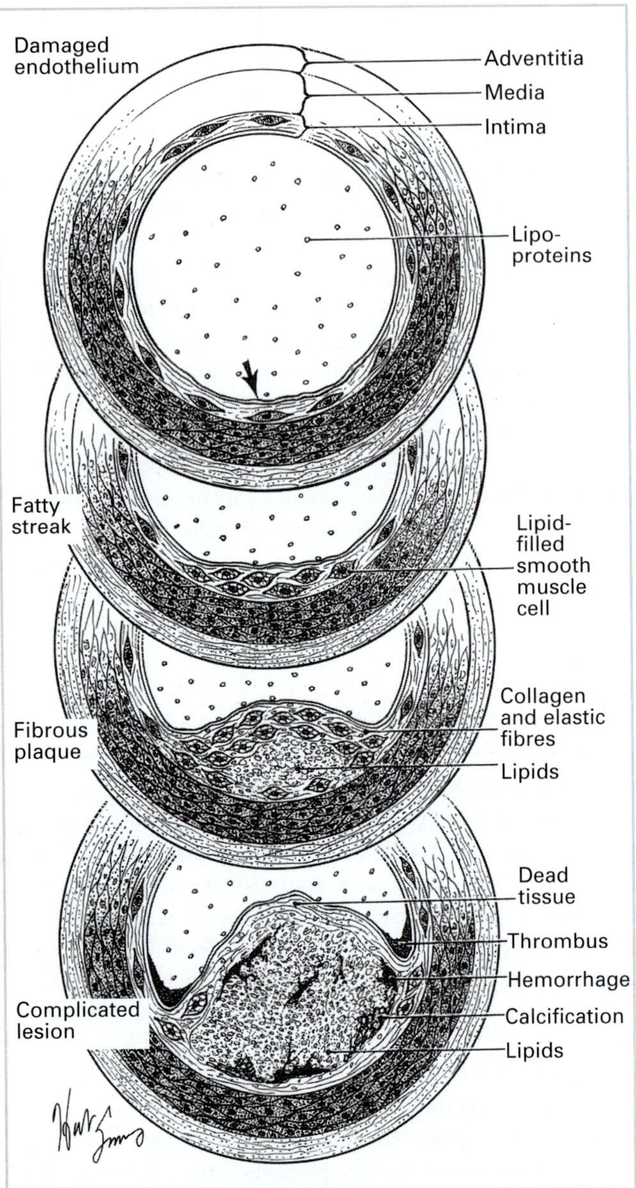

FIGURE 7.9 The Buildup of Atherosclerotic Plaque

Source: DeBakey & Gotto (1977, p. 111).

Blood pressure can vary substantially over the course of a day. Large variations can cause turbulence in the blood vessels, particularly at points where they branch into smaller vessels. This applies *shear stress* powerful enough to damage the cells of the vessel walls. According to one theory of plaque formation, lipids, blood platelets, and other constituents recruited to fix the walls become gathering spots for other atherogenic material. Additionally, circulating catecholamines may contribute to plaque formation by affecting the tendency of blood platelets to "stick" to one another.

Yet another factor that contributes to risk of cardiovascular disease is **hypertension**, a characteristically high level of resting blood pressure (defined as a reading of more than 140/80 in a doctor's office). Hypertension can result from a variety of background causes, but in approximately 90 percent of cases it is "essential," which means that a simple cause cannot be identified.

PSYCHOSOCIAL FACTORS IN CARDIOVASCULAR DISEASE

The activity of the cardiovascular system is clearly and sometimes profoundly altered by psychosocial stimuli. In one study, healthy young men were exposed to four standardized situations (Prkachin, Mills, Zwaal, & Husted, 2001). In one, they squeezed a hand dynamometer for five minutes. In a second, they simply counted forward from the number "1." In a third, they performed mental arithmetic, and in a fourth, they were interviewed about an event that had made them angry. Systolic and diastolic blood pressure increased for all four tasks, most dramatically during the anger interview. This study exemplifies a common method for examining how psychological variables affect physiological responses. Physiological functions such as heart rate or blood pressure are measured while people are exposed to an explicit, psychologically stressful provocation. Hundreds of studies using this **stress reactivity paradigm** have shown that many cardiovascular functions are responsive to changing psychological conditions.

In 1984, David Krantz and Stephen Manuck formally hypothesized that the risk of cardiovascular disease increases with individual differences in **cardiovascular reactivity**, how much an individual's cardiovascular function changes in response to a psychologically significant stimulus. The study of cardiovascular reactivity has provided some important insights. Commonly measured cardiovascular functions like heart rate, blood pressure, and peripheral resistance can be influenced readily by psychological stressors (Turner, 1994), but so, too, can hormones like epinephrine, norepinephrine, and cortisol (Dimsdale & Ziegler, 1991; Kuhn, 1989). More subtle changes in the cardiovascular system, like the percentage of blood pumped by the left ventricle during each beat (Ironson et al., 1992; Legault, Langer, Armstrong, & Freeman, 1995) and even abnormalities in the motion of the heart's chamber walls, can also be produced by psychological stress (Rozanski et al., 1988). Mills and Prkachin (1993), at the University of Waterloo, even found that exposure to psychological stressors could reverse the reduction in "stickiness" of blood platelets produced by dietary supplements containing essential fatty acids.

Manuck and colleagues (Manuck, Kaplan, Adams, & Clarkson, 1989; Manuck, Kaplan, & Clarkson, 1983) have also provided experimental evidence that cardiovascular reactivity contributes to the development of atherosclerosis in Cynomolgus monkeys raised in an experimental colony. The monkeys were fed a high-cholesterol diet. Heart rate was measured at rest and while the monkeys were threatened by a "monkey glove" that had previously been used to capture them. At the end of each study, the researchers measured atherosclerotic deposits on the arteries supplying the animals' hearts. Monkeys that showed a higher increase in heart rate in reaction to threat also showed significantly more atherosclerosis. In other work, Kaplan, Manuck, and colleagues have shown that socially disrupting primate colonies by repeatedly moving the monkeys between groups can promote the development of atherosclerosis, even if the animals are not fed an atherogenic diet (Kaplan et al., 1983).

David Spence and colleagues at the University of Western Ontario found evidence that these findings generalize to humans. In a large sample of middle-aged men and women studied for several years, ultrasound imaging was used to measure plaque buildup in the carotid arteries. The best predictor of worsening atherosclerosis over a two-year period was the magnitude of systolic blood pressure increase during the Stroop colour–word conflict test, in which participants must name the colour of ink in which a colour word is written (Barnett, Spence, Manuck, & Jennings, 1997). Patients highly reactive to this particular psychological stressor showed accelerated development of the disease process underlying heart attack and stroke.

PSYCHOLOGICAL FACTORS IN CARDIOVASCULAR DISEASE The Canadian physician Sir William Osler was one of the earliest students of the modern era to draw attention to the association between styles of behaviour and heart disease. He described the typical patient with atherosclerosis as a "... keen and ambitious man, the indicator of whose engine is always at 'full speed ahead'" (Osler, 1910, p. 839).

Osler's idea that the heart attack is associated with a particular type of personality remained dormant until it was taken up in the mid-twentieth century by a pair of American cardiologists. Friedman and Rosenman (1959) hypothesized the existence of a pattern of behaviour that increases risk of myocardial infarction and death. The pattern involved people who appeared to be "... aggressively involved in a chronic ... struggle to achieve more and more in less and less time, and if required to do so, against the opposing efforts of other things or other persons" (Friedman & Rosenman, 1974, p. 67). Friedman and Rosenman developed an interview to identify people with this behaviour pattern, which they termed **Type A**. This was an important advance because it lent itself to systematic epidemiological investigations. In the landmark Western Collaborative Group Study, Friedman, Rosenman, and others assessed the health and health habits of more than 3000 people, who were followed systematically over the next eight and a half years (Rosenman et al., 1975). Mortality statistics revealed two important findings. First, people assessed as Type A were approximately twice as likely to die from heart disease as people assessed as Type B (that is, those who are more relaxed and calm). Second, the risk associated with Type A behaviour was independent of other risk factors for heart disease, such as smoking. This appeared to be the first clear identification of a psychological characteristic that met conventional criteria for designation as a "risk factor."

Not all studies, however, confirmed an association between Type A behaviour and heart disease. Subsequent evidence indicated that the risk exists in only some of the components of the Type A pattern. Look at the variety of characteristics subsumed under the Type A label: hyperalertness, time urgency, job involvement, competitiveness, and hostility. Do these components always go together? It is possible to imagine someone who is hyperalert but not competitive, or time urgent but not hostile, isn't it? Interest has shifted to identifying which components most directly affect risk of heart disease.

Consistently, measures of hostility have been associated with symptoms of heart disease and death. Hecker, Chesney, Black, and Frautschi (1988) reanalyzed data from the Western Collaborative Group Study, including the Type A interviews, and determined that hostility was the main characteristic accounting for increased risk of heart disease. A number of studies using the Cook-Medley hostility scale (a questionnaire derived from the MMPI; Cook & Medley, 1954) have also documented this association. For example, Barefoot and colleagues (1989) studied the health status of 118 lawyers who had been given the MMPI about 28 years earlier when they were healthy young adults. High hostility scores were associated with a significant increase in the likelihood of death at follow-up.

Although not all studies have confirmed this association, meta-analyses (e.g., Miller, Smith, Turner, Guijarro, & Hallet, 1996) support the conclusion that hostility and related characteristics are a factor in cardiovascular morbidity and mortality. (Meta-analysis is a method of examining the findings of many studies as a whole. See Chapter 17 for a fuller discussion.)

But just what is this characteristic called hostility? The words we use to describe psychological characteristics or behaviours are imperfect and often fail to capture all of their nuances. In the case of hostility, the construct involves several features. Barefoot (1992) emphasized three components: *affective* features involving a tendency to respond to situations with anger and contempt; a *cognitive/attitudinal* dimension involving a tendency to view others with cynicism and to impute bad intentions to them; and a *behavioural* dimension involving direct and subtle aggressiveness and antagonism. Consistent with this analysis, subscales of the Cook-Medley scale measuring cynicism, hostile affect, and aggressive responding predicted likelihood of early death in the study by Barefoot and colleagues (1989).

But how would hostility lead to health risk? What mechanism would apply? In a comprehensive analysis, Timothy Smith (1992) outlined five possible models:

- The **psychophysiological reactivity model** suggests that hostile people are at higher risk because they experience exaggerated autonomic and neuroendocrine responses during stress.
- The **psychosocial vulnerability model** suggests that hostile people experience a more demanding interpersonal life than do others.
- The **transactional model**, a hybrid of the first two models, posits that the behaviour of hostile individuals constructs, by its natural consequences, a social world that is antagonistic and unsupportive. Consequent interpersonal stress and lack of social support increase the vulnerability of these people.

According to recent studies, it is not this man's stressful job and drive to get ahead that put him at risk so much as the hostility he is expressing.

- The **health behaviour model** suggests that hostile people may be more likely to engage in unhealthy behaviours (e.g., smoking, drug use, high-fat diets) and less likely to engage in healthy practices, such as exercise.
- A final theory is that the link between hostility and poor health outcomes is the result of a third variable, **constitutional vulnerability**, with which they are both associated.

It is difficult to pick and choose among these alternatives because there is evidence to support each one. For example, several studies have supported the hypothesis that hostile people show enhanced physiological arousal to psychological stress. Interestingly, however, such responses may occur only when the stressful conditions are relevant to the hostility characteristic. For example, in one study hostile participants differed from non-hostile participants in their cardiovascular responses to a word-identification test only when they were also exposed to social harassment (Suarez and Williams, 1989). Prkachin, Mills, Kaufman, and Carew (1991) found that hostile participants showed a "slow burn" effect. Unlike non-hostile people, their blood pressure increased gradually during a difficult computer task when they were led to believe erroneously that their performance was poor. Both the psychosocial vulnerability and the transactional model derive support from studies showing that hostile people have fewer social supports and more stressful life events than do non-hostile people (Hardy & Smith, 1988; Smith & Frohm, 1985). Prkachin and Silverman (2002) provided support for the transactional model by showing that hostile people are less likely than non-hostile people to engage in tension-defusing behaviour (e.g., social smiling) during stressful interactions. Finally, several studies have shown that hostile people smoke more, use alcohol more, consume more calories, and engage in less exercise than non-hostile people (Smith, 1992).

One relevant set of observations involves physiological response to anger. Studies have shown that recalled experiences of anger elicit distinct and powerful changes in the cardiovascular system (Prkachin et al., 2001). Ironson and colleagues (1992) asked people to recall and describe an event that had made them angry, while measuring the proportion of blood ejected from the left ventricle by an imaging technique called radionuclide ventriculography. Decreased left ventricular ejection fraction (LVEF) is an indicator of compromised cardiovascular function. LVEF decreased during anger recall in coronary artery disease patients, but not in normal controls.

Evidence has increasingly emerged about the importance of another psychological characteristic—depression—in cardiovascular morbidity and mortality. Frasure-Smith, Lesperance, and Talajic (1993), from McGill University, studied more than 200 patients who had recently survived a heart attack. When they had recovered sufficiently, patients were interviewed and categorized as depressed or not according to modified DSM-III-R criteria. You might wonder, wouldn't anybody who has just had a heart attack be depressed? Indeed, sadness and worry are extremely common in such circumstances, but people do vary in their reactions. In this study, only 16 percent of patients met the DSM criteria for a major depressive disorder. The researchers followed up these patients six months later—an important milestone, because most deaths following a heart attack occur within that time. Depression soon after the heart attack was associated with a greater than fivefold increase in the risk of dying within six months, independent of other predictors such as disease severity and history of previous heart attack. Frasure-Smith and colleagues (1999) repeated this observation with a larger sample and a different method of assessing depression. They showed that the elevated risk of mortality associated with depression was approximately the same in men and women.

In the years since the pioneering work of Frasure-Smith and colleagues, many studies have investigated the relationships among depression, heart disease, and death. Rugulies (2002) and Wulsin and Singal (2003) performed meta-analyses of prospective studies of this relationship; that is, of studies that investigated the risk of developing heart disease among people who showed previous evidence of depression. These studies indicate that depression is associated with an approximate 60 percent increase in risk of developing heart disease. Likewise, Barth, Schumacher, and Herrmann-Lingen (2004) performed a meta-analysis of studies that have investigated outcomes of depression among patients who already have coronary heart disease. They found that depression is associated with a two-fold increase in risk of death within approximately two years among people with heart disease (see also Kop & Plumhoff, 2011).

Carney, Freedland, Rich, and Jaffe (1995) have reviewed potential explanations of the impact of depression on cardiovascular disease. Two possible explanations—that the relationship simply reflects the severity of cardiovascular disease (i.e., the worse the heart condition, the more depressed the patient) or that the relationship is a consequence of toxic effects of antidepressant medication—cannot be supported by the available evidence. Three other possibilities each have some support. Like the health behaviour model of hostility, there is some evidence that depression may be associated with other risk factors for heart disease, such as high blood pressure and smoking, and that this association may be responsible for increased mortality. However, in the studies conducted by both Frasure-Smith and colleagues (1993) and Barefoot and Schroll (1996), depression was associated with mortality even when the effects of associated risk factors were taken into account.

Another closely related possibility is that depression may affect the extent to which people follow cardiac treatment plans. A study by Jane Irvine and colleagues (1999) from the Toronto Hospital suggests that this, too, is an unlikely explanation. In an investigation of the effects of medication on patients who had had a heart attack, they found that patients who closely followed the prescribed drug schedule were less likely to die over a two-year period, *whether they received the active drug or a placebo*. Following the treatment regimen, however, was not associated with depression. Yet another possibility that is currently under active investigation is that the relationship reflects alterations in autonomic and neuroendocrine regulation of the heart associated with depression. Depression in cardiac patients has been found to be associated with a number of changes in autonomic function, such as increased heart rate and decreased heart-rate *variability* that are themselves predictors of complications of heart disease (Carney et al., 1995; Krittayaphong et al., 1997). Moreover, post–heart-attack patients whose depression responds favourably to drug therapy show increases, while patients whose depression does not respond favourably show decreases in heart-rate variability (Khaykin et al., 1998).

Greg Miller of the University of British Columbia has provided strong and intriguing evidence that depression may affect the risk of heart disease and death through inflammatory mechanisms, which are increasingly understood as fundamental contributors to atherogenesis (Libby, 2002). In one study (Miller, Stetler, Carney, Freedland, & Banks, 2002), young, otherwise healthy but depressed individuals showed large elevations in C-reactive protein and interleukin 6 compared with controls. C-reactive protein and interleukin 6 are important because they mediate inflammation and have been directly implicated in the development of atherosclerosis. More recently, Miller and his colleagues have shown that, in response to the acute stress of a mock job interview, depressed people show impairments in the ability of their white blood cells to inhibit inflammatory processes (Miller, Rohleder, Stetler, & Kirschbaum, 2005).

As we have seen, research conducted over the last two decades has yielded an abundance of new information about the relationship between psychosocial variables and cardiovascular disease (for a comprehensive review, see Everson-Rose & Lewis, 2005). This section has reviewed some of the psychological characteristics that are currently believed to play a role in the development of heart disease and some of the mechanisms by which psychological variables may exert their effect. But just how important are they? We know, for example, that smoking and a poor diet increase risk for heart disease, and we know that physiological risk factors, such as high blood pressure and diabetes, also play a role. Surely these are much more important and powerful influences, are they not?

In a massive investigation—the INTERHEART study—Salim Yusuf, of McMaster University, and a large team of co-investigators identified more than 15 000 people who had suffered their first heart attack, as well as almost 15 000 controls. Participants were identified in 52 countries on every inhabited continent. For each participant, the investigators performed measurements of a large number of known or suspected treatable risk factors, including smoking, dietary patterns, physical activity, blood constituents, and psychosocial factors. Their measure of psychosocial factors included self-reported stress at home (e.g., irritability, anxiety, sleep loss), work stress, financial stress, major life events, locus of control, and depression. The results of the INTERHEART study (Yusuf et al., 2004) suggested that nine risk factors—smoking, apolipoprotein A/apolipoprotein B ratio (a measure of blood lipids), high blood pressure, diabetes, abdominal obesity, low consumption of fruits and vegetables, lack of consumption of moderate amounts of alcohol, low physical activity, and psychosocial factors—accounted for more than 90 percent of the risk of heart attack. The pattern of associations was generally comparable around the world and in both men and women. Of the nine risk factors, the three that had the greatest impact were raised blood lipids, smoking, and psychosocial factors, in that order. In other words, the influence on cardiovascular disease of psychosocial variables such as those discussed in this chapter is substantial and important in public health terms. As research in this field has progressed, our ideas about the manner in which such influences operate have become more complex and more refined. We will doubtless learn much more as the twenty-first century progresses.

5 BEFORE MOVING ON

Psychophysiological reactivity is a term that can be purely descriptive, in which case it simply refers to physiological reactions to psychological stimuli. On the other hand, it is sometimes used to refer to a variable on which people differ characteristically, with some people being highly reactive, others not reactive at all, and most of us somewhere in between. Describe how psychophysiological reactivity, in either sense of the term, helps to explain the origins of ulcer and cardiovascular diseases.

6 BEFORE MOVING ON

It is important to be able to see the connection between empirical findings and the conclusions they support. In this chapter, we have reviewed evidence that psychological factors can contribute to the onset or exacerbation of infectious, ulcer, and cardiovascular diseases. For each disease-state, pick one empirical study that has been covered and describe how the evidence supports a role for psychological influences. You should also be able to describe some limitations to the conclusions that can be drawn.

Treatment

If psychosocial factors contribute to disease, it seems sensible that psychological approaches would be useful in treatment. A variety of such approaches have been developed, with varied results. Broadly speaking, two classes of intervention characterize work in this field: (1) generic approaches to the management of stress and related problems, and (2) interventions directed toward specific psychosocial variables thought to play a role in the etiology of disease.

Generic stress management programs attempt to address either the physiological arousal response or the behaviours and thought processes believed to play a role in eliciting arousal. Relaxation training is often used to prevent or inhibit stress-induced sympathetic and neuroendocrine responses. Techniques range from teaching the control of specific muscle groups to autogenic training, a multi-faceted procedure that encourages people to invoke images of warmth and heaviness.

Cognitive-behavioural techniques are also commonly used. They focus on helping the individual to identify thinking styles that promote stress, such as negative self-statements, and to devise new ways of thinking and acting to counteract stress (see Chapter 17, and compare with the examples of cognitive-behavioural treatments described in Chapters 5 and 8). Such methods are often informed by Lazarus's transactional model and can be seen as attempts to modify appraisal and coping processes.

An influential series of interventions was performed and evaluated by Dean Ornish and colleagues (Billings, Scherwitz, Sullivan, Sparler, & Ornish, 1996). Patients with evidence of coronary heart disease were given aerobic exercise; a low-fat, low-alcohol, low-sodium vegetarian diet; group support meetings; and stress management strategies involving stretching, relaxation, breathing techniques, meditation, and guided imagery. After one and four years, these interventions were associated with a significant reduction in atherosclerotic lesions of the coronary arteries, compared to controls (e.g., Gould et al., 1995). Of course, with a multifactorial intervention like this, it is difficult to be certain about the specific importance of the stress management aspect of the intervention. However, internal analyses of the data indicated that the amount of practice patients devoted to stress management, along with dietary fat and cholesterol intake, predicted the extent of coronary lesions, suggesting that something about the stress intervention was important.

Linden and Chambers (1994), of the University of British Columbia, reported a meta-analysis of stress management in the treatment of hypertension. Their results indicated that stress management could be as effective as the standard prescription drugs when the interventions were targeted and individualized to the patients' problems. More recently, Linden and Moseley (2006) reported a meta-analysis of controlled trials investigating the effects of psychological treatments such as biofeedback and stress management for hypertension. Their results indicated that such interventions do, in fact, produce significant reductions in systolic blood pressure. Interestingly, these researchers also concluded that interventions that involve multiple components (for example, biofeedback and stress management) or that are individualized based on a patient's specific psychological characteristics produce especially marked reductions.

A variety of treatment techniques have been developed to address specific psychosocial variables. Most of this work has been informed by a cognitive-behavioural, transactional perspective. Probably the best-known example is the Recurrent Coronary Prevention Project (Friedman et al., 1986). Patients who had suffered a heart attack were assigned to one of two conditions. One was a standard cardiac counselling intervention involving education about risks and risk factor control. In the other, patients also underwent intensive counselling to change Type A behaviours. The Type A counselling, which took place in group sessions over four and a half years, included education about Type A behaviour; developing self-awareness about triggers of Type A behaviour; reducing time urgency, anger, and hostility; and increasing patience and empathy. After three years, patients who had received the Type A counselling program showed a reduction in measured Type A behaviour. They also had just over half as many recurrences of cardiac events as the control patients.

Although it is possible that the specific skills targeted in the Recurrent Coronary Prevention Project or in Ornish's intensive lifestyle intervention program may be critically important for therapeutic benefits, it is worth noting that the interventions also address several other relevant

Many people report that meditation or yoga reduces stress, which, in turn, may help to alleviate stress-related medical problems.

psychosocial variables. In particular, the programs emphasize and encourage social support. Indeed, as these types of intervention have evolved, they have begun to place greater emphasis on group interaction and on encouraging emotional communication (Billings et al., 1996). Undoubtedly such experiences can contribute to the development of new ways of appraising and coping. Emotional communication may also enhance the ability to "process" emotional experiences and promote new ways of interacting with others. There is evidence that all of these changes may play a role in promoting health and preventing disease.

7 BEFORE MOVING ON

In this section, we have discussed psychological approaches used in the treatment of somatic diseases. Explain how each of these approaches relates to the etiological theories described in previous sections.

CANADIAN RESEARCH CENTRE

Dr. Jane Irvine

As important as it is to understand how psychosocial factors contribute to disease, it is even more important to discover ways of preventing, treating, or mitigating their negative effects. An exemplary program of research into clinical interventions in cardiac health psychology has been led by Dr. Jane Irvine, a psychologist at York University and Toronto General Hospital, for two decades. Dr. Irvine and her team have been involved in a spectrum of work in cardiac psychology, from basic research into the role of stress and depression to the development of interventions for patients with heart disease. Some of her earliest work involved the development and evaluation of stress-reduction methods to assist patients diagnosed with a major risk factor for heart disease: high blood pressure (Irvine & Logan, 1991).

Among patients who have had a heart attack, good psychosocial care is a key ingredient of recovery and quality of life. These patients are confronted with issues of lifestyle modification (quitting smoking, getting exercise), managing their emotional state (especially depression), and family concerns. Dr. Irvine and associates have investigated the impact of a variety of interventions and programs addressing these issues (e.g., Irvine & Ritvo, 1998).

As you have learned, psychological stress can play an important role in the development and outcome of heart disease. Some effects of stress are more subtle, but equally important. Often the stress of treatment itself can affect the patient's survival and quality of life. As medical technology has improved and made it possible for people to live longer with heart disease, it has often come at a high psychological price.

Take, for example, the life-saving technology known as the implantable cardioverter defibrillator. This is a device used to treat life-threatening arrhythmias—changes in the heart's rhythm that may lead to sudden death. The defibrillators are implanted in the patient's chest and monitor the heart. When they detect the onset of a potentially life-threatening arrhythmia, they administer a shock to the heart, stimulating it to return to a normal rhythm.

Most patients benefit greatly from these devices, but for some the benefit comes with a burden. Imagine the patient's situation. When the heart begins abnormal activity it is shocked. The shock is not benign—for many patients it is quite unpleasant. As well, it is an unmistakable reminder that something that could have killed them just happened. The situation can be very stressful.

Dr. Irvine and her group have developed specific interventions and counselling techniques in research they have performed on patients with implantable defibrillators. These techniques help patients to address issues of stress and helplessness, understand how their responses to defibrillator activity may reflect attempts to control it, and develop more positive coping skills.

One of the most important features of these interventions is that they are designed to meet the needs of patients where they live. The interventions are accompanied by manuals that the patients can use to learn how to regulate their stress levels, and the counselling is delivered, in part, by distance methods such as over the telephone. Given that many patients do not live in close proximity to a specialized treatment centre, this kind of intervention allows access to state-of-the-art care for anyone who can read and has access to a telephone. This is an issue of great importance in a country like Canada that, outside its major cities, is characterized by small populations in massive regions in which remoteness limits access to primary health care.

The work of Dr. Irvine and her team is representative of research and practice in behavioural medicine. It is multidisciplinary, involving the full spectrum of professionals who deal with cardiac patients: cardiologists, nurses, psychiatrists, psychologists, and rehabilitation workers. It addresses basic theoretical questions and practical outcomes. Finally, it is oriented to important issues that affect the lives of cardiac patients.

SUMMARY

- There is a long history of attempts to explain the origin of illness and disease by psychological processes. Advances in psychological and physiological methods have lent a new credibility to these ideas.
- The widespread influence of psychological factors on physical illness is recognized by a distinct axis and diagnostic process in DSM IV-TR. Presently, this system is being considered for substantial revision.
- Biologically plausible mechanisms for the occurrence of certain diseases exist in the physiological changes known to accompany psychological states. Such changes can be mediated in complex ways by the autonomic, neuroendocrine, and immune systems and their interactions.
- Psychological stress, a basic psychological process that stimulates physiological disease mechanisms, is complex and regulated by cognitive, personality, and social variables that can enhance or diminish risk of disease.
- A number of disease states, including the common cold, ulcers, and heart disease, can be understood, at least in part, by examining psychological and psychophysiological variables.
- Theory and findings in this area have contributed to the development of promising psychological treatments for physical disorders.

MySearchLab offers you extensive help with your writing and research projects and provides round-the-clock access to credible and reliable source material. Chapter quizzes and a full electronic version of the text are also provided. Answers to the Before Moving On feature are provided on the MySearchLab. Take a tour at www.mysearchlab.com.

KEY TERMS

dualistic (p. 147)
behavioural medicine (p. 148)
health psychology (p. 148)
mechanism (p. 149)
lesions (p. 149)
nonspecific immune responses (p. 152)
cellular immunity (p. 152)
humoral immunity (p. 153)
psychoneuroimmunology (p. 153)
alarm (p. 154)
resistance (p. 154)
exhaustion (p. 154)
general adaptation syndrome (GAS) (p. 154)
transactional model (1) (p. 155)
appraisals (p. 155)
primary appraisals (p. 155)
secondary appraisals (p. 155)
internal locus of control (p. 157)
external locus of control (p. 157)
longitudinal study (p. 162)
ischemic heart disease (p. 164)
myocardial infarction (p. 164)
stroke (p. 164)
potential years of life lost (PYLL) (p. 164)
vasculature (p. 164)
systolic blood pressure/diastolic blood pressure (p. 165)
cardiac output (p. 165)
total peripheral resistance (p. 165)
arrhythmias (p. 165)
atherosclerosis (p. 165)
atherogenesis (p. 165)
controllable risk factors (p. 165)
protective factor (p. 165)
hypertension (p. 166)
stress reactivity paradigm (p. 166)
cardiovascular reactivity (p. 166)
Type A (p. 167)
psychophysiological reactivity model (p. 167)
psychosocial vulnerability model (p. 167)
transactional model (2) (p. 167)
health behaviour model (p. 168)
constitutional vulnerability (p. 168)

KATE HARKNESS

Chapter 8

Mood Disorders and Suicide

LEARNING OBJECTIVES

AFTER READING THIS CHAPTER, STUDENTS WILL BE ABLE TO:

1. Describe the symptoms and clinical features of the major unipolar and bipolar mood disorders.
2. Explain how biological, psychological, and environmental factors can work together to cause mood disorders.
3. Identify the major classes of medications used to treat unipolar and bipolar mood disorders.
4. Define cognitive-behavioural therapy and describe its basic techniques in treating major depressive disorder.
5. Compare and contrast the three forms of adjunctive psychotherapies for bipolar disorder.
6. Explain how biological, psychological, and social factors can all contribute to suicide.

Lindsey was an "army brat." She moved almost every year as a child and, as a result, never fit in at school. In fact, she was bullied very badly at one school. However, things turned around for Lindsey when she entered high school. Her father had retired from the military by this time and Lindsey was able to spend all four years of high school in the same city. She excelled at sports and formed a strong group of friends. Lindsey married her high school sweetheart, Tom, the summer after graduation. They both enlisted in the military because they thought it would be a fun adventure and would help pay for their post-secondary education. Lindsey completed basic training, but then became pregnant. She and Tom decided that she would leave the military and raise their children. Soon after baby Molly was born, Tom was stationed in an unfamiliar suburb; one month later, he was unexpectedly deployed to Afghanistan.

At this point, things began to fall apart for Lindsey. Housebound with an infant, she missed Tom terribly and felt isolated in her new surroundings. An overwhelming sense of loneliness fell over her and she began to have crying spells several times a day. It became a struggle for her to get out of bed in the morning and she rarely showered or changed out of her pyjamas. She felt worthless in her capacity as a mother and began to resent her daughter. After a particularly difficult night with Molly, Lindsey called her mother and confessed to thoughts of killing herself and her baby. Lindsey's mother took the next flight out and brought Lindsey to the hospital. After two days of inpatient treatment, during which Lindsey was started on citalopram, a selective serotonin reuptake inhibitor (SSRI), Lindsey was sent home in the care of her mother and referred to outpatient treatment at a university hospital. There, she was enrolled in a treatment study investigating the combination of citalopram and interpersonal psychotherapy (IPT) in the treatment of severe major depression.

After four weeks of treatment, Lindsey started sleeping better and saw her energy level improve. In weekly IPT sessions, she explored the difficulty of her role transition to that of wife and mother in the context of her husband's absence. She also worked with her therapist on skills needed to seek support and explored the difficulty of making friends in the context of her early history of bullying. After 20 weeks of treatment, Lindsey felt much better. She had joined a support group for women whose husbands were deployed overseas and had joined a local mommy group in her neighbourhood. Lindsey remains cautiously optimistic about the future. She has finally fallen in love with Molly and is finding new joy in motherhood. Nevertheless, she has decided to put off having another child for a few years and is looking forward to starting university when Tom returns home.

***

Jay's earliest childhood memories are of visiting his mother in the hospital. Jay's mother suffered from bipolar I disorder and was in and out of the hospital for most of his early life. She ended her own life when Jay was 12 years old. Fortunately, Jay had a very strong relationship with his father, and their bond only deepened following his mother's death.

Jay always struggled academically, and in Grade 8 he was given a diagnosis of attention deficit/hyperactivity disorder (ADHD). In high school, his attention and hyperactivity problems increased, and his mood became labile. He was morose and sullen one day and jumping out of his seat, talking a mile a minute, the next. Jay also became more difficult to handle at home and his father was reminded of behaviours he had seen in his late wife—for example, staying up all night making plans to "solve the world's problems" and refusing to go to school because "I'm smarter than all of them." Finally, Jay's guidance counsellor set up an appointment with a psychiatrist.

Jay's father was devastated to learn that Jay was suffering from pediatric bipolar disorder. Jay was placed on carbamazepine (Tegretol), an anticonvulsant medication, and he and his father participated in family-focused therapy (FFT). Through the FFT sessions, Jay became educated about the symptoms of bipolar disorder and the importance of staying on his medication. Together, Jay and his father learned skills to improve their communication. Despite several weeks of treatment, Jay's symptoms did not improve and he slipped into a deep depression. As a result, Jay's psychiatrist increased his dose of Tegretol and added an antidepressant medication, buproprion (Wellbutrin). This combination worked for Jay and his mood stabilized. Jay graduated from high school and enrolled in a local community college. Given the stress of a new school and living independently, Jay's chances of relapse are very high. Jay's father and psychiatrist are trying to ease his transition by setting up disability services with his school and reinforcing with Jay the importance of staying on his medication. With continued support and ongoing treatment, Jay will hopefully avoid his mother's tragic fate.

Historical Perspective

Depression has existed throughout human history. In ancient times, as discussed in Chapter 1, all mental disorders were explained as possession by supernatural forces. By the classical Greek era, however, attempts were made to explain mental disorders using scientific approaches. Hippocrates (460–377 BC), for example, lived at the time of Hellenic enlightenment, when great advances were made in all areas of knowledge. He applied Empedocles' (490–430 BC) humoral theory to mental disorders and proposed that "exaltation" (mania) was caused by an excess of warmth and dampness in the brain and that "melancholia" (depression) was caused by an excess of black bile, which could be seen as a heavy residue in the blood or discolorations on the skin. As late as the seventeenth century, clinicians attempted to cure melancholia by draining blood from patients in an attempt to rebalance the body's humours (i.e., "bloodletting").

Throughout the Roman times, philosophers and physicians came to recognize the importance of emotional factors in causing depression. For example, Cicero (106–43 BC) stated that "perturbations of the mind may proceed from a neglect of reason," and was the first to suggest psychotherapy as a treatment for melancholia.

By the fourth century, the Christian church predominated Western thinking, and supernatural explanations for mental disturbance (e.g., possession by the devil) flourished again for many centuries. Natural theories of mental illness did not re-emerge in any serious way until the seventeenth century. Robert Burton's *Anatomy of Melancholy* was published in 1621 and provided a detailed and scholarly account of the psychological (e.g., fear, solitude) and social (e.g., poverty) causes of depression that is still read today.

The work of Emil Kraepelin (1855–1926) began the modern age of theories about the etiology of depression. Kraepelin coined the term *manic-depression* and described both depressive and manic forms of this disorder. His descriptions formed the basis for the definition of the **mood disorders** contained in the modern diagnostic systems, such as the DSM-IV-TR (American Psychiatric Association [APA], 2000).

The early twentieth century also saw a resurgence of psychological explanations of mental disorders through the work of Sigmund Freud and his student Karl Abraham. Their early psychodynamic model drew a parallel between depression and grief. In a 1917 essay, Freud noted that in mourners who are unable to resolve their grief, the anger they feel toward their lost loved one is turned inward as self-denigration. This leads to symptoms that are similar in both acute grief and depression, including weeping, loss of appetite, difficulty sleeping, loss of pleasure in life, and withdrawal. According to Freud and Abraham, individuals most likely to become depressed following a loss are those whose needs either were not met, or were excessively met, during the oral stage of development. These individuals spend their lives searching for love and approval from others, which then intensifies feelings of loss when a loved one dies (Bemporad, 1992). Freud and Abraham recognized that some individuals develop depression despite the absence of a loss. Therefore, they developed the concept of **imagined loss**, such that the individual unconsciously interprets other types of events as severe loss events (Jackson, 1986). In this formulation, even a failure at work or an argument with a friend could be interpreted as a loss (e.g., loss of esteem, loss of love). Therefore, the impact of these events is more severe for these people than it is for those who do not have this personality tendency to overinterpret events as losses. As such, these events serve as catalysts for the development of depression.

Diagnostic Issues

Have you ever felt sad, depressed, or "down"? Have you felt less interested in the things you usually enjoy doing? Have you ever had times when you felt very tired? What about the opposite: Have you ever felt really good, excited, or "high"? Have you ever been more involved in activities than usual? Have you experienced periods when you needed less sleep than usual to feel rested? These are all symptoms of depression, on the one hand, and mania, on the other, and it is very likely that most people would answer yes to almost all of these questions. Almost everyone goes through transient periods of feeling down and "depressed" as well as through periods of feeling high and "on top of the world." Indeed, life would be very boring if we always felt the same neutral emotion all the time. What distinguishes these very normal mood fluctuations from the changes seen in clinical mood disorders are their *duration* and their *severity*.

For example, whereas most people can point to hours or days here and there when they have felt down or depressed, the DSM-IV-TR criteria for major depressive disorder states that the symptoms of depression must be present for most of the day, more days than not, *for at least two weeks* (duration). Similarly, whereas most people can relate to difficulties falling asleep at night, individuals who meet criteria for this symptom of major depressive disorder require more than an hour to fall asleep nearly every night (severity). Furthermore, to meet DSM-IV-TR criteria for a mood disorder, several symptoms must co-occur. For example, the DSM-IV-TR criteria for major depressive disorder include nine symptoms, of which five must be present to achieve a diagnosis. Therefore, it is only when multiple symptoms co-occur and meet stringent criteria about duration and severity that a mood disorder is present.

It is important to note that the DSM-IV-TR criteria represent arbitrary categorical conventions. There is nothing magical about five symptoms (why not four?) or the duration criterion of two weeks (why not three?). Indeed, American psychiatrist Dr. Kenneth Kendler (1998) has shown that depression, by its nature, is a continuous phenomenon, and that individuals with only four (or three) symptoms may still suffer considerably. Indeed, several researchers have argued that in future editions of the DSM, depression should be defined dimensionally as on a continuum with normal sad mood (e.g., Andrews et al., 2007; Brown & Barlow, 2009). Nevertheless, the DSM-IV-TR is useful because it provides a common language to enable mental health professionals and patients to talk about symptoms.

Mood disorders in the DSM-IV-TR are classified into two broad categories: *unipolar* and *bipolar*. **Unipolar mood disorders** involve a change in mood in the direction of *depression*, whereas **bipolar mood disorders** involve periods of *depression* cycling with periods of *mania*. Each is discussed in turn below.

Unipolar Mood Disorders

A unipolar (one pole) change in mood is a "one-direction" shift that occurs almost exclusively in the negative direction (i.e., depression). Unipolar mania is rarely seen. The two unipolar mood disorders discussed below are major depressive disorder and the less severe, but more chronic, dysthymic disorder.

Major Depressive Disorder

Major depressive disorder (MDD) is often referred to as the "common cold" of mental disorders because it is so prevalent. It is also devastating in its impact. According to the World Health Organization (2008), it is the leading cause of disability worldwide and is the second-leading contributor to the global burden of disease. A 2000 paper by Canadian business and medical leaders reported that depression costs the North American economy $60 billion per year, more than half of that in lost productivity, and named depression an "unheralded business crisis" (Wilson, Joffe, & Wilkerson, 2000).

Depression itself is a very normal human emotion that exists on a continuum from very mild and transient feelings of sadness ("down in the dumps") to the severe, persistent, and debilitating feelings that characterize individuals with major depression. When most of us describe feeling "depressed," we are referring to these mild, transient mood states. However, the use of the word *depression* in this context can make it difficult for people to understand what individuals with MDD experience. Friends and family members may wonder why the depressed person cannot just "get over it." People with MDD may be accused of "faking it" to get attention and may be labelled as "weak" or even morally inferior.

Living with Major Depressive Disorder (MDD)

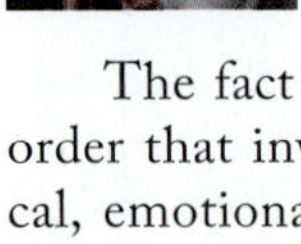

Watch this Speaking Out video at www.mysearchlab.com

Martha: MDD

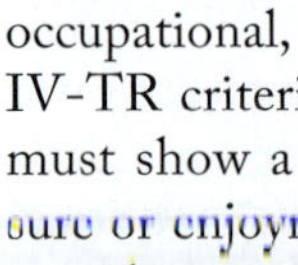

Watch this Speaking Out video at www.mysearchlab.com

The fact is that MDD is a very real and serious disorder that involves abnormalities in all systems (biological, emotional, cognitive, and behavioural) and that can impair functioning in all areas of a person's life (physical, occupational, educational, and relational). To meet DSM-IV-TR criteria for the diagnosis, the depressed individual must show a persistent sad mood and/or a lack of pleasure or enjoyment in activities for at least two weeks. This must be accompanied by at least four additional symptoms, including disturbances in sleeping or eating (either too little or too much), lack of energy, psychomotor retardation or

TABLE 8.1 DSM-IV-TR DIAGNOSTIC CRITERIA FOR MAJOR DEPRESSIVE EPISODE

A. Five (or more) of the following symptoms have been present during the same 2-week period and represent a change from previous functioning; at least one of the symptoms is either (1) depressed mood or (2) loss of interest or pleasure. **Note:** Do not include symptoms that are clearly due to a general medical condition, or mood-incongruent delusions or hallucinations.

1. depressed mood most of the day, nearly every day, as indicated by either subjective report (e.g., feels sad or empty) or observation made by others (e.g., appears tearful). *Note:* In children and adolescents, can be irritable mood.
2. markedly diminished interest or pleasure in all, or almost all, activities most of the day, nearly every day (as indicated by either subjective account or observation made by others)
3. significant weight loss when not dieting or weight gain (e.g., a change of more than 5% of body weight in a month), or decrease or increase in appetite nearly every day. *Note:* In children, consider failure to make expected weight gains.
4. insomnia or hypersomnia nearly every day
5. psychomotor agitation or retardation nearly every day (observable by others, not merely subjective feelings of restlessness or being slowed down)
6. fatigue or loss of energy nearly every day
7. feelings of worthlessness or excessive or inappropriate guilt (which may be delusional) nearly every day (not merely self-reproach or guilt about being sick)
8. diminished ability to think or concentrate, or indecisiveness, nearly every day (either by subjective account or as observed by others)
9. recurrent thoughts of death (not just fear of dying), recurrent suicidal ideation without a specific plan, or a suicide attempt or a specific plan for committing suicide

B. The symptoms do not meet criteria for a Mixed Episode.

C. The symptoms cause clinically significant distress or impairment in social, occupational, or other important areas of functioning.

D. The symptoms are not due to the direct physiological effects of a substance (e.g., a drug of abuse, a medication) or a general medical condition (e.g., hypothyroidism).

E. The symptoms are not better accounted for by Bereavement, i.e., after the loss of a loved one, the symptoms persist for longer than 2 months or are characterized by marked functional impairment, morbid preoccupation with worthlessness, suicidal ideation, psychotic symptoms, or psychomotor retardation.

Source: Reprinted with permission from the *Diagnostic and Statistical Manual of Mental Disorders, Fourth Edition, Text Revision.* (Copyright © 2000). American Psychiatric Association.

agitation (talking or moving more slowly or in a more agitated fashion than usual), difficulty concentrating or making decisions, feelings of worthlessness or guilt, and thoughts of death or suicide.

The criteria for a major depressive episode are presented in Table 8.1. Note that Criterion E specifies that if the symptoms of major depression appear transiently following the death of a loved one, this should be seen as normal grief and not a pathological mood disorder. However, in the proposals for the next edition of the DSM, this criterion has been deleted. That is, according to the proposed DSM-5 (APA, 2010) criteria for MDD, a person could meet criteria for major depression even if his or her symptoms followed the death of a loved one. The decision to remove the bereavement exclusion was based on research showing that bereavement-related depression does not differ from depression resulting from other sorts of loss events that have never been excluded (e.g., divorce) (Zisook & Kendler, 2007). Nevertheless, this decision is contentious, and other researchers have countered that we should not pathologize depressions resulting from other losses either (Horowitz & Wakefield, 2007). What do you think? Should depression symptoms following the death or other loss of a loved one be conceptualized as signs of major depression pathology or are they simply "normal sadness"?

PREVALENCE AND COURSE

MDD affects 1.35 million people in Canada, or 5 percent of the population (Murray & Lopez, 1996). Canadian rates of all mood disorders by age and sex are presented in Figure 8.1. Major depression is a devastating disorder that is associated with significant occupational and interpersonal impairment, physical illness, disability, and death. One of the main factors that accounts for the devastating impact of MDD is the disorder's recurrent course. Approximately 50 percent of individuals who experience one episode of depression will have a second, and up to 90 percent of those who experience two or three episodes will have future recurrences (APA, 2000; Solomon et al., 2000). Furthermore, periods of wellness between episodes become shorter and shorter as the disorder progresses. The episodes themselves last between 6 and 9 months, on average, although they can last for years (APA, 2000).

Average age of first onset of major depression is early to mid twenties (APA, 2000). However, for reasons still unknown, more and more sufferers are having their first onset in childhood and adolescence. Indeed, the incidence of MDD in adolescence is growing faster than in any other age group, and now equals the incidence rate in adults (Birmaher et al., 1996). Adolescence is also the time when sex differences in major depression incidence emerge. Using data from a large-scale study of mental disorders, American epidemiologist Dr. Ronald Kessler reported that rates of

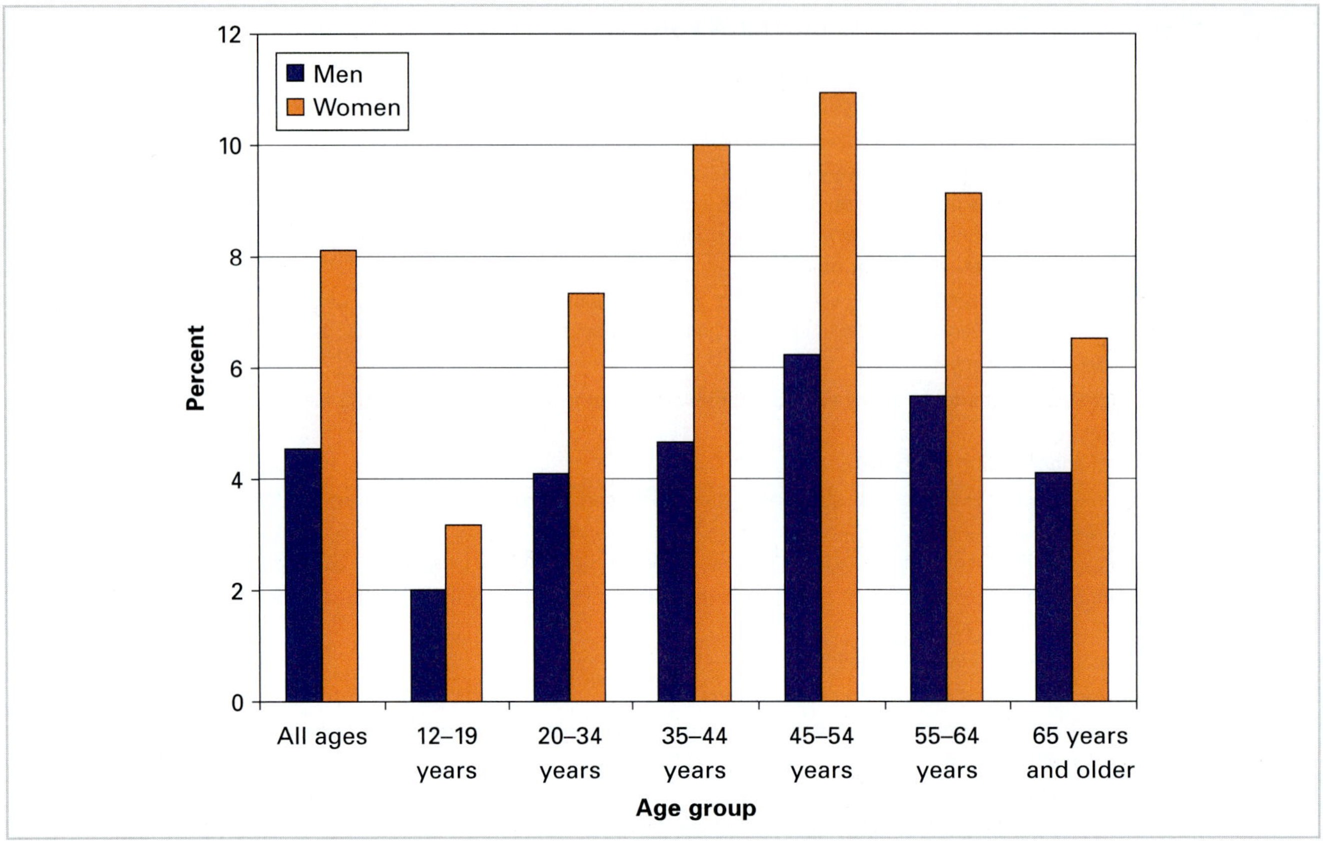

FIGURE 8.1 Percentage Reporting Mood Disorders, by Age Group and Sex, Household Population Aged 12 and Older, Canada, 2009

Source: Statistics Canada, *Canadian Community Health Survey, 2009.* Retrieved from www.statcan.gc.ca/pub/82-625-x/2010002/article/11265-eng.htm

depression grow steadily and equally for both sexes throughout childhood, but then begin to diverge at about age 10. Rates of depression continue to increase dramatically throughout adolescence for girls, whereas they tend to level off for boys (Kessler, McGonagle, Swartz, Blazer, & Nelson, 1993).

Finally, it should be noted that individuals with MDD often suffer from one or more additional (i.e., "comorbid") mental disorders (APA, 2000). The most common class of comorbid disorders is the anxiety disorders, affecting more than 50 percent of patients with MDD (Hirschfeld, 2001). Depressed individuals with comorbid conditions experience a more severe and chronic depression, and they show a slower and less complete response to treatment (Hirschfeld, 2001).

Dysthymic Disorder

Dysthymic disorder, or *dysthymia*, is defined as a chronic low mood, lasting for at least two years, along with at least three associated symptoms (see Table 8.2). The DSM-5 is proposing to rename this disorder chronic depressive disorder. The prevalence of dysthymia in the population is approximately 3 percent (Weissman, Leaf, Bruce, & Florio, 1988). Many individuals with dysthymia also experience recurrent episodes of MDD superimposed on their chronic low mood (i.e., "double depression"; APA, 2000). Other presentations of chronic low mood are seen clinically (see Figure 8.2), including chronic major depression and major depression with poor inter-episode recovery. This latter presentation involves episodes of major depression that fail to remit successfully, thus leading to a chronic dysthymia-like state between episodes. In Figure 8.2, the horizontal line denotes normal mood and the space below the line indicates increasingly depressed mood.

Dr. Daniel Klein and others have found that chronic depression, in all of its manifestations, has higher levels of impairment, a younger age of onset, higher rates of comorbidity, a stronger family history of psychiatric disorder, lower levels of social support, higher levels of stress, and higher levels of dysfunctional personality traits than does episodic major depression (Klein, Taylor, Dickstein, & Harding, 1988; Klein, Taylor, Harding, & Dickstein, 1988). Individuals with chronic depression are also less likely to respond to standard depression treatment than are those with episodic major depression (McCullough, 2005).

Bipolar Mood Disorders

Mania is defined as a distinct period of elevated, expansive, or irritable mood that lasts at least one week and is accompanied by at least three associated symptoms. **Hypomania** is a less severe form of mania that involves a similar number of symptoms, but those symptoms need to be present for only

TABLE 8.2 DSM-IV-TR DIAGNOSTIC CRITERIA FOR DYSTHYMIC DISORDER

A. Depressed mood for most of the day, for more days than not, as indicated either by subjective account or observation by others, for at least 2 years. **Note:** In children and adolescents, mood can be irritable and duration must be at least 1 year.

B. Presence, while depressed, of two (or more) of the following:

1. poor appetite or overeating
2. insomnia or hypersomnia
3. low energy or fatigue
4. low self-esteem
5. poor concentration or difficulty making decisions
6. feelings of hopelessness

C. During the 2-year period (1 year for children or adolescents) of the disturbance, the person has never been without the symptoms in Criteria A and B for more than 2 months at a time.

D. No Major Depressive Episode has been present during the first 2 years of the disturbance (1 year for children and adolescents); i.e., the disturbance is not better accounted for by chronic Major Depressive Disorder, or Major Depressive Disorder, In Partial Remission. **Note:** There may have been a previous Major Depressive Episode provided there was a full remission (no significant signs or symptoms for 2 months) before development of the Dysthymic Disorder. In addition, after the initial 2 years (1 year in children or adolescents) of Dysthymic Disorder, there may be superimposed episodes of Major Depressive Disorder, in which case both diagnoses may be given when the criteria are met for a Major Depressive Episode.

E. There has never been a Manic Episode, a Mixed Episode, or a Hypomanic Episode, and criteria have never been met for Cyclothymic Disorder.

F. The disturbance does not occur exclusively during the course of a chronic Psychotic Disorder, such as Schizophrenia or Delusional Disorder.

G. The symptoms are not due to the direct physiological effects of a substance (e.g., a drug of abuse, a medication) or a general medical condition (e.g., hypothyroidism).

H. The symptoms cause clinically significant distress or impairment in social, occupational, or other important areas of functioning.

Source: Reprinted with permission from the *Diagnostic and Statistical Manual of Mental Disorders, Fourth Edition, Text Revision.* (Copyright © 2000). American Psychiatric Association.

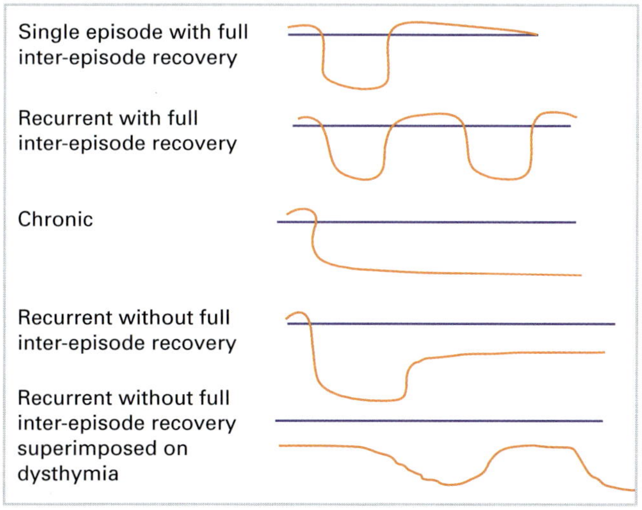

FIGURE 8.2 Types of Chronic Depression

The horizontal line denotes normal mood and the space below the line indicates increasingly depressed mood.

four days. The DSM-5 is proposing to clarify the episodicity of mania and hypomania by requiring that symptoms be "present most of the day nearly every day" and "represent a noticeable change from usual behavior" in order to qualify for the diagnosis. Symptoms of mania include increased energy, decreased need for sleep, racing thoughts, pressured speech, and problems with attention and concentration. Judgment is also impaired, and these patients may go on spending sprees, engage in substance abuse or risky sexual behaviour, or may even become aggressive. Patients in a manic episode may feel that they are special in some way, or that they have been "chosen" to fulfill a special mission. The DSM-IV-TR diagnostic criteria for a manic episode are provided in Table 8.3. Note that some individuals can experience both manic/hypomanic and depressive symptoms at the same time. This is called a "mixed" state. The DSM-5 is proposing adding a "with mixed features" specifier to both manic/hypomanic and depressive episodes. At least three symptoms of the opposing episode state will be required to meet criteria for mixed features.

Bipolar Disorder: Ann

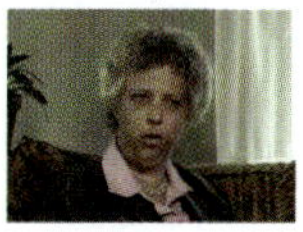

Watch this Speaking Out video at www.mysearchlab.com

At first, the symptoms of mania may be experienced as enjoyable and intoxicating. Patients feel an abundance of energy and report that they are able to get a lot of things done. Their minds may seem clear and sharply focused, allowing them to solve difficult problems and make keen insights. Indeed, this positive side to the manic state may lead some patients to deny the negative impact their symptoms may be having on their lives, delay seeking treatment, or stop taking their medication if they are in treatment. As the noted

TABLE 8.3 DSM-IV-TR DIAGNOSTIC CRITERIA FOR MANIC EPISODE

A. A distinct period of abnormally and persistently elevated, expansive, or irritable mood, lasting at least 1 week (or any duration if hospitalization is necessary).

B. During the period of mood disturbance, three (or more) of the following symptoms have persisted (four if the mood is only irritable) and have been present to a significant degree:

1. inflated self-esteem or grandiosity
2. decreased need for sleep (e.g., feels rested after only 3 hours of sleep)
3. more talkative than usual or pressure to keep talking
4. flight of ideas, or subjective experience that thoughts are racing
5. distractibility (i.e., attention too easily drawn to unimportant or irrelevant external stimuli)
6. increase in goal-directed activity (either socially, at work or school, or sexually) or psychomotor agitation
7. excessive involvement in pleasurable activities that have a high potential for painful consequences (e.g., engaging in unrestrained buying sprees, sexual indiscretions, or foolish business investments)

C. The symptoms do not meet the criteria for a Mixed Episode.

D. The mood disturbance is sufficiently severe to cause marked impairment in occupational functioning or in usual social activities or relationships with others, or to necessitate hospitalization to prevent harm to self or others, or there are psychotic features.

E. The symptoms are not due to the direct physiological effects of a substance (e.g., a drug of abuse, a medication, or other treatment) or a general medical condition (e.g., hypothyroidism).

Note: Manic-like episodes that are clearly caused by somatic antidepressant treatment (e.g., medication, electroconvulsive therapy, light therapy) should not count toward a diagnosis of Bipolar I Disorder.

Source: Reprinted with permission from the *Diagnostic and Statistical Manual of Mental Disorders, Fourth Edition, Text Revision.* (Copyright © 2000). American Psychiatric Association.

psychiatrist, and bipolar disorder sufferer, Dr. Kay Redfield Jamison (1995, p. 67) states in her book *An Unquiet Mind*,

> At first when I'm high, it's tremendous . . . ideas are fast . . . like shooting stars you follow until brighter ones appear. . . . All shyness disappears, the right words and gestures are suddenly there . . . uninteresting people, things become intensely interesting. Sensuality is pervasive, the desire to seduce and be seduced is irresistible. Your marrow is infused with unbelievable feelings of ease, power, well-being, omnipotence, euphoria . . . you can do anything . . . but somewhere this changes.

As the episode progresses, symptoms may become more severe and start to be experienced as disturbing and even frightening: "the fast ideas become too fast, and there are far too many . . . overwhelming confusion replaces clarity . . . you stop keeping up with it—memory goes. Infectious humor ceases to amuse. Your friends become frightened . . . everything is now against the grain . . . you are irritable, angry, frightened, uncontrollable, and trapped" (Jamison, 1995, p. 67). At their most extreme, these patients can experience a break with reality, or psychosis.

BIPOLAR I AND BIPOLAR II

Speaking Out Bipolar Disorder: Living with Bipolar Disorder (Feliziano)

Watch this Speaking Out video at www.mysearchlab.com

In **bipolar I disorder**, an individual has a history of one or more manic episodes with or without one or more major depressive episodes. A depressive episode is not required for the diagnosis of bipolar I disorder, but most patients have both. **Bipolar II disorder** is defined as a history of one or more hypomanic episodes with one or more major depressive episodes. Bipolar II disorder can be more difficult to diagnose than bipolar I because hypomanic episodes are not as severe as manic episodes. Hypomanic episodes may be experienced as a period of successful high productivity, and, indeed, many patients with bipolar II are reluctant to take mood-stabilizing medication because they experience their hypomania as enjoyable. For both disorders, the hypomanic/manic episodes typically last between two weeks and four months, while the depressive episodes last between six and nine months, as in unipolar depression. Rates of suicide range between 10 and 15 percent, similar to those in unipolar depression (APA, 2000). The DSM-5 is proposing to clarify the symptomatic presentation of bipolar disorder by requiring specification of one of the following subtypes: (1) current or most recent episode hypomanic, (2) current or most recent episode manic, (3) current or most recent episode depressed, or (4) current or most recent episode unspecified.

According to a large-scale epidemiological study conducted in the United States, the lifetime prevalence rate in the population of bipolar I disorder is approximately 0.8 percent and of bipolar II disorder is 0.5 percent (Kessler, Rubinow, Holmes, Abelson, & Zhao, 1997). Rates do not differ between men and women. The DSM-IV-TR states that the mean age of onset of bipolar disorder is 20 years, and recent studies have shown that at least 50 percent of adult patients with bipolar disorder report the onset of their symptoms before age 17 (Birmaher et al., 2006). There is now a growing consensus that bipolar disorder has its onset in childhood, and current estimates place the prevalence of bipolar disorder in children at 0.5 percent. Children with bipolar disorder often do not meet the strict DSM-IV-TR definition, and tend to have a rapid-cycling or mixed-cycling pattern. Experts believe that children and adolescents with bipolar disorder are underdiagnosed and undertreated due to a lack of understanding about pediatric bipolar disorder. This is a controversial issue, however, as other experts argue that a focus on pediatric bipolar disorder may lead to overdiagnosis of this condition and the application of inappropriate treatments (e.g., mood stabilizers, antipsychotic medications) to large groups of children who in fact suffer from disorders other than bipolar disorder (e.g., ADHD). Indeed, a recent study found that the number of American children and adolescents treated for bipolar disorder increased fortyfold from 1994 to 2003 and has been increasing ever since (Moreno et al., 2007). The investigators suggested from these findings that doctors have been more aggressively applying the diagnosis to children, and not that the incidence of the disorder in children has increased.

CYCLOTHYMIA

Cyclothymia is to bipolar disorder what dysthymia is to unipolar depression. That is, cyclothymia is a chronic, but less severe, form of bipolar disorder. It involves a history of at least two years of alternating hypomanic episodes and episodes of depression that do not meet the full criteria for major depression. The lifetime prevalence of cyclothymic disorder is 0.4 to 1 percent, and the rate is equal in men and women, though women more often seek treatment. Because the mood swings are relatively mild and the episodes of hypomania may be enjoyable, individuals with cyclothymia often do not seek treatment. However, this group is at risk for developing full-blown bipolar disorder. In particular, antidepressant medication should be used with caution in this group of individuals as these medications can trigger manic episodes in vulnerable patients.

RAPID CYCLING BIPOLAR DISORDER

The DSM-IV-TR defines rapid cycling bipolar disorder as the presence of four or more manic and/or major depressive

APPLIED CLINICAL CASE

Charlie Sheen

Charlie Sheen has always lived life on the edge. He was expelled from high school for low grades and poor attendance, and by his late teens already had a reputation as a hard-partying womanizer. He has been linked with a large number of women, and was married three times. In 1996 he was charged with battery for abusing his ex-girlfriend, Brittany Ashland. In 2005 his then wife, Denise Richards, came forward with allegations of violent threats. Finally, in 2009 he was arrested and charged for assaulting his third wife, Brooke Mueller. Sheen had been in and out of drug rehab since his teens, and in 1998 he was hospitalized for a cocaine overdose at a time when he was already on probation for a previous drug offence. Throughout all this turmoil, however, Sheen maintained a successful acting career, including several Emmy and Golden Globe Award nominations. The most dramatic turn of events for Sheen occurred in January 2011. Sheen used a large ("suitcase") amount of cocaine during a 36-hour bender that resulted in hospitalization. The weeks that followed this event saw the release of several heavily publicized rants by Sheen that seemed to portray a different person. In these televised rants Sheen appeared dishevelled, his speech was pressured and at times incoherent, he had difficulty staying seated, and he appeared agitated. However, it was the grandiosity and floridity of these rants that caught the world's attention: "I was bangin' seven-gram rocks [of crack cocaine] and finishing them because that's how I roll, because I have one speed, one gear. [I survived] because I'm me. I'm different. I have a different constitution, I have a different brain, I have a different heart. I got tiger blood, man. Dying's for fools, dying's for amateurs." To mental health experts, Sheen was clearly suffering from the symptoms of a manic episode, likely induced by his cocaine binge. Sheen rejected this assessment in his most famous quip, "I'm not bipolar, I'm bi-winning." As is very common for individuals with bipolar disorder, Sheen's behaviour was followed by a number of negative consequences. On March 2, 2011, his twin toddler sons were taken from his home, where they had been living with Sheen and his two mistresses. Then, on March 7, 2001, he was fired from the popular television show *Two and a Half Men.* However, Charlie Sheen is a celebrity; as such, he likely remained buffered from the negative consequences of his behaviour by the continued adoration of his many followers. On March 3, 2011, he set a new Guinness World Record for the fastest person to reach 1 million followers on Twitter, and in April 2011 he launched a North American tour to promote his "bi-winning" philosophy. The outcome for Charlie Sheen is not certain, and media coverage of his condition has dropped off. Nevertheless, a positive sidebar may be noted for other sufferers of bipolar disorder: while in Toronto for his tour, Sheen staged a march to raise awareness for bipolar disorder, and pledged to match all contributions to the Alberta-based Organization for Bipolar Affective Disorders "dollar for dollar."

episodes in a 12-month period (APA, 2000). The episodes must be separated from each other by at least two months of full or partial remission, *or* by a switch to the opposite mood state (i.e., mania to depression or vice versa). Patients with a rapid cycling presentation have higher rates of disability and lower rates of response to treatment (Sachs & Gardner-Schuster, 2007). Rapid cycling can be induced, or made worse, by antidepressant medications. Therefore, it is important for patients who are receiving antidepressant treatment to also receive a mood stabilizer (e.g., lithium). Some researchers also identify ultrarapid (cycling every few days) and ultradian (cycling that occurs daily) cycling. However, other investigators believe that these patterns reflect the mood lability inherent in the bipolar disorder diagnosis. Therefore, these additional **specifiers** are not present in the DSM-IV-TR.

Mood Disorder with Seasonal Pattern

Seasonal affective disorder (SAD) can occur in both unipolar depression and bipolar disorder and is characterized by recurrent depressive episodes that are tied to the changing seasons. In northern latitudes, episodes generally occur in the winter months, whereas in southern latitudes they tend to occur in what we consider the summer months (which, after all, are the winter months there). Approximately 11 percent of patients with major depression have SAD. In the general Canadian population, its prevalence is 2 to 3 percent, as compared with 1.3 to 3 percent in Europe and less than 0.9 percent in Asia (Levitt, Boyle, Jofee, & Baumal, 2000).

Early research attempting to explain the seasonal pattern of SAD focused on melatonin, a hormone that is secreted at night by the pineal gland. The normal function of melatonin is as follows. As the sun provides increased light in the morning, melatonin release is lowered. This causes body temperature to rise, triggering the body processes to move to their awake state. Patients with SAD, however, may need more light to trigger decreased melatonin secretion. Therefore, as the nights grow longer in the winter months, melatonin levels remain high, and, thus, there is nothing to prompt the switch from the sleep state to the wake state. As a result, patients continue to sleep, or feel drowsy when awake. This dysregulation of the natural biological pattern of sleep and wakefulness is referred to as a "phase-delayed circadian rhythm" (Lam & Levitan, 2000).

To complicate matters, however, research evidence reviewed by Canadian psychiatrists Lam and Levitan (2000) found that medications that suppress melatonin were not effective in relieving symptoms of SAD. Also, the 24-hour winter melatonin rhythm does not differ between individuals with and without SAD. Therefore, there is likely more to the story than melatonin dysregulation alone. Substantial evidence does indeed suggest, however, that patients with SAD have phase-delayed circadian rhythms (see Lam & Levitan, 2000). Therefore, therapies that "reset" the circadian clock, such as exposure to morning light ("phototherapy"), may work by inducing a "phase advancement" of temperature, melatonin, and other neurochemicals, such as the stress hormone cortisol.

Mood Disorder with Postpartum Onset

While the birth of a new baby is often one of the happiest experiences in a woman's life, as many as 70 percent of women experience mood swings and feelings of depression up to two weeks after childbirth. In most new mothers these symptoms resolve themselves over time and do not impair functioning. In approximately 10 to 15 percent of new mothers, however, the mood swings are chronic and severe enough to meet the criteria for a major depressive or manic episode. In very rare cases (0.1 percent of new mothers), postpartum mood episodes can include psychotic symptoms such as command hallucinations to kill the infant. In 2000 postpartum psychosis was implicated in the tragic suicide of a Toronto-area physician who jumped in front of a subway train while holding her six-month-old baby. Postpartum psychosis has a 5 percent suicide rate and a 4 percent infanticide rate. American actress Brooke Shields documents her struggle with postpartum depression in her 2005 book, *Down Came the Rain.*

Postpartum depression affects women similarly across cultures and socio-economic levels. Risk factors for postpartum depression include a family history of depression, a history of previous depressive episodes, a poor marital relationship and low social support, and stressful life events concurrent with, or immediately following, childbirth (O'Hara, 1995). The hormone progesterone has also been proposed as a causative factor. The waste product ("metabolite") of progesterone acts like a barbiturate drug in the brain, and the very rapid withdrawal of progesterone that occurs with the delivery of the placenta has been significantly associated with depressive symptoms in the week following delivery (O'Hara, 1995). However, the nature of this association beyond the first week is complex and more research is needed.

Mood disorder with postpartum onset affects not only the mother, but also her current and future children. Results of a four-year follow-up study suggest that a mother's postpartum depression is associated with poorer cognitive test scores in her children (O'Hara, Neunaber, & Zekoski, 1984). Another study reported that 32 percent of women with postpartum depression changed their future child-bearing plans significantly, choosing adoption, abortion, or even sterilization (Peindl, Zolnik, Wisner, & Hanusa, 1995). Despite the devastating consequences of this condition, a recent study found that only 46 percent of physicians screened new mothers at well-baby checkups for postpartum mood disorder (Seehusen, Baldwin, Runkle, & Clark, 2005).

1 BEFORE MOVING ON

In the DSM-IV-TR, major depression is defined as a category that is presumed to be qualitatively distinct from normal sadness. However, many researchers have argued that in future editions of the DSM major depression should be defined as a dimensional construct, on a continuum with normal sad mood. What are the advantages and disadvantages of defining depression dimensionally versus categorically?

Etiology

There is no single cause for the mood disorders, and researchers now agree that these disorders are likely caused by an interaction of a number of risk factors at a number of levels of analysis. For example, the mood disorders are highly heritable, but a family history of a mood disorder does not guarantee the presence of disorder. A genetic vulnerability likely needs to be expressed as a vulnerable personality or cognitive trait and triggered by stress in the environment. Similarly, stressful life events are one of the strongest triggers of mood disorders, but again, not everyone who experiences stress becomes depressed. The presence of pre-existing vulnerability factors, such as a family history of depression, a history of poor relationships with early caregivers, or particular personality patterns, may need to be present for individuals to succumb to the effects of stress. Therefore, whereas a number of models of etiology are presented below, it is important to keep in mind that these are not competing models, and that no single model provides a complete account of depression. Instead, they each provide a piece of the puzzle. The most exciting research going on right now is using the latest advances in psychology, genetics, and neuroscience to provide a full and comprehensive model of risk for the mood disorders.

Psychological and Environmental Causal Factors

The psychological level of analysis examines how variables such as temperament and personality, dysfunctional thinking, and maladaptive interpersonal behaviour contribute to the mood disorders. The environmental level of analysis examines the role of external factors, such as stressful or traumatic life events and negative early parental attachments. Over the past century, a number of influential theories have been developed to integrate the above vulnerability factors into models of risk for mood disorders. Four of the most enduring of these theories will be discussed below.

PSYCHODYNAMIC THEORIES

Current psychodynamic theorists no longer subscribe to Freud and Abraham's theory described above that risk for depression is caused by unmet needs during the oral stage of development. Nevertheless, a number of aspects of this theory continue to strongly influence thinking about depression. For example, research has supported the theory that relationships between parents and children are important in shaping a child's temperament, and that neglectful and/or abusive parenting confers a strong risk for later depression (Harkness & Lumley, 2007). In addition, research has confirmed the theory that individuals with a temperamental vulnerability to depression do interpret life events as having a greater impact, and that these events are more strongly related to depression than they are in individuals who do not have this pre-existing vulnerability (Harkness, 2008).

Indeed, the role of personality in depression is still very relevant. In particular, Dr. Sidney Blatt and Canadian psychologist Dr. David Zuroff (McGill University) have discussed two personality patterns that they theorize provide a risk for depression—dependency and self-criticism (Blatt, Quinlan, Chevron, McDonald, & Zuroff, 1982). Dependent individuals rely excessively on their interpersonal relationships for their sense of identity. They are described as being excessively needy, fearing abandonment, and feeling helpless in relationships. In contrast, self-critical individuals are prone to fears of failure, self-blame, inferiority, and guilt, particularly in areas of achievement. Blatt theorized that these personality styles, which develop as a function of maladaptive parenting styles and/or traumas early in development, render people vulnerable to depression when they face a stressful life event that triggers the personality theme. For example, Lindsey, whom we met in the case study above, would likely score high on a measure of dependency given her inconsistent attachments to peers early in life. Therefore, it is not too surprising that she developed depression when her current life situation ("abandonment" by her husband in new surroundings with no friends) mirrored that early life experience. A great deal of research supports the role of these personality styles as predictors of depression in the face of stress (e.g., Blatt, 2004; Bulmash, Harkness, Stewart, & Bagby, 2009).

COGNITIVE THEORIES

The most enduring cognitive theory of the mood disorders was developed by American psychiatrist Dr. Aaron T. Beck in the 1960s. Beck's great insight was in proposing that one's emotional response to a situation is determined by the manner in which that situation is appraised or evaluated (Beck, 1967). For example, imagine that you see an acquaintance on the other side of the street. You wave to her, but she does not wave back. What thoughts are running through your head about this situation? What emotions are you feeling? Different people are likely to appraise this same situation differently. For example, if you thought, "I can't believe she didn't even acknowledge me, how rude of her!" you may feel annoyance or even anger. However, if you thought, "She must not like me, I'm such a loser," you may feel embarrassment, rejection, or sadness. Or, you may have thought, "I guess she didn't see me; oh well, I'll catch up with her later." In this case, you might not feel any particular emotion at all and may just forget the experience altogether. According to Beck, people with depression, and people prone to depression, are more likely to appraise situations negatively than those not prone to depression and, hence, will be more likely to experience negative mood in response to such situations. The important thing to note is that the situations themselves are not necessarily inherently negative (such as in the example above), but they are interpreted negatively by the depression-prone individual. In particular, according to Beck, depressed individuals apply **cognitive distortions** to situations that lead to negative mood. Examples of common cognitive distortions include:

1. *All-or-nothing thinking*: You see things in black-or-white categories. If your performance falls short of perfect, you see yourself as a total failure. Example: When a student got a C on a math exam, she told herself, "I'm a total failure. I'll never get into med school."
2. *Overgeneralization*: You see a single negative event as a never-ending pattern of defeat by using words such as "always" or "never" when you think about it. Example: You are late for a doctor appointment and you tell yourself, "I'm *always* screwing up."
3. *Magnification (catastrophizing)*: You exaggerate the importance of your errors or problems. Example: You forget someone's name when you are introducing him or her, and you tell yourself, "This is *terrible*!"
4. *Jumping to conclusions*: You interpret things negatively when there are no definite facts to support your conclusion. Example: Your girlfriend/boyfriend does not return your call, so you tell yourself, "She/he probably doesn't care about me anymore." You feel so hurt that you mope all day until you discover that she/he was visiting a grandparent in the hospital and did not even get the message that you had called.

According to Beck's model, the foundation of the depressed person's negative cognitive style is the depressive *schema* (Beck, 1976). **Schemas** are hypothetical structures in the mind that contain core beliefs about the self, the world, and the future—the **cognitive triad**. Schemas develop from our early experiences with the world and represent stored memories, images, and thoughts from these experiences. Schemas then guide the selection, encoding, organization, storage, and retrieval of information. We all have schemas and these are central to our understanding of ourselves and our world. The key feature of the depressed individual's schema is its rigidly negative quality (e.g., "I'm a failure," "My future is hopeless," "No one loves me"). It is easy to see that if one has a rigid, pervasive belief that one is fundamentally unlovable, the ambiguous event used as an example above could be interpreted as further evidence of one's unlovability.

Beck's cognitive model is a **diathesis-stress model** (Beck, 1983). Specifically, Beck proposed that the negative cognitive schemas of the depression-prone person remain inactive in the mind, and thus serve as silent vulnerability factors (diatheses) that do not express themselves until activated, or "primed," by a stressful life event that matches the theme of the schema. For example, someone with the schema "I'm a failure" will be at risk for depression when faced with the stress of, say, getting fired from a job or failing a course. In contrast, someone with the schema "I'm unlovable" will be at risk for depression when faced with an interpersonal stress, such as the breakup of an important relationship.

A great deal of evidence has emerged over the past 40 years supporting the cognitive model of depression (see Beck & Dozois, 2011; Dozois & Beck, 2008). Research by Canadian psychologists, including Drs. David Clark (University of New Brunswick), Keith Dobson (University of Calgary), David Dozois (University of Western Ontario), Ian Gotlib (formerly at University of Western Ontario, now at Stanford University), and Zindel Segal (University of Toronto), has provided some of the most compelling and important support for this model, showing that depressed individuals do, indeed, display significantly more negative thinking and engage in negative biases when attending to and remembering information (see Clark & Beck, 1999). Dozois and Dobson (2001b) have also found that the negative schemas of depressed individuals are more tightly organized in the mind than those of non-depressed individuals, whereas their positive schemas have a more diffuse organization than the positive schemas of non-depressed individuals. These findings support Beck's notion that the depressogenic schema structure is rigid and tightly interrelated. Furthermore, American psychologists Drs. Lyn Abramson and Lauren Alloy were the first to show that non-depressed individuals with a negative cognitive vulnerability were significantly more likely to develop a first onset of depression over a subsequent four-year follow-up period than were individuals with a more positive cognitive style (Alloy, Abramson, Whitehouse, Hogan, Panzarella, & Rose, 2006). This study was important in showing that negative cognitive style may be a cause of depression and not just part of the symptom profile once the disorder has started (see Alloy, Abramson, Keyser, Gerstein, & Sylvia, 2008).

INTERPERSONAL MODELS

A key feature of depression is problems in interpersonal relationships. People with depression have deficient social skills in relation to non-depressed people (e.g., Dykman, Horowitz, Abramson, & Usher, 1991; Lewinsohn, Mischel, Chaplin, & Barton, 1980). In addition, their interactions with others are often negative, involving the exchange of angry and depressed feelings (e.g., Coyne, 1976). In terms of the quality of their interactions, depressed people engage in less frequent eye contact, have less animated facial expressions, and show less modulation in their tone of voice than do non-depressed people (e.g., Youngren & Lewinsohn, 1980). These are all social signs that indicate low interest and attachment with one's conversational partner. Therefore, it is no wonder that depressed people would be judged by others as less socially skilled.

While social skills deficits are certainly an important feature of depression, evidence that these deficits *cause* depression is not as compelling. However, there is emerging evidence that a particular type of impaired social skill—*negative feedback seeking*—may serve as a risk factor for depression. According to self-verification theory, **negative feedback seeking** is defined as the tendency to actively seek out criticism and other negative interpersonal feedback from others (Swann, 1990). This theory states that the need to obtain this sort of information, which is consistent with the depressed person's own self-schemas, overrides the pain of receiving negative feedback. Studies by Swann and colleagues have found that depressed individuals do indeed seek more negative feedback from others and are more rejected by others than non-depressed individuals (Swann, Wenzlaff, Krull, & Pelham, 1992; Swann, Wenzlaff, & Tafarodi, 1992). Other research has demonstrated that individuals who are high in negative feedback seeking are at risk for developing future depression (Joiner, Katz, & Lew, 1997; Timmons & Joiner, 2008).

There is also evidence that excessive *interpersonal dependency* serves as a risk factor for depression. That is, an excessive need for interpersonal attachment, support, and acceptance leads to behaviours that cause and maintain depression. One particular behaviour that has received attention in this regard is **excessive reassurance seeking**. This concept is defined as the tendency to repeatedly seek assurance about one's worth and lovability from others, regardless of whether such assurances have already been provided. According to Coyne's (1976) *interpersonal model of depression*, the depression-prone person may excessively seek reassurance after a negative event, such as an argument. Although this reassurance may be provided (e.g., "Yes, I love you"), the depressed person doubts its sincerity and continues to demand more reassurance. As one might expect, this elicits frustration and irritation in others, thus setting the stage for more interpersonal conflict (see Evraire & Dozois, 2011, for review).

Indeed, consistent with Constance Hammen's (1991) **stress generation hypothesis**, depressed individuals have been found to generate stressful life events in the interpersonal domain, including fights, arguments, and interpersonal rejection; that is, depressed individuals contribute to the occurrence of these events due to their maladaptive interpersonal behaviours (Hammen & Shih, 2008). Joiner and his colleagues have found that excessive reassurance seeking, in particular, may be in large part responsible for the generation of interpersonal stressors, which then serve to maintain and perpetuate depression (Potthoff, Holahan, & Joiner, 1995). For example, consider the following short telephone exchange between Lindsey and her husband early during his time in Afghanistan. Think about what effects that this cycle of negative feedback seeking and reassurance seeking might have had on Lindsey and Tom's relationship and on Lindsey's worsening depression:

Tom: So, how are things going?

Lindsey: Pretty bad. I just can't seem to get motivated to do anything with Molly. I'm such a terrible mother, don't you think? [negative feedback seeking]

Tom: No, of course you're not a terrible mother. It's just hard right now. I'm sure you'll feel better soon.

Lindsey: You're just saying that to make me feel better. I'm a terrible mother and a rotten person.

Tom: Don't talk like that.

Lindsey: But do you still love me? [reassurance seeking]

Tom: Of course I still love you.

Lindsey: No you don't. Who could love anyone who feels this way?

Tom: I love you, okay? Look, I'm going through a lot, too.

Lindsey: I'm a terrible mother and a terrible wife. You just don't understand.

LIFE STRESS PERSPECTIVE

From the breakup of one's marriage or the loss of a close friend, to getting fired from one's job or losing one's home, to finding out one's partner has terminal cancer or experiencing the death of a parent, stressful life events tax our psychological and physical resources and can cause significant increases in sadness, anxiety, and irritability. In the long term, most people are resilient in the face of even very severe stress and do not suffer lasting psychological effects. For a significant minority, however, stressful life events can trigger a downward spiral into major depression.

A very large number of studies conducted over the last 40 years have consistently demonstrated that individuals with depression are nearly three times more likely than those without depression to have experienced a stressful life event prior to onset (Harkness, 2008). Hearkening back to Freud, researchers have determined that "severe" life events and events involving themes of loss are of prime relevance to depression (Brown & Harris, 1989). Examples of severe loss events include finding that one's spouse of 20 years has moved out, or learning that one's father has died suddenly of a heart attack. Nearly 75 percent of individuals with major depression have suffered at least one severe loss event in the three to six months prior to onset of their depression (Brown & Harris, 1989).

Researchers have discovered that certain individuals possess characteristics that predispose them to be more sensitive to the effects of stressful life events. These risk characteristics, or diatheses, serve to moderate the effect of life events such that individuals with a particular diathesis are more likely to develop major depression in the face of life events (Monroe & Harkness, 2005; Monroe & Simons, 1991). For example, one study examined monozygotic (identical) and dizygotic (fraternal) twin pairs and found that individuals at the highest genetic risk for depression (i.e., a monozygotic twin whose co-twin was depressed) were more than twice as likely to develop depression in the face of a severe life event than were those at the lowest genetic risk (i.e., a monozygotic twin whose co-twin was not depressed) (Kendler et al., 1995). That is, the genetic risk *sensitized* these high-risk individuals so that they were more likely to develop depression in the face of stress than were those at a lower genetic risk.

CHILDHOOD STRESSFUL LIFE EVENTS A recent review of the literature suggests that children and adolescents who are the victims of physical abuse, sexual abuse, and/or emotional abuse are two to five times more likely to develop depression in young adulthood than are those without this history (Harkness & Lumley, 2007). Why is childhood trauma such a strong predictor of depression? Cognitive theories of depression developed by Drs. Aaron Beck and Jeffrey Young suggest that early maltreatment is internalized by the child in the form of negative cognitive schemas, such as "I'm unlovable," "People are out to hurt me," "The world is a dangerous place" (Young, 1994). As discussed in the earlier section on cognitive theories of depression, these negative schemas then serve as diatheses for depression. Indeed, studies by Dr. Margaret Lumley (University of Guelph) suggest that childhood trauma is related to the development of negative cognitive schemas about the self that are then related to the development of depression (Lumley & Harkness, 2007, 2009).

Biological Causal Factors

The biological level of analysis examines how dysfunction in the brain contributes to the etiology of mood disorders. The biological variables associated with the mood disorders are examined by looking at evidence from genetic, neurochemical, neurophysiological, and neuroimaging studies.

GENETICS

Both unipolar major depression and bipolar disorder run in families, and it is estimated that first-degree relatives of people with unipolar depression are two to five times more likely to develop depression than are individuals from the general population. For bipolar disorder, the link is even stronger: first-degree relatives of people with bipolar disorder have a 7 to 15 times greater risk of developing any mood disorder than does the general population (Alda, 1997; Kelsoe, 1997). These studies show a strong family link in the mood disorders, but they do not prove that this link is genetic; after all, family members also share the same environment, and environmental influences are very strong in promoting risk for mood disorders.

One method that has been used to tease apart family environment from genetic contributions to the mood disorders is the adoption study (see Chapter 4). In an early study using this method, Mendlewicz and Rainer (1977) found rates of 32 percent for bipolar disorder in the biological parents of affectively ill adoptees as compared to 12 percent in the adoptive parents. Twin studies have also been used to support a genetic cause for the mood disorders. Identical, or *monozygotic* (MZ), twins share 100 percent of their genetic material, whereas fraternal, or *dizygotic* (DZ), twins share 50 percent of their genetic material, just like regular siblings. Twins who are both diagnosed with the disorder are said to be concordant. Consistent with a genetic contribution to mood disorders, several studies have found higher concordance rates for unipolar major depression in MZ twins (40 to 59 percent) than in DZ twins (20 to 30 percent). Concordance rates for bipolar disorder are 65 percent in MZ twins and 14 percent in DZ twins (Farmer, 1996; McGuffin, Katz, & Rutherford, 1991; McGuffin, Katz, Watkins, & Rutherford, 1996). A large analysis of all twin studies regarding MDD concluded that the heritability estimate for MDD is .36 (Sullivan, Neale, & Kendler, 2000). Heritability estimates are an indication of the relative contributions of differences in genetic and non-genetic factors to the total variance in the disorder in a population. In its most simplistic sense, imagine a pie divided into slices representing all the different things that could cause depression. The heritability estimate for depression tells us that the genetics slice accounts for 36 percent of the pie. Heritability estimates for bipolar disorder are even higher, at .75. That is a lot of pie!

Jay's case above is a good example of the genetic contribution to bipolar disorder. Jay's mother suffered from bipolar disorder, which helps to explain Jay's vulnerability to the disorder. Of course, genes are likely not the only contributor in Jay's case, but studies have shown that individuals with a family history of the disorder tend to develop the disorder earlier (i.e., in childhood or adolescence) than those without (Strober et al., 1988). Clarifying the role of genetics in causing his disorder will likely help Jay to understand his symptoms better and will emphasize the need for treatment.

Now that the human genome has been mapped, investigators are in the exciting position of specifying the actual genes involved in the risk for mood disorders. There is no single "mood disorder gene," but a number of candidate genes have been examined, and many show significant promise. Genes are located on chromosomes. Humans have 23 pairs of chromosomes; half of each pair is inherited from our mother and half is inherited from our father. Each chromosome may carry several genes. Each gene has two alleles (one copy on each chromosome). These alleles can be the same if we inherit the same copy of the gene from our mother and father (homozygous), or they can be different if we inherit different alleles from our mother and our father (heterozygous). People often wonder how we get from a gene to what you see in a person. The answer is that every single gene codes for a protein, and proteins are the neurochemical basis of all cellular functioning. Therefore, these proteins tell cells how to grow and function throughout life.

The region of a gene that regulates the function of a chemical in the brain called serotonin has received a great deal of attention as a candidate gene in depression. This gene is located on chromosome 17 and is called the serotonin transporter gene (HTT). The alleles of this gene can either be "short" ("s") or "long" ("l"). The "l" allele results in greater activity of the gene and, thus, in higher function of serotonin in the brain. Serotonin is important for regulating mood and is the chemical targeted by many antidepressant medications, such as Prozac. What is most exciting about this gene is that it appears to have its effect on MDD by heightening individuals' reactivity to stress. For example, a recent meta-analysis of 54 studies found that individuals who are homozygous (s/s) or heterozygous (s/l) for the short allele of the HTT gene show higher rates of MDD in response to stressful life events than those who are homozygous for the long allele

(1/1) (Karg, Burmeister, Shedden, & Sen, 2011). Similarly, Dr. Elizabeth Hayden (University of Western Ontario) and her colleagues have recently shown that the "s" allele of the serotonin transporter gene is associated with the sort of negative cognitive style and personality described earlier that indicates a vulnerability to depression (Hayden, Dougherty, Maloney, Olino, et al., 2008; Hayden, Klein, Sheikh, et al., 2010). These findings provide some of the best evidence to date for an interaction between our genes, our psychology, and the environment in causing MDD.

NEUROTRANSMITTERS

Neurotransmitters are chemical substances manufactured at the neuron and released at the *synapse*, or the gap between one neuron and another (see Chapter 2). The synapse is the central point of neural communication; when a neurotransmitter is released, it binds to receptors on the post-synaptic neuron. Neurotransmitters can have excitatory effects on post-synaptic neurons, thus increasing their chances of firing new action potentials, or they can have inhibitory effects, thereby reducing the chances of their firing. In the 1950s, researchers discovered dysfunction in two neurotransmitter systems in depression: the *catecholamine* norepinephrine (NE) and the *indoleamine* serotonin (also known as 5-hydroxytryptamine, or 5-HT). Both of these neurotransmitters were found to be responsible for the functions that are disturbed in depression, such as sleep, appetite, energy, and activity level. Furthermore, the first antidepressant medications (i.e., tricyclic antidepressants and monoamine oxidase inhibitors) worked by increasing levels of these two monoamines. Subsequent research in the early 1970s integrated a third monoamine neurotransmitter, dopamine (DA), into this model. Therefore, at that time, the prevailing biological theory of mood disorders stated that depression was caused by a deficit of 5-HT, NE, or DA activity, whereas mania was caused by too much NE or DA activity in the context of too little 5-HT activity (Schildkraut, 1965).

Since the 1970s, researchers have uncovered great complexities in the neurotransmitter systems related to mood disorders and, thus, the simplistic biological models have been disconfirmed (Thase, Jindal, & Howland, 2002). First, most patients with unipolar depression do not show reductions in NE activity. However, low NE activity appears to be a key feature of both bipolar disorder and severe unipolar depression. Second, brain imaging techniques have shown that depressed individuals have fewer 5-HT receptors. Having fewer receptors means that 5-HT released at a synapse has fewer places to bind on the post-synaptic cell, thus leading to fewer subsequent action potentials and lower 5-HT neurotransmission. Finally, studies have shown that DA neurotransmission partly depends on the level of 5-HT. Therefore, if there are low levels of 5-HT, DA levels will also decrease. DA is strongly implicated in the regulation of reward processing and motor behaviour and, thus, low levels of this neurotransmitter are thought to be responsible for depressed individuals' reduction in the capacity to experience pleasure and their symptoms of psychomotor retardation (Martinot et al., 2001).

NE, DA, and 5-HT are also theorized to play a role in the manic episodes of bipolar disorder. In particular, some researchers theorize that abnormal DA levels may trigger the hyperactivity and psychosis seen in severe mania, whereas abnormal NE levels may trigger euphoria and grandiosity. In terms of 5-HT, normal levels of this neurotransmitter act to inhibit the activity of some neurons, leading to inhibition of certain behaviours. Conversely, low levels of 5-HT can lead to activation (or disinhibition) of a variety of behaviours. Therefore, a defect in the inhibitory effects of serotonin could lead to wide swings between depression and mania.

All the existing medications used to treat unipolar depression and bipolar disorder work by increasing neural levels of 5-HT, NE, and DA to a lesser or greater extent. However, these medications do not work for everyone, and there is wide variability in the type of antidepressant medication that is most effective for a particular individual. This suggests that researchers still have a long way to go before they fully understand the neurochemical basis for the mood disorders.

STRESS AND THE HYPOTHALAMIC-PITUITARY-ADRENAL AXIS

In all mammals, stress is modulated through the **hypothalamic-pituitary-adrenal (HPA) axis** (see Figure 8.3). When one encounters the stress of, say, an oncoming Mack truck (or, in humans' earlier days, an oncoming sabre-toothed tiger), the brain releases a substance called corticotrophin releasing hormone (CRH). This, in turn, leads to the release of adrenocorticotrophic hormone (ACTH) from the pituitary gland and, subsequently, release of the hormone cortisol from the adrenal gland. All of this neurochemical activity is crucial to our survival, as it produces

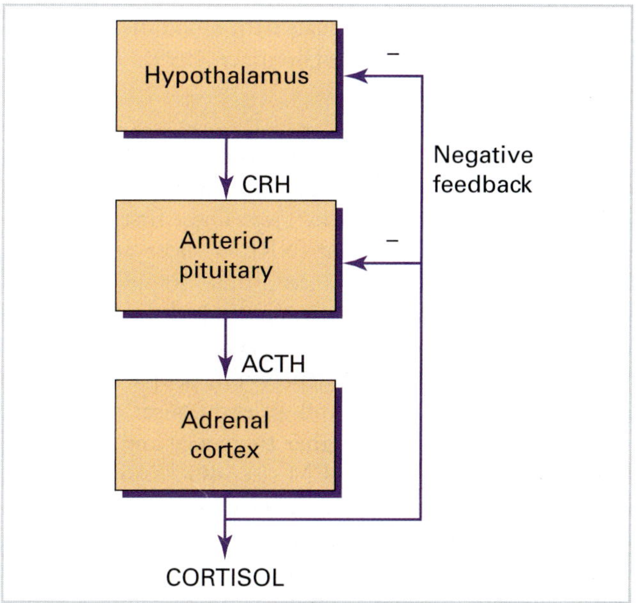

FIGURE 8.3 Hypothalamic-Pituitary-Adrenal Axis

the critical physiological changes that are necessary for our "fight" or "flight." These changes include increased heart rate and blood pressure, anti-inflammatory responses, and increased alertness (Sapolsky & Plotsky, 1990). These response systems have evolved over the millennia to be time-limited. Once we have escaped from the Mack truck, the stress response shuts off. Specifically, cortisol release during stress stimulates receptors in an area of the brain called the hippocampus that inhibit the HPA axis by negative feedback.

The HPA axis worked very well in helping us to deal with the acute dangers we faced in prehistoric times (i.e., stress of the sabre-toothed tiger variety). However, today's stresses are often more chronic, repeated, or uncontrollable (e.g., ongoing relationship problems or financial worries, ongoing physical or sexual abuse). According to noted neuroscientist Robert Sapolsky, these sorts of chronic stressors result in sustained release of cortisol and a breakdown of the negative feedback inhibition of the HPA axis. Prolonged periods of cortisol hypersecretion have been found to kill brain cells and cause permanent damage to the hippocampus (Sapolsky, 2000).

Research has found that depressed individuals, and those who have been exposed to traumatic stressors, such as childhood abuse or military combat, show elevated levels of cortisol in comparison to control groups (Harkness, Stewart, & Wynne-Edwards, 2011; Heim et al., 2000). Further, studies using magnetic resonance imaging (MRI) have found that depressed and traumatized adults have a smaller hippocampal volume in comparison with control groups (e.g., Bremner et al., 1997; Sheline, Sanghavi, Mintun, & Gado, 1999). Depressed patients who experience severely stressful life events have been found to respond more poorly to antidepressant medication than do individuals whose environments are not characterized by severe stress (Bulmash et al., 2009; Monroe, Kupfer, & Frank, 1992). Pharmacological treatments that reduce cortisol secretion have been shown to partly reverse hippocampal volume loss, and may prove to be more effective for individuals with mood disorders who are experiencing severe stress (Bremner, 1999).

SLEEP NEUROPHYSIOLOGY

Human sleep occurs in five recurring stages: stages 1 and 2 are considered "light sleep" and stages 3 and 4 are considered "deep sleep," or *slow-wave sleep*. These first four stages are non-rapid eye movement (NREM) sleep and account for 75 to 80 percent of total sleep time. Rapid eye movement (REM) sleep is the fifth stage, which includes rapid eye movements, low muscle tone, and memorable dreaming. When suffering from depression, people experience a loss of slow-wave sleep and an early onset of the first REM stage, as well as a higher frequency and amplitude of eye movements during REM sleep (Germain & Thase, 2008; Thase & Howland, 1995). These sleep abnormalities appear to be controlled by 5-HT and NE and are genetically mediated, thereby suggesting that they may play a role in causing the disorder (Kupfer & Ehlers, 1989). When patients respond to antidepressant medication, the amount of time spent in REM sleep decreases to normal levels (Wu & Bunney, 1990). Interestingly, the same effect can be achieved by waking a sleeper about to enter the REM phase of the sleep cycle. This delays the onset of REM sleep and also leads to improved mood (Knowles et al., 1979).

Sleep physiology in bipolar disorder has been studied far less. However, a clear connection between the two is evidenced by findings that sleep deprivation triggers the onset of mania in approximately 77 percent of bipolar patients (Jackson, Cavanagh, & Scott, 2003). Frank, Swartz, and Kupfer (2000) suggested that people with bipolar disorder have a genetic vulnerability to sleep–wake cycle disruption. These researchers have found that life events that disrupt one's sleep–wake cycle, such as working the night shift or having to wake two hours early to take a child to hockey practice, predict the onset of manic episodes among individuals with bipolar disorder (Malkoff-Schwartz et al., 1998, 2000). Interpersonal and social rhythm therapy (IPSRT) is a form of psychotherapy developed for patients with bipolar disorder that teaches them to regulate their social routines.

NEUROIMAGING

Over the past 25 years, very sophisticated techniques for examining the brain have been developed. Research using positron emission tomography (PET) has demonstrated that both bipolar and unipolar depression are associated with decreased blood flow and reduced glucose metabolism in the frontal regions of the cerebral cortex, particularly on the left side (Drevets, 2000). Interestingly, there is a reversal of this effect when patients shift from depression into mania, with greater right hemisphere reductions seen in mania. *Increased* glucose metabolism has also been observed in several subcortical regions in depression (Drevets, 2000). Dr. Helen Mayberg, formerly at the University of Toronto, has found that these deficits normalize following treatment with pharmacotherapy and even psychotherapy (Mayberg et al., 2000).

Research using structural and functional MRI has uncovered the neural circuits involved in the cognitive-emotional deficits of depressed individuals. For example, Pezawas and colleagues (2005) found that individuals with the short allele of the serotonin transporter gene discussed above had smaller volumes of the amygdala and the cingulate cortex (see Figure 8.4). These areas may be particularly important for processing emotional information in depression. In particular, Pezawas and colleagues (2005) have proposed that in depression the cingulate cortex is no longer able to exert its "rational" control over the amygdala. As a result, neurons in the amygdala are activated for longer than they should be in the face of emotional information, thereby increasing the salience of that information. Support for this model comes from a study conducted by Siegle and his colleagues (2002). They asked depressed and non-depressed patients to engage in an emotion processing task (rating whether words were emotionally positive, negative, or neutral) and a non-emotion processing task (a memory test) while inside the MRI scanner. The researchers found that

FOCUS 8.1

Sex Differences in Depression

A consistent finding in research on depression is that women are twice as likely as men to develop depression. This sex difference begins in early adolescence and stabilizes by late adolescence. A World Health Organization study of 15 countries on 4 continents concluded that a female preponderance in depression is seen cross-culturally (Gater, Tansella, Korten, Tiemens, Mavreas, & Olatawura, 1998). The gender disparity in depression is seen across all levels of socio-economic status, ethnicity, and marital status, although women with two or more children at home appear to have the highest rates (Gater et al., 1998). Interestingly, gender differences are not seen in bipolar disorder, where rates are consistently equal in men and women.

Is there something fundamentally different, then, about women's biology, psychology, and/or social environment that drives this difference? Several explanations have been offered. For example, the gonadal hormones estrogen and progesterone, which come online at puberty, have been found to make the hypothalamic-pituitary-adrenal axis more reactive to stress in females than in males (Piccinelli & Wilkinson, 2000). Further, not only are women more biologically sensitive to stress, but young women especially are also exposed to higher levels of stress in their environment than are men (Harkness, Alavi, et al., 2010). In addition, differences in social roles, and role strain, may help to account for gender differences in depression. For example, married women with no paid employment must rely on the increasingly devalued role of the housewife, while women working outside the home still face economic discrimination, as well as role conflict if they have young children at home. Evidence for the strong effect of social roles is provided by studies revealing that cultural groups in which a high value is placed on the female role (e.g., in Mediterranean countries, among the Old Order Amish, or among Orthodox Jews) show the lowest gender difference in rates of depression (Hopcroft & Bradley, 2007).

Why are women so much more likely to develop depression than men? Are they just more likely to admit to, and seek help for, their symptoms of depression? A number of studies have found no evidence for this explanation. In fact, men are no less willing to disclose symptoms of depression than are women, and men and women with equal levels of symptoms show a similar likelihood of seeking treatment for, and being diagnosed with, depression (Piccinelli & Wilkinson, 2000).

At present, the reasons for the female preponderance in depressive disorders are still not fully understood. Future research in this area will, it is hoped, produce answers that will lead to the development of treatment and prevention efforts specifically targeted to this group. ●

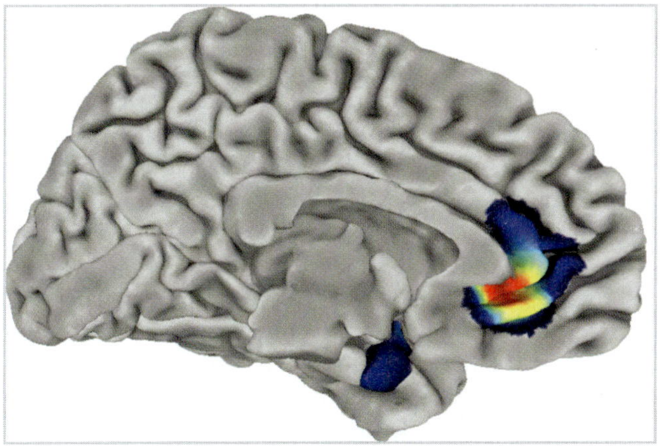

FIGURE 8.4 Areas in the cingulate (*right*) and amygdala (*left*) differed in grey matter volume between subjects with the short and long versions of the serotonin transporter gene.

Source: Reprinted by permission from Macmillan Publishers Ltd: *Nature Neuroscience.* Pezawas, L., Meyere-Lindenberg, A., Drabant, E. M., Verchinski, B. A., Munoz, K. E., Kolachana, B. S., et al. 5-HTTLPR polymorphism impacts human cingulate-amygdala interactions: A genetic susceptibility mechanism for depression. *Nature Neuroscience,* 8.6 (June 2005), 828–834. Copyright 2005.

depressed individuals showed elevated activity in the amygdala when they rated the negative words during the emotion processing task. This elevated brain activity lasted even throughout the non-emotional memory task. The non-depressed participants showed no such amygdala response. These results indicate that a key feature of depression may be the inability to disengage from negative information. That is, depressed individuals cannot shut off their brains when faced with negative information; as a result, they continue to ruminate about this information even after the stimulus itself is no longer present.

The research reviewed above suggests that the mood disorders have a strong neurobiological basis. However, this chapter has hopefully also made clear that the genetic, neurochemical, and neurostructural abnormalities seen in depression are not *sufficient* in causing depression, nor does an examination of etiology in the mood disorders that is limited to these abnormalities provide a full and complete picture of the depressed individual. Future research illuminating causal factors in the mood disorders will be guided by a multidisciplinary mandate to integrate biological, psychological, and environmental levels of analysis.

❷ BEFORE MOVING ON

Research on the role of genes, cognition, and stress in major depression suggests that our biology can change based on input from the environment. Discuss how this is possible using an example of relevance to depression.

Treatment

PSYCHOTHERAPY FOR UNIPOLAR DEPRESSION

In the early 1980s, the American National Institute of Mental Health (NIMH) funded a large multi-site randomized controlled trial that compared cognitive-behavioural therapy (CBT), interpersonal psychotherapy (IPT), an antidepressant medication called imipramine, and a placebo pill condition. This study was called the Treatment of Depression Collaborative Research Program (TDCRP), and it was very important at the time because it was the first to compare all three of these treatments head-to-head using random assignment to treatment condition, a large sample size, and a placebo comparison. The overall results indicated that there were no differences in efficacy among CBT, IPT, and imipramine, and that all the active treatments were significantly superior to placebo (Elkin et al., 1989).

Based primarily on the results of the TDCRP, CBT and IPT are now recommended by the Canadian Psychological Association Task Force on Empirically Supported Treatments as those with the strongest efficacy in the treatment of unipolar major depression (Hunsley, Dobson, Johnston, & Mikail, 1999).

COGNITIVE-BEHAVIOUR THERAPY (CBT) **Cognitive-behaviour (or behavioural) therapy (CBT)** is based on the cognitive theory of depression described earlier, which states that one's emotional reactions to a situation are determined, at least in part, by one's thoughts about that situation (Beck, 1967). Therefore, the goal of CBT is to teach people to become aware of the meanings of and attributions to events in their lives, and to examine how these cognitions contribute to the emotional reactions that follow. CBT was developed by Dr. Beck and is a structured form of treatment that focuses on people's present ways of thinking and behaving. CBT is a time-limited treatment that typically involves 16 to 20 sessions. The goal of CBT is for the therapist to use Socratic-type questions and guided discovery to help clients make their own insights into their thought processes (see Dobson & Dobson, 2009). This is believed to be much more powerful than simply telling the client how to think differently.

The following describes some of the more common interventions used in CBT.

Activity Scheduling. One prominent symptom of depression is a loss of interest, and loss of time spent, in activities that used to be pleasurable. This symptom is likely caused by deficits in the functioning of depressed individuals' dopamine system, which underlies their ability to process reward (Pizzagalli, Iosifescu, Hallett, Ratner, & Fava, 2009). Therefore, an important behavioural technique in treating depression is to encourage clients to start scheduling these activities back into their lives. The theory here is that if depressed people start engaging in these pleasurable activities again, they will correspondingly start to feel pleasure in their lives. During this exercise, clients start by making a list of all the activities they used to engage in that they found pleasurable and/or that gave them a sense of accomplishment, and then rating these activities on a score of 0 to 10 in terms of how much pleasure or accomplishment these activities elicited. These could range from very mundane activities, such as reading, taking a walk, or taking a bath, to activities that involve more time or effort, such as visiting friends, signing up for a yoga class, or taking a trip. Clients then map out their daily schedules on a calendar and work collaboratively with their therapist to gradually schedule in the activities on their list. This exercise serves an additional purpose of testing and challenging the negative cognitions that likely stopped them from engaging in these once-pleasurable activities in the first place (e.g., "There's no point in going out with my friends; I won't have any fun").

Thought Records. The main purpose of CBT is to help clients identify and test their negative thinking patterns. This is often accomplished using a "thought record" (see Figure 8.5). Here, the client is encouraged to focus on a situation that occurred recently and that evoked a strong negative emotion. The client is then encouraged to write down all the thoughts that were running through his or her mind during this situation. Often, these thoughts will include cognitive distortions (e.g., all-or-nothing thinking). The therapist then works collaboratively with the client to evaluate the accuracy of these thoughts by coming up with evidence for and against the thoughts. The client is then encouraged to come up with alternative thoughts that represent a balance of the evidence. Note that these thoughts are not necessarily

Situation	Thoughts	Moods 0–100%	Evidence supporting thought	Evidence against thought	Alternative/more balanced thought	New mood 0–100%
Thursday Judy gives me an odd look when I tell her I'm going to AA on Saturday	She's upset that I'm going to AA on Saturday She doesn't see my recovery program as important She doesn't care about me	Anger 90%	She's not supportive of AA She nags me to do things She yelled at me as I was leaving the house	She stuck with me during all those years of drinking She seemed happy to see me when I came home from work tonight She tells me she loves me.	I know Judy cares about me and wants me to get better. I probably misinterpreted her look and next time I'll ask her if something is up.	Anger 20%

FIGURE 8.5 Sample Thought Record

Source: p. 42: Greenberger, D., & Padesky, C. A. (1995). *Mind Over Mood.* New York: Guilford Press. (pp. 64–65).

the opposite of the negative thoughts, and are not necessarily even positive. The point is simply to encourage depressed clients to consider alternative ways of viewing the situations in their lives that are more realistic and in line with the objective evidence. Eventually, through the course of therapy, the client learns to challenge his or her negative thoughts in the moment without needing to fill out a thought record.

Behavioural Experiments. Another approach that therapists use to help clients challenge their negative beliefs and assumptions about the world is to encourage people to view these thoughts as scientific hypotheses that can be tested in an experiment. For example, the assumption "If I try to talk to new people, I will certainly be rejected" is easy to test empirically. The therapist and client collaboratively design the nature of the experiment and set out clear contingencies. For example, the client might test this thought over the week between sessions by striking up conversations with the people who sit next to him or her in class. The client would then be encouraged to observe and record what takes place. It is very likely that the client will *not* be rejected by these people, thus providing disconfirming evidence for the assumption.

CBT is among the most extensively evaluated of all the psychological treatments for depression, having been studied in more than 80 controlled trials (Beck & Dozois, 2011; Butler, Chapman, Forman, & Beck, 2006; Dobson, 1989). CBT is significantly more effective than minimal or no treatment (Segal & Shaw, 1996). In addition, there is some evidence that CBT may be superior to traditional psychodynamic therapy for depression (Svartberg & Stiles, 1991). A number of randomized clinical trials have also demonstrated that CBT yields comparable results to antidepressant medication for the treatment of depression, with both active treatments producing superior results to placebo control conditions (see Butler et al., 2006). CBT also appears to be as effective as antidepressant medication for the treatment of severe depression (DeRubeis et al., 2005; Fournier et al., 2010). Furthermore, when people who responded to CBT were followed for another one or two years, they had significantly lower relapse rates than those who had responded to antidepressant medication (e.g., Hollon, Thase, & Markowitz, 2002; Hollon et al., 2005).

Researchers have found that therapy focusing solely on the behavioural components of CBT (i.e., behavioural activation therapy [BA]) is just as effective as the full treatment including focus on depression cognitions, both in terms of getting people well and keeping them well over the long term (Dimidjian et al., 2006; Dobson et al., 2008; Jacobson et al., 1996). These studies also found that behavioural activation therapy is just as effective as antidepressant medication in the short term, and is more effective than medication at preventing relapse over two years (Dimidjian et al., 2006; Dobson et al., 2008). This is good news because behavioural activation requires fewer resources in terms of time and therapist training than full CBT, and, thus, may be a cost-effective option for many individuals suffering from MDD (Dobson et al., 2008).

A recent innovative therapeutic adaptation for depression incorporates mindfulness meditation into CBT as a way of preventing depression relapse. This new treatment, Mindfulness-Based Cognitive Therapy (MBCT), was developed by Canadian psychologist Dr. Zindel Segal and his British colleague Dr. John Teasdale (Segal et al., 2002). It is based on traditional Buddhist mindfulness meditation principles that have been more recently articulated by Dr. Jon Kabat-Zinn (Kabat-Zinn, 2003). The purpose of mindfulness is to promote a non-evaluative awareness of the here and now in an effort to help depressed individuals detach from ruminative thinking and cultivate a decentred, detached perspective to depression-related thoughts and feelings. For example, instead of thinking, "I feel sad; I must be getting depressed again. I'll never be healthy," the patient is taught to think, "This is just a transitory emotion; I'm observing it and letting it pass." There is experimental evidence showing that mindfulness meditation does, indeed, decrease ruminative thinking (Williams, 2008). Further, empirical tests of MBCT have produced encouraging results. In the first study of this technique, 145 patients who had recovered from depression were randomized to continue with treatment as usual (e.g., visit their family doctor) or to receive an eight-week course of MBCT. Patients were then followed for a year. Only 40 percent of patients receiving MBCT relapsed in the follow-up period versus 66 percent of those in the treatment-as-usual group (Teasdale et al., 2000). A second follow-up study compared a group of 123 recovered depressed patients, randomized to receive maintenance antidepressant medication (m-ADM) or medication plus MBCT. The MBCT group experienced a significantly lower rate of relapse over the 15-month follow-up period than did the m-ADM group (47 percent versus 60 percent). MBCT was also significantly more effective than m-ADM in reducing residual depressive symptoms, reducing comorbid conditions, and improving quality of life (Kuyken et al., 2008). The results of this latter study were subsequently replicated by Segal and colleagues (2010).

Interpersonal Psychotherapy (IPT). Interpersonal psychotherapy (IPT) was developed in the 1980s by Drs. Gerald Klerman and Myrna Weissman (Klerman, Weissman, Rousanville, & Chevron, 1984). It is based on the early work of psychodynamic theorists that viewed loss and disordered attachment as underlying factors in major depression. In particular, IPT presumes that depression occurs in an interpersonal context and that addressing current problems that depressed clients face in the interpersonal realm is key to relieving symptoms.

IPT is a brief treatment that typically runs from 12 to 16 weekly sessions. Toward the beginning of treatment, the client and therapist work collaboratively to identify the client's source of interpersonal dysfunction with relevance to four areas: (1) interpersonal disputes, (2) role transitions, (3) grief, and (4) interpersonal deficits.

Interpersonal disputes are defined as conflicts in marital, family, or other social relationships. The IPT therapist intervenes by identifying sources of misunderstanding and using communication and problem-solving training to empower the client to change the situation. Role transitions are situations in which the client has difficulty adapting to a life change (e.g., retirement or other job loss, "empty nest," etc.). The IPT therapist intervenes by helping the client to reappraise the old and new roles, identify problems in adapting to the new role, and use cognitive restructuring to alter his or her dysfunctional appraisals of the new role. When the patient's issue is grief, the IPT therapist uses empathic listening to help the client work through the mourning process, and encourages the client to form new relationships. Finally, interpersonal deficits are defined as the main problem for a client who reports either a low number or poor quality of interpersonal relationships. The IPT therapist tries to identify personality issues in the client (e.g., hostility, excessive dependency) that may be interfering with the formation of close relationships, and uses the therapeutic relationship as a model for improving social competence.

The first investigation of this treatment found similar efficacy between IPT and the antidepressant amitriptyline, and both treatments in combination had an additive effect (Weissman et al., 1979). In addition, a more recent study of "maintenance" IPT found that monthly sessions following the remission of depression were effective in preventing depression relapse over three to five years (Frank et al., 2007).

3 BEFORE MOVING ON

How does basic research on cognition and behaviour in depression help to inform the techniques used in CBT and its more recent adaptations (BA and MBCT)?

PHARMACOTHERAPY

MEDICATIONS TO TREAT UNIPOLAR DEPRESSION

Medications to treat unipolar depression were discovered serendipitously in the 1950s by physicians looking for effective drugs to treat tuberculosis. **Tricyclic antidepressants (TCAs)** and **monoamine oxidase inhibitors (MAOIs)** were the first antidepressants introduced on the market, and they resulted in a revolution in the treatment of depression. For the first time, patients who had suffered a lifelong pattern of severe, recurrent disorders saw their symptoms remit due to a simple pill. Controlled efficacy trials of these medications emerged through the 1970s and 1980s, further encouraging their use. The first **selective serotonin reuptake inhibitor (SSRI)**, fluoxetine (Prozac), then burst onto the scene in the late 1980s. Prozac was hailed as a "wonder drug" that could make everyone "better than well." However, the wild claims made about Prozac's success were soon dampened by a 1994 analysis of 13 methodologically rigorous trials comparing fluoxetine to placebo (Greenberg, Bornstein, Zborowski, Fisher, & Greenberg, 1994). This study concluded that "fluoxetine produces modest effects, roughly comparable in magnitude to those of other antidepressants." Nevertheless, several additional SSRIs have entered the marketplace since that time, and newer ones continue to be developed. While none of them works any better than the older antidepressants, they are much better tolerated by patients. A description of the main classes of antidepressants is provided below.

Tricyclics. This oldest class of antidepressants is so called because of its three-ringed chemical structure. Common TCAs include Anafranil (clomipramine), Elavil (amtriptyline), Norpramin (desipramine), Pamelor (nortriptyline), Sinequan (doxepin), and Tofranil (imipramine). These medications work by blocking the reuptake from the synapse of NE and/or, less commonly, 5-HT. This means that more of these neurotransmitters are available in the synapse to bind to post-synaptic receptors and trigger new action potentials. No antidepressant that has been developed since the TCAs has been found to have greater efficacy. However, the TCAs are rarely used as a first-line treatment today because of their many side effects, including dry mouth, blurry vision, constipation, urinary hesitation, dizziness upon standing up, sedation, and weight gain. These drugs can also cause or exacerbate cardiac arrhythmias and thus cannot be used in patients with an existing cardiac condition. Finally, the tricyclics are highly lethal in overdose.

Monoamine Oxidase Inhibitors (MAOIs). As their name implies, the MAOIs work by inhibiting an enzyme (monoamine oxidase) that breaks down monoaminergic neurotransmitters (e.g., dopamine, norepinephrine, serotonin) in the presynaptic cell. This means that more monoamines are available to be released into the synapse, to bind with post-synaptic receptors, and to trigger new action potentials. Common MAOIs include Marplan (isocarboxazid), Nardil (phenelzine), and Parnate (tranylcypromine). The MAOIs are rarely used as first-line treatments because of their potentially dangerous side effects. In particular, because MAOIs inhibit the breakdown of amines, patients taking these medications must limit their intake of foods containing amines, especially tyramine (e.g., aged cheese, chocolate, red wine). Too much tyramine can raise blood pressure to dangerous levels. Patients taking MAOIs also must avoid over-the-counter cold medicines that contain pseudoephedrine (e.g., Sudafed), as well as any drug that works on serotonin, such as another antidepressant.

Selective Serotonin Reuptake Inhibitors (SSRIs). The SSRIs are currently the first-line treatment for unipolar depression because of their relatively mild side effects, their high safety profile (they are not lethal in overdose), and their ease of administration (only one daily dose is required). Common SSRIs include Celexa (citalopram), Paxil (paroxetine), Prozac (fluoxetine), and Zoloft (sertraline). SSRIs work by blocking the reuptake of serotonin into the presynaptic cell. This means that more serotonin is available in the synapse to bind to post-synaptic receptors and trigger new action potentials. Common side effects include nausea, insomnia, sedation, and sexual dysfunction.

Other Classes of Antidepressants. Since the development of the SSRIs, several other classes of antidepressants have emerged. These include (1) serotonin-norepinephrine reuptake inhibitors (SNRIs) such as Wellbutrin (buproprion), Effexor (venlafaxine), Desyrel (trazodone), and Remeron (mirtazapine); (2) medications that work on increasing dopamine transmission, such as Mirapex (pramipexole) and Provigil (mondafinil); and (3) drugs that have other miscellaneous actions on other neurotransmitters such as GABA (e.g., Neurontin [gabapentin]). All of these medications have shown efficacy in comparison with placebo, and they all have slightly different side effect profiles.

A large-scale review of controlled trials of antidepressant medications concluded that approximately 50 to 70 percent of patients who successfully finish a trial of any antidepressant can be expected to respond. This compares to a response rate of 30 percent for placebo (Walsh, Seidman, Sysko, & Gould, 2002). No class of antidepressants has been found to work better than any other, in general, and thus the selection of antidepressant is guided by the drug's side effect profile, its ease of administration, the patient's own history of prior response, any medical issues that might limit use of certain medications, the patient's depressive subtype (e.g., atypical depression), the patient's family history of response, and the drug's cost. Treatment algorithms, such as the Canadian Network for Mood and Anxiety Treatment (CANMAT) guidelines developed by a consensus panel of the Canadian Psychiatric Association, have recently been developed and updated to try to standardize psychiatrists' approach to choosing an antidepressant and deciding what to do if a patient does not respond (Lam et al., 2009).

It should be noted that an important downside of medications is that they are associated with a high risk of relapse. That is, once people stop taking their medication, and even if they keep taking it, there is a strong chance that their symptoms will return. Indeed, a recent survey of 119 psychiatrists in clinical practice treating depressed patients with SSRIs found that most (89 percent) observed the return of depressive symptoms after a favourable SSRI response, *despite continued treatment* (Goldberg & Kocsis, 1996). More than half of these psychiatrists eventually needed to increase SSRI dosages. Therefore, these medications are by no means a "cure" for depression and, as stated above, are significantly less effective in the long run than cognitive-behavioural therapy.

Further, a controversial recent meta-analysis found that the benefit of antidepressant medication over placebo was found only for patients with severe depression (Fournier et al., 2010). For patients with mildly to moderately severe unipolar depression, antidepressant medication was *no more effective than placebo*. Based on these results, do you believe that it is ethical to prescribe antidepressant medication to patients with mild to moderate depression severity?

4 BEFORE MOVING ON

Given what you know about biological treatments for unipolar major depression, what factors might you use to decide which treatment is best for a particular patient?

MEDICATIONS TO TREAT BIPOLAR DISORDER

Lithium. A number of chemical salts of the lithium ion (Li+) have been used as mood-stabilizing treatments for more than 100 years. Indeed, in the mid-nineteenth century, **lithium** was used to treat a range of psychiatric disorders based on theories at the time linking mental illness to an excess in uric acid, which is dissolved by lithium. However, by the turn of the twentieth century, this use of lithium appeared to be forgotten. Lithium was rediscovered in 1949 as a treatment for mania by Australian psychiatrist John Cade. Cade was injecting guinea pigs with lithium in his experiments with uric acid and discovered that the rodents became tranquilized. He soon began successfully using lithium on his own hospitalized manic patients. Researchers still do not know exactly how lithium works in the treatment of bipolar disorder, but there are several theories. For example, lithium deactivates an enzyme called GSK-3B that may be related to the circadian clock. When this enzyme is active, proteins in the body are unable to reset the brain's "master clock," and as a result the body's natural cycles of sleep, metabolism, and activity are disrupted (Yin, Wang, Klein, & Lazar, 2006). In addition, lithium is an antagonist of the neurotransmitter glutamate (Dixon & Hokin, 1998). Glutamate has a general excitatory effect on the brain. Therefore, decreasing the synthesis and/or release of glutamate may account for lithium's stabilizing effect.

The use of lithium requires regular monitoring by a psychiatrist and blood tests because the therapeutic window is very narrow. This means that the dose required to attain a therapeutic effect is only slightly less than the toxic dose. Because lithium interferes with the regulation of sodium and water levels, patients also require regular tests to monitor thyroid and kidney function. Common side effects of lithium include dehydration, weight gain, acne with scarring, thinning of hair, and hand tremor.

Anticonvulsants. Approximately 40 percent of patients with bipolar disorder do not respond to lithium and/or cannot tolerate its side effects. More importantly, lithium often becomes ineffective, resulting in relapse for about 70 percent of people within five years (Gitlin, Swendsen, Heller, & Hammen, 1995). About 20 years ago, doctors discovered that anticonvulsant drugs used in the treatment of epilepsy led to improvements in these patients. Today, they are often prescribed alone, with lithium, or with an antipsychotic drug to control mania. Anticonvulsant drugs include Tegretol (carbamazepine), Depakote (valproate), Lamictal (lamotrigine), Neurontin (gabapentin), Topamax (topiramate), Trileptal (oxcarbazepine), Zonegran (zonisamide), Gabitril (tiagabine), Felbatol (felbamate), Keppra (levatiracetam), Dilantin (phenytoin), and Lyrica (pregabalin).

Many anticonvulsant drugs work by increasing the synthesis and release of the neurotransmitter gamma-aminobutyric acid (GABA), which plays a general inhibitory role in the brain. Others work by *decreasing* the synthesis and release of the neurotransmitter glutamate, which has a general excitatory effect in the brain. Common side effects include dizziness, drowsiness, nausea, tremor, rash, and weight gain. Some anticonvulsants can cause liver or kidney damage or decrease the amount of platelets in the blood. Also, when taken for long periods, anticonvulsants can cause problems with the liver. Finally, pregnant women should not take anticonvulsants because they increase the risk of birth defects.

Antipsychotics. Atypical antipsychotic medications, such as those used to treat schizophrenia, may be used as a short-term treatment during acute manic or severe depressive episodes. These medications may be used to control psychotic symptoms such as hallucinations or delusions and also may be used as sedatives to help with the insomnia and agitation that often accompany manic episodes. Finally, in some people antipsychotic medications have been found to have a mood-stabilizing effect on their own and, thus, can be used for those patients who do not respond to lithium or anticonvulsants.

Antipsychotics used to treat bipolar disorder include Abilify (aripiprazole), Clozaril (clozapine), Geodon (ziprasidone), Risperdal (risperidone), Seroquel (quetiapine), and Zyprexa (olanzapine). These medications are antagonists of multiple neurotransmitter receptors, including serotonin and dopamine. Common side effects include blurred vision, dry mouth, drowsiness, muscle spasms or tremor, facial tics, and weight gain. Antipsychotic medications may also increase the risk of diabetes because they cause rapid weight gain and high cholesterol. Even these newer atypical antipsychotic medications may cause tardive dyskinesia, an irreversible syndrome involving involuntary, dyskinetic movements. The risk of developing tardive dyskinesia increases with the duration and cumulative dose of medication, and it has no treatment. Therefore, antipsychotics should be used only on a very short-term basis, in the smallest dose, and for those patients for whom other mood-stabilizing medications are ineffective.

Antidepressants. The antidepressants discussed in the earlier section on unipolar depression are often used to treat the depressive phase of bipolar disorder. Buproprion appears to be less likely to trigger manic episodes than some of the other antidepressants. In addition, there is some evidence that venlafaxine works more quickly than do other antidepressants. All antidepressants are associated with a risk for triggering mania in bipolar patients, however, so these medications are typically used in conjunction with one of the mood-stabilizing medications discussed above.

Jay was prescribed the anticonvulsant Tegretol to help relieve his symptoms of bipolar disorder. As discussed above, though, his initial dose of Tegretol was not effective and he relapsed into an episode of severe depression. It is very common for patients with bipolar disorder to relapse. When this happens, the prescribing physician must decide what else to do to help the patient. In this case, Jay's psychiatrist did two things: (1) increased the dose of Tegretol, and (2) *augmented* Tegretol with another medication—the antidepressant buproprion (Buspar). This strategy worked for Jay. Unfortunately, bipolar disorder is a chronic illness that requires chronic treatment. However, it is often difficult for people with bipolar disorder to take their medication every day for years, especially when they are feeling well. Have you ever stopped taking medicine, such as an antibiotic, when your symptoms went away, even when your doctor told you to keep taking it? Given Jay's young age and inexperience with bipolar disorder, he is at high risk for stopping his medications. If he does, he will very likely suffer another relapse. Below we will discuss how adding psychotherapy to pharmacological treatments can help patients stay on their medication.

COMBINATIONS OF PSYCHOLOGICAL AND PHARMACOLOGICAL TREATMENTS

COMBINATIONS OF PSYCHOTHERAPY AND MEDICATION FOR UNIPOLAR DEPRESSION Since antidepressant medication, IPT, and CBT have all been shown to be efficacious in treating major depression, shouldn't combining them be even more effective? Not necessarily. In fact, randomized controlled trials of CBT, IPT, medication, and their combination have consistently shown that for non-chronic depression of mild to moderate severity, there is no advantage to combining psychotherapy and medication (Segal, Kennedy, & Cohen, 2001). This means that for most cases of unipolar depression, treatment choice should be based on the relative risks of pharmacotherapy versus psychotherapy (e.g., side effects, cost, time, availability), responses to past treatments, and patient preference (Segal et al., 2001).

Four caveats to this evidence are worth noting. First, for patients with *severe* depression, there is evidence that the combination of IPT and medication is superior to either alone (Thase et al., 1997). Second, for patients with *chronic* depression, there is evidence that the combination of CBASP (a version of CBT modified for chronic depression) and medication is superior to either alone (Keller et al., 2000). Third, there is evidence that *adding* CBT for patients who fail to respond fully to medication improves remission rates and helps in preventing relapse (Fava, Fabbri, & Sonino, 2002). Finally, in the treatment of adolescents with depression there is evidence that a combination of CBT and medication is superior to either alone (Treatment for Adolescent Depression Study Team, 2004).

ADJUNCTIVE PSYCHOTHERAPY FOR BIPOLAR DISORDER The most effective treatment for bipolar disorder is medication. Unfortunately, however, even when these patients receive maximum doses of medications, they are at a high risk for relapse. In addition, these patients often continue to show significant impairments in work, family, and social relationships even while medicated. For this reason, researchers have sought to develop psychological treatments that can be added to the pharmacotherapy of these patients.

Although the mechanism by which it works is still not clearly understood, phototherapy is effective for most people with seasonal affective disorder.

Family-Focused Therapy (FFT). **Family-focused therapy (FFT)** was developed by Dr. David Miklowitz and consists of education for both the patient and his or her family members about the disorder and its effect on the patient's functioning, as well as communication and problem-solving training involving all family members. As discussed above, Jay and his father participated in FFT. This was important for Jay, particularly because his father was his main source of support during his transition to college. It is possible that Jay and his father had some issues to work out regarding what Jay's bipolar diagnosis now means to their relationship, particularly in the context of Jay's mother's illness and suicide. Working through the thoughts and emotions family members have about bipolar disorder in a structured way with a trained therapist will hopefully help Jay and his father to develop positive ways of interacting that keep their relationship supportive over the long term.

In research, a randomized trial comparing FFT to crisis management found that patients randomized to FFT had significantly fewer relapses than those in the crisis management group (Miklowitz, George, Richards, Simoneau, & Suddath, 2003). In addition, the FFT group had fewer new onsets of depression. Importantly, patients in the FFT group were more likely to stay on their medication than were those in the crisis management group. Miklowitz and colleagues concluded that FFT may be a useful adjunctive strategy for patients who are living at home and/or experiencing significant conflict with their family members.

Interpersonal and Social Rhythm Therapy (IPSRT). **Interpersonal and social rhythm therapy (IPSRT)** was developed by Dr. Ellen Frank and is based on the theory that disruptions in daily routines and conflicts in interpersonal relationships can cause relapses of bipolar episodes. Patients are taught to regulate their routines and to cope more effectively with stressful events. A recent randomized controlled trial comparing IPSRT to clinical management found that the group that received IPSRT experienced significantly fewer relapses during the two-year duration of the study (Frank et al., 2005). Furthermore, the strength of this effect was significantly correlated with the extent to which patients were able to regularize their daily routines.

Cognitive Therapy (CT). Cognitive therapy (CT) for bipolar disorder was developed by Dr. Dominic Lam and is very similar to CBT for unipolar depression, described earlier. Patients are taught strategies that address the unique issues faced in bipolar disorder, including (1) how to regularize their sleep and daily routines, (2) how to regularly monitor their mood to help identify early triggers for manic episode relapses, and (3) the importance of medication compliance. A randomized trial comparing CT to clinical management in the adjunctive treatment of bipolar disorder found that patients in the CT group had significantly fewer relapses of their bipolar disorder and significantly fewer hospitalizations during the 12-month study period (Lam et al., 2003). The CT group also reported significantly higher levels of psychosocial functioning, fewer symptoms of depression, and less fluctuation in their manic symptoms.

The Systematic Treatment Enhancement Program (STEP) for bipolar disorder is a large-scale, multi-site, randomized, and controlled study developed to test the efficacy of the above three adjunctive psychosocial treatments head-to-head (Miklowitz et al., 2007). Results so far indicate that patients receiving any one of these psychotherapies were significantly more likely to have recovered after one year of treatment, and they recovered more quickly than patients who received only clinical management with their medication. However, no evidence was found for significant differences among the three psychotherapies. That is, each of these therapies worked equally well when added to medication in the treatment of bipolar disorder.

5 BEFORE MOVING ON

Given what you know about CBT, FFT, and IPSRT for bipolar disorder, what factors might you use to decide which modality to employ for a particular patient?

PHOTOTHERAPY FOR SEASONAL AFFECTIVE DISORDER

As described earlier in this chapter, seasonal affective disorder (SAD) is a mood disorder that affects patients during times of low light (e.g., winter months). Because SAD may be caused by disruptions in individuals' normal circadian rhythms resulting from dysregulations in melatonin production, researchers theorized in the early 1980s that patients with this disorder may be helped by treatments that simulate sunlight. In **phototherapy** (i.e., light therapy), patients sit in front of a small box that contains fluorescent bulbs or tubes. They are exposed to light of a much higher intensity than normal household lighting (2500 to 10 000 lux), thus mimicking sunlight. Patients are instructed to sit in front of the box in the early morning for 30 minutes to 2 hours, depending on the intensity of the light in their box.

While the mechanism by which light therapy works is not entirely understood, it may mimic the natural effects of sunlight on a cascade of neurobiological processes, including gene expression in the adrenal gland, serotonin production in the hypothalamus, and inhibition of melatonin secretion from the pineal gland.

A large analysis of controlled trials involving 332 patients with SAD showed that two hours of daily exposure to a 2500-lux light box resulted in remission in 67 percent of patients with mild depression and in 40 percent of patients with moderate to severe depression (Terman et al., 1989). Based on these results, light therapy is now recommended by the Canadian Psychiatric Association as a first-line treatment for SAD (Lam & Levitt, 1999). A significant advantage of light therapy is that side effects are rare (Lam & Levitt, 1999). However, because phototherapy may precipitate manic episodes in individuals with bipolar SAD, these patients should be maintained on an effective mood stabilizer before starting phototherapy.

NEUROSTIMULATION AND NEUROSURGICAL TREATMENTS

Despite clear data showing the efficacy of psychotherapy and medication in the treatment of depression, approximately 40 percent of patients remain resistant to treatment.

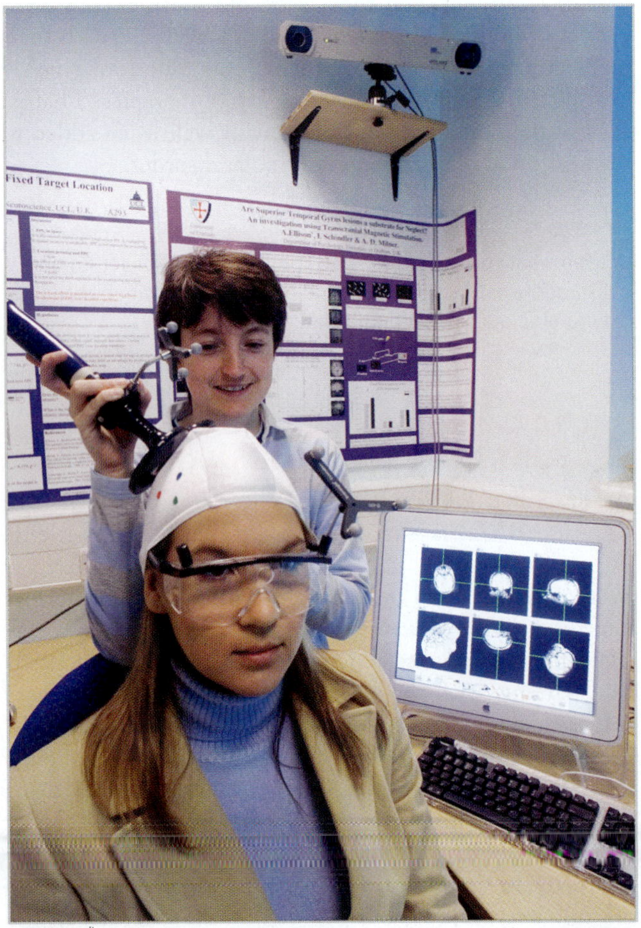

A patient is prepared to receive transcranial magnetic stimulation.

Treatment-resistant depression is defined as a failure to achieve remission following at least two trials of antidepressant medication at an appropriate dose and duration (Thase & Rush, 1997). Many of these patients have failed several treatment trials and have remained chronically depressed for years. Chronic depression is associated with severe impairments in social, educational, occupational, and health functioning, and these individuals have a significantly lower quality of life than non–chronically depressed patients (Petersen et al., 2004). Clearly, then, more drastic measures are needed to relieve suffering in treatment-resistant patients. These more invasive treatment options are described below. Note that none of these are recommended as first-line treatments for depression. They are to be considered only when adequate trials of medication and psychotherapy have failed.

ELECTROCONVULSIVE THERAPY (ECT) **Electroconvulsive therapy (ECT)** still conjures up very negative images from the previous century of patients strapped to beds convulsing, seemingly in pain. Jack Nicholson's chilling performance in *One Flew over the Cuckoo's Nest* portrays a character transformed into a shell of a man after being punished with repeated bouts of ECT. Unfortunately, these early depictions were often accurate. ECT was used indiscriminately from its discovery in the 1930s to the advent in the 1950s of medications used to treat psychological disorders. Furthermore, in these early years it was administered without the use of anaesthetics, and the electrical current used was much higher than the one used today. Patients suffered seizures so violent that they resulted in broken bones.

The reality of present-day ECT is far from these past horrors. Patients are administered a general anaesthetic and muscle relaxant so that they are unaware during the procedure and do not convulse during the seizure. A blood pressure cuff is placed around the patient's ankle, preventing the muscle relaxant from reaching the foot. In this way the physician can ensure that a seizure is occurring by watching the patient's foot move. Patients also wear mouth guards to protect their tongues and teeth from injury. An electrical current is then applied to the patient's brain through electrode pads placed on his or her temples. This induces a seizure that typically lasts for about 25 seconds. After the anaesthetic wears off, patients typically experience a period of confusion that can last up to a few hours. Most patients report persistent memory loss following ECT, involving both retrograde amnesia (forgetting events prior to the seizure) and anterograde amnesia (forgetting events after the seizure). These memory problems usually improve within a couple of months. However, a small proportion of patients complain of continuing memory impairment following ECT. Applying an electrical current to only one side of the brain (unilateral ECT) does appear to be associated with fewer memory problems than is seen with bilateral ECT (Kho, van Vreeswijk, Simpson, & Zwinderman, 2003).

ECT is typically administered 2 to 3 times per week, with a total of between 6 and 12 treatments. An analysis of 73 randomized controlled research trials investigating the efficacy of ECT in severe, treatment-resistant unipolar and bipolar depression concluded that active ECT is significantly more effective than both sham ECT and medication (Carney et al., 2003). In addition, this analysis found that bilateral ECT is more effective than unilateral ECT, and that high-dose electrical stimulus (150 percent above seizure threshold) is more effective than low-dose electrical stimulus (50 percent above seizure threshold). However, these latter two findings need to be considered in light of possible increases in cognitive impairment. ECT is indicated as a first-line treatment only for treatment-resistant depression or depression with severe, life-threatening symptoms where an immediate response is desired (e.g., acute suicidal ideation or psychotic features).

TRANSCRANIAL MAGNETIC STIMULATION (TMS) **Transcranial magnetic stimulation (TMS)** uses magnetic fields to alter brain activity and was approved by Health Canada in 2002. During the procedure, a large electromagnetic coil is held against the patient's scalp. An electric current creates a magnetic pulse that travels through the skull and causes small electrical currents in the brain. These currents stimulate nerve cells in the region of the cortex under the coil. The procedure is non-invasive and painless, although patients sometimes report a tapping or knocking sensation in their head, as well as muscle contractions in their jaw or scalp. The procedure lasts about half an hour and is repeated several times per week.

The exact mechanism of action of TMS is still not completely understood. One possibility is that many patients with depression suffer from low levels of brain activity in the left dorsolateral prefrontal cortex (called "left hypofrontality"). Therefore, applying high-frequency magnetic stimulation leads to increased nerve stimulation and consequent blood flow and glucose metabolism in this area (Gershon, Dannon, & Grunhaus, 2003).

Results of randomized controlled trials comparing active TMS to sham TMS (i.e., the coil is applied, but a magnetic shield against the scalp prevents the magnetic pulse from travelling through the skull) indicate that patients in the active TMS condition were about twice as likely to have achieved remission from their depression after six weeks of treatment than those in the sham condition (Gershon et al., 2003; O'Reardon et al., 2007). Recent trials comparing TMS to ECT have found that TMS may be less effective than ECT, but has fewer adverse effects on cognitive functioning (Hansen et al., 2011).

VAGUS NERVE STIMULATION (VNS) The vagus nerve runs from the brain stem through the neck and down to the chest and abdomen. Information travels through this nerve from the brain to the major organs of the body. In **vagus nerve stimulation (VNS)**, a device called a pulse generator is surgically implanted in the patient's chest on the left side. A lead wire attached to the generator runs under the patient's skin up to the neck and is attached to the vagus nerve. The pulse generator delivers electrical signals through the wire to the vagus nerve, which then delivers them to the brain. The implant is permanent and typically delivers stimulation every 5 minutes for 30 seconds. This stimulation is not felt at all by the patient. VNS has been approved in Canada since 2001 for treatment-resistant unipolar and bipolar depression. Like TMS, the mechanism of action of VNS is still not well understood. VNS leads to increased release of norepinephrine and serotonin, two neurotransmitters known to be important in depression. In addition, VNS leads to increased blood flow in a number of brain regions.

The first large randomized controlled trial comparing active VNS to sham VNS (i.e., a pulse generator is implanted but not turned on) was conducted in 235 patients with treatment-resistant unipolar or bipolar major depression (Rush et al., 2005). After 10 weeks of treatment, there were no significant differences between the active and sham conditions. However, in a second study that followed patients for one year, those receiving standard pharmacotherapy *plus* VNS were twice as likely to show a full response than were those who received pharmacotherapy only (George et al., 2005). Only 13 percent of patients responded in the pharmacotherapy-alone condition versus 27 percent in the condition that also received VNS. Interestingly, the time to attain a response in VNS is long, with a median latency of over 10 months in most studies. At the same time, these patients appear to also maintain their remission status, such that at least 50 percent of patients do not relapse over two years of follow-up (Bajbouj & Grimm, 2010).

DEEP BRAIN STIMULATION Deep brain stimulation is an investigational treatment that involves surgically implanting wires directly into the brain that then run from the head, down the side of the neck, and behind the ear to a pulse generator, which is implanted subcutaneously below the clavicle. The pulse generator is calibrated by a neurologist to deliver a particular dose of electrical current into the brain. The precise area of the brain that is associated with the greatest improvement in patients with depression is still under debate. Areas that have been studied include the subgenual cingulate (Mayberg et al., 2005) and the nucleus accumbens (Bewernick et al., 2010). Deep brain stimulation remains the least well studied of the neurostimulation treatments for treatment-resistant depression, likely due to its highly invasive nature and high cost, and the presence of other equally effective options.

Suicide

Suicide is the intentional taking of one's own life. Views on suicide throughout history have been influenced by themes such as religion, honour, and the meaning of life. The Judeo-Christian religions, Islam, Buddhism, and Hinduism all consider suicide to be a dishonourable act. Indeed, in the West it has been viewed as an offence against both God and the sanctity of life. In many historical European societies, people who died by suicide were buried in unmarked plots on the outskirts of cities. A criminal ordinance issued by King Louis XIV of France in 1670 was even more severe: the dead person's body was dragged face down through the streets and then hanged by a noose or thrown on a garbage heap. In Canada, suicide was decriminalized in 1972, the latest among other Western countries except Ireland (Neeleman, 1996). Aiding and abetting a suicide (i.e., "assisted" suicide) remains a crime in Canada.

In Japanese culture, by contrast, suicide (or *seppuku*) was respected historically as a way to atone for failure. Even today, Japanese suicide rates are among the highest in the world. Attitudes toward suicide in the Western world have changed, and suicide is now viewed as a mental health concern, associated with depression or other psychiatric disorders, inescapable psychological pain, or severe stress. The current focus is on suicide prevention and the treatment of mental disorders associated with suicide.

Nearly a million people worldwide die by suicide annually, and there are an estimated 10 to 20 million attempted suicides every year. In Canada, suicide is among the 10 leading causes of death in the general population, occurring at a rate of 11.3 per 100 000 people (Statistics Canada, 2007). The rate of completed suicide among males (16.7 per 100 000) is more than three times the rate among females (5.3 per 100 000; Statistics Canada, 2007). Among youths aged 10 to 24, suicide is the second-highest cause of death, following traffic accidents; each year, on average, 294 Canadian youths die from suicide. Among Canadian males aged 15 to 19, suicide is the number-one cause of death. It is important to note that for every completed suicide there are 8 to 10 suicide attempts. Suicide is a devastating problem with huge economic and human costs. Indeed, each suicide costs approximately $850 000 in health care services, autopsies, funerals, police investigations, and indirect costs from lost productivity and earnings ("The Quiet Epidemic," 2003). The impact of these deaths on families, friends, and communities is inestimable. For this reason, it is very important to understand the factors that cause suicide in an effort to better prevent and treat suicidal behaviour.

DEFINITION

A number of behaviours fall under the general category of suicide. *Suicidal ideation* refers to thoughts of death and plans for suicide. Many individuals may express suicidal ideation without ever progressing to a suicide attempt. *Suicidal gestures* (parasuicide) are behaviours that look like a suicide attempt, but are clearly not life-threatening (e.g., taking pills, but not enough to overdose). People who engage in suicidal gestures often do not have an intent to die, but may want to alert others to their suffering. A *suicide attempt* is the carrying out of a suicide plan, which is unsuccessful but for which there was a clear intent to die. A *completed suicide* is a successful suicide attempt. Finally, some individuals engage in deliberate, *self-harm* behaviours, such as cutting or burning. People who self-harm often do so in private as a way of coping with extreme emotional distress. This behaviour often follows an extreme trauma, such as a history of severe abuse, and these individuals sometimes report a feeling of dissociation during the self-harm. We will not consider self-harm further in this section.

EPIDEMIOLOGY AND RISK FACTORS

The strongest risk factor for completed suicide is being male. Men in all age groups are over three times more likely than women to complete suicide, whereas women are three times more likely than men to attempt suicide. Differences in rates of completed suicide between sexes are due to the choice of method, as men choose more lethal methods to end their lives than do women. Suicide rates also differ across age categories, with males aged 19 to 24 and over 70 being at greatest risk (see Figure 8.6).

There is considerable cultural, ethnic, and regional variation in suicide rates. Suicide rates in Canada and the United States appear to fall in the mid-range. The highest rates are found in Germany, Scandinavia, Eastern Europe, and Japan, whereas the lowest rates occur in traditionally Catholic countries such as Italy, Spain, and Ireland (Blumenthal, 1990). There are also regional variations within countries. In Canada, Quebec and Alberta have higher-than-average suicide rates for both males and females, while Newfoundland and Ontario have lower-than-average rates (Health Canada, 2003). Aboriginal communities in Canada have suicide rates that are two to four times greater than in the rest of the country, and Inuit and Native men aged 15 to 24 have rates that are five to six times the national average for their age group (Kirmayer, 1994). Indeed, suicide is the leading cause of death for First Nations males between the ages of 10 and 44 (Health Canada, 2003). Inuit communities have been particularly strongly affected by suicide. In Nunavut, the suicide rate is 88 per 100 000, which is eight times the national average (Kral, 2003). A devastating number of suicides occurred in the small and isolated community of Moose Factory in Northern Ontario in 2009. In that year alone, 13 teens committed suicide and another 80 made suicide attempts. These disturbing statistics have been related to a loss of cultural identity and hope, as well as to the disorganization of Aboriginal communities. Poverty, school failure, family violence, and high rates of substance abuse are also strong contributing factors in these communities (Bagley, 1991; Gotowiec & Beiser, 1994). However, First Nations individuals who do not live on reserves have suicide rates equal to those of the general Canadian population (Cooper, Corrado, Karlberg, & Adams, 1992). Marked differences between Aboriginal communities have also been noted. For example, in their study of close to 200 Aboriginal communities in British Columbia, Chandler and Lalonde (1998) found that whereas some communities had suicide rates 800 times the national average, other communities had rates much lower than the national average.

WHAT CAUSES SUICIDE?

THE ROLE OF MENTAL DISORDER The number-one cause of suicide is untreated mental disorder. Former Vancouver Canuck Rick Rypien was suffering from depression when he committed suicide at his home in Alberta in August 2011. Wade Belak, a former Maple Leaf enforcer, also suffered from depression prior to his death by suicide later in the same month. The tragic deaths of these professional athletes show that depression does not discriminate. After mood disorders, the most frequently diagnosed mental disorder in victims of suicide is alcohol and substance abuse. Approximately 25 percent of people who commit suicide have alcoholism, and 46 percent have mixed alcohol and substance use disorders. In youth, the rates are even higher, with 67 percent of adolescents and young adults having a substance use disorder at the time of suicide (Rich, Young, & Fowler, 1986). Approximately 10 percent of persons with schizophrenia complete suicide (Miles, 1977).

SOCIAL CONTEXTUAL FACTORS Nineteenth-century sociologist Emile Durkheim (1897–1951) believed that suicide is caused by a sense of "anomie," or the feeling that one is rootless and lacks a sense of belonging (Durkheim, 1951). He believed that the less people feel integrated in their society, the greater the sense of anomie among society members and, hence, the higher the rate of suicide. As such, Durkheim also believed that suicide rates will differ across cultures, as well as within cultures over time as the values of the society change. The high rates of suicide among young First Nations people, therefore, would be explained by Durkheim as due to a loss of social and cultural identity, disenfranchisement, and the disintegration of support within Aboriginal groups. Durkheim's model could also explain the alarming rise in suicide rates in China. Suicide is now the top cause of death among young adults in China, one of the world's fastest-changing societies (*"Suicide Rates,"* 2004). The disintegration of traditional collectivist culture has been cited as the main contributor to suicide in China, as young people increasingly leave their rural towns to achieve Western values of individual success in the big cities (*"Suicide Rates,"* 2004). Durkheim's theory is very powerful in explaining differences in suicide rates across and within societies. However, it does not explain the root causes of suicide, which account for its existence as a universal human phenomenon. These root causes must be found in our biological and psychological makeup.

BIOLOGICAL FACTORS Because suicide runs in families, genetic factors have been implicated as a risk factor for suicide. Twin studies have shown that the concordance rates for suicide in monozygotic twins are 5 to 10 times higher than for dizygotic twins (Roy, Nielsen, Rylander, Sarchiapone, & Segal, 1999). In addition, an early adoption study found that the rate of suicide in biological relatives of adoptees was more than six times higher for the group of adoptees who had committed suicide (4.5 percent) than for a control group of adoptees who did not commit suicide (0.7 percent; Schulsinger, Kety, Rosenthal, & Wender, 1979). While suicidal behaviour is likely determined by many different genes, the serotonin transporter gene (5-HTT) is one candidate that has received research attention. A recent review of the literature on the relation between the 5-HTT gene and suicidal behaviour found evidence for a significant association (Currier & Mann, 2008).

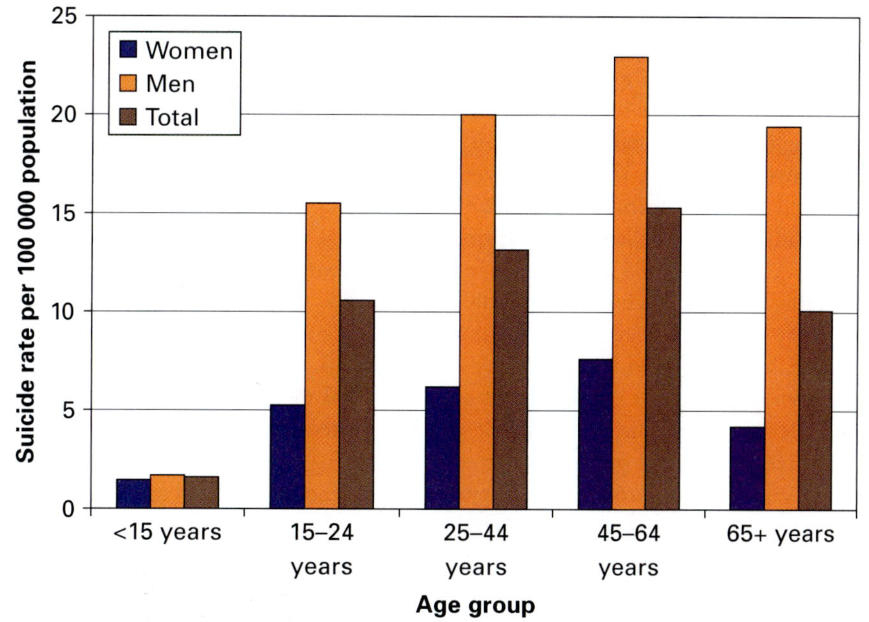

FIGURE 8.6 Age-Specific Suicide Rates, by Sex, in Canada, 2007

Source: Created from raw data from Statistics Canada: www40.statcan.gc.ca/l01/cst01/hlth66a-eng.htm

Low levels of serotonin have been implicated in suicide using other neurobiological techniques as well, including the post-mortem investigation of brains of suicide victims (e.g., Gross-Isseroff, Blegon, Voet, & Weizman, 2002), the cerebrospinal fluid and blood platelets of suicide attempters (e.g., Åsberg, 1976), and PET imaging. Given that both suicidal behaviour and serotonin function are also associated with aggression and impulsivity, researchers have suggested that there is a problem with the mechanism that inhibits impulsivity and aggression, leading to an increased risk of lethal suicidality (Mann et al., 2000).

PSYCHOLOGICAL FACTORS The psychoanalyst Dr. Edwin Shneidman defined **psychache**, or the feeling of unendurable psychological pain and frustration, as the most direct and necessary cause of suicide; that is, when suicide occurs, psychache must also be present. Indeed, Canadian psychologist Dr. Ron Holden (Queen's University) and his students have found that psychache is the end point in a causal chain leading to suicide, and is significantly more strongly related to suicide than a number of other psychological factors previously theorized to confer risk, including hopelessness, depression, and perfectionism (Flamenbaum & Holden, 2007).

MULTIDIMENSIONAL MODEL As with the etiology of major depression and bipolar disorder outlined earlier, it is unlikely that any one factor causes suicide. Therefore, newer models of suicide focus on the role of multiple risk factors at multiple levels of analysis. In particular, the diathesis-stress model of suicide proposes that biogenetic and personality vulnerabilities (diatheses) interact with environmental precipitants, such as stressful life events, to trigger a downward spiral into hopelessness, psychache, and eventual suicidality (e.g., Blankstein, Lumley, & Crawford, 2007).

PREVENTION

The Canadian federal government recently passed legislation supporting a national suicide prevention strategy. The nonpartisan bill was strongly endorsed by interim Liberal leader Bob Rae, who himself struggled with depression. The national suicide prevention strategy, though not yet fully articulated, will be based on input from the Canadian Psychological Association and the Canadian Association for Suicide Prevention (CASP). In 2004 and again in 2009, CASP released its Blueprint for a Canadian National Suicide Prevention Strategy to provincial governments (CASP, 2004, 2009), which has been used by some provinces in developing their own strategies. It is hoped that a national initiative will enable the development and implementation of standardized, research-based prevention programs that are implemented consistently across the country. Research on suicide prevention has focused on primary preventions, which aim to change situations, attitudes, or conditions that predispose individuals toward suicide, and secondary or tertiary interventions, which target individuals who have already made suicidal threats or attempts.

Primary preventions include broad public education programs, which seek to teach the signs of mental/emotional distress and to reduce stigma. However, research examining such programs taught in high schools has found that they are not successful. In fact, although the duration and depth of such programs has been quite limited, some researchers have expressed concern that they actually plant the idea of suicide in vulnerable teens, thus increasing their risk (Shaffer, Garland, Gould, Fisher, & Trautman, 1988).

Other primary prevention strategies have focused on restricting access to suicide means. For example, in Britain in the 1950s, 40 percent of all suicides were committed by self-asphyxiation with household cooking gas. In the 1960s, natural gas replaced coal gas, thus reducing the carbon monoxide content. By 1971, suicides by self-asphyxiation had fallen to less than 10 percent of all suicides (Kreitman, 1976), and this method of suicide had disappeared almost completely by 1990 (Williams, 1997). Similarly, a 1998 review of studies examining the relation of suicide and state-implemented gun control legislations from 1982 to 1998 in the United States found that suicide rates typically decreased following implementation of firearm control laws (Lambert & Silva, 1998). Furthermore, suicidal individuals in these studies rarely substituted other means or acquired firearms illegally to commit suicide. Results of these studies strongly suggest that removing the most lethal means of suicide will improve the chances of prevention.

Secondary/tertiary prevention strategies include suicide prevention centres and telephone hotlines. Telephone hotlines have the advantage of being anonymous and offering immediate support. They also are successful in reaching underserved populations, such as those living in rural areas. Most are staffed by volunteers who are supervised by mental health professionals. Research has shown that telephone hotlines are preferred by consumers over mental health centres, and are particularly successful in helping individuals with suicidal ideation. Their use is also related to decreases in suicide rates among white females under age 25, the most frequent users of hotline services (Centers for Disease Control, 1992). However, other research suggests that hotlines have little impact on general suicide rates because they do not reach the people at highest risk for suicide, specifically young males (Shaffer & Craft, 1999).

TREATMENT

The treatment of suicidality depends on the seriousness of the symptoms. The algorithm recommended by the American Association of Family Physicians is displayed in Figure 8.7. Patients who have a clear suicide plan, access to lethal means, and a clear intent to die, and who cannot guarantee their own safety, should be considered a medical emergency and be hospitalized immediately. This is also one of the few cases in psychiatric care where an individual's rights may be breached. Specifically, suicidal patients who are a danger to themselves may be hospitalized without their consent, and confidentiality may be breached if, for example, the clinician needs to contact the patient's family or other doctor.

In many cases, however, the suicidal individual is not in imminent danger and is suitable for outpatient

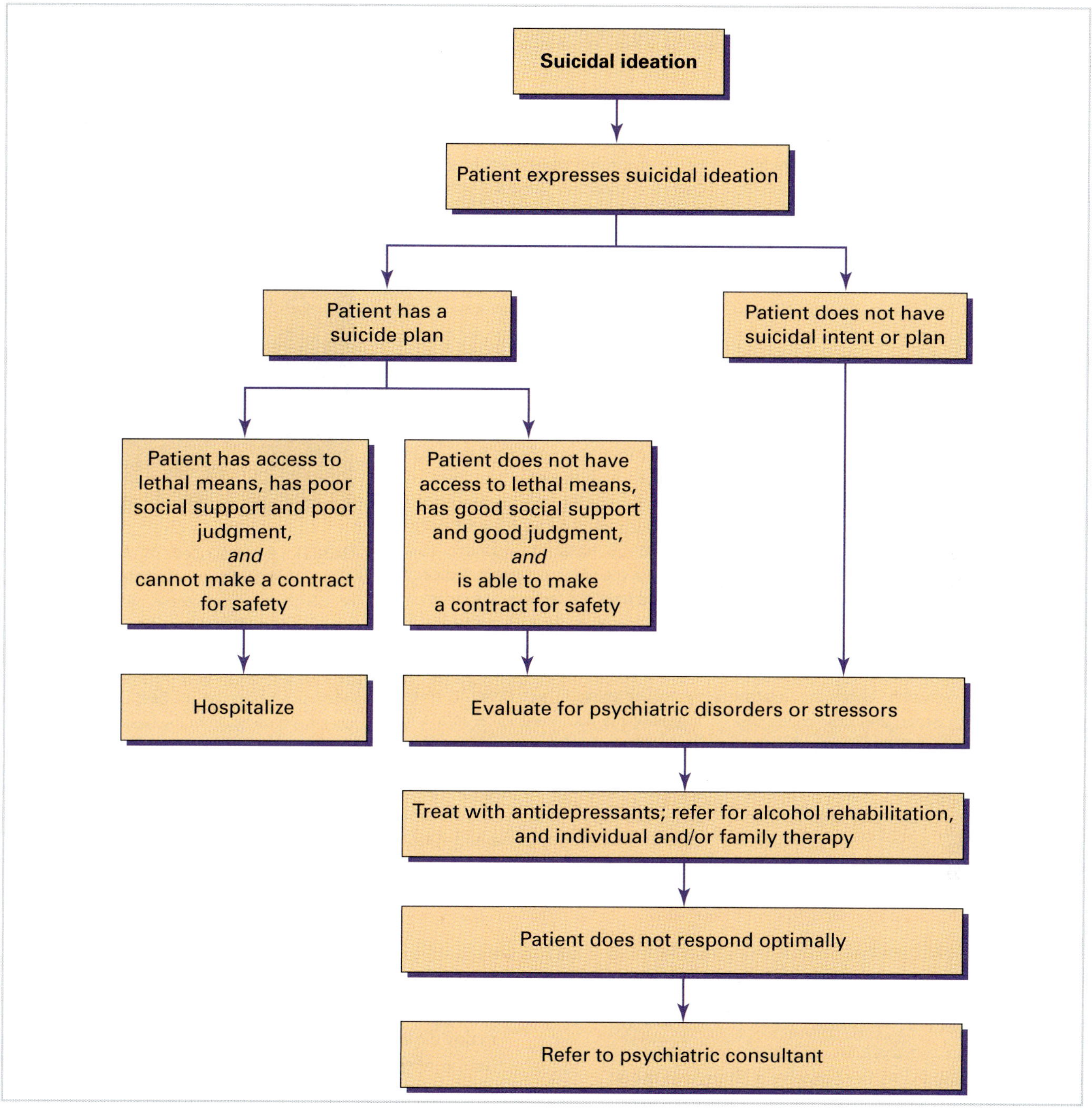

FIGURE 8.7 Algorithm for the Evaluation of Patients with Suicidal Ideation

Source: Adapted with permission from "Evaluation and Treatment of Patients with Suicidal Ideations," March 15, 1999, *American Family Physician.* Copyright © 1999 American Academy of Family Physicians.

treatment. Drs. Gregory Brown and A. T. Beck recently developed a targeted form of cognitive-behavioural therapy to prevent suicide. The central feature of this form of CBT is to identify and modify the thoughts, images, and core beliefs that were activated prior to previous suicide attempts. Therapists also address specific vulnerability factors for suicide, including hopelessness, poor problem solving, poor impulse control, and social isolation. Brown and his colleagues (2005) conducted a randomized trial of this targeted CBT versus usual clinical care in 120 previous suicide attempters. Those randomized to CBT were 50 percent less likely to reattempt suicide over the subsequent 18 months than were participants in the usual clinical care group. The CBT group also had significantly lower depression severity and hopelessness than the usual clinical care group (Brown et al., 2005).

6 BEFORE MOVING ON

How can research on the role of biological, psychological, and social factors in suicide help us to understand the alarmingly high rates of suicide among Aboriginal teenagers?

CANADIAN RESEARCH CENTRE

Dr. Zindel Segal

Dr. Zindel Segal is a professor in the Departments of Psychology and Psychiatry at the University of Toronto, and is the director of the Cognitive Behaviour Therapy Unit at the Centre for Addiction and Mental Health in Toronto. Dr. Segal is providing some of the most important research on cognitive models and treatments for depression. In particular, he is trying to solve the very important problem of depression relapse. Even with today's most effective treatments, the majority of depressed individuals will suffer a return of their symptoms within two years. Indeed, depression is a recurrent condition in at least 50 percent of cases (APA, 1994). Segal's research takes a two-pronged approach to this problem. First, he and his colleagues are using innovative methods to identify individuals who are vulnerable to relapse. Second, he is developing innovative treatment methods that specifically aim to prevent relapse in depression.

In his research identifying relapse vulnerability, Segal and his colleagues have been using PET and mood induction techniques to characterize the unique neural and cognitive profile of individuals who relapse. For example, Segal and colleagues (2006) subjected 99 patients who had all recovered from their depression to a sad-mood induction whereby they listened to sad music and thought about a time in their lives when they felt sad. The researchers then measured patients' cognitive reactivity to the mood induction by having them fill out a measure of dysfunctional thoughts both prior to and following the mood induction. They found that even in this group whose members were *not* currently depressed, those who showed the strongest cognitive reaction to the mood induction were the most likely to suffer a relapse of their depression over the subsequent 18 months (Segal et al., 2006). Segal and his colleagues have theorized that depression relapse vulnerability may be related to the reactivation of negative thinking patterns triggered by transient dysphoric states. That is, in the previously depressed person, mild and transient feelings of sadness may activate negative thinking patterns upon which the patient ruminates (e.g., "I'm sad; my depression must be coming back. I'm never going to get better"), thereby triggering the downward spiral into a full-blown depressive episode.

Based on the above results regarding the *causes* of depression relapse, Segal has helped to develop a treatment specifically geared to preventing relapse: mindfulness-based cognitive therapy (MBCT). As described in more detail above, this treatment integrates elements of CBT with mindfulness, a meditative practice from Buddhism that was refined by Jon Kabat-Zinn (1994).

Segal's work is an example of translational research at its best. That is, he uses his findings from the basic science of psychopathology mechanisms and *translates* the results of that research into the development of a targeted, cost-effective, and empirically supported treatment that prevents the repeated suffering associated with major depression.

SUMMARY

- Unipolar mood disorders involve a change in mood to depression, and include major depressive disorder (MDD) and dysthymia.
- Symptoms of MDD include persistent feelings of sadness, loss of interest in activities, loss of appetite or weight loss, insomnia, low energy, feelings of worthlessness or guilt, difficulty concentrating or making decisions, and suicidality. At least five of these symptoms must be present for at least two weeks, although episodes of MDD typically last for several months.
- Symptoms of dysthymia are chronic feelings of sadness that persist for at least two years, plus an additional two depressive symptoms.
- Bipolar disorders involve alternating periods of depression and mania, and include bipolar I disorder (mania alternating with episodes of major depression), bipolar II disorder (hypomania alternating with episodes of major depression), and cyclothymia (hypomania alternating with minor episodes of depression).
- Mood disorders are caused by the interaction of psychological, environmental, and biological variables.
- Early psychodynamic views of depression saw it as stemming from an unresolved regression to the oral stage of development following a real or imagined loss. More recent psychodynamic theories have focused on disruptions of early parent–child attachment and the development of pathological adult relationships.
- Cognitive models stress the role of negative thinking patterns that derive from rigid and tightly connected negative schemas about the self, world, and future.
- Interpersonal models point to specific maladaptive behaviour patterns that depression-prone individuals engage in, ones that heighten risk for interpersonal conflicts and rejections to trigger depression.

- Life stress models propose that depression occurs when a stressful event in the environment triggers an underlying biological or psychological diathesis.
- Biological models of the mood disorders have focused on the role of genetics, neurochemistry, and brain function and structure. Both major depression and bipolar disorder have a strong genetic component, and this may be mediated at least in part by the role of the serotonin transporter gene in heightening sensitivity to stressful life events. Mood disorders are also associated with disruptions in serotonin, norepinephrine, and dopamine neurotransmission. Techniques that look at the function and structure of the brain have found decreased blood flow in certain cortical regions of the brain, as well as increased activity in limbic areas, such as the amygdala, when processing negative information.
- Psychological treatments for major depression include cognitive-behavioural therapy (CBT) and interpersonal psychotherapy (IPT). These emphasize the role of negative thinking patterns and improving interpersonal relationships and functioning through structured, collaborative, and time-limited therapy sessions.
- Biological treatments for major depression involve medications (monoamine oxidase inhibitors, tricyclics, and serotonin reuptake inhibitors) that increase the availability of one or more neurotransmitters. Other biological treatments include electroconvulsive therapy (ECT), transmagnetic stimulation (TMS), vagus nerve stimulation (VNS), and deep brain stimulation (DBS). All of these more invasive techniques have shown promise for severely and chronically depressed patients who do not respond to psychotherapy or medication.
- Biological treatments for bipolar disorder include lithium, anticonvulsant medication, or antipsychotic medication.
- Adjunctive psychological treatments have recently been developed to help improve remission rates and prevent relapse in bipolar disorder. These include family-focused therapy (FFT), interpersonal and social rhythm therapy (IPSRT), and cognitive therapy (CT).
- Suicide is a devastating problem with huge economic and human costs, and it is now the second-leading cause of death in young people. Men in all age groups are over three times more likely than women to complete suicide, while women are three times more likely than men to attempt suicide. Suicide rates also differ across age categories, with males aged 19 to 24 and over 70 being at greatest risk. Aboriginal communities in Canada have suicide rates two to four times greater than in the rest of the country.
- Suicide is caused by a variety of social, psychological, and biological variables, including genetic predisposition and low serotonin neurotransmission, a sense of detachment from society, psychache (unbearable psychological pain), and severe stress.
- Broad primary prevention strategies have not been effective in reducing suicide rates, although strategies that focus on reducing access to lethal means have shown more promise. Treatment of suicide depends on the severity of the behaviour and can range from inpatient hospitalization to outpatient medication and/or psychotherapy.

MySearchLab offers you extensive help with your writing and research projects and provides round-the-clock access to credible and reliable source material. Chapter quizzes and a full electronic version of the text are also provided. Answers to the Before Moving On feature are provided on the MySearchLab. Take a tour at www.mysearchlab.com.

KEY TERMS

mood disorders (p. 175)
imagined loss (p. 175)
unipolar mood disorders (p. 176)
bipolar mood disorders (p. 176)
major depressive disorder (MDD) (p. 176)
dysthymic disorder (p. 178)
mania (p. 178)
hypomania (p. 178)
bipolar I disorder (p. 180)
bipolar II disorder (p. 180)
cyclothymia (p. 181)
specifiers (p. 182)
seasonal affective disorder (SAD) (p. 182)
cognitive distortions (p. 184)
schemas (p. 184)
cognitive triad (p. 184)
diathesis-stress model (p. 184)
negative feedback seeking (p. 185)
excessive reassurance seeking (p. 185)
stress generation hypothesis (p. 185)
hypothalamic-pituitary-adrenal (HPA) axis (p. 187)
cognitive-behaviour therapy (CBT) (p. 190)
interpersonal psychotherapy (IPT) (p. 191)
tricyclic antidepressants (TCAs) (p. 192)
monoamine oxidase inhibitors (MAOIs) (p. 192)
selective serotonin reuptake inhibitor (SSRI) (p. 192)
lithium (p. 193)
family-focused therapy (FFT) (p. 195)
interpersonal and social rhythm therapy (IPSRT) (p. 195)
phototherapy (p. 195)
electronconvulsive therapy (ECT) (p. 196)
transcranial magnetic stimulation (TMS) (p. 197)
vagus nerve stimulation (VNS) (p. 197)
suicide (p. 197)
psychache (p. 200)

R. WALTER HEINRICHS • ASHLEY MILES • NARMEEN AMMARI • EVA MUHARIB

Chapter 9

Schizophrenia

LEARNING OBJECTIVES

AFTER READING THIS CHAPTER, STUDENTS WILL BE ABLE TO:

1. Explain why schizophrenia is viewed as one of the most serious, disabling, and complex mental disorders.
2. Identify the steps involved in a DSM-IV diagnosis of schizophrenia and the strengths and weaknesses of this approach.
3. Explain why the concept of diathesis, or vulnerability, is so important in theories of schizophrenia.
4. Describe reasons why genes influence but do not determine who develops schizophrenia.
5. Identify the most common cognitive and neurobiological abnormalities associated with schizophrenia.
6. Identify and explain the contributions of antipsychotic medication and psychosocial therapies to the treatment of schizophrenia.

To understand schizophrenia and why it is arguably the most severe and disabling form of mental disorder, try to suspend, at least temporarily, the compelling images, beliefs, and assumptions that tend to crowd in whenever the word *schizophrenia* is mentioned. Concentrate instead on the words of a patient named Ruth as she describes her experience with the disorder:

> *Around my neck, and hanging down from each shoulder there is something like a creature. It comes at night. I know it's there because I can feel weight. It coils around me yet remains invisible. An invisible burden. It feels like an enormous leech on my body and it touches me in familiar ways and in intimate places. It reeks of animal smells. It has a strong smell that rises from its sliding body. It is incredibly powerful and irresistible. I can't resist it* (Heinrichs, 2001, p. 3).

This woman's name is not really Ruth, but she is a real person and the words are her own, drawn from interview and case notes. Imagine what it must be like to feel and smell something alien and disturbing like this creature and to feel that it has power over you. For Ruth it was not a symptom of an illness, it was an utterly convincing experience. It was her "reality." In fact, the experience was so unpleasant that she thought about suicide as a way of freeing herself. However, she went instead to a local hospital and told the nurses that she was thinking about death. This led to an admission of several weeks during which she was treated for depression—not schizophrenia (see Chapter 8). Ruth never actually told anyone about the creature and only described her thoughts of wanting to die. The antidepressant medication she was given helped with the death-feelings, but did not make the "creature" go away. She was eventually given the diagnosis of schizophrenia after describing the creature, reluctantly, to a psychiatrist.

What could do this to a person? Is such a severe mental illness rooted in Ruth's psychological development and background? Unfortunately, the roots of schizophrenia are difficult to find and trace. Ruth was born in an average-size Canadian city, with parents who also seemed to be average in many ways. There is no record of emotional, physical, or sexual abuse in her past, and neither parent was ever treated for psychiatric problems. Ruth had average marks until the second year of high school, when concentration problems began to emerge. Her marks slipped badly and she stopped doing homework. About this time she suddenly decided to drop out of school and marry her boyfriend. But the marriage lasted only a few months because her new husband left and refused to return. A short time later Ruth began to think about death, and it is unclear exactly when the "creature" experience began.

Did rejection cause her disorder? It certainly didn't help, but if emotional pain and rejection were sufficient to cause insanity, wouldn't we all become insane at some time in our lives? In any case, Ruth is just one person with schizophrenia and the disorder has many forms and faces. Consider William, for example, as he describes his experience of schizophrenia:

> *The most hilarious aspect of the hospital is the shower. Why would they ask God to have a shower? This makes me laugh. I have heard the voices of great men in history and seen the rainbow of hope. I am willing to take on da Vinci and beat him, but the rhythm of the building is hypnotic and it unbalances me. If only they would do EEG and IQ tests I could prove that I am God. My beard has grown to fulfill the prophecy of a King of Kings, and I know that my powers will be lost on my 33rd birthday. I anticipate my crucifixion. But I will search for the devil and kill him. Perhaps if I kill my brother I will be the only son in the Father's eye. Yes, I must go and look for my brother the devil* (Heinrichs, 2001, p. 4).

Unlike Ruth's situation and voluntary admission, it was the police who often brought William to hospital. For example, on one occasion the landlord went to William's apartment looking for unpaid rent. The door was wide open and William was running around the rooms smearing excrement on the walls and furniture. On other occasions he became involved with street drugs and alcohol and was charged with assault. Moreover, a look into William's life and background shows that his mother had schizophrenia and attempted suicide. His father seems to have had normal physical and mental health. William's problems began early with learning difficulties and failures in primary school grades. He left after one year of high school and tried to work, but soon drifted into gang organizations and the use of street drugs and spent a year in jail. Indeed, until his mid-twenties he was more likely to be known to police and spend time incarcerated than to have contact with mental health professionals or hospitals. William subsequently had many psychiatric hospital admissions and was extensively assessed and examined. For example, it was found that he had abnormal reflexes even though his brain scan was normal. In addition, his electroencephalogram (EEG) suggested the possibility of a seizure disorder (epilepsy). Nonetheless, his diagnosis was schizophrenia.

Ruth and William are two very different people who share the same diagnosis. Ruth's family background is largely empty of clues about the causes of mental illness, although she did experience a severe and painful personal rejection. William, in contrast, grew up with familial mental illness and experienced many adjustment difficulties and social adversity long before his psychotic symptoms emerged. He also showed "soft" signs of brain damage. There is no shortage of potential clues in William's case. The two patients with schizophrenia also differed in their symptoms. Ruth was convinced that she could smell and feel a "creature," whereas William tried to live out his "divinity" and "heard" and "spoke" with famous historical figures. Ruth felt weak and controlled and William felt strong and powerful. How can patients be so different and still have the same disorder?

(Based on information presented in Heinrichs, 2001.)

Introduction and Historical Perspective

Across the range of abnormal psychology and psychiatry, is there a disorder as strange and challenging, as poorly portrayed and misunderstood as **schizophrenia**? It is difficult to read about this severe form of mental disorder with an open mind and difficult to resist the popular assumptions and widely held beliefs that spring up whenever the puzzling disorder is mentioned. Images of "raving lunatics," so-called crazy people with danger if not murder in mind, people who are completely irrational and unpredictable—these are the associations of the word *schizophrenia*. And then there is the incorrect idea that the disorder involves a "split personality," people within people, perhaps in conflict or completely unaware of each other. Of course, not all preconceptions about schizophrenia are negative and sinister. There is also the notion that a person with the disorder is unusually creative or "spiritual," perhaps misunderstood and alienated, but with special insights into the meaning of life and with special access to sources of inspiration and genius denied to "normal" people. Most of these assumptions and ideas are inaccurate or at most partly true. This chapter will explore what is known about schizophrenia—its characteristic features, possible causes, and current treatments.

The two case studies of Ruth and William illustrate an important and basic fact about the disorder: schizophrenia is a complex condition characterized by **heterogeneity**. In other words, there is a tendency for people with the disorder to differ from each other in symptoms, family and personal background, response to treatment, and ability to live outside of hospital. Heterogeneity makes it difficult to predict how a person will be affected by schizophrenia; what their prospects are for the future; and whether their condition will improve, stabilize, or worsen. For example, a significant proportion of patients, perhaps more than 50 percent, improve over time and in response to treatment (Buchanan & Carpenter, 2000; Möller & Von Zerssen, 1995). Indeed, although there is no cure, the outlook for a person with schizophrenia is better than ever before in terms of treatment options and both drug and psychological therapies. Yet not all patients benefit from medication. For example, up to one-third of patients continue to suffer from positive symptoms like hallucinations or delusions (Tandon, Nasrallah, & Keshavan, 2010), some endure unpleasant side effects, and many are difficult to assist with counselling or rehabilitation. Also, what does "getting better" really mean? Does it mean that symptoms disappear, or should it also mean that a person is able to resume his or her career and educational plans, reconnect with friends and family, and lead a normal life (Shrivastava, Johnston, Shah, & Burueau, 2010)? Which patients will do relatively well, and which will struggle with partly controlled symptoms and persisting distress for most of their lives? There are no clear answers to these questions. Moreover, many patients and their families have to cope with the stigma and negative image associated with serious mental illness (Corrigan, 2004). Hence, it is not surprising that a sense of pessimism and uncertainty still surrounds schizophrenia.

PREVALENCE, AND DEMOGRAPHIC AND SOCIO-ECONOMIC FEATURES

In North America and Europe there is about a 1 percent risk that a person will develop schizophrenia at some point in his or her life. However, the **prevalence**, or total number of cases with the disorder at a given point in time, changes depending on how the diagnosis is made (Government of Canada, 2006; Mueser & McGurk, 2004). If the estimated prevalence rate of 1 percent is accepted, schizophrenia is twice as common as Alzheimer's disease and five times as common as multiple sclerosis. Hence, there may be more than 300 000 people with schizophrenia in Canada. Men and women are at equal risk, but the disorder seems to strike men several years earlier and perhaps more severely than women (Häfner & an der Heiden, 1999; Norquist & Narrow, 2000). In addition, if the disorder develops after age 45, it is more common among women and seems to comprise more emotional and mood-related symptoms (Government of Canada, 2006). Schizophrenia occurs throughout the world, but more frequently in lower socio-economic groups (Bresnahan & Susser, 2003). Once individuals have developed the disorder, they are less likely to complete their education or to find and maintain employment (Müijen & Hadley, 1995). They are more likely to develop additional psychiatric problems, including depression and suicide attempts as well as drug and alcohol abuse (Kendler, Gallagher, Abelson, & Kessler, 1996). These experiences are part of the social drift that affects many patients (Johnson, Cohen, Dohrenwend, Link, & Brook, 1999). And then there are the financial and social costs associated with this disabling and often lifelong condition. According to the Canadian Mental Health Association, schizophrenia rivals stroke and heart disease in terms of hospital care, with 1 out of 12 beds occupied by people with the disorder. In addition, costs to the Canadian taxpayer total approximately $6.85 billion annually in direct and indirect health care, family benefits, social support services, and productivity loss due to morbidity or early mortality (Goeree et al., 2005). More global measures estimate that approximately 3 percent of the total burden of human disease is attributed to schizophrenia. By any measure schizophrenia places a heavy burden on patients, their families, and society.

Over the last three decades, with the rapid growth of knowledge about brain biology and genetics, research on schizophrenia has increased substantially. The number of articles published on the disorder has multiplied since the early 1970s to the current rate of almost 5000 articles a year. Similarly, the International Congress on Schizophrenia Research attracted only 175 attendees when it met for the first time in 1987. By 2011 attendance had grown to more than 1100 researchers, clinicians, and students from over 45 countries and the conference included over 1000 scientific presentations. In Canada, research funding has increased through the Canadian Institutes of Health Research and provincial granting agencies. The National Institute of Mental Health in the United States is directing enormous resources—billions of dollars—to serious mental illness. Yet, despite these efforts, understanding schizophrenia remains a major scientific challenge. It is not even known if the disorder has been part of the human condition for thousands of years or whether it is a latecomer, a "new" disorder that was rare before the year 1800. Could it be that schizophrenia is a "modern" condition and only about 200 years old (see Focus box 9.1)?

1 BEFORE MOVING ON

Why is schizophrenia regarded as so disabling and in need of so much research funding and support?

HISTORICAL PERSPECTIVE: THE MISSING ILLNESS

It is often assumed that schizophrenia-like illness has always existed because "**madness**" and "insanity" have been documented since the beginnings of civilization, medicine, and writing. Certainly, there are many examples of irrational and bizarre behaviour in the Bible, in other ancient texts, and in the writing of many non-Western cultures (Haldipur, 1984; Hershkowitz, 1998; Jeste, del Carmen, Lohr, & Wyatt, 1985). Yet it is a mistake to assume that a disorder akin to modern schizophrenia has always been part of the human condition. In other words, although "madness" in some form existed in the past, it is uncertain whether these historical disturbances included schizophrenia. For example, descriptions of madness and "**lunacy**" before about 1800 suggest that these conditions occurred at any time of life rather than primarily in young people. In addition, experiences like **auditory hallucinations** or "hearing voices" and other sounds occur in up to 70 percent of patients with schizophrenia at some point during their disorder (Andreasen & Flaum, 1991). Yet auditory

FOCUS 9.1

An Eighteenth-Century Sculptor with Schizophrenia

Although at least one review (Hare, 1988) has concluded that no clear examples of schizophrenia-like illness can be found in the eighteenth century, one probable case is well known to historians of European art. Franz Messerschmidt (1736–1783) was born and studied in Munich, Germany, and then found employment at the imperial Austrian court in Vienna. There is no doubt that he was an artist of major talent and many contemporaries recognized his outstanding skills as a sculptor and portraitist (see Pötzl-Malikova, 1982). Yet signs of mental disorder were noted soon after he received a teaching appointment in 1769. Although never described as "insane," he was passed over for promotion because of persisting reports of "confusion" and a "not perfectly healthy imagination." Messerschmidt complained that all other teachers were his enemies and he fled from Vienna, eventually living for many years alone on the outskirts of Bratislava.

It seems clear that Messerschmidt had psychological problems, but did he suffer from schizophrenia? There is no evidence that he was ever hospitalized for insanity, although he may have consulted physicians, including, perhaps, Franz Mesmer, the father of hypnosis (see Pötzl-Malikova, 1987). However, it is possible to make a good case for the disorder even in the absence of hospital or physician records. The evidence takes the form of a visitor's account of Messerschmidt's conversations, living situation, and artistic production, written by Friedrich Nicolai in 1785. Nicolai was a travel writer and apparently gained the sculptor's trust to the point where Messerschmidt was willing to talk about his artwork and creative process. Of special interest from the standpoint of abnormal psychology were the artist's descriptions of nightly visits by demons. These demons tortured him "despite having lived a life of chastity." One demon in particular was troublesome, and was referred to as the "demon of proportion." This demon was envious because the artist had almost achieved perfect proportion in his sculpture. Part of the demon's torture involved causing Messerschmidt pain in his lower abdomen and thighs, especially when he was sculpting a part of the face that "is analogous to a certain part of the lower region of the body." In order to control such demons Messerschmidt pinched himself in the right side under the ribs and simultaneously grimaced into a mirror "in the exact required relationship to the pinching of his flesh." According to Nicolai, the sculptor worked on his piece, looked into the mirror at half-minute intervals, and made "with the greatest exactitude, precisely that grimace which he just needed." An example of one of these sculptures is presented in the photograph.

Franz Xaver Messerschmidt (1736–1783), *Der Gähner* (*The Yawner*). During the years of his illness, Messerschmidt sculpted a series of portrait heads that were given fanciful names after the artist's death. However, it is likely that many were self-portraits and expressed his experience of being tormented by psychotic delusions. Reproduced with permission of the Szépmüvészeti Múzeum, Budapest.

Messerschmidt's experience of being persecuted by envious demons who could be controlled by sculpted facial expressions may represent the kind of **delusional thinking** seen frequently in schizophrenia. In addition, his career decline, increased social isolation, and withdrawal are typical consequences of the modern disorder. Although the biography of Messerschmidt is incomplete, the information on his life and disorder are highly suggestive of a schizophrenia-like condition. And this from a century declared devoid of medical and psychiatric accounts of the condition.

hallucinations are extremely rare in cases of madness prior to 1700 (Hare, 1988; Torrey & Miller, 2001). Moreover, historically documented madness seldom lasted more than a few days, and was often drug and alcohol–induced or related to other diseases. In fact, the first recognizable descriptions of modern schizophrenia did not appear in English or French until the early years of the nineteenth century (Haslam, 1809/1976; Pinel, 1809).

The historical evidence and lack of case material have encouraged the view that a schizophrenia-like disorder was very rare, perhaps even absent, until the late eighteenth century. Then, for some reason, cases of insanity surged, with physicians and asylum custodians unable to cope with the rapid increase in numbers. For example, careful record keeping in Canada's Maritime provinces shows that the number of insanity cases per 1000 people in the population increased by more than 2000 percent between 1847 and 1960 (Torrey & Miller, 2001)! It has been speculated that increasing industrialization, the movement of people to cities from towns and countryside, and environmental changes may have been involved in the sudden and escalating emergence of schizophrenia in modern life.

Of course, the idea that schizophrenia is a recent disorder has many critics. Turner (1992) argued that people in earlier times viewed mental disorder differently and may not have recorded or commented on symptoms and characteristics that help to separate schizophrenia from more generic categories like "lunacy" and insanity. Thus, the disorder existed but was not recognized as a distinct entity until Haslam's (1809/1976) case studies and the later and definitive descriptions of Kraepelin (1896, 1919) and Bleuler (1911/1950). It is important to note, however, that some "modern" psychiatric disorders, including mania and depression (Porter, 1995) as well as mental retardation (Berrios, 1995), are recognizable in historical medical texts and even in ancient writings. Accordingly, there is no easy answer to the question of whether schizophrenia existed in the distant past, and the historical origins of the disorder are likely to remain controversial and uncertain (Heinrichs, 2003).

Typical Characteristics

POSITIVE (PSYCHOTIC) AND NEGATIVE SYMPTOMS

Characteristic symptoms of schizophrenia may be broadly classified as either positive or negative. **Positive symptoms** refer to exaggerated, distorted adaptations of normal behaviour. They include the more obvious signs of **psychosis**, namely, **delusions, hallucinations, thought and speech disorder**, and grossly disorganized or **catatonic behaviour**. **Negative symptoms**, on the other hand, refer to the absence or loss of typical behaviours and experiences. Negative symptoms may take the form of sparse speech and language, social withdrawal, and **avolition** (apathy and loss of motivation). **Anhedonia** (an inability to feel pleasure, as well as lack of emotional responsiveness) and diminished attention and concentration are also considered negative symptoms.

Larry: Schizophrenia

Watch this Speaking Out video at www.mysearchlab.com

HALLUCINATIONS Hallucinations are misinterpretations of sensory perceptions that occur while a person is awake and conscious and in the absence of corresponding external stimuli. In other words, people hear, see, smell, or feel things that are not really present. Alternatively, perhaps they misinterpret normal sensory experiences. Hallucinations occur in all sensory modalities, but auditory hallucinations, in which the person hears voices or noises, are the most common form experienced by patients with schizophrenia. These voices are perceived as distinct from the patient's own thoughts and may include instructions to perform actions that involve self-harm or danger. They may urge the patient to stop fulfilling his or her responsibilities, or the voices may be insulting at one point and complimentary at another. Emil Kraepelin (1919), who first described schizophrenia in detail, mentioned patients who "heard" the roars of Satan, but also whispering children and laughter. One man was told where to stand and when to smile, whereas another heard gossip about his own behaviour.

Research suggests that hallucinations may develop from a "misattribution of sensory experience." This involves an inability to discriminate between internal and external sources of information and experience. Findings by Laroi and Woodward (2007) reveal that patients with schizophrenia who have hallucinations confuse their own responses and the responses of other people. Hence, Ruth, the patient who smelled and felt a creature around her neck, may have failed to recognize her own body and instead experienced its sensations as stemming from somewhere—or something—else. Similarly, hearing voices may result from patients' inability to recognize their own thoughts and a tendency to attribute them to external sources.

DELUSIONS Delusions are implausible beliefs that persist despite reliable contradictory evidence. They reflect a disorder of thought content and may include a complex delusional belief "system" or just a single belief relating to one aspect of daily life. Delusions may reflect persecutory, referential, somatic, religious, or grandiose themes and meanings (see Table 9.1). **Persecutory delusions**, or "paranoid" delusions, in which individuals believe that they are being pursued or targeted for sabotage, ridicule, or deception, are the most common form of delusion. Kraepelin (1919) described patients who were convinced that hospital attendants were poisoning the food and water or that the German emperor's spies were tracking them.

Referential delusions involve the belief that common, meaningless occurrences have significant and personal relevance. The advertisement on the back page of a magazine, for example, may be interpreted as a signal to eat a specific

TABLE 9.1 COMMON DELUSIONS EXPERIENCED BY PATIENTS WITH SCHIZOPHRENIA

Type	Content	Examples
Persecutory	A belief that the individual is being conspired against, deceived, or persecuted	"Strangers on the street are undercover agents following me."
Referential	A belief that events, objects, or other individuals have personally relevant meaning	"Each song that a DJ selects for a radio playlist represents a special truth about my life."
Somatic	Perception of a change or disturbance in personal appearance or bodily function	"My body is inhabited by extraterrestrial beings that give me headaches."
Religious	Unusual religious experiences or beliefs	"Satan is leaving messages for me in television programs and emails."
Grandiose	Possession of special or divine powers, abilities, or knowledge	"I have the power to change the course of history."

cereal for breakfast. In contrast, **somatic delusions** involve beliefs related to the patient's body. Kraepelin (1919) described patients who were convinced that their inner organs had been turned to dust or that they had a special "nerve" of laughter in their stomachs that was the origin of all humour in the world.

A religious delusion often involves the belief that biblical or other religious passages or stories offer the way to destroy or to save the world. The case of William, described at the beginning of the chapter, illustrates how someone can believe that he is living out a biblical prophecy. Similarly, **delusions of grandeur** may entail a belief in divine or special powers that can change the course of history or provide a communication channel to God. For example, Kraepelin (1919) described a patient who believed that all the world's armies were under his personal command.

One theory proposes that persecutory delusions develop in people who make interpretations of experience too quickly and jump to conclusions based on minimal evidence (Freeman, Pugh, & Garety, 2008; Garety & Freeman, 1999). Another theory proposes the existence of a bias in reasoning so that negative events are always perceived as coming from the environment or from other people (Bentall, 1994). Still another theory holds that persecutory delusions reflect an inability to imagine the feelings, perspectives, and experiences of other people (Corcoran, Cahill, & Frith, 1997).

DISORGANIZED SPEECH AND THOUGHT DISORDER Unusual-sounding, nonsensical speech often signifies the existence of a formal thought disorder, a characteristic given great emphasis by the pioneering Swiss psychiatrist Bleuler (1911/1950) in his early descriptions of schizophrenia. The disorganization of speech in patients with schizophrenia presents itself in several ways. **Loosening of associations** and logical connections between ideas occurs and the thought-disordered patient shifts quickly from one topic to another. In addition, answers to questions are "tangential" or hardly related to the original point or request being made. Bleuler gave many examples of this kind of disturbance, including one by a patient who wrote a letter explaining the nature of the Catholic rosary as "a prayer multiplier, and this in turn is a prayer for multiplying and as such is nothing else but a prayer mill, and is therefore a mill-prayer machine which is again a prayer-mill machine" and continued in this way for several pages (Bleuler, 1911/1950, pp. 19, 28). In current practice, a common way to elicit thought and language disorder is to ask a patient to explain a proverb or saying. For example, one man explained the proverb "Don't change horses when crossing a stream" in the following way: "That's wishbell. Double vision. It's like walking across a person's eye and reflecting the personality. It works on you, like dying and going to the spiritual world, but landing in the Vella world" (Harrow, Lanin-Kettering, & Miller, 1989, p. 609). Thought disorder reveals itself in the structure of spoken or written language and therefore provides a more objective index of schizophrenic disturbance than symptoms like hallucinations and delusions. However, it is the least common of the positive symptoms (Andreasen & Flaum, 1991).

Thought disorder may reflect the presence of more basic cognitive problems in symptomatic patients. A reduction in the amount of information a person can hold in immediate memory at one time, distractibility, unawareness of language deviations, and inconsistencies and abnormal "spread" of activated word meanings all seem to associate with this symptom (Kreher, Holcomb, Goff, & Kuperberg, 2008; Kuperberg, McGuire, & David, 1998).

NEGATIVE AND EMOTIONAL SYMPTOMS In contrast to the reality distortion of positive symptoms, the negative symptoms of schizophrenia represent deficits and losses in normal functioning. They include avolition, alogia, and restricted affect. Avolition, or apathy, refers to the inability to initiate and persevere in activities. **Alogia** represents a deficit or reduction in communication whereby questions are answered in a cursory manner with one or two words and no elaboration. In addition, many patients have **affective flattening**—a lack of emotional expressiveness, failing to convey any feeling in their face, tone of voice, or body language. The range and intensity of emotional expressiveness is often restricted in schizophrenia. Anhedonia is consistent with the patient's apathy and denotes a lack of pleasure or reward experiences. Negative symptoms of schizophrenia may also be seen in the deterioration of academic or occupational proficiency that is usually observed, perhaps due to a weakening in cognitive efficiency.

Bleuler (1911/1950) was especially impressed with the apparent lack of emotional response in many patients with schizophrenia when crisis situations or emergencies were encountered. For example, he described an emergency evacuation prompted by fire on the hospital ward and noted a striking lack of interest and concern in several patients. Many also neglected their appearance and seemed to lack any drive or motivation, spending long hours in silent and solitary detachment from other people. Negative symptoms are moderately associated with impairment on objective tests of cognitive abilities, including attention, learning and memory, and mental efficiency, and also relate to everyday functioning and community adjustment (Green, 2001; Harvey, Koren, Reichenberg, & Bowie, 2006).

MOTOR SYMPTOMS AND GROSSLY DISORGANIZED OR CATATONIC BEHAVIOUR These behaviours refer to deficits in motor function ranging from agitation to immobility. Grossly disorganized behaviour also reflects difficulty with goal-directed behaviour. It thus often manifests itself in unpredictable movements; problems performing everyday activities, such as dressing or preserving personal hygiene; and inappropriate sexual behaviour. Catatonic behaviour, in contrast, refers to the other end of the motor spectrum. It involves a significant reduction in responsiveness to the environment wherein patients assume unusual and rigid postures and resist efforts by others to change their position. Alternatively, they may engage in random, undue motor activity, or exhibit **waxy flexibility**, allowing others to move their body and limbs and then maintaining the new position. Catatonic behaviour, especially the rigid maintenance of postures and positions, seems to have been common in the time of Kraepelin (1919) and Bleuler (1911/1950) and is now observed less frequently (Andreasen & Flaum, 1991). However, agitated and disorganized movements and extreme unresponsiveness to the environment are still seen in some patients.

Diagnosis and Assessment

DSM-IV-TR DIAGNOSTIC CRITERIA

The diagnosis of schizophrenia is based on six diagnostic criteria identified by the DSM-IV-TR (American Psychiatric Association [APA], 2000; see Table 9.2). These criteria encompass a combination of symptoms and clinical features that are considered to define the disorder. They include characteristic symptoms (Criterion A), marked social or occupational dysfunction during the course of the disorder (Criterion B), persistence of the disturbance for at least six months (Criterion C), the exclusion of concurrent schizoaffective or mood disorders during the active phase of schizophrenia symptoms (Criterion D), the exclusion of substance use or medical conditions as a causal influence of the disorder (Criterion E), and consideration of any history of autistic disorder or other pervasive developmental disorder (Criterion F). The characteristic symptoms of schizophrenia include delusions (Criterion A1), hallucinations (Criterion A2), disorganized speech (Criterion A3), grossly disorganized or catatonic behaviour (Criterion A4), and negative symptoms (Criterion A5). The first four symptom-related diagnostic criteria for schizophrenia reflect positive symptoms, comprising the more obvious signs of psychosis. The fifth characteristic symptom encompasses negative symptoms. The DSM-IV-TR (APA, 2000) recognizes three negative symptoms, namely, avolition, alogia, and affective flattening.

The DSM-IV-TR (APA, 2000) definition of schizophrenia has been likened to a diagnostic "menu." In other words, the disorder is not defined by any one symptom or cluster of symptoms. Rather, a selection of qualitatively different symptoms is required for a diagnosis and none are unique to schizophrenia. Criterion A specifies that a minimum of two out of the five characteristic symptoms must be present concurrently during the period of acute disturbance referred to as the "active phase" of the disorder. However, the DSM-IV-TR weighs some symptoms more heavily than others so that it is possible to meet Criterion A if specified kinds of hallucinations or delusions are present. These heavily weighted symptoms include the following.

VOICES COMMENTING ON BEHAVIOUR Auditory hallucinations that involve the perception of several voices having a discussion with each other, or providing a running commentary on the individual's actions or thoughts, are sufficient to satisfy Criterion A for the diagnosis of schizophrenia. That is to say, if a person describes or presents with such auditory hallucinations, no other symptoms are needed for the diagnosis. On the other hand, if these hallucinations are not present and the person experiences visual, tactile, gustatory, or olfactory hallucinations, then at least one additional characteristic symptom is required for diagnosis (APA, 2000).

TABLE 9.2 DSM-IV-TR DIAGNOSTIC CRITERIA FOR SCHIZOPHRENIA

A. *Characteristic symptoms:* Two (or more) of the following, each present for a significant period of time during a 1-month period (or less if successfully treated):
   (1) delusions
   (2) hallucinations
   (3) disorganized speech (e.g., frequent derailment or incoherence)
   (4) grossly disorganized or catatonic behavior
   (5) negative symptoms (i.e., affective flattening, alogia, or avolition)

Note: Only one Criterion A symptom is required if delusions are bizarre or hallucinations consist of a voice keeping up a running commentary on the person's behavior or thoughts, or two or more voices are conversing with each other.

B. *Social/occupational dysfunction:* For a significant portion of the time since the onset of the disturbance, one or more major areas of functioning such as work, interpersonal relations, or self-care are markedly below the level achieved prior to the onset (or when the onset is in childhood or adolescence, failure to achieve expected level of interpersonal, academic, or occupational achievement).

C. *Duration:* Continuous signs of the disturbance persist for at least 6 months. This 6-month period must include at least 1 month of symptoms (or less if successfully treated) that meet Criterion A (i.e., active-phase symptoms) and may include periods of prodromal or residual symptoms. During these prodromal or residual periods, the signs of the disturbance may be manifested by only negative symptoms or two or more symptoms listed in Criterion A present in an attenuated form (e.g., odd beliefs, unusual perceptual experiences).

D. *Schizoaffective and mood disorder exclusion:* Schizoaffective Disorder and Mood Disorder With Psychotic Features have been ruled out because either (1) no Major Depressive, Manic, or Mixed Episodes have occurred concurrently with the active-phase symptoms; or (2) if mood episodes have occurred during active-phase symptoms, their total duration has been brief relative to the duration of the active and residual periods.

E. *Substance/general medical condition exclusion:* The disturbance is not due to the physiological effects of a substance (e.g., a drug of abuse, a medication) or a general medical condition.

F. *Relationship to pervasive developmental disorder:* If there is a history of autistic disorder or another pervasive developmental disorder, the additional diagnosis of schizophrenia is made only if prominent delusions or hallucinations are also present for at least a month (or less if successfully treated).

Source: Reprinted with permission from the *Diagnostic and Statistical Manual of Mental Disorders, Fourth Edition, Text Revision.* (Copyright © 2000). American Psychiatric Association.

BIZARRE DELUSIONS Delusions judged to be *bizarre* are also sufficient, by themselves, to meet the symptom criterion for the diagnosis of schizophrenia. As described earlier, a delusion is an implausible belief that ranges from the merely unlikely to the impossible and it may or may not be seen as bizarre. For example, a person may, without any evidence, believe that a roommate is poisoning food and stalking him or her or, in the case of a girlfriend or boyfriend, being unfaithful. Such delusions would be considered implausible but not inconceivable and therefore not bizarre. A bizarre delusion is impossible. A patient may believe that her organs have been removed and replaced without leaving scars. Another patient may believe that ideas were inserted into his brain by aliens or that a central computer in Ottawa is recording all his thoughts. A bizarre delusion is one that conveys this kind of personal loss of control over mind or body. If delusions judged to be bizarre are present, then no other symptoms are needed for the diagnosis of schizophrenia. In the case of a non-bizarre delusion, an additional characteristic symptom is needed.

It is important to distinguish between bizarre delusions and those that are **mood congruent,** or consistent with a person's emotional state, and reflect a mood disorder rather than schizophrenia. For example, a severely depressed person may become convinced that he or she is to blame for all the evil in the world. In a sense, the delusion "fits" or is congruent with the mood state of guilt feelings and self-hatred (see Chapter 8). Bizarre delusions, in contrast, are often incongruent with or seem to contradict a person's predominant mood. Thus, a patient with schizophrenia may seem to enjoy the bizarre delusion of having her or his internal organs replaced by remote-controlled machinery.

CASE EXAMPLES Consider Ruth and William and the way their respective clinical profiles fit into the DSM-IV-TR diagnostic criteria for schizophrenia (APA, 2000). Ruth experienced tactile (touch) and olfactory (smell) hallucinations of an animal, which she believed to be hanging around her neck. She did not hear voices commenting on her behaviour or experience a bizarre delusion. Hence, at least one more characteristic symptom was required for diagnosis. She exhibited withdrawal and affective flattening, which are negative symptoms of schizophrenia. Ruth thus met Criterion A for schizophrenia. William, on the other hand, experienced bizarre religious and grandiose delusions of divinity as well as auditory hallucinations and displayed grossly disorganized behaviour. His symptom picture actually exceeds the number required by the DSM-IV-TR Criterion A.

Both Ruth and William exhibited deterioration in personal, social, and occupation functioning, thus meeting Criterion B for schizophrenia. Ruth neglected her personal hygiene. As well, she was unable to live successfully in supported housing. William was unable to live independently, at times vomiting, defecating, and urinating in his apartment, or engaging in chaotic behaviour. Ruth and William also met Criterion C for schizophrenia, each presenting with more than one month of active symptoms, and experiencing the disturbance for over six months.

It is important and sometimes difficult to distinguish the negative symptoms of schizophrenia from depressive and other mood-related symptoms and also to ensure that positive symptoms do not reflect mood-congruent delusions and hence a mood disorder rather than schizophrenia. Ruth's emotional flatness and withdrawal, thoughts of death, suicidal ideas, hopelessness, and self-deprecation suggest the presence of severe depression with psychotic features. However, careful questioning and review of hospital records and interview notes showed that her hallucinations and withdrawal persisted even when mood-related symptoms improved. This led to the conclusion that she met Criterion D for schizophrenia.

Additional "exclusionary" criteria include elimination of drug effects or coexisting diseases as causes of psychosis or negative symptoms (Criterion E), as well as the possibility of developmental and childhood disorders as contributing causes (Criterion F). William's history of street drug abuse was excluded as a cause of his psychotic episodes because the episodes occurred independently of his drug intake. Further, although William's childhood history included schooling problems and poor social adjustment, there was no evidence of autism or a pervasive developmental disorder. Ruth's history was completely clear of both substance abuse and developmental problems.

SYMPTOM-BASED SUBTYPES

The DSM-IV-TR describes five major subtypes of schizophrenia, including paranoid, disorganized, catatonic, undifferentiated, and residual (APA, 2000). The presenting clinical features at the time of the most recent assessment form the basis for both the diagnosis of schizophrenia and the appropriate subtype. However, the diagnosis of a specific subtype may change over time. It is noteworthy that despite the long history of these subtypes in the diagnosis of schizophrenia, they will be excluded from the next revision of the DSM (DSM-5; APA, 2010).

The **paranoid type** of schizophrenia is indicated by the presence of prominent delusions or auditory hallucinations and the absence of markedly impaired cognitive functioning or affect. As well, the paranoid subtype requires absence of symptoms including disorganized speech and behaviour, catatonia, and flat or inappropriate emotions. Delusions characteristic of paranoid schizophrenia are most commonly persecutory or grandiose. The patient may experience several delusions, but these are typically organized around a central theme. The hallucinations experienced by paranoid patients with schizophrenia are also usually related to the central delusional theme. The paranoid type tends to be the least disabling of the five DSM-IV-TR subtypes and also the most common. Onset of schizophrenia of the paranoid type is typically later and is thought to have a better prognosis than the other subtypes.

The **disorganized type** of schizophrenia is characterized by disorganized speech and behaviour as well as notably flat or inappropriate affect. The disorganized speech may manifest as silliness or laughter unrelated to the content of speech, while the behavioural disorganization refers to an absence of goal orientation and may present as impaired functioning on everyday activities like showering and dressing. Any presenting hallucinations or delusions are disjointed and not structured around a central theme. The criteria for the disorganized type of schizophrenia further require that the criteria for the catatonic type described below are not met. Disorganized schizophrenia tends to be the most disabling of the subtypes. It is typically associated with early onset and is thought to have the poorest prognosis.

The **catatonic type** of schizophrenia is defined by acute psychomotor disturbance, which may present as immobility and extreme negativism and rigidity. Patients with catatonia show peculiarities of voluntary movement. These may include odd postures or purposeless, excessive movements. Additional motor symptoms of this subtype include echopraxia, a repetitive imitation of another person's movements, and echolalia, a pathological, senseless kind of verbal repetition.

The **undifferentiated type** of schizophrenia is seen in patients meeting Criterion A for the disorder, but without sufficient characteristics to satisfy criteria for the paranoid, disorganized, or catatonic subtypes. In contrast, the **residual type** is diagnosed in the case of a patient with at least one prior episode of schizophrenia and with negative symptoms, such as flat affect, poverty of speech, or avolition, as well as attenuated positive symptoms, which may include eccentric behaviour, mildly disorganized speech, or odd beliefs. However, this patient is not currently experiencing prominent positive psychotic symptoms of the disorder, namely, delusions, hallucinations, disorganized speech, or grossly disorganized behaviour.

CRITIQUE OF DSM-IV-TR AND SYMPTOM-BASED DIAGNOSIS

While the DSM-IV-TR diagnosis is currently used as the primary definition of schizophrenia, it is important to be aware of its limitations (Allardyce, Gaebel, Zielasek, & Van Os, 2007; Heinrichs, 2001). The DSM-IV-TR (APA, 2000) relies on a person's presenting symptoms and history as the main indications of disorder. A significant drawback of this approach to diagnosis is its subjectivity. Symptoms are private experiences that a patient describes to a clinician. There are no instruments that can indicate the presence and intensity of a delusion in the way that a thermometer can indicate a fever. Hence, there is also no independent way to confirm a diagnosis of schizophrenia because the DSM-IV-TR system lacks objective signs or laboratory findings. Although clinicians using structured interviews and explicit diagnostic criteria tend to agree on who has or does not have the disorder, the diagnosis may still be inaccurate. In other words, a reliable diagnosis does not necessarily produce a valid diagnosis. Finally, the subtypes of schizophrenia are an attempt to organize the clinical heterogeneity of schizophrenia. Yet they often change over time and only the paranoid type has received some limited research support as a valid distinction. This situation has led many researchers to look for more objective signs that a person has or does not have schizophrenia.

PROPOSED CHANGES IN DSM-5

Several changes to the diagnostic criteria for schizophrenia have been proposed for the upcoming DSM-5 (APA, 2010). These changes have been suggested to ensure that the diagnostic criteria are defined more clearly and reflect the research literature.

The five diagnostic criteria for schizophrenia will remain, and changes will be made only to Criterion A (symptoms). Catatonia will be separated from the disorganized behaviour criterion and added to "grossly abnormal psychomotor behaviour, such as catatonia" (APA, 2010). Examples of negative symptoms will include restricted affect and avolition/asociality, as these are two discernible dimensions of negative symptoms and better define affective abnormalities in schizophrenia (APA, 2010). Additionally, the presence of a bizarre delusion or hallucinations of voices conversing or a voice keeping a running commentary on the individual will no longer be sufficient to satisfy Criterion A. Furthermore, it will be required that at least one of the Criterion A symptoms be delusions, hallucinations, or disorganized speech. The last proposed change includes, as mentioned above, the elimination of all symptom-based schizophrenia subtypes. This has been proposed because subtypes like disorganized or paranoid schizophrenia change over time and have little practical value in terms of treatment or prognosis (APA, 2010). It is likely that further revisions will be made before the release of DSM-5; to view the most up-to-date proposed changes on the diagnostic criteria for schizophrenia, visit www.dsm5.org.

2 BEFORE MOVING ON

> Why would a person who thinks he hears voices not necessarily receive a diagnosis of schizophrenia?

MARKERS AND ENDOPHENOTYPES FOR SCHIZOPHRENIA

What would be required to verify objectively that a person has a disorder like schizophrenia? Objective diagnosis is possible if measurable **disease markers** can be identified, markers that occur in virtually all people with the illness. In principle, a marker is any physical, psychological, or biological characteristic or trait. For example, Alzheimer's disease involves degenerative changes in nerve cells. These changes are observable under a microscope and represent pathological markers that confirm the disease. While symptoms reflect a disturbance in mind and body that is associated with schizophrenia, they are too subjective and private to confirm a diagnosis of the illness. Markers introduce scientific precision into the diagnostic process.

A disease marker for schizophrenia could be any objective psychological as well as physical sign of the illness or of vulnerability to the disorder. For example, Canadian psychologist Richard Steffy argued that the time required to prepare for and respond to simple perceptual events may be an indicator of severe and chronic forms of schizophrenia (Steffy & Waldman, 1993). More generally, a person who exhibits a marker for schizophrenia either has the disorder presently or is likely to develop schizophrenia in the future. A true marker for schizophrenia would be very common among patients with the DSM-IV-TR schizophrenia diagnosis. This high prevalence reflects the marker's **sensitivity** to the disorder. At the same time, the marker must occur very infrequently among healthy people or people with other disorders, reflecting the marker's **specificity** for schizophrenia.

It is possible to further subdivide the marker concept into vulnerability and genetic markers, as well as the closely related concept of **endophenotypes**. A vulnerability marker is a stable and enduring sign or trait of the disorder that occurs before a person actually succumbs to the disorder and experiences symptoms. A vulnerability marker reflects an inherent predisposition to develop the disorder. Such a marker thus allows for the identification of people at risk for becoming ill, even though they may be healthy when the marker is first observed. A genetic marker is a special kind of vulnerability marker. Hence, it is stable and enduring, presents long before onset of the illness, *and* occurs in close relatives of the patient, particularly those who develop schizophrenia. Prevalence among family members implies a genetic component to the marker. Genetic and vulnerability markers may define endophenotypes, which are biological or behavioural predispositions that make the disorder more likely. An endophenotype is "intermediate" between the microscopic world of genes and nerve cells and the experiential and psychological world of symptoms (Braff, Freedman, Schork, & Gottesman, 2007).

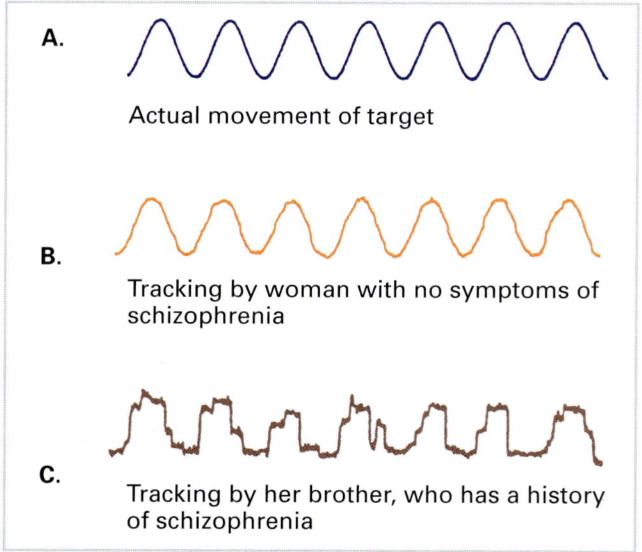

FIGURE 9.1 Samples of Eye-Tracking

Source: Based on Iacono, Bassett, and Jones (1988, p. 1140). Copyright 1988, American Medical Association.

Markers and endophenotypes may work in theory, but do they actually exist for schizophrenia? For example, impairment on the Continuous Performance Test (CPT) has been studied as a **cognitive marker** of the disorder. In the CPT, participants observe a string of numbers and are asked to respond (press a button) whenever two identical numbers occur together. On average, patients with schizophrenia consistently score below healthy people on the CPT (Heinrichs & Zakzanis, 1998). This impairment reflects deficits in attention and an inability to keep a rule in mind (working memory). The CPT is also an example of a test that taps an ability that is in part inherited (Hill, Harris, Herbener, Pavuluri, & Sweeney, 2008). However, CPT performance is deficient in only 50 to 60 percent of diagnosed patients. This limits its efficacy as a marker, because it is not sensitive enough to detect the hypothetical disease defect in a large majority of schizophrenia patients.

Another potential marker of schizophrenia involves smooth pursuit eye movements. Due to the controlling influence of attention, our eyes track—or "pursue"—moving stimuli and duplicate the pattern of a continuously moving stimulus in tiny eye movements. Patients with schizophrenia, however, often exhibit irregularities in these eye movements. Their **eye-tracking** records reveal more deviations from the stimulus path, and thus more errors, when compared to a healthy comparison group (Levy, Holzman, Matthyse, & Mendell, 1993); see Figure 9.1. Deficits in eye-tracking may reflect neurological impairments associated with schizophrenia and a predisposition for the disorder. However, once again, even the best eye-tracking indicators are abnormal in only about 50 percent of patients with schizophrenia. Perhaps this task is better suited as a potential marker for a specific variant of schizophrenia or for a broader classification of impairment that includes other psychiatric disorders.

The above examples of potential markers for schizophrenia highlight the difficulty of finding tasks and indicators that are sufficiently sensitive to the disorder. Yet a researcher would not expect 100 percent of the patients in a sample to be abnormal on any given marker task. After all, there may have been errors in diagnosis and some of the patients may not really have schizophrenia. Therefore, some tolerance or allowance for inaccuracy has to be provided. Despite these uncertainties, there is great interest in the discovery of markers and associated endophenotypes that may help to define the disorder more objectively (Oertel-Knöchel, Bittner, Knöchel, Prvulovic, & Hampel, 2011; Schwarz & Bahn, 2008).

COGNITIVE SUBTYPES OF SCHIZOPHRENIA

Cognitive and biological markers are believed to occur in only some patients with schizophrenia because the disorder exists in several variants, forms, or subtypes

(Heinrichs, 2004). Instead of defining these subtypes with symptoms, researchers have begun to differentiate them in terms of performance on various neuropsychological tests. For example, subgroups of patients have been identified on the basis of impaired problem solving (Goldstein, 1990; Heinrichs & Awad, 1993) and memory deficits (McDermid Vaz & Heinrichs, 2006; Paulsen et al., 1995; Turetsky, Moberg, & Mozley, 2002). York University researchers showed that patients with schizophrenia could be separated into cognitively impaired, cognitively normal, and verbal memory–impaired subtypes (Ammari, Heinrichs, & Miles, 2010). Patients in the generalized cognitive impairment subgroup experienced the most severe negative symptoms and had the most difficulty adjusting to the demands of everyday life. Hence, cognitive measures may replace symptoms as a tool for the discovery and study of variants and subtypes of schizophrenia.

Etiology

The psychiatric pioneers who described modern schizophrenia at the turn of the twentieth century did not formulate or test hypotheses about the causes of the disorder. Kraepelin (1919) noted the hereditary "taint" of dementia praecox and the fact that it "ran" in families. He also thought that the frontal and temporal lobes of the brain must be involved in the disorder, but never developed these notions into a theory or research program. Bleuler (1911/1950) theorized extensively about the mental life and symptoms of people with schizophrenia without ever grappling in detail with what caused the disorder in the first place. He argued, for example, that disconnected or "dissociated" thinking was a fundamental symptom of the disorder, but offered no suggestions about the causes of the symptom. On the other hand, in the first half of the twentieth century, psychoanalysts (see Chapter 2) made a number of suggestions about the causes of schizophrenia. They argued that experiences during infancy, including emotional traumas and inadequate parenting, could lead to a weak and primitive ego that was unable to distinguish wishes and fears from reality (Fromm-Reichmann, 1959; Reichard & Tillman, 1950; Tausk, 1948). It was believed that a severely rejecting mother could be "**schizophrenogenic,**" thereby creating the conditions for a weak and primitive ego—the foundation of schizophrenia—in her children (Diamond, 1997).

The Swiss psychiatrist Carl Jung, working with both Bleuler and Freud, gained considerable experience treating people with schizophrenia. Jung (1956) liked to tell the story of how he "discovered" the connection between psychosis and the **collective unconscious**. One of Jung's patients who had schizophrenia maintained that a swinging penis attached to the sun was the source of the wind. This seemed like just another curious delusion to the psychiatrist until he found a strikingly parallel belief in the ancient Persian religion of Mithraism. The belief held that a swinging tube suspended from the sun caused the wind. Jung became convinced that universal symbols existed in the unconscious mind and erupted into waking life in the course of dreams and mental illnesses like schizophrenia.

In contrast with early views that the disorder primarily reflected internal psychological conflicts and processes, sociological research during the 1930s found connections between schizophrenia and poverty. In particular, first admission rates for the disorder were observed to be four times higher in the slums of central Chicago than in its affluent suburbs (Faris & Dunham, 1939). The relationship between social class and schizophrenia persisted and can be seen in Figure 9.2, which incorporates findings from the 1950s.

One view of the social class–illness link was that the cumulative exposure to poverty, crime, and family disturbances led directly to increased cases of schizophrenia. At the same time, **social drift** explanations held that people from lower socio-economic classes could not rise economically if they had a predisposition for schizophrenia. The predisposition reduced intellectual abilities and motivation even before symptoms occurred, thereby preventing the achievement of educational and occupational goals. While poverty did not turn out to cause the disorder, class-related and other negative social and biological influences may be contributing factors in some cases (Gottesman, 1991). For example, research has revealed that negative immigration

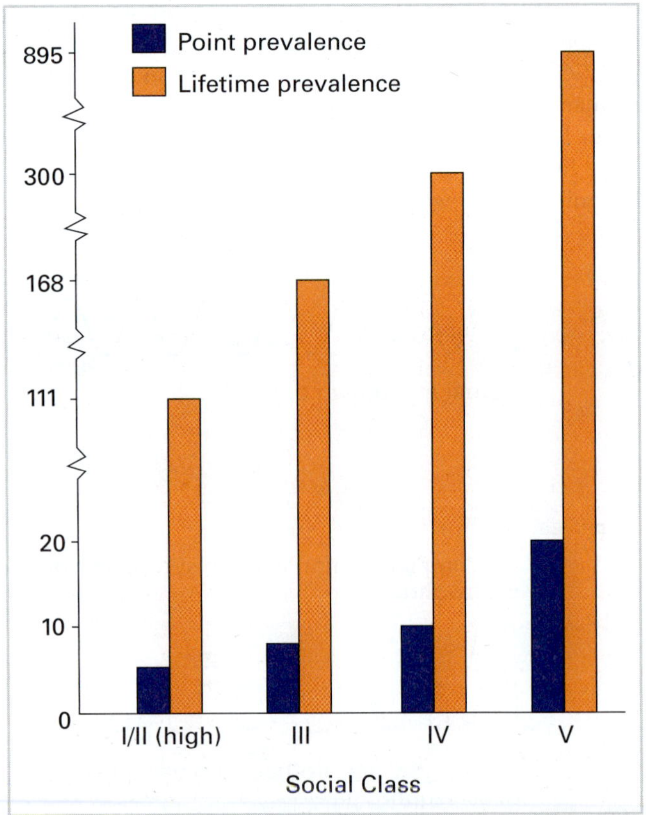

FIGURE 9.2 Prevalence of Schizophrenia by Social Class (rates per 100 000 in New Haven, Connecticut)

Source: Data from Hollingshead & Redlich (1958).

experiences in people of colour may contribute to increased development of schizophrenia (Cantor-Graae, 2007). In addition, there is evidence that living in a city increases the likelihood that a person already vulnerable to mental health problems will go on to experience psychosis (Dragt et al., 2011). Accordingly, social influences remain an important ingredient in the disorder.

THEORIES OF SCHIZOPHRENIA

In contemporary research, almost no one believes that a mother can cause schizophrenia by rejecting her child or that delusions reflect an eruption of the collective unconscious or that poverty adequately explains the occurrence of severe mental disorders. Instead, complex psychiatric conditions are seen as the outcome of inherited, biologically based vulnerabilities that interact with maturation and development and with life and environmental stresses and influences to push people over a threshold into psychosis. The assumption is that vulnerability, or **diathesis**, and disorder-promoting events, or **stress,** are both required. In addition, the causal pathway from diathesis-stress to clinical disorder is complex and extends over at least the first decade and a half of a person's life. American psychologist Paul Meehl (1962, 1990) built on this assumption and proposed a diathesis-stress theory whereby an inherited gene makes a person vulnerable to schizophrenia. However, whether the disorder actually develops depends on the "good" and "bad" effects of other genes, as well as on the social rewards and punishments experienced by vulnerable people as they grow and change from childhood through adolescence to young adulthood.

MEEHL'S THEORY OF SCHIZOTAXIA, SCHIZOTYPY, AND SCHIZOPHRENIA The theory proposes a biological diathesis, termed "**hypokrisia**," that occurs throughout the brain, making nerve cells abnormally reactive to incoming stimulation. A single gene inherited from either parent causes this diathesis. However, the "schizogene" is often expressed weakly in a person and its effects may be compensated by other genes, as well as by experience and environmental influences. Hence, not everyone with the schizogene develops schizophrenia. Moreover, even when the gene is expressed in hypokrisia the defect does not interfere with basic, elementary activities of the nervous system. The brain is still able to regulate bodily processes and register, store, and retrieve information. Hence, hypokrisia does not cause mental retardation or other gross disorders of brain function. What it does produce is a subtler disturbance that Meehl called "**cognitive slippage**." Information is disorganized, incoherent, and "scrambled." In Meehl's theory, high intellectual ability can coexist with hypokrisia and cognitive slippage. Yet these defects do distort thinking by causing an exaggerated and persisting tendency to form haphazard connections between ideas, emotions, and events. This "associative loosening" resembles the thought and language disorder described in the section on symptoms. However, in addition, the unselective neuronal firing that causes cognitive slippage gives rise to a gradual increase in punitive, unpleasant social experiences. The brain amplifies feelings of pain and weakens pleasure, making interpersonal relations difficult. This **"aversive drift"** is related to negative symptoms like social withdrawal and disinterest. As the brain scrambles and distorts rewarding and punitive emotional associations, the vulnerable person begins to find social contact more and more unpleasant. Increasingly, such a person avoids social intercourse and is viewed as strange and subject to disapproval by other people. This negative appraisal in turn accelerates the process of withdrawal and creates a vicious circle.

A person experiencing cognitive slippage and aversive drift is termed a "**schizotype**" in Meehl's theory. But such a person may still be spared the full-blown psychotic disorder of schizophrenia. Schizotypal people suffer from "primary" cognitive slippage, difficulty feeling pleasure, social alienation, and other consequences of aversive drift. However, numerous "moderator" genes that influence everything from intelligence to artistic talent to shyness can prevent or accelerate the development of a person's schizotypy into a schizophrenic disorder. In addition, the environment plays a key role in shaping or limiting the expression of schizotypy. For example, schizophrenia becomes more probable when a schizotypal person inherits tendencies toward shyness; anxiety; low energy; weak motivation; and low ability, talent, or physical attractiveness. Even so, these "polygenic" characteristics still have to combine with the influence of a social world that punishes undesirable traits before a person crosses the threshold into a diagnosable schizophrenia spectrum disorder. Conversely, different polygenes may combine in such a way that a person becomes a "compensated schizotype." This is someone who is able to function in everyday life, although usually at a cost to him- or herself or to other people. Meehl mentioned Adolf Hitler as an example of compensated schizotype: an intelligent and talented but socially fearful and inadequate person, prone to incoherent and irrational thoughts and impulses.

According to Meehl, the development of schizophrenia is understandable only as the product of all of these complex influences. Primary hypokrisia, cognitive slippage, and aversive drift are modified or intensified by personality, temperament, and cognitive traits, and this takes place within stressful or supportive social environments.

NEURODEVELOPMENTAL DIATHESIS-STRESS THEORIES Meehl's formulation has been criticized for its lack of detail on the nature of hypokrisia and cognitive slippage and for not explaining one of the key features of schizophrenia: its occurrence in late adolescence and early adulthood (Heinrichs, 2001). Hence, a number of theorists have accepted the basic diathesis-stress model as a framework and added ideas and detail regarding the nature of what is wrong in the schizophrenic brain, how it got there, and why the disorder occurs primarily in young people.

For example, psychiatrist Daniel Weinberger (1987, 1995) agreed that a person could inherit a genetic defect

APPLIED CLINICAL CASE

John Nash's Beautiful Mind: When Schizophrenia and Genius Coexist

John Nash was born to well-educated parents in 1928; his father was an electrical engineer and his mother a teacher. Nash showed impressive intellectual potential early in life, carrying out sophisticated chemistry experiments in his room by the age of 10 and proving complex theorems by famous mathematicians at the age of 15. Yet, while intellectually gifted, Nash struggled in social situations. His peers nicknamed him "bug brains" and he came to prefer a solitary lifestyle to the rejection and discomfort often experienced with other people.

Nash's intellectual gifts were expressed in educational and scientific accomplishments. He was offered a full scholarship to complete undergraduate studies at Carnegie Mellon University, where his performance was described as exceptional and extraordinary. He earned a master's degree along with his bachelor of science after only three years of university and was subsequently offered fellowships at both Harvard and Princeton. It was his Ph.D. research at Princeton that eventually won him the Nobel Prize from the Royal Swedish Academy of Sciences.

In his personal life, the odd and peculiar behaviour noticed by many people became even more apparent as Nash completed postgraduate work and pursued further academic interests. Throughout his time at Princeton, he refused to attend classes on principle, instead pacing the halls or riding a bicycle in tight concentric circles. Rather than read in the library, he would lie atop the tables with his hands behind his head. According to Sylvia Nasar, author of *A Beautiful Mind*, a biography of Nash that was the basis for the 2001 movie starring Russell Crowe, these strange character traits marked the path from simple quirkiness to frank psychosis. By the age of 30, after accepting a faculty position at the Massachusetts Institute of Technology (MIT), Nash began hearing voices and developed a delusional way of thinking. He believed that a front-page story in *The New York Times* contained coded messages from inhabitants of another galaxy—messages that only he could unscramble. Later, he offered one of his graduate students an "inter-galactic driver's license" and a seat on his newly organized world government. He wrote thousands of letters to the government, newspapers, and colleagues. Nash believed that everything had meaning and nothing was random or accidental. He would spend days making odd calculations like converting contemporary politician Nelson Rockefeller's name to a complex numerical representation and then mathematically factoring the resulting number.

Perhaps surprisingly, this brilliant and severely troubled man was married, although the couple later divorced. His wife initially attempted to hide Nash's psychiatric problems, but ultimately brought him to hospital against his will. Like many people suffering from schizophrenia, Nash denied his illness, convinced that he was being persecuted. At the time of his first hospitalization, he was diagnosed with paranoid schizophrenia. During this time, treatments for psychotic illness were primitive and usually ineffective (see the section "Treatment" later in this chapter). They included psychodynamic psychotherapy, which has since lost favour as a therapy for psychosis, and insulin shock therapy, long abandoned in favour of medication.

Although his groundbreaking research was probably done before his illness, Nash's case illustrates the possibility that exceptional intellectual ability and achievement can exist in people with schizophrenia. The vast majority of patients with the diagnosis are cognitively impaired, but recent studies reveal that a small number have above-average abilities, especially in verbal skills like vocabulary (Heinrichs et al., 2008). Yet, like Nash, these exceptional patients have difficulty functioning normally in the community. It seems that intellectual ability cannot compensate completely for the devastating experience of severe mental illness. Moreover, even the most gifted patients often face social obstacles like stigma. Indeed, the stigma and negative image of schizophrenia almost prevented Nash from being awarded the Nobel Prize. Many involved with the prize were concerned that giving a prestigious award to a "madman" would embarrass and discredit the Academy of Sciences.

John Nash's experience is unique and atypical compared to most people suffering from schizophrenia, but his amazing story is a testimony to hope, courage, and perseverance in the face of both mental illness and social disapproval.

that creates vulnerability for the disorder. But he believed it was also possible that subtle brain injuries during fetal development or birth could become a diathesis. In theory, this early damage or lesion may occur in brain regions that normally mature in adolescence, when they are required by the emerging demands of social life and sexuality. It is the stress of maturational demands on the weakened brain that precipitates a psychotic crisis and initial hospitalization. Psychologist Elaine Walker (Walker & Diforio, 1997; Walker, Mittal, & Tessner, 2008) has gone further and specified hormone producing and regulating mechanisms in the brain that are normally "switched" on by stress experiences in late adolescence. However, people with the biological vulnerability for schizophrenia cannot cope with the effects of surging stress hormones on brain chemistry and begin to develop symptoms and clinical illness.

All of the diathesis-stress theories of schizophrenia hypothesize a biological vulnerability that is either inherited or acquired very early in life. The vulnerability may take the form of neuroanatomical or neurochemical abnormalities, or both. It is the interaction of these abnormalities with maturation, stress, and life events that eventually causes schizophrenia. Yet although the theories explain why the disorder occurs, to what extent are these explanations supported by the facts? We begin with a consideration of genetics and the role of inheritance in the etiology of schizophrenia.

3 BEFORE MOVING ON

How does the concept of diathesis, or vulnerability, differ from the concept of cause?

BIOLOGICAL FACTORS

IS SCHIZOPHRENIA INHERITED? On the basis of shared genes, human characteristics from eye colour and height to illnesses like diabetes and heart disease "run" in families. Indeed, most psychiatric, behavioural, and medical disorders are under at least some genetic influence. This applies to Alzheimer's disease, autism, major mood disorders, and reading disability, as well as to epilepsy, peptic ulcer, and rheumatoid arthritis. In addition, within the spectrum of normal behaviour, genes play a role in cognitive abilities like memory and intelligence and in personality traits like neuroticism. Genes even play a role in vocational interests and scholastic achievement (McGuffin, Owen, O'Donovan, Thapar, & Gottesman, 1994; Whitman, 2008). Nonetheless, the degree to which these complex illnesses and traits are actually controlled by genes seldom exceeds 50 percent. In many cases, heritability is much lower. Accordingly, non-genetic factors must be of roughly equal importance in determining the emergence of many psychiatric disorders and complex behavioural traits.

A familial **genetic contribution** to the development of schizophrenia has been assumed since the time of Kraepelin (1913, 1919) and Bleuler (1911/1950). Schizophrenia is observed to recur in some families, with a risk of about 13 percent to the children of a parent with schizophrenia. This compares with a general population risk for the disorder of only about 1 percent (Gottesman, 1991). Hence, having one parent with schizophrenia increases the risk of developing the disorder 13 times. However, even in this relatively "high-risk" situation, about 87 percent of people with a parent who has schizophrenia will remain free of the disorder. This "**familiality**" effect, summarized in Figure 9.3, shows that the likelihood of a person developing schizophrenia is much higher if a biological relative also has the disorder. The risk is highest for someone with an identical, or monozygotic, twin and then falls off stepwise as the degree of genetic relatedness diminishes.

Yet the genetics of schizophrenia contrast with disorders like Huntington's disease, which has a more straightforward pattern of inheritance. Defects in a single gene cause Huntington's disease, giving rise to a predictable risk: a 50 percent chance of developing the disease if a person has one parent with the disorder, and a 100 percent chance in the unlikely event that both parents are ill. Complex behavioural syndromes, including psychiatric disorders like schizophrenia, do not follow such patterns of inheritance. For example, if a single gene caused schizophrenia, the risk for illness should decrease by a constant factor of 50 percent between different relative classes. This prediction is based on the degree of shared genetic material in relatives, which ranges from 100 percent in the case of identical twins, to 50 percent for parents, to 25 percent for second-degree relatives like aunts and uncles. However, the risk of schizophrenia for someone who has an identical twin with the disorder is only about 48 percent instead of 100 percent. If all genes are in common, including the one that causes schizophrenia, both identical twins should become ill.

Discrepancies between predicted and observed cases of genetic illness can be dealt with through the principle of incomplete "**penetrance**." In other words, it is known that a proportion of people with a dominant gene will fail to show the effect of that gene. As suggested by Meehl's theory, the lack of expression may be due to the environment or to other factors in the person's genetic constitution. Hence, the penetrance of the schizophrenia gene may be much less than 100 percent and closer to about 50 percent. This roughly fits the risk of the disorder in identical twins. However, the single gene model still does not work for the other relative classes. First-degree relatives should have a risk for schizophrenia of about 25 percent, but Figure 9.3 shows that the observed risks are much lower. Similarly, second-degree relatives should have a risk of 12.5 percent and not the 3 to 4 percent actually observed.

SEARCH FOR "SCHIZOGENES" Evidence against simple gene models also comes from attempts by molecular biologists to link schizophrenia with single genes and specific chromosomes. These attempts have been consistently unsuccessful (O'Donovan & Owen, 1992, 1996). All in all, the idea that one major gene causes schizophrenia is both contradicted by the facts and rejected by most researchers.

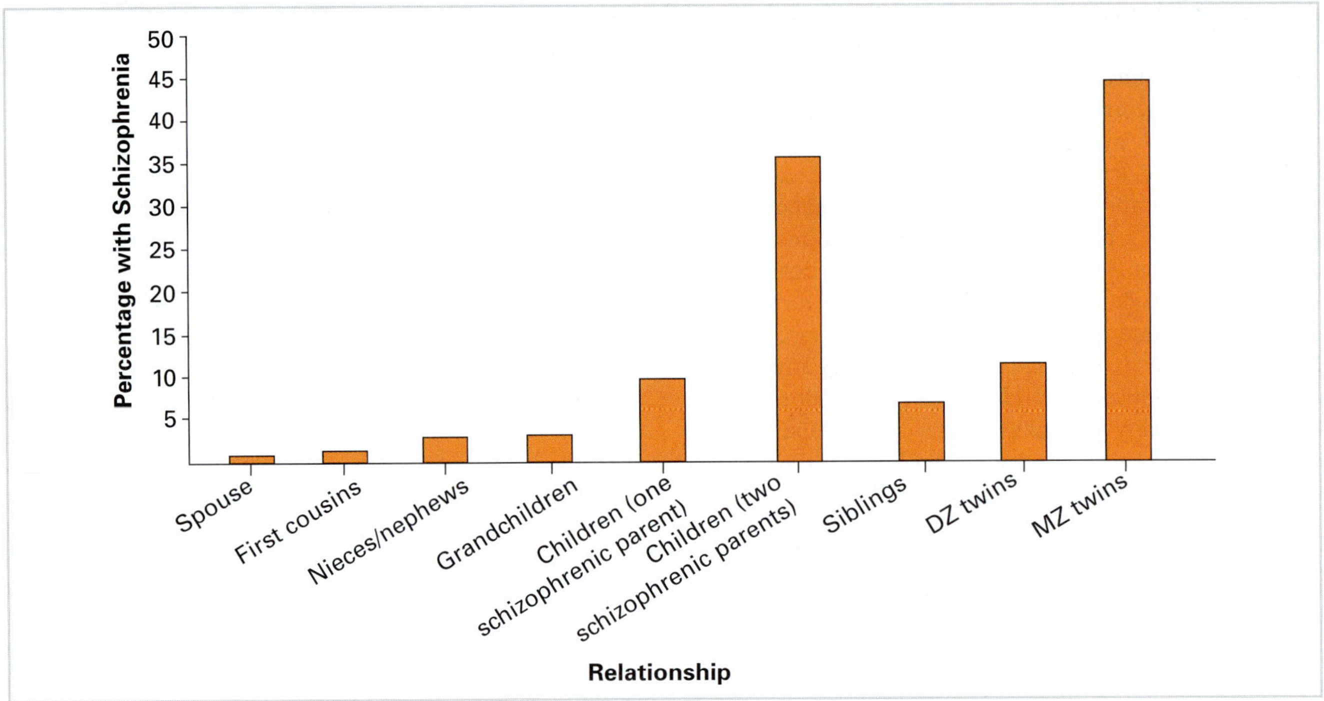

FIGURE 9.3 Prevalence of Schizophrenia Among Relatives of People with Schizophrenia

Source: McGue, M., & Gottesman, I. I. (1989). A single dominant gene still cannot account for the transmission of schizophrenia. *Archives of General Psychiatry*, 46, 478-479; Gottesman, I. I., McGuffin, P., & Farmer, A. E. (1987). Clinical genetics as clues to the "real" genetics of schizophrenia: A decade of modest gains while playing for time. *Schizophrenia Bulletin*, 13, 23-47.

Over the last decade, research has moved increasingly to complex multiple gene models in accounting for the inheritance of schizophrenia (see Gottesman, 1991; Pogue-Geile & Gottesman, 1999; Tiwari, Zai, Müller, & Kennedy, 2010). The field of molecular genetics is considering the possibility that several genes influence the development of schizophrenia. There is evidence for "risk" genes located on chromosomes 1, 2, 3, 4, 5, 6, 8, 9, 11, 13, 15, 16, 17, 18, and 22! Unfortunately, the evidence has sometimes been difficult to reproduce (Kendler, 2000). In addition, individual risk genes have extremely small effects, which means that finding them requires the study of very large numbers of patients (Tandon, Keshavan, & Nasrallah, 2008). For example, any specific gene variant increases the lifetime risk of developing schizophrenia from the general population rate by only about 1 to 1.5 percent. Current approaches compile results from thousands of cases and include the role of environmental influences, while also pursuing new leads like the concept of endophenotypes discussed earlier (Burmeister, McInnis, & Zöllner, 2008). Recent work is considering the possibility that the mechanisms that control or influence genes and their effects may be as important for the etiology of schizophrenia as the genes themselves. These "**epigenetic**" mechanisms may be helpful in explaining why identical twins with the same genes seem to differ in their vulnerability to schizophrenia. For example, Toronto-based researcher Arturas Petronis (2004, 2010) at the Centre for Addiction and Mental Health has identified processes that "turn" genes "on" or "off," and this regulation may be crucial in determining whether a twin actually develops schizophrenia. Accordingly, although schizophrenia is regarded as a highly heritable disorder, unravelling the biological details of the complex genetics involved will challenge researchers for many years to come.

DO PREGNANCY AND BIRTH COMPLICATIONS PLAY A ROLE IN SCHIZOPHRENIA? The diathesis-stress approach to understanding etiology assumes that a genetic predisposition is only part of the pathway that eventually causes an illness. There must be "stressors" as well, including other biological or environmental and social events that accumulate and propel the vulnerable person toward schizophrenia. One possible stressor is a mother's exposure to common viruses like influenza, or "the flu," during pregnancy. Such exposures are linked with increased risk of schizophrenia in the offspring. For example, there is evidence that exposure to the flu virus during the fifth month of pregnancy is associated with an increased risk of schizophrenia in the mother's children later in life (Limosin, Rouillon, Payan, Cohen, & Strub, 2003). However, the incidence of the disorder in people exposed to the virus is still extremely low and some studies have failed to support the relationship (Sacker, Done, Crow, & Goldberg, 1995). Perhaps viral exposure is one of many potential stressors that interact with genetic predisposition and other factors to influence etiology.

Birth-related complications have been proposed as one of these "other" factors. Medical and delivery-related problems at birth may be key environmental and biological events that interact with a genetic diathesis and further predispose a person to schizophrenia. If this idea is true, then high rates of birth complications should occur in children who go on to develop the illness. Birth complications can be studied by interviewing adult patients and their relatives with respect to obstetrical events and by examining birth and health records if these are available. Complications include prolonged labour, preterm delivery, low birth weight, fetal distress, and breathing difficulties. Indeed, it turns out that such complications are more common in the birth records of people with schizophrenia (Cannon, Jones, & Murray, 2002). However, once again, most people with the illness do not have these abnormalities, even though they occur more often than expected by chance or in comparison to healthy people (Heinrichs, 2001; Tandon et al., 2008).

CAN VULNERABILITY TO SCHIZOPHRENIA BE OBSERVED IN CHILDREN? Viral exposure during pregnancy and complications during birth are two possible events that may combine with genetic predisposition to increase the risk for schizophrenia. If genes and physical events in the environment combine to cause a vulnerability to the disorder, perhaps this vulnerability can be seen in children and adolescents before they experience symptoms. The question of whether early signs of eventual schizophrenia exist seems a simple one, but there are many difficulties involved in answering it. The most serious difficulty is the absence of a dependable, accurate way of identifying in advance who will go on to have the clinical disorder. Nevertheless, researchers have useful, if imperfect, ways of identifying children who have a greater-than-average likelihood of developing the disorder.

One strategy makes use of the fact that the child of a parent with schizophrenia has at least 10 times the normal risk of developing the disorder. Yet even with a large number of **"high-risk" children** to maximize the number of eventual patients, a researcher may have to wait for 20 years to discover which children actually develop the disorder. To counter this problem, some researchers use the "follow-back" approach, which begins with patients known to have schizophrenia in adulthood. Developmental histories, archival documents like hospital records, interviews with living relatives, and even early home movies are then employed to look back in time and find evidence of disturbed mental life and behaviour during infancy and childhood. The main disadvantage of the follow-back method is the limited availability and variable accuracy of old records (and old memories).

Nonetheless, despite the procedural challenge, evidence has accumulated that the liability for schizophrenia does manifest itself, albeit weakly and variably, in a variety of early behavioural abnormalities. A few studies suggest that a proportion of children at risk for schizophrenia show early signs of impaired movement and fine motor skills (Walker, Savoie, & Davis, 1994) and have cognitive limitations not shared by children without this risk (Erlenmeyer-Kimling et al., 2000; Steffy, Asarnow, Asarnow, MacCrimmon, & Cleghorn, 1984). Moreover, some children who are vulnerable to schizophrenia are withdrawn and socially reclusive, or more antisocial and aggressive than non-vulnerable children (Davidson et al., 1999). Overall, by the age of 16, nearly a third of individuals who go on to develop psychotic disorder have motor difficulties and deficient IQs (Dickson, Laurens, Cullen, & Hodgins, 2011).

It must also be that experience in some way shapes the mind and behaviour of those children who later become ill and, as Meehl (1990) acknowledged, this experience is partly psychological and social in nature. There is recent evidence that traumatic experiences in childhood are associated with psychotic experiences later in life, especially in adolescents who also use marijuana (Harley et al., 2010). Furthermore, although parenting and family experiences do not *cause* the disorder, there is evidence that family hostility, lack of support, critical attitudes, and over-involvement may make schizophrenia worse, or at least promote relapses and adjustment difficulties (Hooley, 2007). These negative interpersonal communications directed at the family member with the disorder are referred to as **expressed emotion.** However, expressed emotion also occurs in the families of people with mood (Chapter 8) and eating disorders (Chapter 10). This implies that negative family attitudes may make adjusting to psychological problems difficult in general rather than only in relation to schizophrenia.

Overall, the idea of a **cumulative liability** for schizophrenia that shows itself early in behaviour and increases with adverse environmental events and stresses over the course of childhood and adolescence is very appealing. Such a perspective can make up for the apparent weakness of individual stresses and vulnerabilities because it is the accumulation of liability, and not single events, that is causal. However, the research findings do not amount to a very powerful collection of disorder-promoting diatheses and stresses at the present time. Therefore, researchers have looked into the brain to find abnormalities that may contribute to the cause of schizophrenia.

4 BEFORE MOVING ON

If genes have a major influence on who develops the disorder, why do most children of a mother or father with the disorder never develop schizophrenia?

IS SCHIZOPHRENIA A BRAIN DISEASE?

Neuropsychological Tests. If schizophrenia is a brain disorder, then part or all of the brain must be abnormal in some way, giving rise to the typical symptoms of the disorder. One of the first regions that interested researchers was the **frontal**, or prefrontal, **lobe** of the brain. This large region includes about a third of the brain and has extensive connections with other structures and regions. The psychiatric pioneers believed that psychological capacities ascribed to the frontal brain were impaired in schizophrenia (e.g., Kraepelin, 1913, 1919). A series of case studies of neurological patients with frontal brain damage showed that personality change, impaired self-awareness, loss of initiative, disorganized thinking, impulsivity, and inappropriate

FOCUS 9.2

How Different Are Patients with Schizophrenia from Healthy People?

The explosion of research on schizophrenia across many fields from psychology to neurochemistry means that it is often hard, even for researchers, to arrive at a "big picture" of what is known about the disorder. However, the statistical summarizing technique of **meta-analysis** provides a partial solution to this problem. Meta-analysis, also called quantitative research synthesis, compiles all published articles in a field and transforms the individual results into an overall statistic termed the **effect size**. In the case of schizophrenia research, the effect size reflects the degree of difference between patients and healthy people in terms of any selected psychological or biological comparison. Average effect sizes can in turn be used to estimate the proportion or percentage of patients falling outside the healthy range, which is a statistical way of defining "abnormality" (see Chapter 1). A ranked summary of these "abnormality estimates" is presented in Table 9.3.

TABLE 9.3 ASPECTS OF BRAIN AND BEHAVIOUR MOST FREQUENTLY ABNORMAL IN PATIENTS WITH SCHIZOPHRENIA

Rank	Finding	Frequency (%)
1	slowness writing symbols paired with numbers (processing speed)	71–75
2	poor physical coordination and control (neurological soft signs)	68–78
3	impaired ability to filter out redundant information (sensory gating)	63–80
4	impaired learning and recall of words and stories (verbal memory)	62–75
5	increased neurotransmitter receptors in post-mortem brain tissue (dopamine)	47–81
6	blocking of one sensation by the presence of another (backward masking)	46–76
7	impaired ability to attend to one message and ignore another (dichotic listening)	50–71
8	impaired general intellectual ability (IQ)	50–67
9	reduced ability to generate words rapidly (phonemic word fluency)	53–64
10	slow and inaccurate detection of specified letters (Continuous Performance test)	52–62

Source: Chan, Xu, Heinrichs, Yu, & Wang, 2010; Davidson & Heinrichs, 2003; Dickinson, Ramsey, & Gold, 2007; Heinrichs, 2001, 2005; Heinrichs & Zakzanis, 1998).

Note: The table shows frequency estimates of different research findings based on meta-analytic findings and average effect sizes.

social behaviour were common consequences of damage to this brain area (Ackerly & Benton, 1948; Brickner, 1934, 1936; Harlow, 1848, 1868; Hebb & Penfield, 1940). These features echoed the thought and language disorder, bizarre behaviour, and negative symptoms seen in many patients with schizophrenia. At least on the surface, there were impressive similarities between schizophrenia and frontal brain disease.

Although few researchers believe that schizophrenia can be explained completely as a form of frontal brain disorder, the frontal hypothesis remains one of the earliest and most consistent attempts to relate the disorder to a specific brain system. One research strategy is to give patients with schizophrenia cognitive or **neuropsychological tests** that activate and depend on the frontal region (see Chapter 4). Impairment on such a test supports the hypothesis that the frontal brain is defective in the disorder. Some of these tests are relatively simple and others are more complicated and challenging. For example, one common deficit of frontal brain disease is an inability to generate words rapidly and fluently. According to studies with healthy people, the average person can come up with a total of 30 to 35 words that begin with letters like "F," "A," and "S" in three one-minute trials (see Lezak, 1995). Canadian neuropsychologist Brenda Milner (1964), working at the Montreal Neurological Institute, initiated studies showing that patients with surgical removal of frontal brain tissue generated very few words. The "FAS" technique was subsequently applied to patients with schizophrenia and compared to healthy people in 27 separate studies conducted between 1980 and 1997. There was a consistent deficiency in the patient samples, with results suggesting that a clear majority of patients produced fewer words than healthy people (Heinrichs, 2001).

Another neuropsychological test also applied originally by Milner to patients with frontal damage is the **Wisconsin Card Sorting Test** (WCST; Heaton, Chelune, Talley, Kay, & Curtiss, 1993). Most versions involve presenting four "key" cards that depict different shapes, colours, and quantities. The person taking the test is provided with a succession of cards and asked to match each one to a key card. Cards may match on the basis of colour, shape, or number, but only one matching principle is "correct" at a given time. The examiner controls the matching principle and gives feedback about the correctness of each attempted match without ever disclosing the actual principle. Then, after a succession of correct matches, the examiner changes to a new principle (e.g., shape instead of colour) without telling the test-taker. The object of the test is to discover the new principle each time it changes and to respond with correct matches. The WCST is easy for healthy people with average intelligence, but Milner (1963) showed that patients with prefrontal brain damage achieved abnormally few successively correct matches or "categories." They also tended to repeat or **perseverate** erroneous responses.

The WCST has proven to be the most popular neuropsychological measure in schizophrenia research, used in 43 studies published between 1980 and 1997 (Heinrichs & Zakzanis, 1998). Cumulative results from these studies show that at least half of patients with schizophrenia are consistently impaired relative to healthy people. Moreover, this deficiency is similar in severity to the results of studies conducted with neurological patients who had documented damage to their frontal lobes (Heinrichs, 2001).

Despite this impressive evidence, neuropsychological tests do not provide definitive support for the **frontal brain deficiency** hypothesis in schizophrenia. Most tests are sensitive to more than one brain region, so that poor performance does not necessarily mean that the frontal region, or only the frontal region, is defective. Indeed, many neurological patients without frontal damage also find the WCST hard, and some patients with frontal damage manage to obtain surprisingly good scores (Anderson, Damasio, Jones, & Tranel, 1991; Heaton et al., 1993). Another problem is that poor performance on any single test may be a product of a much more general impairment likely to affect most aspects of cognition and performance. As a group, individuals with schizophrenia have lower IQs than the general population, and this broad intellectual disadvantage may also reveal itself in any individual cognitive test result (Heinrichs & Zakzanis, 1998). Thus, at least some of the time, researchers may be measuring a broad ability factor that depends on the whole brain when they think they are measuring only frontal brain abilities. Clearly, the question of whether the frontal brain contributes to schizophrenia cannot be resolved with neuropsychological tests alone. Fortunately, the same question can be addressed with biological methods that offer a much more direct picture of frontal brain structure and physiology.

PICTURES OF THE LIVING BRAIN

Description of Structural Techniques. Developments in brain scanning and imaging over the last three decades provide remarkably accurate ways of studying brain biology (see Chapter 4). First, there are imaging techniques that yield a visual or quantitative display of neuroanatomical structure—a picture of the living brain. These techniques include computerized axial tomography (CT) and **structural magnetic resonance imaging (MRI)**. MRI, in particular, is able to provide clear, detailed images of many brain structures. Since schizophrenia does not involve obvious brain damage like strokes or tumours, most structural brain imaging research compares the volume and shape of different brain regions in patients and healthy people. The assumption is that abnormally small regions must have sustained some kind of damage, including, for example, nerve cell losses. Alternatively, the brain may not have developed normally in the first place, creating vulnerability for schizophrenia later in life.

Findings from CT and MRI Studies. Using these techniques, researchers have found complex patterns of structural abnormalities in patients with schizophrenia, compared with healthy individuals. One of the earliest CT findings suggesting structural alterations in the brains of patients with schizophrenia was that the ventricles are larger than those in non-psychiatric brains (Johnstone, Crow, Frith, Husband, & Kreel, 1976). In particular, the third and lateral ventricles are expanded, which suggests compression or loss of existing nerve tissue. In MRI studies, the most consistent findings include reduced grey matter volumes of the medial temporal, superior temporal, and prefrontal areas (Karlsgodt, Sun, & Cannon, 2010). These are regions on which episodic memory, processing of auditory information, and short-term memory/decision making, respectively, are critically dependent. Other reported structural differences in patients with schizophrenia include parietal lobe, basal ganglia, corpus callosum, thalamus, and cerebellar abnormalities (Kasai et al., 2002; Niznikiewicz, Kubicki, & Shenton, 2003; Shenton, Dickey, Frumin, & McCarley, 2001).

Description of Functional Techniques. More recent advances in imaging technology extend traditional anatomical imaging to include maps of human brain function. These "functional" imaging techniques include **positron emission tomography (PET)** and **functional magnetic resonance imaging (fMRI).** PET scanning involves the introduction of a mildly radioactive tracer into the bloodstream of a person and the use of a sensory apparatus, a kind of camera, to detect the tracer's presence and distribution in the brain. Depending on the type of tracer, this method can furnish a display or readout of changes in blood flow, the metabolism or rate at which energy is used, or the location and density of nerve cells containing specific kinds of chemical receptors. Brain regions with higher activity levels use more blood and will have increased levels of the radioactive tracer that will be detected and imaged by the camera.

On the other hand, fMRI works by detecting the changes in blood oxygenation and flow that occur in response to neural activity. When a brain area is more active, it consumes more oxygen, and to meet this increased demand, blood flow increases to the active area. fMRI techniques allow for the production of activation maps showing which parts of the brain are involved in a particular mental process after controlling for brain activity at rest (see Figure 9.4). These most recent technologies have been applied increasingly to schizophrenia over the last decade (see Huettell, Song, & McCarthy, 2008).

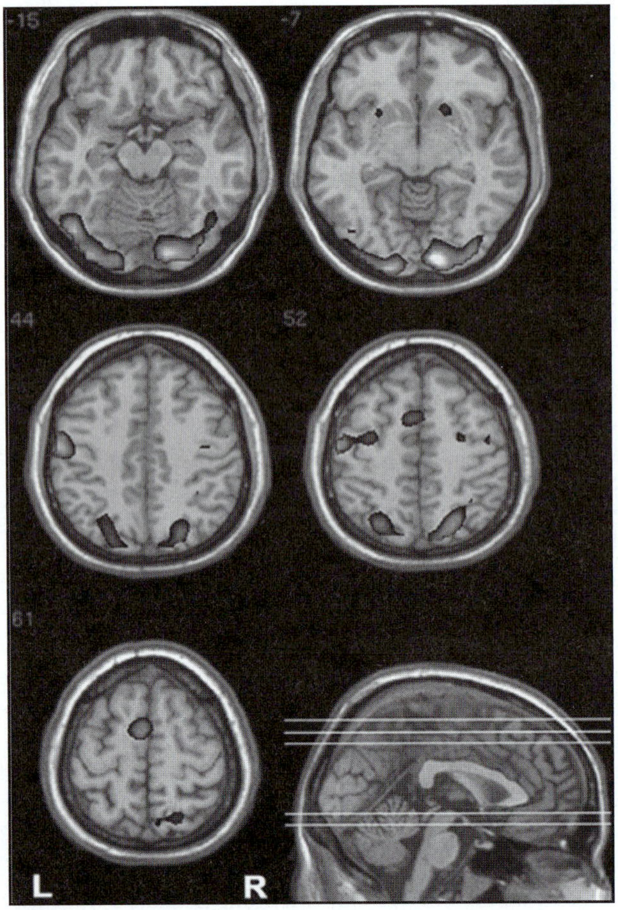

FIGURE 9.4 fMRI Images Showing Regions of Activation During Short-Term Memory Task in Normal Brain

Regions of increased brain activation appear when the person being scanned has to remember small amounts of information over periods of seconds or minutes. Together, these "hot spots" of activity may form a short-term memory network. This network seems to operate less efficiently in people with schizophrenia. The lower-right diagram shows the locations or fMRI "slices" through the brain.

Source: Cairo, Woodward, & Ngan (2006).

Findings from PET and fMRI Studies. In addition to structural changes, functional activation changes, as measured by both fMRI and PET, have been well documented in patients with schizophrenia. To what extent, then, do these brain imaging techniques support the idea that schizophrenia is a disorder of the frontal brain? Lara Davidson, a former graduate student in clinical psychology at York University in Toronto, compiled the findings of all available studies published between 1980 and 2002 (Davidson & Heinrichs, 2003). The results of this meta-analysis showed that only about 25 percent of schizophrenia patients have abnormally reduced frontal brain volumes, and less than 50 percent have reduced blood flow or metabolism in the frontal region when engaged in a mental "activation" task. One way of interpreting this outcome is to say that frontal brain impairment probably affects *some* patients with schizophrenia, but the impairment is not a *necessary* part of the syndrome. It is also possible that only the negative symptoms of the disorder reflect an abnormally working frontal brain. In any case, many patients cannot be distinguished from healthy people with structural MRI or functional PET imaging. Of course, as the use of more accurate and informative techniques like functional MRI increases, the evidence in support of the frontal hypothesis may change. For example, recent findings suggest different patterns of frontal brain activation and deactivation in schizophrenia rather than just an overall reduction (Pomarol-Clotet et al., 2008). Several other brain regions are also of interest in relation to schizophrenia. One of the most researched regions includes the **left temporal lobe** and its many connections with other regions, including the frontal lobes. This is a psychologically vital brain region that controls aspects of attention, the understanding of speech and written language, and interpretation of the visual world. It is in the temporal brain system that sounds are recognized as words, and light patterns as pictures, objects, or human faces. Associated structures like the **amygdala** and **hippocampus** colour these interpretations with emotion and store them in memory. Neurological patients with damage in this region have deficits like receptive aphasia, which means they are unable to understand spoken and written language. Patients with deeper damage affecting the hippocampus are unable to form new memories of events, although memory for the remote past may be relatively intact. Kraepelin (1913, 1919) and other psychiatric pioneers knew the psychological importance of the temporal brain region in broad terms and suggested that, along with the frontal brain, the temporal lobes were the place to look for the causes of schizophrenia.

The evidence compiled and summarized using meta-analysis shows that some psychological abilities associated with the left temporal lobe, especially memory, but also selective attention, are probably deficient in up to 75 percent of individuals with schizophrenia (see Focus box 9.2 and Table 9.3). Conversely, only a small proportion of patients may have normal attention and memory abilities. However, evidence based on brain imaging (MRI, PET) and more direct measurement of the temporal region tells a somewhat different story. None of these comparisons detect abnormalities in a large proportion of patients, and hence they were not included in the summary table. Indeed, meta-analysis shows that the volume of the left temporal lobe is reduced in only about 21 percent of patients, although approximately 38 percent have an abnormally small hippocampus. The results for altered blood flow and metabolism are complex and inconsistent, partly because "resting" and "activation" studies produce different results. Yet here too the evidence in favour of neurobiological abnormalities is not impressive. The average resting activity of the left temporal lobe seems almost the same in patients and healthy people on the basis of PET brain scanning results. Only about 8 percent of patients have truly abnormal blood flow and metabolism. The proportion rises to about 27 percent when temporal lobe activity during a cognitive task is measured. In addition, this proportion of patients seems to have an abnormally

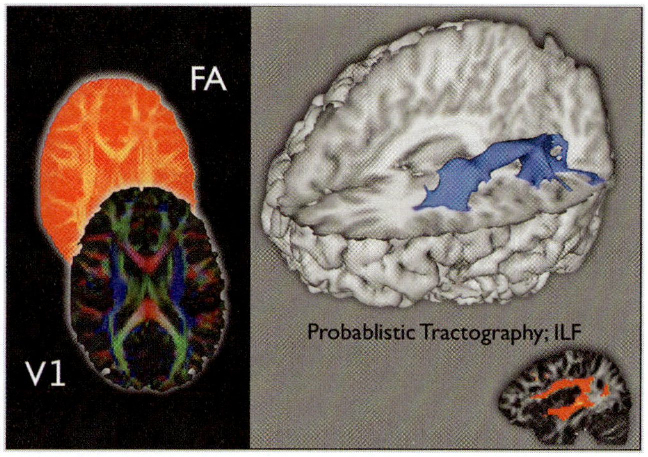

FIGURE 9.5 Diffusion Tensor Imaging (DTI)

DTI allows for the examination of white matter connectivity in the brain. Several techniques are available to analyze the data obtained using DTI. These images include fractional anisotropy (FA) on the left, which indicates the presence and direction of white matter tracts, and a form of brain mapping called tractography on the right, which shows the beginning and end of a predetermined connective tract of interest, in this case the inferior longitudinal fasciculus (ILF).

Source: Images generated using FMRIB Software Library: FSL tools 4.1.9: (FDT & Probabalistic Tractography). Smith, S.M., Jenkinson, M., Woolrich, M.W., Beckmann, C.F., Behrens, T.E.J., Johansen-Berg, H., Bannister, P.R., DeLuca, M., Drobnjak, I., Flitney, D.E., Niazy, R., Saunders, J., Vickers, J., Zhang, Y., De Sefano, N., Brady, J.M., & Matthews, P.M. (2004). Advances in functional and structural MR image analysis and implementation as FSL. *Neuroimage*, 23 (S1), S208-S219.

overactive rather than underactive left temporal lobe. It is noteworthy, however, that many PET findings have poor records in terms of being reproduced by several investigators. In fact, no brain imaging findings make the "top 10" list of findings presented in Table 9.3.

What does this often weak and at times inconsistent evidence indicate about the biology of schizophrenia? It must be that brain regions mediating the perception and storage of meaning and the creation of emotional associations are also the regions involved in schizophrenia. However, research has not demonstrated this involvement in a very convincing way, at least not yet. It is cognitive performance and abilities that appear to be most severely compromised by the disorder, whereas biological findings are often abnormal in only a minority of patients. Is it possible that technical limitations, rather than a faulty hypothesis, underpin the weakness of neurobiological findings on both the frontal and temporal brain hypotheses? Perhaps the brain scanners are at fault. They still lack the degree of accuracy needed to detect the kind of microscopic neural abnormalities that underlie the disorder. However, the near future may hold the answers. For example, recent applications of fMRI indicate that different fronto-temporal brain networks perform abnormally depending on the specific kind of cognitive task presented to patients with schizophrenia (Kuperberg, Lakshmanan, Greve, & West, 2008).

A recent extension of MRI technology, diffusion tensor imaging (DTI), has allowed for the examination of connectivity in the brain (see Figure 9.5). DTI is a critical advancement in neuroimaging, given that brain regions rarely act in isolation. Rather, the brain is a complex organ with component structures that are highly interconnected. The application of DTI to schizophrenia research is fitting because the disorder may involve disturbed communication between and within regions. DTI is based on the idea that water molecules behave differently in connective white matter compared to other brain tissue. Images can be developed using DTI that index white matter fibre tracts that connect brain regions. Recent reviews of DTI studies in schizophrenia have also implicated frontal and temporal regions. Specifically, studies have found that connective tissue or tracts like the corpus callosum, cingulum bundle, and internal capsule are the areas of the brain most affected in schizophrenia (Kyriakopoulos, Bargiotas, Barker, & Frangou, 2008).

The next generation of imaging developments may furnish the powerful evidence of fronto-temporal brain involvement in schizophrenia that is currently lacking. Many brain regions and their connections are under study and the field continues to await a succession of strong findings that converge on the same region (see Harrison, 1999). However, it is also possible that part of the schizophrenia puzzle lies in the brain's chemistry.

IS SCHIZOPHRENIA CAUSED BY A NEUROCHEMICAL IMBALANCE? The arrival of the first therapeutic drug treatments for psychotic symptoms during the 1950s inspired researchers to study schizophrenia as a biological disease. If a chemical agent like a drug was able to reduce symptoms, it might be because brain chemistry was abnormal in the disorder. Perhaps schizophrenia consisted of an abnormality in neurotransmission—the chemical transactions that compose communication between nerve cells at the molecular level. In addition to smaller or malformed brain regions and altered patterns of blood flow and metabolism, the causes of schizophrenia might involve an abnormality or alteration in neurochemistry.

The Dopamine Hypothesis. Researchers in the early 1960s identified a group of brain chemicals involved in the therapeutic effects of antipsychotic drug action. This research showed that **dopamine**, a member of the catecholamine family of **neurotransmitters**, plays a major role in therapeutic drug effects. More specifically, the clinical efficacy of antipsychotic drugs is correlated with their ability to block the effects of dopamine. The hypothesis that dopamine is central to schizophrenia has been one of the most enduring ideas about the disorder. The strongest support for a connection between abnormal dopamine activity or dysregulation and schizophrenia comes from studies showing that antipsychotic drugs like chlorpromazine reduce symptoms by blocking dopamine **receptors**, especially the dopamine D2 receptor subtype. Canadian researcher Dr. Phillip Seeman at the University of Toronto carried out the first studies demonstrating the link between dopamine blockade and symptom reduction (Seeman & Lee, 1975). Seeman used postmortem brain tissue samples from patients with schizophrenia to show that the most effective antipsychotic drugs were chemicals that occupied and blocked receptors for dopamine.

Also supporting the dopamine hypothesis of schizophrenia was the observation that several drugs, including cocaine and amphetamine, accentuate or boost dopamine activity rather than blocking it. This enhancement can induce psychotic symptoms that resemble acute schizophrenic episodes. For example, high doses of cocaine taken by people who do not have schizophrenia may result in persecutory fears and paranoia and create a severely distorted sense of reality (Julien, 2007). Cocaine appears to produce these effects in part by blocking the dopamine transporter, thereby inhibiting reuptake. Concentrations of dopamine in the synaptic space are probably increased in cocaine users, heightening the impact of the neurotransmitter on the postsynaptic neuron. Clearly, there is a correlation between enhanced dopamine activity and psychosis and between blocked dopamine activity and reduced psychotic symptoms.

The evidence on drug effects and dopamine is suggestive, but it does not prove that something is wrong in the dopamine systems of people with schizophrenia or that abnormalities in the neurotransmitter cause the disorder in the first place. However, it is difficult to measure dopamine levels or activity in the brain directly in living people. Therefore, researchers have taken advantage of the fact that the neurotransmitter's byproducts are present in the cerebrospinal fluid (CSF) that surrounds the brain and circulates into the spine. Samples of this fluid can be drawn from the spinal canals of patients and healthy research participants, providing a kind of index of dopamine activity in the brain. The logic is that patients with schizophrenia should have greatly increased levels of these byproducts, reflecting the presence and use of large quantities of dopamine. However, dopamine metabolites were not universally elevated in the CSF of patients with schizophrenia. Furthermore, virtually no differences between patients and healthy people have emerged (Heinrichs, 2001). Accordingly, interest moved to the dopamine receptors that are blocked by antipsychotic drugs. Perhaps schizophrenia does not involve abnormal amounts of dopamine itself as much as it involves abnormal concentrations of dopamine receptors. But how could these microscopic substances be detected and measured?

By the late 1970s, chemical "labels," or **ligands**, that bind selectively with specific receptor sites became available (Seeman, Chau-Wong, Tedesco, & Wong, 1976). This gave rise to a new kind of study, the radioactive binding assay, wherein the density and distribution of various receptors were determined. First, the ligand was labelled with a radioactive isotope. Next, tissue samples from preserved post-mortem brain tissue obtained from schizophrenia patients, or from healthy people who died of natural causes, were prepared in the form of slices. These slices were then exposed to the ligand, which in turn occupied the receptor sites. The end of several technical steps was a display showing the location and density of receptors in the treated brain section. A magnifying glass had been placed over the microscopic world of the dopamine receptor.

Over a 15-year period, researchers looked for evidence that dopamine receptors were abnormally elevated in the brains of people with schizophrenia. Initial findings like those by Lee and Seeman (1980) were promising, with a majority of patient samples showing increased dopamine receptor densities. However, it was also known that these tissue samples were obtained from patients receiving antipsychotic medication prior to death. There was evidence that dopamine-blocking medication stimulated the brain to make more dopamine receptors. Accordingly, chronic exposure to antipsychotic drugs during life may have caused an artificial increase in receptor numbers and distorted the results of receptor assays of schizophrenic brain tissue samples. Although efforts were made to obtain tissue samples from patients who were drug free for weeks or months prior to death, it was hard to completely rule out lifetime drug exposure as an artificial influence on receptor-binding studies. What researchers needed was a way of measuring the density of dopamine receptors in the brains of living patients with schizophrenia.

This possibility was realized with the application of receptor-binding ligands to the field of PET scanning. Instead of injecting tracers that bound to blood cells or glucose, researchers introduced the ligands that bound to dopamine receptors. The innovation not only meant that living people could be studied, but also that individuals who had never been treated with antipsychotic medication could be examined. The PET receptor-binding methods provided the opportunity to determine if schizophrenia involved elevated dopamine receptors without the distorting influence of **dopamine-blocking drugs**. Initial results (Gjedde & Wong, 1987; Wong et al., 1986) confirmed that a large majority of patients with schizophrenia had dopamine receptor densities exceeding the normal range. However, independent researchers failed to support these findings (Martinot et al., 1990) and the field became mired in controversy. It was unclear whether technical properties of different ligands, the imperfect accuracy of PET scanning equipment, or different samples of patients were responsible for the inconsistent results (Sedvall, 1992).

Since the early 1990s, the original form of the dopamine hypothesis has been modified in light of the available evidence and advances in neurobiology and brain imaging technology. Davis, Khan, Ko, and Davidson (1991) reconceptualized the hypothesis to specify excess dopamine neurotransmission in the striatum and reduced dopamine neurotransmission in the frontal lobes of the brain. In the most recent revision of the dopamine hypothesis, Howes and Kapur (2009) hypothesize that multiple "hits" (e.g., pregnancy and obstetric complications, stress and trauma, drug use, and genes) interact to result in dopamine dysregulation. The authors claim that this dysregulation is the "final common pathway" to psychosis in schizophrenia. In sum, what was once a simplistic theory about the role of dopamine in schizophrenia is increasingly complex. It has become progressively more apparent over the past several decades that several neurotransmitter systems are likely involved in schizophrenia. For example, another neurotransmitter, serotonin, has been implicated in some of the therapeutic effects of more recent antipsychotic drugs. Moreover, dopamine interacts with other important neurotransmitters, including glutamate and gamma-aminobutyric acid (GABA), and some researchers suspect that these substances are the true culprits in the story of neurochemistry and schizophrenia (González-Maeso et al., 2008).

5 BEFORE MOVING ON

Is a single biological abnormality found in all patients with the diagnosis of schizophrenia?

Treatment

For many decades following Kraepelin's (1896, 1913, 1919) pioneering descriptions of schizophrenia, there was no effective medical or psychological treatment for the disorder. In fact, use of the term *treatment* to describe what patients endured is highly questionable. Patients with schizophrenia might be subjected to "great and desperate" methods like prolonged barbiturate-induced sleep therapy, **insulin coma,** or **psychosurgery** (Valenstein, 1986). These were "treatments" to be feared and avoided, but patients' rights were seldom at the forefront during the first half of the twentieth century. There were no therapies with proven effectiveness, and experimental procedures were attempted that lacked scientific or medical justification. For example, insulin coma therapy involved creating a hypoglycemic state (low blood sugar) through administration of high doses of insulin. This resulted in loss of consciousness and frequent convulsions. A few reports suggested that a series of such insulin shocks might reduce a patient's psychotic episodes. However, the technique was never carefully evaluated and brought risks to the patient in terms of heart attacks and strokes. Some patients with schizophrenia underwent brain surgery—"psychosurgery"—in the form of **frontal lobotomies** or leukotomies, wherein nerve tracts in the frontal brain were cut. As a hospital psychologist, one of the authors (W. H.) once carried out a neuropsychological assessment with a survivor of this sinister era, an elderly woman who had undergone psychosurgery decades before, in a dim past that she could barely remember. This unfortunate woman was left with brain damage and cognitive deficits due to the surgery—and she retained her schizophrenia. Many thousands of patients were operated on with little demonstrable benefit and little concern for ethical requirements like informed consent to treatment.

By the early 1950s, Canada and the United States had hospitalized on an indefinite basis well over half a million patients with schizophrenia and other severe mental illnesses. Although the psychiatric pioneers had hoped to bring medical science to bear on the problem of schizophrenia, a patient in 1850 may have been better off in terms of quality of life, if not the disease process itself, than a patient in 1950. Fortunately, within a few years this depressing assessment changed as the first genuine treatments for schizophrenia were discovered and developed.

ANTIPSYCHOTIC MEDICATION

The discovery of drugs to treat the symptoms of schizophrenia is a story of accident, dedication, and insight. A young French naval surgeon named Henri Laborit (see Swazey, 1974) was interested in the syndrome of circulatory shock that occurred during and after surgery. The syndrome included depression and apathy, along with marked physical features like shallow breathing and a bloodless, pale appearance. Shock could sometimes progress to death within hours. Laborit and his colleagues began experimenting with a variety of drugs in an attempt to find a compound that might alleviate the shock syndrome in surgical patients. One relatively new agent called promethazine proved to have a number of intriguing and unexpected properties. The drug made patients drowsy, reduced pain, and created a feeling of "euphoric quietude." Hence, promethazine had psychological effects. It was observed that surgical patients receiving the drug remained conscious without signs of pain or anxiety. Laborit realized that if the drug had psychological effects it must be acting on the brain and not just on the circulatory system.

Laborit's (1950) published observations encouraged researchers to modify the formula of promethazine and enhance its curious, brain-related effects. The upshot of these efforts was **chlorpromazine**, the first genuine antipsychotic medication. It was another 10 years before the new drug's specific value in treating schizophrenia was fully recognized and documented. The initial observations of promethazine and chlorpromazine in psychiatric patients reflected the mood-influencing effects that developed over days and initial weeks. Hence, it was thought that the drugs might be most helpful in patients with mood disorders, mania, and agitation. However, it turned out that antipsychotic effects took several weeks to develop fully. A series of drug effectiveness studies or clinical trials was required to demonstrate the full range of clinical applications for the new medication. Canada played an important part in these drug evaluations through studies by Lehmann and Hanrahan (1954) at McGill University in Montreal. Following the large collaborative National Institute of Mental Health study (1964) in the United States, the evidence was finally conclusive. Chlorpromazine reduced more than agitation, mania, and mood disturbances. It also reduced the symptoms associated with schizophrenia.

A large volume of studies now documents the value of chlorpromazine and its chemical relatives, as well as a "new generation" of medications developed in the 1990s, in alleviating the frequency and severity of hallucinations and delusions, thought disorder, and, to a lesser degree, the negative symptoms of the illness. Patients who receive these medications require less time in hospital, have fewer relapses, and enjoy better life functioning when compared to untreated patients (Julien, 2007; Kane, 1989; Meltzer, 1993). However, these drugs are a way of controlling and managing symptoms and not a cure for schizophrenia. Moreover, a minority of patients does not benefit from antipsychotic drugs, and even responsive patients may have to deal with unpleasant and occasionally disabling side effects. This situation has stimulated the development of improved medications, including **risperidone** and **olanzapine**, that provide symptom control with fewer side effects than the older chlorpromazine family of drugs. Still, many patients experience a return of their symptoms if medication is discontinued or find prolonged medication use unpleasant. Moreover, drugs may control symptoms, but they cannot provide the occupational and daily living skills or social supports needed to ensure successful adjustment outside of hospital. In fact, the most disabling aspect of schizophrenia may be the cognitive impairment associated with the disorder rather than the positive and negative symptoms. Cognitive impairment plays a major role in limiting skill learning and everyday life functioning. Perhaps not surprisingly, there is intense interest in the development of "cognitively enhancing" medications that can address these impairments (Harvey & Keefe, 2001). The benefit that current antipsychotics have for cognition is very small, especially in individuals with chronic schizophrenia (Keefe et al., 2007). Additionally, both older and more recent antipsychotic medications produce only extremely small improvements in cognition (Heinrichs, 2007).

Discharging patients from hospital may leave them adrift on city streets with nowhere to go, nothing to do, and no means of support. Too often, ex-patients must struggle with poverty, unemployment, and the negative attitudes of other people, or **social stigma.** These challenges have replaced the confinement and dependency of the pre-medication era, and they are poor alternatives to hospitalization for the person with schizophrenia (see Torrey, 1995).

PSYCHOTHERAPY AND SKILLS TRAINING

The use of psychotherapy in the treatment of schizophrenia has been the subject of considerable controversy. Many pioneers in clinical psychology and psychiatry, including Sigmund Freud, argued that psychoanalysis is ineffective for the treatment of schizophrenia. Several research findings pointing to the poor outcomes of psychotherapy for patients with schizophrenia supported this claim. Further, the established effectiveness of medication as a treatment for schizophrenia in the 1960s contributed to the reluctance to employ psychotherapeutic treatment approaches. At the same time, some researchers and therapists have always insisted on the value and effectiveness of psychoanalytically oriented therapies, leading to lively but inconclusive controversies (Karon & VandenBos, 1981). Adding fuel to the fire, several older literature reviews have noted methodological limitations in previous research, thereby calling into question the value of the studies that rejected psychoanalysis for patients with schizophrenia (Beck, 1978; Mosher & Keith, 1980).

COGNITIVE-BEHAVIOURAL THERAPY More recently, studies of **cognitive-behavioural therapy (CBT)** for patients with schizophrenia have revealed that at least one form of psychotherapy may indeed be helpful in treating this population (Beck, Rector, Stolar, & Grant, 2009; Turkington, Dudley, Warman, & Beck, 2004). Indeed, CBT is now recommended as a standard of care by the National Institute for Clinical Excellence, with a particular focus on four principal problems experienced by psychotic patients: (1) emotional disturbance, (2) psychotic symptoms like delusions and hallucinations, (3) social disabilities, and (4) risk of relapse (Fowler, Garety, & Kuipers, 1995). CBT theory maintains that emotional and behavioural disturbances are influenced by subjective interpretation of life and illness experiences. CBT for schizophrenia integrates analysis and understanding of the patient's symptoms and delusional beliefs through techniques like psychoeducation, belief modification, and coping strategy enhancement (Kingdon & Turkington, 2005). Normalization is one form of psychoeducation, which helps patients understand symptoms by comparing their experiences to those of mentally healthy adults. For example, therapists explain that anomalous experiences can occur in healthy adults who are suffering from sleep or sensory deprivation, or from unusually high levels of stress. Moreover, patients are taught how to interpret correctly relevant environmental events and how to respond appropriately to social cues while interacting and communicating with other people. These techniques are thought to help reduce patients' catastrophic interpretations of symptoms and aid in preventing relapse. Often, therapy develops over a sequence of stages. For example, Canadian psychologist Neil Rector (Beck et al., 2009; Beck & Rector, 2000; Rector, Seeman, & Segal, 2003) focuses initially on engaging the patient with schizophrenia, as a trusting and collaborative therapeutic alliance is critical for success. Establishing this relationship may involve listening, empathic understanding, and gradual exploration of the patient's experiences, combined with gentle questions, which lead to the formulation of a problem list. Next, patients are taught to record and monitor their thoughts and to carry out "homework" assignments. Similar to CBT for depression or anxiety, a thought record or voice diary is often incorporated into treatment to help the patient rationally appraise related symptoms as they occur. For example, recording the intensity and number of voices, affective responses, and self-initiated coping attempts at the time of symptom onset allows the therapist to select novel strategies or improve on existing strategies (i.e., coping strategy enhancement) that will help to reduce symptom severity. Consequently, therapy becomes increasingly focused on the individual's unique clinical presentation, and through careful questioning the patient is encouraged to test the validity of his or her symptoms and to consider their influence on daily life. Alternative explanations are developed for delusions and hallucinations, with belief modification as the final goal of treatment. However, therapists must be careful to maintain a nonconfrontational stance, which often results in therapy progressing at a slow pace. In fact, pushing patients too quickly can result in increases in belief conviction and likelihood of relapse (Nelson, 1997). With respect to negative symptoms, patients are challenged and assisted in identifying the sources of their inactivity or withdrawal, and participate in "experiments" to create alternative and more rewarding experiences and new interests. The last phase in a CBT program may involve patients learning to direct their own cognitive skill development and progress with an eye toward preventing symptom relapses and severe illness episodes. In fact, because relapse is common among patients with schizophrenia, therapists often create reminder coping cards for common delusions or hallucinations that can be referred to when symptom reoccurrence is imminent or occurring (Chadwick, Birchwood, & Trower, 1996).

A recent review of the evolution of CBT in schizophrenia (Tai & Turkington, 2009) summarized findings from a body of evidence that highlighted the efficacy of this intervention. The authors reported that moderate benefits are shown for both positive and negative symptoms and that these benefits are sustained over time (Malik, Kingdon, Pelton, Mehta, & Turkington, 2009). Most recently, clinicians and researchers have used CBT to target low-functioning, chronically disordered patients with schizophrenia. Results from an 18-month clinical trial by Grant and colleagues (2011) found that patients receiving CBT showed gains in their psychosocial functioning and motivation and experienced reduced positive symptoms (e.g., hallucinations, delusions, disorganization). Taken together, the findings from these and other studies are promising. However, research on the predictors of response to treatment (e.g., gender, neurocognitive deficit, insight) is still relatively new and inconclusive (e.g., Brabban, Tai, & Turkington, 2009).

SOCIAL SKILLS TRAINING AND COGNITIVE REMEDIATION **Social skills training** is a learning-based intervention model for the treatment of functional disabilities associated with schizophrenia (Chien et al., 2003). Unlike the symptom-focused CBT approaches, social skills training provides rehabilitation for patients with schizophrenia, fostering the development of practical social and living skills. Patients typically receive training in a variety of functional skills, including carrying out appropriate social interaction, coping with common stressors, dealing with household and residential tasks, and developing employment-related abilities. The social skills training approach thus promotes independence and simultaneously reduces stressors.

A recent meta-analysis of 22 randomized controlled trials, a strict method for evaluating treatments, found that social skills training had moderate effects on social and independent living skills (based on role-play measures), psychosocial functioning, and negative symptoms. Small beneficial effects were observed for relapse rates (Kurtz & Mueser, 2008). These interventions were most effective with younger patients. Continued efforts are needed in developing similarly helpful social skills training for older, more chronic patients who make up a significant proportion of the population with schizophrenia.

Cognitive remediation programs have been used with schizophrenia for the past four decades. Interest in this therapeutic approach followed from emerging research on the relationship between cognitive performance and community outcome. These interventions target specific thinking skills like memory and attention by teaching compensatory strategies, providing practice exercises, and holding group discussions, each with the goal of enhancing cognitive ability. Reviews of this growing body of literature indicate that remediation training has significant benefits for improving cognition in schizophrenia, with medium-range effect sizes that are maintained over an eight-month period (McGurk, Twamley, Sitzer, McHugo, & Mueser, 2007). Cognitive remediation also demonstrated a significant effect on reducing psychiatric symptoms and improving psychosocial outcomes (e.g., obtaining competitive work or more satisfaction with interpersonal relationships). These effects appear to be even stronger when cognitive remediation therapy is combined with social skills training (e.g., Roder, Mueller, Mueser, & Brenner, 2006) or other psychiatric rehabilitation strategies. Indeed, the future of psychological treatment for schizophrenia may involve an integration of interventions that target emotional support, cognitive problems, and functional recovery as well as psychotic symptoms (Dickerson & Lehman, 2011).

FAMILY THERAPY Patients with schizophrenia who have the support of family members may benefit from **family therapy**. This psychosocial intervention conceptualizes the patient as a member of a family system (Kazarian & Malla, 1992) and thus tailors treatment to the family as a whole. Accordingly, therapy aims for active involvement of each member of the family in the treatment process. The family system is of particular importance because of the current focus on deinstitutionalization; patients with schizophrenia struggle in adjusting to community life, which may include residing with family members. Patients are thus subject to the influence of daily family interactions and to the emotional communication or miscommunication (e.g., expressed emotion) embodied in these interactions. Therapy for the family of a schizophrenia patient may also entail psychoeducation (McFarlane, Dixon, Lukens, & Lucksted, 2003) about the clinical presentation of the disorder, theories pertaining to its causes, and available treatment options. Furthermore, family members may be informed of the potential impact of schizophrenia on the family unit and trained in problem-solving and stress-related coping skills. Each individual family member is asked to make a commitment to supporting the treatment process.

EARLY INTERVENTION The importance of early intervention in schizophrenia has emerged as a central area of research over the past two decades and has received worldwide attention through international organizations and dedicated peer-reviewed journals, such as *Early Intervention in Psychiatry*. Canadian researcher Dr. Jean Addington has devoted much of her career to studying people considered at high risk for developing schizophrenia, as well as to those in the prodromal and first episode phases of the disorder. The term *prodrome* refers to the period before the appearance of psychotic symptoms when vulnerable adolescents often become withdrawn and suspicious. Those individuals who progress, or "convert," to psychotic disorder are referred to as "first episode" patients because they are experiencing their first episode of intense and unmistakable symptoms. Results from Addington's work reveal that significant cognitive, social, and functional impairments occur at the beginning stages of the disorder and are not simply a product of many years of hospital admissions or social disadvantage (Addington, 2007). In fact, even those young people at high risk for developing psychosis who do not convert to a full-blown psychotic episode continue to function at a level lower than their nonpsychotic peers (Addington et al., 2011). Symptom improvement is probable following early intervention, but cognitive impairments persist and social and functional skills, as well as quality of life, remain deficient when compared to healthy peers. Early intervention is a promising yet extremely challenging aspect of schizophrenia research and practice.

6 BEFORE MOVING ON

Why is it important not to focus exclusively on psychotic symptoms when developing treatments for schizophrenia?

CANADIAN RESEARCH CENTRE

Dr. Christopher Bowie

Clinical psychologist Dr. Christopher Bowie directs a research program at Queen's University in Kingston, Ontario, that investigates neurocognitive abilities and their relationship to everyday functioning in people with schizophrenia. Dr. Bowie's research has both descriptive and treatment aspects. His descriptive work focuses on how impairments in neurocognitive abilities like attention, memory, and executive functions are associated with deficits in the skills necessary for successful community living.

Although many individuals with schizophrenia have a favourable clinical response—a reduction in the symptoms associated with the condition, like hallucinations and delusions—neurocognitive impairments persist, making a return to optimal living difficult. Neurocognitive impairments are present even before the diagnostic symptoms of schizophrenia emerge and are quite severe. Their early presence and their persistence during remission of symptoms make it difficult for those with schizophrenia to attend to, learn, remember, sequence, and generalize the wide range of living skills that are typically acquired during adolescence and early adulthood. When the acquisition of these critical developmental skills is interrupted early in life, and continuously disrupted throughout adulthood by neurocognitive impairments, living independently, working, and socializing remain a challenge for many patients.

Dr. Bowie's work has identified neurocognitive impairments as a key reason why many people with schizophrenia experience difficulties in many domains of daily life functioning. Building on his correlational research, Dr. Bowie and his team are examining the effects of a psychological treatment called *cognitive remediation*. They are comparing theoretically different types of cognitive remediation in vocational rehabilitation programs to examine which types of changes in brain function are associated with improvements in work skills. Additionally, he is using eye-tracking and neurophysiological techniques to examine the underlying changes in brain function associated with cognitive remediation. The long-term goal of his research program is to find new ways to help individuals with schizophrenia restore their functioning and experience an improved quality of life.

SUMMARY

- Schizophrenia is a psychotic disorder that may affect both men and women in late adolescence and early adulthood.
- The disorder is complex and heterogeneous in its clinical presentation, course, and outcome.
- Approximately 50 percent of patients with schizophrenia improve over time and in response to treatment, but few achieve their social and occupational potential, and many require lifelong support and remain at risk for suicide.
- Direct and indirect social and health care costs of schizophrenia approach $7 billion a year in Canada.
- Schizophrenia involves characteristic symptoms that must be present for diagnosis, including hallucinations, delusions, thought and language disorder, bizarre behaviour, and withdrawal.

- The disorder must be associated with a decline in social and occupational functioning.
- Having psychotic symptoms for one day does not mean a person has schizophrenia; these symptoms must persist for at least a month unless successfully treated.
- Mood disorders like depression and other medical and developmental disorders may complicate the diagnosis of schizophrenia and must be ruled out.
- There is no objective test that confirms whether a person has schizophrenia.
- Disorders like schizophrenia may result from many interacting biological and psychosocial influences rather than from a single cause or event.
- Biological and psychosocial processes may increase or decrease the probability that a vulnerable person develops schizophrenia.
- Most theorists argue that both a vulnerability, or diathesis, and environmental stress are required to cause schizophrenia.
- Having a parent with schizophrenia significantly increases the chances that a young person will develop the disorder.
- The influence of parents on the development of schizophrenia in their children is biological and genetic in nature.
- Many genes are implicated in schizophrenia, but their individual effects are very small.
- Epigenetic processes that turn genes on and off may be as important in causing schizophrenia as the genes themselves.
- Slow processing of information, poor coordination, and deficient attention, perception, and learning are characteristic of most people with schizophrenia.
- Abnormalities of the frontal and temporal lobes of the brain are among the most studied features of schizophrenia, but no single brain abnormality occurs in everyone with the disorder.
- Neuroscience research methods provide increasingly accurate and sophisticated information about the structure and physiology of the brain.
- The most frequently implicated neurochemical abnormality in schizophrenia involves the neurotransmitter dopamine.
- Chlorpromazine was the first effective antipsychotic medication used with schizophrenia patients, reducing the severity of positive and, to a lesser degree, negative symptoms.
- A new, second generation of antipsychotic medications provides therapeutic benefits with fewer side effects.
- Antipsychotic medications have little or no effect on the cognitive impairments associated with schizophrenia.
- Significant advances have been made in the application of psychological interventions, like cognitive-behaviour therapy (CBT), family therapy, and cognitive remediation training.
- Cognitive remediation training has potential value for addressing cognitive impairment and may also reduce positive symptoms and improve social functioning in people with schizophrenia.
- Early intervention, whereby medication and psychological therapies are provided before a person develops prolonged psychosis, has become a new and promising focus for clinical researchers.
- Integrated psychosocial and medical therapies offer the most hope for improving the lives of people with schizophrenia.

MySearchLab offers you extensive help with your writing and research projects and provides round-the-clock access to credible and reliable source material. Chapter quizzes and a full electronic version of the text are also provided. Answers to the Before Moving On feature are provided on the MySearchLab. Take a tour at www.mysearchlab.com.

KEY TERMS

schizophrenia (p. 207)
heterogeneity (p. 207)
prevalence (p. 208)
madness (p. 208)
lunacy (p. 208)
auditory hallucinations (p. 208)
delusional thinking (p. 209)
positive symptoms (p. 210)
psychosis (p. 210)
delusions (p. 210)
hallucinations (p. 210)
thought and speech disorder (p. 210)
catatonic behaviour (p. 210)
negative symptoms (p. 210)
avolition (p. 210)
anhedonia (p. 210)
persecutory delusions (p. 210)
referential delusions (p. 210)

somatic delusions (p. 211)
delusions of grandeur (p. 211)
loosening of associations (p. 211)
alogia (p. 211)
affective flattening (p. 211)
waxy flexibility (p. 211)
mood congruent (p. 213)
paranoid type (p. 213)
disorganized type (p. 214)
catatonic type (p. 214)
undifferentiated type (p. 214)
residual type (p. 214)
disease markers (p. 214)
sensitivity (p. 215)
specificity (p. 215)
endophenotype (p. 215)
cognitive marker (p. 215)
eye-tracking (p. 215)
schizophrenogenic (p. 216)
collective unconscious (p. 216)
social drift (p. 216)
diathesis (p. 217)
stress (p. 217)
hypokrisia (p. 217)
cognitive slippage (p. 217)
aversive drift (p. 217)
schizotype (p. 217)
genetic contribution (p. 219)
familiality (p. 219)
penetrance (p. 219)
epigenetic (p. 220)
birth-related complications (p. 220)
high-risk children (p. 221)
expressed emotion (p. 221)
cumulative liability (p. 221)
frontal lobe (p. 221)
neuropsychological tests (p. 222)
Wisconsin Card Sorting Test (p. 222)
hippocampus (p. 224)
meta-analysis (p. 222)
perseverate (p. 223)
frontal brain deficiency (p. 223)
structural magnetic resonance imaging (MRI) (p. 223)
positron emission (PET) (p. 223)
functional magnetic resonance imaging (fMRI) (p. 223)
left temporal lobe (p. 224)
amygdala (p. 224)
effect size (p. 222)
dopamine (p. 225)
neurotransmitters (p. 225)
receptors (p. 225)
ligands (p. 226)
dopamine-blocking drugs (p. 226)
insulin coma (p. 227)
psychosurgery (p. 227)
frontal lobotomy (p. 227)
chlorpromazine (p. 227)
risperidone (p. 228)
olanzapine (p. 228)
social stigma (p. 228)
cognitive-behavioural therapy (p. 228)
social skills training (p. 229)
family therapy (p. 229)

JENNIFER COELHO • KATHRYN TROTTIER • JANET POLIVY

Chapter 10

Eating Disorders

LEARNING OBJECTIVES

AFTER READING THIS CHAPTER, STUDENTS WILL BE ABLE TO:

1. Describe the symptoms of eating disorders and distinguish between anorexia nervosa, bulimia nervosa, and eating disorder not otherwise specified.
2. Identify the prevalence of anorexia and bulimia nervosa, and illustrate how the prevalence of these disorders has changed over time.
3. Distinguish between the physical/biological factors that are thought to contribute to the development of eating disorders and those that are thought to be a consequence of eating disorders.
4. Outline the primary etiological factors that are involved in eating disorder symptomatology.
5. Compare and contrast biological treatment (i.e., medication), cognitive-behavioural therapy, and interpersonal therapy in the treatment of bulimia nervosa.
6. Describe a prevention program that has been implemented to decrease the risk of developing an eating disorder, and highlight the main findings of the program.

When Becky was 18 years old, her boyfriend broke up with her. Becky, who is now 19, had been dating her boyfriend for two years; after the breakup she found herself feeling depressed, and her self-esteem suffered greatly. Although she was of average weight, Becky thought she might feel better about herself if she lost a few pounds, so she began a strict diet. She cut out all added fats such as butter and mayonnaise, desserts, and fried foods. After successfully losing five pounds and receiving positive comments from her friends and family, Becky thought she might feel even better about herself if she lost a bit more weight. In addition to cutting out foods high in fat, Becky decided to restrict herself to eating fruit, vegetables, diet products, and white meat. However, Becky's weight loss did not seem to be improving her self-esteem, and one evening she found herself home alone, feeling particularly down. She decided to allow herself one piece of cake, but after eating it she felt as though she could not stop eating. She ate several pieces of cake, a bag of chips, and half a bag of cookies. After finishing the food, she felt uncomfortably full and anxious about having consumed so many calories and so much fat. She felt that she had no choice but to vomit the food she had eaten.

In the following weeks, Becky found herself engaging in the same pattern of behaviour. Each morning she made a pact with herself to stick to her diet, but in the evenings when she was feeling tired, alone, and bad about herself she often felt out of control and compelled to eat large amounts of food, which she then felt she had to vomit. Eventually, Becky began to vomit even normal portions of food that she ate during the day. Despite this, she did not lose any more weight and felt worse about herself than before she began to diet.

Introduction and Historical Perspective

If you heard that young girls were voluntarily starving themselves to the point of emaciation and sometimes even death, you would probably conclude that they had anorexia nervosa, an eating disorder characterized by a refusal to eat and a fear of gaining weight (Bruch, 1978). In the Middle Ages, however, such girls were called saints, and were revered for their asceticism. The socio-cultural context of a behaviour can be critical in determining how it is perceived and interpreted (Miller & Pumariega, 2001). Eating disorders such as anorexia nervosa and bulimia nervosa have been described for hundreds, even thousands of years (Bemporad, 1997). Until recently, however, they appear to have been relatively rare, and have not always been seen as evidence of maladjustment (as the fasting saints indicate).

In the 1960s and 1970s, as Western society became increasingly enamoured of the ultra-thin female shape embodied by fashion models such as Twiggy, reports of anorexia nervosa began to increase markedly (Bemporad, 1997). By the late 1970s, a new eating disorder was identified and named bulimia nervosa (Striegel-Moore, 1997). In **anorexia nervosa**, sufferers develop a morbid fear of fatness, perceive themselves as fat, and reduce their food intake to the point of emaciation (American Psychiatric Association [APA], 2000). In **bulimia nervosa**, periods of food restriction alternate with periods of binge eating, wherein excessive amounts of food are consumed. The binges are followed by attempts to compensate by either vomiting, laxative or diuretic abuse, hyperexercising, or starving oneself (APA, 2000). As in anorexia nervosa, there is an overemphasis on shape and weight for determining self-worth. Although these eating disorders have become relatively common in modern Western societies, we should remember that voluntary self-starvation and periods of binge eating and compensatory behaviours (like vomiting) have been reported throughout history. Eating disorders that would be recognizable today as anorexia nervosa and bulimia nervosa have existed since ancient times (Bemporad, 1997).

Typical Characteristics

ANOREXIA NERVOSA

Speaking Out: Anorexia (Natasha)

Watch this Speaking Out video at www.mysearchlab.com

Speaking Out Anorexia: Living with Anorexia

Watch this Speaking Out video at www.mysearchlab.com

Family and friends of individuals with anorexia nervosa may find it difficult to understand why their loved ones are

The fashion model known as Twiggy is often thought to have initiated the idealization of thinness in Western society.

so concerned with weight and shape despite their emaciated appearance. For those who are not familiar with the features of anorexia, and the factors that typically underlie this disorder, it may be difficult to understand the struggle that individuals with anorexia face. Parents are concerned about the serious consequences of their children being so underweight, and often encourage them to eat, as this will seemingly solve their problems. As a result, conflicts with parents about eating are common, and individuals with anorexia may hide or secretly dispose of food, eat alone, or tell others that they have eaten when in fact they have not. To be able to understand and treat this disorder, it is important to recognize that there are a variety of underlying psychological factors associated with anorexia.

Individuals with anorexia have an intense fear of gaining weight, or of becoming fat. This fear is paradoxical, given that they are in fact underweight. To maintain their low weight, they restrict the amount of food they eat. This may begin with a reduction in the total number of calories consumed over the course of a day, and avoidance of foods that are high in calories. However, the number of foods that are avoided often grows to the extent that individuals develop a long list of "feared foods" that they refuse to eat. Individuals with anorexia typically believe that eating feared or forbidden foods will result in significant amounts of weight gain—they might even believe that this weight gain will occur immediately after eating the food. A variety of other maladaptive or ritualistic eating behaviours may also develop. For example, individuals may begin eating foods in a set order (e.g., eating vegetables first and leaving certain types of food on their plate, such as high-protein foods, until last), dissecting food into small pieces, and weighing food or fluids before consumption.

Some people with anorexia engage in excessive exercise as a means of achieving weight loss. General restlessness is also common, as well as pacing back and forth and standing rather than sitting. This restlessness may be driven by a desire to burn additional calories; however, it may also be a result of poor nutrition and starvation. Some individuals with anorexia nervosa achieve and maintain their low body weight through food restriction and exercise. However, others also engage in **purging** behaviours in order to achieve or maintain weight loss. Purging behaviours include self-induced vomiting, laxative abuse, or abuse of enemas or diuretics. These purging behaviours, which result in the direct evacuation of the stomach, bowels, or bladder, are distinct from other compensatory behaviours that can be used to prevent weight gain, such as fasting or excessive exercise. Although purging behaviours can lead to some weight loss, this is primarily due to dehydration (which itself has serious medical consequences).

Many individuals who purge also engage in binge eating. From a clinician and researcher's standpoint, it is important to determine whether a patient is engaging in objective binge eating, or whether binges are subjective. Although both types of binge eating are associated with a lack of control over eating, the amounts of food consumed differ. An **objective binge**, as defined by the DSM-IV-TR, consists of eating a large amount of food (larger than most individuals would eat) in a specific time period (e.g., less than two hours). In contrast, if the individual is in fact eating small or normal amounts of food during these episodes (such as one chocolate bar), these would be considered subjective binge episodes.

Anorexia nervosa involves not only a drive for weight loss and a fear of gaining weight, but also a disturbance in body image. This disturbance may be manifested in several ways. Individuals with anorexia may have a disturbance in their view of their body shape. This may be general body dissatisfaction, in which they view their overall weight or shape to be distressingly unacceptable, or may be dissatisfaction with particular body parts, such as their thighs or hips. Individuals with anorexia often perceive their bodies or parts of their bodies to be much larger than they actually are. This disturbance in body image is often linked with low self-esteem, and individuals may use body weight or shape as one of their primary methods of determining self-evaluation. Individuals with anorexia may be hypervigilant in assessing their bodies, and may employ a variety of methods in their assessments, including repeated weighing, measuring body parts (e.g., measuring stomach or leg circumference), or constant checking of body shape in mirrors or other reflective surfaces.

Although the most striking feature of anorexia nervosa is low body weight, other common features of this disorder may be less immediately apparent. These features may concern cognitive, emotional, and physiological functioning, and include social withdrawal, irritability, preoccupation with food, and depression. However, it is important to note that while these features occur frequently in individuals with anorexia, many seem to be linked to the state of semi-starvation that individuals with anorexia are in, as opposed to being a feature of the disorder itself. In other words, during or after recovery, once an individual with anorexia has gained some weight, many of these features may be less severe, or may no longer be present. In the section on physical and psychological consequences of eating disorders, we will further examine this issue, taking into consideration research that shows that individuals who severely restrict their food intake (but do not have an eating disorder) show many of the same features that are present in anorexia nervosa.

BULIMIA NERVOSA

Bulimia nervosa is characterized by episodes of binge eating followed by compensatory behaviours designed to prevent weight gain. As in anorexia nervosa, individuals with bulimia often have low self-esteem, and use weight and shape information as their primary method of self-evaluation. Other features, such as social isolation and depression, are also common in both anorexia and bulimia nervosa. In contrast to anorexia, however, individuals with bulimia are typically within the normal weight range. This, in conjunction with the fact that binge eating and compensatory behaviours are often conducted in private, may make it harder for friends and family to detect the problem.

Individuals with bulimia engage in objective binge eating and, in order to prevent weight gain, engage in a variety of compensatory behaviours. These compensatory behaviours may include fasting and excessive exercise as well as purging. As mentioned, purging behaviours such as laxative abuse are relatively ineffective at producing significant weight loss, and much of the weight loss that occurs as a result of these behaviours is simply due to dehydration. This, in part, accounts for the fact that many individuals with bulimia are within the normal weight range—the purging and compensatory behaviours they engage in may not be sufficient to produce weight loss, relative to the number of calories that are consumed (some of which are digested before purging begins). These purging behaviours have serious medical consequences, which include, but are not limited to, impaired renal function and cardiovascular difficulties such as arrhythmias. The secretive nature of the binge/purge episodes, in conjunction with the fact that family and friends may not detect a problem, adds to the serious nature of bulimia given the potentially severe medical complications that can arise.

During episodes of binge eating, foods that are high in calories are typically consumed, including cookies, ice cream, and chips. During these episodes, more calories are derived from fat, and less from protein, compared to caloric intake during non-binge-eating episodes (Gendall, Sullivan, Joyce, Carter, & Bulik, 1997). The foods consumed during binge episodes are often considered to be "forbidden foods," and are avoided during periods of dieting and food restriction. This pattern of avoidance may set up a cycle of bingeing and purging. After an episode of binge eating, there is a feeling of physical discomfort (as a result of the large amount of food consumed), in addition to feelings of guilt and worry about weight gain. Many individuals with bulimia engage in self-induced vomiting after binge-eating episodes to relieve this physical discomfort, as well as to compensate for their excessive intake in an attempt to prevent weight gain. After purging, they may begin another period of dieting or restriction, leaving them feeling hungry in addition to feeling guilt and self-hatred about the purging behaviours. This becomes a cyclical pattern of restriction, binge eating, and purging.

In addition to dieting and food restriction, a number of other factors may serve as triggers for binge-eating episodes. Heatherton and Baumeister (1991) have proposed that episodes of binge eating occur in an attempt to escape from high levels of aversive self-awareness. According to this "escape from self-awareness" model, individuals who binge eat tend to have high expectations of themselves, constantly monitor themselves, and often fail to meet the high standards they set for themselves. Awareness of their failures leads to feelings of anxiety and depression and, as a result, individuals become strongly motivated to escape from this negative state. Heatherton and Baumeister propose that binge eating occurs as a result of a shift in attention; attentional focus is narrowed such that it becomes focused on the food present in the situation and on the sensations associated with consuming this food. In other words, binge eating results from shifting the focus of individuals away from their failure to live up to their high standards and toward the behaviour and positive sensations associated with eating.

Upon reviewing the features of anorexia and bulimia nervosa, you might notice that many of them overlap. Individuals with both anorexia and bulimia use their weight and shape as a primary source of self-evaluation, and have low self-esteem. Furthermore, like individuals with bulimia, some individuals with anorexia may engage in binge eating as well as purging behaviours. What, then, is the difference between these groups? One of the primary differences between anorexia and bulimia is body weight; while individuals with anorexia are always underweight, individuals with bulimia are typically within their normal weight range. Furthermore, although all individuals with bulimia engage in binge eating and compensatory behaviours, only some individuals with anorexia exhibit these behaviours. Hence, assessing body weight and eating behaviours can allow clinicians to differentiate between anorexia and bulimia nervosa. We will discuss the diagnostic features of both of these disorders and outline assessment techniques for eating disorders later in this chapter.

TABLE 10.1 PREVALENCE AND INCIDENCE OF ANOREXIA AND BULIMIA NERVOSA

	Prevalence		Incidence
	Females	**Males**	
Anorexia Nervosa	0.3%	0.02%	8 per 100 000 population/year
Bulimia Nervosa	1.0%	0.1%	12 per 100 000 population/year

Source: Adapted from Hoek and van Hoeken (2003); Lucas, Beard, O'Fallon, and Kurland (1991).

Incidence and Prevalence

To determine the prevalence of bulimia nervosa in a Canadian community sample, Garfinkel and colleagues (1995) assessed a total of 8116 individuals living in Ontario. They found that the lifetime prevalence of bulimia nervosa was 1.1 percent for women and 0.1 percent for men. The prevalence of bulimia in Canada is similar to the prevalence in other Western countries. Hoek and van Hoeken (2003) reviewed epidemiological studies conducted in the United States and Western Europe in order to determine the incidence and prevalence of anorexia nervosa and bulimia nervosa (see Table 10.1). Research has suggested that partial syndrome eating disorders (i.e., eating disorder not otherwise specified, or EDNOS; see the section "Diagnosis and Assessment") are even more common than either anorexia or bulimia, with a prevalence rate of 2.37 percent detected in a large community sample of adolescents and young adults (Machado, Machado, Gonçalves, & Hoek, 2007).

There have been reports of an increase in the incidence of anorexia nervosa over the past century (e.g., Eagles, Johnston, Hunter, Lobban, & Millar, 1995), though the incidence appears to have stabilized since the late 1980s (Currin, Schmidt, Treasure & Jick, 2005). For example, in a review of the literature on the incidence rates of anorexia nervosa, Pawluck and Gorey (1998) report that the incidence of anorexia increased by almost threefold among women in their twenties and thirties between 1950 and 1992. The incidence of bulimia nervosa also appears to have been increasing since it was first described in the late 1970s (Turnbull, Ward, Treasure, & Jick, 1996), though some reports indicate that this increase may have peaked in the mid-1990s (Currin et al., 2005). It is unclear to what extent these observed increases in the incidence of anorexia and bulimia are a result of increased awareness and recognition, which formerly would not have been acknowledged (Wakeling, 1996). Fombonne (1995, 1996) has argued that the true incidence of both anorexia and bulimia has not changed. Hoek and van Hoeken (2003) pointed out that regardless of whether the true incidence of anorexia nervosa is increasing, there has been an increase in the incidence of registered cases (and, hence, an increased need for treatment facilities). Despite increased awareness, Hoek and van Hoeken indicate that only about one-third of community-dwelling individuals with anorexia (and less than 10 percent of individuals with bulimia) receive mental health care. Hence, a large proportion of individuals who meet diagnostic criteria for an eating disorder do not receive appropriate mental health care.

PROGNOSIS

Eating disorders have the highest mortality rate of all the psychiatric disorders (Agras et al., 2004). Mortality rates are estimated to be between approximately 5 and 8 percent (e.g., Herzog et al., 2000; Steinhausen, Seidel, & Metzke, 2000). The most common causes of death among individuals with eating disorders are starvation and nutritional complications (e.g., electrolyte imbalance or dehydration) and suicide (Neumärker, 2000). Clearly, eating disorders are serious disorders.

It appears that there is a varied treatment response among individuals with eating disorders. On average, approximately 50 percent of individuals with bulimia nervosa are able to stop binge eating and purging with the current evidence-based individual therapy. Of the other 50 percent, some show partial improvements and others show no change at all in the frequency of binge/purge episodes (Wilson, 1999). In addition, relapse rates are high for eating disorders. One study investigated relapse rates in a group of 240 women who sought treatment for anorexia nervosa or bulimia nervosa, and followed these individuals for up to nine years after their entry into the study (Keel, Dorer, Franko, Jackson, & Herzog, 2005). Relapse occurred in 36 percent of women with anorexia nervosa who had achieved remission, and 35 percent of women with bulimia nervosa. Unfortunately, the high mortality rate in eating disorders exists even among individuals who have received treatment. For example, Herzog and colleagues (2000) report that all the participants who died during the course of their study (5.1 percent of the participants) had received individual psychotherapy and pharmacotherapy.

There is a similar variability in course and outcome in samples of eating-disordered individuals who are not seeking treatment. To study the natural course of bulimia nervosa, researchers conducted a prospective study over a five-year period in which the symptoms and features of eating disorders were assessed in a community-based sample of 102 women with bulimia nervosa (Fairburn, Cooper, Doll, Norman, & O'Connor, 2000). At the five-year follow-up, although only 15 percent of the women continued to meet diagnostic criteria for bulimia nervosa, approximately 50 percent had an eating disorder of clinical severity, and only 35 percent did not meet diagnostic criteria for an eating disorder. Hence, it seems that despite the fact that a substantial minority of individuals continues to have clinically significant eating disorders after receiving treatment, more patients recover after receiving treatment than exhibit spontaneous recovery without treatment. Treatment efficacy will be discussed in greater detail later in the chapter.

1 BEFORE MOVING ON

Over the last half century, our society has preferred increasingly thin women. Do you think this trend is linked to changes in the incidence of eating disorders? Why or why not?

Diagnosis and Assessment

DIAGNOSTIC CRITERIA

Case Notes

Rachel is a 34-year-old woman who works full time and lives on her own in an apartment. Rachel has always been quite thin, and her co-workers have commented to her that they wish they could have her figure. In order to maintain her slim figure, Rachel eats small portions, avoids snacking, and always prepares her own food so that she knows what is in it. Although her co-workers are friendly and sometimes go out together after work for dinner and drinks, Rachel has never joined them. She feels stressed by the idea of ordering at a restaurant and eating in front of other people. She also doesn't want to disrupt her exercise routine, because she is afraid that if she misses one day at the gym, she will fall into a negative spiral and stop exercising completely.

Lately, some of Rachel's friends have noticed that she has been losing weight and looking unwell. Her best friend recently spoke up about her concerns, and Rachel confided to her that it has been difficult to eat normally and maintain her weight since her mother fell ill and passed away last year. She started eating even smaller portions than before, and exercising more, during the stressful period of her mother's illness. She feels better emotionally when she exercises, and has gradually increased her exercise routine to one hour a day, five or six days per week. Although she has noticed her weight loss, she still perceives her stomach and thighs as "too big," and she has found it difficult to eat more because she is concerned about gaining "too much" weight. Her friend suggested that she go to her family doctor to discuss some of her issues with weight and exercise. Rachel reluctantly agreed to do so, and was somewhat alarmed when she found out that she had developed low blood pressure, and that her irregular and missed periods were likely connected with her low weight. Her weight was taken at 49 kilograms, at a height of 170 centimetres, giving her a BMI of 17. Her doctor suggested that he could refer her to a psychiatrist specializing in eating disorders treatment, and she agreed to visit the psychiatrist for further assessment.

ANOREXIA NERVOSA As you have already read, and can observe in the above case example, the central feature of anorexia nervosa is the pursuit and maintenance of an extremely low body weight. The DSM-IV-TR (APA, 2000) defines it as the refusal to maintain one's body weight at a minimal level considered to be normal for one's height and weight (see Table 10.2). The DSM-IV-TR provides two examples of minimal normal weight. The first is defined as 85 percent of one's expected weight based on several versions of published life insurance tables and pediatric growth charts. The second is having a **body mass index (BMI)**—weight in kilograms divided by height in metres squared—of 17.5. The DSM-IV-TR indicates that these criteria are provided only as a guideline for clinicians, as it is unreasonable to specify a single standard for minimally normal weight that applies to all individuals. In fact, for many individuals, a chart average weight of 85 percent corresponds to a BMI higher than 17.5. Most people who develop anorexia nervosa do so in adolescence when they are still growing, with the typical onset between

TABLE 10.2 DSM-IV-TR DIAGNOSTIC CRITERIA FOR ANOREXIA NERVOSA

A. Refusal to maintain body weight at or above a minimally normal weight for age and height (e.g., weight loss leading to maintenance of body weight less than 85% of that expected; or failure to make expected weight gain during period of growth, leading to body weight less than 85% of that expected).

B. Intense fear of gaining weight or becoming fat, even though underweight.

C. Disturbance in the way in which one's body weight or shape is experienced, undue influence of body weight or shape on self-evaluation, or denial of the seriousness of the current low body weight.

D. In postmenarcheal females, amenorrhea, i.e., the absence of at least three consecutive menstrual cycles. (A woman is considered to have amenorrhea if her periods occur only following hormone, e.g., estrogen, administration.)

Restricting Type: during the current episode of anorexia nervosa, the person has not regularly engaged in binge eating or purging behavior (i.e., self-induced vomiting or the misuse of laxatives, diuretics, or enemas)

Binge Eating/Purging Type: during the current episode of anorexia nervosa, the person has regularly engaged in binge eating or purging behavior (i.e., self-induced vomiting or the misuse of laxatives, diuretics, or enemas)

Source: Reprinted with permission from the *Diagnostic and Statistical Manual of Mental Disorders, Fourth Edition, Text Revision.* (Copyright © 2000), American Psychiatric Association.

ages 14 to 18. For these individuals, the criterion is a failure to make expected weight *gain* during a period of growth. Clinicians are instructed to consider an individual's body build and weight history when determining whether an individual meets low weight criteria for anorexia nervosa. Many individuals with anorexia nervosa achieve weights much lower than 85 percent of their expected weights, but some do not get to 85 percent, especially if their weights were high before their symptoms began. For these reasons the DSM-5 will likely remove the specific example of 85 percent and new assessment guidelines will be provided.

The second criterion is an irrational fear of gaining weight or of becoming fat despite being significantly underweight. It is important to note that individuals with anorexia nervosa do not necessarily fear weight gain for aesthetic reasons. Some individuals with anorexia may fear weight gain because they fear losing some of the consequences of their low weights that they view as beneficial. For example, many individuals with anorexia nervosa report that they fear gaining weight because they desire the emotional numbness that is associated with being underweight.

Finally, in order to meet diagnostic criteria, an individual must have a distortion in the experience and significance of body weight. Such distortions can include (1) a disturbance in perception of body weight or shape, such that the individual perceives herself as weighing more than she does or being larger than she is; alternatively, she may recognize that she is underweight but may perceive a particular body part as being larger than it actually is, (2) denial of the seriousness of her current (low) weight, or (3) determining self-worth based primarily on body weight or shape. Canadian researchers Geller, Johnson, and Madsen (1997) developed the Shape and Weight-Based Self-Esteem Inventory (SAWBS) to measure the importance of weight and shape to self-esteem relative to other factors (e.g., personality, relationships, career/school, etc.). Another Canadian research group has recently developed a self-report measure of weight-based self-esteem called the Weight-Influenced Self-Esteem Questionnaire (WISE-Q). The WISE-Q measures the influence of weight on how individuals with eating disorders feel about themselves in various domains of self-evaluation (Trottier, McFarlane, Olmsted, & McCabe, under review). It appears that how individuals with eating disorders feel about their weight influences how they feel about other, unrelated domains of self-evaluation (e.g., morality, performance at work). Research with the WISE-Q found that when weight influences how individuals feel about themselves in domains that realistically should not be linked to weight/shape, relapse following intensive eating disorder treatment is more likely (McFarlane, Olmsted & Trottier, 2008).

The final criterion for anorexia requires that females who are past puberty exhibit **amenorrhea**. Amenorrhea is defined as the absence of three consecutive menstrual cycles. Keep in mind that females who take birth control pills will typically menstruate even if they are significantly underweight. According to the DSM-IV-TR, a woman is also considered to be amenorrheaic if her periods occur only when she takes the birth control pill. However, it is often unclear whether a woman would menstruate if not on the birth control pill. Obviously, this criterion does not apply when considering a diagnosis of anorexia nervosa in males and it is suspected that this criterion will be removed in the DSM-5.

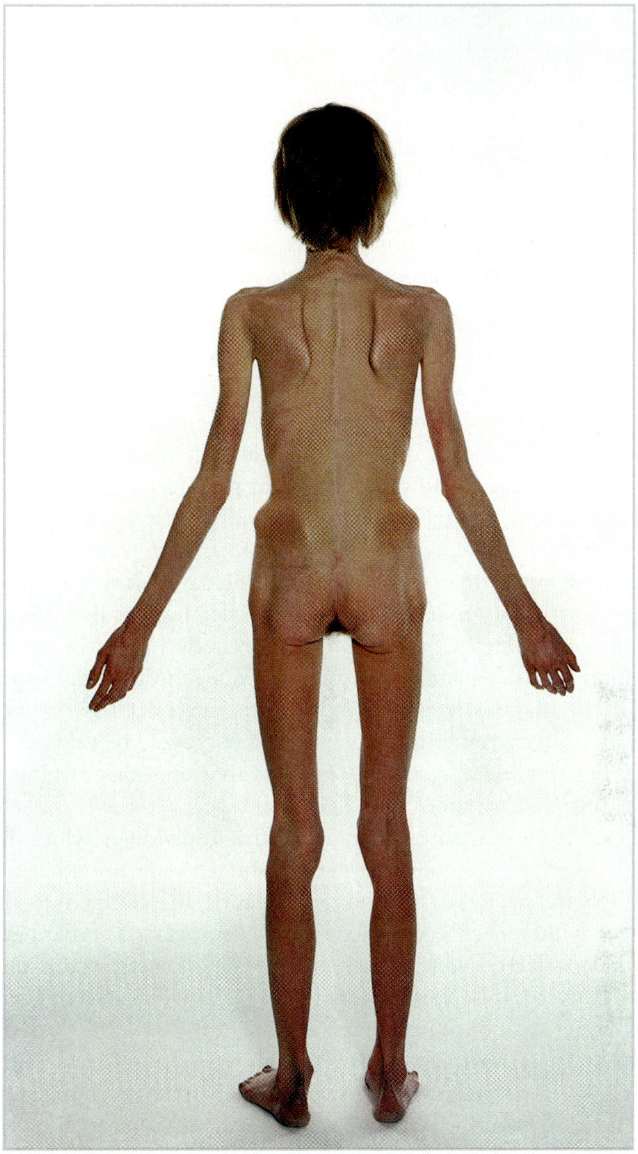

Despite being very thin, individuals with anorexia typically perceive parts of their bodies or their entire bodies as being too large.

The DSM-IV-TR subtypes anorexia into restricting type and binge eating/purging type for both research and clinical purposes. **Restricting type** individuals attain their extremely low body weights through strict dieting and, sometimes, excessive exercise. **Binge eating/purging type** individuals not only engage in strict dieting (and possibly excessive exercise) but also regularly engage in binge eating and/or purging behaviours. The distinction between restricting and binge eating/purging subtypes is important for research and clinical purposes for several reasons. For individuals who engage in binge eating and/or purging, these behaviours are often directly addressed in treatment and have a variety of physical consequences that may require medical attention. Furthermore, there is some evidence to suggest that the binge eating/purging type has a poorer prognosis than the restricting type of anorexia (Steinhausen, Rauss-Mason, & Seidel, 1991). When conducting research, it is important to describe exactly what and whom you are studying. The subtypes allow researchers to describe their participants more precisely.

TABLE 10.3 DSM-IV-TR DIAGNOSTIC CRITERIA FOR BULIMIA NERVOSA

A. Recurrent episodes of binge eating. An episode of binge eating is characterized by both of the following:
   (1) eating, in a discrete period of time (e.g., within any 2-hour period), an amount of food that is definitely larger than most people would eat during a similar period of time and under similar circumstances
   (2) a sense of lack of control over eating during the episode (e.g., a feeling that one cannot stop eating or control what or how much one is eating)

B. Recurrent inappropriate compensatory behavior in order to prevent weight gain, such as self-induced vomiting; misuse of laxatives, diuretics, enemas, or other medications; fasting; or excessive exercise.

C. The binge eating and inappropriate compensatory behaviors both occur, on average, at least twice a week for 3 months.

D. Self-evaluation is unduly influenced by body shape and weight.

E. The disturbance does not occur exclusively during episodes of Anorexia Nervosa.

Purging Type: during the current episode of bulimia nervosa, the person has regularly engaged in self-induced vomiting or the misuse of laxatives, diuretics, or enemas

Nonpurging Type: during the current episode of bulimia nervosa, the person has used other inappropriate compensatory behaviours, such as fasting or excessive exercise, but has not regularly engaged in self-induced vomiting or the misuse of laxatives, diuretics, or enemas

Source: Reprinted with permission from the *Diagnostic and Statistical Manual of Mental Disorders, Fourth Edition, Text Revision.* (Copyright © 2000), American Psychiatric Association.

BULIMIA NERVOSA The DSM-IV-TR defines bulimia nervosa as an eating disorder characterized by recurrent episodes of objective binge eating and inappropriate use of compensatory behaviours such as self-induced vomiting; laxatives, diuretics, or other medications; strict dieting; or vigorous exercise to prevent weight gain (see Table 10.3). In addition, the self-evaluation of individuals with bulimia is unduly influenced by body shape and/or weight. You might notice that this criterion is the same as one of the three criteria for anorexia nervosa, reflecting the distortion in the experience and significance of body weight in these individuals. Whereas this criterion is a central component of the diagnostic criteria for bulimia nervosa, it is one of three alternative criteria for anorexia nervosa. The third criterion for bulimia nervosa requires that episodes of binge eating and compensatory behaviours occur, on average, at least twice a week for three months. Individuals who fail to meet this frequency criterion but who are nonetheless regularly having episodes of binge eating and compensatory behaviour are still considered to have an eating disorder but are not diagnosed with bulimia (see the following section on EDNOS). It is expected that the DSM-5 will recommend a frequency of once per week for three months.

A person diagnosed with bulimia nervosa is further classified as **purging type** (i.e., the person engages in self-induced vomiting or the misuse of laxatives, diuretics, enemas, or other medications) or **nonpurging type** (i.e., the person uses other compensatory behaviours such as fasting or excessive exercise). The distinction between these subtypes of bulimia nervosa is important for the same reasons as in anorexia nervosa.

EATING DISORDER NOT OTHERWISE SPECIFIED (EDNOS) Although the concept of an eating disorder is typically equated with anorexia and bulimia nervosa, EDNOS is more common than either anorexia and bulimia nervosa in community and outpatient settings (Fairburn & Bohn, 2005). Even in a large Canadian tertiary care centre, which provides specialized intensive treatment, 40 percent of the individuals who receive treatment have a diagnosis of EDNOS (Rockert, Kaplan, & Olmsted, 2007). EDNOS encompasses eating disorders of clinical severity that do not meet the specific criteria for anorexia or bulimia (see Table 10.4). In some individuals, the eating disorder resembles the full syndromes of anorexia or bulimia nervosa but does not quite meet the DSM-IV-TR diagnostic criteria (e.g., the case of someone who meets all of the criteria for bulimia nervosa but engages in binge/purge episodes, on average, only once a week). In other individuals, the psychopathological features of the eating disorder combine in a different way than in either anorexia or bulimia nervosa. Recent research has attempted to identify subgroups of individuals within the EDNOS category, with some of these subgroups being considered for possible inclusion in the DSM-5 (APA, 2010). The specific subgroups that are being proposed, along with other possible changes to diagnostic criteria in the DSM-5, will be discussed later in this chapter.

BINGE-EATING DISORDER Binge-eating disorder (BED) characterizes another subgroup of individuals who are diagnosed with EDNOS, though it is also listed as a disorder for further study in an appendix of the DSM-IV-TR (see Table 10.5). There is now a substantial research literature on BED, most of which appeared after it was listed as a disorder for further study. BED involves recurrent episodes of binge eating, as in bulimia nervosa, but these individuals do not engage in inappropriate compensatory behaviours. There has been some disagreement among researchers as to whether BED is itself a discrete disorder or whether it

TABLE 10.4 DSM-IV-TR DIAGNOSTIC CRITERIA FOR EATING DISORDER NOT OTHERWISE SPECIFIED

The Eating Disorder Not Otherwise Specified category is for disorders of eating that do not meet the criteria for any specific eating disorder. Examples include:

1. For females, all of the criteria for Anorexia Nervosa are met except that the individual has regular menses.
2. All of the criteria for Anorexia Nervosa are met except that, despite significant weight loss, the individual's current weight is in the normal range.
3. All of the criteria for Bulimia Nervosa are met except that the binge eating and inappropriate compensatory mechanisms occur at a frequency of less than twice a week or for a duration of less than 3 months.
4. The regular use of inappropriate compensatory behavior by an individual of normal body weight after eating small amounts of food (e.g., self-induced vomiting after the consumption of two cookies).
5. Repeatedly chewing and spitting out, but not swallowing, large amounts of food.
6. Binge eating disorder, recurrent episodes of binge eating in the absence of the regular use of inappropriate compensatory behaviors characteristic of Bulimia Nervosa.

Source: Reprinted with permission from the *Diagnostic and Statistical Manual of Mental Disorders, Fourth Edition, Text Revision.* (Copyright © 2000), American Psychiatric Association.

is a type of bulimia. Some researchers believe that BED should be classified as a subtype of bulimia because both disorders have binge eating as a central feature. Individuals could then be subtyped according to whether they engage in inappropriate compensatory behaviours. Evidence to support this view comes from studies finding few differences between individuals who meet criteria for BED and the nonpurging subtype of bulimia (e.g., Hay & Fairburn, 1998). However, a recent review of the research on BED has helped to resolve some of the discussion about whether this disorder could be considered as a stand-alone eating disorder, by demonstrating that BED appears to be distinct from the other eating disorders (i.e., anorexia nervosa and bulimia nervosa), and that there is notable psychopathology and significant impairments in quality of life associated with BED (Wonderlich, Gordon, Mitchell, Crosby & Engel, 2009). This review has led to the recommendation that BED be considered as a distinct eating disorder in the DSM-5 (APA, 2010).

PROPOSED CHANGES IN DSM-5 As you can see in the notes to the summary tables for the different eating disorders, there are several upcoming proposed changes to the diagnostic criteria of eating disorders. Some of these changes are relatively minor, such as alterations to the wording of some criteria to focus on behaviour instead of weight. Others are more substantial, such as the removal

TABLE 10.5 DSM-IV-TR RESEARCH CRITERIA FOR BINGE-EATING DISORDER

A. Recurrent episodes of binge eating. An episode of binge eating is characterized by both of the following:
   (1) eating in a discrete period of time (e.g., within any 2-hour period) an amount of food that is definitely larger than most people would eat in a similar period of time under similar circumstances
   (2) a sense of lack of control over eating during the episode (e.g., a feeling that one cannot stop eating or control what or how much one is eating)

B. The binge-eating episodes are associated with three (or more) of the following:
   (1) eating much more rapidly than normal
   (2) eating until feeling uncomfortably full
   (3) eating large amounts of food when not feeling physically hungry
   (4) eating alone because of being embarrassed by how much one is eating
   (5) feeling disgusted with oneself, depressed, or very guilty after overeating

C. Marked distress regarding binge eating is present.

D. The binge eating occurs, on average, at least 2 days a week for 6 months.

Note: The method of determining frequency differs from that used for Bulimia Nervosa; future research should address whether the preferred method of setting a frequency threshold is counting the number of days on which binges occur or counting the number of episodes of binge eating.

E. The binge eating is not associated with the regular use of inappropriate compensatory behaviors (e.g., purging, fasting, excessive exercise) and does not occur exclusively during the course of Anorexia Nervosa or Bulimia Nervosa.

Source: Reprinted with permission from the *Diagnostic and Statistical Manual of Mental Disorders, Fourth Edition, Text Revision.* (Copyright © 2000), American Psychiatric Association.

of the amenorrhea criterion in anorexia nervosa and the addition of BED as a distinct disorder. One of the other major changes proposed for the DSM-5 is to merge feeding disorders with the eating disorders section, within the new diagnostic category "Feeding and Eating Disorders." The feeding disorders include pica (repeated eating of non-food substances, such as soil), rumination disorder (repeated regurgitation of food), and avoidant/restrictive food intake disorder (a feeding disturbance that is associated with weight loss or failure to gain weight, or nutritional deficiencies, yet is distinct from anorexia nervosa, as it is not associated with a disturbance in body image). These feeding disorders are classified in the DSM-IV-TR under "Disorders Usually First Diagnosed in Infancy, Childhood or Adolescence" (see Chapter 15), but it has been proposed that they be combined with the eating disorders as they are not restricted to childhood but may occur at any age.

Another substantial change proposed for the DSM-5 is the division of the EDNOS category into "Other Specified Feeding or Eating Disorder" and "Unspecified Feeding or Eating Disorder." Some of the conditions that fall under the "Other Specified Feeding or Eating Disorder" category are similar to those that were listed in the EDNOS category in the DSM-IV-TR, namely atypical anorexia (all criteria for anorexia are met except that weight may be at or above the normal range) and subthreshold bulimia nervosa (binge eating occurs for a limited duration or at a frequency that doesn't meet the criterion). Purging disorder has also been added to this category, although this condition was described in the DSM-IV-TR under the category EDNOS without this term. This condition entails the use of inappropriate compensatory behaviours (such as vomiting or laxative use) in the absence of binge eating by individuals who are within the normal weight range. Night eating syndrome has also been added to the proposed list of conditions in the DSM-5. This syndrome is characterized by repeated nocturnal eating (not better accounted for by BED), which causes significant distress and/or impairment in functioning. Both purging disorder and night eating syndrome lack sufficient research to be classified as distinct eating disorders, although a growing body of evidence suggests that both conditions represent pathological eating behaviour that is associated with significant reductions in quality of life (Keel & Striegel-Moore, 2009; Striegel-Moore, Franko, & Garcia, 2009). It is important to keep in mind that all the proposed changes we have highlighted in this chapter are not yet set in stone, as the revision of the DSM-5 is still under discussion (APA, 2010).

DIAGNOSTIC ISSUES

DIFFERENTIAL DIAGNOSIS As is the case with the diagnosis of all mental disorders, when diagnosing an eating disorder, psychiatrists and psychologists must consider and rule out other possible causes for the patient's symptoms. For example, in the case of someone with a probable diagnosis of anorexia or bulimia nervosa, it is important to establish that the symptoms are not due to a medical condition. Several medical conditions cause significant weight loss (e.g., gastrointestinal disease, acquired immune deficiency syndrome), and some even involve disturbed eating behaviour (e.g., Kleine-Levin syndrome, a sleep disorder characterized by excessive sleep alternating with disinhibited behaviour, such as compulsive overeating). It is also important to rule out major depressive disorder, as it may involve either severe weight loss or overeating. However, individuals suffering from these other disorders and conditions will not exhibit the overconcern with weight and/or shape that is characteristic of eating disorders and they will not engage in inappropriate compensatory behaviours, as in bulimia nervosa.

Once a psychiatrist or psychologist has determined that an individual is suffering from an eating disorder, he or she must then determine which eating disorder the person has. Unlike other disorders, such as anxiety disorders, it is not possible to have more than one eating disorder. Some of the important distinctions to be made are between bulimia nervosa and the binge eating/purging type of anorexia, and between the nonpurging type of bulimia and BED. Someone with the binge eating/purging type of anorexia may differ from someone with bulimia only on whether she is amenorrheaic and whether her weight is below 85 percent of what is expected for her height and weight. Similarly, someone with the nonpurging type of bulimia may differ from someone with BED only on whether she engages in inappropriate behaviours to compensate for binges. If the patient uses only restriction of food intake to compensate for binges, it may be difficult to determine whether the degree of restriction is considered "inappropriate." Due to the fact that only small distinctions often separate individuals in different diagnostic categories, as well as the fact that many individuals change diagnoses over the course of their disorder (Fichter & Quadflieg, 2007), some researchers and clinicians suggest that eating disorders should be considered as one disorder, existing on a continuum of severity. These issues will be addressed further in the next section.

VALIDITY OF DIAGNOSTIC CRITERIA AND CLASSIFICATION As you have just read, some researchers (e.g., Van der Ham, Meulman, Van Strien, & Van Engeland, 1997) have proposed that eating disorders be conceptualized on a spectrum, rather than as separate diagnostic categories. In other words, they suggest that the eating behaviours and other psychopathology of individuals with eating disorders exist on a spectrum of severity. On a spectrum of binge eating, for example, it has been proposed that BED be the least severe and purging type bulimia the most severe pathology (Hay & Fairburn, 1998).

Support for the spectrum view of eating disorders comes from the fact that many individuals move from one diagnostic category to another (and even back again) across time. For example, individuals who at one point met criteria for anorexia may gain weight in the process of recovery but maintain some eating-disordered cognitions and behaviours and later meet criteria for bulimia nervosa. Fairburn and his colleagues (2003) have pointed out that eating disorder diagnoses tend to change in a systematic way over the lifespan. According to Fairburn and his colleagues, in mid-adolescence, eating disorders most typically resemble anorexia nervosa, whereas the eating disorders of late adolescence and early adulthood tend to resemble bulimia nervosa. This transition is so common that it has been suggested that the restricting type of anorexia should be viewed as a "phase" in the course of an eating disorder (Eddy et al., 2002). Furthermore, in a study of individuals who met diagnostic criteria for bulimia nervosa, there was evidence that individuals with a history of anorexia nervosa had lower BMIs and smaller waist and hip circumferences than individuals with bulimia without a history of anorexia (Vaz, Guisado, & Peñas-Lledó, 2003). This finding suggests that subclinical features of anorexia may remain in individuals with bulimia with a history of anorexia and further supports the spectrum view of eating disorders.

A related controversy is about the specific diagnostic criteria for anorexia and bulimia nervosa. For example, there is considerable concern about the validity of amenorrhea and weight loss to a BMI of 17.5 or less than 85 percent of expected weight as diagnostic criteria for anorexia nervosa. As previously noted, the DSM-IV-TR does acknowledge that it is unreasonable to specify a single standard for minimally normal weight that applies to all individuals and it therefore indicates that the 85 percent of chart-average weight and BMI of 17.5 cut-off criteria are provided only as a guideline for clinicians. In the previous section, we discussed how it can be difficult to determine if amenorrhea is present when a woman is taking the birth control pill. However, further controversy surrounds this criterion because each woman has her own threshold for menstruation. Some women may cease menstruation after a minimal amount of weight loss, whereas others may continue to menstruate even when significantly underweight. One study of nearly 300 females with some variant of anorexia compared patients who met diagnostic criteria with those who failed to meet the criteria because they were either menstruating or were above 85 percent of expected weight (Watson & Andersen, 2003). These researchers found few significant differences between these two groups on demographics, illness history, treatment response, psychopathology, or bone density. Studies like this are being carefully considered in the discussion of proposed changes to the diagnostic criteria for the upcoming DSM-5.

ASSESSMENT

Assessment for diagnostic purposes and to guide treatment planning is usually conducted using a structured or semi-structured interview. Many researchers and clinicians use the **Eating Disorder Examination** (**EDE**; Fairburn & Cooper, 1993) to aid their assessments. The EDE is a structured clinical interview for diagnosing eating disorders that has good reliability and validity. It provides numerical ratings of the frequency and degree of eating disorder symptoms and also provides normative data on dietary restraint, bulimic symptoms, and eating, weight, and shape concerns. Conducting a diagnostic interview for an eating disorder involves gathering a great deal of information from the individual being assessed. The interviewer must gather information not only about the current and past frequency and severity of dietary restriction, bingeing, purging, and exercise, but also about distorted attitudes and beliefs about weight, shape, and eating; weight history; and current and past menstrual function. The interview should also explore the patient's interpersonal functioning and potential history of traumatic events. This information is gathered to assess potential factors that may have contributed to the development or maintenance of the eating disorder, as well as the patient's level of available social support.

An additional goal of diagnostic interviews for eating disorders is typically to assess for the presence and absence of other psychological disorders, as other disorders are often present in individuals with eating disorders. Some of the disorders that are often assessed for are substance abuse and dependence disorders, mood disorders, anxiety disorders, and personality disorders.

Another important component of eating disorders assessment is a medical examination, which can determine the presence of any physical and/or medical complications associated with eating disorders. These complications will be addressed in greater detail in the following section. It is important to assess for the medical consequences of eating disorders, as they should be addressed and monitored as part of treatment. Furthermore, for some patients, knowledge of the physical and medical complications of their eating disorders can motivate them to pursue recovery.

A final component of many assessments is the administration of self-report questionnaires to complement the information gathered through the clinical interview. One of the most frequently used self-report questionnaires with patients with eating disorders is the Eating Disorders Inventory, which assesses eating disorder attitudes and behaviours (Garner, Olmsted, & Polivy, 1983). Questionnaires measuring symptoms of depression, general psychopathology, and social support are also often administered.

Physical and Psychological Complications

There are numerous serious medical, psychological, and behavioural effects of eating disorders. In a review of the literature, Agras (2001) indicated that across all the eating disorder subtypes, individuals experience reduced quality of life and their social relationships are negatively affected. In individuals with anorexia, some of the physical and medical complications that may develop include osteoporosis, cardiovascular problems (including lowered heart rate and low blood pressure), decreased fertility, lethargy, dry skin, dry hair and hair loss, and heightened sensitivity to cold. **Lanugo**, a fine downy hair, may grow on the body in order to maintain body warmth. Both cognitive and emotional functioning can also be affected, such as difficulties concentrating and increases in irritability. Severe, potentially fatal medical conditions can arise in anorexia, which are typically attributed to semi-starvation, as well as to the purging behaviours that are sometimes present. These include impaired renal function and cardiac arrhythmia.

In individuals with bulimia, as well as the binge/purge subtype of anorexia nervosa, dental problems (such as erosion of teeth enamel) often develop due to the presence of stomach acid during self-induced vomiting. Similarly, individuals who self-induce vomiting may exhibit **Russell's sign** (scrapes or calluses on the backs of hands or knuckles, named after Gerald Russell, the British clinician who first identified bulimia nervosa). Electrolyte imbalance may occur in individuals with bulimia due to frequent purging. This imbalance may lead to problems with cardiovascular and renal functioning (including gastric rupture and cardiac arrhythmias), which can be fatal. As in anorexia, emotional functioning may also be affected. Furthermore, research indicates that individuals who binge eat (e.g., individuals with bulimia nervosa, or individuals with the binge/purge subtype of anorexia nervosa) are more likely to exhibit comorbid substance abuse (e.g., Corcos et al., 2001). Additional medical problems and complications can arise from drug and alcohol abuse, posing further difficulties for individuals with eating disorders who already have an elevated risk of mortality (Conason, Klomek & Sher, 2006).

One complication involved in studying the physical and psychological symptoms of eating disorders is distinguishing between whether a factor is a *cause* or a *consequence* of the eating disorder. For example, malnutrition may exaggerate certain symptoms of personality disorders, so it can be difficult to determine whether, in the absence of malnutrition, apparent personality disturbances are in fact present in an individual who has been diagnosed with an eating disorder. To investigate whether personality disorders endure after recovery from an eating disorder, or are mainly present during the course of an eating disorder, Matsunaga and colleagues (2000) assessed a group of patients who had recovered from their eating disorders for at least a year. These researchers demonstrated that although treatment for eating disorders seems to attenuate the symptoms of eating disorders, there does indeed seem to be a link between eating disorders and personality disorders, even after recovery. This suggests that personality disorders are not merely a consequence of the disorder.

Without conducting prospective longitudinal studies, it can be difficult to distinguish between the causes and consequences of eating disorders. However, an early study conducted by Franklin, Schiele, Brozek, and Keys (1948) has allowed insight into the physical and emotional consequences of semi-starvation and weight loss, both of which may be present in eating disorders. A group of American conscientious objectors during the Second World War agreed to participate in a study on semi-starvation in lieu of military service. This study was initially conducted to gain insight into how to best renourish civilians in Europe who had starved during the war; however, it has also provided critical insights in the field of eating disorders. The participants were healthy, normal-weight males who restricted their eating and engaged in regular physical activity over the course of 24 weeks in order to lose approximately 25 percent of their initial body weight. This food restriction and weight loss had both psychological and physiological consequences for the participants. The semi-starvation led to decreases in heart rate, increases in emotional instability (including depression and irritability), difficulty concentrating, decreased sex drive, and lethargy. Many participants also exhibited dry skin and hair and increases in hair loss. Almost all of the participants demonstrated an increased focus on food, with food becoming the primary topic of conversation. This increased focus on food continued even after the period of food restriction ended, during the rehabilitation period for weight restoration. However, at the end of the 12-week rehabilitation period, there was improvement in many of the symptoms, and the values for the symptoms had returned to near-normal levels 20 weeks after ending the semi-starvation period. The similarity between these symptoms and those present in the eating disorders is striking. This suggests that malnutrition may lead to several of the symptoms present in eating disorders, and that these symptoms may be alleviated upon re-feeding and improved eating habits.

2 BEFORE MOVING ON

Which conceptualization of eating disorders do you prefer—the categorical view (i.e., the current diagnostic categories) or the spectrum view of eating disorders? What are some of the advantages and disadvantages of the current method of classification?

Etiology

GENETIC AND BIOLOGICAL THEORIES

Despite strong social pressures to be thin and widespread body dissatisfaction among young women, eating disorders remain relatively rare. This, in conjunction with the fact that there appears to be a heritable component to eating disorders, highlights the possibility that biological factors play a role in the etiology of eating disorders (Kaye, 2008). The rate of eating disorders in relatives of individuals with anorexia nervosa is 4.5 times higher than in relatives of a healthy comparison group (Strober, Freeman, Lampert, Diamond, & Kaye, 2000). Reviews of twin studies, family studies, and molecular genetic studies have suggested that genetics play a significant role in the development of eating disorders, with estimates that more than 50 percent of the variance in eating disorders and disordered eating behaviours can be accounted for by genetic factors (Klump, Kaye, & Strober, 2001). Although in recent years numerous genetic studies on eating disorders have emerged, many different genes have been investigated with few replications, which limits our knowledge about the specific influence of genes on eating disorders (Klump & Gobrogge, 2005).

Dysfunctional neurotransmitter activity has also been investigated as another possible contributor to the development of an eating disorder. In particular, a link between serotonin levels and feeding/satiety has been established, and researchers have suggested that a dysregulation of the serotonin system is involved in the pathophysiology of eating disorders (e.g., Brewerton, 1995). Indeed, individuals with anorexia or bulimia demonstrate signs of serotonin dysregulation (e.g., Kaye, Gendall, & Strober, 1998). For example, it appears that anorexia nervosa is associated with reduced serotonin activity (specifically, reduced density of serotonin transporters in women with anorexia nervosa as compared to healthy controls; Bruce, Steiger, Ng Yin Kin, & Israel, 2006).

Further support for the role of serotonin functioning in eating disorders comes from research conducted by Robert Levitan and colleagues (2001) at the University of Toronto. To extend the research demonstrating that individuals with eating disorders have disturbances in their serotonin system, Levitan and colleagues studied polymorphism of the serotonin 1B receptor gene in individuals with bulimia to determine if any association existed between this measure and BMI. They demonstrated that this association does exist—polymorphism of the serotonin 1B receptor gene was associated with a lower minimum lifetime BMI (minimum lifetime BMI was assessed by determining patients' lowest weight since age 17, along with patients' height, to calculate BMI). Hence, individuals with bulimia who exhibited a particular expression of the serotonin 1B receptor gene reported having a lower minimum BMI than individuals with bulimia with different expressions of this gene. These findings support the possible role of genetic factors (in particular, serotonin receptor genes) in bulimia. However, as Klein and Walsh (2004) point out, it is unlikely that eating disorders stem from polymorphism of one gene in particular. It is more likely that sets of genes, interacting with particular environmental factors, are implicated in the development of eating disorders.

Clearly, the development of eating disorders is a complex process, which is not the result of the presence of merely one biological factor. These genetic or biological factors, however, may interact with other factors to precipitate the development of eating disorders. Although it seems that gender differences in eating disorders are in part attributable to socio-cultural factors (which are addressed in the next section), it is also possible that gender differences in biological factors, such as serotonergic functioning and hormonal levels, may also account, in part, for the observed gender differences in the prevalence of eating disorders. Researchers at McMaster University suggest that gender differences in the serotonergic system may make women more susceptible to the development of an eating disorder, as females are more susceptible to dysregulation in the serontonin system than are males (Steiner, Lepage, & Dunn, 1997). For example, it appears that dieting alters brain serotonin function in women, but not in men (Walsh, Oldman, Franklin, Fairburn, & Cowen, 1995). Biological changes occurring at puberty may also contribute to the development of eating disorders through secondary mechanisms (rather than directly influencing the development of eating disorders). Eating disorders typically develop during late puberty, or shortly thereafter. Some researchers have postulated that the hormonal changes associated with puberty in females may activate the development of disordered eating, either directly or indirectly (e.g., hormone levels influence body fat composition or eating behaviour, which in turn increases the risk for disordered eating; Klump et al., 2006). However, until more research is conducted, it is premature to draw conclusions about the causal role of gender differences in biological functioning in the development of eating disorders.

It is important to note that the association that has been established between serotonin functioning and eating disorders should be interpreted with caution. As you read earlier in the chapter, it can be difficult to distinguish between factors that may cause eating disorders and factors that are a consequence of the eating disorder. Part of the difficulty in establishing the role of serotonin in the development of eating disorders is the correlational nature of the studies investigating serotonin function in individuals with eating disorders. It is possible that alterations of serotonergic systems in individuals with eating disorders may simply be a function of low weight (in anorexia) or malnutrition associated with the eating disorder (Wolfe, Metzger, & Jimerson, 1997). However, researchers studying serotonin functioning in individuals who had a history of bulimia nervosa and were no longer symptomatic, compared with individuals with current bulimia nervosa and healthy controls, found that serotonin transporter densities were lower than controls in both individuals with active and remitted bulimia nervosa (Steiger et al., 2005). Steiger and colleagues suggest that serotenergic dysregulation may be a trait that increases the risk of developing bulimia. Further research is necessary in order to conclude that serotonin dysregulation is a contributor to the development of eating disorders, as opposed to a lasting consequence of these disorders.

3 BEFORE MOVING ON

Earlier in the chapter, you read about some of the physical consequences of eating disorders. Compare and contrast these physical symptoms, which are thought to be a consequence of malnutrition associated with eating disorders, with the genetic/biological factors that are thought to contribute to the development of eating disorders.

PSYCHOLOGICAL THEORIES

SOCIO-CULTURAL FACTORS According to the socio-cultural model of eating disorders, these disorders are (to at least some extent) a product of the increasing pressures for women in Western society to achieve an ultra-slim body. The mass media are a ubiquitous source of thin ideal images (see Focus box 10.1). Research has shown that in the last half century, there has been a steady decrease in the body size of the ideal woman. From 1959 to 1988, Miss America contestants became progressively thinner. *Playboy* centrefolds showed a similar pattern (Garner, Garfinkel, Schwartz, & Thompson, 1980; Wiseman, Gray, Mosimann, & Athrens, 1992; see Figure 10.1). Wiseman and colleagues found that most of these models weighed less than 85 percent of what would have been considered normal for their age and height—meaning that these women met the criteria of low body weight for anorexia nervosa. One of the most recent analyses of this type of data examined centrefolds up to

FOCUS 10.1

Thin Ideal Media Images Make Women Feel Bad, Right?

A great deal of research has sought to demonstrate a relation between thin ideal media images and disordered eating behaviours and/or attitudes. A number of correlational studies have found significant relations between mass media consumption and eating disorder–related symptomatology such as body dissatisfaction. For example, Stice and colleagues (1994) found a significant positive correlation between body dissatisfaction, eating disorder symptomatology, and exposure to magazines and television depicting ideal body images during the previous month. That is, women who read more magazines and watched more TV reported having higher levels of body dissatisfaction and other eating disorder symptomatology. In correlational studies, the relation between generalized media consumption and body dissatisfaction (Abramson & Valene, 1991) is similar to that of more specific types of media exposure (e.g., music videos) and body dissatisfaction (Hofschire & Greenberg, 2001). However, correlational studies are not able to demonstrate that exposure to thin body images *causes* body dissatisfaction and other eating disorder–related symptoms. It seems just as likely that individuals who are already dissatisfied with their bodies seek out these images. In response to this problem, a number of experimental studies have manipulated exposure to thin ideal media figures and measured the corresponding effects on body dissatisfaction and other self-perception measures.

The literature suggests that thin media images do have an adverse effect on the body dissatisfaction of some young women. Indeed, a meta-analysis of the literature (Grabe, Ward, & Shibley Hyde, 2008) found that exposure to thin ideal images was associated with higher levels of body dissatisfaction and thin ideal internalization among women compared with exposure to control images. Negative effects were even found on eating beliefs and behaviours. The authors pointed out that it is very concerning that brief experimental exposures to thin ideal images can affect beliefs about eating, dieting, and purging. A previous meta-analysis found that women with pre-existing body image issues were more adversely affected by thin media stimuli than were women who were relatively satisfied with their bodies (Groesz, Levine, & Murnen, 2002).

These frequently observed negative effects of exposure to idealized media images are typically explained using social comparison theory. Studies finding negative effects of idealized media images generally assume that participants are using the thin models as standards of comparison for determining self-evaluations. In line with this hypothesis, studies have shown that when young women engage in upward social comparisons with fashion models on the dimension of attractiveness, decreased appearance satisfaction and increased thin ideal internalization result (e.g., Tiggeman & Polivy, 2010).

Although the majority of studies have found negative effects of thin ideal media exposure, some studies have failed to find any significant effects (e.g., Champion & Furnham, 1999) or have found positive effects on self-perceptions (e.g., Joshi, Herman, & Polivy, 2004). It is likely that a number of studies finding no significant effects have gone unpublished due to the fact that it can be difficult to publish a study with null results. One potential reason why so many studies have found negative effects of thin media exposure is that women are likely to have their own ideas about the effects that thin ideal media images have on them (or are "supposed to have"); they may believe that they *should* feel worse about themselves after viewing these stimuli. In a qualitative interview study, adolescent girls reported that the portrayal of thin models in the media was the major force in creating dissatisfaction with their bodies (Wertheim, Paxton, Schutx, & Muir, 1997). If participants believe that viewing idealized media images should make them feel worse about themselves, then they are likely to respond in a negative way to such images when simply asked how the images make them feel.

One Canadian study directly addressed the issue of these demand characteristics in this area of research. Mills, Polivy, Herman, and Tiggeman (2002) demonstrated that when demand characteristics are present (in that participants were aware that their responses to the media images were the topic of interest to the experimenters), dieters report feeling more depressed following exposure to idealized images; however, when demand characteristics are minimized, chronic dieters rate their current body sizes as thinner following exposure to idealized images. The results of this study suggest that rather than using models as standards of comparison, dieters identified with these thin ideal images and were inspired by them or engaged in a positive fantasy in response to them. These findings may help to explain why many women not only voluntarily expose themselves to thin ideal media images but also seem to enjoy looking at them. Even in the cases where thin ideal media images have immediate positive effects, they may have adverse effects in the long term because positive inspirational effects may encourage dieting, which may worsen self-esteem and body satisfaction in the long run.

1999 (Sypeck et al., 2006). The results of this study suggest that while the *Playboy* models remain underweight, their weights appear to have stabilized over the past two decades.

Internalization of these thin media images is believed to be a causal risk factor for the development of an eating disorder (Thompson & Stice, 2001). Internalization of the thin ideal involves affirming the desirability of socially sanctioned ideals and engaging in behaviours to achieve the ideals (Heinberg, Thompson, & Stormer, 1995). Thin ideal internalization is believed to lead directly to body dissatisfaction (because the cultural ideal is unattainable for most women) and dieting. Both of these variables, in turn, increase the risk for eating disorder psychopathology. Recently, there has been a shift in the ideal female body presented by the media, such that the women are now extremely thin *and* extremely toned (Grogan, 2008). Homan (2010) investigated the longitudinal impact of idealization of these athletic ideal images and found that it predicted change in compulsive exercise over the seven-month study period but not body dissatisfaction or dieting. In contrast, thin ideal internalization predicted change in all three outcomes.

It is interesting that while the ideal body size for women has been getting thinner, women are actually becoming

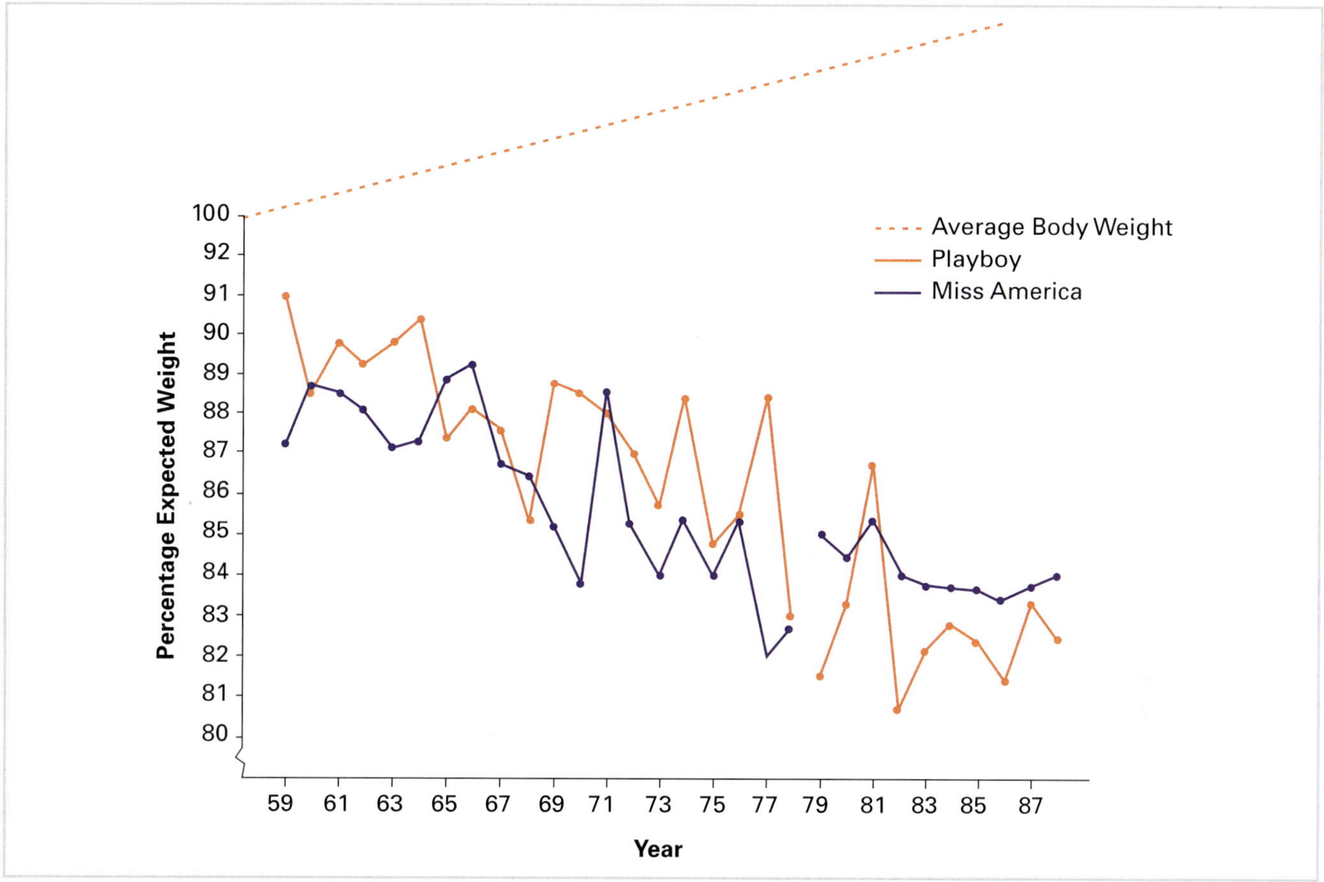

FIGURE 10.1 Average Percentage of Expected Weight of *Playboy* Centrefolds (1959–1978) and Miss America Contestants (1979–1988)

Source: Adapted from Wiseman, Gray, Mosimann, and Ahrens (1992). Cultural Expectations of Thinness in Women: An Update, *International Journal of Eating Disorders*, Vol. 11, No. 1, pp. 85–89, and Garner (1997).

heavier. According to the Women's Health Surveillance Report commissioned by Health Canada, the prevalence of being overweight among women increased from 19 percent in 1985 to 26 percent in 2000/2001, and the prevalence of obesity among women increased from 7 percent to 14 percent during the same time period (Bryan & Walsh, 2003; see Figure 10.2). More recently, the Canadian Community Health Survey found that the prevalence among women of being overweight or obese was 30 percent and 23 percent, respectively, in 2004. The prevalence of being overweight or obese among men has similarly increased.

There also appears to be an increasing discrepancy between the average man and the "ideal" man as depicted in the media, such that the ideal man is becoming more muscular, whereas the average man is developing more body fat (Spitzer, Henderson, & Zivian, 1999). However, pressure to obtain the ideal body appears to be greater for women than for men. According to the socio-cultural model of eating disorders, the greater prevalence of eating disorders among women than among men is a result of the greater pressure on women to obtain the "ideal" body. Nonetheless, a recent meta-analysis suggests that men are indeed susceptible to the potential effects of exposure to idealized male

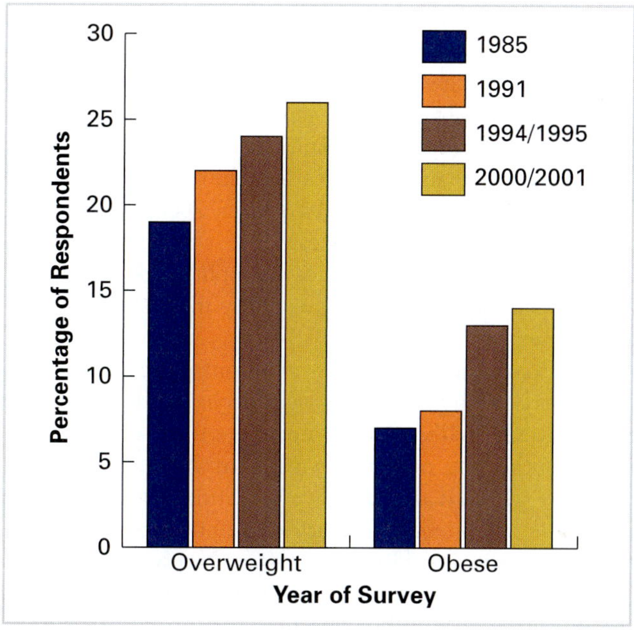

FIGURE 10.2 Percentage of Female Canadians Aged 20–64 Considered Overweight and Obese

Source: Adapted from Bryan & Walsh (2003), pp. 14–15.

media images (Bartlett, Vowels, & Saucier, 2008). Taking the entire published experimental literature into consideration, it appears that exposure to muscular male fashion models leads men to feel worse about their bodies. There is also evidence that exposure to these images is related to negative psychological (e.g., depression) and behavioural (e.g., excessive exercise) outcomes. We further address some of the factors that may play a role in gender differences in eating disorders later in this chapter.

Our society's obsession with thinness for women is so widespread that a moderate degree of body dissatisfaction has been normative among women for some time (Cash, Morrow, Hrabosky & Perry, 2004) and is also prevalent among adolescent girls (Lawler & Nixon, 2011). For example, in a sample of 129 adolescent girls between the ages of 12 and 19, 80 percent reported a desire to change their body size (Lawler & Nixon, 2011). This body dissatisfaction encourages many girls and women to diet in an effort to change their weight or shape. In fact, dieting has become so prevalent that it, too, has been described as "normal" for young women (Polivy & Herman, 1987). The question remains, however, why when almost all women are exposed to socio-cultural pressures to be thin, and many develop body dissatisfaction and engage in dieting behaviours, so few go on to develop eating disorders (Polivy & Herman, 2004).

4 BEFORE MOVING ON

Under what conditions do you think thin ideal media images are more likely to have negative effects on young women? How do you think these images might affect older women or men?

FAMILY FACTORS The family has been identified as an important influence in the development of eating disorders. It can provide cultural transmission of pathological values or be a stressor on its own (by being a source of miscommunication or conflict, or through lack of emotional support). It can also be a protective factor by providing support, identity, and comfort. The way in which families communicate cultural ideas about thinness can potentially contribute to the development of eating disorders (e.g., Haworth-Hoeppner, 2000; Strober et al., 2000). When the family environment is critical or coercive, or the household is dominated by emphases on weight and appearance, the risk of eating disorders increases (Haworth-Hoeppner, 2000).

Both mothers and fathers may contribute to the development of eating disorders. Research has demonstrated that patients with anorexia nervosa often complain that their mothers do not care about them. More importantly, mothers whose daughters have an eating disorder tend to see their daughters as less attractive and needing to lose weight (Polivy & Herman, 2002). Naturally, mothers' comments about weight and shape communicate their feelings and behaviours to their daughters, who often emulate them. Thus, mothers who diet are more likely to have daughters who diet; mothers who are dissatisfied with their own weights may even encourage their daughters to use more extreme weight-loss techniques. Daughters tend to model their mothers' dieting attitudes and behaviours (Smolak, Levine, & Schermer, 1999). Families who focus on physical attractiveness and weight have been shown to have an elevated probability of producing a child with an eating disorder, especially in a child who is more sensitive to family expectations and values (Davis, Shuster, Blackmore, & Fox, 2004).

Even more problematic is the fact that mothers who themselves have eating disorders may transmit their pathological eating behaviours to their young daughters (Polivy & Herman, 2002). The 10-year-old children of mothers who had eating disorders report higher weight and shape concerns and more dietary restraint than do children of mothers without eating disorders (Stein et al., 2006). Furthermore, mothers who have an eating disorder do not feed their children as regularly as do non-disordered mothers, and are more likely to use food for non-nutritive purposes, such as to reward or soothe their children (Agras, Hammer, & McNicholas, 1999). Children of mothers with eating disorders also have higher levels of negative affect (Agras et al., 1999), which itself is a potential risk factor for the development of an eating disorder. When either parent makes critical comments or is generally emotionally negative, this increases the likelihood of a child developing an eating disorder, and predicts a worse prognosis for those who do. For example, when mothers of individuals with eating disorders express primarily negative emotion (especially critical comments), outcomes are worse for these patients (Vanfurth et al., 1996). High parental expectations that are difficult for the child to meet or that do not correspond to the child's own needs or goals decrease the child's feelings of autonomy, and are predictive of the development of eating disorders (Polivy, Herman, Mills, & Wheeler, 2003). These sorts of parent–adolescent conflicts over autonomy and identity tend to be more intense in girls than boys, which may help to explain why eating disorders are so much more common in females than in males (Polivy et al., 2003).

PERSONALITY/INDIVIDUAL FACTORS A number of personality traits appear to characterize patients with eating disorders, both before and during their struggle with the disorder, and some individual difference variables may be influential in the development of the pathology. Personality research is, of necessity, correlational in nature, so it is not possible to conclude that these differences are what cause the development of an eating disorder, but the distinctions are nonetheless suggestive.

Personality traits such as perfectionism, obsessiveness, compliance, lack of awareness of internal feelings, and a sense of ineffectiveness or negative view of self characterize both patients with anorexia nervosa and those with bulimia nervosa (Fairburn, Cooper, Doll, & Welch, 1999; Steiger et al., 2001). In addition, individuals with bulimia are often impulsive. These traits tend to be present both during the disorder and after recovery (Fairburn et al., 1999;

Kaye et al., 1998; Lilenfeld et al., 2000). Some of these characteristics, such as perfectionism, ineffectiveness, and interpersonal distrust, are found in family members of individuals with eating disorders who do not themselves have any symptoms of eating disorders (Lilenfeld et al., 2000). A review that included prospective studies suggested that the presence of these personality factors increases the risk of developing an eating disorder (Lilenfeld, Wonderlich, Riso, Crosby, & Mitchell, 2006).

Other individual differences have been studied as possible risk factors contributing to the development of eating disorders. These include characteristics such as low self-esteem, identity problems, depressive affect, and poor body image, as well as behaviours undertaken in connection with some of these, including dieting and participation in exercising or sports that emphasize the body (Polivy et al., 2003).

Low self-esteem is present in many disorders, not just eating disorders; for example, it is often linked to depression. This lowered self-esteem and identity diffusion may result from traumatic experiences such as sexual, physical, or emotional abuse, though such negative life experiences are not necessary precursors to the development of an eating disorder. Patients with eating disorders, and even non-disordered, chronic weight-loss dieters, suffer from lower self-esteem and more negative affect (Polivy et al., 2003). The lower self-esteem and depressed affect among those with eating disorders have been found to be related to a lack of a cohesive identity and trust in one's body. In general, having a negative body image, being a chronic dieter, and having low self-esteem, depression, and identity problems all seem to be risk factors associated with the development of eating disorders (Polivy & Herman, 2002). Longitudinal studies have indicated that these sorts of factors may predict the development of eating disorders before they appear in a given individual (Thompson & Stice, 2001).

Individuals may try to compensate for these problems by trying to construct an identity focused on weight, shape, and excessive control of one's body, to help create a sense of self. This reliance on one's weight and shape, however, can make one more vulnerable to eating problems in the face of threats to this identity. For example, individuals with eating disorders are overly reliant on the numbers on their bathroom scales to determine their mood and behaviours on a given day (Bruch, 1978). Clinical observations suggest the extent to which an individual's identity can be influenced by an eating disorder, and how difficulties in treatment can arise as a result of this identification with the disorder (e.g., Bulik & Kendler, 2000). There is evidence that individuals with anorexia or bulimia have more negative (and fewer positive) self-schemas than do control individuals without a history of mental disorders (Stein & Corte, 2007). Self-schemas, in turn, are associated with body dissatisfaction, as individuals who have fewer positive self-schemas are more likely to report higher body dissatisfaction. This research supports the notion that identity impairments are associated with eating-disordered symptomatology (Stein & Corte, 2007).

Dieting, and the embracing of society's idealization of thinness for women that dieting reflects, has itself been implicated as a precipitating factor in eating disorders, especially binge eating (Polivy & Herman, 2002). In fact, eating disorders are sometimes referred to as "dieting disorders," although it is clear that very few of the millions of people who are chronic dieters will go on to develop a full-blown eating disorder. Similarly, some sports and activities that place extreme emphasis on body shape (such as gymnastics or ballet dancing) seem to be associated with increased risk for eating disorders (Polivy & Herman, 2002). Thus, certain personality and behavioural patterns appear to be contributors to the development of eating disorders, though none of these is a perfect predictor.

MATURATIONAL ISSUES As children develop into adolescence, physical maturation causes increasing sex differences such that males begin to become more muscular, and females become more curvaceous. For males, this simply pushes them toward the masculine ideal body shape, but for females, pubertal development involves adding body fat, which takes girls further away from the thin ideal female figure (Striegel-Moore, 1993). It may not be an accident, then, that eating disorders are most likely to appear around the time of puberty, at the same time that girls develop feelings of body dissatisfaction and start to diet to lose weight because their level of body fat is increasing. The idealization of a thin body shape by the surrounding culture may push adolescent girls toward dangerous dieting practices and a rejection of one's own body shape that contribute, in susceptible individuals, to the development of eating disorders (Polivy & Herman, 1987, 2002).

In addition, puberty is a time of increasing sex role demands. For girls, this means pursuing the "superwoman ideal" of success in all spheres of life—social, appearance, academic, career, and family. This may require them to attempt to fulfill incompatible role demands, which may be particularly difficult for young girls who have not learned how to prioritize these roles and the demands they make, and which can have negative effects on the girls' identity formation (Polivy et al., 2003). Furthermore, girls must cope with the onset of dating and sexuality, which appears to be more stressful for females than for males (Striegel-Moore, 1993).

ADVERSE EVENTS Traumatic events can certainly have negative effects on an individual's self-esteem, body image, and sense of control. It is therefore not surprising that some researchers have suggested that abuse—in particular, childhood sexual abuse—could cause an individual to develop an eating disorder (e.g., Waller, 1991). Some studies have found a high incidence of sexual abuse among individuals with eating disorders. For instance, a study of eating-disordered patients in Toronto found that 25 percent reported being sexually abused (DeGroot, Kennedy, Rodin, & McVey, 1992). A particularly important point is that an elevated incidence of sexual abuse and other trauma has been found in patients with other psychological disorders such as obsessive-compulsive disorder (e.g., Lochner et al., 2002), suggesting that trauma may elevate the risk of psychological disturbance in general and that the risk is not specific to eating disorders. The spectrum of adverse events found to be associated with eating disorder psychopathology includes not only childhood sexual abuse but also sexual assault in adulthood, physical abuse and neglect, emotional abuse, emotional and physical neglect, teasing, and bullying (Brewerton, 2007).

The research evidence suggests that a trauma history is more frequently associated with development of a bulimic-type eating disorder (i.e., bulimia nervosa, anorexia nervosa—binge eating/purging type, or EDNOS with symptoms of bingeing or purging) than with anorexia nervosa—restricting type or EDNOS characterized by restriction only. For example, in a study conducted at Toronto General Hospital, patients with the binge/purge type of anorexia were more likely to report a history of childhood sexual abuse than were patients with the restricting type of anorexia (Carter, Bewell, Blackmore, & Woodside, 2006).

INTEGRATIVE MODELS

The etiology of eating disorders is multifactorial; no single etiological factor alone can account for the development of an eating disorder. Eating disorders are very complex, and it would be simplistic to suggest that one factor could alone produce an eating disorder in any given individual. Consequently, some researchers have proposed integrative models to describe the development and maintenance of eating disorders. For example, Johnson and Connors (1987) proposed a biopsychosocial model of eating disorder development. This model posits that biological predispositions (e.g., genetic, hormonal, and pubertal), family factors, and cultural pressures to be thin and to fulfill a demanding social role interact to produce an identity-conflicted, vulnerable dieter. Dieters with low self-esteem and affective instability are most susceptible to an eating disorder, particularly following stress or failure. Garner and colleagues (1980) suggest that bulimia nervosa develops due to an interaction of predisposing, precipitating, and perpetuating factors. Predisposing factors include genetic, biological, family, and individual factors. **Precipitating factors** refer to events or situations that trigger the eating disorder (e.g., death of a loved one, transition into puberty, dieting). Finally, **perpetuating factors** refer to the physical and psychological symptoms that serve to maintain the disorder, such as reduced basal metabolic rate, delayed gastric emptying, social isolation, and depression. Striegel-Moore (1993) has suggested that those individuals who are faced with a greater number of simultaneous life challenges are more susceptible to developing an eating disorder. To illustrate, girls who mature early and begin dating at the same time report more disturbed attitudes about eating and body shape. A related theory proposes that the numerous transitions that occur in adolescence (e.g., high school, puberty, dating, conflict in friendships, increased academic and sex role demands) and the restructuring of personality and behaviour demanded by these transitions may overwhelm an adolescent who is already vulnerable because of other interpersonal or intrapersonal problems (e.g., Smolak & Levine, 1996). Although these integrative models and theories attempt to address the complexity of eating disorders and the many identified etiological factors, they have not yet provided predictive power sufficient to identify individuals most likely to develop eating disorders.

Eating Disorders in Males

The main features of anorexia or bulimia are similar in males and females. Likewise, the DSM-IV-TR diagnostic criteria for the different subtypes of eating disorders are identical for both males and females (except for the criterion of amenorrhea in anorexia nervosa in females). However, individuals who are diagnosed with an eating disorder are predominantly female. Reports estimate that for every male who is diagnosed with anorexia or bulimia, there are 10 to 15 females with these disorders (Bramon-Bosch, Troop, & Treasure, 2000; Braun, Sunday, Huang, & Halmi, 1999). Despite these gender differences in the prevalence of eating disorders, however, researchers at the Eating Disorder Program at Toronto General Hospital have reported that the treatment response of male patients to a day hospital program seems to be similar to that of female patients. Furthermore, it appears that male patients are able to be treated effectively in a setting that is composed primarily of females (Woodside & Kaplan, 1994).

A recent review of the literature on eating disorders in males (Jones & Morgan, 2010) suggests that similar factors influence the risk of developing eating disorders in men and women, and that the main factors that could explain the gender discrepancy are unresolved. Eating disorders may occur more frequently in women because the strength, or prevalence, of certain risk factors (such as socio-cultural factors) is higher than for men. For example, Andersen and DiDomenico (1992) found that for every diet-related article or advertisement in men's magazines, there were 10.5 in women's magazines. As the authors point out, this difference is nearly identical to the difference in prevalence of eating disorders across gender! Of course, the fact that women are exposed to more diet-related material than men cannot solely account for why more women develop eating disorders. After all, if this were the case, we would expect to see a higher prevalence of eating disorders in women, given that the majority of women in Western societies are exposed to this type of material.

Within non-clinical populations, there is also evidence that women are disproportionately affected by weight and shape concerns. For example, non–eating-disordered males are more satisfied with their weight than are non–eating-disordered females (Dolan, Birtchnell, & Lacey, 1987), and males are less likely than females to perceive themselves as overweight or report being on a diet (Connor-Greene, 1988).

APPLIED CLINICAL CASE

Sheena Carpenter

Sheena Carpenter was a young woman who struggled with anorexia nervosa up until the time of her death due to starvation at the age of 22. After learning about Sheena's eating disorder, Sheena's mother, Lynn, sought treatment for her daughter but ran into a number of roadblocks: few available treatment resources were available, and her daughter's motivation to recover was low and transient.

At age 14, Sheena went to a modelling agency where she was told that she would be more photogenic if she had a thinner face. In the years that followed, the first signs of her eating disorder emerged—she wore baggy clothes to hide her dropping weight, and she became obsessed with food. By the age of 18, Sheena's weight had dropped to 75 pounds, and her mother discovered that Sheena was inducing vomiting. Over the course of her disorder Sheena was, at times, able to make progress—on two occasions she was able to gain 20 pounds. However, for the most part, her eating disorder increased in severity over time and she developed many complications, including depressed mood, erosion of her tooth enamel, low electrolytes, and seizures. Her heart, liver, and brain were all damaged. At the time of her death, Sheena weighed only 50 pounds.

Sheena's eating disorder was not just about pursuing thinness. Sheena revealed that she had been sexually abused as a child and she struggled with intrusive memories related to this. She also had a very close but difficult relationship with her mother. After Sheena's death, Lynn and two of her friends began work on establishing a not-for-profit support centre for people with eating disorders in Toronto called Sheena's Place. Sheena's Place offers group therapy to people in the community with eating disorders, with the goal of providing hope and support. Sheena's Place has grown tremendously since its inception, offering more than 45 different support groups to people with eating disorders. Other similar support centres can be found in Canada—including Danielle's Place, also in Ontario, and Jessie's Hope Society in British Columbia.

However, despite their healthier attitudes in relation to females, some dissatisfaction in the non–eating-disordered male population emerges across studies, which suggests that the majority of males who are dissatisfied with their weight would like to increase their current weight (e.g., Connor-Greene, 1988; Furnham & Nordling, 1998). This preference is in contrast to the overwhelming desire of women to lose weight (e.g., Dolan et al., 1987). Similarly, the reported body images of college males tended to be distorted toward perceptions of underweight, whereas females' body images were distorted toward perceptions of overweight (Betz, Mintz, & Speakmon, 1994). Hence, it is possible that males are more protected than females against the development of eating disorders, given their different types of weight and shape concerns and less frequent dieting behaviours. However, as discussed earlier in this chapter, this factor alone is unable to account for the development of eating disorders, given that eating disorders are so rare despite the fact that body dissatisfaction is so widespread.

There seem to be some protective factors operating for males; yet, there are still cases of eating disorders in males. Are there certain groups of males that may be more susceptible to developing eating disorders? Some evidence suggests that homosexual males may have a greater risk than heterosexual males for developing eating disorders. Homosexual males are more likely than heterosexual males to be preoccupied with their body size and shape (Strong, Williamson, Netemeyer, & Geer, 2000) and appear to have a higher prevalence of eating disorder symptoms than do heterosexual males (Feldman & Meyer, 2007). Furthermore, researchers have indicated a high prevalence of homosexuality within males seeking treatment for an eating disorder. Carlat and colleagues (1997) indicated that 41 percent of the male eating-disordered patients they treated were heterosexual, whereas 27 percent were homosexual or bisexual, and 32 percent were asexual. In contrast, there do not appear to be any differences between heterosexual and homosexual women with regard to the prevalence of eating disorders (Feldman & Meyer, 2007; Strong et al., 2000).

However, the increased prevalence of homosexuality in eating-disordered males is not ubiquitous. In two studies on eating-disordered populations that included control groups (Mangweth et al., 1997; Olivardia, Pope, Mangweth, & Hudson, 1995), there were no significant differences in the incidence of homosexuality between the males with eating disorders and the control group. Hence, given the inconsistent findings in the literature, it is premature to conclude that there is a strong association between homosexuality and eating disorders in males. In fact, research investigating disordered eating in both heterosexual and homosexual males demonstrated that when males' levels of body dissatisfaction and self-esteem were statistically controlled for, there was no significant association between sexual orientation and eating disorder symptomatology (Hospers & Jansen, 2005). This finding provides support for the suggestion that body dissatisfaction (as opposed to sexual orientation) plays a more central role in the development of eating disorders in males.

Treatment

BIOLOGICAL TREATMENTS

Bulimia nervosa has been treated with antidepressant medication, namely tricyclic antidepressants and selective serotonin reuptake inhibitors. The rationale for treating bulimia with these drugs is that depressive symptoms are common in these patients. Meta-analyses, which systematically and quantitatively review available research evidence, suggest that, overall, fluoxetine (Prozac) produces a moderate initial effect on bulimic symptoms. However, only a small minority of patients recover on these drugs and most patients continue to meet diagnostic criteria (Narash-Eisikovits, Dierberger, & Westen, 2002). Furthermore, meta-analyses have revealed that treatment with antidepressants is inferior to cognitive-behaviour therapy (CBT; described in the next section) at reducing frequency of bingeing and purging, depression, and distorted eating-related attitudes (Whittal, Agras, & Gould, 1999). When CBT is added to antidepressant treatment, it is better than antidepressant treatment alone (Narash-Eisikovits et al., 2002), but not better than CBT on its own (Wilson, 1993). Preliminary evidence exists for other second-generation antidepressants (trazodone and fluvoxamine), an anticonvulsant (topiramate), and a tricyclic antidepressant (desipramine). However, replication for all of these medications is required.

Unfortunately, attempts to treat anorexia nervosa with pharmacological agents have not been successful. Neither antidepressants, antipsychotics, nor any other class of drugs has been found to lead to significant weight gain, improve distorted attitudes or beliefs, or supplement inpatient programs (Bulik, Berkman, Brownley, Sedway, & Lohr, 2007).

PSYCHOLOGICAL TREATMENTS

COGNITIVE-BEHAVIOUR THERAPY (CBT) More than 50 randomized controlled trials of treatments for bulimia nervosa have been conducted. On the basis of this research, CBT is considered the leading evidence-based treatment for bulimia and is widely accepted as the treatment of choice among clinicians (Fairburn, 2008; Whittal et al., 1999). According to the cognitive-behavioural model of the maintenance of bulimia, overvaluation of body weight and shape leads to excessive restriction, which leaves the individual both psychologically and physiologically susceptible to episodes of binge eating. Purging and other excessive means of controlling body weight or shape serve to compensate for binge eating but also maintain binge eating by reducing the individual's anxiety about weight gain and by disrupting learned hunger and satiety cues. Episodes of binge eating and inappropriate compensatory behaviours worsen self-esteem, thereby leading to more dietary restraint and thus more binge eating (Fairburn, 2002).

Individual CBT for bulimia nervosa typically involves three stages that span approximately 20 weeks. In the first stage, the focus is on establishing some control over eating. This is accomplished through psychoeducation about normalized eating and the connection between restricting food intake and binge eating, and teaching patients to use behavioural strategies (e.g., meal planning, distraction, stimulus control) to avoid acting on eating disorder urges. Self-monitoring is also used to help patients normalize their eating and identify triggers for symptoms. The second stage involves a continued focus on normalized eating, especially with respect to eliminating dieting. This stage also focuses on teaching problem-solving skills and identifying and modifying dysfunctional thoughts and beliefs (especially about body weight and shape). The third stage focuses on strategies for maintaining change and preventing relapse (Fairburn, 2008; Fairburn, Marcus, & Wilson, 1993).

Fairburn and his colleagues have also proposed a cognitive-behavioural theory of the maintenance of anorexia (Fairburn, Shafran, & Cooper, 1998). They suggest that the central feature of anorexia nervosa is an extreme need to control eating and that, in Western society, a tendency to determine self-worth based on body weight and shape is superimposed on the need for control (see Figure 10.3). However, very few studies have examined the efficacy of CBT for anorexia nervosa. Research in this area is limited by small sample sizes and relatively large dropout rates (Bulik et al., 2007). One of the first studies that examined the efficacy of CBT for anorexia demonstrated that the control treatment (nonspecific supportive clinical management) was superior to CBT for individuals who completed the 20-session treatment (McIntosh et al., 2005), indicating that CBT does not seem to work as well for anorexia as for bulimia. However, a review of the literature suggests that CBT may be helpful in decreasing the risk of relapse for adults with anorexia (Bulik et al., 2007).

Most recently, Fairburn and colleagues have proposed a transdiagnostic theory and treatment of eating disorders (Fairburn, 2008; Fairburn et al., 2003). This theory argues that anorexia, bulimia, and EDNOS have similar underlying psychopathological processes and maintaining factors and therefore can be treated using similar CBT interventions. The transdiagnostic theory acknowledges that there are typically significant underlying issues in eating disorders other than dysfunctional beliefs about eating, weight/shape, and their control. Specifically, Fairburn and colleagues propose that perfectionism, low self-esteem, mood intolerance, and interpersonal difficulties interact with the core mechanisms that maintain eating disorders. Consequently, CBT for eating disorders has been expanded to address these potential underlying issues. This adapted form of CBT, which can be applied to all individuals with eating disorders, regardless of their specific diagnosis, has been called "enhanced CBT" (Cooper & Fairburn, 2011). Preliminary research shows that this enhanced CBT is an effective treatment for eating disorders (e.g., Byrne, Fursland, Allen, & Watson, 2011; Fairburn et al., 2009).

INTERPERSONAL THERAPY To date, only one other treatment has shown effects on bulimic symptoms that are comparable to those of CBT. In interpersonal therapy (IPT), the focus is on maladaptive personal relationships and ways of relating to others, because difficulties in these areas are thought to contribute to the development and maintenance of eating disorders (Birchall, 1999). In IPT, the major job of the therapist is to identify which problem area is relevant to the patient—grief, role transitions, interpersonal role disputes, or interpersonal deficits—and to work to improve the client's functioning in that area. IPT differs from CBT in that it does not directly target eating-disordered attitudes and behaviours.

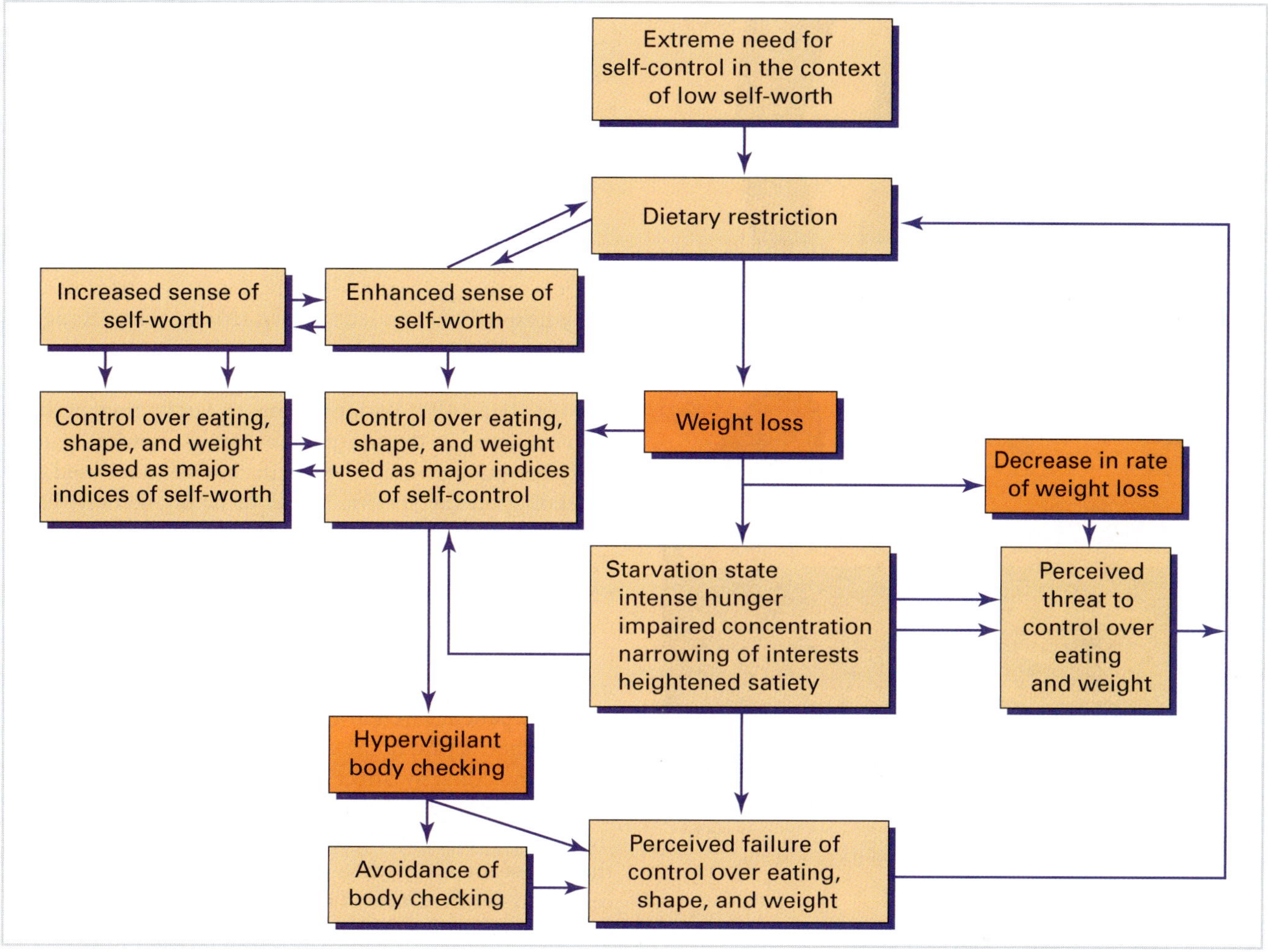

FIGURE 10.3 A Schematic Representation of Core Processes Involved in the Maintenance of Anorexia Nervosa

Source: Reprinted from *Behaviour Research and Therapy*, vol. 37, Christopher G. Fairburn, Roz Shafran, and Zafra Cooper, "A Cognitive Behavioural Theory," p. 6, Fig. 2, © 1999 with permission from Elsevier.

Interpersonal therapy for bulimia nervosa was developed by Fairburn and his colleagues to serve as a comparison treatment to CBT for the purpose of a research trial (Fairburn, Jones, Peveler, Hope, & O'Connor, 1993). In a well-conducted study, Fairburn and his colleagues found that patients with bulimia who received CBT experienced more than a 90 percent reduction in bingeing and purging one year after treatment. Nearly 40 percent of the patients had ceased bulimic symptoms altogether. What was surprising was the finding that IPT produced effects equivalent to CBT at one-year follow-up, although CBT was somewhat better at the conclusion of treatment. In another study, 220 patients with bulimia nervosa were randomly assigned to receive either CBT or IPT (Agras, Walsh, Fairburn, Wilson, & Kraemer, 2000). In line with the results of the previous study, these researchers found that CBT was superior to IPT at the end of the 20-week treatment period. Of the patients who completed treatment, 45 percent in the CBT group and 8 percent in the IPT group were abstinent from bulimic symptoms. Similarly, CBT led to larger reductions in dietary restraint than did IPT (see Figure 10.4). However, at 1-year follow-up there were no significant differences between CBT and IPT. It appears that individuals who received IPT tended to continue improving after the end of treatment, with 27 percent in the IPT group recovered at follow-up (relative to 40 percent of the CBT group, a non-significant difference). Although CBT is still considered the preferred treatment for bulimia nervosa because it reduces symptoms relatively quickly, IPT also appears to be an efficacious option.

NUTRITIONAL THERAPY AND MEAL SUPPORT When a patient has anorexia nervosa, the first priority should be to restore body weight to a minimal healthy level. This is primarily important for medical stability. However, many of the symptoms of anorexia nervosa are due to the effects of starvation. Weight restoration can alleviate many of these symptoms, including cognitive impairments, and is thus typically a prerequisite for psychotherapy. Meal support is often an important component of treatment programs for eating disorders. This involves providing emotional support during or after meals, normalizing eating behaviour,

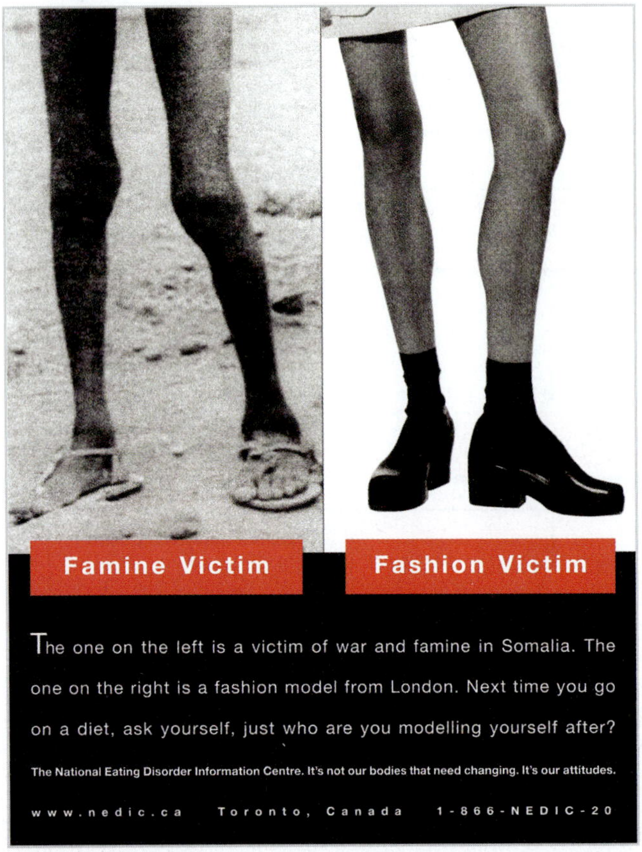

This is one of several public service announcements sponsored by the National Eating Disorder Information Centre in Toronto.

and helping individuals to decrease eating-related rituals (e.g., Leichner, Hall, & Calderon, 2005). Researchers at the British Columbia Children's Hospital have developed meal support training materials for parents of children and adolescents with eating disorders. These materials have been well received by the families, and are being used by clinicians to help involve families in the treatment process (Cairns, Styles, & Leichner, 2007). While these techniques are often integrated into therapy programs, some individuals with eating disorders may seek meal support outside of intensive treatment programs, such as in individual sessions with a dietitian. For example, in a community sample of women with bulimia nervosa, 37 percent of the women who had sought some treatment for their eating disorder had visited a dietitian, whereas only 11 percent had seen a psychiatrist or psychologist, and less than 4 percent had received intensive treatment in a day hospital or inpatient setting (Mond, Hay, Rodgers, & Owen, 2007).

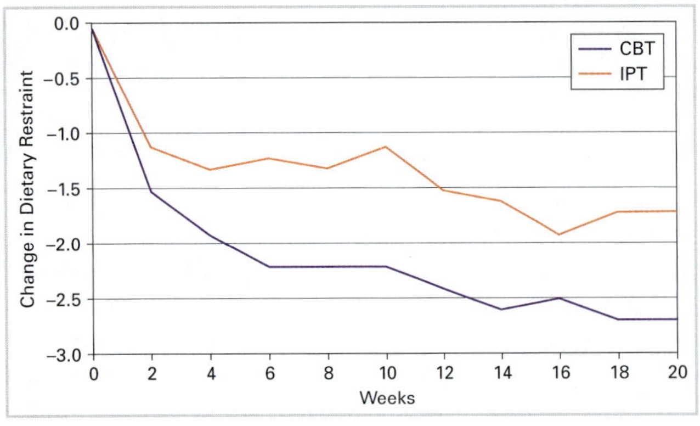

FIGURE 10.4 CBT versus IPT in the Treatment of Bulimia Nervosa

Source: Adapted from Agras, Walsh, Fairburn, Wilson & Kraemer (2000). A Multicenter Comparison of Cognitive-Behavioral Therapy and Interpersonal Psychotherapy for Bulimia Nervosa, *Archives of General Psychiatry,* Vol. 57, pp. 459-466.

FAMILY THERAPY Various forms of family therapy have been employed in the treatment of eating disorders, particularly anorexia nervosa. The specific interventions used vary depending on the specific model of family therapy; however, in general, family therapy focuses on stresses within the family as a whole rather than on individuals, and places responsibility for recovery on both the client and her relatives. Recently, the Maudsley approach has received attention in the research literature. This approach involves an initial focus on recruiting parents to engage actively in managing the patient's weight gain (where relevant) and eating. No attention is paid to the cause of the disorder or to factors that do not directly affect the task of normalized eating. As eating improves and weight approaches normal levels, the therapist helps the family to return control of eating to the adolescent. Only when eating and weight are no longer central to family concerns does the therapist turn to more general adolescent issues independent of the eating disorder (Lock & le Grange, 2005). There is limited evidence of the efficacy of the Maudsley approach. Nonetheless, the available evidence is promising in the treatment of adolescents. For example, one small study of anorexia found significant improvements over time in body weight, menstrual status, and restraint but not in weight and shape concerns (Loeb et al., 2007). With respect to bulimia, a randomized controlled trial found that more adolescent individuals who received family therapy were abstinent from bingeing and purging (even at six-month follow-up) compared to those who received supportive counselling (le Grange, Crosby, Rathouz, & Leventhal, 2007). In contrast, there is not good evidence of the effectiveness of family therapy as a stand-alone treatment in adults.

SELF-HELP Self-help manuals that seek to disseminate information about eating disorders and strategies for overcoming bulimia and BED have been developed in response to the fact that therapists who specialize in eating disorders are in short supply and that large numbers of individuals with eating disorders do not seek treatment. The majority of these manuals are based on cognitive-behavioural principles. Self-help manuals may be used in several different manners, including (1) for provision of an accessible form of information for individuals who might not otherwise have access to expert help, or who may feel too embarrassed to seek treatment; (2) in conjunction with guidance by a non-specialist professional such as a nurse or family doctor; (3) as the first step in a stepped-care approach to treatment delivery, with only those who require further treatment going on to more intensive (and thus more costly) treatments; (4) for administration to patients who are on waiting lists for intensive treatment; and (5) for facilitation of therapist-administered CBT (Carter, 2002).

Published studies of self-help interventions for bulimia nervosa and BED indicate that they provide an efficacious treatment. In a randomized controlled trial conducted at Toronto General Hospital, Carter and colleagues (2003) examined the efficacy of two unguided self-help treatments for bulimia nervosa: a CBT manual and a nonspecific interpersonal treatment manual. These researchers found equivalent significant reductions in frequency of bingeing and vomiting in both of the self-help groups (these reductions did not occur in the control group). Carter and Fairburn (1998) compared the relative effectiveness of guided and unguided self-help for BED in a randomized controlled trial. Participants assigned to the unguided self-help group followed a CBT manual for a period of 12 weeks. Participants assigned to the guided self-help group followed the same treatment manual for the same period of time but also received six to eight brief support sessions with a non-specialist facilitator. Both self-help treatments resulted in statistically significant and equivalent reductions in frequency of episodes of binge eating. There was a similar pattern of results for eating-disordered attitudes.

Self-help treatments are just beginning to be applied to anorexia. A recent study examined the efficacy of cognitive-behavioural guided self-help compared to a waiting list control group before admission to an inpatient unit. Results showed that duration of inpatient treatment was significantly shorter among participants who received guided self-help (Fichter, Cebulla, Quadflieg, & Naab, 2008). It is unlikely that self-help will turn out to be an efficacious stand-alone treatment for anorexia given that individuals typically require high levels of support and guidance to make the behavioural and attitudinal changes necessary for recovery.

5 BEFORE MOVING ON

What are the main differences between the different psychological treatment approaches (i.e., CBT, IPT, and family therapy)? What approach would you recommend to an 18-year-old woman diagnosed with bulimia? Why would you recommend this type of therapy?

PREVENTION

Interventions for eating disorders are predominantly therapeutic. In other words, researchers and clinicians have focused on developing and providing therapies for individuals who have already developed eating disorders. However, some researchers have investigated whether providing preventive intervention programs can decrease the presence of risk factors for the development of eating disorders, and ultimately prevent disordered eating behaviours. One such program, Healthy Schools–Healthy Kids, was applied universally to all Grade 6 and 7 students who participated in the study. This program, developed in Toronto by Gail McVey and her colleagues (McVey, Tweed, & Blackmore, 2007), randomly assigned four schools to either an intervention condition or a control (no intervention) group for comparison. The intervention lasted throughout the school year and incorporated a variety of approaches, including in-class curriculum, a "Girl Talk" peer support group, parent education, and posters, video, and play presentations relating to teasing, peer pressure, size acceptance, and healthy eating. Participants who were exposed to the intervention reported a decrease in internalization of the socio-cultural ideal for weight/shape from baseline to post-intervention, and a further decrease at follow-up (six months post-intervention). In contrast, participants in the control condition exhibited a decrease in internalization from baseline to post-intervention, yet at the six-month follow-up their scores were not significantly different from baseline. This pattern of findings suggests that the intervention was successful in reducing internalization of the socio-cultural ideal. Further supporting the success of the intervention was the finding that disordered eating (measured in girls only) decreased significantly for those in the intervention group from baseline to post-intervention, but increased for those in the control groups.

Other programs have focused their preventive interventions on individuals who have been identified as "high risk" for the development of eating disorders. In one study, a group of young women between the ages of 18 and 30 who reported having high levels of concern about their weight were recruited to investigate the effectiveness of a prevention program (Taylor et al., 2006). A total of 480 women were randomly assigned to either a waitlist control group or an Internet-based prevention program. This prevention program, Student Bodies, was based on cognitive-behavioural strategies, with the aim to decrease body dissatisfaction and weight concerns. Those individuals who took part in the prevention program participated in an eight-week-long structured program in which they logged in once weekly to the program, read new material, and participated in online discussion groups. Participants' eating-disordered attitudes and behaviours were measured before and after the program, as well as one year after the intervention. Participants in the intervention condition reported larger decreases in weight concerns, eating pathology, and drive for thinness after the eight-week program (compared to those in the control group), and these effects remained one year after the end of the program. The success of Internet-based prevention programs is promising, as this type of program may make it easier for individuals who are at risk for developing an eating disorder to access support.

To further investigate the effectiveness of prevention programs and to determine whether certain factors improve the success of an intervention, a meta-analysis evaluated the effectiveness of a total of 38 eating-disorder prevention programs, all of which included a control comparison group (Stice & Shaw, 2004). More than 50 percent of the interventions evaluated in the meta-analysis resulted in significant decreases in at least one risk factor for eating pathology (such as body dissatisfaction). This meta-analysis further suggested that programs that selected "high-risk" participants produced larger decreases in body dissatisfaction, dieting, and eating pathology than did universally

CANADIAN RESEARCH CENTRE

Eating Disorders Program, Douglas Mental Health University Institute (Montreal, Quebec)

Established in 1986, the Eating Disorders Program (EDP) of the Douglas Mental Health University Institute is the largest and best-developed program in Quebec for people with anorexia and bulimia nervosa. Having a province-wide mandate, the EDP serves as a main hub in the effort to care for Quebecers with eating disorders, as well as a centre of clinical and research expertise. The EDP offers cutting-edge care, conducts clinical research to inform future treatment and prevention efforts, and offers training to health care professionals at various nodes in the health care system.

There are four different streams in the EDP's clinical program, each providing a different level of structure and support so as to match different individuals' needs: an outpatient clinic (offering individual, family/couple, and group therapy, as well as nutritional support); a day program (offering an 8-week, structured group therapy program, 4 days a week for 6 hours per day); a day hospital program (offering intensive support for those with severe eating disorders who do not require 24-hour medical support, 4 days a week for 10 hours per day over 8 weeks); and an inpatient unit (offering 24-hour hospitalization for those individuals with severe medical or psychological complications, or for whom outpatient support was not sufficient). Given the limited number of inpatient beds available, and the high costs associated with inpatient treatments, it is advantageous to have a stepped-care approach in which individuals are placed in a therapy that corresponds with the level of structure and support needed. Programs that involve alternatives to inpatient treatment also offer the important advantage of allowing individuals to integrate their behavioural changes within their home environment.

A multidisciplinary team provides clinical care for individuals in the program. This team is led by Dr. Howard Steiger, a clinical psychologist. The other members of the clinical team include two part-time psychiatrists, two additional psychologists, an occupational therapist, a dietitian, three social workers, a counsellor, and several nurses and nursing assistants. Each discipline and individual brings specialized experience and expertise to the team (e.g., the dietitian offers specific knowledge about nutrition, whereas the psychologists have extensive training in assessment and research). However, team members across disciplines also share similar roles in providing psychotherapy sessions, and supervision and coaching during meals that take place in the program. The program offers a multimodal, integrated approach that includes behavioural strategies (e.g., normalizing eating patterns, breaking bingeing/purging cycles), psychoeducation, cognitive interventions (e.g., evaluating thoughts and beliefs and challenging automatic or irrational thoughts that may be linked with maladaptive eating patterns), and techniques oriented toward interpersonal problems and comorbid disturbances (Bruce & Steiger, 2006; Steiger & Israel, 2009).

As the provincial centre for eating disorders in Quebec, the EDP provides specialized training across disciplines as one of its mandates. In addition to clinical care and training provided directly at the Douglas Institute, the program provides support and services throughout Quebec. Specialized knowledge transfer programs provide partnership and support to community health centres around the province. Where the shared-care arrangements have taken hold, waiting times for people in those regions have gone down—individuals in need are now getting informed care in their communities, in the hands of clinicians who are backed up by experts from the EDP.

The Eating Disorders Program aims to provide the best clinical care possible. To maintain this "best practice" culture, it is necessary to conduct research on the effectiveness of the different treatments offered, and on how to improve treatment outcomes. The research program is based on the biopsychosocial model of eating disorders, and involves studies that cut across different themes, including investigating the roles of social factors (such as dieting), psychological traits and individual differences (e.g., personality traits like impulsivity), life stresses, and genetic and biological factors in the risk of developing eating disorders. The ultimate aim of this research is to guide the development of more effective and specialized treatments for individuals with eating disorders. One ongoing project, currently funded by the Klarman Family Foundation Grants Program in Eating Disorders, is investigating the effects of repeated transcranial magnetic stimulation in adults with eating disorders, with the aim of characterizing brain activation patterns in women with anorexia and bulimia nervosa. Another project, funded by the Canadian Institutes of Health Research, is investigating biopsychosocial bases for differences in treatment outcomes in individuals with bulimia nervosa. Results from this project have demonstrated that bulimia nervosa appears to result from an interaction between biological traits (i.e., genetic variations leading to increased reactivity to stress) and stressful life events (such as childhood abuse; Steiger et al., 2011).

applied programs. One possible explanation for the improved success of targeted programs is that high-risk participants may be more motivated by the intervention programs because they experience more weight/shape-related distress, and therefore they may engage more in these programs than do those individuals with low levels of eating pathology (Stice & Shaw, 2004).

6 BEFORE MOVING ON

What are some of the advantages and disadvantages of prevention programs that are targeted toward high-risk groups (as opposed to universally applied)? Do you think more schools should implement eating disorder prevention programs? Why or why not?

SUMMARY

- Eating disorders have been described for hundreds—even thousands—of years, but until recently they appear to have been relatively rare, and they were not always seen as evidence of maladjustment. Although eating disorders have become relatively common in modern Western societies, voluntary self-starvation and periods of binge eating and purging have been reported throughout history.
- According to the DSM-IV-TR, the central feature of anorexia nervosa is refusal to maintain one's body weight at a minimal level considered to be normal for one's height and weight. Individuals with anorexia have an intense fear of gaining weight or becoming fat. They often believe that eating feared or forbidden foods will result in significant amounts of weight gain. In addition, a variety of other maladaptive or ritualistic eating behaviours may be present. Individuals with anorexia nervosa typically achieve and maintain their low body weight through food restriction and exercising (and are classified as "restricting type"). However, some individuals with anorexia also engage in purging behaviours to achieve or maintain weight loss. Many individuals with anorexia who purge also engage in binge eating. These individuals, who engage in binge eating and/or purging, are classified as "binge eating/purging type." Anorexia nervosa also involves disturbed attitudes and beliefs related to body weight and shape. Finally, the DSM-IV-TR requires that females who are past puberty have missed at least three menstrual periods in order to be diagnosed with anorexia nervosa.
- Bulimia nervosa is characterized by fluctuations between episodes of binge eating and engaging in compensatory behaviours to prevent weight gain. As in anorexia nervosa, individuals with bulimia nervosa often have low self-esteem and use weight and shape as a primary method of self-evaluation. Other features, such as social isolation and depression, are also common in both anorexia and bulimia nervosa. However, in contrast to anorexia nervosa, individuals with bulimia are typically within the normal weight range. According to the DSM-IV-TR, episodes of binge eating and compensatory behaviours must occur, on average, at least twice a week for three months in order to give a diagnosis of bulimia nervosa. There are two subtypes of bulimia nervosa: purging type and nonpurging type.
- The DSM-IV-TR also acknowledges eating disorders of clinical severity that do not meet current diagnostic criteria. These eating disorders are classified as "eating disorders not otherwise specified" (EDNOS). In some individuals, these eating disorders resemble the full syndromes of anorexia or bulimia nervosa, and in other individuals the psychopathological features of the eating disorder combine in a somewhat different way. Binge-eating disorder (BED) is currently considered a special case of EDNOS. There have been several proposed changes to the eating disorders section for the upcoming DSM-5, including changes to the diagnostic criteria for anorexia and bulimia nervosa, and the possibility of adding BED as a formal eating disorder.
- There appears to have been an increase in the prevalence of eating disorders over the last several decades, although it is unclear to what extent the increase is due to an enhanced awareness about eating disorders. In Canada, the lifetime prevalence of bulimia nervosa for women is about 1 percent and for men is 0.1 percent. In the United States and Western Europe, the prevalence of anorexia is estimated at 0.3 percent among women and less than 0.001 percent among men. The prevalence of eating disorders in Canada is similar to the prevalence in other Western countries.
- Assessment for diagnostic purposes and to guide treatment planning is usually conducted using a structured or semi-structured interview. Conducting a diagnostic interview for an eating disorder involves gathering information about current and past frequency and severity of dietary restriction, bingeing, purging, and exercise, as well as distorted attitudes and beliefs about weight, shape, and eating, weight history, and current and past menstrual function. Clinicians and researchers often use the Eating Disorder Examination to gather this information.
- Eating disorders are multidetermined. They are very complex disorders, and one factor alone does not produce an eating disorder in any given individual. Our society's preference for thinness has led to a great deal of body dissatisfaction and dieting among young women. In vulnerable individuals, this body dissatisfaction and dieting may precipitate an eating disorder. Factors such as low self-esteem, issues with control, family dysfunction, abuse, and early maturation may leave an individual susceptible to developing an eating disorder. There also appears to be a genetic and

biological predisposition to developing an eating disorder. Although integrative models and theories attempt to address the complexity of eating disorders and the many identified etiological factors, they have not yet provided predictive power sufficient to identify the individuals most likely to develop eating disorders.

- There have been few controlled studies of treatments for anorexia nervosa. Weight restoration to a minimal healthy level is of primary importance. There is some evidence that CBT can be beneficial in preventing relapse in adults, and that family therapy is a good option for adolescents. Although antidepressant medication has not been shown to be effective in the treatment of anorexia nervosa, it is helpful in the treatment of bulimia nervosa. However, research suggests that antidepressants such as Prozac are inferior to CBT in the treatment of bulimia nervosa. CBT is considered the treatment of choice for bulimia nervosa. Nevertheless, IPT produces equivalent effects over the longer term.
- Research on the prevention of eating disorders is emerging, with some promising results. Prevention programs that target "high-risk" participants (such as women with high levels of body dissatisfaction) produced larger decreases in body dissatisfaction, dieting, and eating pathology than did universally applied programs.

MySearchLab offers you extensive help with your writing and research projects and provides round-the-clock access to credible and reliable source material. Chapter quizzes and a full electronic version of the text are also provided. Answers to the Before Moving On feature are provided on the MySearchLab. Take a tour at www.mysearchlab.com.

KEY TERMS

anorexia nervosa (p. 234)
bulimia nervosa (p. 234)
purging (p. 235)
objective binge (p. 235)
body mass index (BMI) (p. 238)
amenorrhea (p. 239)
restricting type (p. 239)
binge eating/purging type (p. 239)
purging type (p. 240)
nonpurging type (p. 240)
Eating Disorder Examination (EDE) (p. 243)
lanugo (p. 243)
Russell's sign (p. 243)
precipitating factors (p. 250)
perpetuating factors (p. 250)

DAVID HODGINS • TERRI-LYNN MACKAY

Chapter 11

Substance-Related Disorders

LEARNING OBJECTIVES

AFTER READING THIS CHAPTER, STUDENTS WILL BE ABLE TO:

1. Explain how substance-related disorders are defined and diagnosed.
2. Understand and describe the effects, etiology, and treatment approaches related to alcohol abuse.
3. Comprehend trends in the prevalence of substance use in Canada.
4. Identify the psychological and physiological effects of various substances of abuse.
5. Describe the most common treatment approaches for substance-related disorders.

At age 39, Gareth found himself in group therapy describing how he had lost his job and almost lost his life. When he thought back to how it had all begun, he found it difficult to pinpoint when using drugs and alcohol ceased to be fun and a social activity and began to be necessary to maintain day-to-day functioning. Somehow, he had gone from having the world by the tail as an executive at a software company to living in a treatment facility, wondering if he would ever be able to stay off drugs and rebuild his life.

At first, Gareth drank to keep up with his co-workers and business clients, many of whom regularly had "liquid lunches." Although he didn't really like the way alcohol made him feel in the afternoon, he soon found that a little of "the hair of the dog that bit you" at the bar after work helped him to feel better for the drive home. He also found alcohol more pleasing at parties and was able to drink more without getting drunk.

At a party held by a business associate, Gareth was introduced to cocaine, which gave him the energy for extended parties and alleviated the hangovers he often experienced after a night of drinking. He was also amazed by the way that cocaine improved his concentration, energy, and creativity. When high on cocaine he could work longer hours without taking a break, and he began to feel as if he could accomplish anything he set his mind to. The only drawback was the cost of the cocaine, but even that he could handle because he was doing so well in his job.

As he began to use cocaine more frequently, Gareth found that he often needed alcohol or "downers" to help him relax and fall asleep in the evenings. His physician was willing to prescribe benzodiazepines when Gareth explained that he was in a high-pressure job and had trouble sleeping because he worked odd hours and travelled to different time zones. Of course, the benzodiazepine and alcohol use at night meant he was often groggy in the morning and needed cocaine to help him function. His co-workers began to notice changes in Gareth's personality and decreased productivity. Gareth was in danger of losing his job.

One night, this cycle of abuse caught up with Gareth. He had been drinking with some customers right after work and came home at about 7:00 p.m. Tired, he decided to skip dinner and have a nap but could not sleep, so he took a couple of sleeping pills and had another stiff drink. The combination of benzodiazepines and a considerable amount of alcohol on an empty stomach resulted in a loss of consciousness. When his wife got home around 8:00 p.m., she found him asleep on the sofa and could not awaken him. She immediately phoned 911, and help arrived in time. The interview in the emergency room later that evening revealed the drug roller coaster that Gareth was on. His physician and wife insisted that he go directly to a treatment facility and he agreed.

Historically, virtually every culture has employed some legally or socially sanctioned drugs to alter moods or states of consciousness. In our culture, the most widely used substances are alcohol, tobacco, and caffeine, all of which are legal and (at least to some extent) socially acceptable. Many people begin their day with a cup of tea or coffee. Other people include a cigarette. Parties and other social events for adults almost always include alcohol. Although the immediate effects of these substances are usually pleasant, history is full of accounts of the devastating long-term impact of addictive substances.

Historical Perspective

Alcohol and drug use have been around longer than recorded history. Mead, an alcoholic beverage naturally formed by the fermentation of honey, was probably the first alcohol that humans consumed. The ancient Egyptians were known for their drinking, and wine was extensively used by the Hebrews.

Opium derivatives were once widely used in Asian cultures, as well as in ancient Greece and Rome. Therapeutically, they were taken to relieve pain or induce sleep; however, the euphoria that these drugs produced resulted in their widespread use to enhance pleasure. In the Andes, for thousands of years, native populations occasionally chewed the leaf of the coca plant to relieve fatigue and increase endurance. The flower of the peyote cactus has long been used by tribes in South and Central America as part of religious ceremonies. The chemical contained in this flower was valued for its ability to alter consciousness and results in hallucinations similar to those caused by LSD.

The effects of substance abuse were particularly grim as the Europeans colonized North and South America. Alcohol, in the form of beer, was widely consumed, in part because of the poor quality of drinking water. The tavern became the hub of social activity in the colonies and alcohol was an integral part of all social and festive occasions. Consumption levels were extremely high by current standards, even among children. When North American Aboriginal people were introduced to European brandy, they discovered a means of being transported into a strange new world of experience. In an inebriated state, people committed crimes and acts of self-destruction previously unheard of (Douville & Casanova, 1967). A hunter might trade his entire winter's catch of furs for a jug or two of whisky, leading to misery and starvation. As a final insult, liquor reduced resistance to many imported diseases (Eccles, 1959).

South American cultures suffered similar effects. Prior to the arrival of the Spanish, alcohol was consumed only collectively, as part of religious ceremonies. A few years after the conquest, Aboriginal people commonly used alcohol to escape from the confusion of their disrupted world (Bethell, 1984). There was also a striking increase in the use of coca leaf in the Andes. Formerly used only with the permission of the Inca king or his governor, coca became indispensable for Quechua mine workers because it enabled them to work almost without eating (Bethell, 1984).

TABLE 11.1 DSM-IV-TR DIAGNOSTIC CRITERIA FOR SUBSTANCE ABUSE

A. A maladaptive pattern of substance use leading to clinically significant impairment or distress, as manifested by one (or more) of the following, occurring within a 12-month period:

(1) recurrent substance use resulting in a failure to fulfill major role obligations at work, school, or home (e.g., repeated absences or poor work performance related to substance use; substance-related absences, suspensions, or expulsions from school; neglect of children or household)

(2) recurrent substance use in situations in which it is physically hazardous (e.g., driving an automobile or operating a machine when impaired by substance use)

(3) recurrent substance-related legal problems (e.g., arrests for substance-related disorderly conduct)

(4) continued substance use despite having persistent or recurrent social or interpersonal problems caused or exacerbated by the effects of the substance (e.g., arguments with spouse about consequences of intoxication, physical fights)

B. The symptoms have never met the criteria for Substance Dependence for this class of substance.

Source: Reprinted with permission from the *Diagnostic and Statistical Manual of Mental Disorders, Fourth Edition, Text Revision.* (Copyright © 2000). American Psychiatric Association.

Alcoholism: Chris

Watch this Speaking Out video at www.mysearchlab.com

Diagnosis and Assessment

DEFINING SUBSTANCE-RELATED CONCEPTS

Several concepts associated with substance-related disorders require explanation. In DSM-IV-TR, the term **substance intoxication** is used to describe a reversible and temporary condition due to the recent ingestion of (or exposure to) a substance. To qualify for this diagnosis, a person must demonstrate clinically significant maladaptive behavioural or cognitive changes, such as belligerence, disturbed perception, altered mood, and impaired thought processes or motor behaviour, as a direct result of the substance.

Substance abuse refers to recurrent substance use that results in significant adverse consequences in social or occupational functioning (see Table 11.1). For example, a person intoxicated by a substance or recuperating from its use may fail to fulfill major obligations, such as a university examination. Interpersonal relationships may deteriorate or come to an end as a result. Substance abuse may also include using the substance in hazardous situations, such as drinking and driving or sexual behaviours that increase the risk for HIV infection. The term *addiction* has commonly been used to describe lack of control over substance use, to the point that a person may feel enslaved. DSM-IV-TR uses the term **substance dependence** to describe this condition (see Table 11.2). However, this terminology will change in the DSM-5 (see Focus box 11.1).

There are two forms of dependence: physiological and psychological. **Physiological dependence** is defined largely in terms of *tolerance* and *withdrawal* symptoms. **Tolerance** means that the person needs increased amounts of the substance to achieve the same effect. Individuals suffering from **withdrawal** experience unpleasant and sometimes dangerous symptoms such as nausea, headache, or tremors when the addictive substance is removed from the body. These physiological events are a result of the changes that the body has undergone in order to adapt to the continued presence of the drug. Specific drugs have predictable groups of symptoms typically characterized by overactivity of the physiological functions that were suppressed by the substance and/or depression of the functions that were stimulated by the substance. Additional ingestion of the specific drug, or one that is closely related, will alleviate these symptoms.

TABLE 11.2 DSM-IV-TR DIAGNOSTIC CRITERIA FOR SUBSTANCE DEPENDENCE

A maladaptive pattern of substance use, leading to clinically significant impairment or distress, as manifested by three (or more) of the following, occurring at any time in the same 12-month period:

(1) tolerance, as defined by either of the following:
 (a) a need for markedly increased amounts of the substance to achieve intoxication or desired effect
 (b) markedly diminished effect with continued use of the same amount of the substance
(2) withdrawal, as manifested by either of the following:
 (a) the characteristic withdrawal syndrome for the substance (refer to Criteria A and B of the criteria sets for Withdrawal from the specific substances)
 (b) the same (or a closely related) substance is taken to relieve or avoid withdrawal symptoms
(3) the substance is often taken in larger amounts or over a longer period than was intended
(4) there is a persistent desire or unsuccessful efforts to cut down or control substance use
(5) a great deal of time is spent in activities necessary to obtain the substance (e.g., visiting multiple doctors or driving long distances), use the substance (e.g., chain-smoking), or recover from its effects
(6) important social, occupational, or recreational activities are given up or reduced because of substance use
(7) the substance use is continued despite knowledge of having a persistent or recurrent physical or psychological problem that is likely to have been caused or exacerbated by the substance (e.g., current cocaine use despite recognition of cocaine-induced depression, or continued drinking despite recognition that an ulcer was made worse by alcohol consumption)

Specify if:

With Physiological Dependence: evidence of tolerance or withdrawal (that is, either Item 1 or 2 is present)

Without Physiological Dependence: no evidence of tolerance or withdrawal (that is, neither Item 1 nor 2 is present)

Source: Reprinted with permission from the *Diagnostic and Statistical Manual of Mental Disorders, Fourth Edition, Text Revision.* (Copyright © 2000). American Psychiatric Association.

Of course, this is part of the vicious circle that maintains dependence.

Psychological dependence, a more recent concept, is also known as **habituation** and refers to being psychologically accustomed to a substance or activity as a consequence of regular usage. When the substance or activity is unavailable, feelings of restlessness, irritability, and uneasiness may be experienced. An indication of psychological dependence

FOCUS 11.1

Back to the Future: Addiction in the DSM-5

A number of significant changes in how we conceptualize substance use disorders are proposed for the DSM-5 (APA, 2010). One major change is in terminology. Since the third edition, the term *dependence* has been used to avoid more pejorative terms like *alcoholic* and *addict*. In the DSM-IV-TR, *dependence* refers to both psychological and physiological aspects of reliance on substances. However, the term is confusing—as in other arenas, tolerance refers to a physiological dependence, which may or may not be related to addiction. For example, an individual prescribed pain medications after surgery quickly develops physical tolerance and typically will experience physiological withdrawal when the medication is discontinued. However, the individual does not show any signs of addiction, such as use of the drug to manage feelings or compulsive use. The proposal for the DSM-5 is that we revert to the use of the term *addiction* and drop the use of *dependence*. The proposed name for the section of the DSM that includes alcohol and other drugs is "Addiction and Related Disorders."

A second major change recognizes that the boundary between substance abuse and substance dependence is often unclear and possibly artificial. The proposal for DSM-5 is for one diagnostic disorder for each substance (e.g., alcohol use disorder) that will be subtyped as moderate or severe depending on the number of diagnostic criteria that an individual shows. DSM-5 will include the current abuse and dependence criteria plus one additional criterion assessing whether a person experiences craving for a substance. The advantage of this proposed change is that it recognizes that substance use problems exist on a continuum from mild to severe.

Another change is related to the broadening of the section to include non-substance-related addictions, often referred to as *behavioural addictions.* At this point, only one behavioural addiction is sufficiently well studied and understood to be included in the DSM-5: gambling disorder. This disorder is labelled pathological gambling in the DSM-IV-TR and is included in a section of the manual called "Impulse Control Disorders" (see Focus box 11.5 for more information on gambling disorders).

Close consideration was given to including Internet addiction as a formal diagnosis as well. However, because research support is limited, a set of tentative diagnostic criteria will be included in the DSM-5 appendix as a way of encouraging further study. It is expected that other behavioural addictions, such as sex addiction and work addiction, will also be candidates for future DSM editions.

Speaking Out Impulse Control: Ed

Watch this Speaking Out video at www.mysearchlab.com

Speaking Out Impulse Control: Living with Impulse Control Disorder

Watch this Speaking Out video at www.mysearchlab.com

is spending increasing amounts of time obtaining or using the substance, and restricting work and social activities that preclude substance use. For example, a person might stay away from an otherwise desirable party if smoking is not allowed. Others may eat only in restaurants where alcohol is served. A core aspect of psychological dependence is **impairment of control** over the use of the substance. Impairment of control is evidenced by exceeding the amounts of a substance or time using a substance than intended by the individual. For example, a man may plan to stop for a quick drink at the neighbourhood pub on his way home to dinner but end up spending a few hours and drinking a number of drinks. In traditional conceptions of alcoholism, impairment of control was referred to as loss of control. Behavioural psychologists have demonstrated that contingencies, rewards, and punishments can influence use of a substance in even the most dependent of individuals, which suggests that control is impaired as opposed to entirely lost.

POLYSUBSTANCE ABUSE

Research into the short-term and long-term effects of substance use and abuse is plagued by the issue of **polysubstance abuse**, the simultaneous misuse or dependence upon two or more substances. In fact, concurrent dependence appears to be the rule rather than the exception. For example, 80 percent of problem drinkers also smoke cigarettes, and many are likely addicted to both (Romberger & Grant, 2004). Research has shown that more than half of cocaine users are dependent on alcohol (Higgins, Budney, Bickel, Foerg, & Badger, 1994), and more than half of all amphetamine users also abuse benzodiazepines (Darke, Ross, & Cohen, 1994). Opioid addicts often abuse alcohol, cocaine-crack, and benzodiazepines, and increasingly illicit use of opioids such as heroin is being augmented with legal prescription opioids such as oxycodone (Oxycontin), codeine, morphine, and hydrocodone (Vicodin; Fischer, Cruz, & Rehm, 2006). Sometimes the pattern is that of concurrent, alternating use. To prevent the excessive excitement, irritability, and insomnia associated with chronic amphetamine use, addicts will often consume barbiturates when they want to "come down" or sleep. Later, amphetamines will be used to reduce the sedative effects or morning drowsiness caused by the barbiturates. Polysubstance abuse appears to be on the rise and is more common in young people (Newcomb, 1994). In a study of Ontario high school students (Paglia-Boak, Mann, Adlaf, & Rehm, 2009), about 6 in 10 reported using alcohol, tobacco, cannabis, or another illicit drug in the past year. Figure 11.1 depicts the overlap of substance use. It appears that alcohol is the most common

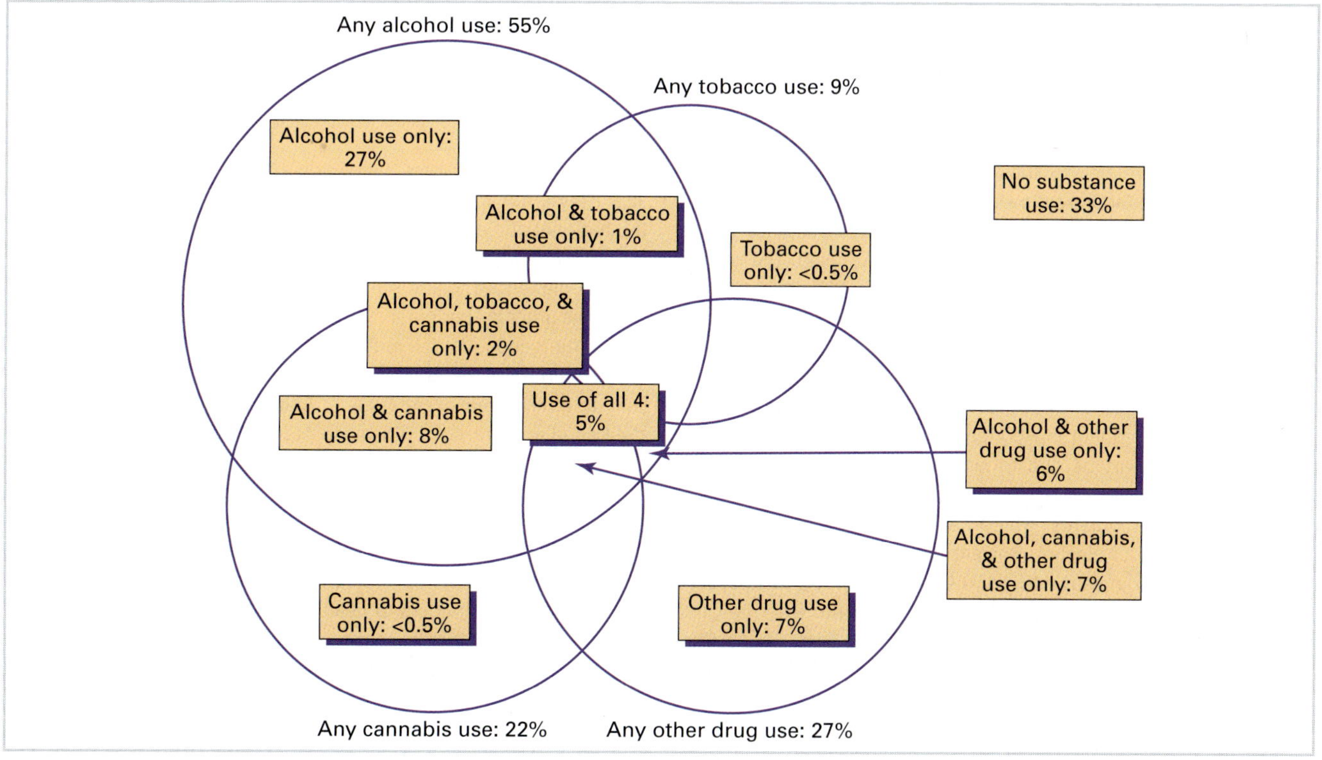

FIGURE 11.1 The Overlap of Alcohol, Cannabis, and Other Drug Use in the Past Year, Ontario Student Drug Use Survey 2009 (Grades 7 to 12)

Source: Ontario Student Drug Use and Health Survey (Paglia-Boak, Adlaf, & Mann, 2011).

element of involvement in other substance use. A very small proportion of students use cannabis exclusively (less than 1 percent), almost no students smoke cigarettes exclusively, and 9 percent use any other drug exclusively.

There are a number of health and treatment concerns related to polysubstance abuse. Combining drugs is physically dangerous because they are often synergistic. That is, the combined effects of the drugs exceed or are significantly different from the sum of their individual effects. For example, mixing alcohol and barbiturates or opioids may depress central nervous system (CNS) functioning to a much greater degree than any of these substances alone. Amphetamines and other stimulants, when combined with alcohol, cause physical damage greater than the damage that would be caused by the drugs if they were taken separately (Comer, 1997). To complicate matters, individuals with a history of polysubstance abuse are likely to have more diagnosable mental problems than individuals who abuse only one substance (Darke et al., 1994). When treatment is considered, the drug that presents the more immediate threat to health (e.g., opioids, cocaine, alcohol) tends to overshadow others (e.g., smoking, marijuana). However, it is not clear which dependence should be treated first, or whether all should be treated at the same time.

Case Notes

"When did things start to fall apart?" thought Marianne. Certainly, the car accident had a lot to do with it. She could still vividly remember that evening five years ago. She was to have gone to Florida with Luc that week, but he told her he wanted to end their relationship. So instead she drove the five hours to Toronto to take a computer graphics course. Driving home after three gruelling days, she fell asleep at the wheel and crashed into a wall of rock. She awoke in the hospital with a fractured spine.

Fortunately, she was able to walk again. Three weeks later, she went back to an empty home and a long recuperation. The medications provided by the hospital helped to control the pain and let her sleep. Combined with alcohol, she discovered, they worked even better. The alcohol also dulled her nagging worries about the future.

Eventually, her injuries healed and she again found employment. She managed to stop taking the pain medication, but kept on drinking. Alcohol dulled her back pain, and it made her feel good. She fell into the habit of having a few drinks alone at home each night, often falling asleep in front of the television. She often resolved not to drink that night, but the loneliness and back pain were too much to bear without alcohol. She convinced herself she was not really an alcoholic because she never drank during the day and was never really drunk. Nevertheless, her concentration was off, her work began to suffer, and her social life dwindled. She finally realized that she had a problem and made inquiries about professional services but, as yet, was too ashamed and frightened to admit that she needed help.

FOCUS 11.2

Aboriginal Canadians

Issues related to substance abuse in Canada's Aboriginal populations are a significant social concern, although there is little specific information about substance abuse and related problems among this group. Although the rate of alcohol use by Aboriginal Canadians does not appear to be greater than that of other Canadians, there is some evidence that the impact of alcohol may be greater in these communities. Health problems associated with alcohol use, including dependency, alcoholic psychosis, and liver disease, are significantly more frequent in Aboriginal populations (Scott, 1994). This may in part be due to significantly higher rates of use for most other drugs, such as nicotine, marijuana, solvents, heroin, and stimulants, which can compound the deleterious health effects of alcohol. Solvent use (e.g., gasoline sniffing), although by no means limited to Aboriginal youth, has become a serious problem in some Aboriginal communities. The First Nations and Inuit Community and Youth Solvent Abuse Survey (Kaweionnehta Human Resource Group, 1993) indicated that one in five Aboriginal youth have tried solvents. Of these, 68 percent are males between 12 and 19 years of age. In British Columbia, however, a full 40 percent of solvent abusers are between the ages of 4 and 11. Solvent use is accompanied by serious medical problems, including respiratory difficulties, liver and kidney problems, blood abnormalities, and CNS damage. Aboriginal adolescent suicide rates are much higher than the national adolescent rate. It appears that fetal alcohol spectrum disorders (FASD) are much more prevalent among Aboriginal people. Tobacco and injection drug use are also particular concerns among Aboriginal populations, with, for example, one in five indigenous street youth in seven major Canadian cities reporting that they had injected drugs (Shields, 2000).

In an overview of the issue of Aboriginal substance abuse, the Canadian Centre on Substance Abuse (2004a) notes:

> Issues of poverty, low education, unstable family structure, unemployment, physical abuse, poor social support networks and involvement with the law are precipitated or aggravated by discrimination, the effects of residential schools, and barriers to health care such as language and the lack of culturally sensitive services. While these issues present a considerable challenge for which substance use is identified as a coping mechanism, many Aboriginal communities have succeeded in preventing or reducing substance use problems among their people. These communities are successfully applying community-wide, culturally-based solutions to problems that are largely socially determined.

1 BEFORE MOVING ON

How does the conceptualization of substance use disorders differ from DSM-IV-TR in the proposed DSM-5 revision?

Alcohol

HISTORY OF USE

Alcohol has been called the "world's number one psychoactive substance" (Ray & Ksir, 1990). By 6400 BC, people had discovered how to make alcohol in the form of beer and berry wine. The distillation process, in which the fermented solution containing alcohol is heated and the vapours are collected and condensed in liquid form again to create what were first called "spirits," is believed to have been discovered in Arabia. In addition to the Egyptians and the Hebrews, there is ample evidence that the Greeks enjoyed wine, and later Roman emperors were notorious for their insobriety. It is reported that the people who met Christopher Columbus in the Caribbean had their own form of beer, and the distillation of whisky was commonplace in Ireland by AD 1500, and occurred on a large scale in America by the eighteenth century. Alcohol was not used by Aboriginal Canadians until the French brought brandy and the British brought rum from Europe.

Concern for overuse of alcohol and attempts to regulate its consumption date back to earliest recordings of its use. All attempts to suppress alcohol in Europe and America from the fourteenth to the twentieth century have failed. In the United States, Prohibition came into effect in 1920, and did effectively reduce overall alcohol intake. Partial or complete prohibition was also introduced into the majority of Canadian provinces around the same time. However, there was widespread disrespect for the laws, leading to the growth of organized crime and bootlegging (illegal production and sale). Much of the bootlegging originated in Canada and was directed to the United States. Concern about this lawlessness, as well as an appreciation of the revenues to be gained by taxing liquor sales, led to the repeal of Prohibition soon after the Great Depression began. As might be expected, there was a gradual increase in alcohol consumption; per capita consumption equalled pre-Prohibition levels by the end of the Second World War, and continued to rise until it peaked in 1980–1981. Consumption dropped between 1981 and the late 1990s but has again begun to rise.

CANADIAN CONSUMPTION PATTERNS

In 2010, 13 615 Canadians aged 15 and older were interviewed about their alcohol use by telephone using a random digit dialing–type survey method (Health Canada, 2010a). This yearly survey was launched in 2008 and is similar to the Canadian Addiction Survey conducted in 1989, 1994, and 2004. In the most recent survey, approximately four out of every five Canadians (77 percent) reported drinking alcohol in the past 12 months, while 12 percent were former drinkers and 11 percent had never imbibed alcohol. These figures are slightly lower than those in the 2004 survey, where 79 percent had consumed alcohol in the past 12 months. The rate of past-year drinking is higher for men than for women (80 percent versus 74 percent).

People who drank alcohol in the past year can be divided into four categories according to the frequency of drinking and the number of drinks consumed (see Table 11.3 for a definition of a standard drink). The largest groups of drinkers are classified as light infrequent drinkers (less than weekly and fewer than five drinks per occasion) at 36 percent, and light frequent drinkers (more than weekly and fewer than five drinks per occasion) at 32 percent. About 5 percent are heavy infrequent drinkers

TABLE 11.3 CONVERTING ALCOHOLIC BEVERAGES INTO STANDARD DRINKS

Beverage (% alcohol)	Usual Bottle Size	Standard Drinks	Usual Serving	Number of Standard Drinks in a Usual Serving
Beer (5%)	340 mL (12 oz.)	1.0	12 oz. (340 mL)	1.0
Wine (12%)	750 mL (26.4 oz.)	5.3	5 oz. (140 mL)	1.0
	1000 mL (35.2 oz.)	7.0		
	1500 mL (52.8 oz)	10.6		
Fortified wine (18%)	750 mL (26.4 oz.)	7.5	3 oz. (85 mL)	1.0
Spirits (40%)	340 mL (12 oz.)	8.0	1.5 oz. (43 mL)	1.0
	710 mL (25 oz.)	16.6		
	1135 mL (40 oz.)	26.6		
Wine coolers (5–7%)	340 mL (12 oz.)	1.0–1.4	12 oz. (340 mL)	1.0–1.4
	variable sizes from 750 mL to 2 L			
Pre-mixed liquor beverages (5–7%)	340 mL (12 oz.)	1.0–1.4	12 oz. (340 mL)	1.0–1.4

Source: Hodgins, D. C., & Diskin, K. M. (2003). Alcohol Problems. In M. Nerson & S. M. Turner (Eds.), *Diagnostic Interviewing* (3rd ed.). New York: Kluwer.

TABLE 11.4 CANADA'S LOW-RISK DRINKING GUIDELINES

Drinking is a personal choice. If you choose to drink, these guidelines can help you decide when, where, why, and how.

Guideline 1

Reduce your long-term health risks by drinking no more than:
10 drinks a week for women, with no more than 2 drinks a day most days.
15 drinks a week for men, with no more than 3 drinks a day most days.
Set aside non-drinking days each week, so you do not develop the habit of drinking.

Guideline 2

Reduce your risk of injury and harm by drinking no more than 3 drinks (for women) and 4 drinks (for men) at any one time. Plan to drink in a safe environment. Stay within the weekly limits outlined in Guideline 1.

Guideline 3

Do not drink when you are driving a vehicle or using machinery and tools; taking medicine or other drugs that interact with alcohol; doing any kind of dangerous (extreme) physical activity; living with mental or physical health problems; living with alcohol dependence; pregnant or planning to be pregnant; responsible for the safety of others; making important decisions

Guideline 4

If you are pregnant, planning to become pregnant, or will soon begin breastfeeding, the safest choice is to drink no alcohol at all.

Guideline 5

If you are a child or youth, you should delay drinking until your late teens. Alcohol can harm the way your brain and body develop. Ask your parents for guidance and follow the local alcohol laws. If you are drinking, plan ahead and stay in control.

Source: Butt, P., Beirness, D., Cesa, F., Gliksman, L., Paradis, C., & Stockwell, T. (in press). *Alcohol and Health in Canada: A Summary of Evidence and Guidelines for Low-Risk Drinking.* Ottawa, ON: Canadian Centre on Substance Abuse.

(less than weekly and five or more drinks per occasion) and 4 percent are heavy frequent drinkers (more than weekly and five or more drinks per occasion).

Young adults are more likely to drink and to drink heavily; consumption peaks in the mid-twenties, then decreases. About 90 percent of youth aged 18 to 24 drink during the course of the year. Single people are more likely to be both casual and heavy drinkers; high-income earners and those with a post-secondary education are also more likely to be current drinkers. However, those with the least education and those out of work reported the heaviest drinking (Canadian Centre on Substance Abuse, 2004a).

Low-risk drinking guidelines have been established by the Canadian Centre on Substance Abuse and endorsed by many professional organizations (e.g., the Canadian Medical Association, the Canadian Paediatric Society, and the Council of Chief Medical Officers of Health) to provide an indication of the *upper limits* on drinking so that drinking is not likely to lead to physical impairment (see Table 11.4). According to low-risk drinking guidelines, daily alcohol intake should not exceed two drinks for women and three drinks for men, and weekly intake should not exceed 10 drinks for women and 15 drinks for men (Butt et al., in press).

Researchers at the CAMH (Adlaf, Demers, & Gliksman, 2005) surveyed alcohol and drug use among university students across the country. Overall, they found that 90 percent of all university students had consumed alcohol at some point in their lives. Eighty-six percent reported drinking in the past 12 months. The rates of drinking were highest in Quebec and the Atlantic provinces (89.7 percent and 85.6 percent, respectively), and were lowest in British Columbia (78.5 percent). Although they represented the highest number of drinkers, students from Quebec universities reported the lowest average weekly intake.

University students are also more likely to consume larger quantities on a single occasion, known as "binge drinking." In the survey of university students, 18.5 percent reported drinking five or more drinks twice per month or more. Male students reported drinking more often and more heavily than female students, and students living on their own or in residence drink more than those living at home.

HIGH-RISK DRINKING Alcohol researchers suggest that there is a direct relationship between the overall level of consumption within a population and the number of alcohol-dependent people. Moreover, there is a relationship between an individual's consumption and that person's risk. In the latest Canadian survey, the Alcohol Use Disorders Identification Test (AUDIT; Babor, de la Fuente, Saunders,

The devastation wrought by alcohol addiction is not a new thing. This woodcut captures the misery suffered by the addicted in eighteenth-century London.

TABLE 11.5 ALCOHOL USE DISORDERS IDENTIFICATION TEST (AUDIT)

Circle the number that comes closest to your actions during the past year.

1. How often do you have a drink containing alcohol?

Never	(0)	2 to 3 times a week	(3)
Monthly or less	(1)	4 or more times a week	(4)
2 to 4 times a month	(2)		

2. How many drinks containing alcohol do you have on a typical day when you are drinking?

1 or 2	(0)	7 to 9	(3)
3 or 4	(1)	10 or more	(4)
5 or 6	(2)		

3. How often do you have five or more drinks on one occasion?

Never	(0)	Weekly	(3)
Less than monthly	(1)	Daily or almost daily	(4)
Monthly	(2)		

4. How often during the past year have you found that you were not able to stop drinking once you had started?

Never	(0)	Weekly	(3)
Less than monthly	(1)	Daily or almost daily	(4)
Monthly	(2)		

5. How often during the last year have you failed to do what was normally expected from you because of drinking?

Never	(0)	Weekly	(3)
Less than monthly	(1)	Daily or almost daily	(4)
Monthly	(2)		

6. How often during the last year have you needed a first drink in the morning to get yourself going after a heavy drinking session?

Never	(0)	Weekly	(3)
Less than monthly	(1)	Daily or almost daily	(4)
Monthly	(2)		

7. How often during the last year have you had a feeling of guilt or remorse after drinking?

Never	(0)	Weekly	(3)
Less than monthly	(1)	Daily or almost daily	(4)
Monthly	(2)		

8. How often during the last year have you been unable to remember what happened the night before because you had been drinking?

Never	(0)	Weekly	(3)
Less than monthly	(1)	Daily or almost daily	(4)
Monthly	(2)		

9. Have you or someone else been injured as a result of your drinking?

No	(0)
Yes, but not in last year	(2)
Yes, during the last year	(4)

10. Has a relative or friend or a doctor or other health worker been concerned about your drinking or suggested you cut down?

No	(0)
Yes, but not in last year	(2)
Yes, during the last year	(4)

Scoring: Each answer is weighted from 0 to 4 as indicated in the brackets. Please note that questions 9 and 10 are scored 0, 2, or 4. A score of 8 or more indicates that a harmful level of alcohol consumption is likely.

Source: Audit from: Babor, T. F., & Higgins Biddle, J. (2002). *AUDIT: The Alcohol Use Disorders Identification Test: Guidelines for Use in Primary Care* (2nd ed.). © World Health Organization.

& Grant, 1992), a 10-question screening tool, was administered to current drinkers (see Table 11.5). The AUDIT was originally developed by the World Health Organization for use in a cross-cultural comparison of brief treatments for alcohol problems. The items were developed to minimize cultural differences in alcohol use and attitudes. The AUDIT has become widely used in surveys of prevalence in different populations, such as medical patients, students, employees, and the general population.

Validation studies of the AUDIT indicate that different cut-off scores are needed for different populations. For the general population, a cut-off of 8 is typically used to indicate high-risk drinking. The AUDIT was used in the 2004 Canadian national study. Among past-year–drinking Canadians, 17 percent of adults were identified as high risk. The proportion of men was 25 percent and of women was 9 percent. More than 30 percent of those under age 25 were high-risk drinkers compared with only 5 percent of people aged 65 and older (Canadian Centre on Substance Abuse, 2004a). The AUDIT was also used in the most recent survey of Ontario high school students (Paglia-Boak et al., 2009). High-risk drinking was reported by 21 percent of students in Grades 7 to 12.

EFFECTS

Ethyl alcohol is the effective chemical compound in alcoholic beverages. It reduces anxiety, produces euphoria, and creates a sense of well-being. It also reduces inhibitions, which adds to the perception that alcohol enhances social and physical pleasure, sexual performance, power, and social assertiveness.

Yet it appears that some of the short-term effects of ingesting small amounts of alcohol are as strongly related to the expectations of the effects of alcohol as they are to its chemical action on the body. In an interesting body of research, participants were told falsely that their drink contained alcohol. These individuals were found to behave more aggressively (Lang, Goeckner, Adessor, & Marlatt, 1975) and to report greater sexual arousal (Wilson & Lawson, 1976) than participants who were not led to believe they were consuming alcohol. It would appear that in some individuals, expectations regarding alcohol's effects are more potent than the actual physical responses.

Unlike most orally ingested psychoactive substances, alcohol does not require digestion to enter the bloodstream. Since ethanol is water-soluble, it can pass directly into the blood from the stomach, although most of it is absorbed from the small intestine. The bloodstream quickly carries it to the CNS. The rate and peak level of absorption depend on how quickly the alcohol gets through the stomach and into the intestine. If alcohol is consumed on a full stomach, such as with a meal, passage to the intestine is more gradual than when consumed on an empty stomach.

Once the alcohol reaches the blood supply, it travels throughout the body and enters most tissues. Alcohol level is usually expressed as a percentage of blood. For example, if there are 80 millilitres of alcohol in 100 000 millilitres of blood, **blood alcohol level (BAL)** is 0.08 percent. Alcohol is removed by the liver at essentially a constant rate of 7 to 8 millilitres of ethanol per hour. Thirty millilitres of liquor, 150 millilitres of wine, and one beer have equivalent absolute alcohol content of 15 millilitres. If rate of intake equals rate of metabolism, then BAL will remain stable. If more than a single standard drink is consumed every two hours, then BAL will climb. Because alcohol does not distribute much into fatty tissues, an 80-kilogram leaner person will have a lower BAL than an 80-kilogram less lean person who drinks the same amount of alcohol. The leaner person has more fluid volume in which to distribute the alcohol. Alcohol is further broken down in the stomach by the enzyme **alcohol dehydrogenase**, and women have significantly less of this enzyme. The lower levels of alcohol dehydrogenase in women and the fact that men tend to have a lower proportion of body fat mean that a woman will usually have a higher BAL (and therefore be more intoxicated) than a man of the same body weight consuming the same quantity of alcohol (Frezza et al., 1990; National Institute on Drug Abuse, 1992).

SHORT-TERM EFFECTS The effects of alcohol vary with the level of concentration of the drug (yes, it is a drug) in the bloodstream. In addition, alcohol has what is termed a *biphasic effect*. The initial effect of alcohol is stimulating, resulting in pleasant feelings as BAL rises. After the blood alcohol level peaks and begins to decline, alcohol acts as a depressant, and many may experience increases in negative emotions. Social drinkers will often have retired to sleep and will, thus, avoid the effects of this negative phase.

Alcohol causes deficits in eye–hand coordination, which can be seen at BALs as low as 0.01 (alcohol only makes one *think* one is the best pool player), and drowsiness shows up on vigilance tasks at levels of 0.06. A 40 percent decrease in steadiness, as measured by the amount of swaying, is evident at a BAL of 0.06. Decreased visual acuity and decreased sensitivity to taste, smell, and pain are evident at BALs as low as 0.08. Furthermore, at BALs of 0.08 to 0.1, reaction time slows by about 10 percent, performance on standard intelligence tests falls, memory is poorer, and perception of time is altered. (Five minutes seems like eight—an interesting challenge to the adage "Time flies when you're having fun.") Alcohol begins to affect driving performance at about 0.05, and the curve starts to rise sharply at about 0.08, the legal limit of impairment in many jurisdictions. At the same time that objective measures show poorer performance, the loss of inhibition often gives a person increased confidence (Wallgren & Barry, 1971).

Not surprisingly, this increased confidence and impaired performance can easily result in accidents. According to the Traffic Injury Research Foundation (2010), approximately 25 percent of Canadians reported that they had driven after consuming alcohol in the past 30 days. This number is a substantial increase from the 15 percent who reported this behaviour in 2005. More than 5 percent of drivers reported having driven at some point in the year before the survey when they were likely over the legal limit, and 38 percent of these drivers admitted to driving with passengers in the vehicle.

Drinking large amounts of alcohol quickly, particularly on an empty stomach, can cause memory **blackouts**, an interval of time for which the person cannot recall key details or entire events. Blackouts are much more common among social drinkers than previously thought. A survey of university students (White, Jamieson-Drake, & Swartzwelder, 2002) found that 51 percent reported "having awoken after a night of drinking not able to remember things [they] did or places [they] went." Among the forgotten events was participation in a wide range of potentially dangerous events, including driving, unprotected sex, and vandalism. Women and men were equally likely to report blackouts in this survey, despite the fact that women drank less often and less heavily, which is likely related to the gender differences in the metabolism of alcohol described above.

Alcohol is often considered a good way to get a good night's sleep. Although alcohol may help a person fall asleep, even low doses of alcohol suppress the rapid eye movement (REM) phase of the sleep cycle. Lighter drinking suppresses REM for the first part of the night, but REM will rebound, or increase, in the latter part of the night to compensate. With heavier drinking, REM is suppressed throughout the night.

The adverse symptoms of "the morning after the night before" are familiar to many, but not well understood. The symptoms of hangovers range from upset stomach, fatigue, headache, thirst, depression, and anxiety to general malaise, and it is possible that these symptoms are a result of withdrawal from the short-term or long-term addiction to alcohol. This notion is supported by the popularly recommended cure of "the hair of the dog that bit you." This remedy may appear to minimize the symptoms, but it really only spreads them out. An analgesic for the headache, and rest and time, are probably the wisest "cures."

The extreme thirst that accompanies a hangover is related to alcohol's ability to cause the fluid inside the body's cells to move outside the cells, causing cellular dehydration. In addition, the diuretic effect that causes the body to excrete more fluid than is taken in (an effect that can be quite inconvenient in certain circumstances) contributes to the increase in thirst. Finally, the nausea and stomach upset result because alcohol is a gastric irritant. In addition, the accumulation of acetaldehyde, a by-product of the metabolism of alcohol, is quite toxic, which contributes to the nausea and headache. The fatigue experienced the next day can often be attributed to alcohol's interference with normal sleep patterns and the increased level of activity during the revelry of the evening before.

LONG-TERM EFFECTS Alcohol is ubiquitous in our society and is therefore rarely considered a dangerous drug. In fact, it is a favourite part of many social activities. However, chronic alcohol consumption is related to many diseases. Because alcohol travels though the body in the bloodstream, it comes in contact with every organ, directly or indirectly affecting every part of the body. Factors related to the severity of damage include an individual's genetic vulnerability, the frequency and duration of drinking, and the severity and spacing of binges (Gutjahr, Gmel, & Rehm, 2001). Alcohol is high in calories and, therefore, heavy drinkers often reduce their food intake or, alternatively, experience increased body fat and weight gain (the "beer belly"). Not only are these calories of little nutritional value, but alcohol interferes with the absorption of nutrients in food that is eaten. Consequently, severe malnutrition and related tissue damage can result. Prolonged alcohol use, with concomitant reduced protein intake, is damaging to the endocrine glands, the pancreas, and especially the liver. Alcohol has also been associated with cancers of the mouth, tongue, pharynx, larynx, esophagus, stomach, liver, lung, pancreas, colon, and rectum. Finally, the effects of alcohol and nicotine are compounded to increase cancers of the oral region (Gunzerath, Faden, Zakhari, & Warren, 2004; Longnecker, 1994).

Heavy alcohol use has been associated with damage to the heart muscle (cardiomyopathy), high blood pressure, and strokes. On the other hand, there is consistent evidence that moderate alcohol consumption is related to a lower incidence of coronary heart disease. This finding has prompted discussions of a possible protective factor. The suggestion is that consuming one to two drinks of alcohol per day may raise HDL cholesterol ("good cholesterol"), which in turn increases blood flow through the coronary vessels (Di Castelnuovo et al., 2006).

It has been a popular belief that consumption of alcohol permanently kills brain cells, and research has demonstrated that the brains of alcoholics demonstrate tissue reduction, particularly in the hypothalamus and thalamus. Cell loss in these areas is associated with **Korsakoff's psychosis**, a chronic disease characterized by impaired memory and a loss of contact with reality. However, research is conflicting and there is some evidence of brain axon regrowth in the cortex following an extended period of abstinence (Bates, Bowden, & Barry, 2002).

FETAL ALCOHOL SPECTRUM DISORDER The relationship between maternal drinking and birth defects was first called **fetal alcohol syndrome (FAS)** in 1973, and described a pattern of facial dysmorphology, growth retardation, and CNS dysfunction (Jones & Smith, 1973). More broadly, the varieties of impact resulting from exposure to prenatal alcohol fall under the umbrella term *fetal alcohol spectrum disorder* (FASD) and include FAS, partial FAS, alcohol-related neurodevelopmental disorder, and alcohol-related birth defects. The most common physical impairments include growth retardation, CNS abnormalities, and a pattern of features of the face and head (see Chapter 14 for further description and a facial diagram). Some children exhibit eye and ear defects, heart murmurs, malformation of organs, undescended testicles, birthmarks, and abnormal fingerprints.

In addition to physical disabilities, individuals with FASD are more likely to experience an increased number of psychological and social problems. High rates of secondary disabilities occur in adults and adolescents, including attention deficit/hyperactivity disorder (ADHD), learning disabilities, disrupted school experience, inappropriate sexual behaviour, mood disorders, alcohol/drug problems, and trouble with the law. Individuals with FASD often demonstrate poor frustration tolerance, distractibility, disorganization, and the inability to predict outcomes accurately, understand consequences, or perceive social cues.

Is there a safe level of alcohol consumption for an expectant mother? There is not a definitive answer to that question. Moderate drinking has been associated with lower birth weight in newborns (Day et al., 2002). Four to six drinks a day led to noticeable mild physical effects and dysfunction. Scientific data do not demonstrate that occasional consumption of one or two drinks definitely causes alcohol-related birth defects, but neither do they indicate any safe level of use (Gunzerath et al., 2004). Contrary to the popular belief that FASD is associated with certain ethnic groups, research has demonstrated that it occurs in a wide range of backgrounds (Astley, Bailey, Talbot, & Clarren, 2000). The most important risk factor is the timing, pattern, and frequency of alcohol use during pregnancy. More recent prevention efforts include advising women to abstain from alcohol altogether if they think they could be pregnant or become pregnant (Tough, Clarke, Hicks, & Clarren, 2004). FASD is the biggest single cause of mental disabilities in most industrialized countries and remains the leading preventable birth defect in North America.

SOCIAL EFFECTS OF ALCOHOL ABUSE In a general survey conducted by Statistics Canada (Health Canada, 2010a), respondents (ages 15+) were asked whether their drinking had adversely affected their friendships and social life, physical health, happiness, financial situation, home life or marriage, work or studies, legal situation, learning abilities, or housing in the previous 12 months. About 5.7 percent of individuals reported at least one of these harms in the past year, with men being more than twice as likely as women to report harm. Youth 15 to 24 years of age reported higher lifetime rates of harm than did adults 25 years and older (13 percent versus 4 percent). These data illustrate some of the direct social consequences of alcohol abuse.

According to a Canadian Centre for Substance Abuse study (Rehm, Baliunas, Brochu, Sarnocinska-Hart, & Taylor, 2006), alcohol use costs Canadians a staggering $14.6 billion a year in increased health care, law enforcement, and reduced productivity (see Table 11.6 for a breakdown of the ways in which alcohol, tobacco, and illicit drugs impose costs on the Canadian economy). In particular, drinking and driving has been recognized as a major social problem. It is estimated that in 2002, 8100 Canadians lost their lives as a result of alcohol consumption. The largest alcohol-related cause of death was liver cirrhosis, followed by motor vehicle accidents and suicide. In addition, there were an estimated 196 000 hospital admissions related to alcohol, the largest number being caused by accidental falls, followed by alcohol dependence and motor vehicle accidents.

ETIOLOGY

The average age at which Canadians start drinking is 13 years and has not changed over the past two decades (Paglia-Boak et al., 2009). Alcohol is advertised on television and radio, and in magazines. It is available in every community, and we are encouraged to imbibe at most social gatherings. There is no stigma attached to drinking alcohol; in fact, people are often pressed to explain why they are abstaining. With such extensive social influence, why do only some people become dependent on alcohol, while others do not? There has been extensive research into the etiology and maintenance of alcohol abuse, and many of these theories have been adopted for other types of substance abuse, so some generalization is possible.

GENETIC FACTORS It is an accepted fact that alcohol abuse and dependence runs in families but, as we have seen in other chapters (see Chapter 4), this does not disentangle the genetic and environmental influences. Twin studies have confirmed that male monozygotic twins are more similar than dizygotic twins in their tendencies to develop problems with alcohol abuse and dependence (Agrawal & Lynskey, 2008). The concordance rate for male monozygotic twins has been found to range from 26 to 77 percent across studies, compared to a range of 12 to 54 percent for male dizygotic twins (McGue, 1999). The results for studies of females are more variable, with about half of the available studies showing a significant genetic effect. The concordance rate for female monozygotic twins has been found to range from 25 to 32 percent, compared to a range of 5 to 24 percent for female dizygotic twins (McGue, 1999). However, these studies fall prey to the criticisms mentioned in Chapter 4. Adoption studies (also explained in Chapter 4) show a similar pattern of consistent results for men but variable results for women (Gelernter & Kranzler, 2009).

Twin and adoption studies provide evidence for a genetic contribution to the development of alcohol disorders, particularly for men, but what exactly is inherited? Given the complexity of alcohol problems, it is unlikely that only one or two of the up to 100 000 genes composing humans are responsible. Instead, it is likely that multiple genes and patterns of genes are important. Research has focused on genes involved in the sensitivity of receptor sites for a number of neurotransmitters that form part of the reward system of the brain. Evidence is accumulating that alcohol produces changes in dopamine, opioid systems, GABA receptors, glutamate, and serotonin, but the relationship between these systems and alcohol use is complex (Gilpin & Koob, 2008).

Another genetic factor that may be involved in alcoholism is the ability to metabolize alcohol. Alcohol is broken down in the liver into a by-product called acetaldehyde, which is further broken down by the enzyme aldehyde dehydrogenase. If acetaldehyde is allowed to build, it causes serious illness. In certain individuals—particularly those of Asian descent—aldehyde dehydrogenase seems to be absent, resulting in unpleasant physiological responses including cutaneous flushing (i.e., facial flushing) and palpitations, perspiration, and headache. These effects provide a biological upper limit on alcohol consumption, which reduces the risk for development of alcohol abuse (Eng, Luczak, & Wall, 2007).

It is important to note that being a son or daughter of an alcoholic does not predetermine alcoholism. Although vulnerable, many offspring of alcoholics do not become alcoholics, and many alcoholics are born to non-alcoholic parents. Undoubtedly, environmental factors and personal choice play significant roles in the development or avoidance of problems with alcohol.

NEUROBIOLOGICAL INFLUENCES Biological marker studies attempt to show that alcoholism is inherited by establishing an association between alcoholism and other inherited characteristics (see also discussions of linkage analysis in

TABLE 11.6 THE SOCIAL COSTS OF TOBACCO, ALCOHOL, AND ILLEGAL DRUGS IN CANADA, 2002

	(in millions of dollars)			
	Tobacco	**Alcohol**	**Illegal drugs**	**Total TAD**
1. Direct health care costs: total	**4360.2**	**3306.2**	**1134.6**	**8800.9**
1.1 Morbidity:				
acute care hospitalization	2551.2	1458.6	426.37	4436.2
psychiatric hospitals	—	19.6	11.5	31.2
1.2 inpatient specialized treatment	—	754.9	352.1	1107.1
1.3 outpatient specialized treatment	—	52.4	56.3	108.7
1.4 ambulatory care: physician fees	142.2	80.2	22.6	245.0
1.5 family physician visit	306.3	172.8	48.8	527.9
1.6 prescription drugs	1360.5	767.6	216.8	2344.9
2. Direct law enforcement costs	**—**	**3072.2**	**2335.5**	**5407.8**
2.1 police	—	1,898.8	1432.0	3330.7
2.2 courts	—	513.1	330.6	843.7
2.3 corrections (including probation)	—	660.4	573.0	1233.4
3. Direct costs for prevention and research	**78.1**	**53.0**	**16.5**	**147.6**
3.1 research	9.0	17.3	8.6	34.9
3.2 prevention programs	69.1	33.9	7.9	110.9
3.3 salaries and operating funds	—	1.8	—	1.8
4. Other direct costs	**87.0**	**996.1**	**79.1**	**1162.2**
4.1 fire damage	86.5	156.5	—	243.0
4.2 traffic accident damage	—	756.9	67.0	823.9
4.3 losses associated with the workplace	0.5	17.0	6.6	24.1
4.3.1 EAP & health promotion programs	0.5	17.0	4.2	21.7
4.3.2. drug testing in the workplace	N/A	—	2.4	2.4
4.4 administrative costs for transfer payments	0.0	65.8	5.4	71.3
4.4.1 social welfare and other programs	—	4.3	—	4.3
4.4.2. workers' compensation	—	61.5	5.4	66.9
5. Indirect costs: productivity losses	**12 470.9**	**7126.4**	**4678.6**	**24 275.9**
5.1 due to long-term disability	10 536.8	6,163.9	4408.4	21 109.1
5.2 due to short-term disability (days in bed)	24.4	15.9	21.8	62.0
5.3 due to short-term disability (days with reduced activity)	36.2	23.6	0.1	59.8
5.4 due to premature mortality	1873.5	923.0	248.5	3045.0
Total	**16 996.2**	**14 554.0**	**8244.3**	**39 794.4**
Total per capita (in $)	**541**	**463**	**262**	**1267**
Total as % of all substance-related costs	**42.7**	**36.6**	**20.7**	**100.0**

TAD: Tobacco, Alcohol, and Illegal Drugs; N/A: not applicable; "–": not available; EAP: Employee Assistance Programs

Categories in italics are sub-categories of immediate prior category.

Source: Canadian Centre on Substance Abuse.

Chapters 8 and 9). Biological processes of alcoholics, of non-problem drinkers, and of children of both are compared to determine markers of vulnerability to alcohol. One such marker is brain wave activity that can be measured by electroencephalographic (EEG) techniques. Sons of alcoholic fathers have higher-than-normal rates of the fast beta wave (Gabrielli et al., 1982) and show less EEG change after alcohol consumption than do sons of non-alcoholic fathers (Ehlers & Schuckit, 1990). Evoked potentials have also been implicated. These are brief changes in EEG responses to external stimuli, such as flashes of light or loud sounds. The P300 response occurs about 300 milliseconds after the presentation of a stimulus and is believed to indicate an individual's attentional abilities. Sons and daughters of alcoholics show smaller P300 amplitudes than do offspring of non-alcoholic fathers (Hill & Steinhauer, 1993; Steinhauer & Hill, 1993). A similar pattern was found in chronic alcoholics who were no longer drinking (Porjesz & Begleiter, 1997). Importantly, longitudinal studies show that P300 response predicts the early onset of alcohol problems (Hill, Steinhauer, Lowers, & Locke, 1995).

Heart rate increases following the consumption of alcohol have also been studied. Men with alcoholic relatives show larger increases in heart rate (Finn, Zeitouni, & Pihl, 1990). In addition, those with the greatest increases in heart rate were more inclined to drink alcohol regularly (Pihl & Peterson, 1991). It has been suggested that heart rate increase is a measure of sensitivity to the stimulating properties of alcohol, and may be viewed as an index of reward (Wise & Bozarth, 1987).

Neurotransmitters such as GABA (gamma-aminobutyric acid), beta-endorphin, and serotonin are other potential markers for alcohol disorders. For example, low levels of serotonin have been associated with alcohol-related characteristics such as impulsivity, aggression, and antisocial behaviour and to alcohol craving in both animals and humans. However, serotonin levels are difficult to measure, making it an impractical marker for alcoholism (Tabakoff & Hoffmann, 1991). Serotonin operates in a complex manner, with more processes involved than simply serotonin level; these include sensitivity and density of receptors, variation in rate of metabolism and reuptake of serotonin in the synaptic cleft, dietary intake of amino acids, and the cell's recent firing history (Neumeister et al., 2006).

Although each of the aforementioned biological markers has shown interesting relationships to alcoholism, none has so far been found clinically useful in diagnosing substance abuse or in predicting which individuals will grow up to be alcoholics. Like the genetic factors discussed earlier, at the present time, these biological markers might be considered indications of a vulnerability to alcoholism and merit further investigation.

PSYCHOLOGICAL FACTORS While one clear profile of an addictive personality has not been established, certain personality characteristics seem to be associated with alcoholism. The strongest association is with the trait of **behavioural disinhibition**. People with alcohol problems tend to have a relative inability to inhibit behavioural impulses (McGue, 1999). They are more rebellious, more impulsive, more aggressive, and more willing to take risks than are non-alcoholics. These differences predate the onset of the alcohol problems and have been observed as early as age three (Caspi, Moffit, Newman, & Silva, 1996). A second trait that has been shown to be associated with alcoholism is **negative emotionality** or neuroticism. Negative emotionality is the tendency to experience psychological distress, anxiety, and depression. Research shows that alcoholics are more likely to have this tendency than are non-alcoholics. However, longitudinal data do not provide evidence that this tendency predates the onset of the alcohol problem. Instead, negative emotionality appears more likely to be a consequence of alcoholism (Sher, Trull, Bartholow, & Vieth, 1999).

The **tension-reduction**, or anxiety-relief, hypothesis suggests that drinking is reinforced by its ability to reduce tension, anxiety, anger, depression, and other unpleasant emotions. However, support for this hypothesis is inconsistent, probably because alcohol has variable effects on tension, depending on how much is consumed, and only certain individuals experience stress reduction after ingesting alcohol. It appears that the subjective effects of alcohol depend largely on the expectancies of the drinker. These expectancies are developed early in childhood by observing adult drinking behaviours and media messages about the feelings and good times that can be had with alcohol. The **alcohol expectancy theory** proposes that drinking behaviour is largely determined by the reinforcement that an individual expects to receive from it. Among the expectancies identified by a group of social drinkers were that alcohol positively transforms experiences, enhances both social and physical pleasure and sexual performance and experience, increases power and aggression, alters personal characteristics and improves social skill, and reduces tension (Goldman, Del Boca, & Darkes, 1999). Nevertheless, most of these subjective experiences are a function of expectation and attitude and not a drug effect. In fact, alcohol's pharmacological effects can have the opposite effect of expectation in regard to tension reduction, mood, sexual performance, and social skills.

In support of the expectancy theory, alcoholics and non-problem drinkers have both been found to drink more when told that their drinks contain alcohol, regardless of the beverage's alcohol content (Marlatt, Demming, & Reid, 1973). Alcoholics and heavy social drinkers can be distinguished by a measure of their alcohol-related beliefs. Alcoholics and heavy social drinkers are more likely than non-problem drinkers to believe that alcohol use will result in positive outcomes (Thombs, 1993). Longitudinal research with adolescents supports the impact of alcohol expectancy on future drinking behaviour. Positive expectancies of alcohol effects predicted higher levels of subsequent alcohol use (Smith, Goldman, Greenbaum, & Christiansen, 1995).

Learning and experience also play a role in the development of tolerance for alcohol and other drugs. Dr. Shep

Siegel from McMaster University in Hamilton originated a line of research that demonstrated that drug tolerance is partially conditioned to the environment in which the substance is used. Traditionally, tolerance was considered to be related entirely to biological process, a cellular adaptation to the substance. Using animal models, Siegel and others demonstrated that through the principles of classical conditioning, cues in the environment can become conditioned stimuli to the effects of drug use. These cues cause the individual to anticipate the drug effects so that when the drug is actually administered the effects are diminished. Over time, as conditioning continues, the drug effects diminish to a greater extent. Tolerance, or the need for a greater amount of drug for the same effect, is greatest when the conditioned environmental cues are present. This **behavioural tolerance** effect accounts for the observation that heroin addicts can use a larger amount of heroin in their typical environment (where tolerance is greatest) but can fatally overdose when they use the same amount in a novel environment (Siegel, 1983).

SOCIO-CULTURAL FACTORS Alcohol use is influenced by such social and cultural factors as family values, attitudes, and expectations that have been passed on from generation to generation. It seems that people who are introduced to drinking as a rite of passage in an environment in which excessive drinking is socially accepted (and, indeed, encouraged by peer pressure) face increased risk of developing alcoholism. In some subcultures, an individual's use of chemicals is seen as a sign of maturity, and this adolescent peer subculture may encourage repeated episodes of substance abuse. Social learning also influences expectancies and, as we have seen, individuals with positive expectancies are most likely to be the heaviest drinkers. Cultural and familial traditions and attitudes toward alcohol use combine to influence the individuals' expectations of the effects of alcohol and their drinking patterns.

Evidence for cultural influence on drinking patterns can be found in comparisons of alcoholism in different countries. While the consumption of alcohol is worldwide, the patterns of alcohol abuse differ from country to country. In France, where daily drinking is common, alcoholics are usually steady drinkers who rarely show a loss of control and are prone to physical disorders rather than social disruptions. Although daily drinking is also acceptable in Italy, drinking is usually restricted to mealtime and consumption is limited, and there is a much lower rate of alcoholism there than in France. In England, Ireland, and North America, alcoholism is often manifested by bouts of extremely heavy drinking and often associated with loss of control and disastrous social consequences. In Muslim countries, where consumption of alcohol is discouraged on religious grounds, alcoholism rates are very low (Rivers, 1994).

Drinking patterns in the home also influence an individual's use of alcohol. Adolescents' drinking tends to mirror that of their parents. If parents use alcohol to cope with stressful situations or associate heavy drinking with celebration, children will likely adopt the same attitudes. In general, the more parents drink, the earlier their children begin to drink. However, there is less linkage between parent and child drinking patterns when parents are either non-drinkers or very heavy drinkers (Barnes, Farrell, & Cairns, 1986; Harburg, Davis, & Caplan, 1982). Children of alcoholics may mimic parents' behaviour or react by being totally abstinent. Children of parents who drink no alcohol also tend to the extremes of drinking behaviour, either drinking heavily or not at all (Lawson, Peterson, & Lawson, 1983).

The exact etiology of alcohol abuse and dependence has yet to be resolved, but many researchers agree that it is

APPLIED CLINICAL CASE

Robert Downey Jr.

Robert John Downey Jr. is a Golden Globe Award–winning and Academy Award–nominated actor who also became infamous for a period of alcohol and other drug abuse during the 1990s. Although he continued his acting career during that time, he was frequently in the news for drug-related incidents that led to arrest, incarceration, and mandated substance abuse treatment. Downey relapsed often and dramatically. In 1999 he explained to a judge: "It's like I have a loaded gun in my mouth and my finger's on the trigger, and I like the taste of the gunmetal" (Reaves, 2001). Over the years, Downey has appeared in more than 70 movies and on various television shows, including *Saturday Night Live*. He has also been arrested on numerous occasions, spent a year in state prison, and is well known for falling asleep in his neighbour's bed while under the influence. In 2001, he was fired from the popular television show *Ally McBeal* after being arrested while on parole for suspicion of being under the influence of drugs. A newly established drug court mandated treatment and probation for Downey, instead of incarceration. Since then, he says he is drug-free and has garnered acclaim for his leading role in the popular movie *Iron Man*. He attributes his recovery to family therapy, 12-step programs, meditation, yoga, and kung fu (Wilde, 2003).

a multidetermined disorder influenced by biological, psychological, and sociological factors. Evidence for a genetic contribution to the development of alcohol abuse and dependence is strong, but it cannot explain why some people with family histories of alcoholism do not develop drinking problems. Nor does it account for the fact that most of the people who develop these disorders do not have family histories of these problems. Individuals develop expectations about alcohol, must choose to use alcohol, and decide on the manner in which it will be used. The individual with biological and/or psychological vulnerabilities may respond to social influences and personal stressors in a manner that promotes

FOCUS 11.3

Non-abstinence Drinking Goals in Treatment

Originally, controlled-drinking research was used to test the critical hypotheses of the popular disease concept of alcoholism (Pattison, Sobell, & Sobell, 1977). Mark and Linda Sobell (researchers who worked for many years at the Centre for Addiction and Mental Health in Toronto) studied a program for teaching alcoholics to drink in moderation in comparison with an abstinence-oriented program similar to Alcoholics Anonymous (Sobell & Sobell, 1973, 1976). Participants in the study were 40 male alcoholics in a treatment program who were thought to have a good prognosis. Overall results over more than two years of follow-up indicated that individuals in the controlled-drinking group were functioning well for 85 percent of the days, as compared to 42 percent of the days for the abstinence group.

These results were challenged in a subsequent paper. Pendery, Maltzman, and West (1982) reported that they had contacted the men in the Sobell study 10 years later and found that only one of the men in the controlled-drinking group continued to maintain a pattern of controlled drinking; four had died from alcohol-induced problems. This re-evaluation made headlines. The Sobells were charged with scientific misconduct and ethical violations. However, these charges were later refuted by several independent investigative committees. Pendery and colleagues (1982) had not provided follow-up data on the abstinence group—who, it turned out, had fared no better than the controlled-drinking group. This controversy has created lasting mistrust between proponents and opponents of controlled-drinking programs.

A number of other lines of evidence point to the viability of non-abstinence treatment goals for some people with alcohol use problems (Hodgins, 2005). First, as early as the 1940s, follow-up studies of alcoholics have revealed that a proportion of patients, albeit a small group, describe successful and sustained non-abstinence outcomes (Ambrogne, 2002). The most widely cited of these studies is the Rand report from the mid-1980s that provided a follow-up of a large national U.S. sample of patients from abstinence-oriented inpatient alcohol treatment programs. Remarkably, about 18 percent of patients were described as drinking moderately and problem-free after four years (Polich, Armor, & Braiker, 1981).

A second line of evidence comes from treatment evaluation studies that have included non-abstinence drinking goals. These studies were reviewed by Ambrogne (2002), who identified 12 studies that consistently found that some patients were able to sustain non-problematic drinking after treatment over follow-up periods of one to eight years.

A number of patient characteristics are found to predict success with non-abstinence outcomes. These include younger age, relatively better social and psychological stability, employment, being female, having less severe alcohol dependence, and having a stronger belief in one's ability to moderate drinking (Saladin & Santa Ana, 2004). In addition, a number of medical factors preclude a non-abstinence goal, including pregnancy and liver disease.

The Centre for Addiction and Mental Health advises that abstinence is clearly the appropriate treatment goal for drinkers who have had a long history of heavy drinking, where drinking has come to be a pervasive and integral part of their lifestyle, or for those who have suffered serious consequences. However, if they are unwilling to accept abstinence as a treatment goal, they may benefit from treatment aimed at harm reduction (Addiction Research Foundation, 1992). What are the implications of assuming the "wrong" goal for an individual? A small group of treatment studies have randomly assigned individuals to either abstinence or non-abstinence drinking goals (Adamson & Sellman, 2001; Ambrogne, 2002). These studies comparing drinking goals do not find differences in outcome, which suggests that it is not harmful to allow individuals to attempt to moderate their drinking instead of abstaining. In fact, there may be an advantage to allowing patients to make their own goal choice. Goals change over time, and treatment can provide experiences that will encourage patients to reconsider and revise their initial goals. In one Canadian study that allowed goal choice among people with severe alcohol dependence, participants choosing moderation initially tended to change their goal to abstinence over time, presumably as a result of lack of success with moderation (Hodgins, Leigh, Milne, & Gerrish, 1997). Choice of abstinence with this group of patients ultimately predicted better outcome at one-year follow-up. In short, the appropriateness of a goal will declare itself over time, and usually in short order.

There is also indirect evidence that individuals can make good choices for themselves. Humphreys (2003) examined the characteristics of people attending Moderation Management, a mutual support group that allows goal choice. In fact, almost all attendees choose a non-abstinence goal. As a group, attendees had characteristics similar to the characteristics that predict success with non-abstinence goals. In particular, they reported less severe problems than individuals who attend formal abstinence-oriented treatment programs. It appears that the right people are choosing this treatment approach.

Humphreys argues that groups like Moderation Management extend the traditional treatment system by attracting people who would not attend traditional treatment. Allowing a choice of goals within treatment systems may be one effective way to increase the numbers of people willing to enter alcohol treatment. It is estimated that as few as 10 percent of individuals with alcohol use disorders attend treatment. More flexibility in goals may appeal to a wider range of people with alcohol use disorders.

the development of drinking problems. Different combinations of risk factors and environmental liabilities create multiple paths to the development of alcohol use disorders.

TREATMENT

Alcohol and other drug abuse have probably been around for as long as the drugs themselves. Early admonitions against the overuse of alcohol were of a moral nature, and those who lacked the fortitude to resist temptation were punished. A more liberal view of alcohol and other drug use arose during the Second World War, when many soldiers engaged in substance abuse. A number of treatment approaches have been developed for alcoholics, each with its own proponents and some evidence of effectiveness. In Canada, there are just over 1000 treatment programs. The differing patterns of alcohol abuse suggest that there are various contributors to alcohol dependence, and it may be that some treatments, or combination of treatments, are better suited for some alcoholics under some conditions. Over the past 25 years, there has been a move toward the use of outpatient treatments from the routine use of the standardized 28-day inpatient program. However, efforts to identify specifically which type of alcoholic does best in which type of approach have met with limited success. Generally, treatments are focused on abstinence, meaning that they help the alcoholic to stop drinking completely (see Focus box 11.3).

RESIDENTIAL TREATMENT: THE MINNESOTA MODEL

The most common residential treatment for alcohol use and dependence is a multimodal approach advocating a 12-step Alcoholics Anonymous philosophy. This model views alcoholism as a disease and is termed the **Minnesota model** because it was popularized by the well-known Hazelden treatment program in that state. For people who show signs of withdrawal, treatment begins in a hospital or detoxification clinic under medical supervision, and often includes prescription drugs. Following detoxification treatment for the physical dependence, treatment of the psychological dependence begins. This component includes education about the consequences of alcohol use and abuse, individual counselling for psychological issues, and group therapy to improve interpersonal skills. Abstinence is the goal, since it is assumed that people with the alcoholism "disease" will never be able to drink in a controlled way. Participants are usually required to attend Alcoholics Anonymous meetings and encouraged to keep going after treatment to address the danger of relapse. Despite the popularity of the Minnesota model, the effectiveness of the approach has not been rigorously evaluated.

PHARMACOTHERAPY Medication has been used in the treatment of alcoholics to assist in detoxification, to reduce the pleasurable effects associated with drinking, and to produce nausea when alcohol is consumed. To make detoxification more bearable, benzodiazepines (tranquilizers) have been administered to alcoholics as a first step in treatment. Since these medications mimic the effects of alcohol, they minimize the effects of withdrawal. Doses are gradually decreased as withdrawal proceeds. The use of benzodiazepines is somewhat controversial because of the danger of substituting one addiction for another, and because most alcoholics do not experience withdrawal symptoms severe enough to warrant this intervention (Wartenberg et al., 1990).

Medication can also be prescribed as a method of reducing the immediate gratification that accompanies drinking. Naltrexone, an **antagonist drug**, targets the neurotransmitters that mediate alcohol's effects on the brain and "blocks" the pleasurable effects of alcohol. In addition, it helps to reduce the sensation of craving. Studies have shown that naltrexone, in combination with psychosocial treatment, does help some alcohol abusers abstain from alcohol use, particularly those who are finding it difficult to initiate abstinence (Killeen et al., 2004; Volpicelli, Alterman, Hayashida, & O'Brien, 1992). Acamprosate is another drug that can be used to reduce craving for alcohol and to reduce distress during early abstinence. It is an **agonist drug** that facilitates the inhibitory action of the neurotransmitter GABA at its receptors. Studies conducted in Europe show that use of Acamprosate in combination with psychosocial treatment doubles the number of people who are successfully abstinent (Swift, 2003). It is likely that these medications will play an increasingly large role in alcohol treatment. However, success depends on the compliance of the individual, which has been a significant concern with these drugs.

Another medication approach is to make the experience of drinking extremely aversive. **Antabuse** (disulfiram) and CCC (citrated calcium carbamate) block the action of the metabolizing enzyme acetaldehyde dehydrogenase, resulting in a buildup of acetaldehyde in the body. Like people who naturally lack this enzyme, people who drink alcohol after taking Antabuse experience increased heart rate, nausea, vomiting, and other unpleasant effects. Patients are instructed to take the medication each morning, before the desire to drink becomes overwhelming. The goal is to deter the individual from drinking, but once again compliance is a major hurdle. It is increasingly common to have a family member administer Antabuse to the alcoholic as part of a treatment program. This approach has the added advantage of helping the family member regain trust in the alcoholic's resolve to not drink.

MUTUAL SUPPORT GROUPS

Alcoholics Anonymous. Alcoholics Anonymous (AA) works with more alcoholics worldwide than any other treatment organization. AA does not use professionally trained staff; it is a self-help group, "a fellowship of men and women who share their experience, strength, and hope with each other that they may solve their common problem and help others to recover from alcoholism" (AA Grapevine, Inc., New York, cited in Rivers, 1994, p. 268). AA got its start in 1935 in a popular Protestant religious following, the Oxford Movement. The movement, dedicated to redeeming humankind through striving for absolute good,

TABLE 11.7 THE 12 STEPS OF ALCOHOLICS ANONYMOUS

1. We admitted we were powerless over alcohol—that our lives had become unmanageable.
2. Came to believe that a Power greater than ourselves could restore us to sanity.
3. Made a decision to turn our will and our lives over to the care of God as we understood Him.
4. Made a searching and fearless moral inventory of ourselves.
5. Admitted to God, to ourselves, and to another human being the exact nature of our wrongs.
6. Were entirely ready to have God remove all these defects of character.
7. Humbly asked Him to remove our shortcomings.
8. Made a list of all persons we had harmed, and became willing to make amends to them all.
9. Made direct amends to such people wherever possible, except when to do so would injure them or others.
10. Continued to take personal inventory and when we were wrong promptly admitted it.
11. Sought through prayer and meditation to improve our conscious contact with God as we understood Him, praying only for knowledge of His will for us and the power to carry that out.
12. Having had a spiritual awakening as the result of these steps, we tried to carry this message to alcoholics, and to practise these principles in all our affairs.

Source: The Twelve Steps are reprinted with permission of Alcoholics Anonymous World Services, Inc. (A.A.W.S.). Permission to reprint the Twelve Steps does not mean that A.A.W.S. has reviewed or approved the contents of this publication.

consisted of small groups that met weekly for prayer, worship, and discussion. Two members, physician Dr. Bob and stockbroker Bill W., had been trying unsuccessfully to quit drinking, and found the fellowship of the group helpful. They invited more and more alcoholics into the group, and when the meetings became too large, they broke away and founded Alcoholics Anonymous.

The AA treatment is based on a disease model and the goal is complete abstinence. AA members believe that there is no cure for alcoholism; there are only alcoholics who drink and alcoholics who do not drink (in recovery). They believe that they are powerless to control their drinking and must rely on a "Higher Power" to help them. Members are encouraged to attend meetings often and regularly, as social support is central to the program, and to follow the "12 steps" of recovery (see Table 11.7). Members who have stayed sober for a period of time serve as sponsors for newcomers. There are more than 65 000 AA groups in the United States and Canada, and more than 100 000 meetings are held each week all over the world. Many of the groups comprise specific types of individuals such as women, gays and lesbians, smokers, non-smokers, and so forth. Active members will often attend more than one group in addition to their "home" group.

AA is an effective treatment for some, and many people credit it with saving their lives. Others find it difficult to embrace because of its reliance on spirituality and its adoption of the disease model. Only a few research evaluations of AA's effectiveness exist, mostly observing the effects when attendance is coerced (e.g., legally mandated by the courts or employers). Results have not been favourable, although the intent of AA is that attendance is voluntary (McCrady, Horvath, & Delaney, 2003). Follow-up studies of alcoholics post-treatment show that those who choose to attend AA have better outcomes than those who do not attend. More rigorous evaluation has been conducted on 12-step facilitation, which involves the use of professionals in encouraging AA attendance with positive results (McCrady et al., 2003).

A number of mutual support groups have been developed to support individuals who do not affiliate with the spiritual aspect of the AA groups. These groups emphasize personal responsibility and rationality as important in recovery. Women for Sobriety and SMART Recovery (Self-Management and Recovery Training) support abstinence from alcohol and other drugs. Moderation Management helps individuals to moderate their drinking versus stopping completely.

PSYCHOLOGICAL TREATMENTS

Behavioural Treatment. The behavioural approach treats alcoholism as a learned behaviour. Alcohol, an unconditioned stimulus, elicits unconditioned responses in the form of pleasant physical reactions. Alcohol becomes associated with these pleasant responses (see Chapter 2 for an explanation of conditioning theory). Therefore, some behavioural interventions attempt to condition an aversive response to alcohol by pairing alcohol with an unpleasant stimulus. For example, the sight, smell, and taste of alcohol may be presented while the alcoholic is nauseated and vomiting as a result of taking an emetic drug. Theoretically, over time the sensation of nausea should be elicited by the presence of alcohol without the emetic drug (a conditioned response), and the previously positive associations with drinking become negative. Even though a number of theoretically sound procedures have been used, aversion therapy alone has had limited success, but it can be combined with other treatments (Costello, 1975; Nietzel, Winett, Macdonald, & Davidson, 1977).

Other behavioural treatments are based on operant conditioning principles (see Chapter 2). *Contingency management* has been used to manipulate reinforcement contingencies for alcohol use. Contracts between patients and treatment programs may be established that specify rewards (or punishments) contingent on small steps toward sobriety. A more comprehensive operant program is the Community Reinforcement Approach (CRA; Azrin, 1976). A spouse, friend, or relative who is not a substance user is recruited to participate in the program; both participants learn behavioural coping skills and how to develop contingency contracts. They learn to identify antecedents to drinking, the circumstances in which drinking is most likely, social reinforcers, and the consequences of drinking. They are also taught how to arrange reinforcement contingencies to reward sobriety rather than reinforce drinking. Finally, this comprehensive intervention program also helps alcoholics to develop new recreational options that do not involve alcohol and reduce stress through improvements in practical areas of life, such as employment, finances, and education.

Behavioural self-management is a treatment approach that teaches alcoholics to manage their own drinking through behavioural contracting, restructuring of thoughts about drinking, and having individuals recognize the patterns in their drinking. This approach has been offered in groups, in individual format, and in the form of self-help workbooks. It has strong research support, particularly for individuals with less severe alcohol problems (Miller, Wilbourne, & Hettema, 2003), and it has been used with the goals of both complete abstinence and moderated drinking.

RELAPSE PREVENTION Whether the goal of treatment for alcoholics is complete abstinence or moderated drinking, the long-term results of most programs are disappointing. Most treated alcoholics eventually relapse and develop problems with alcohol again. Relapse prevention treatment aims to avoid relapses if possible, and to manage a relapse if and when it occurs (Marlatt & Gordon, 1985). **Relapse** is seen as a failure of a person's cognitive and behavioural coping skills to cope with the problems of alcoholism. Maladaptive behaviour is seen as a result of self-defeating thoughts and self-deception that can bring about "inadvertent" slips. Apparently innocent decisions based on distorted beliefs can chain together to create circumstances that increase the risk of drinking. The relapse prevention techniques attempt to help individuals identify these distorted beliefs and replace them with adaptive ones. High-risk situations are identified for each individual and strategies are developed to deal with them. For example, if a person has a history of drinking in response to interpersonal conflict, he or she can be taught to recognize the early stages of an argument and talk issues over more calmly, or to leave and go for a walk before tensions mount too high. People are taught to view lapses not as overwhelming failures that will inevitably lead to more drinking, but as temporary occurrences brought on by a specific situation, from which a person can recover. Evaluations have shown relapse prevention to be useful in treating alcohol dependence (Miller et al., 2003; Witkiewitz & Marlatt, 2004).

MARITAL AND FAMILY THERAPY An individual's pattern of substance abuse is unavoidably linked to close social relationships, though not necessarily caused by these relationships. In family and marital therapy, the relationship, rather than the alcoholic, is seen as the patient. Family therapy focuses on issues of interaction and the notion that a family unit attempts to maintain equilibrium. Established patterns of interaction and resistance to change can inadvertently support alcohol abuse by one member of the family. Family members may have established roles for themselves that are defined by the substance abuse and have become so enmeshed in the drinking problem that they actually prevent changes in the abuse pattern. Such people are described as *codependents*. Even if there is no codependency, marital conflict, such as spousal nagging about drinking, can stimulate bouts of heavy drinking.

In an alcoholic's family, other existing or potential problems are often overshadowed by the alcohol abuse. In a sense, the abuser becomes a scapegoat. When the individual stops drinking, other troubling issues may develop or become evident. For example, a potentially depressed spouse may manage the depression by dealing with the problem of an alcoholic spouse. When this diversion is no longer available, the depression may unfold. Children of alcoholics often try to be "extra good" and supportive during the drinking phase, and may react to a parent's quitting by acting out. Family members may have reduced their communication because of fear of causing the alcoholic to become violent or drink more, and the communication may remain subdued after cessation of drinking. Each of these areas provides potential targets of therapeutic interventions in the families of alcoholics.

Behavioural marital therapies adapted for treatment of couples in which one partner is alcoholic are among the approaches with the strongest empirical support. This approach is focused on teaching communication skills and increasing the levels of positive reinforcement in the relationship. As with the CRA approach described above, the non-alcoholic partner is trained to reward sobriety rather than reinforce drinking.

BRIEF INTERVENTIONS **Brief interventions** are one to three sessions in length, offering time-limited and specific advice regarding the need to reduce or eliminate alcohol consumption. These interventions can be offered opportunistically in settings where the individual is seeking help for a related problem. For example, a family physician may raise the issue of alcohol use in patients with gastrointestinal problems or abnormal liver functioning tests, or an emergency room nurse may approach victims of motor vehicle accidents involving alcohol. Alternatively, brief interventions can be offered to individuals with "concerns" about their alcohol use but who are reluctant to seek more formal treatment. One such program, called the Drinker's Check-up, allows individuals to get feedback on their drinking behaviours. Of the treatment approaches for alcohol problems that have been empirically evaluated, brief interventions are among those that have the largest and strongest support.

Particularly effective are brief approaches that focus on the individual's motivation to make changes in his or her drinking (Miller et al., 2003). **Motivational interviewing** is an approach that can be used with clients who present with varying levels of readiness to change their behaviour. In a non-confrontational, accepting manner, the therapist helps the client to identify and freely discuss both the pros and cons of his or her alcohol use. Motivational interviewing is considered to be a client-centred, semi-directive technique wherein the therapist works to increase the client's awareness of the problems and create a discrepancy between behaviours and goals. The therapist supports the client's self-efficacy and autonomy to move toward change. Motivational interviewing can be used as part of brief interventions or as an adjunct for more comprehensive treatments (see the Canadian Research Centre box at the end of this chapter for the application of a brief motivational treatment approach to problem gambling).

2 BEFORE MOVING ON

What causes one person to develop an alcohol problem, while another does not?

Barbiturates and Benzodiazepines

There are a number of drugs considered to be **depressants** because they inhibit neurotransmitter activity in the CNS. We have seen that alcohol is one of these substances, although it was not developed for this purpose. Barbituric acid, produced in 1903, was one of the first drugs developed as a treatment for anxiety and tension and later for sleep. Since then, there have been many derivatives of this sedative-hypnotic drug, including those with the brand names Seconal, Tuinal, Nembutal, and Fiorinal. Barbiturates were widely prescribed until the 1940s, when their addictive potential became known. Barbiturates are commonly known as "downers," or according to the colour of their brand name versions (e.g., "blues," "yellow jackets," and "red birds"). Now, another group of drugs belonging to the sedative-hypnotic class called benzodiazepines (e.g., Valium, Librium, Xanax, Ativan) are more frequently prescribed for sleep and anxiety problems. Although these are generally thought of as safer alternatives to barbiturates, they too can be addicting if misused. Barbiturates and benzodiazepines are odourless, white, crystalline compounds, usually taken as tablets or capsules. Long-acting forms are available for prolonged sedation. Shorter-acting versions, used to treat insomnia, are thought to be more addicting.

PREVALENCE

The 1999 National Population Health Survey (Statistics Canada, 1999) indicated that the use of tranquilizers (including barbiturates and benzodiazepines) is fairly low in Canada. In this survey, 3.5 percent of women and 1.9 percent of men indicated that they had used prescribed tranquilizers during the past year. In a survey of Ontario high school students (Paglia-Boak et al., 2009), non-medical use of tranquilizers (including benzodiazepines) was 1.3 percent for males and 1.9 percent for females.

EFFECTS

The effects of barbiturates and benzodiazepines are similar except that the anxiolytic effects of the benzodiazepines emerge at lower doses, making them the safer alternative. In small doses, these drugs cause mild euphoria. With larger doses, slurred speech, poor motor coordination, and impairment of judgment and concentration occur. Initially, users may be combative and argumentative, but the larger dosages eventually induce sleep. The behaviour observed at this dosage is similar to that seen in alcohol intoxication. In fact, DSM-IV-TR criteria for sedative, hypnotic, or anxiolytic intoxication are very similar to those of alcohol intoxication. Very large doses of barbiturates lower respiration, blood pressure, and heart rate to dangerous levels. The diaphragm muscles may relax excessively, causing suffocation. Coma is also a common outcome. Many people taking barbiturates and benzodiazepines are unaware that their effects are amplified when mixed with other drugs. As an example, the combination of barbiturates with alcohol greatly increases the sedative qualities of the barbiturate—the effect that nearly killed Gareth in the chapter-opening case. This combination has led to many deaths, both accidental and suicidal.

Chronic use of barbiturates or benzodiazepines can cause what appears to be a constant state of alcohol intoxication. Long-term use causes depression, chronic fatigue, mood swings, and paranoia. It may also result in dramatic personality changes and serious impairments of memory and judgment.

DEPENDENCY

Tolerance to barbiturates develops rapidly. With regular use, increasingly higher doses are needed to achieve sedative effects. Tolerance to the benzodiazepines typically develops much more slowly than tolerance to barbiturates. A user with high tolerance to barbiturates or benzodiazepines attempting to abstain abruptly may experience extreme withdrawal reactions including delirium, convulsions, sleep disruptions, and other symptoms similar to those experienced with alcohol withdrawal. Withdrawal from barbiturates or benzodiazepines takes much longer and is significantly more dangerous than alcohol withdrawal (Cambor & Millman, 1991).

TREATMENT

Treatment for barbiturate or benzodiazepine dependence can be very complicated and may require prolonged hospitalization. Treatment usually involves administering progressively smaller doses of the abused drug to minimize withdrawal symptoms. Many individuals experience **abstinence syndrome**, which is characterized by insomnia, headaches, aching all over the body, anxiety, and depression, and which can last for months (Cambor & Millman, 1991). In addition to the pharmacological interventions, psychological and educational programs are usually advised to treat barbiturate dependency. Narcotics Anonymous mutual support groups, based on the same model as AA, have been set up in most large Canadian cities.

Stimulants

Stimulants are a class of drugs that have a stimulating or arousing effect on the CNS and create their effects by influencing the rate of uptake of the neurotransmitters dopamine, norepinephrine, and serotonin at receptor sites in the brain. The increased availability of these neurotransmitters affects the nucleus accumbens, which is a primary reward centre for the brain. As a group, stimulants are the most commonly used and abused drugs. They include nicotine, amphetamines, cocaine, and caffeine. Medications such as Ritalin that are used to treat attention deficit disorder fall into this drug class.

TOBACCO

Tobacco use (in the form of cigarettes, snuff, chewing tobacco, cigars, and pipes) constitutes one of the leading public health concerns in Canada. The number of Canadian deaths directly attributable to tobacco use is estimated to be approximately 37 000 per year, which is about 17 percent of all deaths (Rehm et al., 2006). This number includes adult smoking-related diseases (e.g., lung cancer and emphysema), childhood illness linked to maternal smoking (e.g., respiratory illness), and deaths due to smoking-related fires. Smoking prevention and cessation programs have become a priority for national health campaigns. Moreover, society bears major costs related to tobacco use. As shown earlier, in Table 11.6, the costs to society related to tobacco are higher than the costs related to alcohol, and much higher than all costs related to illicit drugs.

Nicotine comes from the tobacco plant *Nicotiniana tabacum*, which is a member of the nightshade family. Indigenous to South America, it is now grown in many places throughout the world. In Canada, it was originally grown by the Petun, Neutral, and Huron tribes of southwestern Ontario, who introduced it to French settlers. These colonists began cultivating and trading tobacco as early as 1652. Commercial cultivation began in the 1800s, and Canada now ranks among the top 10 tobacco-producing countries.

PREVALENCE Smoking rates in Canada rose steadily in the 1900s, peaking in the mid-1960s. It is estimated that in 2010, 17 percent of Canadians over the age of 14 smoked cigarettes (Health Canada, 2010b). This represents a decline from 1965, when approximately 50 percent of Canadians smoked regularly, and from 2007, when 19 percent smoked. In 2010, 13 percent reported smoking daily, whereas 4 percent reported smoking occasionally. More males (20 percent) reported smoking than females (14 percent). Daily smokers smoked an average of 15.1 cigarettes per day. There are at present more Canadians who have quit smoking than there are current smokers. Increased awareness about the adverse health effects of tobacco probably has a lot to do with this decline, as well as increasing tobacco prices (Mummery & Hagen, 1996). Many Canadian municipalities have instituted tough smoking bylaws, including reductions or bans in public places such as restaurants, shopping malls, and buses. In addition, it is no longer acceptable to smoke in most workplaces.

Of particular concern to public health officials are the rates of smoking among people under age 20, and efforts have been made to restrict cigarette ads that specifically target young people. The number of teen smokers rose in the 1990s but has been steadily declining since 1997. In 1999 the percentage of teens who smoked was 28 percent; currently, 12 percent of teens smoke (Paglia-Boak et al., 2009).

Other high-risk groups for smoking include people with a lower formal education, blue-collar workers, and Aboriginal Canadians. An estimated 59 percent of the First Nations population (Assembly of First Nations and First Nations Information Governance Committee, 2007) and 71 percent of the Inuit population smoke (First Nations and Inuit Health Branch, 2004).

EFFECTS **Nicotine** is a CNS stimulant related to the amphetamines. It is an extremely potent chemical and the ingestion of only a few drops, in its pure form, can cause respiratory failure. Lower dosages can interfere with thinking and problem solving, and can cause extreme agitation and irritability along with mood changes. However, the very small amount of nicotine present in a cigarette is not lethal and can increase alertness and improve mood. When inhaled, nicotine enters the lungs and reaches the brain in seconds. The pleasure centres of the brain seem to have receptors specific to this chemical (Benowitz, 1990).

Although the short-term consequences of smoking are minimal, the long-term health risks associated with smoking are significant. Smoking has been implicated in the development of lung, esophagus, larynx, and other cancers; emphysema; respiratory illness; heart disease; and other chronic conditions. Most of these illnesses are not caused by the nicotine in cigarettes but by the carbon monoxide and other chemicals found in tobacco. Although many of the health risks associated with smoking can be minimized 5 to 10 years after a person quits, lung damage is often irreversible (Jaffe, 1995). The health hazards of second-hand (or passive) smoke can be even more dangerous. Because there is no filter for these substances, second-hand smoke contains greater concentrations of ammonia, carbon monoxide, nicotine, and tar than the smoke inhaled by the smoker. As a result, passive smoking is associated with significant health risks in non-smokers, including heart disease, lung cancer, and childhood asthma.

Smoking during pregnancy is associated with problems including low birth weight, spontaneous abortion, stillbirth, and infant illness and disability. Women who smoke during pregnancy have double to triple the risk of having an underweight baby and 12 times the risk of delivering prematurely. About 30 percent of Canadian women report that they smoked during their last pregnancy (Statistics Canada, 2003b).

DEPENDENCY Dependence produced by nicotine is thought to be even greater than that produced by other addictive substances, including alcohol, cocaine, and caffeine

TABLE 11.8 RELATIVE ADDICTIVENESS OF COMMONLY USED SUBSTANCES AND ACTIVITIES

This table represents experts' assessment of how easy it is to get hooked on various commonly used substances and activities (both legal and illegal) and how difficult it is to stop using them. The estimates represent the proportion of users who develop an addictive pattern at some point in their lives.

Drug/Activity	Plausible Estimate of "Addictive Potential"
Those with at least some usable data	
Heroin	High
Methadone	High
Nicotine	High
Amphetamines	Moderate
Ecstasy	Moderate
Cocaine	Moderate
Alcohol	Moderate
Marijuana	Moderate
Benzodiazepines	Moderate
Gambling	Low
Those with little usable data	
Inactivity	Moderate
Tasty food	Moderate
Barbiturates	Low
Inhalants	Low
Gammahydroxybutyrate (GHB)	Low
Steroids	Low
Stealing	Low
Violence	Low
Diving	Low
Surfing	Low
Fast driving	Low
Exercise	Very low
Sexual behaviours	Very low
Playing computer games	Very low
Chocolate	Very low
Self-harm	Very low
Caffeine	Very low
Watching TV	Very low
Work	Very low
Shopping	Very low

Source: Adapted from West, R. (2006). *Theory of Addiction*. Oxford, UK: Blackwell Publishing.

(see Table 11.8; West, 2006). Nicotine dependence develops quickly, and although extremely large doses are required to produce intoxication, its behavioural effects are severe enough to classify many tobacco users as having a substance abuse disorder according to DSM-IV-TR criteria. Smokers become addicted not only because of nicotine's mood-enhancing abilities, but to prevent the effects of withdrawal, which can be quite severe.

So, with smoking, we have a situation that is extremely conducive to dependence: heavy nicotine use does not cause intoxication or behavioural impairment, and it is legally available and relatively inexpensive. One can smoke all day and avoid the severe withdrawal symptoms—a perfect recipe for addiction. People addicted to nicotine display behaviours much like those of other substance abusers: they often need a cigarette to start their day, they frequently smoke more than they anticipate, and they often spend a great deal of time looking for more cigarettes. Some smokers change their social plans in order to have continuous access to cigarettes. Furthermore, almost all smokers continue to smoke despite the knowledge that they are seriously damaging their health. There has been some suggestion that some people are more sensitive to the effects of nicotine, and thus become dependent more quickly (Pomerleau, Colins, Shiffman, & Sanderson, 1993). Certainly, people who begin to smoke when they are teenagers tend to be more dependent than those who start smoking in their twenties.

TREATMENT Despite greater restrictions on smoking in public places and ever-increasing knowledge about the health risks associated with smoking, it can be a difficult habit to break. Research in the United States shows that most smokers want to quit and over half have tried to quit in the past year (Center for Disease Control, 2011). Most smokers make three or four quit attempts before achieving lasting success. The majority quit smoking without professional help. Others seek help in the form of widely available self-help materials or through psychological and/or pharmacological treatments.

Psychological Treatments. Psychological interventions have increasingly become conceptualized and organized as an integrated system that includes a range of interventions varying in terms of intensity. Examples include formal face-to-face psychological interventions, brief counselling provided by health care professionals, telephone counselling, online support groups for quitting, and provision of self-help materials for quitting. A review of the research on effectiveness of psychological treatments concluded that there is consistent evidence that counselling is associated with increased quitting. The use of self-help materials without counselling or medication is not effective at improving quit rates (Ranney et al., 2006).

The psychological interventions designed to help people stop smoking are usually behavioural or cognitive in nature. As such, they typically help individuals develop skills such as self-monitoring, goal setting, and reinforcement. Some interventions attempt to reduce the pleasure experienced by smokers by forcing them to smoke far more cigarettes than they would normally. The adverse nature of these programs has probably contributed to their lack of success (Sobell, Toneatto, & Sobell, 1990). Other smoking cessation programs involve abrupt abstinence ("cold turkey") or include a period of reduction before the individual quits for good.

Pharmacological Treatments. Smoking cessation medications fall under two main categories: over-the-counter nicotine replacements and medications that are available only by prescription. Nicotine replacement in the form of gum, lozenges, inhalers, or skin patches helps to reduce cravings and other physiological withdrawal symptoms by maintaining a steady level of nicotine in the system. The idea is to break the behavioural habits associated with smoking while simultaneously reducing craving.

Prescription-only medications include bupropion hydrochloride and varenicline tartrate. Both of these drugs work by targeting receptors in the brain and do not deliver any nicotine to the body. Bupropion hydrochloride (Wellbutrin, Zyban) was originally prescribed as an antidepressant but was subsequently found to be effective in aiding smoking cessation. It works by reducing the severity of nicotine cravings and withdrawal symptoms. Varenicline tartrate (Chantix, Champix) is a prescription drug that was approved by Health Canada in 2007 and works by reducing cravings and decreasing the pleasurable effects of nicotine. There has been some evidence to suggest an association between varenicline and suicidal ideation. It is recommended that health care professionals and patients be very attentive to mood and behavioural changes when taking varenicline. Success rates of pharmacological treatments are greatly enhanced when used in conjunction with psychological therapies (Alberta Alcohol and Drug Abuse Commission, 2004).

3 BEFORE MOVING ON

> Despite the relative addictiveness of tobacco, the prevalence of smoking has decreased in recent years. What are some explanations for this trend?

AMPHETAMINES AND DESIGNER DRUGS

Amphetamines and related drugs have effects on the body similar to those of the naturally occurring hormone adrenalin. The two most commonly abused forms of amphetamine are methamphetamine (with street names such as "speed" when injected, and "ice" or "crystal" when smoked in a purified form) and dextroamphetamine (a legally prescribed medication sold under the name Dexedrine). Other street names for these drugs are "bennies," "uppers," "glass," "crank," and "pep pills." Methylphenidate (Ritalin) is used to treat ADHD but can also be abused. Methylated amphetamines, referred to as designer drugs, have both stimulant and hallucinogenic properties. Methylenedioxymethamphetamine (MDMA), known as "Ecstasy" (or simply "E"), has had recent popularity, particularly among young people at raves. Methylene-dioxyamphetamine (MDA) and para-methoxyamphetamine (PMA) are other examples of designer drugs.

Amphetamines were originally developed as a nasal decongestant and asthma treatment in the 1930s. It was discovered that, in addition to shrinking mucous membranes and constricting blood vessels, they also increased alertness and concentration. Consequently, they were used to treat narcolepsy (a sleeping disorder) and later ADHD. Later, the appetite-suppressant qualities of amphetamines also led to their use as a treatment for obesity. Currently, only dextroamphetamine (or Dexedrine, used in the treatment of ADHD) is legally manufactured in Canada. Other amphetamines and related drugs, referred to as "designer drugs," are manufactured illegally in home laboratories.

Mali: Living with Narcolepsy

Watch this Speaking Out video at www.mysearchlab.com

Mali Sleep Disorder: Narcolepsy

Watch this Speaking Out video at www.mysearchlab.com

PREVALENCE The rate of amphetamine and other illicit drug use in Canada is difficult to determine for a number of reasons. First, unlike alcohol and tobacco (which can be measured by the standard drink or the cigarette), most drugs have no accepted units of measurement. Moreover, because the majority of sales of such drugs are illegal, there are no consumer records or indexes of availability. Consumers may not even know what they are using. Because many are manufactured in illegal laboratories, the contents vary considerably. For example, the RCMP conducted an analysis of Ecstasy tablets seized at Vancouver raves (Royal Canadian Mounted Police, 2000). Only 24 percent of the tablets were pure MDMA; the other tablets were mixtures of other substances with or without MDMA. More than one-third contained no MDMA. Thus, it is difficult to define and monitor addiction, or to gauge the social impact of illicit drug use.

Between 1950 and 1970, stimulants were widely consumed by truckers, athletes, students, and others wishing to increase alertness and enhance performance. Since then, amphetamine use in Canada has declined markedly. In the Canadian Centre on Substance Abuse (2004a) national survey, 6 percent of respondents (aged 15+) reported using amphetamines at some time in their life. Ecstasy use was reported by 4 percent. Use is somewhat higher among youth in Grades 7 to 12—lifetime use among Ontario high school students was 4.8 percent for stimulants (non-cocaine), 3.2 percent for Ecstasy, 1.4 percent for methamphetamine, 0.5 percent for crystal methamphetamine ("ice"), and 1.6 percent for non-medical use of ADHD-type drugs (Paglia-Boak et al., 2009).

EFFECTS At low doses, amphetamines increase alertness and allow the user to focus attention effectively, offering improved performance on cognitive tasks. At higher doses, they induce

Crack, a fast-acting and highly addictive form of cocaine, is smoked with a special pipe.

feelings of exhilaration, extroversion, and confidence, and at very high doses, restlessness and anxiety can occur.

Chronic amphetamine use is associated with feelings of fatigue and sadness, as well as periods of social withdrawal and intense anger. Repeated high doses can cause hallucinations, delirium, and paranoia, a condition known as **toxic psychosis**. To combat undesirable effects such as sleeplessness, many amphetamine users also become dependent upon depressant drugs such as tranquilizers, barbiturates, and alcohol to induce sleep. This can lead to a roller coaster–like vicious circle of drug use (Stein & Ellinwood, 1993).

The physical effects of amphetamines include increased or irregular heartbeat, fluctuations in blood pressure, hot or cold flashes, nausea, weakness, and dilation of pupils. Prolonged use usually leads to weight loss. At very high doses, amphetamines can induce seizures, confusion, and coma. The periods of intense anger associated with prolonged amphetamine use may also contribute to the prevalence of violent death in Canada such as suicides, homicides, and violent accidents (Gourlay, 2000).

The long-term effects of Ecstasy have received considerable attention. Based on animal studies, there is a concern that moderate or greater use can lead to permanent depletion of serotonin. There have been reports of long-term neuropsychiatric problems in users, although the specific role of Ecstasy in producing these effects is unclear.

DEPENDENCY Amphetamine tolerance and dependence develops very quickly. The effects of amphetamines do not last long, and users often experience a post-high "crash" marked by feelings of fatigue, irritability, sadness, and craving. Withdrawal from amphetamines also often causes periods of apathy and prolonged sleeping.

COCAINE

Cocaine comes from the *Erythroxylon coca* bush, indigenous to various areas in South America. Its stimulating effects have long been known to the people of these regions, who chew on the leaves to reduce fatigue and induce euphoria. Throughout the 1800s, cocaine was viewed as harmless; it was sold in cocaine-laced cigarettes, cigars, inhalants, and crystals, and was the principal ingredient in a variety of commercial products, including Coca-Cola (Musto, 1992). In 1911 cocaine use was restricted in Canada, and it is now only occasionally used legally as a local anaesthetic for minor surgeries.

In the 1960s and 1970s, cocaine became a popular recreational drug. Due to the high cost, its use was generally limited to those in middle- and upper-income groups. Recently, however, cocaine has fallen in price as cheaper forms such as crack have been introduced.

Cocaine is usually sold on the street in powder form. This powder is often snorted, but can also be rubbed into the skin or mixed with water and injected. Another method of cocaine ingestion is called "freebasing" and involves purifying cocaine by heating it and smoking the residue. (See Table 11.9 for a comparison of methods of taking substances.) Crack is made by dissolving powdered cocaine in a solvent, combining it with baking soda, and heating it until it forms a crystallized substance (a "rock"), which is then smoked. The process itself is potentially dangerous, because the solvents are highly flammable. It is popular, however, because of its cheapness, since the cocaine used need not be as refined as cocaine for snorting. This method of ingestion also increases the rate of metabolizing the drug and makes it more addictive.

TABLE 11.9 METHODS OF TAKING SUBSTANCES

Method	Route	Time to Reach Brain
Inhaling	Drug in vapour form is inhaled through mouth and lungs into circulatory system.	7 seconds
Snorting	Drug in powdered form is snorted into the nose. Some of the drug lands on the nasal mucous membranes, is absorbed by blood vessels, and enters the bloodstream.	4 minutes
Injection	Drug in liquid form directly enters the body through a needle.	20 seconds (intravenous)
	Injection may be intravenous or intramuscular (subcutaneous).	4 minutes (intramuscular)
Oral ingestion	Drug in solid or liquid form passes through esophagus and stomach and finally to the small intestines. It is absorbed by blood vessels in the intestines.	30 minutes
Other routes	Drugs can be absorbed through areas that contain mucous membranes. Drugs can be placed under the tongue, inserted anally and vaginally, and administered as eyedrops.	Variable

Source: Reprinted with permission from Landry, M. J. (1994). *Understanding drugs of abuse: The process of addiction, treatment and recovery.* Washington, DC: American Psychiatric Press.

The short-term effects of cocaine appear soon after its ingestion and wear off very quickly. Crack is especially fast-acting, and may wear off in a few minutes. In small amounts, cocaine use in any form produces feelings of euphoria, well-being, and confidence. Users become more alert and talkative, and experience reduced appetite and increased excitement and energy, due to the stimulation of the higher centres of the CNS. It appears that these effects are primarily achieved by increasing the availability of dopamine at important neuronal sites in the brain. With high doses, the CNS is overstimulated, leading to poor muscle control, confusion, anxiety, anger, and aggression. Continuous use may result in mood swings, loss of interest in sex, weight loss, and insomnia. As with amphetamines, chronic use of cocaine can also lead to toxic psychosis experienced as delusions and hallucinations.

Physical symptoms of cocaine use include increased blood pressure and body temperature, as well as irregular heartbeat. Users may also experience chest pain, nausea, blurred vision, fever, muscle spasms, convulsions, and coma. Death can occur as a result of cocaine's impact on the brain centres that control respiration.

PREVALENCE The restriction on cocaine use by the Canadian government in the early 1900s led to a decline in its use throughout the first half of the century. This decline coincided with an increase in amphetamine use. When amphetamine use waned in the 1950s and 1960s, cocaine's popularity again increased (Addiction Research Foundation, 1997).

In a 2010 survey, about 0.7 percent of Canadians reported having used cocaine or crack in the past year (Health Canada, 2010a). Among high school students, lifetime use was reported as 3.4 percent for cocaine and 1.5 percent for crack. Use in the past year was reported as 2.6 percent for cocaine and 1.1 percent for crack (Paglia-Boak et al., 2009).

DEPENDENCY Cocaine produces intense psychological dependence and results in severe withdrawal symptoms. Cocaine users often feel a crash as the drug begins to wear off, which results in intense craving, depression, and paranoia, followed by fatigue. The craving for cocaine experienced during withdrawal gradually diminishes in intensity, but can take more than a month to disappear completely (Gawin & Kleber, 1986; Weddington et al., 1990).

TREATMENT FOR AMPHETAMINE AND COCAINE ABUSE

Treatment for stimulant abuse is complicated by several factors. Stimulant users are also likely to use other drugs to counteract some of the effects of the stimulants. As a result, many are dependent on alcohol or other depressants, making it difficult to decide which dependency to treat first. In addition, people who abuse more than one drug often have comorbid mental disorders, and it is difficult to determine whether one of these conditions predates the other.

Psychological Treatments. Psychological treatments for stimulant abuse developed in the 1980s were often modelled after the 12-step programs for alcohol. Intervention programs, which normally have abstinence as a goal, have also focused on group therapy, individual counselling, and developing relapse prevention skills (McClellan, Arndt, Metzger, Woody, & O'Brien, 1993). Cognitive-behavioural interventions examine the thoughts and behaviours that precede and maintain stimulant abuse (Joe, Dansereau, & Simpson, 1994). Recently, community outpatient programs have become popular, in which individuals are rewarded with money and social outings if they remain drug-free. There is some evidence that these programs are superior to 12-step programs (Higgins et al., 1993). Treatment programs have also been developed that integrate the treatment of the drug and comorbid mental health disorders. This integrated approach is considered superior to sequential treatment of the various concerns. Cocaine Anonymous and Narcotics Anonymous mutual support groups are often recommended to complement the formal treatment program.

Biological Treatments. Biological treatments are usually used as adjuncts to psychological interventions for stimulant abuse. Antidepressants may be prescribed to combat the depression that frequently occurs during withdrawal. In addition, dopamine-enhancing drugs (for example, bromocriptine) may be given in order to reduce cravings. So far, studies have not found that these medications alone improve outcomes (Gourlay, 2000). Again, they are probably most beneficial when used in conjunction with a good psychological treatment program.

CAFFEINE

Caffeine, the world's most popular stimulant, was first isolated from coffee beans in 1820. However, it had been used for centuries before that. Tea was drunk in China at least as early as the ninth century, but tradition places its discovery much earlier. Coffee was recorded in Ethiopia in the fifteenth century, and was then stated to have been drunk from time immemorial. Soon after that time, the substance became controversial among Muslims in North Africa and Arabia; some used it to keep awake during long religious ceremonies, although others claimed that it was an intoxicating beverage and thus forbidden by the Quran. Nevertheless, coffee became the national beverage of the region. Both coffee and tea were introduced to Europe in the seventeenth century. Coffee houses played an important social role in seventeenth- and eighteenth-century England, and tea had become a staple of British life by the end of the eighteenth century. So-called energy drinks are increasingly popular among young people in North America.

Caffeine is found in a variety of other foods and beverages (see Figure 11.2). It is also a common ingredient in many over-the-counter pain medications, cough and cold remedies, and diet pills. Like other stimulants, it produces a release of the neurotransmitters dopamine, serotonin, and norepinephrine.

EFFECTS In general, caffeine is less harmful than other stimulants. Health Canada (2010c) recommends that

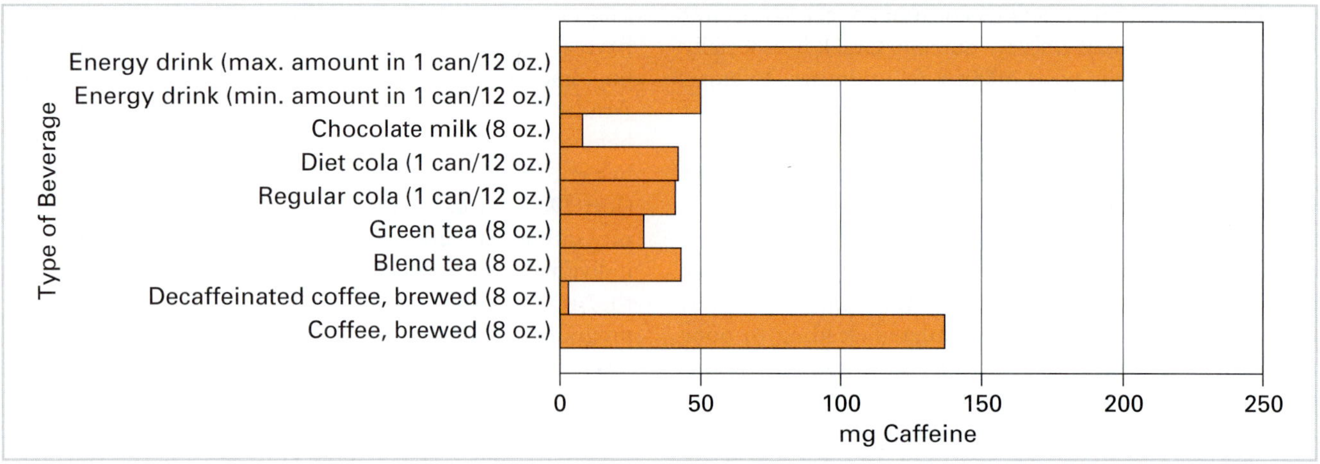

FIGURE 11.2 Amounts of Caffeine in Common Beverages

Source: Health Canada. (2011). Caffeine in Food. Retrieved from http://www.hc-sc.gc.ca/fn-an/securit/addit/caf/food-caf-aliments-eng.php

healthy adults do not exceed 400 mg of caffeine per day. This amount equals about three cups (237 ml) of brewed coffee per day. At low doses (100–150 milligrams, approximately one cup of brewed coffee), caffeine can increase attention, improve problem-solving skills, and improve mood. Higher doses cause increased jitteriness, nervousness, gastrointestinal discomfort, and insomnia. At doses exceeding 1000 milligrams per day, caffeine can cause muscle tremors, agitation, excessive talkativeness, disorganized thinking, and rapid or irregular heartbeat. Prolonged use of 350 milligrams per day or more can result in physical dependence. Long-term consumption of more than 650 milligrams per day may cause chronic insomnia, persistent anxiety and depression, and irregular heartbeat. Approximately 20 percent of Canadians are described as physically dependent on caffeine (that is, they consume 350 milligrams per day or more), and roughly 4 percent consume more than 650 milligrams per day. Cessation of caffeine use can cause withdrawal symptoms that include headaches (which can be relieved only by caffeine consumption), drowsiness, and irritability (Silverman, Evans, Strain, & Griffiths, 1992).

DSM-IV-TR has several classes of caffeine-related disorders, including caffeine intoxication, caffeine-induced anxiety disorder, and caffeine-induced sleep disorder.

Opioids

Opioids (also known as narcotics) are a class of CNS depressants—drugs whose main effects are the reduction of pain and sleep inducement. Opium, the alkaloid from which opioids are derived, comes from the seeds of the opium poppy, which is indigenous to Asia and the Middle East. Natural opiates (e.g., morphine, codeine) are refined directly from opium, whereas semi-synthetic opiates (e.g., heroin, oxycodon) are derived from natural opiates. Synthetic opiates (e.g., methadone, Darvon, Demerol) are drugs manufactured to have effects similar to those of the other opiates.

Opioids can be taken as tablets, capsules, suppositories, syrups, or in the form of an injection. In pure form, heroin appears as a white, odourless, bitter-tasting powder that can also be snorted. Most heroin users, however, prefer to mix heroin with water and inject it to produce a more intense high. This is known as "mainlining."

Heroin, the most commonly abused opioid, was originally introduced in 1898 as a replacement for morphine and was viewed as relatively harmless. Not until the early 1900s was it discovered that heroin is even more addictive than morphine. Morphine and codeine are the only naturally derived opioids in common clinical use in North America. Morphine remains a mainstay of analgesia for severe pain, such as that experienced by terminally ill cancer patients, and codeine is present in many common medications, such as cough syrups and painkillers. Although synthetic opiates are used frequently today as analgesics, they can also produce dependence.

PREVALENCE

In 2010 less than 1 percent of Canadians reported ever having tried heroin (Health Canada, 2010a). Among high school students in Ontario, 0.8 percent reported using it sometime in their life and 0.7 percent reported using it in the past year. Rates have been generally low but have dropped in the past decade (Paglia-Boak et al., 2009).

Even if the street use of heroin is not a major Canadian problem, the use of prescription forms of opioids by Canadians is of considerable concern. Surveys of adults have found that 8 percent report using prescription forms of codeine, morphine, or Demerol in the previous month (Adlaf, Ivis, & Smart, 1994). Opioids were most likely to be used in British Columbia (12 percent) and least likely to be used in Quebec (3 percent); those between the ages of 25 and 34 were most likely to use prescription opioids (11 percent), and women report greater use than do men (9.0 percent versus 7.4 percent; Single, MacLennan, & MacNeil, 1994). In the most recent Canadian survey, one in five (20.6 percent) of Canadians aged 15 years and older reported using opioid pain relievers in the previous 12 months. Students are also reporting high levels of use, with 19.8 percent of Ontario students in Grades 7 to 12 reporting lifetime use and 17.8 percent reporting past-year use (Paglia-Boak et al., 2009).

EFFECTS

Opioids mimic the effects of **endogenous opiates**, or the body's natural painkillers. Known as **exogenous opiates**, narcotics affect receptor sites located throughout the body, including the brain, spinal cord, and bloodstream. The narcotics bind to receptor sites at these locations and, in turn, reduce the body's production of endogenous opiates. Thus, someone who stops using exogenous opiates may experience increased pain sensitivity (Cambor & Millman, 1991).

Heroin is perhaps the most addicting of all opiates, in part due to the sensations associated with using the drug. About one minute after injecting heroin, the user experiences an intense pleasurable rush. After this subsides, a euphoria characterized by dulled sensations and dream-like sedation is produced, and the user may appear drunk. Heroin also acts as an appetite suppressant, and even small doses can cause restlessness, nausea, and vomiting (Addiction Research Foundation, 1997).

At higher doses, heroin has extremely dangerous effects: pupils constrict, the skin may turn blue and feel cold and clammy, breathing slows, and coma and respiratory depression causing death can occur. A major problem is that the impact of any dose can be difficult to determine. In fact, heroin addicts sometimes die from a dosage level that they had previously tolerated. It appears that this is more likely to occur when the drug is taken in an environment that is different from the one in which the drug is usually taken, although it is not clear why this is so (Szabo, Tabakoff, & Hoffman, 1994). In addition, because heroin is produced in an uncontrolled manner and sold on the street, it is often cut with other drugs and its purity is difficult to determine. Many deaths have resulted when, for

FOCUS 11.4

Needle Exchange Programs: An Effective Harm Reduction Strategy

Almost any psychoactive drug can be liquefied and injected into the body. Because the substance enters the bloodstream very quickly, injection is often the preferred method of drug-taking, particularly for the hardcore drug user. In Canada, frequently injected drugs include cocaine, heroin, amphetamines, opioids, and anabolic steroids. It is difficult to get a clear picture of the extent of injection drug use, although attention has focused on Vancouver, Montreal, and Toronto as having significant problems. In Vancouver, for example, it is estimated that about 15 000 people inject (Millar, 1998). Street youth, both male and female, make up a substantial proportion of daily injectors (Shields, 2000).

Among the other health risks of drug abuse, injection drug use puts the user at risk of contracting HIV or hepatitis C through the use of contaminated needles or other injection equipment such as spoons or containers. Users inject many times per day, so the risk to the individual over time is high. In Vancouver, a study of users found that 28 percent were HIV positive and 86 percent were hepatitis C positive (Spittal et al., 1998).

THE HARM REDUCTION APPROACH

Whereas treatment for drug abuse focuses on reducing or eliminating the use of the drug, **harm reduction approaches** focus on reducing the consequences of the use. In the 1980s, the Public Health Department in Rotterdam began to distribute clean needles to a semi-organized group of heroin addicts. Since then, a number of countries, including Canada, have established increasingly organized needle exchange services. Canada has 30 needle exchange programs operating across the country (Riley, 1994). These programs are often implemented along with counselling, education, and outreach efforts attempting to encourage addicts to participate more fully in treatment programs. Often the service is mobile, with a van travelling to particular convenient meeting points with the addicts.

Research demonstrates that needle exchange programs accomplish their harm reduction goals. Users who attend programs compared to those who do not attend reduce their risk behaviours and infection rates (Hurley, 1997) and are more likely to attend treatment programs (United States Department of Health and Human Services, 2000).

Despite these positive effects, concerns about needle exchange programs continue to be voiced. Many are concerned about the risk to the public of providing extra needles to addicts. However, no large public health risks have emerged. For example, the rate at which needles are turned in exceeds the rate at which they are handed out in Vancouver (Vancouver Coastal Health, 2003). There is no evidence of an increase in needle stick accidents in public places such as playgrounds and parks. There is also no evidence that drug dealers are drawn to areas with programs because of a perceived availability of clientele or that crime rates increase (Videnieks, 2003).

Perhaps the largest objections are to the harm reduction philosophy itself. The harm reduction policy is seen as supporting illicit drug use by providing drug use paraphernalia. As a result of these concerns, the U.S. federal government has a constitutional ban on the use of federal funds to support needle exchange programs and research on their effectiveness (Vernick, Burris, & Strathdee, 2003). In Canada, the police community has expressed concerns at times, although generally a positive working relationship between the police and programs has developed (Canadian Centre on Substance Abuse, 2004b). The establishment of needle exchange programs in Canadian prisons, where injection drug use rates and rates of HIV and hepatitis C infection are far higher than those in the general population, has been more controversial. Despite their successful introduction in prisons in many other countries, there are currently no programs in Canadian correctional institutions (Canadian Centre on Substance Abuse, 2004b).

Source: Adapted from the Canadian Centre on Substance Abuse (2004b).

some unknown reason, the heroin that is sold at a street level is purer than usual, so that the user unwittingly injects too high a dose.

Chronic users may develop a number of physical conditions. Chronic respiratory and pulmonary problems may develop as a result of the effects of heroin on the respiratory system.

Endocarditis, an infection of the lining of the heart, occurs as a result of the use of unsterilized needles. The use of unsterilized injection equipment can also cause abscesses, cellulitis, liver disease, and brain damage. The risk of HIV infection among intravenous drug users is significant, although the introduction of needle exchange programs seems to have been successful at reducing the spread of HIV through needles (see Focus box 11.4; Hurley, 1997).

DEPENDENCY

The withdrawal symptoms associated with heroin and other opioids are extremely severe and begin about eight hours after the last dose. Along with increased pain sensitivity, the user may experience dysphoria, a dulling of the senses, anxiety, increased bodily secretions (runny eyes and nose), pupil dilation, fever, sweating, and muscle pain. Thirty-six hours after a dose, muscle-twitching, cramps, hot flashes, and changes in heart rate and blood pressure can occur, in addition to sleeplessness, vomiting, and diarrhea. These symptoms gradually diminish over a 5- to 10-day period. Partly because of the intensity of these symptoms, relapse of opioid abuse is extremely common (Addiction Research Foundation, 1997).

TREATMENT

The treatment for opioid abuse typically involves the use of medications. Drugs such as naltrexone act as opioid antagonists and help to alleviate initial symptoms of withdrawal, while **methadone**, a heroin replacement, is often used to reduce the craving after initial withdrawal symptoms have abated. Higher doses are given in the early stages of treatment and are then gradually decreased. The methadone is either tapered out completely or is maintained at a steady dose to allow individuals to improve their functioning in other areas of their lives, such as employment and social relationships. People receiving methadone maintenance therapy are less likely to commit crimes to support their habit (Bertschy, 1995) and are at less risk of HIV infection than people using heroin (Rosenbach & Hunot, 1995). Most experts agree that methadone therapy works best in conjunction with good individual and group psychological programs, as well as ongoing peer support.

4 BEFORE MOVING ON

Why do opioids such as heroin and oxycodone have a high addictive potential?

Cannabis

Case Notes

When Derek was 16 years old and in Grade 11, his older brother turned him on to grass, and he liked it. Derek began to smoke occasionally with his brother during the week. He could get marijuana for other kids from his brother, which made him very popular.

Although Derek's parents and brother had dropped out of school early, Derek seemed academically gifted. However, as his smoking became more frequent, his work habits deteriorated and his attendance dropped. Within a few months, he met suppliers who could provide him with cheaper marijuana and other drugs as well. Derek was now spending more time dealing than doing schoolwork, and he failed his year. But he was earning as much in a day or two as his father did in a week of casual labour.

By the end of the next school year, word of his services reached the ears of the principal. Derek's apartment was raided and a sizable cache of drugs was seized. Derek was sentenced to 18 months in prison.

Upon release six months later, Derek was adamant about going straight. He returned to school and got a job waiting tables. But grades did not come as easily as before, the other students were all much younger, and the double workload was tiring. He slowly slipped into seeing some of his old acquaintances and smoking the odd joint. When other students asked for drugs, he found it hard to refuse. Derek soon gave up his job and started selling, and using, a variety of drugs.

Derek was referred to one of the authors for a pre-sentencing report after being found guilty of possession of a variety of drugs for the purpose of trafficking. This time, he was also charged with possession of a large number of stolen goods, including a very expensive stereo system. Derek claimed he had received the goods as payment for drugs and did not know that they had been stolen.

Marijuana and hashish come from the hemp plant *Cannabis sativa*, indigenous to Asia but now grown in many parts of the world. The hemp plant was originally (and still is) cultivated for its strong fibres, which can be processed into cloth and rope. However, its psychotropic and medicinal properties soon became known, and it was used for pleasure as well as to treat rheumatism, gout, depression, and cholera. Marijuana consists of the leaves and flowers of this plant, which are dried and crushed. Hashish, made from the resin produced by the plant, is a much stronger form of **cannabis**. Although both forms are most often smoked in cigarette form (called a "joint") or in a pipe, they can also be chewed, added to baked goods, or prepared in a tea. Other names for marijuana and hashish are "pot," "weed," "grass," "dope," "reefer," and "bud." Cannabis does not fit into the usual classification of drug groups. It generally has depressant effects, yet it increases the user's heart rate like a stimulant. It can also produce hallucinations when consumed in large doses, but this is not a usual effect.

PREVALENCE

Marijuana is the most commonly used and most widely available illicit drug in Canada. In 2010, 42 percent of Canadians aged 15 and over reported using cannabis at least once in their lives and 11 percent reported using it in the year before the survey (Health Canada, 2010a). Rates are higher among males and for younger people. Rates of lifetime and past-year use are lower than those reported in 2004, when the lifetime and past-year rates were 44.5 percent and 14.1 percent respectively.

Among high school students in Ontario, overall 25.6 percent reported use in the 12 months before the survey. This figure includes 14.5 percent who reported using marijuana frequently (six or more times in the past year). Use increases with each grade from 7 to 12, with 45.6 percent of people in Grade 12 reporting last-year use. Males were more likely than females to use marijuana, with 28.8 percent of males reporting past-year use compared to 22.2 percent of females (Paglia-Boak et al., 2009).

Although rates of marijuana use among adults appear to be rising, use among high school students has been fairly stable since 1999 (Paglia-Boak et al., 2009). Use among university students is similar to that of Grade 12 students. A survey by researchers at the CAMH (Adlaf et al., 2005) found that more than half (51 percent) of university students across Canada reported using cannabis at some point in their lives. About a third (32 percent) had used it during the past 12 months, and this varied by region. Students in Quebec reported the highest rates of cannabis use in the previous 12 months (39 percent), followed by the Atlantic provinces (37 percent), Ontario (33 percent), and British Columbia (30 percent). University students in the Prairie provinces reported the lowest rates of cannabis use (19 percent).

EFFECTS

The psychoactive effects of cannabis are caused primarily by the chemical delta-9-tetrahydrocannabinol (**THC**). Although the exact mechanisms by which THC exerts its influence are not fully understood, it appears that it acts upon specific cannabinoid receptors in the body and mimics the effects of naturally occurring substances, including the endogenous opiates (Bouaboula et al., 1993). The concentration of THC in marijuana and hashish has increased about fivefold since the 1960s and 1970s, making it difficult to measure accurately the effect of specific doses.

Cannabis involves mild changes in perception along with enhancement of physical experiences. With relatively small doses, most users report feeling mildly euphoric and sociable. A sense of well-being and relaxation usually begins within minutes of ingesting the drug and lasts for two to three hours. Some people, however, find the drug stimulating, and occasionally panic or anxiety is also experienced. At high doses, cannabis has been known to cause hallucinations, although it seems that this most often occurs when the user has a pre-existing mental disorder. Individuals under the influence of marijuana show deficits in complex motor skills, short-term memory, reaction time, and attention. Physical effects include itchy, red eyes, and both increased blood pressure and appetite (Wilson, Ellinwood, Mathew, & Johnson, 1994). Cannabis has clear effects on ability to drive. Although detection of impairment is considerably more complex than alcohol impairment, a standardized roadside assessment called the Drug Evaluation and Classification (DEC) program has been used throughout Canada since 2008. DEC, which detects use of other psychoactive drugs in addition to cannabis, involves a series of coordination tests, an eye examination, behavioural observations, and toxicology analysis. Drug Recognition Experts (DREs) are individuals trained and certified in conducting DEC evaluations. Certification is essential because of the large number and complexity of factors that need to be considered in each appraisal. A review of DEC evaluation studies found the overall accuracy of DEC evaluations of suspected impaired drivers to be greater than 80 percent (Beirness, LeCavalier & Singhal, 2007). An analysis of 1400 DEC evaluations conducted in Canada revealed that DREs are extremely accurate (95 percent) in detecting drivers who are impaired by drugs (Beirness, Beasley, & LeCavalier, 2009).

Long-term users often suffer greater lung problems than tobacco smokers, including deterioration in the linings of the trachea and bronchial tubes, which may be a result of holding unfiltered smoke in their lungs for long periods of time. In addition, marijuana and hashish contain much greater concentrations of some known carcinogens (e.g., benzopyrene) than does tobacco, and there is also some evidence that chronic marijuana use can result in fertility problems for both men and women.

Some long-term users develop **amotivational syndrome**, a continuing pattern of apathy, profound self-absorption, detachment from friends and family, and abandonment of career and educational goals. Although the amotivational syndrome is thought to be related to the alteration of brain function caused by chronic cannabis use (Musty & Kabak, 1995), it may also be related to depression in long-term users. There is evidence that about 30 percent of regular cannabis users also have symptoms of depression (American Psychiatric Association, 2000; Cambor & Millman, 1991). It is unclear whether depression leads to increased cannabis consumption, or whether it is a result of prolonged use.

THERAPEUTIC EFFECTS OF MARIJUANA Marijuana has been used in the treatment of several diseases, including cancer, AIDS, and glaucoma. It has been shown that THC can help to alleviate nausea and encourage eating in cancer and AIDS patients. In the treatment of glaucoma, THC has been used to relieve pressure within the eyes. Because it

Timothy Leary was one of the leaders of a movement that extolled hallucinogens as part of a quasi-spiritual quest to expand consciousness and live life on a higher plane.

is both illicit and thought to be "bad for one's health," most jurisdictions do not currently allow marijuana consumption for therapeutic use, even in extreme cases. However, as of 2001, the Canadian government changed regulations on the possession and production of marijuana for medical purposes so that those with a terminal illness, and those with severe pain from medical conditions (including severe pain associated with multiple sclerosis, spinal cord injury, AIDS/HIV, severe arthritis, and epilepsy), can apply to the Office of Cannabis Medical Access to possess the drug legally. All applications must be supported by declarations from medical practitioners. Patients can also apply for a licence to grow their own marijuana for the above purposes (Munroe, 2002).

DEPENDENCY

It has long been believed that marijuana is not addictive, but there is recent recognition that regular marijuana use results in both tolerance and withdrawal symptoms, although withdrawal is milder than with other addictive substances. Symptoms include irritability, nervousness and anxiety, loss of appetite, restlessness, sleep disturbances, and anger/aggression (Budney, Moore, Vandrey, & Hughes, 2003). According to the recent adult survey, about 1 in 20 Canadians report a cannabis-related concern. The most common concerns were impaired control over use and a strong desire to use (Canadian Centre on Substance Abuse, 2004a). Adlaf and Paglia-Boak (2007) estimate that about 1 in 10 Ontario high school students have a dependence problem (daily uncontrolled use or attempts to reduce use).

Most marijuana abusers in Canada are placed in generalized treatment programs, although there are also efforts to develop cannabis-specific treatment approaches using a cognitive-behavioural treatment model (e.g., Stephens, Roffman, & Curtin, 2000).

Hallucinogens

Hallucinogens are drugs that change a person's mental state by inducing perceptual and sensory distortions or hallucinations. They are also called *psychedelics*, which comes from the Greek words for "soul" and "to make manifest." Hallucinogens have been used in religious or spiritual ceremonies for thousands of years. Many of these drugs are derived from plants, but others are produced in the laboratory. There are many different kinds of hallucinogens, but the most well known are lysergic acid diethylamide (LSD or "acid"), mescaline, and psilocybin (magic mushrooms). Methylene-dioxymethamphetamine (MDMA) or Ecstasy (described under "Amphetamines and Designer Drugs" earlier in this chapter) is sometimes included in this category as well. Phencyclidine (PCP or "angel dust"), which was very popular in the 1980s but has declined in use recently, is a dissociative anaesthetic used for its hallucinogenic properties. Ketamine (K or Special K) is a close analogue to PCP, used as a veterinary anaesthetic. Salvia (*Salvia divinorum*) is a plant native to southern Mexico containing powerful psychoactive chemical properties that lead to hallucinations.

LSD was first discovered in 1938 by Swiss chemist Albert Hoffman, who was investigating ergot—a fungus that affects cereal plants such as wheat and rye. In 1943 he accidentally ingested some of the compound he had isolated from this fungus, and subsequently had the first recorded "acid trip." Later, he also extracted psilocybin from a mushroom called *Psilocybe mexicana*.

Hallucinogens can be ingested in capsule or tablet form, or as a liquid applied to small pieces of paper (for example, stamps or stickers) and then placed on the tongue. Mescaline is found in the head of the peyote cactus and is chewed or mixed with food or water. Psilocybin is also chewed or swallowed with water. PCP is produced in a laboratory and is typically smoked. Ketamine, also produced in a laboratory, is injected, snorted, or taken orally. Salvia was traditionally ingested by chewing the plant leaves but is more commonly smoked. The effects of hallucinogens usually begin within an hour of ingestion or sooner and last between 6 and 12 hours.

PREVALENCE

In Canada, the use of hallucinogens peaked in the 1960s. According to the latest adult survey (Health Canada, 2010a), 11 percent reported using hallucinogens sometime in their life, although use in the year before the survey was rare (less than 1 percent). Use is slightly higher among high school students in Ontario than among Canadian adults. Past-year use of LSD was 1.8 percent, of other hallucinogens was 5.0 percent, of PCP was 0.8 percent, of salvia was 4.4 percent, and of ketamine was 1.6 percent (Paglia-Boak et al., 2009).

EFFECTS

The subjective effects of hallucinogens depend on a number of variables, including the personality of the user and the amount of drug ingested. People's expectations regarding the effects of hallucinogens appear to play a large role in determining their reaction. In addition, the setting in which the hallucinogens are taken appears to be very important. Users who feel uncomfortable or unsafe in their environment may experience anxiety and fear, which can sometimes escalate into panic or psychotic-like episodes. A very small number of individuals are left with a prolonged psychotic disorder long after the drug has worn off.

People taking hallucinogens report a number of sensory experiences, including vivid visual hallucinations. Objects may waver, shimmer, or become distorted (for example, limbs may appear very long). People commonly see colourful "halos" around objects; moving objects leave visible trails. Users may also experience *synesthesia*, a transference of stimuli from one sense to another, such as "hearing" colours or "feeling" sounds.

Hallucinogens have an excitatory effect on the CNS and mimic the effects of serotonin by acting upon serotonin receptors in the brain stem and cerebral cortex. LSD, for example, affects the sympathetic nervous system and causes dilated pupils, increased heart rate, elevated blood pressure, and increased alertness. Most hallucinogens are not physiologically dangerous even in high doses. However, hallucinations may lead to a risk of injury if there are extreme distortions in sense of distance, depth, or speed. PCP has effects that are more variable, and larger doses have been

FOCUS 11.5

Gambling: An Addiction?

Social gambling has been part of many societies; it can be recreational and provide exciting and exhilarating entertainment. In Canada, a large expansion in gambling opportunities occurred in the 1990s when provincial governments began legalizing video lottery terminals (VLTs) and permanent casinos to supplement lottery, bingo, and horse racing gambling. Most Canadians are social gamblers. They limit the frequency of their gambling, and the time and money spent on gambling, and suffer no repercussions from their gambling. However, there is another group of gamblers who will "risk their reputation, their family's security, their life's savings, their work, their freedom, or their safety on the turn of a card, a roll of the dice, or the legs of a horse" (Custer, 1982). They are preoccupied with gambling and unable to resist despite staggeringly negative consequences. Such people are commonly called "compulsive gamblers"; mental health professionals refer to them as *pathological gamblers.*

The Canadian Community Health Survey (Marshall & Wynne, 2003) provided a national perspective on gambling problems, including pathological gambling. As shown in Figure 11.3, gambling was identified as a problem or a potential problem for about 5 percent of the population. Risk factors for problem gambling included being male, being Aboriginal, and having a low level of education. Daily gamblers and VLT players were at particularly high risk for problems. In contrast, lottery tickets were associated with the smallest risk for problem gambling (Marshall & Wynne, 2003).

The Canadian Community Health Survey and other surveys also found an association between gambling problems and alcohol problems. Many parallels between pathological gambling and alcohol/drug dependencies have been noted. Some pathological gamblers have such great difficulty quitting that they even experience withdrawal-like symptoms when attempting to stop. In fact, DSM-IV-TR diagnostic criteria for pathological gambling were intentionally patterned after those for substance dependence. It has been suggested that gambling and other addictive disorders are functionally equivalent forms of behaviour that satisfy similar needs and that these behaviours may be regarded as cross-addictions. As a result, an addiction model of pathological gambling has gained increasing acceptance among clinicians. The methods of Gamblers Anonymous, established in Los Angeles in 1957, were fashioned after the 12-step model of Alcoholics Anonymous.

Gambling shares many characteristics with substance use. Both generate short-lived pleasurable feelings and provide relief from negative feelings, and both ultimately create cravings to repeat the behaviour. Both have the ability to alter mood and level of arousal and, arguably, to induce an altered state of perception. When engaged in excessively, both behaviours lead to harmful consequences for the individual and society. Yet certain individuals are unable to control the frequency or amount of the behaviour.

The issue of whether addiction can occur without the ingestion of a substance is a topic of lively debate. Some researchers argue in favour of a physiological definition of dependence that requires neurophysiological changes in response to the presence of a foreign substance, while others adhere to the psychological aspect of dependence. DSM-IV-TR criteria for diagnosis of substance dependence can be with or without physiological dependence. DSM-IV-TR has categorized pathological gambling as a disorder of impulse control, yet has patterned the diagnostic criteria for this disorder after those for substance dependence.

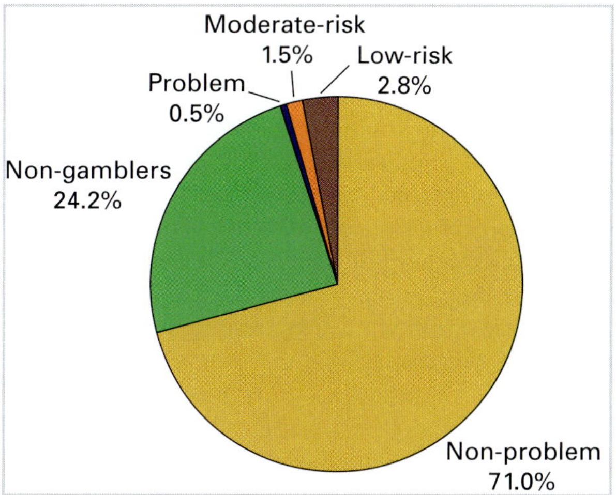

FIGURE 11.3 Prevalence of Gambling Among the Canadian Adult Population, 2002

Source: From the Statistics Canada publication *Perspectives on Labour and Income*, Catalogue 75-001, December 2003, p. 5.

CANADIAN RESEARCH CENTRE

Promoting Self-Recovery from Gambling Problems

Canadian psychologists are widely recognized for their contribution to the development of empirically based treatments for problem gambling. Only a few years ago, little was known about how to best treat such individuals. Often, substance abuse treatment programs were slightly modified for use with problem gamblers. Today, research groups across the country are tackling the issue of developing gambling-specific treatment approaches. Robert Ladouceur and his group at Laval University have developed cognitive treatment programs. At McGill University, Jeffery Derevensky and Rina Gupta are working on adolescent treatment approaches. Tony Toneatto and colleagues at the University of Toronto are looking at the effectiveness of treatment for co-occurring mental disorders and gambling problems. At the Addictive Behaviours Lab in the Department of Psychology at the University of Calgary, the authors of this chapter and colleagues have developed brief treatment approaches using a motivational approach.

Our brief treatment development work has three underlying assumptions. First, we know that many people recover from substance abuse and other addictions without the help of formal treatment. For example, it is clear that the most common pathway out of an alcohol problem for Canadians is "self-recovery" (Cunningham & Breslin, 2004). We assume that this is also true for people with gambling problems, although we know that people will often not initiate the process of changing until they have suffered significant problems for a significant period of time (Hodgins & el-Guebaly, 2000).

Second, we also know that very few problem gamblers, as few as 3 percent, will attend formal treatment (Hodgins, Currie, & el-Guebaly, 2001). Third, we know from studies of self-recovered gamblers that the change strategies they use (e.g., avoiding cues to gamble, self-instruction) are similar to those used by individuals attending treatment (Hodgins & el-Guebaly, 2000).

The challenge in helping greater numbers of problem gamblers than currently attend formal treatment is to foster the early use of these strategies without requiring that an individual attend a program. Our strategy has been twofold: we have incorporated practical information about recovery strategies into a brief self-help workbook and we have provided individuals interested in using a self-help approach with brief telephone support that focuses on their motivation to implement the change strategies. We know that brief treatments that focus on motivational issues are effective for other addictive disorders (Miller & Rollnick, 2003).

We have conducted a number of clinical trials of this brief intervention (Hodgins, Currie, Currie, & Fick, 2009; Diskin & Hodgins, 2009). Newspaper and television ads are used to recruit problem gamblers who want to recover on their own. In one trial, we followed participants for 24 months and found that those who received the workbook–motivational intervention had better outcomes than those who received the workbook only. About 37 percent were abstinent from gambling, and an additional 40 percent had significantly reduced their expenditures on gambling (Hodgins, Currie, el-Guebaly, & Peden, 2004). Future research will focus on determining more specifically what type of individual with which type of gambling problem is best helped by "promoting natural recovery."

linked to convulsions, coma, and death. Individuals often purchase PCP unknowingly under the guise of other drugs such as mescaline.

One of the most frightening and inexplicable consequences of hallucinogen use can be the occurrence of "**flashbacks**," unpredictable recurrences of some of the physical or perceptual distortions experienced during a previous trip. DSM-IV-TR includes a diagnosis called *hallucinogen persisting perception disorder*, which is applied if flashbacks cause significant distress or interfere with social or occupational functioning.

DEPENDENCY

It is widely thought that hallucinogens have little addictive potential, although they may induce psychological dependence. Even heavy users of hallucinogens rarely consume the drug more than once every few weeks, partly due to the fact that tolerance develops within a few days of continuous use. When this occurs, a user no longer experiences the hallucinogenic effects of the drug, although the physiological effects are still manifested. Abstinence from the drug for a few days to a week lowers tolerance to normal levels. Hallucinogens do not appear to cause noticeable withdrawal effects, even after long-term use.

Because hallucinogens do not appear to be addictive, few programs have been developed specifically to treat hallucinogen dependence. Those that have been developed generally focus on addressing the user's psychological dependence on the drug.

5 BEFORE MOVING ON

What are the benefits of brief treatment, self-recovery, and harm reduction approaches?

SUMMARY

- DSM-IV-TR sets out the criteria for substance intoxication, substance abuse, and substance dependence. In the DSM-5, it is proposed that this terminology be dropped and replaced with the term *addiction*. The alcohol use disorders will be included in the "Addiction and Related Disorders" section, which will also include behavioural addictions such as gambling disorder.
- Alcohol is the world's number one psychoactive substance, with almost 80 percent of Canadians reporting drinking in the past year. Alcohol may result in positive feelings in the short term, but over time it acts as a depressant. Alcohol causes deficits in coordination, vigilance, and reaction time. These physical and psychological effects can result in negative consequences economically, socially, and medically. Treatment for alcohol use disorders includes abstinence-based treatments (AA, Minnesota model), pharmacotherapy medication (benzodiazepines, Naltrexone, Acamprosate, Antabuse), and psychological treatments (behavioural interventions, relapse prevention, marital and family therapy, brief interventions).
- One of the major problems in treating substance abusers is the phenomenon of polysubstance abuse. Research has demonstrated that concurrent dependence may be the rule rather than the exception.
- The use of tranquilizers (including barbiturates and benzodiazepines) is fairly low in Canada. Barbiturates and benzodiazepines are considered depressants because they inhibit neurotransmitter activity in the CNS. The euphoria produced by small doses turns to poor motor coordination at higher doses, and can prove fatal in too large a dose. Treatment usually involves pharmacological treatment (progressively smaller doses of the abused drug) in combination with psychological and educational programs.
- In 2010 it was estimated that 17 percent of Canadians over the age of 14 smoked cigarettes. Nicotine is a CNS stimulant. Lower dosages can interfere with thinking and problem solving, and can cause extreme agitation and irritability along with mood changes. The small amount of nicotine present in a cigarette is not lethal and can increase alertness and improve mood. Treatments for smoking cessation include psychological (behavioural or cognitive) and pharmacological (nicotine replacement and prescription medication) interventions.
- Six percent of Canadians report having used amphetamines at least once in their life. Short-term effects of low dosages of amphetamines include increased alertness and ability to focus attention. This may lead to enhanced cognitive performance. Higher dosages, preferred by drug addicts, may produce feelings of exhilaration, but restlessness and anxiety may also be present. Prolonged use may lead to paranoia, toxic psychosis, periods of chronic fatigue, or a "crash" when the drugs wear off.
- In 2010 about 0.7 percent of Canadians reported having used cocaine or crack in the past year. The short-term effects of cocaine appear soon after its ingestion and wear off very quickly. Crack is especially fast-acting, and its effects may wear off in a few minutes. In small amounts, cocaine use in any form produces feelings of euphoria, well-being, and confidence. Continual use may result in mood swings, loss of interest in sex, weight loss, and insomnia.
- Treatments for stimulant abuse developed in the 1980s were often modelled after the 12-step programs for alcohol. They include psychological (cognitive behavioural) and pharmacological (e.g., antidepressants) interventions.
- At low doses, caffeine can increase attention, improve problem-solving skills, and improve mood. Higher doses cause increased jitteriness, nervousness, gastrointestinal discomfort, and insomnia. At doses exceeding 1000 milligrams per day, caffeine can cause muscle tremors, agitation, excessive talkativeness, disorganized thinking, and rapid or irregular heartbeat.
- Opioids are a class of CNS depressant drugs whose main effects are the reduction of pain and sleep inducement. Heroin is the most commonly abused opioid. In 2010 less than 1 percent of Canadians reported ever having tried heroin. Opioids mimic the effects of endogenous opiates, or the body's natural painkillers. The treatment for opioid abuse typically involves the use of medications (naltrexone, methadone).
- In 2010, 42 percent of Canadians aged 15 and over reported using cannabis at least once in their lives and 11 percent reported using it in the year before the survey. Cannabis involves mild changes in perception along with enhancement of physical experiences. With relatively small doses, most users report feeling mildly euphoric and sociable. At high doses, cannabis has been known to cause hallucinations, although it seems that this most often occurs when the user has a pre-existing mental disorder. Most marijuana abusers in Canada are placed in generalized treatment programs, although there are also efforts to develop cannabis-specific treatment approaches using a cognitive-behavioural treatment model.
- In 2010 approximately 11 percent of Canadian adults reported using hallucinogens sometime in their life, although use in the year before the survey was less than 1 percent. People taking hallucinogens report a

number of sensory experiences, including vivid visual hallucinations. Hallucinogens have an excitatory effect on the CNS and mimic the effects of serotonin by acting upon serotonin receptors in the brain stem and cerebral cortex. Because hallucinogens do not appear to be addictive, few programs have been developed specifically to treat hallucinogen dependence.

It is clear that alcohol, tobacco, and illicit drugs are a major health hazard and cost our country billions of dollars annually, in direct and indirect expenses. There is evidence that educating communities has had some positive effects with alcohol and tobacco use, but there is a disturbing trend toward increased use of several illicit drugs, particularly by teenagers and young adults.

MySearchLab offers you extensive help with your writing and research projects and provides round-the-clock access to credible and reliable source material. Chapter quizzes and a full electronic version of the text are also provided. Answers to the Before Moving On feature are provided on the MySearchLab. Take a tour at www.mysearchlab.com.

KEY TERMS

substance intoxication (p. 261)
substance abuse (p. 261)
substance dependence (p. 261)
physiological dependence (p. 261)
tolerance (p. 261)
withdrawal (p. 261)
psychological dependence (p. 262)
habituation (p. 262)
impairment of control (p. 263)
polysubstance abuse (p. 263)
low-risk drinking guidelines (p. 266)
ethyl alcohol (p. 268)
blood alcohol level (BAL) (p. 268)
alcohol dehydrogenase (p. 268)
blackouts (p. 269)
Korsakoff's psychosis (p. 269)
fetal alcohol syndrome (FAS) (p. 269).
behavioural disinhibition (p. 272)
negative emotionality (p. 272)
tension-reduction (p. 272)
alcohol expectancy theory (p. 272)
behavioural tolerance (p. 273)
Minnesota model (p. 275)
antagonist drug (p. 275)
agonist drug (p. 275)
Antabuse (p. 275)
relapse (p. 277)
brief intervention (p. 277)
motivational interviewing (p. 277)
depressants (p. 278)
abstinence syndrome (p. 278)
stimulants (p. 279)
nicotine (p. 279)
amphetamines (p. 281)
toxic psychosis (p. 282)
opioids (p. 284)
endogenous opiates (p. 285)
exogenous opiates (p. 285)
harm reduction approaches (p. 285)
methadone (p. 286)
cannabis (p. 286)
THC (p. 287)
amotivational syndrome (p. 287)
hallucinogens (p. 288)
flashbacks (p. 290)

STEPHEN PORTER • PAMELA BLACK • NATASHA KORVA

Chapter 12

The Personality Disorders

LEARNING OBJECTIVES

BY THE END OF THIS CHAPTER, STUDENTS WILL BE ABLE TO:

1. Differentiate between personality traits and disorders in accordance with the *Diagnostic and Statistical Manual* (DSM-IV-TR).
2. Understand how Axis II personality disorders differ from Axis I disorders, and define *egosyntonic* and *egodystonic*.
3. Identify the three clusters of personality disorders, and define each disorder.
4. Understand the proposed changes to the DSM-5, and identify the four personality disorders that will likely not be included in the newest DSM.
5. Differentiate between antisocial personality disorder and psychopathy.
6. Understand how obsessive-compulsive personality disorder (OCPD) differs from the Axis I condition called obsessive-compulsive disorder (OCD).
7. Identify and summarize the four main etiological perspectives of personality disorders.

George is 20 years old and lives in his parents' basement in Ottawa. He has no interest whatsoever in socializing with family or making friends. His parents are alarmed that he has never expressed any desire to go on dates and almost always keeps to himself. Although he is not shy, he prefers to be alone and all of his hobbies and activities are solitary. Because of his lack of interest in being around others, he hardly ever leaves the house, which is affecting his health. He responds coldly and dismissively when his parents confront him with their concerns. In general, he acts with a cold indifference to everyone. George is relatively intelligent and has no other mental health concerns.

***

Joanna has been hospitalized in Halifax as a result of slashing her wrists. She engaged in this self-harm behaviour in front of her boyfriend after he told her he was leaving her. The doctors find numerous cuts on her wrists and arms, all superficial. In addition, she has many scars that reveal previous incidents of slashing. In her initial interactions with others, Joanna can seem charming and attractive. However, during her many romantic relationships with both men and women, Joanna shows a pattern of quickly falling in love and idolizing her partner followed by expressing bitter anger and hatred toward the person when he or she inevitably rejects Joanna because of her extreme mood swings. Following the end of some of her relationships, she stalked the person for months, sometimes leaving nude photos of herself and, at other times, leaving threatening notes.

***

James enjoyed a good upbringing in a well-to-do family in British Columbia. His family reports that he was a likeable child, but that he lied frequently from a young age and was "like Jekyll and Hyde," changing from being friendly to aggressive in an instant. As he got older, he was seen as charming and engaging, and was very popular with women. He became a musician in a rock band. James has a long history of violence against both men and women. His pattern of violence is diverse such that some of his violent acts were highly premeditated (including sexual assaults, an attempted murder, and a robbery), while many others seemed spontaneous. In fact, he once put his "friend" in a wheelchair over a poker hand. He is now an incarcerated serial rapist.

Although George, Joanna, and James seem to be reasonably "normal" in some respects, they also have a personal style (or personality) that upsets or harms others, interferes with their social interactions, and may cause them some personal problems. James, while likeable, shows a pattern of attitudes and behaviours that is extremely destructive to those around him and has resulted in periods of incarceration, even though he may see nothing wrong with his lifestyle. None of them has any one of the clinical disorders identified on Axis I, but each has an inability to function in a manner that is adaptive and flexible, and each seems to be dominated by a single main negative feature (aloofness in George's case, emotional instability in Joanna's, and the utter selfishness seen in James) that dominates his or her behaviour and thinking. All three people would very likely meet the diagnostic criteria for an Axis II personality disorder.

The Concept of Personality Disorder

How would you describe your best friend? Your answer will likely focus on his or her personality characteristics, or on the manner in which he or she consistently behaves and thinks. Perhaps your friend is friendly, outgoing, confident, and charismatic. Or maybe he or she is shy, quiet, and passive. All people display some consistency in their behaviour and thinking, and this consistency is the basis for describing people as having a particular "personality." We readily describe people we know as being meek or aggressive, friendly or hostile, kind or cruel, shy or outgoing, sensitive or easygoing, et cetera. There are, in fact, many adjectives used to describe a person, but all of us sometimes display variations of these features. For example, you may usually be an outgoing, talkative person, but you may feel great distress or even "clam up" during a public presentation. Further, you are likely to be quiet and restrained at a funeral. However, we describe someone as having a personality characteristic only if that feature is typically displayed over time and in various situations. These cross-situationally consistent and persistent features are described by personality theorists as **traits**. Each person possesses several traits, the combination of which describes his or her personality. The focus of this chapter is on patterns of highly maladaptive personality traits known as **personality disorders**.

According to the DSM-IV-TR, personality traits are "enduring patterns of perceiving, relating to, and thinking about the environment and oneself that are exhibited in a wide range of social and personal contexts" (American Psychiatric Association [APA], 2000, p. 686). While this definition is similar to those found in most textbooks on personality, it does ignore the fact that the behaviour of most of us is also modified by context. One feature of people with personality disorders, however, is that their personality is more rigid and inflexible, and is displayed, to a large extent, independently of context. In a given situation, their behaviour often seems highly inappropriate to most others. Alternatively, they may initially display appropriate behaviour in a given situation but cannot typically sustain it for long periods or when under stress. In fact, DSM-IV-TR asserts that personality traits constitute a personality disorder only when they are *inflexible* and *maladaptive*. People with personality disorders also show a far more restricted range of traits than do most people. Whereas we would describe most people we know well as having a variety of key traits (e.g., generous, friendly, ambitious, etc.), personality-disordered individuals are more likely to be characterized by a single dominant, dysfunctional trait.

All the mental disorders described on Axis I, such as depression, schizophrenia, or the phobias, are associated with subjective distress. That is, they are maladaptive and harmful primarily for the person afflicted with the condition. Interestingly, however, the personality disorders include conditions that cause distress primarily for other people. For example, someone with antisocial personality disorder (APD) or narcissistic personality disorder may see nothing wrong with him- or herself, or even believe that other people have the problem. Someone with APD, in particular, can wreak havoc on the lives of those around him or her through persistent violence, lying, and manipulation. George, described above, may warrant a diagnosis of schizoid personality disorder but he feels little distress about his lack of interactions with others.

As a reader, you justifiably may ask why we need to "pathologize" or diagnose a condition that causes the affected person little distress. This issue is highly controversial. On the one hand, the field of abnormal psychology does not wish to cause harm to a person through the stigma of a diagnostic label such as "personality disorder." Further, we run the risk of circular logic with such labels by implying that they have some explanatory power. For example, if we explain the destructive behaviour of someone with APD as resulting from his or her condition or "illness," we are using circular reasoning (because we diagnose the condition based on such behaviour). On the other hand, abnormal psychology seeks to classify these conditions in order to aid in the diagnosis, treatment, and prediction of behaviour. Psychopathy is a good example of a construct that helps to predict behaviour. For example, knowing that a criminal offender is psychopathic allows us to predict that he or she is far more likely to perpetrate predatory violence than are his or her counterparts. Moreover, three large-scale prospective longitudinal studies, known as the Children in the Community Study of Developmental Course of Personality Disorder (Cohen, Crawford, Johnson, & Kasen, 2005), the Collaborative Longitudinal Personality Disorders Study (Skodol et al., 2005), and the McLean Study of Adult Development (Zanarini, Frankenburg, Hennen, Reich, & Silk, 2005), have been consistent in their conclusions that personality disorders represent a significant health problem for those with the condition. Personality disorders were found to be associated with various forms of personal impairment—including subsequent Axis I disorders, interpersonal conflict, suicide attempts, and violent and criminal behaviour—and were also associated with extensive treatment use.

1 BEFORE MOVING ON

How does the DSM-IV define personality traits and personality disorders? When do personality traits constitute a personality disorder? How do the Axis II personality disorders differ from the Axis I disorders?

This chapter reflects the model for personality disorders advocated by the DSM-IV-TR; however, it is important to note that the foundational model currently used to diagnose personality disorders will be fundamentally different in the DSM-5. In fact, personality disorders may be the category of disorders that will be most affected by the release of the DSM-5. There are a number of reasons for the personality disorders to be revised, including the excessive co-occurrence of personality disorders and comorbidity among Axis I disorders, the poor temporal stability of diagnoses, and the use of arbitrary thresholds for diagnosis (Bornstein, 2011). After a thorough review of the personality disorder literature, the work group responsible for suggesting amendments to the diagnosis of personality disorders decided that four of the current personality disorders should be removed from the DSM-5 completely: schizoid personality disorder, histrionic personality disorder, paranoid personality disorder, and dependent personality disorder. Further, as discussed later in the chapter, this group proposed adding a "Personality Disorder Trait Specified" (PDTS) category to account for the disorders that are being removed.

In addition to the removal of four of the personality disorders, a change to the way in which clinicians diagnose personality disorders also has been proposed. Since the first version of the DSM, the diagnosis of personality disorders has been categorical; individuals have to meet a certain number of the criteria to reach the cut-off to be diagnosed with a personality disorder. The proposed change for DSM-5 is to shift to a hybrid dimensional-categorical model for personality disorders and personality disorder assessment. This shift will involve a completely new method for diagnosis, replacing the categorical method with a measure of self and interpersonal functioning, as well as a continuum of personality traits. Clinicians will have to assess a client's overall personality functioning by assessing self-functioning, characterized by impairments in identity and self-direction, and interpersonal functioning, characterized by impairments in empathy and intimacy. Similar to the current model, clinicians must also assess whether the client possesses the pathological personality traits associated with the personality disorder in question. It is expected that this shift to a dimensional-categorical model will reduce the amount of concurrent personality disorders and comorbidity with Axis I disorders (Samuel, Lynam, Widiger, & Ball, 2011). While the proposed revisions to the model of personality disorders have not yet been officially accepted into the DSM-5, it is likely that these changes will occur and so they are discussed throughout the remainder of the chapter.

The DSM-IV-TR provides five formal criteria in defining personality disorders:

- Criterion A states that the pattern of behaviour must be manifested in at least two of the following areas: cognition, emotions, interpersonal functioning, or impulse control.
- Criterion B requires that the enduring pattern of behaviour be rigid and consistent across a broad range of personal and social situations.
- Criterion C states that this behaviour should lead to clinically significant distress.
- Criterion D requires stability and long duration of symptoms, with onset in adolescence or earlier.
- Criterion E states that the behaviour cannot be accounted for by another mental disorder.

Along with numerous changes to the personality disorders themselves, the general criteria for defining personality disorders have also been revised to the following five criteria:

- Criterion A requires significant impairments in self-identity or self-direction and interpersonal (empathy or intimacy) functioning.
- Criterion B requires one or more pathological personality trait domains or trait facets.
- Criterion C requires that the impairments in personality functioning and the individual's personality trait expressions be relatively stable across time and situations.
- Criterion D requires the impairments in personality functioning and personality trait expression to not be better understood as normative for the individual's developmental stage or socio-cultural environment.
- Criterion E requires the impairments in personality functioning and personality trait expression to not be solely due to direct physiological effects of a substance (e.g., drug abuse, medication) or a general medical condition (e.g., severe head trauma).

DSM-IV-TR lists the specific personality disorders according to three broad **clusters**:

- **Cluster A** *odd and eccentric disorders* (paranoid, schizoid, and schizotypal);
- **Cluster B** *dramatic, emotional, or erratic disorders* (antisocial, borderline, histrionic, and narcissistic); and
- **Cluster C** *anxious and fearful disorders* (avoidant, dependent, and obsessive-compulsive).

In addition to these three clusters, the manual also includes *personality disorder not otherwise specified.* Not only will four of these personality disorders (paranoid, schizoid, histrionic, and dependent) cease to exist in the DSM-5, but it has been proposed that the clusters of personality disorders be abolished as well. However, it has been suggested that a new category, *personality disorder trait specified* (PDTS), be created. The purpose of PDTS is to account for the disorders that are being removed, including "personality disorder not otherwise specified." This will be achieved by assessing personality disorders that do not fall within the remaining six categories by assessing the core impairments in personality functioning and combining them with the individual's unique set of personality traits (Skodol et al., 2011). Any individual who presents with pathological personality traits in the domain of negative affectivity, detachment, antagonism, disinhibition vs. compulsivity, and psychoticism that are not accounted for by the remaining six personality disorders and who demonstrates impairment in self and interpersonal functioning will be diagnosed with PDTS (APA, 2011).

2 BEFORE MOVING ON

Some psychologists believe in a dimensional classification of personality disorders, whereas others argue for a categorical classification. Given what you know about personality disorders, which scheme do you believe is better? How is the DSM-5 accommodating this diagnostic issue? Which of the DSM-IV-TR disorders are being excluded from the DSM-5, and what is the explanation for the exclusion? Which other diagnostic issue is the DSM-5 addressing?

Table 12.1 presents the clusters with characteristic features. While Clusters A and C appear to have enough features in common to make reasonably cohesive groups, Cluster B is a somewhat heterogeneous—even confusing—group (Frances, 1985). Perhaps this is one reason that personality disorders are a somewhat neglected diagnostic category.

While their definitional problems should be acknowledged, the assessment of these pathological conditions should be an important concern in clinical and forensic settings. For one thing, when someone has a personality

TABLE 12.1 PERSONALITY DISORDERS LISTED IN DSM-IV-TR

Paranoid Personality Disorder is a pattern of distrust and suspiciousness such that others' motives are interpreted as malevolent.

Schizoid Personality Disorder is a pattern of detachment from social relationships and a restricted range of emotional expression.

Schizotypal Personality Disorder is a pattern of acute discomfort in close relationships, cognitive or perceptual distortions, and eccentricities of behavior.

Antisocial Personality Disorder is a pattern of disregard for, and violation of, the rights of others.

Borderline Personality Disorder is a pattern of instability in interpersonal relationships, self-image, and affects, and marked impulsivity.

Histrionic Personality Disorder is a pattern of excessive emotionality and attention seeking.

Narcissistic Personality Disorder is a pattern of grandiosity, need for admiration, and lack of empathy.

Avoidant Personality Disorder is a pattern of social inhibition, feelings of inadequacy, and hypersensitivity to negative evaluation.

Dependent Personality Disorder is a pattern of submissive and clinging behaviour related to an excessive need to be taken care of.

Obsessive-Compulsive Personality Disorder is a pattern of preoccupation with orderliness, perfectionism, and control.

Personality Disorder Not Otherwise Specified is a category provided for two situations: 1) the individual's personality pattern meets the general criteria for a Personality Disorder and traits of several different Personality Disorders are present, but the criteria for any specific Personality Disorder are not met; or 2) the individual's personality pattern meets the general criteria for a Personality Disorder, but the individual is considered to have a Personality Disorder that is not included in the Classification (e.g., passive-aggressive personality disorder).

The Personality Disorders are grouped into three clusters based on descriptive similarities. Cluster A includes the Paranoid, Schizoid, and Schizotypal Personality Disorders. Individuals with these disorders often appear odd or eccentric. Cluster B includes the Antisocial, Borderline, Histrionic, and Narcissistic Personality Disorders. Individuals with these disorders often appear dramatic, emotional, or erratic. Cluster C includes the Avoidant, Dependent, and Obsessive-Compulsive Personality Disorders. Individuals with these disorders often appear anxious or fearful. It should be noted that this clustering system, although useful in some research-and educational situations, has serious limitations and has not been consistently validated. Moreover, individuals frequently present with co-occurring Personality Disorders from different clusters.

Source: Reprinted with permission from the *Diagnostic and Statistical Manual of Mental Disorders, Fourth Edition, Text Revision.* (Copyright © 2000). American Psychiatric Association.

disorder it can greatly complicate the treatment of Axis I disorders. Personality disorders can easily disrupt the alliance between a therapist and a client. Sometimes a personality disorder can even be mistaken for an Axis I condition. For example, schizotypal personality disorder shares features (although less severe) with the Axis I condition of schizophrenia. A wrong diagnosis could lead to the wrong treatment plan, or possibly a mistaken drug prescription. In addition, while the treatment of personality disorders has been traditionally viewed as difficult and the prognosis poor, the situation is improving with the development of more effective therapeutic approaches.

Studies examining the **prevalence** of personality disorders have examined rates among inpatient samples, among outpatients, and among the community. Depending on the sample and method of diagnosis, prevalence rates vary considerably. For example, relative to structured interviews, self-report measures will likely yield underestimates of APD because individuals are reluctant to admit that they engage in antisocial behaviours. Other disorders, such as those in Cluster C, may be overrepresented by self-report questionnaires; patients may endorse particular items, even though the severity of the associated symptoms may not be sufficient to merit a clinical diagnosis. The issue of multimethod assessment, then, is relevant to broader diagnostic issues as well as to treatment and prediction issues. For example, Klein (2003) evaluated patients' and informants' (e.g., intimate partners, relatives, friends) reports of personality disorders in predicting outcome in a 7.5-year follow-up of 85 depressed outpatients. Both informants' and patients' reports uniquely predicted depression symptoms and global functioning at follow-up. Interestingly, only informants' reports made an independent contribution to predicting social adjustment, suggesting that patients with personality disorders may not be cognizant of the negative impact they have on those close to them.

Unfortunately, little research has examined the prevalence of personality disorders among the general Canadian population. Epidemiological studies here have typically measured the prevalence of APD. For example, a 1991 Ontario survey estimated that the one-year prevalence rate of APD in the general population was 1.7 percent (Offord et al., 1996). According to a 1980s Edmonton study, 1.8 percent of the population had APD in the six-month period before

TABLE 12.2 LIFETIME PREVALENCE IN A COMMUNITY SURVEY

Disorder	Percentage
Cluster A	**3.6***
Paranoid	0.4
Schizoid	0.7
Schizotypal	3.0
Cluster B	**1.5***
Antisocial	3.0
Borderline	1.7
Histrionic	3.0
Narcissistic	(None found)
Cluster C	**2.7***
Avoidant	1.3
Dependent	1.7
Obsessive-Compulsive	1.7
Overall Average	**6.1***

Source: Adapted from Zimmerman and Coryell (1990).

* From Huang et al. (2009).

the survey, and 3.7 percent reported a personality disorder at some point in their lives (Bland, Newman, & Orn, 1988; Bland, Orn, & Newman, 1988). As reported by the Public Health Agency of Canada (2002), there has been Canadian research examining personality disorders among institutionalized patients. However, it should be kept in mind that these data have major limitations because most people hospitalized with personality disorders are a risk to themselves or to others. Most others are untreated or treated in the community rather than in hospitals. Among both women and men, the highest rates of hospitalization for personality disorders in 1999 were in people between 15 and 44 years of age. More than three-quarters (78 percent) of all admissions were between these ages and rates were higher among women than men. In all age groups, personality disorders were more likely to be a contributing rather than the main factor determining length of stay in hospital. This is because personality disorders are associated with other conditions, such as suicidal behaviour, that lead to hospitalization. The average length of stay in hospitals due to personality disorders was 9.5 days. Séguin and colleagues (2006) conducted "psychological autopsies" on 102 cases of completed suicide in New Brunswick and found that 52 percent of the cases involved personality disorders, half of which were Cluster B type. These data give us only a small part of the picture; it is clear that data concerning the prevalence of these disorders in community samples in Canada are greatly needed!

Table 12.2 lists lifelong prevalence data from a community study conducted in the United States. Studies in Europe reveal rates different from those observed in the United States, with the lifetime prevalence for most of the disorders being somewhat lower (Maier, Lichtermann, Klingler, Heun, & Hallmayer, 1992). Comparisons of these and other findings suggest that about 6 to 9 percent of the entire population, including community, hospitalized, and outpatient samples, will have one or more personality disorders during their life (Merikangas & Weissman, 1986). Samuels and colleagues (2002) had clinical psychologists assess personality disorders in 742 adult participants living in Maryland. They found that the overall prevalence of all personality disorders was 9 percent. The authors also examined various demographic characteristics associated with personality disorders. Cluster A disorders were most prevalent in men who had never married. Cluster B disorders were most prevalent in poorly educated men, and Cluster C disorders were most common among those who had graduated from high school but who had never married (but see Lenzenweger, Lane, Loranger, & Kessler, 2007, for a critique of the study).

Studies published in the *Journal of Clinical Psychiatry* and the *Journal of Personality Disorders* provide some of the highest estimates of personality disorders to date. Conducted by the National Institute on Alcohol Abuse and Alcoholism and the National Institutes of Health, the first study focused on a representative community survey of 43 000 American adults. The authors (Grant et al., 2004) estimated that in 2001–2002, 14.8 percent of American adults (30.8 million) met the diagnostic criteria for at least one DSM-IV-TR personality disorder. Overall, the risk of having avoidant, dependent, and paranoid personality disorders was greater for females than for males, whereas the risk of having APD was greater for males than for females. The authors found no gender differences in risk for obsessive-compulsive, schizoid, or histrionic personality disorders. Other risk factors included being Native American or black, being a young adult, having low socio-economic status, and being divorced, separated, widowed, or never married. This study must be considered with caution, as it has been criticized for relying on a new diagnostic interview administered by laypersons instead of a well-validated interview by trained clinicians (Lenzenweger et al., 2007). In the second study, based on a community sample of 644 children tracked from early childhood through adolescence and into early adulthood, Crawford and colleagues (2005) estimated the prevalence of any personality disorder to be 15.7 percent. Specifically, 5.1 percent of this sample had paranoid personality disorder, 1.7 percent had schizoid personality disorder, 1.1 percent had schizotypal personality disorder, 1.2 percent had APD, 3.9 percent had borderline personality disorder, 0.9 percent had histrionic personality disorder, 2.2 percent had narcissistic personality disorder, 6.4 percent had avoidant personality disorder, 0.8 percent had dependent personality disorder, and 4.7 percent had obsessive-compulsive personality disorder. As with the Samuels and colleagues (2002) study, however, the Crawford and colleagues (2005) sample has been criticized for not being representative of the greater U.S. population (Lenzenweger et al., 2007).

In an effort to address some of these methodological limitations and present nationally representative estimates of clinician-diagnosed personality disorders in the general population of the United States, Lenzenweger and colleagues (2007) examined the responses to questions from the International Personality Disorder Examination administered to 5692 participants. The results from a sub-sample of more than 200 participants who were administered the complete measure led to the following population prevalence estimates: 5.7 percent for Cluster A disorders, 1.5 percent for Cluster B disorders, 6.0 percent for Cluster C disorders, and 9.1 percent for any personality disorder. Cluster B was negatively associated with age and education, APD was less prevalent among women, and borderline personality disorder was positively associated with unemployment. Gender, race/ethnicity, family income, and marital status were not significantly related to any of the personality disorder measures.

Generally speaking, prevalence rates are higher among inpatient psychiatric patients than among outpatients. For example, borderline personality disorder, the most commonly diagnosed personality disorder among patients in treatment, was reported in 11 percent of outpatients and 19 percent of inpatients (Widiger & Frances, 1989). Similarly, outpatient prevalence rates for schizotypal personality disorder range between 10 and 15 percent (Bornstein, Klein, Malon, & Slater, 1988), whereas 20 to 30 percent of inpatients display this disorder (Widiger & Rogers, 1989). The rates for APD vary depending on whether psychiatric patients or criminal offenders are surveyed. In psychiatric outpatients, the prevalence rates are near 5 percent, but jump to 12 to 37 percent for psychiatric inpatients. In prison populations, the rates range from 30 to 70 percent (Widiger & Rogers, 1989).

The personality disorders are distinct from other forms of psychopathology in DSM-IV-TR and appear on Axis II rather than Axis I, where most of the other disorders are clustered. Relative to the personality disorders, the so-called *clinical disorders* (i.e., Axis I disorders) have more pronounced symptomatology, leading to a greater likelihood of referral to mental health professionals. Axis I disorders are more likely to be referred to as "mental illnesses" than are personality disorders. While older research indicated that 80 percent or more of people with personality disorders never seek treatment for their problems (Drake & Vaillant, 1985), results from the National Comorbidity Survey Replication (Lenzenweger et al., 2007) suggested that 39 percent of people with a personality disorder receive treatment for their mental health or substance abuse difficulties. Those with Cluster B disorders sought treatment the most (49.1 percent), followed by those with Cluster C disorders (29 percent) and Cluster A disorders (25 percent). Most of the respondents sought treatment from general medical providers (19 percent), followed by psychiatrists (14 percent) or other mental health professionals (17 percent). An important distinction between Axis I and Axis II is that most individuals suffering from Axis I disorders have far more impaired functioning than do most personality-disordered patients. An objective evaluation of personality-disordered patients indicates impaired life circumstances, but their actual abilities appear relatively intact compared to those with Axis I disorders (Millon, 1996). Also, as mentioned, for many people with personality disorder, their functioning is **egosyntonic**; that is, they do not view it as problematic. In contrast, the Axis I disorders are generally considered **egodystonic** (they cause distress and are viewed as problematic by the individual sufferer). Intervention for individuals with personality disorders, then, must initially address the issue of motivation for treatment and treatment readiness. It should be mentioned that there have been numerous debates on whether the distinction between Axis I and II should even be made in future editions of the DSM. Some argue that certain personality disorders co-occur with specific Axis I disorders so frequently that they may be better classified on Axis I (Nakdimen, 1986). Further, many insurance companies will not assist clients with the cost of treatment for personality disorders, leading some to suggest that removing the distinction between the Axes may remedy the situation (Cohen et al., 2005).

Diagnostic Issues

The personality disorders have traditionally presented more diagnostic problems than most of the Axis I disorders because of the lower reliability of their diagnosis (Rogers, Duncan, Lynett, & Sewell, 1994), their poorly understood etiology (Marshall & Barbaree, 1984), and weak treatment efficacy (Kelly et al., 1992). With respect to diagnosis, two indices of reliability are important. Inter-rater reliability—that is, the agreement between two raters—ranges from 0.86 to 0.97 for the personality disorders (Maffei et al., 1997). Test-retest reliability—that is, agreement in diagnosis over time—has traditionally been much weaker, ranging from 0.11 to 0.57 (Zimmerman, 1994), although the situation seems to have been improving in recent years (see below).

There are, however, other challenges to the DSM's definitions of personality disorder and questions of whether a "diagnosis" is even warranted. For example, Canadian researcher John Livesley and his colleagues (Livesley, 1986; Livesley, Schroeder, Jackson, & Jang, 1994) have argued that personality disorders are better viewed as constellations of traits, each of which lie along a continuum, rather than as disorders that people simply have or do not have. This conceptualization of personality disorders as traits along a continuum will be acknowledged in the DSM-5, as the model of personality disorders has been revised. In addition, others have suggested that the diagnostic criteria for some personality disorders are gender-biased (Kaplan, 1983b), or that their application permits the gender biases of the diagnostician to influence diagnosis (Ford & Widiger, 1989).

There are, in fact, many problems with the notion of personality disorder that have not been resolved, and it is clear that further research is needed before a clearly defined set of criteria is developed. Nonetheless, most clinicians agree that some people consistently show maladaptive, inflexible, and restricted ways of behaving and thinking that are best described as relating to personality. The problem is not so much whether these syndromes exist, but rather how they can be defined in a way that is unbiased, reliable, and leads to effective treatment or prediction.

Among the various diagnostic issues, researchers have identified gender and cultural bias in the diagnostic criteria as subjects of concern. These biases, it is suggested, contribute to the broader problem of unsatisfactory reliability.

GENDER AND CULTURAL ISSUES

DSM-IV-TR requires diagnosticians to ensure that the client's functioning does not simply reflect normative responding in the client's culture. As our populations become increasingly culturally diverse, clinicians may misdiagnose if they do not take adequate precautions to determine whether certain attitudes and behaviours are appropriate for distinct cultures or societal subgroups. For example, economically disadvantaged children living in inner cities may learn self-interested strategies in order to survive. These strategies may, in the eyes of a more privileged clinician, appear to reveal psychopathology, whereas in reality they are adaptive given the environmental context.

Similar concerns exist for gender biases in the diagnosis of personality disorders. Sex role stereotypes may influence the clinician's determination of the presence of personality disorders (Pantony & Caplan, 1991). For example, clinicians have been shown to be reluctant to diagnose males with histrionic personality disorder and are unlikely to consider females as having APD (Samuel & Widiger, 2009; Widiger & Spitzer, 1991). The emphasis on aggression in the criteria for APD may result in underdiagnosing in females because of gender differences in the prevalence and expression of aggression. In addition, Henry and Cohen (1983) have suggested that clinicians typically overdiagnose borderline personality disorder in women. Widiger and Trull (1993) found that an average of 80 percent of people identified as borderline by structured interviews were women. It is difficult to know whether these results reflect a true gender difference in the occurrence of the disorder, or whether they reflect inappropriately gender-biased criteria or application of the criteria. A more recent study conducted by Boggs and colleagues (2005) discovered that the diagnosis of borderline personality disorder (BPD) in females (more than males) may be due to the criteria themselves. This study revealed that there was a gender bias in the criteria for BPD and that borderline personality disorder manifests differently in men than in women. Finally, this study concluded that this gender difference in the symptoms of BPD is not reflected in the existing DSM-IV criteria for the disorder; the existing criteria do not address the symptoms characteristic of BPD in men. Researchers in the field of domestic violence seem to be exceptional in recognizing the importance of studying borderline personality disorder in males. This research focus led to the finding that violent males with borderline personality disorder have been found to experience significant attachment problems resulting from childhood abuse and neglect that may have placed them at risk to stalk, assault, or sometimes even kill their intimate partners when they perceive that they are being abandoned (Dutton, 2002; Dutton & Starzomski 1993).

Other attempts have been made to address the biases mentioned. For example, histrionic personality disorder used to be called "hysterical personality." *Hysterical* is a descriptor that has traditionally been applied to women, so it was thought that changing the name to reflect the actual behaviour (*histrionic* means "excessively theatrical") might reduce diagnostic biases. However, the impact does not seem to have been substantial. Histrionic personality disorder has long been diagnosed more commonly in females than in males (Reich, 1987), and studies asking participants to rate the diagnostic criteria indicate that most people view the features of the disorder as decidedly feminine (Sprock, Blashfield, & Smith, 1990). In an interesting examination of gender bias, Warner (1978) had 175 mental health professionals make a diagnosis after reading a case history. The patient was described as a woman in half of the cases and as a man in the other half, but the case description remained the same. Of those clinicians who were given the "female" case, 76 percent diagnosed the patient as suffering from a hysterical personality disorder (the earlier name for histrionic personality disorder), while only 49 percent applied that diagnosis when the patient was described as a man.

Ford and Widiger (1989) also examined these issues, but looked at gender bias both in the diagnostic criteria and in the diagnosis of histrionic personality disorder. They found that, while the specific diagnostic criteria for histrionic personality disorder were found with equal frequency among men and women, women were more likely to be diagnosed with the disorder. In another study of histrionic personality disorder, women were more commonly diagnosed, whereas an epidemiological survey of more than 3000 community adults revealed the same prevalence (2.2 percent) in males and females (Nestadt et al., 1990). This finding suggests either biases in referrals to psychiatric clinics for people with histrionic features or gender bias in the application of the diagnosis among those who are referred.

The gender biases witnessed in diagnosing personality disorders have sometimes become "systemic," such that large numbers of males or females are virtually excluded from a diagnosis category because of their gender. For example, psychopathy—one of the most harmful personality disorders, although not yet formally listed in DSM-IV-TR—is diagnosed in approximately 15 to 25 percent of male federal inmates in Canada (translating into thousands of men). However, very few female federal inmates ever receive this classification because the Correctional Service of Canada apparently views being female as largely incompatible with being psychopathic, a belief that is not in accordance with research. For example, Rutherford, Cacciola, and Alterman (1999) examined the prevalence of psychopathy in a group of 137 women seeking treatment for cocaine dependency. The findings showed that 19 percent of the women scored in the moderate to high range on the Psychopathy Checklist–Revised, 12 of whom were diagnosed with APD according to the DSM-IV. Clearly, psychopathy can occur in women, despite the reluctance—perhaps politically driven—of some agencies to concur with the research.

It is difficult to determine whether differences in the prevalence of personality disorders across genders and ethnic groups represent biases in diagnosis or perhaps reflect *true differences*. One study looked at this issue by examining ratings of both diagnosticians and the patients themselves. Grilo and colleagues (2003) compared the distribution of borderline (BPD), schizotypal (STPD), avoidant (AVPD), and obsessive-compulsive (OCPD) disorders across three ethnic groups: Caucasians, African-Americans, and Hispanics. The researchers used both a clinician-administered diagnostic interview and a self-report instrument. The results indicated higher rates of BPD in Hispanic than in Caucasian and African-American participants, and higher rates of STPD among African-Americans than Caucasians. Self-report data reflected the same patterns, suggesting that there may be true cultural differences in the risk for certain disorders.

RELIABILITY OF DIAGNOSIS

Concerns regarding cultural and gender insensitivity in diagnostic strategies underscore larger issues related to the reliability and validity of personality disorder diagnoses. These are not new concerns and they have governed revisions to the DSM since 1980. For instance, the early field trials with DSM-III (APA, 1980) revealed rather poor reliability for the personality disorders, suggesting that clinicians often fail to agree on a particular diagnosis for a specific patient. Specific to the diagnosis of APD, Rogers, Dion, and Lynett (1992) found that only 3 of 13 studies provided evidence for satisfactory reliability. Strategies such as using structured interviews and expanding the breadth of information collected appear to increase reliability. Millon (1996) has highlighted that personality disorders require a very thorough and careful consideration of the potential disorder's pervasiveness and severity, as well as the client's personality style and motivation. He points out that a diagnosis should be much more than a simple compilation of behaviours or symptoms. However, these procedures take longer, and many clinicians may be unwilling or unable to spend the necessary extra time. On the other hand, some personality disorders can be diagnosed with a high level of reliability with a file review followed by an hour to two-hour interview with the client (Hare, 1991, 2003). In other words, it is likely that most personality disorders can be reliably diagnosed given enough information and effort. Imagine if oncologists or cardiologists did not "have time" to diagnose cancer or heart disease reliably! Sometimes, the consequences of a missed personality disorder can be as destructive.

The situation may be improving, however. More recent studies suggest that personality disorder diagnoses may be becoming more reliable. Zanarini and colleagues (2000) examined both the inter-rater and the test-retest reliability of Axis I and II disorders using structured DSM-IV-based interviews. The results indicated at least "fair to good" inter-rater reliability for all personality disorders diagnosed by experienced clinicians. In addition, all personality disorders, except for narcissistic personality disorder and paranoid personality disorder, showed "fair to good" test-retest reliability. Inter-rater and test-retest dimensional reliability figures for Axis II were generally higher than those for their categorical counterparts; most were in the "excellent" range.

A major goal of the above-mentioned research was to determine the stability of personality disorders over time. It is possible that these conditions may not be as chronic as once believed (Bornovalova, Hicks, Iacono, & McGue, 2009; Ericson, Tuvbald, Raine, Young-Wolff, & Baker, 2011). For example, Skodol and colleagues (2005) reported that fewer than half of the personality-disordered patients in their large sample remained at or above the diagnostic criteria for their initial diagnosis every month for a follow-up period lasting two years. These findings were consistent with those of two other large-scale longitudinal studies, the Children in the Community Study of Developmental Course of Personality Disorder (Cohen et al., 2005) and the McLean Study of Adult Development (Zanarini et al., 2005), which found that personality disorders were not as enduring as was once thought.

COMORBIDITY AND DIAGNOSTIC OVERLAP

One further problem with the diagnosis of personality disorders concerns their independence from each other and from Axis I disorders. The terms *comorbidity* and *overlap* are often used synonymously in the literature when, in fact, they refer to two conceptually distinct features of diagnosis. **Comorbidity** should be used to describe the co-occurrence in the same person of two or more different disorders. **Overlap**, on the other hand, refers to the similarity of symptoms in two or more different disorders (i.e., some of the same criteria apply to different diagnoses). Diagnostic criteria for different disorders should be distinct, but for some personality disorders the criteria remain sufficiently vague or require such significant inference by the clinician that overlap seems likely. For example, narcissistic personality disorder (NPD) and antisocial personality disorder (APD) are both associated with a lack of empathy or concern for others.

Research has indicated problems with overlap between specific disorders. Patients diagnosed as borderline have commonly been found to have schizotypal features, and considerable overlap has been observed between borderline diagnoses and other personality disorders (Pfohl, Coryell, Zimmerman, & Stangl, 1986). For example, in one study, 47 percent of those diagnosed as borderline met the criteria for APD and 57 percent met the criteria for histrionic disorder (Widiger, Frances, & Trull, 1987). Similarly, Morey (1988) reported high diagnostic overlap in individuals with borderline personality disorder, with paranoid, histrionic, narcissistic, avoidant, and dependent personality disorder diagnoses. Overlap also occurs between other personality disorders. A recent study found that schizotypal personality disorder was associated with both borderline personality disorder and narcissistic personality disorder (Lentz, Robinson, & Bolton, 2010). Another example is a study that revealed that psychopathic individuals with antisocial personality disorder often show overlapping symptoms with both schizoid personality disorder and narcissistic personality disorder (Coid & Ullrich, 2010). A third example is the high level of comorbidity between the construct of histrionic personality disorder and borderline, narcissistic, and dependent personality disorder (Bakkevig & Karterud, 2010).

Comorbidity also exists between personality disorders (Axis II disorders) and Axis I disorders. A recent World Health Organization study estimated that worldwide, over half (51.2 percent) of the individuals diagnosed with personality disorders meet the criteria for at least one Axis I disorder (Huang et al., 2009). A specific example is the comorbidity between borderline personality disorder and mood disorders. This comorbidity has led to suggestions that borderline disorder might best be classified as a subtype of affective disorder (Nakdimen, 1986). The Collaborative Longitudinal Personality Disorders Study (Skodol et al., 2005) established, however, that the diagnostic criteria for the individual personality disorders related better with one another than with criteria from other personality disorders, leading those researchers to conclude that the diagnostic criteria of each of the disorders do show some discriminant validity.

In recent revisions of the DSM, clinicians have been encouraged to consider multiple diagnoses to be applied to the same individual. However, a specific diagnosis often implies a course of treatment and differential prognosis, and this is complicated by the use of multiple diagnoses. This similarity of symptoms across disorders also results in blurred boundaries between diagnoses, perhaps confusing clinicians. One of the goals of changing the model for diagnosis in DSM-5 is to reduce the amount of overlap between diagnoses by including a continuum of personality traits. This will restrict the overlap of diagnoses and encourage a more individualized treatment plan.

Historical Perspective

Historically, there has been greater attention to what we now call antisocial personality disorder, or the related condition psychopathy, than to any other personality disorder. For thousands of years, characters with such traits have been witnessed. The ancient Greek philosopher Theophrastus described a "man without moral feeling" in one of his 30 character profiles of human nature.

The well-known writings of Niccolò Machiavelli (1469–1527) advocated for the use of unscrupulous, manipulative, amoral, and deceptive behaviour in achieving power in politics and society (Campbell, 2003). In *The Prince*, Machiavelli expressed this view in his description of the ideal qualities of a successful political ruler! Based on his writings, the term *machiavellianism* has become synonymous with callous, manipulative, and deceptive personality characteristics (see Campbell, 2003; Fehr, Samson, & Paulhus, 1992; Wilson, Near, & Miller, 1996). Machiavellianism, in addition to subclinical narcissism and subclinical psychopathy, make up the "Dark Triad." The Dark Triad is a constellation of personality traits that are deemed to be socially aversive (Paulhus & Williams, 2002).

In the nineteenth century, scholars continued to describe people who engaged in antisocial behaviour in the absence of obvious cognitive or psychiatric dysfunction. Such discussions emphasized definitions and diagnostic symptoms of a poorly understood phenomenon. One of the first written descriptions of the condition was by Pinel (1809), whose work was discussed in Chapter 1. Pinel described a psychiatric condition associated primarily with amorality rather than psychosis. He referred to this condition as *manie sans délire*, or madness without delirium. In such patients, he observed profound deficits in emotion but no apparent reasoning/intellectual dysfunction. Such patients were prone to stealing, violence, and lying, but seemed to have no other mental health issues.

Similar to Pinel's notion, British psychiatrist James Pritchard (1835) coined the term *moral insanity* to delineate a mental condition characterized by an absence of morality, rather than the "madness" seen in other psychiatric patients. Like Pinel, Pritchard observed that while there clearly was emotional dysfunction in such patients, their cognitive abilities were intact. Pritchard (1835) further discussed how individuals suffering from moral insanity seemed to completely disregard the moral, ethical, and cultural norms of society. He thought that the "moral principles of the mind" were "perverted or depraved" in these men. Koch (1891, as cited in Millon, Simonsen, & Birket-Smith, 1998) objected to the term *moral insanity* and gave the opinion that a more appropriate term would be *psychopathic inferiority*. In his view, the condition of psychopathy stemmed from a type of biological abnormality that resulted in personality anomalies such as extreme selfishness. This conceptualization of psychopathy, with its focus on personality pathology, was more closely aligned to the modern conceptualization of psychopathy than were earlier views.

Sociologists began to take an interest in this problem in the early part of the twentieth century, and they, not surprisingly, saw social conditions as the critical factors. Accordingly, they replaced the term *psychopath* with the descriptor *sociopath* (Birnbaum, 1914). Partridge (1930) argued that individuals with this psychopathic inferiority were exhibiting a "social" disorder and coined the term *sociopath*, reflecting the idea that the condition involved an "anti-society" view of life. Such views were eventually incorporated into the APA's first edition of the DSM in 1952, which described a "sociopathic personality disturbance, antisocial reaction."

The current conceptualization of psychopathy is founded largely in the clinical observations of psychiatrist Hervey Cleckley. With a series of clinical case vignettes presented in his classic text *The Mask of Sanity* (1941), Cleckley proposed that there are a number of defining characteristics of the disorder, including emotional, interpersonal, and behavioural elements. Cleckley observed that psychopaths were unresponsive to social control and behaved in a socially inappropriate manner. Further, he described a profound emotional deficit, such that deep emotion and anxiety were missing in the psychopath. In fact, he theorized that a lack of emotion was at the core of the disorder, with other symptoms following from this emotional shallowness. For the past four decades, Dr. Robert Hare and colleagues at the University of British Columbia have worked toward operationalizing Cleckley's criteria for psychopathy, aimed at the generation of a highly reliable diagnostic tool for researchers: the Psychopathy Checklist (Hare, 1980), revised in 1991 and 2003 (Psychopathy Checklist–Revised; Hare, 1991, 2003).

Etiology

Aside from mentions of "hereditary taint" in prominent psychiatric texts (e.g., Krafft-Ebing, 1886/1939), little consideration was given to potential causes of personality disorders in the nineteenth century (e.g., Porter, 1996). This trend began to change with the development of the psychodynamic school and the publication of the first etiological theories of psychopathy in the 1920s (e.g., Partridge, 1928, 1929). During and after the 1940s, many causal theories were published, from learning theorists (e.g., Schachter & Latane, 1964), psychoanalysts (e.g., Arieti, 1963), and psychophysiologists (e.g., Hare, 1970). In fact, in a 1967 bibliography (Hare & Hare, 1967), 218 studies fell under the category of etiology—more than any other topic on psychopathy.

Unfortunately, despite the proliferation of theories, to this day there have been no firm conclusions about the factors that cause personality disorders. In this section, we will briefly cover the main current theories about the etiology of these problems. Where there are more detailed accounts and evidence (i.e., in antisocial and borderline disorders), we will cover this in more detail in the section on the specific disorders.

PSYCHODYNAMIC VIEWS

Psychoanalysts see personality disorder as resulting from disturbances in the parent–child relationship, particularly in problems related to separation-individuation (Mahler, Pine, & Bergman, 1975). This refers to the process by which the child learns that he or she is an individual separate from the mother and other people and, as a result, acquires a sense of him- or herself as an independent person. Thus, difficulties in this process, according to psychodynamic theorists, result in either an inadequate sense of self (e.g., borderline, narcissistic, or histrionic personality disorders) or problems in dealing with other people (e.g., avoidant or antisocial personality disorders). There is clear evidence that personality-disordered adults are far more likely than other people to have had disrupted childhoods, including the loss of a parent through death, divorce, or abandonment (Pert, Ferriter, & Saul, 2004; Robins, 1966) or parental rejection (McCord & McCord, 1964; Russ, Heim, & Westen, 2003). This evidence has also served to bolster other environmental theories of personality disorders, particularly attachment theory (Ainsworth & Bowlby, 1991) and learning-based theories (Turkat & Levin, 1984).

ATTACHMENT THEORY

As we have seen with many of the mental disorders, dominant thinking on the nature/nurture debate has undergone dramatic shifts over time. During the 1990s, it became somewhat unfashionable to explain personality pathology as being rooted in childhood (Porter, 1996), with biology being seen by many as the primary cause, especially for APD and psychopathy (e.g., Hare, 1993; Livesley, Jang, & Vernon, 2003). More recently, the Children in the Community Study of Developmental Course of Personality Disorder established that "PD symptom constellations identified in adulthood have their origins in childhood" (Cohen et al., 2005, p. 481).

Many theorists are again turning to the role of early relationships in contributing to personality pathology in adulthood. **Attachment theory** asserts that children learn how to relate to others, particularly in affectionate ways, by the way in which their parents relate to them. When the attachment bond between parents and the child is positive (i.e., the parents are loving, encouraging, and supportive), the child will develop the skills and confidence necessary to relate effectively to others. The parent–child bond serves as a template for all later relationships (Bowlby, 1977). When this bond is poor, children will lack confidence in relations with others (i.e., they will be afraid of rejection by others, and they will not have the skills necessary for intimate relationships). This analysis has been applied to various personality disorders (Links, 1992; Patrick, Hobson, Castle, & Howard, 1994), and the evidence appears to support the role of disrupted attachments in the etiology of these disorders (Coons, 1994; Torgersen & Alnaes, 1992; West, Keller, Links, & Patrick, 1993).

Researchers at the University of British Columbia (Bartholomew, 1990; Dutton, Saunders, Starzomski, & Bartholomew, 1994) have shown that if parent–child attachments are poor, the child will typically develop adult relationship styles that are characterized by ambivalence, fear, or avoidance. Poor attachments typically lead to deficits in developing intimacy (Marshall, Hudson, & Hodkinson, 1993), such that various maladaptive ways of dealing with interpersonal relationships are likely (Marshall & Barbaree, 1984). Levy (2000) has argued that poor attachment bonds are an antecedent to violence and antisocial patterns in children. The fact that personality disorders usually become obvious during late adolescence when the demands for social interaction become pre-eminent lends some support to the importance of attachment deficits in the origin of these disorders. Consistent with these claims, Goldberg, Mann, Wise, and Segall (1985) found that patients with personality disorders typically described their parents as either uncaring or overprotective, or both.

Battle and colleagues (2004) examined the childhood histories of 600 patients diagnosed with a personality disorder or major depressive disorder, in a multi-site investigation. The study confirmed that rates of childhood maltreatment among individuals with personality disorders are generally high (73 percent reporting abuse; 82 percent reporting neglect). As expected, borderline personality disorder was more consistently associated with childhood abuse and neglect than were other disorders. Of course, it is not possible to establish causation (only correlation) using this approach, but the findings show the very high prevalence of negative childhood experiences in those with a personality disorder.

COGNITIVE-BEHAVIOURAL PERSPECTIVES

Theorists of the cognitive-behavioural bent have suggested a variety of factors that may contribute to the emergence of personality disorders. Cognitive strategies or schemas (e.g., beliefs, assumptions, and attitudes) are said to develop early in life, and in personality-disordered individuals these schemas become rigid and inflexible (Beck, Freeman, & Davis, 2004; Shapiro, 1981; Young, 1999; Young, Klosko, & Weishaar, 2003). Young defined schemas as broad and pervasively maladaptive themes that people hold about themselves and their relationships with others. Because they form early in life as a result of damaging experiences (e.g., abandonment), Young believed that schemas are comfortable and familiar. The views of new events become distorted to maintain the validity of the schemas. People cope with their schemas in ways that may have been adaptive when they were children trying to survive in a damaging environment (e.g., by surrendering or overcompensating), but they continue coping in this same manner into adulthood. Linehan (1987, 1993) argued that these people come from families who consistently invalidate the emotional experiences of the child and oversimplify the ease with which life's problems can be solved. Accordingly, they learn that the way to get their parents' attention (and, as a consequence, the attention of others) is through a display of major emotional outbursts. Linehan's theory has been applied primarily to borderline patients, but it could apply to other types of personality disorder, particularly to all Cluster B disorders (i.e., the dramatic, emotional, or erratic disorders).

Of course, parents may also model inappropriate personal styles themselves, and there is considerable evidence that modelling is a powerful influence on children's behaviour (Bandura, 1976). In addition, parents may inappropriately reward or punish behaviour and the expression of attitudes. Parents of children who engage in antisocial behaviour, for example, have been shown to reward or punish their children non-contingently (Bauer & Webster-Stratton, 2007; Snyder, 1977); that is, their responses are not related to the child's behaviour.

BIOLOGICAL FACTORS

Biological accounts of personality disorders have been most thoroughly explored with APD, and we will discuss them in more depth when we describe that disorder later in this chapter. Basically, however, biological theorists have claimed that there is either brain dysfunction or a genetic or hormonal basis for these conditions. Cloninger, Svrakic, and Przybeck (1993), for example, have proposed that specific disturbances in neurotransmitter systems in the brain characterize particular types of personality disorders. Similarly, Siever and Davis (1991) suggest that different biological processes are associated with four dimensions (i.e., cognitive-perceptual organization, impulsivity-aggression, affective stability, and anxiety-inhibition) that together determine personality. Disruptions in the biological underpinnings of these four factors, then, might be expected to produce the unique personality disorders.

Although the evidence showing the value of these general theories is limited, there has been some support for biological factors in personality disorders (Depue, Luciana, Arbisi, Collins, & Leon, 1994). The strongest support, as we will see, comes from research with antisocial personality theories. But more recent work also suggests the likelihood of biological influences on other disorders, such as schizotypal personality disorder. Hans, Auerbach, Styr, and Marcus (2004) examined lifetime Axis I and II diagnoses for 116 young people (ages 12 to 22). Forty-one participants had a parent with schizophrenia, 39 had a parent with a mental disorder other than schizophrenia, and 36 had parents with no mental disorder. One central finding was that both schizophrenia and schizotypal personality disorder occurred exclusively in children of parents with schizophrenia. Children of parents with schizophrenia also were at increased risk for avoidant personality disorder but not paranoid personality disorder. These relationships were particularly strong for males. These findings strongly suggest that there is a familial vulnerability to schizophrenia spectrum disorders (especially schizotypal personality disorder) that is observable before adulthood.

Raine and colleagues (2002) took a different approach to examining biological correlates of personality disorders. These researchers focused on a brain region known as the prefrontal cortex. It was already known that structural prefrontal deficits existed in some patients with schizophrenia. The authors examined whether such deficits would also be found in patients with schizophrenia spectrum personality disorders. They assessed prefrontal grey and white volumes using magnetic resonance imaging (MRI) in a community sample of 16 individuals with schizotypal/paranoid personality disorder, 27 healthy control individuals, and 26 psychiatric controls. The personality disorder group showed reduced prefrontal volume and poorer frontal functioning compared to both other groups. More recently, functional MRI (fMRI) studies on patients with borderline personality disorder have begun to appear. These studies have mapped both the structure and the functioning of the brains of people with borderline personality disorder while they engage in emotion-inducing tasks, such as recalling emotional autobiographical events or viewing various emotional expressions on faces. The studies have implicated dysregulated responding of the prefrontal areas of the brain as well as fronto-limbic dysfunction in the form of overactivation of the amygdala (Beblo et al., 2006; Minzenberg, Fan, New, Tang, & Siever, 2007; Schnell, Dietrich, Schnitker, Daumann, & Herpertz, 2007; Schnell & Herpertz, 2007; Silbersweig et al., 2007).

Examining concordance rates among twins provides another approach to test the role of biology in personality disorders. Coolidge, Thede, and Jang (2001) investigated the heritability of personality disorder features in 112 pairs of 4- to 15-year-old twins: 70 monozygotic and 42 dizygotic. The children's parents provided information about the children's features using a tool measuring 12 personality disorders according to the criteria in DSM-IV-TR. The analyses showed that the median "heritability coefficient" for the 12 scales was .75 (ranging from a high of .81 for the dependent and schizotypal personality disorder scales to .50 for the paranoid personality disorder scales). The results suggested that childhood personality disorders may have a substantial genetic component.

SUMMARY OF ETIOLOGY

There are various theories regarding the causes of personality disorders. In keeping with most other disorders, some synthesis of these theories seems to make the most sense. There is clear correlational evidence of biological, family, and learning processes, and there is some (limited) support for psychodynamic accounts. With respect to Cluster A disorders, the most prominent observations are genetic links with both schizophrenia and mood disorders. Biological variables such as impaired eye-tracking, as measured by smooth-pursuit eye movements, have also been investigated as signs of biological bases for Cluster A disorders (Zemishlany, Siever, & Coccaro, 1988). For Cluster B disorders, the two etiological factors that have received the best support are biological factors and attachment problems. Investigations of causal factors specifically with Cluster C disorders have been very limited, despite the prevalence of the disorders (Morey, 1988). In general, causes of the personality disorders remain murky; longitudinal (lifespan) approaches are essential to resolve the lingering mysteries and are currently being conducted (see Cohen et al., 2005; Skodol et al., 2005; Zanarini et al., 2005).

3 BEFORE MOVING ON

What are the four main perspectives used to explain the etiology of personality disorders? Are there any definite causes of personality disorders? After reviewing each theory, which perspective appears to be the most legitimate? Do certain theories seem more fitting for some personality disorders than others? Why or why not?

The Specific Disorders

Two personality disorders have received the bulk of research attention over the past several years: antisocial personality disorder and borderline personality disorder. Accordingly, our primary focus will be on these, with briefer descriptions of the remaining disorders. Additionally, a short discussion of proposed changes for the DSM-5 will be provided for all personality disorders.

Cluster A: Odd and Eccentric Disorders

PARANOID PERSONALITY DISORDER

Pervasive **suspiciousness** concerning the motives of other people and a tendency to interpret what others say and do as personally meaningful in a negative way are the primary features of someone with paranoid personality disorder. These individuals consistently misread the innocent actions or comments of others as being threatening or critical, and they expect other people to exploit them. Consequently, individuals with paranoid personality tend to be hypervigilant, and they take extreme precautions against potential threats from others. They believe that other people intend to hurt them, and they are reluctant to share anything personal for fear it might be used against them. In addition, they are typically humourless and eccentric, and are seen by others as hostile, jealous, and preoccupied with power and control. Not surprisingly, they have numerous problems in relationships; most people cannot tolerate their need to control and particularly their jealous and suspicious nature. Frequently, patients who are paranoid become socially isolated, and this seems only to add to their persecutory ideas.

These features, identified both in the diagnostic criteria and in clinical reports, have been confirmed in research. For example, compared with non-psychiatric participants, individuals with paranoid personalities experience far more paranoid thoughts both currently and during their school days (Turkat & Banks, 1987), have greater difficulty dealing with ambiguity and are more suspicious (Thompson-Pope & Turkat, 1988), and are more likely to misread social cues as evidence of hostility by others (Turkat, Keane, & Thompson-Pope, 1990).

Since paranoid personality occurs quite commonly in the relatives of individuals with schizophrenia, a genetic link with schizophrenia has been proposed. Kendler, Masterson, and Davis (1985) even suggested that paranoid personality disorder may be a subtype of schizophrenia. A more common view is that it is a related disorder, or a "cousin" of schizophrenia. The main difference in paranoid personality and paranoid schizophrenia is the severity (e.g., in terms of bizarreness, extension) of the paranoid belief. In schizophrenia, the paranoid belief is sufficiently bizarre and ingrained that it is considered "psychotic"—a **delusion**. In paranoid personality, the individual's paranoid beliefs are non-bizarre, within the realm of possibility, and pertain to general suspiciousness, even though they are mistaken.

There is also significant diagnostic overlap between paranoid personality and both avoidant and borderline personality disorders (Morey, 1988). Further, in a large-scale study among adolescents in New York, paranoid personality disorder was one of the four most persistent types of personality disorder identified (Bernstein et al., 1993). Recent data also suggest that paranoid personality disorder is one of the most commonly diagnosed personality disorders in community samples (Edens, Marcus, & Morey, 2009). You might imagine that attempting to provide treatment to someone who distrusts everyone, including the clinician, is very difficult. In fact, it is likely that only a very small proportion of individuals with this disorder would seek or accept treatment.

Despite recent research that has demonstrated that paranoid personality disorder is best represented as a continuum of personality traits (Edens et al., 2009), it appears that paranoid personality disorder will not be included in the DSM-5 (APA, 2011).

SCHIZOID PERSONALITY DISORDER

Individuals with this condition—such as George, introduced early in this chapter—seem completely uninterested in having any sort of intimate involvement with others, and they display little in the way of **emotional responsiveness**. They come across as being detached and self-absorbed. These individuals often report that they rarely experience intense emotions and may be puzzled by the passions of others. Individuals with schizoid personality disorder are typically loners who are cold and indifferent toward others. In fact, they seem not to enjoy relationships of any type, apparently preferring to be alone. Unlike most of us, they avoid social activities and do not seek or seem to desire sexual relations. There seems to be little doubt that most do not have the skills necessary for effective social interaction, but they also appear uninterested in acquiring such skills.

Morey's (1988) examination of the impact on diagnostic practices of the changes from DSM-III to DSM-III-R revealed that the frequency of schizoid diagnoses increased significantly (from 1.4 percent of patients to 11 percent). This was apparently due to a reduction in the frequency of the diagnosis of schizotypal disorder with a corresponding increase in diagnosing schizoid personality. Unfortunately, this makes it difficult to compare research on schizoid personality conducted before and after the publication of DSM-III-R.

One of the main problems with this diagnostic category is that it has been the focus of little methodologically sound research. Not surprisingly, it is difficult to find research participants in the community. As a consequence, little more is known about this disorder than was true several years ago. Perhaps as a result of the changes in diagnostic criteria, published studies frequently confound schizoid and schizotypal features, and do not, therefore, permit any definitive conclusions. More recently, data from the Children in the Community Study of Developmental Course of Personality Disorder led Cohen and colleagues (2005) to conclude that schizoid personality disorder appeared to be distinct from paranoid personality disorder and schizotypal personality disorder. They suggested that the disorder may be more related to asocial disorders (e.g., Asperger disorder). At this time it appears that schizoid personality disorder will not be included in the DSM-5 (APA, 2011).

SCHIZOTYPAL PERSONALITY DISORDER

The major presenting feature of individuals with schizotypal personality disorder is **eccentricity** of thought and behaviour; many are extremely superstitious and may believe in magic. Their ideation and behaviour are peculiar, and these features tend to turn other people away so that schizotypal patients are typically socially isolated. No doubt this isolation from others increases the likelihood that they will have unusual thoughts and perceptions, since they have little opportunity to check the accuracy of their cognitions. Their thinking tends to be permeated by odd beliefs. They typically believe in magical thinking and paranormal phenomena such as telepathy and clairvoyance, and may see such skills in themselves.

Like paranoid personality disorder, this condition has some similarities with schizophrenia. Again, the difference lies in the severity and quality of the symptoms. Although their beliefs, perceptual experiences, speech, and behaviours are odd and tend to isolate them from others, they are not usually considered to be so eccentric as to meet the criteria for delusional or hallucinatory psychotic experiences. There is, however, considerable disagreement on this issue. For example, McGlashan (1994) claimed that transient psychoses characterize these patients, and Kendler (1985) concluded that schizotypal disorder is simply a subtle form of schizophrenia. Research examining biological features has found strong similarities between patients with schizotypal personality disorder and those with schizophrenia (Siever, 1985). In addition, many family members of patients with schizophrenia exhibit schizotypal symptoms (Kendler, 1985). More recent research has revealed that, while the symptoms of SPD remain the same, the severity of the symptoms varies depending on sex and age (Fonseca-Pedrero, Lemos-Giráldez, Muñiz, García-Cueto, & Campillo-Álvarez, 2008; Paíno-Piñeiro, Fonseca-Pedrero, Lemos-Giráldez, & Muñiz, 2008).

Diagnostic overlap between schizotypal disorder and other Cluster A disorders—as well as avoidant personality disorder and, to a lesser degree, borderline personality disorder—is also considerable (Morey, 1988). Thus, the meaningfulness and value of the distinctions among Cluster A diagnoses have been criticized (Livesley & West, 1986).

The literature regarding treatment of schizotypal personality disorder mirrors the approach taken with etiology; that is, the emphasis is on the schizophrenic-like features. Low doses of antipsychotic drugs relieve the cognitive problems and social anxiety apparent in these patients (Goldberg et al., 1986), and antidepressant medication has also produced positive effects (Markovitz, Calabrese, Schulz, & Meltzer, 1991). Overall, medication has positive, although modest, effects (Gitlin, 1993). Finally, controlled studies of psychological forms of treatment have not been reported, and generally the long-term prognosis for schizotypal patients is poor.

Schizotypal personality disorder will most likely be included in the DSM-5. The diagnostic criteria for schizotypal personality disorder in the DSM-IV-TR requires at least five of the following criteria: ideas of reference (excluding delusions of reference), odd beliefs or magical thinking, unusual perceptual experiences, suspiciousness or paranoid ideation, inappropriate or constricted affect, odd or eccentric behaviour or appearance, a lack of close friends, and excessive social anxiety that does not diminish with familiarity and tends to be associated with paranoid fears. In line with the proposed changes to the model of personality disorders in the DSM-5, significant impairments must be present in both self and interpersonal functioning, and personality traits in a number of different domains must be present as well. In relation to self-functioning, the individual must have impairments in identity (such as confused boundaries between self and others and/or a distorted self-concept) or self-direction (such as unrealistic or incoherent goals). The individual must experience impairments in interpersonal functioning, either with the ability to empathize or the ability to be intimate with others. Finally, the individual must display specific personality traits in a number of domains, such as psychoticism, detachment, and negative affectivity (APA, 2011).

Cluster B: Dramatic, Emotional, or Erratic Disorders

As noted earlier, the four disorders in Cluster B do not seem to have as much in common with each other as is implied by their collective grouping in DSM-IV-TR. Whereas histrionic and borderline disorders may be perceived as dramatic, it is hard to see what this descriptor has to do with antisocial personality disorder. Indeed, except for a limited range of emotional expression among these patients, none of the descriptors of Cluster B seem to fit the antisocial patients. In fact, it has been suggested that antisocial patients belong to a separate category of personality disorders (Lykken, 1995).

ANTISOCIAL PERSONALITY DISORDER AND PSYCHOPATHY: A CONFUSION OF DIAGNOSES

You were introduced to James at the beginning of this chapter. People like James are among the most dangerous individuals in society, as reflected by a consistently higher rate of criminal behaviour than other offenders throughout adulthood (e.g., Harpur & Hare, 1994; Porter, Birt, & Boer, 2001).

James's personal style occurs often in individuals who are diagnosed as having APD. On the surface, he is charming and persuasive, but this masks a self-centred and, in his case, criminal lifestyle. Not all patients with antisocial personalities commit crimes, although most of them who are so diagnosed by clinicians have a criminal record. This may simply reflect the fact that it is their criminal behaviour that brings them to the attention of psychiatrists or psychologists. However, the behavioural features of APD do predispose these patients to crime, and unlawfulness is one of the examples that DSM-IV-TR provides of the disregard that those with antisocial personalities display toward others.

DESCRIPTION OF THE DISORDER Individuals thus identified have been referred to as **psychopaths**, **sociopaths**, or dyssocial personalities, with these terms sometimes being used interchangeably. In fact, in correctional settings, the terms *psychopathy* and *APD* have been confused for decades. Many researchers and clinicians continue to use the concept of psychopathy rather than following DSM-IV-TR criteria, or vice versa.

However, it is important to recognize that APD and psychopathy are *not* the same disorder (e.g., Hart & Hare, 1997). Psychopathy incorporates a richer set of emotional, interpersonal, and behavioural features than the DSM-IV-TR definition of APD, which focuses on observable behaviour. The relatively few criteria reflecting emotional and interpersonal processes in the diagnostic manual, as well as the results of studies (Rogers et al., 1994) comparing DSM-IV and other measures of APD (e.g., PCL-R and the ICD-10 of the World Health Organization, 1992), underscore this concern. However, there is some overlap between APD and psychopathy, such that only a small proportion of individuals who qualify for a diagnosis of APD are psychopathic, whereas most individuals who are psychopathic would qualify for an APD diagnosis (Hare, 2003; Hart & Hare, 1997). Coid and Ullrich (2010) reveal that APD and psychopathy are in fact related, but that psychopathy is more severe than APD. In other words, APD and psychopathy have an asymmetric relationship. As such, we will consider APD and psychopathy to be related but separate entities in the following sections.

The debate regarding the differential utility of the concepts of APD and psychopathy has led to some confusion. Central to this issue is whether DSM-IV-TR criteria sufficiently reflect the personality domain of the disorder. Employing essentially behavioural criteria may increase diagnostic reliability, but may also yield a group of antisocial individuals who are markedly variable in terms of personality traits (Blackburn, 1992). The advantage of using the most widely accepted measure of psychopathy—the Psychopathy Checklist–Revised (PCL-R; Hare, 1991, 2003)—is that it specifies both behaviour and personality as features to be considered. Studies of the PCL-R have revealed that two factors, personality traits and lifestyle instability, are *necessary and sufficient* for a diagnosis (Hare, Hart, & Harpur, 1991). Further, the PCL-R emotional/affective criteria (such as shallow affect) are highly reliable if the rater has the appropriate training (e.g., Hare, 2003).

Unlike the other personality disorders, the essential feature of APD is a pervasive pattern of disregard for and violation of the rights of others that begins in childhood or early adolescence and continues into adulthood. The increasing reliance on behavioural indices of the disorder introduced since DSM-II has raised concerns regarding the relationship of the diagnostic criteria to clinical conceptions of the related construct of psychopathy (Hare et al., 1991). The notion of psychopathy as a destructive constellation of personality characteristics has, as we saw earlier, a long history and, in fact, was the clinical concept that originally led to the definition of APD. Again, it is important to highlight that the DSM-IV-TR criteria for APD are a highly reliable set of indicators of a socially deviant lifestyle; however, they are not the best criteria for tapping the core features of psychopathy (e.g., shallow affect, lack of empathy), which are best measured by the Psychopathy Checklist–Revised. It should be noted that incorporating core features of psychopathy into the diagnosis for APD has been recommended for the fifth version of the DSM.

ANTISOCIAL PERSONALITY DISORDER (APD) The DSM-IV-TR criteria for the diagnosis of APD include seven exemplars reflecting the violation of the rights of others: nonconformity, callousness, deceitfulness, irresponsibility, impulsivity, aggressiveness, and recklessness. Sean Penn gave a remarkably accurate portrayal of APD in the movie *Dead Man Walking*. Reflecting a **polythetic** approach (meaning only a subset of symptoms or behaviours is required for a diagnosis, unlike most medical diagnoses), three or more of the above symptoms must be met for the diagnosis to be applied.

At this time it appears that antisocial personality disorder will be included in the DSM-5. To be diagnosed with APD according to the criteria of the DSM-5, the individual must demonstrate significant impairment in self-functioning, reflected by impairments in identity (such as self-esteem derived from personal gain or power) and self-direction (absence of prosocial internal standards associated with failure to conform to lawful, ethical behaviour). The individual must also present with impairment in interpersonal functioning, reflected by a lack of empathy after mistreat-

FOCUS 12.1

Paul Bernardo and Karla Homolka

Serial offenders who commit sexual assaults and/or homicides continue to be a major concern to the public. Paul Bernardo, known as the "Scarborough Rapist" and a diagnosed psychopath, sexually assaulted numerous Ontario women over the course of several years in the early 1990s. Although he was a suspect in the investigation of the rapes, he was not arrested and his violence escalated until he—along with his wife, Karla Homolka—raped and murdered three young women, including Homolka's own sister. Bernardo and Homolka abducted two teenage girls and held them captive for several days while they repeatedly and brutally sexually assaulted them, and videotaped their actions. After several days of torture, the girls were murdered and their bodies were disposed of. When these callous crimes were revealed, the public was outraged—all the more so because a woman was involved. In one of the most notorious plea bargains in Canadian legal history, Homolka entered into a deal with the Ontario Crown Attorney's office on May 14, 1993, in which she agreed to plead guilty to two counts of manslaughter in return for a 12-year sentence (see Galligan, 1996). During the sentencing hearing, evidence was presented that she had played a direct role in the drugging, sexual assault, and death of her 15-year-old sister. Prior to the plea bargain, Homolka had been assessed by several mental health professionals. In March 1993 she had been admitted into a hospital where she underwent lengthy evaluations by two psychiatrists and two psychologists. The clinical reports include numerous diagnoses and clinical descriptions, from stress, anxiety, and depression to learned helplessness, post-traumatic stress disorder, lack of affect, and other indicators of "battered woman syndrome," whereas little evidence was found for psychosis or sexual deviance. The domestic violence she had experienced at the hands of Bernardo had reportedly left her like a "concentration camp survivor," and had contributed to her involvement in the murders (Galligan, 1996).

However, the true extent of Homolka's culpability in the murders was revealed in the videotapes that were later recovered. Her claims of being under her husband's control—central to the plea bargain—appeared to be blatantly false (see Wrightsman & Porter, 2005). On the videotapes they had made of their violence, these predatory offenders clearly derived enjoyment from the suffering of the victims. It was reported that Homolka spoke with and sexually assaulted the victims with a smile on her face. As a student of psychology, how helpful do you think the descriptions provided by the mental health professionals were in helping the court make the right decisions? Did Homolka successfully deceive the court? How does this case inform your opinion of the reliability and validity of DSM disorders and the diagnostic process?

ing others as well as an inability to be intimate with others. Finally, he or she must possess pathological personality traits such as antagonism and disinhibition (APA, 2011).

Prevalence. DSM-IV-TR reports lifetime prevalence rates for APD of approximately 3 percent in males and 1 percent in females for community samples. These results are not quite comparable to the United States National Comorbidity Survey Replication (Lenzenweger et al., 2007), which reported a prevalence rate of 0.6 percent in males and females combined. The discrepancy may reflect variability in the sampling methods between the National Comorbidity Survey Replication and the studies relied on when the DSM-IV-TR was authored. The incidence in forensic settings can be expected to be higher, since, as we have seen, criminal behaviour is a dominant feature of APD. Yet contemporary estimates are unavailable for DSM-IV-TR. Estimates in Great Britain (Chiswick, 1992) indicate a prevalence rate of approximately 25 to 33 percent of patients in Special Hospitals. This high number presumably occurs because criminals who are considered to have a psychiatric disorder are diverted to these Special Hospitals, whereas those who do not are simply imprisoned. Hare (1983, 1985) reported higher estimates in Canadian prisons using DSM-III-R, where approximately 40 percent of offenders were diagnosed as having APD. Similar data from another correctional sample were provided by Hart and Hare (1989), reflecting the relative overdiagnosis using DSM-III criteria (50 percent incidence of APD) compared with an early version of the Personality Checklist (12.5 percent incidence of psychopathy). These rates are slightly lower than estimates provided by Quebec researchers Côté and Hodgins (1990), who used yet another assessment strategy, the Diagnostic Interview Schedule (Robins, Helzer, Croughan, & Ratcliff, 1981). In a random sample of 495 male inmates, Côté and Hodgins diagnosed 61.5 percent as having APD using the diagnostic interview criteria.

Etiology of APD. Several lines of investigation have been pursued in an attempt to explain the essential characteristics of antisocial persons: callous disregard for others, impulsivity and poor self-regulation, rule breaking and criminality, and exploitation of others. Social and family factors were initial explanations (Robins, 1966), with the view being that parental behaviours can influence the development of antisocial functioning. This led to the application of family systems approaches to treatment, with which empirically determined risk factors are targeted within a family-centred model of service delivery (Henggeler & Schoenwald, 1993). This multi-systemic therapy approach has produced some promising outcome data (Borduin et al., 1995) and this has further encouraged the idea that disruptive families are causal factors in the disorder. Moffit's (1993) work on developmental trajectories indicates that a minority of youth become involved in rule breaking and delinquent behaviour at an early age and that this is sustained throughout their lifespan in one form or another. This research also suggests the importance of familial/parental factors and genetic features as risk factors for developing APD. There have been two major systematic literature reviews (Miles & Carey, 1997; Rhee & Waldman, 2002) that collectively analyzed a relatively large body of empirical studies on the genetic influences on antisocial and aggressive behaviour. Both of these reviews incorporated twin and adoption studies in their analyses and both converged on the importance of genetics in the development of aggressive and antisocial behaviour. This literature has yielded heritability estimates for measures of antisocial behaviour/aggression ranging from 44 percent to 72 percent (Blair, Peschardt, Budhani, Mitchell, & Pine, 2006).

However, while a strictly biological explanation has been found to be insufficient to account for the etiology of antisocial behaviour (Raine, 1993), such factors appear to interact with childhood experiences to produce criminality. There appear to be neuropsychological markers that, in combination with specific environmental circumstances (e.g., criminogenic environment, poor parenting, neglect, and physical abuse), interact to make children vulnerable to developing an antisocial lifestyle and personality (Mealey, 1995).

The final line of research to be discussed here concerns the examination of potential psychological explanations of the inadequate self-regulation shown by individuals with APD. Lykken (1957), for example, suggested that such individuals are essentially fearless. This **fearlessness hypothesis** claims that those with APD have a higher threshold for feeling fear than do other people. Events that make most people anxious (e.g., the expectation of being punished) are thought to have little or no effect on those with APD. A recent study provided support for this hypothesis by confirming that there appears to be an attentional mechanism that reduces the fear response in individuals with APD (Dvorak-Bertsch, Curtin, Rubinstein, & Newman, 2009).

Subsequently, however, some social learning theorists questioned the validity of the fearlessness hypothesis. Schmauk (1970), for example, suggested that, since Lykken's research (see Figure 12.1) and other studies used

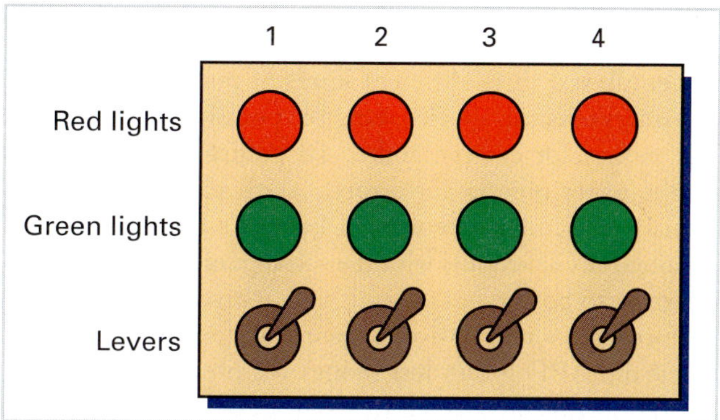

FIGURE 12.1 Lykken's Lever Apparatus to Test Avoidance Learning

Lykken (1957) devised this apparatus for his study of avoidance learning in individuals with APD. The participants had to learn a sequence of 20 correct lever presses.

Source: Lykken (1957).

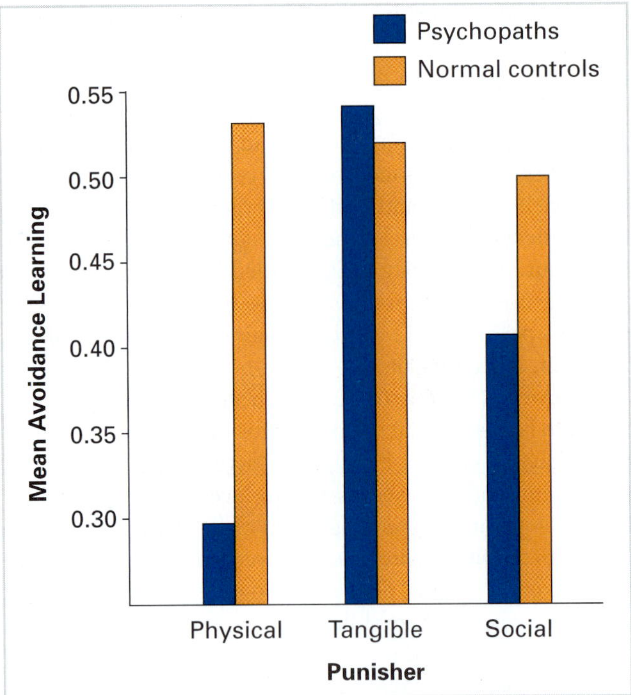

FIGURE 12.2 Effects of Different Types of Punishment on Psychopaths

Source: Adapted from Schmauk (1970).

an electric shock as a punisher, the findings might only be relevant to shocks and other types of physical punishment. Schmauk pointed out that, as children, individuals with APD appear to have been exposed to severe physical punishment from their parents or guardians that was frequently not contingent upon their behaviour. As a result, Schmauk suggested that these individuals might have learned to be either indifferent to physical punishment or oppositional to such attempts at controlling them. **Oppositional behaviour** has been thoroughly examined in children (Campbell, 1990) and refers to a tendency to do the opposite of what is being asked of the person. In the present case, oppositional behaviour would result in the punished behaviour showing an increase rather than the expected decrease.

To test this idea, Schmauk repeated Lykken's study but employed three different kinds of punishers: physical punishers (electric shocks), tangible punishers (participants lost money for errors), and social punishers (reprimands by the experimenter for errors). With electric shocks as punishers, Schmauk replicated Lykken's findings, and he obtained similar results with the social punishers. That is, in response to both types of punishers, individuals with APD performed poorly relative to their counterparts. However, when the APD group lost money for pressing the wrong lever, they quickly learned to avoid the shocked levers and, in fact, did so more successfully than had their counterparts under any of the punishment conditions (see Figure 12.2). Schmauk concluded that individuals with APD were differentially responsive to different kinds of punishment as a result of early learning experiences, rather than completely fearless or unresponsive to all punishment.

Newman and his colleagues have described the pathology of psychopaths (as measured by the PCL-R) as due primarily to information processing deficiencies (Wallace, Schmitt, Vitale, & Newman, 2000). Through a series of laboratory and process-based investigations, they concluded that psychopaths suffer from a generalized information processing deficiency involving the *automatic* directing of attention to stimuli that are peripheral to ongoing directed behaviour. That is, once engaged in reward-based behaviour, the psychopath is less likely to attend to other cues to modulate his or her ongoing response. In contrast, the antisocial and criminal behaviour exhibited by those diagnosed as having APD involves schema-based deficits. These deficits comprise antisocial schemas and cognitive distortions not requiring automatic attentional cueing. Such research supports the idea that psychopathy and APD are different diagnoses implying different etiology, intervention, and prognosis.

Course and Prognosis of APD. Robins and Regier (1991) reported that the average duration of APD, from the onset of the first symptom to the end of the last, was 19 years. This remittance over time of symptoms has been described as the *burnout factor*, with the expectation being that symptoms will disappear by the fourth decade of life. However, Arboleda-Florez and Holley (1991) have presented data refuting the view that individuals with APD do burn out. These conflicting data are confusing and it is hard to make sense of them. Correctional Service Canada researchers Porporino and Motiuk (1995) found that when APD and substance use are comorbid conditions, the post-release performance is poorer than in those offenders who have only one or the other disorder.

Treatment for APD. Reviews of treatment efficacy for patients with APD have been generally pessimistic (Reid & Gacono, 2000; Suedfeld & Landon, 1978). Many of the early studies, however, suffered from poor methodology. As pointed out by Dr. Paul Gendreau (1996) of the University of New Brunswick, programs delivered in previous decades did not reflect contemporary knowledge of effective treatment programs for resistant clients, so it may be premature to discount the potential for modifying the destructive behaviours of these clients. Attrition from treatment programs is also high, and this has proved to be predictive of subsequent reoffending. Lastly, in substance abuse treatment, individuals with APD fare more poorly than do other patients (Alterman & Cacciola, 1991). Surprisingly, therapeutic hope has not vanished. Approximately two-thirds of psychiatrists think that individuals with APD are sometimes treatable (Tennent, Tennent, Prins, & Bedford, 1993). Despite a poor response to hospitalization, prognosis is improved for these clients if there is a treatable anxiety or depressive feature to their behaviour (Gabbard & Coyne, 1987) or if they can be convinced to form an effective therapeutic alliance (Gerstley et al., 1989). According to current views, treatment should be aimed at symptom reduction and behaviour management rather than at a cure (Quinsey, Harris, Rice, & Cormier, 2006).

Treatment of other groups of resistant clients suggests a **responsivity factor**. That is, treatment must be responsive (or matched) to a particular patient's needs and interpersonal style. Poor treatment performance may, in part, be caused by an intervention that is of insufficient intensity (Gendreau, 1996), viewed by patients as irrelevant (Miller & Rollnick, 1991), or seen as involuntary (Gabbard & Coyne, 1987). Several of these issues have been specifically considered in the context of the provision of treatment, yet they remain untested hypotheses. Researchers at the Oak Ridge Mental Health Centre in Ontario (Rice, Harris, & Quinsey, 1996) have pointed out that treatment programs vary for these clients according to the extent that either personality or criminality is emphasized, and yet a problems-based approach would appear to enhance compliance and efficacy.

Many of the more recent developments in treatment programs for criminal populations have involved significant contributions from Canadian researchers in forensic hospitals (e.g., Quinsey et al., 2006) and in prisons (e.g., Serin & Kuriychuk, 1994). While treatment targets for these samples have sometimes obscured the distinction between criminality and antisocial personality, they typically include a focus on some combination of aggressive and antisocial attitudes and beliefs, impulsivity or poor self-regulation, social skills, anger, assertiveness, substance abuse, empathy, problem solving, and moral reasoning (Serin & Preston, 2001). For many of these targets, there are structured program materials; however, the technology to measure treatment gains remains relatively unsophisticated. Furthermore, the over-reliance on self-report assessment methods is problematic in a population for whom honesty is suspect.

Another strategy for managing antisocial or acting-out behaviour, particularly in closed settings, has been pharmacotherapy. Short-term use of psychopharmocological agents is most often used to manage difficult or threatening behaviour. However, the side effects of long-term drug use and problems of noncompliance have been noted in forensic patients (Harris, 1989). While short-term use of antipsychotic, anti-anxiety, and sedative medications is not uncommon, symptom alleviation is rarely sustained, and patients are typically provided with no new skills to improve their ability to deal with future situations. For some patients, medication may reduce arousal level sufficiently for them to participate more fully in cognitive-behavioural treatment (Rice & Harris, 1993).

Summary of APD. The goal of DSM-IV-TR to develop simplified yet reliable criteria for APD appears to have been reasonably well met. These changes, however, have not served to bridge the conceptual differences between divergent views regarding the preferred diagnostic criteria or the assessment of these clients. It is important to note that alternatives to the diagnostic criteria, such as the PCL-R and ICD-10, may yield better assessments, in the view of experienced clinicians.

Currently, treatment initiatives can be only partly guided by theory (Rice & Harris, 1997b; Serin & Preston, 2001). Prognosis even after treatment remains relatively poor for patients with APD. For example, Hanson and Morton-Bourgon (2005) collectively analyzed the results of 82 studies examining persistent sexual offending (n = 29 450 sexual offenders) and found that the major predictors of future sexual offences by both adolescents and adults were an antisocial orientation and deviant sexual preferences. An antisocial orientation was also a major predictor of future non-sexual violent offences. Interestingly, many of the variables traditionally targeted in sexual offender treatment programs (e.g., psychological distress) showed little or no relationship with future sexual offences. Conceptualizing treatment as a management strategy rather than as a cure is perhaps a more helpful framework, and likely to protect clinicians from undue optimism. Further, targeting responsivity factors (i.e., those factors that are related to the antisocial behaviour) may yield enhanced treatment efficacy, but this remains an empirical question.

PSYCHOPATHY Although psychopathy is not yet listed on Axis II of the DSM-IV-TR (and will likely not be included as an independent personality disorder in the DSM-5), an enormous amount of research has been devoted to the disorder in the past two decades, probably more than to APD, or all other personality disorders combined. Psychopaths are a distinctive subgroup of offenders best described by their unique interpersonal and affective disposition. They are egocentric, deceptive, callous, manipulative individuals who lack remorse and emotional depth. Readers interested in viewing a film depiction of a psychopath might consider *The Last King of Scotland,* in which Forest Whitaker plays the role of Ugandan dictator Idi Amin. Whitaker effectively conveys the superficially charming, charismatic, and grandiose qualities of the disorder that are often used to mask a selfish, deceitful, callous, and antisocial lifestyle. He received the Best Actor award at the 79th Academy Awards for his portrayal of Amin.

Psychopaths commit a disproportionate amount of antisocial and violent behaviour in society, extending to both nonsexual and sexual violence (Hart & Hare, 1997; Porter et al., 2000). In addition to their aggression and violence, psychopaths are chronic deceivers, often but not always lying for instrumental reasons such as to escape punishment. Häkkänen-Nyholm and Hare (2009) revealed that offenders with high PCL-R scores are more likely to deny charges or claim self-defence. These offenders are also likely to be convicted of a less serious crime than the one they committed, be granted an appeal of their sentence, and be granted undeserved conditional release. Psychopathic non-sex offenders were the most successful at garnering conditional release, but even the psychopathic sex offenders were more successful than non-psychopathic non-sex offenders (Porter, ten Brinke, & Wilson, 2009). They are "users" of others, in their attempts to obtain money, drugs, sex, or power (e.g., Hart & Hare, 1997; Porter & Woodworth, 2007; Woodworth & Porter, 2002). Many psychopaths are con artists with a long history of frauds and scams; some even become cult leaders, corrupt politicians, or successful corporate leaders, before their frequent downfall (e.g., Babiak & Hare, 2006).

Not only are psychopaths successful scam artists, they also appear to have a heightened ability to discern vulnerable individuals from non-vulnerable individuals. To successfully dupe someone, it is important to target an individual who is easy to manipulate. There are many characteristics associated with vulnerability, including low self-esteem, low assertiveness, and increased depression and anxiety (Egan & Perry, 1998). Psychopaths have demonstrated a keen ability to detect these signs of vulnerability among others in a number of studies. Book, Quinsey, and Langford (2007) found that psychopathic individuals were better able than are non-psychopaths to sense a lack of assertiveness after simply viewing a two-minute video of a vulnerable target. Wheeler, Book, and Costello (2009) revealed that psychopaths were able to detect vulnerability based on gait and non-verbal cues alone. Finally, Wilson, Demetrioff, and Porter (2008) discovered that men who possessed a high number of psychopathic traits had nearly perfect recall for sad and unsuccessful females, who are likely to be highly vulnerable. It is unknown at this time how psychopaths detect vulnerability in others, but the authors of this chapter are currently investigating this phenomenon.

It is important to note that diagnostic strategies other than those outlined in DSM-IV-TR are gaining prominence in the forensic literature. For example, the PCL-R (Hare, 1991) enjoys international popularity as both a research instrument and a clinical tool (e.g., Hemphill & Hare, 2004). Psychopathy, as measured by the PCL-R, is characterized by 20 criteria scored from 0 to 2 for a maximum score of 40. As recommended in the manual, a minimum score of 30 is the cut-off for classifying psychopathy. The PCL-R score is highly reliable over time and has a high level of validity according to much research (e.g., Fulero, 1995; Stone, 1995). Increasingly, the PCL-R is used in assessments to inform judicial decisions, principally because of its predictive validity in terms of recidivism (i.e., the commission of new criminal offences following some previous involvement in the criminal justice system) (Douglas, Vincent, & Edens, 2007; Serin & Brown, 2000).

Despite the definitional differences between APD and psychopathy, little distinction has been made between APD and psychopathy in the legal system (Lyon & Ogloff, 2000). Some authors (e.g., Harding, 1992) suggest that the reluctance to use the term *psychopathic* stems from its pejorative connotations. Psychopathy, however, is a resilient term that has enjoyed a relative resurgence in use in correctional and forensic settings (Hare, 2003). In the media, psychopathy has been prominent in descriptions of infamous offenders such as Clifford Olson and Paul Bernardo. Such sensationalism, however, does little to inform the public or clinicians regarding the disorder, as many or most psychopaths are not serial rapists or murderers. Many "white-collar psychopaths" are successful in business or politics (e.g., Babiak & Hare, 2006).

Psychopathy and Aggression. As outlined by Porter and Porter (2007), research has established a strong link between psychopathic traits and aggression or violence in both adult offenders and psychiatric patients. Porter, Birt, and Boer (2001) found that psychopaths incarcerated in Canadian correctional institutions had perpetrated an average of more than seven violent crimes, nearly twice the average of their counterparts. This link helps us predict whether an offender is likely to commit future violent behaviour (e.g., Harris, Rice, & Quinsey, 1993; Hemphill, Hare, & Wong, 1998; Rice & Harris, 1997a; Salekin, Rogers, & Sewell, 1996). For example, Canadian researchers Serin and Amos (1995) found that psychopaths were about five times more likely than their counterparts to engage in violent reoffending within five years of their release from prison. Although the prevalence of psychopathy in civil psychiatric patients is low compared to that among criminal offenders (e.g., Douglas, Ogloff, Nicholls, & Grant, 1999), a consideration of psychopathy still helps to predict future aggression in this population. Skeem and Mulvey (2001) examined future violence in 1136 psychiatric patients from the MacArthur Violence Risk Assessment project, and found that PCL-R scores predicted future serious violence, despite a low base rate (8 percent).

Not only do psychopaths commit more violence, they commit particularly heinous violence. Williamson, Hare, and Wong (1987) found that psychopaths' violent crimes were more likely to have a motive of material gain (45.2 percent) than were non-psychopaths' (14.6 percent). Further, non-psychopaths (31.7 percent) were more likely to display high levels of emotion in their offences than were psychopaths (2.4 percent). Cornell and colleagues (1996) found that offenders who had committed at least one previous act of instrumental (planned with an external goal) violence had higher PCL-R scores than offenders who had only committed acts of reactive violence. In addition, Juodis, Starzomski, Porter, and Woodworth (2012) discovered that psychopaths adhere to the selective impulsivity theory. That is, psychopaths are not out of control, but are able to quickly weigh the pros and cons of their actions. They will act impulsively only if the consequences are worth the risk. Woodworth and Porter (2002) examined the relationship between psychopathy and homicide. In a sample of 125 incarcerated homicide offenders from two Canadian federal institutions, psychopaths were more likely to have engaged in "cold-blooded" predatory homicides (93.3 percent) than were non-psychopathic offenders (48.4 percent). Research has revealed that psychopaths are likely to commit a number of other violent crimes including spousal abuse (Shaw & Porter, 2012) and rape (Porter et al., 2001).

In addition to committing more cold-blooded violence, psychopaths may even enjoy inflicting the violence. Research has addressed the possible link between psychopathy and sadistic interests. Holt, Meloy, and Stack (1999) found that sadistic traits were more common in violent psychopaths than in violent non-psychopaths. Further, there is a modest correlation (.21 to .28) between PCL-R scores and deviant sexual arousal (e.g., Barbaree, Seto, Serin, Amos, & Preston, 1994). A team of Canadian researchers (Porter, Woodworth, Earle, Drugge, & Boer, 2003) examined the relationship between PCL-R scores and the types of aggression evidenced during the crime in a sample of 38 Canadian sexual murderers. Homicides committed by psychopaths showed a higher level of both gratuitous and sadistic violence than did homicides perpetrated by non-psychopathic offenders. In fact, most psychopaths (82.4 percent) had committed sadistic acts on their victims, compared to 52.6 percent of the non-psychopaths.

Prevalence of Psychopathy. Hare (1996, 2003) estimates that 1 percent of the population is psychopathic (meaning that we have more than 300 000 psychopaths in Canada). However, it is very difficult, if not impossible, to determine definitively the prevalence of psychopathy in the community. Imagine psychopaths receiving a survey questionnaire in which they are asked whether they lack remorse, lie frequently, are callous individuals, et cetera. The researcher is unlikely to receive many honest responses!

However, there is a wealth of research to allow conclusions about the prevalence of psychopathy in forensic populations. In federal correctional settings, approximately 15 to 25 percent of inmates are psychopaths, according to the PCL-R (e.g., see Hare, 2003). Rates of psychopathy among Canadian offenders also appear to vary according to security level, with psychopaths being overrepresented in maximum-security prisons (Wong, 1984).

Research with female inmate samples (outside Canada) indicates a base rate of psychopathy of 9 to 31 percent (e.g., Kennedy, Hicks, & Patrick, 2007; Vitale, Smith, Brinkley, & Newman, 2002; Warren et al., 2003).

Etiology of Psychopathy. There has been an abundance of etiological theories concerning psychopathy, ranging from evolutionary (Lalumière, Harris, & Rice, 2001; Mealey, 1995; Quinsey, 1995) and neurobiological (Raine, Lencz, Bihrle, LaCasse, & Colletti, 2000) explanations to environmental models involving early childhood trauma or maltreatment (McCord & McCord, 1964; Porter, 1996). However, at present, the data are primarily correlational in nature and it is not possible to offer a definitive causal account.

Biological theorists have observed that psychopaths tend to differ from non-psychopaths in terms of their underlying biological functioning and neurological processing. Psychopaths are insensitive to the emotional content of information, especially language (Hancock, Woodworth, & Porter, 2011; Willamson, Harpur, & Hare, 1991) and emotional pictorial information (Christianson et al., 1996). The limited existing neuroimaging studies implicate brain abnormalities in psychopaths. Such abnormalities have been identified in the prefrontal cortex, hippocampus, angular gyrus, basal ganglia, and amygdala (e.g., Abbott, 2001; Blair, 2001, 2003; Brower & Price, 2001; Deeley et al., 2006; De Oliveira-Souza et al., 2008; Kiehl et al., 2004; Mitchell, Colledge, Leonard, & Blair, 2002; Stevens, Charman, & Blair, 2001; Yang et al., 2005). For example, because of an apparent dysfunction of the amygdala, psychopathic individuals appear to use alternative (primarily cognitive) means of processing emotional material to compensate for the absence of appropriate limbic input (which normally provides prompt information about the affective characteristics of stimuli).

Neurotransmitters have also been implicated in psychopathic behaviour. Soderstrom, Blennow, Manhem, and Forsman (2001) found that PCL-R scores were predicted by lower 5-HIAA concentrations (a metabolite of serotonin) and high catecholaminergic activity (HVA) in the cerebral spinal fluid of violent forensic inpatients. The authors concluded that the impulsive aggression of psychopaths may be linked to serotonergic hypofunctioning in combination with a high dopamine activity. Despite these compelling findings, the data are correlational, and much more research is required to establish whether such biological correlates are causal factors.

Three relatively recent studies have reported important data on the genetic contributions to psychopathy. Blonigen, Carlson, Krueger, and Patrick (2003) had 353 male adult twins complete a self-report measure of psychopathic traits and found moderate levels of heritability for the subscales measuring affect-related traits of the disorder. Blonigen, Hicks, Krueger, Patrick, & Iacono (2005) examined 626 pairs of 17-year-old male and female twins and found significant heritability on measures of fearless dominance and impulsive antisocial behaviour. Viding, Blair, Moffit, and Plomin (2005) published data on 3500 twin pairs of children from the Twins Early Development Study. These researchers indexed the callous and unemotional component of psychopathy at age seven and found significant group heritability and no environmental influence on this component of psychopathy. Such findings have led some researchers to argue that there is a stronger genetic cause as opposed to social cause of psychopathy (Blair et al., 2006).

As with most mental disorders, it is unlikely that biology tells the whole story of how psychopathy develops. Almost certainly, environmental factors play a role. More than 40 years ago, McCord and McCord (1964) argued that there is an association between early emotional deprivation (i.e., parental neglect, erratic punishment) and psychopathic characteristics in adulthood. There are some data to speak to their claim. Weiler and Widom (1996) found that children who were abused or neglected went on to have higher PCL-R scores than matched controls who had not been maltreated. Using a retrospective design, Marshall and Cooke (1995, 1999) found that psychopaths had experienced a more negative upbringing (e.g., poor discipline, emotional abuse/neglect) and negative school experience than had non-psychopaths. More recently, Campbell, Porter, and Santor (2004) examined the criminal, clinical, and psychosocial correlates of psychopathy in a sample of 226 incarcerated adolescents. Only 9.4 percent of the sample showed a high level of psychopathic traits. Thirty-three percent of the sample had a history of experiencing physical abuse and 50 percent had a history of non-parental living arrangements such as foster care. High psychopathy scores in these adolescents were associated with both the experience of physical abuse and disrupted living arrangements.

Porter (1996) has suggested that there are in fact two pathways that can lead to the development of psychopathy. In the case of *fundamental psychopathy*, the disorder is the inevitable result of a biological (probably polygenic) predisposition within the individual that hinders the development of affective bonds. In the case of *secondary psychopathy*, the development of the disorder is heavily dependent on and the result of negative environmental experiences during the formative years of childhood, such as extreme neglect or abuse. With secondary psychopathy, the profound affective deficit may be the result of the individual's ability to detach him- or herself from his or her emotions, as opposed to an inability to actually experience emotions, as is the case with fundamental psychopathy. More recent research has generated some evidence in support of this existence of, and distinction between, primary and secondary psychopaths (Skeem, Johansson, Andershed, Kerr, & Louden, 2007). Further, another recent study that used a large sample of inmates found support for dissociation as a mediator between childhood maltreatment and higher PCL-R scores measuring an impulsive and antisocial lifestyle (Poythress, Skeem, & Lilienfeld, 2006). Thus, it is possible that psychopathy may have its roots in biological predispositions and/or environmental experiences, depending on the individual.

Course and Prognosis of Psychopathy. Like all personality disorders, psychopathy is typically a lifelong condition. Precursors to psychopathy emerge early in childhood as "callous/unemotional" traits (Frick, 2006; Frick, Bodin, & Barry, 2000; Frick & Ellis, 1999; Lynam, 2002), which map closely onto adult psychopathic traits (Frick, 2002; Munoz & Frick, 2007; Salekin & Frick, 2005). As outlined by Campbell and colleagues (2004; Hare & Neumann, 2009), although the existence of psychopathy in adults is generally accepted, the appropriateness of diagnosing psychopathy in children and youths is much more controversial, with a host of ethical concerns. Nonetheless, it is important to focus on the presence of psychopathic traits in this group, given their associations with specific patterns of future antisocial behaviour (Forth, Kosson, & Hare, 2003).

Campbell and colleagues (2004) note that adolescents with a high level of psychopathic traits are more likely to have an earlier onset of conduct problems and to present with a greater variety and severity of delinquent behaviours (e.g., Smith, Gacono, & Kaufman, 1997). Such adolescents are also more likely to have symptoms and diagnoses of conduct disorder, narcissistic personality disorder, and oppositional defiant disorder (e.g., Murrie & Cornell, 2000). In addition, such adolescents have been found to score high on measures of impulsivity (Stanford, Ebner, Patton, & Williams, 1994) and sensation seeking (Vitacco, Rogers, Neumann, Durrant, & Collins, 2000). Research conducted in Canada revealed that psychopathy has a moderate to high level of stability, with behavioural and interpersonal factors having the greatest stability (Lee, Klaver, Hart, Moretti, & Douglas, 2009).

Treatment of Psychopaths. One of the key requirements for successful psychological treatment is motivation on the part of the client. Not surprisingly, observations on the effectiveness of treatment with psychopaths have not been encouraging (Hare, 1998; Lösel, 1998; Rice, 1997; Rice, Harris, & Cormier, 1992). For example, Richards and colleagues (2003) evaluated the role of psychopathy in treatment outcome in a large sample of adult female offenders. Psychopaths showed poorer response to substance abuse treatment in terms of noncompliance, violent and disruptive rule violations, avoidance of urinalysis testing, poor treatment attendance, and low therapist progress ratings. Using a sample of adult male offenders, Hobson, Shine, and Roberts (2000) found that higher PCL-R scores were associated with a higher incidence of misbehaviours (e.g., lying, verbal outbursts) in a treatment group.

APPLIED CLINICAL CASE

Diane

In the journal *Clinical Case Studies*, Katz and Cox (2002) presented the case of "Diane," a chronically parasuicidal adolescent admitted to a psychiatric ward after an attempted overdose following an argument with her sibling. In the past, Diane had cut herself more than 100 times, frequently burned herself, and tried to strangle herself. She had no history of psychosis or medical problems. Diane reported physical abuse by her father and was sexually assaulted once by a third party. Her diagnosis was major depressive disorder with borderline personality features and she reluctantly participated in dialectical behaviour therapy (DBT). In a group that met daily, Diane was taught mindfulness meditation techniques to help her identify emotion dysregulation, distraction and self-soothing techniques to manage crises, and emotion regulation skills to assist her in managing her mood. Interpersonal skills were taught to alleviate social skills deficits. Diane also participated in biweekly individual psychotherapy sessions to review thought records and perform behavioural analyses of maladaptive events, so that cognitive restructuring could be practised and alternative coping strategies could be learned. At a one-year follow-up, Diane had discontinued her outpatient psychotherapy; however, her scores on self-report measures of depression and suicidal ideation had dropped substantially from her initial assessment. She had one new emergency room contact but was not rehospitalized. At contact, Diane had been off her medication for two months and had not harmed herself for two months.

Despite the huge obstacles, some researchers remain optimistic that an effective intervention strategy with psychopathic individuals can be devised with further research. Skeem, Monahan, and Mulvey (2002), for example, found that longer involvement in outpatient treatment (at least seven sessions) reduced the risk of violence among psychopathic individuals discharged from a non-forensic inpatient setting when compared to those who received less than seven sessions of treatment.

Any way you look at it, adult psychopaths represent a unique group of offenders who can be expected to be resistant to treatment. According to leading researchers, programs should focus on changing and managing behaviour rather than on changing the core personality characteristics of the psychopath (Quinsey et al., 2006; Wong & Hare, 2005). Behaviourist techniques (e.g., the use of token economies) that are strictly defined and implemented by institutional staff have shown some success within institutions; however, the gains observed within institutions may not generalize to the community for many of those who are eventually released (Quinsey et al., 2006). Intense supervision in the form of probation or parole is often necessary, and in some extreme cases preventive detention is warranted (i.e., long-term/indeterminate incarceration) (Quinsey et al., 2006). Treatment providers must be especially careful not to be deceived into perceiving progress when they are really observing a performance worthy of an Academy Award.

4 BEFORE MOVING ON

What are the key differences between psychopathy and antisocial personality disorder? If you were to see a client in a forensic setting, what symptoms or behaviours would you look for to differentiate between the two? What tools would you use to aid in your diagnosis?

BORDERLINE PERSONALITY DISORDER

Borderline personality disorder (BPD) may be one of the most poorly named personality disorders. Historically, the diagnostic label was meant to describe a person on the border between neurosis and psychosis. Many laypersons assume that the term refers to someone on the "border" of psychosis or "going crazy," which is not typically the case. Most people with BPD do not experience psychotic symptoms.

Liz: Borderline Personality Disorder

Watch this Speaking Out video at www.mysearchlab.com

Fluctuations in mood, an unstable sense of their own identity, and **instability** in their relationships characterize BPD patients. For a compelling movie example, readers might wish to view the thriller *Fatal Attraction*, in which Glenn Close effectively portrays a woman with BPD. Another is Winona Ryder's character in the film *Girl, Interrupted*.

This overriding instability in all aspects of their functioning makes individuals with BPD unpredictable and impulsive, and these features, along with their irritability and argumentative style, tend to seriously interfere with their relationships (Stepp, Hallquist, Morse, & Pilkonis, 2011). However, they seem unable to tolerate being alone and accordingly become desperate about relationships, although they typically alternate between idealizing and devaluing their partners.

In addition to the typical symptoms of BPD, there are also several associated features that may or may not be present in patients with the disorder. Patients with BPD may blame their relationship problems on others instead of accepting any personal responsibility, and they may also attempt to undermine their achievements when they have nearly succeeded in reaching their goals (such as dropping out of university shortly before graduation). In addition, a few BPD patients may experience psychotic-like symptoms at times of stress. These symptoms are not usually sufficiently severe to require an additional Axis I diagnosis (APA, 2001).

Millon (1992) has described the origins of the present conceptualization of BPD. In an examination of four influential reports on what was variously called *borderline personality organization* (Kernberg, 1967), the *borderline syndrome* (Grinker, Werble, & Drye, 1968), *borderline states* (Knight, 1953), and simply *borderline patients* (Gunderson & Singer, 1975), Perry and Klerman (1978) found that more than half of the different criteria were present in only one of the four articles. Only one criterion (the patient's maladaptive and inappropriate behaviour at interview) appeared in all four reports. Spitzer, Endicott, and Gibbon (1979) concluded that the label *borderline* had been used up to that time to identify two different constellations of symptoms: (1) instability and vulnerability, and (2) a set of features that had been described as borderline schizophrenia. The former constellation provided the basis for identifying BPD in DSM-III, while the latter became schizotypal personality disorder. Perhaps not surprisingly, there have been consistent observations ever since of considerable overlap and even confusion between these two disorders (Rosenberger & Miller, 1989; Serban, Conte, & Plutchik, 1987). Oddly enough, the DSM-III characteristic (intolerance of being alone) that most accurately distinguished individuals with BPD from those with schizotypal personality disorder (McGlashan, 1987) was dropped from the diagnostic criteria in DSM-III-R and DSM-IV.

BPD has a lifetime occurrence in approximately 2 percent of the population and is thought to be more common in women than in men, with an estimated ratio of 3 to 1 (APA, 2001). This disorder, which typically begins in adolescence, has been shown to display reasonable stability over time (Barasch, Frances, Hurt, Clarkin, & Cohen, 1985). However, Stone (1993) reported that, of patients diagnosed during early adulthood as borderline, only 25 percent still met the diagnostic criteria in middle age.

Debate continues concerning the nature of borderline disorders. Millon (1986), in particular, has expressed strong disagreement regarding the appropriate diagnostic criteria. Widiger, Miele, and Tilly (1992) reviewed the various alternative perspectives on the diagnosis and found considerable inconsistencies in the research aimed at evaluating the diagnostic formulations. They attribute these inconsistencies in findings to differences in the research samples across different settings and, most importantly, to variability in the interpretations of the diagnostic criteria. Linehan's (1987, 1993) biosocial theory (described below) posited that the core feature of the disorder was an emotionally dysregulated system that underlies interpersonal dysregulation (interpersonal problems), self-dysregulation (confusion about the self), cognitive dysregulation, and behavioural dysregulation (impulsivity).

These disagreements about the appropriate criteria for BPD, and the unreliability of the application of diagnostic criteria, challenge the value of attempting to integrate research findings. In fact, raters tend to vary in their identification of the presence or absence of each of the diagnostic criteria (Angus & Marziali, 1988). When researchers report satisfactory inter-rater reliability, it is apparently due to establishing clear, but local, operational definitions that unfortunately vary across settings (Widiger et al., 1992). Once again, reliability has been shown to be superior when dimensional ratings (using rating scales and structured interviews) are used rather than simply making categorical diagnoses (Widiger et al., 1992). Interestingly, in a sample of incarcerated women, a greater degree of affect dysregulation—notably, poor anger modulation—was significantly related to APD where controlling for BPD and trauma (Zlotnick, 1999). This suggests that, for distinct samples where BPD is frequently comorbid with other Axis II diagnoses, treatment planning must be carefully considered.

ETIOLOGY OF BPD The etiology of BPD has been debated for many years, with the different views emphasizing childhood experiences, biological factors, psychodynamic processes, or social learning. Certainly, the evidence strongly implicates disruptions in the family of origin and childhood abuse and neglect as very significant factors in the development of borderline personality disorder (Links, 1992; Marziali, 1992). Patients with BPD typically recall their parents as either neglectful (Paris & Frank, 1989) or abusive (Bryer, Nelson, Miller, & Krol, 1987). Briere and Zaidi (1989), in a study of 100 females seen at an emergency service, found that females who had been sexually abused during their childhood were five times more likely to be given a diagnosis of BPD than were female patients who had not been sexually abused.

Despite problems with determining the accuracy of traumatic childhood recollections (e.g., Loftus, 2003; Porter, Yuille, & Lehman, 1999), the findings to date suggest that attachment problems with parents may be an etiological factor in BPD. Patients with BPD have major problems with adult relationships, and this may be understood to result from a fear of, or ambivalence about, intimacy. People who have problems with adult intimacy are considered to have developed these difficulties as a result of poor parent–child attachments (Berman & Sperling, 1994), which fail to instill the self-confidence and skills necessary for effective intimacy (Bartholomew, 1989) and fail to provide an adequate template for adult intimate relationships (Bowlby, 1988). For example, many adults who as children had poor relationships with their parents have an interpersonal style that is described as **anxious ambivalent**. These adults often harbour intense fears of abandonment but they strongly desire intimacy with others and, consequently, persistently seek out romantic partners. However, once they begin to get close to their partner, they become anxious and begin to back away from the relationship. While they desire closeness, they appear to be afraid of it. This is precisely the relationship style that characterizes borderline patients. The features of BPD may then be seen as attempts to adjust to their desire for, but distrust of, intimacy.

Murray (1979) has suggested an association between minimal brain dysfunction and the development of BPD. He proposed that the distorting effects of minimal brain dysfunction on perceptual processes may interfere with effective parent–child relationships and that these effects may continue to disrupt relationships throughout the lifespan. Confused perceptions, emotional instability, and poor impulse control typical of minimal brain dysfunction are said by Murray to lead to the development of borderline behaviour. A recent study that examined the brains of individuals with BPD revealed that these individuals have significantly reduced right hippocampal volumes compared to healthy participants (Sala et al., 2011). A similar study discovered that individuals with BPD also have reduced volumes of grey matter in the dorsolateral prefrontal cortex (DLPFC) (Brunner et al., 2010). The hippocampus and the DLPFC both play a pivotal role in the sustaining and controlling (or lack thereof) of impulsive and aggressive behaviour (Bellani et al., 2010; Sala et al., 2011). Research that has examined this claim has generally supported the idea that a subset of individuals with borderline personality disorder have soft neurological signs (Marziali, 1992), but the evidence is certainly far from convincing at this time.

Available evidence suggests a relatively high incidence of borderline features in the first-degree relatives of patients with BPD (Links, 1992), and this has been taken by some to suggest familial transmission of the disorder (Baron, Risch, Levitt, & Gruen, 1985). Of course, familial transmission of a disorder may be the result of environmental rather than genetic factors. Torgersen (1984) found no support for a genetic contribution to the development of either BPD or schizotypal disorder in a study of Norwegian twins, but the number of participants was very small.

Linehan's (1987, 1993) biosocial theory describes BPD primarily as dysfunction of the emotion regulation system. According to the theory, people with BPD have a biologically predisposed difficulty in regulating their own emotions. Individuals who are biologically vulnerable may include those who experience emotional reactions more intensely, those who are more sensitive to various emotional stimuli, or those who take longer to return to a baseline level of emotional arousal after an emotional reaction. This vulnerability interacts with exposure to a pervasively invalidating environment (i.e., one that minimizes, rejects, blames, or attributes pejorative characteristics to an individual's responses) to result in an emotionally dysregulated system that is believed to underlie the aforementioned symptoms. Treatment for BPD is often challenging because the etiology of the disorder is still largely unclear (Paris, 2009).

At this time it appears likely that borderline personality disorder will be included in the DSM-5. To receive a diagnosis of BPD, based on the DSM-IV-TR, an individual has to meet five of the following criteria: frantic efforts to avoid real or imagined abandonment, a pattern of unstable and intense interpersonal relationships characterized by extremes of idealization and devaluation, identity disturbance, impulsivity in two areas that are self-damaging (such as spending, sex, or substance abuse), recurrent suicidal behaviour, affective instability, chronic feelings of emptiness, inappropriate or intense anger, and stress-related ideation. Under the proposed DSM-5 criteria, the individual will have to demonstrate impairments in self-functioning, such as a poorly developed identity or instability in goals, values, and self-direction. Further, the individual will need to demonstrate impairment in interpersonal functioning characterized by a compromised ability to empathize with others and intense, unstable, and conflicted relationships that prevent the individual from being genuinely intimate with another person. Finally, the individual must also present with the following pathological personality traits: negative affectivity, disinhibition, and antagonism (APA, 2011).

HISTRIONIC PERSONALITY DISORDER

People with histrionic personality disorder (HPD) can sometimes be "the life of the party." Attention-seeking behaviours distinguish people with this disorder. In fact, there seems to be little that someone with HPD will not do to solicit attention. They are overly dramatic in their emotional displays, self-centred, and constantly attempting to be the centre of attention. They may dress provocatively and be overly sexual in inappropriate contexts such as a job interview. The flamboyant displays of individuals with HPD are apparently intended to make others focus on them, as they seem unable to tolerate being ignored. They can become quite annoyed at the perception that another person in a group is receiving more attention than they are. Associated with this tendency is the over-responsiveness of patients with HPD to what others might consider insignificant events. Their insincerity and shallowness, however, make it difficult for them to hold other people's attention for long, and as a consequence, they typically have few friends. Because of their strong need for attention, they tend to be very demanding and inconsiderate, and not surprisingly, their relationships are often short-lived and tumultuous. Again, as a result of their need to be the centre of attention, patients who are histrionic are often flirtatious, and they seem unable to develop any degree of deeper intimacy in relationships. Their behaviour causes considerable distress to themselves and to others with whom they become involved. For an excellent movie depiction of this disorder, you may consider watching the 1953 classic *A Streetcar Named Desire*, in which the character of Blanche Dubois is a prototypical case of HPD.

According to Greek myth, the beautiful youth Narkissos fell in love with his own reflection in a spring; to punish him for his excessive self-love, the gods transformed him into the flower called the narcissus.

There is considerable overlap between this condition and BPD. Widiger and Trull (1992), for example, found that 57 percent of patients with BPD also meet the criteria for HPD. Much more research is needed for the field to gain a comprehensive understanding of the etiology of this condition.

At this time, it appears that histrionic personality disorder will not be included in the DSM-5.

NARCISSISTIC PERSONALITY DISORDER

Patients who are narcissistic are grandiose and consider themselves to have unique and outstanding abilities. They have an exaggerated sense of self-importance; indeed, egocentricity is the hallmark of these individuals. In a conversation with a narcissist, you will get the impression of "me me me," with every topic somehow being turned to the person's own greatness. They are so preoccupied with their own interests and desires that they typically have difficulty feeling any concern for others, like the empathy deficit seen in APD or psychopathy. However, unlike the latter disorders, individuals who are narcissistic are easily hurt by any perception that their greatness is not being recognized. Similarly, their self-esteem is readily shattered by negative feedback from others, presumably because they desire only admiration and approval. The self-absorption of these patients frequently leads to an obsession with unrealistic fantasies of success. They expect, and demand, to be treated as "special," and this, along with their lack of empathy, leads them to exploit others. Like histrionic patients, the typical behaviour of narcissistic individuals alienates others, and they are frequently lonely and unhappy. When frustrated or slighted, they can become vengeful and verbally or physically aggressive.

Ronningstam and Gunderson (1990) claim that research has validated these features as characteristic of narcissistic personality disorder. However, while Morey (1988) has reported a remarkable increase (from 6.2 percent of patients to 22 percent) in the application of the diagnosis from DSM-III to DSM-III-R, Zimmerman and Coryell (1989) could find no cases of narcissistic personality disorder in a sample of 800 community subjects. When narcissism is diagnosed, there is considerable overlap with BPD (Morey, 1988).

Although encountering an individual with narcissistic personality disorder is rare, one of the authors of this chapter recently experienced the behaviour of a narcissist while completing a practicum in a forensic setting. During the brief consultation, the individual displayed all the characteristic personality traits associated with narcissistic personality disorder, including grandiosity, egocentricity, and an elevated sense of self-importance. Specifically, the individual paid very little attention to the professional during the interview. While this individual was being questioned about a previous offence and his current progress, he assumed superiority and spoke in a condescending manner to the interviewer. Further, the individual spent the majority of the consultation answering text messages on his phone; when he did acknowledge the professional, he was extremely patronizing. By behaving in this way, the individual revealed his strong feelings of superiority and high levels of egocentricity. Although this individual proved to be a perfect exemplar of narcissistic personality disorder, he was a less than perfect client to have in treatment.

With the increasing popularity of the Internet and social media, research has begun to focus on the types of individuals most likely to use these media outlets. One such study revealed that a high degree of narcissism was related to increased overall Internet use (Mehdizadeh, 2010). Specifically, narcissistic individuals used social networking sites to promote themselves and were most likely to change their photos, write status updates, and write notes. A similar study discovered that individuals who possess a high number of narcissistic traits displayed more self-promoting and sexy images of themselves on their Facebook profiles (DeWall, Buffardi, Bonser, & Campbell, 2011). Although personality disorders are characterized as egosyntonic, a recent review of narcissism across a wide range of traits revealed that narcissistic individuals are often aware that others perceive them less favourably than they perceive themselves, that they are able to make positive first impressions that eventually deteriorate, and that they do appear to have some insight into their narcissistic traits (Carlson, Vazire, & Oltmanns, 2011).

Contrary to the original recommendations forwarded by the Personality Work Group, narcissistic personality disorder will likely be featured in the DSM-5 (APA, 2011). As with all the other personality disorders, the criteria for a diagnosis of narcissistic personality disorder will require impairments in personality functioning. Specifically, the individual must demonstrate impairment in self-functioning characterized by either an issue with identity, including relying on others to define self and self-esteem, or issues with self-direction, including setting unreasonably high personal standards in order to see oneself as exceptional. There must also be evidence of impairment in interpersonal functioning characterized by difficulty empathizing with others or maintaining largely superficial relationships to serve as self esteem regulation. Finally, the individual must demonstrate the following pathological personality traits: antagonism, characterized by grandiosity and feelings of entitlement, and drastic attention seeking (APA, 2011).

5 BEFORE MOVING ON

What are the general themes of each of the three personality disorder clusters? Define each of the DSM-IV-TR personality disorders and explain some of the key symptoms. How are histrionic personality disorder and narcissistic personality disorder different? How are they similar?

Cluster C: Anxious and Fearful Disorders

Although avoidant and dependent personality disorders appear to share anxieties and fears as primary features, obsessive-compulsive personality disorder seems to be characterized more by a preoccupation with orderliness and rules. Again, there seems to be little value in clustering these disorders in the same category. Information regarding etiology and effective intervention specific to these disorders is sparse.

AVOIDANT PERSONALITY DISORDER

A pervasive pattern of avoiding interpersonal contacts and an extreme sensitivity to criticism and disapproval characterize individuals with avoidant personality disorder. These individuals actively avoid intimacy with others, although they clearly desire affection (unlike schizoid personality disorder). As a result, they frequently experience terrible loneliness. Social discomfort and a fear of negative evaluation are common features, but the fundamental fear of those with avoidant personality disorder is that of rejection. Avoidant clients restrict social interactions to those they trust not to denigrate them; however, even with these people, they refrain from getting too close for fear of ultimate rejection. These fears cause many problems for individuals with avoidant personality, disrupting interpersonal relationships and severely restricting their job options, academic pursuits, and leisure activities. Their avoidance of intimacy also distresses other people who may wish to form a close relationship with them.

People with avoidant styles were identified in the literature for many years prior to the inclusion of this personality disorder in the diagnostic manual. For instance, in 1945, Horney noted that there were people who found interpersonal relationships of any kind to be such an intolerable strain that "solitude becomes primarily a means of avoiding it" (p. 73). Millon (1969) was the first to use the term *avoidant personality* to describe people who actively avoided social interactions. He suggested that a child rejected by his or her parents would lack self-confidence and would, as a consequence, avoid others for fear of further rejection (Millon, 1981). This notion fits with the extensive literature on parent–child attachments and the consequences of parental rejection for adult relationships. While some children who have poor parental bonds develop an anxious/avoidant relationship style, others grow up to be so afraid of intimate relationships that they become avoidant of any depth in whatever relationships they form. These are just the characteristics that identify avoidant personality clients.

Trull, Widiger, and Frances (1987) found considerable overlap between avoidant personality disorder and dependent disorder, and Morey (1988) reported overlap with borderline disorder. There is also a problem distinguishing between avoidant disorder and social phobia. In particular, Turner, Beidel, Dancu, and Keys (1991) found considerable overlap between these two disorders; they appear to differ only in the severity of their symptoms (Cox, Pagura, Stein, & Sareen, 2009; Holt, Heimberg, & Hope, 1992).

At this time, it appears that avoidant personality disorder will be included in the DSM-5. A significant impairment in self-functioning must be present, characterized by low self-esteem associated with a poor self-identity, or unrealistic standards for behaviour associated with reluctance to pursue goals. There must also be impairments in interpersonal functioning characterized by a preoccupation with criticism and rejection and a reluctance to get involved with someone without certainty of being liked. Finally, the individual must present with the following pathological personality traits: detachment and negative affectivity (APA, 2011).

DEPENDENT PERSONALITY DISORDER

These patients appear to be afraid to rely on themselves to make decisions. They seek advice and direction from others, need constant reassurance, and seek out relationships where they can adopt a submissive role. Dependent patients not only allow other people to assume responsibility for important aspects of their lives, but also seem to desperately need to do so. They seem unable to function independently, and typically ask their spouse or partner to decide what job they should seek or what clothes they should purchase; indeed, they defer to others for most, if not all, of the decisions in their lives. Patients with dependent personality disorder (DPD) subordinate their needs to those of other people, even people they hardly know. This style often gets them involved in abusive relationships or destroys relationships with partners who could be beneficial to them.

Reich (1990) observed that the relatives of male dependent patients were likely to experience depression, whereas the relatives of female dependents were more likely to have panic disorder. Panic-disordered patients have also been found to have comorbidity with various personality disorders, including dependent disorder (Johnson, Weissman, & Klerman, 1990). DPD is arguably the most culture-laden of the personality disorders. This disorder is rooted in the individualistic culture of North America, but is not as prevalent in collectivist cultures (Chen, Nettles, & Chen, 2009).

At this time it appears that dependent personality disorder will not be included in the DSM-5.

OBSESSIVE-COMPULSIVE PERSONALITY DISORDER

Inflexibility and a desire for perfection characterize this disorder. It is the centrality of these two features, and the absence of obsessional thoughts and compulsive behaviours, that distinguish this personality disorder from the Axis I obsessive-compulsive disorder (discussed in Chapter 5). Preoccupation with rules and order makes these patients rigid and inefficient as a result of focusing too much on the details of a problem. Individuals with obsessive-compulsive personality disorder (OCPD) also attempt to ignore feelings, since they consider emotions to be unpredictable. They tend to be moralistic and judgmental, and this causes them problems in dealing with others.

Knock, knock, knock, Penny? A popular example of a television character with many features of OCPD is Dr. Sheldon Cooper, played by Emmy winner Jim Parsons, on *The Big Bang Theory*. Sheldon demonstrates many of the pathological personality traits associated with OCPD, including a preoccupation with details, lists, rules, and order (i.e., his strict adherence to eating specific take-out meals depending on the day of the week), rigidity and stubbornness (i.e., his insistence that he alone is the only individual who is allowed to sit on the left side of the couch), and his unreasonable insistence that others submit exactly to his way of doing things (i.e., the roommate agreement). Although Sheldon has never been officially diagnosed with OCPD, and often claims on the show "I'm not crazy. My mother had me tested," he does provide an excellent example of the behaviour of an individual who possesses characteristics of OCPD.

Turkat and Levin (1984) could find no empirical reports in the literature that they considered at all helpful in understanding obsessive-compulsive personality disorder. Most of the research they reviewed was concerned with the psychoanalytic notion of the anal retentive character, which was thought to be related to obsessive-compulsive personality. It is not clear, however, that the results of this research are helpful in understanding the personality disorder.

Very little research on this disorder has emerged over the years since DSM-III-R was published, except that which concerns distinguishing this personality disorder from obsessive-compulsive disorder. Studies using objective measures have found a clear independence, whereas those using projective techniques or clinical interviews found co-occurrence of the two disorders (Cawley, 1974; Slade, 1974). In fact, Joffe, Swinson, and Regan (1988) found that other personality disorders (e.g., avoidant, dependent, and schizotypal) were more likely to co-occur with obsessive-compulsive disorder than was obsessive-compulsive personality disorder. More recently, Lochner and colleagues (2011) revealed that OCPD is not phenomenologically different from OCD, and that OCPD is simply a marker of obsessive-compulsive severity. Further, Garyfallos and colleagues (2010) discovered a high rate of comorbidity between OCD and OCPD and suggested that individuals with both of these disorders should constitute a subtype of OCD.

It appears likely that obsessive-compulsive personality disorder will be included in the DSM-5. To obtain a diagnosis of OCPD, there must be evidence of impairment in self-functioning characterized by constricted experience and expression of strong emotions or difficulty completing tasks and realizing goals associated with rigid and unreasonably high internal standards. Impairment in interpersonal functioning, characterized by difficulty understanding and appreciating the ideas and feelings of others or the belief that relationships are secondary to work and productivity, must also be present. Finally, the individual must demonstrate a number of pathological personality traits, including compulsivity and negative affectivity (APA, 2011).

6 BEFORE MOVING ON

> How does obsessive-compulsive personality disorder differ from obsessive-compulsive disorder? What differences would you expect to see in the symptoms of clients with each of these disorders, and how would their treatment plans differ?

Treatment

There are numerous obstacles to providing effective treatment to clients with personality disorders. As Gorton and Akhtar (1990) observed, two important factors make it difficult to evaluate treatment with the personality disorders: (1) many of these patients are not themselves upset by their characteristic personality style and so do not seek treatment, and (2) the dropout rates from treatment among these patients is extremely high. There is no doubt that these patients constitute a serious challenge for the therapist. All of them have considerable difficulties with relationships and this affects the therapeutic alliance. For some clients, the treatment context itself is a barrier to treatment. Most treatment provided to an individual with APD or psychopathy is court-ordered or provided in prison, not exactly the best environment for developing a trusting therapeutic alliance. Also, most have problems maintaining focus on the therapeutic process between sessions. Even when the focus in treatment is on an Axis I disorder, those patients who also have a personality disorder do more poorly than those who are free of such problems (Reich & Green, 1991). In recent years, however, far more effort has been devoted to developing treatment programs specifically for these patients, although to date outcome data are limited.

According to Sperry (2003), five basic premises can be considered essential to achieving effective treatment outcomes with patients diagnosed with a personality disorder: (1) these disorders are best conceptualized in a way that considers both biological and psychological factors and the more effective treatment will reflect this approach; (2) before treatment, it is important to assess the individual's amenability to treatment; (3) effective treatment is flexible and tailored to the individual client; (4) the lower the level of treatability in the client, the more the therapist must combine multiple treatment approaches; and (5) the basic goal of treatment should be to help the client move from personality-disordered functioning to personality style functioning.

In line with Sperry's recommendations, three main approaches have been developed: (1) object-relations therapy, (2) cognitive-behavioural approaches, and (3) the use of medications.

OBJECT-RELATIONS THERAPY

Leading proponents of an object-relations approach have been Kernberg (1975) and Kohut (1977). In their view, treatment should be aimed at correcting the flaws in the self that have resulted from unfortunate formative experiences. The relationship between patient and therapist serves as a vehicle for confronting, in a supportive way, the patient's defences and distortions. This process is slow and, if successful, produces gradual changes. Thus, treatment is seen as necessarily long term.

In the only controlled evaluation of this approach, Stevenson and Meares (1992) treated 30 patients with BPD, and followed them up for one year. At follow-up, 30 percent of the patients no longer met DSM criteria for BPD. Single-case reports of similar treatment programs with narcissistic patients have also provided encouraging results (Kinston, 1980), but more extensive and more rigorous evaluations are required to determine the true value of this approach.

Although Walsh (1990) has suggested that a psychotherapeutic approach emphasizing a supportive relationship and aimed at enhancing social skills may be useful with schizotypal personality disorder, no controlled evaluations of such an approach have been conducted as yet.

COGNITIVE-BEHAVIOURAL APPROACHES

Dr. Aaron Beck and his colleagues have extended his cognitive analyses to the personality disorders and suggested that treatment must correct the cognitive distortions of these patients in order to be successful (Beck et al., 2004). Beck's treatment is directed at challenging the core beliefs that are thought to underlie the problems of personality-disordered patients. **Cognitive restructuring**, as this challenging of core beliefs is called, provides the basis for change, along with skills training and behavioural practices (see Chapter 17). To date, however, adherents of this promising approach have not produced controlled evaluations. This appears to be at least partly explained by the relatively recent development of this approach and the claim by Beck and colleagues (1990) that, unlike the application of cognitive therapy to other problems, treatment of personality disorders will take far longer. Schema therapy, developed by Jeffrey Young (Young, 1999; Young et al., 2003), involves a cognitive-behavioural approach to the treatment of personality disorders; however, it also incorporates gestalt, object-relations, and psychodynamic treatment techniques while placing a heavy emphasis on clients' early damaging life experiences and on their current therapeutic relationship. A review of treatment efficacy for personality disorders suggests that CBT significantly reduces symptoms and enhances outcomes for all the personality disorders (Matusiewicz, Hopwood, Banducci, & Lejeuz, 2010). A randomized trial of schema-focused therapy (SFT) versus transference-focused therapy (TFT) for 88 patients with severe BPD symptomatology demonstrated that SFT patients had a significantly lower dropout rate compared to TFT patients over three years (27 percent versus 50 percent) and that SFT patients showed greater improvements on all clinical and quality-of-life measures administered compared to TFT patients (Giesen-Bloo et al., 2006).

The **dialectical behaviour therapy** (DBT) developed by Linehan (Linehan & Heard, 1992) is attracting major international attention in the treatment of BPD. Originally developed as a treatment for parasuicidal women (Robins & Chapman, 2004), the approach now targets patients with BPD, although its application has been expanding. One of the main features of this approach is the acceptance by the therapist of the patient's demanding and manipulative behaviours. In addition, several standard behavioural procedures are used, such as exposure treatment for the external and internal cues that evoke distress, skills training, contingency management, and cognitive restructuring. The dialectical process describes "both the coexisting multiple tensions and the thought processes and styles used and targeted in the treatment strategies" (Linehan & Heard, 1992, p. 249).

According to Robins and Chapman (2004), DBT is the only outpatient psychotherapy that has been shown to be effective with patients with BPD. Linehan and colleagues (1991) compared the treatment outcome of 22 female borderline patients assigned to DBT with 22 patients who were provided with "treatment as usual." At the end of one year of treatment, those assigned to DBT had made fewer suicide attempts and had spent less time in hospital than those allocated to the other treatment program. An important additional observation was that while only 17 percent of the dialectically treated patients dropped out, almost 60 percent of the other group withdrew prior to treatment termination. Although both groups displayed less depression and hopelessness after treatment, there were no group differences on these measures. In a more recent study, Linehan and colleagues (2006) reported the results of a two-year randomized controlled trial (101 women) for suicidal behaviours and BPD comparing DBT to therapy provided by experts. Compared to the therapy provided by the experts not using DBT, patients who received DBT were half as likely to make a suicide attempt, made fewer visits to psychiatric emergency departments, required less hospitalization for suicidal thoughts, and were less likely to drop out of treatment. A more recent study with a Canadian sample compared the effectiveness of DBT to general psychiatric management among individuals with BPD (McMain et al., 2009). The results of this study demonstrate that both DBT and general psychiatric management significantly reduced common symptoms of BPD,

CANADIAN RESEARCH CENTRE

Dr. Robert Hare

Dr. Robert Hare is emeritus professor of psychology, University of British Columbia, where he has taught and conducted research for some 35 years, and president of Darkstone Research Group Ltd., a forensic research and consulting firm. He has devoted most of his academic career to the investigation of psychopathy, examining its nature, assessment, and implications for mental health and criminal justice. He is the author of several books, including *Without Conscience: The Disturbing World of the Psychopaths Among Us*, and more than 100 scientific articles on psychopathy. He developed the Psychopathy Checklist–Revised (PCL-R) and co-authored its derivatives, the Psychopathy Checklist: Screening Version, the Psychopathy Checklist: Youth Version, the Antisocial Process Screening Device, and the P-Scan (for use in law enforcement). Dr. Hare's assessment tools are used in every developed country. In addition to his extensive research activities, he consults with many law enforcement agencies, including the FBI and the RCMP, sits on the Research Advisory Board of the FBI Child Abduction and Serial Murder Investigative Resources Center (CASMIRC), and is a member of the FBI Serial Murder Working Group. He was also a member of the advisory panel established by Her Majesty's Prison Service to develop new programs for the treatment of psychopathic offenders. His current research on psychopathy includes assessment issues, developmental factors, neurobiological correlates, risk for recidivism and violence, and the development of new treatment and management strategies for psychopathic offenders. More recently, Dr. Hare has extended the theory and research on psychopathy to the business and corporate world with the development of the B-Scan-360, an instrument used to screen for psychopathic traits and behaviours.

Dr. Hare continues to lecture widely on psychopathy and on the use and misuse of the PCL-R in the mental health and criminal justice systems. Among his most recent awards are the Silver Medal of the Queen Sophia Centre in Spain; the Canadian Psychological Association Award for Distinguished Applications of Psychology; the American Academy of Forensic Psychology Award for Distinguished Applications to the Field of Forensic Psychology; the Isaac Ray Award, presented by the American Psychiatric Association and the American Academy of Psychiatry and Law for Outstanding Contributions to Forensic Psychiatry and Psychiatric Jurisprudence; and the B. Jaye Anno Award for Excellence in Communication, presented by the National Commission on Correctional Health Care. He was also made an affiliate member of the International Criminal Investigative Analysis Fellowship.

including psychological distress, degree of suicidality, and health care utilization.

DBT has since been adapted for use with a variety of other patients, including those who have eating disorders, patients with attention deficit/hyperactivity disorder, elderly depressed patients, inmates in correctional settings, and individuals in couples therapy, although little is known about their efficacy with these conditions (Robins & Chapman, 2004). However, even though its use has been expanded, to date no work on the application of DBT to other personality disorders has been published; there does not seem to be any compelling reason why this has not happened.

Canadian therapist Ariel Stravynski and his colleagues (Stravynski, Lesage, Marcouiller, & Elie, 1989) have applied behavioural approaches employing social skills training and desensitization to the problems of patients with avoidant personality disorder. However, the benefits of these programs have not been evaluated at long-term follow-up, and Alden (1989) observed that most of the treated patients remained socially uncomfortable.

PHARMACOLOGICAL INTERVENTIONS

Patients with BPD have been treated using a variety of pharmacotherapy treatments, including antidepressants (e.g., SSRIs, tricyclics, MAOIs), mood stabilizers (e.g., lithium carbonate), anxiolytics (e.g., anti-anxiety medications), opiate antagonists, and neuroleptics. These pharmacological agents have varying degrees of effectiveness (APA, 2001). Overall, these patients have been successfully treated with some level of success with such medications as amitriptyline (an antidepressant), thiothixene and olanzapine (both antipsychotics), and carbamazepine and lamotrigine (both anticonvulsants). Different subtypes of BPD may be differentially responsive to either antipsychotic or antidepressant medications. Goldberg and colleagues (1986), for example, found that antipsychotics were most effective with individuals with BPD who also displayed psychotic-like features. Cole and colleagues (1984) found maximal improvements with antidepressants for those borderline patients who also met the criteria for major depression. Reich, Zanarini, and Bieri (2009) found that anticonvulsants were effective at reducing affective instability and impulsivity in individuals with BPD.

Goldberg and colleagues (1986) also found low doses of thiothixene to be beneficial with schizotypal-disordered patients. Also, individuals with schizotypal personality disorder seem to respond to antidepressants (Markovitz et al., 1991); however, the benefits of any medications with schizotypal personality disorder are modest at best (Gitlin, 1993). Medication has been used with antisocial patients for short-term management of problematic and threatening behaviour. However, long-term side effects, lack of symptom alleviation, and noncompliance indicate that this approach has, at best, a modest impact. In combination with other intervention strategies, however, it may prove helpful.

7 BEFORE MOVING ON

Many patients who have a personality disorder do not believe that there is anything wrong with them. Do these patients exhibit egosyntonic or egodystonic symptoms? Considering the various forms of treatments that are available, which would be most effective for dealing with this type of patient, and how would you attempt to deal with his or her resistance? How might this method differ from treatment of an Axis I disorder?

SUMMARY

- Personality disorders are essentially maladaptive personality traits. All people have relatively consistent characteristics that make up their personality. Personality disorders are distinguished from normal personality traits by being rigid, maladaptive, and monolithic. People with personality disorders typically have many intact abilities but have impaired functioning (especially socially) because of their disorder. Personality disorders (i.e., psychopathy or APD) were first clearly described in the early nineteenth century. The present set of personality disorders first appeared in DSM-III as Axis II, separate from the Axis I "clinical" disorders.
- Personality disorders are more rigid and often more difficult to treat than are Axis I disorders. Axis I disorders are primarily considered to be egodystonic because they cause distress and are viewed as problematic by the individual sufferer. Axis II disorders are often considered to be egosyntonic. In fact, most individuals diagnosed with personality disorders do not report experiencing any distress in interpersonal relations or daily functioning (with exceptions, of course, e.g., borderline personality disorder). It is often the family and friends of an individual with a personality disorder who seek help for the individual, because the effects of personality disorders are felt most often by those closest to the individual.
- The DSM-IV-TR lists 10 disorders, grouped into 3 clusters: odd and eccentric disorders (paranoid, schizoid, schizotypal); dramatic, emotional, or erratic disorders (antisocial, borderline, histrionic, narcissistic); and anxious and fearful disorders (avoidant, dependent, obsessive-compulsive). Axis II diagnoses tend to have lower reliability than those of Axis I, and there is considerable comorbidity as well as overlap among these disorders. Further, many have argued that the diagnostic criteria reflect cultural and gender bias, although it is possible that a particular gender or culture could actually place an individual at higher risk for a disorder.
- To address this issue of comorbidity, the Personality and Personality Disorders Work Group has recently

conducted a comprehensive literature review of all the personality disorders. Based on this research, they have made a number of recommendations for changes to the DSM-5. The recommendations are quite drastic and include abolishing four of the existing personality disorders (schizoid personality disorder, histrionic personality disorder, paranoid personality disorder, and dependent personality disorder), as well as adding a new diagnosis of personality disorder trait specified. They have also proposed to change the model used to diagnose personality disorders from categorical to a hybrid dimensional-categorical model. This shift will involve a completely new method for diagnosis, replacing the categorical method with a measure of self and interpersonal functioning, as well as a continuum of personality traits.

- The essential feature of APD is a pervasive, ongoing disregard for the rights of others. Special diagnostic issues and confusion over prevalence and research outcomes arise because APD is similar in some respects to the related construct of psychopathy. The latter, as measured by PCL-R, focuses on core emotional and interpersonal processes as well as behaviour, whereas the DSM-IV-TR's criteria for APD are largely behavioural. Social and family factors have been cited as etiological factors for APD; there is some support for genetic factors as well. Studies have shown that psychopaths are at high risk for future violence and that treatment outcomes are generally poor. BPD is characterized by fluctuations in mood, an unstable sense of identity, and instability in relationships. Diagnostic criteria are still debated. Disruptions in the family of origin are the most common etiological explanation. Treatment for personality disorders in general is difficult to evaluate, because many patients never seek treatment. Three main approaches have been tried: object-relations therapy, cognitive-behavioural approaches, and medications. There are few well-controlled studies of any treatments for most of these disorders.
- Obsessive-compulsive personality disorder and the more commonly known obsessive-compulsive disorder are distinct constructs. OCD is an Axis I disorder, whereas OCPD is an Axis II disorder. These disorders can be distinguished by the symptoms displayed; due to these differences, OCD and OCPD require different interventions.
- Etiological explanations have focused on psychodynamics, attachment theory, cognitive-behavioural perspectives, and, most recently, biological factors such as genetics, neurotransmitters, or brain dysfunction. Unfortunately, the majority of the data are correlational. Of the 10 DSM-IV-TR disorders, APD has received the bulk of research attention due to the harm caused by those with the disorder.

MySearchLab offers you extensive help with your writing and research projects and provides round-the-clock access to credible and reliable source material. Chapter quizzes and a full electronic version of the text are also provided. Answers to the Before Moving On feature are provided on the MySearchLab. Take a tour at www.mysearchlab.com.

KEY TERMS

traits (p. 295)
personality disorders (p. 295)
clusters (p. 296)
prevalence (p. 297)
egosyntonic (p. 299)
egodystonic (p. 299)
comorbidity (p. 301)
overlap (p. 301)
attachment theory (p. 303)
suspiciousness (p. 305)
delusions (p. 305)
emotional responsiveness (p. 306)
eccentricity (p. 306)
psychopaths (p. 307)
sociopaths (p. 307)
polythetic (p. 308)
fearlessness hypothesis (p. 309)
oppositional behaviour (p. 310)
responsivity factor (p. 311)
instability (p. 315)
anxious ambivalent (p. 316)
cognitive restructuring (p. 320)
dialectical behaviour therapy (p. 321)

CAROLINE F. PUKALL • PHILIP FIRESTONE

Chapter 13

Sexual and Gender Identity Disorders

LEARNING OBJECTIVES

AFTER READING THIS CHAPTER, STUDENTS WILL BE ABLE TO:

1. List and provide examples of each phase of the sexual response cycle as developed by Masters and Johnson.
2. Compare and contrast lifelong versus acquired sexual dysfunction, and generalized versus situational sexual dysfunction. Provide one example of each of the following: a lifelong generalized male sexual dysfunction, a lifelong situational female sexual dysfunction, an acquired generalized male sexual dysfunction, and an acquired situational female sexual dysfunction.
3. Describe the rationale for sensate focus, and describe the stages of this treatment tool for a couple in which the male partner has been diagnosed with erectile dysfunction.
4. Identify the different dimensions of gender and explain how inconsistencies among them can result in sexes other than male or female.
5. Compare and contrast the following paraphilias: exhibitionism, voyeurism, and frotteurism. Provide an example of each.
6. Explain how a clinician currently makes a diagnosis of "rapist" using the DSM-IV-TR, and describe how this diagnostic procedure will change with the proposed DSM-5 revisions.

When David phoned for an appointment, he asked whether he could arrange to arrive at the office unseen by other clients to avoid recognition. He said that his problem was "impotence," so the therapist encouraged him to bring his wife to the initial interview.

David had always doubted the adequacy of his sexual responsiveness. He had first tried to have intercourse at age 20 while on a road tour with his university football team. After a night of drunken revelry, some of the guys hired a prostitute for the night. Rather than admit to being a virgin, David went along, despite his anxiety. He tried to take his turn with the woman, but could not. He was so ashamed that he begged the prostitute not to tell anyone, but later he boasted about his prowess.

Although he could masturbate to orgasm and develop an erection when he did so, David believed that he wasn't "highly sexed" like most guys, because he did not share his classmates' fascination with pornography and ribald jokes. He became upset by his continued masturbation, believing that it was an abnormal sexual outlet, and worried about whether he could have intercourse. The episode with the prostitute confirmed David's worst fears. To avoid facing such embarrassment again, he broke off relations with women as soon as they made any sexual overtures. Eventually, he stopped dating entirely.

David had graduated and was working as an engineer when he began to develop a strong friendship with Alicia, a colleague in his office. He admired her for bucking the establishment in a male-dominated field, and they often talked over coffee or lunch. Eventually she made it clear that she was interested in more than friendship. Before he knew it, David had agreed to marriage. He felt that he had led her on by allowing such a close bond to develop and hoped that in the security of a caring relationship, his capacity for a sexual relationship with a woman would grow.

David was nevertheless panicked by the thought of meeting his wife's sexual demands. Alicia did not seem to expect sex before marriage and, to his relief, when he finally admitted his problem to her the week before their marriage, she understood and was calm, stating that they would work it out together. On their honeymoon, David found that he was able to have intercourse on several occasions. Many more times, however, Alicia was interested but David could not get an erection and quickly backed out of the encounter.

As the years passed, Alicia remained the sexual initiator, and David grew more and more anxious. He began to stay up late, working until Alicia was asleep. Gradually, conflict between them increased. Alicia, who was thinking about having children, began to press David "to do something about [his] impotence." David became more anxious about failure with each unsuccessful attempt, and he would sometimes try to satisfy Alicia with oral sex. This always left him feeling inadequate, and he withdrew emotionally, leaving her upset.

By the time they sought therapy, David and Alicia felt quite hopeless. They saw therapy as a last-ditch effort to save their marriage, but they were also motivated by the joint desire to have children.

This case illustrates a particular type of sexual dysfunction (i.e., erectile disorder) that represents a persistent failure to achieve satisfaction in sexual relations. Other sexual dysfunctions will be described, as will specific paraphilias (i.e., a redirection of sexual desires toward inappropriate objects, people, or behaviours). This chapter will also describe what are called *gender identity disorders:* the condition of people who feel ill at ease with their biological sex.

Historical Perspective

Conceptions of the appropriateness or deviance of human sexual behaviours have varied considerably throughout history (Bullough, 1976). Sex is one of the most discussed human behaviours, although these discussions are often superficial and skirt substantive issues. For example, sex education often takes the form of a recitation of knowledge about physiological functioning and anatomical facts rather than a discussion of actual behaviours and their associated thoughts and feelings.

Brown (1985) suggests that the Judeo-Christian tradition has had a significant influence on notions about appropriate and inappropriate sexual behaviours within our society. He contends that the prevailing attitudes at the time the Bible and the Talmud were written condoned "sex between men and very young girls in marriage, concubinage, and slavery" (p. 23). Not surprisingly, some of the remarks in these historical documents are in conflict with today's values. Christian notions of acceptable sexual behaviour evolved in the West primarily through the teachings of St. Augustine, who declared that sexual intercourse was permissible only for purposes of procreation, only when the male was on top, and only when the penis and vagina were involved. Thus, oral-genital sex, masturbation, anal sex, and presumably all forms of precoital activities were considered sinful, as were sexual activities with someone who could not conceive, such as a child or a same-sex partner.

Science in the sixteenth and seventeenth centuries offered support for these Christian teachings by attributing all manner of dire consequences to so-called excessive sexual activity. These views were popularized in 1766 by Tissot in his treatise on the ills of onanism (solitary masturbation). Tissot attributed a whole variety of ills to masturbation and recommended that the state establish controls on sexuality, although just how these controls were to be enacted was not made clear. Popular writers on sex in the nineteenth century took up Tissot's claims with gusto. The Reverend Sylvester Graham and Dr. John Harvey Kellogg published treatises declaring that masturbation caused numerous problems, including lassitude, dullness, defective development, untrustworthiness, and even ill health and rounded shoulders. Parents were warned to watch for these signs and prevent the destructive behaviour at all costs. Excessive sexuality could be counteracted by healthy activities and a diet of bland foods. Graham developed Graham Crackers and Kellogg developed Corn Flakes to meet this need.

Krafft-Ebing (1901) published the first strictly medical textbook on sexual aberrations, called *Psychopathia Sexualis*. Again, masturbation was blamed for numerous illnesses. The range of sexual behaviours considered to be deviant was initially extremely broad, including whatever was thought to differ from prevailing beliefs about acceptable practices. Accordingly, up to the early part of the twentieth century, the list of deviant activities included a variety of sexual practices that are no longer officially listed as abnormal.

Research on sexuality has not progressed at the same rate as has research on other human problems, apparently as a result of notions concerning the privacy of sex. Such notions have encouraged the general public to view sex researchers with suspicion. The publication of Alfred Kinsey's research (Kinsey, Pomeroy, & Martin, 1948; Kinsey, Pomeroy, Martin, & Gebhard, 1953) investigating human sexual practices was greeted with animosity by the general public, the media, and many of his scientific colleagues because his findings upset established beliefs about sexuality. His data revealed that masturbation, oral-genital sex, and homosexuality, for example, were engaged in by far more people and with far greater frequency than was previously believed. Masters and Johnson's (1966) study of human sexual response was greeted with much the same animosity. Starting in the 1990s and continuing today, several sexuality studies in the United States were stopped as a result of political pressure, despite the fact that they had already been carefully screened and approved by scientific communities (Udry, 1993). Perhaps even more illustrative are the funding levels provided by the National Institute of Mental Health (NIMH), the primary source of research funding in the United States. Despite the well-established damage that sexual offenders cause to society, in 1993 NIMH devoted $1.2 million to research on this topic, while spending $125.3 million on studies of depression (Goode, 1994). Although less of an issue in Canada, some studies have come under scrutiny by the government, resulting in loss of research funds and less funding available to researchers. However, in general, the lay public and governmental agencies in Canada demonstrate greater tolerance of sexuality research.

Diagnostic Issues

As in all other areas of human functioning, it is necessary to have at least an approximate idea of what is normal (including some indication of the frequency of behaviours) in order to define abnormal functioning. Simple frequency, however, will not always do. Premature ejaculation, for example, is subject to both parties' perception of the act, and can therefore cause problems based on this perception (Byers & Grenier, 2003). Even if most men ejaculated rapidly upon being sexually aroused, would this be considered normal? It certainly would be from a statistical point of view, but if the man and his partner were dissatisfied and sought help, the diagnosis of a problem would nevertheless be likely from a clinical standpoint.

Satisfaction with present functioning is an important diagnostic criterion, reflected in DSM-IV-TR's definition of sexual dysfunctions. A problem for reliable diagnoses is that DSM-IV-TR's criteria require diagnosticians to make somewhat subjective judgments: to decide, for example, whether a client's experiences are "persistent," "recurrently deficient," "minimal," "delayed," or cause "marked distress or interpersonal difficulty." There are no perfectly objective standards for these qualities, which will in any case vary within the same individual from one time and setting to another.

For the paraphilias, on the other hand, the question of satisfaction, or distress, of the person suffering from the disorder is not quite so straightforward. Presumably a person could have a fetish (or some other odd sexual interest that did not hurt anyone) and not be upset by it. In that case, would the person have a diagnosable problem? Not according to DSM-IV-TR, which requires that the individual experience distress. Clinicians, however, characteristically apply a diagnosis of fetishism whether or not the person is distressed by the behaviour. In fact, it appears that the majority of fetishists are only occasionally distressed by their sexual interests—when a friend or family member finds out, for example.

For the other paraphilias, such as sadism, exhibitionism, and pedophilia, DSM-IV was not clear about *who* must experience distress for the diagnosis to be made. Need the person with the paraphilia feel distress? Or does the distress of victims count? In DSM-IV-TR, the notion of distress has been modified specifically for these particular paraphilias (i.e., sadism, exhibitionism, and pedophilia) by changing the criterion to read: "The person has acted on these sexual urges, or the sexual urges or fantasies cause marked distress or interpersonal difficulty" (American Psychiatric Association [APA], 2000, pp. 569, 572, 574). These changes have made the diagnostician's task easier.

Surprisingly, perhaps, many men who sexually molest children do not meet DSM-IV-TR criteria for pedophilia because they do not *persistently* molest (or persistently imagine molesting) children. Similarly, most men who rape women do not engage in or fantasize about sadistic acts with their victim, which is a necessary DSM-IV-TR criterion for sexual sadism, the only relevant diagnosis in these cases. The diagnostic criteria for paraphilias, then, seem to reflect an insensitivity to public concerns about sexual abuse and to ignore the fact that most people consider sexual offenders to be distinctly aberrant.

Of course, just because the public thinks an act, such as murder, is aberrant does not mean that the person committing the act is mentally disordered. A distinction here between the requirements for legal insanity and DSM-IV-TR disorders may be helpful. The only DSM-IV-TR disorders that are relevant to the legal notion of insanity are those that involve a loss of contact with reality or impairment in the person's ability to recognize an act as wrong. Paraphilia does not fit this description; sexual offenders know what they are doing and know that it is wrong. They must therefore be held responsible for their crimes.

At the same time, research has revealed that sexual offenders differ from normal people in many aspects of their functioning, and they clearly upset others with their behaviour. It seems sensible, therefore, to consider all sexual offenders to be in need of corrective interventions, whether or not they have a diagnosable disorder. However, these corrective interventions are best seen as rehabilitative rather than as treatment.

Although homosexuality will not be discussed as a topic in this chapter, the history of homosexuality as a disorder is of relevance in terms of the role of the prevailing mindset of society in determining what "problems" are considered mental disorders. Homosexuality (that is, sexual relations between persons of the same sex) is no longer identified in the diagnostic manual as a disorder. Up to and including DSM-II (APA, 1968), homosexuality was listed as a disorder, and people (mostly males) with this sexual orientation were subjected to treatment aimed at changing their attraction from same-sex to opposite-sex partners. Homosexuality was also illegal, and all too often homosexuals were imprisoned. In 1973 the APA's Nomenclature Committee recommended that homosexuality be eliminated from the list of disorders. However, this committee also suggested the addition of "sexual orientation disturbance" to refer to those homosexuals who experienced conflict with their sexual orientation or who wished to change their orientation. Accordingly, DSM-III (APA, 1980) included **egodystonic homosexuality** to refer to conflicted homosexuals and, although this category was dropped from DSM-III-R (APA, 1987) and DSM-IV (APA, 1994), both included, as one possible form of a sexual disorder not otherwise specified, "persistent and marked distress about sexual orientation" (APA, 1994, p. 538). These remarks about sexual orientation are not included in the DSM-IV-TR or upcoming DSM-5.

Sexual Response

It is difficult to gain an understanding of what most people "do" sexually and how often people engage in various kinds of sexual activity. There are wide ranges in types and frequency of sexual behaviour, and differences can be seen within an individual depending on age, sexual experience, partner status, length of relationship, and many other factors. Also, sex is a private topic for most people, so simply asking the people we know may not give us accurate information (or any information at all!). Research can sometimes shed light on questions related to sexuality (e.g., how does sexuality differ between men and women?), but we also have to keep in mind that people who participate in sexuality studies likely differ from those who do not. Regardless, research has shown some interesting differences in frequency of fantasies and sexual behaviour patterns between men and women. In an investigation into the sexual activity of Canadians (Fischtein, Herold, & Desmarais, 2007), results indicated that adult men fantasized about sex much more frequently than did women (see Table 13.1). Not surprisingly, in another survey, 61 percent of men compared to only 38 percent of women reported masturbating during a specified one-year period (Das, 2007). Furthermore, of those who do report masturbating, men do so over three times more frequently than women (Laumann, Gagnon, Michael, & Michaels, 1994). In addition, men report an earlier age at first intercourse and a greater number of sexual partners (Smith, 1992). All of this makes intuitive sense; these patterns fall right into the sex stereotypes we all have

TABLE 13.1 RESPONSE TO THE QUESTION: "HOW OFTEN DO YOU THINK ABOUT SEX?"

	"Several times per day"	"A few times per week"	"A few times per month"
Men	46.1%	25.0%	4.6%
Women	10.6%	42.3%	18.3%

Source: Adapted from Fischtein, Herold, and Desmarais (2007).

that men are more sexually permissive and less discriminating and women are more sexually cautious. But if men are consistently reporting a higher number of sexual partners than women, who exactly are these men having sex with?

In an ingenious experiment devised to investigate this issue, Alexander and Fisher (2003) used the bogus pipeline to examine sex differences in self-reported sexuality domains. Male and female participants were randomly assigned to one of three conditions: the bogus pipeline condition, in which participants were given a false polygraph test while they answered questionnaires after being told that the polygraph would detect dishonest responding; the anonymous condition, in which participants were asked to fill out the questionnaires privately and leave them in a locked box; and the exposure-threat condition, in which participants were asked to give their names to the experimenter and complete the questionnaires while the experimenter was in the room. Results indicated that the smallest sex differences in behaviour were found in the bogus pipeline condition; the authors suggest that the participants were motivated to answer honestly given the belief that false responding would be detected. Slightly larger sex differences were found in the anonymous condition, and the largest differences were found in the exposure-threat condition. Interestingly, although women underreported sexual behaviours in the anonymous and exposure-threat conditions as compared to the bogus pipeline condition, men's responses were consistent across conditions. Specifically, women underreported frequency of masturbation and pornography use; in the bogus pipeline condition, however, the results for these behaviours were similar for men and women. It appears as though sex differences in reported sexual behaviours may at least be partly explained by sex differences in reported as opposed to actual sex differences. So it is important to keep a critical eye when drawing conclusions about sex differences in the domain of sexuality.

To emphasize this point, a recently published meta-analytic study demonstrated that sex differences were typically small in such behaviours as petting, intercourse incidence, younger age at first intercourse, and number of sexual partners (Petersen & Hyde, 2010), indicating that men and women are more similar than different for most behaviours reported.

The issue of sex differences aside, research has revealed considerable cultural differences in sexuality. For example, Canadians tend to have more permissive sexual attitudes than do Americans; 29 percent of Americans as compared to 12 percent of Canadians feel that premarital sex is morally wrong (Widmer, Tread, & Newcomb, 1998). Furthermore, certain countries have sexual norms that differ considerably from those of Canadians. On the island of Inis Beag off the coast of Ireland, for example, the citizens have no knowledge of sexual practices; in fact, during sexual intercourse both parties keep their underwear on, and a female orgasm is unheard of (Messenger, 1993). However, there are some common sexual trends across cultures. Kissing is the most common sexual technique in nearly all cultures, whereas incest is considered universally taboo (Firestone, Dixon, Nunes, & Bradford, 2005).

Sex therapists Virginia Johnson and William Masters.

Some norms for sexual behaviour also change with time. Beginning in the mid-1960s, liberalization of attitudes toward sexuality appeared to be accompanied by greater sexual experience (there are few earlier statistics available). A study of Canadian university students reported that, from 1968 to 1978, the percentage of female students who had had intercourse increased from 32 to 58 percent, and of male students from 40 to 62 percent (Barrett, 1980). More current estimates suggest that the trend is continuing for both genders: 10 to 13 percent of 14-year-olds, 20 to 25 percent of 15-year-olds, 40 percent of 16-year-olds, and 50 percent of 17-year-olds have engaged in penile–vaginal intercourse (Maticka-Tyndale, 2001).

Interestingly, people have different views of what constitutes sex. Canadian sex researcher Sandra Byers (University of New Brunswick) and her colleagues surveyed students' definitions of "having sex" (Byers, Henderson, & Hobson, 2009). Not surprisingly, less than 5 percent of students defined behaviours that did not include genital touching as "having sex." Only 12 to 15 percent included manual genital touching in their definition of having sex, and 24 to 25 percent included oral genital stimulation. Ninety percent of students agreed that vaginal–penile intercourse was having sex, but only 83 percent agreed that anal–penile intercourse was sex.

William Masters and Virginia Johnson (1966) were the first investigators to study and document the physiological stages that take place in human sexual response. They noted the changes that occur in the body during sexual arousal, orgasm, and the return to the unaroused state, and referred to this sequence as the **sexual response cycle**. Masters and Johnson divided the sexual response cycle into four stages: excitement, plateau, orgasm, and resolution.

During the *excitement* stage, the genital tissues of both males and females swell as they fill with blood (vasocongestion). This causes erection of the penis in men and engorgement of the clitoris and vaginal lubrication in women. Furthermore, the testes and nipples become engorged, muscular tension and heart rate increase, and breathing becomes more rapid and shallow. See Focus box 13.1 for the role of thermal imaging in measuring sexual response in current studies in males and females.

The *plateau* stage consolidates this arousal, with additional swelling of the penis and vaginal tissues. In men, the testes become elevated and may reach one and a half times their unaroused size. In women, the clitoris retracts underneath the clitoral hood and the inner part of the vagina expands. During *orgasm*, both sexes experience rhythmic, muscular contractions at about eight-second intervals. In men, orgasm comprises two stages, which quickly follow one another. First, seminal fluid collects in the urethral bulb, at the base of the penis. As this happens, there is a sense of orgasmic inevitability and nothing can

FOCUS 13.1

A Hot Topic: Measuring Sexual Arousal in Men and Women

To date, the psychophysiological measurement of sexual arousal, and by extension, our understanding and treatment of sexual arousal problems, has differed between men and women. While the measurement of male erectile functioning in a laboratory setting has led to clinical guidelines and pharmaceutical treatment options for erectile dysfunction (Connoly, Boriakchanyavat, & Lue, 1996; Goldstein et al., 1998), similar studies in women have not been successful (Graham, 2010a, 2010b). Part of the issue is that different instruments have been used to measure physical sexual response in men and women, making it impossible to directly compare male and female sexual arousal. Furthermore, the numerous practical and quantitative limitations with widely used instruments for the measurement of female physiological sexual arousal have limited the use of these devices in clinical settings and have not made it possible to quantify physical parameters for arousal disorders (Prause & Janssen, 2006).

Researchers in Canada, however, may be close to solving these problems through the use of thermographic imaging to assess physiological sexual response. Thermography cameras, similar to night vision goggles, pick up infrared emissions from the human body through remote sensing and provide temperature readings of the target in focus. As temperature is directly related to blood flow, and genital blood flow is a physical marker of sexual response, thermography offers a unique way to examine sexual arousal in men and women through the measurement of genital temperature. Because the camera does not require any physical contact with participants, the same methodology can be used for both sexes, allowing for a direct comparison of sexual arousal between men and women.

During her Ph.D. studies at McGill University, Dr. Tuuli Kukkonen, an assistant professor at the University of Guelph, assessed the validity of thermography to measure and compare sexual arousal in men and women. By recording genital and thigh temperature while participants watched sexually arousing, neutral, anxiety-provoking, or humorous film clips, Kukkonen and colleagues found that temperature increases were specific to the genitals during the sexual arousal condition only (Kukkonen, Binik, Amsel, & Carrier, 2007, 2010a). Of interest is that both men and women had significant correlations between their self-reported sexual arousal and genital temperature, indicating that this physical measure matched how participants were feeling, a finding that goes against most previous research on women. In addition, a comparison of men and women demonstrated that the sexes did not differ in the time it took them to reach a peak sexual response, a finding that might contradict popular culture assumptions regarding sexual response. Finally, research across multiple testing sessions demonstrated that these results are consistent across time, providing support for the use of thermography in longitudinal studies (Kukkonen, Binik, Amsel, & Carrier, 2010b).

Although all this research was conducted on sexually healthy individuals, a significant decrease in physical sexual arousal with age for both men and women was noted, suggesting that the development of age-appropriate parameters for normative sexual response might be worthwhile before examining clinical populations (Kukkonen, Binik, Amsel, & Carrier, 2009).

Clearly, thermography holds great potential as a tool to measure physiological sexual response. These initial studies have laid the groundwork for examining clinical issues of sexual arousal in women by demonstrating the reliability and validity of thermography in sexually healthy individuals. Furthermore, by having an instrument that can be used for both men and women, researchers can address issues of sex differences and similarities in sexual arousal, which might answer the age-old question of whether men and women really are that different.

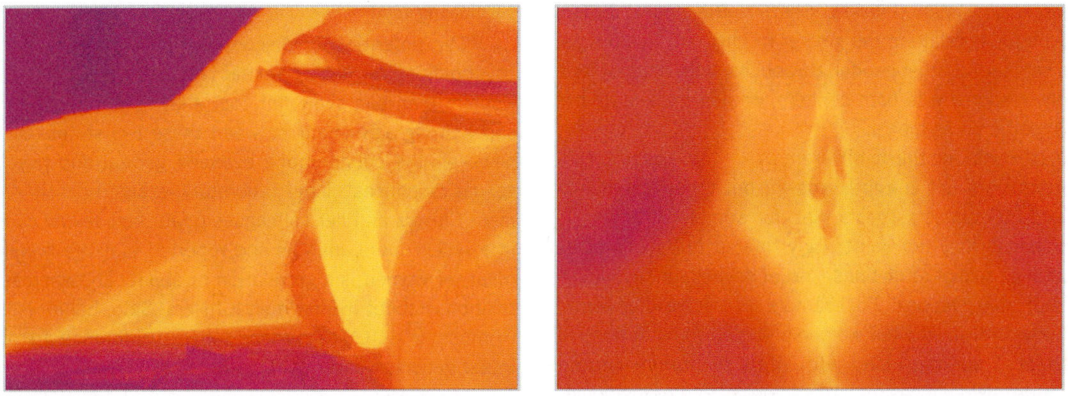

Source: Contributed by Dr. Tuuli Kukkonen of the University of Guelph.

prevent ejaculation from following. Within two or three seconds, contractions lead to expulsion of the ejaculate from the penis. Women experience contractions of the uterus and of the muscles surrounding the vagina during orgasm. Blood pressure and heart rate reach a peak during orgasm, and there are involuntary muscular contractions. Following orgasm, the body gradually returns to its pre-aroused state, in the stage that Masters and Johnson called *resolution*. Shortly after ejaculation, men experience what is called a *refractory period* during which they are unresponsive to sexual stimulation. Women, however, may be able to experience multiple orgasms without any refractory period. Although Masters and Johnson did not include homosexual individuals in their sample, it is likely that the physiological responses of same-sex partners follow similar patterns as described above. Or do they? See Focus box 13.2 for research examining sexual arousal in same-sex partners and heterosexual men and women. Figure 13.1 depicts the sexual response cycles of men and women derived from Masters and Johnson's research.

Helen Singer Kaplan (1979) proposed an alternative model of sexual stages, consisting of desire, excitement, and orgasm. An important contribution of her work was the distinction of desire as primarily a psychological component to sexual response. She also treated the stages as independent components, and noted that normal sexual experiences do not necessarily follow the full sequence described by Masters and Johnson. Thus, a couple's sexual encounter may sometimes involve excitement followed by diminished arousal without orgasm. This information is valuable in that it suggests that many sequences of sexual response exist and each of them is normal.

Many older individuals engage in sexual intercourse well into their eighties and nineties, although the frequency of sex decreases with age (Kessel, 2001). It is also evident that as women experience menopause, interest in sexual activity and sexual intercourse usually decreases (Palacios, Menendez, Jurado, Castano, & Vargas, 1995), which is associated with a more general reduction in sexual interest (Dennerstein, Smith, Morse, & Burger, 1994). These

FOCUS 13.2

Nonspecificity of Sexual Response in Women

Research by Dr. Meredith Chivers at Queen's University in Kingston, Ontario, suggests that the patterns of sexual response in women and men are not opposite sides of the same coin. By studying the relationship between people's sexual attractions (to women, men, or both) and sexual responses in the laboratory to stimuli depicting women or men, Chivers has discovered a compelling gender and sexual-orientation difference: whereas men's physiological and psychological sexual responses are strongly related to their sexual attractions to women or men, a pattern of response described as *category specific*, heterosexual women's are not—they are *nonspecific* (Chivers, Reiger, Latty, & Bailey, 2004). Women who report sexual attractions exclusively to men show physiological sexual responses to stimuli depicting women and men; their self-reported arousal (that is, how sexually aroused they report that they feel) is, however, more strongly related to their sexual attractions. Women who are sexually attracted to women, on the other hand, do show greater arousal to sexual stimuli depicting women than men, suggesting that their arousal patterns are more category specific than those of heterosexual women (Chivers, Seto, & Blanchard, 2007). These results may relate to the greater fluidity and flexibility in women's same- and other-gender attractions; with a capacity to be sexually responsive to both genders, women's sexuality may not be as restricted as men's.

The reasons for these differences in the *specificity* of sexual arousal are not currently known, but other research by Chivers and colleagues suggests that, for women, physiological sexual response may not be strongly related to psychological states, such as sexual attractions, sexual desires, or psychological states of sexual arousal. For example, in a somewhat controversial study, Chivers showed women and men films of bonobos (chimpanzees) mating, along with films of human couples engaged in sex, while measuring physiological and psychological sexual responses. Only women showed significant increases in physiological responses to the bonobo film, though both women and men reported not feeling aroused by this unusual stimulus (Chivers & Bailey, 2005). These results suggest that, despite being an unarousing film psychologically, something about watching bonobos have sex was sufficient to cause women to experience an increase in genital vasocongestion.

Chivers and colleagues have proposed that women's genital responding to a broader range of sexual cues may have very little relationship to a woman's sexual desires or attractions and is, instead, an automatic, protective response. Vaginal lubrication, necessary to reduce the likelihood of genital injury and to make sexual penetration more comfortable, is thought to result from a process called *transudation*—fluid passing into the vaginal canal caused by genital vasocongestion. So even though a woman might not feel sexually aroused, her body is prepared for the possibility of sex, similar to how even vegetarians might find themselves salivating to the smell of a cooking steak: they may not actually want to eat the steak, but the smell is a powerful cue that leads to an automatic reflex that aids in chewing and swallowing food.

The potential for disconnect between physiological and psychological states of sexual responding is not exclusive to women; men can show this too, and, conversely, some women show strong agreement between these two states. On average, however, the concordance between genital and psychological sexual responses in the laboratory is significantly greater for men; Chivers and her colleagues quantified *sexual concordance* in a recent meta-analysis and reported that the average agreement for women is a correlation of about .26, whereas the correlation is about .66 for men (Chivers, Seto, Lalumière, Laan, & Grimbos, 2010). The reasons for this difference are still under investigation by several laboratories.

Source: Contributed by Dr. Meredith Chivers of Queen's University.

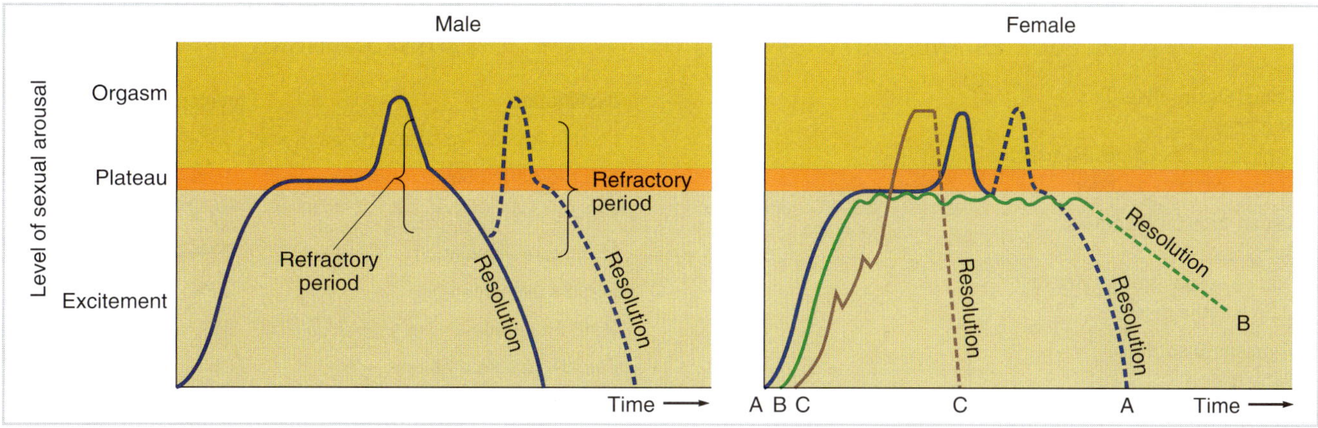

FIGURE 13.1 Levels of Sexual Arousal During the Phases of the Sexual Response Cycle

Masters and Johnson divided the sexual response cycle into four phases: excitement, plateau, orgasm, and resolution. During the resolution phase, the level of sexual arousal returns to the pre-aroused state. For men there is a refractory period following orgasm. As shown by the broken line, however, men can become re-aroused to orgasm once past the refractory period and their levels of sexual arousal have returned to pre-plateau levels. Pattern A for women shows a typical response cycle; the broken line indicates multiple orgasms, should they occur. Pattern B shows the cycle of a woman who reaches the plateau phase but for whom arousal is "resolved" without orgasm. Pattern C shows the sexual response of a highly aroused woman who passes quickly through phases.

Source: Masters et al., Human Sexuality, 2 Figs. "Male Sexual Response Cycle" and "Three Possible Female Sexual Response Cycles," © 1995 Pearson Education, Inc. Reproduced by permission of Pearson Education, Inc.

effects were demonstrated to be attributable to menopause independently of the effects of aging (Dennerstein, Dudley, Lehert, & Burger, 2000). However, Dennerstein and colleagues also showed lowered levels of sexual responsivity with age in women who were not menopausal.

1 BEFORE MOVING ON

It is important to note that people's sexual response cycles vary immensely; for example, men can have multiple orgasms, although this feature was not captured in the Masters and Johnson model. What are some of the advantages and disadvantages of models that combine hundreds of responses into a general representation?

Sexual Dysfunctions

As the following case illustrates, multiple factors (for example, shame and ignorance about sex, anxiety about sex, lack of experience with physical affection, and low self-confidence) may contribute to the development of sexual dysfunctions. Joan's problem clearly developed over time, becoming worse the more she worried about it. By the time someone like Joan consults a therapist, the problem has typically become more complex and involves secondary difficulties, such as relationship problems and low self-esteem.

Case Notes

Joan sought help at the insistence of her best friend, in whom she had confided. Recently, Joan had become interested in a man. Ron, she believed, was gentle and caring, and she wanted to return his affection. Joan had never had an orgasm, and she thought that this had contributed to the breakdown of her only previous relationship and was afraid it would mar things with Ron.

Joan had been reared in a strict religious family in which the word *sex* had never been spoken. Anything to do with the body was held to be shameful and disgusting. Joan had never touched her own body except while washing, and felt uncomfortable even seeing herself undressed in a mirror. Her parents never showed open affection, and, although her mother hugged her, her father merely shook her hand when she left home for university.

Joan was sexually inexperienced, and tolerated Ron's advances because she was too embarrassed to protest. She believed that she should stop him from making love to her, but could not find the words to say no. She grew very fond of him and enjoyed the tenderness he showed her, although she found the intensity of his sexuality frightening and completely foreign to her own experience.

Joan felt constricted by Ron's needs, which she felt obliged to satisfy but resented. She was completely unable to express her own wishes, but expected him to know what she wanted. Finally, in frustration, she broke off her relationship with him, refusing to return his phone calls or open his letters.

Joan had read some popular materials about sexuality in the last several years and had begun to think that there was something wrong with her. The books suggested that she should not be afraid or ashamed of her own sexuality, but she could not shake these negative feelings.

The DSM-IV-TR (APA, 2000) uses an amalgamation of Masters and Johnson's (1966) and Kaplan's (1979)

TABLE 13.2 SEXUAL DYSFUNCTIONS: CATEGORIES AND SUBTYPES

Sexual Desire Disorders
Subtypes
Hypoactive sexual desire disorder
Sexual aversion disorder

Sexual Arousal Disorders
Subtypes
Female sexual arousal disorder
Male erectile disorder

Orgasmic Disorders
Subtypes
Female orgasmic disorder
Male orgasmic disorder
Premature ejaculation

Sexual Pain Disorders
Subtypes
Dyspareunia
Vaginismus

Source: American Psychiatric Association.

TABLE 13.3 LIFETIME PREVALENCE OF SEXUAL DYSFUNCTIONS

Dysfunction	Prevalence
Female hypoactive sexual desire	33%
Erectile difficulties	10%
Female arousal problems	20%
Premature ejaculation	27%
Female dyspareunia	15%
Male dyspareunia	3%
Female orgasm problems	25%
Male orgasm problems	10%

Source: Reprinted with permission from the *Diagnostic and Statistical Manual of Mental Disorders, Fourth Edition, Text Revision.* (Copyright © 2000). American Psychiatric Association.

components of the sexual response in classifying sexual dysfunctions. It categorizes them according to which of the three stages is affected: desire, arousal, or orgasm. A separate category deals with instances in which pain is the primary complaint (see Table 13.2).

Each of the sexual dysfunctions can be further classified into several subtypes. For example, if the person has always experienced the problem, the disorder is called **lifelong sexual dysfunction**; if it is of fairly recent onset, it is said to be an **acquired sexual dysfunction**. In addition, sexual dysfunctions may be apparent with all partners and even during solitary sexual activity, in which case they would be termed **generalized sexual dysfunctions**; when the problems are apparent in only one situation (for example, with the client's spouse, or only during masturbation), they are known as **situational sexual dysfunctions**.

The Sexual and Gender Identity Disorders Work Group for the DSM-5 has proposed retaining the subtypes mentioned above, and has suggested that the following factors be specified for each sexual dysfunction: partner aspects, relationship factors, individual vulnerability issues or psychiatric comorbidity, cultural/religious factors, and medical concerns relevant to prognosis, course, or treatment. Five of the sexual dysfunctions also have the additional specifier of whether the individual is also presenting with concomitant problems in sexual interest and/or arousal. In addition, symptoms must be present for a minimum of six months and be experienced on most sexual activity occasions (Zucker, 2010b). Given that the DSM-5 diagnoses have not yet been formally accepted, the DSM-IV-TR terms will be used when sexual and gender identity disorders are discussed outside of the proposed changes for the DSM-5.

We know very little about the prevalence of sexual dysfunctions and even less about their incidence (Simons & Carey, 2001; Spector & Carey, 1990). Existing epidemiological studies are few and suffer from methodological shortcomings. Table 13.3 shows estimates of the prevalence of sexual problems, although these problems were not defined in DSM-IV-TR terms. More recent data reveal lifetime prevalence rates for sexual dysfunctions of 43 percent for females and 31 percent for males (Laumann, Paik, & Rosen, 1999) and incidence rates (i.e., currently has a disorder) of 23 percent among women (Bancroft, 2000).

In reviewing reports from a wide variety of studies, Bancroft (1989) found that a lack of sexual interest was the most common complaint of women attending sex therapy clinics, whereas Kaplan (1974) reported orgasmic dysfunction to be the most common problem among women.

Altogether, the evidence suggests that some degree of sexual dysfunction is very common: "The lifetime prevalence of sexual dysfunctions may be so high that almost every man or woman who lives a long life can be expected to qualify for a diagnosis at some time" (Levine, 1989, pp. 215–216). However, the authors who published one of the most frequently cited surveys suggest caution in interpreting survey findings, as individuals may experience sexual difficulties without necessarily being dissatisfied with their marriages or even with their sexual relations (Laumann et al., 1994).

2 BEFORE MOVING ON

Think about the specifiers of lifelong versus acquired sexual dysfunction, and generalized versus situational. Which combination do you think would be most difficult to treat? Most easy? Which ones would most likely have a biological or psychological basis?

SEXUAL DESIRE DISORDERS

Both Kinsey and Masters and Johnson found that the frequency of masturbation among men varied from less than once per month to several times per day. However, all of these men regarded their own frequency as "normal"; they thought that a man with higher frequencies was "abnormal," and they considered lower frequencies to be indicative of "low sex drive." These two examples illustrate both the differences among individuals in sexual behaviours and associated desire and the subjective nature of people's definition of the "normal" frequency of sexual desires.

In the DSM-IV-TR, sexual desire disorders are subdivided into two categories: **hypoactive sexual desire disorder** and **sexual aversion disorder**. For a diagnosis of hypoactive sexual desire disorder, DSM-IV-TR requires a persistent or recurrent deficiency of sexual fantasies and desire for sex, causing marked distress or interpersonal difficulty. Note that the DSM-IV-TR treats desire as separate from arousal; according to this conceptualization, it is not just the presence or absence of a physiological response that is of concern. The focus is on whether the person "just doesn't feel like it." In the DSM-5, this distinction will be retained for men in the newly named diagnosis of "hypoactive sexual desire disorder in men"; however, a combination of "lack of sexual interest" and "arousal disorder" has resulted in a proposed diagnosis of "sexual interest/arousal disorder in women." The main rationale for this amalgamation is based on findings from several studies indicating that the processes of desire and arousal overlap for many women (Brotto, 2010a; Graham, 2010b). Unfortunately, similar data do not yet exist for men.

Hypoactive desire is among the most difficult dysfunctions to define, because of the importance of context. Desire may occur in some situations but not in others, and sexual activity may occur without desire, in both males and females. The discrepancy between partners' desire can create a circular problem, affecting the quantity and quality of both the sexual and the personal relationship (Clement, 2002). Furthermore, social pressure for high levels of sexual interest may play a role in elevating performance pressure and creating unrealistic expectations.

In fact, some have criticized the existence of such a diagnosis as a reflection of culturally imposed standards that are typically male-centred and hypersexual. The very term *hypoactive* implies an established standard—but whose? A population average? A clinical consensus? However it is defined, a standard of desire is value-laden and many question its appropriateness.

Nevertheless, a substantial number of people attending sexual dysfunction clinics report a problematic lack of sexual desire and meet diagnostic criteria for this disorder (Donahey & Carroll, 1993). The majority of these clients (85 percent of the males and 75 percent of the females) also reported other sexual dysfunctions (Donahey & Carroll, 1993).

Sexual aversion disorder is diagnosed if there is persistent or recurrent extreme aversion to, and avoidance of, almost all genital sex with a partner, causing marked distress or interpersonal difficulty. Sexual aversion disorder may also include characteristics of panic attacks, extreme anxiety, and avoidance of partners. The DSM-5 proposes to exclude sexual aversion as a stand-alone diagnosis, as it is a rare and poorly researched condition (Brotto, 2010a).

SEXUAL AROUSAL DISORDERS

Sexual arousal disorders involve difficulty becoming physically aroused when the person desires such arousal. In males, sexual arousal or lack of arousal is usually gauged by penile erection, not the only physiological response but certainly the most obvious. Female sexual arousal, however, is less directly evident, and women can have intercourse without arousal. Perhaps for this reason, female sexual arousal disorder may be the least understood sexual dysfunction (Spector & Carey, 1990). Note that we are not discussing the person who is "not in the mood," but someone who is emotionally and mentally interested in sex but who does not become physiologically aroused.

The DSM-IV-TR diagnostic criteria for **female sexual arousal disorder** include a persistent or recurrent inability to attain or maintain arousal during sexual activity and the presence of marked distress or difficulty. DSM-IV-TR defines the presence and maintenance of arousal in terms of genital vasocongestion. Several studies investigating female sexual arousal have found that there is a low correlation between measures of subjective arousal and genital response (Polan et al., 2003), suggesting that some women may be aroused but may be unaware of it. Since this criterion of arousal is rarely measured directly, and typically rests on a woman's reported arousal, misdiagnosis may occur. Approximately 20 percent of women report difficulty with arousal and lubrication during sexual activities (Laumann et al., 1999). As mentioned above, arousal disorder in women is not proposed as a distinct diagnosis in the DSM-5 (APA, 2010).

Male erectile disorder characterizes a persistent or recurrent inability to reach or sustain an erection "until completion of the sexual activity" and resultant distress. The previous term for this problem, *impotence*, acquired such negative connotations that it has been abandoned in the official nomenclature, although it is still widely used by the general public and by many practitioners. The DSM-5 proposes to retain the indicators of difficulty with obtaining and/or maintaining an erection for this diagnosis and adds a third possibility—that of a decrease in erectile rigidity that interferes with sexual function.

Erectile disorder is the second most commonly reported male sexual dysfunction (after premature ejaculation). In their large-scale empirical review, Simons and Carey (2001) found a community prevalence rate, based on 10 studies, ranging from 0 to 10 percent. In general mental health settings, the rates ranged from 0.4 to 37 percent, whereas in sexuality clinics, the proportion was as high as 53 percent. Several factors can influence the rates of erectile disorder, including smoking, heart disease, and age, the last factor being particularly salient.

Erectile problems, while certainly not new, have gained increased public attention, partly because of current expectations for lifelong sexuality, women's increased expectations of sexual satisfaction, and media attention (Wincze & Carey, 2001). Erectile problems can be psychologically devastating for men and can contribute to significant relationship problems. Difficulty attaining or maintaining an erection often leads to embarrassment, depression, and even suicidal inclinations. Not surprisingly, erectile disorder has a high comorbidity with depression (Seidman & Roose, 2000). Because the problem carries such connotations about masculinity, men with erectile difficulty are likely to delay seeking help and to avoid confronting the problem, and may try home remedies before approaching a professional. The relationship with a sexual partner is likely to be affected, not just by the erectile problem, but also by the avoidance, depression, and other secondary problems that follow. As a result, by the time a man and his partner seek help, the problem is likely to seem overwhelming and to be much more complex and intractable than it might have been had he sought help earlier.

ORGASMIC DISORDERS

Orgasmic disorders are some of the most commonly reported sexual dysfunctions. Both males and females may experience difficulty in reaching orgasm.

The DSM-IV-TR diagnostic criteria for **female orgasmic disorder**, also known as **anorgasmia**, require a persistent or recurrent delay in, or absence of, orgasm following normal excitement, causing marked distress or interpersonal difficulty. As with other sexual dysfunctions, this diagnosis requires subjective judgments, such as what constitutes persistent and recurrent. The DSM-5 proposes to clarify the issues related to the use of subjective judgments present in the DSM-IV-TR by indicating that at least one of two of the following indicators must be present for at least six months and be experienced on most sexual occasions: marked delay in, marked infrequency of, or absence of orgasm; and/or markedly reduced intensity of orgasmic sensation (Graham, 2010a).

Kinsey was the first researcher to pay attention to female orgasms, counting them for women as he did for men (Kinsey et al., 1953). In his work, Kinsey noted that women were more likely to experience orgasm through masturbation than with a partner, a finding that has since been replicated (Spector & Carey, 1990). These observations led to marked changes in the way women's sexual functioning was viewed, and today, female orgasmic disorder is typically cited as the most common sexual problem presented at sex clinics. The rates among clinical samples range from 18 to 76 percent (Spector & Carey, 1990).

Male orgasmic disorder is defined in the same way as female orgasmic disorder, but it is much less common. DSM-IV-TR criteria require a persistent or recurrent delay in, or absence of, orgasm following normal excitement, causing marked distress or interpersonal difficulty. In these men, orgasm may be possible only with oral or manual stimulation or only during erotic dreams, but not during intercourse. The DSM-5 proposes a new term for this disorder, "delayed ejaculation."

Community estimates for male orgasmic disorder have reportedly been as high as 3 percent, whereas in sexuality clinics estimates have been as high as 38 percent. However, the dysfunction appears to be much more frequent (up to 39 percent) among gay males and men with HIV (up to 38 percent; Simons & Carey, 2001).

Premature ejaculation, also referred to as early ejaculation and rapid ejaculation, is defined as a persistent or recurrent inability to control ejaculation upon minimal sexual stimulation, before, on, or shortly after penetration (APA, 2000). It is a highly prevalent male sexual dysfunction and affects approximately 20 to 40 percent of sexually active men (Althof, 2007) and 75 percent of men during at least one point in their lifetime (Wang, Kumar, Minhas, & Ralph, 2005).

The current definition of premature ejaculation is purposely vague and subjective, as it relies on the clinician's judgment as to what constitutes "before, on, or shortly after penetration." In response to this problem, several investigators have objectively measured the average duration of sexual intercourse to determine an appropriate cut-off with which to categorize this disorder. Specifically, duration is measured using the time interval between penetration and ejaculation, known as intravaginal ejaculatory latency time (IELT; Waldinger, 2005). Normative IELT data have been obtained and results generally indicate that the average duration is between five and six minutes (Waldinger, 2005; Waldinger, Hengeveld, Zwinderman, & Olivier, 1998). In an attempt to operationally define this criterion, Waldinger and colleagues (1998) interviewed 110 individuals diagnosed with premature ejaculation and found that 90 percent of men ejaculated within 1 minute of penetration, and 60 percent ejaculated within 15 seconds; therefore, it was suggested that premature ejaculation should be defined as ejaculating in less than 1 minute in greater than 90 percent of episodes of sexual intercourse (Wang et al., 2005). Consistent with this body of research, the proposed DSM-5 criteria for the newly termed "early ejaculation" diagnosis use the qualifier of "within approximately one minute of beginning of sexual activity and before the person wishes it" (APA, 2010).

Undoubtedly, IELT provides a simple and objective method to assist in the diagnosis of premature ejaculation (Jannini, Lombardo, & Lenzi, 2005). However, some suggest that solely focusing on latency is one-dimensional and ignores several essential features of this disorder (Wang et al., 2005). Indeed, an adequate assessment should be multi-dimensional and, as such, include objective data (i.e., IELT) in addition to other features, such as voluntary control over ejaculation, sexual satisfaction in both partners, and the presence of distress.

SEXUAL PAIN DISORDERS

Dyspareunia refers to genital pain associated with intercourse in males or females, although painful intercourse is rare among men and is usually associated with infections, inflammation of the prostate (i.e., prostatitis), or physical anomalies. In the DSM-IV-TR, dyspareunia must cause marked distress or interpersonal difficulty and must not be caused exclusively by lack of lubrication or by vaginismus. Dr. Irv Binik, at McGill University's Department of Psychology, has been one of the leading researchers on sexual pain disorders for many years. Dr. Binik and colleagues (Binik, Bergeron, & Khalifé, 2007; Meana, Binik, Khalifé, & Cohen, 1997) have been highly critical of the current definition and diagnosis of dyspareunia. Empirical investigations have shown that pain is of primary importance and should be covered in a comprehensive assessment (Pukall, Payne, Binik, & Khalifé, 2003). Interestingly, in their samples, the location and pattern of pain allowed the researchers to differentiate among several subtypes of dyspareunia (e.g., vulvar vestibulitis, currently termed provoked vestibulodynia; Meana et al., 1997). Provoked vestibulodynia is one of the most common forms of painful intercourse in young women. It is characterized by a severe sharp and burning pain at the entrance of the vagina when vaginal penetration is attempted and affects many aspects of women's lives other than sexuality (e.g., relationship adjustment, mood) (Pukall & Binik, 2009; Pukall, Smith, & Chamberlain, 2007).

The true incidence and prevalence of dyspareunia is difficult to determine, given significant methodological problems, including varying definitions of the disorder. Studies have indicated prevalence rates ranging from 3 to 18 percent in the general population and up to 46 percent in primary care settings (Simons & Carey, 2001). It has been claimed that dyspareunia is the second most common female dysfunction and that it is increasingly reported in clinics. One study in New York (Glatt, Zinner, & McCormack, 1990) surveyed 324 women in their early thirties. Thirty-three percent of these women had persistent dyspareunia at the time of the study; in addition, almost 30 percent had previously experienced dyspareunia. In 34 percent of the cases of dyspareunia, the women reported an important adverse effect on their relationships, and 48 percent reported a decrease in frequency of intercourse as a result. Fewer than half of those still experiencing dyspareunia had ever consulted a health care professional about the problem.

Vaginismus is primarily defined as the involuntary contraction of the pelvic muscles that surround the outer third of the vagina upon attempts at penetration. The DSM-IV-TR further specifies that the spasms are recurrent or persistent and interfere with the penetration of a penis, or, in more extreme cases, the insertion of tampons, fingers, or a speculum during gynecological examination. Currently, the diagnostic focus is on the interference with intercourse and not on the experience of pain, despite the fact that it is classified as a sexual pain disorder (Binik et al., 2007). Moreover, studies (e.g., Reissing, Binik, Khalifé, Cohen, & Amsel, 2004) have demonstrated that women with vaginismus and dyspareunia show significant overlap on measures of pain and pelvic muscle tension, suggesting that pain is an important but neglected criterion. In addition to pain, distress involving penetration and avoidance-based behaviours seem to be characteristic of vaginismus. In the Reissing and colleagues study, for example, 73 percent of women with vaginismus refused to participate in vaginal surface electromyography evaluations, whereas none of the participants in either the dyspareunia group or the control group refused this test.

Criticisms have been directed at the lack of research investigating vaginismus, and serious problems with the diagnostic criteria of this disorder have been noted. In particular, vaginal spasm characterizing the disorder was neither a reliable nor a valid feature, such that only 28 percent of women presented with this criterion (Reissing et al., 2004). Given some of the problems with the criteria, it is not surprising that clinicians are unable to reliably differentiate vaginismus from dyspareunia (Binik et al., 2007) and that there is difficulty arriving at reliable estimates for general incidence and prevalence of the disorder. John Lamont (1978) reported that, at the Human Sexuality Clinic at McMaster University in Hamilton, 47 percent of all patients seen between 1972 and 1976 received a diagnosis of vaginismus. Other epidemiological reports obtained from various clinics have varied between 12 and 55 percent (Spector & Carey, 1990).

Given the overlap between many features of dyspareunia and vaginismus, the DSM-5 proposes a single category of genito-pelvic pain/penetration disorder that incorporates symptoms of both conditions (Binik, 2010a, 2010b). Affected women may experience pain, increased pelvic floor muscle tension, and/or fear or anxiety during attempted or completed vaginal intercourse activities; a possible additional indicator is the complete inability to be penetrated vaginally.

HYPERSEXUAL DISORDER

The concept of **hypersexuality**, or sexual addiction, is not new. In his eighteenth-century *Mémoires écrits par lui-même*, Giovanni Jacopo Casanova De Seingalt (known simply as Casanova) provided clear illustrations of an intense preoccupation with pursuing sex with women. Later, Richard von Krafft-Ebing, in *Psychopathia Sexualis* (1901), described what he called "hyperaesthesia" (i.e., abnormally increased sexual desire). Krafft-Ebing labelled this disorder as either "nymphomania" (excessive desire in women) or "satyriasis" (excessive desire in men). However, the modern conceptualization of hypersexuality is most often credited to Patrick Carnes, an American psychologist, who described a series of patients suffering from an addiction to sex (Carnes, 1983, 1989).

The notion of hypersexuality has been widely criticized (for summaries of these criticisms, see Orford, 2001, and Walters, 1999). While there is disagreement regarding terminology (e.g., sexual addiction, sexual compulsivity), there is some consistency with regard to the essential features of the disorder. In other words, sexual addicts typically experience a loss of control over sexual urges, fantasies, and behaviours, and they often engage in sexual activity to regulate negative emotional states (e.g., anxiety, depression).

The behavioural component of sexual addiction has received increasing attention and has been suggested as an essential feature of this disorder. To quantify sexual frequency, researchers rely on an index, termed *total sexual outlet* (TSO), initially described by Kinsey and colleagues (1948). TSO was based on the number of orgasms achieved through any combination of methods (e.g., intercourse, masturbation) during a specific week. Research has suggested that few males (approximately 5 to 10 percent) report a sexual outlet of seven or more times per week and that this level of sexual activity is rarely maintained over time (e.g., Janus & Janus, 1993; Kinsey et al., 1948). Based on such evidence, Kafka (1997) proposed that hypersexuality should incorporate TSOs of at least seven times per week, over a period of at least six months. While this definition is useful, it is clearly not sufficient. For example, the applicability of this criterion to women is problematic, given research suggesting that a significant proportion of women have difficulty reaching orgasm (Laumann et al., 1994). Additionally, there is some dissension as to whether excessive levels of sexual behaviour are, in fact, pathological.

Although hypersexuality has never been included as an official diagnostic category in any of the DSM versions, Kafka (2010b) has proposed the inclusion of "hypersexual disorder" in the DSM-5 as "a sexual disorder associated with increased or disinhibited expressions of sexual arousal and desire in association with a dimension of impulsivity" (p. 393). He characterizes it as including at least four of the following: (1) spending excessive time consumed by sexual fantasies and urges, and in planning for and engaging in sexual behaviour; (2) repetitively engaging in these sexual fantasies, urges, and behaviours in response to dysphoric mood states or (3) stressful life events; (4) making repeated but unsuccessful efforts to control or significantly reduce these fantasies, urges, and behaviours; and (5) repetitively engaging in sexual behaviours while disregarding the risk for physical and emotional harm to self or others.

Hypersexual disorder has been identified in approximately 3 to 6 percent of the general population (Black, 2000) and is associated with a variety of emotional and physical problems, including depression, relationship instability, and sexually transmitted infections (Kafka, 2007).

ETIOLOGY OF SEXUAL DYSFUNCTIONS

Most of the research conducted on the causes of sexual dysfunctions has focused on specific disorders, although all of these disorders possess common factors to some degree. Early reports in the literature expressed the belief that most female sexual dysfunctions were the result of some interference with psychological functioning (Berman, Berman, Chhabra, & Goldstein, 2001). However, Berman and colleagues' review of recent findings indicates that, in many instances, these dysfunctions are secondary to medical problems and appear to have an organic basis. Consistent with this, Guay (2000) found that both premenopausal and postmenopausal women suffering some form of sexual dysfunction had unusually low androgen levels. Guay also found that treatment with androgens alleviated the problems of these women. In addition, Korenman (1998) reported that men with erectile disorder say they experience sexual arousal despite the fact that their penis does not respond, suggesting problems with the vascular reflex mechanism that normally generates an erection. Finally, people who rate their physical health as excellent report markedly fewer sexual problems than those who rate their health as poor (Laumann et al., 1994). Clearly, both physical and psychological factors are involved in the development of most, if not all, sexual dysfunctions, although one factor or another may be more important in a given case.

Almost everyone experiences some sort of sexual performance difficulty at some point. Excessive alcohol, for example, may cause a temporary lessening of desire or interfere with erection or orgasm. After a long period without sex, or during the first time with a new partner, a man may ejaculate prematurely. Usually the problem disappears with the situation that caused it. However, a person who is very upset by such an experience may carefully monitor his or her responses during the next sexual encounter. This second perceived failure, of course, only leads to greater anxiety, and a chronic dysfunction may emerge.

Research findings are consistent with the idea that the person's perspective plays a part in the development or maintenance of sexual dysfunction. For example, men with erectile disorder typically do not pay attention to the arousing properties of sex but rather focus on the threatening consequences of their likely failure to produce an erection (Bach, Brown, & Barlow, 1999). Canadian researchers have found that women who suffer from vaginismus report being afraid of intercourse (Reissing, Binik, & Khalifé, 1999). Whether these psychological factors in erectile disorder or vaginismus precede or follow the development of clients' problems is irrelevant for treatment purposes, since it is the maintenance factors that are important for change. Let us now consider etiological factors associated with some of the specific sexual dysfunctions.

SEXUAL DESIRE DISORDERS People with sexual desire disorders are generally not interested in sexual activity, a pattern sometimes evident in depressed patients. This similarity has led to speculation that hypoactive sexual desire may result from depression. Cyranowski and colleagues (2004), for example, found a correlation between high levels of depressive symptoms and reduced levels of sexual desire. In another investigation, Hartmann, Heiser, Ruffer-Hesse, and Kloth (2002) found that a significant number of women with sexual difficulties also satisfied the diagnostic criteria for a mood disorder. With the widespread use of SSRI antidepressants, there is evidence that hypoactive sexual desire may result from depression or from the medication used to treat it (Renshaw, 1998).

Kaplan (1979) emphasized other psychological factors in sexual desire disorders, such as dysfunctional attitudes about sex, relationship problems, and a strict upbringing that associated sexual pleasure with guilt. Indeed, these appear to be factors in all sexual dysfunctions (also see Wincze, Bach, & Barlow, 2008).

In addition to psychological difficulties that may precipitate sexual dysfunctions, abnormal hormonal functioning may cause problems. Certainly, hormones such as **estrogen** (the so-called female sex hormone), **testosterone** (the so-called male sex hormone), and **prolactin** are involved in sexual activity and desire, and variations in the levels of these hormones can lower or increase sex drive (Rosen & Leiblum, 1995). However, the evidence suggests that abnormal hormonal levels contribute to only a few cases of sexual desire disorder (Kresin, 1993).

SEXUAL AROUSAL DISORDERS Perhaps the most commonly reported factor associated with arousal disorders, and to some extent all sexual dysfunctions, is what Masters and Johnson (1970) originally called performance anxiety. **Performance anxiety** is the response of individuals who feel that they are expected to perform sexually. Worried that their performance will not be up to the expectations of their partner, they become *spectators* of their own behaviour, monitoring their own sexual performance and the perceived responses of their partner. When this happens, the person's focus is on the performance rather than on enjoyment of the sexual experience. Like the watched pot that never boils, the spontaneous sensory response of sexual arousal is blocked. However, anxiety can affect sexual functioning simply as a result of increased activity in the sympathetic branch of the autonomic nervous system. When sympathetic activity occurs, as happens when someone is anxious, its activity inhibits the parasympathetic branch. Since sexual arousal is associated with activation of the parasympathetic branch, inhibition of this branch by sympathetic activity will interfere with sexual arousal and may, as a result, cause sexual dysfunction.

Weisberg and his colleagues (Weisberg, Brown, Wincze, & Barlow, 2001) examined this idea in a laboratory study. Fifty-two sexually functioning men were instructed to watch two erotic films. Following the viewing of these films, the men were given bogus feedback indicating that they had a low erectile response. The men were divided into two groups. Group I was given an external fluctuating attribution (i.e., the films were poorly made), while Group II was given an internal, stable attribution (i.e., problematic thoughts about sex). The participants were then instructed to watch a third erotic film. Individuals in Group II, who were given the problematic sexual thoughts feedback, experienced lower erectile responses than Group I, who attributed their reported sexual malfunctioning during the first films to external factors (i.e., poor videos). This study suggested that the attributions we make regarding our sexual performance may affect our future ability to perform.

Erectile dysfunction or male erectile disorder involves a complex interplay between physiological and psychological factors. Physiological factors include cardiovascular disease, neurological diseases, or various medications, whereas psychological factors include performance anxiety (described above), depression, problems in the relationship, and psychological traumas. Other risk factors for male erectile disorder include age, diabetes, hypertension, cigarette smoking, and alcoholism (Russell & Nehra, 2003). Hormonal factors have been proposed, where a loss of androgens may ultimately lead to erectile dysfunction. In fact, Gilna (2004) demonstrated that testosterone replacement therapy improved erectile rigidity in men experiencing erectile dysfunction. Masters and Johnson (1970) estimated that psychological factors were primary in 95 percent of the cases of erectile dysfunction, although more recent estimates suggest something closer to a 50/50 split between biogenic and psychogenic origins (Everaerd, 1993). However, methodological problems within these studies make such estimates unreliable. Nevertheless, both psychological and organic causes are important and should be considered in a comprehensive assessment.

ORGASMIC DISORDERS Orgasmic disorders are generally thought to involve primarily psychological factors, but certain medical conditions (for example, heart or circulatory problems) and some medications can cause anorgasmia in women. Again, relationship difficulties are common, although it is often hard to know whether these difficulties preceded or were caused by the sexual dysfunction. Limited sexual techniques, a lack of understanding of their own response, and partners who do not understand their needs may all play a role, as does an inability to let go and allow the natural response to sexual stimulation to occur. As shown in the case of Joan, these barriers are more difficult to overcome if a woman feels constrained in discussing sex with her partner or in exploring techniques.

PREMATURE EJACULATION Two types of premature ejaculation have been identified: primary and secondary. Secondary premature ejaculation occurs in men who previously had ejaculatory control. In such cases, Metz, Pryor, and Nesvacil (1997) found that premature ejaculation could be caused by trauma to the sympathetic nervous system, abdominal or pelvic injuries, prostatitis, urethritis, or, as Althof (1995) found, withdrawal from narcotics. Grenier and Byers (1995) determined that hormones do not play a role in premature ejaculation. Primary premature ejaculation could be caused by various problems. It may be a conditioned response to rapid ejaculation from the age when boys masturbated and ejaculated rapidly out of convenience (as cited in Carver, 1998), or when young men attempt sexual intercourse under pressure or once again in situations where they had to ejaculate fairly rapidly. With repeated experiences, the conditioning effect becomes stronger. Men may also avoid sex due to feelings of guilt and shame, and thus in clinical situations may be more likely to be diagnosed with low sexual desire when they are simply trying to avoid premature ejaculation. Thus, it is evident that premature ejaculation is largely thought to be psychological in nature, based around men's sensations and perceptions (Byer, Shainberg, & Galliano, 2002). However, it is evident that some men have a low threshold for physical stimulation and therefore are thought to be physiologically predisposed to premature ejaculation (Crooks & Baur, 1996).

VAGINISMUS/DYSPAREUNIA There is a paucity of research investigating etiological markers of both vaginismus and dyspareunia (Beck, 1993; Binik et al., 2007). Most studies have investigated psychogenic mechanisms and have reported several potential causal factors such as negative sexual attitudes, lack of sexual education, unpleasant or traumatic sexual experiences such as rape or childhood sexual abuse, and various cognitive styles associated with anxiety (Binik et al., 2007; Reissing et al., 2004). Studies have indicated that women diagnosed with either vaginismus or dyspareunia present with significantly more distress and avoidance behaviours pertaining to expected pain than do women without these disorders (Reissing et al., 2004). While this highlights the importance of conditioned responses, further research on causal mechanisms is necessary.

TREATMENT OF SEXUAL DYSFUNCTIONS

PSYCHOLOGICAL INTERVENTIONS Until the publication of Masters and Johnson's (1970) book describing their treatment approach, there was very little literature on therapy for sexual dysfunctions. Masters and Johnson described a comprehensive and intensive approach that required couples to live in their clinic for two weeks. Many aspects of Masters and Johnson's approach have been retained or modified at other clinics, so that most programs now share a number of common elements. Most programs see sexual dysfunctions as involving two people and, as a consequence, they typically insist that both partners attend treatment.

Communication and Exploration. The majority of programs begin with an extensive assessment of the couple, including a detailed sexual history (see Wincze et al., 2008). This is typically followed by sex education, where information is provided and maladaptive ideas about sex are challenged. Procedures are provided for enhancing communication between the partners, not only about sexual matters, but about all issues that may cause disharmony. Effective sexual communication first requires each partner to develop an understanding of his or her own sensations and bodily response. Acceptance of their own bodies may be limited because of embarrassment or guilt. Accordingly, sex therapists often suggest exercises in which clients privately explore their own bodies and use masturbation to become aware of their own arousal response. Clients also learn to communicate their specific sexual preferences to one another so that they can give each other sexual pleasure.

Sensate Focus. An important component in sex therapy programs is what Masters and Johnson (1970) called **sensate focus**, essentially a form of desensitization applied to sexual fears. It is assumed that once the sexual dysfunction has emerged, the person develops performance anxiety or fear, which serves to worsen and entrench the problem.

Given that many sexual dysfunctions are associated with anxiety or fear and performance anxiety, sensate focus is often employed to redirect attention away from the specific sexual response and toward the sexual interaction (Wincze et al., 2008). Sensate focus involves a series of exercises where partners engage in predetermined stages of sexual interaction. In the first step, they undress together with the light on to desensitize any embarrassment they may have about being naked together. They next take turns at massaging or touching one another all over, except for the genital or breast areas. They are learning to enjoy touching and being touched without any fear of imminent demands for sex. After several sessions of this, each person begins to tell the partner during the touching exercises what he or she enjoys. All of these sessions are interspersed with discussions with their therapist, which is meant to enhance communication skills and to identify and deal with any problems that arise during the touching sessions. As the couple becomes comfortable and they begin to expand their enjoyment of the associated physical pleasures, they progress to the next stage: genital and breast touching. There is still, however, a moratorium on sexual intercourse to allow the couple to enjoy sexual sensations and arousal without the fear of having to perform. The aim is to eliminate "spectatoring," allowing each partner to relax and focus on his or her own pleasure. Once the couple can maintain their pleasure without fear, they are advised to enter the last stage of sensate focus, which is designed specifically for the problem that brought them to the clinic. In this final stage, the ban on sexual intercourse is lifted. However, the couple is instructed to progress slowly and they follow a particular gradual program aimed at overcoming the specific dysfunction.

In addition to sensate focus, there are several behavioural exercises aimed at particular sexual dysfunctions. The stop-start and squeeze techniques, for example, are behavioural approaches used to treat premature ejaculation, and can be used either with or without a partner. With the stop-start technique, the partner manually stimulates the man until he feels the earliest signs of approaching orgasm, at which point the partner ceases the stimulation. After a period of time (approximately 40 seconds to 1 minute), the partner begins masturbating him again. This procedure is repeated so that the entire process lasts approximately 15 minutes (employing as many stops as is necessary). Sometimes, just stopping is not enough to prevent the man from ejaculating. In those cases, the squeeze technique is employed by squeezing around the coronal ridge of the penis. Although it is not painful, the squeeze technique diminishes arousal and prevents ejaculation. When the individual can last approximately 15 minutes with only 1 or 2 "stops," the couple can proceed to more arousing stimulation methods (e.g., oral sex). One advantage of the stop-start method is that it can be practised with or without a partner and used with manual, oral, or vaginal sex.

EVALUATION OF PSYCHOLOGICAL TREATMENT Masters and Johnson (1970) claimed that more than 80 percent of their clients were successfully treated for their various dysfunctions. However, they used a rather loose criterion of success and did not follow up with their clients for long enough to properly evaluate the maintenance of their gains.

More recent and careful evaluations have shown that premature ejaculation and vaginismus are most successfully treated with the type of therapy outlined above (Beck, 1993). Success rates as high as 80 percent for vaginismus and 90 percent for premature ejaculation have been reported. Treatment for erectile dysfunction has not fared as well, although as many as 70 percent of men with this disorder reported that they recovered sufficient erectile capacity to have intercourse (Hawton, Catalan, & Fagg, 1992). For problems such as low desire or orgasmic dysfunction in women, directions to engage in self-masturbation appear to enhance the effects of comprehensive therapy (LoPiccolo, 1990).

Overall, psychological sex therapy has been quite successful in treating sexual dysfunctions. Some cases in which it is not successful may be attributable to undetected physical problems.

PHYSICAL TREATMENTS Physical treatments are best used in conjunction with psychological approaches, even in cases where there is a clear organic cause. In erectile disorder that has a physical basis, for example, there are nevertheless psychological features once the disorder is established. In these cases, the man will very likely become afraid of failing and develop performance anxiety, which may remain a problem even after the physical cause has been corrected.

Medications of one kind or another have been shown to be helpful in some cases of sexual dysfunction. With regard to erectile dysfunction, several muscle relaxants, including Phentolamine, Papaverine, and Alprostadil, can be self-injected into the corpus cavernosum of the penis, which facilitates an erection by relaxing isolated human penile erectile tissue and cavernous arteries (El-Sakka, 2006). Alprostadil, in particular, represents the most common form of **intracavernous treatment** for erectile dysfunction and, upon administration, erections may last for an hour or longer, irrespective of whether there is direct sexual stimulation. Intracavernous treatment using Alprostadil is extremely efficacious, particularly for men who experience problems with the transmission of nerve signals that regulate their erections.

Efficacy rates for intracavernous therapy are extremely high, such that up to 94 percent of individuals undergoing this treatment have reported subsequent sexual activity (Hatzimouratidis & Hatzichristou, 2005; Mohr & Beutler, 1990). However, complications include penile pain, the development of scar tissue, prolonged erections (i.e., priapism), and fibrosis. Despite the positive results of this treatment, the fact that many men find this procedure painful, or at least unpleasant, has led to high discontinuation rates and limited treatment compliance (Althof & Turner, 1992).

Antidepressants have also been used, typically in the treatment of premature ejaculation, as they have demonstrated the ability to delay the ejaculatory response and have led to improved sexual satisfaction in some men (Althof & Seftel, 1995). Aphrodisiacs have also been historically implicated in sexual arousal. The first kind of aphrodisiac is psychophysiological, affecting one's five senses—the idea being that one's senses can be stimulated to heighten sexual awareness. The second kind of aphrodisiac is internal and based on the old belief that certain products have sexually stimulating qualities. Examples include various foods, herbal remedies (e.g., Ginkgo biloba), alcohol, and "love potions" (Slovenko, 2001). However, the positive effects of these aphrodisiacs have not been supported by research.

Considerable publicity has accompanied the announcement of the phosphodiesterase inhibitors (PDE5 inhibitors) designed to treat erectile disorders. The three agents within this class are Sildenafil (marketed under the trade name Viagra), Tadalafil (marketed under the trade name Cialis), and Vardenafil (marketed under the trade name Levitra), and all restrict the breakdown of cyclic guanine monophosphate, which leads to increased blood flow and stronger erections. Each medication has been approved by Health Canada, although some adverse side effects have been noted (e.g., problems with vision). Some patients prefer one type over another, given differences with regard to duration of action (Viagra has the shortest duration at 4 to 6 hours and Cialis has the longest duration at up to 36 hours) and interactions with fatty foods (Ashton, 2007).

Among these agents, Viagra, in particular, has been subjected to well-controlled and systematic research. In one of the early investigations, Goldstein and colleagues (1998) evaluated its effects on more than 850 men who could not generate and maintain an erection of sufficient quality to have intercourse. Their careful examination of these men revealed that some had an organic basis to their problem, others had psychogenic causes, and some had both organic and psychogenic problems. Sixty-nine percent of all attempts at intercourse were successful for the men taking Viagra, while only 22 percent of the attempts were successful on the placebo. Furthermore, increased doses were associated with improved erectile functioning. These findings were essentially confirmed by Mitka (1998), who found that Viagra generated erections in two-thirds of men with severe erectile problems.

PDE5 inhibitors are generally safe, and side effects are typically mild (e.g., headache, flushing, visual disturbances); however, these medications are contraindicated in men who use nitrates to manage cardiovascular disease. Additionally, given the paucity of research, it is still too early to rule out the possibility of more problematic effects with long-term use. Nevertheless, given the encouraging results and typically mild side effects, the administration of these drugs for erectile disorder has become common.

Interestingly, use of PDE5 inhibitors in women with sexual arousal disorders has been described in several case reports (Ashton, 2007). In a double-blind crossover design, Caruso, Intelisano, Lupo, and Agnello (2001) investigated the utility of Viagra in 51 women experiencing arousal disorders. Compared to placebo treatment, women treated with Viagra showed significant increases in sexual arousal and in the frequency of orgasm, as well as increases in the frequency of sexual fantasies and intercourse; they also reported marked improvements in their enjoyment of sex. Unfortunately, other studies have not demonstrated such positive changes, and research on the use of PDE5 inhibitors in women has essentially been abandoned at present. Not surprisingly, other treatments (e.g., testosterone gel) have been touted to treat low desire/arousal in women; however, none of these has been approved by the appropriate regulatory boards to date.

Pelvic floor physiotherapy has emerged as a potential treatment for men with erectile dysfunction (primarily in the UK; Dorey et al., 2004)—although the use of vacuum erection devices is more common—and for women with a common form of dyspareunia, provoked vestibulodynia. Both retrospective (Bergeron et al., 2002) and prospective studies (Goldfinger, Pukall, Gentilcore-Saulnier, McLean, & Chamberlain, 2009) have documented positive outcomes in terms of pain reduction and improvements in sexual function after treatment.

Surgical interventions are also recommended for some individuals with sexual dysfunctions. For example, vestibulectomy (surgical removal of the superficial vestibule) for women with provoked vestibulodynia is the most commonly reported treatment and has positive outcomes (Bergeron, Pukall, & Mailloux, 2008). Surgery can be helpful for males with erectile dysfunction when the cause has been identified as a vascular blockage preventing adequate blood flow to the penis (Mohr & Beutler, 1990).

The most common physical treatment for sexual dysfunctions is penile implants for men with erectile disorder. While a number of different implants were used in the past, currently the most popular approach is to implant inflatable silicone cylinders in the penis (see Figure 13.2). These cylinders are joined to a reservoir of fluid that has been inserted into the man's abdomen along with a tiny pump in the scrotum. To produce an erection, the man presses the pump, which pushes fluid from the reservoir into the cylinders. As the cylinders fill, they cause the penis to become erect. These implants have been very popular, and the early evidence indicated that the patients and their partners were quite satisfied (Anderson & Wold, 1986). However, follow-up studies have shown that 40 percent of such men and their partners are not satisfied, in the long term, with the results. Fears associated with silicone implants and concerns about the invasiveness and irreversibility of the procedure appear to have reduced the popularity of this approach in recent years (Thomas & LoPiccolo, 1994).

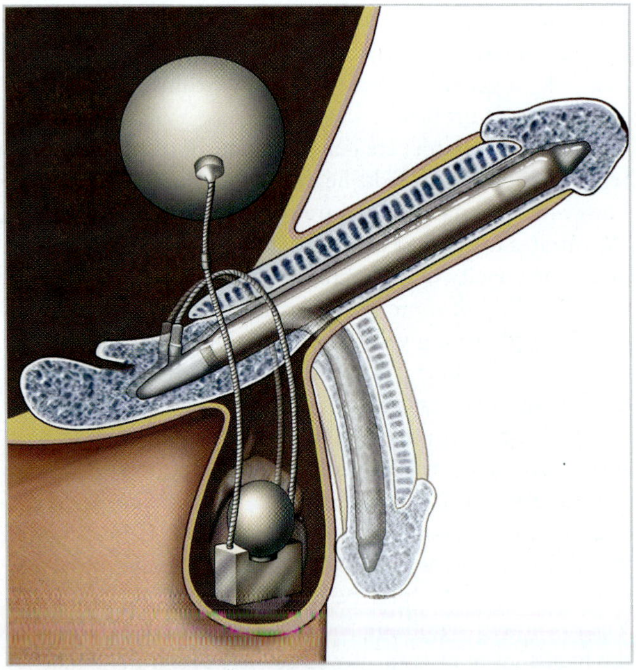

FIGURE 13.2 Penile Implant

Source: Courtesy of Dr. Jan Looman, Regional Treatment Centre, Kingston, Ontario.

3 BEFORE MOVING ON

Imagine a heterosexual couple presenting to a sex therapy clinic in which the male has severe erectile dysfunction. Intercourse is impossible and their main goal is to be able to have intercourse again. Their therapist assigns them the first two steps of sensate focus. The couple is baffled. Why is their therapist asking them to not have sex when their goal is exactly that? How would you explain this apparent paradox to this couple?

Gender Identity

Boys are expected to act like boys, and they are allowed little latitude before they are labelled "sissies." Girls who play hockey and prefer trucks to dolls are tolerated much better. Indeed, Western society presents a very rigid view of what is considered "male" or "female" and offers very little room for expressions outside of these two extremes, especially for males. In many non-Western cultures, however, the existence of individuals who are neither traditionally masculine nor traditionally feminine has long been recognized and accepted; in fact, such gender-variant individuals may be given a specific name and accorded a distinct role in society. In several Native cultures, rituals conducted at or before puberty give a boy the option to choose between the status of a conventional male or that of a transgendered male—a "two-spirit" (male–female) person, or *berdache*. Berdaches wear special clothing fashioned from male and female attire, practise mostly female occupations, and engage in sexual relationships with conventional men. They are often shamans (healers who derived their curative powers from their knowledge of the spirit world), chanters, dancers, or mediators. Such latitude in creating room for a third sex is lacking in Western society; although some individuals resist categorization by "gender-bending" (i.e., actively transgressing expected gender roles), some transpeople may feel forced to "fit" into either the male or female category, and others may simply choose to "switch" their sex through a lengthy, painful, and difficult process of sex reassignment.

Despite the greater latitude offered to women in expressing male behaviours, when Leslie Feinberg was growing up, she was such a tomboy that she was rejected on all sides (Gilbert, 1996). As she matured, the female role chafed so much that eventually Feinberg moved to New York and began to pass as a man. She dressed like a man, acted like a man, and expected others to treat her like a man.

In making this transition, Feinberg identified herself as "transgendered," or simply "trans." She rejected her categorization as female and insisted on having the right to live as she pleased without harassment. Her transformation dealt with more than gender: Feinberg became a spokesperson for a new movement of those in society who have been marginalized. These are the women and men who feel that they are the victims of cruel accidents of biology—that they were born the wrong sex.

Despite many people's assumption that gender is a clear-cut concept, there are many different dimensions of gender, including the following: chromosomal gender (XY in males and XX in females), gonadal gender (testes in the male and ovaries in the female), prenatal hormonal gender (testosterone and anti-Mullerian hormone in the male but not in the female), internal accessory organs (e.g., prostate in the male and Fallopian tubes in the female), external genital appearance (e.g., penis in the male and vulva in the female), assigned gender (based on the external genital appearance at birth, resulting in the "it's a boy" or "it's a girl" announcement that then affects society's labelling of that child and the gender in which the child is raised), and **gender identity** (a person's basic sense of self as male or female, the first signs of which appear between 18 and 36 months of age) (Money, 1987). **Gender role** is the collection of those characteristics that a society defines as masculine or feminine. Because roles relate to social standards, ideas about gender role change over time and from culture to culture. In some instances, these "variables of gender" do not all coincide. In rare cases where the actual biological variables are discordant, **hermaphroditism** occurs, with the reproductive structures being partly female and partly male. When the biological variables are consistent, but are discordant with the person's sense of self, **gender identity disorder** occurs.

GENDER IDENTITY DISORDERS

A "trans" activist, such as Leslie Feinberg, might appear to fulfill the DSM-IV-TR criteria for gender identity disorder (GID, previously known as *transsexualism*—see Table 13.4). She has experienced a "strong and persistent cross-gender identification" and reported "persistent discomfort with . . . her sex or sense of inappropriateness in the gender role of that sex" (APA, 2000, p. 576). This latter feature (that is, discomfort with biologically endowed sex) is referred to as **gender dysphoria**. Thus, if a biological male says that he does not feel like a male but rather feels like a female trapped in a man's body, he would be experiencing gender dysphoria. The diagnosis of GID, however, also requires that there be "clinically significant distress or impairment in social, occupational, or other important areas of functioning" (APA, 2000, p. 576). Feinberg argues that she is perfectly well adjusted to her transgendered life, although society may have difficulty with it. Such individuals may fulfill some of the cross-gender requirements for the diagnosis, but they do not completely fit the criteria because their gender identity appears not to result in severe distress.

TABLE 13.4 DSM-IV-TR DIAGNOSTIC CRITERIA FOR GENDER IDENTITY DISORDER

A. A strong and persistent cross-gender identification (not merely a desire for any perceived cultural advantages of being the other sex).
In children, the disturbance is manifested by four (or more) of the following:
(1) repeatedly stated desire to be, or insistence that he or she is, the other sex
(2) in boys, preference for cross-dressing or simulating female attire; in girls, insistence on wearing only stereotypical masculine clothing
(3) strong and persistent preferences for cross-sex roles in make-believe play or persistent fantasies of being the other sex
(4) intense desire to participate in the stereotypical games and pastimes of the other sex
(5) strong preference for playmates of the other sex

In adolescents and adults, the disturbance is manifested by symptoms such as a stated desire to be the other sex, frequent passing as the other sex, desire to live or be treated as the other sex, or the conviction that he or she has the typical feelings and reactions of the other sex.

B. Persistent discomfort with his or her sex or sense of inappropriateness in the gender role of that sex.

In children, the disturbance is manifested by any of the following: in boys, assertion that his penis or testes are disgusting or will disappear or assertion that it would be better not to have a penis, or aversion toward rough-and-tumble play and rejection of male stereotypical toys, games, and activities; in girls, rejection of urinating in a sitting position, assertion that she has or will grow a penis, or assertion that she does not want to grow breasts or menstruate, or marked aversion toward normative feminine clothing.

In adolescents and adults, the disturbance is manifested by symptoms such as preoccupation with getting rid of primary and secondary sex characteristics (e.g., request for hormones, surgery, or other procedures to physically alter sexual characteristics to simulate the other sex) or belief that he or she was born the wrong sex.

C. The disturbance is not concurrent with a physical intersex condition.

D. The disturbance' causes clinically significant distress or impairment in social, occupational, or other important areas of functioning.

Source: Reprinted with permission from the *Diagnostic and Statistical Manual of Mental Disorders, Fourth Edition, Text Revision.* (Copyright © 2000). American Psychiatric Association.

In the DSM-5, two separate diagnoses have been proposed to replace GID based on the age of the individual presenting with the complaint: gender dysphoria in children (Zucker, 2010a) and gender dysphoria in adolescents and adults (Cohen-Kettenis & Pfäfflin, 2010). Both have two possible subtypes (with or without a disorder of sex development, e.g., Turner syndrome), and the diagnosis pertaining to older individuals has an additional specifier of whether the individual is post-transition (i.e., has undergone at least one form of cross-sex treatment and is living full time as the desired gender).

Because they feel as if they are physically the wrong sex, people with GIDs may cross-dress or attempt to rid themselves of secondary sex characteristics in other ways. They may request hormonal treatment or other physical alterations, such as electrolysis to remove facial hair, in attempts to assume the role of the other sex. In some instances, they undertake surgery to change their anatomy and are then known as transsexuals.

Green and Blanchard (1995) reported that GID occurs more commonly in children than in adults, with 3 percent of boys and 1 percent of girls identified as having the disorder. In fact, the gender dysphoria associated with GID most commonly begins in childhood; most adults having this disorder report gender-role conflicts and transsexual feelings occurring at a very early age (Tsoi, 1990). However, in adults the prevalence of GID is quite low: approximately 1 in 30 000 men and 1 in 100 000 to 150 000 women (APA, 2000).

ETIOLOGY OF GENDER IDENTITY DISORDERS

Very little is known about the origins of GID. Unfortunately, what data are available present a rather confusing picture, although most authorities in the field consider the problem to result from some as yet unspecified combination of biological and psychological factors.

A tragic Canadian "test case" that offers some insight into the nature/nurture debate emerged accidentally when one of a pair of male monozygotic twins had his penis cut off during a botched circumcision (Colapinto, 2000). Instead of undertaking the repeated, difficult, and possibly unsatisfactory surgeries necessary to reconstruct a penis, sexologist John Money persuaded the parents to have the boy surgically "reassigned" as a girl. Thus, nature (that is, the hereditary component) was held constant between the twins because of their identical genetic makeup. Only the nurture component varied for the two: one twin was subsequently reared as a girl, the other as a boy. The reports indicated that the reassigned twin became feminine in behaviour and interests. At puberty, she was given hormonal replacement therapy in order to develop breasts and other female secondary sex characteristics. This case is still cited by many writers as evidence that "gender identity is something one *learns* at a very young age" (Barlow & Durand, 1995, p. 419). Such conclusions overlook follow-up information on the reassigned twin (Colapinto, 2000). The professionals who studied this case maintained that, as a young adolescent, the child was extremely masculine (Diamond, 1982). It was clear that this child had not adjusted well to being a female. When the child was told at age 14 of the botched circumcision, it devastated him. He adopted the male role, changed his name to David, and later married. Tragically, he committed suicide in 2004, just two years after his twin brother overdosed on antidepressant medication and as his own marriage was dissolving. The many years he suffered attempting to adapt to the role of a female apparently had no effect on his gender identity, and although this is only a single case, it supports the idea that gender identity is minimally influenced by environmental experiences.

Some theorists have suggested that disturbances in gender identity may be caused by either genetically influenced hormonal disturbances or exposure during fetal development to inappropriate hormones. It has been proposed that an excess or absence of testosterone during a critical point in fetal development may affect the individual's gender identity. Thus, males who were not prenatally exposed to testosterone will act in a feminine manner, whereas females who were exposed prenatally to excess testosterone will be "tomboyish" (Cohen-Kettenis & Gooren, 1999).

One of the most predominant neurobiological theories for the development of GID has focused on the role of prenatal hormones. In particular, prenatal exposure to male-typical levels of androgens masculinizes postnatal behaviour, whereas underexposure to male-typical levels of androgens has the opposite effect (Zucker, 1990). Although theoretically complex and not frequently studied, some investigators have pointed to the overrepresentation of left-handed individuals presenting with GID compared to non-disordered individuals as evidence for instability in neurodevelopment and a general biological marker (see Zucker, Bealieu, Bradley, Grimshaw, & Wilcox, 2001). Other evidence has come from heritability studies. Several studies have reported evidence indicating a significant heritable pattern for children with GID (Zucker, 2005; Zucker & Bradley, 1995). In one study, Coolidge, Thede, and Young (2002) examined the heritability and prevalence of GID in a non-retrospective study of 314 child and adolescent twins. Results indicated that GID within this sample was highly heritable.

A problem with this type of research concerns the issue of what constitutes masculine or feminine behaviour. Certainly, it is common for children to show some supposedly gender-atypical behaviours and interests, and in today's more tolerant climate more parents are comfortable with boys playing with dolls or girls engaging in rough-and-tumble play. In any event, some reviews have cautioned against the hormonal hypothesis (Bancroft, 1989; Bradley & Zucker, 1997; Carroll, 2007).

Psychodynamic and social learning theories of human behaviour emphasize the importance of early childhood experiences and the family environment. For psychoanalytic theory, the basic conflict resulting from a boy's failure to separate from the mother and develop an independent identity creates a gender identity problem (Meyers & Keith,

1991). Behavioural theory (Bernstein, Steiner, Glaiser, & Muir, 1981) suggests that the basis of GID lies in encouragement by parents of gender-inappropriate behaviours, combined with the lack of a same-sex adult model and overprotection by the opposite-sex parent. Some believe that parental characteristics might give children insufficient means to identify with the same-sex parent or to interact in cross-gender reinforcement situations. However, it is important to consider that child-related factors may be evoking certain parental responses—for example, femininity encouraged in a son by an unstable, vulnerable parent (Cohen-Kettenis & Gooren, 1999). Cohen-Kettinis and Arrindell (1990) conducted retrospective studies on the child-rearing practices of the parents of adult gender dysphorics and non-gender dysphorics. Those males who became females reported their fathers as less emotionally warm, more rejecting, and more overly controlling. Females who became males reported that both parents were less emotionally warm, but stated that only their mothers were more overprotective, as compared to the controls. Studies of the importance of the influence of parental behaviours during this developmental period have so far been somewhat supportive of a relationship between parental child-rearing behaviour and adulthood gender dysphoria.

TREATMENT OF GENDER IDENTITY DISORDERS

Dr. Kenneth Zucker has worked extensively with GID children at the Centre for Addiction and Mental Health in Toronto. When parents present cross-gender–identified children for treatment, the clinician faces a difficult issue. Some feel it is inappropriate to try to change gender identity, but increasing evidence has indicated that these individuals experience significant distress (Zucker, 1990; Zucker, 2005). The most systematic information on associated problems in these children has come from parent-report data using the Child Behaviour Checklist (Achenbach & Edelbrock, 1983). Several studies have shown that boys and girls diagnosed with GID display more behavioural problems and experience more social ostracism than do same-sex siblings and age-matched controls (Cohen-Kettenis, Owen, Kaijser, Bradley, & Zucker, 2003; Zucker, 2005). Consequently, attempts have been made to encourage gender-appropriate behaviour and to discourage cross-gender behaviour among these children through various psychotherapeutic techniques. In the short term, these interventions may affect cross-gender behaviour, but little is known about their long-term impact on gender disorders of children.

APPLIED CLINICAL CASE

Dr. Richard Raskin

Dr. Richard Raskin was born in New York City in 1934. He was the captain of Yale University's tennis team and went on to become an ophthalmologist and professional tennis player. Richard had been dressing as a woman since he was a child. He married in the early 1970s and had one child. After 10 years of psychoanalysis and a marriage that ended in divorce, Richard underwent sex-reassignment surgery and became Dr. Renée Richards.

Renée is noted for her impact on the "courts." When a number of female professional tennis players complained that her participation in the U.S. Open would result in unfair competition, the U.S. Tennis Association denied her entry. When they told her that she could not play, she suddenly became "the world's activist for the sexually disenfranchised" (Giltz, 2007). In 1977 the New York Supreme Court overturned this policy and ruled in favour of transsexual rights. Renée went on to reach the women's double finals, continued to play tennis until 1981, and ranked twentieth overall. She has published two autobiographies, one in 1986 (*Second Serve*) and another in 2007 (*No Way Renée: The Second Half of My Notorious Life*).

Portrayals of transpeople in the media can be seen in movies such as *The Crying Game*, *Breakfast on Pluto*, *Boys Don't Cry*, *Normal*, *Transamerica*, and *Hedwig and the Angry Inch*, and in television shows such as *Bones*, *Dirty Sexy Money*, *The L Word*, *Nip/Tuck*, and *Ugly Betty*.

Dr. Richard Raskin/Dr. Renée Richards before (left) and after (right) sex-reassignment surgery.

Some heterosexual but more homosexual gender dysphorics eventually request hormonal treatment or surgery to "reassign" them to the opposite sex (Lawrence, 2003). Jeremy Baumbach, a psychologist at the Yukon Family Services Association in Whitehorse, and Louisa Turner, at Case Western Reserve University School of Medicine (Baumbach & Turner, 1992), noted that not all gender dysphorics request hormonal or surgical reassignment. Those with the highest desire for surgical sex reassignment appear to be those who are the most sexually aroused by imagining themselves as having the sexual organs of the opposite sex (Blanchard, 1993). The most recent edition of the HBIGDA Standards of Care, Version 6 (Meyer et al., 2001), includes the following minimum eligibility criteria for sex-reassignment surgery: (1) "12 months of successful continuous full time real-life experience," (2) "usually 12 months of continuous hormonal therapy for those without a medical contraindication," and (3) "if required by the mental health professional, regular responsible participation in psychotherapy throughout the real-life experience at a frequency determined jointly by the patient and the mental health professional" (p. 28; as cited in Lawrence, 2003). This "real-life test" helps to ensure that patients are able to function fully in the desired gender role before potentially irreversible measures are undertaken.

Toronto researchers have found that hormonal therapy assists in developing the desired secondary sex characteristics (Dickey & Steiner, 1990). Males treated with feminizing hormones show breast enlargement, increased fat deposits, and decreased muscle mass, as well as decreased facial and body hair. Their capacity to have erections and to ejaculate diminishes. Treatment of women with testosterone leads to an increase in muscle bulk and facial hair, deepening of the voice, enlargement of the clitoris, and suppression of ovarian function.

Currently, there are more than 80 empirical studies and reviews reporting outcome data on gender reassignment surgery and, while methodological concerns are evident, these procedures have resulted in satisfactory outcomes in approximately 90 percent of patients (Carroll, 2007). More specifically, patients usually experience satisfaction with interpersonal functioning and general psychological health but have reported negative effects on cosmetic results and sexual functioning. One study conducted by Lawrence (2003) examined factors associated with satisfaction and regret following sex-reassignment surgery in 232 male-to-female patients where the surgeon and his surgical technique are the same across all participants. One year after the operation, patients were asked to complete a questionnaire evaluating their attitudes and experiences. Most patients were very satisfied, claiming that it improved their quality of life. Only a few patients experienced regret, and that was only on an occasional basis. Dissatisfaction was usually associated with unsatisfactory physical or functional results of the surgery. Yet, psychological issues can still occur and, as such, most clinics now offer psychotherapy and counselling both before and after surgery for their transsexual clients. Clients who receive such counselling appear to do better than clients who do not receive assistance with the transition from one gender to another (Green & Fleming, 1990).

4 BEFORE MOVING ON

Consider just one of the unique challenges that a person with GID may experience. Although this individual's experience of maleness or femaleness is in his or her head and part of a constant inner reality, society sees only the physical body of this person and treats him or her accordingly. The larger society is only acting on what is observable without any regard for that person's inner experience. Indeed, the person with GID considers this treatment unwanted, ignorant, and offensive as it is not part of his or her reality. What do you think would be easier—to change the inner experience of the person with GID, to change the physical appearance of the person with GID, or to change society's perception?

The Paraphilias

Case Notes

Shortly after his fiftieth birthday, Joseph Fredericks was sent to prison for life for the murder of an 11-year-old boy. Fredericks had kidnapped the boy from a shopping mall in Brampton, Ontario, and then repeatedly raped him before stabbing him to death.

Fredericks's history revealed that in his second year at school, he had been assessed by a school psychologist who concluded that his intelligence was extremely low. Fredericks was taken from his poverty-stricken parents and placed in an institution for the retarded (as they were then called), where he knew no one and lost all contact with the parents he loved. Many years later, it was discovered that Fredericks's intelligence was normal.

Fredericks was introduced to sexual activities by older residents of the institution. Frightened at first, he soon sought out other boys for sex. There was little else to do in the institution and sex became his only pleasure.

At age 17, Fredericks was considered too old for the institution and sent out into the world with some money in his pocket but no idea what to do with it. He did not know how to find a room or a job. Because he was assumed to be incapable of learning, he had not been taught any job skills. He went on welfare until he found casual work. Since he had no friends or relatives that he knew of, Fredericks soon began to seek out the company of young boys, the only people he had ever learned to relate to. He was arrested for sexual molestation soon after leaving the institution and repeated this behaviour over the next 30 years. In 1985, he was sent to Kingston Penitentiary for five years, but was released after serving two-thirds of his sentence because he was considered to pose no great risk to the community.

Evidently, this conclusion was disastrously mistaken, for within a few weeks he had murdered the little boy.

DSM-IV-TR describes unusual sexual interests as **paraphilias**, which means "beyond the usual" (*para*) form of love (*philia*). According to the diagnostic manual, paraphilias are characterized by "recurrent, intense, sexually arousing fantasies, sexual urges, or behaviours" (APA, 2000, p. 566) concerning the particular focus of the paraphiliac's desire (Tables 13.5–13.12). In practice, however, people have usually been diagnosed as having a paraphilia only if they are considered to actually prefer the eccentric sexual behaviour over more normative sexual behaviours. This is because prior versions of the diagnostic manual appeared to require the presence of this preference or, at least, were interpreted that way by diagnosticians. The changes introduced in DSM-IV (APA, 1994) and retained in DSM-IV-TR (APA, 2000) to include actual sexual behaviours are an improvement and may lead to changes in diagnostic practices more consistent with the range of behaviours dealt with by clinicians. To date, however, clinicians have treated numerous sexual aberrations despite the fact that many of these clients (for example, most rapists and many child molesters) did not meet DSM diagnostic criteria. Clinicians prefer to deal with harmful behaviours whether or not these are driven by abnormal preferences.

The DSM-5 Work Group suggests significant changes to the conceptualization and terminology of the paraphilias, as well as some modifications to the specific diagnoses. The first significant change is to create a distinction between paraphilias and paraphilic disorders; this proposal would distinguish between normative and non-normative sexual behaviours, such that paraphilias would no longer be viewed as psychiatric disorders. According to this perspective, if a clinician ascertained the presence of a paraphilia, it would not necessarily require psychiatric diagnosis or intervention. Only in the case that this paraphilia caused distress to the individual experiencing it or harm to others would it then be diagnosed as a paraphilic disorder. Second, the criterion for the paraphilic disorders that involves nonconsenting persons is more specific in terms of the number of nonconsenting persons involved, and this number varies depending on the paraphilic disorder. This information, as well as any changes to the specific diagnoses, is detailed below. Note that all disorders specify a period of at least six months' duration and need to be manifested by fantasies, urges, or behaviours in order for the diagnosis to be made.

PARAPHILIC DISORDERS THAT INVOLVE CONSENTING ADULTS

FETISHISM The DSM-IV-TR describes **fetishism** as sexual behaviours in which the presence of non-living objects elicits sexual arousal and is usually required or strongly preferred for sexual excitement. Most researchers and clinicians also include an excessive attraction to a particular body part (e.g., feet, breasts) as a type of fetishism called *partialism*. The proposed DSM-5 diagnosis of fetishistic disorder includes both of these elements (Kafka, 2010a).

TABLE 13.5 DSM IV TR DIAGNOSTIC CRITERIA FOR FETISHISM

A. Over a period of at least 6 months, recurrent, intense sexually arousing fantasies, sexual urges, or behaviors involving the use of nonliving objects (e.g., female undergarments).

B. The fantasies, sexual urges, or behaviors cause clinically significant distress or impairment in social, occupational, or other important areas of functioning.

C. The fetish objects are not limited to articles of female clothing used in cross-dressing (as in Transvestic Fetishism) or devices designed for the purpose of tactile genital stimulation (e.g., a vibrator).

Source: Reprinted with permission from the *Diagnostic and Statistical Manual of Mental Disorders, Fourth Edition, Text Revision.* (Copyright © 2000). American Psychiatric Association.

Since it is mostly men who appear at clinics for treatment of fetishisms, it is often presumed that these fixations are primarily found in males, although there is no clear evidence that this is so. Of the fetishistic objects that have been reported in the literature, women's underwear or women's shoes appear to be among the most common, but there are reports of fetishisms for leather, rubber, plastic, babies' diapers, furs, and purses. Indeed, almost any object, or even behaviour, can become a fetish. For example, apotemnophilia is the disturbing fetish for amputation and genital mutilation. One case was even documented where a man cut off his own penis due to a genital mutilation fetish (Lowenstein, 2002).

The fetishist typically likes to smell or rub the object against his or her body or, in some cases, wear the article or have his partner wear it. When the articles worn by the fetishist are clothes of the opposite sex, it should be called *transvestic fetishism*, which we will describe in more detail in a moment. Some fetishists are driven to steal their desired objects. It is often this theft rather than their actual sexual behaviour that gets them into trouble with the law.

Very little is known about the psychological adjustment of fetishists, but many of those who enter treatment appear in all other aspects to be quite normal. A fetishist who accepts his own feelings, odd though they may seem to others, and who has found ways of meeting his desires in ways that do not harm others and do not interfere with his social functioning, does not seem to pose a problem. And indeed, since he would not meet the criterion of distress, he would not be diagnosed by DSM-IV-TR standards as having a disorder.

We know very little about the origin of fetishes, although many fetishists report that their unusual sexual attraction began in childhood. Massie and Szajnberg (1997), for example, reported a case study of a man who recalled having sexual fetishes at age 5 or 6, and Gosselin

Transvestic fetishists like this man are sexually aroused by cross-dressing.

and Wilson (1980) reported that, in their sample, sexual fetishes developed between ages 4 and 10.

In considering possible etiological mechanisms, early hypotheses were based on the psychoanalytic perspective but, unfortunately, it is not clear how such theories can be empirically tested (Lowenstein, 2002). More recently, classical conditioning and social learning perspectives were advanced, highlighting the importance of early childhood events and social interaction. However, as Baron and Byrne (1977) pointed out, if it was simply fortuitous associations between sexual arousal and some object, then there should be many fetishists who are attracted to pillows or ceilings since sexual arousal occurs very frequently at bedtime or upon waking. There are, however, no reports in the literature of such fetishisms. Finally, a number of authors have considered biological factors and their association with fetishism, with most focusing on temporal lobe abnormalities. El-Badri and Robertshaw (1998), for example, conducted a study in which they found that temporal lobe epilepsy or a disturbance in the temporal area was associated with fetishism.

TRANSVESTIC FETISHISM A person who cross-dresses—wears the clothing associated with the opposite sex—to produce or enhance sexual excitement is said to be a **transvestite** (or to have a transvestic fetish) in the DSM-IV-TR and the proposed DSM-5 (Blanchard, 2010b). This disorder has only been described in men (APA, 2000), and previous studies have never identified females reporting sexual arousal from cross-dressing. Evidence from the first population-based study (Långström & Zucker, 2005) of 2450 randomly selected men and women indicated that 2.8 percent of men and only 0.4 percent of women reported episodes of transvestic fetishism, suggesting that this is primarily a male sexual disorder.

TABLE 13.6 DSM-IV-TR DIAGNOSTIC CRITERIA FOR TRANSVESTIC FETISHISM

A. Over a period of at least 6 months, in a heterosexual male, recurrent, intense sexually arousing fantasies, sexual urges, or behaviors involving cross-dressing.
B. The fantasies, sexual urges, or behaviors cause clinically significant distress or impairment in social, occupational, or other important areas of functioning.

Source: Reprinted with permission from the *Diagnostic and Statistical Manual of Mental Disorders, Fourth Edition, Text Revision.* (Copyright © 2000). American Psychiatric Association.

People cross-dress for various reasons. Performers who earn their living impersonating people of the opposite sex are not transvestites unless they are sexually excited by their work, which few seem to be. Men who wear women's clothing to attract other men are better understood as homosexuals who adopt a particular style to make themselves appealing (called "drag queens" in the argot of the street). Most transvestites, on the other hand, are clearly heterosexual. Docter and Prince (1997) conducted a study of 1032 male transvestites and found that 87 percent identified themselves as heterosexual, 83 percent were married or had married at some point during the survey, and 69 percent had fathered children. Similarly, Långström & Zucker (2005), in their large sample, indicated that no man reported a primary same-sex sexual orientation.

In general, most transvestites state that cross-dressing allows them to express themselves, although significant proportions of these men seek therapy or counselling to help them with the effects of cross-dressing—for example, anxiety and depression (Docter & Prince, 1997), which, it should be noted, may not result from transvestism directly but from being social outcasts.

SADISM AND MASOCHISM **Sexual sadism** (or sexual sadism disorder in the DSM-5; Krueger, 2010b) describes a sexual preference toward inflicting pain or humiliation on others and can be considered either a sexual variant (if it involves co-operative, willing partners) or a sexual offence (if it involves unwilling partners). **Sexual masochism** (or sexual masochism disorder; Krueger, 2010a), on the other hand, describes individuals who enjoy experiencing pain or humiliation from another individual. Sexual masochism can range from harmless behaviour, such as being restrained, to potentially dangerous activity, such as **hypoxyphilia** (also known as **autoerotic asphyxia** or **asphyxiophilia**). This particular behaviour involves the deliberate induction of unconsciousness by oxygen deprivation, chest compression, strangulation, enclosing the head in a plastic bag, or various other techniques. Oxygen deprivation is usually self-induced and follows a ritualistic pattern, terminating just prior to losing consciousness. Unfortunately, when miscalculations occur, they sometimes result in death.

TABLE 13.7 DSM-IV-TR DIAGNOSTIC CRITERIA FOR SEXUAL SADISM

A. Over a period of at least 6 months, recurrent, intense sexually arousing fantasies, sexual urges, or behaviors involving acts (real, not simulated) in which the psychological or physical suffering (including humiliation) of the victim is sexually exciting to the person.
B. The person has acted on these sexual urges with a nonconsenting person, or the sexual urges or fantasies cause marked distress or interpersonal difficulty.

Source: Reprinted with permission from the *Diagnostic and Statistical Manual of Mental Disorders, Fourth Edition, Text Revision.* (Copyright © 2000). American Psychiatric Association.

Jocelyn: Exploring Sadism and Masochism

Watch this Speaking Out video at www.mysearchlab.com

More about Jocelyn

Watch this Speaking Out video at www.mysearchlab.com

In North American nosology, sexual sadism and masochism are separate diagnostic entities (Berner, Berger, & Hill, 2003; Kingston & Yates, 2008), whereas the nomenclature used in the rest of the world (i.e., ICD-10; WHO, 1992) advocates a dimensional approach to classification, combining both submissive (masochism) and dominant (sadism) elements within the same classification. As evidenced by these two nosological systems, there is some dissension as to whether these disorders are, in fact, mutually exclusive. In other words, some researchers suggest that sadistic and masochistic partners routinely switch roles (Reinisch & Beasley, 1990), whereas others (e.g., Kingston & Yates, 2008) report that individuals typically adopt one specific role.

In addition to the characteristics of pain and humiliation, several other features have been associated with sadism and masochism, such as fantasy and ritualization (Santtila, Sandnabba, Alison, & Nordling, 2002). Sadistic and masochistic fantasies are common and, in a study conducted at the University of New Brunswick, Renaud and Byers (1999) indicated that 65 percent of students reported fantasies of being tied up, while 62 percent had fantasies of tying up someone else. Participants in sadomasochistic behaviour also often engage in elaborate rituals and use a variety of equipment (e.g., handcuffs, masks). Ritualistic patterns of sexual behaviour involve the assignment of roles to partners and require them to engage in specific sequences of behaviours. Among the variety of role plays enacted, the "master and slave" game, wherein the sadist leads the masochist around by a leash and requires him or her to perform degrading activities, seems to be the most commonly performed (Sandnabba, Santtila, Alison, & Nordling, 2002). For most, sadistic elements are ritualized and symbolic rather than actual painful experiences, and extreme forms of pain and torture are rare. However, some sadists find ritualized sadism with a willing partner to be unsatisfying and seek out nonconsenting partners, thus satisfying the definition of a sexual offence. These sadists will be considered in more detail in the later section dealing with rape.

TABLE 13.8 DSM-IV-TR DIAGNOSTIC CRITERIA FOR SEXUAL MASOCHISM

A. Over a period of at least 6 months, recurrent, intense sexually arousing fantasies, sexual urges, or behaviors involving the act (real, not simulated) of being humiliated, beaten, bound, or otherwise made to suffer.
B. The fantasies, sexual urges, or behaviors cause clinically significant distress or impairment in social, occupational, or other important areas of functioning.

Source: Reprinted with permission from the *Diagnostic and Statistical Manual of Mental Disorders, Fourth Edition, Text Revision.* (Copyright © 2000). American Psychiatric Association.

The causes of sadism and masochism are unclear, although several theories have been advanced, including psychodynamic, behavioural, social learning, and physiological perspectives. While some have highlighted the importance of early negative childhood experiences (Blum, 1991), others have suggested that this conclusion is premature (Sandnabba et al., 2002) and needs further investigation. Other evidence has pointed to biological mechanisms and highlights the release of endorphins (which produce feelings of euphoria) in the brain in response to pain. While this area undoubtedly requires further research, it is important to note that many sadists and masochists are generally well-adjusted individuals with otherwise conventional lifestyles.

UNUSUAL SEXUAL VARIANTS New Zealand–born psychologist John Money (1984) claims that there are many more paraphilias than are listed in the diagnostic manual. He suggests that there are at least 30 or more different types, although DSM-IV-TR has a category that would accommodate these, called "paraphilias not otherwise specified." Sexual satisfaction derived from receiving enemas (klismaphilia), as well as urination (urophilia) or defecation (coprophilia), occurs frequently enough that pornographers cater to such interests. Some less frequent paraphilias, however, involve activities that break the law, such as sex with corpses (necrophilia) or with animals (zoophilia or bestiality), or that take the form of obscene telephone calls (scatologia). All of these unusual sexual variants, although occasionally described in the literature, are far too infrequently seen at clinics to permit adequate descriptive research.

PARAPHILIC DISORDERS THAT INVOLVE NONCONSENTING PERSONS

The DSM-IV-TR lists four specific paraphilias involving sexual desires that, if enacted, constitute a criminal offence. **Exhibitionism** (exhibitionistic disorder in the DSM-5) involves exposure of the genitals to an unsuspecting stranger, **voyeurism** (voyeuristic disorder) entails secretly

TABLE 13.9 DSM-IV-TR DIAGNOSTIC CRITERIA FOR EXHIBITIONISM

A. Over a period of at least 6 months, recurrent, intense sexually arousing fantasies, sexual urges, or behaviors involving the exposure of one's genitals to an unsuspecting stranger.
B. The person has acted on these sexual urges, or the sexual urges or fantasies cause marked distress or interpersonal difficulty.

Source: Reprinted with permission from the *Diagnostic and Statistical Manual of Mental Disorders, Fourth Edition, Text Revision.* (Copyright © 2000). American Psychiatric Association.

looking at naked people, and **frotteurism** (frotteuristic disorder) is touching or rubbing against a nonconsenting person for the purpose of sexual pleasure. **Pedophilia** (pedohebephilic disorder) describes recurrent fantasies or behaviours involving sexual activity with prepubescent children, and paraphilic coercive disorder (new in the DSM-5) involves sexual arousal from sexual coercion.

EXHIBITIONISM Exhibitionism is the most frequently occurring sexual offence in Western countries. According to one survey, 33 percent of university women have been the victims of an exhibitionist (Cox, 1988). Yet Byers and colleagues (1997) found that only 6 percent of arrested sex offenders in New Brunswick were exhibitionists. Abel and colleagues (1987) found that exhibitionists committed in excess of 70 000 acts of exposure, for an average of 514 acts per offender. Furthermore, exhibitionists have the highest rate of reoffending, with up to 57 percent being reported again within four years of being originally convicted (Marshall, Eccles, & Barbaree, 1991). Freund (1990) found that many exhibitionists also peep into windows to watch women undressing or having sex (voyeurism), and as many as 12 percent had also committed rape. Dr. Philip Firestone and his research group at the University of Ottawa (Firestone, Kingston, Wexler, & Bradford, 2006; Rabinowitz Greenberg, Firestone, Bradford, & Greenberg, 2002) have investigated the characteristics of various types of sexual offenders, including exhibitionists. They found that a substantial number of exhibitionists go on to commit more serious "hands-on" sexual offences and that such individuals are at greater risk for committing another offence when compared to other types of sexual offenders. In addition, standardized psychological tests have indicated that these men score in the lowest fifth percentile of general sexual functioning and demonstrate significant levels of deviant sexual arousal, as indicated by phallometric assessments. The DSM-5 specifies exhibitionists according to preferred age of victim: under the age of 15, age 15 and over, or both (Långström, 2010).

5 BEFORE MOVING ON

How many people do you know who have been the victim of exhibitionism, for example? How common do you think this is? For females? For males? What reaction is expected from the victims when the exhibitionist "flashes" that person? What is the best way to respond to this kind of situation?

TABLE 13.10 DSM-IV-TR DIAGNOSTIC CRITERIA FOR VOYEURISM

A. Over a period of at least 6 months, recurrent, intense sexually arousing fantasies, sexual urges, or behaviors involving the act of observing an unsuspecting person who is naked, in the process of disrobing, or engaging in sexual activity.
B. The person has acted on these sexual urges, or the sexual urges or fantasies cause marked distress or interpersonal difficulty.

Source: Reprinted with permission from the *Diagnostic and Statistical Manual of Mental Disorders, Fourth Edition, Text Revision.* (Copyright © 2000). American Psychiatric Association.

VOYEURISM Voyeurs or "Peeping Toms" are individuals who experience recurrent and intense sexually arousing urges/fantasies or behaviours involving the observation of unsuspecting individuals who are naked, disrobing, or engaged in sexual activity (APA, 2000; Långström, 2010). An essential feature of this disorder is that the person of interest must be unaware that he or she is being watched. Usually, voyeurs do not seek sexual relations with the person being watched and will often masturbate while engaged in the voyeuristic activity or later in response to the memory of what the person has witnessed.

The available research on voyeurs is quite limited. Most research has identified that voyeuristic activity occurs prior to age 15 (Abel & Rouleau, 1990; APA, 2000). Moreover, while most voyeurs are not dangerous, some do commit "hands-on" sexual offences and many present with comorbid paraphilias. As examples, Abel and Rouleau (1990) found that 37 percent of their sample of voyeurs (n =62) had been involved in sexual assault and more than half in child molestation, whereas Freund (1990; n = 94) found that 19 percent had engaged in sexual assault.

FROTTEURISM Almost all detected frotteurs are male. Frotteurism (or *frottage*—from the French *frotter*, "to rub"), according to the DSM-IV-TR and proposed DSM-5, refers to touching or rubbing up against a noncompliant person so that the frotteur can become sexually aroused and, in many cases, reach orgasm. The DSM-5 specifies that three or more nonconsenting persons must be affected in order for this diagnosis to be made (Långström, 2010).

TABLE 13.11 DSM-IV-TR DIAGNOSTIC CRITERIA FOR FROTTEURISM

A. Over a period of at least 6 months, recurrent, intense sexually arousing fantasies, sexual urges, or behaviors involving touching and rubbing against a nonconsenting person.
B. The person has acted on these sexual urges, or the sexual urges or fantasies cause marked distress or interpersonal difficulty.

Source: Reprinted with permission from the *Diagnostic and Statistical Manual of Mental Disorders, Fourth Edition, Text Revision.* (Copyright © 2000). American Psychiatric Association.

These offences typically occur in crowded places such as busy sidewalks, stores, or shopping malls, or on packed public transport. The impersonal nature of this type of sexual contact is considered by some authorities (Money, 1987) as essential to the pleasure of the frotteur. Abel and colleagues (1987) found that while some frotteurs keep the contact brief and furtive to make it appear accidental, others seem unconcerned about being detected and are more intrusive and aggressive, fondling the victim's genitals, buttocks, or breasts, or rubbing the penis vigorously against the victim until orgasm occurs. Observations like these encouraged Langevin (1983) to view frotteurism as a form of sexual aggression belonging to the same category as rape. He pointed out that both are aggressive forms of direct sexual touching without the consent of the victim.

PEDOPHILIA Pedophilia is a sexual disorder evident most often in males and describes individuals who exhibit a predominant sexual interest in, or preference toward, prepubescent children (Freund, 1981; Marshall, 1997). Specifically, this paraphilia is characteristic of recurrent, intense sexually arousing fantasies, sexual urges, or behaviours involving sexual activity with a prepubescent child (generally aged 13 years or younger). Additionally, either the individual must have acted on these sexual urges or the sexual urges/fantasies have caused marked distress or interpersonal difficulty. Lastly, the individual being assessed is at least 16 years old and at least 5 years older than the victim (APA, 2000). The DSM-5 specifies that one or more of the following symptoms must be present for a diagnosis of pedohebephilic disorder: the sexual urges cause the individual distress; the person has sought sexual stimulation on separate occasions from two or more children (if prepubescent) or from three or more children (if one or more are pubescent); and/or there is repeated use of and greater arousal from pornography depicting prepubescent or pubescent children than from pornography depicting physically mature persons (Blanchard, 2010a).

TABLE 13.12 DSM-IV-TR DIAGNOSTIC CRITERIA FOR PEDOPHILIA

A. Over a period of at least 6 months, recurrent, intense sexually arousing fantasies, sexual urges, or behaviors involving sexual activity with a prepubescent child or children (generally age 13 years or younger).
B. The person has acted on these sexual urges, or the sexual urges or fantasies cause marked distress or interpersonal difficulty.
C. The person is at least age 16 years and at least 5 years older than the child or children in Criterion A.

Note: Do not include an individual in late adolescence involved in an ongoing sexual relationship with a 12- or 13-year-old.

Source: Reprinted with permission from the *Diagnostic and Statistical Manual of Mental Disorders, Fourth Edition, Text Revision.* (Copyright © 2000). American Psychiatric Association.

It is important to note that the terms *pedophile* and *child molester* are often used interchangeably, which creates confusion among professionals who work with these individuals (Barbaree & Seto, 1997; Kingston, Firestone, Moulden, & Bradford, 2007). In the literature on sexual offending, a **child molester** is described as an individual who has engaged in a sexually motivated act against a prepubescent child, without an indication of preference, whereas a **pedophile** is described as an individual who has displayed a preference for sexual behaviour with a child (O'Donohue, Regev, & Hagstrom, 2000). This distinction is important, as not all child molesters are pedophiles, and some pedophiles may not have committed a sexual offence against a child (Konopasky & Konopasky, 2000).

The purpose of diagnosis is to categorize individuals into homogeneous subgroups, which is intended to promote accurate prognosis and effective treatment. However, several problems associated with the diagnosis of pedophilia have been identified, and researchers have questioned the value added by the use of such a label (Marshall, 1997; O'Donohue et al., 2000). For example, specific concerns have included the ambiguous nature of the terms *recurrent* and *intense* within the diagnostic criteria, which possibly contributes to reduced reliability. In fact, one study (Levenson, 2004) evaluated the reliability of various diagnoses in a sample of 295 adult incarcerated sexual offenders, and results indicated that the diagnosis of pedophilia was clearly below acceptable standards (kappa = .65). In addition to problems with reliability, the diagnosis of pedophilia has shown poor criterion-related validity and predictive validity. Kingston and colleagues (2007), for example, found that the construct of pedophilia, according to the DSM, was unrelated to other measures purported to assess the same paraphilia. Finally, in two studies (see Moulden, Firestone, Kingston, & Bradford, 2007, and Wilson, Abracen, Picheca, Malcolm, & Prinzo, 2003), a DSM diagnosis of pedophilia was unrelated to long-term recidivism.

Based on the problems indicated above, some (e.g., Marshall, 2007; Marshall, Marshall, Serran, & Fernandez, 2006) have questioned the value of providing a diagnosis of pedophilia. In fact, research conducted with child molesters irrespective of diagnosis has contributed more to our understanding of these individuals. While the diagnosis of pedophilia is limited, this is not to say that there are not individuals who demonstrate a preference toward children. Clearly, such information is important when implementing effective treatment and case management strategies.

RAPE The term *rape*, in its traditional sense, refers to forced penetration of an unwilling female's vagina by a male assailant's penis. Not only did this definition exclude the rape of males, it placed quite unnecessary emphasis on penile–vaginal intercourse. In terms of legal processes, this requirement of demonstrated forced vaginal intercourse in order to obtain a conviction of rape caused so many problems that Canadian legislators decided to change the law.

Rape, as a criminal offence, and various other sexual crimes were replaced in 1983 in Canadian law by three crimes of *sexual assault*. These three types of sexual assault are defined by varying levels of forcefulness by the offender and incur, upon conviction, increasing lengths of possible sentences. These improvements in the law served to make clear the intrusiveness of these crimes, and to diminish the legal relevance of whether penetration had occurred. This is quite reasonable, since the severity of psychological damage caused by an incident of sexual assault does not depend only on whether the vagina was penetrated, but on many other factors as well. Over and above sexual objectification, many offenders also make a point of degrading and humiliating their victims and may physically hurt them. The current Canadian laws better reflect the reality of sexual assault than did the earlier rape laws.

Because sexual assault laws have not been similarly modified in most jurisdictions of the United States, nor in other countries, most researchers continue to use the terms *rape* and *rapist*. For convenience, we will use these terms, but this should not be taken to imply support for the old laws. The current Canadian laws, we believe, are superior to any in the world in terms of encouraging victims to report and in having the courts focus on the appropriate issues.

Because of these changes, and because there are now restrictions on questioning the victim in court about previous sexual experiences, more victims are coming forward. Nevertheless, sexual assault remains a markedly underreported crime. Koss (1992), from a thorough analysis of survey data, concluded that the real rate of rape was 6 to 10 times as high as the officially recorded statistics. Relying on estimates such as these, Marshall and Barrett (1990) took the official Canadian figures for 1988 and multiplied them by four (a conservative strategy) to estimate the true frequency of rape in Canada. This calculation suggested that more than 75 000 women are raped in Canada every year, at the frightening rate of one every seven minutes. As Figure 13.3 reveals, strangers actually constitute a very small percentage of rapists.

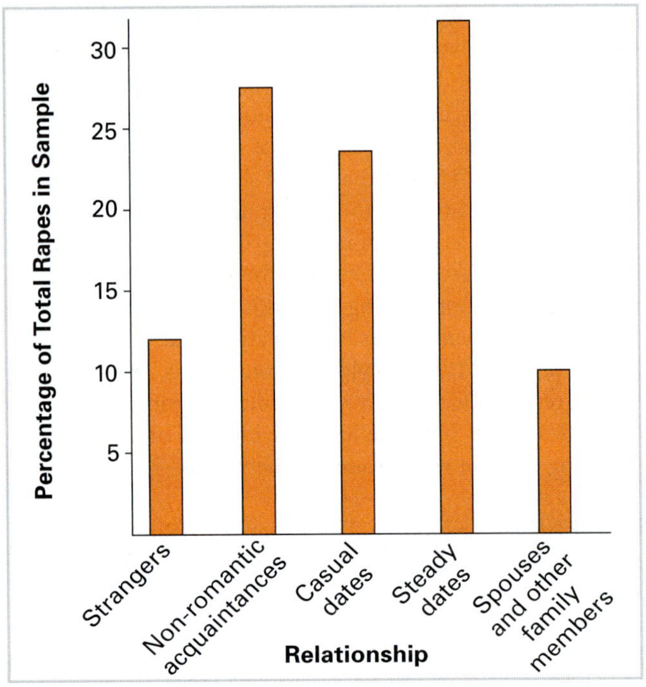

FIGURE 13.3 Relationships of Rapists to Their Victims

Source: Adapted from Koss (1988).

Note: These data are drawn from a large-scale survey of women attending colleges in the United States.

Until quite recently, forcible sex by a spouse was not covered by the sexual assault laws of most countries, and it is still excluded from these laws in many places. In addition to rape being an underreported crime, several studies have investigated the rate at which sexual offenders with adult victims reoffend after serving a period of incarceration (i.e., recidivism). Several studies have demonstrated that after 5 to 10 years in the community, more than 25 percent of rapists will commit another sexual assault, and that this rate is typically higher than what is found among child molesters (Firestone et al., 1998; Harris et al., 2003).

In contrast to pedophilia, there was no formal paraphilic diagnosis to identify men who prefer sexual activity with a nonconsenting partner in the DSM-IV-TR. As such, clinicians required to diagnose these individuals often used the diagnosis of paraphilia not otherwise specified and listed the descriptor of rape to explicate the type of mental disorder (Doren, 2002). Obviously, this omission was unfortunate, as it was not very useful in defining relevant treatment needs (Marshall, 2007). The DSM-5, however, proposes to add the diagnostic term *paraphilic coercive disorder* (Quinsey, 2010) to explicitly define rapists in order to address the issues with the lack of such a term in the DSM-IV-TR (Thornton, 2010).

In addition to paraphilia not otherwise specified, some evaluators have diagnosed rapists as sexual sadists. In an interesting analysis of a 27-year-old man serving a 7-year sentence for rape in a Canadian penitentiary, Barbaree (1990) found that the man showed greater sexual arousal to both rape and non-sexual assault on a woman than he did to consenting sex. This pattern is just what we would expect of a sadistic rapist, and the details of this man's offence revealed that it was particularly vicious. Furthermore, he described himself as having enjoyed hurting his victim.

Although cases like the one described by Barbaree (1990) are clear-cut examples of sexual sadism, the number of rapists who meet the criteria for a diagnosis of sadism is likely to be small (Kingston & Yates, 2008) and several problems with the diagnosis have been noted (Marshall, 2007).

For example, in a review of the literature, Marshall and Kennedy (2001) found substantial differences across studies in how they defined the diagnosis, such that some research centres defined sadists in terms of their desire to exercise control over their victims, while others considered violence to be the crucial feature, and yet others considered humiliation of the victim to be the primary factor. Unfortunately, these criteria did not exhaust the various definitions that Marshall and Kennedy identified. Even more problematic is the fact that all rapists display these features to some degree. Rape is, by definition, an exercise in control and involves some degree of violence. Also, Darke (1990) found that more than 60 percent of rapists reported deliberately humiliating their victims. In fact, in one study, Marshall, Kennedy, and Yates (2002) found that they could not distinguish rapists diagnosed as sadists from those who were said not to be sadists on any of the above features nor on any other feature. Furthermore, internationally renowned experts could not agree on the diagnosis of sexual sadism applied to 12 quite violent and brutal rapists (Marshall, Kennedy, Yates, & Serran, 2002).

The primary problem facing diagnosticians in deciding whether a rapist meets the criteria for sexual sadism is that the diagnosis must be based on the offender being sexually aroused by the idea of physically or psychologically hurting another person. Unless the offender tells the diagnostician that he is aroused by these characteristics (or any other feature), there is little alternative for the clinician except to guess what arouses the offender. Phallometric assessment could answer this question, but to date no one has demonstrated that phallometric testing can identify sadists, although some researchers have tried (Seto & Kuban, 1996). These problems with the diagnosis of sexual sadism are also true for other paraphilias (Marshall, 1997). This, in part, has led many clinicians and researchers working with sexual offenders to eschew diagnoses and to simply describe their clients in terms of their offending behaviours—for example, calling them child molesters rather than pedophiles, and dangerous or violent rapists rather than sadists.

While most rapists do not exhibit a sexual preference toward nonconsenting sexual activity, clearly some do. An interesting hypothesis has been proposed, which differentiates among three distinct sexual arousal patterns seen in rapists (Lalumière, Quinsey, Harris, Rice, & Trautrimas, 2003). The three profiles include **biastophilia**, a sexual preference toward nonconsenting and resisting but not necessarily physically suffering victims; *sadism*, a preference toward the suffering or humiliation of others; and *antisociality*, a marked sexual indifference to the interests and desires of others. Studies reporting on sexual preferences have indicated some support for the above categories (Lalumière et al., 2003).

6 BEFORE MOVING ON

Consider the following legal definition of rape in Canada that was in effect prior to 1983: forced heterosexual intercourse of a woman by a man outside of marriage. In addition, a victim's prior sexual experience could be considered as evidence of her consent. What implications does this definition have for married versus single women, for female versus male victims, and for women with prior sexual experience?

ETIOLOGY OF SEXUAL OFFENDING Over the years, many theorists have speculated about the origins of sexual offending. Behaviourists have tended to view such offending as being sexually motivated, and consequently they have offered explanations that focus on the misdirection of sexual desires. As we saw with fetishes, the most frequently cited of these explanations is the claim that accidental sexual experiences result in classical conditioning processes making deviant sexual practices attractive.

Conditioning Theories. McGuire, Carlisle, and Young (1965) were the first to propose that conditioning was the basis of acquired preferences motivating men to engage in unusual or offensive sexual behaviours. A young male, for example, might be caught in the act of masturbating by an attractive woman, and this association between high sexual arousal and a woman seeing his exposed penis might, according to this conditioning account, serve to entrench an attraction to (or preference for) exposing his penis to women. Similar accidental associations between sexual arousal and seeing younger children were said to be the conditioning bases of future child molestation, while masturbating to pornographic images of, or to thoughts of, sexually assaulting a woman were said to instill a preference for rape.

A similar theory, which assumes that sexual offenders are aroused by their deviant acts, was advanced by Kurt Freund, who began his outstanding career in his native Czechoslovakia but lived and worked in Toronto from the 1960s until he died in 1996. Freund outlined what he called a **courtship disorder theory** of sexual offending. Freund (1990) suggests, by analogy with animal courtship behaviour, that there are four phases in human sexual interactions: (1) looking for and appraising a potential partner, (2) posturing and displaying oneself to the partner, (3) tactile interaction with the partner, and (4) sexual intercourse. Freund's notion of courtship disorder suggests that fixation at any one of these stages produces sexual offending. Fixation at stage 1 would result in voyeurism; at stage 2 in exhibitionism; at stage 3 in frotteurism; and at stage 4 in rape.

These theories have some intuitive appeal as long as we accept that these offensive behaviours are sexually motivated. However, not everybody accepts that sexual crimes are driven exclusively by sexual desires. Indeed, Marshall and Eccles (1993), in their review of the relevant literature on animal and human sexual behaviour, found little supporting evidence for conditioning theories.

Feminist Theories. Feminist theories of sexual offending are quite diverse, but they do have common threads. Most feminists vigorously hold men to be personally, as well as collectively, responsible for sexual assault. Feminist theorists typically see sexual abuse as arising naturally out of the socio-cultural environment of our societies, which they see as essentially patriarchal (Brownmiller, 1975; Clark & Lewis, 1977). In this context, these theorists point to the differential ways in which parents and other influential people (e.g., peers, teachers) respond to boys and girls. According to this analysis, girls are encouraged to be submissive, co-operative, nurturing, and emotional, whereas boys are encouraged to be dominant and competitive and are discouraged from displaying any emotions (other than perhaps anger). Feminists see this difference as setting up women and children to be dominated by, and to be subservient to, adult males. Such a power differential provides few constraints on men's behaviour toward women and children that may facilitate sexual abuse.

Feminist theorists typically see rape as a non-sexual, or pseudo-sexual, offence. They emphasize instead offenders' apparent anger toward women, as seen in their efforts to humiliate the victims and to exercise power and control. Canadian psychologist Juliet Darke (1990) examined both what rapists said about their own motives and victims' perceptions. Both sources revealed that more than 60 percent of rapes involved some form of intentional humiliation of the victims. Consistent with feminist analyses, Seidman and colleagues (1994) found that rapists attending community clinics were angrier toward women than were matched, non-offending males.

Consistent with the idea that patriarchal structures encourage rape, Sanday (1981), in her examination of data from 156 tribal societies, found higher rates of rape in societies characterized by patriarchal systems. In these rape-prone societies, women were seen as the property of men and were excluded from all positions of power and influence. These societies, where violence was endemic, had far higher rates of sexual assault than did societies where both sexes were treated more equally. Rape was less common in societies in which women were respected and had an equal say in religious, political, and economic matters.

In terms of men's likelihood to rape, there is a fairly extensive body of literature indicating that approximately 30 percent (and even higher in some studies) of non-offending males acknowledge that they would rape a woman if they knew they could get away with it (Malamuth, 1986; Malamuth, Heavey, & Linz, 1993). These figures, taken at face value, are quite startling and appear to strongly support feminist claims. However, it is difficult to determine how to rate a response that amounts to a guess about what the respondent might do in a purely hypothetical situation.

Despite some problems with the evidence taken to support feminist views of sexual assault, the analyses offered by feminists have radically changed and expanded our understanding of these crimes. They have made it clear that these are primarily crimes committed by men (which needs explaining in any theory of sexual assault) and that there are clear socio-cultural bases to sexual offending. Most importantly, lobbying by feminists has changed the way we deal with sexual abuse as a society. The investigation and prosecution processes have been made far easier on victims than they were just a few years ago, and the offenders who are identified are more likely to be convicted and jailed than excused and let go, as so many were in the past.

Comprehensive Theories. Marshall and his colleagues (Marshall & Barbaree, 1990; Marshall, Hudson, & Hodkinson, 1993; Marshall & Marshall, 2000) have integrated a broad range of evidence to suggest that the childhoods of sexual offenders create a predisposition for aggression and a social inadequacy that makes them readily attracted to deviant sexual behaviours. These deviant acts, unlike prosocial sexual behaviours, require little social skill, have no built-in obligations to others, and do not require the offender to be concerned about the other person's needs or rights. Deviant sexual acts, then, might appeal to males who are lacking in social skills and who are self-centred. Also, sexual offences provide the opportunity to exercise power and control over others, and this is particularly satisfying to powerless males who lack self-confidence.

As we have seen, sexual offenders do typically have disrupted childhoods, and there is clear evidence that such experiences leave a child feeling unlovable, lacking in self-confidence, with poor social skills, and with a propensity for antisocial behaviour (Loeber, 1990). In this theory, however, it is not just poor parenting that produces sexual offending.

Socio-cultural factors, accidental opportunities, and transitory states all contribute to the complex array of influences that set the stage for sexual offending. Sanday's (1981) research revealed that those societies with high rates of sexual assaults were characterized by an acceptance of violence and by male dominance over women and children. Violence is all too frequently presented by the media in our society as an acceptable way to solve problems (Cantor, 2000), and men are still portrayed in many popular sitcoms as the dominant figures. A vulnerable young male would be expected to find these images of males (as dominant and violent) attractive, and he might subsequently look for ways to act as powerfully as the men in the stories. Sexually assaulting a woman or a child certainly puts the offender in a position of power over the victim and allows the offender to control what happens—and, of course, it produces the added satisfaction of sexual gratification.

Transitory states such as anger, depression, intoxication, and boredom have been found to immediately precede sexual offending (Pithers, Beal, Armstrong, & Petty, 1989), but Marshall's theory suggests that it is only vulnerable males who will respond in abusive ways to such circumstances. Even under these conditions, a vulnerable male cannot offend unless he has an opportunity, or creates one.

The implications of Marshall's account that have been examined have generally been confirmed. In addition, the general theory has led to more precise sub-theories, including the role of self-esteem (Marshall, Anderson, & Champagne, 1997), empathy (Marshall, Hudson, Jones, & Fernandez, 1995), and relationship functioning (Ward, Hudson, Marshall, & Siegert, 1995).

There are other comprehensive accounts of sexual offending (e.g., Finkelhor, 1984; Hall & Hirschman, 1991; see Ward, Polaschek, & Beech, 2006, for summaries) that have the same advantages as Marshall's theory—that is, they integrated a breadth of currently available knowledge, have generated clearly testable implications, and have contributed to the development of effective treatment programs. Most recently, Ward and Beech (2006) have developed an integrated theory of sexual offending, which possesses many of the strengths of other sexual offending theories (e.g., Marshall's theory) and accounts for some of their weaknesses. The theory is extremely broad and complex and accounts for the dynamic interaction among neuropsychological systems as well as ecological factors to explain both the onset and the maintenance of sexual offending. Further investigation is necessary to determine the utility of this theory to the understanding of sexual offenders and the development of effective treatment programs.

TREATMENT OF SEXUAL OFFENDERS Prior to the 1970s, most treatment programs for sexual offenders were derived from some form of psychoanalytic theory. However, the programs were not very effective (Furby, Weinrott, & Blackshaw, 1989), so clinicians turned to other models for direction.

Medical Interventions. The early medical treatment of sexual offenders involved surgical castration, whereas more recent methods consisted of either pharmacological treatments designed to reduce levels of testosterone or various antidepressant medications, particularly selective serotonin reuptake inhibitors (SSRIs). The aim of most of these treatment approaches was either to eliminate or to reduce sexual drive so that the person will be uninterested in sex or will easily be able to control the expression of his or her deviant interests.

The first, and most extensively employed, procedure used to achieve this goal of reduced sexual drive was physical castration. Physical castration refers to the surgical removal of the testicles, thereby essentially eliminating the body's production of testosterone, the sex steroid that primarily activates sexual drive. Some 3600 male sexual offenders were castrated in Germany during the period 1934–1977 (Heim & Hursch, 1979), and similar numbers were castrated in various other European countries as well as in North America. Efficacy studies, despite some methodological problems, have demonstrated that castration was associated with lower recidivism rates in offenders (Bradford, 2001). However, given the irreversible nature of this approach and the significant side effects, there is considerable controversy surrounding this procedure (it is not permitted in Canada except to save a person's life when it is endangered by disease).

Chemical castration (i.e., the reduction in testosterone resulting from the action of pharmacological treatment) has not drawn the same ethical criticisms, presumably because the changes it produces are reversible when the drug is withdrawn. The principal androgen related to sexual development and activity is testosterone, and its relationship to sexual aggression is well established (Bradford, 2000). The primary anti-androgens are Cyproterone Acetate (CPA) and Medroxyprogesterone Acetate (MPA). CPA can be used as a chemical castration agent or, at lower doses, to reduce deviant sexual fantasies (Rösler & Witztum, 2000). CPA and MPA have been shown to reduce sexual interest, fantasies, and behaviours in sexual offenders (Rösler & Witztum, 2000). Of note, the side effects of both medications are considerable and include diabetes mellitus, dyskinetic and feminization effects, and increased blood pressure. In terms of outcome, given that anti-androgens are typically administered in conjunction with psychological treatment, it is difficult to determine whether the drug, psychotherapy, or the synergistic effects of both have contributed positively to the decreased recidivism rates among treated offenders.

Alternatives to anti-androgens have been proposed, including SSRIs and luteinizing hormone-releasing hormone agonists (LHRH agonists). SSRIs, originally used to treat depression and obsessive-compulsive disorders, appear to give sexual offenders a sense of control over their deviant urges that they did not previously have, although most data have come from clinical case reports (e.g., Fedoroff, 1993). LHRH agonists have also demonstrated an ability to reduce or alleviate sexual fantasy, urges, and behaviours (Briken, Nika, & Berner, 2001; Rösler & Witztum, 1998) without causing significant side effects.

The evidence appears to demonstrate a valuable role for medications in the treatment of sexual offenders. However, as noted, these have typically been administered while the offender was involved in psychological treatment and, as we will see, psychological interventions have been effective with sexual offenders. It is therefore somewhat difficult at present to identify the contribution of medications to the effectiveness of treatment with these offenders.

Behaviour Therapy. In the late 1960s, behaviour therapists were just beginning to extend their treatment theories to sexual offenders. Bond and Evans (1967), for example, developed a simple approach to treatment based on the assumption that these offensive behaviours were driven by deviant sexual preferences. They thought that all that was necessary in treatment was to eliminate these deviant preferences (e.g., a sexual attraction to children, or to forced sex, or to exposing oneself) and the offending behaviour would disappear. Typically, sexual preferences in these early studies were modified by associating the deviant thoughts with a strongly aversive event, such as an electric shock to the calf muscles. Rice, Quinsey, and Harris (1991) examined this treatment program, offered at the Oak Ridge Mental Health Centre in Ontario during the 1970s and early 1980s, and found that it was ineffective.

Comprehensive Programs. As a result of the lack of benefits from these early behavioural interventions, more comprehensive approaches began to emerge based primarily on a cognitive-behavioural perspective. American psychiatrist Gene Abel and his colleagues (Abel, Blanchard, & Becker, 1978) were among the first to develop such programs, and similar programs have been developed in Canada (Lang, Pugh, & Langevin, 1988; Marshall, Earls, Segal, & Darke, 1983; Yates et al., 2000).

These comprehensive programs typically address sexual offenders' tendency to deny or minimize their offending. They work to improve self-esteem and social and relationship skills, to enhance empathy, and to alter offence-supportive attitudes and deviant sexual preferences. Various other offence-related problems are also addressed, such as substance abuse, anger, and an inability to handle stress. Sexual offenders are trained to identify factors that might increase their risk of reoffending, and they are taught ways to deal with these problems should they arise. In addition to the above, current programs (e.g., Marshall, Marshall, Serran, & Fernandez, 2006; Yates et al., 2000) emphasize the role of positive psychology in the treatment of sexual offenders, which takes into account the offenders' strengths and helps them to construct a meaningful and prosocial life.

Benefits of Treatment. To evaluate the effects of treatment, it is necessary to follow treated offenders for several years after their discharge from treatment or release from prison, and to compare their reoffence rates with a matched group of untreated offenders. The ideal treatment outcome design would require the random allocation of those who volunteered for treatment—to either treatment or no treatment (Quinsey, Harris, Rice, & Lalumière, 1993)—but unfortunately this ideal study cannot easily be implemented for a variety of ethical reasons. As such, treatment evaluators have adopted alternative strategies, such as incidental matching procedures, where treated participants are matched with untreated sexual offenders on demographic features and offence characteristics.

Two large-scale meta-analyses have evaluated the extent to which sexual offender treatment is associated with lowered recidivism rates. First, Hanson and colleagues (2002) reviewed the sexual offender treatment outcome literature and found 42 studies, with a total of 9316 participants. Results indicated that treatment was associated with reductions in both sexual and general recidivism (i.e., the percentage who reoffended). These beneficial effects were found to be greatest among those programs that employed the broad cognitive-behavioural approach described in the previous subsection. Furthermore, these benefits were evident whether the program was based in the community or in an institutional setting. Second, Lösel and Schmucker (2005) have provided the largest and most recent meta-analyses of sexual offender treatment outcome. Specifically, this review included published and unpublished studies that were reported in a variety of languages. The final review consisted of 80 comparisons derived from 69 studies (n = 22 181). With regard to sexual, violent, and criminal recidivism, the treatment group displayed reductions of 37, 44, and 31 percent, respectively, compared to the base rates of the control groups. As such, the results indicated a positive treatment effect for all types of recidivism.

TABLE 13.13 REOFFENCE RATES FROM CURRENT COGNITIVE-BEHAVIOURAL TREATMENT PROGRAMS

	Treated	Untreated
Sexual recidivism	9.9%	17.3%
General recidivism	32.3%	51.3%

Source: Adapted from Hanson, R. K., Gordon, A., Harris, A. J., Marques, J. K., Murphy, W., Quinsey, V. L., & Seto, M. (2002). "First report of the collaborative outcome data project on the effectiveness of psychological treatment for sex offenders," *Sexual Abuse: A Journal of Research and Treatment, 14*(2), 169–194. Reprinted by permission of Kluwer Academic/Plenum Publishers.

Table 13.13 summarizes the data generated by Hanson's analyses. Clearly, treatment can be effective, but this is not to say that all treatment programs reduce sexual offender recidivism. In Hanson and colleagues' study, those programs based on approaches other than cognitive-behavioural ones were ineffective, although Hanson did not evaluate any medically based treatments.

Two other ways to look at the benefits of treatment for sexual offenders is to consider the reduction in the number of innocent victims harmed by these offenders and the financial savings associated with treatment benefits. In a study of the effects of their community-based program, Marshall and Barbaree (1988) found that each recidivist sexually abused at least two further victims. Marshall and Barbaree's results indicated that 13 percent of the treated offenders reoffended, compared to 34 percent of the untreated offenders. This is a difference of 21 percent, which, given that the recidivists abused at least two victims each, means that for every 100 treated offenders more than 42 innocent people were saved from suffering. In addition, Marshall (1992) calculated the costs incurred by police investigations, the prosecution of an offender, and his imprisonment. He found that it costs taxpayers $200 000 to convict and imprison each sexual reoffender. Table 13.14 presents a calculation of the estimated financial benefits of treating sexual offenders by subtracting the costs of treating 100 offenders from the savings resulting from the reductions in recidivism produced by treatment. Obviously, treating sexual offenders can be effective and, when it is, fewer victims suffer and taxpayers are saved considerable money.

CANADIAN RESEARCH CENTRE

Dr. Elke Reissing, Human Sexuality Research Laboratory

Dr. Elke Reissing is an associate professor at the University of Ottawa and the assistant director of the School of Psychology. She is the director of the Human Sexuality Research Laboratory (HSRL) and supervisor for sex therapy at the Centre for Psychological Services and Research (CPSR).

Originally, Dr. Reissing came to Canada from Germany to complete one year of undergraduate studies at Concordia University in Montreal, but she stayed for her Ph.D. studies at McGill University and accepted a faculty position at the University of Ottawa. At McGill, she worked with Irv Binik and a close cohort of graduate students, which included Marta Meana, Sophie Bergeron, and Caroline Pukall—all groundbreakers in the study of sexuality who inspired her work with sexual pain disorders in general and vaginismus in particular.

Dr. Reissing joined the University of Ottawa for a pre-doctoral, clinical internship at the Centre for Psychological Services in 2001 and as faculty the following year. She developed the HSRL, which is home to clinical and experimental graduate students in sexuality and various research collaborators. Current research programs in the lab include two applied areas—vaginismus, and sexuality and aging—and two experimental/sexological research areas—uncommitted sexual relationships and bisexuality. Dr. Reissing also treats sexual pain disorders and other sexual dysfunctions. She has a small private practice but works with more clients through her supervision of sex therapy training at the CPSR. Services there are provided by senior Ph.D. students in clinical psychology who are supervised session-by-session by Dr. Reissing. Sex therapy is based on the scientist-practitioner model and, because the clinic is a training site, it is one of the few places that offer sex therapy at greatly reduced fees. Dr. Reissing has also served on the executive committee of the Canadian Sex Research Forum and on the editorial boards of journals covering first-rate research topics related to sexuality and psychology.

Dr. Reissing's main research interest lies in the examination of women who have such severe difficulties with vaginal penetration that they cannot experience intercourse, use tampons, or have a gynecological examination. This may be due to pain with attempted penetration or fear of possible pain. Difficulties may also be due to fear and/or disgust related to vaginal penetration. All women seem to share one aspect: a very tense pelvic floor that makes penetration attempts painful and ultimately impossible. In the past, the diagnosis of vaginismus focused solely on pelvic floor pathology, but increasingly, psychological factors are being taken into account. This is not to pathologize women but rather to understand the scope of the problem and the severity of their suffering, and to come up with more effective treatment solutions. Dr. Reissing's current projects focus on examining the necessary and sufficient elements of psychological interventions (e.g., components of sex therapy and cognitive-behavioural treatment) for problem-focused and successful—yet short-term—treatment of women with vaginismus. The goal is to combine these with physiological treatment approaches, in particular pelvic floor physiotherapy, in order to provide a multidisciplinary, multimodal treatment package for women with vaginismus.

TABLE 13.14 COST-BENEFIT ANALYSIS OF TREATING SEXUAL OFFENDERS

		Rate of Reoffence		
		Treated	**Untreated**	**Reduction in Reoffenders**
Prison program		24%	52%	28%
Reduction in number of victims per 100 offenders treated (i.e., 28 x 2 victims per reoffender)	=	56		
Cost per reoffender (to convict and imprison)	=	$200 000		
Cost to prison service to treat and supervise 100 offenders	=	$1 000 000		
Savings per 100 offenders treated:				
Savings (28 x $200 000)	=	$5 600 000		
Less costs	=	$1 000 000		
TOTAL SAVINGS	**=**	**$4 600 000**		

Source: Reoffence data are from Hanson and colleagues (2002) and cost-benefit analysis is derived from Marshall (1992). Adapted from Kluwer Academic Publishers, *Sexual Abuse: A Journal of Research and Treatment, 14*(2), 2002, 169–194, "The 2000 ATSA report on the effectiveness of treatment for sex offenders" by Hanson et al.

SUMMARY

- Masters and Johnson developed the sexual response cycle based on their research examining the physiological correlates of human sexual response.
- During the excitement stage, the genital tissues of both males and females swell as they fill with blood, causing penile erection and vaginal lubrication, among other changes.
- The plateau stage involves additional swelling of the penis, vaginal tissues, and other areas as the body gets ready for orgasm.
- During orgasm, both sexes experience rhythmic, muscular contractions of the pelvic and genital areas, and males ejaculate.
- Following orgasm, the body returns to its pre-aroused state during the resolution stage. Males experience a refractory period, although women have the capacity to be multiply orgasmic.
- Several sexual dysfunctions are listed in the DSM that can affect men and women in the following areas: desire, arousal, orgasm, and pain.
- Lifelong sexual dysfunctions have always been experienced by the individual, and acquired sexual dysfunctions are those that are of recent onset.
- If sexual dysfunctions are apparent in all sexual situations, they are categorized as generalized, whereas when the problems are apparent in only one situation, they are known as situational.
- Sensate focus is a form of desensitization applied to sexual fears and anxiety.
- Gender can differ on many dimensions, including the following: chromosomal gender, gonadal gender, prenatal hormonal gender, internal accessory organs, external genital appearance, assigned gender, gender identity, and gender role.
- There are several paraphilias that involve nonconsenting persons. Exhibitionism involves exposure of the genitals to an unsuspecting stranger, voyeurism entails secretly looking at naked people, and frotteurism is touching or rubbing against a nonconsenting person for the purpose of sexual pleasure.
- The DSM-IV-TR does not include a formal paraphilic diagnosis to identify men who prefer sexual activity with a nonconsenting partner.
- To diagnose these individuals, clinicians often used the diagnosis of paraphilia not otherwise specified and listed the descriptor of rape to explicate the type of mental disorder.
- The DSM-5, however, proposes to add the diagnostic term *paraphilic coercive disorder* to explicitly define rapists.

MySearchLab offers you extensive help with your writing and research projects and provides round-the-clock access to credible and reliable source material. Chapter quizzes and a full electronic version of the text are also provided. Answers to the Before Moving On feature are provided on the MySearchLab. Take a tour at www.mysearchlab.com.

KEY TERMS

egodystonic homosexuality (p. 327)
sexual response cycle (p. 328)
lifelong sexual dysfunction (p. 332)
acquired sexual dysfunction (p. 332)
generalized sexual dysfunctions (p. 332)
situational sexual dysfunctions (p. 332)
hypoactive sexual desire disorder (p. 333)
sexual aversion disorder (p. 333)
female sexual arousal disorder (p. 333)
male erectile disorder (p. 333)
female orgasmic disorder (p. 334)
anorgasmia (p. 334)
male orgasmic disorder (p. 334)
premature ejaculation (p. 334)
dyspareunia (p. 334)
vaginismus (p. 335)
hypersexuality (p. 335)
estrogen (p. 337)
testosterone (p. 337)
prolactin (p. 337)
performance anxiety (p. 337)
sensate focus (p. 338)
intracavernous treatment (p. 339)
gender identity (p. 341)
gender role (p. 341)
hermaphroditism (p. 341)
gender identity disorder (p. 341)

gender dysphoria (p. 341)
paraphilias (p. 345)
fetishism (p. 345)
transvestite (p. 346)
sexual sadism (p. 346)
sexual masochism (p. 346)
hypoxyphilia (p. 346)
autoerotic asphyxia (p. 346)
asphyxiophilia (p. 346)
exhibitionism (p. 347)
voyeurism (p. 347)
frotteurism (p. 348)
pedophilia (p. 348)
child molester (p. 349)
pedophile (p. 349)
biastophilia (p. 351)
courtship disorder theory (p. 351)

PATRICIA M. MINNES • MARJORY L. PHILLIPS

Chapter 14

Developmental Disorders

LEARNING OBJECTIVES

AFTER READING THIS CHAPTER, STUDENTS WILL BE ABLE TO:

1. Explain the challenges of assessing the abilities of individuals with developmental disabilities.
2. Identify ways that the impact of intellectual disabilities can be reduced or prevented.
3. Identify variables that need to be measured when evaluating community integration and inclusion.
4. Explain varying prevalence rates for autism spectrum disorders.
5. Explain the cognitive impairments that are viewed as the defining features of learning disorders.
6. Identify the similarities and differences between nonverbal learning disability and Asperger disorder.

Joe proudly points to his baseball cap bearing a picture of Niagara Falls. He eagerly announces that he took a boat ride to the bottom of the Falls, went to the top of a tower in an elevator with windows, and had his own motel room next to Jim and Mary's room. Joe's delight is contagious; one cannot help but smile as he talks about the trip organized to celebrate his fiftieth birthday.

At age 12, Joe was institutionalized when his parents could no longer manage his behaviour. His parents were older and lived in the country, a three-hour drive from the institution. Joe saw little of his family, and after a few years he lost contact altogether. He attended the institutional school and later worked in the workshop. A psychological assessment at age 37 found Joe to have a mild developmental handicap. He was able to read, spell, add, and subtract at a primary school level. Joe had fairly well developed verbal skills and good comprehension and could manage personal care with limited supervision. Joe's major problem was his temper. Whenever his routine was changed, Joe would start shouting, swearing, and threatening. When Joe became particularly upset, he would bang his head and scratch himself. After taking psychotropic and neuroleptic medication for many years to control these outbursts, Joe developed coordination and visual problems that were thought to be drug-related.

Joe's institution was scheduled to close in a few years, and his assessment indicated that he would be a good candidate for community living. So, after 25 years in the institution, he was moved to a new group home. He still worked in the institution's workshop, and he would hang around the institution and hide from group home staff when it was time to go home. He had outbursts of temper, and his shouting and screaming disturbed the neighbours. He would "borrow" other residents' things and become upset if they did not want to watch his television programs or listen to his favourite music. Joe would also bully a younger resident and would bother one of the female residents by standing close to her, stroking her arm, and staring at her.

Joe was enrolled in a program called Living with Others, through which he learned the importance of personal space and strategies to manage anger. He practised relaxation exercises and met regularly with a psychologist to talk about his fears and concerns. The psychologist found that change and unexpected events triggered feelings of loss of control related to Joe's long history of abandonment. Joe's outbursts improved to the point where he no longer required medication.

Since he was unhappy at the group home, Joe was considered for a new program called Homeshare, in which adults with developmental disabilities live with families in the community. On Joe's first weekend visit with Jim and Mary, he was anxious and became agitated on three occasions, but he was able to cool off in their large garden. After three more visits over the next two months, Joe asked if he could move in with Jim and Mary. Finding their house too quiet since their youngest son had left for university, Jim and Mary agreed. They were pleased with Joe's progress over the next few months and came to consider him a member of the family.

Historical Perspective

Throughout history, and particularly since the mid-nineteenth century, changing attitudes toward people with developmental disabilities have been reflected in policies and models of service delivery (Wolfensberger, 1975).

For centuries, such people were regarded as subhuman, a menace, or an object of dread. In ancient Greece, handicapped infants were left on mountaintops to die or were thrown from the cliffs. While this practice is abhorrent to modern sensibilities, some people argue that a similar view of disability is reflected in the common current practice of aborting a fetus shown at prenatal screening to have Down syndrome or spina bifida. Moreover, people with developmental disabilities may be given lower priority than others for medical and surgical intervention. Some people support euthanasia in cases of severe disability.

Between 1870 and 1890, attitudes shifted toward viewing people with disabilities as objects of pity, burdens of charity, and "holy innocents" (Wolfensberger, 1975). Asylums were built to protect them. However, in the later nineteenth and early twentieth century, genealogical studies by Goddard (1912) and others emphasized that mental retardation was inherited. People with disabilities came to be viewed as a threat to the moral and intellectual fibre of society; the growing *eugenics movement* called for sterilization, the restriction of marriages, and institutionalization to protect society from this threat.

The *medical model* dominated the first half of the twentieth century. Increasing numbers of individuals were viewed as needing medical care and were thus institutionalized. Psychologists played an important role in the diagnosis and classification process through intelligence testing. However, few institutions were able to provide more than custodial care for the growing numbers of residents. As institutions became more crowded, challenging behaviours became increasingly difficult for staff, and medication became the treatment of choice.

The late 1950s and early 1960s represented a time of major change in the field of developmental disabilities. It was the time of the civil rights movement in the United States, when freedom from oppression was a major theme. The publication of *Christmas in Purgatory* (Blatt & Kaplan, 1966), a photographic essay about the appalling living conditions of persons with developmental disabilities in institutions, led to litigation and public outcry. In 1968 the International League of Societies for the Mentally Handicapped adopted the *developmental model* to guide educational programming.

At the same time, interest in environmental influences on behaviour and the rise of behaviourism led to the application of operant conditioning techniques in educational programs. For the first time, people with mental retardation were viewed as having potential, and as capable of some learning and development regardless of the degree of disability.

New initiatives were stimulated by the interest shown by U.S. President John F. Kennedy, who had a sister with a developmental disability. Gradually, the medical model was replaced by the philosophy of *normalization,* and changing attitudes were reflected in policies promoting the use of least restrictive practices and environments.

From the 1960s to the present, deinstitutionalization, educational mainstreaming, and community-based service delivery have been major goals. People with disabilities have gained increasing visibility through media coverage of the Special Olympics and through television and films that increase public awareness. In the 1990s advocacy became an important theme, including self-advocacy through organizations such as People First and the National Association of Retarded Citizens in the United States (Shogren & Broussard, 2011). Since 2000, people with intellectual disabilities have become increasingly visible in the community, engaging in socially valued roles. Actors with intellectual disabilities have appeared in films and on television programs (see the Applied Clinical Case). It is important to note that positive and negative attitudes toward persons with intellectual disabilities have coexisted throughout history and continue today (Brown & Radford, 2007). While attitudes toward people with intellectual disabilities seem to be increasingly positive, negative attitudes continue to occur and reflect the need for ongoing education to reduce stigma.

A Note About Terminology

Developmental disorders may be manifested in a number of ways. There may be unusual physical features; deficits in language, motor ability, and other skills; and patterns of behaviour such as hyperactivity, aggressiveness, or **stereotypy** (the repetition of meaningless gestures or movements). The terminology associated with developmental disorders varies and can be confusing. In recent years, the term **intellectual disability** has been adopted in Canada, Europe, and Australia. The United States adopted the

APPLIED CLINICAL CASE

Actors with Disabilities

Chris Burke was one of the first people with Down syndrome to work as an actor. Burke first acted in the ABC movie *Desperate* and then played the main role of Corky in the television show *Life Goes On.* He also made guest appearances on *Touched by an Angel* as Taylor, an angel who has Down syndrome.

Burke is a frequent inspirational speaker and travels as a goodwill ambassador for the National Down Syndrome Society (NDSS). He is also editor-in-chief of the NDSS quarterly magazine, *Straight Talk.* Burke wrote his autobiography, *A Special Kind of Hero,* in 1991 as well as a chapter entitled "Believe in Yourself" in the 1999 book *Down Syndrome: A Promising Future, Together,* edited by T. J. Hassold & D. Patterson.

Source: http://en.wikipedia.org/wiki/Chris_Burke_(actor)

term *intellectual disability* relatively recently after widespread debate (Schalock, 2002; Smith, 2002; Turnbull, Turnbull, Warren, Eidelman, & Marchand, 2002; Walsh, 2002; Wolfensberger, 2002). The term *mental retardation* continues to be used for diagnostic purposes, at least by countries using the *Diagnostic and Statistical Manual of Mental Disorders* (DSM-IV-TR). However, this term will be replaced in the DSM-5 by *intellectual developmental disorder* under the umbrella category of neurodevelopmentaldisorders (APA, 2010). In Britain, the term *learning disability* has replaced the term *mental handicap*. This term can be particularly confusing, as the term *learning disability* when used in North America refers to normal intelligence with specific learning problems (e.g., in reading, writing, arithmetic), whereas in Britain it refers to significantly subaverage intellectual dysfunction. The term *developmental disability* is often used interchangeably with *intellectual disability*, but in the United States the term *developmental disability* has a broader definition in that individuals may have mental or physical impairments or a combination of these. For the purposes of this section, assume that the terms *intellectual disability*, *developmental disability*, and *mental retardation* are synonymous.

Intellectual Disability

PREVALENCE

The prevalence of intellectual disability is difficult to determine. Many studies report "ascertained" prevalence rates, which refer to the numbers of cases found in official records. However, these numbers are not accurate in that they do not include the total number of persons with developmental disabilities in the population but rather those who are known to service agencies. To determine true prevalence, the number of individuals born with developmental disabilities and mortality rates are required (Roeleveld, Zielhuis, & Gabreels, 1997). The data available are also problematic due to the varying definitions used and differences as a result of age, gender, and ethnicity (Leonard & Wen, 2002). The majority of statistics are based on U.S. samples, and statistics also vary depending on the classification system and the measures used. The World Health Organization (WHO) cites the true prevalence rate of mental retardation in industrialized countries as 3 percent. However, American researchers disagree on whether the figure should be 1 percent or 3 percent (Munro, 1986). The data from Canadian studies (Health and Welfare Canada, 1988; Ouellette-Kuntz et al., 2009) suggest a prevalence of at least 8 per 1000 altogether across all age groups, with approximately half (4 per 1000) falling within the mild range (IQ 50–70) and the other half falling within the severe range of mental retardation (IQ less than 50). A cross-sectional survey in the Maritime provinces (McQueen, Spence, Garner, Pereira, & Winsor, 1987) determined that the prevalence of major mental retardation in children aged 7 to 10 years was 3.65 per 1000. A recent study in Manitoba (Ouellette-Kuntz et al., 2009) reported estimates of 4.7 per 1000.

Diagnostic Issues

Although IQ as measured by standardized intelligence tests is the most basic criterion for mental retardation, there have been important changes in the definition over the years.

These comprise the level of IQ required and the inclusion of deficits in adaptive behaviour. In North America, the American Association on Mental Retardation (AAMR), founded in 1876 and now known as the American Association on Intellectual and Developmental Disabilities (AAIDD), has strongly influenced the definition and classification of mental retardation through the publication of classification manuals since 1921. More recently, the AAMR definition (Grossman, 1983) has been incorporated into the DSM criteria (see Table 14.1).

According to the 1983 classification manual (Grossman, 1983), mental retardation refers to significantly subaverage intellectual functioning with onset before age 18. However, it must also be accompanied by significant limitations in two or more areas of adaptive behaviour as expressed in conceptual, social, and practical adaptive skills, such as communication; self-care; academic, domestic, social, or community skills; leisure; and work. Traditionally, intellectual functioning has been determined on the basis of

TABLE 14.1 DSM-IV-TR DIAGNOSTIC CRITERIA FOR MENTAL RETARDATION

A. Significantly subaverage intellectual functioning: an IQ of approximately 70 or below on an individually administered IQ test (for infants, a clinical judgment of significantly subaverage intellectual functioning).

B. Concurrent deficits or impairments in present adaptive functioning (i.e., the person's effectiveness in meeting the standards expected for his or her age by his or her cultural group) in at least two of the following areas: communication, self-care, home living, social/interpersonal skills, use of community resources, self-direction, functional academic skills, work, leisure, health and safety.

C. The onset is before age 18 years.

Code based on degree of severity reflecting level of intellectual impairment:

317	**Mild Mental Retardation:**	IQ level 50–55 to approximately 70
318.0	**Moderate Mental Retardation:**	IQ level 35–40 to 50–55
318.1	**Severe Mental Retardation:**	IQ level 20–25 to 35–40
318.2	**Profound Mental Retardation:**	IQ level below 20 or 25

319 Mental Retardation, Severity Unspecified: when there is strong presumption of Mental Retardation but the person's intelligence is untestable by standard tests

Source: Reprinted with permission from the *Diagnostic and Statistical Manual of Mental Disorders, Fourth Edition, Text Revision.* (Copyright © 2000). American Psychiatric Association.

IQ scores (see Chapter 4). As shown in Figure 14.1, IQ scores are normally distributed, with a mean of 100 and a standard deviation of 15.

The choice of cut-off point, however, has been somewhat arbitrary and has changed several times over the years (Zigler & Hodapp, 1991). For example, for many years, IQ scores falling two standard deviations below the mean were considered to be within the mentally retarded range. Scores within this range were divided into four subcategories: mild (IQ 50–55 to 70), moderate (IQ 35–40 to 50), severe (IQ 20–25 to 35), and profound (IQ less than 20). In 1959 the fifth edition of the AAMR classification manual (Heber, 1959) raised the cut-off to one standard deviation below the mean (IQ less than 85) and created a fifth level called "borderline." These changes raised the prevalence of mental retardation from approximately 3 percent to 16 percent of the population, leading to increased demands on services for persons with disabilities. In 1973 the cut-off was returned to 70; in 1992 it was raised slightly to 75 to accommodate errors in measurement.

A number of other changes were introduced in the ninth edition (AAMR, 1992). While the age of onset, significantly subaverage intelligence, and limitations in adaptive functioning remain the same, the new classification approach is more positive, in that it addresses the person's strengths and capabilities. Furthermore, the criteria represent a broader, more ecological perspective; level of functioning is seen to represent not only the abilities of the individual but also the environmental support or services available to that person (Schalock et al., 1994). Thus, rather than diagnosing someone as having "moderate mental retardation," which gives the impression of a fixed state, the diagnosis might read, in part, "able to complete activities of daily living with limited support." In 2002 the AAMR introduced its most recent definition of mental retardation that highlights the multi-dimensional relationships among individual functioning, support, participation, health, and environment (Luckasson et al., 2002). The DSM has not as yet incorporated the updated approach used in the new AAMR manual, but the new system is being used increasingly by Canadian clinicians.

THE CHALLENGES OF ASSESSING INTELLIGENCE

Although classification systems such as those adopted by the DSM and AAMR place heavy emphasis on IQ, the use of IQ tests has been the subject of considerable controversy in recent years. First, such tests were not devised to take into account sensory, motor, and language deficits, which may contribute to poor performance. Second, when people have had limited experiences because of their disability or when they have lived in institutions, their performance may be limited because the test situation is unfamiliar and overwhelming. They may not understand what is expected of them or may not take the initiative to solve problems (Zigler, Hodapp, & Edison, 1990). For these reasons, IQ scores may not accurately reflect people's cognitive abilities. Moreover, it is questionable whether scores on the lower end of the scale are meaningful because the major intelligence tests such as the Wechsler Scales and early editions of the Stanford-Binet were not standardized on people with developmental disabilities with IQ scores lower than 70. However, a number of changes to the fifth edition of the Stanford-Binet Intelligence Scales (Roid, 2003) have made it a more useful instrument in evaluating older children and adults with developmental disorders. The Leiter International Intelligence Scale may be better suited to individuals with limited verbal abilities as it requires no spoken language from the person being tested or from the person administering the test.

MEASURING ADAPTIVE BEHAVIOUR

The assessment of adaptive behaviour has added greatly to the utility of psychological assessments. Measures used to assess adaptive behaviour include the Vineland Adaptive Behavior Scales Second Edition (Vineland II; Sparrow, Cicchetti, & Balla, 2006), the Adaptive Behavior Assessment System (2nd ed.; Harrison & Oakland, 2003),

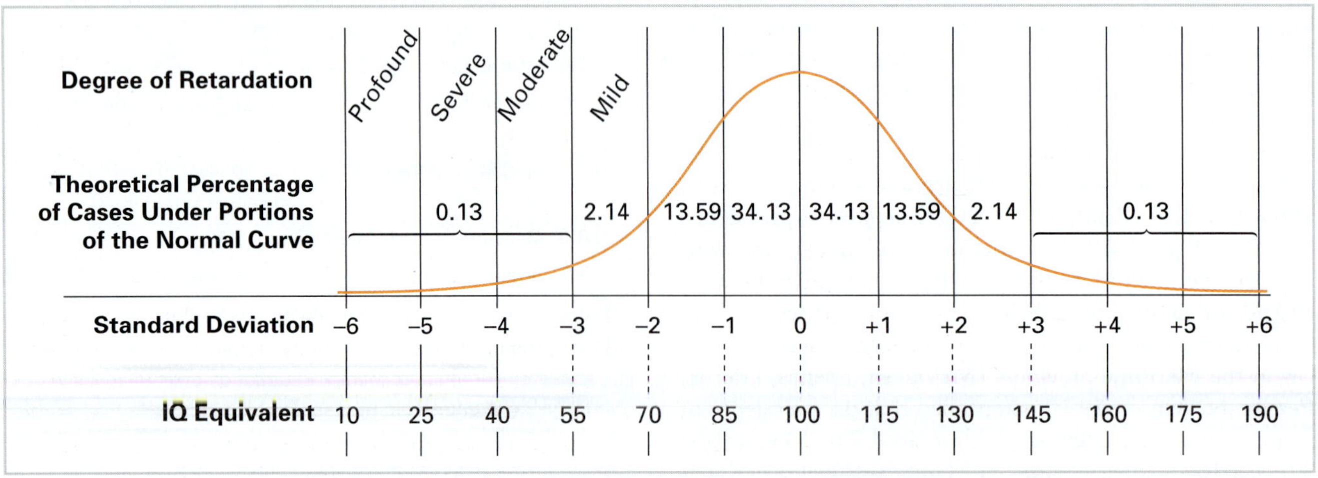

FIGURE 14.1 Distribution of IQ Scores

and the Scales of Independent Behavior–Revised (Bruininks, Woodcock, Weatherman, & Hill, 1996). Most scales may be completed during interviews with parents, teachers, or caregivers, but some versions can be filled in by these individuals as a checklist.

Adaptive behaviours are generally clustered under four domains: communication (i.e., expressive, receptive, and written language), daily living or personal living skills (e.g., eating, dressing, personal hygiene, domestic and community living skills), socialization or social interaction skills (e.g., interpersonal relationships, coping, leisure skills), and motor skills (e.g., movement, coordination, ability to manipulate objects using fingers and hands). Challenging behaviours are also identified.

The Vineland Scales have norms up to age 18. The Scales of Independent Behavior–Revised have norms up to age 80 and include a scale measuring the intensity of support needed in each domain. The Adaptive Behavior Assessment System (ABAS) has norms for adaptive behaviour and related skills from ages 5 to 89. The ABAS can be used to assess individuals with different disabilities, including Alzheimer's disease, attention deficit/hyperactivity disorder, autistic disorder, pervasive developmental disorders, and learning disabilities. Given the problems of assessing intelligence, the assessment of adaptive skills is particularly important.

PROPOSED CHANGES TO DIAGNOSTIC CRITERIA IN THE DSM-5

A number of the issues discussed above are being addressed in the changes proposed for the DSM-5 (APA, 2010). For example, one recommendation is that the term *mental retardation* be changed to *intellectual developmental disorder* to promote more consistent use internationally. In addition, less emphasis is placed on IQ level, more attention is paid to cultural issues, and more detail is provided regarding adaptive behaviour. To date, information regarding classification of severity levels is not available.

INTERVIEWING STRATEGIES

Gathering information from people with developmental disorders is an important aspect of any assessment. However, the reliability of the information gathered is critical (Finlay & Lyons, 2001). Unfortunately, it is often assumed that people with disabilities cannot give reliable information. On the other hand, some may err by assuming the opposite (Wyngaarden, 1981). When the person himself or herself is the best, or the only, source of information, it is up to the interviewer to adapt the questions to the person's level of functioning (Booth & Booth, 1996). One area of concern is acquiescence, or the tendency of individuals with developmental disorders to agree in interviews (Finlay & Lyons, 2002). Several factors can contribute to acquiescence, including social desirability, motivational and personality factors, as well as cognitive and linguistic limitations. However, the wording used in questions may also play an important role. For example, research has shown that acquiescence occurs more frequently in situations where the answers to questions are not known or when questions are vaguely worded. To improve the reliability of answers given in interviews, research has indicated that interviewers should use different types of questions, such as yes–no and open ended, while also giving the person an opportunity to answer "I don't know" (Finlay & Lyons, 2002). Alternative formats such as picture response cards also can be helpful. At the same time, it is important to systematically check for response bias (Sigelman et al., 1981).

1 BEFORE MOVING ON

Intelligence testing and standardized interviews have frequently been criticized as putting individuals with developmental disabilities at a disadvantage compared to their non-disabled peers. Given what you know about the abilities of people with different types of developmental disabilities, what precautions would you suggest that clinicians take when assessing such individuals?

Etiology

Developmental disorders have many causes. Some have clear organic causes; some relate to environmental factors; some reflect an interaction between genetics and environment. For example, damage due to an environmental toxin will have different effects on a child, depending on inherited factors such as temperament or birth weight. Conversely, genetically based disorders can have different outcomes depending on the availability of medical and educational services. It is not possible in this chapter to provide comprehensive coverage of all causes of developmental disorders. Therefore, a number of disorders have been selected to represent different types of damage occurring at different stages of development. A more detailed list of examples is outlined in Table 14.2.

GENETIC CAUSES

In recent years, the field of genetics has become very active, with increasing understanding of the processes of genetic transmission and the identification of genes associated with particular disorders. New developments in genetic screening techniques have important implications for the field of developmental disabilities, as increasing numbers of developmental disabilities are being found to be related to genetic abnormalities. For example, genetic links have now been identified in more than 70 percent of intellectual and developmental disabilities (Percy, Lewkis, & Brown, 2007). Approximately 45 percent of developmental disabilities associated with severe intellectual deficits are caused by chromosomal abnormalities and genetic mutations that are either inherited or spontaneous. Approximately 14 percent of developmental disabilities associated with mild intellectual deficits also have a genetic basis (Percy, Lewkis, & Brown, 2003).

With greater understanding of the genetic causes of developmental disabilities, researchers and clinicians hope to be able to develop improved diagnostic procedures.

TABLE 14.2 DISORDERS ASSOCIATED WITH INTELLECTUAL DISABILITY

Prenatal Causes	**Prenatal Causes**	**Postnatal Causes**
A. Chromosomal Abnormalities	**A. Intrauterine Disorders**	**A. Head or Brain Injuries**
1. Autosomes	1. Placental insufficiency	1. Cerebral concussion
Trisomy 21 (Down syndrome)	a. Placenta previa/hemorrhage	2. Cerebral contusion or laceration
Translocation 21 (Down syndrome)	b. Toxemia/eclampsia	3. Intracranial hemorrhage
Tuberous sclerosis	2. Abnormal labour/delivery	**B.Infections**
2. X-Linked	a. Prematurity	1. Encephalitis
Fragile X syndrome	b. Premature rupture of membranes	a. Herpes simplex
3. Other X chromosome disorders	c. Abnormal presentation, for example, breech	b. Measles
XO syndrome (Turner)	3. Obstetrical trauma	c. HIV
XYY syndrome	4. Multiple birth	2. Meningitis
XXY syndrome (Klinefelter)	**B. Neonatal Disorders**	a. Streptococcus pneumonia
B. Metabolic Disorders	1. Hypoxia	b. Influenza type B
1. Amino acid disorders	2. Intracranial hemorrhage	**C. Seizure Disorders**
Phenylketonuria (PKU)	3. Neonatal seizures	**D. Toxic-Metabolic Poisons**
2. Carbohydrate disorders	4. Respiratory disorders	1. Lead
Galactosemia	5. Infections	2. Mercury
3. Nucleic acid disorders	a. Meningitis	**E. Malnutrition**
Lesch-Nyhan disease	b. Encephalitis	**F. Environmental Deprivation**
C. Neural Tube Defects	c. Septicemia	1. Abuse
1. Anencephaly	6. Head trauma at birth	2. Neglect
2. Spina bifida		
D. Environmental Factors		
1. Intrauterine malnutrition		
a. Maternal malnutrition		
b. Placental insufficiency		
2. Drugs, toxins, teratogens		
a. Thalidomide		
b. Alcohol		
c. Cocaine		
d. Methylmercury		
e. Radiation		
3. Maternal diseases		
a. Diabetes mellitus		
b. Rubella		
c. Syphilis		
d. Toxoplasmosis		
e. Cytomegalovirus		
f. Hypothyroidism		

Source: Adapted from American Association on Mental Retardation (1992).

However, such advances also raise complex ethical, legal, and social issues associated with new approaches to prevention and intervention (Percy et al., 2003). Research has highlighted behavioural and neurocognitive patterns as well as different developmental pathways for different genetically related disorders (Dykens, Hodapp, & Finucane, 2000). In addition, **behavioural phenotypes** (the pattern of social cognitive, and behavioural abnormalities) have been described for particular disabilities. Current research is now focused on neuropathological mechanisms related to specific behavioural characteristics and potential pharmaceutical treatments (Hagerman, River, & Hagerman, 2008).

AN OVERVIEW OF GENETICS Basically, the traits we inherit from our parents are carried by thousands of genes found in each of our cells. Genes are found in specific positions on chromosomes. Each human cell contains 23 pairs of chromosomes, each pair including one chromosome from each parent. Forty-four of these are matching and called autosomes. The additional two are called the sex chromosomes. Females have two X chromosomes; males have an X and a Y chromosome. An X chromosome is contributed during conception by the mother, and either an X or a Y may be contributed by the father (Patton, Payne, & Beirne-Smith, 1986).

Developmental disorders may be caused by single or multiple genes alone or in association with environmental factors. Single gene disorders are less common than disorders caused by multiple genes (Percy et al., 2007).

There are three types of inheritance: dominant, recessive, and sex-linked or X-linked. In dominant inheritance, if one parent of either sex has a defective gene, that gene "assumes 'control' over or masks its partner gene and therefore will operate whether an individual gene pair is similar or dissimilar" (Patton et al., 1986, p. 164). A child has a 50 percent chance of inheriting either the defective or the normal gene from the parent with the defective gene. Examples of dominant inheritance that may lead to intellectual disability are tuberous sclerosis and neurofibromatosis. In recessive inheritance, genes "in a sense 'recede' when paired with a dissimilar mate and therefore only are influential when matched with another recessive gene" carrying the same trait (Patton et al., 1986, p. 164). Therefore, both parents need to carry a defective gene for the disorder to occur. There is a 25 percent chance that two copies of the defective gene will be inherited and the child will be affected, a 50 percent chance that the child will be a carrier of the disorder (i.e., the child carries one defective gene but may not display signs of the disorder), and a 25 percent chance that the child will not be affected and not be a carrier (Percy et al., 2007). Disorders associated with recessive inheritance include phenylketonuria, Tay-Sachs disease, and galactosemia.

In X or sex-linked inheritance, the abnormal gene is carried on the X chromosome. In females, the gene is generally recessive and will operate only when it appears on both X chromosomes. Disorders transmitted in this way therefore primarily affect males, who have only one X chromosome; the Y chromosome is not able to dominate or override the trait. A male child has a 50 percent chance of being affected. There is a 50 percent chance that a female child will carry the defective gene, but the degree to which she is affected is relatively limited. X-linked disorders associated with intellectual disability include Fragile X syndrome (described later in this chapter) and Lesch-Nyhan syndrome.

Inherited disorders can be identified through a blood test. Genetic screening can also determine whether both parents (in the case of recessive disorders) or the mother (in the case of X-linked disorders) carries an abnormal gene and runs the risk of bearing a child with the disorder. For example, since Tay-Sachs disease is found largely among Jews of Eastern European descent, some Jewish couples will undergo testing before trying to conceive.

CHROMOSOMAL ABNORMALITIES Chromosomal disorders occur as a result of a structural alteration in the chromosome or due to a person having a greater or smaller number of chromosomes. Although chromosomal abnormalities are genetically related, they are not inherited and occur spontaneously at conception. The best-known chromosomal abnormality associated with intellectual disability is **Down syndrome**, first described by Langdon Down in 1866. In 1959 the genetic link was discovered by Jerome Lejeune and his colleagues. There are three types of Down syndrome. The most common is **trisomy 21**, which occurs in 95 percent of cases of Down syndrome. Whereas the normal human cell has 23 pairs of chromosomes, one chromosome in each pair provided by each parent, in Down syndrome there is an extra chromosome on pair 21. Thus, persons with Down syndrome have 47 rather than 46 chromosomes. Trisomy 21 occurs in approximately 1 in 700 live births, with a larger proportion occurring in older mothers. The incidence increases dramatically from approximately 1 in 350 for women between the ages of 35 and 39 to 1 in 100 after age 40 (Baroff, 1986). More recently, research has indicated that the risk of Down syndrome may increase when the father is over 40, regardless of the mother's age (Hook, Cross, & Regal, 1990; see Figure 14.2). Down syndrome is discussed in more detail later in this chapter.

Two other causes of Down syndrome are **translocation** and **mosaicism**. In the former, part of the twenty-first chromosome breaks off and attaches to another. This occurs in approximately 4 percent of cases. This type of anomaly is not associated with maternal age. In mosaicism, cell division occurs unevenly, so that some cells have 45 chromosomes

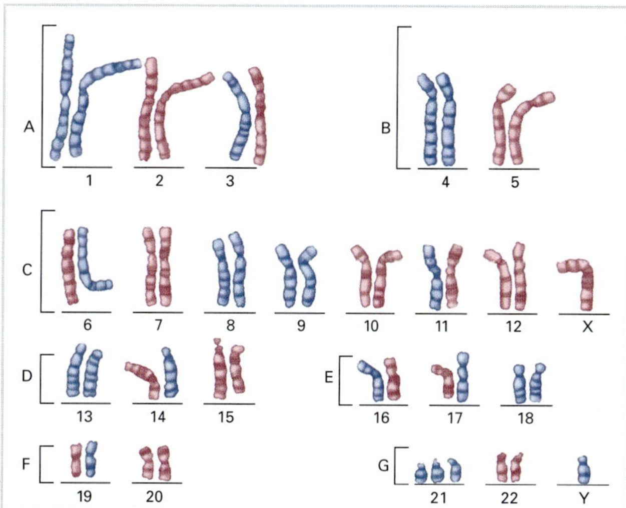

FIGURE 14.2 Chromosomes of a Person with Down Syndrome

Karyotype (a type of diagram developed from photomicrographs of chromosomes) of a person with the most common type of Down syndrome, showing the third chromosome at pair 21.

and some have 47. This type occurs in only 1 percent of cases. Whereas individuals with Down syndrome due to translocation have all the features found in trisomy 21, people with mosaic Down syndrome may have fewer physical characteristics, better speech, and higher intellectual functioning, depending on the number of cells affected.

PRENATAL SCREENING Prenatal screening for chromosomal and other abnormalities is possible through a number of methods. Maternal serum screening (MSS) is carried out through a blood test 15 to 20 weeks into the pregnancy. MSS detects alpha-fetoprotein (AFP) as well as two hormones produced by the placenta. The levels of these substances can help identify women at higher risk of having babies with chromosomal abnormalities like Down syndrome or neural tube defects like spina bifida (Wald et al., 1992).

The nuchal translucency (NT) test may also be carried out with women who are at risk of having a baby with Down syndrome (e.g., women over 35 years). The test is usually done between 10 and 14 weeks. The test involves measurement of the amount of fluid at the back of the fetus's neck through ultrasound. If increased levels of AFP following MSS or increased fluid levels following NT are detected, indicating greater risk of fetal abnormality, follow-up tests such as amniocentesis are usually recommended (Borruto, Comparetto, Acanfora, Bertini, & Rubaltelli, 2002).

Amniocentesis is a procedure conducted between the eleventh and eighteenth weeks of pregnancy. With the assistance of ultrasound, a needle is inserted into the amniotic sac via the pregnant woman's abdomen. A small amount of amniotic fluid is withdrawn, and cells contained in the fluid are then cultured in the lab. Studies of amniocentesis indicate diagnostic accuracy of up to 99.4 percent, with the estimated risk of complications such as infection or miscarriage being approximately 0.5 percent greater than in pregnancies without amniocentesis (Baroff, 1986).

A more recently developed test known as **chorionic villus sampling (CVS)** involves obtaining cells from the placenta. Minor complications such as cramping or vaginal bleeding occur more frequently following CVS than amniocentesis and the overall miscarriage rate is somewhat higher (2 to 5 percent) than after amniocentesis. However, figures for transcervical as opposed to transabdominal CVS are quite low at approximately 1 percent (Machalek, Brown, Birkan, Fung, & Percy, 2003). This test can be carried out earlier, between the tenth and twelfth weeks of pregnancy, but may be less accurate than amniocentesis. If a chromosomal abnormality is found, the parents may choose to terminate the pregnancy.

These techniques can also identify inherited genetic abnormalities. Prenatal screening techniques are advocated by those in favour of preventing developmental disabilities, but opposed by many others who advocate for the basic rights of people with disabilities. The use of microchip assays is a new screening approach currently being developed. Microchips containing information about different genetic disorders are used to detect disorders in DNA samples. The high cost of such technology and problems of storing large data sets have yet to be addressed (Green & Pass, 2005).

METABOLIC DISORDERS **Phenylketonuria (PKU)** is the best known of several rare metabolic disorders that can cause intellectual disability. PKU has been described as an "inborn error of metabolism." It is caused by an autosomal recessive gene occurring in approximately 1 in 10 000 to 15 000 live births in North America (Harris, 1995). As a result of a recessive gene passed on from each parent, a liver enzyme localized on chromosome 12 is inactive, causing an inability to process or metabolize the amino acid phenylalanine. This substance builds up in the brain to toxic levels, leading to intellectual disability (Cheetham, Gitta, & Morrison, 2003).

PKU is now detected through a blood test shortly after birth. Affected infants are given a low-phenylalanine diet, which includes primarily fruits and vegetables and eliminates most protein-rich foods such as fish, meat, and eggs. Protein required for development is provided through a special dietary supplement. Follow-up studies indicate that children started on the diet before three months of age will function intellectually within the normal range, with IQs in the 90s, whereas untreated children often have moderate to severe intellectual disability (Dobson, Kushida, Williamson, & Friedman, 1976). Although there is general agreement that a low-phenylalanine diet should be started as soon as possible within the first few weeks of life, there is little agreement regarding when to stop the diet. As many foods contain phenylalanine, it is difficult for school-aged children and adolescents to adhere to the diet, but if the diet has been followed during the preschool years, the most damaging effects of the disorder will have already been prevented. However, research has documented reduction of abilities following discontinuation of the diet (Koch et al., 1996) and British medical researchers have begun to recommend that the diet be maintained across the lifespan (Merrick, Aspler, & Schwartz, 2001).

Other metabolic disorders include congenital hypothyroidism, hyperammonemia, Gaucher's disease, and Hurler's syndrome. Congenital hypothyroidism occurs in approximately 1 in 4000 newborns and may be detected through a screening test at birth. If not treated through replacement of the hormone thyroxine, children will be small and have poor muscle tone and severe intellectual disability (Cheetham et al., 2003). Hyperammonemia, which occurs in 1 in 30 000 children, involves a deficiency in the enzyme that normally transforms the neurotoxic ammonia (produced when protein is broken down into component amino acids) into urea, which is excreted in the urine. If this process does not take place, ammonia builds up and brain damage or death may occur. Treatment through dietary regulation is less effective than in PKU. Gaucher's disease and Hurler's syndrome also involve deficient enzymes. Both are progressive neurological disorders associated with intellectual disability and early death. Treatment through enzyme replacement frequently has only limited success (Cheetham et al., 2003).

ENVIRONMENTAL CAUSES

THE PRENATAL ENVIRONMENT Developmental disability can result if the fetus is exposed to toxins or infections or if the blood supply lacks nutrients or oxygen. Maternal health, therefore, is very important. Inadequate nutrition; the use of alcohol, tobacco, or drugs; infections such as rubella or AIDS; and exposure to radiation can all affect infant development (Durkin, 2002).

Maternal Infections. **Rubella** (also known as German measles) during the first three months of pregnancy can lead to intellectual disability, visual defects, deafness, heart disease, and other problems. Fortunately, rubella-related problems have declined with routine vaccination.

HIV. In the past 20 years, the number of children reported to have **HIV** has increased dramatically. Developmental delays or disabilities occur in 75 to 90 percent of children with HIV who do not receive appropriate treatment (Durkin, 2002; Renwick, Goldie, & King, 1999). HIV may be transmitted from mother to infant during pregnancy, delivery, or through breast milk. According to Canadian statistics, HIV was transmitted from mother to child in 78 percent of children with HIV from birth to age 14 (Health Canada, 1998). A child with HIV may display symptoms including poor growth, recurring diarrhea and fevers, feeding problems, respiratory problems, and pain. Other symptoms affecting the brain and spinal cord include delayed growth and development, cognitive delays and memory problems, distractibility, language and motor impairments, social skill deficits, behavioural problems, and loss of earlier attained developmental milestones (Renwick et al., 1999). HIV can be controlled in children through the use of various medications; however, to date a cure is not available. Immunizations to limit other infections and interventions to address the child's physical and cognitive needs can be helpful. However, other more challenging issues such as future planning, especially if one or both parents are also infected, confidentiality, and dealing with the stigma associated with HIV also need to be addressed (Renwick et al., 1999).

Fetal Alcohol Spectrum Disorder (FASD) Including Fetal Alcohol Syndrome and Fetal Alcohol Effects. Alcohol consumption during pregnancy can lead to a number of defects of varying degrees. Prenatal and postnatal growth retardation and central nervous system dysfunction are common. Figure 14.3 shows the typical facial features of **fetal alcohol syndrome (FAS)**, including short eye openings, an elongated, flattened area between the mouth and nose, thin upper lip, and flattened cheeks and nasal bridge. Head circumference is frequently below the third percentile. Cleft palate, heart and kidney damage, and vision defects are also found (Chudley et al., 2005).

FAS is one of the most common known causes of intellectual disability, found in 1 to 3 per 1000 live births (Streissguth & O'Malley, 2000). **Fetal alcohol effects (FAE)**—also referred to as alcohol-related birth defects (ARBD) and alcohol-related neurodevelopmental disorder

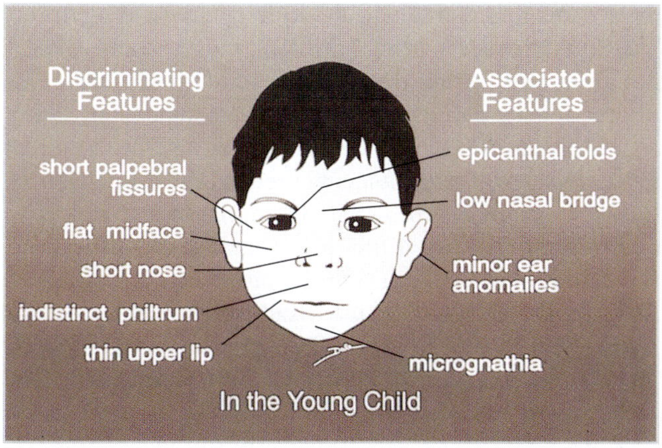

FIGURE 14.3 The Facial Features of Fetal Alcohol Syndrome

Source: A. P. Streissguth & R. E. Little (1994). Unit 5: Alcohol, Pregnancy, and the Fetal Alcohol Syndrome (2nd ed.). Biomedical Education: Alcohol Use and Its Medical Consequences.

(ARND)—is a term used to describe children who display some of the symptoms of FAS without meeting all diagnostic criteria. ARBD and ARND can be related to "lower doses" of teratogen in utero and the timing of exposure, as well as genetic factors affecting the metabolism or susceptibility of the mother or the fetus (Sampson et al., 1997). The fact that infants born to alcoholic mothers do not always exhibit FAE or FAS reflects the complex interplay of genetic and environmental factors contributing to these disorders, including socio-economic status, pattern of consumption, nutritional status, and the use of tobacco and drugs such as cocaine and marijuana (Nulman, Ickeowicz, Koren, & Knittel-Keren, 2007). FAE are estimated to occur approximately three times as often as FAS (3 to 5 per 1000 live births). The incidence of FAS among alcoholics is estimated to be 25 per 1000 (Abel, 1984). A study in Seattle (Sampson et al., 1997) gives a conservative estimate that the combined rate of FAS and ARND is at least 9.1 per 1000, which is almost 1 in every 100 live births.

In an effort to address the lack of consensus on prevalence, Canadian diagnostic guidelines have been developed that recommend a multidisciplinary approach to assessment, diagnosis, and intervention as best practice. Early diagnosis is critical to promote early intervention and support, not only for affected children but also for their parents and siblings who may have similar undiagnosed challenges (Chudley et al., 2005). Appropriate supports can also help to reduce the risk of secondary disabilities frequently found in individuals with FASD (Clark, Lutke, Minnes, & Ouellette-Kuntz, 2004).

Binge drinking has been shown to have a particularly significant impact on fetal development (Gladstone, Nulman, & Koren, 1996; Streissguth, Barr, & Sampson, 1990). Children of women who drank five or more drinks on one occasion were more likely to have developmental delays of up to three months in reading and arithmetic and to require special educational support. This study suggests that heavy drinking on even a few occasions may be more damaging than moderate drinking over a longer time. The link between paternal drinking patterns and FAS is not clear, and further research is required to determine its impact on fetal development (Jenkins & Culbertson, 1996).

Children with FAS exhibit a range of problems at varying stages of development. Prenatal exposure to alcohol is associated with deficits in cognitive and executive functioning that last a lifetime (Wass, 2008). Cognitive functioning varies from relatively minor learning problems to severe intellectual disability (Kalberg & Buckley, 2007). Individuals with FASD may have behavioural challenges, including problems with impulse control, attention deficit/hyperactivity disorder, social difficulties (Bishop, Gahagan & Lord, 2007), eneuresis (bedwetting), and eating and sleeping difficulties (Noland et al., 2003).

It is difficult, however, to distinguish such inherited tendencies from the effects of environmental deprivation resulting from ongoing alcoholism in the family. The effects of FAS are not confined to childhood. Secondary disabilities continue into adulthood, with problems such as poor judgment, inappropriate sexual behaviour, drug problems, delinquency, unemployment, and a variety of psychiatric problems (Streissguth, Bookstein, & Barr, 1996).

Other Drugs. Early development of the fetus can also be severely affected by certain drugs. The anticonvulsant Dilantin, chemotherapy, and hormone therapy have all been found to have teratogenic effects, including facial anomalies, malformed limbs, and a risk of later cancer (Batshaw & Perret, 1986). Congenital limb deficiency, although rare, is one of the best-known examples of teratogenic effects. It received a great deal of attention in the 1950s and 1960s when **thalidomide**, a drug prescribed by European physicians for nausea (Tausig, 1962), was found to cause limb deficiencies or malformations in infants (McBride, 1961). Alcohol and cigarette smoking have been found to be associated with a higher risk of low birth weight, microcephaly, and hearing deficits (Olsen, Pereira, & Olsen, 1991).

BIRTH-RELATED CAUSES Advances in obstetric and neonatal intensive care in recent years have reduced the risk of brain damage and intellectual disability as a result of birth-related trauma. Nevertheless, extreme prematurity or a lack of oxygen during prolonged or complicated labour and delivery can result in developmental problems including visual deficits, cerebral palsy, and speech and learning difficulties.

POSTNATAL ENVIRONMENTAL FACTORS: PSYCHOSOCIAL DISADVANTAGE

Childhood environment can have an important effect on cognitive as well as physical and emotional development. Psychological and social deprivation due to lack of stimulation and care can impair intellectual development. Poverty, poor nutrition, large family size, lack of structure in the home, and low expectations for academic success may all be contributing factors. Children learn by experience and by modelling adult behaviour; if they are given little opportunity to practise cognitive skills or to watch adults practising them, it seems reasonable that they would not develop as rapidly as children given ample opportunity and encouragement to practise reasoning and communication skills.

In approximately 75 percent of people diagnosed with a developmental disability, no organic cause or brain dysfunction has been identified (Zigler, 1967). Most people within this group function intellectually within the mild range. They are found more frequently within lower socioeconomic groups, and commonly have at least one parent and possibly one or more siblings with developmental delays. More recent research (Emerson & Hatton, 2007) has revealed that children with intellectual disabilities are significantly more likely to come from socially disadvantaged families. The incidence of developmental disabilities in Aboriginal groups in Canada is thought to be higher than in the general population. Poverty has been identified as a major risk factor for developmental disabilities among Aboriginal families but other factors may also contribute, including high incidence of prenatal trauma due to physical abuse of mothers, FASD, poor housing, malnutrition, disease, limited access to services and supports, large families, and high numbers of single-parent families (Fudge Schormans & Mandamin-Cameron, 2007).

As with other disorders (see, for example, the discussion of conduct disorder in Chapter 15), the latter finding can be read in two ways: Do children inherit low intelligence from their parents, or do parents with low intelligence create a deprived environment? Debate continues as to the relative contributions of genetic and environmental factors.

Canadian research conducted with infants and children adopted from Romanian orphanages (Ames, 1992) explored the effects of environmental and social deprivation experienced by children institutionalized in Romanian orphanages. This longitudinal study documented the devastating effects of poor nutrition and limited physical and social stimulation (Ames et al., 1997). All of the 46 children were found to be delayed in developmental milestones and intelligence at the time of adoption; 78 percent were also delayed in gross and fine motor skills, personal–social skills, and language. Fewer areas of delay were found among children who had spent less time in institutions, who had access to toys, who were favourites among the caregivers, and who had been kept clean (Morison, 1997).

The orphans who entered an infant development program after adoption were found to progress rapidly. However, approximately three years after adoption, 17 percent of the Romanian children at four and a half years of age (those who had been adopted young) and 56 percent of the older children were not ready for the school grade appropriate to their age. The children who had been in the orphanage longest had the lowest IQs, with a mean score in the low-average range. The mean score for children in the early-adopted group was within the average range. The Canadian-born children in the comparison group had the highest IQ scores, with a mean score in the high-average range.

Physical growth was also affected. Eighty-five percent of the Romanian children at adoption were below the tenth percentile for weight. Three years after adoption, the Romanian children weighed 2.5 kilograms less, on average, than the Canadian-born children and were approximately 5 centimetres shorter than the Canadian-born children and 2.5 centimetres shorter than the early-adoption group.

Behavioural and social problems were reported to be more common in the older adoptees than in the Canadian-born and early-adoption groups. These problems included eating difficulties (either refusing solids or not knowing when to stop eating), stereotyped movements (e.g., rocking), social withdrawal, being slow to attach, not making needs known, and being indiscriminately friendly.

At follow-up, the older Romanian children continued to display significantly more behaviour problems than did the Canadian-born children and those in the early-adoption group. Three years after adoption, 36 percent of the Romanian children had behaviour problems that required professional assistance, including crying, problems with peers, hyperactivity and distractibility, and disobedience or defiance. Children who spent less time in the orphanage, and were adopted by families with more time and energy to spend working with them, tended to do better.

PREVENTION AND EARLY INTERVENTION PROGRAMS

Research conducted with children living with their natural families has also confirmed the effect of environmental factors on development. Prevention and early intervention programs were first developed in the late 1940s and 1950s with early support for mothers and children, including prenatal care, immunization, and nutritional advice. In the 1960s such programs expanded to include daycare and community mental health centres and stimulating early childhood education programs (the U.S. Head Start program being the best known of the latter; Crocker, 1992). Several major studies investigated whether intellectual disability related to inadequate environmental conditions could be prevented. Intensive preschool programming, including medical care and nutritional support, was provided to children from infancy until age five (e.g., Martin, Ramey, & Ramey, 1990; Wasik, Ramey, Bryant, & Sparling, 1990).

Currently, the importance of early intervention for infants, toddlers, and preschoolers at risk for developmental delays is recognized internationally (Odom, Teferra, & Kaul, 2004). Evaluative reviews of early intervention and prevention programs (Frankel & Gold, 2007; Ramey & Ramey, 1992) indicate that they can significantly improve intellectual performance and levels of academic achievement as well as developmental outcomes, including greater engagement and social competence, independence, and mastery. Additional outcomes include preparation for inclusive education and community experience and prevention of behavioural challenges (Wolery & Bailey, 2002). In a summary of the results of early intervention studies, Ramey and Ramey (1992) outlined a number of "essential daily ingredients" for the development of young children. These include

- **a.** encouragement of exploration;
- **b.** assistance in basic skills such as labelling, sorting, sequencing, comparing, and noting means–end relations;
- **c.** reinforcement of developmental achievements;
- **d.** guided rehearsal and extension of new skills;
- **e.** protection from inappropriate disapproval, teasing, or punishment;
- **f.** a rich and responsive language environment; and
- **g.** a supportive and predictable environment in terms of opportunities for learning and patterns of interaction.

More recent research on best practices also highlights the importance of following principles of inclusion, family-centred practice, and collaborative work across professional disciplines involved with the child and family throughout the intervention process (Frankel & Gold, 2007).

2 BEFORE MOVING ON

What are three ways that the impact of intellectual disabilities can be reduced?

Two Specific Disorders

DOWN SYNDROME

Case Notes

Jessica is 14 years old and has Down syndrome. She lives with her parents and a younger brother. Since her birth, Jessica's parents have been determined to give her the best possible opportunities for learning and to integrate her into the community. They were actively involved in an early intervention program focusing on language and motor development. When she was two, they enrolled her in an integrated daycare. Jessica attended regular primary school classes, but received some help from an educational assistant and a resource consultant. However, her only real friend was Jan, another girl with Down syndrome. The other children tended to avoid Jessica and Jan unless specifically asked by the teacher to do something with them.

Jessica attended Brownies and sang in the church choir, but her favourite activity was swimming with the Special Olympics team. At age 12, a psychological assessment found that Jessica was functioning intellectually in the upper half of the moderate range, but had significantly higher adaptive skills. She could complete most activities of daily living independently or with minimal supervision. She liked to help her mother with the cooking and laundry and liked to watch television or play computer games with her younger brother. Jessica was able to use money and enjoyed shopping for clothes. She could read at a Grade 4 level and do Grade 6 arithmetic.

At age 14, Jessica is preparing to enter high school, but the special education consultant was unsure whether she should be fully integrated. It was decided that she would attend a special class for her weaker subjects (English, history, and geography) but would be integrated for math, music, and physical education. Social isolation continues to be a challenge for Jessica; however, her activities with Special Olympics have provided her with a close circle of friends who also have disabilities.

The physical features of Down syndrome are widely recognized. These include short stature; slanted eyes with an epicanthic fold of skin over the inner corner; a wide and flat bridge of the nose; a short, thick neck; stubby hands and fingers; a large, protruding tongue; and poor muscle tone. Other associated problems include congenital heart disease (Reilly, Huws, Hastings, & Vaughan, 2010), gastrointestinal abnormalities, and congenital cataracts (Lovering, 2003). The degree of intellectual impairment can range from mild to severe, with the largest proportion functioning within the mild to moderate range. Particular difficulties in expressive language are common. Despite a number of methodological challenges, research has begun to provide evidence for a behavioural phenotype for Down syndrome. Characteristics vary according to age. In young children these characteristics include delayed nonverbal cognitive development, and deficits in verbal abilities and auditory short-term memory. In approximately half of adults over 50 years with Down syndrome, symptoms of dementia occur (Chapman & Hesketh, 2000).

Early intervention and education have been shown to contribute to the development and adaptive functioning of people with Down syndrome. Indeed, while the range of intellectual ability is broad, many individuals with Down syndrome are able to attain basic reading, number, and writing skills, and considerable independence in activities of daily living in the community (Cicchetti & Beeghly, 1990). Some individuals with Down syndrome are able to function at a much higher level. One example is Christopher Burke, an actor with Down syndrome who became well known for his role in the television program *Life Goes On*.

Life expectancy for people with Down syndrome has increased in the past three decades due to more frequent use of antibiotic medications to reduce infections (e.g., chest, ear, nose, and throat) and surgical treatment of congenital heart disease, both of which are common in individuals with Down syndrome (Pueschel, 2006). However, other health problems occur more frequently in people with Down syndrome than in the general population. These include hypothyroidism, diabetes, obesity, and leukemia (Lovering & Percy, 2007).

Although life expectancy is currently higher for people with Down syndrome than it used to be, adults with Down syndrome are at high risk for developing Alzheimer-type dementia (Dalton & McLachlan, 1986). Research has shown that individuals with Down syndrome over the age of 40 generally show the neuropathological indicators of that dementia (Zigman, Schupf, Lubin, & Silverman, 1987). However, its associated behavioural deterioration (e.g., cognitive and visual memory deficits, declines in daily living skills and adaptive behaviour) appears in only 15 to 40 percent of cases (Zigman et al., 1987). The Dementia Scale for Down Syndrome (DSDS), developed by Angela Gedye (1995) in British Columbia, is designed to detect and rate the severity of dementia among people who are not verbal and cannot follow test instructions. Information is gathered through informant-based interviews. Research findings suggest that the instrument has considerable utility, especially when individuals are reassessed every six months.

FRAGILE X SYNDROME

Case Notes

Ryan is a 10-year-old boy with Fragile X syndrome. He lives at home with his parents and older brother Kurt, who also has Fragile X. Ryan's mother has a brother with Fragile X, and her sister has a daughter who is affected. Ryan attends a class for children with disabilities at the local school. He reads at a Grade 3 level and can do simple addition and subtraction. Ryan has a well-developed vocabulary, but he tends to repeat particular phrases from commercials and songs he has heard, and his speech becomes especially repetitive when he is agitated. Ryan enjoys being active. He and his brother like to ride their bikes and to go bowling. They are both on a basketball team organized through the Special Olympics. At home, computer games are a favourite activity.

Both Ryan and Kurt are able to take care of their personal hygiene with relatively little supervision. They make their own beds and help with chores such as washing the dishes, mowing the lawn, and shovelling snow. They are able to use the microwave to make simple meals and enjoy helping their mother with baking.

Ryan's new teacher was concerned about his limited attention span and frequent outbursts, especially during transitions from one task or setting to another. Ryan's parents were also concerned that he was increasingly irritable; if his routine changed unexpectedly, he would have tantrums, swearing repeatedly and sometimes becoming physically aggressive.

After consulting with his parents, the school referred Ryan to the school board's psychologist, who observed Ryan at home and at school. She noted that he was distracted in class by other children's activities and by the

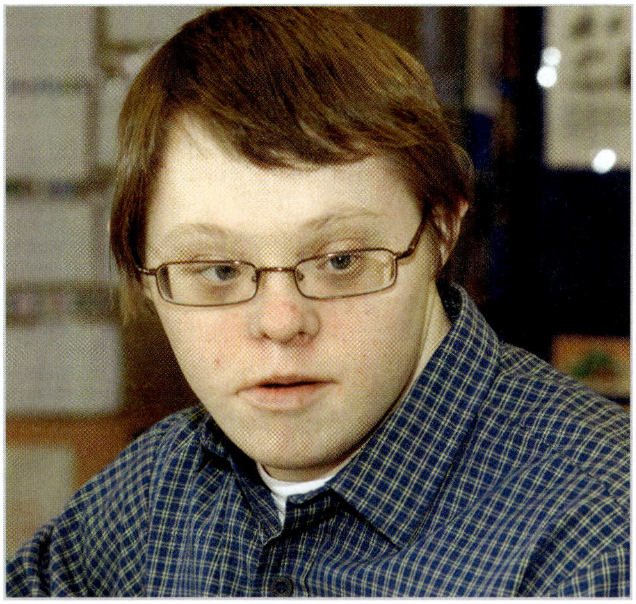

A person with Down syndrome.

many pictures and notices on the walls, arts and crafts materials, and books on the shelves, and that he had the most difficulty remaining seated and attentive during class discussions or unstructured time. The teacher rearranged the desks and created some quiet areas set apart by low room dividers. Ryan's desk was placed against the wall, and he was given frequent opportunities to sit in one of the quiet areas. A token program was also devised where Ryan could collect stickers for paying attention and staying in his seat during structured class activities. These could be "cashed in" for computer time during unstructured periods.

The psychologist also suggested that Ryan's parents and his teacher develop a pictorial schedule of daily activities, with a copy kept at Ryan's desk and another posted on the refrigerator at home. Reviewing the schedule for the next day helped to prepare Ryan for changes in routine and reminded his parents and teachers to anticipate changes that might trigger extreme responses by Ryan.

Fragile X syndrome, first described by Martin and Bell (1943), was identified as an X-linked chromosomal abnormality in the late 1960s (Lubs, 1969), and the mutation for the gene causing the disorder (FMR-1 gene) was discovered in 1991 (Oberle et al., 1991; Yu et al., 1991). It is characterized by a weakened or "fragile" site on the X chromosome, as shown in Figure 14.4. Everyone has a copy of the FMR-1 gene on the X chromosome; however, the gene is larger in persons with Fragile X syndrome. DNA molecules are made up of nucleotides, each of which contains a chemical base. The four bases in DNA are adenine (A), cytosine (C), guanine (G), and thymine (T). In Fragile X syndrome, there are extra pairs of cytosine and guanine, called *triplet repeats*. In a normal FMR-1 gene, the range of CGG repeats is between 6 and 50. Individuals with the *full mutation* have more than 200 repeats, whereas individuals with between 60 and 200 repeats are said to have a *premutation*. A person who inherits a Fragile X gene may not be directly affected, but may be a genetic carrier, transmitting the disorder to his or her offspring. Almost all males who have a full mutation are affected, whereas approximately 50 percent of females will be affected by a full mutation. If a female carrier of a premutation passes this gene to her sons, there is an 80 percent chance that the gene will expand to become a full mutation (Lee, MacKenzie, & Holden, 2003).

Fragile X syndrome is the second-most frequently occurring chromosomal abnormality causing intellectual disability after Down syndrome, and the most common hereditary cause of intellectual disability (Dykens, Hodapp, & Leckman, 1994). As this is a relatively recently discovered disorder, prevalence rates vary. Among females, approximately 1 in 400 is estimated to be an unaffected carrier, and approximately 1 in 2000 is directly affected. Rates for males with the full mutation range from 1 in 700 to 1 in 1000; approximately 1 in 2000 males is an unaffected carrier.

Physical features include a high forehead, elongated face, large jaw, large underdeveloped ears, and (in males) enlarged testes. Individuals with Fragile X syndrome display a number of cognitive, behavioural, and physical symptoms, but the degree to which they are affected in any of these varies (Dykens, Leckman, Paul, & Watson, 1988). Moreover, these characteristics are often less pronounced in carrier females. For example, intellectual levels in males vary from moderate intellectual disability to within the normal range, with declines in IQ appearing around puberty.

Males show a particular pattern of cognitive functioning, with weaknesses in sequential processing of information in a particular order (e.g., words in a sentence, a sequence of tasks) but strengths in simultaneous processing of information in a more holistic fashion (e.g., visuo-spatial tasks, recognizing a picture despite

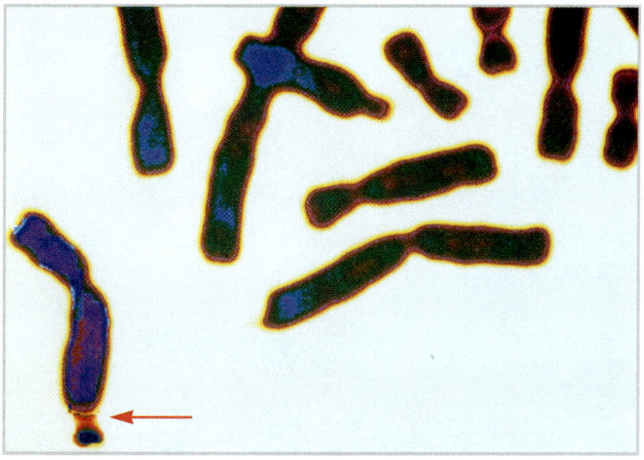

FIGURE 14.4 Schematic Drawing of the Fragile X Syndrome

Source: R. J. Hagerman & P. M. Boggs, *The Fragile X Syndrome* (1983). Dillon, CO: Spectra. Permission granted by Spectra Publishing.

missing parts) (Dykens, Hodapp, & Leckman, 1987). In contrast, only approximately one-third of females are mildly mentally retarded, and most display only learning difficulties involving attention, short-term memory, planning, problem solving, and understanding mathematical concepts (Dykens et al., 1994).

Receptive language may be relatively well developed in relation to expressive language in males with Fragile X syndrome. Their speech has been described as "jocular, staccato, perseverative and sing-songy" (Dykens et al., 1994). Vocabulary may be well developed and individuals may be able to express themselves relatively well in certain familiar contexts. Males with Fragile X often have particular problems with communication and socialization, but may show greater strengths in adaptive behaviour, particularly in activities of daily living. Fragile X syndrome is associated with attention deficits, hyperactivity, anxiety, and aggression. Autistic-type behaviours such as hand flapping, hand biting, poor eye contact, and an aversion to being touched or oversensitivity to certain textures may also occur (Hagerman, 1987). Approximately 25 percent of males with Fragile X syndrome also meet the criteria for a diagnosis of autism (Mazzocco & Holden, 2007). A national survey focusing on the nature and impact of Fragile X syndrome for individuals and their families (Bailey Jr., Raspa, & Olmstead, 2010) has yielded important new information regarding the occurrence of seizures (Berry-Kravis et al., 2010), self-injurious behaviour, sleep difficulties (Symons, Byiers, Raspa, Bishop, & Bailey Jr., 2010), obesity, and sensitivity to textures and foods (Raspa, Bailey Jr., & Bishop, 2010). In addition, recent research has documented phenotypical characteristics associated with the Fragile X premutation. These characteristics include the development of motor tremors and ataxia associated with dementia in 4 to 5 percent of older carriers of the FMR-1 premutation (Kogan, Turk, Hagerman, & Kornish, 2008) and premature ovarian failure in women under the age of 40 (Holoch, Stein, Flanagan, & Hansen, 2008).

A boy with Fragile X syndrome.

People with Fragile X often exhibit behaviours similar to those diagnosed with autism. The diagnosis is easily made by blood test. If the person seems to show any of the facial features suggestive of Fragile X, it is worthwhile testing, both for the guidance of relatives considering childbearing and because the diagnosis may allow access to specialized intervention programs.

Children with Fragile X, like children with autism, can benefit from structured educational programs that limit distractions, include regular routines, and provide a good deal of visual information (Braden, 1989).

The Effect of Developmental Disorders on the Family

Over the past three decades, the experiences and needs of families of children with disabilities have been the focus of numerous publications and research studies—for example, *American Journal of Mental Retardation, 94*(3) (1989), Special issue on research on families; *Journal of Intellectual Disability Research, 47*(4 & 5) (2003), Special issue on family research; and *Journal of Applied Research in Intellectual Disability, 16*(3) (2003), Special issue on family perspectives on services. While there is little doubt that parents of children with disabilities do experience more stress than other parents, research has investigated the presence of positive perceptions and outcomes in parents of children with disabilities (Hastings & Taunt, 2002). The experiences of parents can be affected by factors such as the type and degree of disability. Recent research describing more positive outcomes for families of children with Down syndrome supports the existence of a "Down syndrome advantage" (Corrice & Glidden, 2009). However, the child's behaviour can also be a major predictor of outcome for families (Nachshen, Garcin, & Minnes, 2005). While informal social support from friends, family members, and neighbours can help to mediate family stress (Flynt, Wood, & Scott, 1992; Minnes, 1998), more formal support from professionals and social service agencies has not been consistently shown to contribute to positive outcomes. Indeed, parents frequently report interactions with professionals to be stressful (Baxter, 1989; Turnbull, Summers, & Brotherson, 1986).

Family cohesion, open communication patterns, and patterns of organization and control can also help a family cope (Minnes, 1998; Perry, Harris, & Minnes, 2004). Studies of siblings of children with disabilities have yielded conflicting results; some report adverse effects (Cuskelly & Dadds, 1992) and others do not (Dyson, Edgar, & Crnic, 1989). Further research is needed on the relationships and interactions between disabled and non-disabled siblings within the family system at different stages of the family life cycle (Skrtic, Summers, Brotherson, & Turnbull, 1984). A study by Orsmond and Seltzer (2000) indicates that there are differences in involvement of brothers and sisters of adults with developmental disabilities, with sisters being more highly involved in caregiving and companionship than are brothers. Brothers were more involved with brothers rather than sisters with developmental disabilities, and their degree of involvement depended on the health of their mother.

Parental reactions to the birth of a child with a disability have been likened to those found in bereavement; however, they have also been described as "chronic sorrow" (Olshansky, 1966). In contrast to the view that incomplete resolution of grief is evidence of pathology, Olshansky normalized parental reactions, describing them as an understandable reaction to an unexpected and upsetting situation. Today, there is concern that research tends to pathologize parents by focusing only on the stresses and challenges of having a child with a disability (Glidden, 1993). Parental stress associated with having a child with a disability is viewed as a periodic rather than a continuous phenomenon (Wikler, Wasow, & Hatfield, 1981). Adjustment is interrupted by emotional stress and upheaval at significant transition points when progress in the child's development might be expected to occur and in association with significant events (e.g., diagnosis of the disability) or ongoing activities (e.g., dealing with health care professionals or teachers, and the reactions of family and people in the community) (Minnes & Woodford, 2004; Nachshen, Woodford & Minnes, 2001). As a result of this changing perspective, research has begun to focus on positive outcomes as well. Many parents report positive impacts (Hastings & Taunt, 2002), including opportunities for personal growth, improved relations with others, changes in philosophical or spiritual values (Scorgie & Sobsey, 2000), satisfaction with providing care (Rapanaro, Bartu, & Lee, 2008), and empowerment (Nachshen & Minnes, 2005).

Deinstitutionalization and Community Integration or Inclusion

Since the 1970s, services for people with developmental disabilities have been guided by the normalization principle, a concept introduced in Scandinavia by Bengt Nirje (1969), which suggested that the lives of individuals with disabilities should be as normal as possible. This principle was applied to services for persons with disabilities in North America by Wolfensberger (1972). Normalization, as defined by Wolfensberger, recommended "utilization of means which are as culturally normative as possible, in order to establish and/or maintain personal behaviours and characteristics which are as culturally normative as possible" (Wolfensberger, 1972, p. 28). In other words, people with disabilities should be given the opportunity to have as normal a lifestyle as possible through participation in activities common to members of society of similar age (Zigler, Hodapp, & Edison, 1990). The United Nations Convention on the Rights and Dignity of Persons with Disabilities, signed by Canada in 2007 and ratified in 2010, highlights the importance of participation and inclusion in society as well as independence of persons with disabilities (United Nations, Article 4).

The influence of these changing views has been widespread, contributing to the **deinstitutionalization** of thousands of people with disabilities and the provision of community-based accommodation and services. The evolution of Canadian policies regarding integration can be traced through a review of documents about services for people with developmental disabilities. For example, as early as 1973, the importance of being involved in one's community was recognized by the Ontario Ministry of Health in a report called *Community Living for the Mentally Retarded in Ontario: A New Policy Focus*. In 1974, the mandate of the Developmental Services Act was to help people with disabilities live in their own homes. Since then, the policy focus has been on moving people from institutions into the community and supporting people to remain in the community. In Ontario alone, nine institutions were closed between 1974 and 1996, with the number of people with developmental disabilities served in the community increasing from approximately 4600 in 1974 to more than 50 000 in 1996. Since 2000, moves from institutions to communities have been completed for most of the people with intellectual disabilities in Ontario, with closure of the last of the institutions in 2009. Similar trends are occurring across Canada. Currently, the social and cultural contexts beyond the immediate home, such as family, friends, work, and leisure, are becoming the focus of research and service delivery. However, the need to evaluate objectives and outcomes has been recognized only recently.

Community integration has been measured in a variety of ways. Cummins and Lau (2003) have summarized several relevant variables in order of frequency of use (see Table 14.3). These researchers see the inclusion of subjective well-being as a positive step forward; however, they note that the majority of studies have measured community integration from an objective perspective rather than from the subjective or personal experience perspective of individuals with intellectual disability. They add that the views of parents, staff, or caregivers are frequently measured, but the views of individuals with intellectual disability are overlooked.

TABLE 14.3 WHAT IS COMMUNITY INTEGRATION?

Variables Measured in Studies to Date	Variables Needing More Research Attention
Number of activities within the community	How much individuals with intellectual disability value or desire community integration
Number of personal relationships	Satisfaction obtained as a result of community integration
Frequency of access to community resources	Nature of the communities individuals wish to be integrated into
Number of leisure activities outside the home	Subjective well-being

MAINSTREAMING AND INCLUSION OF STUDENTS WITH DISABILITIES IN EDUCATIONAL SETTINGS

Although there are many definitions, inclusion is most often defined as occurring in a *place* where individuals with developmental disabilities are served with their non-disabled peers to the greatest extent possible. However, social inclusion is a complex, multidimensional concept that also refers to an active *process* that can promote development and facilitate participation of individuals with developmental disabilities (Ainscow, 2000). Since the 1980s, inclusion has been accepted in both Canada (e.g., Ontario Bill 82, 1980) and the United States as best practice for children with disabilities in the classroom. The goal of full inclusion in social and recreational as well as educational contexts, however, has not been achieved in many sectors. Challenges have been related to early identification of developmental disabilities and limited availability of interventions to address disabilities and associated behaviours, but also to a lack of knowledge transfer among parents, health care providers, and educators in different contexts (Smith, 2007).

PREPARATION FOR COMMUNITY LIVING

As more people with disabilities live in the community, it becomes especially important for them to learn to look after their own needs as much as possible. Awareness of the importance of adaptive behaviour has also been heightened with its inclusion in the AAIDD classification system. Many educational programs for people with developmental disabilities have focused on developing social skills and independent living skills and on reducing or managing challenging or maladaptive behaviours. These programs often use systematic observation, task analysis, and various shaping and prompting procedures and reinforcement contingencies. Operant conditioning has been found to be very successful in teaching not only basic self-help skills such as feeding and dressing (Hughes, Schuster, & Nelson, 1993), but also more complex skills such as social interaction, meal planning, vocational skills, personal hygiene, use of public transport, and use of money (Reid, Wilson, & Faw, 1983).

Audiovisual and computer technology have facilitated the development of innovative approaches to teaching work-related and social skills, food preparation, and cleaning skills (Wehmeyer et al., 2006). A recent study used GPS technology to support independent use of public transportation, which is often necessary for individuals to access social and recreational activities and employment in the community (Davies, Stock, Holloway, & Wehmeyer, 2010).

In recent years, however, more person-centred models guiding service delivery have shifted from focusing on skills deficits to the supports needed to promote full participation of persons with disabilities in society. The Supports Intensity Scale (SIS) is now being used internationally to assist with the assessment of medical and behavioural needs and with planning for appropriate supports (Thompson et al., 2009).

EVALUATING QUALITY OF LIFE

In addition to changing views on approaches to supporting individuals with disabilities, the concept of **quality of life** has been the topic of considerable discussion over the past 15 years. Research in Canada, the United States, and Australia alone has led to numerous publications on this topic (e.g., Brown, 1997; Brown & Brown, 2004; Schalock, 1996, 1997). However, researchers do not always agree on the factors contributing to quality of life for individuals with disabilities. In a summary of definitional dimensions of quality of life in the literature, McVilly and Rawlinson (1998) highlight the importance of including both subjective and objective indicators in the measurement of quality of life.

In Canada, an approach developed at the Centre for Health Promotion in Toronto (Renwick, Brown, & Raphael, 1994) divides quality of life into three components: (1) "Being" in physical, psychological, and spiritual domains; (2) "Belonging" in physical, social, and community environments; and (3) "Becoming," focusing on strategies to achieve hopes and goals related to practical issues, leisure, and personal growth.

More recently, the focus of research has expanded from the quality of life of individuals with developmental disabilities to the quality of life of their families and caregivers (Turnbull, Brown, & Turnbull, 2003). Important aspects of individuals' lives for family quality of life include physical well-being, emotional well-being, environmental well-being, and social well-being. Important aspects of quality of life for the whole family include financial well-being, support from others, support from services, and support from society (Brown & Brown, 2004).

3 BEFORE MOVING ON

Inclusion and integration of individuals with developmental disabilities in schools and other community activities have been supported by legislation in Canada and the United

States. However, research has not provided consistent results favouring such approaches. What factors need to be considered when evaluating the success of inclusion and integration programs?

THE ISSUE OF SEX EDUCATION

Since the 1970s, there has been much debate about whether people with developmental disabilities should have the right to enjoy sexual activity, marriage, and children.

Studies in Canada and Scotland have indicated a range of attitudes among residential staff and other professionals working in the field (Murray & Minnes, 1994a, 1994b), and research in Australia indicates that parents tend to have more conservative attitudes than do staff. Younger and more highly educated individuals are generally found to be more accepting, and professionals are frequently more accepting than direct care staff. Parents and staff were found to express less positive attitudes toward adults with intellectual disability becoming parents and more cautious views regarding sexual freedom for women with intellectual disabilities than for women without disabilities (Cuskelly & Bryde, 2004; Gilmore & Chambers, 2010). Such differences in attitudes highlight the importance of assessing attitudes to avoid confusion for individuals with intellectual disabilities who may be receiving mixed messages about their behaviour.

With increasing numbers of people with developmental disabilities living in the community, both children and adults with developmental disabilities are at considerable risk for sexual assault and sexual abuse (McCarthy & Thompson, 1997; Sobsey, Gray, Wells, Pyper, & Reimer-Heck, 1991). A survey of women with intellectual disabilities living in community residences reported that 75 to 80 percent had been sexually assaulted (Davis, 1989). Such figures may reflect individuals' limited ability to make informed decisions and to give consent to sexual contact (Dukes & McGuire, 2009). Furthermore, inadequate staff screening, environmental factors such as understaffing, staff burnout, limited staff education, and isolation can increase the risk of abuse of individuals with disabilities (White, Holland, Marsland, & Oakes, 2003). There is an urgent need for specialized sex education programs for people with intellectual disabilities, especially as those who are living more independently in the community are at increasing risk of contracting HIV infections and AIDS (Murray & Minnes, 1994b). Individuals with intellectual disabilities, unlike typically developing individuals, often have limited opportunities for education about sexuality and relationships (Bazzo, Nota, Soresi, Ferrari, & Minnes, 2007). Although counselling and psychotherapy have often been seen as inappropriate for people with developmental disabilities, recent initiatives have demonstrated that adaptations can be made to accommodate limited expressive and receptive language skills (Lynch, 2004; see below under "Challenging Behaviours and Dual Diagnosis"). Furthermore, programs to help survivors of sexual abuse who have intellectual disabilities (e.g., Mansell, Sobsey, & Calder, 1992) are now being introduced through interactive-behavioural group therapy, which involves intensive support and the use of role-playing exercises (Tomasulo, 1994; Tomasulo, Keller, & Pfadt, 1995).

With greater freedom through community living, more adults with ID are having children. Although the issue of whether individuals with ID should become parents continues to be a topic of debate (as in the film *I Am Sam*), research and practice have emphasized the need to focus on developing parenting skills programs, implementing home-based interventions (Wade, Llewellyn, & Matthews, 2008), and providing support rather than constraint to reduce the risk of child abuse and neglect and to promote child development (Reinders, 2008).

Challenging Behaviours and Dual Diagnosis

Case Notes

Kevin was a 27-year-old man who had lived in the community since completing a school-to-community program at the local high school six years ago. He lived with his parents until he was 24 and then moved into his own apartment. He continued to have regular, frequent contact with his parents, but was able to manage cooking, cleaning, and other activities of daily living without much supervision. Kevin had two volunteer jobs. Three days a week he helped the cleaners at the local school, and on Fridays he did grocery shopping for an elderly neighbour.

Kevin had been assessed as functioning at the top of the mild range of developmental handicap. He could read at a Grade 4 level and understood money fairly well. One of his favourite activities was to take the bus to the mall and hang out. Kevin had been involved in social activities organized by the Association for Community Living but had to stop going because of poor frustration tolerance and angry outbursts. These outbursts tended to occur in unstructured situations; when Kevin did not have a clear idea of what to expect, he could become agitated and would shout and sometimes strike passersby.

Kevin longed to have friends, but his behaviour often alienated them. A recent outburst at the grocery store raised concerns about his ability to keep his volunteer jobs. Without such activities during the day, Kevin would be even more socially isolated.

Kevin had recently become involved with a group of teens, some of whom had been charged with shoplifting.

His parents were concerned that his new friends may have been encouraging Kevin to join them on shoplifting sprees and that Kevin might be easily led because he was so eager for acceptance. Whenever they tried to discuss his friends and activities, Kevin became very angry and clammed up.

Until the 1980s, it was rare for a person with intellectual disability to be diagnosed with a psychiatric disorder. Emotional and behavioural difficulties were often attributed to lower intelligence and psychosocial problems (Borthwick-Duffy, 1994). People with intellectual disability who have limited communication skills often express physical or psychological distress through their behaviour (Dykens, 2000). On the other hand, perceiving deviant behaviours to be a function of the developmental disorder may cause real psychiatric disorders to be missed (Bradley et al., 2007). This phenomenon is called **diagnostic overshadowing**. It is now generally recognized that people with intellectual disabilities are at increased risk of developing emotional and behavioural problems similar to psychiatric disorders. Epidemiological studies indicate that they can develop all types of psychiatric disorders, including less common ones (Dykens, 2000). Furthermore, individuals with particular syndromes such as Fragile X, as well as individuals with autism, are at great risk (Bradley, Bolton, & Bryson, 2004; Dykens et al., 2000).

The co-occurrence of serious behavioural or psychiatric disorders in people with intellectual disability has been labelled **dual diagnosis**. Prevalence rates of dual diagnosis, obtained primarily in the United States, vary widely. Recent estimates of the numbers of children and adults with intellectual disabilities with a psychiatric diagnosis range from 14 to 39 percent (Emerson & Hatton, 2007). Although they have not been given a formal psychiatric diagnosis, up to 40 percent are receiving medication, counselling, or therapy from a mental health professional for behavioural challenges (Davidson et al., 1994; Reiss, 1990). A Canadian survey of individuals with intellectual disabilities found clinically significant aberrant behaviour in 52.9 percent of children between the ages of 4 and 11, and in 46.8 percent of adolescents and adults (Atkinson & Feldman, 1994). The most frequently reported behaviours found in the children included inadequate self-control or anger control, attention deficit, withdrawal, toileting problems (i.e., enuresis/encopresis), and pica (eating inedible substances). The type and intensity of behaviour varied according to the degree of disability and the age and sex of the child. Aggression and depression were the most common psychological problems reported in the older group. The frequency of these behaviours diminished with age and varied according to sex.

Behavioural approaches are generally the intervention of choice for challenging behaviours such as aggression, destructiveness, and self injury. The use of intrusive procedures such as timeout (seclusion), physical or mechanical restraint, and other approaches focusing on punishment has decreased since the 1980s due to concerns regarding the negative impact on the dignity and freedom of persons with intellectual disabilities and on community attitudes (Condillac, 2007). Positive behavioural support techniques that focus on positive reinforcement, natural consequences, and changes to the environment where the behaviour occurs have been successfully used in the treatment of aggressive, self-injurious, and disruptive behaviour (Feldman, Condillac, Tough, Hunt, & Griffiths, 2002). The use of psychotherapeutic interventions with higher-functioning individuals with intellectual disabilities has grown since the 1980s. A British survey (Nagel & Leiper, 1999) indicated that behavioural interventions continue to be used most frequently (81 percent), however; 35 percent of respondents reported using cognitive-behavioural therapy, 31 percent reported using humanistic or person-centred therapy, and 17 percent reported using psychodynamic approaches. These numbers may reflect the challenges of using psychotherapeutic approaches such as cognitive therapy with individuals who have comprehension and attention deficits, expressive and receptive language deficits, and other behavioural issues such as a tendency to acquiesce or respond repeatedly in the same way, as well as the need for a support person to be present during sessions. Nevertheless, strategies to facilitate the process have been developed and demonstrated (Lynch, 2004). These include simplifying the language, presenting information more slowly, using nonverbal communication, checking regularly for comprehension, allowing more time for the client to respond, and repeating the information in different ways. In addition, sessions need to be more structured, shorter, and goal-focused with individuals with intellectual disabilities. Therapists may also need to be more directive, using visual aids, role-playing, and real-life situations, and caregivers may need to be involved to facilitate generalization. Assessment and teaching of core skills prior to beginning therapy is recommended (Joyce, Globe, & Moody, 2006). Such prerequisite skills include the ability to identify and differentiate between emotions and beliefs or cognitions and to link emotions and cognitions with an event.

Bradley and Summers (2003) highlight the need for a biopsychosocial approach to treatment and interventions for individuals with dual diagnosis. These include (1) decreasing organic or biological contributors to mental health problems to reduce the risk of secondary disorders developing; (2) decreasing stress that may be caused by environmental or interpersonal factors and increasing support systems; (3) increasing coping skills, self-esteem, and social supports; and (4) developing interdisciplinary support teams and plans for crisis management. They also recommend interventions at several levels, including (1) behavioural support and skills development, including assistance with communication; (2) environmental assessment and change according to the needs of the client; (3) education and support for the client, family, and caregivers; (4) broader interventions at the system or organization level (e.g., education, agency); (5) counselling or psychotherapy for the client and family; and (6) appropriate use of psychopharmacology.

Community-based crisis intervention services are needed for individuals with dual diagnoses (Davidson et al., 1995). In the absence of such services, families of individuals with dual diagnosis in crisis may have to rely upon emergency departments at their local hospital, where staff may have limited training in this field (Lunsky, Tint, Robinson, Khodaverdian, & Jaskulski, 2011). Their special needs can be met only if service providers in the fields of mental health and developmental disability combine their resources and expertise. Although the majority of services would be community-based, short stays in inpatient facilities may be required for assessment and treatment of serious crises.

Pervasive Developmental Disorders: Autism

Case Notes

Stevie was a four-year-old boy who had been diagnosed with autism. He had been referred to a community behaviour management team because of frequent tantrums, in which he screamed and hit his head and jaw. His parents were concerned that Stevie would seriously injure himself, and were finding it difficult to manage his behaviour. He was on a waiting list for intensive behavioural intervention, and the daycare has indicated that they may have to limit his attendance to three days per week because of his disruptive behaviour.

From the beginning, Stevie's parents knew that there was something different about their son. Stevie was described as a "good" baby. He resisted cuddling and seemed to be quite happy to be left alone. As a toddler, Stevie rarely interacted with his older sister and did not play with toys like other children. He liked to spin the wheels on his toy cars, tricycle, and wagon. He rarely used these toys in the conventional way and would scream if pushed to do so. Stevie's parents also noted his lack of language. Stevie would make repetitive sounds and imitate what was said to him, but he did not make spontaneous comments or ask questions.

When Stevie was enrolled in daycare at age four, the director recommended contacting a psychologist. The psychologist observed Stevie at home and at the daycare centre, recording the frequency and duration of Stevie's outbursts, and their antecedents and consequences. A pattern emerged: when Stevie became frustrated for some reason, perhaps because a wheel on a toy had fallen off or another child had taken one of his toys, he would scream and hit his jaw; restraint or comforting by his parents did not help.

The psychologist concluded that Stevie was frustrated by his inability to communicate his needs. She felt that once he was able to communicate and reinforced for doing so appropriately, his tantrums and hitting would gradually decrease. The psychologist referred Stevie to a speech pathologist, who taught him and his parents some basic sign language. In addition, the psychologist wrote a letter requesting that Stevie be enrolled in an intensive behavioural intervention program as soon as possible.

Xavier: Autism

Watch this Speaking Out video at www.mysearchlab.com

Autism (from the Greek *autos*, meaning "self") is the best known of the **pervasive developmental disorders**. Others include Asperger disorder, Rett syndrome, and child disintegrative disorder. Autism was first identified as a childhood disorder in 1943 by Leo Kanner. He described a sample of 11 children who exhibited a number of distinct characteristics, including a lack of social responsiveness or extreme autistic aloneness and significantly limited or unusual communication patterns. In addition, Kanner noted unusual patterns of behaviour, such as a lack of eye contact; self-stimulation, including rocking, spinning, or flapping; self-injury, including head banging or hand biting; an obsessive interest in particular objects; and an obsessive need for sameness (see Table 14.4). Early terms for this disorder included Kanner's syndrome and childhood psychosis, the latter reflecting the notion of an association with schizophrenia. However, clinical research has shown that autism and childhood schizophrenia are very different in their clinical features. Childhood schizophrenia, unlike autism, typically involves hallucinations and delusions, normal language skills, normal IQ, normal development until after age six, and frequent remissions and relapses. In addition, schizophrenia, unlike autism, shows a pattern of heritability and is equally distributed between males and females (Volkmar, Carter, Grossman, & Klin, 1997).

PREVALENCE

Since the 1990s, prevalence estimates of autism have risen steadily (Wing & Potter, 2009). Canadian estimates of the prevalence of autism range from 1 to 3 per 1000 live births (Fombonne, 2003). International epidemiological studies from Canada, the United States, England, France, Scandinavia, and Asia (Troyb, Knoch, & Barton, 2011) indicate that autism is found at similar rates around the world. Higher estimates of 1 in 150 births (Kuehn, 2007) may reflect changes in diagnostic criteria, including a broader range of disorders in the autism spectrum, as well as the use of different diagnostic measures and increasing awareness among the general public and professionals (Wing & Potter, 2002). Autism occurs three to four times as often in males as in females. The sex difference appears to occur among

TABLE 14.4 DSM-IV-TR DIAGNOSTIC CRITERIA FOR AUTISTIC DISORDER

A. A total of six (or more) items from (1), (2), and (3), with at least two from (1), and one each from (2) and (3):

(1) qualitative impairment in social interaction, as manifested by at least two of the following:

(a) marked impairment in the use of multiple nonverbal behaviors such as eye-to-eye gaze, facial expression, body postures, and gestures to regulate social interaction

(b) failure to develop peer relationships appropriate to developmental level

(c) a lack of spontaneous seeking to share enjoyment, interests, or achievements with other people (e.g., by a lack of showing, bringing, or pointing out objects of interest)

(d) lack of social or emotional reciprocity

(2) qualitative impairments in communication as manifested by at least one of the following:

(a) delay in, or total lack of, the development of spoken language (not accompanied by an attempt to compensate through alternative modes of communication such as gesture or mime)

(b) in individuals with adequate speech, marked impairment in the ability to initiate or sustain a conversation with others

(c) stereotyped and repetitive use of language or idiosyncratic language

(d) lack of varied, spontaneous make-believe play or social imitative play appropriate to developmental level

(3) restricted repetitive and stereotyped patterns of behavior, interests, and activities, as manifested by at least one of the following:

(a) encompassing preoccupation with one or more stereotyped and restricted patterns of interest that is abnormal either in intensity or focus

(b) apparently inflexible adherence to specific, nonfunctional routines or rituals

(c) stereotyped and repetitive motor mannerisms (e.g., hand or finger flapping or twisting, or complex whole-body movements)

(d) persistent preoccupation with parts of objects

B. Delays or abnormal functioning in at least one of the following areas, with onset prior to age 3 years: (1) social interaction, (2) language as used in social communication, or (3) symbolic or imaginative play.

C. The disturbance is not better accounted for by Rett's Disorder or Childhood Disintegrative Disorder.

Source: Reprinted with permission from the *Diagnostic and Statistical Manual of Mental Disorders, Fourth Edition, Text Revision.* (Copyright © 2000). American Psychiatric Association.

people with higher IQs; no such sex difference is found among individuals functioning at a lower level (Lord & Schopler, 1987). Approximately one third of individuals with autism do not speak, and up to half exhibit significant psychiatric and/or behavioural problems, including depression, anxiety, and aggression toward self or others. Epilepsy and sensory impairments are also common (Bryson, 1996). The strongest single predictor of functional outcome among people with autism has consistently been found to be the development of functional speech by age five.

Description

Autism spectrum disorders are characterized by deficits in three major areas: social interaction, verbal and nonverbal communication, and behaviour and interests.

SOCIAL INTERACTION

Two critical features of autism are social dysfunction and unusual responses to the environment. Such deficits, while frequently described, are less understood than other aspects of autism (Lord, 1993). From infancy, parents often note the lack of attachment and comfort-seeking behaviours. The child does not anticipate being picked up and does not seek physical contact. Indeed, autistic children will often stiffen their bodies or scream in response to being picked up or may seem indifferent. Social interactions are characterized by a lack of reciprocity.

The nature of the social interactions of autistic individuals differs according to developmental level; however, they continue to be deficient or unusual. For example, young children with autism frequently display relatively little interest in social interaction and prefer solitary activities. They may respond with relative indifference to strangers and even to their parents (Volkmar, Carter, et al., 1997). Abnormal or absent social behaviours are noted in the first two years of life of most children with autism.

Whereas the social environment is of particular interest to normally developing infants and young children, as well as to some children with intellectual disabilities, children with autism are often much more responsive to the nonsocial environment. Minor changes in the environment (e.g., routines, arrangement of furniture or objects) can lead to emotional outbursts. Over time, older individuals with autism may display some attachments to family members and show differential awareness of strangers, but they will rarely initiate social interaction (Sigman & Mundy, 1989). Autistic individuals without expressive language often do not use the nonverbal signals (e.g., eye contact) that usually guide social interaction.

Studies of social orientation indicate that children with autism show little interest in the human face and often avoid eye contact. In addition, subsequent preverbal social communication skills such as smiling, pointing, and joint attention are frequently absent or significantly delayed. The lack of these skills hampers subsequent symbolic development, including imitation and symbolic play. Whereas normally developing children, and some older children with intellectual disability, readily imitate actions involved in interactive games such as "peekaboo" and "pat-a-cake," children with autism rarely initiate social interaction, preferring solitary activities involving repetitive or stereotyped actions with objects (Stone, Lemanek, Fishel, Fernandez, & Altemeier, 1990).

VERBAL AND NONVERBAL COMMUNICATION

The first three years of life see rapid development of expressive language. In normally developing children, verbal skills begin with babbling and progress to single words, short but meaningful phrases, and then sentences. However, approximately 50 percent of children with autism are mute. Those who do develop speech often do not communicate meaningfully. Moreover, those who do develop language often have speech that is abnormal in tone and content. As a result, two-way conversations are difficult. There is some evidence to suggest that children with fluent speech (i.e., three-word phrases produced spontaneously and regularly in an effort to communicate) by age five are more likely to have higher academic achievement and better-developed adaptive skills by adolescence than are children without such speech by age five (Venter, Lord, & Schopler, 1992). This measure was found to be as effective in predicting outcome as early IQ or language tests (Lord & Paul, 1997). Nonverbal joint attention and play skills prior to age five have also been found to predict the acquisition of language (Mundy, Sigman, & Kasari, 1990).

Echolalia is a common characteristic of speech in children with autism. In this condition, the child will repeat another person's words or phrases, using the same or similar intonation. **Pronoun reversal** is also common; autistic individuals often refer to themselves as "he" or "she" rather than "I," perhaps because they have trouble shifting reference between speaker and listener or a third party. This aspect of language is thought to be related to deficits in joint attention and to difficulties in understanding the perspectives of others and the distinction between self and other (Lord & Paul, 1997).

Although articulation is often clear and there may be quite a good vocabulary, meaningful, spontaneous speech is rare among individuals with autism. Receptive language can also be affected. People with autism may understand relatively short requests but fail to understand more complex information.

Other skills related to communication and social interaction that are limited in individuals with autism include imitation and imaginative play.

BEHAVIOUR AND INTERESTS

Children with autism are often recognized by their restricted, repetitive, and unusual behaviours and interests. Hand flapping, rocking, and unusual repetitive movements are often seen as forms of self-stimulation. Individuals with autism also tend to focus on particular aspects of their environment to the exclusion of others and may engage in stereotyped behaviours such as spinning and tapping objects in a repetitive and non-functional way. They may also be preoccupied with objects or patterns (e.g., toys organized in a particular way, routines carried out in a particular sequence). Change in such patterns or routines can be particularly stressful (Johnson, Myers, & the Council of Children with Disabilities, 2007).

Approximately 25 percent of individuals with autism function within the normal range of intelligence. These individuals often have some meaningful speech and are ultimately able to function more independently, although social difficulties limit the degree of community integration possible. Among the remaining 75 percent, a small proportion, often called **savants**, display islets of exceptional ability in areas such as mathematics, music, or art, or unusual feats of memory. This combination of extraordinary skills and significant social deficits was well portrayed by Dustin Hoffman in the widely acclaimed film *Rain Man*. Hoffman's character, Raymond, could memorize all the numbers in the telephone book and remember all the cards played in a poker game.

Diagnostic Issues

The classification of autism has evolved since it was first included as a diagnostic category in DSM-III in 1980. The wide range of intellectual, social, and language deficits has made diagnostic reliability problematic. To clarify diagnostic categories, several changes were made to the DSM-IV criteria. Subgroups were classified according to a number of criteria, including level of intelligence, social functioning, and the presence of organic features (Volkmar & Schwab-Stone, 1996). Subgroups included the "core syndrome" of autism, Rett syndrome, and Asperger disorder. Debate continues as to whether autism and Asperger disorder represent points on a continuum of severity, or whether they are different but related disorders (Waterhouse et al., 1996).

Although clinicians are able to reliably differentiate between individuals with autism and individuals who are typically developing, there is often diagnostic confusion between Asperger disorder and high-functioning individuals with autism. As a result, a single diagnostic category of Autism Spectrum Disorder has been proposed for the DSM-5, focusing on common behaviours and specific clinical characteristics, such as severity, verbal abilities, epilepsy, and intellectual disability (APA, 2010).

ASPERGER DISORDER

Case Notes

Matthew was an 18-year-old man with Asperger disorder. He was relatively high functioning, with fairly well-developed expressive language, and was able to read and write. He was not echolalic in the traditional sense but did exhibit other features of autism, such as hand flapping and obsessive behaviour. He was able to interact socially to some extent but in a rather rigid, stilted fashion. In addition, his way of approaching individuals, especially young women, was often intrusive and inappropriate.

Matthew had always lived at home with his parents. He took the bus to school, where he was integrated for computer and physical education and spent the rest of the day in a special class for students who were relatively high functioning but needed learning support for a variety of reasons. Matthew enjoyed sports, especially swimming and playing basketball with his classmates. He also liked to go to the mall, where he could spend his allowance on CDs and computer games. In the past year, he had become very involved with the Internet and spent hours surfing.

Through the school-to-community transition program, Matthew was assigned to a job coach who helped him develop his computer skills to prepare for a work placement at the local library gathering research information from the Web.

Speaking Out Asperger's: Living with Asperger's (David)

Watch this Speaking Out video at www.mysearchlab.com

Speaking Out Asperger's (David)

Watch this Speaking Out video at www.mysearchlab.com

Unlike those with autism, individuals with **Asperger disorder** do not have significantly delayed cognitive development. Except for social skills, their adaptive behaviour and interest in the environment are age appropriate, and they may indicate particular interest in social interaction. However, their interactions are frequently odd or eccentric (Volkmar, Carter, et al., 1997). The most commonly cited social deficits include

- failure to establish a joint frame of reference for interaction (i.e., they may begin to speak seemingly in mid-thought);
- failure to observe social norms or to show awareness of the listener's feelings (e.g., making inappropriate personal remarks to strangers); and
- repeated reference to preoccupations in conversation (e.g., the Internet) and use of stereotyped phrases, often related to these limited areas of interest (e.g., "Do you have a Web page?").

The symptoms of Asperger disorder were noted in the literature long before the disorder was recognized. In 1944, a year after Kanner first described autistic children, Hans Asperger described a group of children with similar characteristics. Controversy has been ongoing as to whether the disorders described by Kanner and by Asperger are separate conditions diagnostically or represent different parts of a continuum of "autistic spectrum disorders." Generally, Asperger disorder has been viewed as a mild version of autism associated with higher intellectual functioning (Gillberg & Gillberg, 1989; Waterhouse et al., 1996).

In recent years, people with Asperger syndrome or with similar traits have been portrayed in the media. For example, think of Sheldon on *The Big Bang Theory*. Do you think that Sheldon's affected speech patterns, his limited interests, and his difficulties in social interactions meet the criteria for Asperger syndrome? A more extreme example is Jerry Espenson, an attorney on *Boston Legal* who becomes very anxious when dealing with people and exhibits a number of unusual behaviours (e.g., purring, walking with hands on his lap) that are not necessarily typical of Asperger syndrome. There has also been considerable speculation as to whether a number of famous people had Asperger syndrome (e.g., Canadian pianist Glenn Gould, Albert Einstein).

CHILD DISINTEGRATIVE DISORDER

Child disintegrative disorder (CDD), although described in the literature in the early 1900s, continues to be less frequently reported and less well understood than autism. The major distinguishing feature of CDD is later onset; after a period of several years of normal development, marked deterioration occurs. The ability to speak in sentences is present before onset of the disorder. Individuals with CDD exhibit behaviours and deficits in social skill and communication similar to those found in autism. The etiology of CDD has not been determined, although it is thought that a neurobiological cause is likely (Volkmar, Klin, Marans, & Cohen, 1997).

RETT SYNDROME

Rett syndrome was first described in the 1960s by Andreas Rett in a German report of 22 cases. However, the syndrome did not receive much recognition until several papers were published in the 1980s by Hagberg in Sweden (Hagberg, Aicardi, Dias, & Ramos, 1983). Rett syndrome is a distinct disorder primarily affecting females. Incidence is approximately 1 in 15 000. Rett syndrome is often confused with autism due to similarities in speech problems, lack of social responsiveness, stereotyped behaviours, and, in some cases, screaming and self-injurious behaviour. However, in Rett syndrome, a unique pattern of cognitive and functional deterioration occurs, including loss of interest in social contact and repetitive hand wringing (Perry, 1991).

Although the etiology of Rett syndrome is not known, it is thought to be related to a metabolic problem. Brain imaging studies indicate the presence of mild diffuse cerebral atrophy.

ASSESSMENT

Due to the multi-faceted nature of autism spectrum disorders, assessments are usually carried out by a multidisciplinary team, including a psychologist, psychiatrist, speech and language specialist, occupational and physical therapist, and teacher. Audiological and neurological assessments may also be conducted. A comprehensive developmental approach to assessment is strongly recommended to obtain or clarify an initial diagnosis, which is necessary before parents can apply for funding or obtain specialized services, and to permit accurate documentation of strengths and deficits in various areas of functioning related to adaptation in day-to-day life (Perry, Condillac, & Freeman, 2002). The Autism Diagnostic Observation Schedule (ADOS-G; Lord et al., 2000) and the Autism Diagnostic Interview–Revised (ADI-R; Lord, Rutter, & Le Couteur, 1994) are now highly recommended as the diagnostic instruments of choice. They were originally created for research, but have been adapted for clinical use. In addition to diagnosis, the use of these instruments can help parents to understand the nature of autism and to begin to plan for their child. Both instruments operationalize the DSM-IV-TR criteria focusing on social reciprocity, communication, and restricted repetitive behaviours and interests. The ADI-R is a structured interview that takes about 90 minutes to complete, whereas the ADOS-G is a standardized observational measure with different activities according to the age and language abilities of the child. The ADOS-G takes approximately 30 to 45 minutes to complete.

Etiology

Since Kanner (1943) first presented his 11 cases in the 1940s, the etiology of autism has been a topic of considerable debate (Glidden, 2001). In the past 30 years, the focus of research has shifted from psychogenic to biological factors (see Table 14.5). There is no empirical evidence that the personality characteristics described by Kanner (e.g., obsessive, rigid, lacking in warmth) occur more frequently in parents of children with autism than in other parents (Cantwell, Baker, & Rutter, 1978).

Genetic factors are now considered to play a considerable role in the development of autism. The relatively high frequency of autism among siblings of a person with autism (3 to 5 percent); the frequent occurrence of autistic features in individuals with Fragile X syndrome, phenylketonuria (PKU), and tuberous sclerosis; and evidence that the phenotype (the pattern of social, cognitive, and behavioural abnormalities) extends beyond autism support a strong genetic component (Rutter et al., 1997). However, the genetic links are very complex. For example, gene-mapping research has found evidence of autism foci on 20 different chromosomes (Muhle, Trentacosta, & Rapin, 2004; Sebat et al., 2007), although other factors may also contribute (Smalley & Collins, 1996).

For the past decade, there has been a great deal of media attention concerning a link between the measles/mumps vaccine (MMR) and autism (Wakefield et al., 1998). This concern continues despite the lack of research to support this link (DeStefano, Bhasin, Thompson, Yeargin-Allsopp, & Boyle, 2004) and strong scientific evidence pointing to genetic causes of autism. Parents continue to express considerable concern to the point that they are refusing to have their children vaccinated. The official withdrawal of the original article by the journal publishers and the fact that Wakefield lost his licence to practise in Britain after charges of professional misconduct (Burns, 2010) do not seem to have had much impact on the concerns of parents and the general public regarding the safety of vaccines. Indeed, concerns were raised further when it was suggested that the chemical thimerosol or other preservatives in vaccines

TABLE 14.5 EVIDENCE SUPPORTING ORGANIC-BASED ETIOLOGY

Potential Causes	Explanation
Neurological	Approximately 1 in 3 adolescents with autism have epileptic seizures (Perry, Dunlap, & Black, 2007).
	New brain imaging technology has shown the brains of people with autism to be slightly larger and heavier.
	Abnormalities have been found in a number of brain structures (e.g., amygdala, hippocampus, septum, mamillary bodies, frontal lobes, and basal ganglia; Denckla, 1996).
	Difficulties are commonly found with executive functions controlled by the frontal lobes (e.g., inhibition, flexibility, planning, and organization; Ozonoff, Pennington, & Rogers, 1991).
	Considerable variability is found within different functional domains (attention, language, memory), including problems orienting to social stimuli, motor imitation, joint attention, and empathy. Also found are an ability to focus on minute details to the exclusion of other cues, a complete absence of expressive language to hyperlexia, and islets of ability often related to memory in savants.
Neurochemical	Abnormal levels of the neurotransmitter serotonin are found in 30 to 50 percent of children with autism (Chugani, 2002).
Infection	A history of prenatal infections such as rubella and problems during pregnancy and delivery are fairly common among mothers of children with autism.
Genetics	A relatively high frequency of autism among siblings of a person with autism (3 to 5 percent) suggests a strong genetic component, although other factors may also contribute (Smalley & Collins, 1996).
	There is frequent occurrence of autistic features in individuals with Fragile X syndrome, phenylketonuria (PKU), and tuberous sclerosis, among several other disorders (see Joshi, Percy, & Brown, 2002).
	Evidence that the phenotype (the pattern of social, cognitive, and behavioural abnormalities) extends beyond autism suggests that a number of interacting genes are likely to be involved (Rutter, Bailey, Simonoff, & Pickles, 1997).

were causal agents. Again, concerns continued despite the removal of thimerosol from all vaccines and despite court rulings that denied the links between the MMR vaccine or thimerosol and autism (Fombonne, 2008).

4 BEFORE MOVING ON

Media coverage of the rising rates of autism has fuelled the concerns of parents and the general public. Describe reasons for the varying prevalence rates. How might you address this problem?

Treatment and Intervention

MEDICATIONS AND NUTRITIONAL SUPPLEMENTS

Although biological factors in the etiology of autism have received the most attention in recent years, no medications have been developed specifically to treat autism (Posey & McDougall, 2001). Nevertheless, the prescription of medications for individuals with autism spectrum disorders has increased significantly in recent years (Filipek, Steinberg-Epstein, & Book, 2006), with a threefold increase in the use of antidepressants, particularly related to prescription of SSRIs for perseverative behaviour (Aman, Lam, & Collier-Crespin, 2005). A survey indicated that 70 percent of children with autism over age eight are receiving some psychoactive medication (Oswald & Sonenklar, 2007).

Drugs are generally used to regulate levels of neurotransmitters (e.g., serotonin, dopamine, norepinephrine) thought to contribute to abnormal behaviours frequently associated with autism. Preliminary research evidence summarized by McDougle, Price, and Volkmar (1994) suggested that drugs that increase 5-HT neurotransmission (e.g., clomipramine) may facilitate reduction of repetitive behaviours and aggression and help improve social skills. Dopamine receptor antagonists such as haloperidol are effective in reducing challenging behaviours, but extrapyramidal side effects and tardive dyskinesia (although less with rispridone) can be problematic (Joshi et al., 2002). Stimulants such as methylphenidate (Ritalin) and clonidine may help to reduce distractibility and hyperactivity. Studies of naltrexone (Neo-Synalar, Nupercainal) have shown some benefit in reducing hyperactivity but little effect on social skills and self-injurious behaviour and aggression. While there was considerable interest in fenfluramine in the treatment of social and sensory functioning, more recent controlled studies have not demonstrated significant effects on the core symptoms of autism. In addition, research data on the six most frequently prescribed medications—methylphenidate (Ritalin), thioridazine (Mellaril), diphenhydramine (Benadryl), phenytoin (Dilantin), haloperidol (Haldol), and carbamazepine (Tegretol)—indicate benefits in less than one-third of cases and adverse reactions in almost half of cases (Rimland & Baker, 1996).

Alternative approaches, including nutritional supplements such as megadoses of vitamin B6 and magnesium, vitamin C, and folic acid, have become popular because they do not have the side effects of prescription drugs (Rimland & Baker, 1996). Well-controlled research on their effectiveness, however, is extremely limited (see Kidd, 2002, for a review). A recent randomized, double-blind, placebo-controlled study, however, provided some support for the effectiveness of omega-3 fatty acid supplements in reducing hyperactivity and stereotyped behaviours (Amminger et al., 2007).

BEHAVIOURAL INTERVENTIONS

Behavioural interventions focusing on cognitive, communication, and behavioural challenges have been demonstrated to be effective with children with autism for many years. In the 1970s, Ivor Lovaas and colleagues began the Young Autism Project at the University of California Los Angeles, which offered behavioural programs designed to alleviate symptoms of autism. Such programs, which were also used with individuals with developmental disorders, focused on developing self-help skills, language, appropriate social interactions, and academic skills and on reducing maladaptive behaviours, including self-stimulation, stereotyped actions, self-injury, and aggression (Lovaas, Koegel, Simmons, & Long, 1973; Lovaas & Smith, 1988).

Reviews of behavioural intervention studies (Horner, Carr, Strain, Todd, & Reed, 2002; Matson, Benavidez, Compton, Paclawskyj, & Baglio, 1996) highlight tantrums, aggression, stereotypy, and self-injurious behaviour as the most frequently addressed challenging behaviours among people with autism. Prior to the 1990s, interventions tended to be primarily consequence-based. Since the 1990s, however, the focus has changed to stimulus- and instruction-based interventions. Furthermore, evidence is strong for the effectiveness of positive interventions, with reductions in challenging behaviours occurring in 80 to 90 percent of cases (Horner et al., 2002). Such high success rates depend upon comprehensive functional assessment of reinforcement contingencies and other environmental factors prior to implementation of the intervention (Carr et al., 1999).

Improvements in behavioural approaches over the years have led to increasingly positive results; thus, early intensive behavioural intervention (EIBI) programs, along with government funding, have expanded across North America. Some studies indicate that 75 to 95 percent of children who participated in EIBI programs developed useful speech by age five (McGee, Morrier, & Daly, 1999). In addition, follow-up studies involving well-controlled, relatively intense (25 hours per week) programs have reported significant gains (Smith, Groen, & Wynn, 2000). Although some outcome studies have reported that some clients were able to function at a normal level (Green, 1996; Howard, Sparkman, Cohen, Green, & Stanislaw, 2005; Sallows & Graupner, 2005), an evaluation of a large publicly funded and community-based EIBI program in Ontario suggests that outcomes of such programs are variable. In this project, although EIBI was found to lead to successful outcomes for the majority of children, with 75 percent showing some gains during EIBI and 11 percent achieving average functioning, many children made no improvements or exhibited more symptoms after receiving the intervention (Perry et al., 2008).

In a special issue of the *Journal of Autism and Developmental Disorders* focusing on treatment approaches, Schreibman (2000) concluded the following about intensive behavioural interventions:

1. Intensive interventions can be extremely effective in developing a wide range of skills and in reducing challenging behaviours.
2. Such interventions are most successful when introduced when children are very young (i.e., under three to four years).
3. The inclusion of carefully controlled structure in the learning environment is critical.
4. Effective interventions take into account the attentional patterns of children with autism and maximize learning by carefully planning how stimuli will be presented.
5. Generalization and maintenance of treatment effects need to be actively addressed using naturalistic and child-initiated strategies as part of the intervention.
6. Parent training and active involvement in intervention contributes significantly to generalization and maintenance.
7. Child responses to intervention vary widely. Different approaches may work better with some children than with others.

A more recent systematic review of EIBI (Howlin, Magiati, & Charman, 2009) also found strong evidence supporting its use; however, the authors note that the greatest treatment gains occur in the first 12 months and that response to intervention varies widely. The continuing need for randomized control trials to clearly demonstrate the efficacy of EIBI was emphasized. It is important to note that nonintensive interventions focusing on communication and social interaction skills are also supported by evidence from randomized control trials (e.g., Howlin, Gordon, Pasco, Wade, & Charman, 2007; Kasari, Freeman, & Paparella, 2006).

Communication and social skills are strongly interrelated, and evidence suggests that improved communication skills are often associated with reduced challenging behaviours, such as tantrums, aggression, and self-injury (Donnellan, Mirenda, Mesaros, & Fassbender, 1984). As a result, communication and social skills training are important components of early intervention. Studies have demonstrated that children with autism who begin EIBI before the age of five can develop verbal communication skills (Koegel, 1995). Many programs continue to use traditional operant conditioning principles, shaping and modelling to teach verbal imitation, labelling, asking questions, and appropriate verbal responding (Lovaas, 1977). However, the pragmatics of communication in social situations, including eye contact, appropriate affect, inflection, and conversational skills, also need to be included in such training programs (Koegel, 2000).

For individuals with autism who do not have functional expressive language, other augmentative communication systems have been developed. Although early studies suggested that manual sign language might be an effective approach, alone or as part of a "total communication" approach (Mirenda & Schuler, 1988), a critical review of the research literature (Schwartz & Nye, 2006) concludes that there is limited evidence that manual sign language training provides substantial improvements in either oral or sign language with individuals with autism. The use of picture exchange communication systems (PECS) has grown in recent years. This approach has the advantage of promoting initiated interaction with a variety of communication partners (i.e., the child hands a person a picture to make a request or comment) and motivation due to natural reinforcement. A recent review of empirical research (Preston & Carter, 2009) provides preliminary support indicating that individuals with little or no speech can learn to use PECS; however, to date there is only limited empirical evidence indicating related improvements in challenging behaviour, social skills, or speech development.

Computer technology has provided new possibilities for augmentative or alternative communication strategies. For example, persons with autism have been taught to touch pictures on a speech-generating device to make requests or to answer questions. A critical review of the literature highlights initial evidence supporting the use of such devices with individuals with autism (Van der meer & Rispoli, 2010). (See Focus box 14.1 for an example of an approach that did not fulfill its promise.)

Helping people with autism to develop social competence is another important area of intervention. *Social competence* refers to a complex set of skills and competencies needed to navigate social relationships and includes social skills; an ability to regulate one's emotions and behaviours; and an understanding of the social environment, including having theory of mind (Stichter et al., 2010). Group intervention targeting specific social skills and social competence is associated with gains in positive peer interactions, reduced anxiety, and improvements in specific skills such as active listening (Cotugno, 2009). The most frequently addressed social skills behaviours include initiating contact, responding appropriately, and engaging in reciprocal interactions. In a majority of studies, the operant conditioning principles have been the foundation for interventions using positive reinforcement (i.e., using praise, tokens, stickers, etc.) for appropriate behaviour (Matson et al., 1996). Through the use of task analysis, target behaviours are broken down into steps, including prerequisite skills. For example, eye contact and joint attention would be taught as precursors to asking and responding to questions (Goldstein & Wickstrom, 1986). Skills taught in this way need to be generalized to other individuals and other environments. One successful way of address-

FOCUS 14.1

The Dangers of Hope: Lessons from Facilitated Communication and Other Miracle Cures

For decades, alternative approaches to overcoming various forms of disability have passed in and out of fashion. The success of such movements has been described as a function of "the unhappiness of clients and the vividness of their dreams" (Toch, 1971, p. 44). Parents and caregivers who become strong proponents of alternative approaches frequently ignore concerns raised by professionals and "non-believers." Furthermore, the beliefs of such supporters tend not to change despite strong research evidence disconfirming their views. Families of children with autism seem to be particularly vulnerable to the claims made about unvalidated interventions (Jacobson, Mulick, & Schwartz, 1995).

One of the recent techniques to attract such attention is facilitated communication (FC). Claims of dramatic and rapid improvements in behaviour and functioning gave parents great hope. However, research findings have not supported the continued use of this type of communication training.

Facilitated communication (FC) training, developed in Australia in the 1970s, was introduced to Canada and the United States in 1990 by Douglas Biklen from Syracuse University. The technique is described as a "teaching strategy used with people with severe communication impairment requiring aided communication who are not yet able to access a communication aid independently but for whom direct access with their hands is a realistic and desirable goal" (Crossley, 1992). Individuals with communication difficulties are taught to point to pictures, letters, or objects by a facilitator who provides various types of support to the hand or forearm. Physical support, it was suggested, can overcome neuromotor problems that limit the individual's ability to initiate movements, thus interfering with communication. Letterboards, typewriters, or talking computers are often used as part of this process.

The technique aroused great excitement and controversy in Canada, Australia, and the United States (Minnes, 1992; Prior & Cummins, 1992). Remarkable success stories emerged of apparently low-functioning children with autism who suddenly demonstrated the ability to read and produce sentences expressing sophisticated ideas and feelings. However, concerns were soon raised about the "ouija board" effect: Were these really the child's own thoughts, or were facilitators unintentionally influencing the child's choice of symbol through subtle body movements (Rimland, 1991)?

Despite the absence of empirical evidence to confirm independent communication, countless parents, caregivers, and educators became strong proponents of the technique. It became even more important to determine the reliability and validity of this technique when numerous reports were published of people around the world using their new-found communication channel to describe physical and sexual abuse.

Over the next few years, dozens of well-controlled studies on FC (see Green, 1994) were conducted. The results indicated that, in the majority of cases, messages were not being communicated independently; rather, facilitators were unwittingly influencing the messages being communicated (Rimland, 1993; Wheeler, Jacobson, Paglieri, & Schwartz, 1993). The results of an intensive, multi-method validation study conducted in Toronto by Adrienne Perry, Susan Bryson, and James Bebko did not provide support for the emergence of hidden literacy skills. Moreover, they noted an "abdication effect," whereby students who could perform basic communication tasks independently became passive when a facilitator became involved (Bebko, Perry, & Bryson, 1996; Perry, Bryson, & Bebko, 1993).

Auditory integration training developed by Berard (1993) is another treatment approach that has excited parents. This technique requires the child with autism to listen to specially modulated and filtered music through headphones for 30 minutes twice a day for 10 days. Although much has been written about auditory integration, only six studies have been published to date, and beneficial effects have not been demonstrated (Dawson & Watling, 2000; Mudford et al., 2000). Indeed, some authors have suggested that auditory integration training could be harmful if potentially damaging sound levels (.130 dB) are used; if large amounts of money are spent on ineffective interventions; if parents are discouraged by poor results and do not pursue more beneficial approaches; and if involvement with providers of one ineffective or invalidated intervention introduces parents to other ineffective or potentially harmful approaches (Mudford et al., 2000).

These and other results point to a number of risks associated with the use of such interventions. A review of the Canadian Code of Ethics for Psychologists (Dayan & Minnes, 1995) raised serious ethical questions about choosing approaches without well-documented effectiveness.

ing this challenge is the use of typically developing peers as tutors or mediators in school and community settings (McConnell, 2002; Rogers, 2002).

Learning Disorders

Case Notes

Justin is a 13-year-old boy in Grade 8 who was diagnosed with a reading disorder at age 8. As a preschooler, Justin received speech and language intervention to address his language delays and difficulties with the articulation of speech sounds. In kindergarten, Justin's teacher noted that he had more trouble than most children in the class in learning his alphabet. By Grade 1, he still could not print his name, nor could he recognize letters or numerals consistently. Justin's parents were perplexed because Justin seemed very bright. For example, he took an interest in the solar system and had memorized the names of the planets. Justin was mechanically inclined and he loved to figure out how to reassemble his family's appliances.

By Grade 3, Justin's struggles with reading and writing affected all areas of school functioning. He read slowly and laboriously, often guessing at a word by using the first letter. The results of a comprehensive psychological assessment revealed that Justin's overall level of intelligence fell in the high-average range, ranking above 86 percent of his peers. He showed specific deficits in phonological processing, which affected his ability to read and to produce written work. Justin began to see himself as stupid and was bullied at school. However, in Grade 8, he was introduced to adaptive technology, including a computer software program that read aloud text as he followed along. He learned keyboarding skills and how to use software effectively to organize his ideas and to check his spelling and grammar. With the aid of a teacher who took a particular interest in him, Justin began to experience greater success at school, although he continued to require more time and effort at homework than did his peers.

HISTORICAL PERSPECTIVE

Learning disorders were first identified in the nineteenth century when physicians observed patients who appeared to be intelligent and physically healthy yet were unable to read and to write. The terminology used to reflect this presentation has varied over the years, as have beliefs about the mechanisms underlying the learning impairments. For example, in the early years, most understood reading disorders to reflect a visual/perceptual impairment with difficulties in perceiving and processing letters and words (Snowling, 1996). In 1887, German ophthalmologist Rudolf Berlin coined the term *dyslexia* from the Greek words for "impaired word," while in 1886, British physician W. Pringle Morgan published a case study in the *British Medical Journal* using the term *congenital wordblindness* (Shaywitz, Morris, & Shaywitz, 2008). Popular theories included the belief that individuals with dyslexia perceived letters backwards. However, advances in neuroimaging techniques and in reading research have given support to newer theories stating that reading disorders stem from a core deficit in **phonological processing** (Lonigan, 2006; Mody, 2003; Vellutino, Fletcher, Snowling, & Scanlon, 2004). In 1963, Samuel Kirk introduced the broader term *learning disabilities* to include individuals with difficulties in other arenas, such as mathematics and writing. In Canada, the Education Act (1990) included the term *learning disability* to define a subset of students with exceptionalities that required special education programming. In current classification systems, such as ICD-10 and the DSM-IV-TR, learning disabilities are thought to reflect poor academic performance that cannot be explained by intelligence or external factors (Buttner & Hasselhorn, 2011).

DIAGNOSTIC CRITERIA

The DSM-IV-TR subdivides learning disorders (LD) by functional impairment, including Reading Disorder, Mathematics Disorder, Disorder of Written Expression, and Learning Disorder Not Otherwise Specified (for example, see Tables 14.6 and 14.7). According to the DSM-IV-TR criteria, an LD diagnosis is made on the basis of a substantial discrepancy between academic achievement in the particular area of function, as measured by individually administered standardized tests, and a person's measured intelligence. The discrepancy must not be due to cultural or educational factors, impairments in hearing or vision, or other neurological condition. "Abnormalities in cognitive processing" are identified as an "associated feature" of the disorder (APA, 2000).

However, a growing body of empirical data suggests that the specific impairments in cognitive processing are the defining features of learning disorders (Mammarella et al., 2006; Mody, 2003; Shaywitz et al., 2008) and that the discrepancy between intelligence and achievement is less relevant to the diagnosis (Burns, Jacob, & Wagner, 2008; Gonzalez & Espinel, 1999; Siegel, 1999). Clinically, a learning disability is widely recognized as "a neurobiological disorder of cognitive and/or language processing caused by atypical brain functioning" (Silver et al., 2008, p. 217). In Canada, the Learning Disabilities Association of Ontario (LDAO) published an inclusive definition that suggests that learning disabilities affect how individuals

TABLE 14.6 DSM-IV-TR DIAGNOSTIC CRITERIA FOR READING DISORDER

A. Reading achievement, as measured by individually administered standardized tests of reading accuracy or comprehension, is substantially below that expected given the person's chronological age, measured intelligence, and age-appropriate education.

B. The disturbance in Criterion A significantly interferes with academic achievement or activities of daily living that require reading skills.

C. If a sensory deficit is present, the reading difficulties are in excess of those usually associated with it.

Source: Reprinted with permission from the *Diagnostic and Statistical Manual of Mental Disorders, Fourth Edition, Text Revision.* (Copyright © 2000). American Psychiatric Association.

TABLE 14.7 DSM-IV-TR DIAGNOSTIC CRITERIA FOR MATHEMATICS DISORDER

A. Mathematical ability, as measured by individually administered standardized tests, is substantially below that expected given the person's chronological age, measured intelligence, and age-appropriate education.

B. The disturbance in Criterion A significantly interferes with academic achievement or activities of daily living that require mathematical ability.

C. If a sensory deficit is present, the mathematical difficulties are in excess of those usually associated with it.

Source: Reprinted with permission from the *Diagnostic and Statistical Manual of Mental Disorders, Fourth Edition, Text Revision.* (Copyright © 2000). American Psychiatric Association.

acquire, understand, retain, or organize information; are specific rather than global deficits; and result from impairments in one or more psychological processes related to learning (LDAO, 2007). These psychological or cognitive processes include phonological processing, language, perceptual-motor skills, visual-spatial skills, processing speed, memory, and attention.

CONTROVERSY IN DIAGNOSIS

There have been increasing challenges to the use of an IQ/achievement discrepancy in the diagnosis of learning disabilities (Mayes & Calhoun, 2005; Vellutino et al., 2004). First, intelligence and academic achievement are continuously distributed variables. Selections of a cut-off point for a discrepancy score are arbitrary and inconsistent (Fuchs, Mock, Morgan, & Young, 2003). Second, recent studies in cognitive processing suggest that processes such as working memory and phonological processing are associated with learning disabilities irrespective of intelligence level (Maehler & Schuchardt, 2011). Third, the intelligence/achievement discrepancy approach may exclude gifted children with high levels of intelligence whose academic achievement scores may be within normal limits yet who show processing deficits that result in functional impairments (Buttner & Hasselhorn, 2011). Fourth, there is no clear evidence that an intelligence/achievement discrepancy is related to learning intervention outcome (Buttner & Hasselhorn, 2011). Lastly, Shaywitz, Morris, and Shaywitz (2008) characterize the discrepancy approach to LD diagnosis as a "wait-to-fail model." In particular, in order to demonstrate a discrepancy between measured intelligence and academic achievement, there needs to be time for the child to gain academic skills and for the gap between intellectual potential and achievement to widen. However, with growing understanding of the cognitive processes that contribute to the neurobiologically based LDs, Shaywitz and colleagues argue that we can identify children who are struggling with reading as early as four or five years of age.

PROPOSED CHANGES FOR THE DSM-5

In the proposed DSM-5, learning disorders will be classified as a neurodevelopmental disorder (APA, 2010). The DSM-5 will likely include one overarching category called "Learning Disorders," which recognizes that learning disorders are identified by persistent patterns of deficits in achievement and related psychological processes. In addition, clinicians will likely have a new opportunity to identify "specifiers" such as descriptive features (e.g., problems with accurate or fluent word reading, a.k.a. dyslexia) and level of severity of learning disorders.

5 BEFORE MOVING ON

Explain the intelligence/achievement discrepancy approach to the diagnosis of learning disorders and provide three reasons why this approach is problematic.

READING DISORDER

There is general agreement that the core deficit underlying a reading disorder (also known as **dyslexia**) is an impairment in phonological processing (Lonigan, 2006; Mody, 2003; Shaywitz et al., 2008; Vellutino et al., 2004). Reading requires an understanding that spoken words are composed of the smallest segments of language (phonemes) and that there is a connection between elements of printed words (letters) and phonemes (Sandak, Mencl, Frost, & Pugh, 2004). Poor readers compensate for phonological weaknesses by overrelying on contextual cues to read individual words (Perfetti & Bell, 1991). Individuals with a reading disorder may also have difficulties with reading fluency, resulting in reading skills that are accurate but effortful and slow (Katzir, Youngsuk, Wolf, O'Brien, & Kennedy, 2006).

MATHEMATICS DISORDER

In contrast to the consensus regarding the mechanisms of reading disorders, the nature of mathematics disorders (also known as **dyscalculia**) is less well understood and more controversial (Geary, 2011; Gersten, Clarke, & Mazzacco, 2007; Swanson, 2007). Individuals with a math learning disability (MLD) show impairments in computational and or procedural skills, reflecting deficits in working memory (Chong & Siegel, 2008; Geary, 2011) and executive function (Geary, Hoard, Nugent, & Byrd-Craven, 2008). However, a number of behavioural factors complicate the identification and diagnosis of math disabilities. For example, low performance in math may reflect factors such as anxiety about performance or a deliberate avoidance of math (Ashcroft, Krause, & Hopko, 2007). Despite a perception that males may be better at math than females, the evidence suggests that there are no sex differences in math performance over time, although females report less motivation and confidence in self-concept regarding math (Royer & Walles, 2007). As is true for all subtypes of learning disorders, a comprehensive psychological assessment of intelligence, cognitive processes, academic achievement, and social-emotional or behavioural factors is required for diagnosis (see Table 14.7).

DISORDER OF WRITTEN EXPRESSION

Disorder of written expression is the least well understood and most controversial of all the learning disorder subtypes (Mayes & Calhoun, 2007; Wakely, Hooper, de Kruif, & Swartz, 2006). Usually, written language problems occur in the context of problems with reading or mathematics disorders. Siegel (1999) argued that the existence of a separate written language disability has not been clearly established or defined. In contrast, research by Mayes and Calhoun suggests that research outcomes may reflect different testing methodologies: using tests that measure written compositional skills results in a higher prevalence of disorders of written expression than does using tests that assess single-word writing or spelling (Mayes & Calhoun, 2007; Mayes, Calhoun, & Lane, 2005).

NONVERBAL LEARNING DISABILITIES

In the 1970s, Johnson & Myklebust (1971) described a group of children with a "social perception" disability characterized by average verbal intelligence yet impairments in many nonverbal aspects of daily living, such as difficulties in reading facial expressions and body language, interpreting maps, and learning to tell time. Dr. Byron Rourke, a neuropsychology professor at the University of Windsor in Ontario, studied a similar cluster of children, noting that this clinical presentation was consistent with right hemisphere deficits. Rourke became a leading researcher studying the construct he first labelled a "nonverbal perceptual-organization-output disability" (Rourke & Finlayson, 1978) and later called a **nonverbal learning disability (NLD)** (Rourke, 1989). In 2002 Rourke characterized the NLD profile as including deficits in tactile perception, psychomotor coordination, and visual-spatial organization; difficulty managing novelty and/or complexity; poor nonverbal problem solving; poor sense of time; strong decoding yet weak reading comprehension; poor language pragmatics; poor arithmetic; and poor social interaction. In contrast to the left hemisphere deficits of reading disorders, NLD is associated with impairment in the right hemisphere and in the white matter of the brain (Rourke, Ahmad, Hayman-Abello, & Warriner, 2002; Semrud-Clikeman & Hynd, 1990).

There has been controversy regarding the differentiation between NLD and Asperger disorder. The two disorders share common features, including a history of advanced verbal skills, difficulties in processing nonverbal social cues and adapting to new situations, impairments in executive function, and problems with handwriting and organization (Stein, Klin, & Miller, 2004). However, Asperger disorder is characterized by restricted repetitive and stereotypic interests (according to the DSM-IV-TR), which is not a hallmark feature of NLD. NLD is characterized by visual-spatial cognitive deficits that are not consistently present in Asperger disorder (Semrud-Clikeman & Fine, 2011). Joseph Palombo (2006) also argues that children with NLD show a higher level of motivational desire to connect in social relationships than do children with Asperger disorder. However, an explosion of research in the field challenges Palombo's assertion and suggests that children with Asperger disorder often do make attempts to connect with others (Ghaziuddin, 2008).

6 BEFORE MOVING ON

What are your thoughts about the nonverbal learning disability label? Why do you think it is not included as a distinct diagnosis in the DSM classification system?

PREVALENCE

Learning disorders are persistent and continue over the lifespan. General prevalence rates are estimated at about 8 percent of the general population (Lerner & Lerner, 1991). Rates for reading disorders are estimated to be as high as 10 to 15 percent among school-aged children (Vellutino et al., 2004) and are the most common form of LD, accounting for 80 percent of learning disabilities (Fletcher et al., 1999; Lerner, 1989; Shaywitz et al., 2008). Mathematics learning disorders have a prevalence rate of about 7 percent (Geary, 2011). More boys than girls are identified with reading disorders (Shaywitz, Shaywitz, Fletcher, & Escobar, 1990), although the issue is complicated by a referral bias for identification and diagnosis in favour of boys whose learning challenges may come to the attention of educators because of disruptive classroom behaviours (Shaywitz et al., 2008). The view that specific reading disorders are predominant has been called into question by Mayes and Calhoun (2007), who studied a clinical group of 485 children with learning problems and found that 50 percent of the sample had disorders of written expression. In this sample, learning disorders in reading or mathematics alone were uncommon, reflecting only 4 percent of the sample. The researchers concluded that difficulties with compositional writing skills are the most common type of learning disabilities in children (Mayes & Calhoun, 2007).

ETIOLOGY

The etiology of learning disorders is multifactorial. Dyslexia, for example, is both familial and hereditary (Shaywitz, 2008). Evidence from twin studies suggests that 50 to 60 percent of the variance in reading is explained by genetics (Olson & Byrne, 2005; Vellutino et al., 2004). Similarly, 50 to 67 percent of the individual differences in mathematics achievement is attributable to genetic variation (Geary, 2011). However, research in the field of response-to-intervention (RTI) approaches to reading disorders (Fuchs & Fuchs, 2006) suggests that environmental changes in the form of specific reading instruction can influence neural systems in the brain (Shaywitz, 2008; Temple, Deutsch, Poldrack, Miller, & Tallal, 2003). There is converging neurological evidence that skilled word recognition involves three subsystems in the left hemisphere: ventral (occipitotemporal), dorsal tempoparietal, and inferior frontal gyrus (Sandak et al., 2004). Functional magnetic resonance imaging (fMRI) studies suggest that poor readers show less activation in these left hemisphere regions during reading activities and greater reliance on right and frontal hemispheres (Sandak et al., 2004). Research in the field of mathematics disorders suggests that posterior parietal areas of the brain are associated with numerical competence (Simon & Rivera, 2007).

SOCIAL AND EMOTIONAL WELL-BEING OF CHILDREN WITH LEARNING DISORDERS

In a meta-analysis of social skills research, Kavale and Forness (1996) found that 75 percent of students with

FOCUS 14.2

Youth at Risk

Why are there so many youth with learning disabilities in the justice system? A number of theories attempt to explain the high correlation between learning difficulties, academic failure, and offences. The "school failure" hypothesis states that having a learning disability places a youth at higher risk for academic failure, leading to negative self-image, increased risk of school dropout, and higher rates of delinquency (Shelton, 2006). Alternatively, the "susceptibility theory" suggests that youth with learning disabilities and problems with impulse control, hyperactivity, and behavioural regulation are more vulnerable to opportunities to engage in delinquent behaviour (Grigorenko, 2006; Rasmussen, Almvik, & Levander, 2001).

LDs have lower levels of social competence than do comparison children, as assessed by teachers, peers, and themselves. Perhaps unsurprisingly, children and youth who are intelligent but who have specific difficulties in processing information often have difficulty with tasks such as understanding sarcasm, reading body language, recalling information about social situations, or engaging in effective social problem solving (Bauminger, Edelsztein, & Morash, 2005; Elksnin & Elksnin, 2004). Without the protective factors of positive social relationships, children and youth with LDs experience greater peer victimization and bullying (Baumeister, Storch, & Geffken, 2008; Mishna, 2003), social rejection (Bryan, Burstein, & Ergul, 2004; Kavale & Forness, 1996), and feelings of loneliness (Valas, 1999). Chronic social and academic failures are associated with decreased feelings of self-worth (Bender & Wall, 1994). If unrecognized and unremediated, learning disabilities can lead to academic failure and dropout from high school (Pearl & Bay, 1999) and an increased risk of involvement with the youth justice system (Grigorenko, 2006; Shelton, 2006; see Focus box 14.2).

INTERVENTION

Evidence-based reading interventions target phonemic awareness, phonics, vocabulary development, reading fluency, and reading comprehension strategies, with a focus on explicit instruction, close monitoring of progress, and opportunities for supervised practice (Reschly, 2005). A response-to-intervention approach to reading identification and remediation uses a multi-tiered approach to instruction in which reading strategies are taught to children who are screened to be "at risk" for reading difficulties (Tran, Sanchez, Arellano, & Swanson, 2011). Those who continue to struggle are provided with a more intensive intervention. "Non-responders" to the second tier of intensive reading remediation are likely to be diagnosed with learning disabilities (Buttner & Hasselhorn, 2011). Interventions to support math-based learning disabilities are beginning to follow the response-to-intervention format to teach fundamental math skills (Geary, 2011).

Having learning disabilities complicates the efficacy of evidence-based mental health therapies. For example, cognitive-behavioural therapy to treat anxiety needs to be tailored for the individual who struggles with reading and writing and has trouble producing written thought records. However, there is a paucity of research on effective mental health interventions for children and youth with learning disabilities (Mishna, Muskat, & Wiener, 2010).

Outcome research for youth with LD highlights the important role of schools and educators in promoting resiliency and a successful transition to adulthood. Key factors that predict success include providing students with a clear knowledge of LD and compensatory strategies (Skinner & Lindstrom, 2003) in order to promote self-advocacy skills (Test, Fowler, Wood, Brewer, & Eddy, 2005), a supportive school environment (Cruise, Evans, & Pickens, 2011; Malian & Nevin, 2002), and positive relationships with effective teachers (Mather & Goldstein, 2001). As Focus box 14.3 shows, with the right support, people with learning disabilities can be successful.

FOCUS 14.3

Famous People with Learning Disabilities

Throughout history, persons of interest and importance have overcome the challenges of suspected or identified learning disabilities to achieve success in their respective fields. These include historical figures such as Hans Christian Anderson (writer), Thomas Edison (inventor), and Woodrow Wilson (American president); business leaders such as Charles Schwab; scientists such as William Hewlett (Hewlett-Packard computers); actors and television personalities such as Tom Cruise, Orlando Bloom, Whoopi Goldberg, and Jay Leno; musical artists such as Cher and Joss Stone; and athletes such as Bruce Jenner, Billy Blank, and Magic Johnson (www.schwablearning.org; Aaron, Phillips, & Larsen, 1988).

CANADIAN RESEARCH CENTRE

Jean Vanier, Founder of L'Arche

Jean Vanier (1928–) has been described as a social visionary with a keen sense of what makes a compassionate society. He has received many honours for his humanitarian efforts on behalf of individuals with developmental disabilities, including the Order of Canada. Jean Vanier is the son of former Canadian Governor General Georges P. Vanier and Pauline Vanier. He was educated in England and Canada, and after several years serving with the British and later the Canadian Navy he completed a doctorate in philosophy at the Institut Catholique de Paris. In 1964, Jean Vanier founded the first L'Arche community in Trosly, France, northeast of Paris, when he welcomed Raphael Simi and Philippe Seux, two men with disabilities, into his home. The first Canadian L'Arche community was established in 1969, and since that time 130 other L'Arche communities have been established on five continents. Philippe describes his early days with Vanier:

> The first time I met Jean Vanier, it was in a centre where we weren't allowed to leave. I saw him in the chapel, then he gave out soup. He impressed me right away. The table looked really small in front of him because he was so big. . . . Before, for me, [in the institution] that wasn't a life: all day sitting in a room. We couldn't do anything, we couldn't go outside, it was so boring, nothing to do, nothing. I even cried. I didn't feel good at all. Little by little, things got better at L'Arche. We started off doing things however we could. We cooked meals together, we helped with the food. (www.larchecanada.org/pseux1.htm)

The L'Arche Mission includes three tenets: (1) to create homes where faithful relationships based on forgiveness and celebration are nurtured, (2) to reveal each person's unique value and the gift that each person has to offer to others, and (3) to change society by choosing to live relationships in community as a sign to the wider society that hope and love are possible. L'Arche recognizes the ability of many people with developmental disabilities to welcome and accept others and to gather a diversity of people together around them in harmony. L'Arche communities are ecumenical and interfaith, encouraging members of their communities to grow in their own faith tradition. L'Arche also welcomes people who do not have a religious affiliation.

Vanier, now in his eighties, has passed along his administrative responsibilities within L'Arche to others; however, he continues to live in one of the L'Arche communities in France, where he acts as a mentor to assistants. He is also a frequent speaker at conferences and meetings around the world.

Source: Adapted from www.larche.org.

SUMMARY

- Intellectual disorders are associated with varying degrees of damage to the brain occurring at different stages of development before, during, or after birth.
- Damage is manifested in a number of ways depending on the condition, including unusual physical features; particular types of cognitive, language, motor, or other deficits; and patterns of behaviour (e.g., hyperactivity, stereotypy, aggressiveness).
- IQ as measured by standardized intelligence tests is the most basic criterion for intellectual disability; adaptive behaviour is another important component. It is important to address not only individuals' deficits but also their strengths and capabilities, and the supports needed to function well in a given environment.
- The etiology of developmental disorders in general and intellectual disability in particular is complex. In some disorders, the cause is clearly genetic (e.g., chromosomal abnormality). Intellectual disabilities can also be caused by environmental factors at different stages of development (e.g., maternal malnutrition, toxins, or maternal infections; oxygen deprivation; prematurity; or birth-related trauma. The postnatal environment can also significantly affect development. Intervention strategies for people with intellectual disabilities tend to focus on developing social and community living skills and reducing or managing challenging behaviours. Pharmaceutical interventions for some severe behavioural problems associated with dual diagnosis are recommended. Sex education, while controversial, can reduce the risk of abuse while promoting more successful integration into the community. Genetic and supportive counselling for

family members and parent training can reduce family stress and improve quality of life for individuals with developmental disorders and their families.

- The deinstitutionalization and mainstreaming movements have emphasized the importance of community integration. Evaluation of community-based care and quality of life has become an important area of work for psychologists.
- Autism is characterized by a lack of social responsiveness, unusual responses to the environment, and absent or unusual expressive language. Higher-functioning individuals with higher IQ, more expressive language, and fewer other symptoms are often categorized as having Asperger disorder.
- Neurobiological and genetic factors are currently considered to play important roles in the development of autism, although the causal processes are still not clearly understood.
- Systematic intensive early intervention programs applying operant conditioning principles have been found effective in developing language and social skills and in managing challenging behaviour.
- Neurologically based disorders affect one or more ways in which a person takes in, stores, or uses information.
- Individuals with learning disorders are of at least average intelligence, yet they experience specific impairments in one or more of the cognitive processes related to learning.
- Cognitive processes include
  - phonological processing;
  - working memory;
  - processing speed;
  - language processing;
  - visual-spatial processing;
  - executive functions; and
  - visual-motor processing.
- Learning disorders can impede academic achievement in the areas of reading, writing, or mathematics. They can also impact daily life, such as having difficulty with organization, following multi-step instructions, or understanding sarcasm.
- Individuals with learning disorders may have greater difficulty with social relationships and may be at risk for bullying or may experience problems of mental health, such as anxiety or low self-esteem.
- Early identification by means of a comprehensive psychological assessment, academic remediation and accommodations in the school setting, and support or therapeutic intervention where appropriate, is vital for enabling individuals with LD to accomplish goals and to engage in fulfilling and productive lives.

MySearchLab offers you extensive help with your writing and research projects and provides round-the-clock access to credible and reliable source material. Chapter quizzes and a full electronic version of the text are also provided. Answers to the Before Moving On feature are provided on the MySearchLab. Take a tour at www.mysearchlab.com.

KEY TERMS

stereotypy (p. 360)
intellectual disability (p. 360)
behavioural phenotype (p. 364)
Down syndrome (p. 365)
trisomy 21 (p. 365)
translocation (p. 365)
mosaicism (p. 365)
amniocentesis (p. 366)
chorionic villus sampling (CVS) (p. 366)
phenylketonuria (PKU) (p. 366)
rubella (p. 367)
HIV (p. 367)
fetal alcohol syndrome (FAS) (p. 367)
fetal alcohol effects (FAE) (p. 367)
thalidomide (p. 368)
deinstitutionalization (p. 373)
quality of life (p. 374)
diagnostic overshadowing (p. 376)
dual diagnosis (p. 376)
autism (p. 377)
pervasive developmental disorders (p. 377)
echolalia (p. 379)
pronoun reversal (p. 379)
savants (p. 379)
Asperger disorder (p. 380)
child disintegrative disorder (CDD) (p. 380)
Rett syndrome (p. 380)
facilitated communication (FC) (p. 384)
learning disorders (p. 385)
phonological processing (p. 385)
dyslexia (p. 386)
dyscalculia (p. 386)
nonverbal learning disability (NLD) (p. 387)

TRACY VAILLANCOURT • KHRISTA BOYLAN

Chapter 15

Behaviour and Emotional Disorders of Childhood and Adolescence

LEARNING OBJECTIVES

AFTER READING THIS CHAPTER, STUDENTS WILL BE ABLE TO:

1. Identify the current issues associated with assessing and treating children and adolescents with mental health problems.
2. Describe the prevalence of common childhood mental disorders (ADHD, disruptive behaviour disorders, and anxiety disorders) and their comorbidities.
3. Identify the symptoms and clinical features of common childhood mental disorders.
4. Explain how biological, psychological, and environmental factors can work together to cause these common childhood mental disorders.
5. Identify evidence-based psychological and pharmacological treatments for common childhood mental disorders.

When Sam was 4, his mother could not leave him alone with his younger sister, Ellie. It was too dangerous, because Sam always hit or pinched her. Reprimanding Sam seemed to do little to discourage his aggressive ways. When Sam entered kindergarten, his teacher raised concerns about his behaviour, indicating that he could not sit still and seemed to enjoy bullying his classmates. When Sam was seven, he started his first fire—a small one—at the park close to his house. By age 10, Sam was sneaking alcohol from his mother's liquor cabinet. By age 12, he was a habitual glue sniffer, regularly truant from school, and still lighting fires and getting into fights at school and at home. Teachers described Sam as cruel and impulsive. His mother described him as angry and jaded.

Sam was finally seen by a clinician at age 13, after his school insisted he be assessed before they would allow him to return from his latest suspension. During the assessment, Sam acknowledged that he was angry and irritable most of the time. He also admitted that he liked to "sneak drinks" and that "life was boring." Sam seemed to have little insight into how his behaviour affected those around him. He was not concerned about his poor grades or his family's distress over his behaviour. He just wanted to be "left alone"; he also wanted to find his father so that he could live with him. Under no circumstances was Sam willing to entertain the idea that he had any real problems and he promptly refused to return to see the clinician again.

Unfortunately, youth like Sam are common in the mental health system. They present to mental health clinics because someone is concerned about them, yet they themselves are unwilling to get help. Youth like Sam are challenging to assess and they have many signs of current or insidious mental health problems. It is clear that Sam's mental health profile is multi-faceted. He has a smattering of symptoms that are consistent with several different disorders, including conduct disorder (early onset), attention deficit/hyperactivity disorder, substance abuse, and perhaps a learning disorder. The complexity of Sam's case seems to be the norm and not the exception in children's mental health. Indeed, in our clinical experience working in child psychology and psychiatry, we most often see children who present with a variety of different symptoms. These children, and their families, are often distressed by the way they are feeling and behaving. Their family lives tend to be complicated, and their social and academic lives are compromised. What is especially disconcerting is that for many of these children and adolescents, their current mental health problems represent the beginning of a lifelong trajectory of psychological disturbances. Although this point is daunting and not very encouraging, what is hopeful is that many efficacious treatments are available for behavioural and emotional disorders of childhood and adolescence and much is being learned about the etiology and developmental course of these disorders.

Historical Perspective of Child and Adolescent Mental Health

As noted by Neve and Turner (2001) in their review of the history of child psychiatry, "History dictates how the child is perceived." With now available means to study children and families using genetic, neuroimaging, and other scientific methods, scientists and clinicians are helping to expand our knowledge of the complexity of mental disorders in children. Today, most researchers study child psychopathology within a framework that stipulates that mental disorders have some biological basis. However, this has not always been the case, and it is important to appreciate the significant progress that has been made in understanding mental disorders and psychopathology in children over the past centuries.

The recognition of mental disturbance or psychopathology in children has a history that dates to the early nineteenth century; however, the study of children's mental states has evolved most rapidly over the past three decades. Initial accounts of abnormal child behaviour were attributed to inadequate parenting, which meant insufficient moral discipline in upbringing. Because children were thought to be incapable of self-reflection and reason, their behavioural problems were seen as a reflection of their environments, hence they were not seen as having problems with their brain functions. The advent of mandatory schooling for children created the opportunity to identify those who had intellectual delays—the first problems to be identified and studied. Treatment reflected the (then-recognized) importance of providing quality care in early life for children through adequate hygiene, nutrition, exercise, and teaching of moral well-being to parents to improve their children's behaviour.

At the end of the nineteenth century, attention turned to causes of behaviour as related to abnormal brain functioning, based on observations that many disordered children had parents who were unwell or low in intellectual functioning (Still, 1932). A few prominent child psychiatrists advocated for the need for psychiatric assessment and hospitalization for some very dysfunctional or dangerous children. In the twentieth century, Leo Kanner's (1935) first textbook of child psychiatry provided a framework for assessing children and adolescents. This book included sections on (1) personality problems arising from physical illness, (2) psychosomatic problems, (3) problems with behaviour, and (4) practical guidance on how to obtain a mental health history and the use of psychotherapy as a form of treatment. At that time, child guidance clinics were being introduced in schools in the United States and England. These clinics employed child psychiatrists, psychologists, and social workers, reflecting the developing knowledge in the field of educational psychology.

The first forms of research in children's mental disorders were descriptions of children with *infantile autism* and behavioural manifestations of deficient maternal care and overprotection. It was not until the 1960s that epidemiological studies of mental disorders in children began to document the prevalence of common child behavioural problems. The first comprehensive population survey, the Isle of Wight Study (Rutter, Tizard, Yule, Graham, & Whitmore, 1976), included 9- to 11-year-olds, and the Ontario Child Health Study in the early 1980s addressed questions that have continued to be of importance to child psychiatry—for example, What are the rates of youth psychiatric disorders? What is the role of intellectual development, physical impairment, and potential social influences on the diagnosis and prevalence of children's disorders? These works were influential because the researchers demonstrated that some childhood disorders persist into adolescence, and do so in characteristic ways.

The main diagnostic text for psychiatric disorders used in North America, the *Diagnostic and Statistical Manual of Mental Disorders* (DSM), has evolved over the years to include child psychiatric disorders (American Psychiatric Association [APA], 1980). While it has become clear that some disorders have an onset only in childhood (e.g., pervasive developmental disorders, mental retardation, genetic syndromes; see Chapter 14), other disorders commonly diagnosed in children (e.g., anxiety disorders, mood disorders) may have an onset or occur only in childhood or in adulthood. It remains to be demonstrated whether the manifestations and symptoms of childhood- versus adult-onset mood and anxiety disorders are the same, but most research to date supports the hypothesis that they are.

Treatments in child psychiatry encompassed mostly family therapy and psychoanalytic therapy, influenced by the teachings of Anna Freud and Melanie Klein, prior to the discovery of medications to treat hyperactivity in the 1960s. Since that time, there has been increasing emphasis on the use of medications in children and adolescents, with consideration of not only their efficacy for the disorders in question, but in particular their safety and side effects on behaviour and cognition in the developing person.

CURRENT ISSUES IN ASSESSING AND TREATING CHILDREN AND ADOLESCENTS

Issues that continue to challenge and stimulate research in child psychology and psychiatry include the imperative to study age-specific variation in symptoms and to establish what is normal behaviour or emotion for a child based on his or her age. This is not only because children may present with different symptoms based on their cognitive stage, but also because change and development of new skills or brain maturation may be adaptive to children and reduce their impairments, or symptoms, substantially. This latter feature begs the question: What constitutes disorder in children and how long and how severe must it be to merit treatment? The answer to this question will require complex and challenging longitudinal research studies that examine the persistence and continuity of psychopathology across childhood and adolescence.

More so than adults, youth are influenced by their environments and the lives of others around them because they have less autonomy for their decisions. This reality can also influence the presentation of impairment or symptoms. Furthermore, those who report a child's problems are typically parents or teachers, and not the child per se. What is challenging about the gathering of information from different sources is that those rating child psychological symptoms rarely agree with each other (De Los Reyes & Kazdin, 2005; Offord et al., 1996), a lack of concordance that may be clinically relevant.

Factors particular to child and adolescent mental assessment, including developmental variation in symptoms as well as impairment and informant bias, emphasize the importance of comprehensive diagnostic assessment of the youth. Psychologists and psychiatrists therefore aim to identify mental disorder symptoms in patients, but seek additional information about developmental, medical, social, and educational functioning to obtain a more global picture of the child. Such information is required to direct the development and implementation of treatment plans for the child and his or her family.

In summary, the process of providing a diagnosis for a given clinical presentation and determining whether this diagnosis is valid and reliable is an ongoing effort in the case of adults, and even more so in the case of youth (Jensen, 2003; Wakefield, 1993). Research studies designed to measure continuity and change in children's psychological symptoms are required to support the possibility that some childhood problems do represent severe or long-term impairments and therefore may merit diagnosis. Such research will be more robust when biologically based indicators of impairment (cognitive testing, genetic markers, physiological parameters) are also measured.

1 BEFORE MOVING ON

The assessment and treatment of children and youth with mental health issues are associated with many challenges that are specific to this pediatric population. What are some of the current issues associated with child and adolescent mental health assessment and treatment? How are these issues different from those that arise when assessing and treating adults?

Prevalence of Childhood Disorders

Mental disorders in childhood are typically divided into **externalizing problems**, including attention deficit/hyperactivity disorder (ADHD), oppositional defiant disorder (ODD), and conduct disorder (CD); and **internalizing problems**, including separation anxiety disorder (SAD), selective mutism, reactive attachment disorder (RAD), anxiety disorders, and mood disorders. Externalizing problems are also referred to as *disorders of undercontrolled behaviour*, whereas internalizing problems are also referred to as *disorders of overcontrolled behaviour*. In the DSM-IV-TR (APA, 2000), externalizing problems and some internalizing problems are described in the section "Disorders Usually First Diagnosed in Infancy, Childhood, or Adolescence" (see Table 15.1). However, anxiety and mood disorders are not included in this section because it is generally assumed that these disorders are fundamentally the same disorder in both childhood and adulthood. Although a distinction between externalizing and internalizing disorders is made, it is important to note that this distinction does not mean that the two types of disorders cannot coexist in the same person. In fact, **comorbidity** (the co-occurrence of two or more disorders or diseases) is the rule rather than the exception in mental health (see Angold, Costello, & Erkanli, 1999). Results from the recent National Comorbidity Survey Replication–Adolescent Supplement (NCS-A), a study of 10 123 American youth aged 13 to 18 years, confirm this point. In this nationally representative study, about 40 percent of youth with one psychiatric disorder met diagnostic criteria for another psychiatric disorder (Merikangas et al., 2010). Moreover, longitudinal studies show that not only do children typically receive more than one diagnosis at a given time, but their current diagnosis is often predictive of their receiving the same diagnosis in the future (**homotypic continuity**) or receiving a different psychiatric diagnosis in the future (**heterotypic continuity**). For example, Costello et al. (2003) found that children with a history of a psychiatric disorder were three times more likely to have a diagnosis at follow-up compared to those with no previous disorder. They also found that panic disorders, psychosis, verbal tics, encopresis (boys only), and enuresis showed the highest level of homotypic continuity. In terms of heterotypic continuity, they found strong evidence from depression to anxiety and from ADHD to ODD.

TABLE 15.1 DISORDERS USUALLY FIRST DIAGNOSED IN INFANCY, CHILDHOOD, AND ADOLESCENCE

Mental Retardation
Learning Disorders (e.g., Reading Disorder, Mathematics Disorder)
Motor Skills Disorder (e.g., Developmental Coordination Disorder)
Communication Disorders (e.g., Phonological Disorder, Stuttering)
Pervasive Developmental Disorders (e.g., Autistic Disorder, Asperger Disorder)
Attention Deficit and Disruptive Behaviour Disorders (e.g., ADHD, Conduct Disorder, Oppositional Defiant Disorder)
Feeding and Eating Disorders of Infancy and Early Childhood (e.g., Pica)
Tic Disorders (e.g., Tourette's Disorder)
Elimination Disorders (e.g., Encopresis, Enuresis)
Other Disorders of Infancy, Childhood, or Adolescence (e.g., Separation Anxiety Disorder, Selective Mutism)

The prevalence of child and youth mental disorders has been estimated in several large Canadian (Breton et al., 1999; Meltzer, Gatward, Goodman, & Ford, 2000; Offord et al., 1987) and American (Costello et al., 1996; Shaffer et al., 1996; Simonoff et al., 1997) epidemiological studies. These particular studies have more recently been combined, and disorder-specific prevalence rates have been calculated (Waddell, McEwan, Shepherd, Offord, & Hua, 2005; Waddell, Offord, Shepherd, Hua, & McEwan, 2002). Importantly, only studies that (1) assessed symptoms and impairment using a standardized assessment protocol, (2) included multiple informants such as children, parents, and teachers, and (3) assessed at least 1000 children were included in the summary prevalence rates. As seen in Figure 15.1,

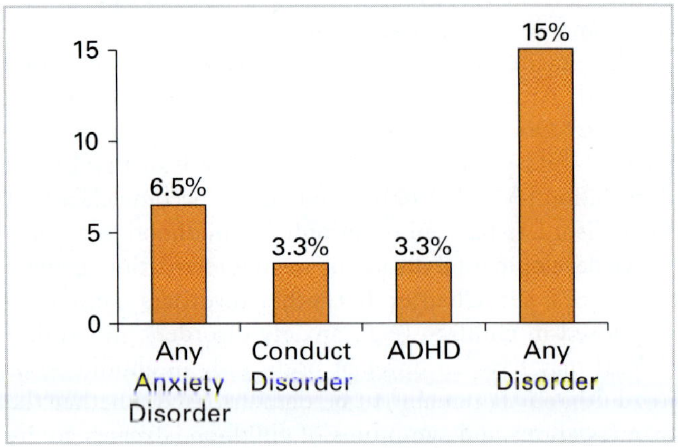

FIGURE 15.1 Prevalence of Selected Mental Disorders in Children and Youth

anxiety disorders, conduct disorder, and ADHD are the most common psychiatric disorders among children and youth using data from North America. Keeping in mind that many children and youth have comorbid conditions, it is not surprising that the average community prevalence rate is 14.3 percent. This means that over 800 000 children and youth in Canada have a mental disorder that causes them significant distress and is associated with noteworthy impairment in their social, school, community, and/or family functioning (Waddell et al., 2005). Recent epidemiological studies point to the fact that this rate is likely underestimated, at least for American children and youth. In the NCS-A study, approximately 1 out of every 4 to 5 youth met criteria for a mental disorder "with severe impairment across their lifetime" (Merikangas et al., 2010, p. 980). In another American study, the past-year prevalence data in the early elementary school years was also 1 in 5 (Carter et al., 2010).

The prevalence of mental disorders varies by the sex and age of the child. For example, children under the age of 8 rarely meet diagnostic criteria for conduct disorder, a disorder that is more common in boys than in girls (Loeber, Burke, Lahey, Winters, & Zera, 2000). Results from the NCS-A study showed that the median age of onset for disorders varied considerably by type of disorder (Merikangas et al., 2010). Anxiety disorders emerged by age 6, behavioural problems by age 11, mood disorders by age 13, and substance use disorders by age 15. In this study, females were more likely than males to be

APPLIED CLINICAL CASE

Bullying and Children's Mental Health

Shortly after creating a MySpace account, 13-year-old Megan Meier from Dardenne Prairie, Missouri, received a friendly message from 16-year-old Josh Evans. The two teens quickly hit it off and began an online romance that soon turned ugly. Josh told Megan that he did not want to continue the relationship because he had heard that she was not a good friend to others. Many other hurtful things were said online, including the suggestion that everyone hated Megan and that the world would be a better place without her in it. Megan was so upset by Josh's rejection that she took her own life on October 17, 2006. In the aftermath of her death, a disturbing twist was revealed: Josh Evans was not a real person, but rather had been co-created by Megan's former friend and that friend's mother, Lori Drew, age 47. The two invented Josh with the intention of soliciting information from Megan about her feelings toward Lori's daughter and to "mess with Megan."

Unfortunately, Megan's case is not an isolated incident—far from it. In 1982 three Norwegian boys aged 10 to 14 took their lives in response to bullying. These untimely deaths attracted media and public attention, which led to the initiation of a nationwide campaign against school bullying. Although the suicide of a Japanese 13-year-old in 1986 in response to bullying drew public attention to the issue, it was not until the suicide of another bullied youth in 1994 that Japan's Ministry of Education initiated its own efforts to address bullying in schools (Hymel, Schonert-Reichl, Bonanno, Vaillancourt, & Rocke-Henderson, 2009).

Closer to home, the start of the 2011 school year was rung in with horror as Ontario students Mitchell Wilson (age 11), Jamie Hubley (age 15), and Christopher Howell (age 17) all committed suicide in response to bullying. Despite these tragedies and other youth suicides, Canada's response to "bullycide" has been slow. In fact, with the exception of Manitoba and Ontario, none of the provinces or territories has formally addressed bullying in its Safe School or Education Acts. This lack of response is problematic given that bullying represents a formidable threat to children's and youth's mental well-being. In fact, studies have shown that bullied children experience more internalizing disorders than do non-bullied children. They are also at risk for poor educational attainment and report experiencing more health-related concerns. Importantly, longitudinal studies of peer-victimized children have shown that while some experience bullying as a consequence of poor adjustment and behaviour, for most, peer abuse *causes* maladjustment (see Vaillancourt, Clinton, McDougall, Schmidt, & Hymel, 2009). What's more, a recent study by Vaillancourt and colleagues (2011) showed that being bullied affects the brain. Using a longitudinal design in which Canadian children were assessed four times over a two-year period, these researchers found that peer victimization predicted elevated symptoms of depression, which in turn predicted dysregulation of the hypothalamic-pituitary-adrenal (HPA) axis (stress system). They also found that depression and HPA axis dysregulation predicted memory deficits in a manner that was consistent with published research on depressed adults. These results underscore the aversive nature of bullying that pervasively impacts the individual across multiple domains of functioning.

Cyberbullying and other forms of bullying are serious threats to mental well-being in youth.

diagnosed (lifetime prevalence) with a mood disorder (18.3 vs. 10.5 percent), anxiety disorder (38.0 vs. 26.1 percent), or eating disorder (3.8 vs. 1.5 percent), whereas males were more likely than females to be diagnosed with a behaviour disorder (23.5 vs. 15.5 percent) or a substance use disorder (12.5 vs. 10.2 percent).

2 BEFORE MOVING ON

Research about the prevalence and course of childhood psychopathology is burgeoning. Are the rates of psychiatric disorders in childhood increasing, decreasing, or staying the same? Moreover, what are the most common comorbid patterns in children and youth (hint: comorbid patterns are described in each disorder subsection)?

Attention Deficit/Hyperactivity Disorder

CLINICAL DESCRIPTION

ADHD: Jimmy

Watch this Speaking Out video at www.mysearchlab.com

Attention deficit/hyperactivity disorder (ADHD) is one of the most common psychiatric disorders in childhood and adolescence. Children with ADHD are motorically and often verbally hyperactive; they have problems maintaining their focus in conversations and activities; and they show impulsive or erratic behaviours. These symptoms almost always emerge in early childhood (Greenfield-Spira & Fischel, 2005) and, although some aspects of the disorder improve with age and brain maturation (Halperin & Schulz, 2006), at least one-third of children with ADHD in childhood retain this diagnosis in adulthood (Spencer, Biederman, & Mick, 2007).

CLASSIFICATION OF SUBTYPES Following the current DSM-IV-TR criteria, ADHD symptoms are grouped into three categories—*hyperactivity*, *inattention*, and *impulsivity* (see Table 15.2)—considered to be the three primary symptoms of ADHD (Barkley, 1997). Based on the main type of symptom that the child presents with, he or she will receive one of the following diagnoses: ADHD inattentive type (ADHD-I), ADHD hyperactive-impulsive type (ADHD-H), or ADHD combined type (ADHD-HI).

ADHD-I is more common in girls than in boys and is associated with a greater number of academic problems, especially in the area of mathematical achievement, than are the other two subtypes (Milich, Balentine, & Lynam, 2001). The inattentive symptoms are reflected more in areas such as listening, learning, and remembering. As well, children with ADHD-I subtype tend to have problems with organization and motor control. Accordingly, these children often have messy handwriting and problems eating neatly, for example. Social problems with peers are also common, and seem to increase the risk of development of other types of psychiatric issues not related to ADHD per se (Nijmeijer et al., 2008). ADHD-H and ADHD-HI are three times more common in boys than in girls and are associated with higher rates of comorbid conduct problems than is the ADHD-I subtype (Milich et al., 2001). Children and youth with ADHD-H and ADHD-HI tend to get into trouble, talk to themselves and others, interrupt others, move and fidget, and react more than do children with ADHD-I. Although the motor hyperactivity symptoms associated with ADHD-H and ADHD-HI often reduce over time, the fidgeting and restlessness often persist into adulthood (Willoughby, 2003).

VALIDITY OF ADHD SUBTYPES There is some debate in the literature about the validity of subtyping, with some critics arguing against this approach because subtypes are unstable over time (Lahey, Pelham, Loney, Lee, & Willcutt, 2005), arbitrarily divide a continuous trait into categories, and create threshold artifacts (APA, 2010). The ADHD and Disruptive Behaviours Disorder Work Group for DSM-5 suggest that the subtyping of ADHD may be removed in the next version of DSM. Instead, the DSM may recommend (1) classifying all youth with ADHD as having the combined type, (2) specifying clearly what the predominant subtype presentation has been over the past six months, or (3) providing no subtype coding, but rather guidance on how to code the predominant symptom type.

COMORBIDITY Children with ADHD, especially those with the hyperactive and combined subtypes, come to the attention of clinicians because of the impact their behaviour has on others, their parents' or teachers' frustration, and, in later years, their own academic, employment, or relationship struggles. Children with ADHD have higher rates of grade retention, suspension, and dropout, and are less likely to graduate from high school. As well, children with ADHD tend to have other mental health problems. In fact, 50 percent of children with ADHD have at least one other psychiatric disorder (Spencer et al., 2007). The most common comorbid conditions are oppositional defiant disorder (ODD) or conduct disorder (40 to 60 percent), learning disorders (25 percent), anxiety disorders (25 percent), and, in later years, depression (30 percent) and substance abuse disorders (40 percent).

PREVALENCE The prevalence of ADHD in the general population is about 2 percent among preschool-aged children (Lavigne et al., 1996), 6 percent among children and adolescents (Polancyzk, de Lima, Horta, Biederman, & Rohde, 2007), and 4 percent among adults (Polancyzk & Rohde, 2007). This rate, however, increases tenfold in psychiatric populations. Overall, more boys than girls are affected by ADHD, but when subtypes are taken into account, more girls than boys are affected with ADHD-I and more boys than girls are affected with ADHD-H and ADHD-HI.

DEVELOPMENTAL TRAJECTORY Most children with ADHD continue to have symptoms that require a chronic approach to management throughout adolescence and into

TABLE 15.2 DSM-IV-TR DIAGNOSTIC CRITERIA FOR ATTENTION DEFICIT/HYPERACTIVITY DISORDER

A. Either (1) or (2):

(1) six (or more) of the following symptoms of **inattention** have persisted for at least 6 months to a degree that is maladaptive and inconsistent with developmental level:

Inattention

(a) often fails to give close attention to details or makes careless mistakes in schoolwork, work, or other activities
(b) often has difficulty sustaining attention in tasks or play activities
(c) often does not seem to listen when spoken to directly
(d) often does not follow through on instructions and fails to finish schoolwork, chores, or duties in the workplace (not due to oppositional behavior or failure to understand instructions)
(e) often has difficulty organizing tasks and activities
(f) often avoids, dislikes, or is reluctant to engage in tasks that require sustained mental effort (such as schoolwork or homework)
(g) often loses things necessary for tasks or activities (e.g., toys, school assignments, pencils, books, or tools)
(h) is often easily distracted by extraneous stimuli
(i) is often forgetful in daily activities

(2) six (or more) of the following symptoms of **hyperactivity-impulsivity** have persisted for at least 6 months to a degree that is maladaptive and inconsistent with developmental level:

Hyperactivity

(a) often fidgets with hands or feet or squirms in seat
(b) often leaves seat in classroom or in other situations in which remaining seated is expected
(c) often runs about or climbs excessively in situations in which it is inappropriate (in adolescents or adults, may be limited to subjective feelings of restlessness)
(d) often has difficulty playing or engaging in leisure activities quietly
(e) is often "on the go" or often acts as if "driven by a motor"
(f) often talks excessively

Impulsivity

(g) often blurts out answers before questions have been completed
(h) often has difficulty awaiting turn
(i) often interrupts or intrudes on others (e.g., butts into conversations or games)

B. Some hyperactive-impulsive or inattentive symptoms that caused impairment were present before age 7 years.

C. Some impairment from the symptoms is present in two or more settings (e.g., at school [or work] and at home).

D. There must be clear evidence of clinically significant impairment in social, academic, or occupational functioning.

E. The symptoms do not occur exclusively during the course of a Pervasive Developmental Disorder, Schizophrenia, or other Psychotic Disorder and are not better accounted for by another mental disorder (e.g., Mood Disorder, Anxiety Disorder, Dissociative Disorder, or a Personality Disorder).

Code based on type:

314.01 Attention-Deficit/Hyperactivity Disorder, Combined Type: if both Criteria A1 and A2 are met for the past 6 months

314.00 Attention-Deficit/Hyperactivity Disorder, Predominantly Inattentive Type: if Criterion A1 is met but Criterion A2 is not met for the past 6 months

314.01 Attention-Deficit/Hyperactivity Disorder, Predominantly Hyperactive-Impulsive Type: if Criterion A2 is met but Criterion A1 is not met for the past 6 months

Coding note: For individuals (especially adolescents and adults) who currently have symptoms that no longer meet full criteria, "In Partial Remission" should be specified.

Source: Reprinted with permission from the *Diagnostic and Statistical Manual of Mental Disorders, Fourth Edition, Text Revision.* (Copyright © 2000). American Psychiatric Association.

adulthood. The most important long-term issue for youth with ADHD is increased risk for developing another psychiatric disorder (Biederman, Petty, Evans, Small, & Faraone, 2010). For example, 40 to 50 percent of adults with ADHD have a mood or anxiety disorder at some point in their lives, and one-third of these adults have one or more substance abuse disorders (Gibbins & Weiss, 2007). Research that studies patterns of substance use in youth with ADHD into adulthood has shown that these youth begin substance use earlier than youth who do not have ADHD; the earlier this substance use begins, the worse is the long-term mental health outcome (Molina et al., 2007). Other health and lifestyle challenges are associated with ADHD in adulthood, including a four times greater risk of serious injury, particularly in motor vehicle accidents. Despite comparable education and IQ, adults with ADHD have lower occupational attainment and greater academic problems (Seidman, 2006). Adults with ADHD become parents at an earlier age, have four times as many sexually transmitted diseases in adolescence, and have higher rates of divorce and separation (Flory, Molina, Pelham, Gnagy, & Smith, 2006).

ETIOLOGY

ADHD is the most well-studied child psychiatric condition. Currently, most research focuses on understanding the genetics of ADHD and how brain development in children with ADHD differs from that of children without this disorder (e.g., Halperin & Schulz, 2006). There is a strong biological basis for ADHD in that many of the symptoms are related to delays or abnormalities in the development of the connections between emotional and motor areas of the brain (Halperin & Schulz, 2006). Fortunately, medication and psychosocial treatments are quite effective as they focus on the well-characterized functional and biological deficits of the brain. As such, research on ADHD is a success story with a long history.

The earliest descriptor of the disorder currently known as ADHD was *minimal brain dysfunction*, followed by *hyperkinetic syndrome of childhood*. By the 1970s, it was recognized that hyperactive and disorganized children also had problems sustaining and organizing their attention. As such, in 1970, the syndrome was renamed *attention deficit disorder* (ADD) in the DSM-II. At that time, the diagnosis was made on the basis of three types of symptoms: inattention, impulsivity, and hyperactivity. In the revised edition of DSM-III (APA, 1987), the syndrome was renamed ADHD, and two new diagnostic features were required: *functional impairment* and *symptoms being present before age seven*. The validity of the three subgroups of symptoms began to be tested in the first large prospective treatment study of ADHD in children called the Multimodal Treatment Study of ADHD (Richters et al., 1995). This ongoing study, supported by the National Institutes of Mental Health, involves 579 children and families at seven sites across Canada and the United States.

Over the decades, the literature base on ADHD has expanded substantially. Although we now know more about the long-term course and impairments of ADHD than we do about any other childhood disorder, its effects on the family and child, and some successful treatments, the causes of ADHD are still elusive. This is because the disorder commonly co-occurs with other psychiatric disorders of childhood and involves perhaps the most complicated of brain functions: sustained attention (Barkley, 1997).

Because the causes of ADHD are largely unknown, a discussion of risk factors for ADHD is an important step in finding the true cause(s) of this disorder. The risk factors for ADHD can be categorized accordingly: (1) brain structure and function, (2) genetics, (3) neurotransmitters, and (4) environmental factors. It is well recognized that risk factors interact to cause a given psychiatric condition; thus, the multifactorial causation for ADHD is discussed.

BRAIN STRUCTURE AND FUNCTION Several studies have found that children with ADHD, compared to those without ADHD, generally have reduced brain size (3 to 8 percent reduction), abnormalities in the metabolism of dopamine and noradrenergic neurotransmitters, and abnormalities in the functioning of genes that regulate these neurotransmitter systems (Faraone & Khan, 2006; Halperin & Schulz, 2006). Several magnetic resonance imaging (MRI) studies have shown that ADHD is associated with abnormalities of the prefrontal cortex and basal ganglia. The prefrontal cortex is an area of the brain associated with executive functioning while the basal ganglia is associated with higher motor control, learning, memory and cognition, and emotional regulation. In a large prospective study of 223 children with ADHD and 223 typically developing controls, Shaw and colleagues (2007) found a marked delay in when children with ADHD attained peak thickness throughout their cerebellum (10.5 years for children with ADHD vs. 7.5 years for typical controls). The cerebellum is responsible for motor control such as coordination and precision but is also involved in cognitive functions such as attention. These findings are consistent with the clinical presentation of ADHD. Individuals with ADHD tend to have poor executive functioning skills, they tend to be clumsy, and they tend to have poor emotional self-regulation. These differences converge on a common problem in ADHD: the regulation of attention by the neurotransmitter dopamine in the prefrontal cortex and basal ganglia.

GENETICS Family and twin studies allow for the examination of differences between genetic and environmental causes of disorders. These studies have shown that more than half of the risk for ADHD in offspring is due to purely genetic factors, with some studies suggesting that the heritability of ADHD is as high as 77 percent (Banerjee, Middleton, & Faraone, 2007; Faraone & Khan, 2006). Genes that have been extensively studied are those responsible for the recycling and transportation of the neurotransmitter dopamine in the synaptic cleft (dopamine receptor 4 and 5; DRD-4, DRD-5), dopamine beta-hydroxylase (DBH), synaptosomal associated protein 5 (SNAP 5), and serotonin receptor 1B (HTR1B). Although much progress has been made in this area of study, a particular gene specific to ADHD has not been identified to date.

PRENATAL RISK FACTORS A number of recent reviews have described the prenatal environmental risk factors associated with ADHD and other disorders of childhood (e.g., Banerjee et al., 2007; Eubig, Aguiar, & Schantz, 2010; Froehlich et al., 2011, Williams & Ross, 2007, Winzer-Serhan, 2008). These reviews point convincingly to the fact that prenatal toxin exposure is related to mental health problems in offspring, in particular to ADHD. The "toxins" include poor diet, exposure to antidepressants, antihypertensives, illicit drugs, alcohol, tobacco, caffeine, mercury, and lead, and pregnancy or delivery complications. More recently, increased risk for ADHD has been linked to exposure to manganese, organophosphates, and phthalates, which may be particularly problematic for boys (Froehlich et al., 2011). However, as Williams and Ross (2007) point out, the prenatal risk factor findings are difficult to interpret because risk factors tend to co-occur and interact together.

PSYCHOSOCIAL RISK FACTORS Psychosocial risk factors include low socio-economic status, large family size, paternal criminality, poor maternal mental health, child maltreatment, foster care placement, and family dysfunction (Banerjee et al., 2007). The role of family dysfunction as a risk factor in ADHD is hard to assess, as the families of many children with ADHD report high levels of distress. However, work by Hechtman (1996) has shown that treatment of ADHD improves family stress and that family stress also decreases as the child grows older or moves out of the home.

GENE–ENVIRONMENTAL INTERACTIONS The current state of knowledge in the field of psychopathology is that psychiatric disorders are not the result of nature *or* nurture, but rather the result of nature via nurture. **Gene–environment interactions** (G × E) describe "any phenotypic event" that is the result of an interaction between genes and the environment (Banerjee et al., 2007, p. 1272). G × E is similar to the **diathesis-stress perspective** of disease, which postulates that environmental stressors should exact their greatest toll on individuals who have an underlying genetic vulnerability (Monroe & Simons, 1991). For example, Martel and colleagues (2011) found that homozygosity for a certain type of dopamine receptor gene that is expressed in the prefrontal cortical regions of the brain was associated with greater risk for ADHD and ODD only when children were also exposed to inconsistent parenting.

An example of a gene–environment interaction in the area of ADHD was uncovered by Khan and colleagues (2003), who found that ADHD symptoms were present in children with the 480-bp DAT 1 risk allele *only when* their mothers smoked during pregnancy. Becker and colleagues (2008) found that for males but not females, prenatal smoke exposure was associated with higher hyperactivity-impulsivity in those who were homozygous for the DAT 10r allele. As another example, Neuman and colleagues (2007) found that the odds of being diagnosed with ADHD combined subtype were much higher (2.9 times greater) in twins with a DAT1 440 allele who were exposed prenatally to smoke than among twins without the exposure and risk gene. It is not surprising, then, that Winzer-Serhan (2008), in a review of this literature, concluded that *maternal smoking* during pregnancy is an environmental factor that increases the risk of developing ADHD *in those with a genetic predisposition,* even after controlling for known confounding factors such as maternal age, low birth weight, lower parental education, parental ADHD, and income.

ASSESSMENT AND TREATMENT

Treatments are required to address the different symptom clusters of ADHD and the domains of impairment in both the child and his or her family. Comprehensive assessments of the child's development and academic, social, and family functioning are required to make a diagnosis. Hallmarks of assessment include reports from more than one informant, in ideally two or more contexts, using valid and reliable assessment tools. Clinicians need to identify the severity of impairment and potential worsening factors (e.g., learning disability or anxiety at school may make symptoms worse, or perhaps better) when assessing children. This information is also important to gauge treatment response over time.

Basic assessment requires administering a rating to parents and teachers that covers the symptoms of ADHD and their related impairments. As children approach adolescence, self-report may be helpful (see Snyder, Hall, Cornwell, & Quintana, 2006, for a review of rating scales for ADHD). In addition to symptom surveillance, a clinical interview is required to understand the developmental history of the child, the onset of problems and the degree of impairment from symptoms across multiple settings, differential psychiatric and medical diagnosis (e.g., toxin exposure, head injury), possible psychosocial issues that contribute to the presentation, and family mental health history. Usually, direct communication with teachers is required to understand both classroom behaviour and academic abilities. When the latter is in doubt, psychoeducation testing is required to explore the possibility of a learning disability.

PHARMACOLOGICAL TREATMENT The mainstay of treatment for ADHD is the use of stimulant medication (see Table 15.3), which has been shown to be effective in approximately 80 percent of children with ADHD symptoms (Prince, 2006). These medications work by increasing the release of dopamine and norepinephrine from storage sites in nerve terminals and by blocking their reuptake by inhibition of the dopamine transport protein. A new medication, atomoxetine, alters levels of brain norepinephrine. Several randomized controlled trials covering 8 to 10 years of follow-up demonstrate efficacy and effectiveness of stimulant medications for all subtypes of ADHD (Spencer et al., 2007).

Stimulant medications include short-acting or long-acting **methylphenidate (Ritalin)**, dextroamphetamine, and amphetamine. Stimulant medications such as atomoxetine act on other neurotransmitters (noradrenaline and serotonin). These medications have been shown to increase vigilance, reaction time, short-term memory, and learning of new material in children with ADHD (Prince, 2006). They also show beneficial effects on other associated problems relating to impulsivity, such as aggressive behaviour, noncompliance, noisiness, and peer relationships. Atomoxetine has been shown to have additional benefits in reducing ODD and anxiety symptoms in ADHD children.

Side effects of stimulant medications are common and include decreased appetite and weight loss, trouble falling asleep, headaches, and increases in pulse and blood

TABLE 15.3 SUMMARY OF DRUGS USED TO TREAT CHILDHOOD DISORDERS

Disorder	Drug Category	Generic Names	Trade Name
Attention Deficit/Hyperactivity Disorder	Psychostimulant	Methylphenidate	Ritalin, Concerta
		Amphetamine	Adderall
		Dextroamphetamine	Dexedrine
		Atomoxetine	Strattera
Conduct Disorder	SSRI	Fluoxetine	Prozac
	Mood Stabilizer	Carbemazepine	Tegretol
		Lithium carbonate	Lithium
	Antipsychotic	Risperidone	Risperidone
		Quetiapine	Seroquel
		Perphenazine	Perphenazine
	Psychostimulant	See above	
Separation Anxiety Disorder	SSRI*√	Fluoxetine	Prozac
Generalized Anxiety Disorder	SSRI	Fluoxetine	Prozac

*Serotonin specific reuptake inhibitor. While fluoxetine is the only SSRI indicated for use in children and adolescents in Canada, others commonly used are fluvoxamine (Luvox), citalopram (Celexa), and sertraline (Zoloft).

√ Behavioural therapy is the first treatment for SAD and GAD in all cases. However, many highly anxious children with GAD may require medication in combination with behavioural therapy at the beginning of treatment.

pressure. Some children can become more irritable or angry. These side effects are usually short-lived and reverse when the medications are reduced or stopped (Prince, 2006). However, children who take stimulant medications for several years have been shown to have slightly lower height and weight than those who do not take these medications (Swanson et al., 2007). Clinicians recommend that children and adolescents with ADHD remain on stimulant medications throughout childhood and adolescence. Although previously a common practice, drug holidays or periods off medications on weekends or during the summer are not recommended, as they do not help to improve growth and weight gain in children who regularly take stimulant medications (Wilens et al., 2005). Regular follow-up with a clinician to monitor growth, cardiac and developmental milestones, and comorbid conditions is crucial.

Despite the use of stimulants, most children with ADHD will continue to have social, academic, and emotional difficulties. For example, a review of 14 long-term childhood ADHD treatment studies by Schachar and colleagues (2002) found that stimulant medications improved both ADHD symptoms and social behaviours, with one study showing additional benefit in these areas by the addition of other psychosocial treatments. Their review found no benefits of medication on academic functioning and only a minor effect on emotional functioning. As such, emotional and behavioural deficits should be expected to persist following medication treatment alone, and additional treatments that target the acquisition of social and learning strategies are required for the child and his or her parents.

PSYCHOEDUCATIONAL INTERVENTIONS Research supports the benefit of caregiver psychoeducation about ADHD (Cunningham, Bremner, & Boyle, 1995). In this intervention, adults responsible for the child (parents and teachers) are educated about the symptoms, course of the disorder, and deficits associated with ADHD and how they can facilitate the use of the child's strengths to his or her advantage. For example, parents learn about the importance of routines, physical exercise, and supervised or planned activities to occupy the child. They also learn about what to expect in terms of tempers and other intrusive impulsive behaviours so that the parent can identify what is within the child's control. Such information helps parents and teachers to feel that they have a role to play in facilitating the child's development, which is associated with better outcomes in ADHD symptoms (Cunningham, 2007).

ACADEMIC SKILL FACILITATION AND REMEDIATION School-focused interventions for ADHD symptoms are usually required to ensure that the child is achieving the academic and social skills appropriate for his or her age and developmental level. Liaison with teachers or school guidance counsellors helps to identify areas in the child's school day where modifications can occur to accommodate the ADHD symptoms. For example, scheduled breaks from classroom activities, the use of reward systems, appropriate positioning of the child's desk, auditory versus written instructions, and the use of agendas can all help to improve the child's academic performance. Psychoeducational testing to identify learning disorders or attentional and behavioural challenges that may stress children's ability to learn is recommended for most children with ADHD. Such specific interventions around academic organization and remediation have been shown to be most helpful for children with severe ADHD (Chatfield, 2002).

PARENT TRAINING Parent education groups have been shown to help parents develop skills to manage their

Parent training is associated with more positive parent–child interactions.

child's ADHD-related problem behaviours (Cunningham, 2007). Parent training works when parents learn contingency management; specifically, parents learn techniques to help the child modify his or her own behaviours by providing consistent rewards and attention when the child completes a task or ceases a negative behaviour. For example, parents are taught to recognize and then acknowledge when the inattentive child pauses before interrupting a conversation, or asks if he or she can speak prior to doing so. In groups, parents are taught how to identify target behaviours to work on with their child and are given instruction on how to modify the behaviours. Parent training appears to be more useful for younger children, and may need to be repeated for parents as the child grows older to maintain the skills. Examples include the Community Parent Education Program (COPE) developed by Dr. Charles Cunningham and colleagues (1995) at McMaster University in Hamilton, Ontario; Dr. Carolyn Webster-Stratton's (1996) *The Incredible Years*; and Drs. Russell Barkley and Christine Benton's (1998) *Your Defiant Child*. A recent meta-analytic review of the effectiveness of various parent training components showed that larger effects were associated with fostering increased positive parent–child interactions and communication skills, teaching parents appropriate use of timeouts and encouraging consistency, and having parents practise new skills with their child during the training sessions (Wyatt Kaminski, Valle, Filene, & Boyle, 2008).

OTHER TREATMENTS There is less convincing evidence for family therapy, cognitive-behavioural therapy, individual psychotherapy, or social skills training in helping a child's ADHD symptoms. This suggests that the most effective treatments are those that help children to enhance their deficient self-motivation and working memory to show what they know as opposed to teaching them something or having them learn a new skill. The current gold standard in the treatment of ADHD is multimodal—a combination of stimulants and some targeted combination of the non-drug interventions discussed above (Daly, Creed, Xanthopoulos, & Brown, 2007). In particular, behavioural parent training and behavioural classroom management are the most well-established non-drug treatments for ADHD (Pelham & Fabiano, 2008).

3 BEFORE MOVING ON

> ADHD is a condition associated with specific cognitive deficits and various forms of social, academic, and family impairment. Describe the evidence-based treatment of stimulant medication and what aspects of impairment it is intended to treat. As well, describe the side effects associated with stimulant use.

Oppositional Defiant Disorder and Conduct Disorder

CLINICAL DESCRIPTION

Children with **oppositional defiant disorder (ODD)** frequently argue with adults, have many temper tantrums, deliberately annoy others, and are spiteful and vindictive. They do not take responsibility for their actions, blaming others for their outbursts and rude behaviour. Children who display symptoms such as these do not have a developmental disability like the ones described in Chapter 14; rather, these children meet diagnostic criteria for ODD. ODD is generally diagnosed by the time children are eight years old (see Table 15.4). Children with ODD are very difficult to manage—their negativistic behaviours and poor attitude are obvious and taxing to parents, teachers, and peers.

Some researchers have argued that ODD is simply an earlier expression of **conduct disorder (CD)** (e.g., Loeber, Keenan, Lahey, Green, & Thomas, 1993), which is also characterized by a pattern of hostile behaviour. In fact, one in four boys diagnosed with ODD will eventually be diagnosed with CD (Hinshaw & Anderson, 1996; Loeber et al., 1993), although the majority of children with ODD do not develop CD. Despite this overlap, what differentiates CD from ODD is that the behaviours displayed by the child or youth with CD *violate the basic rights of others or major societal norms or rules* (APA, 2000). The DSM-IV-TR organizes CD behaviours into four major groups: (1) aggression directed toward people and animals; (2) destruction of property; (3) deceitfulness or theft; and (4) serious violations of rules, such as being chronically truant from school before age 13 (see Table 15.5).

The ADHD and Disruptive Behaviour Disorder Work Group for DSM-5 have proposed that ODD symptoms be organized into groupings to distinguish irritable mood from defiant behaviours. This suggestion follows research findings that these groupings predict different mental health outcomes. Specifically, the irritable mood symptoms are substantially more predictive of later mood and anxiety dis-

TABLE 15.4 DSM-IV-TR DIAGNOSTIC CRITERIA FOR OPPOSITIONAL DEFIANT DISORDER

A. A pattern of negativistic, hostile, and defiant behavior lasting at least 6 months, during which four (or more) of the following are present:

(1) often loses temper

(2) often argues with adults

(3) often actively defies or refuses to comply with adults' requests or rules

(4) often deliberately annoys people

(5) often blames others for his or her mistakes or misbehavior

(6) is often touchy or easily annoyed by others

(7) is often angry and resentful

(8) is often spiteful or vindictive

Note: Consider a criterion met only if the behavior occurs more frequently than is typically observed in individuals of comparable age and developmental level.

B. The disturbance in behavior causes clinically significant impairment in social, academic, or occupational functioning.

C. The behaviors do not occur exclusively during the course of a Psychotic or Mood Disorder.

D. Criteria are not met for Conduct Disorder, and, if the individual is age 18 years or older, criteria are not met for Antisocial Personality Disorder.

Source: Reprinted with permission from the *Diagnostic and Statistical Manual of Mental Disorders, Fourth Edition, Text Revision.* (Copyright © 2000). American Psychiatric Association.

TABLE 15.5 DSM-IV-TR DIAGNOSTIC CRITERIA FOR CONDUCT DISORDER

A. A repetitive and persistent pattern of behavior in which the basic rights of others or major age-appropriate societal norms or rules are violated, as manifested by the presence of three (or more) of the following criteria in the past 12 months, with at least one criterion present in the past 6 months:

Aggression to people and animals

(1) often bullies, threatens, or intimidates others

(2) often initiates physical fights

(3) has used a weapon that can cause serious physical harm to others (e.g., a bat, brick, broken bottle, knife, gun)

(4) has been physically cruel to people

(5) has been physically cruel to animals

(6) has stolen while confronting a victim (e.g., mugging, purse snatching, extortion, armed robbery)

(7) has forced someone into sexual activity

Destruction of property

(8) has deliberately engaged in fire setting with the intention of causing serious damage

(9) has deliberately destroyed others' property (other than by fire setting)

Deceitfulness or theft

(10) has broken into someone else's house, building, or car

(11) often lies to obtain goods or favors or to avoid obligations (i.e., "cons" others)

(12) has stolen items of nontrivial value without confronting a victim (e.g., shoplifting, but without breaking and entering; forgery)

Serious violations of rules

(13) often stays out at night despite parental prohibitions, beginning before age 13 years

(14) has run away from home overnight at least twice while living in parental or parental surrogate home (or once without returning for a lengthy period)

(15) is often truant from school, beginning before age 13 years

B. The disturbance in behavior causes clinically significant impairment in social, academic, or occupational functioning

C. If the individual is age 18 years or older, criteria are not met for Antisocial Personality Disorder

Code based on age at onset:

312.81 Conduct Disorder, Childhood-Onset Type: onset of at least one criterion characteristic of Conduct Disorder prior to age 10 years

312.82 Conduct Disorder, Adolescent-Onset Type: absence of any criteria characteristic of Conduct Disorder prior to age 10 years

312.89 Conduct Disorder, Unspecified Onset: age at onset is not known

Specify severity:

Mild: few if any conduct problems in excess of those required to make the diagnosis **and** conduct problems cause only minor harm to others

Moderate: number of conduct problems and effect on others intermediate between "mild" and "severe"

Severe: many conduct problems in excess of those required to make the diagnosis **or** conduct problems cause considerable harm to others

Source: Reprinted with permission from the *Diagnostic and Statistical Manual of Mental Disorders, Fourth Edition, Text Revision.* (Copyright © 2000). American Psychiatric Association.

orders than are defiant behaviours (Stringaris & Goodman, 2009). Another proposal is that ODD be diagnosed even in the presence of conduct disorder as the research evidence suggests they are sufficiently distinct conditions.

Children and youth who meet diagnostic criteria for CD often display other problems. Like children with ODD, children with CD often have ADHD and learning difficulties (Hinshaw & Lee, 2003; Loeber et al., 2000). Some children with CD display *psychopathic* tendencies (Blair, Peschardt, Budhani, Mitchell, & Pine, 2006; Lynam, 1996). That is, these children show a general disregard for others and are not distressed by their negative behaviour, showing little, if any, remorse for their indiscretions. They are often described as egocentric, manipulative, and cold-hearted and are often extremely violent (Lynam, 1996). For example, one of the authors of this chapter met Jake, a 16-year-old boy who disclosed that on weekends he would drive around town looking for cats for his "experiment." This "experiment" involved calculating how long it took, on average, for a cat's tail to detach from its body when it was slammed repeatedly against the door of his truck. Given the strong evidence that the presence of psychopathic traits in youth with conduct disorder predicts more persistent, severe, and violent conduct behaviours, the addition of a callous and unemotional traits specifier is being considered for the DSM-5 (APA, 2010). The specifier asks clinicians to consider if the child or youth shows at least two or more of the following characteristics, which are persistent over 12 months and occur in more than one relationship or setting: (1) lack of remorse or guilt, (2) callous lack of empathy, (3) absence of concern about performance (at school, at work, or in other important activities), and (4) shallow or deficient affect. Clinicians are encouraged to consider multiple sources of information to determine the presence of these traits.

CLASSIFICATION OF SUBTYPES The DSM-IV-TR includes three subtypes of CD: (1) childhood-onset type, (2) adolescent-onset type, and (3) unspecified onset (age of onset is unknown). Individuals diagnosed with childhood-onset CD have at least one core symptom before the age of 10. Severity of CD is also specified in terms of mild, moderate, and severe.

SEX DIFFERENCES Boys are three to four times more likely than girls to meet the diagnostic criteria for CD (Loeber et al., 2000), girls are more likely to be diagnosed with CD at a later age than boys (Burke, Loeber, & Birmaher, 2002), and slightly more boys than girls are diagnosed with ODD (Boylan, Vaillancourt, Boyle, & Szatmari, 2007; Loeber et al., 2000). Although more boys than girls have conduct problems, it is nevertheless important to note the fact that many girls do have disorders of conduct (Zoccolillo, 1993). Conduct problems in girls are strongly associated with problematic outcomes such as teen pregnancy (Pedersen & Mastekaasa, 2011; Zoccolillo & Rogers, 1991) and suicidal behaviour (Cairns, Cairns, Neckerman, Gest, & Gariepy, 1988), issues that become particularly pronounced if girls with CD become involved with antisocial partners. Unfortunately, studies have shown that females with CD tend to date (and marry) males with CD, termed **assortative mating** (Farrington, Jolliffe, Loeber, Stouthamer-Loeber, & Kalb, 2001). Romantic relationships between two antisocial individuals are associated with more severe negative behaviour, discord in the relationship, and poor parenting of future offspring, who, incidentally, have a higher genetic load for conduct problems (see "Genetics" below).

COMORBIDITY The comorbid conditions associated with ODD and CD tend to be externalizing in nature, although internalizing problems are also linked to ODD and CD. For example, in one study, 92.4 percent of those with lifetime ODD met criteria for another lifetime DSM-IV-TR disorder (45.8 percent mood, 62.3 percent anxiety, 68.2 percent impulse control, 47.2 percent substance abuse) (Nock, Kazdin, Hiripi, & Kessler, 2007). ODD and CD are highly comorbid with ADHD (Loeber et al., 2000; Offord et al., 1992), with as many as 40 percent of children with ADHD meeting diagnostic criteria for CD (Szatmari, Boyle, & Offord, 1989). Studies have shown that youth who have conduct problems and ADHD started their trajectory of inappropriate behaviour at a much earlier age than did youth with only CD (Moffitt, 1990a, 1990b). In addition, these children are more likely to exhibit more severe and protracted symptoms than are those with CD alone (Farrington et al., 1990; Magnusson, 1988; Magnusson & Bergman, 1990). This large body of evidence lends strong support to the idea that the combination of CD and ADHD is synergistic and not additive—these children have an earlier onset of CD that is more entrenched, and their symptoms tend to be more aggressive in nature. Perhaps not so surprising, CD is also strongly linked to substance use (Boyle & Offord, 1991), with most studies providing evidence that CD precedes substance use. Although it may seem illogical, ODD and CD are also linked to internalizing disorders such as anxiety and depression (Angold & Costello, 1996; Boylan et al., 2007; Loeber et al., 2000), which have been shown to protect children and youth from future antisocial behaviours, but not improvement in psychopathology overall.

PREVALENCE The prevalence of ODD in preschool is 9 to 12 percent; across childhood and adolescence, the rate falls to between 3 and 6 percent (Boylan et al., 2007). The lifetime prevalence of ODD is estimated at 10.2 percent (Nock et al., 2007). The prevalence rate for CD has been estimated at 6.6 percent in children aged 4.5 to 5 with moderate symptoms, and at 2.5 percent in preschool-aged children with severe symptoms using DSM-IV criteria (Kim-Cohen et al., 2005). Among school-aged children and adolescents, the prevalence of CD ranges from 1 to 10 percent (Hinshaw & Lee, 2003). DSM-IV-TR notes that the prevalence rates fall to between 6 and 16 percent for boys and between 2 and 9 percent for girls (APA, 2000). Canadian researchers have estimated the prevalence rate to be 8.1 percent for boys and 2.8 percent for girls (Offord, Alder, & Boyle, 1986) using DSM-III criteria.

Why is there such a large range in prevalence rates? The establishment of a true prevalence rate for ODD and CD has been hampered by changes in the DSM criteria. In the past decade, there has been a noted drop in the prevalence rates of ODD and CD. This decline is thought to be associated with changes in DSM criteria for these disorders. For example, the DSM-III-R required an additional 3 symptoms out of a possible 13 for a CD diagnosis, and these symptoms needed to be present for at least 6 months (Hinshaw & Lee, 2003). Using DSM-IV-TR criteria, it is expected that the prevalence rates may begin to increase (Lynam, 1996). This hypothesis is based on the following: (1) that a diagnosis for CD using the DSM-IV-TR criteria now only requires that 3 of 15 symptoms be present, as opposed to 3 of 13 using the DSM-III-R criteria, and (2) the 2 new symptoms (threatening and breaking curfew) that were added to the DSM-IV-TR are less severe in nature and hence presumably more common.

DEVELOPMENTAL TRAJECTORY Symptoms associated with externalizing disorders follow a clear developmental sequence. Looking retrospectively (backwards), to be diagnosed with antisocial personality disorder (APD; see Chapter 12), there must be evidence of conduct disorder before age 15 (APA, 2000, p. 292). As well, looking backwards, most children with CD had ODD (although perhaps not formally diagnosed). However, looking forward, the developmental progression from ODD to CD to APD is less stable. Still, for children with conduct issues that begin early in life and are severe in nature, the aforementioned trajectory from ODD to CD to APD is robust (Loeber et al., 1993; Loeber et al., 2000), especially for boys (Rowe, Costello, Angold, Copeland, & Maughan, 2010). Clinically, this means that psychologists and psychiatrists would be less concerned with a 15-year-old who just started to skip school, shoplift, and break curfew than they would with a 5-year-old who has started a fire in his backyard, told his kindergarten teacher to go to hell, and has seriously injured the family hamster. The latter represents an early extreme, whereas the former is, to some extent, developmentally normative.

Given the developmental progression associated with conduct issues, one might ask whether ODD, CD, and APD are simply the same disorder that manifests differently over time. Although the stability of conduct problems over time is high (Cohen, Cohen, & Brook, 1993; Cote, Vaillancourt, Barker, Nagin, & Tremblay, 2007; Offord et al., 1992), most empirical studies support a distinction between ODD and CD (Biederman et al., 2008; Loeber et al., 2000; Rowe et al., 2010). For example, a recent 10-year prospective longitudinal study showed that ODD and CD predicted different types of future impairment. ODD was linked to major depression and to some extent CD and antisocial personality disorder; however, CD conferred a much higher risk for antisocial personality disorder, substance abuse issues, and bipolar disorder (Biederman et al., 2008). In another longitudinal study, Rowe and colleagues (2010) found that childhood ODD showed stronger predictive associations with emotional disorders in early adulthood, whereas CD in childhood largely predicted behavioural issues in later life.

FOCUS 15.1

A New Childhood Disorder in DSM-5? Disruptive Mood Dysregulation Disorder

There has been recent interest in identifying a childhood form of bipolar disorder upon which to focus early intervention efforts. Studies have shown that indeed some children present with a pattern of mood instability that is severe and consists of episodes of manic and depressive symptoms. However, the majority of children with extreme moodiness present with irritable, angry mood of a mostly chronic nature (Leibenluft, Blair, Charney, & Pine, 2003). These children are not being distinguished from youth with bipolar disorder and hence are being treated, potentially unnecessarily, with mood stabilizing medications. To facilitate classification and treatment of youth with unstable mood, criteria have been developed for a diagnosis initially called *severe mood dysregulation* (SMD), later modified to *temper dysregulation disorder with dysphoria*, and recently renamed *disruptive mood dysregulation disorder* (APA, 2010). Essentially, the criteria for this diagnosis describe a pattern of persistent and severe anger outbursts interspersed with symptoms of arousal or agitation that are not typically found in other disorders.

Although studies showed that children with SMD were equally impaired as those with pediatric bipolar disorder, they did not appear to develop bipolar disorder, but instead unipolar depression (Brotman et al., 2006). One treatment study suggested that they did not respond to medication (e.g., lithium) for bipolar disorder (Dickstein et al., 2009). The challenge with this group is that they also all met criteria for ODD, and likely also ADHD. Accordingly, many critics of the diagnosis have suggested that these children have a behaviour disorder and not a mood disorder. The consensus now is that they have features of behavioural as well as mood dysregulation, although the predominant mood is anger rather than sadness.

Proponents of the diagnosis argue for its importance for inclusion in DSM-5 mostly for clinical reasons. For example, children with these features will receive more than a diagnosis of ODD or ADHD, which is important in the American privately funded health care system, where eligible treatment services are linked to the diagnosis made by the clinician. However, the proposed diagnosis as it stands has some major problems. Specifically, there is insufficient evidence of its validity and no studies have been conducted to examine whether treatment brings about better outcomes. Perhaps the most important learning point from this effort is that many children and youth have mood dysregulation or instability that is not captured by existing DSM-IV-TR diagnoses. It remains to be shown whether these difficulties should be best understood within a categorical framework or as a specifier for other disorders (i.e., ODD or conduct disorder with mood dysregulation).

ETIOLOGY

As is the case with ADHD, the real cause of ODD and CD remains elusive, and these disorders are not likely to be the result of any one factor. Accordingly, a discussion of key risk factors associated with conduct problems is presented and not a discussion of the "causes" of ODD and CD per se.

GENETICS Conduct problems tend to run in families, providing some support for a genetic influence on ODD and CD (Burke et al., 2002; see meta-analysis by Rhee & Waldman, 2002). For example, in one retrospective twin study, the genetic influence on the risk for CD was 71 percent (Slutske et al., 1997). Other twin studies, including the Quebec Longitudinal Twin Study, have demonstrated that there is a strong genetic basis for antisocial and aggressive behaviour (e.g., Brendgen, Vitaro, Boivin, Dionne, & Perusse, 2006). The heritability estimates for conduct problems that include aggression range from 44 to 72 percent in adults (Blair et al., 2006), with a higher risk present for male than female offspring (D'Onofrio et al., 2007). Other support for the genetic argument comes from studies demonstrating that children with parents who have a history of antisocial behaviour are more likely to be diagnosed early with CD than are children without an antisocial parent (Burke et al., 2002). Caution must be heeded when interpreting these findings, however, as antisocial parents are not only contributing their genes to their offspring, but also raising them in environments that tend to be less than nurturing. For example, Offord and Bennett (1994) found that among children with CD, 69 percent of the fathers and 43 percent of the mothers had a substance abuse problem. Importantly, it is not only antisocial tendencies in parents that confer a risk; other types of psychopathology have been shown to contribute to conduct disturbances. For example, Silberg, Maes, and Eaves (2010) showed that parental depression had both an environmental (the effects of living with a person with a significant mood disorder) and a genetic (inheriting risk genes) impact on the offspring's behaviour.

NEUROBIOLOGY It is important to recognize that most studies investigating the biological correlates of ODD and CD have, in effect, focused on the biological correlates of *violence* and *aggression*. With this in mind, it has been demonstrated that aggression is associated with decreased glucose metabolism in the frontal lobe (Burke et al., 2002; Moffit, 1993; Raine, 2002) and damage to the orbital and ventrolateral prefrontal cortex (Anderson, Bechara, Damasio, Tranel, & Damasio, 1999; Grafman et al., 1996). This latter finding is interesting because the orbital and ventrolateral prefrontal cortex regulates the neural systems that mediate the basic reaction to threat. Damage to the amygdala, the emotion centre of the brain, has also been linked to impulsive aggressive behaviours (van Elst, Woermann, Lemieux, Thompson, & Trimble, 2000). As well, evidence suggests that aggression is associated with serotonergic abnormalities such as reduction in the turnover of serotonin (Coccaro, 1996). Low norepinephrine has been linked to conduct disorders (Rogeness, Cepeda, Macedo, Fischer, & Harris, 1990), as has low salivary cortisol (McBurnett, Lahey, Rathouz, & Loeber, 2000; van Goozen et al., 1998). Although most people assume that high testosterone is associated with aggressive behaviour, in truth this association is modest at best (Archer, 1991). What has been shown consistently is that aggression is related to the underarousal of the autonomic nervous system (low heart rate and lower skin conductance), especially among psychopaths (see Hinshaw & Lee, 2003).

NEUROLOGICAL Several individual factors have been linked to conduct problems. These include early difficult temperament, poor executive functioning, low IQ, reading disorders, lack of empathy, and poor social cognition (Burke et al., 2002; Hinshaw & Lee, 2003; Lovett & Sheffield, 2007). What many studies have failed to consider, however, is the moderating role of ADHD. In other words, it is not clear whether these associations would be as strong (or weaker) if ADHD was controlled for statistically in the analyses.

PRENATAL RISK FACTORS The in utero environment been has consistently linked to conduct problems. Maternal smoking is predictive of CD (Wakschlag et al., 1997), as is substance abuse (Loukas, Fitzgerald, Zucker, & von Eye, 2001) and pregnancy and birth complications (Arseneault et al., 2002; Raine, Venables, & Mednick, 1997). In a recent large-scale cohort study of 2868 children born in Australia, Robinson and colleagues (2008) found that the most important risk factors for behaviour problems in early childhood were maternal stress and smoking during pregnancy.

PSYCHOSOCIAL RISK FACTORS Psychosocial factors have been studied extensively in relation to conduct problems. These studies have consistently demonstrated that poor parenting, which includes low monitoring, harsh and inconsistent discipline, and child abuse, is strongly linked to externalizing difficulties in children and youth. Other psychosocial correlates include peer rejection, associating with deviant peers (McDougall, Hymel, Vaillancourt, & Mercer, 2001; Poulin, Dishion, & Haas, 1999; Vitaro, Brendgen, & Tremblay, 2000; Vitaro, Trembay, Kerr, Pagani, & Bukowski, 2007), parental psychopathology, lone-parent families, large family size, and teenage parenthood (Hinshaw & Lee, 2003). Children and youth who live in poverty are more likely to display conduct problems than their more affluent peers (Burke et al., 2002; Loeber et al., 2000), but keep in mind that poverty is strongly linked to high-violence neighbourhoods, public housing, lone parenthood, et cetera, factors that tend to exacerbate pre-existing negative attitudes and behaviours.

GENE–ENVIRONMENT INTERACTIONS One of the best illustrations of G × E comes from a study conducted by Caspi and colleagues (2002), who found that about 80 percent of individuals who were severely maltreated in childhood *and* had low monoamine oxidase A (MAOA) activity had conduct disorder in adulthood as compared to about 40 percent

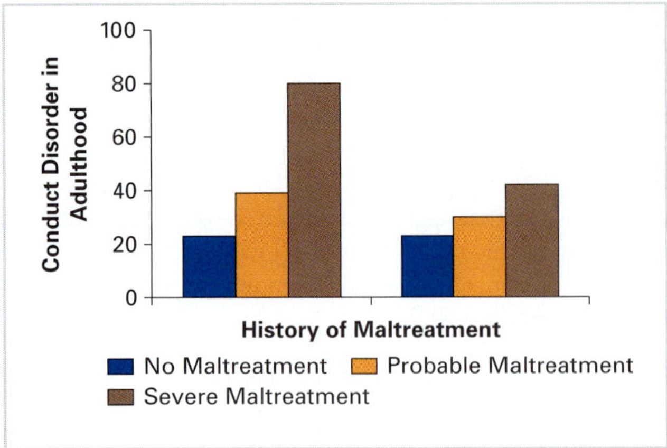

FIGURE 15.2 Conduct Disorder by MAOA Activity Level and Childhood Maltreatment

Source: Adapted from Caspi et al. (2002).

of individuals maltreated in childhood who had high MAOA activity (see Figure 15.2). MAOA is a gene that produces the enzyme that breaks down neurotransmitters like serotonin (5-HT), norepinephrine (NE), and dopamine, and, in doing so, renders them inactive. 5-HT plays an important role in the modulation of aggression, NE is implicated in the fight-or-flight response, and dopamine is associated with the pleasure system of the brain. Another example comes from the work of Jaffee and colleagues (2005), who found that physical maltreatment in childhood alone hardly predicted conduct disorder; however, when it was coupled with a high genetic risk for conduct disorder, it did predict conduct disorder. Taken together, these two studies demonstrated that childhood maltreatment alone is a weak predictor of conduct problems, but when combined with a pre-existing genetic vulnerability, the relationship is dauntingly robust.

TREATMENT

Four diverse treatment methods used for ODD and CD have been examined in controlled trials. These methods include (1) problem-solving skills, (2) pharmacological interventions, (3) parent management training, and (4) school- and community-based treatments. Although many "programs" claim to be effective in the treatment of conduct problems, caution must be heeded as CD in adolescence has been shown to be very resistant to treatment (Kazdin, 1997; Kazdin, Mazurick, & Siegel, 1994), highlighting the need for early intervention.

PROBLEM-SOLVING SKILLS TRAINING Deficits in problem-solving skills, social perception, and social attributions have been consistently found in children with aggressive conduct problems (Crick & Dodge, 1994; Dodge, 1986). These children are more likely to interpret ambiguous situations as being hostile. For example, if pushed, their first interpretation would be that another person did something on purpose, never considering that it may, in reality, have been an accident. These children also have a limited repertoire of behavioural responses, and the strategies they do have tend to be aggressive. Several interventions have been designed with these deficits in mind. Problem-solving skills training typically combines several different procedures, which include modelling and practice, role-playing, and reinforcement contingencies (Firestone & Ledingham, 2007). There is evidence to suggest that this type of intervention is effective at reducing problematic behaviour (Kazdin, Esveldt-Dawson, French, & Unis, 1987a, 1987b), although children never really reach normal levels of functioning even after intervention (Kazdin, 1992).

PHARMACOLOGICAL TREATMENT There is some suggestion that **mood stabilizers**, typical and atypical **neuroleptics** (antipsychotic medication), and stimulants may help children and adolescents with CD (see Table 15.3). Randomized controlled trials comparing lithium, a type of mood stabilizer, to a placebo found that lithium was an effective short-term therapy for *inpatient* aggressive children and adolescents (Campbell et al., 1995; Malone, Delaney, Luebbert, Cater, & Campbell, 2000). Risperidone, a type of neuroleptic, has been shown to be associated with improved symptoms in a small group of outpatients (Findling et al., 2000), as has the stimulant methylphenidate (Klein et al., 1997). A review by Gerardin and colleagues (2002) indicates that although lithium is the most documented treatment, typical neuroleptics have been most commonly prescribed and atypical neuroleptics appear to be the most promising pharmacological intervention. Moreover, methylphenidate has been shown to improve some symptoms of CD even when ADHD is not present.

PARENT TRAINING Parent training (PT) programs are based on a *social learning causal model* whereby interactions between the parent and the child are considered to maintain and promote conduct problems inadvertently (Firestone & Ledingham, 2007), termed the **coercive process** (Patterson, 1982, 1986). During the coercive process, the child's negative behaviour functions to diminish the negative behaviour of the parent. For example, in the early years, children use aversive strategies such as whining or crying to successfully terminate conflicts with family members (Dishion & Patterson, 1996). The purpose of PT is to develop a new skill set in parents that promotes prosocial behaviour while also applying effective discipline techniques to minimize the negative behaviour. One example, mentioned in the previous section on ADHD, is the Incredible Years Parent Program by Webster-Stratton (1996), a program geared toward children two to eight years of age. To date, several randomized control group evaluations have investigated the effectiveness of this program in treating conduct problems (e.g., Spacarelli, Colter, & Penman, 1992; Taylor, Schmidt, Pepler, & Hodgins, 1998). Results have consistently shown a general increase in positive parenting, a decrease in harsh discipline, and, importantly, reductions in conduct problems associated with this program. Interestingly, the Incredible Years Parent Program has also been used with teachers, with evidence demonstrating positive changes in their disciplinary practices and classroom management skills, as well as decreases in classroom aggression and increases in prosocial behaviour (Webster-Stratton & Reid, 2008).

SCHOOL- AND COMMUNITY-BASED TREATMENT Clinic-based treatment, like that described in the pharmacology section above, is limited by the fact that it is available to only a minority of individuals, who often represent the extreme end of the continuum on impairment. Without a doubt, the children and youth we have seen and continue to see in clinical practice tend to receive our care because something extreme—such as a serious violation of the law or a suicide attempt—has happened. When you consider the correlates of ODD and CD, such as poverty, lone-parent families, maternal psychopathology, et cetera, it is easy to see why clinical intervention is highly skewed toward the most severe cases. Data on who receives mental health treatment supports our anecdotal observation. For example, according to the Ontario Child Health Study, only one in six children who suffer from a psychiatric disorder receives services (Boyle & Offord, 1990). Complicating matters is the fact that the people who we most want to engage in services such as parent training are the least likely to attend and the least likely to benefit from programs (Cunningham et al., 1995; Cunningham et al., 2000; Kazdin, 1993; Kazdin, Siegel, & Bass, 1990).

Recognizing these realities, several programs targeting families through schools and the community have been developed. The Community Education Training Program (COPE), developed by Cunningham (2006), is one example. COPE has been successfully used to reduce symptoms of ADHD and conduct problems in preschoolers, children, and adolescents (e.g., Cunningham et al., 1995). The structure of the training sessions is described in detail in Table 15.6.

TABLE 15.6 COPE: STRUCTURE OF LARGE-GROUP SESSIONS

Phase 1:	Informal social activities.
Phase 2:	Leader outlines session plan.
Phase 3:	Subgroups review homework* successes.
Phase 4:	Large-group discussion of homework projects.
Phase 5:	Subgroups discuss errors made by videotaped coping model.
Phase 6:	Large discussion of errors.
Phase 7:	Subgroups formulate alternatives to videotaped errors.
Phase 8:	Large-group discussion of proposed solutions.
Phase 9:	Leader models group's solution.
Phase 10:	Subgroup brainstorm application.
Phase 11:	Dyads rehearse strategies.
Phase 12:	Homework planning.
Phase 13:	Leader closes session.

Source: Cunningham, C. E. (2006). COPE: Large-Group, Community-Based, Family-Centered Parent Training. In R. A. Barkley (Ed.), *Attention-Deficit Hyperactivity Disorder: A Handbook for Diagnosis and Treatment* (p. 487). New York: Guilford Press.

*Homework refers to therapy work. Participants are assigned activities to work through at home with their child.

An example of a school-based intervention program is one that was developed by Dr. Cunningham and colleagues (1998). In this program, called peer mediation, student volunteers are trained to identify conflict among peers and to intervene (i.e., mediate conflict) quickly and appropriately. The idea is that intervening early in the cycle of conflict should help to reduce the chances of it escalating into something far more serious. Peer mediators monitor the school playground and classroom during times of low surveillance by adults. Results of a randomized controlled trial provide impressive results—a 50 percent reduction in the amount of physical aggression displayed at school (Cunningham et al., 1998).

Programs like COPE and peer mediation are community-based intervention programs that offer important advantages over traditional clinic-based treatment options (Firestone & Ledingham, 2007). Because they are available to all children, these programs increase the likelihood of reaching those who are difficult to engage in children's mental treatment. As well, because they are universal, everyone gets the treatment. These programs also reduce the stigmatization or labelling of children with mental health issues because no one child is singled out for treatment (Offord & Bennett, 1994).

4 BEFORE MOVING ON

It is well recognized that multiple risk factors interact to cause a given psychiatric condition. Describe the multifactoral etiology of the disruptive disorders ODD and CD, paying specific attention to factors that may modify an individual's risk.

Anxiety Disorders

Case Notes

Hannah was eight years old when her parents brought her in for a psychological assessment. Her parents were very concerned because she was refusing to go to school, had no friends, and was "stuck" to her mother at all times.

When asked about her early development, Hannah's parents described a child who was always "clingy" and "fearful." Entry into kindergarten was a disaster because Hannah would not let go of her mother's hand. In fact, her mother had to remove herself forcefully from Hannah's grip every day at school drop-off. At school, Hannah cried the whole day. When her mother asked the kindergarten teacher about Hannah's behaviour and obvious distress, she was told that "many kids do this and within a few weeks she'll stop and start having fun." After several months of intense struggle, Hannah's parents took her out of school. They hoped that by the following year, with increased maturity, Hannah would be ready for school. This did not prove to be the case, however. At the time of her assessment, Hannah was absent from school an average of three days per week. She was so determined to not attend school that she would vomit if forced to go. Hannah also complained more often than not that she had a headache and/or stomach problems.

In addition to her refusal to attend school, Hannah was described by her father as being "worried about everything" and being excessively preoccupied with the idea that something terrible would happen to her mother. She wanted her mother by her side at all times and so she constructed a "rope" made out of towels to connect them. When Hannah was in a different room in the house, she made her mother hold the end of this rope. Her mother called the rope her daughter's "umbilical cord."

Every night, Hannah fought with her parents about where she would sleep. She refused to sleep in her own room. Because her father would not allow her to sleep in the bed with them, Hannah slept on the floor at the foot of their bed.

Needless to say, Hannah's emotional and behavioural issues were taxing to her parents, who worried about their daughter's future and about their marriage. Hannah's dependency on her mother was proving to be a formidable source of stress between Hannah's parents.

After her assessment, Hannah was diagnosed with separation anxiety disorder and generalized anxiety disorder.

Having fears and worries in childhood is common. For example, in a large community study, 90 percent of children aged 2 to 14 and 3 to 5 percent of adolescents reported at least one specific fear (Lichtenstein & Annas, 2000). The most common fears reported were of animals, mutilation (blood, accidents), and environmental threats (heights, weather).

Anxious children are often reluctant to separate from their caregivers, especially their mothers.

When fear is age-specific and the intensity is proportional to the perceived threat, it is considered developmentally appropriate. However, many children show excessive levels of fear from their preschool years onward into childhood and, for some, fearfulness can persist throughout their lives. The majority of these excessively fearful children will develop atypical patterns of fears and worries that impair their ability to develop normally. Many of these very fearful children develop anxiety disorders that require clinical intervention.

Although the DSM-IV-TR (APA, 2000) lists a number of anxiety disorders, with regard to children, only **separation anxiety disorder (SAD)** is listed separately in the childhood disorders section. One of the main reasons for this differentiation is that SAD is thought to be unique to childhood. However, the fact that only SAD is listed in the childhood disorders section does not imply that children do not suffer from other types of anxiety disorders—far from it. Anxiety disorders are among the most common psychiatric disorders affecting children and adolescents. Moreover, children and adolescents can be diagnosed with any of the anxiety disorders listed in the DSM-IV-TR (see Chapter 5). In this section, we focus on the most common anxiety disorder of childhood, SAD, and of adolescence, generalized anxiety disorder (GAD).

CLINICAL DESCRIPTION

The most obvious symptom associated with SAD is *distress* when separated from the attachment figure. It is not uncommon for the distress to culminate into a full-blown panic. Like Hannah, children with SAD constantly worry that something terrible will happen to their parents or other family members. They are fearful of new situations and of meeting new people, as these are unknowns that create a heightened sense of insecurity. Children with SAD also have a difficult time with transitions such as changing activities with the family or going to school on Mondays, after the weekend. Many children with this disorder feel fearful or on edge most of the time, not just in times of transition and stress. They can, however, be calmed when in the presence of their caregiver. Most children with SAD withdraw or appear timid as a means of reducing their exposure to distressing situations, but others can become angry and irritable or throw tantrums when forced to confront situations that heighten their fear.

Specific to SAD are hallmark features of at least three of the following symptoms for a minimum of four weeks: recurrent distress upon separation from a parent; excessive worry about losing a parent; excessive worry that an event will lead to harm to the parent; reluctance to go places without the parent in proximity; reluctance to sleep away from the parent; and nightmares about separation or complaints about physical symptoms when separation is anticipated (APA, 2000; see Table 15.7). In one study, the most frequently occurring symptoms in young children were worries about something happening to their attachment figure;

TABLE 15.7 DSM-IV-TR DIAGNOSTIC CRITERIA FOR SEPARATION ANXIETY DISORDER

A. Developmentally inappropriate and excessive anxiety concerning separation from home or from those to whom the individual is attached, as evidenced by three (or more) of the following:
   (1) recurrent excessive distress when separation from home or major attachment figures occurs or is anticipated
   (2) persistent and excessive worry about losing, or about possible harm befalling, major attachment figures
   (3) persistent and excessive worry that an untoward event will lead to separation from a major attachment figure (e.g., getting lost or being kidnapped)
   (4) persistent reluctance or refusal to go to school or elsewhere because of fear of separation
   (5) persistent and excessively fearful or reluctant to be alone or without major attachment figures at home or without significant adults in other settings
   (6) persistent reluctance or refusal to go to sleep without being near a major attachment figure or to sleep away from home
   (7) repeated nightmares involving the theme of separation
   (8) repeated complaints of physical symptoms (such as headaches, stomachaches, nausea, or vomiting) when separation from major attachment figures occurs or is anticipated

B. The duration of the disturbance is at least 4 weeks.

C. The onset is before age 18 years.

D. The disturbance causes clinically significant distress or impairment in social, academic (occupational), or other important areas of functioning.

E. The disturbance does not occur exclusively during the course of a Pervasive Developmental Disorder, Schizophrenia, or other Psychotic Disorder and, in adolescents and adults, is not better accounted for by Panic Disorder With Agoraphobia.

Source: Reprinted with permission from the *Diagnostic and Statistical Manual of Mental Disorders, Fourth Edition, Text Revision,* (Copyright © 2000). American Psychiatric Association.

in middle-aged children, excessive distress upon separation from their attachment figure was the most common symptom; and in adolescence it was physical complaints on school days (Last, Strauss, & Francis, 1987).

Children with SAD tend to recover within the first year of its onset; however, a three-year follow-up study found that one-third of children develop other anxiety or mood disorders (Foley, Pickles, Maes, Silberg, & Eaves, 2004). Most children are diagnosed with SAD before puberty (Bowen, Offord, & Boyle, 1990) and the qualifier *early onset* is made if SAD occurs before age six using the DSM-IV-TR. However, the proposed change for the DSM-5 is to drop this specifier because there is no evidence to support its inclusion. The argument is that for all anxiety disorders, "the age of onset could be specified as a continuous variable" (APA, 2010).

GAD, previously termed *overanxious disorder of childhood* in the DSM-III (APA, 1980), is diagnosed when (1) the child has many different types of worries or apprehensions, (2) he or she finds it very difficult to control his or her worries, and (3) his or her worries are accompanied by physical symptoms of being tired, restless, easily fatigued, irritable, or tense. For this diagnosis to be made, the child must have these problems for a six-month period and, unlike with adults, only one accompanying physiological symptom is required. In adults, three or more physiological symptoms are needed to meet diagnostic criteria. The most common worries expressed by teens with GAD are uncertainties about their grades and school performance and fears about natural disasters, being physically attacked, and being bullied by peers (Weems, Silverman, & LaGreca, 2000).

The primary difference between SAD and GAD is that, with GAD, the distress and uncertainty the child feels becomes directed outward to the world around them. They may become concerned about whether others like them, worry about doing badly at school and being uncomfortable, worry that a storm may come and cause damage to their home, or worry that something from outer space will apprehend them. Typically, the physical symptoms become the main source of distress for the child and family, and limit participation in normal activities such as attending school or parties.

When determining the type of anxiety disorder in youth, it is important to note the pervasive, persistent, and impairing nature of the symptoms. Also, the possibility that there are realistic triggers of anxiety (e.g., death, birth, a move, a new school) should be considered. If the stressor persists during the time that the anxiety is experienced, an adjustment disorder should also be considered.

COMORBIDITY Children with anxiety disorders often meet the diagnostic criteria for a mood disorder (Angold et al., 1999; Kovacs & Devlin, 1998). In one epidemiological study that examined comborbidity, 71.4 percent of 11-year-olds met the diagnostic criteria for depression and anxiety (Anderson, Williams, McGee, & Silva, 1987). In clinical populations, 70 percent of children with anxiety disorders are clinically depressed and about 80 percent are reluctant to attend school (Gittelman et al., 1980). Moreover, 70 percent of children with an anxiety disorder show somatic complaints, and test anxiety is common in these children (Biedel & Turner, 1988). About one-third of children with SAD

FOCUS 15.2

Suicidal Thoughts and Self-Harm in Youth

Fact: Suicide is the second-leading cause of death among Canadian youth aged 10 to 19 (Health Canada, 1999).

Deliberate self-harm (DSH), a term used to describe purposeful attempts to injure oneself without causing death, and suicide ideation or attempts, meaning that a deliberate plan or attempt to cause an end to one's life has occurred, are unfortunately common events for children and teens. A recent meta-analysis of studies including more than 500 000 teens reported a suicide attempt rate of 9.7 percent and a 29.9 percent rate for suicidal thoughts. Males are more likely to complete suicide and females are four times more likely to participate in DSH (Hawton & Harriss, 2007). However, do these behaviours and thoughts indicate risk for mental disorder, and which youth should caregivers be most concerned about?

Although DSH or thoughts of suicide may occur during a short period of distress, recent studies suggest that they are important indicators that mental health problems such as depression, substance abuse, and anxiety disorder are present. In the Great Smokey Mountains Study of more than 1400 youth, almost all youth who reported suicidal thoughts had important psychiatric problems: a diagnosable disorder (61 percent), a sub-threshold diagnosis (31 percent), or only significant impaired functioning at home or school (8 percent; Costello et al., 1996). This large study, consistent with many others, showed that the highest risk for self-injury was associated with having depression and one other psychiatric disorder concurrently. Youth who self-harm without the intent of suicide may be a different group, often having exposure to peers or family members who also participate in such behaviour, as opposed to having a psychiatric disorder (De Leo & Heller, 2008). The most important predictor of future self-harm or suicidal behaviours is having a history of these behaviours; however, abusing drugs and/or access to a firearm increases the risk of completing suicide. As such, youth with suicidal ideation require specific attention, and no suicidal youth should be left alone. Evidence suggests that cognitive-behavioural therapy for suicidal and self-harming youth may reduce future attempts by helping youth think of other options (Brown et al., 2005); however, few additional controlled studies can inform treatment of these youth at this time.

Your Life Counts is a registered charitable organization that helps youth aged 13 to 24 to change self-destructive behaviours that can lead to suicide. This organization has an interactive youth-focused website (www.yourlifecounts.org) with an email response facility geared toward listening and steadying youth through their moments of crisis and referring them to professional help in their communities when they are often not strong enough to reach out for such help themselves.

present with a concurrent diagnosis of GAD, and another third eventually develop GAD (Last et al., 1987). A recent study on comorbidity among anxiety disorders in a Danish national cohort of psychiatrically referred children and youth revealed that **homotypic comorbidity** (one anxiety disorder with another anxiety disorder) was low, at 2.8 percent, whereas **heterotypic comorbidity** (e.g., an anxiety with an externalizing problem) was high, at 73.6 percent (EsbjØrn, Hoeyer, Dyrborg, Leth, & Kendall, 2010).

PREVALENCE The most common types of pathological anxiety are SAD (5 percent), GAD (3 percent), social anxiety disorder (1 percent), and simple phobias (2.5 percent; Lichtenstein & Annas, 2000). Significantly fewer children experience other common anxiety disorders of adulthood—namely, obsessive-compulsive disorder (OCD), panic disorder, and post-traumatic stress disorder. In childhood and adolescence, anxiety disorders are equally common in both boys and girls. These anxiety disorders have different primary symptoms, but all imply that the child is suffering from impairment in functioning in his or her daily life and that the symptoms have been present for a certain period of time. Studies have shown that many anxious children have multiple types of anxiety. It is generally agreed that these symptoms are similar to those in the adult diagnoses, except for SAD, which is not currently diagnosed in the DSM-IV-TR in adults.

DEVELOPMENTAL TRAJECTORY Although most children with anxiety disorders develop normally and achieve age-appropriate academic and social goals, a significant proportion continue to struggle with anxiety over time. In fact, the homotypic continuity of anxiety disorders is robust, as is heterotypic continuity. For example, in one large longitudinal study, anxiety at age 11 was a very strong predictor of anxiety at age 15 for girls only (McGee, Feehan, Williams, & Anderson, 1992; see also Cohen et al., 1993). In a recent longitudinal study of children diagnosed with an anxiety disorder before age 13 who were reassessed at age 19, Bittner and colleagues (2007) found that SAD in childhood predicted SAD in adolescence, whereas overanxious disorder (now termed GAD) predicted GAD, panic attacks, depression, and CD in adolescence. Other evidence for the stability of anxiety disorders comes from an 18-month follow-up study of children and adolescents with SAD (Foley et al., 2004). In this study, 80 percent of participants no longer had an anxiety disorder at the end of the study. Those who were still anxious had significantly more depression, oppositional and hyperactive symptoms, and parents with marital distress than those who did not have persisting anxiety. One-third of children with SAD develop GAD, depression, or substance abuse problems, and these particular children appear to have more severe SAD and other mental health problems earlier in their lives (Manassis & Monga, 2001). Suicidal ideation and suicide attempts are reported to be increased in youth with anxiety disorders (Brent et al., 1996; see Focus box 15.2). A recent study of French-Canadian children followed from the time they were in kindergarten until they were young adults found that anxious-disruptive girls (and disruptive boys) were far more likely than their peers to attempt suicide by the time they had reached adulthood (Brezo et al., 2008). These studies suggest that youth with anxiety disorders that persist beyond one year of treatment require monitoring for depression and substance abuse in particular.

5 BEFORE MOVING ON

Many children have fears and phobias in childhood. What are some factors that may influence whether these fears develop into an anxiety disorder?

Research suggests that the developmental chronology of childhood disorders is one that begins with anxiety in early childhood, is followed by behavioural issues in middle childhood, and is then followed by depressive disorders in late childhood (Kovacs & Devlin, 1998). This research suggests that early psychopathology is a strong predictor of later mental health issues. Therefore, although many children grow out of their anxiety disorders, it is nevertheless important to monitor these children, given evidence for both homotypic and heterotypic continuity among a subset of this population.

ETIOLOGY

Compared to externalizing disorders, far less is known about the etiology of anxiety in children and adolescents, despite the fact that they are common to these age groups and are associated with significant distress, impairment, and disability.

TEMPERAMENT Most children with anxiety disorders have a history of anxious temperament in infancy and early childhood. This anxious temperament is described as **behavioural inhibition**, where children display withdrawal or fear behaviours in novel situations (Kagan, 1995; Kagan, Reznick, Clarke, Snidman, & Garcia-Coll, 1984). This temperament style has been shown to persist throughout life in most affected children, and their risk of developing one or more anxiety disorders in later life is two to four times that of children who are not behaviourally inhibited (Chronis-Tuscano et al., 2009; Essex, Klein, Slattery, Goldsmith, & Kalin, 2010; Hisfield-Becker, Micco, Simoes, & Henin, 2008).

BRAIN STRUCTURE AND FUNCTION Brain imaging and physiology research has shown that children and adults with behavioural inhibition or other anxiety disorders have abnormal functioning in a temporal lobe brain structure (the amygdala) that alerts a person to threat and orchestrates the response to it. In addition, they have higher resting heart rates and blood pressure (called physiological hyperarousal) and abnormal stress hormone regulation, which changes in an atypical way with age (see Pine, 2007).

GENETICS As with other mental disorders of childhood, anxiety disorders seem to have a heritable component. Turner, Beidel, and Costello (1987) found that 38 percent of children of parents with an anxiety disorder also had an anxiety disorder. Although anxiety disorders seem to run in families, it is important to bear in mind that this type of familial clustering can also be explained by shared environmental factors such as parenting practices or socio-economic status (Thaper & McGuffin, 1995). Twin studies help disentangle shared environmental influences from the influences of genes. Although many studies have been conducted on adults (e.g., Kendler, Heath, Martin, & Eaves, 1986; Kendler, Neale, Kessler, Heath, & Eaves, 1992), studies examining the heritability estimate in children are few and far between. In one British study, the heritability estimate was 59 percent using parent reports (Thaper & McGuffin, 1995). Interestingly, however, when self-rating of symptoms was used to index anxiety, familial transmission could only be accounted for by shared environmental factors. In a more recent longitudinal twin study, Trzaskowski and colleagues (2011) found that genetic factors explained most (68 percent) of the stability in anxiety symptoms, whereas shared and non-shared environmental influences were modest (18 percent and 28 percent, respectively). However, using data from eight different samples of monozygotic twins, Kendler and colleagues (2011) found that the environment does indeed play an important role in the development of anxiety. In this study, researchers found that as children aged, their environmental experiences contributed to stable and predictable differences in levels of anxiety and depression. In fact, on the basis on their findings, these researchers went as far as to reject the hypothesis that genetic factors alone were responsible for the temporal stability of internalizing disorders. As mentioned above in this paragraph, and in other sections, the current school of thought regarding psychopathology is one that includes G × E interactions.

PRENATAL RISK FACTORS A large body of evidence reviewed by Talge, Neal, and Glover (2007) suggests that if a mother experiences considerable enduring stress while pregnant, her child is significantly more likely to have problems with anxiety, and also with learning and attention problems. This is thought to be related to the effect of elevated levels of maternal stress hormone, or cortisol, on the developing brain.

PSYCHOSOCIAL RISK FACTORS Genetic studies of anxiety disorders in children have shown that it is not typical for the same anxiety disorder to be passed from parent to child, suggesting that the genetic risk for anxiety may be channelled by the type of environment in which the child grows up. Seminal research by Dr. Stanley (Jack) Rachman at the University of British Columbia has shown that the child learns what and how to fear from the parent either vicariously (by observing the parent) or through instructions given by the parent (Rachmann, 1977). Children can also learn to fear directly based on experiences in which they have been hurt or frightened (classical conditioning). The effect of the child's anxiety on the parent is not to be ignored, however, as bidirectional effects amplifying the parental experience and distress associated with child anxiety have been noted (Fisak & Grills-Taquechel, 2007).

Although they are likely very relevant, other psychosocial factors such as socio-economic status or parental education have not been studied extensively as risk factors for anxiety disorders. Using data from the U.S. National Comorbidity Survey Replication study, McLaughlin and colleagues (2011) found a strong relationship between child poverty and the onset of child psychopathology, especially anxiety disorders.

GENE–ENVIRONMENT INTERACTIONS Pine (2007) has proposed a model to describe how anxiety disorders develop in susceptible children. Most anxiety can be theorized to result from "fear conditioning." Here, the brain is engaged by threats (aversive stimuli) that the person would naturally want to avoid, and often a neutral stimulus becomes paired—or conditioned—with the threat to induce a similar fear and avoidance response. This pairing, along with its pattern of reinforcement, is largely influenced by the amygdala; hence, people with a genetic predisposition to amygdala dysfunction (i.e., those at risk for anxiety disorders or who have behavioural inhibition) would be more prone to be threatened, or fooled, by non-noxious stimuli. Such stimuli become the focus of childhood fears. Fears diminish over time in most children as the circuitry develops more elaborate connections with the prefrontal (inhibitory) cortex. However, fears persist in those children with behavioural inhibition.

The type of anxiety and the timing of its onset may be related to a combination of genetic susceptibility and environmental exposures. Consistent with this, many anxiety disorders are noted to begin following a period of life stress, and most research on families of anxious children suggests that they are close-knit and that parents are over-involved. It is difficult to disentangle this presentation from the parents' own high levels of anxiety (or of anxiety disorders); thus, additional research in this area is required. Recent work by Kendler and colleagues (2008) suggests that the genetic or biological component of risk for anxiety may diminish as the child ages, suggesting further the importance of studying the environmental causes of anxiety, particularly in adolescents.

TREATMENT

The primary aim of treatment of anxiety is reduction of children's physical symptoms and their pattern of avoidance of situations or things that provoke their fear symptoms and thoughts. This reduction in physical symptoms of anxiety will help the children think more clearly about their anxieties and, depending on their age, begin to think more probabilistically or neutrally about the fears so that they function more normally. However, modification of the behavioural avoidance is also central. For example, if school avoidance exists, this should be addressed as an urgent issue. Typically, multiple people are involved in any treatment plan for child anxiety disorder.

Treatment of anxiety disorders includes first providing psychoeducation about the causes of anxiety and which of the child's behaviours are most likely related to anxiety. This is provided to the child, parents, and teachers. Behavioural assessment of how the parents and teachers handle the anxiety is required because the way in which adults manage the symptoms often unintentionally reinforces a child's avoidance behaviours. Taking a life history of the child to understand his or her development and its normalcy is important in that a child who has social or language delays will have additional challenges in responding optimally to treatment, and often adults are protective of these children. In most instances of severe child anxiety, ongoing monitoring of how the parents are managing the anxiety is required. Some very anxious parents may require treatment for underlying anxiety disorders themselves.

COGNITIVE-BEHAVIOURAL TREATMENT The most robust evidence for treatment of childhood anxiety disorders exists for cognitive-behavioural therapy (CBT; Cartwright-Hatton, Roberts, Chitsabesan, Fothergill, & Harrington, 2004), with one of the most widely used methods being the Coping Cat program (Kendall & Hedtke, 2006). Components of CBT include extensive education about anxiety and its treatment approach, helping the parents and child learn new ways to cope with anxiety (skills building), and systematic and gradual exposure to anxiety-provoking situations in which they can practise their skills. How children are exposed to anxiety-provoking situations depends on how anxious or functionally impaired they (or the parents) are. For example, children who cannot go to school or want to call their parents every hour would be expected to go to school and remain there until they were less upset prior to calling the parents (or not call the parents at all), or they could call their parents only once a day for a few weeks. In CBT, it is important that all parties agree on what behaviour is acceptable or unacceptable. In addition, after the behavioural intervention, there is an opportunity to debrief with the child about his or her success, or to discuss how to make it more successful next time (mastery).

Many anxious children have a parent who is also anxious. Accordingly, there is evidence to support the inclusion of a parent component when using CBT. For example, Cobham, Dadds, and Spence (1998) found that the efficacy of child-focused CBT was reduced among children whose parents were anxious. However, the provision of a parental anxiety management component enhanced the treatment efficacy among these children.

Some children are so anxious that they cannot succeed with CBT. In these instances, medications can be useful. Indeed, a recent randomized controlled trial of anxious children aged 7 to 17 found that a combination of CBT and the selective serotonin reuptake inhibitor sertraline (Zoloft) produced the best response rates (Walkup et al., 2008).

PHARMACOLOGICAL TREATMENT Similar pharmacological treatments (see Table 15.3) are recommended for SAD and GAD because they probably target similar underlying physiological processes, and because most

CANADIAN RESEARCH CENTRE

Selective Mutism Service, McMaster Children's Hospital

Selective mutism is classified in the DSM-IV-TR in the childhood disorders section with no revision recommended for the DSM-5. Children with selective mutism often do not speak in social situations despite speaking in other situations, such as at home with their parents. Although these children rarely have speech problems, they do experience such heightened anxiety in social situations that they are unable to speak. For this reason, experienced clinicians in the field have conceptualized selective mutism as a type of social phobia (see Chapter 5) and treat it as such (Anstendig, 1999; Black & Uhde, 1995). Like children with social phobia, those with selective mutism often have other anxiety-related conditions (Cunningham, McHolm, Boyle, & Patel, 2005).

In Canada, a treatment program for selectively mute children has been developed by Drs. Angela McHolm and Charles Cunningham at McMaster University (McHolm, Cunningham, & Vanier, 2005). The Selective Mutism Service at McMaster Children's Hospital in Hamilton, Ontario, offers assessment, school-based consultation, and individual and group treatment to youth with selective mutism (aged preschool to 18). Parents, educators, and involved mental health professionals are often the primary recipients of clinical services given their critical roles in supporting these children, the early age of onset for the condition, and the fact that the youth's speaking inhibition often becomes a barrier to a more conventional "talk therapy" approach. The program centres on a school-based, collaborative approach to assessment and treatment with psychoeducation and skills training of parents and professionals as key components in the intervention. Given that selective mutism is viewed as an anxiety-based condition, behavioural principles (e.g., exposure training and the use of a hierarchy, shaping, fading) guide the systematic intervention program, with particular consideration of anxiety-provoking speaking situations within the school setting. Older youth may also be offered CBT to address comorbid forms of anxiety such as social anxiety, separation anxiety, or generalized anxiety.

The Selective Mutism Service serves as a regional centre that provides support to families across southwestern Ontario, and it is the only comprehensive mental health service of its kind known to exist in North America. In recent times, other mental health agencies within Ontario and beyond have borrowed aspects of the program to develop additional local services for this special population of children.

randomized controlled trials in children include children with both, or more, disorders. Three placebo-controlled studies report significant benefits of the **selective serotonin reuptake inhibitors**, or SSRIs (fluvoxamine, paroxetine, and fluoxetine), emerging by approximately four weeks of treatment (Clark et al., 2005; Rynn, Siqueland, & Rickels, 2001; Wagner et al., 2004). The largest randomized controlled study (128 youth) of longest duration (6 months) found a significant reduction in anxiety symptoms with the drug fluvoxamine after eight weeks (Walkup et al., 2002). At the end of the study, they found that 92 percent of those taking medications stayed well. To date, no studies have been conducted to determine whether youth relapse, or become unwell again, after stopping SSRI medications. These studies, although few in number, suggest that SSRI medications are efficacious at reducing anxiety symptoms in children with these types of anxiety disorders (Walkup et al., 2008), but more studies are required to determine whether medications are better than CBT alone.

The most common side effects of SSRIs are gastrointestinal complaints, headaches, and drowsiness. Concerns about increased risk of suicidal ideation in SSRI anxiety trials cannot be answered, as most children with suicidal ideation or depression are excluded and the studies do not include enough participants. For all children or teens taking SSRI medications, close monitoring of suicidal thoughts or feelings of agitation is necessary, as some youth taking such medications may develop these problems (Hetrick, Merry, McKenzie, Sindahl, & Proctor, 2007). Medications with a poor risk–benefit profile include benzodiazepines and tricyclic antidepressants, and these are not recommended for the treatment of anxiety in youth.

SUMMARY

- More so than adults, children and youth are influenced by their environments and the lives of others around them because they have less autonomy for their decisions. This reality can also influence the presentation of impairment or symptoms.
- It is important to consider the impact of life stressors and family context on a child's symptoms. The impact of treatment or cognitive and emotional development on symptom persistence is also important to consider as children continue to grow and mature.
- The opinion of the child's difficulties can differ by the informant. Teachers have been shown to be better

respondents than parents about severity of ADHD and social functioning. Parents have been shown to be the most comprehensive respondents about disruptive behaviours, although they under-report conduct symptoms compared to the child. Adolescents are the most accurate respondents with respect to anxiety.

- These developmental and informant factors specific to children and youth emphasize the importance of comprehensive assessment of symptoms and global functioning from multiple informants in this population.
- One in five youth have a psychiatric disorder. Forty percent of these youth have multiple disorders (comorbidity). Having a childhood disorder substantially increases the risk for developing another disorder (heterotypic continuity) or continuing to have the same disorder (homotypic continuity).
- Some disorders appear to be more common in boys prior to puberty (ADHD) and in girls following puberty (anxiety disorders). Although conduct disorders are more common in boys before puberty, the rates are more similar across sex in adolescence.
- ADHD can be diagnosed in 2 percent of preschoolers and 6 percent of children and adolescents. ADHD is 10 times as prevalent in clinical samples. The prevalence of ODD (3 to 6 percent) and CD (1 to 10 percent) is similar to ADHD, although more difficult to estimate as many studies do not clearly distinguish the prevalence of ODD from CD (and many do not account for the comorbid condition ADHD). Anxiety disorders are also common, but rates vary by disorder, with the most common presentation being separation anxiety disorder (5 percent of children) and the least common being social anxiety disorder (1 percent of children).
- Regardless of the type of disorder, all diagnoses require that the child show evidence of persistent impairment in multiple settings, which can be directly attributed to the symptoms of disorder.
- ADHD is a neuropsychiatric disorder that reflects problems with executive functions, such as the regulation of attention, behaviour, and motivation. The two broad areas of symptom impairment are hyperactivity/impulsivity and inattention. The DSM recognizes ADHD subtypes where some children appear more hyperactive or more inattentive and can be classified as such, although most children with ADHD have both hyperactivity/impulsivity and inattention.
- ODD and CD describe youth who have persistent difficulties of reacting negatively toward others with hostility or defiance as a primary problem (ODD) or engaging in behaviours that result in deliberate physical or emotional harm to others (CD). It is clear that these diagnoses describe the behaviours of the youth and not so much their underlying difficulties, such as comorbid disorders (ADHD, anxiety, or learning disabilities) or the difficult social circumstances they live in. For example, recent research suggests there may be a subgroup of ODD youth who struggle with high levels of irritable mood, and a group of CD youth who have psychopathic tendencies.
- Children with anxiety disorders experience all of the following difficulties: mental preoccupations with worries or fears, behavioural or mental actions directed toward avoidance of the perceived source of fear or worry, and physical distress (headaches, tension) because of the worry. What differs across the types of anxiety disorders is the focus of the fear or worry. For example, being worried about a parent's safety is consistent with separation anxiety, being worried about potential embarrassment is consistent with social anxiety, and being worried about unpredictable events is consistent with generalized anxiety.
- Mental disorders present as a result of multiple risk processes that involve components of disturbed biology, environment, and psychological factors. The timing of occurrence of disorder and the severity of the disorder are related to the ways these factors exert their effects for a particular child. It is therefore false to assume that any one factor is causal. When describing a mental disorder and its presentation, it is important to consider how biological, environmental, and psychological factors are of relevance for that child. For example, most children with ADHD have a family history, attesting to its inherited genetic component, and their symptoms typically respond to stimulant medication, suggesting a biological basis for the disorder. Symptoms of ADHD are worse in unstructured environments (such as lunchtime versus in class), attesting to the influence of context in shaping behaviour. Many children with ADHD are difficult to parent or teach and experience difficulties with peers, and their self-esteem is often affected. It is important to intervene in all these areas to help the child with ADHD.
- ADHD: Evidence-based psychological interventions should be provided to all families who have a child with ADHD. These include caregiver psychoeducation, parent training programs to help parents facilitate more functional behaviour patterns, and school-focused interventions including psychoeducational testing for learning difficulties and providing classroom modifications to facilitate attention. Pharmacological treatments for ADHD include short- and long-acting derivatives of methylphenidate, dextroamphetamine, and amphetamine. These compounds work by increasing the sensitivity of dopamine receptors in the prefrontal cortex. Children treated with these medications require close medical monitoring. These treatments do not cure ADHD but help reduce symptoms and should be used in concert with psychological interventions.
- ODD and CD: Four diverse treatment methods have been shown to be helpful for ODD and CD: (1)

teaching problem-solving skills, (2) pharmacological interventions, (3) parent management training, and (4) school- and community-based treatments. With the exception of pharmacological interventions, these methods help to break the coercive effect of the youth's behaviour on families and peers by teaching others how to respond to the behaviour or increasing the youth's sensitivity to the effects of his or her behaviour on others. Pharmacological interventions are generally focused on the treatment of comorbid conditions (ADHD or anxiety).

- Anxiety disorders: Cognitive-behavioural therapy (CBT) has been shown to be effective for the treatment of childhood anxiety disorders. CBT should include a parent component as many parents have anxiety themselves or reinforce the child's avoidance behaviours. Medications for treatment of anxiety in children and youth include antidepressant medications (serotonin specific reuptake inhibitors), and are used as an adjunct to CBT or as a means of reducing anxiety sufficiently to allow participation in CBT.

MySearchLab offers you extensive help with your writing and research projects and provides round-the-clock access to credible and reliable source material. Chapter quizzes and a full electronic version of the text are also provided. Answers to the Before Moving On feature are provided on the MySearchLab. Take a tour at www.mysearchlab.com.

KEY TERMS

externalizing problems (p. 394)
internalizing problems (p. 394)
comorbidity (p. 394)
homotypic continuity (p. 394)
heterotypic continuity (p. 394)
attention deficit/hyperactivity disorder (ADHD) (p. 396)
gene–environment interactions (p. 399)
diathesis-stress perspective (p. 399)
methylphenidate (Ritalin) (p. 399)
oppositional defiant disorder (ODD) (p. 401)
conduct disorder (CD) (p. 401)
assortative mating (p. 403)
mood stabilizers (p. 406)
neuroleptics (p. 406)
coercive process (p. 406)
separation anxiety disorder (SAD) (p. 408)
homotypic comorbidity (p. 410)
heterotypic comorbidity (p. 410)
deliberate self-harm (DSH) (p. 410)
behavioural inhibition (p. 411)
selective serotonin reuptake inhibitors (p. 413)
selective mutism (p. 413)

COREY S. MACKENZIE • KRISTIN A. REYNOLDS

Chapter 16

Aging and Mental Health

LEARNING OBJECTIVES

AFTER READING THIS CHAPTER, STUDENTS WILL BE ABLE TO:

1. Explain how Canada's population is aging, why it is aging, and what effect our aging population will have on mental health professionals.
2. Describe the commonly held myth about treating mental disorders among older adults and list reasons for why this myth exists.
3. Describe how the three primary lifespan theoretical models of aging view successful aging.
4. Summarize the various factors that complicate the diagnosis and treatment of sleep disorders in older adults.
5. Briefly summarize what current research tells us about the effectiveness of psychological and pharmacological treatment of mood, anxiety, and sleep disorders for older versus younger adults.
6. List the primary risk factors for developing Alzheimer's disease.

Just after Laura retired at age 65, her only daughter, Stephanie, died in a mountain-climbing accident. Laura and her daughter, a single pediatrician, had always been very close, and people often remarked that they seemed more like sisters than like mother and daughter. Immediately after hearing the terrible news, Laura began a whirlwind of activity. First, she arranged single-handedly to have Stephanie's body returned home from Nepal. Next, she planned an elaborate funeral. During these few days, Laura barely slept and never shed a tear. She displayed no sadness, and showed anxiety only about funeral details. Laura wanted everything to be perfect for Stephanie. Her friends praised her strength of character, but her husband, Mark, was silently worried about her frantic pace of activity. For a few weeks after the funeral, Laura's state of agitation persisted. She could not sleep and usually declined food at mealtimes. Migraine headaches, an occasional problem for her before, became almost daily occurrences.

Then, just when Mark had convinced himself that Laura's reactions were normal in the face of such a terrible loss, she began to behave in ways that caused him serious concern. Laura had not cried to this point, but now she began to cry often, sometimes for hours at a time. She still could not sleep well, but now when she was awake she seemed to have little energy for anything that Mark might suggest. Mark was also concerned about how forgetful his wife had suddenly become. She preferred to sit alone in the den doing nothing at all. Laura talked of nothing but Stephanie and of her desire to be reunited with her daughter. Often she said that she, not Stephanie, should have been the one who died.

At other times she would say that Stephanie was with them, that she could see Stephanie sitting in a chair next to hers. When Laura began to speak to Stephanie as though she were really in the room, Mark decided it was time to seek professional help. He did not understand what was happening. He knew that Laura was probably depressed, but he was also afraid that her recent memory problems and hallucinations might be the start of Alzheimer's disease.

Mark made an appointment for Laura with a clinical psychologist, who first conducted a thorough diagnostic workup and then met with the couple. The psychologist reassured them that Laura was not mentally ill. Rather, she was suffering from normal bereavement, particularly because her daughter's death was premature and unexpected. Mark was especially relieved to learn that neither memory problems nor hallucinating the presence of Stephanie was an unusual reaction within the first months after a death. When the psychologist learned that Stephanie's birthday was two weeks away, she pointed out that such anniversaries are commonly times at which symptoms of bereavement worsen. She recommended that Laura begin bereavement counselling right away.

Changing Demography

Around the world, the number of older adults is increasing at an unprecedented rate. Although different chronological ages are used to define "older adults" for different purposes, we will use the most conventional dividing line and say that an older adult is anyone over age 65. The global population of people aged 65 and over was estimated to be 506 million in 2008 (7 percent of the world's population). By the year 2040 this number is expected to grow to a staggering 1.3 billion (14 percent of the world's population; Kinsella & He, 2009). Canada is no exception to this population aging trend. In fact, our population is aging at an even faster rate. Figure 16.1 shows that compared to the early 1980s, when older adults made up about 10 percent of the population, more than one in five Canadians are expected to be over the age of 65 by 2031. The figure also indicates that the fastest growth among individuals over age 65 is occurring among the oldest Canadians, those aged 75 to 84 and 85-plus.

There are two primary reasons for these trends, the most important of which is the aging of the **baby boomers**—people who were born within 20 years following the end of the Second World War in 1945 (Statistics Canada, 2006). In 2011 the oldest of the baby boomers started to turn 65. Because this group of individuals spans

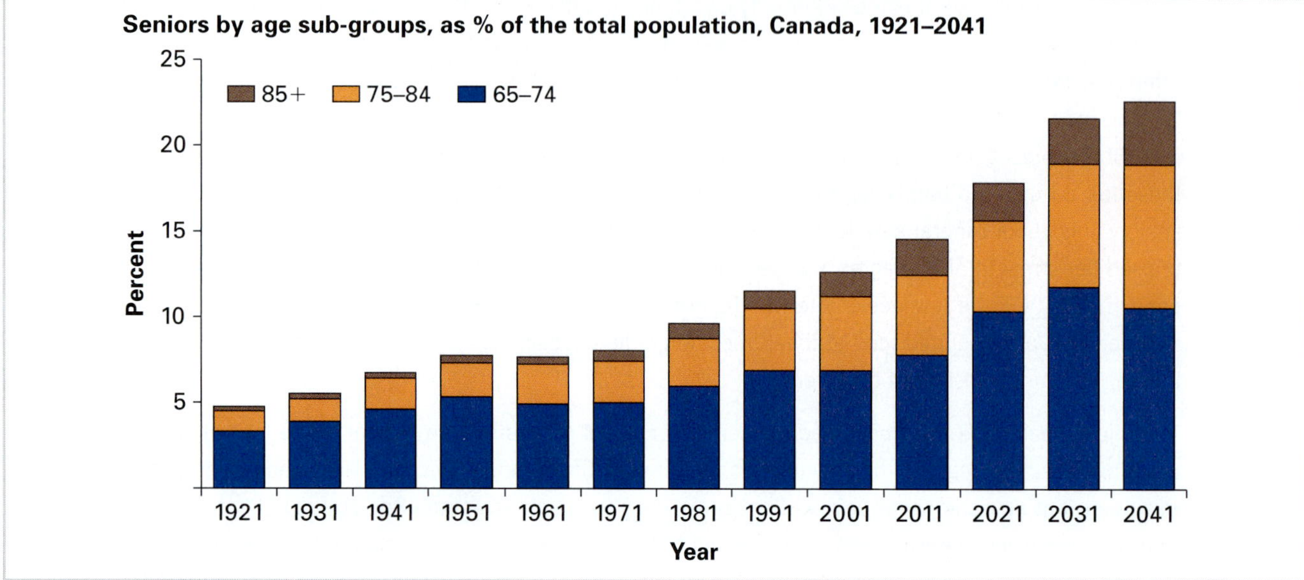

FIGURE 16.1 Older Adults by Age Group, as Percentage of Total Canadian Population

Source: Canada's Aging Population, Public Health Agency of Canada, 2002. Reproduced with the permission of the Minister of Public Works and Government Services Canada, 2008.

two decades, Figure 16.1 shows especially sharp rises in the proportion of older adults in Canada in 2021 and 2031. The second primary reason for our aging population is that Canadians are living longer than ever. Canadians have one of the longest life expectancies in the world; in 2001 men were expected to live to age 77 and women to age 82 (up from age 69 for men and age 76 for women in 1970; Belanger, Martel, & Caron-Malenfant, 2005). Reductions in mortality among both younger and older adults are due to advances in public health (e.g., immunization, safer drinking water), workplace safety, and newly developed and more effective medications and surgical procedures. In addition, factors such as greater affluence and higher levels of education are thought to contribute to longevity, presumably because more affluent, better-educated people are likely, for example, to have less dangerous jobs that require less physical wear and tear on their bodies, better nutrition, and better health care.

What do these changing demographics mean for the mental health field? As the proportion of older adults in the population increases, so will the number of older adults with mental disorders. This increase will pose a number of challenges for mental health professionals that are addressed in the section "Age-Specific Issues of Diagnosis and Treatment." This shift will also result in a number of new opportunities for mental health professionals with interest and expertise in treating older individuals.

1 BEFORE MOVING ON

The number of older Canadians will increase substantially in the next several decades. Some individuals think that this demographic shift will overwhelm our health care system, including mental health care. Others think that this shift will have relatively modest effects on our physical and mental health care systems. What do you think will happen, and why?

VULNERABILITY VERSUS RESILIENCE IN OLD AGE

A person is more likely to develop a mental disorder at times of increased vulnerability (Gatz, Kasl-Godley, & Karel, 1996). When people are vulnerable, they may become unable to cope with previously manageable problems or situations. Have you ever found that something as simple as a cold or a headache has reduced your ability to cope with a difficult situation, perhaps an exam? To take a more dramatic example, a person might be able to cope with being laid off from work, or with a spouse being diagnosed with a terminal illness; however, if both happened close together, the person might be overwhelmed and might begin to show signs of depression or anxiety. The first blow may be said to have increased the person's emotional vulnerability to the point that he or she is unable to cope with the second blow. As people age, they are more likely to experience increased vulnerability—both physically, as various organ systems begin to be compromised, and psychologically, with losses in areas such as social support (due to deaths of friends and relatives) and independence (due to lost driver's licences, increased hospitalizations, or relocations from home to institution).

The increased vulnerability that older adults are likely to face suggests that they should also be more likely to experience mental health problems. Although this chapter focuses on mental disorders among older adults, there is good evidence to suggest that old age is generally a time of psychological resilience rather than poor mental health. In addition to evidence of decreases in the prevalence of most mental disorders with age (which we outline in the upcoming prevalence section), an impressive review of life satisfaction among individuals from 40 nations found remarkable stability in well-being across the lifespan (Diener, Suh,

Lucas, & Smith, 1999). Impressively, data from Statistics Canada indicate that in 2009, 97 percent of older adults reported being satisfied with life and 70 percent reported having either good or excellent mental health (Butler-Jones, 2010). These findings support a growing body of evidence suggesting that psychological well-being may even increase from middle age to old age (Blanchflower & Oswald, 2008; Isaacowitz, 2005; Phillips, Henry, Hosie, & Milne, 2006; Stone, Schwartz, Broderick, & Deaton, 2010). Finally, a number of personality characteristics that are associated with positive health, such as conscientiousness, agreeableness, and emotional stability, appear to increase across the adult lifespan (Roberts, Walton, & Viechtbauer, 2006). Together, this evidence of positive mental health among older adults who would normally be considered vulnerable has been coined the **paradox of aging** (Baltes & Baltes, 1990). Of course, it is important for us to keep in mind that older adults do tend to experience multiple losses and that there are wide individual differences in how loss is dealt with. As we will see in the next section, although older adults tend to be resilient in the face of these losses, many do go on to develop mental health problems.

Prevalence of Mental Disorders in Older Adults

Although we will discuss prevalence rates for individual disorders later in the chapter, it is helpful to begin with an understanding of age differences in overall rates of mental health problems. Awareness of both overall prevalence and prevalence rates for specific disorders can help practitioners, researchers, and policy-makers understand how common mental health problems are so that they can make informed decisions about how best to target prevention and treatment strategies to improve older people's mental health. The best evidence concerning the prevalence of mental disorders across the lifespan comes from large-scale community surveys conducted in the United States (Kessler et al., 2005; Mackenzie, Pagura, & Sareen, 2010), Australia (Henderson, 2002), Europe (Alonso & Lepine, 2007), and Canada (Streiner, Cairney, & Veldhuizen, 2006).

These surveys have provided three very important pieces of information. First, mental health problems are extremely common in the general population. Although there is variability across studies, they suggest that 25 to 50 percent of people will have a mental disorder in their lifetimes, and 12 to 30 percent will have a mental disorder in a given year. Second, these surveys suggest that, with the exception of dementia and sleep disorders, mental disorders are less common among older adults. For example, the European Study of the Epidemiology of Mental Disorders found the highest 12-month prevalence of any mental disorder among 18- to 24-year-olds (16.5 percent), rates of about 12 percent among middle-aged Europeans, and the lowest prevalence (7.8 percent) among those aged 65 and older. In Canada, the best prevalence data come from the Canadian Community Health Survey of 36 984 adults from across the country. As shown in Figure 16.2, data from this survey for adults aged 55 and older indicate a linear decrease with age in lifetime prevalence rates of combined major depression, bipolar disorder, social phobia, agoraphobia, and panic disorder. Third, gender differences occur in the prevalence of mental health problems. Women are more likely to have diagnosable mental health problems across the lifespan. However, as is evident in Figure 16.2, some studies find that gender differences decrease with increasing age.

Before leaving this section on prevalence rates, it is important that we critically examine one of the key findings

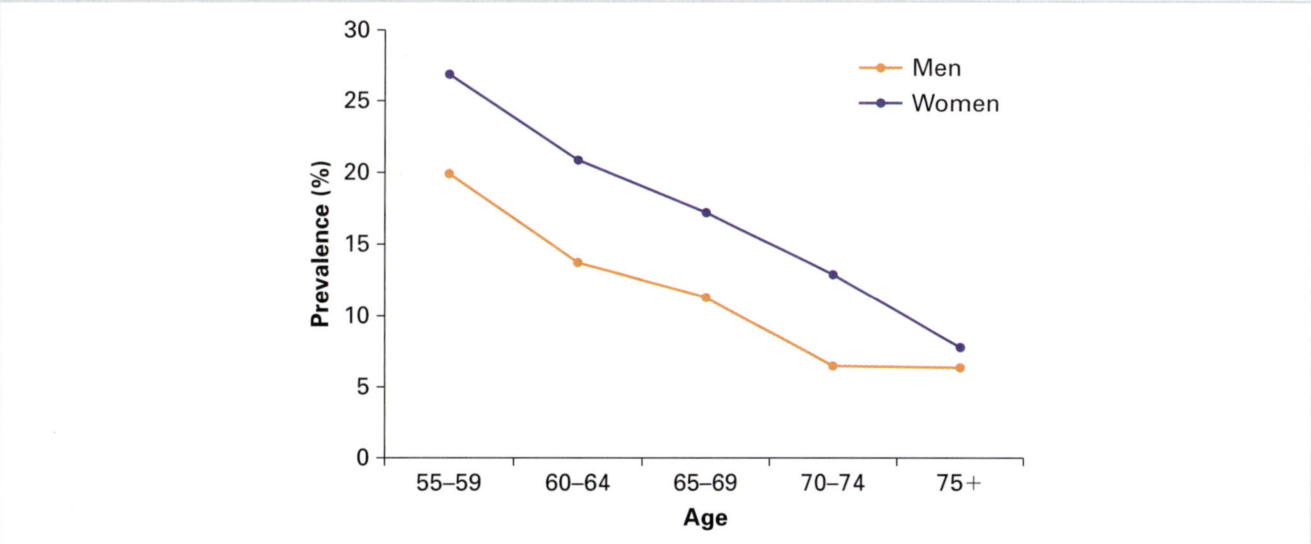

FIGURE 16.2 Prevalence of Lifetime Mental Disorders for Men and Women Aged 55 and Older

Source: Adapted from Streiner et al. (2006).

from community surveys—that most mental disorders become less prevalent with increasing age. On the one hand, this may be a true finding reflecting the resiliency of older individuals discussed earlier in the chapter, although these cross-sectional surveys cannot determine whether people become more resilient over time (referred to as a **period effect** in the aging literature) or whether certain cohorts of individuals born at particular times are more resilient (referred to as a **cohort effect**). For example, it may be that the cohort of adults who were born prior to 1920 and who lived through the Great Depression and both world wars are more psychologically resilient than are individuals born after 1950 because of their experiences coping with these difficult times. It may also be, however, that the process of aging brings with it perspective, wisdom, and good mental health. On the other hand, there are good reasons to be cautious about the findings from these surveys, which suggest that mental disorders are less prevalent among older adults. There are at least three reasons why large community surveys almost certainly underestimate mental disorders in older people. First, older individuals may be less likely than younger individuals to remember having symptoms of disorder, less likely to report them, or more likely to express psychological symptoms in somatic ways (e.g., as aches and pains rather than as depression). Second, older adults with severe mental health problems may be excluded from surveys or refuse to participate in them because of homelessness or institutionalization. Finally, there is likely a survivor effect in these surveys due to the fact that individuals with mental disorders have higher mortality rates, so that only the healthiest members of society survive to old age (Streiner et al., 2006). So, despite the consistent findings of decreasing prevalence of most mental disorders with age, it is quite likely that the downward slope in Figure 16.2 is exaggerated, although the degree of that exaggeration is unknown at the present time.

Historical Perspective

Historically, older adults with mental disorders were typically seen as eccentric rather than ill. Their "eccentricities" were generally tolerated by those around them as long as their aberrant behaviour did not seriously interfere with the family or the occupational commitments of others. When older adults became too disruptive, they were isolated, either in a variety of institutions or at home. Such eccentricities were seen both as part of normal old age and as something about which nothing could be done. Starting in the 1930s, psychiatric treatment—psychosurgery and psychopharmacological agents—became available, although limited to the most disruptive of older adults suffering from mental disorders. More commonly, however, "treatment" for such people continued to be isolation in some form of institution.

The idea that mental disorders in older adults can and should be treated is relatively new. Kermis (1984) argued that as recently as 1972 the clinical psychology of aging was virtually nonexistent, and that even the most widely used assessment tools were not normed for people over age 65. Today, there is growing acceptance in clinical psychology of the value of treating older adults with mental disorders and of assessing them using appropriate age-normed methods.

MISCONCEPTIONS ABOUT TREATING OLDER ADULTS

Gerontologists are professionals from a wide variety of disciplines with expertise in aging. In addition to treating older adults with health concerns, these professionals help dispel myths about aging. One such myth that is particularly common is that treatment for mental health problems in late life is unnecessary and/or ineffective. This myth exists for a number of reasons. First, consider the following commonly held (and untrue) negative stereotypes about older adults: (a) they are rigid and set in their ways, (b) you cannot teach an old dog new tricks, and (c) the lights are on but no one is home. It is easy to see why people who mistakenly view older adults as being stuck in their ways, unable to learn new information, and cognitively impaired would not believe that therapy could be effective for them. Second, many people mistakenly believe that the development of pathology must be accepted as a part of **normal aging** and therefore need not be treated (Birren & Renner, 1980). It is not uncommon for people to think that aging is a sad, unfortunate process during which individuals experience physiological, cognitive, and social losses. Why wouldn't an 82-year-old man who has disabling arthritis and mild memory problems and has attended the funerals of two close friends in the past year be depressed? Third, the notion that aging is a sad process is strongly reinforced by our societal emphasis on youth and "anti-aging" marketing. Fourth, current thinking may be influenced by early lifespan developmental theories, which suggested that emotional experiences paralleled changes in cognition and physiology, peaking in the early twenties and then deteriorating (Banham, 1951; Frenkel-Brunswik, 1968). Finally, one of Freud's unfortunate legacies was his explicit position that psychotherapy with older adults was ill-advised. As a result of factors like this, as discussed in detail in Focus box 16.1, research in Canada and elsewhere has demonstrated that younger and older adults in the community (including older adults themselves) and mental health professionals have inaccurate beliefs and ageist attitudes concerning older adults' ability to benefit from treatment for mental disorders.

The belief that older adults cannot benefit from treatment is simply false. There is increasing evidence that psychotherapy and other psychosocial interventions are just as effective for older adults as for younger adults (Bartels et al., 2003). There is also strong evidence that pharmacological treatments are equally effective for older and younger adults, although some antidepressant and antipsychotic medications tend to be tolerated less

FOCUS 16.1

Older Adults: The Missing Clients

By any measure—admissions to psychiatric facilities, attendance at community health clinics, representation in therapist caseloads—older adults are disproportionately underrepresented as users of mental health services. Recent research conducted with a representative sample of community-dwelling adults from the United States indicates that in comparison to middle-aged adults aged 35 to 64, older adults aged 65+ are approximately two times less likely to seek help for anxiety and mood disorders (Mackenzie, Reynolds, Cairney, Streiner, & Sareen, in press). These findings indicate that low levels of help-seeking among older adults extend to the Canadian population, with only 37 percent of older adults with one or more disorder reporting the use of at least one mental health service in the past year (Cairney, Corna, & Streiner, 2010). According to Gatz and colleagues (1985), there are three possible reasons for this unsettling finding: client barriers, therapist barriers, and systemic barriers.

Client barriers are reasons why older adults might contribute to their own low rates of mental health service use due to factors such as negative attitudes toward seeking help, stigma, and lack of knowledge about where to go for help. Until fairly recently, gerontologists assumed that older people were more likely to experience stigma about mental health problems because they grew up in an era when seeing a psychiatrist, psychologist, or social worker was uncommon. Interestingly, research from our laboratory, shown in Figure 16.3, suggests that older adults' attitudes toward seeking psychological help are actually more positive than those of younger adults (Mackenzie, Scott, Mather, & Sareen, 2008). This finding, and similar findings from other research labs, is calling into question the previously held belief that older adults are largely responsible for not seeking psychological help when they need it.

Therapist barriers are reasons why mental health professionals may be less willing or able to treat older adults due to factors such as lack of geriatric training and ageist attitudes, beliefs, and treatment practices. More support exists for this barrier to older adults' service use. It is well documented that psychologists and psychiatrists are reluctant to treat older adults and prefer to work with younger clients (Zivian, Larsen, Knox, Gekoski, & Hatchette, 1992). Unfortunately, older clients are not likely to be better served by the next generation of therapists. DeRyck, Gekoski, Knox, and Zivian (1996) found that graduate students training as clinical psychologists underestimated the benefit of treatment for older adults and rated them as their least preferred client group. There is some room for optimism, though: the more professional experience students had with older clients, the more positive they were about them.

Mental health professionals are not, however, the only providers of mental health services. In fact, family physicians provide the majority of these services in North America. Not only that, but they are the gatekeepers to the mental health system—in Canada, family physicians are an important source of referrals to mental health specialists. And there is reason to think that they, too, contribute to the greater underservice of the older segment of the population. We surveyed Canadian family physicians, who indicated that they were less likely both to treat older patients and to refer them to mental health professionals (Mackenzie, Gekoski, & Knox, 1999). This finding is not surprising considering that these physicians reported being less prepared to identify and treat mental disorders in older adults than in younger adults.

Finally, systemic barriers are practical reasons why access to mental health services is limited, including government policies and regulations that disadvantage older mental health service users (Karlin & Duffy, 2004), logistic impediments to using services such as transportation and mobility issues, and the help-seeking attitudes and beliefs of people in older adults' social support networks (Mackenzie, Knox, Smoley, & Gekoski, 2004). A particularly important systemic barrier to meeting older adults' mental health needs is an insufficient number of mental health professionals who specialize in assessing and treating them. Fortunately, there is growing awareness of the need to improve our detection and treatment of mental health problems among older adults. To address the growing demand for psychologists and other mental health professionals with expertise in aging, guidelines and models of geropsychology training have been published (American Psychological Association, 2004; Knight, Karel, Hinrichsen, Qualls, & Duffy, 2009) and the need for increased training opportunities for geropsychologists has been highlighted internationally by a number of scholars and the World Health Organization (Pachana, Emery, Konnert, Woodhead, & Edelstein, 2010). Unfortunately, in Canada there are no doctoral programs with a formal concentration in geropsychology, and faculty resources and practicum experiences in clinical psychology programs are sparse (Konnert, Dobson, & Watt, 2009). The situation is somewhat better when clinical psychology graduate students go on internship, 40 percent of whom have a major rotation and a further 48 percent a minor rotation in geropsychology. So although there are training opportunities in geropsychology in Canada and internationally, it is very clear that there is and will continue to be a severe shortage of geriatric mental health professionals for the foreseeable future. Students thinking about career opportunities after graduation should take note!

well in later life (Meyers & Jeste, 2010; Wolitzky-Taylor, Castriotta, Lenze, Stanley, & Craske, 2010). Finally, we published a recent study of 12 792 Canadians 55 years of age and older in which we found that the 664 older adults who used mental health services in the past year reported very good treatment outcomes. The majority were satisfied with treatment (88.5 percent) and perceived it as effective (84 percent), which is likely why only 15.5 percent dropped out of treatment in the past year (Lippens & Mackenzie, 2011).

2 BEFORE MOVING ON

We have just reviewed several stereotypes of older adults, including the belief that older people are rigid and set in their ways, or that they cannot benefit from mental health services. What other stereotypes of older adults have you encountered—both negative and positive? In what way are these stereotypes helpful and harmful?

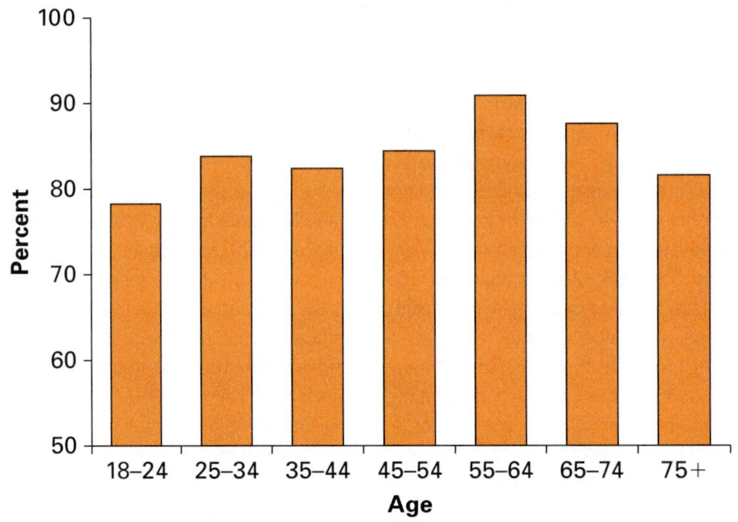

FIGURE 16.3 Prevalence of Positive Help-Seeking Attitudes Across the Adult Lifespan

Age-Specific Issues of Diagnosis and Treatment

Recognizing and treating mental disorders in older adults is complicated by a number of factors particularly relevant to this population. Several of these factors are discussed in Focus box 16.1, including ageist attitudes and a dearth of mental health professionals with geriatric expertise. At least three other factors that can complicate diagnosis and treatment are worth mentioning. First, symptoms of mental disorders can be attributed to age-related rather than psychological factors. For example, vegetative symptoms of depression, such as difficulty sleeping and loss of energy, that are likely to be accurately diagnosed in younger adults can be missed in older adults because of the perception that they are a "normal" part of aging. Second, correctly recognizing and diagnosing mental disorders in older adults is more difficult because they are more likely to have comorbid chronic physical illnesses (e.g., cardiovascular disease, arthritis, and gastrointestinal disease). Not only can mental and physical health problems result in similar symptoms (e.g., fatigue caused by depression, sleep disorders, thyroid problems, chronic pain), but they also directly and indirectly influence one another (Lu & Ahmed, 2010). A recent study from our laboratory found that a number of chronic pain conditions and other commonly occurring diseases increased the likelihood that older adults met criteria for an anxiety disorder in the past year by 1.7 to 2.8 times, and that as the number of health conditions increased so did the likelihood of experiencing clinical anxiety (El-Gabalawy, Mackenzie, Shooshtari, & Sareen, in press). Finally, because health problems are increasingly common with advancing age, older adults are especially likely to be taking multiple medications for such illnesses. This concurrent use of multiple medications is known as **polypharmacy**. Both the symptoms of physical illness and the side effects of their treatments may mimic, or obscure, symptoms of mental disorders, making recognition and diagnosis more difficult. Comorbidity can also lead to problems for older adults if the appropriate treatment for one disorder is incompatible with the otherwise optimal treatment for the second. For example, a possible (anticholinergic) side effect of certain antidepressant medication is cognitive slowing and memory problems. For individuals who have both dementia and depression, these medications should be either avoided or used cautiously.

Another recent advance related to the increasing mental health needs of older adults has to do not only with treating mental illness, but also with preventing it. There is increasing recognition of the importance of supplementing treatment with efforts to prevent age-related mental health problems and to promote older adults' mental health (Smyer, 1995; van't Veer-Tazelaar et al., 2009; Waters, 1995).

Theoretical Frameworks of Aging

Because the way we conceptualize things has a strong influence on our actions, it is useful to look at theories that have been used or could be used to help us better understand mental health in older adults. There are two ways to approach the task of looking at theoretical frameworks for understanding mental health in later life. The first involves considering general theories that have been developed in an attempt to understand the causes of mental disorders, and asking what these theories have to say about mental disorders in older adults. The second approach involves considering theories developed specifically to understand aging and older adults, and asking what light they might shed on our understanding of mental disorders in older adults. Chapter 2 outlines several different theoretical frameworks for thinking about mental disorders, including biological, psychodynamic, behavioural, cognitive, humanistic, and existential.

With few exceptions, theorists have not extended, adapted, or refined any of the approaches in Chapter 2 to specifically fit the clinical experience of older adults. It is not clear whether they have concluded that a particular framework can be applied without adaptation to older adults, or whether they have simply not asked the question. Much of psychoanalytic theory, for example, deals with how the early development of personality structures and unconscious processes can lead to mental disorders later in life. However, nothing in this approach differentiates between mental disorders in 25-year-olds and 75-year-olds.

In contrast, Erik Erikson (1950) extended psychoanalytic theory in a number of ways, one of which was to suggest that the critical issues for successful functioning vary at different points in development across the lifespan. Erikson did not, however, focus on the implications of his lifespan approach for understanding mental disorders at different points in the life course.

Let us turn to an examination of theoretical approaches to understanding aging and old age. A number of approaches focus on how older adults adjust to or cope with age-related changes and may inform our thinking about mental disorders in older adults, as well as what factors are important in order to age successfully. Three approaches are of particular interest here: the theory of selective optimization with compensation, socio-emotional selectivity theory, and strength and vulnerability integration theory. Let us look at each of these in turn.

SELECTIVE OPTIMIZATION WITH COMPENSATION

This theoretical framework (Baltes & Baltes, 1990) is one of the leading models in the field of gerontology in general, and successful aging in particular. The selective optimization with compensation (SOC) model holds that even within the context of normal aging and in the absence of pathology, old age brings losses of abilities and skills. According to SOC, successful aging entails (1) selecting goals and goal priorities, (2) optimizing resources that facilitate these goals, and (3) compensating for losses by creatively using alternative means to achieving one's goals despite limited capacities. For example, now that she is in her seventies, former concert pianist Janine might decide that continuing to play piano is an important goal despite the fact that arthritis and slower reaction time are preventing her from playing pieces that she used to be able to play. To achieve this goal, she might optimize her playing by practising often and exercising, and compensate for her arthritis and psychomotor slowing by playing more slowly.

The SOC framework could be used to maximize functioning in people with mental disorders by building on strengths and avoiding weaknesses. For example, activities that do not make heavy demands on memory, such as bingo, will afford greater gratification to patients with dementia. This theoretical framework is especially attractive, as it seems to be equally appropriate for dealing with all older adults, whether or not they suffer from physical or mental pathology. A review of nine studies using the SOC model with older adults found that compensation and optimization in particular were strongly associated with successful aging (Ouwehand, de Ridder, & Bensing, 2007).

SOCIO-EMOTIONAL SELECTIVITY THEORY

A second lifespan theory was originally developed to explain age differences in motivation, but has since been employed to better understand age differences in other factors such as mental health, emotion regulation, physical health, and cognitive functioning (Carstensen, Issacowitz, & Charles, 1999). The fundamental assumption of this theory is that when we perceive time as unlimited (as younger adults tend to), our goals will be future-oriented and we will focus our energy on seeking information and expanding our knowledge and horizons. In contrast, when we perceive time as limited (as older adults tend to), our goals become focused on short-term and emotionally meaningful matters. Figure 16.4 shows that as individuals progress from adolescence to middle age and eventually to old age, their goals shift from being knowledge focused to meaning focused, which has benefits for mental health.

A great deal of research supports socio-emotional selectivity theory (SST). In one study, younger and older adults were shown two advertisements for a camera store that had a slogan at the top and various pictures below it. The posters were identical except that they had different slogans: one emphasized expanding horizons ("capture the unexplored world") and one emphasized emotional rewards ("capture those special moments"). Not only did older adults prefer the emotional advertisements, but they also remembered significantly more pictures from them. Another interesting aspect of SST is the "positivity effect," whereby younger adults tend to focus on negative information whereas older adults tend to focus on positive information. Recent neuroscience research, using brain imaging technology, suggests that older participants actually process negative information less deeply than they do positive information (Carstensen, 2006).

STRENGTH AND VULNERABILITY INTEGRATION THEORY

Building on the components of SST, Charles and Piazza (2009) proposed the strength and vulnerability integration (SAVI) theory. This theory posits that aging is associated with an increased ability to regulate emotions. Reasons for this include the possession of a time-limited perspective characterized by a greater emphasis on emotionally

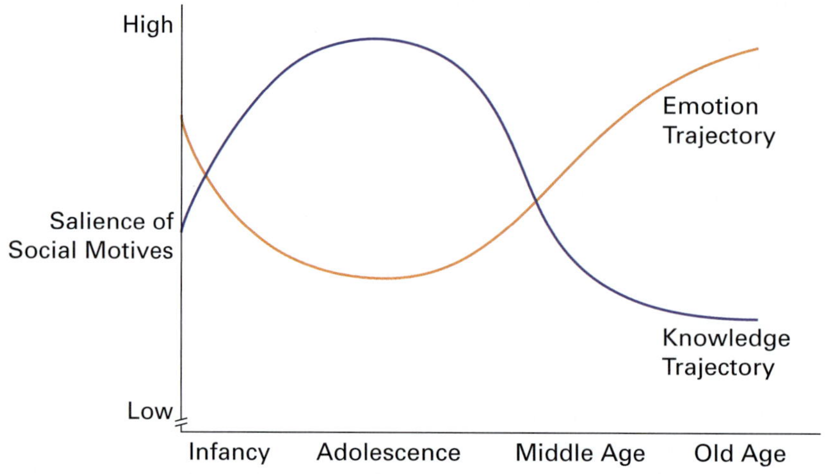

FIGURE 16.4 Age Differences in Social Goals Across the Lifespan According to Socio-Emotional Selectivity Theory

Source: Adapted from "The Social Context of Emotion" by L. Carstensen, J. Gross, & H. Fung (1997). *Annual Review of Geriatrics and Gerontology, 17,* p. 331. Reproduced with the permission of Springer Publishing Company, LLC, New York, NY 10036.

meaningful goals; an increased present-moment awareness, which promotes strength-based appraisals of information and same-age social comparisons; a decrease in interpersonal conflict due to avoidance of difficult situations and the intentional pruning of peripheral social network members; and a greater focus on positive information and experiences. So far, these attentional and appraisal strategies have all been indicated in the SST described above. SAVI includes the idea that older adults have had more opportunities to practise these strategies in dealing with the stress of daily life, and are therefore more effective and successful at applying them than younger and middle-aged adults. Both the change in perspective (time limited, present awareness, positive focused) and successful use of emotion regulation strategies (attentional and appraisal) allow older adults to avoid negative experiences and enhance their well-being, accounting for the gains in affective well-being across the lifespan (Charles, 2010). On the other hand, SAVI also indicates that old age is associated with decreased physiological tolerance to stress, resulting in dysregulation of immune functioning and increases in blood pressure and fibrinogen. This leads to greater difficulty regulating emotional arousal and prolonged recovery from the stressful event. When negative experiences are unavoidable, are accompanied with high levels of arousal, and occur over a sustained amount of time (e.g., loss of a spouse, relative, or close friend; caregiver stress; illness), age-related advantages in emotion regulation and well-being dissipate (Charles, 2010).

3 BEFORE MOVING ON

Which of these theoretical models do you think best explains why the prevalence of mood and anxiety disorders is lower among older adults than among middle-aged and younger individuals? What does your favourite model have that the others seem to be missing?

The remaining sections of this chapter focus on specific mental disorders, with an emphasis on disorders that are common in old age or that manifest differently in later life.

Mood Disorders

Case Notes

Mrs. Sharma, aged 73, was referred to an outpatient psychological clinic by her family physician with symptoms of sleeplessness, appetite loss, and feelings of hopelessness and despair. Mrs. Sharma lost her husband of nearly 50 years about 18 months ago. Shortly thereafter, at her children's urging, she moved from the family home to a seniors' apartment complex. Now she thinks that the move might have been a mistake. Compared to her house, the apartment feels tiny and holds no fond memories. Mrs. Sharma reports that she is still depressed over her husband's death. She had spent much of the last several years caring for him and now feels that she has too little to occupy her time. Mrs. Sharma worries that her memory might be failing, though tests show this not to be the case. She is also concerned that her children seem too busy with their own lives to spend enough time with her.

Perhaps because of the belief that older people have a lot to be depressed about—declining health, loss of those close to them, shrinking resources, reduced options—it is commonly assumed that they are most likely to experience mood disorders. Yet the data show that quite the opposite is true for the major DSM-IV-TR mood disorders (i.e., major depression, bipolar disorder, dysthymic disorder). Major depressive disorder is nearly 4 times as common in younger adults as in older adults, and bipolar disorders are 16 times as common. The milder form of depression, dysthymic disorder, is approximately twice as common among younger than older adults (Weissman et al., 1988). We recently published a study of 8012 older adults interviewed twice over a three-year period. Of all the mood and anxiety disorders in this study, the most likely disorder to have a new onset for the first time in the participants' lives within this three-year period was major depression; 3.3 percent of older adults had incident major depression, whereas only 0.3 percent had incident bipolar II disorder (Chou, Mackenzie, Liang, & Sareen, 2011).

Depression in people over age 60 is more likely to be chronic than it is in younger adults (Benazzi, 2000). In fact, researchers at McGill University and the University of Montreal reviewed a dozen studies of depression in elderly community-residing populations and found that, overall, only 33 percent were well after two years (Cole, Bellavance, & Mansour, 1999). However, most of these people were not treated for their depression after it was detected. If they had been, the picture would likely have been better because older adults respond at least as well as younger people to most treatments for depression—a point we touch on elsewhere in the chapter. Nonetheless, the outlook for elderly depressed people is poorer than for younger individuals because of concurrent physical diseases, a higher death rate, and development of dementia (Tuma, 2000). See Chapter 8 for a full discussion of mood disorders and their symptoms.

SUICIDE

The risk of suicide is elevated in individuals with a variety of mental health problems, although it is a particular concern for those who are severely depressed (CCSMH, 2006a). How common is suicidal behaviour (a term that includes suicidal ideation or thoughts, as well as successful and unsuccessful attempts) among older adults? Before answering this question it is important to acknowledge that rates are likely underestimates as a result of reluctance to discuss this topic and to label deaths this way. If we begin with a broad definition of suicidal thoughts, research from the Canadian Community Health Survey found that more than 2 percent (n = 246) of the 12 792 adults aged 55 and older endorsed suicidal ideation in the past year (Corna, Cairney, & Streiner, 2010). With respect to rates of successful suicides, in 2002 Statistics Canada reported that 430 older Canadians committed suicide, 361 of whom were older men (CCSMH, 2006a). These numbers are consistent with earlier Canadian data indicating that older men were five times more likely than older women to commit suicide, with an even larger sex ratio of 8:1 among adults 75 years of age and older (Heisel, 2006). Alarmingly, although younger people are more likely to attempt suicide, with 10 or more attempts per completed suicide, older individuals are more likely to be successful, with approximately 4 attempts per completed suicide (Blazer, 2003). There are a number of potential explanations for increasing suicide success with age. In comparison to younger adults, older adults may have a greater intent to die; they often use more lethal methods; and they are more socially isolated, which decreases the chance of others intervening or rescuing them (Heisel, 2006; McIntosh, Santos, Hubbard, & Overholser, 1994).

Among older individuals, a number of factors increase the risk of suicide. The Canadian Coalition for Seniors' Mental Health (CCSMH, 2006a) guidelines for the assessment of suicidal risk and prevention of treatment outline the following risks: prior suicidal behaviour, mental illness and addiction, personality disorders, poor social support including being divorced or widowed, recent negative life events such as financial or social losses, and impairment in the ability to carry out the activities of everyday life. In addition, the Canadian Community Health Survey found that chronic pain conditions, which are more common among older adults, were associated with both suicidal thoughts and attempts (Ratcliffe, Enns, Belik, & Sareen, 2008). Identification of these risk factors is extremely important for suicide prevention initiatives. For example, research indicates that those who die from suicide are 30 times more likely than controls to have a history of suicidal behaviour. Thus, taking threats to commit suicide seriously, detecting and treating depression, and reducing access to firearms have been identified as some of the most important ways of preventing suicide in older adults (Unützer, 2007).

ETIOLOGY

What predisposes an older adult to depression? It seems that both physical health and social supports are involved; the combination of a weak support network and poor physical health places older individuals at particular risk (Blazer, 2003). However, the etiology of depression is not a simple matter. A variety of biological, psychological, social, and spiritual factors may play a greater or lesser role, depending on the particular depressive disorder and the age of the individual (see the discussion of risk factors in Chapters 2 and 7). For example, heredity has been shown to be important in the development of major depression and especially bipolar disorder (Escamilla & Zavala, 2008). However, when either of these disorders occurs for the first time later in life, hereditary factors are less likely to be a primary cause (Fiske, Wetherell, & Gatz, 2009). In contrast to the decreasing role of heredity in the etiology of late-life depression, there is an increasing role for medical illnesses such as cardiovascular disease, pain, and Parkinson's disease. These conditions increase the risk of depression across the lifespan and are more prevalent among older adults (Blazer, 2003; Lu & Ahmed, 2010). Stressful life events can also influence older adults differently than they do younger adults. For instance, an older person who loses a loved one is less likely to become depressed than is a younger widow or widower (George, Blazer, & Hughes, 1989). Whereas death can seem like a bolt out of the blue to younger adults, older people's resilience in the face of death is likely the result of the emotion regulation strategies outlined in strength and vulnerability integration (SAVI) theory (Charles, 2010).

Let us turn now to a consideration of what we know about the main DSM-IV-TR mood disorders in older individuals.

DEPRESSIVE DISORDERS

Blazer's (2003) review of late-life mood disorders begins by saying that "depression is perhaps the most frequent cause of emotional suffering in later life and significantly decreases the quality of life in older adults" (p. 249). This review goes on to say that although symptoms of depression are common, rates of clinically diagnosed major depressive disorder (MDD) are less common, ranging from 1 to 4 percent of community-dwelling older adults. Rates jump dramatically, however, when older adults with health problems are considered. Approximately 5 to 10 percent of older adults who visit their family physicians have MDD, 10 to 12 percent of older adults hospitalized for medical concerns have this diagnosis, and 11 to 14 percent of institutionalized older adults in long-term care facilities have MDD. In each case, minor, subsyndromal, or subthreshold rates of depression are much higher.

Dysthymic disorder is chronic depression that has lasted at least two years but is not severe enough to warrant a diagnosis of MDD (see Chapter 8). As with MDD, dysthymic disorder is more common in younger than older adults, and more common in women than men. Among women over age 65, prevalence is 2.3 percent as compared to 1 percent among males in the same age range (Weissman et al., 1988). Again, rates are much higher—between 4 and 8 percent—among the institutionalized (Blazer, 2003). Interestingly, research from our laboratory indicates that individuals with dysthymia are even more likely than those with major depression to seek professional help (Mackenzie et al., in press). Although this finding may seem curious because this disorder is less severe than major depression, the most likely reason for it is the chronic nature of the mood problems that significantly reduce quality of life.

DIAGNOSTIC ISSUES What does MDD look like in older individuals? You will recall from Chapter 8 that, in addition to dysphoria (feeling sad) or anhedonia (a lack of ability to take pleasure in things), a diagnosis of MDD requires that four other symptoms be present from a list of affective (e.g., feelings of worthlessness or guilt), cognitive (e.g., difficulty concentrating or making decisions), and somatic (e.g., weight gain or loss, primary insomnia, fatigue) symptoms. MDD often looks different in older adults than it does in younger adults. Older clinically depressed individuals are more likely to report weight loss and other somatic symptoms and less likely to report feelings of sadness, worthlessness, or guilt (Blazer, 2003; Wallace & Pfohl, 1995). Given that either sadness or anhedonia is required for a diagnosis of MDD, older adults' reduced likelihood of reporting sadness when depressed may contribute to why they are less likely than younger adults to meet diagnostic criteria for this disorder.

In addition to the challenge of diagnosing depression in the absence of sadness, the Canadian Coalition for Seniors' Mental Health (CCSMH, 2006b) guidelines for the assessment and treatment of depression identify three other difficulties that clinicians face when assessing mood disorders in older adults. First, it can be difficult to diagnose depression among individuals with cognitive impairment. Depression and early-onset dementia are very difficult to distinguish from one another because both have prominent mood and memory problems. Also, these disorders often coexist, and we now know that having a first depressive episode late in life is a risk factor for developing cognitive impairment (Chodosh, Kado, Seeman, & Karlamangla, 2007) and even dementia (Green et al., 2003). Second, it is difficult to diagnose depression among individuals with somatic or physical problems, and older adults are at greater risk than younger adults for developing depression as a result of medical conditions. Depression can be found in 33 percent of stroke sufferers (Hachett, Yapa, Parag, & Anderson, 2005) and 20 to 40 percent of individuals with Parkinson's disease (Lieberman, 2006). Third, although most people experience symptoms of depression following the loss of a loved one, certain symptoms, such as suicidal ideation, are not typical and might indicate the presence of major depression. Differentiating a mood disorder from normal or complicated grief is nonetheless a very difficult undertaking.

Because most older adults who seek mental health treatment start by visiting their family physician, it is important to consider factors that might make diagnosing depression especially difficult. Mitchell (2011) outlines the following five major diagnostic issues faced by physicians: (1) time constraints, which make it difficult to attend to verbal and nonverbal signs of depression; (2) complexity of late-life depression, including vague symptoms and patients' lack of knowledge about depressive symptoms; (3) lack of specific diagnostic criteria for older adults; (4) physical comorbidity masking depressive symptoms; and (5) lack of knowledge about available and effective treatment options for older adults, which leads physicians to question the utility of diagnosis.

TREATMENT Both MDD and dysthymic disorder are typically treated with psychotherapy, drug therapy, or some combination of these. Earlier in this chapter, we made the point that, despite evidence to the contrary, older patients are commonly assumed to be poor candidates for psychotherapy. Meta-analyses (e.g., Cuijpers, van Straten, & Smit, 2006) and expert consensus statements (e.g., Alexopoulous, Katz, Reynolds, Carpenter, & Docherty, 2001) converge to suggest that a variety of psychotherapeutic approaches are highly effective for depressed older adults, and that overall effectiveness of treatments is similar for older and younger individuals. Also, for individuals who require more intensive treatment, we have shown that depressed older adults attending a day hospital program at Toronto's Baycrest Centre for Geriatric Care for 3.5 days per week for 4 months experienced clinically significant improvement in mood (Mackenzie, Rosenberg, & Major, 2006).

As for drug therapy for late-life depression, reviews by Canadian researchers Alastair Flint (1994) at the University of Toronto and Marie-France Tourigny-Rivard (1997) at the University of Ottawa suggest that antidepressants and other chemical treatments are as effective in older patients as they are in younger ones. As these reviews also point out, however, these drugs often produce side effects that are tolerated less well, particularly among the frail elderly, than among younger patients. Natural age-related changes such as reduced renal clearance and more sensitive drug receptor sites in the brain can increase side effects and reduce drug tolerance. Furthermore, when polypharmacy is an issue for older adults, the interactive effects of multiple medications (referred to as **drug interactions**) can have unknown and dangerous consequences.

Another biological therapy that has proven to be quite effective for treating severe and treatment-resistant MDD in older adults is electroconvulsive therapy (ECT), with response rates of 60 to 80 percent (Unützer, 2007). Despite its effectiveness and usefulness in situations where the risk of harm is high due to factors such as suicidal ideation and psychosis, ECT often has side effects—most commonly headaches, temporary confusion, and memory impairment, but also occasionally amnesia for events surrounding treatment and falls immediately after sessions. Fortunately, a recent study of 380 patients with a mean age of 51 (30 percent of the sample was 60+) found good evidence of ECT effectiveness, excellent tolerability among the older subsample, and only transient and not life-threatening adverse events (Damm et al., 2010).

Given the potential problems with use of drugs and ECT, you might expect there to be a bias in favour of psychotherapy for this patient group. This is not so. Research from the United States found that 74 percent of older adults receiving treatment for depression received antidepressant medications (Marcus & Olfson, 2010). This strong bias toward biological treatments exists despite a recent meta-analysis which found that antidepressant medications and structured psychotherapy are equally effective in older and younger adults (Pinquart, Duberstein, & Lyness, 2006). In addition, older adults prefer psychotherapy over medication for the treatment of depression (Landreville, Landry, Baillargeon, Guerette, & Matteau, 2001).

Sleep Disorders

Case Notes

All her life Rose slept soundly, got up early, and was energetic. Now, in her seventies, things have changed. She often finds it hard to fall asleep and then often awakens in the middle of the night, worrying about her husband's worsening angina attacks, her daughter's marriage, and her son's difficulty finding a good job. Sometimes her husband wakes her because she is snoring. She feels guilty about her snoring waking him and yet resents being woken once she has finally fallen asleep. At the suggestion of friends, she has experimented with eating and drinking various supposedly sleep-inducing things before bed. So far, nothing has helped. Rose tries to sleep in, but finds it hard to sleep once it is light outside. When she gets up, she feels tired and often finds herself dozing off during the day. This has happened in church and in social situations, and has been very embarrassing. To avoid dozing off she has started to take naps during the day, but doing so has made it even more difficult to fall asleep at night. Finally, at her husband's urging, she has made an appointment to discuss the problem with her physician.

It is clear from the literature on sleep and sleep disorders that older adults report much greater levels of dissatisfaction with the quality of their sleep than do younger adults. Epidemiological research suggests that between 30 and 60 percent of older adults complain of sleep problems (McCurry, Logsdon, Teri, & Vitiello, 2007; Stepanski, Rybarczyk, Lopez, & Stevens, 2003; Vitiello & Prinz, 1994). The primary complaints reported are light sleep, frequent awakenings during the night, decreased time spent asleep, awakening too early in the morning, and sleepiness during the day (Crowley, 2011). One reason why sleep problems appear to be more prevalent among older adults is that sleep disturbances often appear as a result of medical problems that are more common in later life (McCurry et al., 2007). The literature also confirms that older adults use more sedatives or hypnotic medications than do younger adults. In the United States, 40 percent of the sedative or hypnotic medications prescribed were for the 12 percent of population who were older adults (Moran, Thompson, & Nies, 1988).

Importantly, sleep problems among older adults affect more than just their sleep. Individuals who fail to get the rest they need experience poorer daytime cognitive and functional performance, which can have serious consequences such as motor vehicle and other accidents (Stepanski et al., 2003). In addition, individuals with chronic sleep problems are more likely to have poor physical health and poor mental health, including an increased risk for developing depression, anxiety, and suicidal ideation (McCurry et al., 2007). The high prevalence of sleep problems in old age, and their negative consequences, highlights the importance of detecting and treating these conditions.

DIAGNOSTIC ISSUES

Unfortunately, most patients with sleep problems do not report them to their family physicians (Ancoli-Israel & Roth, 1999). This may be especially true for older adults. When sleep problems are reported, decisions about whether

TABLE 16.1 DSM-IV-TR DIAGNOSTIC CRITERIA FOR PRIMARY INSOMNIA

A. The predominant complaint is difficulty initiating or maintaining sleep, or nonrestorative sleep, for at least 1 month.

B. The sleep disturbance (or associated daytime fatigue) causes clinically significant distress or impairment in social, occupational, or other important areas of functioning.

C. The sleep disturbance does not occur exclusively during the course of Narcolepsy, Breathinq-Related Sleep Disorder, Circadian Rhythm Sleep Disorder, or a Parasomnia.

D. The disturbance does not occur exclusively during the course of another mental disorder (e.g., Major Depressive Disorder, Generalized Anxiety Disorder, a delirium).

E. The disturbance is not due to the direct physiological effects of a substance (e.g., a drug of abuse, a medication) or a general medical condition.

Source: Reprinted with permission from the *Diagnostic and Statistical Manual of Mental Disorders, Fourth Edition, Text Revision.* (Copyright © 2000). American Psychiatric Association.

they warrant the diagnosis of sleep disorder depends on the quantity (intensity and/or persistence) and quality of the sleep disturbance. DSM-IV-TR identifies 10 sleep disorder categories and provides diagnostic criteria for them. Several are extremely rare in older adults (e.g., narcolepsy, sleepwalking disorder), and so we will not discuss them here. Criteria for the most common sleep disorder among older adults, insomnia, are presented in Table 16.1.

Diagnosing and treating sleep disorders in older adults is complicated by a number of factors (Vitiello & Prinz, 1994; Woodhouse, 1993) that must be considered before a diagnosis of primary sleep disorder can be made.

- Information about sleep quantity and quality typically comes from self-reports, and so there is always a question as to whether they are distorted by unrealistic expectations.
- Sleep disturbance can be secondary to a host of physical and mental disorders and medications for such disorders. Treating the disorder or changing the medication may alleviate the sleep disturbance.
- There are age-related changes in sleep that appear to be universal, and thus might be considered normal.
- Sleep characteristics and patterns vary widely between individuals; such differences may be especially great among older people.
- Sleep is affected by what sleep researchers and clinicians call sleep hygiene, which refers to habits surrounding sleep such as what time you go to bed, where you sleep, who you sleep with, and how much eating, drinking, and exercising you engage in prior to going to sleep. These habits may change with age; for example, retirement may change an individual's bedtime. On the other hand, established sleep habits may no longer be conducive to quality sleep. For example, because sleep is lighter in older adults, sleeping with someone else in the bed may become a cause of frequent awakening and difficulty falling back to sleep.

Because of the multitude of factors that can affect sleep in older adults, it is essential that the complete 24-hour sleep–wake cycle be assessed when the diagnosis of insomnia is being considered. Unfortunately, such a thorough examination is rarely conducted.

NORMAL CHANGES IN SLEEPING PATTERNS

Sleep comprises five stages (Daly, 1989; Fetveit, 2009). In rapid eye movement (REM) sleep, electroencephalographic (EEG) activity is similar to that which occurs during waking activity, rapid conjugate eye movements occur (that is, the eyes move together), and muscle tone is decreased. Non-rapid eye movement (NREM) sleep is divided into the remaining four stages. In stage 1, low-amplitude, fast-frequency, irregular EEG activity occurs. In stage 2, the activity is more synchronous (regular). Stages 3 and 4 are marked by slow EEG waves. Stage 4 is deemed to be the deepest level of sleep, because more intense stimulation is required to rouse someone at this stage. Laboratory studies have shown age-related changes of three types:

- *Changes in EEG activity.* Stage 2 EEG activity is less synchronous than in young adults; the slow waves in stages 3 and 4 are lower in amplitude and there are fewer of them.
- *Changes in the organization of sleep stages.* For example, although the number of REM sleep periods does not change, successive REM periods no longer increase in length.
- *Changes in the circadian rhythms, or sleep–wake cycles.* For example, older people may nap more and get up earlier in the morning than younger adults.

With respect to this third change, University of Toronto researcher Lynn Hasher and her colleagues (Hasher, Goldstein, & May, 2005) have demonstrated that there are changes with age in people's optimal times of day—the times at which they are most alert and functioning at the highest level both physically and cognitively. Their research indicates that only 6 percent of university-aged students consider themselves to be morning types (i.e., most alert and awake in the morning). The majority of young adults function better in the evening, which is why 8 a.m. classes in university are so unpopular. In contrast, nearly 75 percent of older adults in Hasher and colleagues' research classify themselves as morning types, reflecting a marked shift in circadian patterns with age.

Vitiello and Prinz (1994, p. 640) conclude:

> Each of these age-related sleep changes—decreases in total sleep time, stage 4 sleep, and REM sleep; increases in wakefulness during the night, frequency of stage shifts, and sensitivity to environmental stimuli—may contribute

to the characterization of the sleep of the elderly as "lighter" or more fragile than that of younger individuals. All of these changes may reflect normal, age-related neuronal alterations in brain areas controlling sleep physiology.

It is in distinction from these well-documented age-related changes in sleep that we must try to identify sleep disorders—pathologies that go beyond the normal age-related changes. The three most common sleep disorders in older adults are primary insomnia, restless legs syndrome, and sleep apnea. We will now consider each of these in turn.

PRIMARY INSOMNIA

Primary insomnia is typically defined in terms of both nocturnal and daytime symptoms. Nocturnal symptoms include difficulty falling asleep, frequent awakenings, shortened sleep, and non-restorative sleep. Daytime symptoms include fatigue, sleepiness, depression, and anxiety (Ancoli-Israel, 1989; Daly, 1989; Fetveit, 2009; Vitiello & Prinz, 1994). DSM-IV-TR diagnostic criteria (see Table 16.1) require that symptoms persist for at least one month, are perceived as stressful, and are not secondary to any other disorder. The prevalence of insomnia is thought to increase with age, with approximately half of all older adults complaining of significant sleep disturbances (Fetveit, 2009) and especially high prevalence rates found among the oldest group of older adults (Crowley, 2011; Vitiello & Prinz, 1994).

ETIOLOGY Primary insomnia can result from a wide variety of causes, occurring either singly or in combination. Bootzin and Perlis (1992) group the various possible causes into the categories shown in Table 16.2: physical disorders, substances, circadian rhythm problems, psychological factors, and poor sleep environment or habits.

TABLE 16.2 CAUSES OF PRIMARY INSOMNIA

Physical disorders Periodic movements during sleep, restless legs, gastroesophageal reflux, sleep apnea, fibromyalgia, arthritis, chronic pain, cardiac problems, renal disease, nocturia, cerebrovascular disease, gastrointestinal disease, respiratory disorders, neurological diseases, menopause, cardiovascular disease

Substances Caffeine, nicotine, alcohol, hypnotics, tranquillizers, other prescription medication, substances of abuse

Circadian rhythm problem Shift work, jet lag, delayed sleep phase syndrome, advanced sleep phase syndrome

Poor sleep environment or habits The disturbance is not due to the direct physiological effects of a substance (e.g., a drug of abuse, a medication) or a general medical condition

Sources: Causes of Primary Insomnia from Bootzin, R. R., & Perlis, M. L. (1992). Nonpharmacological treatments of insomnia. *Journal of Clinical Psychiatry, 53* (Suppl. 6), 37–41. Copyright 2009, Physicians Postgraduate Press. Reprinted by permission. Crowley, K. (2011). Sleep and sleep disorders in older adults. *Neuropsychology Review, 21*, 41–53.

Given that many of the symptoms of primary insomnia are the same as those characteristics of sleep that normally change as we age, drawing a line between normal and pathological is difficult if not arbitrary.

TREATMENT Unfortunately, although primary insomnia is more common among older adults, they are less likely than younger adults to be referred to sleep disorder clinics for full assessment and appropriate treatment. Instead, they are commonly treated with sedatives or hypnotics prescribed by their family physicians. A national community survey by Stewart and colleagues (2006) found that whereas 5 percent of adults aged 25 to 34 with a diagnosis of insomnia received an anxiolytic or hypnotic prescription for sleep, that rate jumped to 16 percent among adults aged 65 to 74. Although a wide variety of medications are prescribed for insomnia in older adults (e.g., benzodiazepines, barbiturates, antihistamines), most are contraindicated for this age group. This is because older adults are "at particularly high risk for drug tolerance, dependence, drug interactions, hangover effects, and severe withdrawal reactions" (Daly, 1989, p. 485). Researchers have found that the number of medications consumed by older adults correlates positively with the severity of their sleep-disordered symptoms (Bliwise, 2004). In addition to using prescription and over-the-counter drugs for sleep problems, many older adults self-medicate with alcohol because of the common misconception that it is an effective treatment for insomnia. Although alcohol can help individuals fall asleep, it disrupts the normal sleep cycle discussed above and reduces the quality of sleep (Morin, Mimeault, & Gagne, 1999). In addition, alcohol is contraindicated if an individual is taking any of a wide variety of medications. Indeed, 20 percent of all drug-related accidental or suicidal deaths are estimated to be the result of combining alcohol and drugs.

Fortunately, there is an alternative to medication for sleep problems. Dr. Charles Morin and his colleagues at Laval University have published extensively on the treatment of insomnia for younger and older adults. In their 1999 review, they highlight that cognitive and behavioural strategies for late-life insomnia are as effective as similar treatments for younger adults, produce reliable and lasting improvements in sleep efficiency and satisfaction with sleep, and reduce the use of sleep medications among older adults who are dependent on them. Generally, these approaches involve education (providing information about normal age-related changes in sleep and good sleep habits and hygiene), cognitive therapy (correcting dysfunctional thoughts and attitudes about sleep), stimulus control (strengthening the association between the bedroom and sleep by getting out of bed rather than tossing and turning, using the bedroom only for sleep and sex, etc.), sleep restriction (restricting the amount of time spent in bed to the actual amount of time the insomniac is sleeping), and relaxation. Examples of recommended sleep hygiene tips for Rose, the woman described at the beginning of this section, might include limiting naps, relaxing and avoiding stimulants or beverages before bed, making sure her bedroom is dark and comfortable, and exercising earlier in the day but not late in the evening. At the moment, sleep restriction therapy and multi-component cognitive-behavioural treatments have the greatest research support for older adults with insomnia, with some research indicating that CBT is more effective in managing insomnia than the more commonly administered pharmacotherapy treatment (Sivertsen, 2007). Other promising treatments that require additional research include relaxation training, physical activity, bright light therapy, and massage (McCurry et al., 2007; Teodorescu & Husain, 2010).

RESTLESS LEGS SYNDROME

The second most common sleep disorder in older adults is **restless legs syndrome (RLS),** otherwise known as nocturnal myoclonus. This disorder is characterized by (1) the urge to move one's legs, accompanied by unpleasant sensations in them, (2) the urge and unpleasant sensations being worse during periods of inactivity, (3) movement relieving the urge and unpleasantness, and (4) the urge to move and unpleasant sensations being worse in the evening and night (Bliwise, 2006). In some cases, the leg movement wakes the individual and thus leads to insomnia.

There is a great deal of variability in studies examining the prevalence of RLS among older adults, although most report rates ranging from 10 to 20 percent. Even more common, with estimated rates ranging from 29 to 85 percent, is the less severe form of RLS, known as periodic leg movements in sleep (PLMS). The majority of epidemiological studies suggest that the prevalence of both RLS and PLMS increases with age (Bliwise, 2006; Vitiello & Prinz, 1994). RLS is more common in women (Innes, Selfe, & Agarwal, 2011). This disorder is not recognized as such in the DSM-IV-TR, but it is routinely diagnosed and treated at sleep disorder clinics. Although not yet approved, the DSM-5 Sleep-Wake Disorders Work Group is proposing the addition of RLS diagnostic criteria in the upcoming version of the DSM (APA, 2010). Very little is understood about the etiology of nocturnal myoclonus.

Treatment has been almost exclusively pharmacological to date, with the drug treatments of choice being the same dopaminergic drugs used to treat tremors and other symptoms in patients with Parkinson's disease. The American Academy of Sleep Medicine review of evidence since 2002 clearly indicates that these drugs are effective for the treatment of both PLMS and RLS (Bliwise, 2006). Importantly, however, the side effects of these medications are substantial. RLS often occurs in conjunction with the third most common sleep disorders in older adults: sleep apnea.

SLEEP APNEA

Sleep apnea involves episodes of cessation of breathing (apnea) that last at least 10 seconds (Ancoli-Israel, 1989; Vitiello & Prinz, 1994). Diagnosis requires that there be at least five such episodes per hour of sleep.

This disorder results in hypoxemia (low blood oxygen saturation) and awakenings from sleep. Because quality and quantity of nighttime sleep is disturbed, during the day sufferers will typically have difficulty staying awake, take frequent naps, have difficulty waking up and getting going in the morning or after a nap, and often have a headache for an hour or two in the morning. Difficulty concentrating and remembering may also occur. If the disorder is severe or left untreated, weakened cardiac functioning can occur and can be fatal.

Between 25 and 36 percent of older adults have this disorder (Hoch et al., 1992; Young et al., 2002), and it is markedly more common in men than in women and with increasing age (Vitiello & Prinz, 1994).

ETIOLOGY Three types of sleep apnea have been identified: (1) obstructive apnea due to blockage of the upper airways, generally indicated by snoring; (2) central apnea due to impairment of activation in the medullary respiratory centre in the central nervous system; and (3) mixed apnea, in which both obstructive and central apnea are present. Although excessive body weight contributes to obstructive apnea, the etiology of central apnea is unclear.

DIAGNOSIS Obstructive apnea is the most common form and is easily recognized. During sleep, the sufferer will have periods of no breathing followed by a restorative gasp and then a snore and sometimes a sharp muscle movement. Severity is typically related to obesity. This disorder is likely substantially underdiagnosed and undertreated in older adults (Ancoli-Israel, 1989). Importantly, it is also likely to become increasingly prevalent given that the incidence of obesity in older adults has been increasing over time (Arterbutrn, Crane, & Sullivan, 2006).

TREATMENT For the most part, treatments for sleep apnea are identical for younger and older adults; they involve losing weight, learning to avoid sleeping on one's back (e.g., by wearing a T-shirt with tennis balls sewn into the back), and avoiding respiratory depressants such as alcohol and hypnotic medication. In addition, respiratory stimulants are often helpful. Treatment may also involve continuous positive airway pressure (CPAP), which involves wearing a mask attached to an air compressor to keep the upper airways open while sleeping. As a last resort, surgery can modify the upper airway structures. Treatment can be effective, although compliance can be a problem with respect to weight loss and use of CPAP (Stepanski et al., 2003).

4 BEFORE MOVING ON

Given that diagnosing and treating sleep disorders such as insomnia is often especially complicated when working with older adults, what kind of training do you think you would need above and beyond that needed to work with younger adults?

Anxiety Disorders

Case Notes

Mr. Wallace, a 68-year-old widower, came to the psychological clinic at the insistence of his sister. Since shortly after his retirement three years ago, he has been experiencing what he calls "attacks." During these attacks, his heart pounds and sometimes he has pain in his chest and trouble breathing. He trembles all over and feels that he is going to die. According to Mr. Wallace, the attacks were infrequent at first, occurring no more than once a month. Two years ago his wife died, and since then the attacks have become more frequent, averaging one or two a week. His sister says that Mr. Wallace seems totally preoccupied with these attacks, worries continually about when the next one might occur, and has started leaving the house less and less. Their father died of a heart attack and Mr. Wallace is convinced that sooner or later one of his attacks will prove fatal too. A recent medical examination found no evidence of heart disease, blood pressure problems, or other medical conditions that might be producing his symptoms. Nonetheless, Mr. Wallace remains convinced that he has an undiagnosed life-threatening disorder and anticipates the next attack with dread.

Large community surveys in Canada and the United States that were reviewed in the prevalence section suggest that anxiety disorders occur approximately twice as often as mood disorders among older adults. Whereas about 4 percent of adults 55 and older had a mood disorder (major depression, dysthymia, or bipolar) in the past year, somewhere between 7 and 12 percent had an anxiety disorder (generalized anxiety disorder, panic disorder with or without agoraphobia, social phobia, specific phobia, or post-traumatic stress disorder) (Byers, Yaffe, Covinsky, Friedman, & Bruce, 2010; Mackenzie, Pagura, & Sareen, 2010). Significant symptoms of anxiety and anxiety disorders are among the most common psychiatric problems experienced by older adults (Nordhus & Pallesen, 2003). Unfortunately, they are also among the least studied in this age group (Stanley & Beck, 2000). These prevalent disorders are associated with a number of negative outcomes. For example, Wetherell and colleagues (2011) found that chronic anxiety in older adults can lead to an increased risk of age-related conditions such as Alzheimer's disease.

DIAGNOSTIC ISSUES

Accurately detecting and diagnosing anxiety disorders in adults can be problematic for a number of reasons. One reason is that anxiety disorders can sometimes be overshadowed by depression. Research from Canada and Europe suggests that among older adults in the community with a diagnosis of major depression in the past year, between 23 and 46 percent also had a comorbid anxiety disorder (Ayers, Sorrell, Thorp, & Wetherell, 2007; Cairney, Corna, Veldhuizen, Hemnann, & Streiner, 2008). A second related reason is that anxiety is associated with a range of physical and psychological issues, and it is often difficult to determine which of these problems are causing anxiety, or vice versa (Ayers et al., 2007; Wolitzky-Taylor et al., 2010). A third reason is that a common method of assessing anxiety symptoms involves having individuals complete questionnaires (e.g., Beck Anxiety Inventory). Most of the available scales have been normed and validated with younger adults, and so it is not clear that a score obtained by an elderly individual should be interpreted in the same way as it is for a younger person. For example, many of the symptoms on the typical anxiety scale are somatic (feelings of dizziness, heart palpitations, and so forth). These symptoms are not exclusively those of anxiety; they can also be the result of neurological, cardiovascular, respiratory, and endocrine disorders. Given that these medical problems are more common in older people, they may endorse somatic symptoms on anxiety scales for the "wrong" reasons. We need scales developed especially for older people, but they have not yet been created (Stanley & Beck, 2000). Despite the challenges of accurately diagnosing anxiety disorders in older adults, doing so is especially important considering that they are an independent risk factor for suicidal behaviour, especially when they co-occur with mood and psychotic disorders (Hawgood & De Leo, 2008).

TREATMENT

How should anxiety disorders be treated in older patients? Unfortunately, this is a difficult question to answer, because despite a wealth of research examining treatments for anxiety among younger adults, much less research has been conducted with older adults (Sheikh & Cassidy, 2000). Furthermore, much of the research that has been done is not methodologically rigorous, preventing confident conclusions from being drawn. Nevertheless, there have been several recent reviews and meta-analyses of high-quality studies with anxious older adults randomly assigned to control groups or psychological treatments. This research suggests that cognitive-behavioural, supportive, and relaxation-based therapies are significantly more effective than wait-list or active controls (Ayers et al., 2007; Nordhus & Pallesen, 2003). Research by Mohlman and colleagues (2003) suggests that cognitive-behavioural therapy for older adults with anxiety might be more effective if tailored to suit the unique needs of older adults (e.g., by conducting reminder calls and weekly reviews of important concepts, strategies, and homework assignments). More recently, mindfulness training and acceptance and commitment therapy have been shown to be effective in the treatment of anxiety disorders among older adults (Lenze & Wetherell, 2011).

Despite the apparent benefit of psychological treatment, benzodiazepine medications are most often used to treat anxiety among older individuals, even though they increase older adults' risk for falls and can cause cognitive and psychomotor impairment (Wolitzky-Taylor et al., 2010).

The newer selective serotonin reuptake inhibitors (SSRIs) are becoming increasingly common, although little is known at the present time about their long-term risks and benefits for older people (Ayers et al., 2007; Sheikh & Cassidy, 2000; Stanley & Beck, 2000). Despite the proven benefits of psychotherapy for anxiety and the known risks of pharmacological treatments, research suggests that elderly patients with anxiety disorders are roughly five times more likely to receive prescriptions for benzodiazepines than to receive psychotherapy (Hendriks, Oude Voshaar, Keijsers, Hoogduin, & van Balkom, 2008). Research from our laboratory also indicates that whereas 73 percent of older adults with both depression and anxiety sought professional help in the past year, only 43 percent with just a mood disorder alone sought help, and less than half that number (21 percent) with an anxiety disorder sought professional treatment (Scott, Mackenzie, Chipperfield, & Sareen, 2010).

Of the various anxiety disorders discussed in Chapter 5, the three most common in later life are social phobia, specific phobia, and generalized anxiety disorder (GAD; Mackenzie, Reynolds, Chou, Pagura, & Sareen, 2011). Although there has been far less research on anxiety than on mood disorders in later life, most of the anxiety disorder research has focused on GAD. GAD is a chronic and recurrent disorder with symptoms often lasting decades. Approximately half of the cases of GAD among older adults have their first onset later in life (Chou, 2009). Our recent study of 12 312 American adults 55 years of age and older found that 3 percent met criteria for GAD in the past year, but most of those individuals also had another anxiety, mood, or personality disorder (only 0.5 percent had GAD alone). Despite the fact that older individuals with this disorder in our study had significantly reduced physical and mental health–related quality of life, only 28 percent sought professional help in the past year (Mackenzie et al., 2010). Cognitive-behavioural and relaxation therapies are effective for older individuals with this disorder. Unfortunately, research evidence is limited or nonexistent with respect to therapy effectiveness for older adults with phobias, panic disorder, obsessive-compulsive disorder, and post-traumatic stress disorder (Ayers et al., 2007).

5 BEFORE MOVING ON

Research now shows that for mood disorders, anxiety disorders, and sleep disorders, psychotherapy and pharmacotherapy appear to be equally effective. What are some of the reasons why psychotherapy would be a preferable option to pharmacotherapy for older adults with these disorders? Conversely, what are some of the reasons why pharmacotherapy would be preferable? Would your reasons be the same for younger patients?

Schizophrenia

As you will recall from Chapter 9, schizophrenia typically begins to manifest itself in the late teens or twenties. The typical early-onset schizophrenia can be distinguished from the late-onset form of the disorder, which first appears after the age of 40 or 45. There are important differences between the two, as we will see in a moment.

Early-onset schizophrenia becomes relevant to this chapter when these people grow into old age. Unfortunately, many do not. People with early-onset schizophrenia have a higher death rate than the general population, largely because of increased suicide rates (Allebeck, 1989). It was believed for many years that the disease followed a deteriorating course with age, so that those who did survive would have a poor long-term prognosis. More recent longitudinal studies do not support this view. On the contrary, it appears that symptoms of schizophrenia either disappear or decrease substantially over time in a significant number of patients (Harding, Brooks, Ashikaga, Strauss, & Breier, 1987; Harvey, 2001; Jeste, Manley, & Harris, 1991; Ruskin, 1990). In particular, as people with schizophrenia age, it appears that there is a decrease in positive symptoms, such as delusions and hallucinations, and an increase in negative symptoms, such as withdrawal and flattened affect (Ruskin, 1990).

Late-onset schizophrenia is less common than the early-onset variant; nearly one-quarter of those with this diagnosis develop it after age 40 (Broadway & Mintzer, 2007). In one Canadian study, only 2.4 percent of all individuals admitted to a psychogeriatric unit over a four-year period had a diagnosis of schizophrenia (Yassa, Dastoor, Nastase, Camille, & Belzile, 1993). In contrast to early-onset schizophrenia, the majority of individuals with the late-onset variant of this disorder are women (Broadway & Mintzer, 2007).

DIAGNOSTIC ISSUES

The diagnostic criteria for late-onset schizophrenia are the same as those for early-onset schizophrenia, but the particular symptoms are likely to be different. Late-onset cases are less likely to have disorganized speech, lack of logical thought, and flattened affect (Jeste et al., 1991). Late-onset patients are more likely than early-onset individuals to have hallucinations (Broadway & Mintzer, 2007), and their hallucinations and delusions are likely to be more florid and bizarre (Rabins, 1992). The content of these delusions and hallucinations is commonly persecutory, so people with late-onset schizophrenia are most likely to resemble the paranoid schizophrenic subtype. Because delusions of persecution are associated with a number of disorders that occur in older individuals—dementia and delusional disorders, for example—differential diagnosis can be a problem (Howard, Castle, Wessely, & Murray, 1993; Jeste et al., 1988; Pearlson et al., 1989). To complicate matters, psychotic symptoms in this age group can also be caused by a number of medical illnesses, including Addison's disease, Parkinson's disease, and brain tumours.

TREATMENT

Neuroleptic (antipsychotic) drugs are the treatment of choice for schizophrenia and other causes of psychosis across the lifespan. Continuing with a common theme in this chapter, most of the research on antipsychotic medications has focused on younger adults. Several recent studies of both typical and the newer atypical antipsychotics with older adults suggest that they are generally well tolerated and effective (Broadway & Mintzer, 2007). Research on the effectiveness of cognitive-behavioural skills training for older adults with schizophrenia has shown increases in social activities, cognitive insight, and mastery of skills, as compared to an age-matched control group (Granholm et al., 2005). Similarly, a social skills intervention study carried out by Bartels and colleagues (2004) found evidence of increased social functioning and health management and decreases of inappropriate behaviour that remained one year following their intervention.

Delirium

Case Notes

Mrs. Chen is a 77-year-old woman who lives alone. She was brought to hospital by ambulance after she was found wandering and talking incoherently in a downtown department store. Her dazed appearance, and the fact that she was engaged in a rambling "conversation" with no one in particular, had attracted the attention of a security guard. When he attempted to question Mrs. Chen, she was unable to provide either her name or address or say why she was in the store. The security guard phoned 911 and an ambulance arrived. The ambulance attendants were also unable to obtain clear answers to their questions. She appeared anxious, confused, and frightened. When they arrived at the hospital, a nurse found several bottles of medication on Mrs. Chen, as well as her daughter's phone number. Consultation with her daughter and her primary care physician established that Mrs. Chen suffered from thyroid problems, and that her nutritional statuswas poor. Emergency room physicians diagnosed Mrs. Chen as suffering from delirium brought on by her poor nutritional status, in conjunction with her failure to take her thyroid medication. After several days in hospital, her symptoms began to abate. She was released to her daughter's care, with instructions to monitor her food and fluid intake, and her medication regimen.

Although delirium can occur at any age, it is most common in older adults, as they are more likely to suffer from the various conditions that can precipitate its onset. As shown in the case example above, delirium is especially common among medically ill older adults. According to the Canadian Coalition for Seniors' Mental Health National Guidelines for the Assessment and Treatment of Delirium (CCSMH, 2006c), this disorder has been found in up to 50 percent of older people admitted as inpatients to acute care settings. Surgery is also a risk factor for the development of delirium; it has been reported in 10 to 15 percent of older adults undergoing general surgery, in as many as 30 percent of older adults undergoing open-heart surgery, and in 50 percent of older adults receiving hip replacements. In a review of this disorder, Marin Cole (2004) at McGill University reports that delirium is typically characterized by an acute onset (developing over days or even hours) of disturbances in consciousness, orientation, memory, thinking, perception, and behaviour. In some cases, however, there is a more gradual prodromal phase during which individuals experience mild, transient symptoms of fatigue, poor concentration, restlessness, and mild cognitive impairment. These disturbances may remain at this subacute level or progress to a full delirium.

The hallmark symptom of delirium is reduced or clouded consciousness, including fluctuating impairments in attention and orientation. The individual may move back and forth from lucidity to severe confusion. In addition to disorientation, delirium may also be manifested in incoherent speech, marked memory impairment, and confusion over simple things. Behaviourally, hallucinations, aggression, restlessness, and a dazed expression may be present.

Typically, delirium is of short duration (usually less than a week). Despite the brevity of this disorder, however, it has serious consequences and a poor prognosis. Experiencing a delirium increases one's risk for functional disability, longer hospital stays, admission to long-term care institutions, or worse. If untreated, delirium can result in rapid deterioration and premature death; even with accurate diagnosis and treatment, the death rate is about 40 percent.

ETIOLOGY

Although the exact cause of delirium is undetermined, known risk factors include a wide variety of organic factors that can be categorized as metabolic (e.g., hypothyroidism, nutritional deficits), infectious (e.g., tuberculosis, HIV-related dementia), or structural (e.g., Parkinson's disease, dementia, head injury). Other organic possibilities include drug overdose or withdrawal, acute strokes, and exposure to toxic substances. Delirium can also accompany functional disorders such as psychotic depression, mania, and schizophrenia.

DIAGNOSTIC ISSUES

Despite the rather striking symptoms associated with delirium, it is often undetected or misdiagnosed as dementia or another psychiatric disorder such as depression (Cole, 2004). Because of the potentially lethal consequences of untreated delirium, the diagnostic challenge is to identify the underlying condition leading to the delirium in the individual case. Thus, it is essential that someone (family or friend) provide a detailed history of the patient to the diagnostician. The DSM-5 Neurocognitive Disorders Work Group has proposed a new category of neurocognitive disorders, which will replace the previous categories of delirium, dementia, amnestic, and other geriatric cognitive disorders (APA, 2010). The three proposed diagnostic categories are delirium, major neurocognitive disorder, and mild neurocognitive disorder. The proposed changes to the DSM-IV-TR delirium criteria include more specific wording to improve diagnostic clarity.

TREATMENT

There are essentially two phases to the treatment of this disorder, according to the Canadian Coalition for Seniors' Mental Health National Guidelines (CCSMH, 2006c). Psychotropic medications are sometimes needed for individuals who are agitated or psychotic in order to carry out a thorough assessment and to prevent delirious patients from endangering themselves or others. When this is the case, the treatment of choice is usually the antipsychotic medication Haloperidol, although the more recent atypical antipsychotic medications are now being used (Broadway & Mintzer, 2007). The second and arguably more important phase of treatment, according to Cole (2004), is "the diagnosis and treatment of the conditions predisposing to, precipitating, or perpetuating the delirium" (p. 14). For example, in the case of Mrs. Chen, compliance with the medication regimen for her thyroid problem is essential. In many cases, if treatment is appropriate and timely, virtually complete recovery is possible. Because patients may fade in and out of delirium, are not likely aware of their own needs, and are easily upset or agitated, the general approach to treating delirium includes maintaining a carefully controlled and simple environment, monitoring the patient's nutritional and fluid status, and minimizing the number and amount of medications being taken, in addition to whatever specific treatment is necessary to deal with the presumed cause. There is also emerging evidence that supportive care may be helpful, that systematic detection and treatment programs can improve outcome for surgical patients, and that prevention programs might reduce the prevalence of delirium for surgical and medical patients (Popeo, 2011).

Dementia

Case Notes

Mrs. Lorenzo was 76 when she and her family first noticed that she was beginning to be forgetful. In conversations, she would repeat things and be unable to answer questions about recent events. Soon she noticed that she was beginning to make errors at work, and so she retired from a part-time bookkeeping job that had been a great source of satisfaction for her. Mrs. Lorenzo's children convinced her and her husband to move from the family home to an apartment in a life care centre. The children were surprised that their mother showed little emotion as she disposed of treasured possessions and left her home of many years. In the new apartment, Mrs. Lorenzo's forgetfulness worsened. Once a voracious reader, she stopped reading entirely and spent her days playing game after game of solitaire. Less than two years after the move, Mrs. Lorenzo's husband died. Although they had been married for 59 years and had been very close, she did not appear to grieve. She had trouble remembering that her husband was no longer alive. When her children phoned her, she would ask the same two or three questions over and over. Once fastidious, Mrs. Lorenzo no longer bathed or changed her clothes without prompting. In the year following her husband's death, she was able to remain in her apartment with daily assistance from a homemaker and close monitoring by the life care centre staff. This was not expected to be possible for very much longer, as her children were increasingly concerned about her health and safety.

Dementia is the most common mental disorder in older adults and, many argue, the cruellest, gradually robbing sufferers of their memory, judgment, and reason; their personal dignity; and, finally, their very sense of self. In the early stages, it may be almost as difficult for loved ones to stand helplessly by as it is for the sufferer; in the later stages, it is almost certainly more distressing for family, friends, and even professional caregivers.

Dementia, from the Latin *de* ("from" or "out of") and *mentis* ("mind"), refers to a large category of disorders that have in common the individual's loss of his or her former level of cognitive functioning—that is, loss of memory, language, visuospatial, and reasoning abilities. The causes of this loss and the specific patterns of loss differ for various specific disorders grouped together in the general category of dementia.

For a long time, dementia was commonly known as senility or senile dementia because the mental deterioration was thought to be simply the result of the normal aging process (Blazer, 1990). We now know that this is not the case, and that dementia is a pathology that, although relatively common in older adults, is not universally present. Consequently, the terms *senile dementia* and *senility* are, quite appropriately, out of favour.

Although dementia occurs in younger people, it is rare and generally secondary to another disorder such as substance abuse or AIDS. As a primary mental disorder, dementia is clearly a disorder of old age. The Canadian Study of Health and Aging has made significant contributions to our understanding of the prevalence of dementia. More than 10 000 older Canadians living in the community (9008) and institutions (1255) were surveyed to identify its prevalence. The key findings from this survey, summarized in Table 16.3, are that (1) 8 percent of Canadians over the age of 65 have some form of dementia, (2) prevalence rates increase sharply with age, and (3) women are about twice as likely as men to have dementia (Canadian Study of Health and Aging Working Group, 1994). Because of the

TABLE 16.3 PREVALENCE OF DEMENTIAS BY AGE IN CANADA

Age Group	All Dementias	Alzheimer's Dementia	Vascular Dementia
65–74	2.4	1.0	0.6
75–84	11.1	6.9	2.4
85+	34.5	26.0	4.8
85–89	22.8	16.7	3.4
90–94	40.4	32.3	4.6
95+	58.6	43.3	6.7

Source: First three rows based on report of Canadian Study of Health and Aging Working Group (1994); last three rows based on Ebly, Parhad, Hogan, and Fung (1994).

dramatic growth of the older-adult segment of the population, unless prevalence rates change, we can expect about 600 000 cases of dementia in the over-65 population by 2021. The prevalence of dementia is even more startling on a global level. Current estimates suggest that about 24 million people have dementia worldwide, with the number projected to double every 20 years (Qiu, de Ronchi, & Fratiglioni, 2007).

There are many forms of dementia—the DSM-IV-TR lists 13—and so it is not surprising that attempts have been made to categorize or classify the different types. The previously mentioned DSM-5 Neurocognitive Disorders Working Group has proposed to split the DSM-IV-TR dementia category into separate major neurocognitive disorder and mild neurocognitive disorder categories.

Dementias may be classified by such aspects as etiology, prognosis, symptoms, and treatments. No system is uniformly accepted, and the DSM-IV-TR uses no categorization system. One classification scheme distinguishes dementias that are reversible from those that are irreversible. The term **pseudo-dementia** is sometimes used to describe disorders that produce cognitive impairment similar to dementia but that can be reversed (Foster & Martin, 1990). Depression, nutritional deficiency, thyroid disorder, and a number of other diseases can cause symptoms that mimic dementia, such as forgetfulness, inability to concentrate, poor judgment, faulty reasoning, and lability or flattening of affect. Such symptoms may also occur as side effects from many medications, such as hypnotics, but are transient and disappear when their underlying cause is treated.

Another common way to distinguish among the various types of dementia focuses on the areas of the brain that are primarily affected. Cummings and Benson (1992) separate cortical dementias, which primarily attack the cerebral cortex or grey matter, from subcortical dementias, which primarily attack the white matter and more primitive parts of the brain that are closer to the brain stem. This distinction is useful clinically because depending on what brain regions are affected by the dementia, different symptoms will be prominent. In cortical dementias (e.g., Alzheimer's disease, frontotemporal dementia), the primary symptoms include problems learning new information and loss of short-term memory ability, visuospatial problems, language problems, and eventually poor reasoning and judgment. In subcortical dementias (e.g., vascular dementia, Lewy body dementia), the primary symptoms are cognitive slowing, problems retrieving information from memory, and difficulty with executive functioning (i.e., reasoning, judgment, and mental flexibility).

The remainder of this section will focus on the two most common types of dementia: Alzheimer's disease (AD) and vascular dementia. It is estimated that 50 to 60 percent of dementias are due exclusively to AD, 12 to 17 percent are due to vascular insults, 8 to 18 percent are due to a combination of AD and vascular pathology, and 10 to 20 percent are due to other causes (Zarit & Zarit, 1998). Two additional types of dementia—dementia with Lewy bodies and frontotemporal dementia—are being recognized as distinct forms of disease that were formerly misclassified as AD (Kukull & Bowen, 2002). We will also discuss these types of dementia briefly.

MILD COGNITIVE IMPAIRMENT (MCI)

Before discussing specific forms of dementia, however, we will focus briefly on a relatively new concept that is receiving a great deal of attention from clinicians and researchers—**mild cognitive impairment (MCI)**. The reason why this concept has generated such clinical and theoretical interest is that, as shown in Figure 16.5, it is thought to represent a transitional state between normal aging and dementia (Knopman, Boeve, & Petersen, 2003). Individuals who have MCI are between 5 and 10 times more likely to develop dementia than are cognitively healthy adults. Another way of stating this is that healthy adults develop dementia at a rate of about 1 to 2 percent per year. In comparison, individuals with MCI develop dementia at a rate of about 10 to 15 percent per year, so that after five years, more than half of individuals diagnosed with MCI will progress to a diagnosis of dementia (Petersen et al., 2001).

What exactly is MCI? According to Ronald Petersen and his colleagues (2001) at the Mayo Clinic, diagnostic criteria include (1) memory complaints that are corroborated by family members or other informants, (2) objective evidence of impaired short-term memory, (3) otherwise

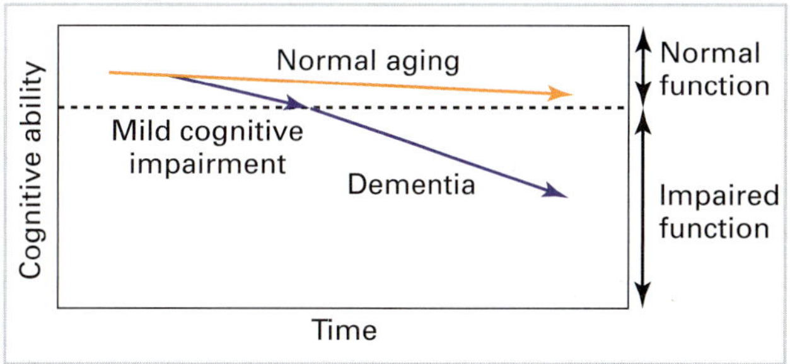

FIGURE 16.5 Theoretical Progression of Cognitive Ability over Time for Adults with Good Health, MCI, and Dementia

normal cognitive functioning, (4) unimpaired social or occupational functioning, and (5) no dementia. Diagnosis is important because individuals with MCI are at very high risk of developing dementia, so identifying these individuals early in the process can help patients and their families begin to prepare for the likely onset of dementia. In addition, MCI is an obvious target for treatments aimed at improving symptoms and even preventing dementia. As we will discuss below, there are medications that can slow the progression of dementia. Unfortunately, the first wave of clinical trials examining the ability of these drugs to slow the progression of MCI to dementia has been largely unsuccessful; additional trials are currently under way (Wilson, Peters, Ritchie, & Ritchie, 2011). In a recent review, Wilson and colleagues concluded that although an effective drug-based intervention to slow the progression of dementia has yet to be solidified, lifestyle modifications such as avoiding high blood pressure; maintaining low levels of cholesterol; eating a healthy, balanced diet; and engaging in exercise may have an impact in lowering the risk of developing dementia (Wilson et al., 2011).

ALZHEIMER'S DISEASE

Alzheimer's disease (AD) is the most common cause of dementia, and one of the most common mental disorders among older adults. It is a progressive, fatal, neurological disease with an average course of at least six years from diagnosis to death (Knopman et al., 2003), with some patients surviving after diagnosis for as long as 20 years (Zarit & Zarit, 1998). Although the course of the disease is progressive, slow, and steady, it is often helpful to conceptualize this decline in terms of three stages. The Alzheimer's Society of Canada refers to these as early, middle, and late stages.

Speaking Out Dementia: Living with Dementia

Watch this Speaking Out video at www.mysearchlab.com

Speaking Out Dementia: Alvin

Watch this Speaking Out video at www.mysearchlab.com

In the early stage, individuals with AD exhibit memory difficulties, problems with concentration, unclear thinking, and mild difficulty finding words. The initial signs are first recognized sometimes by the afflicted individual and sometimes by those close to him or her. Isolation and marital and/or family strain are common during the first stage. Estimates of depression in AD patients are as high as 25 percent (Foster & Martin, 1990), although mood disorders are more common in the early to middle phases of the disease; with progression of AD, patients typically lose insight into their difficulties so that later in the process the disease is more difficult for caregivers.

During the middle stage, existing symptoms become more severe and a wide range of additional symptoms may occur: short-term memory problems worsen (amnesia); language difficulties become more pronounced (aphasia); difficulty with purposeful motor movements appear so that individuals may have difficulty eating or getting dressed by themselves (apraxia); individuals have difficulty recognizing or naming people or things (agnosia); and problems with judgment, reasoning, and mental flexibility emerge (executive dysfunction). In addition, individuals with AD have problems in orientation as to time and place, sleep difficulties, difficulties in social situations, urinary incontinence, feelings of helplessness, flattening of affect, agitation, irritability, and wandering. Although at this point individuals with the disease are not yet bedridden, the caregiver's role becomes quite demanding.

TABLE 16.4 DSM-IV-TR DIAGNOSTIC CRITERIA FOR DEMENTIA OF THE ALZHEIMER'S TYPE

A. The development of multiple cognitive deficits manifested by both
   (1) memory impairment (impaired ability to learn new information or to recall previously learned information)
   (2) one (or more) of the following cognitive disturbances:
      (a) aphasia (language disturbance)
      (b) apraxia (impaired ability to carry out motor activities despite intact motor function)
      (c) agnosia (failure to recognize or identify objects despite intact sensory function)
      (d) disturbance in executive functioning (i.e., planning, organizing, sequencing, abstracting)

B. The cognitive deficits in Criteria A1 and A2 each cause significant impairment in social or occupational functioning and represent a significant decline from a previous level of functioning.

C. The course is characterized by gradual onset and continuing cognitive decline.

D. The cognitive deficits in Criteria A1 and A2 are not due to any of the following:
   (1) other central nervous system conditions that cause progressive deficits in memory and cognition (e.g., cerebrovascular disease, Parkinson's disease, Huntington's disease, subdural hematoma, normal-pressure hydrocephalus, brain tumor)
   (2) systemic conditions that are known to cause dementia (e.g., hypothyroidism, vitamin B12 or folic acid deficiency, niacin deficiency, hypercalcemia, neurosyphilis, HIV infection)
   (3) substance-induced conditions

E. The deficits do not occur exclusively during the course of a delirium.

F. The disturbance is not better accounted for by another Axis I disorder (e.g., Major Depressive Disorder, Schizophrenia).

Code based on presence or absence of a clinically significant behavioral disturbance:

294.10 Without Behavioral Disturbance: if the cognitive disturbance is not accompanied by any clinically significant behavioral disturbance.

Source: Reprinted with permission from the *Diagnostic and Statistical Manual of Mental Disorders, Fourth Edition, Text Revision.* (Copyright © 2000). American Psychiatric Association.

In the late stage, language and memory impairments are profound. A variety of physical symptoms develop: stooped posture, increasing immobility, total incontinence, and increasing vulnerability to conditions such as pneumonia and congestive heart failure. In this stage, challenging behaviours include extreme symptoms such as delusions and hallucinations that occur in 30 to 50 percent of individuals with AD (Broadway & Mintzer, 2007).

DIAGNOSTIC CRITERIA Because AD is distinguished by distinct changes in the brain that are discussed in the next section, the gold standard for diagnosis is a histological examination at autopsy. However, neurologists, neuropsychologists, and other dementia specialists have been shown to be quite accurate in their clinical diagnoses (Knopman et al., 2003). Table 16.4 lists the DSM-IV-TR criteria used, but in many cases a definitive diagnosis is difficult because the same individual can suffer from multiple forms of dementia (mixed dementia). The most significant proposed change to the diagnostic criteria for AD in the DSM-5 (APA, 2010) includes specifying it as either (1) major neurocognitive disorder that requires impairment in memory and one other cognitive domain, including language, motor functioning, object recognition, and executive functioning, or (2) mild neurocognitive disorder that requires strong evidence for AD (e.g., genetic test) but does not require impairment in cognitive domains outside of memory.

ETIOLOGY What causes the devastation of AD? It seems clear that the etiology is physiological. There are two dramatic differences between the brains of individuals with and without AD (Foster & Martin, 1990). The first is the presence of excessive amounts of plaques (collections within a nerve cell of nerve cell and supportive tissue debris suspended in a protein substance called amyloid) and neurofibrillary tangles (clusters of intertwined filaments in nerve cells that in the normal brain are not tangled). Greater numbers of plaques and tangles are related to poorer functioning and even death of nerve cells. The second difference, as shown in Figure 16.6, is substantial atrophy of the cortex in AD brains.

The question, of course, is what causes these changes. One hypothesis is genetic. The evidence for genetic involvement is twofold (Raskind & Peskind, 1992). First, individuals with Down syndrome (a genetic disorder) who live beyond age 40 generally show neuropathological indicators of AD. Second, AD has been shown to run in families. In such families, about 50 percent of those at risk develop the disease. The genetic influence is even stronger among identical twins, evidenced by a concordance rate of 78 percent (Bergem, Engedal, & Kringlen, 1997). However, familial AD is estimated to make up only 15 percent of all cases. Initially, there was thought to be an AD gene on chromosome 21, but more recent evidence has implicated chromosomes 1, 4, 9, 10, 11, 12, 14, 18, and 20 as well (Padilla & Isaacson, 2011; Rogaeva, Kawarai, & St. George-Hyslop,

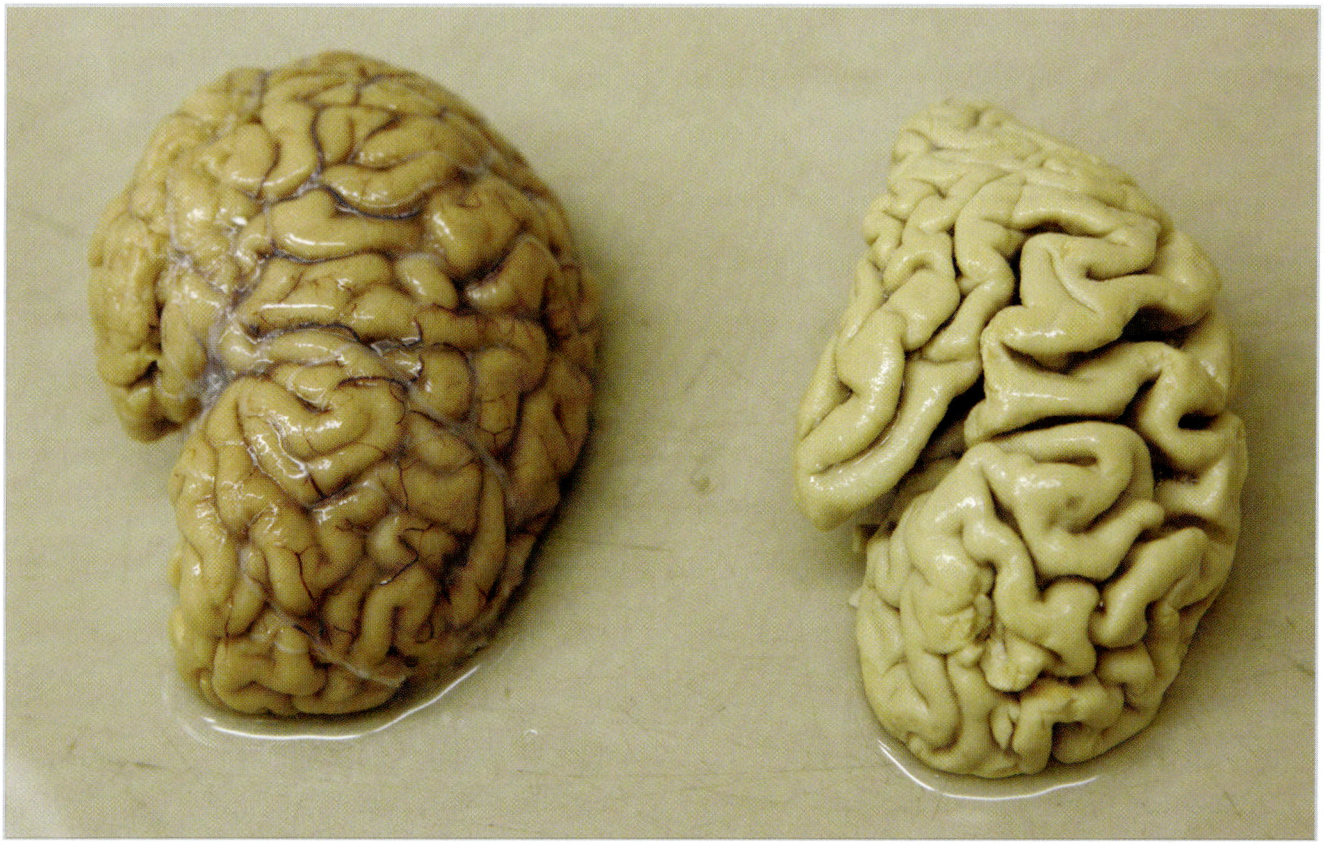

FIGURE 16.6 Normal Brain Tissue Contrasted with That of a Patient with Alzheimer's Disease
The slide on the left shows a normal brain; the slide on the right shows a brain from a person with Alzheimer's disease.

2006; St. George-Hyslop, 2006). A certain form of the Apolipopritein E (APOE) gene, 4, has also been shown to increase the risk of developing AD, especially among women (Tsuang & Bird, 2002). Although researchers have discovered many genes that are linked with AD, APOE remains the most reliable genetic association (Rogaeva et al., 2006). Of course, AD may have a number of forms, each associated with different genes or gene combinations.

A second hypothesis regarding the cause of AD involves environmental and medical factors. Epidemiological research has identified numerous non-genetic risk factors for AD, many of which are preventable or reversible. These risk factors include vascular-related factors (e.g., high blood pressure, high cholesterol, cardiovascular problems, diabetes, stroke), depression, head trauma, lifestyle factors (e.g., poor nutrition, alcoholism, lack of regular physical activity, smoking), exposure to environmental toxins (e.g., pesticides, solvents, aluminum, mercury), lower levels of education, and manual labour jobs (Patterson, Feightner, Garcia, & MacKnight, 2007; Qiu et al., 2007).

With the exception of genetic causes of the relatively rare form of familial AD, there is still no known definite cause of the disease. It is important to highlight that genetic and environmental factors need not work in isolation. The interaction of these factors will likely receive increasing attention from researchers in years to come (Kukull & Bowen, 2002). In addition to efforts aimed at finding the cause or causes of AD, research has also focused on possible protective factors. Many protective factors are simply the reverse of the risk factors identified above (e.g., whereas a high-fat diet is a risk factor, a low-fat vegetarian diet is considered protective). Additional protective factors identified in the literature include regular and moderate consumption of red wine, dietary antioxidants such as vitamins C and E, exposure to certain prescription medications (e.g., lipid-lowering drugs and non-steroidal anti-inflammatory drugs such as Aspirin), and inoculations and vaccinations (e.g., tetanus, influenza). Interventions designed to prevent or delay dementia by focusing on remediable risk and protective factors represent an exciting direction for future research (Kukull & Bowen, 2002; Patterson et al., 2007; Qiu et al., 2007).

TREATMENT One approach to treating dementia has been to seek drugs that will reverse, stop, or at least slow its progression. Emphasis on seeking effective treatment has focused on AD because it is the most common type of dementia. Progress has been limited, and a "cure" remains elusive, but in recent years a particular class of drugs, cholinesterase inhibitors (ChEIs; e.g., Aricept), has been developed that may slow the progression and treat the symptoms of AD (Ihl et al., 2011). The benefit of the three "second-generation" ChEIs that have been approved for use in Canada (donepezil, galantamine, and rivastigmine) was examined by Dr. Krista Lanctot and her colleagues (2003) at Sunnybrook and Women's College Health Sciences Centre in Toronto. The outcome of their review and meta-analysis of 5159 treated patients compared to 2795 controls who received a placebo was that "treatment with ChEIs results in a modest but significant therapeutic effect and modestly but significantly higher rates of adverse events and discontinuation of treatment" (p. 557).

An additional approach to treatment has been to focus on secondary symptoms common in dementia, such as agitation, anxiety, and depression. For the most part, the antidepressants, antipsychotics, and neuroleptics that ameliorate these symptoms in other populations also work with AD patients. Some are contraindicated, however, because of undesirable side effects. For example, some drugs cause hyperactivity, which worsens AD symptoms such as wandering or agitation.

In addition to pharmacological approaches to treating secondary symptoms, effective non-pharmacological interventions have been developed to manage some of the challenging behaviours associated with AD and other dementias (Cohen-Mansfield, 2001). A recent review of evidence-based treatments for behavioural disturbances in older adults with dementia found the most support for behavioural problem-solving therapies that increase pleasant activities and identify antecedents and consequences of challenging behaviours in patients with dementia (Logsdon, McCurry, & Teri, 2007). These interventions not only decrease challenging behaviours, but also reduce caregiver stress.

6 BEFORE MOVING ON

Recent research has demonstrated that individuals who have a particular genotype (APOE) are at increased risk for developing AD, although being APOE-positive does not mean that an individual will develop the disease. Would you want this test if it were available to you? What are arguments for and against genetic testing for a trait that increases your risk for developing a disease such as Alzheimer's, considering that no curative treatment is currently available?

VASCULAR DEMENTIA

The second most common cause of dementia is cerebrovascular damage. In vascular disease, the arteries that supply the brain are partly blocked. When blood flow is reduced beyond a certain point, a stroke occurs (Read, 1996). The area affected by a stroke can be large or small. An area of damaged cortex due to vascular damage, referred to as a **brain lesion** or infarction, can lead to dementia. As shown in Table 16.3, the prevalence of **vascular dementia** increases with age and is higher among men than women.

DIAGNOSTIC ISSUES Vascular dementia can be diagnosed clinically and with the aid of neuroimaging (e.g., CT, PET, or MRI scans). Evidence of focal lesions or infarctions on scans is a telltale sign, although numerous small infarcts (transient ischemic attacks, or TIAs) can be hard to detect on neuroimaging. Clinically, the onset of vascular dementia is often sudden (in comparison to the slow onset of AD) and patients will experience stepwise progression as they experience additional vascular insults. These individuals will also often have a history of stroke or stroke risk factors, such as obesity, diabetes, and being a smoker. The prognosis of vascular dementia is somewhat worse than for AD, with a faster progression and shorter survival times (Knopman et al.,

APPLIED CLINICAL CASE

Ronald Reagan

The most famous person to be affected by Alzheimer's disease is Ronald Reagan, the 40th president of the United States. Reagan left office in 1989 at age 78. Five years later, he issued a handwritten letter to the American public informing them of his diagnosis. Given the insidious and progressive nature of AD, there was speculation about whether he had exhibited early signs of the disease while he was president. Although his White House physicians stated publicly that they saw no evidence of the disease while he was in power, it is quite possible that Reagan experienced some degree of brain changes and clinical symptoms of the disease before he left office. Two factors complicate this issue. First, individuals who are highly intelligent are likely able to hide the effects of the disease longer than less intelligent people can. Second, six months after Reagan left office, he suffered significant head trauma after being thrown from a horse while in Mexico. As discussed earlier in this section, head trauma is a risk factor for dementia. As a result, it is possible that he showed no signs of the disease until this trauma, which may have triggered it or hastened its progression.

2003). As mentioned above, vascular dementia is a subcortical disease in which the first symptoms include cognitive slowing, problems retrieving short-term memories (that improve with cues, reminders, etc.), and executive dysfunction. As a result, its symptoms can be distinguished from "pure" AD, which is a cortical dementia in which the first symptoms are problems forming and recalling short-term memories (that do not improve with cues) and word-finding problems. Unfortunately, this distinction is frequently blurred by the fact that vascular dementia and AD often co-occur.

TREATMENT The most effective way of treating vascular dementia is by managing the risk factors for future cerebrovascular events. Such treatments include lifestyle changes as well as medications. Evidence suggests that the cholinesterase inhibitors also appear to benefit individuals with vascular dementia (Knopman et al., 2003). In addition, blood-thinning medication is often prescribed for vascular disease to lessen the likelihood of further strokes (Foster & Martin, 1990). In other respects, treatment focuses on management and is similar to that for AD.

OTHER FORMS OF DEMENTIA

Although AD and vascular disease account for 80 to 90 percent of all dementia diagnoses, and certain types of dementia are exceedingly rare (e.g., Creutzfeldt-Jakob disease), we will discuss two forms of dementia in this section that are not uncommon, and in which memory problems are not necessarily a key clinical feature: Lewy body dementia and frontotemporal dementia.

Dementia is now recognized as occurring relatively frequently among older adults with Parkinson's disease. A key pathological change in the brains of patients with Parkinson's disease is filaments of protein with a dense core called Lewy bodies. Increasing awareness of a unique dementia syndrome associated with these pathological changes has led to the use of the term **Lewy body dementia**. Like AD and vascular dementia, a diagnosis of Lewy body dementia requires a progressive cognitive decline that interferes with social or occupational functioning. The diagnosis of this disorder differs from the others in that one or more of the following key symptoms are evident: (1) fluctuating cognition with pronounced variations in alertness and attention; (2) recurrent well-formed hallucinations; and (3) spontaneous features of Parkinsonism, including slowed body movement, muscle rigidity, resting tremor, and postural instability. In addition, patients with this type of dementia have neuroleptic sensitivity, meaning that they have extreme reactions to antipsychotic medications. Because of this feature, proper diagnosis is crucial due to the fact that if antipsychotics are prescribed to treat hallucinations, these patients can experience neuroleptic malignant syndrome, which can result in death (Ross & Bowen, 2002). As is the case with vascular dementia, the prognosis of Lewy body dementia is poorer than for AD. Treatments for this type of dementia often focus on the proper medication management of Parkinson's symptoms with levodopa. In addition, the cholinesterase inhibitors have shown promise for patients with this disease (Zarit & Zarit, 1998).

Frontotemporal dementia (FTD) is a term used to describe a heterogeneous group of disorders, including Pick's disease (characterized by "Pick" bodies, spherical protein deposits found within neurons primarily in the frontal lobes of the brain at autopsy), that affect the frontal and temporal lobes of the brain. The key features of this type of dementia are changes in personality and judgment (Knopman et al., 2003). Patients with FTD often have relatively intact memory

CANADIAN RESEARCH CENTRE

Baycrest Centre for Geriatric Care

Baycrest is an academic health sciences centre affiliated with the University of Toronto. It began as the Toronto Jewish Old Folks Home in 1918 and has developed into one of the leading centres in North America with a focus on older adults' health, mental health, and cognitive functioning. Key to the success of Baycrest's mission of improving the quality of life of the elderly are its efforts to integrate clinical care, research, and education. Clinically, Baycrest provides inpatient, outpatient, and day program services to more than 3000 older adults every day. As is the case in other university-affiliated hospitals in Canada and around the world, these clinical services both inform and are informed by a dizzying array of research activities.

In addition to research activities within many Baycrest departments, including psychology, psychiatry, medicine, and social work, the centre houses two research facilities: the internationally renowned Rotman Research Institute and the Kunin-Lunenfeld Applied Research Unit (KLARU). The Rotman's focus is on changes in cognition and other mental processes with age. In particular, scientists at the institute study normal age-related changes in cognition, as well as the effects of abnormal processes such as dementia, stroke, traumatic brain injury, and other neuropsychiatric illnesses. The focus of KLARU is to work closely with clinicians to close the gap between research and clinical care.

In one example of a groundbreaking research carried out at the Rotman Research Institute, Ellen Bialystock, Fergus Craik, and Morris Freedman (2007) looked at the effects of speaking more than one language on the development of dementia. These scientists examined the clinical records of 184 patients referred to Dr. Freedman's memory clinic with memory complaints, half of whom were bilingual. Remarkably, patients who spoke only English developed dementia an average of four years sooner than those who spoke more than one language. Although this study did not examine why bilingualism appears to offer some protection against developing dementia, the researchers speculate that changes in the brain due to language learning enables it to better tolerate accumulated pathologies that eventually lead to diseases such as Alzheimer's. In another example of a groundbreaking research carried out at KLARU, Dr. Nicholaas Verhoeff and his colleagues (2004) succeeded in using a novel positron emission tomography (PET) brain scanning technique to detect beta-amyloid plaques, one of the telltale signs of AD in the brain. Advances such as this may lead to ways of detecting the earliest changes in the disease in order to understand and treat it more effectively.

function until later in the disease process. In contrast to other types of dementia, they exhibit striking behaviour and personality changes such as disinhibition, impulsiveness, repetitiveness, poor judgment, social inappropriateness, loss of empathy, apathy, and reclusiveness. Patients with FTD may also develop a taste for sweet foods, and overeating is common. Because of their striking personality changes and lapses in judgment, individuals with FTD are often mistaken for having a psychiatric disorder, leading to under-recognition of this type of dementia. Age of onset tends to be younger than for AD and the course of FTD is variable, with certain patients living only three or four years and others living more than a decade.

CAREGIVER STRESS

Finally, it is important to recognize the impact that dementia has on family members, friends, and professional caregivers. Family caregivers, in particular, live their daily lives under chronically high levels of stress due to a variety of unpredictable physical and psychosocial demands. A growing body of research is clearly showing that caregivers have heightened levels of clinical depression and anxiety (Alzheimer's Disease International, 2009). In addition, caregivers have a higher risk of physical health problems (Vitaliano, Zhang, & Scanlan, 2003) and even premature mortality (Schulz & Beach, 1999). Finally, a small number of recent studies, including several from our laboratory, are finding that caregivers' cognitive abilities are also compromised by the daily stress they encounter (Mackenzie, Wiprzycka, Hasher, & Goldstein, 2009). Importantly, the consequences of caregiving affect large numbers of North Americans; there are an estimated 6 to 7 million caregivers of older adults with dementia in the United States alone (Schulz & Martire, 2004), and the direct costs of dementia caregiving are estimated at more than $50 billion per year south of the border (Leon, Cheung, & Neumann, 1998). The number of individuals providing care and the negative impact of this care are expected to grow as demographic shifts result in greater numbers of older adults over the next two decades. Fortunately, there is accumulating evidence of the effectiveness of cognitive-behavioural and multi-component programs aimed at reducing caregiver stress (Gallagher-Thompson & Coon, 2007). Our own research has demonstrated the effectiveness of self-efficacy and mindfulness-based interventions for professional caregivers (Mackenzie & Peragine, 2003; Mackenzie, Poulin, & Seidman-Carlson, 2006) and expressive writing for family caregivers (Mackenzie, Wiprzycka, Hasher, & Goldstein, 2007, 2008). The focus of recent research in caregiving interventions has been on the implementation of technology and the Internet. Although the effectiveness of these tools has yet to be determined, preliminary evidence suggests that their use will be of value in reaching a broader sample of caregivers and in decreasing the cost of treatment programs (Marziali & Garcia, 2011; Schulz & Martire, 2004). More generally, recent Canadian research has highlighted the association between older adults' use of the Internet and greater feelings of self-efficacy, indicating its potential application in the treatment of a wide range of disorders among older adults (Erickson & Johnson, 2011).

SUMMARY

- People are living longer than they ever have, and baby boomers have started to turn 60.
- Older adults are the fastest-growing segment of the population, and by 2031 about one in every five Canadians will be 65 or older.
- As the number of older Canadians continues to grow, the physical and mental health of this segment of the population will become an increasingly important issue.
- A majority of health professionals, family members, and older people believe that mental disorders such as depression are a normal and expected part of growing old, and that treatments for mental disorders are ineffective in older adults.
- Historical factors (e.g., the influence of Freud and early lifespan developmental theories), a societal emphasis on youth, and ageist beliefs on the part of older adults and health care professionals have all contributed to this inaccurate belief.
- The theoretical approaches to mental disorders covered in Chapter 2 typically do not take age into account and therefore provide little assistance in understanding mental health problems in older adults.
- In contrast, lifespan approaches such as Baltes and Baltes' (1990) selective optimization with compensation framework, Carstensen and colleagues' (1999) socioemotional selectivity theory, and Charles and Piazza's (2009) strength and vulnerability integration theory offer testable hypotheses about how aging affects mental health that will help researchers better understand and improve older adults' mental health.
- Mental disorders are generally more complicated to diagnose and treat in later life for a variety of reasons, including the tendency to attribute symptoms to age rather than to disorders, the fact that chronic physical health problems interact closely with mental health problems, and the possibility that medications used to treat health problems will mimic or obscure symptoms of mental disorders.
- There are also specific challenges in diagnosing and treating sleep disorders, including the fact that self-reports of sleep problems are unreliable, that universal age-related changes in sleep are not always well understood, and that sleep characteristics and patterns vary widely, especially among older adults.
- Although more research has focused on mood disorders than on anxiety and sleep disorders among older adults, it is clear that depression, anxiety, and sleep problems are highly treatable. Psychological and pharmacological treatments appear to be just as effective for older adults as they are for younger adults.
- The final disorder we discussed in this chapter, dementia, is truly a disorder of aging, and the most prevalent form of dementia is Alzheimer's disease (AD).
- Risk factors for developing AD, and its precursor, mild cognitive impairment, are important for helping researchers, clinicians, and policy-makers target groups of people most likely to develop this disease so that they can develop prevention and early intervention programs for them and their caregivers.
- Certain known risk factors are not modifiable (e.g., chromosomes and genes that are implicated in the disease), some are more difficult to modify (e.g., exposure to environmental toxins, levels of education, and head trauma), and others are more easily modifiable (e.g., obesity, diet, activity levels, access to inoculations and vaccinations).

MySearchLab offers you extensive help with your writing and research projects and provides round-the-clock access to credible and reliable source material. Chapter quizzes and a full electronic version of the text are also provided. Answers to the Before Moving On feature are provided on the MySearchLab. Take a tour at www.mysearchlab.com.

KEY TERMS

baby boomers (p. 417)
paradox of aging (p. 419)
period effect (p. 420)
cohort effect (p. 420)
gerontologists (p. 420)
normal aging (p. 420)
polypharmacy (p. 422)
drug interactions (p. 427)
primary insomnia (p. 429)
restless legs syndrome (RLS) (p. 430)
sleep apnea (p. 430)
late-onset schizophrenia (p. 432)
dementia (p. 434)
pseudo-dementia (p. 435)
mild cognitive impairment (MCI) (p. 435)
Alzheimer's disease (AD) (p. 436)
brain lesion (p. 438)
vascular dementia (p. 438)
Lewy body dementia (p. 439)
frontotemporal dementia (FTD) (p. 439)

Chapter 17

Therapies

LEARNING OBJECTIVES

AFTER READING THIS CHAPTER, STUDENTS WILL BE ABLE TO:

1. Describe issues in the use of electroconvulsive therapy for the treatment of depression.
2. Explain how psychoactive drugs are used in the treatment of different types of mental disorders.
3. Define psychotherapy and describe how the major theoretical approaches explain the development of problems and the strategies they use to facilitate change.
4. Identify the different modalities by which psychotherapy can be offered.
5. Explain how meta-analysis is used to synthesize results of several studies.
6. Explain how the effects of psychotherapy have been evaluated and give an overview of the conditions for which psychotherapy is helpful.
7. Identify the key issues in the development of evidence-based psychological practice.

When Jessica was 17 years old, her mother contacted a psychologist over concerns that Jessica was depressed: she had scratch marks on her forearms, always dressed in black, listened to music full of themes of despair and destruction, and had written about death in her personal diary.

Jessica's parents divorced when she was 10. She had appeared to adjust very well to the divorce; her school grades had remained excellent, she helped around the house, and her mother considered her to be a perfect child. Both of Jessica's parents remarried—her father when she was 13 and her mother when she was 14.

Jessica's mother and stepfather reported that since starting high school, Jessica had become moody and easily burst into tears. She accused them of being controlling and unreasonable about chores, and they now felt that they "walked on eggshells" around her. Jessica's father reported that she no longer seemed interested in visiting him and was disrespectful and sullen toward his new partner.

Jessica agreed to attend a first therapy session with her mother. When asked about herself, she gave only brief answers and seemed uncomfortable. She did, however, agree to meet individually with the psychologist. Jessica acknowledged that she was dissatisfied with her life, felt irritable and moody, and did not get along well with her family. She showed the psychologist scars on her arm from using a nail file to hurt herself. She said that she sometimes had thoughts that life was not worth living, but did not have plans to kill herself.

The psychologist first worked with Jessica to develop a safety plan, including crisis and emergency services she could phone if she had thoughts of hurting or killing herself. Jessica next began to monitor her mood. Together with the psychologist, she began to notice that her mood fluctuated with her activities, school pressures, tiredness, and family interactions.

The psychologist helped Jessica plan her weeks so that there was a mixture of work and enjoyable activities. She learned to problem-solve to manage the demands of schoolwork. Next, the psychologist invited Jessica's parents to attend a session. The family talked about reasonable expectations for a 17-year-old. When the parents became aware that they continued to negotiate and monitor chores as they had when Jessica was much younger, they were willing to experiment with discussing issues in regular household meetings. In one session, the family discussed how they could maintain contact in a way that fit Jessica's developmental needs for greater autonomy and more time with her friends. They began to experiment with developing a more mutually respectful style of interaction.

Over several months, Jessica's mood improved and family members found her more pleasant to be around. In therapy, Jessica worked to identify stressors that might make her prone to slip back into depression. She developed awareness of the early signs and planned ways to get back on track quickly. Short-term therapy that focused on Jessica's feelings, behaviours, and thoughts was successful in lifting her depression and helping her fight depression in the future.

Throughout this book, treatments have been discussed in relation to the various disorders. In this chapter, to more fully explore issues related to treatment, we re-examine the range of therapies available to treat mental disorders and the context within which these therapies are offered. Consistent with the tenets of evidence-based practice in health care (Sackett, Straus, Richardson, Rosenberg, & Haynes, 2000), we will focus on the research evidence regarding the effects and outcomes of common treatments for mental disorders.

Biological Treatments

The first treatments for psychological disorders were biological (see Chapter 1). Practices such as bleeding, often by cuts to the body or application of leeches, were designed to correct biological imbalances presumed to underlie psychological symptoms. In the latter part of the nineteenth century, there was a proliferation of physical strategies designed to calm disturbed behaviour. For example, disturbed patients were protected from self-harm by physical restraints and were subjected to prolonged warm baths, or were placed under cold packs designed to pacify them.

Far more efficacious treatments are now available, and considerable attention is now paid to possible negative side effects of biological treatments. In the following sections, we will focus on two current treatment options, including one of the most controversial, electroconvulsive therapy, and the most common, psychopharmacology. However, there is a host of other biological treatment options that are the focus of intense research activity. For example, in the treatment of depression, light therapy, repetitive transcranial magnetic stimulation, and deep brain stimulation have all shown some encouraging results (e.g., Jorge, Moser, Acion, & Robinson, 2008; Kennedy et al., 2011; Meesters, Dekker, Schlangen, Bos, & Ruiter, 2011).

ELECTROCONVULSIVE THERAPY

In the 1930s, clinicians noticed that patients with schizophrenia who spontaneously experienced epileptic seizures subsequently showed a reduction in schizophrenic symptoms. They reasoned, therefore, that if seizures could be provoked, psychotic symptoms would be reduced. Seizures were provoked by the application of an electrical current to the patient's temples in a procedure now known as electroconvulsive therapy (ECT).

With the advent of effective antipsychotic medication, ECT was abandoned in the treatment of schizophrenia, but it is still used to treat severe depression that has not responded to other treatments, especially with older adults and medically ill patients (Kennedy & Giacobbe, 2007). ECT used to be associated with serious side effects, including considerable disorientation and memory loss, broken bones, and in rare cases (1 in 10 000), death due to cardiac failure (Avery, 1993). Recently, however, adverse effects have been minimized through less intense, briefer currents, often on only one side of the brain, and shorter courses of treatment. Now, the most commonly reported side effect is retrograde amnesia, and the mortality rate has been reduced to 2 deaths per 100 000 (Fink & Taylor, 2007; Scott, 2010). Anaesthesia and muscle relaxants reduce distress and the risk of injury. Patients receive a full medical and neurological evaluation before receiving ECT and are monitored during the procedure. The reduced risks set the stage for an increase in the use of ECT in Canada. For example, in Ontario from 1999 to 2005, the number of patients receiving ECT rose from 7800 to 10 800 (Hoag, 2008).

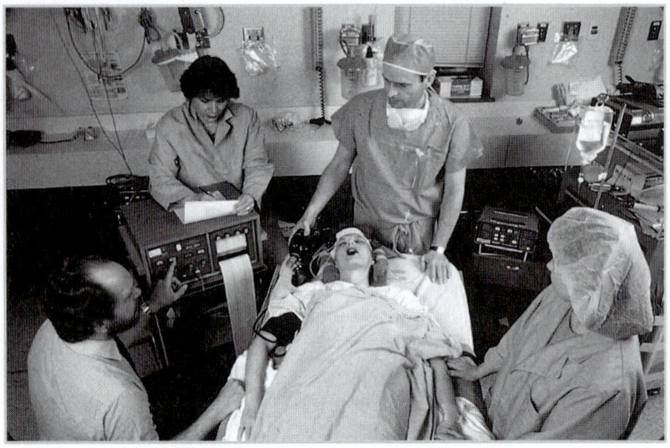

Electroconvulsive therapy (ECT) involves the application of an electrical current to the patient's temples.

A comprehensive review of randomized controlled trials found consistent evidence of the short-term efficacy of ECT in treating adult patients with depressive disorders (UK ECT Review Group, 2003; see Chapter 8). However, research has found that more than 50 percent of those treated with ECT are likely to relapse (Sackheim et al., 2000). A further dilemma facing practitioners is that the most effective types of ECT delivery are those associated with the greatest risk of cognitive impairment (UK ECT Review Group, 2003). Given these concerns, ECT is considered appropriate only in the treatment of life-threatening severe depression that has not responded to other treatment (National Institute for Health and Clinical Excellence, 2010).

1 BEFORE MOVING ON

ECT may be seen by some people as a crude treatment with the risk of serious side effects, but by others as a life-saving intervention. What are the advantages and disadvantages of ECT in the treatment of depression?

PSYCHOPHARMACOLOGY

Pharmacological agents that affect the individual's psychological functioning are known as **psychoactive agents**. A total of 64 853 000 prescriptions for psychotherapeutic drugs were issued in Canada in 2010, second only to the number of prescriptions issued to treat cardiovascular problems (IMS Brogan, 2011). A trend for increases in the prescription of psychotropic medication is found in many countries (e.g., Mojtabai & Olfson, 2010).

The ideal method for developing new medications is first to understand the pathological process by which a disorder develops, then to identify an agent that will change that process. In reality, things do not always work out so neatly. Science has not clearly established biochemical mechanisms that account for most psychological disorders, and the discovery of classes of psychoactive drugs has often occurred serendipitously; that is, physicians carefully monitoring a patient's reaction to a drug have observed unanticipated benefits in other areas. After case studies

TABLE 17.1 MEDICATION TRIALS

- **Placebo:** An inert substance associated with alleviation of symptoms through expectancy effects
- **Active placebo:** A therapeutically inert substance with the same side effects as the medication
- **Placebo washout:** The first phase of a clinical trial, in which all participants are given a placebo and those who respond to the placebo are dropped from the study
- **Single-blind trial:** A clinical trial in which patients are unaware of whether they are receiving medication or placebo, but the clinician is aware
- **Double-blind trial:** A clinical trial in which both the patient and the clinician are unaware of whether the patient is receiving medication or placebo
- **Randomized controlled trial:** A clinical trial in which patients are randomly assigned to either a placebo or a medication condition, and the results of the two conditions are statistically compared

show beneficial effects, medication trials are conducted to systematically assess drug efficacy (see Table 17.1; see also Chapter 4 for further discussion and example of blind trials). Nevertheless, there are important differences between the conditions in medication trials and the conditions in which these medications are subsequently prescribed (Verdoux & Bégaud, 2004; Zimmerman, Mattia, & Posternak, 2002). As a result, we cannot assume that drugs will have the same effects in general practice as they do in clinical trials. There is also evidence that some drugs that are effective in one age group may not be suitable for administration to other age groups, such as older adults (Fick et al., 2003).

Drugs can be classified in many ways. We group them here according to their application in the treatment of different types of disorder: antipsychotic, antidepressant, anxiolytic (anti-anxiety), mood-altering, and psycho-stimulant. However, as you can see in the following sections, many drugs are efficacious for disorders other than those for which they were originally prescribed. Commonly prescribed examples of these medications are listed in Table 17.2.

ANTIPSYCHOTICS Prior to the development of this class of drugs in the 1950s, patients diagnosed with schizophrenia typically spent their lives confined in psychiatric institutions. Those receiving chronic care had their physical needs met and were restricted to hospital grounds. The chances of return to the community were slender and, by the time their symptoms abated in middle and later life, they were ill-equipped for life in the community.

The development of phenothiazines and related major tranquilizers offered the possibility of reducing psychotic symptoms such as hallucinations. Freedom from debilitating and alarming symptoms offered relief to many patients. Following stabilization on the drug, formerly institutionalized patients were able to return to the community. This made possible the policy of deinstitutionalization, in which hospital stays were reserved only for the acute phase of the disorder and patients were rapidly returned to the community. The economic benefits of this process are clear, and the advent of antipsychotic medication was heralded as a major breakthrough.

Because schizophrenia is a chronic disorder, patients must adhere to a long-term medication regimen. Antipsychotics do not cure schizophrenia; instead, they control its symptoms. Dosage must be carefully calibrated to maximize symptomatic control and to minimize side effects. Although drug maintenance reduces the risk of relapse, many patients are tempted to discontinue their medication when they are feeling symptom-free, increasing the risk of a relapse. To address this concern, medication can be delivered via long-acting intramuscular injection rather than as oral medication (Tiihonen et al., 2011).

Unfortunately, after a few weeks of taking major tranquilizers, some patients experience **extrapyramidal effects** similar to the symptoms of Parkinson's disease, including stooped posture, muscular rigidity, a distinctive shuffling gait, and occasional drooling. These side effects may be relieved by anti-Parkinsonian drugs, which in turn may have their own unpleasant side effects. After prolonged administration, patients may begin to show strange muscular movements such as eye twitching and tongue thrusting, which are evidence of another extrapyramidal effect known as tardive dyskinesia. Of concern, these symptoms may persist even after the medication has been discontinued.

A new generation of antipsychotic medications such as clozapine and olanzapine have fewer extrapyramidal effects, but are associated with other side effects such as weight gain. Although these second-generation antipsychotics were initially thought to be superior to the first-generation antipsychotics (e.g., Keck & McElroy, 1997; Wahlbeck, Cheine, Essali, & Adams, 1999), the majority of studies comparing first- and second-generation antipsychotics yielded no evidence that the newer generation of drugs was more efficacious than the older (and less expensive) antipsychotics (Crossley, Constante, McGuire, & Power, 2010). The second-generation antipsychotics have mood-stabilizing properties, which may make them effective in the treatment of bipolar disorder (Suppes et al., 1999; Tohen et al., 2000). Evidence-based guidelines for the pharmacological treatment of schizophrenia indicate that the choice of antipsychotic medication should be based on side effects in the individual patient (Barnes & the Schizophrenia Consensus Group of the British Association for Psychopharmacology, 2011).

ANXIOLYTICS Anxiolytics are used to alleviate symptoms of anxiety and muscle tension by reducing activity in parts of the central nervous system, which lowers activity in the sympathetic nervous system, leading to lower respiration and heart rate and decreased muscle tension. An unfortunate property of barbiturates, the first class of anxiolytic drugs, is that patients develop tolerance for them, requiring larger doses over time to achieve the same effects. Large doses of barbiturates are highly toxic, which make them a common choice for suicide attempts.

TABLE 17.2 COMMONLY PRESCRIBED PSYCHOTROPIC MEDICATIONS

Type/Generic Name	Brand Name	Treats	Side Effects
Antipsychotics			
Phenothiazines			
chlorpromazine thioridazine fluphenazine trifluoperazine	Thorazine Mellaril Prolixin Stelazine	Psychotic symptoms (agitation, delusions, hallucinations, violent or aggressive behaviour), schizophrenia, possibly bipolar disorder	Variable effectiveness, uncomfortable side effects, long-term possibility of tardive dyskinesia
Butyrophenone			
haloperidol	Haldol		
Dibenzodiazepine			
clozapine olanzapine risperidone	Clozaril Zyprexa Risperdal		
Anxiolytics			
alprazolam chlordiazepoxide diazepam lorazepam oxazepam busiprone propranolol meprobamate	Xanax Librium Valium Ativan Serax BuSpar Inderal Equinil, Miltown	Anxiety, tension, panic attacks	Drowsiness, lethargy, variable effectiveness
Antidepressants			
MAO Inhibitors			
isocarboxazid phenelzine tranylcypromine selegiline	Marplan Nardil Parnate Eldepryl	Depression, panic disorder	Dizziness, sleep disturbances, headaches, may be dangerous, special diet necessary
Tricyclics			
amitriptyline clomipramine doxepin imipramine nortriptyline	Elavil Anafranil Sinequan Tofranil Pamelor	Depression, panic disorder, OCD	Effects may take time, may cause discomfort
SSRIs			
fluoxetine sertraline paroxetine fluvoxamine	Prozac Zoloft Paxil Luvox	Depression, OCD, panic disorder, eating disorders	Relatively few side effects
SNRIs			
venlafaxine duloxetine	Effexor Cymbalta	Depression, OCD	Relatively few side effects
buproprion	Wellbutrin	Depression	Relatively few side effects
Mood Stabilizers			
lithium carbonate lithium citrate	Eskalith, Lithane Cibalith-S	Bipolar dsorder	Possibility of toxicity
divalproex carbamazepine lamtrogine	Depakote Tegretol Lamictal	Bipolar disorder	Nausea, dizziness, visual problems
Stimulants			
dextroamphetamine methylphenidate pemoline	Dexedrine, Adderall Ritalin Cylert	Hyperactivity, distractibility, learning disorders	Nervousness, insomnia, loss of appetite

A second class of anxiolytics, the benzodiazepines, offer effective control of anxiety without toxicity at high doses (see Chapter 5 for a discussion of possible mechanisms). Of concern, benzodiazepines are also addictive. After prolonged use of this class of drugs, sudden withdrawal can provoke convulsions that may be life-threatening. Consequently, as the dose is gradually reduced, patients must be monitored carefully. Like barbiturates, benzodiazepines are dangerous when taken in combination with alcohol. Clinical guidelines suggest that benzodiazepines should be used only for brief periods in the treatment of anxiety disorders (National Institute for Clinical Excellence, 2004).

ANTIDEPRESSANTS Drugs used in the treatment of depression fall into four major categories (see Chapter 8): the monoamine oxidase inhibitors (MAOIs), the tricyclics (TCAs), the selective serotonin reuptake inhibitors (SSRIs), and the serotonin-norepinephrine reuptake inhibitors (SNRIs). A major drawback of MAOIs is the severe dietary restrictions they impose. In combination with MAOIs, common foods such as yeast, chocolate, and beer that contain the enzyme tyramine can cause a life-threatening increase in blood pressure. The TCAs, although commonly used for many years, provoke many unpleasant side effects such as dry mouth, blurry vision, constipation, and light-headedness.

The most recently developed groups of antidepressants are the SSRIs and SNRIs, of which Prozac is the best known. Extensive evidence suggests that, for adults, SSRIs are comparable in efficacy to TCAs (Bech et al., 2000). Although SSRIs may be better tolerated than TCAs (McGrath et al., 2000), they still cause side effects such as nausea, diarrhea, headache, tremors, and sleepiness. Similar side effects can occur with SNRIs, and flu-like symptoms can occur if SNRIs are stopped abruptly. Recent research has raised concerns that the risk of adverse outcomes in older adults is greater with SSRIs than with TCAs (Coupland et al., 2011). Nevertheless, taking into account demonstrated treatment efficacy and common side-effect profiles, Canadian guidelines for the pharmacotherapy of depression recommend SSRIs and SNRIs as first-line medication options (Lam et al., 2009).

Antidepressants take time to reach beneficial levels in the blood, so improvement is typically evident only after one to two weeks of treatment, with optimal response by the third or fourth week. Thirty to 50 percent of patients do not respond favourably to antidepressants, which may partly explain why most people discontinue using antidepressants within three months of starting the medication (Olfson, Marcus, Tedeschi, & Wan, 2006). However, 30 to 50 percent of those who do not respond to one class of antidepressants will respond favourably to another. Antidepressants bring symptomatic relief to many adults in the acute phase of a depressive disorder, but there is less evidence of their influence on relapse. Although the prescribing of antidepressant medication has markedly increased (Olfson & Marcus, 2009), the precise mode of action for antidepressants remains unclear. Furthermore, the benefits of antidepressants are most pronounced in those with severe depression, but only minimal or nonexistent at mild and moderate levels of symptom severity (Barbui, Cipriani, Ayuso-Mateos, & van Ommeren, 2011; Fournier et al., 2010). Importantly, Health Canada has advised of potential risks to newborns when pregnant women are prescribed SSRIs (Health Canada, 2006). There is evidence that SSRIs may provide substantial relief for adults suffering from eating disorders such as bulimia nervosa and binge-eating disorder, and from anxiety disorders such as social phobia, panic disorder, and obsessive-compulsive disorder (Hoehn-Saric et al., 2000; McElroy et al., 2000; Walsh et al., 2000).

As depression is a major risk factor for suicidal ideation and suicidal behaviour, considerable attention has been focused on suicidal risks in patients taking antidepressant medication. Ironically, because TCAs are toxic in overdose, a medication prescribed to alleviate depression can be used to attempt suicide. A major advantage of the SSRIs is their lower toxicity in overdose, but there have been suggestions in some research that the medication itself may increase the likelihood of suicidal ideation and behaviour. In particular, a number of studies showed that depressed children and adolescents were at greater risk for suicidal behaviour when taking SSRIs than when taking a placebo. As a result, drug regulatory agencies, including Health Canada, issued warnings about the use of SSRIs for depressed youth. Although these warnings were designed to protect children and adolescents, there are indications that they had unintended negative outcomes. In Canada, the rate of antidepressant prescriptions for youth dropped, but the total number of visits made to physicians because of depression also dropped and the number of completed suicides among children and adolescents rose (Katz et al., 2008). A similar drop in the rate of SSRI prescriptions for youth occurred in the United States; the American data also showed that the change in prescription patterns was not offset by an increase in referrals for psychotherapy (Libby et al., 2007). A recent review of the treatment research indicated that the benefits of antidepressants for youth appear to outweigh the risks of suicidal behaviour (Bridge et al., 2007).

MOOD STABILIZERS Although lithium salts have long been the medication of choice for bipolar disorder (see Chapter 8), their use has decreased in favour of other mood stabilizers (e.g., divalproex, carbamazepine, lamotrigine) and the newer antipsychotics (Scherk, Pajonk, & Leucht, 2007; Young & Hammond, 2007). Lithium and related mood stabilizers reduce rapid cycling between depressive and manic or hypomanic states. A review of five randomized controlled trials revealed that lithium reduces the risk of relapse in patients who have bipolar disorder—with clear protective effects with respect to manic episodes and less clear effects with respect to subsequent depressive episodes (Geddes, Burgess, Hawton, Jamison, & Goodwin, 2004). Side effects of lithium at therapeutic dosages may include nausea, dizziness, weight gain, and mild diarrhea. Of greater concern, however, is the fact that lithium has a narrow window of effectiveness, with low doses being ineffective and high doses being highly toxic. Physicians must carefully monitor patients' blood lithium levels. On the other hand, other mood stabilizers may have less of an effect on depressive symptoms, thus requiring the addition of an antidepressant for the patient.

STIMULANTS Stimulants are the class of drugs most commonly used in the treatment of children and adults with attention deficit/hyperactivity disorder (ADHD; see Chapter 15). They are short-acting compounds with an onset of action within 30 to 60 minutes and peak clinical efficacy 1 to 5 hours after administration. Stimulants such as Ritalin reduce hyperactive and impulsive behaviour, permitting the child to sustain attention. Compared to other classes of drugs, stimulants have received intense study. A review of 153 studies including 5768 participants (Spencer et al., 1996) found a 70 percent response rate in the treatment of uncomplicated ADHD. A meta-analytic study on the use of Ritalin for the treatment of adult ADHD found effects comparable to results in the treatment of child and adolescent patients (Faraone, Spencer, Aleardi, Pagano, & Biederman, 2004). Common side effects are appetite suppression and sleep disturbance. Less frequently, patients report mood disturbance, headaches, abdominal discomfort, and fatigue. Evidence-based clinical guidelines for the management of ADHD indicate that stimulants combined with psychological treatment should be the first-line treatment for severe ADHD in children and for moderate and severe ADHD in adults (National Institute for Health and Clinical Excellence, 2008).

LIMITS ON EFFICACY It is clear that several classes of drugs have demonstrated efficacy in controlling diverse psychological symptoms. However, no class of drugs is efficacious for all people with a particular disorder, and it is not possible to predict who will respond to a particular class of drugs (Simon & Perlis, 2010). Psychoactive medication has freed many people from debilitating symptoms. However, medication does not necessarily enable the individual to learn new skills or to process information in a different way. Medication may be helpful in symptom control, but without concomitant psychological interventions, the person may be prone to relapse and chronic disorder (Biederman, Spencer, & Wilens, 1997) (see Focus box 17.1 for a discussion of whether psychologists should have the authority to prescribe medications).

2 BEFORE MOVING ON

> Psychoactive medications are prescribed at unprecedented rates to treat a range of debilitating mental disorders. It is impossible to predict who will respond positively to a particular drug. What issues should an informed consumer consider in making decisions about the advantages and disadvantages of taking a particular medication?

Psychotherapy: A Definition

Psychotherapy is defined as a process in which a professionally trained therapist systematically uses techniques derived from psychological principles to relieve another person's psychological distress or to facilitate growth. Psychotherapy is practised by professionals from many disciplines, including psychology, psychiatry, social work, medicine, and nursing. In most jurisdictions in Canada, the title *psychotherapist* is not licensed or restricted in any fashion; anyone can advertise his or her services as a psychotherapist. In the future this situation may change. For example, in Ontario, the Psychotherapy Act defined the professions that are authorized to practise psychotherapy and established a new College of Registered Psychotherapists and Registered Mental Health Therapists of Ontario.

Theoretical Orientations

Which types of psychotherapy are practised by therapists today? Surveys show the major schools of psychotherapy to be psychodynamic, cognitive-behavioural (including behavioural and cognitive approaches), humanistic-experiential, and integrative or eclectic (Cohen, Hunsley, Westmacott, & Flear, 2008; Norcross, Karpiak, & Santoro, 2005). The theoretical assumptions of each approach were presented in Chapter 2. As approaches to psychotherapy are constantly evolving, criticisms that may apply to an early form of a therapy may no longer apply to later forms of the therapy. As approaches evolve, there is considerable "cross-pollination" so that ideas from one approach are integrated into other approaches (e.g., Greenberg, 2008). The current emphasis on identifying and disseminating treatments that work represents a shift in attention from theoretical debates toward a search to ensure that psychological interventions are helpful. So, instead of defending their own beliefs, psychologists focus on identifying what will help the patient. In the following pages, we provide an overview of some key aspects of common approaches to psychotherapy.

PSYCHODYNAMIC APPROACHES

Freud developed a theory that psychological problems have their roots in very early childhood and in unconscious conflicts (see Chapter 2). The main goal of Freudian psychoanalysis is to help patients understand the unconscious factors that drive and control their behaviour. Classic psychoanalysis is an intensive process, generally entailing several visits each week over a period of years during which patients obtain insight into the nature of their problems and how past conflicts continue to affect them. Classic psychoanalysts rely heavily on five basic techniques:

1. *Free association.* The analyst requires the individual to say everything that comes to mind without censoring seemingly unimportant or embarrassing thoughts. The analyst helps the patient recognize unconscious

FOCUS 17.1

Should Psychologists Prescribe Medication?

Since the 1980s, psychologists in the United States have debated the advantages and disadvantages of appropriately trained psychologists having the right to prescribe psychoactive medication. Some American jurisdictions (Louisiana, New Mexico, and Guam) and government departments now allow psychologists to prescribe psychoactive medication. Advocates of prescription privileges for psychologists argue that

1. Many major mental disorders (such as schizophrenia) are best treated with medication.
2. It might be more cost-effective for psychologists to prescribe for their patients rather than referring patients to psychiatrists or physicians.
3. Underserved groups such as the elderly, the chronically mentally ill, and those living in rural areas would benefit from expanded opportunities to receive pharmaceutical treatment from mental health professionals.
4. Psychologists can be at least as competent as other health care professionals in prescribing medication for psychological disorders. Most psychoactive medications are prescribed by general practitioners whose training in mental health issues is limited to a few weeks of placement with a psychiatrist.

Physicians have strongly opposed the extension of prescription privileges to psychologists, citing the importance of full medical training to understand the impact of psychoactive medication on other physical systems. Within psychology, critics argue that psychologists' distinctive expertise is in the development and application of evidence-based assessment and psychological interventions. They express concern that the inclusion of adequate training in psychopharmacology would inevitably come at the expense of training in psychological issues.

Under Canada's publicly funded health care system, it is likely that the federal government would have concerns that additional numbers of practitioners eligible to prescribe expensive psychopharmacological treatments would contribute to mushrooming health care costs (Romanow & Marchildon, 2003). A Canadian Psychological Association (CPA) task force on prescriptive authority for psychology affirmed the importance of a biopsychosocial approach to the science and practice of psychology and emphasized the necessity for psychologists to work in a collaborative fashion with other health care professionals (CPA Task Force on Prescriptive Authority for Psychologists in Canada, 2010). The CPA task force recommended that training and continuing education in professional psychology ensure a basic understanding of psychopharmacology so that psychologists are equipped to work collaboratively with other professions in providing evidence-based services.

There is no plan for psychologists to seek prescriptive authority in Canada in the near future. A survey of Canadian students and professionals in psychology revealed that fewer than half of the clinical students polled (72 of 164) indicated that they would seek prescription privileges if they were made available; among clinically oriented professionals, a little more than one-third (149 of 418) indicated that they would seek prescription privileges (St. Pierre & Melnyk, 2004). The survey did not address the question of how much additional time students and professionals in psychology were willing to devote to acquiring competence in this field. However, these points were considered in an American survey of psychology interns, residents, and psychologists (Fagan, Ax, Liss, Resnick, & Moody, 2007). Consistent with prior research, many respondents favoured psychologists having prescriptive authority and many were interested in obtaining this authority. However, respondents' interest in obtaining prescription privileges dropped dramatically when they were told that the required training would take two years or more and cost more than $10 000!

motives and conflicts expressed in the spontaneous speech.

2. *Dream interpretation.* The analyst distinguishes between the manifest content of the dream (which is consciously remembered by the client) and the more important latent content (the unconscious ideas and impulses that have been disguised).
3. *Interpretation.* The analyst interprets what the client says or does. Slips of the tongue, forgetfulness, and the client's behaviour are presumed to reveal unconscious impulses, defence mechanisms, or conflicts. First, the analyst interprets behaviour that the client is already on the verge of understanding. Later, the therapist interprets the unconscious conflicts that induce defence mechanisms.
4. *Analysis of resistance.* During the process of free association or dream interpretation, clients may become resistant—for example, being unwilling to discuss certain topics, missing or arriving late for appointments, joking during the session, or remaining silent. Resistance prevents painful or difficult thoughts from entering awareness; thus, therapists must determine the source of resistance if the client is to deal effectively with the problem.
5. *Analysis of transference.* The core of psychoanalytic therapy is **transference**, which occurs when the client responds to the therapist as he or she responded to significant figures from his or her childhood (generally the parents). Freud believed that individuals unconsciously re-experience repressed thoughts during transference, making it essential to the resolution of the client's problems. By recognizing the transference relationship and remaining neutral, the therapist helps the client work through the conflict. The analyst is careful not to allow personal feelings, needs, or fears to interfere with the relationship with the client (counter-transference).

Throughout his life, Freud continued to modify his theories and his therapeutic strategies. In addition, many of his former disciples developed their own modifications of his work. This family of therapies is referred to as *psychoanalytic psychotherapy*, *psychoanalytically oriented therapy*, or *psychodynamic therapy*. Naturalistic observations have shown that, across these approaches, therapists engage in a blend of interpretive and supportive statements (Henry, Strupp, Schacht, & Gaston, 1994). The following are some examples of psychodynamic therapies.

BRIEF PSYCHODYNAMIC PSYCHOTHERAPY Primarily developed by Alexander and French (1946), this psychoanalytically oriented therapy uses Freudian techniques in an active, flexible manner. Therapy tends to be short term: sessions occur twice a week rather than daily. Goals are concrete, conversation replaces free association, therapists are empathic rather than emotionally detached, and interpretations focus on current life events rather than on childhood fears and conflicts.

EGO ANALYSIS Ego analysts, such as Karen Horney, Erik Erikson, Anna Freud, and Heinz Hartmann, argued that Freudian analysis was too focused on the unconscious sexual and aggressive motivation. They believed that individuals are capable of controlling their own behaviour. **Ego analysts** use Freudian techniques to explore the ego rather than the id. Therapists help clients understand how they have relied on defence mechanisms to cope with conflicts.

ADLER'S INDIVIDUAL PSYCHOLOGY Alfred Adler proposed that sexual and aggressive instincts are less important than the individual's striving to overcome personal weakness. Adler's individual psychology was based on the assumption that mental disorders are the consequence of deeply entrenched mistaken beliefs, which lead individuals to develop a maladaptive style of life that protects them from discovering their own imperfections. Adlerian therapists interpret dreams in terms of current behaviour, offer direct advice, and encourage new behaviours.

INTERPERSONAL PSYCHODYNAMIC PSYCHOTHERAPY Harry Stack Sullivan, the American psychiatrist who developed **interpersonal psychodynamic psychotherapy**, believed that mental disorders resulted from maladaptive early interactions between child and parent. This type of therapy is a variation of brief psychodynamic therapy and emphasizes the interactions between the client and his or her social environment. Interpersonal therapists provide feedback to help the client understand how his or her interpersonal styles (such as hostility or dependence) are perpetuating or provoking conflicts. The therapist also helps the client learn to interact with others in more flexible and positive ways and must be careful not to reinforce the client's maladaptive behaviours.

TIME-LIMITED DYNAMIC PSYCHOTHERAPY More recent psychodynamic approaches, such as **time-limited dynamic psychotherapy (TLDP)** (Binder, Strupp, & Henry, 1995), tend to be briefer and to involve the client in face-to-face contact with the therapist, but retain Freud's emphasis on analysis of transference as a central mechanism of therapeutic change. The TLDP therapist also helps identify patterns of interaction with others that strengthen unhelpful thoughts about self and others. Research in psychodynamic therapy has underlined the importance of the **therapeutic alliance**. The quality of the relationship between therapist and client is recognized to be a predictor of therapy outcome. Consequently, approaches such as TLDP place greater emphasis on interpersonal processes than did early psychoanalytic formulations.

HUMANISTIC-EXPERIENTIAL APPROACHES

Whereas psychodynamic approaches focus on the person's unconscious processes, humanistic and experiential approaches focus on the person's subjective experience, giving particular attention to emotional aspects of experience (Greenberg, 2008). Humanistic-experiential approaches place emphasis on the person's current experience rather than on the past. In contrast to psychoanalytic formulations that view individuals as dominated by primitive urges that must be constrained, humanistic-experiential approaches value the individual's free will and encourage the client to take responsibility for personal choices. In addition to the growing evidence base for the efficacy of some humanistic approaches, a major contribution of the humanistic approaches has been the emphasis on the human qualities of the therapist. Research has established that therapists working with different approaches are more effective when their clients feel that they are genuine, that they make efforts to understand their experience, and that they accept them despite their problems (e.g., Greenberg, Elliott, & Lietaer, 1994).

CLIENT-CENTRED THERAPY Carl Rogers developed client-centred therapy in the 1940s as an alternative to psychoanalysis. **Client-centred therapy** emphasizes the warmth and permissiveness of the therapist and the tolerant climate in which the feelings of the client can be freely expressed. Rogers believed that psychological problems arise when personal growth is stunted by judgments imposed by others (see Chapter 2 for more on Rogers's theories). This creates conditions of worth in which the client believes that he or she must meet the standards of others in order to be a worthwhile person. Rogers defined the therapist qualities that facilitate the client's growth: genuineness, empathy, and "unconditional positive regard." The therapist strives to provide an environment in which the client feels accepted. It is theorized that self-acceptance follows, and this in turn leads to self-knowledge and dissipation of bad feelings. In the client-centred approach, clients are not diagnosed, evaluated, or given advice; rather, they are valued as unique individuals.

EXISTENTIAL THERAPY Existential therapists are inspired by the work of existential philosophers such as Sartre and Kierkegaard. Existential therapy focuses on the importance of the human situation as perceived by the individual, with the ultimate goal of making the client more aware of his or her own potential for growth and capacity for making choices. Existential therapists do not follow any particular procedures but emphasize the uniqueness of each individual. They challenge and confront the client on past and present choices. The therapist helps the client relate authentically to others through the therapeutic encounter. Existential therapists share themselves, their feelings, and their values with the client. This type of therapy examines the lack of meaning in a person's life, and is assumed to work best with those who are having conflicts regarding their existence, or those with anxiety or personality disorders rather than psychoses.

GESTALT THERAPY Gestalt therapy, developed by Frederich (Fritz) Perls, emphasized the idea that individuals have a distorted awareness of genuine feelings that leads to impairments in personal growth and behavioural problems. Gestalt therapists help clients become aware of feelings and needs that have been ignored or distorted and recognize that these needs are a part of themselves and should be accepted. The key goal of Gestalt therapy is client awareness. To become aware, clients must integrate both their inner feelings and their external environments. Therapists encourage clients to experience what is going on in the here and now by asking questions such as "How do you feel when you think about that?" or "What thoughts are running through your head now?" Clients are instructed to communicate directly by talking *to* people rather than *about* them (using "I" statements). One of the most popular Gestalt techniques is the *empty chair technique*, used to make the client more aware of his or her genuine feelings. For example, a young woman with an unresolved conflict with her ex-boyfriend would be instructed to face an empty chair and imagine that her boyfriend was in it, and speak as though she were talking directly to him. Gestalt therapists often interpret dreams, looking at the importance of the dream to the client at that moment. They also attend to nonverbal cues and ask clients to focus on their body and the meaning that these paralinguistic cues are communicating.

EMOTION-FOCUSED THERAPY In recent years, there has been substantial growth in the range of humanistic-experiential approaches. Psychologist Les Greenberg and his colleagues at a number of Canadian universities, including the University of Ottawa, the University of Windsor, and York University, have developed an **emotion-focused therapy**, in which the client enters into an empathic relationship with a therapist who is directive and responsive to his or her experience (Elliot & Greenberg, 1995; Greenberg, 2008). These psychologists have developed treatments that address common psychological problems such as depression, trauma, and marital distress by enhancing and then focusing on clients' emotional reactions.

COGNITIVE-BEHAVIOURAL APPROACHES

Although the distinctions between behavioural, cognitive, and cognitive-behavioural therapies continue to be debated, the overlap between them in both techniques and theoretical underpinnings is so great that the leading professional association in the area (the Association of Behavioral and Cognitive Therapies and the newly founded Canadian Association of Cognitive and Behavioural Therapies) view them as a single orientation. The term *behaviour therapy* was first used in the 1950s to describe an operant conditioning treatment for psychotic patients (Lindsley, Skinner, & Solomon, 1954). Skinner's work produced dramatic changes in the behaviour of populations previously considered untreatable, such as the chronically mentally ill and individuals with mental retardation. Behavioural approaches emphasize that problem behaviours are learned behaviours and that faulty learning can be reversed through the application of learning principles (see Chapter 2).

From its roots in the application of classical and operant conditioning, the field of behaviour therapy has broadened to include research findings from areas such as perception, cognition, and the biological bases of behaviour. Behavioural therapists focus primarily on present thoughts and behaviours as opposed to childhood history. Accordingly, behavioural interventions focus on specific targets, such as dealing with social phobia, reducing the frequency of bulimic symptoms, and changing a host of other maladaptive behaviours. An essential feature is the application of scientifically derived principles in the treatment of problems. Throughout therapy, progress is assessed to determine whether the strategy should be modified. Behavioural treatment requires clear identification of goals and is oriented toward the future. Behaviour therapists are very active in evaluating the outcome of their interventions, but until the past two decades have devoted less attention to studying the process of therapy or the role of the therapeutic relationship (Emmelkamp, 1994).

The idea that the way we think and feel influences our behaviour is not new. From the writings of the ancient Greeks onward, writers have suggested that the way we interpret our experience affects how we feel and behave (Meichenbaum, 1995). Albert Bandura drew attention to ways that learning could take place by observation and imitation (see Chapter 2). Bandura's work was first applied to children, but has been found to have important applications for adults as well. Bandura also focused on internal processes that facilitate skill development. He noted that in helping an individual to develop new behaviours, it is important to reward coping as well as mastery. For example, a person making fumbling attempts to learn to skate should be encouraged for persistence and effort, even in the absence of an accomplished performance. Self-efficacy, which refers to a person's sense of his or her own competence to learn and perform new tasks, is often found to be the best predictor of behaviour, such as approaching a phobic stimulus or attempting a new behaviour. Bandura's work laid the foundation for approaches that emphasize the importance of cognitions in mediating behavioural responses (Craighead, Craighead, & Ilardi, 1995).

Other, more purely cognitive approaches, such as Albert Ellis's rational-emotive therapy and Aaron Beck's cognitive therapy (see Chapter 2), are based on the assumption that an individual's perception of events, rather than the events themselves, affects adjustment. Consequently, they focus on identifying automatic thoughts and changing maladaptive patterns of thinking that are associated with distress, anxiety, and depression (Hollon & Beck, 1994). Like their behavioural "relatives," cognitive and cognitive-behavioural approaches rely on the application of empirically derived strategies in the treatment of diverse disorders, including depression, anxiety disorders, eating disorders, attention deficit/hyperactivity disorder, chronic pain, personality disorders, bipolar disorder, substance abuse, schizophrenia, and couple distress (Beck & Dozois, 2011; Beck et al., 2009). Cognitive approaches foster a collaborative relationship in which the therapist and client work together to identify problems, test hypotheses, and re-evaluate beliefs. Treatment response is continuously monitored and treatment is tailored to the needs of individual clients. Chapter 5 discusses in more detail cognitive techniques in the treatment of anxiety; Chapter 12 describes cognitive and behavioural treatments for personality disorders; and Chapter 8 discusses a cognitive approach to depression.

Several developments in cognitive-behavioural approaches have shifted the focus away from an exclusive emphasis on challenging or disputing maladaptive thoughts to an alternative emphasis on attending to and accepting the presence of such thoughts (Dozois & Beck, 2011; Hayes, Villatte, Levin, & Hildebrandt, 2011). These contextual approaches focus on the way the person experiences and reacts to his or her thoughts. As part of promoting the client's awareness of the experience of the thoughts, they are also helped to disengage from automatically responding to the thoughts. For example, rather than learning to challenge a self-critical thought, a client would be encouraged to be fully aware of the thought, understand its meaning and purpose, and then determine whether or not to take any action in response to the thought.

We now present examples of some commonly used behavioural, cognitive, and cognitive-behavioural interventions (Dobson & Dobson, 2009).

REINFORCEMENT Building on the robust phenomenon that a behaviour that is followed by a reward is more likely to be repeated, efforts to reinforce desirable behaviours are at the heart of behavioural approaches. They form the essence of treatments in which parents learn to attend selectively to and reinforce appropriate behaviours in their children and to ignore undesirable behaviours. Systematic programs that use reinforcement to encourage and maintain effective behaviour work well in situations such as schools, residences, and institutions.

RESPONSE SHAPING Because many news skills are acquired gradually, **response shaping** is used to shape behaviour in gradual steps toward a goal. This method is used extensively with behaviour problems or difficulties across the lifespan. For example, a child with mental retardation who is unable to get dressed independently can be taught the process gradually by being rewarded for putting on one item at a time until he or she is eventually able to handle the entire task. The method would also be used in treating a young child presenting with school refusal.

BEHAVIOURAL ACTIVATION Extensive research has demonstrated that depressed individuals are limited in the scope and nature of positive reinforcers. For example, they typically minimize interactions with others and avoid engaging in activities that they previously found enjoyable. The essence of behavioural activation in the treatment of depression is to help patients develop strategies to increase their overall activity and to counteract their tendencies to avoid activities. As patients begin to experience more natural reinforcers in their lives (such as enjoying going for a walk, watching a movie with a friend, going for coffee while shopping), their depressive symptoms begin to diminish (Dimidjian, Barrera, Martell, Muñoz, & Lewinsohn, 2011).

RELAXATION TRAINING Helping clients to relax, both physically and mentally, is a component of many treatments for anxiety disorders, as well as for interventions focused on helping people to cope with pain or manage stress. A range of relaxation strategies can be used with both children and adults, including visualization, breathing retraining, biofeedback, and progressive muscle relaxation. A key issue in all forms of relaxation training is ensuring that clients develop skills that are practical, so that they can be quickly and easily used when needed.

EXPOSURE Also called in vivo exposure, exposure involves gradually exposing the client to a series of increasingly anxiety-provoking situations or stimuli. This is the most commonly used technique based on the concept of extinction. Related to **exposure therapy** is systematic desensitization. Joseph Wolpe's work drew on classical conditioning processes, reasoning that pairing anxiety-provoking stimuli with responses incompatible with anxiety would eliminate the anxiety response. In the process of **systematic desensitization**, fear-inducing stimuli are arranged in a hierarchy. Next, individuals are trained in techniques to achieve deep muscle relaxation. They are then required to imagine the first item on the hierarchy while remaining relaxed. They gradually progress through the hierarchy while maintaining their relaxed state. If they become anxious, they stop visualizing until they have regained their relaxed state (see Chapter 5). Systematic desensitization is not used as frequently as it once was because in vivo exposure produces a better outcome than imaginal exposure and the addition of relaxation is no more effective than exposure alone (Antony & Barlow, 2002).

ASSERTIVENESS TRAINING Assertiveness training is designed to help clients who have difficulty in conflict situations. The desired behaviours are first rehearsed in the therapy session and are later applied in real-life situations. The therapist's role is to encourage and guide the client in practising new, more appropriate assertive behaviours and more effective interpersonal skills. For example, clients may learn "refusal skills," conversational skills, social problem solving, and appropriate responding to insults. Assertiveness training is offered to couples experiencing relationship problems, to aggressive individuals, and to shy, socially awkward individuals.

PROBLEM SOLVING Using models developed in information processing, D'Zurilla and Goldfried (1971) introduced a **problem-solving approach** that was applied in the treatment of diverse problems such as weight control, clinical depression, and social skills deficits. The key elements of problem solving in cognitive-behavioural treatments are problem definition and formulation, generating alternative solutions to deal with the problem, deciding on the best solution to implement, and implementing and evaluating the solution (D'Zurilla & Nezu, 2010).

COGNITIVE RESTRUCTURING Based on the assumption that many psychological and interpersonal problems are related to assumptions, expectations, attributions, and automatic thoughts, cognitive-behavioural therapists have developed a range of strategies for testing and changing people's thoughts and beliefs. The initial step of **cognitive restructuring** involves having people become more aware of their thoughts when they are experiencing strong emotions. The nature and accuracy of these thoughts are questioned by the therapist, and patients are encouraged to conduct behavioural experiments to determine the validity and accuracy of these thoughts.

MINDFULNESS Drawing on well-established yoga and meditation techniques, mindfulness-based strategies are designed to help the person focus on the present moment. This focused awareness on current experience is nonjudgmental and open. Open awareness of one's experience is presumed to facilitate self-management and successful coping, in part by altering the person's usual unsuccessful attempts to avoid, ignore, or eliminate negative thoughts, memories, or emotions.

ECLECTIC AND INTEGRATIVE APPROACHES

So far, we have highlighted the distinctive features of each approach to psychotherapy. This "compare and contrast" strategy illustrates how therapists who were dissatisfied with the dominant theories of the time split off from the mainstream and started new schools of thought. Ironically, the history of psychotherapy, a discipline devoted to helping people, has been marked by some bitter competition and intolerance of opposing views.

Over the years, a number of therapists have observed the similarities and overlaps between apparently different approaches. In his 1961 book, *Persuasion and Healing*, Jerome Frank looked not only at twentieth-century psychotherapy, but also at primitive shamanism, religious conversion experiences, and placebo effects in drug treatment. He defined psychotherapy as a process whereby a person who was demoralized about some part of life sought help from a socially sanctioned healer. This separates psychotherapy from the conversations we may have with a friend or a hairdresser or in an online chat room. The first ingredient in healing is hope: either explicitly or implicitly, the therapist conveys an expectation that the client's life will change as a result of the psychotherapeutic process (Roberts, Kewman, Mercier, & Hovell, 1993). The second ingredient is an alternative explanation for the problem. Within specific orientations, the types of explanation differ; so, for example, a psychodynamic therapist works on the assumption that distress is related to early childhood experiences, whereas a cognitive therapist emphasizes the way the client thinks about the situation. According to Frank, these interpretations offer a way to understand the problems that the person is facing. The third ingredient is that the client is expected to think, feel, or act in a different way. Changes in thoughts, feelings, or behaviours have been found to have ripple effects, so that a person who engages in more pleasant activities may be less likely to feel depressed, or a person who thinks that a poor grade is unfortunate but not disastrous may be less likely to feel hopeless, et cetera.

Frank was influential in promoting the development of new therapeutic practices and frameworks that draw on selected aspects of various dominant schools of therapy. The appeal of the resulting eclectic (that is, using techniques stemming from diverse orientations) or integrative (that is, developing a conceptual model to guide treatment based on elements of diverse orientations) approaches is evident in surveys of psychotherapists. Across numerous surveys in recent decades, at least one-third of therapists identify themselves as disciples of a particular school of therapy, but claim to have integrated aspects of diverse approaches (e.g., Cassin, Singer, Dobson, & Altmaier, 2007). In a climate of fiscal restraint, when health service providers are required to be accountable and furnish evidence that the service they offer is effective, therapists are increasingly motivated to attend to research findings (Goldfried & Norcross, 1995) and to combine the best elements of different schools of therapy.

As psychological treatments require the person to make lifestyle changes, a key component of many approaches involves assessing the client's readiness to embark on changes. Motivational interviewing has been found to be efficacious in addressing ambivalence to adopt lifestyle changes among people with diverse problems, including anxiety, depression (Arkowitz, Westra, Miller, & Rollnick, 2008), eating disorders (e.g., Cassin, von Ranson, Heng, Brar, & Wojtowicz, 2008), and substance abuse (D'Amico, Miles, Stern, & Meredith, 2008).

3 BEFORE MOVING ON

Given what you have learned about different theoretical approaches and their associated treatments, if a friend asked you what to expect in cognitive-behavioural therapy for the treatment of anxiety, what would you say?

Psychotherapy: Treatment Modalities

In addition to different theoretical approaches to therapy, there are distinctive modalities of delivering therapy—to individuals, couples, families, and groups.

INDIVIDUAL THERAPY

Early therapy was conducted exclusively in an individual format, with one person (the client or patient) and one therapist. Contacts with other family members were strictly avoided lest they contaminate the all-important therapeutic relationship. Individual therapy remains the most common treatment modality. Nevertheless, many psychologists find it useful to sometimes invite the client to include his or her significant others in treatment. Individual therapy is also practised with children and adolescents. Some forms of individual child psychotherapy appear very similar to adult "talk" therapy, whereas other approaches use activities and children's play as the medium of communication.

COUPLES THERAPY

In the nineteenth century, marriage was considered a lifetime commitment to live together and to raise a family. The personal qualities of each partner and the couple's enjoyment of life together were not relevant to the stability of the marriage. At the beginning of the twenty-first century, marriage is considered to be a partnership based on mutual interests and companionship. With the liberalization of Canadian divorce laws in 1968 and 1985, it became possible for one partner to end an unsatisfying marriage. At the same time as divorce became easier in Western countries, there was increased interest in developing therapies to help couples resolve their difficulties. Partners (who may be married, cohabiting, or dating, and may be of any sexual orientation) may have conjoint sessions but may also each meet separately with the therapist.

The goal in most forms of couples therapy is to enhance each partner's satisfaction with the relationship. Couples therapy is most effective when it is an early response to developing relationship problems. Couples treatments have also been found to be effective for problems originally thought of as individual, such as depression or alcoholism in adults and conduct disorder in children (Hunsley & Lee, 1995; Rohrbaugh, Shoham, Spungen, & Steinglass, 1995). Couples therapy may be based on different theoretical orientations, with the cognitive-behavioural forms of couples therapy having the most supporting research evidence (Shadish & Baldwin, 2005). In this form of treatment, therapists seek to enhance communication and conflict resolution skills, to help both partners to be realistic in their expectations about their relationship, and to promote intimacy. Canadian psychologists Sue Johnson and Les Greenberg have developed and evaluated an **emotionally focused couples therapy**. Drawing on elements of experiential

The goals of family therapy are to improve interactions in the family.

therapy and structural family therapy, the goal of the therapy is to modify distressed couples' constricted interaction patterns and emotional responses by fostering the development of a secure emotional bond (Johnson, Hunsley, Greenberg, & Schindler, 1999).

FAMILY THERAPY

Family therapy originated in social work and in the child guidance movement (Clarkin & Carpenter, 1995), but is now practised by therapists of diverse orientations, including cognitive-behavioural and psychodynamic. Although early family approaches viewed the family as the source of a family member's problems, many current family approaches make no such assumption but consider the family to be an important part of the solution to problems. A common goal of family approaches is to identify interactions between family members that may inadvertently contribute to problems. Family approaches often involve **reframing** the problem—or presenting a novel explanation for it—after which family members are required to carry out various tasks designed to change their ways of interacting with one another (Seaburn, Landau-Stanton, & Horwitz, 1995). The goals of family therapy are to enhance interactions in the family, so that each family member's well-being is promoted.

GROUP THERAPY

The cost of psychotherapy reduces its accessibility for many people. One obvious way to reduce the cost is to work with several clients in a group format. After the Second World War, therapy groups were developed to address the needs of various underprivileged groups. Many current cognitive-behavioural treatments, originally developed for use in individual therapy, have been modified for use in a group format. In addition to cost savings, there are important theoretical reasons for seeing clients in a group. In addition to the shared therapeutic experience of hope for change, the group context offers feedback from other people (Rosenbaum & Patterson, 1995) and a place to practise ways of relating to others. *Universality*—the awareness that other people share similar experiences or feelings—can reduce feelings of stigma (Ballinger & Yalom, 1995). Participation in a group offers exposure to solutions that have worked for others and may also lead to feelings of cohesion or belonging.

4 BEFORE MOVING ON

Psychotherapy can be offered in different modalities. What are the advantages and disadvantages of each?

The Context of Psychotherapy

WHO PROVIDES PSYCHOTHERAPY?

Clinical psychologists are among the main providers of psychotherapy. Surveys over the years have found that most clinical psychologists are actively involved in offering some form of therapeutic service, be it individual, couple, family, or group therapy. Although many clinical psychologists identify themselves as practising from a single orientation, many practise in a more eclectic manner. For example, in their survey of Canadian clinical psychologists, Cohen and colleagues (2008) found that 84 percent described themselves as cognitive-behavioural, 24 percent as psychodynamic, and 23 percent as humanistic-experiential. As the total exceeds 100 percent, it is clear that many psychologists see themselves as having an eclectic or integrative orientation. On average, survey respondents reported that they spent 37 percent of their professional time providing treatment services, with 80 percent of psychologists reporting that they provided individual psychotherapy services (other treatment modalities were offered by less than a third of respondents).

Research, to date, does not provide much evidence that therapists' professional training or years of experience are directly related to the outcome of treatment, although professionally trained therapists are more effective than non-professional therapists when therapy is shorter than 12 sessions (Beutler, Machado, & Neufeldt, 1994). Because most clients attend fewer than 12 sessions of psychotherapy, there may be substantial advantages to selecting a trained mental health professional as a therapist. Accordingly, people seeking psychotherapy should adopt a "consumer rights" attitude, and before treatment they should question therapists about their training, experience, and therapeutic methods. Also, though many potential clients do not ask about confidentiality issues, financial arrangements, or treatment alternatives (Braaten, Otto, & Handelsman, 1993), they should raise these matters. Table 17.3 offers suggested questions to ask when seeking services.

WHO SEEKS PSYCHOTHERAPY?

People seek therapy for a multitude of reasons. Many have significant emotional distress that interferes with their daily functioning; previous chapters have described the range of disorders such individuals may be experiencing. Some seek therapy for advice and assistance in coping with the demands of social roles, such as parent, spouse, or employee. Some people may come to therapy for aid in coping with recent trauma (e.g., rape) or loss (e.g., death of a loved one). Some seek assistance in addressing questions related to personal identity, values, or self-knowledge. The use of mental health services has risen since the early 1980s, with approximately 13 percent of the American population using such services during a 12-month period (Kessler et al., 1999). However, much of the increase in mental health service use is associated with the use of medication rather than psychotherapy (Olfson & Marcus, 2010). In a telephone survey conducted in Alberta, Esposito and colleagues (2007) examined the pattern of mental health treatment provided for depression. Among survey respondents meeting the diagnostic criteria for major depression, approximately 40 percent reported using antidepressant medication, whereas only 14 percent reported receiving some form of counselling or psychotherapy.

TABLE 17.3 INFORMED CONSUMERS: QUESTIONS TO ASK A POTENTIAL THERAPIST

1. What are your professional qualifications?
2. Have you worked with this kind of problem?
3. How would you describe the way you work?
4. How many times do you think it will be necessary for me to see you?
5. What are the treatment options for me? Are there clinics or other practitioners who also work with problems like this?
6. What is the research evidence on the best type of treatment for my problem?
7. What can I expect from treatment? How will I be different at the end of treatment?
8. How much do you charge? Do you have a sliding fee scale?
9. How soon can I see you? How long is your waiting list?

American epidemiological surveys indicate that some groups of people are more likely than others to seek psychotherapy (Vessey & Howard, 1993). For example, two-thirds of psychotherapy clients are female, half have university education, half are married, and the majority are young to middle-aged adults. Unfortunately, Vessey and Howard's analysis also suggested that many of those most in need of such services (that is, those suffering from a psychological disorder) never seek professional help. A similar picture is evident in Canada. Responses to the National Population Health Survey (NPHS) showed similar socio-demographic characteristics among those who reported consulting a psychologist for health or mental health reasons (Hunsley, Lee, & Aubry, 1999), as shown in Table 17.4. Users of psychological services experienced more stress and distress than did the population at large and were less satisfied with their life situation. Consistent with American data, Hunsley and colleagues' analysis found that, unfortunately, many who could benefit from therapy had not received it. For example, many Canadians suffering from depression had received neither therapy (from a psychologist, social worker, or other kind of counsellor) nor antidepressant medication. Data from the 2002 Canadian Community

TABLE 17.4 CHARACTERISTICS OF CANADIANS WHO RECEIVE PSYCHOLOGICAL SERVICES

1. Women are twice as likely as men to consult a psychologist.
2. Although Canadians with university education make up 13 percent of the population, they make up 22 percent of the clientele of psychologists.
3. Although parents and children in single-parent families make up 8 percent of the Canadian population, they make up 20 percent of the clientele of psychologists.
4. People who experience pain that interferes with their daily lives are twice as likely as other Canadians to seek psychological services.
5. Canadians who receive psychological services also tend to be frequent users of other health care services.
6. Canadians who feel so unhappy that they believe life is not worthwhile are five times as likely as other Canadians to seek psychological services.
7. Whether measured by the number of stressful events in their past or the number of ongoing current stressors, users of psychological services are more likely than other Canadians to report high levels of stress.

Health Survey examining the reasons why Canadian adults consulted a health professional for mental health reasons show that low income was a significant barrier to accessing the services of a psychologist (Vasiliadis, Tempier, Lesage, & Kates, 2009).

THE DURATION OF TREATMENT

For many people, the word *psychotherapy* conjures up notions of an ongoing lifestyle of regular and frequent sessions with a therapist. Nothing could be further from the truth. The majority of people who receive psychotherapy attend fewer than 10 sessions! Across a range of therapy clinics, across European and North American settings, across a range of clients presenting problems, and over the past 60 years, the picture of the duration of psychotherapy is remarkably consistent (Garfield, 1994; Phillips, 1991). A large minority of clients come for only one or two sessions, and the median number of therapy sessions ranges from 5 to 13 sessions.

Although many of the currently used psychotherapies are designed to be short term in nature (that is, 20 or fewer sessions), there is obviously some concern that many people who start treatment may terminate prematurely, thereby receiving less than optimal benefit from therapy. A number of researchers have attempted to understand the phenomenon of premature termination, with strikingly little success. Although a host of client characteristics have been hypothesized to contribute to premature termination or to treatment failure, many have failed to be empirically confirmed or have been found to contribute very little to the prediction of termination (Hatchett & Park, 2003; Wierzbicki & Pekarik, 1993).

Evaluating the Effects of Psychotherapy

HISTORICAL CONTEXT

With growing awareness of health care costs and a more sophisticated clientele, service providers face increasing demands to be accountable—to demonstrate that the services they offer are effective in treating the problem for which the person sought therapy. The history of research evaluating the effectiveness of psychotherapy is relatively brief; little empirical evidence was available prior to the 1960s. Since that time, though, there has been a veritable explosion in this line of research, so that there are now literally thousands of studies examining the effects of many different forms of therapy for many different types of problems. An important distinction that is now being made in the research literature, and one that we shall use in the following sections, is one between efficacy and effectiveness. **Treatment efficacy** is defined as evidence of treatment effects when delivered in the context of a controlled study, whereas **treatment effectiveness** is defined as the evidence of effects when the treatment is evaluated in a "real-world" context. Thought of in another way, efficacy relates to studies designed to maximize internal validity, and effectiveness relates to studies designed to maximize external validity.

As is often the case in science, research attention to a phenomenon is sparked by a controversy or a challenge to the accepted view. The current abundance of psychotherapy outcome research is due, in large part, to Hans Eysenck's 1952 article in which he argued that the rates of improvement among clients receiving psychodynamic or eclectic therapy were comparable to rates of remission of symptoms among untreated clients. On the basis of his review of the limited data available, he contended that about two-thirds of people with neurotic disorders (e.g., anxiety disorders, depression) would improve within two years, regardless of whether they were treated by psychotherapy. In other words, Eysenck argued that there was no evidence that psychotherapy had any demonstrable effect!

Not surprisingly, Eysenck's review evoked strong reactions from psychotherapists and psychotherapy researchers. Many critical responses to his review were published in scientific journals by leading proponents of psychotherapy. Perhaps the most important result of the ensuing debate was the emerging emphasis on the need for solid research design in evaluating psychotherapeutic effects. Vocal critics of Eysenck's position, such as Luborsky (1954) and Bergin (1971), claimed that Eysenck erred in comparing improvement rates across studies. For example, they argued that adequate control groups (that is, clients who did not receive treatment) were not available in many studies and that Eysenck's criteria for establishing clinical improvement were arbitrary and biased against finding positive therapeutic effects. These criticisms were, in turn, addressed by Rachman (1971) in his review of the growing empirical evidence. Like Eysenck, he concluded that there was no evidence to substantiate the claims of efficacy or effectiveness made by psychotherapy proponents.

Throughout the 1970s, the debate about the impact of psychotherapy grew, as did the number of published studies on therapy outcome. By this time, behavioural therapies were being used by a growing number of psychologists. As empirical verification of outcome was a key element of the behavioural approach to treatment, there were soon many published studies examining the effect of these therapies. Researchers attempting to understand and integrate the burgeoning number of empirical articles on psychotherapy (including psychodynamic, behavioural, and other approaches) faced a formidable challenge in attempting to draw reasonable conclusions. As a result, the debate about the efficacy and effectiveness of therapy was muddied by the fact that proponents and critics of psychotherapy often drew on different studies to support their respective positions.

META-ANALYSIS

Chapter 4 reviewed the procedures generally used to evaluate the results of interventions in single studies. In attempting to reach conclusions derived from several studies, researchers typically employ qualitative (that is, non-numerical) methods. In these, the reviewer provides a narrative account of the various studies—their strengths, weaknesses, and findings—and then draws conclusions about the state of knowledge. However, these methods were limited in their ability to synthesize information across numerous studies using a number of different patient populations and a wide variety of outcome measures. As a response to this challenge, "meta-analytic" techniques were developed. **Meta-analysis** is simply a method of quantitatively reviewing previous research. An analogy to a typical research study may be helpful in understanding the nature of meta-analysis. As described in Chapter 4, a typical psychotherapy outcome study involves the collection of data from multiple research participants. These data are then summed and overall trends in the group of participants are examined with the use of statistical procedures such as analysis of variance. The same general process occurs in meta-analysis, except that the "participants" in a meta-analysis are research studies rather than individual clients.

In a single research study, similar data are collected from all participants. Obviously this is not possible in a meta-analysis, for the original research studies are likely to have employed a range of measures for assessing outcome. Therefore, in meta-analysis, the results of prior research are combined by developing a common metric (basically a z transformation) to be used across the studies. The metric is called an **effect size** and is calculated as the difference between the means of the experimental (that is, the treatment) group and the control group, divided by the standard deviation of either the control group or the pooled sample of both groups. In some instances, where two treatments are compared to one another, the effect size is the difference between the two treated groups, divided by the standard deviation of the control group or the pooled standard deviation of all groups (treated and untreated) in the study. Effect sizes can be calculated from raw data, group means, and standard deviations, or from inferential statistics reported in the original research studies (e.g., correlations, F-tests, t-tests).

Meta-analysis offers numerous advantages over traditional research reviews or single empirical studies. For example, statistical analyses, rather than the author's impressions, guide conclusions about a body of literature. Moreover, by including data from many studies, the number of research participants on whom conclusions are based is dramatically increased. This greatly enhances the meta-analyst's power to detect an effect in the literature and the generalizability of the conclusions drawn on the basis of the literature. As a result of these methodological and statistical strengths, meta-analysis is increasingly used to determine the current state of knowledge about the impact of psychotherapy and to assist in the development of health care policies regarding the provision of psychotherapy.

A BRIEF REVIEW OF META-ANALYTIC EVIDENCE

In the first meta-analysis of the treatment literature, Smith, Glass, and Miller (1980) reviewed 475 controlled studies of psychotherapy, including both studies published in scientific journals and unpublished dissertations. They concluded that psychotherapy, in general, was clearly efficacious, with an average effect size of 0.85; that is, the difference in the dependent variables (such as measures of symptomatology) between the treated and untreated groups was 0.85 standard deviation units. This value means that the average person receiving therapy was better off after therapy than 80 percent of people who did not receive therapy.

A subset of the studies they reviewed included direct comparisons of different forms of treatment. For example, there were 57 studies in which therapies they termed "verbal" (including psychodynamic, cognitive, and humanistic therapies) were compared with "behavioural" (behavioural and cognitive-behavioural therapies) treatments. An analysis of this subset of studies yielded an effect size of 0.77 for the verbal therapies and 0.96 for the behavioural therapies. Caution is required, however, in interpreting the differences among therapies, because clients treated by each differ in the type and severity of problems.

Since the initial meta-analysis of the effectiveness of psychotherapy, dozens of meta-analytic studies have been published. Initially, these studies focused on replicating the findings of Smith and colleagues (1980), and, indeed, other researchers obtained similar findings. Subsequent meta-analyses have had a narrower focus. For many researchers, the question of whether psychotherapy is efficacious has been answered with a resounding yes. Attention has therefore turned to the different effects of treatments on specific disorders (that is, what works for whom) and the effects of therapist and client characteristics on the process and outcome of treatment.

In an influential review of the literature, Luborsky, Singer, and Luborsky (1975) concluded that all psychotherapies produce equivalent effects. Quoting the dodo bird in *Alice in Wonderland*, they pronounced that "[e]verybody has won, and all must have prizes." Since the Luborsky and colleagues review, many psychotherapists and researchers have endorsed this view, citing meta-analytic findings such as Smith and colleagues (1980). More recently, Wampold and colleagues (1997) conducted a meta-analysis that included data from studies published between 1970 and 1995 that compared at least two bona fide treatments (i.e., the treatments were intended to be therapeutic and not simply to serve as a control condition). They reported an average effect size of 0.19 and suggested that this indicated that real treatments, regardless of orientation, do not differ in their efficacy. However, as the majority of studies included in the meta-analysis dealt with forms of cognitive-behavioural treatments, it would be more accurate to conclude that different cognitive-behavioural treatments have similar efficacy (Hunsley & Di Giulio, 2002).

Careful examination of comparative efficacy is crucial, because the acceptance of the equivalence of psychotherapies is tantamount to accepting the null hypothesis. Yet the failure to find a significant difference does not necessarily mean that no difference exists. Methodological limitations, such as small sample sizes, may limit the ability to draw conclusions. In fact, Kazdin and Bass (1989) found that almost half of the studies that found no differences between treatments had too few research participants to detect differences that may have existed. Other methodological aspects of treatment studies can also be examined with meta-analysis. For example, in a series of meta-analyses, Westen and colleagues (e.g., Westen & Morrison, 2001) emphasized the importance of considering the number of potential participants excluded from studies because they failed to meet inclusion criteria. This type of information can be critical in determining the likely generalizability of the research findings.

Meta-analysis has also been used to evaluate the effects of psychological treatments for youth. Weiss and Weisz (1995) evaluated the relative efficacy of behavioural (including cognitive) versus non-behavioural (psychodynamic and humanistic) treatments for children and adolescents. Their meta-analysis examined 105 studies of treatments for problems including anxiety disorders, depression, and social skills deficits. Past reviews of the literature had found that behavioural treatments tend to be superior to non-behavioural ones, but some researchers suggested that this may be due to superior study design rather than to the true strength of the behavioural treatment. When Weiss and Weisz statistically controlled for methodological quality of the studies, the effect sizes of the behavioural and non-behavioural treatments were 0.86 and 0.38, respectively. The difference was even stronger in the 10 studies in their sample that directly compared behavioural and non-behavioural treatments.

Can we conclude, then, that cognitive-behavioural therapies are always the most effective? Not necessarily. It is accurate to say that there is more evidence to support the efficacy of this group of treatments than there is for any other approach. However, this is due, in large part, to the fact that cognitive-behaviourists have a tradition of empirically substantiating treatment effects. There may well be other effective approaches that have not been the object of as much empirical investigation.

Psychodynamic therapies, in particular, despite their widespread use, have received very little empirical attention. This has begun to change, largely through the efforts of prominent psychodynamic researchers/therapists such as Lester Luborsky and Hans Strupp (cf. Henry et al., 1994). Reviews and meta-analyses of a growing number of studies in which short-term psychodynamic therapy is systematically evaluated have yielded encouraging results (Gerber et al., 2011; Gibbons, Crits-Christoph, & Hearon, 2008; Leichsenring et al., 2009). Researchers have been actively evaluating interpersonal therapy in the past few years, and indications are that it is an efficacious treatment for depression and social phobia (e.g., Cuijpers et al., 2011; Lipsitz, Markowitz, Cherry, & Fyer, 1999; Mufson, Weissman, Moreau, & Garfinkel, 1999; O'Hara, Stuart, Gorman, & Wenzel, 2000). Finally, meta-analytic evidence suggests that experiential therapies that are structured, directive, and short term can be efficacious for treating symptoms of depression, anxiety, trauma, and marital distress (Elliott, Greenberg, & Lietaer, 2004).

5 BEFORE MOVING ON

> Clinicians who wish to offer services need to keep up with the research literature. There are, however, so many studies that it can be bewildering to make sense of the results. How has meta-analysis been used in synthesizing results?

EFFECTS OF PSYCHOTHERAPY FOR SPECIFIC DISORDERS

Let us now turn to the effects of psychotherapy for specific disorders. There is now extensive evidence that there are effective psychotherapeutic treatments for many Axis I disorders and other health problems (Nathan & Gorman, 2007). In this section, we provide only a glimpse of the range of problems that can be treated with psychotherapy.

ANXIETY DISORDERS It is now commonly accepted that efficacious treatment for specific phobias must involve an element of exposure. That is, the individual with a phobia must begin to confront the object of the phobia. The person is also encouraged (in various ways, depending on the exact nature of the treatment) to accept that the surge of anxiety he or she feels is normal, not life-threatening, and will soon diminish (see Chapter 5).

There are many efficacious cognitive-behavioural treatments for other anxiety disorders (Deacon & Abramowitz, 2004; Norton & Price, 2007). For example, in the treatment of panic disorder, cognitive-behavioural treatments that combine cognitive restructuring (that is, challenging the beliefs and expectations held by the patient) and

The individual with a phobia must begin to confront the object of the phobia.

interoceptive exposure (that is, exposing the patient to bodily symptoms similar to those experienced in a panic disorder) are highly efficacious. Indeed, it is common to find that approximately 75 percent of patients treated in this manner are panic-free by the end of treatment—and that this improvement is typically long term. Interestingly, the addition of medication to these forms of therapy does not appear to improve outcome rates (Furukawa, Watanabe, & Churchill, 2006). Large effect sizes for two types of treatment of obsessive-compulsive disorder have been reported. The first involves a combination of exposure to the object of the obsession or compulsion and response prevention (e.g., the patient is encouraged to abstain from rituals such as washing or checking); the other is cognitive therapy. Cognitive-behavioural treatments (CBT) have also been found to be efficacious in treating generalized anxiety disorder (GAD). Given the high level of comorbidity associated with GAD, it is encouraging to note a "ripple effect"; Borkovec, Abel, and Newman (1995) found that other symptoms decreased when the GAD symptoms were treated. Finally, evidence to date suggests that, in the treatment of post-traumatic stress disorder (PTSD), trauma-focused CBT and a form of treatment known as eye movement desensitization and reprocessing (EMDR) are the treatments of choice (Bisson et al., 2007). It is worth noting that many PTSD researchers have suggested that, as is the case for many forms of CBT for anxiety disorders, the critical component of EMDR is the use of exposure.

Efficacious treatments are also available for childhood anxiety disorders. Both group and individual CBT are helpful in treating social phobia (Silverman, Pina, & Viswesvaran, 2008). Individual exposure-based CBT is efficacious in treating obsessive-compulsive disorder in children and adolescents (Barrett, Farrell, Pina, Persis, & Piacentini, 2008), and trauma-focused CBT is efficacious in the treatment of children and youth exposed to traumatic events (Silverman, Ortiz, et al. 2008).

MOOD DISORDERS Researchers have found a number of psychologically based interventions to be efficacious in the treatment of clinical depression. In general, extensive research suggests that cognitive (and cognitive-behavioural) therapy is efficacious in treating depression (Dobson, 1989), as is interpersonal psychotherapy, which helps the person learn new ways of interacting with others (Frank & Spanier, 1995; see also Chapter 8). Indeed, the major National Institute of Mental Health Treatment of Depression Collaborative Research Program found comparable results for these two treatments (Elkin, 1994). Importantly, there is also emerging evidence that cognitive therapy is efficacious in preventing relapse and recurrence of depression (Hollon, Stewart, & Strunk, 2006; Vittengl, Clark, Dunn, & Jarrett, 2007). A number of treatments have been found to be efficacious in treating depression in older adults (Scogin, Welsh, Hanson, Stump, & Coates, 2005). These include several forms of CBT, brief psychodynamic therapy, and reminiscence therapy (in which clients are encouraged to review their life and the ways in which they have dealt with challenges and stresses). In practice, it is relatively common for patients to receive both an antidepressant and some form of psychotherapy. The research evidence indicates that such combined treatments can be slightly more efficacious than either treatment on its own, although this may be primarily true for patients who have chronic depression (de Maat, Dekker, Schoevers, & de Jonghe, 2007; Pampallona, Bollini, Tibaldi, Kupelnick, & Munizza, 2004).

Many Canadian psychologists have been involved in developing cognitive-behavioural treatments for depression and for other disorders. After establishing the efficacy of this form of treatment, investigators attempted to separate the components of cognitive therapy to determine the "essential ingredient." Keith Dobson of the University of Calgary collaborated with American colleagues in a study that randomly assigned people with major depression to one of three treatment conditions (Jacobson et al., 1996). A behavioural activation treatment focused only on increasing patients' physical activity, social interactions, et cetera. The second treatment added interventions to help patients modify negative automatic thoughts. The full cognitive therapy condition included both of these components as well as work to alter the underlying dysfunctional beliefs that are hypothesized to make someone vulnerable to depression. Much to the researchers' surprise, there were no discernible differences between the three treatments, in either the short term or the long term, leading them to conclude that the active ingredient of cognitive therapy for depression may be behavioural activation (Gortner, Gollan, Dobson, & Jacobson, 1998). These findings have led to a dramatic growth in interest in developing and evaluating behavioural activation treatments for a range of client populations.

CHILDHOOD DISORDERS Psychosocial interventions have been demonstrated to help children and adolescents who are dealing with diverse disorders and problems. A special series in the *Journal of Clinical Child and Adolescent Psychology* included reviews of the usefulness of psychosocial treatments for DSM-IV Axis I disorders such as autism (Rogers & Vismara, 2008), anxiety disorders (Barrett et al., 2008; Silverman et al., 2008), depression (David-Ferdon & Kaslow, 2008), ADHD (Pelham & Fabiano, 2008), disruptive behaviour disorders (Eyberg, Nelson, & Boggs, 2008), and substance abuse (Waldron & Turner, 2008), as well as issues in primary care or medical practice such as adherence to treatment of chronic health conditions (Kahana, Drotar, & Frazier, 2008). This encouraging picture must be balanced by the fact that, unfortunately, efficacious psychological treatments for various problems of childhood and adolescence are not routinely offered in standard care (Connor-Smith & Weisz, 2003). In a meta-analysis of 32 studies comparing evidence-based treatments to usual clinical care, Weisz, Jensen-Doss, and Hawley (2006) found superior results for evidence-based treatment compared to usual clinical care; furthermore, the evidence-based treatment outperformed usual clinical care in the treatment of minority youth and youth with the most severe problems. Efficacious treatments for children and youth often include the same core components as similar treatments for adult disorders, such as exposure for anxiety symptoms. Many treatments for children and youth disorders also involved training parents to respond in a way that encourages positive behaviour and discourages problematic behaviour.

SLEEP DISORDERS Psychotherapy researchers have been actively involved in devising interventions for sleep disorders. To date, much of their attention has been devoted to insomnia. As sedatives can lead to poor-quality sleep, possible addiction, and rebound insomnia on withdrawal, there is a pressing need for effective psychological interventions, especially for older adults (see Chapter 16). Treatments include strategies such as relaxation training, sleep restriction (that is, limiting the time spent in bed to the time one is asleep), and stimulus control (e.g., going to bed only when sleepy, getting out of bed if unable to fall asleep). Canadian psychologist Charles Morin of Laval University has been at the forefront of work with adults suffering from insomnia (e.g., Morin, 2006). Given the very substantial effects that CBT interventions have on sleep disorders, a great deal of attention is now focused on streamlining the treatments to make them as user-friendly as possible. For example, a randomized controlled trial found that a brief (two-hour) cognitive-behavioural intervention for young and middle-aged adults was more efficacious than either pharmacotherapy or combined cognitive-behavioural treatment and pharmacotherapy in the treatment of insomnia (Jacobs, Pace-Shott, Stickgold, & Otto, 2004).

AXIS II DISORDERS Despite impressive breakthroughs in the treatment of psychological distress for Axis I disorders, the majority of Axis II disorders have received little or no attention from psychotherapy researchers. Some evidence, primarily based on uncontrolled observational studies, suggests that both psychodynamic and cognitive-behavioural treatments may be beneficial for these disorders (Crits-Christoph & Barber, 2007; Leichsenring & Rabung, 2008). The one major exception to this neglect of treatments for Axis II disorders is Linehan's multi-component cognitive-behavioural treatment (including training in emotional awareness and control, problem solving, and stress management) for borderline personality disorder (e.g., Linehan, 1993; see Chapter 12). The development of efficacious and effective interventions for individuals with personality disorders continues to be a priority for many psychotherapy researchers.

SERIOUS MENTAL ILLNESS There is growing evidence that, for people with bipolar disorder, the addition of psychological interventions to the prescription of a mood stabilizer can enhance treatment outcome: CBT and group psychoeducation (and possibly family therapy) are efficacious in preventing relapse (Beynon, Soares-Weiser, Woolacott, Duffy, & Geddes, 2008). It appears that treatments focusing on medication adherence and the recognition of mood changes reduce manic symptoms, whereas treatments focusing on cognitive and interpersonal coping strategies reduce depressive symptoms (Miklowitz, 2008). There is evidence that the inclusion of CBT and family-based services in the treatment of early psychosis contributes to positive outcomes (Bird, Premkumar, Kendall, Whittington, Mitchell, & Kuipers, 2010). Psychological interventions have also been found to be important adjunctive treatments for individuals with schizophrenia (Wykes, Huddy, Cellard, McGurk, & Czobor, 2011). Given the severity of the deficits associated with this diagnosis, it is not surprising that no single form of psychotherapy has a positive impact on all aspects of a patient's psychosocial functioning. Nevertheless, when combined with efficacious medication, specific therapies yield important specific effects: social skills training improves social functioning, CBT reduces positive symptoms, cognitive remediation leads to improved cognitive functioning, and psychoeducational interventions with families decrease hospitalization and relapse rates (Pfammatter, Junghan, & Brenner, 2006).

COUPLE DISTRESS

The most widely studied couples therapy is behavioural marital therapy, developed by Jacobson and Margolin (1979). This therapy focuses on improving the communication between partners and encouraging more constructive interactions. Although this treatment has been found to have relatively large effect sizes (0.95) in meta-analytic studies (Hahlweg & Markman, 1988), evidence indicates that fewer than 50 percent of treated couples maintain happy marriages in the years following treatment (Jacobson & Addis, 1993). Interestingly, behavioural marital therapy, used as a treatment for depressed clients who are maritally distressed, appears to be efficacious in diminishing depressive symptoms (Beach & O'Leary, 1992). Research indicates that, for mildly to moderately distressed couples, emotionally focused marital therapy is efficacious in reducing conflict and distress (effect size of 1.31; Johnson et al., 1999).

GENERALIZING TO CLINICAL SETTINGS

The evidence we have presented on the impact of psychotherapy in the preceding sections has one major potential limitation: almost all studies were conducted in a controlled research context. To meet the requirements of increasingly demanding experimental designs, researchers must carefully screen potential research participants to ensure that they fit criteria for their study, randomly assign participants to conditions, provide thorough training to therapists, and monitor the adherence of these therapists to the model of therapy they are supposed to use. The most important question, of course, is whether the results of such experimental studies generalize to the "real world" of clinical services. In the "real world" patients often have multiple problems rather than a single diagnosis, and they may receive services that are untested from therapists who are unlikely to be supervised as closely as those involved in randomized clinical trials.

Several reviews and analyses of the published literature have attempted to determine the extent to which the effects of research trials on psychotherapy for children, adolescents, and adults generalize to real clinical settings. Jensen-Doss and Weisz (2006) examined 325 clinically referred young people aged 7 to 17 and found no evidence of poorer outcome in youth with multiple problems. Similarly, Kazdin and Whitley (2006) found that the presence of comorbidity was associated with greater change in young people with disruptive behaviour disorders who received evidence-based parent training or problem-solving treatments. These findings are encouraging in suggesting that evidence-based services are useful to those with more serious problems.

To determine whether such a conclusion applies also to treatments for adults, a group of psychotherapy researchers who had previously published meta-analytic studies joined forces to review the pertinent literature (Shadish et al., 1997). They were able to identify only 56 studies (out of approximately 1000 included in their own and other meta-analyses) that met criteria for clinical relevance (that is, treatment provided in a non-university setting, with

FOCUS 17.2

Technological Advances in the Provision of Psychological Treatments

Although there are now evidence-based treatment protocols for many disorders and conditions, only a small proportion of those who could potentially benefit from services actually seek treatment. Those who do request services often face barriers such as long waiting lists and the high costs of services. In many countries there is a serious lack of trained practitioners who can deliver evidence-based psychological treatments (e.g., Hollinghurst et al., 2010). In this context, technological innovations that have become an integral part of the way we communicate, gather information, shop, and plan our activities also offer an intriguing opportunity to make effective psychological services available to large numbers of people, who can then access services at a time and location that is convenient to them.

Computerized and Internet-based interventions that deliver evidence-based services with minimal contact with a clinician have produced promising results in the treatment of a range of disorders, including anxiety (Reger & Gahm, 2009), insomnia (Ritterband et al., 2009), and post-traumatic stress disorder (Amstadter, Broman-Fulks, Zinzow, Ruggiero, & Cercone, 2009). Titov and his colleagues (2011) also obtained positive results for the Wellbeing Program, which is designed to treat anxiety disorders and depression over 8 sessions in a 10-week program. Although clinicians in this program spent an average of only 85 minutes with each client, participants found the procedures acceptable, and they sustained the positive gains over time. A survey of university students found that although students were less likely to seek help the more psychologically distressed they felt, the pattern was reversed for online services, with distressed students being more likely to express their intention to seek online services than traditional services (Ryan, Shochet, & Stallman, 2010).

Several randomized controlled trials have now been conducted examining computerized treatments of anxiety for children (Khanna & Kendall, 2010) and adolescents (Spence et al., 2011; Stallard, Richardson, Velleman, & Attwood, 2011). Similar to the results with adults, these investigations found encouraging evidence that computerized and online services produce equivalent gains to those in individual CBT, with evidence that gains are maintained and sometimes enhanced at follow-up. Ratings of acceptability and satisfaction are comparable to regular CBT.

Smartphone technology offers intriguing possibilities as an adjunct to psychological services. Rizvi, Dimeff, Skutch, Carroll, and Linehan (2011), for example, developed software called the DBT Coach that could be accessed via smartphone. Participants in a pilot project who were given smartphones with the DBT Coach app for a period of 10 to 14 days used the DBT Coach an average of 15 times, and found it helpful and user-friendly; furthermore, use of the DBT Coach was associated with positive changes such as decreased emotional intensity and reduced urges to engage in maladaptive behaviour. Moving to a different problem area, Jones, Forehand, McKee, Cuellar, and Kincaid (2010) outlined numerous potential uses of smartphones as an adjunct to parenting interventions.

It is clear that we have only begun to explore the potential uses of communications technology in extending evidence-based psychological services to a wider population in a manner that is engaging, is cost-effective, and yields sustained gains. ●

referred patients and experienced, professional therapists). Of those, only 15 met additional criteria for "treatment as usual." They did find a significant positive effect for psychotherapy for adults (effect sizes of 0.68 and 0.58 for the sets of 56 and 15 studies, respectively).

These studies pointed out a glaring gap in our knowledge of the benefits of psychotherapy. Researchers have steadily improved the internal validity of treatment studies by using randomized clinical trials and homogeneous groups of patients, and by training and monitoring the therapists. However, maximizing the internal validity of a study always comes with a cost—namely, a reduction in external validity (see Chapter 4 to review these concepts of validity). Psychotherapy researchers are increasingly aware of the need for research that has reasonable external validity without entirely sacrificing the controls necessary for sufficient internal validity. Accordingly, in a growing number of treatment studies, investigators conduct little or no screening of patients or provide no ongoing supervision of therapists (beyond an initial training workshop). These effectiveness trials are designed to explore treatment effects under truly "real-world" conditions.

A recent review examined the results of these effectiveness studies. Using a benchmarking strategy in which the results of efficacy trials are used as a point of comparison, Hunsley and Lee (2007) examined the results of effectiveness studies for adults and youth. Using benchmarks for treatment completion and treatment outcome derived from meta-analyses of efficacy studies, they reported that, for the treatment of adult depression and anxiety disorders, it was typical for more than 75 percent of patients to follow the course of services to completion. This was comparable to completion rates reported in efficacy trials. With respect to treatment outcome, most of the effectiveness studies reported results that were comparable or superior to those obtained in efficacy studies. Almost identical results were obtained for effectiveness studies for child and adolescent mood and anxiety disorders. Consistent with these findings, a meta-analysis of effectiveness studies of CBT for adult anxiety disorders found that the mean outcome of treatment in over 50 effectiveness studies was consistent with results obtained in efficacy studies (Stewart & Chambless, 2009). Thus, the evidence to date from various countries indicates that many evidence-based treatments for adults and youth can be very effective when used in regular practice settings.

6 BEFORE MOVING ON

What are the common disorders for which there are efficacious treatments? Additionally, what are the common disorders with which we do not yet have efficacious treatments?

EVIDENCE-BASED PRACTICE

Over the past two decades, health care systems in most Western countries have been restructured. Governments, insurance companies, and hospital health care professionals have recognized the importance of basing health care services on established scientific findings rather than on practitioners' assumptions. Psychotherapy is not exempt from this trend, and there is growing pressure to develop standards for **evidence-based practice**.

In 1993 the American Psychological Association's first Task Force on Promotion and Dissemination of Psychological Procedures set out to (1) develop criteria to determine whether a psychosocial intervention has been demonstrated empirically to be effective; and (2) suggest methods for educating clinical psychologists, third-party payers, and the public about effective psychotherapies. The criteria introduced by this task force for obtaining the designation as an **empirically supported therapy** (Chambless et al., 1996) are presented in Table 17.5. The first task force, along with two subsequent task forces, also released a list of treatments that were considered to have met these criteria. In the UK, a group of psychotherapy researchers working with the National Health Service developed similar criteria and lists of treatments (Roth & Fonagy, 1996). Subsequently, an American Psychological Association (APA) presidential task force was struck to recommend APA policies and practices with respect to evidence-based practice (APA Presidential Task Force on Evidence-Based Practice, 2006). In its report, the task force defined evidence-based practice as the integration of the best available research and clinical expertise within the context of patient characteristics, culture, values, and treatment preferences. To provide you with a sense of the evidence-based treatments available for psychologists to use, Tables 17.6 and 17.7 summarize the disorders and conditions for which

TABLE 17.5 CRITERIA FOR DESIGNATION AS AN EMPIRICALLY SUPPORTED THERAPY

One of two sets of studies are necessary:

I. At least 2 group design studies (that is, randomized clinical trials), demonstrating efficacy by being:
   A. Superior to pill, psychological placebo, or another treatment
   B. Equivalent to an already established treatment, in studies with adequate statistical power (that is, at least 30 participants per group)

II. At least 10 single-case-design studies demonstrating efficacy. These studies must have:
   A. Used good experimental designs
   B. Compared the intervention to another treatment, as in I (A)

Furthermore, for both criterion I and criterion II:

A. Studies must be conducted with treatment manuals.
B. The characteristics of the participants must be clearly described.
C. Treatment effects must have been found by at least two different researchers or research teams.

Source: Adapted from Chambless et al. (1996).

TABLE 17.6 CHILD AND ADOLESCENT DISORDERS/CONDITIONS FOR WHICH THERE ARE EVIDENCE-BASED TREATMENTS

Anxiety disorders
- Post-traumatic stress disorder

Obsessive-compulsive disorder
- Separation anxiety disorder
- Specific phobias

Autism

Disruptive behaviour disorders
- Attention deficit/hyperactivity disorder
- Oppositional defiant disorder
- Conduct disorder

Elimination disorders
- Encopresis
- Enuresis

Major depressive disorder

Pain disorders

Substance abuse disorders

Other conditions
- Distress due to medical procedures
- Obesity

evidence-based psychotherapies are available (Chambless & Ollendick, 2001; Nathan & Gorman, 2007; Silverman & Hinshaw, 2008).

The momentum for evidence-based practice in psychology continues to grow. For example, the APA and the Canadian Psychological Association require that clinical psychology training programs and internships train students in some evidence-based treatments. However, not all psychologists are supportive of such moves. Some researchers feel that the criteria for evidence-based or empirically supported treatments are too lax. Conversely, some practitioners object to this development, fearing that health care agencies and companies will refuse to support any other therapies.

Drawing upon the substantial research base on the process of psychotherapy, the APA Division of Psychotherapy commissioned a task force to evaluate and disseminate information on **empirically supported therapy relationships (ESR)**. The two major aims of the ESR task force were to identify elements of effective therapy relationships and to determine efficacious methods of individually tailoring therapy to patient characteristics. A summary of this work was published in a book that provided the full research reviews, detailed therapeutic practices, and task force recommendations (Norcross, 2002). A decade after this groundbreaking work, the APA Division of Psychotherapy and the Division of Clinical Psychology collaborated in commissioning a task

TABLE 17.7 ADULT DISORDERS/CONDITIONS FOR WHICH THERE ARE EVIDENCE-BASED TREATMENTS

Anxiety disorders
- Panic disorder with and without agoraphobia
- Blood-injection-injury phobia
- Generalized anxiety disorder
- Obsessive-compulsive disorder
- Post-traumatic stress disorder
- Social phobia
- Specific phobias

Dementia

Eating disorders
- Anorexia nervosa
- Bulimia nervosa
- Binge-eating disorder

Mood disorders
- Bipolar disorder
- Major depressive disorder

Paraphilias

Personality disorders
- Avoidant personality disorder
- Borderline personality disorder

Schizophrenia

Sexual dysfunction
- Female orgasmic disorder
- Hypoactive sexual desire
- Male erectile dysfunction
- Premature ejaculation
- Vaginismus

Sleep disorders

Somatoform disorders
- Body dysmorphic disorder
- Hypochondriasis
- Pain disorders

Substance-related disorders
- Alcohol abuse and alcohol dependence
- Benzodiazepine withdrawal for panic disorder
- Cocaine abuse
- Opiod dependence

Other conditions/disorders
- Geriatric caregivers' distress
- Irritable bowel syndrome
- Marital distress
- Obesity
- Side effects of chemotherapy
- Smoking cessation
- Stress management

force to update the findings on evidence-based therapy relationships (Norcross, 2011). They concluded that the following elements of the therapeutic relationship are demonstrably or probably effective in influencing treatment outcome: therapeutic alliance (in individual adult therapy, therapy for youth, and family therapy), cohesion in group therapy, therapist empathy and positive regard, monitoring of client treatment progress, and patient–therapist goal consensus and collaboration. With respect to patient behaviours or characteristics, the task force found evidence that patient resistance, readiness for change, treatment preferences, cultural background, copying style, and treatment expectations were demonstrably or probably effective as factors for customizing therapy. Finally, one of the task force's main recommendations was that the concurrent use of evidence-based therapy relationship factors within the context of providing evidence-based treatments is likely to generate the best clinical outcome for patients.

Organizations such as the American Psychological Association and the Canadian Psychological Association have published guidelines on working with specific populations. Another important initiative with respect to evidence-based treatments is the development of **clinical practice guidelines**. Practice guidelines often draw together the research evidence for the assessment, diagnosis, and treatment of a specific disorder. Usually developed by an expert working group, these guidelines are meant to be used as tools for clinical training and service delivery. Such guidelines have been developed by a number of psychiatric associations and some government-sponsored health agencies. Most recently, the American Psychological Association has begun to develop practice guidelines for specific disorders.

When people suffering from a psychological disorder decide to seek treatment, they often face a difficult decision—whether to take medication or to begin psychotherapy. As we have indicated in this chapter, there is evidence that both options can be helpful. Conversely, it is clear that neither option works for all people. Evidence-based clinical guidelines for the management of depression and anxiety offer authoritative recommendations on the treatment options (National Institute for Health and Clinical Excellence [NICE], 2009, 2011). A key element of these guidelines is that the foundation of good treatment includes early detection, sound assessment, and person-centred care involving treatments that have been shown to be helpful for each level of symptom severity. For example, after reviewing the best available research on pharmacological treatment, psychological treatment, and combined treatments for depression, NICE made the following recommendations: (1) antidepressants should not be offered as the first treatment for mild depression, because the risk–benefit ratio is poor; (2) in the treatment of mild to moderate depression, patients should be offered a low-intensity cognitive-behavioural treatment that is delivered as individual guided self-help, computerized CBT, or a structured group physical activity program; and (3) patients with moderate or severe depression should receive combined medication (SSRI) and high-intensity psychological intervention (CBT or IPT). In the treatment of anxiety, it is recommended that the first step is to communicate the diagnosis and explain the disorder. Next, individuals are offered a low-intensity psychological intervention, which could include self-help, with or without brief facilitation, or participation in a psychoeducational group. Only individuals with more severe symptoms or those who have not responded to low-intensity psychological interventions are offered high-intensity cognitive-behavioural treatment or medication with an SSRI for anxiety disorders.

These guidelines do not assume that medication should be the first line of treatment for most psychological disorders. Although a pharmacological intervention may be the best first-line treatment for disorders such as schizophrenia and bipolar disorder, there is reason to be cautious in drawing this conclusion about psychopharmacological treatment in general. Moreover, psychotropic medication is commonly prescribed for conditions for which there are no supporting efficacy data. In the final analysis, it is unwise to think too generally about whether pharmaceutical or psychological treatments are best—instead, the evidence for the various treatment options must be examined. People's preferences must also be considered. Some individuals may not be good candidates for psychological interventions on the basis of their personal characteristics and social conditions. Likewise, some people may not be good candidates for psychotropic medication or may decide to discontinue medication because of side effects. A most reasoned, evidence-based approach to patient care should consider what treatment, or combination of treatments, might work best for a given individual at a particular point in time. In other words, research evidence, clinical expertise, and patient preferences are all key components of evidence-based practice for mental disorders that should be considered in any treatment decision.

In the eyes of many clinical psychologists, the field of psychotherapy research has matured sufficiently to warrant the promotion of psychotherapy as an evidence-based health service for many conditions and disorders. When combined with empirical evidence on important aspects of the therapeutic relationship, evidence-based treatments have a great deal to offer many people suffering from a range of health and psychological problems. In the relatively short time since Freud, psychotherapy has moved from being an esoteric set of practices based entirely on speculation and supposition to an essential health care service with substantial foundations in solid scientific knowledge.

7 **BEFORE MOVING ON**

For psychologists who wish to offer evidence-based services, which lines of research are most relevant?

CANADIAN RESEARCH CENTRE

Dr. Keith S. Dobson

Keith Dobson, Ph.D., is a professor of clinical psychology at the University of Calgary. His research is in the area of cognitive aspects of clinical depression and cognitive-behavioural therapy. He has co-authored or co-edited numerous books, including *Handbook of Cognitive-Behavioral Therapies, The Prevention of Anxiety and Depression,* and *Evidence-Based Practice of Cognitive-Behavioral Therapy.* He has also published more than 180 research articles and chapters, and has participated widely in conferences, both locally and abroad. Dr. Dobson has also served as a member or chair of a large number of committees of national and international organizations, including a term as president of the Canadian Psychological Association. In 2001 he was awarded the CPA Professional Award for Distinguished Contributions to the Profession of Psychology.

Clinical depression is one of the more common and debilitating mental disorders. Identifying effective treatments is an important task; however, because depression is often a recurrent problem, it is necessary to examine the long-term effects of treatment. Dr. Dobson was involved in a clinical trial that examined these issues, in conjunction with collaborators at the University of Washington and Vanderbilt University in the United States.

A total of 151 depressed patients were carefully assessed, and then randomly assigned to one of three active treatments (cognitive therapy, behavioural activation therapy, SSRI medication [Paxil]) or to a medication placebo condition. Patients treated with medications had better outcomes than did those assigned to receive a placebo, which confirmed that the treatments overall were efficacious. Patients receiving the three active treatments did not differ on most outcome measures, suggesting a relatively equal benefit from each treatment (although significantly more medicated patients dropped out of the study, mostly due to adverse side effects).

At the end of the active phase of psychological treatment, the medication group was divided into a group that continued to receive medication and a second group that was switched to the placebo. Relapse rates were higher in the continued medication group than in the two groups that had received psychological treatment; those on placebo had the poorest outcome. In the second year of follow-up, when medications were withdrawn, the previously medicated patients deteriorated rapidly, whereas those previously treated with psychological interventions maintained their gains. Cost estimates showed that although medication was a cheaper alternative in the first part of the study, the costs of maintaining patients on medication in the first year of follow-up were substantial. Further details on these and other results can be found in Dimidjian and colleagues (2006) and Dobson and colleagues (2008).

SUMMARY

- ECT is a last-resort treatment for severely depressed individuals who have not responded to other treatment and are at suicidal risk.
- It is associated with short-term benefits, but these must be balanced with cognitive side effects.
- Psychoactive drugs have proven to be effective in treating a wide range of disorders.
- Psychopharmacological treatment includes phenothiazines, used to treat psychotic disorders; anxiolytics for anxiety disorders; MAOIs, TCAs, SRRIs, and SNRIs for depression; mood stabilizers for bipolar disorders; and stimulants for ADHD.
- Psychotherapy is offered by diverse mental health professionals using a variety of theoretical orientations.
- It has been shown to be effective in the treatment of many Axis I and some Axis II disorders.
- Psychodynamic approaches assume that much of the client's distress stems from patterns developed early in life.
- Humanistic-experiential approaches focus on emotional aspects of subjective experience, highlighting the impact of affect in the client's current life situation.
- Cognitive-behavioural approaches focus on internal (thoughts, images, emotions, bodily sensations) and external (fear-arousing objects, interpersonal interactions) stimuli in shaping the client's adaptive and maladaptive reactions.
- Individual therapy is the most common.
- Couples therapy can be effective in treating relationship difficulties.

- Family therapy addresses the way that family patterns maintain or resolve problems.
- Group therapy is a cost-effective way to deliver services.
- Efficacy trials use highly controlled randomized clinical trials to establish that the treatment works.
- Effectiveness research examines whether the treatment can be just as useful when transported to a real-world context.
- Meta-analyses are an efficient way to synthesize results from diverse studies.
- Clinical practice guidelines are based on the best available data and often use a stepped-care approach.

MySearchLab offers you extensive help with your writing and research projects and provides round-the-clock access to credible and reliable source material. Chapter quizzes and a full electronic version of the text are also provided. Answers to the Before Moving On feature are provided on the MySearchLab. Take a tour at www.mysearchlab.com.

KEY TERMS

psychoactive agents (p. 444)
extrapyramidal effects (p. 445)
transference (p. 449)
ego analysts (p. 450)
interpersonal psychodynamic psychotherapy (p. 450)
time-limited dynamic psychotherapy (TLDP) (p. 450)
therapeutic alliance (p. 450)
client-centred therapy (p. 450)
emotion-focused therapy (p. 451)
response shaping (p. 452)
exposure therapy (p. 452)
systematic desensitization (p. 452)
problem-solving approach (p. 453)
cognitive restructuring (p. 453)
emotionally focused couples therapy (p. 454)
reframing (p. 454)
treatment efficacy (p. 456)
treatment effectiveness (p. 456)
meta-analysis (p. 457)
effect size (p. 457)
evidence-based practice (p. 462)
empirically supported therapy (p. 462)
empirically supported therapy relationships (p. 463)
clinical practice guidelines (p. 464)

GEOFFREY NELSON • ISAAC PRILLELTENSKY • JULIAN HASFORD

Chapter 18

Prevention and Mental Health Promotion in the Community

LEARNING OBJECTIVES

AFTER READING THIS CHAPTER, STUDENTS WILL BE ABLE TO:

1. Define and distinguish the major types of prevention and mental health promotion.
2. Provide a historical perspective on the field of prevention.
3. Explain and give examples of how the concepts of risk, resilience, and protection are important for prevention.
4. Describe the Strengths, Prevention, Empowerment, and Community Change conceptual framework for prevention.
5. Give examples of research on the high-risk and universal approaches to prevention.
6. Understand Canadian policy on prevention and mental health promotion.
7. Note some of the key issues in program implementation, dissemination, and social justice.

The birth of a baby is typically a joyous event for a family. However, after giving birth, some mothers become depressed, experiencing a condition commonly known as postpartum depression. This form of depression can be treated in various ways: with medication, talk therapies, diet and nutrition, home visitation by nurses, or other forms of social support. But can some of the far-reaching adverse consequences of postpartum depression be prevented? In seven Ontario communities, Dennis and colleagues (2009) studied a one-to-one peer support program designed to prevent postpartum depression. Women at risk for postpartum depression were randomly assigned to either standard postnatal care or standard postnatal care plus telephone-based peer support from a mother who previously experienced postpartum depression. Twelve weeks after the program started, 14 percent of the women who received peer support experienced high levels of depression, which was a significantly lower rate than the 25 percent of those who received only standard care.

In the field of abnormal psychology, the dominant emphasis has been on expanding our understanding of the nature and etiology of mental disorders and on developing effective treatments. Throughout this book, we have considered the manifestations and effects of specific disorders on individuals. But people do not live in isolation; they belong to families, communities, and societies. In this chapter, we consider the mental health not only of individuals but also of whole communities. We begin by briefly outlining the field of community psychology, which has highlighted the need for the prevention of mental disorders and the promotion of mental health.

Community Psychology

The term **community psychology** was first coined by Canadian psychologist William Line in 1951. In the United States, community psychology had its roots in clinical psychology. Some clinically trained psychologists began to question the appropriateness of an exclusive reliance on treatment approaches. They recognized that the prevalence of mental disorders far outstrips the availability of professional help.

Epidemiological studies have shown that the one-year prevalence rate of mental disorders for adults (Offord et al., 1994) and the six-month prevalence rate for children (Offord et al., 1987) in Ontario is about 18 percent of the population. Waddell and colleagues (2005) estimate that at any given time 14 percent of Canadian children aged 4 to 17 (i.e., more than 800 000) suffer from a mental disorder. What is more, as discussed in Chapter 15, childhood disorders can often set the stage for ongoing problems in adulthood, which cause great misery to those afflicted and to their families and cost Canadians \$11 billion to \$15 billion annually.

There are not, and never could be, enough trained mental health professionals to provide therapeutic interventions for the large number of children and adults worldwide who are afflicted with mental disorders (Albee, 1990). Moreover, as is clear from Chapter 17, no therapeutic intervention is 100 percent effective. Furthermore, most children with mental disorders do not receive treatment for their mental health problems (only 17 percent do, according to the findings of the Ontario Child Health study; Offord et al., 1987). As well, more than half of mental, emotional, and behavioural disorders begin in childhood or adolescence (O'Connell, Boat, & Warner, 2009). As Waddell, McEwan, Peters, Hua, and Garland (2007, p. 174) state:

> It is increasingly evident that treatment services alone cannot reduce the burden of illness. As well, the understanding that many mental disorders arise during childhood has encouraged a shift toward considering prevention. Preventing mental disorders requires placing children at the centre of a public mental health strategy.

For these reasons, much of the prevention and mental health promotion literature discussed in this chapter focuses on children and youth. It is important for the reader to know that only methods oriented toward prevention have been successful in reducing rates of health problems: "[A]s the history of public health methods (that emphasize social change) has clearly established, no mass disease or disorder afflicting humankind has ever been eliminated by attempts at treating affected individuals" (Albee, 1990, p. 370).

In addition to its emphasis on prevention, community psychology has a number of other identifying features that distinguish it from clinical psychology (Nelson & Prilleltensky, 2010). Whereas clinical psychology has historically focused on the individual or micro level (e.g., the family) in diagnosis and treatment, community psychology applies an ecological perspective that stresses the interdependence of the individual, the family, the community, and society. Community psychologists believe that interventions for many problems should address multiple levels of analysis. For example, psychotherapy may be somewhat helpful to a family living in poverty, but social policies that reduce poverty may play an even more important role. Sensitivity to a person's social context and appreciation of diversity are key themes of community psychology (Reich, Riemer, Prilleltensky, & Montero, 2007).

Another difference is that, in contrast to the clinical psychology focus on deficits and on reducing maladaptive behaviours, community psychology tends to pay more attention to people's strengths and to the promotion of mental health and well-being (Prilleltensky & Prilleltensky, 2006). The community psychologist often functions as an enabler, a consultant, or a planner, rather than as an expert in diagnosis and treatment. The working style of the community psychologist emphasizes collaboration and participation of diverse groups from the community in planning, implementing, and evaluating interventions.

Community psychologists believe in the importance of informal social supports rather than an exclusive reliance on professional help. So, for example, community psychologists may help people who are experiencing a problem, such as depression, to form self-help/mutual aid groups. Research has shown that this alternative approach of supporting one another can be quite effective (Pistrang, Barker, & Humphreys, 2010).

Finally, with its U.S. roots in the 1960s, community psychology is oriented to social justice and social change. Community psychologists do not see themselves as value-neutral scientists, because to do so would be to accept the status quo of unjust social conditions. Rather, community psychology has a clear emphasis on values and social ethics (Nelson & Prilleltensky, 2010). The elimination of poverty, racism, sexism, and other forms of social injustice are viewed not only as important in preventing problems, but also as moral imperatives in the work of community psychology.

Prevention and Mental Health Promotion: Some Definitions

PRIMARY, SECONDARY, AND TERTIARY PREVENTION

Historically, the concept of **prevention** of mental disorders developed from the fields of physical disease, public health, and epidemiology. Graham (1994, p. 815) distinguished three levels of prevention:

> By convention, three types of preventive activity are recognized. **Primary prevention** involves intervention that reduces the incidence of disorder. **Secondary prevention** comprises treatment that reduces the duration of the disorder, and **tertiary prevention** covers rehabilitative activity that reduces the disability arising from an established disorder.

In secondary prevention, the disorder has already occurred, but its duration is reduced through early detection and effective treatment (Caplan, 1964).

In this chapter, we use the term *prevention* to mean primary prevention. There are three key features in our definition of prevention:

1. With successful prevention, new cases of a problem do not occur.
2. Prevention is not aimed at individuals but at populations; the goal is a decline in rates of disorder.
3. Preventive interventions intentionally focus on preventing mental health problems (Cowen, 1980).

UNIVERSAL, SELECTIVE, AND INDICATED PREVENTION

The typology of primary, secondary, and tertiary prevention has given way to a new typology of universal, selective, and indicated prevention developed by the U.S. Institute of Medicine (1994). The **universal approach** is designed to include all individuals in a particular geographical area (e.g., neighbourhood, city, province) or particular setting (e.g., school, workplace, public housing complex).

In contrast to universal prevention, **selective prevention**, also known as the high-risk approach, is based on the assumption that there are known risk factors for certain mental health problems, and prevention has the greatest effect in targeting individuals most exposed to these risk factors. Selective prevention targets participants on the basis of characteristics external to the participant (e.g., children whose parents have divorced) and/or on internal characteristics of the participant (e.g., cognitive vulnerability to anxiety or depression). Finally, several programs have selected participants who show mild or early-developing mental health problems (e.g., young children showing antisocial behaviour). These programs are sometimes referred to as **indicated prevention** programs, but might more appropriately be called early intervention, or what was previously called secondary prevention programs. In contrast, universal and selective prevention approaches are examples of what was previously called primary prevention.

MENTAL HEALTH PROMOTION

Complementary to prevention is the concept of **mental health promotion**. Whereas prevention, by definition, focuses on reducing problems, promotion focuses on enhancing well-being. Many people think of **mental health** in negative terms, as the absence of disorder. However, a broader view defines mental health, or well-being, in positive terms, as the presence of optimal social, emotional, and cognitive functioning (Peters, 1988). According to the Epp (1988, p. 7) report *Mental Health for Canadians: Striking a Balance*:

> Mental health is the capacity of the individual, the group and the environment to interact

with one another in ways that promote subjective well-being, the optimal development and use of mental abilities (cognitive, affective, and relational), the achievement of individual and collective goals consistent with justice and the attainment and preservation of conditions of fundamental equality.

In the Epp report, mental health and mental disorder are viewed as conceptually distinct. There is a mental disorder continuum ranging from severe mental disorder (e.g., florid schizophrenia) to the absence of mental disorder, and a mental health continuum ranging from minimal mental health (e.g., poor coping skills, low self-esteem) to optimal mental health (e.g., good coping skills, high self-esteem). Recent research in the United States has confirmed that mental health and mental disorder are two different dimensions (Keyes, 2010).

The Canadian Population Health Initiative (Canadian Institute for Health Information, 2009) has operationalized positive mental health in terms of five components: (1) the ability to enjoy life, (2) the ability to deal with life's challenges, (3) emotional well-being, (4) spiritual well-being, and (5) social connections and respect for culture, equity, social justice, and personal dignity.

Having identified the qualities of positive mental health, the question arises as to how mental health can be promoted. Cowen (1996) identifies four key characteristics of mental health promotion.

1. It is proactive; it seeks to promote mental health before mental health problems have taken root.
2. It focuses on populations, not individuals.
3. It is multi-dimensional, focusing on "integrated sets of operations involving individuals, families, settings, community contexts, and macrolevel societal structures and policies" (Cowen, 1996, p. 246).
4. It is ongoing, not a one-shot, time-limited intervention.

In practice, prevention and mental health promotion go together, and a program will normally involve elements of both, inextricably intertwined. Enhancing well-being will often prevent problems, and preventing problems may enhance well-being. The Canadian Institute for Health Information (CIHI, 2009, p. 47) has described mental health promotion as follows:

> Mental health promotion typically emphasizes supporting individual resilience, creating supportive environments and addressing the influence of the broader determinants of mental health. Specific goals of mental health promotion include enhancing protective factors that help individuals, families and communities to deal with events, and increasing conditions, such as social cohesion, that reduce risk factors for diminished mental health among individuals, families and communities.

Moreover, CIHI emphasizes an **ecological approach** to mental health promotion, asserting that strategies to promote mental health can be implemented at the societal, community, and individual levels of analysis.

1. *Societal-level strategies.* The CIHI (2009) report underscored the importance of changing social policies to promote mental health. Two different policy streams were identified. One stream involves social policies that indirectly affect positive mental health through distal socio-political conditions, such as economic inequality, housing, education, racism, and sexism (Joffe & Albee, 1981). The other policy stream involves identifying the characteristics of more proximal supportive environments associated with positive mental health and instituting policies that create or enhance the supportive qualities of these environments (Cowen, 2000; Moos, 1996). This policy stream is aimed at more local settings, such as schools, neighbourhoods, churches, and workplaces.
2. *Community-level strategies.* The CIHI (2009) report suggests that empowering community residents is an important community-level strategy for promoting mental health. *Empowerment* refers to perceived and actual control over one's life (Rappaport, 1987; also see Chapter 7 for a discussion of the relationship between stress and control). Empowering interventions are those that enhance participants' "voice and choice" (self-determination and democratic participation) and that are directed and controlled by citizens (Prilleltensky, 1994a). The Better Beginnings, Better Futures project in Ontario, which is discussed later in the chapter, is a good example of how community residents can be empowered to improve their communities and the lives of their children and families (Peters, Bradshaw, et al., 2010). Building a strong sense of community and social support is also important for the promotion of mental health. Family, school, and workplace programs are important settings in which mental health can be enhanced (CIHI, 2009).
3. *Individual-level strategies.* The development of age-appropriate skills and competencies is an individual-level strategy for the enhancement of mental health (CIHI, 2009). Social competencies (e.g., social problem-solving skills, assertiveness, interpersonal skills), academic competencies, and work competencies are all important for mental health. Comprehensive, well-integrated, ongoing programs that are institutionalized in social settings show the most promise for the promotion of social competence and mental health (Weissberg & Greenberg, 1998). Also, the ability to cope effectively with stressful life events and conditions is another key pathway to mental health. Throughout life, we face both expected stressors, such as life transitions, and unexpected stressful events. Therefore, skills and resources to meet the challenges posed by stressors

are essential for mental health. Research has demonstrated that some individuals are extremely resilient and able to withstand life stressors (e.g., Luthar, Cicchetti, & Becker, 2000). Moreover, stressors are often seen as presenting an opportunity for growth. Programs that build up resources to cope with stress can potentially promote mental health.

1 BEFORE MOVING ON

A program to prevent postpartum depression was described at the beginning of the chapter. What type of prevention program was this, and how might this program also promote mental health?

Historical Perspective

PRE–GERM THEORY ERA

In the eighteenth century, people believed that disease resulted from "miasmas," or noxious odours, that emanated from soil polluted with waste products. Miasmatists believed that the way to prevent disease was to clean up the environment (Bloom, 1984). Through the development of sewage disposal and sanitation campaigns, the rates of many diseases (e.g., typhoid fever, yellow fever, typhus) dropped dramatically. Some nutritional diseases were reduced without knowledge of the precise cause of the disease. For example, British sailors became known as "limeys" because they learned to prevent scurvy by eating citrus fruits, long before it was known that this disease resulted from a deficiency of vitamin C. This is a useful perspective for mental health, a field in which, as we have seen in almost every chapter of this book, etiology is usually complex and impossible to completely pin down.

PUBLIC HEALTH APPROACH

The next major impetus to the field of prevention was the public health approach, based on epidemiology (the study of the distribution and determinants of disease in a population; see Chapter 4).

The traditional **public health approach** is characterized by the following steps:

1. identifying a disease and developing a reliable diagnostic method (descriptive epidemiology);
2. developing a theory of the disease's course of development based on laboratory and epidemiological research (analytic epidemiology); and
3. developing and evaluating a disease prevention program (experimental epidemiology) (Bloom, 1984).

Public health researchers tend to focus on three components: (1) characteristics of the host (that is, the person who contracts the disease); (2) characteristics of the environment (that is, stressors); and (3) the agent (that is, the manner in which the disease is transmitted to the host). The thrust of public health promotion is generally twofold: to reduce environmental stressors while enhancing people's capacities to withstand those stressors. In the mental health field, for example, one could attempt to prevent substance abuse problems by strengthening the host (e.g., teaching teens how to deal with peer pressure to drink or take drugs), changing the environment (e.g., providing good alternative activities in the community for youth), and targeting the agent (e.g., regulating sales and reducing access to alcohol and drugs).

The public health approach has been very successful in reducing the incidence of many problems, including some mental health problems. For example, the incidence of general paresis, an organic psychosis resulting from syphilitic infection (see Chapter 1), has been greatly reduced as a result of this approach. Yet this approach is effective only with diseases that have a single identified precursor or cause, be it a vitamin deficiency or a germ. As shown throughout this book, very few mental health problems have a single cause (Albee, 1982).

EDUCATIONAL APPROACH

While prevention of mental disorders was strongly influenced by the field of public health, prevention and mental health promotion have shifted more toward an educational approach. More specifically, there has been a great deal of interest recently in early childhood development (ECD) programs for preschool children as a method of prevention (Barnett, 2011). While ECD programs have been found to be successful in reaching their explicit goal of enhancing children's cognitive and academic outcomes (Camilli, Vargas, Ryan, & Barnett, 2010), long-term follow-up studies have found that these programs also have profound impacts on health (O'Nise, Lynch, Sawyer, & McDermott, 2010) and socio-emotional development, including lower rates of crime (Manning, Homel, & Smith, 2010). While there are several examples of effective selective, or high-risk, ECD approaches in the United States (Camilli et al., 2010; Manning et al., 2010), some European countries have implemented ECD programs universally (Melhuish, 2011). For example, France has had universal, free preschool programs (l'école maternelle) starting at age three since the 1960s and 1970s. Not only has this program been effective in promoting success in school and the labour market, but it has also been shown to have a greater impact on children from economically disadvantaged families (Melhuish, 2011). ECD research has also had impacts on policies, with governments viewing ECD programs as a sound way to invest in the future (Gormley, 2011). For example, in 2010 the Ontario government began implementing a universal, full-day early learning program for kindergarten-age children.

2 BEFORE MOVING ON

The history of public health suggests that some health problems can be effectively prevented without knowing the precise cause of the problems. What are the implications of this observation for the prevention of mental health problems?

Resilience, Risk, and Protection

RESILIENCE, RISK, AND PROTECTIVE FACTORS

As discussed in Chapter 2, as knowledge of any mental disorder grows, single-factor explanations are generally replaced by interactionist explanations that view behaviour as the product of the interaction of a variety of factors. The resilience approach reflects this complexity, focusing not on single factors but on many risk and protective factors. **Resilience** refers to the process of positive adaptation to significant adversity through the interaction of risk and protective factors (Luthar et al., 2000). **Risk factors** are the conditions or events that increase the likelihood of negative mental health outcomes, whereas **protective factors** are assets or resources that help to offset, or buffer, risk factors (Fergus & Zimmerman, 2005). For example, a person with a good social support network or good coping skills may adjust well to a stressful life event such as marital separation or job loss.

Over the past 30 years, a substantial amount of research has confirmed that most mental health problems are associated with many different risk and protective factors—most of which are, in turn, associated with many different types of mental health problems. Researchers have recognized the need to go beyond identifying general risk and protective factors to understanding how these factors operate and how they interact in context. Ecological studies of resilience have examined the interaction of risk and protective factors in context at the **microsystem** (e.g., small settings in which a child directly participates) and **macrosystem** (larger social systems of culture, norms, etc.) levels of analysis (Sandler, 2001). For example, in a review of environmental and social influences on mental health, Shinn and Toohey (2003) demonstrated the powerful effects of neighbourhood context. They cite studies in which children who moved from the inner city to affluent suburbs did much better in school than children who remained in deprived neighbourhoods. No attempts were made to modify children's behaviour in the new environment. The new context of better-equipped schools with norms of high achievement accounted for the positive outcomes displayed, such as better rates of graduation, better college attendance, and better employment records. They also emphasize the impact of context on parenting. In high-risk contexts, a controlling parenting style is more protective than is a permissive attitude toward teens. Contexts influence mental health in diverse ways, and the wisdom lies in crafting interventions that attend to the changing nature of social conditions.

Risk factors and protective factors do not affect everyone in the same way. Resilience researchers have considered how dimensions of human diversity shape resilience, and have found that characteristics such as gender, age, and ethnicity can influence the interactions between risk factors, protective factors, and mental health outcomes. For instance, it has been suggested that divorce affects young boys more strongly than it does young girls in the short term, but that girls suffer from "sleeper effects": they feel the consequences of parental divorce later in adolescence (Gore & Eckenrode, 1994). Another illustration of diversity concerns early parental loss. Losing a parent at a young age has been implicated in vulnerability to later psychiatric disorder. Brown and his colleagues found that girls who lost their mothers before age 11 were likely to experience depression later in life, but only if they did not have adequate care after the loss. This finding suggests that it is not so much the grief of losing a parent that predisposes children to psychiatric disorders as the fact that a child who has lost a parent is likely to receive poor care (Brown, Harris, & Bifulco, 1986).

At this point in our knowledge, it is difficult to connect specific risk factors and protective factors with specific forms of abnormal behaviour (see the discussion of the diathesis-stress and biopsychosocial models in Chapter 2 for an indication of how complex the relationships among factors can be). Furthermore, not all risk factors and protective factors have a direct impact on a person's mental health. Some have an immediate impact; others influence functioning indirectly. Some common risk factors and protective factors for mental health are presented in Tables 18.1 and 18.2.

CUMULATIVE RISK

The effects of risk are cumulative: the more of these factors that are present, the more vulnerable a person is to a wide range of mental health problems. Research on **cumulative risk** has shown that the number of risk factors experienced

TABLE 18.1 SOME GENERAL RISK FACTORS

Ecological Level	Domain	Risk Factor
Individual	Socio-emotional	Anxiety Social incompetence
	Cognitive	Attentional deficits Learning disabilities
	Biological	Sensory disabilities Perinatal complications
	Behavioural	Aggression Delinquency
Microsystem	Peers	Peer rejection Delinquent peers
	Families	Hostile parenting Single-parent status Mental illness in the family Family dysfunction Child abuse by parents Parental unemployment
	Schools	Poor school quality Scholastic demoralization
	Neighbourhood/ Community	Neighbourhood disorganization Neighbourhood disadvantage
Macrosystem	Socio-political	Social inequality Systemic discrimination

TABLE 18.2 SOME GENERAL PROTECTIVE FACTORS

Ecological Level	Domain	Protective Factor
Individual	Socio-emotional	Self-esteem Aspirations and an inclination to plan for the future
	Cognitive	High IQ Problem-solving abilities
	Biological	Attractiveness to peers and adults Easy temperament
	Behavioural	Prosocial behaviour
Microsystem	Relational	Positive role models
	Peers	Positive peer relations
	Families	Parental monitoring Parental education
	Schools	Positive school climate Positive classroom psychosocial environment
	Neighbourhood/ Community	Social capital (feelings of trust and connection with people in the community) Community participation
Macrosystem	Socio-political	Democracy Healthy public policy

by an individual often accounts for a greater proportion of the variation in outcomes than the sum of individual risk factors. In a study of rural children in the United States, Evans (2003) found that children with a greater number of environmental risk factors experienced higher levels of physiological and psychological distress and lower levels of self-worth than those exposed to fewer risk factors. Findings from a number of cumulative risk studies suggest that the likelihood of negative outcomes increases considerably when an individual has been exposed to three or more risk factors (e.g., Forehand, Biggar, & Kotchick, 1998).

MECHANISMS OF RISK AND PROTECTION

Understanding the mechanisms of risk, protection, and resilience has important implications for prevention and promotion. According to Rutter (1987), there are four central mechanisms that can help people cope with adversity and develop positive mental health: (1) reducing risk impact; (2) interrupting unhealthy chain reactions stemming from stressful life events; (3) enhancing self-esteem and self-efficacy; and (4) creating opportunities for personal growth.

Risk impact may be reduced either by altering the risk factor itself or by altering exposure to the risk. Altering the risk means changing it in some way to minimize effects. For instance, facing a separation or a new situation without preparation constitutes a risk for young children. The risk for children who need hospitalization can be altered by taking them to visit the hospital before admission and by "practice separations" from parents in secure circumstances. Altering exposure means keeping the person away from the risky situation, or reducing involvement in its riskier aspects. For example, Rutter (1987) found that, in high-risk communities, strict parental supervision of children's activities outside the home can reduce the risk for delinquent behaviour. Placing limits on what children can do and how long they can stay outside the home minimizes exposure to the risky environment.

The mechanism of breaking a potentially damaging chain reaction can be seen in Brown and colleagues' (1986) study of parental loss: ensuring sustained, adequate care breaks the chain of harmful consequences. A nurturing environment can protect children from the consequences of loss, separation, and other risks. *Self-efficacy* can be fostered in children by offering age-appropriate tasks and sufficient rewarding experiences of control (see Chapter 2 for a fuller discussion of this concept). Finally, opportunities for personal development may be created by teaching youth social skills that they can apply in various settings, and by preventing school dropout. This last mechanism may be conceptualized as promoting beneficial chain reactions. A good education can lead to attractive jobs, a higher income, and the like. Similarly, adequate social skills can lead to friendships, which translate into social supports that have the effect of buffering stress (Gore & Eckenrode, 1994).

IMPLICATIONS OF RESILIENCE, RISK, AND PROTECTION FOR PREVENTION

Albee (1982) views the incidence of mental health problems as an equation involving risk and protective factors:

$$\text{Incidence} = \frac{\text{Risk factors}}{\text{Protective factors}} = \frac{\text{Organic causes} + \text{Stress} + \text{Exploitation}}{\text{Coping skills} + \text{Self-esteem} + \text{Support systems}}$$

Prevention can be approached from both sides: by reducing risk factors and by increasing protective factors. Elias (1987), noting that Albee's equation tends to focus on the individual, formulated a prevention equation that focuses more on the social environment. Elias's equation is as follows:

$$\frac{\text{Stressors} + \text{Risk factors in the environment}}{\text{Positive socialization experiences} + \text{Social support resources} + \text{Opportunities for positive relatedness and connectedness}}$$

The important implication for prevention from Elias's equation is that interventions designed to reduce the likelihood of behavioural and emotional problems should strive to change the social environment rather than the individual. For example, prevention programs should strive to reduce risk factors in the environment

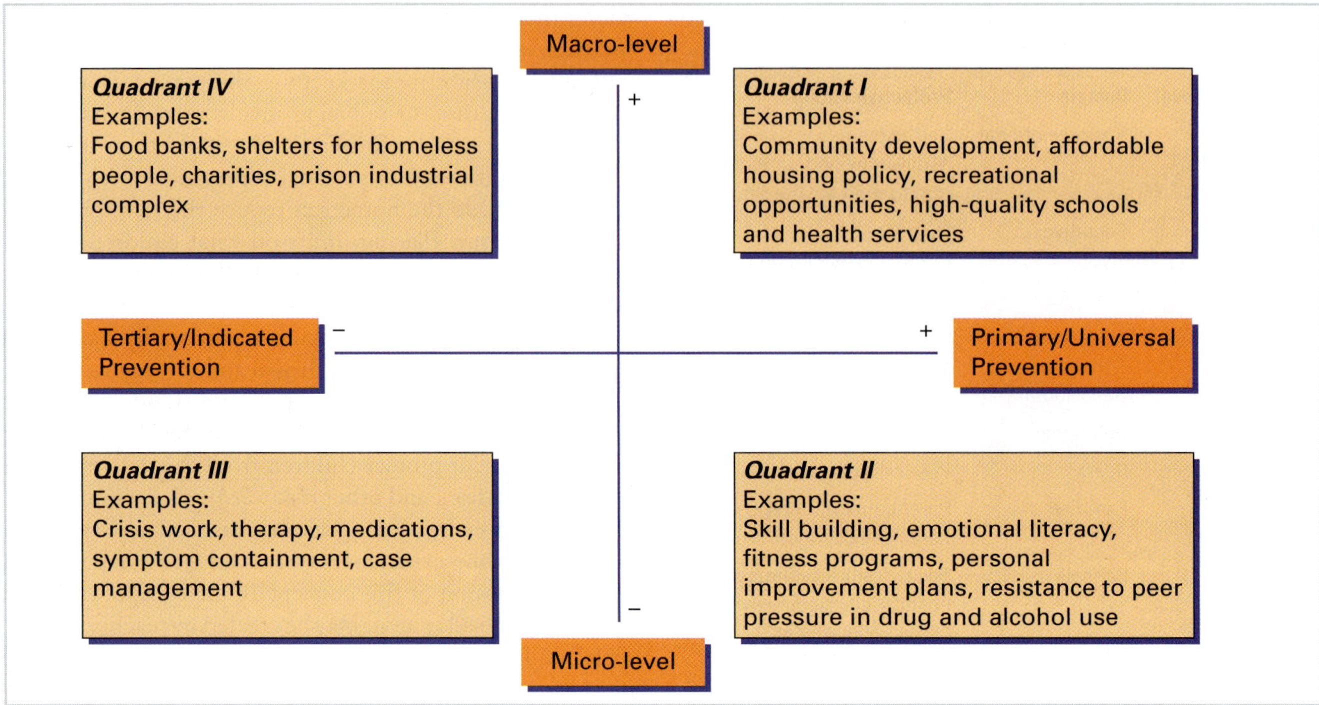

FIGURE 18.1 The Contextual Field: Intersection of Ecological and Temporal Dimensions in Prevention and Promotion

Source: Adapted from Prilleltensky (2005).

and increase the social support resources for people. The basic idea of this approach is that creating healthy environments will promote the healthy development of people and prevent mental health problems.

3 BEFORE MOVING ON

Define risk factors, protective factors, and resilience, and give an example of how these concepts are important for prevention.

A Conceptual Framework for Prevention and Promotion

Prilleltensky (2005) developed a framework for the prevention of mental health problems and the promotion of well-being consisting of four complementary dimensions: ecological, temporal, capabilities, and participation. He has called this framework *SPEC*, which stands for Strengths, Prevention, Empowerment, and Community Change. The four dimensions belong in two fields. The contextual field consists of intersecting continua of temporal and ecological dimensions, creating four contextual quadrants. The affirmation field reflects the intersections of the participation and capabilities dimensions.

THE CONTEXTUAL FIELD

A contextual approach to well-being must account for the role of temporal and ecological variables. The ecological dimension covers the full range of interventions—from micro to macro levels (see "Ecological Dimension" below). The temporal dimension, in turn, ranges from tertiary or indicated prevention to universal or primary prevention (see "Temporal Dimension" below). When the two dimensions intersect, as illustrated in Figure 18.1, a contextual field with four quadrants is formed.

ECOLOGICAL DIMENSION Some prevention and mental health promotion programs focus narrowly on a small number of influences on behaviour, or on a tightly defined set of target outcome behaviours. A growing trend, however, is for more comprehensive programs that address a broad range of personal and environmental factors as well as a broad range of outcomes (Durlak et al., 2007). These comprehensive programs are based on an **ecological perspective**, which considers multiple levels of analysis (Bronfenbrenner, 1977). Thus, mental health problems are viewed in the context of characteristics of the individual (e.g., coping skills, personality traits), the microsystem (e.g., the family, the school), and the macrosystem (e.g., social norms, social class). The levels are nested like Russian dolls: the individual within the microsystem within the macrosystem. Thus, this dimension ranges from the individual to the macrosystem.

TEMPORAL DIMENSION The timing of the intervention is another important dimension of the conceptual framework of prevention and promotion. The early concepts of primary, secondary, and tertiary prevention capture the issue of timing quite well. Primary prevention occurs before a problem has developed; secondary prevention involves early identification and intervention, as the problem is in its incipient stages of development; and tertiary prevention (treatment or rehabilitation) occurs well after the problem has developed. Thus, this dimension ranges from tertiary or indicated to primary or universal.

CONTEXTUAL QUADRANTS As seen in Figure 18.1, four quadrants are formed by the intersection of the temporal and ecological dimensions. Clockwise, Quadrant I is formed by the intersection of the positive ends of the x and y axes. Examples of collective and preventive approaches include affordable housing policies; provision of high-quality health care; incentives to achieve high educational standards; investments in education, family planning, and mental health; and progressive taxation policies that distribute wealth among the population.

Quadrant II represents interventions that are preventive but person-centred. Examples include skills building, emotional literacy, and education for proper eating and exercise to prevent physical illness. Many drug prevention programs that teach youth resistance skills and knowledge about the effects of alcohol, smoking, and illicit drugs fit into this quadrant.

Quadrant III reflects the medical model tradition whereby the intervention is aimed at containing symptoms and managing crises. Medications, therapy, and crisis intervention are the prototypical approaches in this quadrant. Practitioners wait until patients, clients, or community members complain of an ailment before intervening, usually in a medical clinic or a community agency setting.

Quadrant IV is created by the intersection of collective and indicated approaches. Food banks, shelters for homeless people, and charity efforts are aimed at alleviating the ill effects of social injustice or the unpredictable outcomes of economic downturns for certain groups.

THE AFFIRMATION FIELD

To experience well-being, human beings must first experience affirmation. Affirmation comes from an acknowledgment of a person's strengths, voice, and choice. Health and human services have been notorious for concentrating on deficits and for creating *clienthood* and *patienthood* instead of citizenship (McKnight, 1995). The focus on weaknesses and the insistence that patients passively acquiesce to professional dictates run against affirmation of strengths, voice, and choice. When empowerment and strengths are promoted, on the contrary, the experience of affirmation grows. The affirmation field consists of two intersecting continua: the capability dimension (see "Capability Dimension" below) and the participation dimension (see "Participation Dimension" below). Together, they create four distinct approaches to helping and healing.

CAPABILITY DIMENSION This dimension ranges from an exclusive focus on risk reduction and the prevention of deficits to an exclusive focus on the enhancement of protective factors and the promotion of strengths. Of course, it is possible to focus simultaneously on both prevention and promotion, which is captured by the middle range of the continuum.

PARTICIPATION DIMENSION Both the process and the content of prevention and promotion programs are typically controlled by researchers and human service professionals. Although community members increasingly participate in design and implementation, they still take a back seat. Professionals often operate on the basis of an expert model that (1) takes control away from the community, (2) promotes a power imbalance between professionals and citizens, (3) emphasizes deficits instead of strengths, and (4) limits the ability of people to help themselves (McKnight, 1995). A sense of ownership is important for the best outcomes (e.g., Peirson & Prilleltensky, 1994; Prilleltensky, 2005). This dimension ranges from expert-driven to community-driven participation.

AFFIRMATION QUADRANTS Quadrant I in Figure 18.2 represents interventions aiming to promote voice and choice in celebrating and building competencies. People are given an opportunity to exercise control over decisions affecting their lives, whereas modes of help build on former experiences of success.

Quadrant II affords community members voice and choice in methods of deficit reduction. Citizens are made partners in the struggle to combat depression, stress, obesity, or infectious diseases.

Quadrant III is the epitome of clienthood and patienthood. Not only are people deprived of an opportunity to participate in helping and healing, but most of the focus is on diagnosis of pathology and labelling of maladaptive behaviour. Quadrant IV represents the unique combination of approaches that strives to be positive while keeping the person detached from the change process. Popular yet ineffective campaigns such as "just say no to drugs," or cheerleading efforts such "you can do it if you want" represent vacuous promises of better health. While positive and effusive, such strategies fail to connect with the real-life experiences of youth growing up in drug-infested communities or with the struggle of many people to lower their weight despite lack of access to affordable and nutritious foods and vegetables.

4 BEFORE MOVING ON

> The conceptual framework for prevention and promotion that was presented includes four dimensions: an ecological dimension, a temporal dimension, a capability dimension, and a participation dimension. Discuss how each of these elements is relevant to prevention and promotion.

Research and Practice in Prevention and Promotion

Prevention activities may be either biological or psychological. As an example of biological primary prevention, encouraging pregnant women to avoid alcohol can prevent fetal alcohol syndrome (see Chapters 11 and 14). In fact,

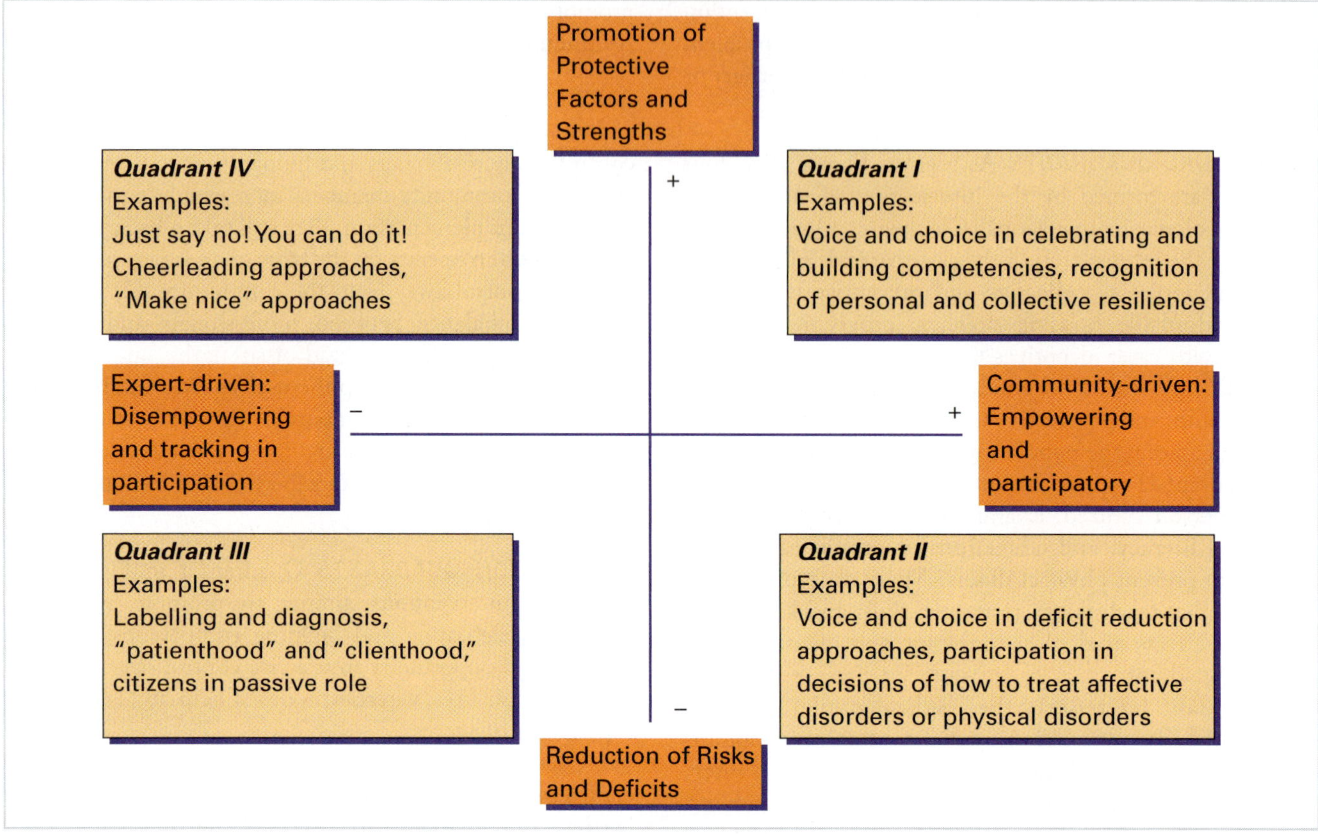

FIGURE 18.2 The Affirmation Field: The Intersection of the Capabilities and Participation Dimensions in the Promotion of Well-Being

Source: Adapted from Prilleltensky (2005).

many prevention programs start with pregnant women, and include counselling on nutrition and substance use. An example of biological secondary prevention is the administration of special diets to children born with phenylketonuria (a genetic disorder characterized by an inability of the body to use an essential amino acid). As described in Chapter 14, this diet cannot correct the basic metabolic disorder, but it can prevent its most serious consequence, mental retardation. Most prevention and mental health promotion programs, however, are primarily psychological or social in nature, and that is the type of program we will be discussing in this chapter.

Prevention may target children, adolescents, or adults; however, because so many mental health problems have roots in childhood, most prevention programs work with children or youths and their families (Weissberg, Kumpfer, & Seligman, 2003).

Case Notes

The south side of Ypsilanti, Michigan, in the 1960s was a slum as one probably pictures slums in the United States; in fact, it was described as "one of the most congested slum areas in the state" (Schweinhart & Weikart, 1988). The children of the neighbourhood—black and very poor—had difficulties when they entered school. They grew up into poverty and high rates of unemployment and imprisonment. The Perry Preschool Project set out to see whether the picture could be changed through a preschool educational program designed to give children the intellectual and social skills they needed for school. Selected participants were very poor three- and four-year-old children, with IQs between 60 and 90 (well below average), randomly assigned to experimental and control groups. For two school years, the children in the experimental program had two and a half hours a day of well-organized classroom activities. Each teacher worked with a group of five or six children. Also, every week during the school year, the teacher made a one-and-a-half-hour home visit to every mother and child, offering the mothers guidance in child-rearing skills.

What happened when these children started school? Initial results were encouraging: in kindergarten and Grade 1, the children in the experimental group showed more academic readiness and intellectual skills than those the control group. Disappointingly, by the time the children had reached Grades 3 and 4, differences in academic performance between the two groups had vanished.

Fortunately, the researchers continued to follow the children through their school-aged years and adulthood. The long-term effects of the Perry Preschool Project have been most interesting. At age 19, twice as many program participants as control children were employed, attending college, or receiving further training. High school graduation rates were 30 percent higher, and arrest and teen pregnancy rates were 40 percent lower. At age 27, program participants scored significantly higher than controls on literacy tests, and they were more likely to be employed (69 percent versus 56 percent) and own their own homes (27 percent versus 5 percent) (Schweinhart et al., 2005). Remarkably, the researchers were able to follow the participants in the Perry Preschool Project to age 40. Compared with participants in the control group, program participants at age 40 were less likely to be arrested five or more times (36 percent versus 55 percent) and more likely to be employed (70 percent versus 50 percent), earn $20 000 or more (60 percent versus 40 percent), and have a savings account (76 percent versus 50 percent). Moreover, the program was cost-effective. For every dollar invested in the 30-week program, there was a $14 return in savings from decreased special education, criminal justice, and welfare costs. The interested reader can learn more about this project from one of its founders, Dr. Larry Schweinhart, at the following website:

www.pdkintl.org/research/rbulletins/resbul32.htm

The Perry Preschool Project, described above, is one of the best known of the pioneering "first-generation" prevention and mental health promotion programs that began in the 1960s and 1970s. These early programs were often small and poorly funded and were rarely evaluated (Price, Cowen, Lorion, & Ramos-McKay, 1989). In 1982, the American Psychological Association established a task force to study these prevention programs. The report of this task force profiled 14 soundly researched programs that had been effective in preventing a number of different problems (Price, Cowen, Lorion, & Ramos-McKay, 1988). These served as models for planning and redesigning "second-generation" programs in the 1980s and 1990s.

HIGH-RISK (SELECTIVE) PREVENTION PROGRAMS

Like the Perry Preschool Project, most of the early prevention programs—and, in fact, most programs being implemented today—are **high-risk programs**. The short-term and long-term results of the Perry Preschool Project have received extensive attention over the years and are consistent with several other studies involving enriched preschool experiences for high-risk children. That is, structured preschool experiences can give high-risk disadvantaged children a head start on their early academic performance. Although these gains in cognitive skills and academic performance diminish after several years, there are still enduring academic, health, and social impacts over the long term (Barnett, 2011; Camilli et al., 2010; D'Onise, Lynch, Sawyer, & McDermott, 2010; Manning et al., 2010; Melhuish, 2011).

Can these benefits be classed as prevention in the field of mental health? There were no specific measures of the incidence of mental disorders in the Perry Preschool Project. However, teen pregnancies, unemployment, arrests, and incarceration are related to a number of mental disorders, including depression and antisocial personality disorder. More generally, if we look at the definition of mental health provided earlier in the chapter, as not merely the absence of disorder but optimal social, cognitive, and emotional functioning, it seems clear that the measures of life success reflect improved mental health. Finally, another preschool prevention program in North Carolina, called the Abecedarian Project, has been found to significantly reduce symptoms of depression when the participants reach 21 years of age (McLaughlin, Campbell, Pungello, & Skinner, 2007).

On the basis of the Perry Preschool Project and several other demonstration projects started in the early 1960s, the national Head Start project was established in the United States in 1966. This initiative provided one or two years of preschool experiences for nearly 1 million disadvantaged children. Although funding for the Head Start project has decreased over the years, and only one in five eligible disadvantaged children in the United States participates in the program, the long-term prevention effects of the Perry Preschool Project and other well-researched preschool projects have provided protection for Head Start through the period of severe cuts to social programs in the late 1980s and 1990s. In fact, the Head Start program has been extended to provide services to high-risk children from birth to three years of age (Early Head Start Benefits Children and Families, 2006; Ounce of Prevention Fund, 1994).

Another first-generation high-risk prevention project that has been well researched is the Prenatal Early Infancy Project. This project was initiated by David Olds in 1977 in Elmira, New York, a small, semi-rural community in upstate New York that was rated in the 1980 census as the most economically depressed area in the United States, and that had the highest rates of child abuse and neglect in the state. A major focus of the project was to prevent child abuse and neglect; it consisted of trained registered nurses carrying out home visits with first-time mothers from pregnancy through the child's second year of life (Olds, 1988, 1997).

Four hundred women were enrolled in the project before the thirtieth week of pregnancy, 85 percent of whom were considered to be high risk because they were low-income, unmarried, or teenaged. They were randomly assigned to the home visit program or to a control group that received transportation for health care and screening for health problems but no home visits.

The home visitation program was designed to improve three aspects of maternal and child functioning: (1) the outcomes of pregnancy, (2) quality of parenting, and (3) the mother's life course development (e.g., helping the mothers to return to school, find work, and plan future pregnancies).

The nurses completed an average of 9 home visits during pregnancy, and 23 visits from birth through the second year of the child's life. Olds attempted to apply the ecological model described earlier in this chapter. Thus, the nurses were trained to attend to the immediate day-to-day needs of the mother and the child, as well as to other family and community concerns. This resulted in a very comprehensive program for fostering maternal and child development: nurses helped mothers learn about pregnancy, infant health, and child-rearing; helped them obtain support from families, friends, and community health and human services; and provided them with direct personal and emotional support.

The results of the evaluation research were striking. During the prenatal period, the women who received home visits improved the quality of their diets to a greater extent than did the women in the non-visited comparison group. By the end of pregnancy, nurse-visited women had fewer kidney infections, experienced greater informal social support, and made better use of formal community services. Two particularly high-risk groups showed especially strong benefits: among women who smoked, those who received home visits had 75 percent fewer preterm deliveries than did those in the control group, and among very young adolescents (aged 14 to 16), those who were nurse-visited had babies who were nearly 400 grams heavier.

During the first two years after delivery, 14 percent of the poor, unmarried teen mothers in the control group abused or neglected their children, as opposed to only 4 percent of the poor, unmarried teens visited by a nurse. Over a four-year period, the children of nurse-visited women were less likely to visit a physician or emergency department for injuries or ingestions. Among low-income, unmarried women, the rate of subsequent pregnancy was reduced by 42 percent, and the number of months that nurse-visited women participated in the workforce was increased by 83 percent. Children born to women who were moderate to heavy smokers when they registered in the program during pregnancy and who received home visits had significantly higher IQ scores at three to four years of age than did their counterparts in the control group. Kitzman, Olds, and colleagues (1997, 2000) conducted a replication of the Elmira study in Memphis, Tennessee, with a sample of predominantly African-American mothers, and reported similar positive results for the home visitation program (Olds, Kitzman, et al., 2004). In a nine-year follow-up of the Memphis study, Olds, Kitzman, and colleagues (2007) reported that nurse-visited women had longer intervals between the births of their first and second children and used welfare and food stamps less often than did women in the control condition. Moreover, the children born to nurse-visited women who were at particularly high risk (those with low psychological resources) had better grade point averages and test scores in reading and math than did control children.

Moreover, in a 15-year follow-up of the Elmira study, Olds and colleagues (1997) found that the nurse-visited women had higher rates of employment than did the women in the control group, as well as lower rates of substance abuse, verified child abuse or neglect, arrests, convictions, days in jail, use of welfare, and subsequent pregnancies. Also, when the children were 15 years old, those whose mothers had participated in the home visitation program had significantly fewer problems of antisocial criminal behaviour than did those whose mothers were in the control group and had not received sustained home visiting (Olds et al., 1998). In the most recent follow-up of this sample when the youth were 19 years of age, Eckenrode et al. (2010) reported significantly lower rates of arrests and convictions for girls, but not boys, in the nurse home visitation group compared with the control group.

In general, the effects of the Prenatal Early Infancy Project on preventing adverse outcomes tended to be concentrated on groups who were at highest risk for these problems—namely, poor, unmarried teenaged mothers and their children. The results of this project have fostered great interest in the use of home visits as an effective prevention approach for high-risk mothers and children. Subsequent reviews of the literature have reported positive impacts of home visitation programs in preventing child maltreatment (Geeraert, Van de Noortgate, Grietans, & Onghenea, 2004; MacLeod & Nelson, 2000; Sweet & Appelbaum, 2004).

It is important to note that the home visitors in Olds's program were professionally trained registered nurses. Many subsequent home visit programs have been staffed by visitors who often reside in the communities they serve and who have no formal professional training in health or human services. Olds and colleagues (Olds, Robinson, et al., 2002, 2004) are currently conducting a study comparing the effectiveness of professional and paraprofessional home visitors in Denver, Colorado, with a sample of women who are economically disadvantaged and of diverse racial and ethnic backgrounds. The initial findings suggested that women who are visited by paraprofessionals do not achieve the same beneficial outcomes as women visited by nurses (Olds, Robinson, et al., 2002), but the results of a follow-up with the mothers and children two years after the intervention ended (i.e., when the children were four years old) found more encouraging results for the paraprofessional home visitors (Olds, Robinson, et al., 2004). Women who were visited by paraprofessionals worked more, reported a higher sense of mastery and mental health, had fewer subsequent miscarriages and low-birth-weight babies, and showed greater sensitivity and responsiveness to their children.

UNIVERSAL PREVENTION AND PROMOTION PROGRAMS

A good example of a universal program is currently being implemented with children and families living in socioeconomically disadvantaged neighbourhoods in eight communities in Ontario. This program, called Better Beginnings, Better Futures, is described in the Canadian Research Centre box. The Early Head Start Project (Ounce of Prevention Fund, 1994), which is being implemented nationally in the United States, is another example. This program is large-scale, involving thousands of children and families; is very comprehensive ecologically in its focus on

CANADIAN RESEARCH CENTRE

Better Beginnings, Better Futures

The Better Beginnings, Better Futures project was announced in 1991 by the Ontario government as a 25-year longitudinal prevention research project focusing on children from birth to eight years of age and their families. The project has three major goals:

1. *Prevention.* To prevent serious social, emotional, behavioural, physical, and cognitive problems in young children.
2. *Promotion.* To promote the social, emotional, behavioural, physical, and cognitive development of these children.
3. *Community development.* To enhance the ability of socio-economically disadvantaged families and communities to provide for their children.

Funding was provided by the Ontario and federal governments to eight communities to provide services tailored to local circumstances for four years of program implementation. To determine both short-term and long-term effects, researchers will follow the progress of the children, their families, and their neighbourhoods until the children reach their mid-twenties. Five communities focused their programs on children from conception to four years of age (younger child sites), and three concentrated on the four- to eight-year age range (older child sites). Children and families from three communities that did not receive program funding are also being evaluated for comparison purposes. All communities offering programs followed the same model—one that is unique in several aspects:

- *A comprehensive ecological model.* An ecological perspective of child development recognizes that children live and grow in families, within neighbourhoods and cultures. Better Beginnings programs attempted to address this broad range of ecological influences on children. Unlike most prevention programs, the project was designed to address child development, parent/family development, and community development. In their review of universal competence-promotion programs for children and adolescents, Durlak and colleagues (2007, pp. 276–277) noted: "The Better Beginnings, Better Futures Project is unique in our review as a large-scale community based intervention that uses participatory research methods to target all three mesosystems: families, schools, and community-based organizations."

People participating in the Family Resource Centre, Highfield Community Enrichment Project (Better Beginnings, Better Futures) in Etobicoke, Ontario.

- *Local responsibility and significant parent–community involvement.* In most prevention projects, professionals plan, manage, and deliver services to parents, who are seen as receiving help. In Better Beginnings projects, professionals, parents, and other local community members worked collaboratively. Parents and other community members were actively involved in all decisions about the local project, including program development, organization and management, staff hiring, and budgets. The transfer of this level of control and responsibility has the potential to empower community residents, who may have felt little control, individually or collectively, over their own lives and the lives of their children.

Project funding began in 1991, but it took each community at least two and a half years to develop such a comprehensive program, establish organization and management structures, and hire and train program staff, many of whom were local residents. Programs were implemented for four years from 1993 to 1997. Although the specific program activities differed somewhat across the eight communities, they generally had the following elements:

- *Home visits.* All projects for zero- to four-year-olds included home visits to families during pregnancy and infancy. Drawing on Olds's work (described above), home visitors assisted all families in the neighbourhood with children four years of age or under who agreed to participate. Most of the home visitors were residents of the local neighbourhoods, and they worked with the families to meet basic needs, provide parent training and child development information, and link families with community health and social services and informal support resources.
- *Classroom enrichment.* The three project sites for the four- to eight-year-olds enriched children's formal educational experiences with social skills training, academic tutoring, and teacher support.
- *Child care enrichment.* All projects supplemented existing community child care with additional staff, resources, drop-in centres for at-home care providers, toy-lending libraries, et cetera.
- *Other child-focused programs.* Other program elements, tailored to needs in each community, included playgroups, breakfast programs, and school-based anti-bullying programs.
- *Family/parent-focused programs.* Again, a variety of activities were designed to meet community needs, including parent training and parent support groups, cooking classes, prenatal programs, and fathers' groups.
- *Community-focused programs.* A wide range of program activities were designed to create new resources in the community (e.g., food banks, crosswalks); activities for community members at large, designed to improve the quality of life in the community; and improved cultural awareness, relations, and pride. Included were such activities as neighbourhood safety working groups, cultural workshops and celebrations, and, for Aboriginal people, a variety of healing activities and programs.

The Better Beginnings, Better Futures project is considered to be universal because it was offered to all children in a given age range and their families. The neighbourhoods selected for the program are "high risk" because they all have high concentrations of socio-economically disadvantaged families, but all residents, regardless of

(Continued)

(Continued)

their socio-economic status, are actively encouraged to participate.

To adequately evaluate a program as comprehensive and broad-based as Better Beginnings requires a multidisciplinary approach. Project research includes extensive home interviews with parents; teacher ratings and direct assessments of the children's physical, cognitive, social, and mental development; descriptions of program activities and costs; and an evaluation of how well the programs were developed and implemented and whether they successfully involved community members as active decision makers.

Research on the short-term and medium-term impacts of the Better Beginnings Project at Grades 3, 6, and 9 indicated improved emotional, behavioural, and school functioning among children, and improved health for children in the older child sites (Peters, Bradshaw, et al., 2010). Also, parents reported better marital satisfaction and family functioning, improved social support, and improved neighbourhood quality. The percentage of students receiving special education services decreased, while the percentage of such students in schools in the control neighbourhoods increased. All Better Beginnings sites achieved at least 50 percent community member participation on planning and implementation committees. Community members from the eight sites volunteered 40 000 hours of their time in a year to local Better Beginnings projects. Follow-up research on the children and parents in the older child sites at Grades 6 and 9 also demonstrates some positive impacts of Better Beginnings on children, parents, and the communities.

The average cost of offering the Better Beginnings projects was between \$1200 and \$2000 per child per year. These expenditures are quite modest in comparison to other well-known prevention projects such as the High/Scope Perry Preschool Project, which averaged \$8600 per child per year, and the Elmira nurse home visitation program, which averaged \$4300 per child per year for two years (all costs are in 1997 Canadian dollars). Many prevention research projects have not reported average costs, making decisions by government policy-makers about which projects to fund at what cost very difficult. By Grade 12, it was estimated that for every dollar invested in Better Beginnings, there was a \$2.50 savings in government spending (Peters, Nelson, et al., 2010).

The Better Beginnings, Better Futures project model appears to be an effective and affordable strategy for governments to counter the negative impact of disadvantaged neighbourhoods on child development and community spirit. For current information on the Better Beginnings programs and current research results, see the Better Beginnings, Better Futures website: http://bbbf.queensu.ca.

FOCUS 18.1

Preventing Substance Abuse and Dependence Among Canadian Children and Youth: Policy and Programs

Many children and youth experiment with drugs and alcohol. A study of nearly 30 000 youth in Grades 7 to 12 in British Columbia found that 54 percent had used alcohol and 30 percent had used marijuana (Smith et al., 2009). Excessive drug and alcohol use can lead to substance abuse, which involves clinical impairment and distress, as well as dependence, including tolerance and withdrawal (Children's Health Policy Centre, 2010). Within Canada's National Anti-drug Strategy, 70 percent of the funding goes toward law enforcement, and only 4 percent is allocated to prevention programs (Debeck, Wood, Montaner, & Kerr, 2009). However, other universal and selective prevention programs have been developed in Canada to prevent substance abuse disorders (Shamblen & Derzon, 2009).

We know from research what types of programs are ineffective and what types are effective in reducing rates of substance abuse (Fox, Ireland, Lister-Sharp, & Breen, 2003). Programs inspired by former U.S. First Lady Nancy Reagan's approach of "just say no to drugs" do not work (Tobler, 2000; Tobler et al., 2000). In spite of their popularity, noninteractive approaches in which adults lecture youth about drugs and alcohol to raise their awareness and knowledge (e.g., the police-developed project Drug Abuse Resistance Education [DARE]) have not been found to have any impact on youth's drug or alcohol use (West & O'Neal, 2004). What does work? Programs that are effective in reducing substance abuse use interactive formats with youth, including active participation with peers and youth-generated role plays, that focus on (1) knowledge and attitudes, including a critique of media influences; (2) drug-refusal interpersonal skills, such as assertiveness and communication skills; and (3) intrapersonal skills like goal setting, problem solving, and stress reduction (Tobler, 2000; Tobler et al., 2000).

One evidence-based approach to substance abuse prevention is the Life Skills Training (LST) program (Botvin, 2000). LST is a universal prevention program that focuses on both general life skills and drug-refusal skills. Botvin, Baker, Dusenbury, Tortu, and Botvin (1990) evaluated LST in a randomized controlled trial of more than 4400 predominantly white Grade 7 students from 56 schools. The Grade 7 students attended 15 class periods during or after school, with ten booster class sessions in Grade 8 and five in Grade 9. At Grade 9, significant prevention effects were found for cigarette smoking, marijuana use, and immoderate alcohol use, and improvements were found in knowledge concerning substance use, interpersonal skills, and communication skills. Three years later, at Grade 12, more than 3500 students from the initial Grade 7 sample (60 percent of the original sample) were assessed again, and significant prevention effects were found for both drug and polydrug use (Botvin, Baker, Dusenbury, Botvin, & Diaz, 1995). Positive impacts of the LST combined with a universal, family-based program, the Strengthening Families Program, have also been reported (Spoth, Redmond, Trudeau, & Shin, 2002), and the economic benefits of LST have been found to outweigh its costs (Aos, Lieb, Mayfiel, Miller, & Pennucci, 2004).

If programs to prevent substance abuse and other mental, emotional, and behavioural problems are effective and save money in the long run, why do government policies like the National Anti-Drug Strategy underinvest in them?

children, families, and communities; and has shown positive results (Early Head Start Benefits Children and Families, 2006). For example, Love et al. (2005) randomly assigned more than 3000 low-income families with three-year-old children to either Early Head Start or a control group. The Early Head Start group participated in centre-based programs for the children and/or home-based programs for the parents over a two-year period prior to the children enrolling in elementary school. The children who participated in Early Head Start exhibited better cognitive and language development and lower levels of aggressive behaviour than did controls. In addition, the parents of these children were more emotionally supportive of, and intellectually stimulating with, their children, reading to them more often and spanking them less frequently. The best results were achieved by programs that included both centre-based and home-based components. Early Head Start is less universal than the Better Beginnings model, because only families that fall below the poverty line qualify.

In his review of the literature on mental health promotion and primary prevention, Cowen (1977) referred to progress as being made in "baby steps." Twenty years later, Cowen (1996) spoke of "lengthy strides." Clearly, the past few decades have seen tremendous growth in the research and practice bases of mental health promotion and prevention. In a meta-analytic review (see Chapter 17 for a discussion of meta-analysis) of 526 prevention and promotion programs for children and youth, Durlak and colleagues (2007) reported positive preventive impacts of these programs on children's emotional and behavioural problems.

Nation and colleagues (2003) conducted a review of prevention programs for children and youth. They concluded that the most effective prevention programs are those that

- are *comprehensive*;
- use *varied teaching methods*;
- provide *sufficient "dosage"* (i.e., the program is long and intensive enough to make a difference);
- are *theory-driven*;
- promote *positive relationships with adults and peers*;
- are *appropriately timed*;
- are *socio-culturally relevant*;
- use *outcome evaluation*; and
- have *well-trained staff*.

In Canada and the United States, prevention programs have been applied in a wide variety of settings to address many different problems and disorders, including youth violence and bullying (Craig, Pepler, & Cummings, 2009; Crooks, Wolfe, Hughes, Jaffe, & Chiodo, 2008); criminal behaviour and conduct disorder (Waddell, Hua, Garland, Peters, & McEwan, 2007); and depression and anxiety problems in adults (Dozois & Dobson, 2004; Muñoz, Cuijpers, Smit, Barrera, & Leykin, 2010), children, and youth (Beardslee, Wright, Gladstone, & Forbes, 2007; Waddell, Hua, et al., 2007; Waddell, McEwan, et al., 2007). In the United States, three influential reports, one by the Institute of Medicine (1994), one by the National Institute of Mental Health (Reiss & Price, 1996), and a recent report by the National Research Council and Institute of Medicine (O'Connell et al., 2009), have outlined how prevention strategies can be applied to a range of mental, emotional, and behavioural disorders.

5 BEFORE MOVING ON

Describe one universal prevention program and one selective (high-risk) program, and report the findings from research on each of these programs.

Prevention and Promotion Policy in Canada

THE FEDERAL ROLE

Canada has been a leader in promoting the concept of prevention. In 1974, then federal Minister of Health Marc Lalonde released a report entitled *A New Perspective on the Health of Canadians*, which recognized the influence of biological, lifestyle, and environmental factors on disease rates and argued for an increased emphasis on prevention and health promotion. The main message of the report was re-emphasized and expanded upon in two reports by subsequent federal Minister of Health Jake Epp, *Achieving Health for All* (1986) and *Mental Health for Canadians: Striking a Balance* (1988).

However, critics have argued that despite the rhetoric of prevention apparent in federal documents, little has changed in Canadian health systems (Wharf, 1989). Beginning in the late 1980s, the federal government began to drastically reduce transfer payments to the provinces, which are primarily responsible for health, education, and social services policies and programs. As Canada entered the twenty-first century, the federal government realized large budget surpluses and, under pressure from the public and the provinces, began to restore funding for health, education, and social services. In a review of Canadian programs, Waddell, Hua, and colleagues (2007) found that while there are several national and provincial ECD initiatives, only the Better Beginnings project has explicitly focused on the prevention of mental health problems and the promotion of mental health, and it is the only well-researched program that has demonstrated positive mental health outcomes for children.

When we compare Canada with several Western European countries, we find that Canada lags behind such countries in social policies that support families and children (Peters, Peters, Laurendeau, Chamberland, & Peirson, 2001). For example, France, Germany, the Netherlands, and the Scandinavian countries have implemented universal child care policies and, through various tax and transfer mechanisms, have dramatically reduced rates of child poverty, which is a significant risk factor in children's mental, emotional, and behavioural disorders. To address the gaps in Canadian mental health policy, the federal government created the Mental Health Commission of Canada in 2007. While one of 16 chapters of the Kirby and Leon (2006) report focuses on mental health promotion and prevention, the bulk of the report focuses on treatment and rehabilitation. In contrast, the Canadian mental health strategy document produced by the commission includes prevention and mental health promotion as one of seven goals of a transformed mental health system (Mental Health Commission of Canada, 2009). This report states: "[T]o address underlying risk and protective factors, mental health promotion and mental illness prevention must be integrated not only into mental health policy but also more broadly into public health and social policy" (p. 41). These observations reinforce Albee's (1996) argument that rather than an exclusive focus on the prevention of clinical disorders, prevention also requires social and political change that is reflected in our nation's social policies. However, Canada has no national policy or funding mechanism for prevention or mental health promotion.

THE PROVINCIAL ROLE

Nelson, Prilleltensky, Laurendeau, and Powell (1996) surveyed mental health promotion and prevention in all provinces and territories. They found a good deal of support on paper for prevention, and many interesting projects. Nevertheless, they also reported that health funding has not been reallocated from treatment to prevention, and that funding for prevention remains very low in all provinces and territories. More recently, Kutcher, Hampton, and Wilson (2010) reported that while 4 of the 10 provinces have a child and adolescent policy or plan, little emphasis is placed on prevention and mental health promotion, except for suicide prevention.

There are more visible signs of prevention initiatives in some of the provinces, indicating that prevention is beginning to take root in provincial health, education, and social services. For example, Quebec has developed an infrastructure to support the growth of child care and prevention programs for children and youth (Laurendeau & Perreault, 1997), which has resulted in a diverse array of prevention programs being implemented (Chamberland et al., 1998). Several provinces have implemented home visitation programs (Waddell, McEwan, et al., 2007). In Ontario, McCain and Mustard (1999) completed a report entitled *Reversing the Real Brain Drain: Early Years Study—Final Report*, in which they advocated for early child development centres. A central argument of this report and a more recent updated report (McCain, Mustard, & Shanker, 2007) is that infant nurturing during the preschool years is essential for healthy child development and that preschool intervention programs can help parents provide such nurturing. Following from this report, Ontario Early Years Centres have been developed in many Ontario communities.

RETURN ON INVESTMENT

The sciences of prevention and early intervention have matured to the extent that it is now possible to compute the **return on investment (ROI)** of various programs and policies. Various states, such as Michigan, Connecticut, and Washington, have commissioned studies on the economic returns of high-quality programs in early childhood (see Focus box 18.2 for a list of reports on ROI).

Very reputable institutions such as the Brookings Institute, the Rand Corporation, the Federal Reserve Bank of Minneapolis, the Institute of Child Development at the University of Minnesota, and the Washington Institute for Public Policy have conducted state and national studies that demonstrate the human and financial benefits of investing in prevention.

In general, the research indicates that the economic returns for a variety of early intervention programs with families and children at risk range from $1.50 to $17.00 for every dollar invested. The savings come in the form of reduced attendance in costly special education programs, less contact with expensive social services, lower rates of incarceration and delinquency, and increased tax contributions through steady employment.

These findings, documented extensively in the reports listed in Focus box 18.2 and other academic publications,

FOCUS 18.2

Reports Documenting Return on Investment in Prevention

The following reports document the positive economic returns of early intervention and prevention programs in various American states. Returns usually vary from $1.50 to $17.00 for every dollar invested. They are presented alphabetically by state or by organization publishing the study.

1. Brookings Institution, www3.brookings.edu/views/papers/200701isaacs.pdf
2. Chicago Parenting Centers, http://www.waisman.wisc.edu/cls/cbaexecsum4.html
3. Connecticut, www.cga.ct.gov/COC/stockportfolio.htm; www.cga.ct.gov/COC/PDFs/prevention/040207_stockpor tfolio_v1.pdf
4. Economic Policy Institute, http://www.epi.org/publication/book_enriching
5. Michigan, www.michigan.gov/documents/0-3_ROI_Report-WEB_158972_7.pdf
6. Minneapolis, Federal Reserve Bank, http://www.minneapolisfed.org/publications_papers/studies/earlychild/highreturn.pdf
7. Rand Corporation, http://www.rand.org/pubs/research_briefs/2005/RAND_RB 9145.pdf
8. Washington State Institute for Public Policy, http://www.wsipp.wa.gov/pub.asp?docid=04-07-3901

demonstrate that, indeed, one ounce of prevention is worth a pound—or more—of cure. Connecticut has passed a law requesting that all programs and agencies serving children invest at least 10 percent of their budgets in prevention.

A review of the economic benefits of early childhood development (ECD) programs came to the following conclusion:

> Investments in high-quality ECD programs consistently generate benefit-cost ratios exceeding 3-to-1—or more than a $3 return for every dollar invested—well above the 1-to-1 ratio needed to justify such investments. Even economists who are particularly skeptical about government programs make an exception for high-quality ECD programs. . . . This study demonstrates, for the first time, that providing all 20 percent of the nation's three- and four-year-old children who live in poverty with a high-quality ECD program would have a substantial payoff for governments and taxpayers in the future. (Lynch, 2004, pp. vii–viii)

6 BEFORE MOVING ON

How well do national and provincial policies in Canada support prevention and mental health promotion? Give an example to support your response.

Implementation, Dissemination, and Social Justice

While the outcomes of many prevention programs have been well documented, there is growing attention to three issues: program implementation, program dissemination, and social justice.

IMPLEMENTATION

Durlak (1998) has argued that **implementation** is important for understanding outcomes. If the outcomes of a prevention program are not achieved, this could be due either to problems with the program's theory of change or to poor implementation. Thus, it is important to determine how well a program is implemented. The study of implementation has been concerned with a program's fidelity, which has been defined as "the extent to which the innovation corresponds to the originally intended program" (Durlak & DuPre, 2008, p. 329), and a program's dosage, or the amount of the intervention that is delivered. Based on their review of prevention program implementation, Durlak and DuPre (2008) found that both program fidelity and dosage were related to outcomes. The higher the degree of fidelity and the more intensive the program, the better were the outcomes of the prevention program.

While fidelity appears to be important for outcomes, concern has been expressed that rigid adherence to a program model may lead to inappropriate applications of the program in some contexts. For example, suppose that a program has been developed to prevent problems in a predominantly Caucasian, rural population. The question arises as to how applicable, culturally sensitive, or relevant this model may be for other populations or communities, such as urban black children or First Nations children living on or off reserves. Some would argue that it is not only important but necessary to adapt and tailor programs to local conditions in order for them to be successful (Durlak & DuPre, 2008). While the debate about fidelity and adaptation has typically been framed as an "either-or" issue, it may be possible to ensure both fidelity and adaptation. Hawe, Shiell, and Riley (2004) have made a distinction between the form and function of a program, with form focusing on the specific way that the program is operated and function referring to the purpose or principles of the program. According to Hawe et al. (2004), this distinction suggests that it is possible to do the same program differently. For example, a parenting intervention might be delivered in different languages with unique cultural referents, while having a common set of principles. This distinction suggests that it is possible to have both fidelity and adaptation at the same time. Both are important, as Durlak and DuPre's (2008) review found that both fidelity and adaptation are associated with positive outcomes.

DISSEMINATION

Wandersman and colleagues (2008) have developed a model for the dissemination and adoption of prevention programs. They argue that **dissemination** is influenced by three inter-related systems: the prevention synthesis and translation system, the prevention delivery system, and the prevention support system.

First, the prevention synthesis and translation system acknowledges that scientific reports and journal articles are insufficient tools for transmitting knowledge about effective prevention programs. Rather, such information must be translated for practitioners, lay audiences, and policy-makers into user-friendly materials, as suggested by social marketing theory (Flay et al., 2005; Gormley, 2011; Wandersman et al., 2008). A good example of this knowledge synthesis and translation is the Triple P (Positive Parenting Program) that was developed in Australia (Sanders, 2010). While Triple P started as a clinical intervention for children with conduct or oppositional defiant disorders, it has been adapted for use as a universal prevention and promotion program. Universal Triple P was used in the state of South Carolina and has been shown in rigorously controlled research to prevent child maltreatment (Prinz, Sanders, Shapiro, Whitaker, & Lutzker, 2009). The adoption of the Triple P program for universal promotion, prevention for high-risk groups, and treatment for children with existing behavioural problems in South Carolina and in the province of Manitoba (http://www.gov.mb.ca/healthychild/triplep/) has been enabled in part by the production of a variety of training materials.

Second, the prevention delivery system includes individual, organizational, and community supports for prevention at the local level. The "readiness for change" of individuals, organizations, and communities is important for the dissemination of prevention programs (Feinberg, Greenberg, & Osgood, 2004). Third, there is growing evidence of the importance of the prevention support system for the adoption of prevention programs (Flay et al., 2005; Wandersman et al., 2008). Good training materials and readiness for change are important, but must be reinforced by technical assistance and capacity-building. Important in this regard are education, networking, and consultation for settings that wish to adopt a prevention program. The adoption of Triple P in Manitoba and South Carolina was enhanced with substantial technical assistance by the developers of the program.

SOCIAL JUSTICE

Ample evidence suggests that many social and psychological ills can be traced to social injustice. If not the sole source, social injustice is at least a contributing factor; however, rarely do prevention or mental health promotion programs address issues of social justice (Prilleltensky, 1994b). **Social justice** "deals with the fair and equitable allocation of resources, obligations, and bargaining powers in society" (Prilleltensky & Nelson, in press). A focus on social justice draws attention to issues of economic inequality, racism, sexism, and other societal sources of injustice. Joffe and Albee (1981) refer to these injustices as the "causes of the causes." The late George Albee (1996) was an outspoken advocate for the use of social and political action as a prevention tool. To date, however, most prevention programs focus on the individual or micro levels of analysis to the neglect of macro-level social injustices. In a review of 526 prevention studies, Durlak and colleagues (2007) found that none of the studies attempted to change community conditions.

Despite the call for a social justice approach to prevention (Albee, 1996; Joffe & Albee, 1981), to date there has been a lack of practical program models that exemplify such a perspective. A special issue of the *Journal of Primary Prevention* on social justice (Kenny & Hage, 2009) and a chapter by Prilleltensky and Nelson (in press) have attempted to bring together the concepts of social justice and prevention. Examples of this integration include Matthews and Adams's (2009) description of a project to prevent the negative consequences of heterosexism that included civic action and political awareness; Kivnick and Lymburner's (2009) description of a community program to promote social justice consciousness with youth through the arts; and Buhin and Vera's (2009) intervention to prevent racism at both the individual and policy levels. While research is needed on prevention programs that strive to create social justice, this is an important future direction for the field of prevention.

In summary, Canadian community psychologist, prevention researcher, policy advocate, and former Quebec politician Camil Bouchard (1994) noted the limitations of prevention programs that do not tackle issues of social injustice:

> Canadian families and children suffering the consequences of poverty are growing in number. In this context, the sole use of preventive psychosocial programs to counter the consequences of poverty without an equally important global strategy to reduce economic inequality or poverty itself seems incomplete, inefficient, and even cynical. (p. 44)

7 BEFORE MOVING ON

Using an example, describe the three systems that are important for program dissemination.

SUMMARY

- Universal, selective, and indicated prevention are approaches to prevent mental, emotional, and behavioural disorders. Mental health promotion strives to promote the ability to enjoy life, the ability to deal with life's challenges, emotional well-being, spiritual well-being, social connections, and respect for culture, equity, social justice, and personal dignity.
- Historically, the field of prevention has shifted from a pre–germ theory period to a public health approach to an educational approach.
- Risk, resilience, protection, and ecological levels of analysis are important theoretical constructs that serve to focus the strategies and goals of prevention programs.
- The Strengths, Prevention, Empowerment, and Community Change (SPEC) framework includes a contextual field, with ecological and temporal dimensions, and an affirmation field, with capability and participation fields, which are important for conceptualizing prevention programs.
- Both selective (high-risk) and universal approaches to prevention have been developed and found effective in preventing mental, emotional, and behavioural problems through evaluation research.
- While there is much rhetoric about the value of prevention and mental health promotion in federal and provincial policy in Canada, and considerable research attesting to the effectiveness of prevention programs, prevention and mental health promotion remain underfunded and underdeveloped.
- Issues in program implementation, program dissemination, and social justice are growing concerns in the prevention field that need further attention.

MySearchLab offers you extensive help with your writing and research projects and provides round-the-clock access to credible and reliable source material. Chapter quizzes and a full electronic version of the text are also provided. Answers to the Before Moving On feature are provided on the MySearchLab. Take a tour at www.mysearchlab.com.

KEY TERMS

community psychology (p. 468)
prevention (p. 469)
primary prevention (p. 469)
secondary prevention (p. 469)
tertiary prevention (p. 469)
universal approach (p. 469)
selective prevention (p. 469)
indicated prevention (p. 469)
mental health promotion (p. 469)
mental health (p. 469)
ecological approach (p. 470)
public health approach (p. 471)
resilience (p. 472)
risk factors (p. 472)
protective factors (p. 472)
microsystem (p. 472)
macrosystem (p. 472)
cumulative risk (p. 472)
ecological perspective (p. 474)
high-risk programs (p. 477)
return on investment (ROI) (p. 482)
implementation (p. 483)
dissemination (p. 483)
social justice (p. 484)

STEPHEN D. HART • RONALD ROESCH

Chapter 19

Mental Disorder and the Law

LEARNING OBJECTIVES

AFTER READING THIS CHAPTER, STUDENTS WILL BE ABLE TO:

1. Describe the basic structure of the Canadian legal system, including the primary sources of law in Canada.
2. Explain the law's assumptions regarding human nature and how mental disorder challenges these assumptions.
3. Explain the common law principles of police powers and *parens patriae* and how they provide a rationale for Canadian civil mental health law with respect to involuntary hospitalization and treatment.
4. Define and differentiate the concepts of mental state at the time of the offence and mental state at the time of trial in Canadian criminal law.
5. Describe some of the general and special ethical problems faced by psychologists who become involved in legal proceedings.

Scott Jeffery Schutzman was a man of considerable charm, intelligence, and creativity. Born in the United States, he moved to Canada with his family when he was about 13 years old. He skipped two grades in school, graduating from Ryerson (then a polytechnical school) with a diploma in electronics technology. He became a top salesman for an electronics firm. He was also an avid and skilled skier and a talented amateur physicist—yes, physicist. Despite a lack of formal education, he studied topics such as time measurement, anti-gravity, and relativity. He even collaborated with academics, such as a professor at Stanford University's SLAC National Accelerator Laboratory in the United States, who described his thinking as "years ahead of its time." He was given the nickname "Professor."

The "Professor" also had a serious mental disorder. Starting in 1985, when he was about 29 years old, he started to exhibit symptoms of psychosis. For example, he held some beliefs that were odd or eccentric, and others that were outright delusional. At various times, he claimed that he placed the last antenna on top of the CN Tower in Toronto; was married to celebrities such as Joan Rivers and Joan Collins; operated a business, the Starson Corporation, that was building a "starship"; communicated with extra-terrestrials; and was the next head of NASA. He considered himself to be the "son of the stars" and eventually changed his surname from Schutzman to Starson. His behaviour was also disorganized. He was overactive and had frequent outbursts of shouting and inexplicable laughter. He lost his job and his personal relationships suffered. He made repeated threats to kill others and engaged in other fear-inducing behaviour, including stalking Joan Rivers. He was hospitalized, arrested, and charged with criminal offences on many occasions. His symptoms improved when he was treated with antipsychotic medications, but he found that these medications also impaired his ability to think creatively. He considered this side effect "worse than death" and so refused treatment. His mental disorder worsened over the years.

***

In November 1998, Professor Starson was found not criminally responsible on account of mental disorder (NCRMD) on two counts of uttering death threats toward fellow residents of the Toronto townhouse in which he resided, and was subsequently detained in a secure facility. His psychiatrists proposed to treat him with medications, but he refused. The psychiatrists sought approval from the Ontario Consent and Capacity Board to treat Professor Starson involuntarily under that province's Health Care Consent Act (1996), arguing that he was not capable of making his own decisions about treatment—that is, unable to understand information relevant to making a decision about the treatment and to appreciate the reasonably foreseeable consequences of a decision. The board granted approval for involuntary treatment, finding that Professor Starson was in "almost total" denial of his mental disorder and failed to appreciate the consequences of his decision to refuse treatment. The board concluded that treatment was in Professor Starson's own best interests.

Professor Starson refused to accept the board's decision. He sought judicial review, first before the Ontario Superior Court of Justice, then the Court of Appeal of Ontario, and finally the Supreme Court of Canada (*Starson v. Swayze*, 2003). These courts reviewed the evidence and found the board had erred in its decision. First, although Professor Starson did not accept that his condition was a mental disorder, he recognized that his brain did not function normally. Second, there was no evidence that he failed to appreciate the potential risks and benefits of treatment (or lack thereof). Consequently, the board was wrong to conclude that he lacked the capacity to make a decision regarding his treatment. Furthermore, the courts found that the board, when it considered what was in his best interests, overstepped its legislative authority. Put simply, the board had no right to consider the wisdom of his ultimate decision regarding treatment, only to consider whether he was capable to make such a decision. The law must respect the dignity and autonomy of all Canadians, including those with mental health problems, by allowing them the freedom to make decisions that others might regard as foolish unless it is proven they are incapable of making such a decision.

The court decisions in this case, including the final one by the Supreme Court of Canada to uphold those by the lower courts, were praised by some as protecting the rights of those with mental disorder, and condemned by others as permitting mental disorder to ruin the lives of people who suffer from it. But the decisions were not easy for the courts to make. For example, the Supreme Court of Canada decision was split: six justices voted with the majority, but three dissented. One of the dissenters was the Chief Justice, the Right Honourable Beverley McLachlin, P.C. She later made a rare public commentary about the challenges posed by this case (McLachlin, 2005):

> Professor Starson may well never recover from the illness that afflicts him and may spend the rest of his life in custody or under the significant control of the criminal justice system. Hence the cruel paradox—freedom to refuse "medication" may in fact result in institutional confinement and continued debilitation. . . . [O]ur law governing hospitalization and consent continues to grapple with the challenges of appropriately balancing the autonomy and dignity of mentally ill persons with their right to treatment and the important objective of protecting the public from dangerous individuals. . . . Laws cannot heal people . . . [b]ut the law can create a social and regulatory environment that assists medical professionals in delivering their services in a manner that is both ethical and respectful of the rights and needs of the mentally ill.

The comments of Chief Justice McLachlin may strike some as idealistic rather than realistic. It came as little surprise to many that in the wake of the Supreme Court of Canada's decision, Professor Starson's symptoms persisted and worsened without treatment; he even began to refuse food. The hospital once again went before the Ontario Consent and Capacity Board, this time gathering and presenting incontrovertible evidence that he was incapable of making decisions about treatment and should be medicated involuntarily. The treatment led to a marked improvement in Professor Starson's mental health. He also regained his physical health. Once he was well enough to be deemed capable of making treatment decisions, he no longer resisted medications. With continued treatment, he eventually improved to the point that the Ontario Review Board was able to relax his conditions of detention and allow him greater freedoms. With the benefit of hindsight, then, we may conclude that Chief Justice McLachlin's comments were prescient. Ultimately, the law actually helped to make sure that Professor Starson received appropriate treatment, in a manner that respected his wishes as much as possible and that protected both his rights and freedoms and those of the public.

(Based on information presented in McLachlin, 2005; O'Neill & Fischer, 2005; Seymour, 2006; *Starson v. Swayze*, 2003.)

As the previous chapters have made clear, many forms of mental disorder are associated with social dysfunction or disability—problems getting along with other people, problems fulfilling social roles and obligations, and so forth. It should come as no surprise, then, that many people suffering from mental disorder find themselves in conflict with the law or involved in disputes with other people that end up in court. In many different societies and for many years, legal traditions have recognized this fact and made special provisions for handling disputes that involve people suffering from mental disorder. These legal traditions have also come to recognize that mental health professionals can play an important role by providing information about mental disorder to legal decision makers. In fact, all the major mental health professions—clinical psychology, psychiatry, social work, and nursing—now have forensic specialists, people whose work focuses primarily on topics related to mental disorder and the law.

The Starson case raises some fascinating questions about mental disorder and the law in Canada, as well as the role of psychologists in court. Should people suffering from mental disorders be held responsible for their behaviour and punished, or should they be found not responsible and treated? How should decisions of this sort be made? How much confidence should we have in psychologists when they state that people suffer from mental disorder that makes them incapable of making decisions about their own health care, not criminally responsible, or a risk of harm to others? How much weight should be accorded to the evidence presented by psychologists in court? Is the state of the science in psychology sufficiently developed to be used as the basis for making decisions that change the lives of others? Who do psychologists work for when they participate in legal proceedings—the people who are parties to a proceeding, the lawyers who represent them, or perhaps even the judges who preside over the proceedings?

To answer these and related questions, we will examine Canadian law as it relates to mental disorder and the practice of psychology in legal settings. The first part of the chapter is devoted to the issue of law. We start by outlining the structure of the Canadian legal system and discussing what various sources of law (constitutional, statutory, and common) have to say about mental disorder. We then take a closer look at two types of statutory law: civil mental health law and criminal law. We discuss the nature of the problem that the law is trying to address, the provisions it makes for special care and control of people suffering from mental disorder, and what research has revealed about the issue. The second part of the chapter is devoted to an examination of the role of psychology in the legal system. We begin by discussing the ways in which psychologists may become involved in legal proceedings. Next, we review ethical codes of psychology, focusing in particular on the ethical codes of forensic psychology, to see what guidance they offer. Finally, we examine the status of psychology in the law.

Mental Disorder in Canadian Law

Canadian law assumes that people can (and typically do) think and act in a reasoned, deliberate manner. People may be treated differently under the law when it is demonstrated that their thinking is irrational or their behaviour is involuntary. The inability to perceive accurately or reason correctly about the outside world is referred to as cognitive impairment; the inability to exert adequate controls on one's behaviour is sometimes referred to as volitional impairment (Hart, 2001b). Canadian law recognizes that, in some cases, mental disorder may cause cognitive or volitional impairment. Courts and tribunals often call on mental health professionals to render opinions concerning the existence and impact of mental disorder in a given case, recognizing that they have special expertise in evaluating people and understanding human behaviour, especially abnormal behaviour.

1 BEFORE MOVING ON

Why is mental disorder relevant in Canadian law?

The legal concept of mental disorder is not bound by psychological or medical definitions. The law typically defines mental disorder as any impairment of psychological functioning that is internal, stable, and involuntary in nature—that is, not a reflection of situational or contextual factors, not an ephemeral or transient state, and not a self-induced condition. Legal definitions of mental disorder, then, typically focus on acute and severe disturbances in thought, affect, or behaviour. Examples include cognitive disorders such as dementia; psychotic disorders such as schizophrenia; mood disorders such as major depressive disorder; developmental disorders such as autistic disorder; and mental retardation. Mental disorders of this sort have been recognized in medicine and in law for millennia.

Although quite broad or general, the legal definition of mental disorder is much narrower than that used by mental health professionals. This means that some mental disorders that are recognized by mental health professionals and even included in the fourth edition (text revision) of the *Diagnostic and Statistical Manual of Mental Disorders* (DSM-IV-TR; American Psychiatric Association [APA], 2000) may not meet the legal definition of a mental disorder. One example is substance-related disorders, such as alcohol intoxication. Alcohol intoxication can result in severe disturbance of thought, affect, and behaviour. In most cases, however, intoxication is the result of voluntary behaviour—a conscious and deliberate decision to drink alcoholic beverages—and the disturbance in psychological functioning is temporary. For these reasons, the law typically does not consider alcohol intoxication to be a mental disorder. But what if the intoxication was involuntary? Perhaps a man who attends a party is given alcohol without his knowledge, or a woman who consumes a single drink of alcohol has an extreme reaction due to undiagnosed liver problems or the unanticipated effects of a new medication she is taking. And what if the intoxication is not temporary? It is possible that a person who drinks sufficient alcohol may suffer severe and long-lasting—even permanent—effects. In these latter scenarios, the law may consider people to have been suffering from a mental disorder.

In legal proceedings, triers of fact—those responsible for making decisions, such as judges, juries, or review boards—must determine whether or not a person who is party to the proceedings has a mental disorder, according to how mental disorder is defined in the relevant law. Mental health professionals act merely as consultants to triers of fact, providing expert observations and opinions. It is irksome to mental health professionals, but a fact of life, that their opinions may be accorded relatively little weight by triers of fact, or even disregarded entirely. The opinions of mental health professionals are most likely to be given weight when those opinions are based on an accurate understanding of the relevant law. We turn now to an overview of the Canadian legal system.

2 BEFORE MOVING ON

What are the primary differences between legal and psychological definitions of mental disorder in Canada?

The Canadian Legal System

Law, most generally, is a set of rules and procedures designed to regulate the behaviour of people (Melton, 1985). The fundamental goal of the law is to prevent and resolve, in a principled manner, conflicts among people. When people think about the law, they typically imagine lawyers arguing in front of a judge or jury in criminal court; yet people's encounters with the law take place, for the most part, outside court. Indeed, the law is so much a part of day-to-day life in modern society that we are rarely conscious of the extent to which it influences our actions. In Canada, there are three primary sources of law. **Constitutional law** comprises rules that govern the administration of Canada as a nation state. It both authorizes and limits the powers of the government vis-à-vis its citizens. **Statutory law** comprises written codes enacted by legislative authorities. Various statutes establish the law with respect to specific issues. **Common law** comprises legal precedent. It is the body of decisions made in past cases with respect to specific issues. Other sources of law include such things as international conventions and treaties.

CONSTITUTIONAL LAW

The development of Canada's legal system was strongly influenced by its historic ties to the United Kingdom. Canada has the same form of government as the United Kingdom, known as a constitutional monarchy. Under this system, the head of state is a monarch (king or queen), but day-to-day administration of the country is carried out by a government of parliamentary executives, who are in turn elected by the citizenry. The rights and responsibilities of the monarch, parliamentary executives, and citizenry are set out in a constitution. The Canadian constitution is a work in progress, with some parts as old as the country itself and other parts written and adopted within the last 25 years or so, but it enshrines the principles and precedents that were established in British law over the past thousand years and more. When questions arise about whether the government is living up to its responsibilities to care and provide for citizens, or whether it is overstepping its role and interfering in the private lives of citizens, it is the constitution that determines the answers. For this reason, constitutional law may be considered the single most important source of law in Canada.

The *Charter of Rights and Freedoms* (Constitution Act, 1982) sets out the fundamental freedoms of citizens, including freedom of conscience and religion; freedom of thought, belief, opinion, and expression; freedom of peaceful assembly; and freedom of association. It also sets out basic rights, including democratic rights, mobility rights, legal rights, equality rights, and language rights. Importantly, the *Charter* guarantees that the rights and freedoms enjoyed by ordinary citizens cannot be denied to others simply because they suffer from mental disorder. (Canada is unusual in this respect; even the *Universal Declaration of Human Rights of the United Nations* does not make such a guarantee.) Under the Equality Rights provision, section 15(1) of the Charter:

> Every individual is equal before and under the law and has the right to the equal protection and equal benefit of the law without discrimination and, in particular, without discrimination based on race, national or ethnic origin, colour, sex, age or mental or physical disability.

For people with mental disorders, the implications of section 15(1) are profound. Because the *Charter* prohibits discrimination on the basis of mental disability, they cannot be held against their will, prevented from expressing themselves, or denied opportunities for such things as employment or housing solely on the basis that they suffer from mental disorder. This minimizes the harm that may stem from stereotypical attitudes—sweeping and inaccurate generalizations—such as, "All people with mental disorder are at risk for violence" or "All people with mental disorder are incapable of making decisions about their health care." Thus, infringement of rights requires demonstration of a functional link—sometimes referred to in law as a causal nexus—between a person's mental disorder and some legally relevant impairment of cognitive or volitional capacity.

Constitutional law thus permits restriction of the rights and freedoms of people suffering from mental disorder. If people suffering from mental disorder are found to be incompetent to make important decisions about their lives—such as how to raise their children, what to do with their money, and how to care for their health and well-being—or incapable of controlling their behaviour, then others may make such decisions on their behalf or they may be detained and treated involuntarily (as we will discuss later). But at the same time, the constitution places strict limits on the extent to which rights and freedoms can be restricted, as well as the manner in which they can be restricted. The nature of the restrictions must be justified in light of any cognitive or volitional impairment resulting from mental disorder; they cannot be arbitrary or excessive. Also, the restrictions must be imposed in accord with the principles of fundamental justice, so that people are informed of the reasons for the restrictions and have the opportunity to challenge their imposition. In essence, the *Charter* demands that people suffering from mental disorder are treated fairly and retain as many of their rights and freedoms as possible.

STATUTORY LAW

In Canada, statutes are written and enacted by the government, with the support and approval of the monarch. If one considers federal, provincial, and municipal statutes together, there are literally hundreds of statutes in Canada that contain many thousands of rules governing the actions of citizens. Statutes set out what should and should not be done with respect to trade and commerce, health and safety, education, taxation, the environment—in fact, it is not an exaggeration to state that statutory law governs every aspect of the lives of Canadians, and every moment of their lives, from birth to death. Statutes are continually revised and updated to take into account changes in the world and the opinions and desires of citizens, but they must always be consistent with the constitution. Mental disorder plays an important role in two types of statutory law in Canada: civil mental health law and criminal law. Civil mental health law differs across the provinces and territories, but criminal law does not (this is because the Canadian constitution gives the federal government primary authority with respect to setting criminal law, but gives provinces and territories primary authority with respect to health care).

Civil mental health law sets out the procedures under which people suffering from mental disorder can be involuntarily hospitalized or treated. These laws attempt to strike a balance between, on the one hand, the right of people suffering from mental disorder to receive the treatment of their choice—including the right not to receive treatment at all—and, on the other hand, the responsibility of the government to protect its citizens from harm. Although at first glance the mental health laws of the provinces and territories appear very similar, there are important differences among them. In fact, the same person would be treated in very different ways across the country, depending on the province or territory in which he or she lived.

Criminal law—specifically, the *Criminal Code* (R.S.C. 1985, c. C-46)—defines various criminal offences and sets out the procedures under which people can be arrested, tried, and sentenced for those offences. The *Criminal Code* includes provisions for dealing with people who may suffer from mental disorder that renders them not criminally responsible (i.e., not morally blameworthy and therefore undeserving of punishment) or that renders them unfit to stand trial (i.e., incapable of participating in the trial process). The provisions set out procedures for detaining people for assessment of their mental state, specify the nature of the impairment that must be evident before someone is deemed not criminally responsible or unfit to stand trial on account of mental disorder, and specify what happens to people who are found not criminally responsible or unfit to stand trial on account of mental disorder. The *Criminal Code* is intended to deal with people who are aged 18 or older; people in conflict with the law who are between the ages of 12 and 17 inclusive are dealt with under the *Youth Criminal Justice Act* (R.S.C. 2002, c. 1), which is similar to the *Criminal Code* but has a more rehabilitative philosophy in recognition of the special status and needs of young people.

COMMON LAW

Written laws, both constitutional and statutory, have important limitations. For example, it is impossible to anticipate every conflict that might arise between citizens, and so gaps in existing law become apparent over time. Also, it is impossible to write laws that are perfectly clear and unambiguous, so all existing laws must be interpreted and re-interpreted continually. What courts, tribunals, and review boards do on a day-to-day basis—the decisions they reach in particular cases, and the reasoning underlying those decisions—comprises common law, and is written down in legal journals. Decisions made at a local level may be reviewed by courts at a higher level; for example, the decision of a judge sitting on the bench of a provincial superior court may be reviewed by colleagues who sit on the provincial appellate court, or the decisions of a provincial appellate court may be reviewed by the highest court in the land, the Supreme Court of Canada. The outcomes of these reviews also become part of common law.

Common law may eventually become enshrined in statutory or even constitutional law. For example, common law has long recognized that the monarch has the duty—in reality, both the responsibility and the authority—to arrest, prosecute, and punish those who breach the peace and disturb subjects of the realm. In Canada, this common law principle of the police powers of the state is enshrined in constitutional and statutory law. Another ancient common law principle, ***parens patriae***, recognizes that the monarch or state has the duty—again, both the responsibility and the authority—to care for citizens when they are unable to care for themselves. Historically, the monarch's duty extended to three major groups of people: children, those with mental retardation (or what will likely be called intellectual developmental disorder in DSM-5; APA, 2010), and those with serious mental disorders. The "care" offered by the monarch or state to people with mental retardation or serious mental disorder could include involuntary detention in a hospital or asylum. In Canada, this common law principle is, in part, enshrined in the civil mental health laws of the provinces and territories.

In the domain of civil law, Quebec differs from the rest of Canada. It relies on a **civil code** instead of common law. The civil code is a comprehensive set of legal rules and principles that guides legal proceedings and decision making. Quebec's civil code was based on the Napoleonic code and reflects that province's historic ties to France. As in common law jurisdictions, previous court decisions may be considered when the law is silent or unclear regarding a particular issue.

A Closer Look at Civil Mental Health Law

Virtually every Canadian is touched by mental disorder in some way. According to the epidemiological research (Health Canada, 2002), at some point in our lives about 20 percent of Canadians—about five to six million of us—will experience a serious mental disorder, perhaps one as common as a major depressive disorder (lifetime prevalence of about 10 percent to 15 percent) or one as rare as a schizophrenic disorder, a bipolar mood disorder, or mental retardation (each with a lifetime prevalence of about 1 percent). National surveys indicate that almost 1 in 10 Canadians reported their mental health was only "fair" or even "poor" during the past year (Government of Canada, 2006), and about the same number reported they were in need of or had sought services to deal with mental or emotional problems (Sareen, Cox, Afifi, Clara, & Yu, 2005; Sareen, Cox, Afifi, Yu, & Stein, 2005). Even Canadians who do not suffer from a mental disorder will probably have a family member, friend, or co-worker who does.

Mental disorder is often associated with a call to action—it provokes in others the desire to help people who are suffering from mental disorder. Most of the time, people with mental disorder can and do function adequately while living in the community, either on their own, with personal support from family and friends, or with the assistance of health care professionals. But what happens when mental disorder is so serious that it impairs people's daily functioning? Some people lack insight and cannot recognize that they suffer from mental disorder and may reject treatment or other assistance; others have symptoms so severe that they are unable to make rational decisions about their own care or unable to provide for themselves the necessities of life, such as food, clothing, or even basic hygiene. There are no good estimates of the number of Canadians who are unable to care for themselves or to make decisions regarding their own care due to mental disorder, but anyone who has visited a big city like Montreal, Toronto, or Vancouver has seen some of these people living on the street or panhandling. What are we to do with people in this position—simply leave them to suffer on their own, or force care on them against their wishes?

As discussed above, each province and territory has a statute that enshrines the *parens patriae* powers of the state to care for people suffering from mental disorder who are unable to care for themselves (Douglas & Koch, 2001; Gray & O'Reilly, 2001, 2005). Civil mental health law gives the provinces and territories tremendous powers to interfere in the lives of citizens, including the authority to detain people against their will. The mental health acts of the 10 provinces and 3 territories are summarized in Table 19.1. The statutes deal with three major issues: involuntary hospitalization, including conditional leave; involuntary treatment, including community treatment orders; and procedures for reviewing and appealing decisions with respect to involuntary hospitalization and treatment.

INVOLUNTARY HOSPITALIZATION

Involuntary hospitalization, also known as **civil commitment**, is the process of detention of people against their will on the grounds that they pose a risk to themselves or others on account of mental disorder (Winick, 2008). The issue is, in essence, one of public safety: governments have a legal responsibility to protect citizens, and this includes the responsibility to protect them from the harmful consequences of physical or mental illness (Gostin, 2005). In a very real sense, then, civil commitment is about containing dangerous illnesses, rather than dangerous people.

Laws that allow involuntary hospitalization and treatment of physical illness or mental disorder clearly infringe on the basic rights and freedoms of citizens. This infringement may be legally justified on two grounds (Melton, Petrila, Poythress, & Slobogin, 2007; Morse, 2002, 2004; Schopp, 2001). First, governments have *parens patriae* powers to act as guardian or caretaker for people who are deemed unable to make decisions about their own health and welfare because they are physically or mentally ill. Second, governments have police powers to control people who threaten public order, whether or not they are physically or mentally ill.

Involuntary hospitalization on the grounds of mental disorder, then, is very different from **criminal commitment**, detention following conviction for a criminal offence. Criminal commitment is inherently and deliberately punitive. It is intended to make people suffer for harms they have perpetrated and for which they are morally culpable. In this respect, it is focused on the past, on what has already happened. But involuntary hospitalization as a form of civil commitment is preventive. It is intended to minimize potential harm, and so has its eye toward the future. Laws regarding involuntary hospitalization make no assumption that people are morally culpable for the risks they pose, and may even assume that people are not culpable for the illnesses they suffer. For this reason, involuntary hospitalization is not punitive in nature, and in fact the procedures for and conditions of involuntary hospitalization must not be punitive if it is to be legally justified.

Although the specific legal requirements for involuntary hospitalization vary across provinces and territories, they are very similar in general terms. People may

TABLE 19.1 COMPARISON OF THE MENTAL HEALTH ACTS OF CANADIAN PROVINCES AND TERRITORIES

	Criteria for Commitment				Length of Commitment				
Province/ Territory	**Definition of Mental Disorder**	**Definition of Harm to Others**	**Include Deterioration**	**Include Need for Treatment**	**Short Term**	**Initial**	**Subsequent**	**Patient Has Right to Refuse Treatment**	**Permits Conditional Release**
Alberta	Narrow	Narrow	No	No	24 hrs.	1 mo.	1–6 mos.	No	Yes
British Columbia	Narrow	Broad	Yes	Yes	48 hrs.	1 mo.	1–6 mos.	No	Yes
Manitoba	Narrow	Narrow	No	Yes	72 hrs.	3 wks.	3 mos.	Yes	Yes
New Brunswick	Narrow	Broad	No	Yes	72 hrs.	1 mo.	2–3 mos.	No	Yes
Newfoundland & Labrador	Broad	Broad	Yes	Yes	72 hrs.*	1 mo.	1–3 mos.	No	No
N.W.T.	Narrow	Narrow	Yes	No	48 hrs.	2 wks.	1–6 mos.	No	Yes
Nova Scotia	Broad	Broad	Yes	Yes	48 hrs.	1 wk.	1–6 mos.	Yes	Yes
Nunavut	Narrow	Narrow	Yes	No	48 hrs.	2 wks.	1–2 mos.	No	Yes
Ontario	Broad	Narrow	No	Yes	72 hrs.	2 wks.	1–3 mos.	Yes	Yes
Prince Edward Island	Narrow	Broad	No	Yes	72 hrs.	1 mo.	3 mos.–1 yr.	No	Yes
Quebec	Broad	Broad	No	No	48 hrs.	3 wks.	3–6 mos.	No	Yes
Saskatchewan	Narrow	Broad	No	Yes	24 hrs.	3 wks.	3 wks.–1 yr.	No	No
Yukon	Narrow	Narrow	No	No	24 hrs.	3 wks.	3 wks.	No	Yes

Source: After Douglas and Koch (2001) and Gray and O'Reilly (2001, 2005); updated to include changes to provincial mental health legislation in Newfoundland and Labrador in 2006, Nova Scotia in 2007, and Nunavut in 2010.

*Can be extended up to 7 days in exceptional circumstances.

be involuntarily hospitalized only if each of the following three criteria is met:

1. People must be suffering from a mental disorder. In most jurisdictions, the definition of mental disorder is narrow and the mental disorder must be severe (i.e., one that causes serious impairment) and treatable (i.e., one that is likely to be successfully managed or improved by treatment). In a few jurisdictions the definition is broad and not limited to severe or treatable conditions.
2. People must be either unwilling to consent or incapable of consenting to hospitalization on a voluntary or informal basis. It is simply unnecessary to involuntarily hospitalize people who want treatment and are capable of giving their consent. This requirement prevents the state from needlessly exercising its powers and infringing on people's rights.
3. People must be at risk for causing harm to self (i.e., suicidal behaviour) or others (i.e., violent behaviour) due to the mental disorder. The risk must be acute in terms of severity, imminence, or likelihood. With respect to severity, most jurisdictions require that the risk involves serious physical injury to self or others; people at risk for causing fear or for minor physical assault may not be committable in some provinces. With respect to imminence, some jurisdictions require that the person must be at risk for harm in the near future—that is, in the next few hours or days rather than in the coming weeks, months, or years. Finally, with respect to likelihood, there must be a substantial probability that the harm may occur. Commitment cannot be based on remote or trivial probability of harm. As an alternative to this criterion of risk for harm to self or others, some jurisdictions also allow commitment based on the need for treatment, lack of capacity to make treatment decisions, or risk for deterioration in physical or mental health due to failure to obtain treatment. In some respects, these alternatives may be seen as a logical extension of the "risk for harm to self" criterion.

The process of involuntary hospitalization sometimes starts with emergency or short-term detention. Most often, this is ordered by a physician who has evaluated the patient. In most jurisdictions, peace officers have the right to apprehend people suffering from mental disorder, if they have reasonable grounds to believe that those people may meet the criteria for civil commitment under the relevant mental health act, and then to detain the person for a short period of time, typically 24 to 72 hours, for evaluation by a physician. In most jurisdictions, people have a specified right to be informed of the reasons for their detention. If, after the emergency or short-term detention for evaluation, it is determined that the person meets criteria in the mental health act, then the person may be certified and committed for a longer period of time, typically 2 to 4 weeks. In other cases, the process of involuntary hospitalization begins with certification and commitment. This typically happens when people are already being assessed or treated for mental disorder—and in fact may have been admitted to hospital already—and thus there is no need to detain the person for (further) evaluation by physicians. Once the initial period of commitment is over, people may be recommitted if they continue to meet the criteria in the mental health act. The second commitment is often for a longer period than was the initial commitment, typically 1 to 3 months. Subsequent recommitments may be even longer, for periods as long as 6 to 12 months.

Release from involuntary hospitalization typically occurs in one of two ways. First, people may get better as a result of treatment or due simply to the passage of time (i.e., spontaneous remission). The improvement may reflect a clinically significant reduction in either mental disorder or functional impairment. This means that the causal nexus between mental disorder and functional impairment has been broken, and there is no basis for commitment. The statutes of most jurisdictions provide criteria to help judge when patients are ready for release. In some jurisdictions, patients are given an unconditional release or absolute discharge from hospital, and so their full rights and freedoms are returned to them. In other jurisdictions, patients may be given a conditional release that requires them to receive specified outpatient treatment. Second, people may be released by a review board or panel despite a lack of improvement.

3 BEFORE MOVING ON

Someone who suffers from a mental disorder and is believed to pose an imminent risk for serious harm to others may be involuntarily hospitalized for days or weeks—in theory, even for months or years. Isn't it simply unfair or unreasonable to punish someone for something he or she *hasn't done* but *might do*? How can this be justified?

INVOLUNTARY TREATMENT

Everyone committed to hospital receives a clean and safe place to stay where he or she is provided with the necessities of life, such as food, clothing, and care for physical illnesses or injury. In this sense, commitment may be considered therapeutic. But some people refuse active treatment in the form of psychoactive medications or psychotherapy.

When patients are committed and deemed incapable of making decisions about treatment, someone must make treatment decisions on their behalf. This person is sometimes referred to as a **temporary substitute decision maker**. In some jurisdictions, the temporary substitute decision maker is an appointee of the state, such as a physician, the director of a psychiatric unit, or a court or tribunal. In other jurisdictions, the temporary substitute decision maker is a private representative of the patient. Private representatives may be people appointed by patients when they were mentally healthy and competent to make decisions, or they may be guardians or family members; if no private representative is available, then the Public Trustee, an appointee of the state, makes the decision.

Regardless of who they are and how they were appointed, temporary substitute decision makers must exercise their judgment according to principles outlined in the mental health act. Two principles are used most commonly. The first is known as the **best interests principle**. Briefly, it holds that the temporary substitute decision maker should choose the treatment that maximizes the chances of a good outcome for the patient, taking into account the risks and benefits of all available treatments. At least implicitly, a patient's personal wishes regarding treatment must be taken into account at some point in the decision-making process. The second principle is known as the **capable wishes principle**. It holds that a patient's personal wishes regarding treatment should be given the greatest weight in the decision-making process, especially when these wishes were expressed previously when the patient was competent to make decisions about treatment. In fact, some jurisdictions hold that a wish applicable to the circumstances expressed while a patient was capable cannot be overridden. One jurisdiction uses the capable wishes principle except when the patient's wish would endanger the health or safety of people, in which case the best interests principle is used.

A relatively new trend in mental health law is the option of **compulsory treatment orders**, involuntary treatment on an outpatient basis (Gray & O'Reilly, 2005). Currently, three provinces (Newfoundland and Labrador, Ontario, and Saskatchewan) have mental health acts that permit compulsory treatment orders; all require that the person has a history of recent psychiatric hospitalization (compulsory treatment orders differ from conditional leaves in that the latter require that a person was first involuntarily hospitalized and then released on the condition of continuing treatment in the community upon discharge).

A potential strength of compulsory treatment orders is that they provide a means of ensuring that patients will receive treatment that may relieve their distress and reduce the chances of relapse or re-hospitalization in a way that is less restrictive than involuntary hospitalization (Gray & O'Reilly, 2005). But compulsory treatment orders have several potential limitations as well. First, they are still coercive: people are legally required to receive a treatment they do not want, and face the threat of involuntary hospitalization if they fail to comply. In other jurisdictions, people under compulsory treatment orders may even lose their residence or financial support if they fail to comply (Bonnie & Monahan, 2005). Coercion may impair attempts to establish and maintain supportive and effective treatment relationships between people and their health care providers (Winick, 2008). Second, critics have expressed concern that compulsory treatment orders are used to coerce people into treatment who do not meet criteria for involuntary hospitalization because they pose a relatively low risk of harm to self or others. This means that compulsory treatment orders may actually increase, rather than decrease, the frequency with which people are subjected to coercive treatment, a result sometimes referred to as "net widening" (Geller, Fisher, Grudzinskas, Clayfield, & Lawlor, 2006). Finally, there is no convincing evidence from systematic reviews that compulsory treatment orders are effective in reducing health service use or improving clinical outcome and social functioning relative to traditional forms of treatment, voluntary or involuntary (Kisely, Campbell, Scott, Preston, & Xiao, 2006; Swartz & Swanson, 2004). Adequate mental health services must be available in the community for compulsory treatment orders to be effective, and it may be that providing high-quality voluntary outpatient services reduces or even eliminates the need for compulsory treatment orders (Greenfield, Stoneking, Humphreys, Sundby, & Bond, 2008).

REVIEWS AND APPEALS

Consistent with the *Charter*, every jurisdiction provides for quasi-judicial review of decisions regarding involuntary hospitalization and involuntary treatment. With respect to involuntary hospitalization, reviews typically take place at the end of each period of commitment and also, under certain circumstances, at the request of patients. The review board or panel will convene a hearing to consider evidence presented by the hospital to which the person was committed, as well as any evidence presented by the patients themselves; in most jurisdictions, patients have a specified right to be represented by legal counsel at the hearing. Patients or people acting on their behalf usually have the specified right to appeal their commitment to a court. Patients do not, however, have the right to be released from hospital while their commitment is under review or appeal. With respect to involuntary treatment, the procedures are very similar, except that treatment cannot begin until the matter is resolved, including any appeal.

SOME EXAMPLES OF RESEARCH ON MENTAL HEALTH LAW IN CANADA

WHO IS INVOLUNTARILY HOSPITALIZED? Somewhat surprisingly, no good statistics are readily available in Canada regarding the number of people who are involuntarily hospitalized or involuntarily treated. Better statistics are available concerning any hospitalization due to mental disorder. According to statistics for 2005–2006 collected by the Canadian Institute for Health Information, the hospitalization rate for mental disorder was 600 separations (that is, discharges from or deaths in hospital) per 100 000 people in the general population per year. About 1 in every 200 Canadians was released from the psychiatric ward of general hospitals, where the average length of stay was 16 days; and about 1 in 1200 was released from a specialized psychiatric hospital, where the average length of stay was 100 days (Canadian Institute for Health Information, 2008). (Comparing these statistics to those collected over the past 30 years or so, there has been a major decrease in the rate of long-term hospitalization for mental disorder, referred to as **deinstitutionalization**, and a substantial increase in short-term and community-based treatments; see Canadian Institute for Health Information, 2008; Sealy & Whitehead, 2004; Stefan, 2006.) Based on older national statistics (e.g., Riley & Richman, 1983) and studies that compared voluntary and involuntary admissions in smaller samples (e.g., Crisanti & Love, 2001; Malla, Norman, & Helmes, 1987; Tremblay, King, & Baines, 1994), it appears that up to 15 to 20 percent of all hospitalizations for mental disorder in Canada are involuntary. If this estimate is accurate, then the rate of involuntary hospitalization may be between 90 and 120 commitments per 100 000 people per year, or as many as 30 000 committals annually.

Comparisons of voluntary and involuntary admissions have found relatively few differences between the two groups. In one such study, Annette Crisanti and Edgar Love (2001) examined admissions to a psychiatric unit at Calgary General Hospital between 1987 and 1995. They reviewed the hospital records of large, representative samples of patients admitted either voluntarily ($n = 1007$) or involuntarily under Alberta's *Mental Health Act* ($n = 711$).

Their results are summarized in Table 19.2. They found that the groups differed significantly with respect to age, length of stay, primary diagnosis, and criminal record: involuntary patients were more likely to be male, stayed in the hospital longer, were more likely to be diagnosed as schizophrenic (and less likely to be diagnosed as personality disordered), and more frequently had a criminal record prior to admission. The groups did not differ with respect to age, and also did not appear to differ with respect to education or employment history (although it was difficult to test these differences due to missing information).

A similar profile of involuntarily hospitalized patients has emerged from studies of patients who applied for a review of their detention. For example, Grant, Ogloff, and Douglas (2000) studied 279 patients at Riverview Hospital, a large psychiatric hospital in British Columbia that serves the entire province. They found that 60 percent of the patients were male, the average age was about 39 years, and 67 percent had a primary diagnosis of a psychotic disorder. Most also had a history of serious employment problems; in fact, only 4 percent were working prior to their admission. Consistent with a history of serious mental disorder, 91 percent of patients had a history of prior psychiatric hospitalizations. Grant and colleagues were also able to collect information about risk for harm to self or others. They found that 68 percent of the patients had a history of suicidal or other self-injurious behaviour prior to hospitalization, and 23 percent had engaged in self-harmful behaviour while hospitalized. Similarly, 64 percent of patients had a history of violence, including 23 percent with a history of arrests for violent offences and 49 percent who had committed violence in the two weeks prior to hospitalization.

TABLE 19.2 COMPARISON OF VOLUNTARILY AND INVOLUNTARILY HOSPITALIZED PATIENTS ADMITTED TO CALGARY GENERAL HOSPITAL, 1987–1995

	Voluntarily Hospitalized (n = 1007)	Involuntarily Hospitalized (n = 711)
Sex		
Male	42%	54%
Female	58%	46%
Age (mean)	39 years	37 years
Length of Stay (median)	12 days	19 days
Primary Diagnosis		
Psychotic Disorder	23%	54%
Mood Disorder	36%	28%
Personality Disorder	28%	12%
Other Disorder	13%	6%
Criminal Record	16%	19%

Source: International Journal of Law & Psychiatry, Vol. 23, 2001, pp. 399–401, Crisanti et al., "Characteristics of Psychiatric Inpatients Detained Under Civil Commitment Legislation: A Canadian Study." With permission from Elsevier.

What happens to people who are involuntarily hospitalized? A number of studies have examined the frequency with which patients apply for review of their committal. Gray, Clark, Higenbottam, Ledwidge, and Paredes (1985) examined 487 involuntary patients in British Columbia who applied for review and 2966 who did not. This suggests that in only 14 percent of cases was a review requested. Gray and colleagues also found some differences between people who applied for review and those who did not with respect to demographic characteristics and mental health history. For example, those who applied for review were more often male, were younger, and had a history of more serious education and employment problems. Also, those who applied for review were more likely to have a diagnosis of schizophrenic disorder (and less likely to have a diagnosis of mental retardation) and had more previous hospitalizations. Similar findings were reported by Komer, O'Reilly, Cernovsky, and Dunbar (1999), who examined involuntarily hospitalized patients in Ontario. During a six-year period from 1987 to 1993, there were 31 124 involuntary hospitalizations in the 10 provincial psychiatric hospitals in Ontario. A surprisingly small number of patients—4953, or 16 percent of all those involuntarily hospitalized—requested a review. Komer and colleagues also examined the outcome of the involuntary hospitalizations. Many of the cases in which applications were made were resolved prior to review: in 18 percent of cases, patients withdrew their request; in another 25 percent, physicians transferred patients to voluntary status; and in 1 percent, the period of commitment expired. Of the cases that actually went to review, the outcome was known in 2680 cases, and in only 343 cases was the patient released. This latter number reflects a tiny percentage of all involuntary hospitalization (1 percent); even looking only at cases that proceeded to review that had known outcomes, it reflects a very low "success rate" (13 percent).

Research by Higgenbottam et al. (1985) compared patients in British Columbia who were released after review to those who were not released. They found that patients who were released appeared to have less serious mental disorder, spent less time hospitalized, and were perceived to be at lower risk for harm to self. Also, they had better plans for release, insofar as they were more likely to be on the waiting list for placement in a boarding home. Furthermore, they were more likely to have been represented by legal counsel at the review.

Finally, there has been follow-up research examining the community adjustment of patients released from involuntary hospitalization. For example, Ledwidge and colleagues (1987) compared the post-release adjustment of 47 involuntary patients from British Columbia who were released after review with 47 patients released by their attending physicians. The two groups were matched on a number of key variables, including sex, age, primary diagnosis, and length of stay. The adjustment of both groups was rather poor: 45 percent were readmitted to hospital within a year, and most patients continued to have serious problems with employment and personal relationships. Poor adjustment after release was associated with more serious mental disorder and poor response to treatment before release. On a positive note, few patients engaged in suicidal or violent behaviour after release. Douglas and colleagues (Douglas, Ogloff, Nicholls, & Grant, 1999) conducted a retrospective file review of 193 involuntarily hospitalized patients who applied for review of their detention and were subsequently released, either after review or at the end of the period of committal. They examined adjustment in the community over a period of 20 months following release, focusing on violent acts that were documented in clinical files or resulted in arrest. Of the 193 patients, 38 percent committed at least one documented act of violence in the 20 months after their release from hospital, including 19 percent who committed at least one act of physical violence and 10 percent who were arrested for at least one violent criminal offence.

HOW CAN VIOLENCE RISK BE EVALUATED? Violence risk is a key element in decision making with respect to involuntary hospitalization. It is also important when making decisions about mentally disordered offenders (as we will discuss shortly). Until recently, psychologists trying to assess the violence risk posed by patients had few resources to guide them: little was known about the frequency of violence among psychiatric patients, the most important risk factors for violence, or the best ways to gather and combine information to reach decisions about violence risk. But the past decade has seen major developments in this field, and Canadian researchers have made important contributions, including the development of procedures for the systematic assessment of violence risk.

There are two basic approaches to violence risk assessment: discretionary and nondiscretionary (see Hart, 2001a; Monahan, 1981/1995). The discretionary approach is sometimes referred to as clinical, informal, or intuitive, whereas the nondiscretionary approach is sometimes referred to as actuarial, mechanistic, or algorithmic. The discretionary approach permits mental health professionals to exercise judgment in gathering relevant information and combining the information to make decisions about what kind of violence a patient might commit and how best to prevent the occurrence of violence or minimize the harm caused by the violence. The nondiscretionary approach imposes strict rules on the assessment process, instructing mental professionals as to exactly which information can and must be considered and exactly how the information should be weighted and combined to make decisions. The decisions here are typically estimates of the absolute or relative likelihood that someone will commit violence (e.g., the specific probability that someone will be arrested for a violent offence within six months of release from an institution). The two approaches have complementary strengths: the discretionary approach is flexible, or easily adapted to new and unusual situations, and idiographic, or responsive to the unique characteristics of the case at hand, whereas the nondiscretionary approach encourages consistency across cases.

One example of the discretionary approach to violence risk assessment is the HCR-20, developed at Simon Fraser University by Christopher D. Webster, Kevin S. Douglas, Derek Eaves, and Stephen D. Hart (1997). The HCR-20 is a set of structured professional guidelines for assessing violence risk that was based on a comprehensive review of the scientific, professional, and legal literatures. The HCR-20 is a book or manual that discusses the concept of violence, recommends procedures for gathering relevant information, and describes 20 major risk factors for violence that should be considered, at a minimum, in every risk assessment. Related publications discuss how this information can be used to develop treatment or management plans for individual cases (e.g., Douglas, Webster, Hart, Eaves, & Ogloff, 2001). The 20 risk factors in the HCR-20 fall into three categories: there are 10 **H**istorical factors that reflect past or long-term functioning; 5 **C**linical factors that reflect recent or current functioning; and 5 **R**isk management factors that reflect potential adjustment problems based on the patient's plans for the future. The HCR-20 risk factors are summarized in Table 19.3.

Research indicates that the HCR-20 helps professionals make reliable judgments of violence risk. Not only are judgments concerning individual risk factors made reliably, but overall or integrative judgments based on the individual factors are made reliably; these judgments also have predictive validity with respect to violence committed while institutionalized as well as violence committed after discharge into the community (see Douglas & Reeves, 2010; Yang, Wong, & Coid, 2010, for reviews). For example, in their study of involuntarily committed civil psychiatric patients who were treated and then released, Douglas and colleagues (1999) found that ratings made using the HCR-20 had moderate to high predictive validity with respect to violent behaviour in the community. This was true when violence was defined broadly to include threatening or intimidating behaviour, and when it was defined more narrowly to include only physical violence or violence that resulted in criminal charges or convictions. They used a simple median split procedure to divide the patients into two groups: low risk (those with few HCR-20 risk factors) and high risk (those with many HCR-20 risk factors). Based on event history analyses, they estimated that only 20 percent of the low-risk patients would commit violence within two years

TABLE 19.3 THE HCR-20 RISK FACTORS

Historical Factors	Clinical Factors	Risk Management Factors
H1. Previous violence	C1. Lack of insight	R1. Plans lack feasibility
H2. Young age at first violence	C2. Negative attitudes	R2. Exposure to destabilizers
H3. Relationship instability	C3. Active symptoms of major mental illness	R3. Lack of personal support
H4. Employment problems	C4. Impulsivity	R4. Noncompliance with remediation attempts
H5. Substance use problems	C5. Unresponsive to treatment	R5. Stress
H6. Major mental illness		
H7. Psychopathy		
H8. Early maladjustment		
H9. Personality disorder		
H10. Prior supervision failure		

Source: Webster, C. D., Douglas, K. S., Eaves, D., & Hart, S. D. (1997). *HCR-20: Assessing risk for violence*, version 2. Burnaby, BC: Mental Health, Law, & Policy Institute, Simon Fraser University.

of release, compared to 60 percent of the high-risk patients. Based on these and similar findings, it is not surprising that the HCR-20 has been translated into more than a dozen languages and is used widely in civil psychiatric, forensic psychiatric, and correctional settings around the world.

A Closer Look at Mentally Disordered Offenders

People suffering from mental disorder are overrepresented among those who are arrested, charged with, or convicted of criminal offences. For example, Roesch and his colleagues (Roesch, 1995; see also Corrado, Cohen, Hart, & Roesch, 2000b; Hart, Roesch, Corrado, & Cox, 1993) conducted large-scale epidemiological research at a pretrial jail in Vancouver, British Columbia. They screened 881 consecutive admissions to the institution in 1989 and 1990, all adult males. A total of 684 were willing and able to complete various interview-based screens for mental disorder; the findings indicated that about 10 to 20 percent of all admissions appeared to be suffering from symptoms of a serious mental disorder (Hart et al., 1993). A subsample of admissions completed the Diagnostic Interview Schedule, Version III-A (DIS; Robins & Helzer, 1985), which was used to make current and lifetime diagnoses of selected mental disorders according to the criteria contained in DSM-III (American Psychiatric Association, 1980). According to the DIS, 94 percent of admissions met diagnostic criteria for at least one DSM-III mental disorder, including 16 percent who met the criteria for at least one serious mental disorder (Corrado et al., 2000b; see also Table 19.4). People diagnosed with serious mental disorder were more likely to receive health care in the jail, including psychological counselling, psychoactive medications, transfer to the medical unit of the jail, and transfer out of the jail to a psychiatric hospital (Corrado et al., 2000b). Similar findings have been reported in epidemiological studies of people sentenced to provincial prisons (e.g., Bland, Newman, Dyck, & Orn, 1990) or federal penitentiaries (e.g., Brink, Doherty, & Boer, 2001; Hodgins & Côté, 1990; Porporino & Motiuk, 1995).

TABLE 19.4 LIFETIME PREVALENCE OF MENTAL DISORDERS AMONG 192 ADULT MALES ADMITTED TO THE VANCOUVER PRETRIAL SERVICES CENTRE, 1989–1990

Disorder	Lifetime Prevalence
Major mental disorders	15.6% (2.6%)
Cognitive impairment	0.5% (0.5%)
Schizophrenic disorders	4.9% (1.6%)
Bipolar affective disorder	4.1% (1.4%)
Major depressive disorder	6.0% (1.7%)
Substance use disorders	85.9% (2.5%)
Alcohol use disorders	77.6% (3.0%)
Drug use disorders	63.7% (3.5%)
Other mental disorders	88.0% (2.4%)
Anxiety disorders	41.1% (3.6%)
Dysthymia	7.2% (1.9%)
Somatization disorder	0.7% (0.6%)
Bulimia	0.3% (0.4%)
Sexual disorders	27.0% (3.2%)
Antisocial personality disorder	64.3% (3.5%)
Any disorder	93.6% (1.8%)

Source: Corrado, R. R., Cohen, I., Hart, S. D., & Roesch, R. (2000). Comparative examination of the prevalence of mental disorders among jailed inmates in Canada and the United States. *International Journal of Law and Psychiatry, 23*,633–647.

The Correctional Investigator of Canada has commented that the number of mentally ill offenders in Canada's correctional system currently exceeds the capacity of the Correctional Service of Canada (Sapers, 2010). This situation may be exacerbated in the future due to recent and proposed changes to criminal justice policy that have been introduced by the Conservative Party, the current government of Canada. These changes, which have sometimes been referred to as "tough on crime" policies, are likely to result in increases in the number of incarcerated individuals, including those with mental health problems. Cook and Roesch (in press) have critiqued these policies, arguing that research shows that these types of reforms will come at a substantial financial and human cost, and will not lower crime rates or better protect the public. Cook and Roesch also note that the high costs associated with expanding the prison system will siphon funds away from prevention and early intervention programs that psychological research shows can be more beneficial in preventing crime in the long term as well as being more cost effective.

Municipal police are recognizing that a high proportion of police time is spent on responding to calls involving persons with mental health problems. The city of Vancouver conducted a study in 2007 to assess the extent of this involvement (Wilson-Bates, 2008). Police contact data were obtained over a 16-day period. Police officers responding to the calls indicated whether the call involved a person with mental health problems. They found that of 1154 calls, 31 percent involved at least one mentally ill person. Certain areas of Vancouver, such as the Downtown Eastside, had percentages close to 50 percent. Many of these individuals are arrested due at least in part to the lack of alternative services in the community.

The fact that so many people who come into contact with police suffer from serious mental disorder poses tremendous problems for those responsible for the institutional and community management of offenders. But it also poses a problem for the police, prosecutors, and triers of fact who are responsible for making decisions about when to arrest, charge, or convict people who suffer from mental disorder. Criminal law gives the state awesome powers, including the power to punish its citizens by stripping them of their fundamental rights and freedoms for the rest of their lives. But criminal law is only intended to be used when people have committed acts that deserve punishment. It may not serve the public good to devote resources to punishing a crowd of ecstatic fans who hold an impromptu parade when their hockey team wins the league championship, someone who burns a flag during a political demonstration, or a person who "moons" someone in public on a dare, even though each of these things may technically constitute a criminal offence. Similarly, it may not serve the public good to punish a depressed person who creates a public disturbance while attempting to commit suicide by jumping off a bridge; a woman who kills her children while suffering from the delusion that they were possessed by the devil; or a man who walks naked in public while suffering from dementia but does not know the date, his wife's name, or where he resides. The Criminal Code includes special provisions for deciding whether people who committed offences while suffering from mental disorder should be held criminally responsible, as well as whether people currently suffering from mental disorder should be put on trial.

CRIMINAL RESPONSIBILITY: MENTAL STATE AT THE TIME OF THE OFFENCE

Under Canadian law, people can be convicted of criminal offences only when they commit a prohibited act with bad intention. The prohibited act is known as the ***actus reus***; the bad intention as the ***mens rea***. Among other things, the Criminal Code sets out the *actus reus* and the *mens rea* that constitute each criminal offence. It also sets out certain defences that might serve as acceptable explanations or excuses for what would otherwise be a criminal offence. A good example is self-defence; section 34 of the Criminal Code authorizes people to use force to protect themselves when they are unlawfully assaulted by another person; they are even authorized to cause the death of someone, if they have reasonable grounds to believe that person is attempting to kill them or to cause them grievous bodily harm. Similarly, section 16 of the Criminal Code sets out the defence of mental disorder, known popularly as the "insanity defence":

> 16. (1) No person is criminally responsible for an act committed or an omission made while suffering from a mental disorder that rendered the person incapable of appreciating the nature and quality of the act or omission or of knowing that it was wrong.
>
> (2) Every person is presumed not to suffer from a mental disorder so as to be exempt from criminal responsibility by virtue of subsection (1), until the contrary is proved on the balance of probabilities.
>
> (3) The burden of proof that an accused was suffering from a mental disorder so as to be exempt from criminal responsibility is on the party that raises the issue.

According to the Criminal Code, some people suffering from mental disorder, through no fault of their own, may have inaccurate perceptions of or irrational beliefs about the world that led them to commit a prohibited act, but without any bad intention—exactly in the same way that someone who raises the defence of self-defence admits the act, but denies the intent. In short, section 16 recognizes that mental disorder may negate or rule out *mens rea*.

The history of section 16 can be traced back across several millennia of European history (e.g., Zapf, Golding, & Roesch, 2005). The laws of ancient civilizations, such as the Greeks and the Romans, as well as the philosophies of the Jewish, Christian, and Muslim faiths, recognized that people suffering from mental disorder are deserving of special care. This view was incorporated into English common law as far back as 1505, which was the first documented case of a person being found not guilty by reason of insanity. But the current language of section 16, as well as the inclusion of provisions in the Criminal Code for the detention of people found legally insane—what we now call a finding of **not criminally responsible on account of mental disorder**, or **NCRMD**—dates back to the 1800s. That century saw two important cases in England involving people suffering from serious mental disorders who attempted to assassinate public figures, including the monarch and the prime minister. In the first, James Hadfield attempted to shoot King George III (*R. v. Hadfield*, 1800). He was charged with high treason but later acquitted due to mental disorder by a jury, after the defence led evidence indicating that he suffered from religious and nihilistic delusions that by killing the king he would hasten the end of the earthly world and the Second Coming of Jesus. In response to Hadfield's case, the English parliament passed the Criminal Lunatics Acts of 1800, which required that people acquitted due to mental disorder be detained in a secure facility for the rest of their lives. In the second case, Daniel M'Naghten attempted to shoot the prime minister, Robert Peel, mistakenly killing Peel's private secretary instead (*R. v. M'Naghten*, 1843). Like Hadfield before him, a jury heard evidence that M'Naghten was suffering from delusions—persecutory delusions that the government was involved in a conspiracy against him—and found him not guilty by reason of insanity. But following M'Naghten's acquittal, there was public outrage that he got away with murder. A panel of judges was convened to clarify the law, and the result was known as the **M'Naghten standard**. Briefly, it held that people could be acquitted due to mental disorder only if they suffered from a mental disorder that caused a specific cognitive impairment—namely, the inability to understand the nature and quality of their acts or the inability to understand that the acts were wrong. The original M'Naghten standard was included almost verbatim in the first Canadian Criminal Code in 1894 and has survived, virtually intact, to the present day. The M'Naghten standard also formed the basis for the insanity provisions of the criminal codes in most common law jurisdictions around the world, including the federal and most state codes in the United States.

Although the wording of section 16 has changed little in the last hundred years, there have been important developments in the insanity defence in Canada. One development was cases that led to clarification of key concepts in section 16(1). For example, in the Supreme Court of Canada's judgments in *Cooper v. R.* (1980) and *R. v. Rabey* (1980), it was confirmed that mental disorder includes any disturbance of the mind or its functioning that is internal (i.e., not the result of situational factors), intransient (i.e., not temporary or ephemeral), and involuntary (i.e., not self-induced). Thus, the law's definition of mental disorder is broad, and legal arguments therefore tend to focus on whether a person's mental disorder causes cognitive impairment, rather than whether the person's mental disorder is real or valid according to the law. In the cases of *Cooper v. R.* (1980), *Kjeldsen v. R.* (1981), and *R. v. Abbey* (1982), it was confirmed that appreciating the nature and quality of an act requires full comprehension or understanding of the act's physical consequences. It is irrelevant, for example, if people suffer from a personality disorder that makes them unable to appreciate the emotional harm their victims suffer. And most recently, in the case of *R. v. Chaulk* (1990), it was confirmed that knowing an act is wrong requires simple understanding or recognition that an act is legally and morally wrong.

A second development was major changes in the Criminal Code concerning the disposition of people detained for evaluation of criminal responsibility or found NCRMD. Until 1992, defendants who were referred for evaluation of criminal responsibility were committed to a secure facility for 30 days, and they could easily be recommitted for further evaluation. Those acquitted by reason of insanity were committed to a secure facility indefinitely, or "at the pleasure of the Lieutenant Governor," according to the review procedures set out by each province or territory. In the case of *R. v. Swain* (1991), the Supreme Court of Canada held that these procedures violated the *Charter*. In April 1992, Parliament passed Bill C-30, which addressed defects in the Criminal Code identified by the Supreme Court. There were four major amendments. First, the Criminal Code now places a five-day limit on assessment orders, unless the defendant and prosecutor agree to a longer period not exceeding 30 days. Compelling circumstances can extend this to a maximum of 60 days. These evaluations can take place in a jail, an outpatient clinic, or an inpatient facility. Second, there have been changes to the disposition of an accused following a finding of NCRMD. People who are committed must undergo a regular review of their detention by a board, the composition and procedures of which are established under the provision of the Code. People may be committed only if they still present a risk of harm—in the case of *Winko v. B.C. (Forensic Psychiatric Institute)* (1999), defined as a "significant threat" to public safety—due to mental disorder. At the initial disposition or after review, people found to be NCRMD may be detained in hospital, given a conditional discharge according to certain restrictions or requirements set out by the review board, or given an absolute or unconditional discharge. Third, there were changes regarding who may argue for acquittal under section 16. The Criminal Code now prohibits the prosecution from raising the issue of the accused's mental state unless the defence raises it at the time of the offence, or until after the accused is found guilty of an offence. This change recognizes that accused people should have the right to choose their own defence at trial. Finally, the Criminal Code amendments established "caps" or upper limits on the maximum length of time that people may be detained following a finding of NCRMD. In theory, this should prevent the possibility that people will be detained indefinitely for minor offences. The capping provisions, however, have not yet been proclaimed.

COMPETENCY TO MAKE LEGAL DECISIONS: MENTAL STATE AT THE TIME OF TRIAL

According to principles of fundamental justice, people accused of crimes have the right to be present at their trial, to confront their accusers, and to make full answer and defence to the accusations against them (e.g., Zapf & Roesch, 2009). Proceeding to trial when people are suffering from a serious mental disorder and not fully "present" or lacking the capacity to defend themselves is not in the interests of justice: the risk of mistaken conviction increases, and even when people are guilty any deterrent impact of punishment is diminished. When accused individuals suffer from a serious mental disorder, their trials may be suspended temporarily while they are transferred to hospital and treated.

Like the insanity defence, the doctrine of fitness or competency to stand trial has a long history in English common law. In the case of *R. v. Pritchard* (1836), it was clarified that accused people must be able to make a plea to the indictment against them and must be of sufficient intellect to comprehend the course of the trial proceedings and the details of the evidence against them. In Canadian law, people who are unable to participate actively and effectively in their own defence due to mental disorder are referred to as **unfit to stand trial (UST)**. According to section 2 of the Criminal Code,

> "[U]nfit to stand trial" means unable on account of mental disorder to conduct a defence at any stage of the proceedings before a verdict is rendered or to instruct counsel to do so, and, in particular, unable on account of mental disorder to
>
> (a) understand the nature or object of the proceedings,
>
> (b) understand the possible consequences of the proceedings, or
>
> (c) communicate with counsel.

Only limited cognitive capacity is required for a person to be considered fit to stand trial (*R. v. Taylor*, 1992; *R. v. Whittle*, 1994). Defendants need to be able to recount to their attorneys the necessary facts relating to their offence in such a way that the attorneys can properly present their cases; it is not necessary that defendants have a rational understanding of their situation or that they can act in their own best interests.

The procedures governing the evaluation of fitness and the disposition of people who were found to be UST were revised in 1992 following the Supreme Court of Canada's decision in *Swain*. Briefly, defendants are presumed fit unless the court is satisfied, on the balance of probabilities, that they are UST. The issue of fitness can be raised before trial or at trial by the defendant, the prosecution (under certain circumstances), or the trial judge. Courts can order evaluations to assist in the determination of whether the defendant is UST. As is the case for criminal responsibility evaluations, there is a five-day limit on assessment orders, unless the defendant and Crown agree to a longer period not exceeding 30 days; compelling circumstances can extend this to a maximum of 60 days. These evaluations can take place in a jail, an outpatient clinic, or an inpatient facility, although there is a presumption against custody. Despite this presumption, the majority of the evaluations are conducted in inpatient facilities, although the number of outpatient evaluations has increased since the passage of the 1992 Criminal Code revisions. The issue of unfitness is tried separately from the trial on the charge itself, and may be tried by judge or jury. If they are found fit to stand trial, defendants proceed to trial, although courts may order them to be detained until their trials are over to prevent deterioration of their mental state. If they are found to be UST, any pleas defendants may have made are set aside and they may be ordered to undergo inpatient or outpatient treatment. The cases of defendants found to be UST are considered by a review board formed under the Criminal Code at least once every two years. Defendants who become fit to stand trial are returned to court for the disposition of their case. At that point, defendants may go to trial, may plead guilty, or if sufficient evidence to obtain a conviction no longer exists, may be acquitted and released.

4 BEFORE MOVING ON

A psychologist evaluates a person who has been arrested to determine if he is unfit to stand trial (UST). The psychologist concludes that the person is UST because he is experiencing severe symptoms of psychosis (e.g., conceptual disorganization, incoherent speech) that render him incapable of communicating with counsel. Does this mean that the psychologist should also conclude that the person was also not criminally responsible on account of mental disorder (NCRMD)? Why or why not?

SOME EXAMPLES OF RESEARCH ON MENTALLY DISORDERED OFFENDERS IN CANADA

HOW ARE FITNESS EVALUATIONS CONDUCTED? In Canada, as in other common law jurisdictions, research suggests that the opinions of mental health professionals regarding fitness are virtually dispositive—that is, courts rarely disagree with the opinions expressed by professionals (e.g., Hart & Hare, 1992; see also Cox & Zapf, 2004). But although the concept of fitness to stand trial is an old one, its definition has never been explicit in the law. This raises some interesting questions. How do mental health professionals interpret the law when determining whether a particular defendant is fit or unfit? What kinds of assessment techniques or procedures should be used?

Early research conducted in Canada and the United States suggested that mental health professionals based opinions regarding competency or fitness to stand trial on the seriousness of the mental disorder from which defendants were suffering, rather than on the seriousness of the functional deficits that stemmed from the mental disorder, such as inability to understand the proceedings or communicate with counsel. In fact, many evaluators seemed to equate psychosis with incompetency or unfitness (Roesch & Golding, 1980). These and similar findings prompted Canadian researchers to devote considerable effort to improving fitness evaluations over the past 25 years.

One example of how research has improved the practice of forensic psychology and psychiatry is the development of the revised Fitness Interview Test, or FIT-R, developed by Ron Roesch, Patricia Zapf, Christopher Webster, and Derek Eaves (1998). The FIT-R is a manual or reference book that presents guidelines concerning how to conduct brief evaluations of competency or fitness to stand trial, either in institutional or community settings. The FIT-R takes approximately 30 minutes to administer. It requires evaluators to make ratings of the defendant's functioning with respect to a number of specific psycholegal abilities, each of which is defined in the manual. The FIT-R manual also presents questions that can be posed to defendants to help evaluators make their ratings. The items in the FIT-R fall into three main areas, consistent with the Criminal Code: (1) ability to understand the nature or object of the proceedings, or factual knowledge of criminal procedure, such as the defendant's understanding of the arrest process and the nature and severity of current charges; (2) the ability to understand the possible consequences of the proceedings, or the appreciation of personal involvement in and importance of the proceedings, such as the defendant's appreciation of the range and nature of possible penalties if found guilty; and (3) the ability to communicate with counsel, or to participate in the defence, such as the defendant's capacity to communicate facts to a lawyer. Each item is rated on a 3-point scale, where 2 means *definite or serious impairment*, 1 means *possible or mild impairment*, and 0 means *no impairment*. A sample item from the FIT-R is presented in Focus box 19.1.

In a number of studies, the FIT-R has been shown to help evaluators make reliable and valid decisions about fitness with adults. In one study, Zapf, Roesch, and Viljoen (2001) used the FIT-R to evaluate 145 defendants who had been remanded to an inpatient facility for a fitness evaluation. FIT-R evaluations were typically conducted within 24 hours of admission, and the interviews lasted less than

FOCUS 19.1

A Sample Item from the FIT-R Manual

ITEM 12. CAPACITY TO PLAN LEGAL STRATEGY

This item calls for an assessment of the degree to which the accused can understand and cooperate with his/her counsel in planning a strategy for the defence that is consistent with the reality of his/her circumstances. Strategic issues such as agreeing to enter a guilty plea to a lesser offence, or the decision as to whether or not the accused should testify, may arise and require some participation from the accused.

- If your lawyer can get the Crown counsel [prosecutor] to accept a plea bargain wherein you plead guilty to a less serious charge in return for the Crown dropping a more serious charge, would you agree to it? Why/why not?
- If your lawyer decides that you should not testify, would you go along with him/her?
- What will you do if you disagree with your lawyer about how to handle your case?
- Should you talk with a lawyer before pleading guilty?
- What questions should you ask your lawyer if you are thinking about pleading guilty?
- Do you understand the consequences of being found unfit to stand trial?

Source: Roesch et al. (1998).

1 hour. Zapf and colleagues compared judgments based on the FIT-R with the clinical judgments of the forensic psychiatrists, made independent of the FIT-R. The clinical judgments were reached after an average length of stay of 21 days. Of the 145 evaluations, the FIT-R judgment and the hospital judgment were in full agreement that 106 of the defendants were fit to stand trial. Of the remaining 39 defendants, the FIT-R and the hospital agreed that 9 defendants were unfit. The other 30 defendants were considered possibly unfit by the FIT-R but were found to be fit by the hospital psychiatrists. The results show that the FIT-R works well as a screening instrument, in that it correctly identified defendants who were clearly fit and did not misclassify any defendants who were subsequently found to be unfit by the hospital evaluators. This study also shows that 73 percent (106 of 145) of the defendants could have been assessed without the need for inpatient evaluation, as the assessment can take place in a jail or other community setting rather than a forensic hospital. Defendants remanded to the forensic hospital were held an average of about 17 days. If decisions about a substantial portion of the defendants could be made on the basis of a brief assessment, the cost savings would be substantial—the cost of community-based evaluations is only a fraction of the cost of inpatient evaluations (see also Zapf & Roesch, 1997). More recently, the FIT-R has been shown to be useful in evaluating juveniles who have been charged with crimes (Viljoen & Roesch, 2007). Ensuring that the legal rights of adolescents are equally protected has become increasingly important due to changes in Canadian laws allowing for the imposition of adult sentences on juveniles convicted of certain offences.

WHO IS REFERRED FOR EVALUATION OF FITNESS OR CRIMINAL RESPONSIBILITY? Accused referred for fitness evaluations are often marginalized individuals. The majority are male, single, unemployed, with prior criminal histories, prior contact with mental health services, and past psychiatric hospitalizations (Zapf & Roesch, 1998; Zapf, Roesch, & Viljoen, 2001). Viljoen and Zapf (2002) compared 80 defendants referred for fitness evaluations with 80 defendants not referred and found that referred defendants were significantly more likely to meet diagnostic criteria for current psychotic disorder, be charged with a violent offence, and have impaired legal abilities, and less likely to have had previous criminal charges.

The public often views the Criminal Code provisions regarding mental disorder skeptically, believing they are used too frequently. This is a misconception; in fact, very few people charged with criminal offences raise the issue of mental disorder. Roesch and his colleagues (Roesch et al., 1997) examined patterns in the number of people in British Columbia who underwent evaluations of criminal responsibility or fitness in a two-year period between 1992 and 1994. In total, 653 defendants were referred for evaluation: 15 percent for evaluation of NCRMD, 61 percent for evaluation of fitness, and 24 percent for evaluation of both. In most of these evaluations, the outcome was a finding that the defendant was *not* NCRMD (recommended in about 61 percent of evaluations) or was *not* UST (recommended in about 79 percent of cases). A study by Grant (1997) found that fewer than 100 people were actually found NCRMD by courts in British Columbia in 1992 and 1993. In 1992 and 1993, the total number of charges laid for Criminal Code offences was more than 500 000 annually in British Columbia; thus, there were about 65 evaluations of mental state per 100 000 criminal charges per year, and the rate of "successful" NCRMD defences was about 10 per 100 000 criminal charges per year. This estimate is consistent with the findings of Hylton (1995), who estimated that a section 16 defence was raised in less than 0.2 percent of all cases coming before the courts in British Columbia.

Another misconception is that people found NCRMD or UST somehow "get off easy." In fact, the reality is that whereas virtually all defendants found guilty are given a fixed or determinate sentence, there is no limit on the length of time someone may be detained if found NCRMD or UST. Also, many people found NCRMD or UST will spend as much or even more time in a secure hospital than they would have spent in prison if they had been convicted. For example, Harris, Rice, and Cormier (1991) compared the length of detention among a cohort of insanity acquittees in Ontario to that of a group of men arrested for similar offences and with similar offence histories who were not found legally insane. They found that, on average, the insanity acquittees were detained for about 60 months whereas the men sentenced to prison were detained for about 50 months. Length of detention was similar for those men who had been arrested for serious offences such as murder or manslaughter, but men found legally insane for less serious offences were detained much longer than the sentenced men (e.g., 34 months versus 12 months, respectively, for those initially arrested for property crimes).

Despite a popular belief that the typical insanity acquittee has been charged with murder, research has demonstrated that only a minority has actually committed murder or even attempted murder. In Canada, a review of all insanity evaluatees in the province of British Columbia over a two-year period showed that although the majority of defendants had been charged with violent offences, less than 10 percent had been charged with murder or attempted murder (Roesch et al., 1997). More notably, in addition to the finding that murder charges are rare for insanity acquittees, approximately 35 percent of all charges in this population are for nonviolent minor offences, such as uttering threats, breach of probation, mischief, and possession of stolen property (Roesch et al., 1997).

The 1992 amendments to the Criminal Code appear to have had a small but significant impact on evaluations for NCRMD and UST. The number of evaluations appears to have increased in some provinces (e.g., British Columbia; see Grant 1997; Roesch et al., 1997) but not in others (e.g., Alberta; see Stuart, Arboleda-Florez, & Crisanti, 2001). A more consistent finding is that the number of short-term evaluations has increased, and an increasing number of evaluations are conducted in the defendant's community or in jail rather than a central forensic facility (Roesch et al., 1997; Stuart et al., 2001; Zapf & Roesch, 1998).

Psychology in the Legal System

Two types of psychologists are involved in the legal system. The first group comprises "accidental visitors" who are asked to provide opinions to a court or tribunal due to their specialized knowledge. For example, clinical or counselling psychologists who treat families may be subsequently called to court and asked to summarize the assessment findings and treatment outcome as part of custody and access hearings; or industrial-organizational psychologists may be asked to evaluate the hiring and promotion procedures of large companies as part of a sexual discrimination hearing. The second group comprises specialists in **forensic psychology**, whose work is primarily intended to assist proceedings in criminal or civil courts, or in front of quasi-judicial bodies such as administrative boards and tribunals. (Forensic—which derives from the Latin *forensis*, meaning forum—is an umbrella term used to describe any sort of legal proceeding.)

The field of forensic psychology is currently in a period of tremendous growth and expansion (for an overview, see Melton et al., 2007). Although its origins can be traced back more than hundred years, it is only in the past 30 years or so that it has become recognized and accepted as a formal specialization. The field is very diverse, differing with respect to the primary focus (e.g., civil versus criminal issues) and the nature of the work (e.g., research versus practice). For example, forensic psychologists may

- Conduct a custody evaluation to determine what residential and access or visitation arrangements are most appropriate for children whose parents are in the midst of a divorce.
- Design a program for training correctional officers at a provincial prison to identify offenders who may be suicidal and in need of special care.
- Study the abilities of young children to accurately perceive and recognize faces in stressful situations, to help understand and improve the accuracy of their courtroom testimony.
- Evaluate the hiring and promotion practices of large organizations to determine whether there is evidence of discrimination on the basis of gender or age.
- Provide expert evidence in court concerning the assessment and management of violence risk in forensic psychiatric patients.

Psychological Ethics

GENERAL ETHICAL PRINCIPLES OF PSYCHOLOGY

The law is, in general, concerned with minimal standards of conduct: it focuses on identifying what constitutes bad or inappropriate behaviour and what actions should be taken in response to such behaviour. Put simply, the law tells us what *not* to do. To determine what psychologists *should* do in a given situation, they turn to **ethical codes**. Ethical codes are a fundamental part of the profession of psychology: they set out the core values that underlie the practice of psychology, thereby establishing an implied social contract between the psychologists and the public (Truscott & Crook, 2004). Ethical codes are primarily descriptive, in the sense that they reflect the actual or existing values of psychologists. But they are also aspirational, in the sense that they reflect the preferred values and highest ideals of psychologists. Similar to ethical codes in some respects are **professional standards**, which put forward expectations regarding the day-to-day practice or conduct of psychologists.

In Canada, the primary ethical code is the third edition of the *Canadian Code of Ethics for Psychologists*, published by the Canadian Psychological Association (2000). The *Code of Ethics* sets out four fundamental ethical principles, defines and discusses the principles, and presents a method for making ethical decisions. The four principles are as follows:

I. *Respect for the Dignity of Persons*. Psychologists strive to recognize and demonstrate their regard for the innate worth of every human being.

II. *Responsible Caring*. Psychologists strive to minimize risks and maximize benefits for others, particularly vulnerable people.

III. *Integrity in Relationships*. Psychologists strive to be honest, open, straightforward, and unbiased in their interactions with others.

IV. *Responsibility to Society*. Psychologists strive to promote the welfare of all people.

The principles in the *Code of Ethics* are, in many respects, a restatement of more general ethical principles: the **principle of autonomy**, or respect for self-determination; the **principle of nonmaleficence**, or avoiding harm; the **principle of beneficence**, or maximizing good; the **principle of fidelity**, or personal reliability; and the **principle of justice**, or fairness (e.g., Truscott & Crook, 2004). What makes the *Code of Ethics* different is that it ranks the principles in order of importance: Principle I is considered the most important, Principle II the next most important, and so forth. This ranking is useful when deciding what to do in situations where the principles are or may be in conflict.

The *Code of Ethics* presents many specific ethical standards derived from the four fundamental principles. Of most relevance to the practice of forensic psychology are ethical standards stating that psychologists should respect the legal rights of others (Ethical Standard I.5); clarify situations in which they have professional relationships with multiple parties, including situations in which the parties may include courts or police (Ethical Standard I.26); be aware of the knowledge and skills of other disciplines, including law (Ethical Standard II.20); do everything possible to prevent harm to others, including notification of police or potential victims (Ethical Standard II.39); and familiarize themselves with relevant laws and regulations (Ethical Standard IV.17).

5 BEFORE MOVING ON

For the past year, a psychologist has been providing supportive psychotherapy to a client, the mother of two young children, to help her deal with adjustment problems related to marital and child rearing stress. One day, the client informs the psychologist that she is seeking a divorce from her husband and sole custody of her children. She asks the psychologist to write a report assessing her parenting capacity for use in legal proceedings. What ethical concerns does this request raise? What should the psychologist do?

SPECIALIZED ETHICAL GUIDELINES

The *Code of Ethics* is very helpful for dealing with general ethical issues, but it does not deal much with the practice of forensic psychology or the special ethical dilemmas faced by forensic psychologists. Fortunately, two major professional organizations of forensic psychologists, the American Academy of Forensic Psychology and the American Psychology-Law Society (Division 41 of the American Psychological Association), collaborated to fill this gap. Based on their work, the American Psychological Association developed and adopted the *Specialty Guidelines for Forensic Psychology* (American Psychological Association, in press). As stated in the introduction, the goals of the *Specialty Guidelines* are to "improve the quality of forensic psychological services; enhance the practice and facilitate the systematic development of forensic psychology; encourage a high level of quality in professional practice; and encourage forensic practitioners to acknowledge and respect the rights of those they serve."

The *Specialty Guidelines* have a dual nature: they are a blend of ethical principles and professional standards. They are intended to assist psychologists in applying more general ethical codes to the practice of forensic psychology. Several major themes are apparent in the *Specialty Guidelines*; we will focus our discussion on three of them. The first is the importance of objectivity and neutrality. Although psychologists in other areas of practice are expected to advocate for the people they are evaluating and treating, forensic psychologists are expected to reason, act, and communicate in an unbiased manner. This is reflected in statements such as, "Forensic practitioners strive for accuracy, honesty, and truthfulness in the science, teaching, and practice of forensic psychology and they strive to resist partisan pressures to provide services in any ways that might tend to be misleading or inaccurate" (Specialty Guideline 1.01) and "Forensic practitioners recognize the adversarial nature of the legal system and strive to treat all participants and weigh all data, opinions, and rival hypotheses impartially" (Specialty Guideline 1.02).

A second major theme is the importance of establishing, maintaining, and practising within one's area of competence. This is reflected in statements such as, "Forensic practitioners make ongoing efforts to develop and maintain their competencies" (Specialty Guideline 2.02) and "[F]orensic practitioners adequately and accurately inform all recipients of their services (e.g., attorneys, tribunals) about relevant aspects of the nature and extent of their experience, training, credentials, and qualifications, and how they were obtained" (Specialty Guideline 2.03).

A third major theme is the need for forensic psychologists to know and respect the laws that govern their areas of practice. Psychologists who do not know the law often fail to recognize that what may be acceptable in general practice may be unacceptable in forensic practice—indeed, it may even violate fundamental principles of law. One example here is the reliance of psychologists in general practice on oral or written self-report methods, such as interviews and questionnaires, in their assessments. In the law, it is a highly questionable practice to rely on uncorroborated statements made by parties to legal proceedings; key statements should be corroborated with third-party information obtained from collateral informants, official records, and so forth. Another example is the need to avoid asking unnecessary questions in certain situations, such as evaluating fitness to stand trial. Defendants should not be asked whether they "did it"—that is, committed the offence(s) with which they have been charged. Not only is the answer irrelevant to the legal issue, but the question itself asks defendants to give up their constitutional rights against self-incrimination. The importance of understanding the law is reflected in statements such as, "Forensic practitioners recognize the importance of obtaining a fundamental and reasonable level of knowledge and understanding of the legal and professional standards, laws, rules, and precedents that govern their participation in legal proceedings and that guide the impact of their services on service recipients" (Specialty Guideline 2.04).

The practice of forensic psychology is a high-stakes arena. The potential consequences for parties to legal proceedings, as well as for the public, may be profound. Forensic psychologists must be familiar not only with general ethical codes, but with specialized ethical and professional standards. It is not sufficient for forensic psychologists to be "adequate" or "competent" with respect to their level of knowledge, skills, or expertise; they must be judged according to a higher standard of practice.

The Status of Psychology in the Legal System

Psychologists are often asked to give evidence before courts and tribunals as professionals (e.g., after conducting psychological assessments of such things as criminal responsibility, violence, risk, or parenting ability) or as scientists (e.g., after conducting research personally, or after preparing an *amicus curiae* brief that summarizes psychological research on a legal issue, such as the capacity of minors to consent to abortion or the impact that testimony might have on a child sexual abuse victim). But the role of psychologists is limited by law, and medical practitioners play a more dominant role in many areas in which mental health input is needed.

For example, in every province and territory, decisions regarding involuntary hospitalization and treatment must be made by one or more physicians—not necessarily psychiatrists, but any qualified medical practitioners. In no jurisdiction do psychologists have the legal authority to involuntarily hospitalize people. This is a rather curious state of affairs: psychologists—whose expertise in assessing, diagnosing, and treating mental disorder is recognized in law—cannot play a role in civil commitment; yet in some jurisdictions any physician, including a general practitioner, anaesthesiologist, or dermatologist, can involuntarily hospitalize someone under civil mental health law. This would seem to be of no benefit to citizens in terms of ensuring that they have access to appropriate health care.

The situation is similar with respect to criminal law, at least until recently. The Criminal Code had excluded psychologists from conducting court-ordered assessments of criminal responsibility and fitness to stand trial. Section 671.1 specified that these assessments must be conducted by "medical practitioners." The definition of "medical practitioners" includes both psychiatric and nonpsychiatric physicians, although in practice it is rare for a nonpsychiatric physician to evaluate criminal responsibility or fitness in Canada. The rationale for including nonpsychiatric physicians is that a psychiatrist may not be available in small or remote communities. A recent change to the Criminal Code allows the possibility that psychologists can conduct assessments of fitness and NCRMD. Section 671.1 now indicates that an assessment can be made by a medical practitioner or any other person who has been designated by the Attorney General as being qualified to conduct an assessment of the mental condition of the accused. Thus, if the Attorney General of a province designates psychologists as being qualified, they could then independently conduct these assessments.

The recent Criminal Code changes suggest that psychology's role in mental disorder assessments may gradually change in the coming years; it is important to note that psychologists have already been involved in evaluations related to involuntary hospitalization, fitness, or criminal responsibility (Viljoen, Roesch, Ogloff, & Zapf, 2003). In some cases, they are asked by psychiatrists to conduct an evaluation and prepare a report, which is in turn cited in or submitted together with a psychiatric report (Pollack & Webster, 1993). Although this role has sometimes been equated to playing "handmaiden" to psychiatrists (Bartholomew, Badger, & Milte, 1977), it is an important and valuable one that also serves as an opportunity for interdisciplinary collaboration (see Grisso, 1993).

Why have Canadian courts been reluctant to recognize the expertise of psychologists? It appears that they have doubts about the ability of psychologists to diagnose mental disorders. The case of *R. v. F. D. M.* (1987) illustrates this concern. When asked about the defendant's sanity, a psychologist opined that the defendant had paranoid schizophrenia and was legally insane at the time of the crime. A psychiatrist diagnosed the same defendant with paranoid psychosis. Although these diagnoses are essentially equivalent in terms of symptomatology, the court emphasized the discrepancy. Monnin J., for the majority, stated, "Dr. Shane, a psychiatrist, did not support the schizophrenia portion of Dr. Ellis' assessment. Who are we to believe and whose testimony are we to accept—the psychologist or the psychiatrist? In my view, the only one qualified to testify is the psychiatrist" (p. 123). Surprisingly, in arguing that psychologists were unable to testify on the presence of mental disorder and the issue of criminal responsibility, he noted, "A general practitioner would not venture in this field. Nor would much weight be given to his testimony" (p. 123). Yet the Criminal Code itself permits general practitioners to make the venture!

Exclusion of psychological testimony with the claim that psychologists are unable to diagnose mental disorders is contrary to several provincial statutes governing the profession of psychology. Explicit references to the ability of psychologists to diagnose mental disorder are made in the psychology acts of Alberta, British Columbia, Nova Scotia, Ontario, Prince Edward Island, and Saskatchewan (Viljoen et al., 2003).

Although *R. v. F. D. M.* (1987) did not recognize the ability of psychologists to diagnose schizophrenia, other cases have reached different conclusions. In *R. v. J. A. P.* (2000, para. 33), Wheelan J. acknowledged the court's previous rejection of psychological testimony in *R. v. F. D. M.* (1987) but noted:

> In this case the concern is with mental functioning due to brain injury and there has been ongoing reliance on the tests routinely used in assessing his level of functioning, including the ability to learn. This is a field in which it would seem that psychologists are particularly qualified.

Wheelan J. (para. 41) went on to say:

> Indeed it is my observation that the two disciplines in this case, psychiatry and psychology, have not communicated well and the gap in their approaches and opinions remains unexplained. I am particularly struck by the lack of objective testing by the psychiatrist and the routine way in which such tests were relied upon by the psychologists who found consistent results over several years and several occasions . . .

R. *v*. *J. A. P.* (2000) appears to be an important case for Canadian psychologists, and may mark the era of expansion in the role of psychologists in legal proceedings.

CANADIAN RESEARCH CENTRE

Dr.Christopher Webster

Chris Webster received his Ph.D. in experimental psychology from Dalhousie University in 1967. After a few further years researching animal learning at the Addiction Research Foundation and teaching at the University of Toronto, he became interested in childhood autism and conduct disorder. This meant taking advantage of an offer by the Clarke Institute of Psychiatry to lead a program of research and clinical service for children suffering from autism and conduct disorders. In 1975 he became Director of the School of Child and Youth Care at the University of Victoria in British Columbia. The idea behind the school was, and remains, to prepare undergraduates from a variety of disciplines for careers in treatment centres, community projects, and remedial programs in schools and juvenile detention facilities.

A different kind of research opportunity beckoned in 1977 with the introduction of a new law and mental health assessment and treatment service within the Clarke Institute (now the Centre for Addiction and Mental Health). It was there that Chris began to undertake research and clinical work within the area of forensic psychology, clinical criminology, and psychiatry. This meant studying how to assess fitness for trial, criminal responsibility, and potential for violence.

In 1993 Chris became chair of the Department of Psychology at Simon Fraser University and began his collaboration with Steve Hart, Kevin Douglas, Derek Eaves, Randy Kropp, and others. Over the next four or five years the small group, aided by some prominent international researchers and clinicians, published what has become known as the Historical/Clinical/Risk Management-20 (HCR-20). This clinical guide has now been researched extensively and has found practical application in the forensic and mental health fields, as well as in specialized aspects of correctional services.

In 1997 Chris again returned to Toronto. There he was able to return to his roots by joining a small group of clinicians and researchers at the Child Development Institute, all of whom were intent on creating structured professional judgment guides for use with under-12 boys and girls with conduct disorders. These have become known as the Early Assessment Risk Lists (EARLs). He continues to research risk assessment issues and has become increasingly involved in devising and researching assessment schemes that are usable on an interdisciplinary basis, which are helpful to courts and review boards, and ethically sound. Chris believes that advances in his area of specialization are most likely to succeed when carried out by means of sustained, intense collaborations between researchers, clinicians, and policy-makers.

SUMMARY

- The fundamental goal of the law is to prevent and resolve, in a principled manner, conflicts among people. In Canada, which has a form of government known as a constitutional monarchy, there are three primary sources of law: constitutional law, statutory law, and common law (except in Quebec, which relies on a civil code). Each of these sources of law recognizes the potential relevance of mental disorder.
- Although Canadian law assumes that people typically think and act in a reasoned, deliberate manner, they may be treated differently when it is demonstrated that their thinking is irrational or their behaviour is involuntary. The legal concept of mental disorder is not bound by psychological or medical definitions. The law typically defines mental disorder as any impairment of psychological functioning that is internal, stable, and involuntary in nature. This definition of mental disorder is much narrower than that used by mental health professionals, so that some disorders that are recognized by mental health professionals may not meet the legal definition of a mental disorder. In legal proceedings, triers of fact must determine whether or not a person who is party to the proceedings has a mental disorder, according to how mental disorder is defined in the relevant law. Mental health professionals act merely as consultants to triers of fact, providing expert observations and opinions.
- Two common law principles are important with respect to mental health law in Canada. The first, the principle of police powers, recognizes that the state has the duty to protect its citizens from threats to their safety and security. The second, the principle of *parens patriae*, recognizes that the state has the duty to care for citizens when they are unable to care for themselves. These principles provide a justification for the involuntary hospitalization and treatment of people suffering form mental disorder. Involuntary hospitalization, or civil commitment, is most often based on the patient's risk of harm to self or others; in some jurisdictions, it may also be based on the need for treatment, lack of capacity to make treatment decisions, or risk for deterioration in physical or mental health. When patients are committed and deemed incapable of making decisions about treatment, a temporary substitute decision maker may make treatment decisions on their behalf. Temporary substitute decision makers most often follow the best interests or capable wishes principles. Up to 15 to 20 percent of all hospitalizations for mental disorder in Canada may be involuntary.
- The Criminal Code includes special provisions for dealing with people suffering from mental disorder who are charged with offences. One important issue concerns whether these people are not criminally responsible on account of mental disorder (NCRMD). According to the Criminal Code, some people suffering from mental disorder, through no fault of their own, may have inaccurate perceptions of or irrational beliefs about the world that led them to commit a prohibited act, but without any bad intention—exactly in the same way that someone who raises the defence of self-defence admits the act, but denies the intent. Another important issue concerns whether people suffering from mental disorder are unfit to stand trial (UST). According to the Criminal Code, some people suffering from mental disorder are unable to participate actively and effectively in their own defence. The key distinction is that decisions regarding NCRMD are based on mental disorder at the time an offence was committed (i.e., in the past), whereas decisions regarding UST are based on mental disorder at the time of trial (i.e., in the present).
- There are some ethical special challenges faced by psychologists whose work takes them inside the legal system. Ethical codes for psychologists set out the core values that underlie the practice of psychology, thereby establishing an implied social contract between the psychologists and the public. In Canada, this is the *Canadian Code of Ethics for Psychologists*, which sets out four fundamental ethical principles, defines and discusses the principles, and presents a method for making ethical decisions. Although ethical codes generally expect psychologists to advocate for the people they are evaluating and treating, psychologists who work in the legal system are expected to reason, act, and communicate in a neutral, unbiased manner. For this reason, specialty ethical guidelines for forensic psychologists have been developed.

MySearchLab offers you extensive help with your writing and research projects and provides round-the-clock access to credible and reliable source material. Chapter quizzes and a full electronic version of the text are also provided. Answers to the Before Moving On feature are provided on the MySearchLab. Take a tour at www.mysearchlab.com.

KEY TERMS

constitutional law (p. 490)

statutory law (p. 490)

common law (p. 490)

parens patriae (p. 491)

civil code (p. 492)

civil commitment (p. 492)

criminal commitment (p. 492)

temporary substitute decision maker (p. 494)

best interests principle (p. 494)

capable wishes principle (p. 494)

compulsory treatment orders (p. 494)

deinstitutionalization (p. 495)

actus reus (p. 499)

mens rea (p. 499)

not criminally responsible on account of mental disorder (NCRMD) (499)

M'Naghten standard (p. 499)

unfit to stand trial (UST) (p. 500)

forensic psychology (p. 503)

ethical codes (p. 503)

professional standards (p. 503)

principle of autonomy (p. 504)

principle of nonmaleficence (p. 504)

principle of beneficence (p. 504)

principle of fidelity (p. 504)

principle of justice (p. 504)

Glossary

A

ABAB Also called *reversal design*; a non-experimental investigative method, a variety of ***single-subject design***, that requires the quantification of behaviour in its naturally occurring environment prior to any intervention. This constitutes the A phase or the baseline of the procedure. Next, in the B phase, the treatment is introduced in a controlled manner for a period of time. The next A phase constitutes the reversal, during which time the treatment is not provided, and the subject is exposed to the original baseline conditions. Finally, in the final B phase, the treatment is provided once again.

abstinence syndrome A reaction that many individuals experience during treatment for barbiturate abuse. It occurs at the stage at which the user is no longer dependent, and is characterized by insomnia, headaches, aching all over the body, anxiety, and depression, and can last for months.

acquired sexual dysfunction Any sexual dysfunction that the sufferer has not always experienced.

actuarial approach An approach to evaluating and interpreting the data on patients, making predictions, and coming to decisions that relies exclusively on statistical procedures, empirical methods, and formal rules. *See also* ***clinical approach***.

actus reus In Canadian criminal law, the prohibited physical act that, together with the ***mens rea***, defines a criminal offence.

affective flattening Lack of emotional expression and response.

agonist drug A neurotransmitter that facilitates the inhibitory action of the neurotransmitter GABA at its receptors. Used as a pharmacological agent for the treatment of alcohol dependence.

agoraphobia An irrational fear of being in a situation where escape might be difficult or impossible.

alarm The first phase of the ***general adaptation syndrome (GAS)***, a concept that was the first formal description and definition of stress as a consequence of adaptation to demands placed on the body. In the alarm phase, the body, faced with an adaptive challenge, mobilizes its defences. *See* ***also resistance*** and ***exhaustion***.

alarm theory This theory proposes that a "true alarm" occurs when there is a real threat—our bodies produce an adaptive physiological response that allows us to face the feared object or flee from the situation. In some instances, this alarm system can be activated by emotional cues (in which case it is a "false alarm.")

alcohol dehydrogenase An enzyme that helps break down alcohol in the stomach. Women have significantly less of this enzyme than men.

alcohol expectancy theory A theory that proposes drinking behaviour is largely determined by the reinforcement that an individual expects to receive from it. Most of the subjective experiences actually felt are a function of expectation and attitude and not an effect of the alcohol.

alogia Loss or reduction in speech and verbal expression.

alter One of two or more unique personalities in a single individual who has ***dissociative identity disorder (DID)***. Alters may be almost polar opposites, requiring different eyeglass prescriptions and having different allergies. Alters may also differ in the age, sex, race, and family history they claim to have.

alternate-form reliability An attribute of a test demonstrated by a high correlation between scores on two versions of a test. To circumvent the problem that one may improve on a test the second time around because of practice, test designers may prepare two forms of the same test—that is, they decide what construct they want their test to measure, think up questions (or items) that would test that construct, and then word those questions in a slightly different way in order to create a second test that measures the same construct as the first.

Alzheimer's disease The most common of the *primary dementias*. It progresses through three stages: *forgetfulness*, in which there are memory difficulties, problems with concentration, unclear thinking, difficulty finding words, and errors in judgment; *confusion*, in which existing symptoms become more severe and additional symptoms occur such as language difficulties, problems in time and place orientation, sleep difficulties, employment or social difficulties, incontinence, feelings of helplessness, flattening of affect, agitation, irritability, and wandering; and ***dementia***, in which the ability to communicate is lost, memory impairment is profound, and a variety of physical symptoms develop such as stooped posture, increasing immobility, total incontinence, increasing vulnerability to pneumonia, congestive heart failure, etc.

amenorrhea Failure to menstruate, a medical effect of ***anorexia nervosa*** and ***bulimia nervosa***.

amniocentesis A procedure for prenatal screening for chromosomal abnormalities conducted between the eleventh and eighteenth weeks of pregnancy. With the assistance of ultrasound, a needle is inserted into the amniotic sac via the abdomen and a small amount of amniotic fluid withdrawn. Cells contained in the fluid are then cultured in the lab.

amotivational syndrome A continuing pattern of apathy, profound self-absorption, detachment from friends and family, and abandonment of career and educational goals evident in some long-term users of ***cannabis***.

amphetamines Drugs that have effects on the body similar to those of the naturally occurring hormone adrenaline. Originally developed as a nasal decongestant and asthma treatment in the 1930s. In addition to shrinking mucous membranes and constricting blood vessels, they increase alertness and concentration. Chronic amphetamine use is associated with feelings of fatigue and sadness, as well as periods of social withdrawal and intense anger.

amygdala A small almond-shaped structure in the tip of the temporal lobe that plays a role in emotional behaviour.

analogue observational setting An artificial environment set up in an office or laboratory to elicit specific classes of behaviour in individuals. Used when ***in vivo observation*** in the natural environment is impractical because of time constraints and the unpredictability of modern family life.

anhedonia A loss of pleasure or interest in almost all activities or a lack of reactivity to usually pleasurable events.

anorexia nervosa An eating disorder characterized by the pursuit of thinness to dangerously low weight levels.

anorgasmia *See* ***female orgasmic disorder***.

Antabuse Disulfiram, a drug that is used to make the experience of drinking extremely aversive. It blocks the action of the metabolizing enzyme acetaldehyde dehydrogenase, resulting in a build-up of acetaldehyde in the body. Like people who naturally lack this enzyme, people who drink alcohol after taking Antabuse experience increased heart rate, nausea, vomiting, and other unpleasant effects.

antagonist drug A neurotransmitter that inhibits the production of acetylcholine, a bodily substance that mediates the transmission of nerve impulses within the brain. Used as a pharmacological agent.

anxiety An emotion that leaves an individual feeling threatened by the potential occurrence of a future negative event.

anxiety sensitivity The tendency to catastrophically misinterpret arousal-related bodily sensations because one believes the sensations to have harmful consequences, such as death, insanity, or loss of control.

anxious/ambivalent *See* ***anxious/ambivalent attachment***.

anxious/ambivalent attachment The interpersonal style of persons who strongly desire intimacy with others and persistently seek out romantic partners, but who, once they begin to get close to their partner, become anxious and back away; while they desire closeness, they appear to be afraid of it. People are considered to have developed these difficulties as a result of poor parent–child attachments that fail to instill the self-confidence and skills necessary for intimacy. Because this relationship style characterizes *borderline personality disorder (BPD)* patients, the features of borderline disorder may be seen as attempts to adjust to a desire for but distrust of intimacy.

appraisals In the ***transactional model*** *of stress*, evaluations that people constantly make about what is happening to them and its implications for themselves.

arrhythmias Disturbances in the normal pumping rhythm of the heart. Can result in ***myocardial infarction***.

Asperger disorder A developmental disorder similar to ***autism*** but associated with fewer symptoms, higher functioning, and higher IQ. It is not known whether "core autism" (the full range and severity of symptoms) and Asperger disorder represent points on a continuum of severity, or whether they are related but different disorders.

asphyxiophilia *See* ***autoerotic asphyxia***.

assessment A procedure in which information is gathered systematically in the evaluation of a condition; it serves as the preliminary to a *diagnosis*. A psychiatric assessment may include interviews with the patient or the patient's family, medical testing, psychophysiological or psychological testing, and the completion of self-report scales or other report rating scales.

assortative mating When individuals tend to mate with people who are like themselves in some respect.

asylum A place for treatment of the mentally ill. Units for the mentally ill were established within the great Arab hospitals in Baghdad in AD 800 and asylums were created in other Arab cities some 500 years before Europeans built their first asylums. Treatment in Arab asylums followed the tradition of care, support, and compassion.

atheoretical Not based on or concerned with a particular theory.

atherogenesis The development of ***atherosclerosis***. Can occur as early as two years of age.

atherosclerosis A build-up of deposits, known as *plaques*, on the walls of the blood vessels. Atherosclerosis can narrow the openings of arteries enough to compromise the blood supply to the heart or the brain, leading to ***myocardial infarction*** or ***stroke***.

attachment theory A development of the psychoanalytic approach by John Bowlby. According to this view, children form attachments with their parents that become the child's internalized model for all subsequent relationships. Difficulties in such attachments form the basis for later problems.

attention deficit/hyperactivity disorder (ADHD) A childhood disorder characterized by disruptive behaviour, an inability to control activity levels or impulses, or difficulty concentrating.

auditory hallucinations The experience of hearing sounds like voices that do not actually exist. A common symptom of schizophrenia.

autism The best known of the ***pervasive developmental disorders***. Autistic children exhibit a lack of social responsiveness or extreme autistic aloneness; very limited or unusual communication patterns; unusual patterns of behaviour such as a lack of eye contact; self-stimulation including rocking, spinning, or flapping; self-injury including head-banging or hand-biting; an obsessive interest in particular objects; and an obsessive need for sameness. From the Greek *autos*, "self."

autoerotic asphyxia A self-administered procedure for suppressing breathing so that unconsciousness occurs. Usually releasing procedures are built in to reinitiate breathing upon unconsciousness. This loss of consciousness is sexually arousing to the participant.

aversive drift In Meehl's theory, the tendency for people with a genetic predisposition for schizophrenia to be perceived negatively and subjected to personal rejection, leading progressively to social withdrawal and alienation.

avolition A loss of energy, motivation, or interest in activities, including grooming, education, or physical exertion.

B

baby boomers A person who was born during the post–Second World War baby boom between 1946 and 1964.

bedlam Any form of rowdy, chaotic behaviour. The noise and disruption among the residents of Bethlem Royal Hospital (as it is now known) prompted the use of the word (the local corruption of "Bethlem"). This asylum was established by Henry VIII in 1547 when he had the monastery of St. Mary of Bethlehem in London converted.

behavioural avoidance test (BAT) An assessment of a patient's avoidance whereby the person determines how close he or she can come to a feared object. During their approach, patients also provide ratings of their fear. This test is used to assess initial avoidance and behavioural change through therapy.

behavioural disinhibition A personality trait describing an inability to inhibit behavioural impulses, rebelliousness, aggressiveness, and risk-taking that are associated with the development of alcohol problems.

behavioural genetics The study of the way in which inherited features interact with the environment to produce behaviour.

behavioural inhibition A temperament in early childhood that may be related to anxiety disorders later in life, characterized by profound avoidance of others in preschool, and atypical autonomic nervous system responses to novelty.

behavioural medicine Application of the methods of behaviour modification to the treatment or prevention of disease—for example, the use of psychological techniques to control pain in patients undergoing medical procedures, or interventions to improve the diabetics' ability to control their blood glucose.

behavioural phenotype Characteristic patterns of motor, cognitive, linguistic, and social abnormalities commonly displayed by individuals with certain genetic disorders.

behavioural tolerance Through the principles of classical conditioning, cues in the environment can become conditioned stimuli to the effects of drug use. These cues cause the individual to anticipate the drug effects so that when the drug is actually administered the effects are diminished. Tolerance, or the need for a greater amount of drug for the same effect, is greatest when the conditioned environmental cues are present.

behaviourism A psychological approach to understanding abnormal behaviour devised by John B. Watson (1858–1935), which declared that psychology must be restricted to the study of observable features, that is, the behaviour of organisms. Watson considered abnormal functioning to be learned and so believed it could be unlearned. His model for learning was derived from Ivan Pavlov's (1849–1936) studies of classical conditioning.

Bender Visual-Motor Gestalt Test The oldest and most commonly used of neuropsychological assessments often used to screen children for neuropsychological impairment. The test consists of a series of nine cards containing lines and shapes drawn in black on a piece of white cardboard. Children are asked first to copy the images on another card and then to draw them from memory. Errors in reproducing these lines and shapes may indicate neurological problems.

best interests principle In provincial mental health law, the doctrine that decisions made by others about the treatment of people suffering from mental disorders should maximize the chances of a good outcome, taking into account the risks and benefits of all available treatments.

biastophilia From Greek *biastes*, meaning rape; also referred to as paraphilic rape.

binge eating/purging type A subtype of ***anorexia nervosa*** in which the afflicted person's dietary restraint breaks down fairly regularly and she/he binges and/or purges. About half of anorexia nervosa patients are of the binge eating/purging type. *See also* ***restricting type***.

biological preparedness Refers to the idea that humans and animals are biologically prepared to fear certain stimuli as opposed to others. That is, evolution has "hard-wired" organisms to easily learn those associations that facilitate species survival.

biopsychosocial model A model proposing that behaviour is the result of the combined influence of biological, psychological, and social factors. Thus genetic endowment, neurological damage, and life experience (personal and social) all play a role in the emergence of behaviour.

bipolar disorders Mood disorders in which the change in mood occurs in both directions; that is, the patient at one time or another experiences both depression (mood lowering) and ***mania*** (mood elevation).

bipolar I disorder A subtype of the ***bipolar mood disorders*** in which there are one or more manic episodes and usually one or more depressive episodes. *See also* ***bipolar II***.

bipolar II disorder A subtype of the ***bipolar mood disorders*** in which there is at least one hypomanic episode and one or more episodes of major depression. *See also* ***bipolar I***.

birth-related complications Minor abnormalities at the time of birth, including extended labour, forceps delivery, and low weight, that may predispose a person to later illness.

blackouts Memory deficit caused by alcohol intoxication in which an interval of time passes for which a person cannot recall key details or entire events.

blood alcohol level (BAL) Alcohol level expressed as a percentage of blood volume. For example, if there are 80 milligrams of alcohol in 100 000 milligrams of blood, BAL is 0.08 percent.

body dysmorphic disorder (BDD) A ***somatoform disorder*** characterized by an individual's being unusually and excessively preoccupied with some aspect of his or her personal appearance—an imagined defect or an exaggeration of an existing trait.

body mass index (BMI) A person's weight in kilograms over his or her height in metres squared, an indicator of how much fat one has on one's body.

brain lesion An area of brain tissue that appears abnormal.

brain plasticity The ability of intact brain cells to compensate for damaged cells and take over their function.

brief intervention One- to three-session treatments, offering time-limited and specific advice regarding the need to reduce or eliminate alcohol and other drug consumption or gambling behaviour.

bulimia nervosa An eating disorder characterized by a binge-purge syndrome in people who are generally in the normal weight range.

C

cannabis Hashish, which comes from the hemp plant *cannabis sativa*, indigenous to Asia but now grown in many parts of the world. Has psychoactive effects caused primarily by the chemical ***THC***.

capable wishes principle In provincial mental health law, the doctrine that decisions made by others about the treatment of people suffering from mental disorders should reflect their personal wishes.

cardiac output The amount of blood pumped by the heart. One of the two major variables that determine blood pressure. Cardiac output is itself determined by two other variables: the rate at which the heart beats (commonly measured in beats per minute) and the amount of blood ejected from the heart (stroke volume). *See also* ***total peripheral resistance***.

cardiovascular reactivity The degree of change in a cardiovascular function that occurs in response to psychologically significant events.

case study A non-experimental investigative method resulting in a description of the past and current functioning of a single individual, generally the result of information gathered through intense interactions over long periods. Variables such as family history, education, employment history, medical history, social relationships, and the patient's level of psychological adjustment are described. The goal is a description of an individual's current problem, and its relation to his or her past. A case study seeks to provide a theory concerning the etiology of a patient's problem or psychological makeup, and/or a course of treatment and outcome. The oldest approach to the study of abnormal behaviour.

catastrophic misinterpretation In the context of panic, when one misinterprets normal bodily sensations as signals that one is going to have a heart attack, go crazy, lose control, or die.

catatonic behaviour Rigid body positions assumed by people with schizophrenia.

catatonic type One of the five official types of ***schizophrenia***, characterized by stupor, rigidity, negativism, odd posturing, excitement, and echopraxia (imitation of someone else's movements) or ***echolalia***.

categorical approach The diagnostic approach taken by the DSM, in which an individual is deemed either to have a disorder or not have a disorder.

cellular immunity One of the three general categories of immune response, based on the action of a class of blood cells called T-lymphocytes. The "T" designation refers to the locus of their production, the thymus gland. Cellular immunity results from a cascade of actions of various types of T-lymphocytes.

child disintegrative disorder (CDD) A developmental disorder evinced by behaviours and deficits in social skill and communication similar to those found in ***autism***. The major distinguishing feature is later onset; after a period of several years of normal development, marked deterioration occurs. The ability to speak in sentences is present before onset.

child molester An individual who abuses children for sexual gratification.

chlorpromazine The first true antipsychotic medication, introduced in the early 1950s.

chorionic villus sampling (CVS) A procedure for prenatal screening for chromosomal abnormalities that involves obtaining cells from the vagina and cervix. This test can be carried out earlier than amniocentesis—between the eighth and twelfth weeks of pregnancy—but may be less accurate.

civil code The written statement of law used in some jurisdictions to deal with matters of private law (i.e., disputes between individuals); in Canada, Quebec uses a civil code, whereas the other provinces and territories use common law.

civil commitment In provincial mental health law, the involuntary hospitalization of people suffering from mental disorder.

classical conditioning A type of learning described by the Russian physiologist Ivan Pavlov (1849–1936). In classical conditioning, a response is transferred from one stimulus to another. John B. Watson, an early behaviourist, took the view that classical conditioning was the basis for human behaviour, including abnormal behaviour. *See also* ***operant conditioning***.

client-centred therapy A type of therapy developed by Carl Rogers as an alternative to psychoanalysis, based on his belief that psychological problems arose when personal growth was stunted by judgments imposed by others.

clinical approach An approach to evaluating and interpreting the data on patients, making predictions, and coming to decisions that relies on the clinician's experience and personal judgment, guided by intuition honed with professional experience rather than by formal rules. *See also* ***actuarial approach***.

clinical practice guidelines Guidelines based on the best available empirical evidence that translate the knowledge gained from research into concrete guidelines intended to inform clinical practice.

clinical psychologists Persons who are initially trained in general psychology and then receive graduate training in the application of this knowledge to the understanding, diagnosis, and amelioration of disorders of thinking and behaviour. They have a thorough grounding in research methods, and some spend their careers doing research on abnormal functioning, although many also provide treatment. The treatment methods of clinical psychologists primarily involve psychological interventions of one kind or another.

clinical significance An attribute of research results, referring to the practical utility of the treatment studied, which does not follow automatically from the results' ***statistical significance***.

clusters Groups of personality disorders. DSM-IV-TR lists 10 personality disorders in three clusters: (A) odd and eccentric disorders (paranoid, schizoid, and schizotypal); (B) dramatic, emotional, or erratic disorders (antisocial, borderline, histrionic, and narcissistic); and (C) anxious and fearful disorders (avoidant, dependent, and obsessive-compulsive).

coefficient alpha A method for evaluating ***internal consistency***, calculated by averaging the intercorrelations of all the items on a given test. The higher the coefficient alpha, the higher the internal consistency.

coercive process A process in relationships in which aversive reactions are used to control the behaviour of another individual.

cognitive-behavioural theory A psychological theory that reflects the view that both thinking and behaviour are learned and can, therefore, be changed. It assumes that the way people view the world, including their beliefs and attitudes toward the world, themselves, and others, arises out of their experience and that these patterns of thinking and perceiving are maintained by consequences in the same way overt behaviour is maintained. While this treatment approach incorporates some procedures derived from strictly cognitive therapy, it essentially follows the views expressed by Bandura's ***social learning theory***.

cognitive-behaviour (behavioural) therapy (CBT) A form of psychotherapy that attempts to change maladaptive thoughts and behaviours.

cognitive distortions Thoughts about the self, world, or future that are distortions of the true state of affairs.

cognitive marker A disease marker that is cognitive in nature, typically involving a test of attention, memory, or reasoning.

cognitive restructuring A technique used by cognitive-behavioural therapists to encourage clients to become aware of, and to question, their assumptions, expectations, attributions, and automatic thoughts.

cognitive slippage The mental consequence of ***hypokrisia***, namely loss of integrated thinking and coherent mental life.

cognitive triad Negative views of the self, world, and future, as part of Beck's cognitive model of depression.

cohort effect A cohort refers to people born at roughly the same time, and a cohort effect refers to differences in age cohorts (e.g., people born in 1930 versus those born in 1980) as a result of unique social and historical events they have experienced.

collective unconscious The concept that symbols and myths are shared among people in a culture, but remain beneath awareness. The Swiss psychiatrist C. G. Jung developed this concept more fully in his approach to dreams.

common law The law as stated in the decisions of the judges from the earliest times to the present.

community psychology A field of psychology that has highlighted the need for the prevention of mental disorders and the promotion of mental health, as opposed to exclusive reliance on treatment approaches; applies an ecological perspective that stresses the interdependence of the individual, the family, community, and society; embodies sensitivity to a person's social context and appreciation of diversity; pays more attention to people's strengths and the promotion of wellness, in contrast to the clinical psychology focus on deficits and reduction of maladaptive behaviours; stresses the importance of informal social supports, rather than relying solely on professional help; and is oriented to social justice and social change.

comorbidity The common situation in which an individual meets the criteria for more than one diagnostic condition. *See also* ***overlap***.

compulsions Repetitive behaviours (overt actions or cognitive acts) performed in response to an obsession, or according to certain rules or in a stereotyped manner.

compulsory treatment order A court order requiring an individual to undergo treatment for his or her mental disorder.

computerized axial tomography (CAT) A brain imaging technique in which a narrow band of X-rays is projected through the head. The X-ray source and detector rotate very slightly and project successive images. The exposures are combined by a computer to produce a highly detailed cross-section of the brain.

concordance A concept used in behavioural research into the genetic bases of psychiatric disorders. When the disorder that characterizes one person, called the *index case* or ***proband***, also occurs in another person, the two are said to display concordance. The degree of concordance is thought to reveal the influence of genetics.

concordant The similarity of diagnosis in a pair of twins—they are concordant if they both exhibit the same trait or disorder.

concurrent validity The ability of a diagnostic category to estimate an individual's present standing on factors related to the disorder but not themselves part of the diagnostic criteria. One of the major criticisms of the DSM is that it sheds little light on the non-symptom attributes of people with a given diagnosis.

conduct disorder (CD) A disorder of children who show a pattern of violating the rights of others and major age-appropriate societal norms or rules in a variety of settings.

confound In an experiment, what occurs when two or more variables exert their influence at the same time, making it impossible to accurately establish the causal role of either variable.

conscious In ***psychodynamic*** theory, the conscious contains information of which we are currently aware.

constitutional law The written statement of law that, among other things, defines the powers and limits of powers that can be exercised by the different levels and branches of government; in Canada, set out primarily in the *Constitution Act.*

constitutional vulnerability One model of how hostility might lead to health risk, which suggests that the link between hostility and poor health outcomes is the result of a third variable, constitutional vulnerability, with which they are both associated.

construct validity The validity of a test assuming a specific theoretical framework that relates the item the test measures, often rather abstract, to some other item that is more easily assessed. If the two sets of measurements correlate, the test is said to have construct validity.

content-specificity Distinct cognitive content is related to different types of disorders. For example, depression is related to thoughts of deprivation and loss, whereas anxiety is related to themes of threat and potential harm.

content validity When the content of a test includes a representative sample of behaviours thought to be related to the construct (that is, the concept or entity) the test is designed to measure.

control group In an experiment, the group that experiences all aspects of the experiment, including assessments, in a manner identical to the ***experimental group***, except for the manipulation of the ***independent variable***.

controllable risk factors Factors increasing the likelihood of disease, such as poor diet or smoking, that are under the control of the individual.

conversion disorder A ***somatoform disorder*** characterized by motor symptoms or disturbances in sensory functioning that appear to be a result of a neurological problem, but for which no physical cause can be found. Previously known as "hysteria," from the Greek *hystera* ("uterus").

correlational method A nonexperimental investigative method that measures the degree of relationship between two variables; behaviour is not manipulated but quantitatively measured and then analyzed statistically. Following the measurement of the variables, a statistical quantity called a *correlation coefficient* is computed. Generally requires a large number of participants.

courtship disorder theory A theory of sexual offending advanced by Kurt Freund that holds it is produced when a person's sexual behaviour becomes fixated at one of the four phases of human sexual interactions: (1) looking for and appraising a potential partner; (2) posturing and displaying oneself to the partner; (3) tactile interaction with the partner; and (4) sexual intercourse. Fixation at stage 1 results in ***voyeurism***; at stage 2 in ***exhibitionism***; at stage 3 in ***frotteurism***; and at stage 4 in *rape*.

criminal commitment A custodial sentence, or detention in a correctional facility following conviction for a criminal offence.

criterion validity An attribute of a test, when it gives higher scores to people already known to have greater ability in the area it tests. The concept arises because some qualities are easier to recognize than to define completely, such as artistic ability.

cross-fostering A type of adoption study in which one group comprises adopted children whose biological parents have a disorder and whose adoptive parents demonstrate no psychopathology, and the other group comprises adopted children whose biological parents have no disorder but whose adoptive parents develop psychopathology. The comparisons available in this design allow statements concerning the relative impact of genes and environment. Regarded as an improvement on the traditional adoption study.

culturally relative The functions and acceptability of various behaviours vary by culture, rather than being universal truths; as such, an individual's beliefs and activities should be understood in terms of his or her own culture.

cumulative liability The combined risk for developing an illness that accumulates over multiple factors and over time.

cumulative risk The summation of a person's risk for a disorder or disease up to a specified age.

cyclothymia *See* ***cyclothymic disorder***.

cyclothymic disorder Mood disorder characterized by long-term (i.e., at least two years) repeated fluctuations in mood, varying from hypomanic symptoms to depressive symptoms that do not meet diagnostic criteria for ***major depressive disorder***.

D

defence mechanisms According to Sigmund Freud, mechanisms through which the ego allows the expression of libidinal desires in a distorted or symbolic form.

deinstitutionalization The removal of people with disabilities from institutions and the provision of community-based accommodation and services.

deliberate self-harm (DSH) When someone injures or harms him- or herself on purpose.

delusional thinking Implausible and unfounded beliefs and convictions not based in reality, as often experienced by people with schizophrenia and other psychotic disorders.

delusions False beliefs that are strongly held, even in the face of solid contradictory evidence. Such beliefs usually involve a misinterpretation of one's experiences.

delusions of grandeur False and implausible beliefs that focus on the possession of special powers, divinity, or fame.

dementia The most common mental disorder in older adults, in which sufferers lose their memory, judgment, reason, personal dignity, and finally their sense of self.

dependent variable In an experiment, the behavioural response on measures the researchers hypothesize would be affected by the manipulation of the ***independent variable***.

depersonalization The feeling that one is an observer, rather than an initiator, of one's own behaviour.

depersonalization disorder A dissociative disorder characterized by a feeling of detachment from one's self or surroundings. People with this disorder often describe themselves as feeling like robots who are able to respond to those nearby without feeling connected to their actions.

depressants Drugs that inhibit neurotransmitter activity in the central nervous system. Examples are alcohol, barbiturates ("downers"), and benzodiazepines.

derealization A dissociative symptom where the external world is experienced as strange or unreal.

description The specification and classification of clinical phenomena; one of the primary goals of clinical research.

diagnosis In the realm of medicine and abnormal psychology, a determination or identification of the nature of a person's disease or condition, or a statement of that finding. A diagnosis is made on the basis of a ***diagnostic system***.

diagnostic overshadowing The problem of attributing emotional and behavioural difficulties of people with mental retardation to the developmental disorder, causing real psychiatric disorders to be missed. The fact is that such people can develop all types of psychiatric disorders, including less common ones.

diagnostic system A system of rules for recognizing and grouping various types of abnormalities. Forms the basis for ***diagnosis***.

dialectical behaviour therapy One of the cognitive-behavioural approaches to treatment of *borderline personality disorder (BPD)*, one of whose main features is the acceptance by the therapist of the patient's demanding and manipulative behaviours. In addition, several standard behavioural procedures are used, such as exposure treatment for the external and internal cues that evoke distress, skills training, contingency management, and cognitive restructuring.

diathesis A predisposition or vulnerability for the development of an illness or disorder.

diathesis-stress model A model that recognizes the combination of a diathesis (i.e., vulnerability) and sufficient amounts of life stress that, combined, are likely to produce a disorder.

diathesis-stress perspective The view that a predisposition to develop a disorder (the "diathesis"), interacting with the experience of stress, causes mental disorders. According to this perspective, the interaction underlies the onset of all disorders, although either the predisposition or the stress may be more important in a particular disorder, or in a particular person.

dimensional An approach to diagnosis that examines constructs on a continuum rather than as discrete categorical entities.

disease markers Objective biological or behavioural traits or features of an individual that reliably reflect the presence of a medical or psychiatric disease or a predisposition to develop such a disease.

disgust sensitivity The degree to which people are disgusted by a variety of stimuli, such as bugs, types of food, and small animals.

disorganized type One of the five official types of *schizophrenia*, characterized by disorganized speech, clearly disorganized behaviour, and markedly flat or inappropriate affect. Generally viewed as the most severe subtype.

dissemination Scaling up of program to other settings for widespread adoption.

dissociation The disruption of mental processes involved in memory or consciousness that are normally integrated.

dissociative amnesia Complete memory loss for extensive and important actions and/or personal information. Characterized by a sudden onset, typically in response to a traumatic event or extremely stressful experience, and by an equally sudden return of memory.

dissociative disorders Psychological problems characterized by ***dissociation***.

dissociative fugue Loss of memory with the added feature of physical flight. For diagnosis, there must be (1) sudden and unexpected travel away from home or work and (2) an inability to recall one's past and confusion about personal identity. A sufferer leaves the comfort of home and familiar surroundings and assumes a completely new identity, one that can be quite elaborate and last for years. The person may also display behaviour very different from previous habits. From the Latin *fugere*, "to flee."

dissociative identity disorder (DID) The most severe and chronic of the dissociative disorders, characterized by the existence of two or more unique personalities in a single individual. Each personality may have its own constellation of behaviour, tone of voice, and physical gestures. *See also* ***alter***.

dizygotic (DZ) twins Non-identical (or fraternal) twins, which result when two independent sperm separately fertilize two independent ova at approximately the same time. DZ twins, like non-twin siblings, have, on average, just 50 percent of their genes in common. From *di*, meaning "two."

dopamine A neurotransmitter associated with movement, attention, learning, and the brain's pleasure and reward system.

dopamine-blocking drugs Medication that acts by occupying receptors for dopamine in the brain, thereby reducing psychotic symptoms.

double-blind A procedure to help ensure that expectations of the subjects of a study do not influence the outcome, according to which neither the subjects nor the experimenters know who is getting the substance in question and who is getting a ***placebo***.

Down syndrome The best-known chromosomal abnormality associated with mental retardation.

drug interactions When another substance affects the activity of a drug (e.g., by increasing or decreasing its activity).

dual diagnosis The co-occurrence of serious behavioural or psychiatric disorders in people with developmental disabilities.

dualistic A view of mind and body as separate entities, subject to different laws. Nowadays avoided in DSM terminology, hence the substitution of the term *psychophysiological* for *psychosomatic*.

dyscalculia A learning disorder that involves problems with recognizing and understanding numerical symbols, sequencing problems, and attention deficits. Also known as *mathematical disorder*.

dyslexia A reading disorder that involves difficulties not only in the recognition but also in the comprehension of words. Reading is often very slow and characterized by omitted, substituted, or distorted words. Such difficulties often extend to spelling as well. Also referred to as *reading disorder*.

dyspareunia A sexual dysfunction characterized by genital pain associated with intercourse. Some experts claim lack of lubrication is the most common cause of the problem. Among men, it is rare and usually associated with infections, inflammation, or physical anomalies.

dysthymia *See* ***dysthymic disorder***.

dysthymic disorder A ***unipolar mood disorder*** that manifests many of the same symptoms as major depression, except that they are less severe. It persists for at least two years, with only brief interludes of normal mood. Also known as ***dysthymia***.

E

Eating Disorder Examination (EDE) A structured clinical interview for diagnosing eating disorders.

eccentricity Generally describes behaviour that deviates from the norm and would be considered odd or whimsical.

echolalia One of the common characteristics of speech in autistic children, in which the child repeats another person's words or phrases, using the same or similar intonation.

ecological perspective A perspective on health promotion that considers nested levels of analysis, viewing mental health problems in the context of characteristics of the individual (for example, coping skills, personality traits); the ***microsystem*** (that is, the family and social network); the ***exo-system***, which mediates between the individual, the family, and the larger society (for example, work settings, schools, religious settings, neighbourhoods); and the ***macrosystem*** (for example, social norms, social class).

effect size A common metric used to summarize the meaning of diverse studies in a ***meta-analysis***. It is calculated as the difference between the means of the experimental (that is, the treatment) group and the control group, divided by the standard deviation of either the control group or the pooled sample of both groups.

ego In Sigmund Freud's theory, the structure that begins to develop in response to the fact that instinctual demands of the ***id*** are not always immediately met. The ego develops to curb the desires of id so that the individual does not suffer any unpleasant consequences.

ego analysts Psychoanalytically oriented therapists who use Freudian techniques to explore the ego rather than the id, and try to help clients understand how they have relied on defence mechanisms to cope with conflicts.

egodystonic Thoughts and behaviours that do not coincide with one's self-image (ego).

egodystonic homosexuality A type of ***gender identity disorder (GID)*** in which the afflicted person is attracted to people of the same sex, but experiences conflict with his or her sexual orientation or wishes to change it.

egosyntonic Lack of emotional responsiveness to events or situations that would normally elicit a strong negative emotional response such as heightened anxiety or depression.

Electra complex The condition in which, according to Sigmund Freud, girls want to seduce their fathers to gain what they truly desire: a penis. By analogy to a character in several Greek tragedies.

electroconvulsive therapy (ECT) The use of electricity to induce a seizure in mental patients by placing electrodes on the skull and administering a convulsive rather than a lethal shock intensity.

emotional numbing The perception that one lacks, is without, or can't feel emotions; instead one feels "numb."

emotional responsiveness Reflecting a range of appropriate and contextual emotions to different situations and individuals.

emotionally focused couples therapy An experiential approach to couples therapy that aims to modify constricted interaction patterns and emotional responses by fostering the development of a secure emotional bond.

emotion-focused therapy A short-term psychotherapy approach that purports that emotions themselves are inherently adaptive and can help clients to change problematic emotional states or unwanted self-experiences.

empirically supported therapy Psychotherapeutic intervention that has been demonstrated empirically to be effective.

empirically supported therapy relationships (ESR) A task force of the APA Division of Psychotherapy reviewed the research literature to identify elements of effective therapy relationships and determine methods of tailoring therapy to individual patient characteristics.

endogenous opiates The body's natural painkillers. ***Opioids*** mimic their effects.

endophenotypes A hereditary characteristic that is normally associated with some condition but is not a direct symptom of that condition.

epidemiology The study of the ***incidence*** and ***prevalence*** of disorders in a population.

epigenetic Biological regulation of the activity and expression of genes.

equipotentiality premise The presumption that all stimuli have an equal chance of becoming acquired phobias.

estrogen A hormone (the so-called female sex hormone) involved in sexual activity and desire, variations in the level of which can lower or increase sex drive.

ethical codes Written statements that set out the core values that should guide decision making by members of a profession or other group.

ethyl alcohol The effective chemical compound in alcoholic beverages, which reduces anxiety and inhibitions, produces euphoria, and creates a sense of well-being.

etiology Causes or origins, especially of disease.

evidence-based practice Health care based on established scientific findings rather than practitioners' assumptions.

excessive reassurance seeking Part of Coyne's model of depression where a depressed person seeks reassurance about him- or herself from non-depressed people.

exhaustion The third phase of the ***general adaptation syndrome (GAS)***, a concept that was the first formal description and definition of stress as a consequence of adaptation to demands placed on the body. If the challenge persists beyond the ***resistance*** phase, the body can no longer maintain resistance, and characteristic tissue changes occur. At this point, the organism may succumb to a disease of adaptation, such as an ulcer. *See also* ***alarm***.

exhibitionism A form of ***paraphilia*** that is also a criminal offence, in which a person exposes his or her genitals to an unsuspecting stranger.

Exner system A way of standardizing the scoring of responses in a Rorschach examination in order to increase its reliability and validity. The Exner system may have greater clinical validity for testing schizophrenia than depression or personality disorders.

exogenous opiates Narcotics, which bind to receptor sites throughout the body, including the brain, spinal cord, and bloodstream, and reduce the body's production of ***endogenous opiates***.

experiment A scientific procedure in which variables are manipulated and the effects on other variables are gauged. Large groups of subjects are generally used, and the results are analyzed statistically. In a true experiment, subjects are randomly assigned to ***experimental*** and ***control groups***.

experimental effect The difference obtained in the dependent variable that occurs as a function of the manipulation of the ***independent variable***.

experimental group In an experiment, the group exposed to a variable that is manipulated, the ***independent variable***.

exposure therapy Any therapeutic procedure that repeatedly confronts the person with a stimulus that typically elicits an undesirable behaviour or an unwanted emotional response until the behaviour or response no longer occurs.

expressed emotion A measure of the amount of emotion displayed, typically within a family.

externalizing problems A type of disruptive behaviour disorder under the DSM-IV classification exhibited by children who behave disruptively, cannot control their activity levels or impulses, or have difficulty concentrating. These behaviours are usually more disturbing to others than to the children themselves.

external locus of control A belief that the determinants of one's life reside outside oneself. People who have an external locus of control see themselves as being buffeted by the random events of the world. *See also* ***internal locus of control***.

external validity The generalizability of the findings in an investigation, or the degree to which the findings apply to other individuals in other settings.

extrapyramidal effects Severe side effects of the major tranquilizers.

eye-tracking The measurement of movements of the eyes as they follow a point of light or a waveform. Patients with schizophrenia often show jerky or irregular eye-tracking.

F

face validity An attribute of a test, when the items on it resemble the characteristics associated with the concept being tested for.

facilitated communication (FC) An alternative approach to teaching people with severe communication impairment, such as low-functioning children with ***autism***. In FC, subjects pointed to pictures, letters, or objects while a facilitator provided various types of support to the hand or forearm, on the theory that physical support could overcome neuromotor problems. However, concerns were soon raised about the "ouija board effect"—that is, that facilitators were unintentionally influencing the subject by subtle body movements. Controlled studies confirmed that this was occurring and did not provide support for the emergence of hidden literacy skills.

factitious disorder Faking or bringing on symptoms of illness to gain a doctor's attention and thus satisfy a need to play the role of patient. Not to be considered a ***somatoform disorder***, in which the sufferer truly believes there is a serious physical problem.

false memory syndrome Said to be exhibited by persons who claim to remember events that did not really take place, due to the influence of therapists who use leading questions, repeated suggestion, visualization, and hypnosis with the aim of recovering repressed memories.

familiality The extent to which a disorder occurs in members of the same family, including previous generations.

family-focused therapy (FFT) Adjunctive psychotherapy for bipolar disorder that focuses on educating the patient's family about the disorder and improving family communication.

family therapy A form of psychotherapy that focuses on work with families and couples in intimate relationships.

fear An emotion that occurs in response to a real or perceived current threat.

fear hierarchy A fear hierarchy is a list of feared situations or objects that are arranged in descending order according to how much they evoke anxiety. This list is then used in therapy for exposure exercises.

fearlessness hypothesis A theory that suggests that ***psychopaths*** have a higher threshold for feeling fear than other people. Events that make most people anxious (such as the expectation of being punished) seem to have little or no effect on psychopaths.

female orgasmic disorder A sexual dysfunction characterized by a woman's persistent or recurrent delay in, or absence of, orgasm following normal excitement, causing marked distress or interpersonal difficulty. Also known as ***anorgasmia***.

female sexual arousal disorder A sexual dysfunction characterized by a woman's persistent or recurrent inability to attain or maintain arousal until completion of her sexual activity, and the presence of marked distress or difficulty.

fetal alcohol effects (FAE) Defects shown by children who display some of the symptoms of ***fetal alcohol syndrome (FAS)*** without meeting all diagnostic criteria.

fetal alcohol syndrome (FAS) Prenatal and postnatal growth retardation and central nervous system dysfunction due to alcohol consumption during pregnancy.

fetishisms Sexual behaviours in which the presence of nonliving objects is usually required or strongly preferred for sexual excitement. Most researchers and clinicians also include an excessive attraction to certain parts of the body.

"fight or flight" response A term commonly used to describe the behavioural options of individuals (or organisms) experiencing fear; specifically, to either flee from a dangerous situation, or stand and fight.

flashback Unpredictable recurrences of some of the physical or perceptual distortions associated with drug use that occur when the person is no longer using the drug.

flooding (intense exposure) Flooding is intense exposure. This involves facing one's fears at a very high level of intensity rather than working gradually through the fear hierarchy.

forensic psychology An area of specialization in psychology that focuses on the application of research and practice to matters of law, including proceedings in criminal or civil courts or in front of quasi-judicial bodies such as administrative boards and tribunals.

frontal brain deficiency The idea that the frontal brain region is damaged or dysfunctional in schizophrenia.

frontal lobe The large brain region underlying the frontal part of the skull.

frontal lobotomy The surgical cutting of connecting fibres within the frontal brain.

frontotemporal dementia (FTD) A subtype of ***dementia*** characterized by striking changes in personality or social conduct (e.g., loss of initiative, lack of empathy, lapses in judgment) as well as deficits in higher-order cognitive abilities (i.e., executive functions).

frotteurism A form of ***paraphilia*** that is also a criminal offence, in which a person touches or rubs against a nonconsenting person for the purpose of sexual pleasure.

functional magnetic resonance imaging (fMRI) A technique that allows observation of neurophysiological activity accompanying specific cognitive tasks.

G

gender dysphoria Discomfort with one's biologically endowed sex.

gender identity One of the three aspects of the development of gender, referring to a person's basic sense of self as male or female, the first signs of which appear between 18 and 36 months of age. *See also* ***sexual orientation*** and ***gender role***.

gender identity disorder (GID) A condition in which a person experiences strong and persistent identification with the other sex, ***gender dysphoria***, and significant distress or impairment in social, occupational, or other important areas of functioning. Previously known as *transsexualism*.

gender role One of the three aspects of the development of gender identity, referring to the collection of those characteristics that a society defines as masculine or feminine. Because roles relate to social standards, ideas about gender role change over time and from culture to culture. *See also* ***gender identity***.

gene–environment interactions A term used to describe the phenotypic effects (i.e., observable characteristics) that are due to interactions between the environment and genes.

general adaptation syndrome (GAS) A stereotyped pattern of bodily changes that occur in response to diverse challenges to the organism, first described by Hans Selye. The syndrome comprises three stages: ***alarm***, ***resistance***, and ***exhaustion***. The GAS was the first formal description and definition of stress.

generalized sexual dysfunctions Any sexual dysfunction that is apparent with all the sufferer's sexual partners and even during solitary sexual activity.

general paresis of the insane (GPI) A disorder evidenced by mania, euphoria, and grandiosity, followed by a progressive deterioration of brain functioning (called ***dementia***) and paralysis. Now known to result from untreated infections by the syphilis spirochete.

genetic contribution The influence of genes on the development of a mental illness or disorder.

genetic linkage studies Studies in which researchers examine families that have a high incidence of a particular psychiatric disorder. Within these extended families the researchers look for the presence of particular traits (called genetic markers) that can be linked to the occurrence of the disorder.

genotype–environment interaction Refers to the fact that genes may influence behaviours that contribute to environmental stressors, which, in turn, increase the risk of psychopathology. In other words, there is a reciprocal relationship between genetic predisposition and environmental risk.

gerontologist A specialist in gerontology (a branch of science that deals with the study of the elderly).

glove anaesthesia A sensory symptom of conversion disorder where a lack of sensation exists in the part of the arm that would usually be covered with a glove.

H

habituation *See* ***psychological dependence***.

hallucinations False perceptions occurring in the absence of any relevant stimulus. Auditory hallucinations are the most common form, but they may occur within any sensory modality.

hallucinogens Drugs that change a person's mental state by inducing perceptual and sensory distortions or hallucinations. Also called *psychedelics*, from the Greek for "soul" and "to make manifest."

harm reduction approaches Approaches to treatment for alcohol and other drug abuse that focus on reducing the consequences of the use versus reducing or eliminating use.

health behaviour model One model of how hostility might lead to health risk, which suggests that hostile people may be more likely to engage in unhealthy behaviours (for example, smoking, drug use, high-fat diets) and less likely to have healthy practices, such as exercise.

health psychology Any application of psychological methods and theories to understand the origins of disease, individual responses to disease, and the dimensions and determinants of good health.

hermaphroditism A condition in which a person's reproductive structures are partly female and partly male.

heterogeneity The variability and diversity of clinical and biological features seen in schizophrenia.

heterosexual gender dysphoria A type of ***gender identity disorder (GID)*** in which the afflicted person is attracted to people of the opposite sex.

heterotypic comorbidity A disorder that is comorbid with another disorder in a different class of disorders (e.g., ODD and GAD).

heterotypic continuity An underlying (developmental) process or impairment stays the same, but how it is manifested may be different (e.g., prediction of a disorder by another disorder); in ***homeotypic continuity***, by contrast, the manifestations stay the same, but the underlying process changes.

high-risk children The children of parents with schizophrenia or other genetically influenced disorders who therefore have an increased risk of developing the disorder themselves.

high-risk program An intervention or prevention program that targets individuals (usually children or adolescents) at high risk for disorder or disease.

hippocampus A region of the middle part of the temporal lobe involved with memory formation.

HIV Human immunodeficiency virus (HIV) is a chronic disease that affects the immune system. Under normal circumstances, the immune system protects against infections and diseases; however, it becomes less efficient when weakened by HIV. The rate of deterioration of the immune system varies from rapid to slow. As the immune system deteriorates, other health problems, including opportunistic infections, are increasingly likely to occur.

homotypic comorbidity A disorder that is comorbid with another disorder in the same class of disorders (e.g., ODD and CD).

homotypic continuity An underlying (developmental) process or impairment may change, but the way it is manifested stays the same (e.g., the prediction of a disorder by the same disorder).

humoral immunity One of the three general categories of immune response, in which invading antigens are presented by macrophages to B-lymphocytes. ("B" stands for *bursa*, an organ in which such cells are produced in birds. B-lymphocytes derive from the liver and bone marrow in humans.) This causes the B-cells to reproduce—a process reinforced by the lymphokine secretion from the helper T-cells. Some of the activated B-cells remain as memory B-cells. Others go on to be plasma cells, secreting antibodies called immunoglobulins that neutralize antigens in a number of different ways, such as clumping, presenting the antigen to phagocytic cells, or rupturing the antigen.

humours Bodily fluids, disturbances of which, according to Hippocrates, resulted in psychological dysfunctioning.

hypersexuality Excessive interest or involvement in sexual activity at levels high enough to become clinically significant.

hypertension A characteristically high level of resting blood pressure (defined as a ***systolic blood pressure/diastolic blood pressure*** reading of more than 140/80 under precisely defined conditions). Can result from any of variety of causes, but in about 90 percent of cases it is "essential," meaning a simple cause cannot be identified. Hypertension is a *risk factor* for death due to cardiovascular disease.

hypoactive sexual desire disorder A sexual dysfunction characterized by persistent or recurrent deficiency of sexual fantasies and desire for sex, causing marked distress or interpersonal difficulty.

hypochondriasis A ***somatoform disorder*** characterized by excessive preoccupation with fears of having a serious illness when there is no underlying illness. The most common diseases people worry about are cancer and heart disease. Often leads to "doctor shopping." From the Greek *hypochondria* for the region below the ribs, thought to be linked to changes in mood and mental functioning.

hypokrisia In Meehl's theory, the reduced selectivity with which nerve cells respond to stimuli, especially as seen in schizophrenia.

hypomania A less severe, less disruptive, and often shorter version of a manic episode.

hypothalamic-pituitary-adrenal (HPA) axis The biological stress response system responsible for the fight-or-flight response. It is overactive in major depression.

hypoxyphilia The practice of heightening the sexual experience by deliberately inducing unconsciousness in oneself by oxygen deprivation, produced by chest compression, strangulation, enclosing the head in a plastic bag, or various other techniques. Also known as ***autoerotic asphyxia*** and ***asphyxiophilia***.

hysteria A condition characterized by emotional excitability and a physical or sensory deficit, without an organic cause.

I

iatrogenic Negative side effects of treatment (literally meaning "produced by treatment").

id In Sigmund Freud's theory, the structure present at birth that contains, or represents, the biological or instinctual drives that are not constrained at birth, demanding instant gratification without concern for the consequences either to the self or to others.

illness phobia An intense fear of developing a disease that the individual does not currently have. It is different from hypochondriasis, where the person believes that he or she *currently* has a disease or medical condition.

imagined loss Freudian theory that the individual unconsciously interprets all types of loss events (e.g., job loss) in terms of grief, thereby raising the risk for depression.

impairment of control A core symptom of substance dependence referring to a pattern of using more of the drug or using it longer than planned.

implementation How well a program is put into practice in a particular setting.

incidence The number of new cases of a disorder in a particular population over a specified time period, usually a year.

independent variable In an experiment, the variable that is manipulated.

indicated prevention Interventions that target high-risk individuals who have minimal but detectable symptoms of a disorder, or who exhibit vulnerability markers that indicate a predisposition to a disorder but do not currently meet diagnostic levels for the disorder.

instability In the context of personality disorders, describes an individual who has maladaptive interpersonal relationships and decisions and is generally unable to effectively regulate emotions or behaviour.

insulin coma A seizure and loss of consciousness induced by administration of insulin.

intellectual disability Significant limitations in intellectual functioning (i.e., IQ < 70; below the 2nd percentile) and adaptive behaviour, including communication, social, and community skills (i.e., below the 2nd percentile). The disability occurs before the age of 18.

intelligence quotient (IQ) A test of judgment, comprehension, and reasoning invented by the French psychologist Alfred Binet (1857–1911), in which a child's mental age, determined by the child's successful performance on age-grouped tests that had been normed, was divided by the child's chronological age, and the quotient multiplied by 100. Theoretically, IQ was a reflection of that person's performance compared with that of others the same age.

interactionist explanation A theory that views behaviour as the product of the interaction of a variety of factors.

internal consistency The degree of reliability within a test—the extent to which different parts of the same test yield the same results.

internalizing problems Problems such as anxiety, depression, shyness, social withdrawal, and somatic complaints that are problematic for the individual who experiences them but pose few problems for the social partners surrounding that person.

internal locus of control A belief that the determinants of one's life reside inside oneself. People who have an internal locus of control see themselves as the masters of their own destiny and seem to be protected against the harmful effects of stress on their health. *See also* ***external locus of control.***

internal validity The degree to which the changes in the ***dependent variable*** of an experiment are a result of the manipulation of the ***independent variable***. If no alternative explanations are possible, the experiment has strong internal validity.

interoceptive exposure Interoceptive exposure is exposure to bodily sensations (e.g., dizziness, shortness of breath, increased heart rate). It is a technique used to treat panic disorder.

interpersonal and social rhythm therapy (IPSRT) Adjunctive psychotherapy for bipolar disorder that focuses on regularizing patients' daily rhythms and routines.

interpersonal psychodynamic psychotherapy A variation of brief psychodynamic therapy that emphasizes the interactions between the client and his or her social environment.

interpersonal psychotherapy (IPT) A therapy that uses a medical model to understand interpersonal conflicts and transitions as they relate to depression.

inter-rater reliability The extent to which two or more clinicians agree on the ***diagnosis*** of a particular patient.

intolerance of uncertainty (IU) An individual's discomfort with ambiguity and uncertainty.

intracavernous treatment Medication injected directly into tissue or taken as a suppository.

in vivo exposure (in vivo, "in the living being") A therapeutic technique for overcoming anxiety. In in vivo ("real life") exposure, patients face their feared objects or situations directly (this is often used gradually, whereby patients work their way progressively through their fear hierarchy).

in vivo observation (in vivo, "in the living being") A method used by behaviourally oriented therapists to determine how environmental variables affect a behaviour of concern, in which a clinician may record a running narrative of events, using pencil and paper, video, or still camera, in the client's everyday environment. More commonly, observations are made by *participant observers*, key people in the client's environment, and reported to the clinician. *See also* ***analogue observational setting***.

ischemic heart disease A condition in which blood supply to the heart becomes compromised, leading to a *myocardial infarction*. One of the leading causes of death from diseases of the cardiovascular system in Western societies.

K

Korsakoff's psychosis A chronic disease related to alcohol dependence characterized by impaired memory and a loss of contact with reality.

L

la belle indifférence Surprising unconcern about the severity of their symptoms frequently shown by people with ***conversion disorder***.

labelling theory A point of view that suggests that when a person is identified as having a disorder, other people, particularly mental health workers, perceive that person as dysfunctional and different. This perception, which tends to persist even after recovery, results in these people being treated disadvantageously and even disrespectfully.

lanugo The fine white hair that grows on individuals with anorexia when they have no body fat left to keep themselves warm.

late-onset schizophrenia A type of ***schizophrenia*** that first appears after the age of 45. Diagnostic criteria are the same as those for ***early-onset schizophrenia***, the more common type, but late-onset cases are less likely to have disorganized speech, lack of logical thought, and flattened affect, and hallucinations and delusions are likely to be more florid and bizarre. The content of delusions and hallucinations is commonly persecutory, so people with this disorder are most likely to resemble the ***paranoid type*** of schizophrenia.

learning disorders A group of developmental disorders that include reading disorders, mathematics disorders, and disorders of written expression. Communication disorders and problems related to poor motor skills may also be included. Frequently referred to as *learning disabilities*.

left temporal lobe The brain region immediately beneath the left side of the skull and just above the ear.

lesions Disruptions of bodily tissue or of the normal function of a bodily system.

Lewy body dementia A subtype of ***dementia*** characterized by at least two of the following symptoms: (1) Parkinsonism (e.g., resting tremor, muscular rigidity, unstable posture); (2) visual hallucinations; (3) fluctuating alertness or cognition; and (4) rapid eye movement sleep disorder.

lifelong sexual dysfunction Any sexual dysfunction that the sufferer has always experienced.

ligands Chemical labels that identify the presence of specific types of receptors in brain tissue.

lithium Lithium salt, used to treat mania and depression. Has the effect of flattening out the peaks and valleys of the illness, allowing sufferers to achieve some stability in their lives with less disruption for family members. Apparently lithium has preventive effects for both ***unipolar mood disorders*** and ***bipolar mood disorders***, and lithium is considered the treatment of choice for bipolar disorder.

lobotomy ***Psychosurgery*** consisting of surgical removal, or disconnection, of the frontal lobes of the brain, intended to relieve all manner of mental and emotional disorders.

longitudinal study A scientific study in which a large number of people are evaluated with respect to the existence of psychological or behavioural features and are then followed up, often years or decades later, to determine whether they have developed a disease.

loosening of associations Loss of logical or conventional connections between ideas or words.

low-risk drinking guidelines A research-based definition of the ***upper limits*** on drinking that is not likely to lead to physical impairment in people in general.

lunacy A historical term for madness rooted in folk beliefs that the moon influenced mental states.

M

macrosystem A level of analysis in the ***ecological perspective*** that consists of social norms and social class.

madness A common term for irrational or uncontrolled behaviour as well as conditions like schizophrenia and bipolar disorder.

magnetic resonance imaging (MRI) Also called *nuclear magnetic resonance imaging*. A noninvasive technique for examining the structure and the functioning of the brain. A strong homogeneous magnetic field is produced around the head and brief pulses of radio waves are introduced. When the radio waves are turned off, radio waves of a characteristic frequency are emitted from the brain itself, which can be detected. The information gathered is integrated into a computer-generated image of the brain.

major depressive disorder (MDD) A ***unipolar mood disorder*** characterized by persistent feelings of sadness, loss of interest or ability to feel pleasure, unexplained weight loss, difficulty sleeping, fatigue, difficulty concentrating, feelings of worthlessness or guilt, suicidal thoughts, and either agitation or slowing down. The person must not be suffering from other disorders that may present as depression, such as *schizoaffective disorder* or a *delusional disorder*.

male erectile disorder A sexual dysfunction characterized by a man's persistent or recurrent inability to reach or sustain an erection until completion of his sexual activity and resultant distress. Also known informally as *impotence*.

male orgasmic disorder A sexual dysfunction characterized by a man's persistent or recurrent delay in, or absence of, orgasm following normal excitement, causing marked distress or interpersonal difficulty. Much less common than ***female orgasmic disorder***.

malingering Pretending to be ill in order to achieve some specific objective. Not to be considered a ***somatoform disorder***, in which the sufferer truly believes there is a serious physical problem.

mania A ***bipolar mood disorder*** characterized by flamboyance and expansiveness. A person experiencing a manic episode may go on shopping sprees, engage in sexually promiscuous behaviour, take on numerous, unrealistic work commitments, brag, and dominate others socially. In general, the person shows intolerance when the world does not cooperate with his or her momentary needs. Extreme or prolonged cases of mania are considered bona fide psychotic states, implying that the person is experiencing a break with reality. From the Greek *mainomai*, "to be mad." *See also* ***hypomania***.

maternal serum screening (MSS) A blood test conducted during the second trimester of pregnancy. MSS detects alpha-fetoprotein (AFP), as well as two hormones produced by the placenta. The levels of these substances can help identify women at higher risk of having babies with chromosomal abnormalities like Down syndrome or neural tube defects like spina bifida. This test may be used to select women for diagnostic amniocentesis, which is a more invasive procedure.

mechanism In *psychophysiological* medicine, a process—an activity of a living system—that mediates the influence of an antecedent factor on disease.

mens rea In Canadian criminal law, the guilty mind or bad intent that, together with the ***actus reus***, defines a criminal offence.

mental health Narrowly, the absence of disorder. In a broader view, the presence of optimal social, emotional, and cognitive functioning—also known as *wellness*.

Mental Health Commission of Canada (MHCC) A non-profit organization created to focus national attention on mental health issues and to work to improve the health and social outcomes of people living with mental illness.

mental health promotion A concept complementary to the concept of ***prevention*** in ***community psychology*** that focuses on the idea of enhancing the functioning of people.

mental hygiene movement A movement started by Dorothea Dix (1802–1887), a Boston schoolteacher, characterized by a desire to protect and provide humane treatment for the mentally ill. Her campaign resulted directly in the opening of 32 state hospitals, including 2 in Canada. Despite the noble aims, the asylums were overcrowded and the staff had no time to do more than warehouse and restrain the patients.

mental illness Often used to convey the same meaning as ***psychological abnormality***, but implies a medical rather than psychological cause.

mental status examination The most frequently used semi-structured interview in psychiatric settings. Screens for patients' emotional, intellectual, and neurological functioning. Used in formal diagnosis or to plan treatment.

meta-analysis A method of quantitatively summing up previous research studies that have used different patient populations and outcome measures. The research results are combined by developing a common metric called an ***effect size***.

methadone A heroin replacement used to treat heroin addicts, often to reduce the craving after initial withdrawal symptoms have abated. Methadone therapy appears to work best in conjunction with good individual and group psychological intervention programs, as well as ongoing peer support.

methylphenidate (Ritalin) The most frequently prescribed stimulant medication for children with ***attention deficit hyperactivity disorder (ADHD)***.

microsystem A level of analysis in the ***ecological perspective*** that consists of the family and the social network.

mild cognitive impairment (MCI) The boundary zone between normal cognitive functioning and dementia. Individuals with mild cognitive impairment have deficits in one cognitive domain (usually memory) but are able to function independently.

Millon Clinical Multiaxial Inventory (MCMI) An objective test of personality developed to help clinicians make diagnostic judgments within the multiaxial DSM system, especially in the personality disorders found on Axis II.

Minnesota model A residential treatment for alcohol dependence advocating a 12-step Alcoholics Anonymous philosophy and viewing alcoholism as a disease.

Minnesota Multiphasic Personality Inventory (MMPI) The most widely used objective test of personality. The adjective "multiphasic" means that it assesses many aspects of personality. The test contains 567 questions grouped to form 10 content scales plus additional scales to detect sources of invalidity such as carelessness, defensiveness, or evasiveness. The revised and updated version, called the MMPI-2, focuses primarily on Axis I disorders.

M'Naghten standard A standard of insanity defined by the case of *Regina v. M'Naghten* (1843) that became the accepted rule in England, the United States, and Canada. In today's interpretation of the standard, (1) the accused must have been suffering from a mental disorder, and (2) he or she must not have known at least one of two things: the nature and quality of the act and that what he or she was doing was wrong. That is, inability to understand that an act is wrong can be sufficient even if the accused understands the act itself. Because the second element requires determination of the accused's thinking, the M'Naghten standard is referred to as a "cognitive" test of insanity.

molecular biology A field in which researchers have been able to compare specific DNA segments, identify the genes that determine individual characteristics, and pinpoint the defective genes that cause various medical and psychological disorders.

monoamine oxidase inhibitors (MAOIs) A class of medications used to treat major depression by inhibiting the enzyme monoamine oxidase, which breaks down monoamines such as dopamine and norepinephrine, thus allowing more of these neurotransmitters to accumulate in the presynaptic cell.

monozygotic (MZ) twins Identical twins, which result from the fertilization by a single sperm of a single ovum. This is followed by an unusual extra division into exactly matched zygotes, which subsequently develop into genetically identical fetuses. MZ twins have 100 percent of their genes in common. From *mono* meaning "one" and *zygote* meaning "fertilized egg."

mood congruent Consistent with a person's mood state. For example, a person's belief that he or she is rotting inside may be mood congruent with severe depression. In contrast, a person with schizophrenia may have a mood incongruent delusion, wherein laughter and smiling occur despite a belief in impending torture and execution.

mood disorder An altered mood state severe enough to interfere with a person's social and occupational functioning (for example, ability to work or go to school) and whose range of symptoms is not limited to the person's feelings, but affects other bodily and behavioural systems as well.

mood stabilizers Psychotropic medication used to treat mood disorders characterized by extreme and sustained mood shifts. These medications tend to stabilize one's mood state.

moral therapy A form of treatment advocated by Philippe Pinel and his followers that held that the insane could be controlled without the use of physical or chemical restraints, by means of respect and quiet and peaceful surroundings, plenty of rest, a good diet, moderate exercise, and activities.

mosaicism A cause of ***Down syndrome*** in which cell division occurs unevenly, so that some cells have 45 chromosomes and some have 47. People with mosaic Down syndrome may have fewer physical characteristics, better speech, and higher intellectual functioning, depending upon the numbers of cells affected.

motivational interviewing A therapeutic approach that is client-centred and helps to engage intrinsic motivation for changing behaviour by creating discrepancy and exploring and resolving ambivalence within the client.

multiaxial A DSM diagnosis has five parts. Each part, called an *axis*, provides a different type of information about the diagnosis.

myocardial infarction Heart attack.

N

natural causes Causes that can be observed and examined. When mental afflictions are seen as being due to natural causes, they are treated in a way that addresses such causes.

negative emotionality A personality trait describing the tendency to experience psychological distress, anxiety, and depression that is associated with the development of alcohol problems.

negative feedback seeking The tendency to actively seek out criticism and other negative interpersonal feedback from others.

negative symptoms Features of schizophrenia that comprise behavioural deficits including loss of motivation, lack of emotional expression, and lack of interest in the environment.

neuroleptics Antipsychotic medication.

neuropsychological tests Tests of cognitive and motor ability that are sensitive to damage or dysfunction in different brain regions.

neurosis A nineteenth-century term for anxiety disorders and several other psychological problems (plural *neuroses*). Still in popular usage.

neurotransmitters The chemical substances that carry the messages from one neuron to the next in the complex pathways of nervous activity within the brain.

neutralizations Behavioural or cognitive acts used to prevent, cancel, or "undo" the feared consequences and distress caused by an obsession. While neutralizations can resemble ***compulsions***, they are not the same thing (e.g., neutralizations are not necessarily repetitive).

nicotine An extremely potent central nervous system stimulant related to the ***amphetamines***. The very small amount present in a cigarette is not lethal, and can increase alertness and improve mood. The pleasure centres of the brain seem to have receptors specific to it.

nocturnal panic Panic attacks that occur during the night and awaken sufferers from their sleep.

nocturnal penile tumescence (NPT) A measure of nighttime erections in which the client sleeps in a laboratory over several nights with a device attached to his penis that records changes in its circumference as a result of blood inflow. The measurement technique is called *phallometry*.

nonassociative model A theory proposing that the process of evolution has endowed humans to respond fearfully to a select group of stimuli (e.g., water, heights, spiders), and thus no learning is necessary to develop phobias.

nonpurging type A subtype of ***bulimia nervosa*** characterized by the afflicted person's compensating for overeating by fasting or exercising to excess. The nonpurging type is encountered far less frequently than the *purging type*.

nonspecific immune responses One of the three general categories of immune response, in which circulating white cells called granulocytes and monocytes identify invading antigens and destroy them by *phagocytosis*: engulfing and digesting them. *See also* ***cellular immunity*** and ***humoral immunity***.

nonverbal learning disability (NLD)A term used to reflect a cognitive and behavioural profile characterized by impairments in visual-spatial skills, motor skills, and social skills, with strengths in language abilities and reading.

normal aging A normal process of bodily systems slowing down that ultimately causes some systems to stop functioning, so that the person dies of old age rather than of any particular disease.

normative comparison An investigative approach meant to control for the potential irrelevance of statistical significance in research, in which treatment results are compared to those of non-disturbed samples.

not criminally responsible on account of mental disorder (NCRMD) In Canadian criminal law, not morally culpable for committing a prohibited act due to mental disorder at the time the act was committed.

null hypothesis Proposes that a prediction made from a given theory is false. Experiments (and other research strategies) are set up not to prove the worth of a theory, but rather to reject (or fail to reject) the null hypothesis. Thus, theories gain in strength because alternative explanations are rejected.

O

objective binge A large amount of food (larger than most individuals would eat) that is consumed in a specific time period (e.g., less than two hours).

obsessions Recurrent and uncontrollable thoughts, impulses, or ideas that an individual finds disturbing and anxiety-provoking.

occupational therapists (OTs) Therapists who may practise in Canada with a baccalaureate degree along with field-training experience. OTs are sometimes involved in providing mental health care. These individuals may provide a broad range of services on rehabilitation teams and typically focus on helping clients to improve their functional performance (e.g., training in community living skills).

Oedipal complex According to Sigmund Freud, a condition that occurs during the ***phallic stage***, when boys are presumed to develop sexual desires for their mother and see their father as a competitor for their mother's love. The term is a reference to the character of Oedipus in the play by the Greek tragedian Sophocles.

olanzapine An "atypical" antipsychotic medication introduced in the late 1990s.

operant conditioning An idea developed by Burrhus F. Skinner (1904–1990), according to which it is the consequences of behaviour that are important. Some consequences encourage the repetition of the behaviour that produces them, while other consequences result in the opposite effect. *See also* ***classical conditioning***.

opioids Also known as *narcotics*. A class of central nervous system ***depressants*** whose main effects are the reduction of pain and sleep inducement. Opium, the alkaloid from which opioids are derived, comes from the seeds of the opium poppy, which is indigenous to Asia and the Middle East.

oppositional behaviour Deliberate flouting of the expectations of others, even when it means certain punishment, and perhaps even because of it.

oppositional defiant disorder (ODD) A disorder of children who, more frequently than is usual, refuse to follow instructions, argue apparently just for the sake of arguing, and show hostility toward parents and teachers.

overlap The similarity of symptoms in two or more different disorders (that is, some of the same criteria apply to different diagnoses), which creates problems with diagnosis. *See also* ***comorbidity***.

P

pain disorder A ***somatoform disorder*** characterized by chronic pain with no known organic cause.

panic An extreme fear reaction that is triggered even though there is nothing to be afraid of (it is essentially a "false alarm").

panic attack A discrete period of intense fear or discomfort accompanied by at least 4 of 13 specific somatic, behavioural, and cognitive symptoms such as palpitations, shaking, chest pain, and fear of dying, going crazy, or losing control.

paradox of aging Positive mental health among older adults who would normally be considered vulnerable.

paranoid type One of the five official subtypes of ***schizophrenia***, characterized by preoccupation with one or more ***delusions*** or by frequent auditory ***hallucinations***, and by an absence of prominent disorganized speech, disorganized behaviour, catatonic behaviour, and flat or inappropriate emotions. Thought to be the least severe of the five subtypes.

paraphilia A redirection of sexual desires toward what is generally considered to be an inappropriate object, or person, or behaviour.

parens patriae The common law principle that recognizes the duty of the monarch or the state to care for citizens who are unable to care for themselves.

pedophile An adult who is sexually attracted to children.

pedophilia A form of ***paraphilia*** that is also a criminal offence, in which a person has recurrent fantasies or behaviours involving sexual activity with prepubescent children.

penetrance In genetics, the proportion of people with a given genetic endowment that actually express the effects of this endowment.

performance anxiety The anxiety of dysfunctional people who feel they are expected to perform sexually, and hence do not because they are too busy worrying about and monitoring their own sexual performance and the perceived responses of their partner, and the spontaneous sensory response of sexual arousal is blocked.

period effect The influence of particular historical periods or events on people, such as the Great Depression or the September 11, 2001, attacks on the World Trade Center and the Pentagon.

perpetuating factors Factors that serve to maintain a particular disorder.

persecutory delusions False and implausible beliefs that focus on being followed, chased, harassed, or threatened by other people or unseen forces.

perseverate To repeat mistakes or incorrect responses.

personality disorders Personality styles that are characterized by inflexible and pervasive behavioural patterns, often cause serious personal and social difficulties, and impair general functioning.

person by situation interaction The impact of a person's surroundings on his or her behavioural characteristics, according to Walter Mischel's view that predicting a person's behaviour requires knowledge of both the person's typical behaviour patterns and the characteristics of the setting.

pervasive developmental disorders Developmental disorders whose manifestations are more profound than either mental retardation or learning disorders. ***Autism*** is the best-known pervasive developmental disorder; others are ***Asperger disorder***, ***Rett syndrome***, and ***child disintegrative disorder***.

phallic stage In this stage, according to Sigmund Freud, boys become focused on their penis and girls become aware that they do not have one. Girls are said to develop penis envy (that is, they desire to have a penis and feel cheated).

phenotype Any *observable* characteristic or trait of an organism.

phenylketonuria (PKU) The best known of several rare metabolic disorders that can cause mental retardation. As a result of a recessive gene passed on from each parent, a liver enzyme is inactive, causing an inability to process or metabolize the amino acid phenylalanine. This substance builds up in the brain to toxic levels, leading to retardation.

phonological processing An auditory processing skill that involves detecting and discriminating differences in speech sounds under conditions of little or no distraction or distortion.

phototherapy Treatment for seasonal affective disorder that involves exposure to high-intensity full spectrum lighting.

physiological dependence A persistent need to administer an intoxicating substance to oneself, with ***tolerance*** and ***withdrawal*** symptoms.

placebo A substance that looks and feels like the substance being tested in an experiment, but does not contain the active ingredient.

placebo effect The phenomenon that individuals in treatment programs expect to get better, and as a result may feel an improvement, or that they report improvement to please the experimenter. From the Latin word meaning "I shall please."

polypharmacy Taking multiple medications concurrently, often practised by older adults.

polysubstance abuse The simultaneous misuse or dependence upon two or more substances.

polythetic An individual may be diagnosed with only a certain subset of symptoms without having to meet all criteria.

positive symptoms Abnormal additions to mental life, including the hallucinations, delusions, and disordered thought frequently experienced by schizophrenia patients.

positron emission tomography (PET) A combination of ***computerized axial tomography*** and radioisotope imaging. Radiation is generated by injected or inhaled radioisotopes—that is, common elements or substances with the atom altered to be radioactive. As the substance is used in brain activity, radiation is given off and detected, allowing measurement of a variety of biological activities as the processes occur in the living brain.

post-test In an experiment, assessment of the subjects on several dependent variables judged to be important, in order to get a comprehensive picture of the effects of manipulating the ***independent variable***.

potential years of life lost (PYLL) A measure of the impact of death on someone's lifespan calculated by subtracting age of death from his or her life expectancy.

precipitating factors Events or situations that trigger or cause a given disorder.

preconscious In ***psychodynamic*** theory, the preconscious holds information that is not presently within our awareness but can readily be brought into awareness.

predictive validity The ability of a test to predict the future course of an individual's development. An essential requirement of a good ***diagnostic system***.

premature ejaculation A sexual dysfunction characterized by a man's ejaculating after minimal stimulation and often before or immediately following entry of the penis into the vagina, with marked distress or interpersonal difficulty.

pretest In an experiment, an assessment of subjects on many measures prior to manipulation of the ***independent variable***. Done for descriptive purposes.

prevalence The frequency of a disorder in a population at a given point or period of time.

prevention A concept borrowed from the fields of physical disease, public health, and epidemiology and applied to mental disorders by ***community psychology***. There are three categories of prevention activities: ***primary prevention***, ***secondary prevention***, and ***tertiary prevention***.

primary appraisals In the *transactional model* of stress, an *appraisal*, which may occur quite unconsciously, that takes place when a person is faced with an event that may have adaptational significance. It is as if the individual asks: "Is this a threat to me?" The primary appraisal sets the stage for further events that may or may not lead to stress.

primary insomnia The most common sleep disorder in older adults, with nocturnal symptoms of difficulty falling asleep, frequent awakenings, shortened sleep, and non-restorative sleep, and daytime symptoms of fatigue, sleepiness, depression, and anxiety. DSM-IV diagnostic criteria require the symptoms to persist for at least one month, to be perceived as stressful, and to not be secondary to any other disorder.

primary prevention A type of ***prevention*** practised prior to the biological origin of the disease (for example, immunization). *See also* ***secondary prevention*** and ***tertiary prevention***.

principle of autonomy In ethics, the doctrine that stresses the importance of respect for people's right to self-determination when making decisions.

principle of beneficence In ethics, the doctrine that stresses the importance of maximizing good when making decisions.

principle of fidelity In ethics, the doctrine that stresses the importance of personal reliability when making decisions.

principle of justice In ethics, the doctrine that stresses the importance of fairness when making decisions.

principle of nonmaleficence In ethics, the doctrine that stresses the importance of avoiding or minimizing harm to people when making decisions.

proband In family studies, the patient, or the person who has come to the attention of the clinician or researcher. Also called the *index case*.

problem-solving approach A cognitive-behavioural treatment that involves the client in determining the problem definition and formulation, generating alternative solutions to deal with the problem, deciding on the best solution to implement, and then implementing and evaluating the solution.

professional standards Written statements that set out expectations regarding the day-to-day practice or conduct of members of a profession or other group.

projective test A type of psychological test that reveals information the person being tested cannot or will not report directly. Used to help clinicians form hypotheses about an individual's personality. *See also* ***Rorschach inkblot test***.

prolactin A hormone involved in sexual activity and desire, variations in the level of which can lower or increase sex drive.

pronoun reversal One of the common characteristics of speech in autistic children, in which the child often refers to him- or herself in the third person, perhaps because of trouble shifting reference between speaker and listener or a third party.

protective factors Events or circumstances that help to offset, or buffer, ***risk factors***. Anything that lessens the likelihood of disease. For example, exercise is thought to be a protective factor for cardiovascular disease.

pseudo-dementia Cognitive impairment similar to that of ***dementia*** but reversible. May be brought on by depression, nutritional deficiency, thyroid disorder, or any one of a number of other diseases; symptoms may also occur as side effects from medications.

psychache Unbearable psychological and emotional pain that strongly predicts suicide.

psychiatric nurses Persons who have received formal training in nursing before completing a specialization in psychiatric problems and who typically work in hospital settings where they manage the day-to-day care of mentally disordered patients.

psychiatric social workers Persons who attend to the influence of the social environment on disordered clients. They usually have a graduate degree in social work and provide assistance to clients in adjusting to life within their families and the community.

psychiatrists Persons trained in medicine prior to doing specialized training in dealing with mental illness. This specialized training focuses on diagnosis and medical treatment that emphasize the use of pharmacological agents in managing mental disorders. Most psychiatrists attend to the medical aspects and biological foundations of these disorders, although they usually also consider psychological and environmental influences.

psychoactive agents Pharmacological agents found to affect the individual's psychological functioning.

psychodynamic Denoting a school of psychology founded by Sigmund Freud. Psychodynamic theories claim that behaviour is controlled by unconscious forces of which the person is unaware.

psychological abnormality Behaviour, speech, or thought that impairs the ability of a person to function in a way generally expected of him or her, in the context in which the unusual functioning occurs.

psychological assessment A systematic gathering and evaluation of information pertaining to an individual with suspected abnormal behaviour.

psychological dependence The state of being psychologically accustomed to a substance or activity as a consequence of regular usage. Also known as ***habituation***. Evinced by feelings of restlessness, irritability, and uneasiness when the substance or activity is unavailable.

psychological disorder A specific manifestation of mental illness as described by some set of criteria established by a panel of experts.

psychoneuroimmunology A new field that studies the responsiveness of the immune system to psychosocial influences, and that has shown that the immune system can be affected by learning experiences, emotional states, and personal characteristics.

psychopathology Both the scientific study of psychological abnormality and the problems faced by people who suffer from such disorders.

psychopaths People who are considered to be predisposed via temperament to antisocial behaviour and whose primary characteristics include callousness and grandiosity combined with a history of poor self-regulation.

psychophysiological reactivity model One model of how hostility might lead to health risk, which suggests that hostile people are at higher risk for various diseases because they experience exaggerated autonomic and neuroendocrine responses during stress.

psychosis A mental state characterized by severe impairment or distortion in the experience of reality as seen in disorders like ***schizophrenia***.

psychosocial vulnerability model One model of how hostility might lead to health risk, which suggests that hostile people experience a more demanding interpersonal life than others.

psychosurgery The use of brain surgery to alter behaviour, especially in relation to psychiatric disorders.

public health approach An approach to ***community psychology*** characterized by the following steps: (1) identifying a disease and developing a reliable diagnostic method (descriptive epidemiology); (2) developing a theory of the disease's course of development on the basis of laboratory and epidemiological research (analytic epidemiology); and (3) developing and evaluating a disease prevention program (experimental epidemiology). The thrust of the approach is to reduce environmental stressors while enhancing people's capacities to withstand those stressors.

public stigma The typical societal response that people have to stigmatizing attributes.

punishment In ***operant conditioning***, what occurs when a behaviour decreases in frequency as a result of its consequences.

purging The engagement of compensatory behaviour intended to "undo" calories that have been consumed (e.g., vomiting, misuse of laxatives).

purging type A subtype of ***bulimia nervosa*** characterized by the afflicted person's compensating for overeating, most typically by self-induced vomiting or the use of laxatives, diuretics, or enemas. The purging type is encountered far more frequently than the nonpurging type.

Q

quality of life A recognized desirable goal in the field of developmental disabilities, about which there is a great deal of disagreement. What constitutes quality of life and how can it be measured? A number of different approaches have been taken. For example, the Quality of Life Interview Schedule (QUOLIS), designed specifically to address the needs of adults with severe and profound disabilities, involves interviews with two informants who know an individual well in different contexts, and quality of life is measured under 12 domains, such as health services and housing and safety. A second approach is reflected in the Quality of Life Project, a conceptual framework that includes three major components of quality of life, each divided into subcomponents.

quasi-experimental study One in which the subjects in the experimental group are not randomly assigned but selected on the basis of certain characteristics, and in which there is no manipulation of an ***independent variable***.

R

random assignment A procedure that ensures each subject in an experiment has an equal probability of being in either the ***experimental*** or the ***control group***, guaranteeing the equivalence of these groups.

rapport Mutual understanding or trust between people.

rational-emotive behaviour therapy A form of therapy developed by Albert Ellis that is concerned with how people interpret events and how these interpretations influence their responses. These interpretations, or mediating processes, are cognitive and result from the person's belief systems.

reactivity The change in behaviour often seen when people know they are being observed or filmed. One of the difficulties inherent in ***in vivo observation*** and ***analogue observational settings***.

receptors Patches of sensitive membrane on nerve cells that bind to neurochemical messages from other nerve cells.

referential delusions The belief that common, meaningless occurrences have significant and personal relevance.

reframing A strategy in which problems are restated so that they can be more easily dealt with.

reinforcement In ***operant conditioning***, what occurs when a behaviour increases in frequency as a result of consistent consequences.

relapse The return of an illness or disorder after a recovery.

reliability The ability of a measurement tool to give the same measurement for a given thing every time. Its usefulness partly depends on this attribute. *See also* ***validity***.

religious delusions The belief that religious passages offer the way to destroy or save the world.

repressed Said of memories that a person cannot call into awareness, but which remain in the person's subconscious and can be retrieved under certain conditions or with the help of a psychotherapist.

residual type One of the five official types of *schizophrenia*, diagnosed when a person who previously met the criteria for one of the other four types has no current ***delusions, hallucinations***, *disorganized speech*, *grossly disorganized behaviour*, or ***catatonic behaviour***, but nevertheless continues to show evidence of disturbance by the continuation of either negative symptoms or very mild levels of earlier positive symptoms, which have lessened either with the passage of time or through treatment.

resilience The capacity of people to "bounce back" and cope with stress and catastrophe.

resistance The second phase of the ***general adaptation syndrome (GAS)***, a concept that was the first formal description and definition of stress as a consequence of adaptation to demands placed on the body. In the resistance phase, if the challenge of the ***alarm*** phase persists, the body actively fights or copes with the challenge through immune and neuroendocrine changes. These adaptive responses enhance the body's ability to ward off threats in the short term. *See also* ***exhaustion***.

response shaping A process of shaping behaviour by gradual approximations of what is expected. For example, a child who is mentally retarded and may be unable to get dressed independently can be taught the process gradually by being rewarded for putting on one item at a time until he or she is eventually able to handle the entire task.

responsivity factor The circumstance that treatment must be responsive (or matched) to a particular client's needs and interpersonal style—that is, it must be of sufficient intensity and relevance, and seen by the patient as voluntary. Apparently, the efficacy of the treatment programs tend to be determined more by the orientation of the therapist or director.

restless legs syndrome (RLS) Characterized by an intense urge to move one's body to stop uncomfortable or odd sensations.

restricting type A subtype of ***anorexia nervosa*** in which the afflicted person relies on a rigidly controlled, very low intake of food to maintain her low weight. About half of anorexia nervosa patients are of the restricting type. *See also* ***binge eating/purging type***.

Rett syndrome A ***pervasive developmental disorder*** that is diagnosed primarily in females. Development before birth and up to the age of 5 months appears to be normal. However, between the ages of 5 and 30 months, the progress of development, including growth rate, slows, and the child loses speech and motor skills that have already developed. Social interaction diminishes and stereotyped wringing movements in the hands occur. Motor coordination problems increase and both expressive and receptive language are significantly impaired.

return on investment (ROI) A measurement used to evaluate the efficiency of an investment.

reversal design *See* ***ABAB***.

risk factors Events or circumstances that increase the likelihood of later pathology.

risperidone An "atypical" antipsychotic medication with fewer side effects than ***chlorpromazine***. It was introduced in the 1990s and is believed to influence serotonin as well as dopamine.

ritual prevention Intentionally refraining from maladaptive coping patterns. By doing so, the patient gradually and with repeated exposures experiences anxiety climb, peak, and then subsidence.

Rorschach inkblot test The oldest and probably the best known ***projective test***. Based on the idea that people see different things in the same inkblot and that what they see reflects their personality. The blots are presented on separate cards and handed to the subject in a particular sequence.

rubella German measles, an infection that can affect infant development and cause mental retardation. Rubella-related problems have declined with routine vaccination.

Russell's sign An indication of bulimia in which scrapes or calluses occur on the back of the hands as a result of manually induced vomiting.

S

St. Vitus' dance An epidemic of mass hysteria, wherein groups of people would suddenly be seized by an irresistible urge to leap about, jumping and dancing, and sometimes convulsing.

savants Mentally deficient persons who nevertheless display islets of exceptional ability in areas such as mathematics, music, or art, or unusual feats of memory. A small proportion of those persons with ***autism*** who do not fall within the normal range of intelligence are savants.

schemas Mental structures used to organize information about the world.

schizophrenia One of the most serious psychological disorders, characterized by ***delusions, hallucinations***, and *disorganized speech*. There are overall, adverse changes in thought, perception, emotion, and motor behaviour, and a feeling of *depersonalization*. Behaviour in some instances appears to be "autistic," in the sense of being governed by internal stimuli or private events. The individual may be unresponsive to environmental stimuli that would normally prompt reactions, or may respond in a way that suggests a distorted interpretation of the stimuli. Ordinary objects or events seem to take on a marked personal significance. There is pronounced disruption of cognitive transactions: thought and language appear to become loosened from the normal constraints that make for coherent sequences of ideas and distinguish fantasy from reality. Often, some notion or theme involving malevolent forces or inordinate personal power increasingly commands the individual's attention. Many people with schizophrenia appear to lose their intensity. Language may become impoverished, with little apparent effort or success at communication. They may become withdrawn socially and exhibit little interest in formerly enjoyable pursuits. Attention span may be markedly reduced. From the Greek *schizein*, "to split," and *phrenos*, "mind."

schizophrenogenic The unsupported theory that cold and rejecting behaviour causes ***schizophrenia***.

schizotype In Meehl's theory, a person with the genetic liability for ***schizophrenia***, but who may or may not progress to the full-blown psychotic illness.

science Knowledge obtained by observation and experimentation, critically tested, systematized, and brought under general principles. From the Latin *scientia* ("knowledge").

seasonal affective disorder (SAD) A ***unipolar mood disorder*** characterized by a vulnerability to environmental sunlight changes and a pattern of cyclic and time-limited mood problems.

secondary appraisals In the ***transactional model*** of stress, a set of ***appraisals*** that occur after a ***primary appraisal*** if the individual concludes there is an element of threat, equivalent to the question: "Is there anything I can do about this?"

secondary prevention A type of ***prevention*** practised after the disease is identified but before it has caused suffering and disability (for example, the control of blood sugar early in the course of diabetes to prevent systemic damage). *See also* ***primary prevention*** and ***tertiary prevention***.

selective mutism A social anxiety disorder in which a person normally capable of speech is unable to speak in given situations, or to specific individuals.

selective serotonin reuptake inhibitors (SSRIs) One of the three known major classes of antidepressants. SSRIs, as their name suggests, delay the process of reuptake of neurotransmitters so that they remain available longer to maintain optimal neuronal firing rates. They include fluoxetine (Prozac), sertraline (Zoloft), and paraxetine (Paxil). *See also* ***tricyclic antidepressants***.

selective prevention Interventions that target individuals whose risk of developing a disorder is greater than the average risk for that disorder within the general population.

self-actualization In Abraham H. Maslow's theory, an actualization of one's potential arrived at by satisfaction of a hierarchy of needs visualized as a pyramid. At the base are biological or survival needs; the next step up is the need for friendship and affiliation; finally, there is an assurance of self-worth, which comes from giving and receiving love and from an internalized sense of self-esteem. In Maslow's view, abnormal or dysfunctional behaviour results from a failure to attain the self-esteem necessary to achieve self-actualization.

self-stigma The internalized psychological impact of public stigma.

sensate focus The final component in sex therapy programs, essentially a form of desensitization applied to sexual fears.

sensitivity The accuracy or ability of a test to detect what it was designed to detect.

separation anxiety disorder (SAD) A children's disorder characterized by severe and excessive anxiety, even panic, at the prospect of separation from parents or others to whom the child is emotionally attached.

sexual aversion disorder A sexual dysfunction characterized by persistent or recurrent extreme aversion to, and avoidance of, almost all genital sex with a partner, causing marked distress or interpersonal difficulty. May also include panic attacks, extreme anxiety, and avoidance of partners.

sexual masochism A sexual preference that involves experiencing pain or humiliation inflicted by others.

sexual response cycle The sequence of changes that occur in the body with increased sexual arousal, orgasm, and the return to the unaroused state, noted by William Masters and Virginia Johnson.

sexual sadism A sexual preference that involves inflicting pain or humiliation on others.

single-factor explanation A theory that attributes the supposed causal chain of dysfunctional behaviour to a single factor.

single-subject design A nonexperimental investigative method that, like the ***case study***, is based on the intense investigation of an individual subject, but avoids many criticisms of the case study by using experimentally accepted procedures. It uses observable behaviours that are quantifiable, quantifies the presence of the behaviour prior to any intervention, systematically applies readily observable and quantifiable interventions, and measures the effects of the intervention on the behaviours of the subject.

situational sexual dysfunctions Any sexual dysfunction that is apparent only with a certain sexual partner of the sufferer (for example, the client's spouse).

sleep apnea A sleep disorder characterized by episodes of cessation of breathing (apnea) that last at least 10 seconds. Diagnosis requires that there be at least five such episodes per hour of sleep.

social drift The tendency for people vulnerable to schizophrenia to "drift" down to lower social and economic levels.

social justice The fair and equitable allocation of burdens and privileges, rights and responsibilities, and pains and gains in society.

social learning theory As originally outlined by Bandura and Walters (1959), a theory that suggested that while ***classical*** and ***operant conditioning*** experiences are important, the majority of such experiences are primarily acquired vicariously—that is, by observation of others rather than direct personal experience. This theory has been extended to include not only direct observation of others but also information derived from books, movies, and television.

social skills training The teaching of appropriate and effective social communication and interpersonal behaviour.

social stigma The negative perceptions and judgments made about people with mental illness.

social support An individual's perceived quality of support from close others (e.g., partner, friends, parent).

socio-cognitive model The theory that dissociative identity disorder is a form of role-playing in which individuals come to construe themselves as possessing multiple selves and then begin to act in ways consistent with their or their therapist's conception of the disorder.

sociopaths People who are considered to have normal temperament but who are weakly socialized because of environmental failures, including poor parenting, antisocial peers, and disorganized home and school experiences.

somatic delusions Beliefs related to the body.

somatization disorder A ***somatoform disorder*** characterized by multiple complaints of physical ailments that do not appear to have any organic basis. These symptoms must cause significant impairment in social and occupational functioning.

somatoform disorders A set of disorders marked by physical symptoms for which there is no known physical cause, excessive preoccupation with minor physical symptoms, or excessive concern about normal bodily functioning.

somatogenesis The idea that psychopathology is caused by biological factors—*soma* meaning "body" in Latin.

SORC Four sets of variables that behavioural and cognitively oriented clinicians are concerned with. S stands for *stimuli*, environmental situations that preceded the problem, or in which the problem arose; O stands for *organismic*, factors within the individual that might increase the probability of a behaviour; R stands for overt *responses*—the problem behaviour itself; C stands for *consequences* of the behaviour, particularly those that might reinforce or punish it.

specificity The extent to which a trait or feature occurs selectively in the target group under study as opposed to its occurrence in other groups or in the general population.

specifiers Further descriptors of a patient's condition that capture the natural variation in the expression of affective disturbances, and therefore increase the specificity of diagnoses by conveying important information about salient features that might be otherwise overlooked. For example, one specifier used in conjunction with a diagnosis of ***major depressive disorder*** is "with melancholic features."

split-half reliability A measure of ***internal consistency***, often ascertained by comparing responses on odd-numbered test items with responses on even-numbered test items and seeing if the scores for these responses are correlated.

Stanford-Binet Intelligence Scales An intelligence test whose most recent version assesses four general kinds of ability: verbal reasoning, quantitative reasoning, abstract/visual reasoning, and short-term memory. It produces separate scores for each of these functions as well as a global IQ score that summarizes the child's ability. Developed from the work of French psychologist Alfred Binet (1857–1911).

statistical significance An attribute of research results when it is extremely unlikely that they could have occurred purely by chance. The standard by which most research is judged as valuable or worthy of being published.

statutory law A written or codified statement of the law in a given area, enacted by government.

stereotypy The repetition of meaningless gestures or movements. One of the manifestations of a developmental disorder.

stimulants A class of drugs that have a stimulating or arousing effect on the central nervous system, and create their effects by influencing the rate of uptake of the neurotransmitters dopamine and norepinephrine and serotonin at receptor sites in the brain.

stress Environmental and life events or stimuli that influence the development and onset of an illness or disorder.

stress generation hypothesis A theory of depression recurrence, which states that individuals with a history of depression have higher rates of stressful life events that are at least in part dependent on their own behaviour or characteristics than non-depressed individuals.

stress reactivity paradigm A viewpoint that sees the reaction to stress as important to an understanding of cardiovascular disease.

stroke A loss of brain functions that results from interruption of blood supply to the brain or hemorrhage of blood vessels in the brain and consequent death of the neural tissue on which the brain functions depend.

structural magnetic resonance imaging (MRI) A brain scanning technique that provides detailed pictures and information on neuroanatomical structures.

substance abuse Recurrent substance use that results in significant adverse consequences in social or occupational functioning, or use of a substance that impairs one's performance in hazardous situations, for example drinking and driving.

substance dependence Lack of control over substance use, to the point that a person feels enslaved. Commonly known as *addiction. See also* ***physiological dependence*** and ***psychological dependence***.

substance intoxication A reversible and temporary condition due to the recent ingestion of, or exposure to, a substance, and characterized by significant maladaptive behavioural or cognitive changes, such as belligerence, disturbed perception, altered mood, and impaired thought processes or motor behaviour.

subtle avoidance Engaging in safety behaviours that serve to maintain anxiety. For example, an individual may be able to go into a movie theatre only if he or she sits in the back near the exit or is accompanied by a significant other. These subtle behaviours need to end in order for anxiety to really diminish over the long term.

suicide The intentional taking of one's life.

superego In Sigmund Freud's theory, the internalization of the moral standards of society inculcated by the child's parents.

supernatural causes Causes beyond the understanding of ordinary mortals, such as the influence of gods, demons, or magic. Psychological dysfunction in various historical periods was thought to result from either possession by demons or the witchcraft of evil people.

suspiciousness A generalized distrustful view of others and their motivations, but not sufficiently pathological to warrant a clinical diagnosis of paranoia.

switching The transition from one ***alter*** to another. Occurs suddenly and is often precipitated by stress or some other identifiable cue in the surrounding environment.

syndromes Groups of symptoms that tend to occur together.

synergistic Said of drugs whose combined effects exceed or are significantly different from the sum of their individual effects.

systematic desensitization A therapeutic technique whereby patients imagine the lowest feared stimuli and combine this image with a relaxation response. Patients gradually work their way up the fear hierarchy so that they can learn to handle increasingly disturbing stimuli.

systems theory A theory proposing that multiple interacting factors generate all behaviour, and that the effects of these factors are bidirectional; that is, the influence of each factor on another changes the other factors, which in turn then influence the original factor. The overall effect of these influences is said to be greater than the sum of the influence of each of the factors.

systolic blood pressure/diastolic blood pressure A measure of the pressure of the blood flowing through the vasculature. It is obtained by finding the number of millimetres of mercury displaced by a sphygmomanometer (blood pressure cuff).

T

temporary substitute decision maker In provincial mental health law, someone authorized to make treatment decisions on behalf of a person who is civilly committed and deemed incapable of making such decisions.

tension-reduction A hypothesis which suggests that drinking is reinforced by its ability to reduce tension, anxiety, anger, depression, and other unpleasant emotions.

tertiary prevention A type of ***prevention*** practised after suffering or disability from the disease is being experienced, with the goal of preventing further deterioration. *See also* ***primary prevention*** and ***secondary prevention***.

test-retest reliability The degree to which a test yields the same results when it is given more than once to the same person. Test-retest reliability can be evaluated by correlating a person's score on a given test with the same person's score on the same test taken at a later time. The higher the correlation between the two scores (as expressed in terms of a correlation coefficient) the more ***reliable*** it is.

testosterone A hormone (the so-called male sex hormone) involved in sexual activity and desire, variations in the level of which can lower or increase sex drive.

thalidomide A drug prescribed for nausea in the 1950s and 1960s by European physicians that was found to cause limb deficiencies or malformations in infants.

THC The chemical delta-9-tetrahydrocannabinol, which causes the psychoactive effects of ***cannabis***. Although the exact mechanisms by which THC exerts its influences is not fully understood, it appears as if it acts upon specific cannabinoid receptors in the body and mimics the effects of naturally occurring substances, including the ***endogenous opiates***.

thematic apperception test (TAT) A psychological test using drawings on cards depicting ambiguous social interactions. Those being tested are asked to construct stories about the cards. It is assumed their tales reflect their experiences, outlook on life, and deep-seated needs and conflicts. Validity and reliability of scoring techniques are open to the same criticisms as those of the ***Rorschach inkblot test***.

therapeutic alliance The relationship between therapist and client, recognized to be a predictor of therapy outcome. Recent research in psychodynamic therapy has underlined its importance.

thought-action fusion (TAF) The irrational tendency for individuals to believe their thoughts will increase the probability that a certain event will occur (Likelihood TAF), or to believe that their thoughts are the moral equivalent of actions (Moral TAF).

thought and speech disorder A psychotic symptom, often reported in schizophrenia, that involves disorganized and incoherent ideas and language, a kind of nonsensical "crazy talk."

time-limited dynamic psychotherapy (TLDP) A psychodynamic approach that tends to be brief and involve the client in face-to-face contact with the therapist. The TLDP therapist helps identify patterns of interaction with others that strengthen unhelpful thoughts about oneself and others.

tolerance The need of a person for increased amounts of an addictive substance to achieve the desired effect.

total peripheral resistance The diameter of the blood vessels; one of the variables affecting blood pressure.

toxic psychosis Hallucinations, delirium, and paranoia caused by repeated high doses of ***amphetamines***.

trait A personal quality that is characteristic of someone ("generous," "creative," etc.); that is, it is persistently displayed over time and in various situations. Every person manifests several traits, the combination of which makes up his or her personality.

transactional model (1) A model of stress that conceives of stress as a property neither of stimulus nor of response, but rather as an ongoing series of transactions between an individual and his or her environment. Central to this formulation is the idea that people constantly evaluate what is happening to them and its implications for themselves.

transactional model (2) One model of how hostility might lead to health risk, which suggests that the behaviour of hostile individuals constructs, by its natural consequences, a social world that is antagonistic and unsupportive, so that both interpersonal stressors and the lack of social support increase vulnerability. A hybrid of the ***psychophysiological reactivity model*** and the ***psychosocial vulnerability model***.

transcranial magnetic stimulation (TMS) Treatment for severe depression that uses a magnet to excite neurons in the brain.

transference In the psychodynamic approach to therapy, the client's action of responding to the therapist as he or she responded to significant figures from his or her childhood (generally the parents). Considered the core of psychoanalytic therapy.

translocation A cause of ***Down syndrome*** in which part of the 21st chromosome of the human cell breaks off and attaches to another. Individuals with Down syndrome due to translocation have all of the features found in trisomy 21.

transvestite A person who wears the clothing associated with the opposite sex—in order to produce or enhance sexual excitement.

trauma model The theory that dissociative identity disorder is caused by severe childhood trauma, including sexual, physical, and emotional abuse, accompanied by personality traits that predispose the individual to employ dissociation as a defence mechanism or coping strategy.

treatment effectiveness Evidence that a treatment has been shown to work in real-world conditions (i.e., an emphasis on external validity).

treatment efficacy Evidence that a treatment has been shown to work under research conditions that emphasized internal validity.

trephination A prehistoric form of surgery possibly intended to let out evil spirits; it involved chipping a hole into a person's skull.

tricyclic antidepressants (TCAs) One of the three known major classes of antidepressants. Tricyclics enable more neurotransmitters to be released into the synaptic cleft. They include amoxapine (Asendin), amitriptyline (Elavil), imipramine (Tofranil), and doxepin (Sinequan).

trisomy 21 The most common type of ***Down syndrome***, in which there is an extra chromosome on pair 21 of the 23 pairs of chromosomes in the human cell.

two-factor theory The most influential theory of fear and phobias during the 1960s and 1970s. The model proposed that fears are acquired by ***classical conditioning***, but maintained by ***operant conditioning***.

Type A A syndrome of behaviours that includes hyperalertness and arousability, a chronic sense of time-urgency, competitiveness, hostility, and job-involvement.

U

unconscious In ***psychodynamic*** theory, the unconscious contains the majority of our memories and drives, which can only be raised to awareness with great difficulty and typically only in response to special techniques (that is, psychoanalytic procedures).

undifferentiated type One of the five official types of ***schizophrenia***, a general category for patients who display prominent symptoms but do not fall easily into the *paranoid*, the *disorganized*, or the *catatonic* category.

unfit to stand trial (UST) In Canadian criminal law, incapable of participating in the trial process due to mental disorder at the time of trial.

unipolar mood disorders Mood disorders in which the change in mood is only in the direction of depression or lowered mood, followed by a return to normal mood with recovery. *See also* ***bipolar mood disorders***.

universal approach An approach to ***prevention*** programs designed to include all individuals in a certain geographical area (for example, the neighbourhood, the city, the province) or a certain setting (for example, school, the workplace, a public housing complex).

V

vaginismus A sexual dysfunction characterized by persistent involuntary contraction of the muscles in the outer third of the vagina upon attempts at penetration by the penis, preventing it from occurring.

vagus nerve stimulation (VNS) Treatment for severe depression that electrically stimulates the vagus nerve by way of an implanted stimulator.

validity The ability of a measurement tool to measure what it purports to measure. A rigid ruler would be ***reliable***; but it would be useless as a measure of temperature.

vascular dementia The second most common cause of ***dementia*** (second to ***Alzheimer's disease***) that results from brain damage due to cerebrovascular disease.

vasculature The system of arteries, arterioles, capillaries, venules, and veins responsible for circulation of the blood to all parts of the body and its return to the heart.

vicarious learning Learning that takes place by observing others. Also called *modelling*.

voyeurism A form of ***paraphilia*** that is also a criminal offence, in which a person secretly looks at naked people.

W

WAIS-IV The most recent version of the ***Wechsler Adult Intelligence Scale***, published in 2008.

waxy flexibility A state wherein a person's limbs and posture can be "moulded" into different positions as if the person were made of wax. Occasionally seen in ***schizophrenia***.

Wechsler Adult Intelligence Scale, or WAIS. The most widely used IQ tests, designed to measure diverse aspects of intelligence. Developed by David Wechsler (1896–1981). *See also* ***WAIS-IV***.

Wisconsin Card Sorting Test A neuropsychological test that requires sorting cards into categories based on colour, shape, or quantity depending on corrective feedback from the examiner. One of the most frequently used tests in schizophrenia research.

withdrawal Unpleasant and sometimes dangerous symptoms such as nausea, headache, or tremors experienced when an addictive substance is removed from the body.

worry imagery exposure Identifying the patient's main areas of worry, vividly imagining these unpleasant scenes, and concentrating on them while conjuring up images of the worst possible outcome. After holding these graphic images in their minds for a period of time, patients are then encouraged to generate as many alternatives as possible to the worst scenario.

References

Aaron, P. G., Phillips, S., & Larsen, S. (1988). Specific reading disability in historically famous persons. *Journal of Learning Disabilities, 21* (9), 523–538.

Abbott, A. (2001). Into the mind of a killer. *Nature, 410,* 296–298.

Abel, E. L. (1984). *Fetal alcohol syndrome and fetal alcohol effects.* New York: Plenum Press.

Abel, G., & Rouleau, J.-L. (1990). The nature and extent of sexual assault. In W. L. Marshall, D. R. Laws, & E. H. Bartarce (Eds.), *Handbook of sexual assault* (pp. 9–21). New York: Plenum.

Abel, G. G., Becker, J. V., Mittelman, M. S., Cunningham-Rathner, J., Rouleau, J. L., & Murphy, W. D. (1987). Self-reported sex crimes of nonincarcerated paraphiliacs. *Journal of Interpersonal Violence, 2,* 3–25.

Abel, G. G., Blanchard, E. B., & Becker, J. V. (1978). An integrated treatment program for rapists. In R. T. Rada (Ed.), *Clinical aspects of the rapist* (pp. 161–214). New York: Grune & Stratton.

Abramowitz, J. S. (2008). Obsessive-compulsive disorder. In W. E. Craighead, D. J. Miklowitz, & L. W. Craighead (Eds.), *Psychopathology: History, diagnosis, and empirical foundations* (pp. 159–197). Hoboken, NJ: Wiley.

Abramowitz, J. S., Deacon, B. J., & Whiteside, S. P. H. (2011). *Exposure therapy for anxiety: Principles and practice.* New York: Guilford Press.

Abramson, E. E., & Valene, P. (1991). Media use, dietary restraint, bulimia and attitudes towards obesity: A prelimary study. *British Review of Bulimia & Anorexia Nervosa, 5,* 73–76.

Achenbach, T. M., & Edelbrock, C. (1983). *Manual for the child behavior checklist and revised child behavior profile.* Burlington, VT: University of Vermont.

Achenbach, T. M., & Rescorla, L. A. (2001). *Manual for ASEBA school-age forms & profiles.* Burlington, VT: University of Vermont, Research Center for Children, Youth, & Families.

Ackerknect, E. H. (1968). *Short history of psychiatry.* (S. Wolff, Trans.). New York: Hafner.

Ackerly, S. S., & Benton, A. L. (1948). Report of a case of bilateral frontal lobe defect. *Research and Publications of the Association for the Research of Nervous and Mental Disease, 27,* 479–504.

Adamson, S. J., & Sellman, J. D. (2001). Drinking goal selection and treatment outcome in out-patients with mild-moderate alcohol dependence. *Drug and Alcohol Review, 20,* 351–359.

Addiction Research Foundation. (1992). Abstinence and reduced drinking: Two approaches to alcohol treatment. *Best advice.* Toronto: Author.

Addiction Research Foundation. (1997). *Addiction Research Foundation website.* Retrieved from http://www.arf.org. Now Centre for Addiction and Mental Health, http://www.camh.net

Addington, J. (2007). The promise of early intervention. *Early Intervention in Psychiatry, 1,* 294–307.

Addington, J., Cornblatt, B. A., Cadenhead, K. S., Cannon, T. D., McGlashan, T. H., Perkins, D. O., . . . Heinssen, R. (2011). At clinical high risk for psychosis: Outcome for nonconverters. *American Journal of Psychiatry, 168* (8), 800–805.

Ader, R., Felten, D. L., & Cohen, N. (Eds.). (2001). *Psychoneuroimmunology* (Vols. 1–2, 3rd ed.). San Diego, CA: Academic Press.

Adlaf, E., Ivis, F. J., & Smart, R. (1994). *Alcohol and other drug use among Ontario adults in 1994 and changes since 1977.* Toronto: Addiction Research Foundation.

Adlaf, E. M., Demers, A., & Gliksman, L. (Eds.). (2005). *Canadian campus survey 2004.* Toronto: Centre for Addiction and Mental Health.

Adlaf, E. M., & Paglia-Boak, A. (2007). *Drug use among Ontario students: OSDUHS highlights 1977–2007.* Toronto: Centre for Addiction and Mental Health.

Adler, D. A., Drake, R. E., & Teague, G. B. (1990). Clinicians' practices in personality assessment: Does gender influence the use of DSM-III axis II? *Comprehensive Psychiatry, 31,* 125–133.

Adler, N. E., Boyce, T., Chesney, M. A., Cohen, S., Folkman, S., Kahn, R. L., & Syme, S. L. (1994). Socioeconomic status and health: The challenge of the gradient. *American Psychologist, 49,* 15–24.

Agras, S., Brandt, H. A., Bulik, C. M., Dolan-Sewell, R., Fairburn, C. G., Halmi, K. A., et al. (2004). Report of the National Institutes of Health Workshop on overcoming barriers to treatment research in anorexia nervosa. *International Journal of Eating Disorders, 35,* 509–521.

Agras, S., Hammer, L., & McNicholas, F. (1999). A prospective study of the influence of eating-disordered mothers on their children. *International Journal of Eating Disorders, 25,* 253–262.

Agras, W. S. (2001). The consequences and costs of the eating disorders. *Psychiatric Clinics of North America, 24,* 371–379.

Agras, W. S., Walsh, T., Fairburn, C. G., Wilson, G. T., & Kraemer, H. C. (2000). A multicenter comparison of cognitive-behavioral therapy and interpersonal psychotherapy for bulimia nervosa. *Archives of General Psychiatry, 57,* 459–466.

Agrawal, A., & Lynskey, M. T. (2008). Are there genetic influences on addiction: Evidence from family, adoption and twin studies. *Addiction, 103,* 1069–1081.

Ainscow, M. (2000). Reaching out to all learners: Some lessons from international experience. *School Effectiveness and School Improvement, 11,* 1–9.

Albee, G. W. (1982). Preventing psychopathology and promoting human potential. *American Psychologist, 37,* 1043–1050.

Albee, G. W. (1990). The futility of psychotherapy. *Journal of Mind and Behavior, 11,* 369–384.

Albee, G. W. (1996). Revolutions and counterrevolutions in prevention. *American Psychologist, 51,* 1130–1133.

Alberta Alcohol and Drug Abuse Commission. (2004). *Tobacco basics handbook.* Edmonton: Author.

Alda, M. (1997). Bipolar disorder: From families to genes. *Canadian Journal of Psychiatry, 42,* 378–387.

Alden, L. (1989). Short-term structured treatment for avoidant personality disorder. *Journal of Consulting and Clinical Psychology, 57,* 756–764.

Alden, L. E., & Taylor, C. T. (2004). Interpersonal processes in social phobia. *Clinical Psychology Review, 24,* 857–882.

Alexander, F. (1950). *Psychosomatic medicine: Its principles and applications.* New York: Norton.

Alexander, F., & French, T. M. (1946). *Psychoanalytic therapy: Principles and application.* New York: Ronald Press.

Alexander, M. G., & Fisher, T. D. (2003). Truth and consequences: Using the bogus pipeline to examine sex differences in self-reported sexuality. *The Journal of Sex Research, 40* (1), 27–35.

Alexopoulous, G. S., Katz, I. R., Reynolds, C. F., Carpenter, D., & Docherty, J. P. (2001). The Expert Consensus Guideline Series: Pharmacotherapy of depressive disorders in older patients. *Postgraduate Medicine, 110,* 1–86.

Alford, B. A., & Beck, A. T. (1997). *The integrative power of cognitive therapy.* New York: Guilford Press.

Allardyce, J., Gaebel, W., Zielasek, J., & Van Os, J. (2007). Deconstructing Psychosis Conference, February 2006: The validity of schizophrenia and alternative approaches to the classification of psychosis. *Schizophrenia Bulletin, 33,* 863–867.

Allebeck, P. (1989). Schizophrenia: A life-shortening disease. *Schizophrenia Bulletin, 15,* 81–90.

Alloy, L. B., Abramson, L. Y., Keyser, J., Gerstein, R. K., & Sylvia, L. G. (2008). Negative cognitive style. In K. S. Dobson & D. J. A. Dozois (Eds.), *Risk factors in depression* (pp. 237–262). Oxford, UK: Elsevier/Academic Press.

Alloy, L. B., Abramson, L. Y., Whitehouse, W. G., Hogan, M. E., Panzarella, C., & Rose, D. T. (2006). Prospective incidence of first onsets and recurrences of depression in individuals at high and low cognitive risk for depression. *Journal of Abnormal Psychology, 115,* 145–156.

Alonso, J., & Lepine, J. (2007). Overview of key data from the European Study of the Epidemiology of Mental Disorders. *Journal of Clinical Psychiatry, 68* (Suppl. 2), 3–9.

Alterman, A. I., & Cacciola, J. S. (1991). The antisocial personality disorder diagnosis in substance abusers. *Journal of Nervous and Mental Disease, 179,* 401–409.

Althof, S. (2007). Treatment of rapid ejaculation: Psychotherapy, pharmacotherapy and combined therapy. In S. R. Leiblum (Ed.), *Principles and practices of sex therapy* (4th ed., pp. 212–240). New York: Guilford Press.

Althof, S. E. (1995). Pharmacologic treatment of rapid ejaculation. *Psychiatric Clinics of North America, 18* (1), 85–94.

Althof, S. E., & Seftel, A. D. (1995). The evaluation and management of erectile dysfunction. *Psychiatric Clinics of North America, 18,* 171–192.

Althof, S. E., & Turner, L. A. (1992). Self-injection therapy and external vacuum devices in the treatment of erectile dysfunction: Methods and outcome. In R. C. Rosen & S. R. Leiblum (Eds.), *Erectile disorders: Assessment and treatment* (pp. 283–309). New York: Guilford Press.

Alzheimer's Disease International. (2009). *World Alzheimer report 2009.* Retrieved from http://alz.co.uk/research/worldreport

Aman, M. G., Lam, K. S. L., & Collier-Crespin, A. (2003). Prevalence and patterns of use of psychoactive medicines among individuals with autism in the Autism Society of Ohio. *Journal of Autism & Developmental Disorders, 33,* 527–534.

Ambrogne, J. A. (2002). Reduced drinking as a treatment goal: What clinicians need to know. *Journal of Substance Abuse Treatment, 22,* 45–53.

American Association on Mental Retardation. (1992). *Mental retardation: Definition, classification and systems of support* (9th ed.). Washington, DC: Author.

American Psychiatric Association. (1968). *Diagnostic and statistical manual of mental disorders* (2nd ed.). Washington, DC: Author.

American Psychiatric Association. (1980). *Diagnostic and statistical manual of mental disorders* (3rd ed.). Washington, DC: Author.

American Psychiatric Association. (1987). *Diagnostic and statistical manual of mental disorders* (3rd ed. rev.). Washington, DC: Author.

American Psychiatric Association. (1994). *Diagnostic and statistical manual of mental disorders* (4th ed.). Washington, DC: Author.

American Psychiatric Association. (2000). *Diagnostic and statistical manual of mental disorders* (4th ed. rev.). Washington, DC: Author.

American Psychiatric Association. (2001). *Practice guidelines for the treatment of patients with borderline personality disorder.* Washington, DC: Author.

American Psychiatric Association. (2010). DSM-5: The future of psychiatric diagnosis. *American Psychiatric Association DSM-5 development.* Retrieved from http://www.dsm5.org/Pages/Default.aspx

American Psychiatric Association. (2011). *DSM-5 development.* Retrieved from http://www.dsm5.org/Pages/Default.aspx

American Psychological Association. (2004). Guidelines for psychological practice with older adults. *American Psychologist, 59,* 236–260.

American Psychological Association. (in press). Specialty guidelines for forensic psychology. *American Psychologist.*

American Psychological Association Presidential Task Force on Evidence-Based Practice. (2006). Evidence-based practice in psychology. *American Psychologist, 61,* 271–285.

American Psychosomatic Society. (1996). Special Issue: Animal models in psychosomatic research. *Psychosomatic Medicine, 58,* 521–632.

Ames, E. (1992). Development of Romanian orphanage children adopted to Canada. *Canadian Psychology, 33,* 503.

Ames, E., Chisholm, K., Fisher, L., Morison, S. J., Thompson, S., Mainemer, H., Carter, M., Ebbern, H., Ellwood, A. L., Ferrari, M., Gilman, L., Lukie, S., & Savoie, L. A. (1997). *The development of Romanian orphanage children adopted to Canada.* [Final report to National Welfare Grants Program, Human Resources Development Canada]. Burnaby, BC: Simon Fraser University.

Amir, N., Beard, C., & Bower, E. (2005). Interpretation bias and social anxiety. *Cognitive Therapy and Research, 29,* 433–443.

Ammari, N., Heinrichs, R. W., & Miles, A. A. (2010). An investigation of 3 neurocognitive subtypes in schizophrenia. *Schizophrenia Research, 121,* 1–3.

Amminger, G. P., Berger, G. E., Schafer, M. R., Klier, C., Friedrich, M. H., & Feucht, M. (2007). Omega 3 fatty acids supplementation in children with autism: A double-blind, randomized, placebo-controlled pilot study. *Biological Psychiatry, 61,* 551–553.

Amstadter, A. B., Broman-Fulks, J., Zinzow, H., Ruggiero, K. J., & Cercone, J. (2009). Internet-based interventions for traumatic-stress related mental health problems. *Clinical Psychology Review, 29,* 410–420.

Ancoli-Israel, S. (1989). Epidemiology of sleep disorders. *Clinics in Geriatric Medicine, 5,* 347–362.

Ancoli-Israel, S., & Roth, T. (1999). Characteristics of insomnia in the United States: I. Results of the 1991 National Sleep Foundation Survey. *Sleep, 22(Suppl. 2),* 347–353.

Andersen, A. E., & DiDomenico, L. (1992). Diet vs. shape content of popular male and female magazines: A dose-response relationship to the incidence of eating disorders? *International Journal of Eating Disorders, 11,* 283–287.

Anderson, B. J., & Wold, F. M. (1986). Chronic physical illness and sexual behavior. *Journal of Consulting and Clinical Psychology, 54,* 168–175.

Anderson, J. C., Williams, S., McGee, R., & Silva, P. A. (1987). DSM-III disorders in preadolescent children: Prevalence in a large sample from the general population. *Archives of General Psychiatry, 44,* 69–76.

Anderson, S. W., Bechara, A., Damasio, H., Tranel, D., & Damasio, A. R. (1999). Impairment of social and moral behaviour related to early damage in human prefrontal cortex. *Nature Neuroscience, 2,* 1032–1037.

Anderson, S. W., Damasio, H., Jones, R. D., & Tranel, D. (1991). Wisconsin Card Sorting Test performance as a measure of frontal lobe damage. *Journal of Clinical and Experimental Neuropsychology, 13,* 909–922.

Andreasen, N. C., & Flaum, M. (1991). Schizophrenia: The characteristic symptoms. *Schizophrenia Bulletin, 17,* 27–49.

Andrés, S., Lázaro, L., Salamero, M., Boget, T., Penadés, R., & Castro-Fornieles, J. (2008). Changes in cognitive dysfunction in children and adolescents with obsessive-compulsive disorder after treatment. *Journal of Psychiatric Research, 42,* 507–514.

Andrews, G., Brugha, T., Thase, M. E., Duffy, F. F., Rucci, P., & Slade, T. (2007). Dimensionality and the category of major depressive episode. *International Journal of Methods in Psychiatric Research, 16,* S41–S51.

Andrews, G., Goldberg, D. P., Krueger, R. F., Carpenter, W. T., Jr., Hyman, S. E., Sachdev, P., & Pine, D. S. (2009). Exploring the feasibility of a meta-structure for DSM-V and ICD-11: Could it improve utility and validity? *Psychological Medicine, 39,* 1993–2000.

Andrews, G., Hobbs, M. J., Borkovec, T. D., Beesdo, K., Craske, M. G., Heimberg, R. G., et al. (2010). Generalized worry disorder: A review of DSM-IV generalized anxiety disorder and options for DSM-V. *Depression and Anxiety, 27,* 134–147.

Angold, A., Costello, E. J., & Erkani, A. (1999). Comorbidity. *The Journal of Child Psychology and Psychiatry, 40,* 57–87.

Angold, A., & Costello, J. (1996). Toward establishing an empirical basis for the diagnosis of oppositional defiant disorder. *Journal of the American Academy of Child & Adolescent Psychiatry, 35,* 1205–1212.

Angus, L. E., & Marziali, E. (1988). A comparison of three measures for the diagnosis of borderline personality disorder. *American Journal of Psychiatry, 145,* 1453–1454.

Anstendig, K. D. (1999). Is selective mutism an anxiety disorder? Rethinking its DSM-IV classification. *Journal of Anxiety Disorders, 13,* 417–434.

Antony, M. M., & Barlow, D. H. (2002). Specific phobias. In D. H. Barlow (Ed.), *Anxiety and its disorders* (2nd ed., pp. 380–417). New York: Guilford Press.

Antony, M. M., McCabe, R. E., Leeuw, I., Sano, N., & Swinson, R. P. (2001). Effect of distraction and coping style on in vivo exposure for specific phobia of spiders. *Behaviour Research & Therapy, 39,* 1137–1150.

Antony, M. M., Orsillo, S. M., & Roemer, L. (2001). *Practitioner's guide to empirically based measures of anxiety.* New York: Kluwer Academic/Plenum.

Antony, M. M., Purdon, C. L., Huta, V., & Swinson, R. P. (1998). Dimensions of perfectionism across the anxiety disorders. *Behaviour Research & Therapy, 36,* 1143–1154.

Antony, M. M., Rowa, K., Liss, A., Swallow, S. R., & Swinson, R. P. (2005). Social comparison processes in social phobia. *Behavior Therapy, 36,* 65–75.

Antony, M. M., & Swinson, R. P. (1996). *Anxiety disorders and their treatment: A critical review of the evidence-based literature.* Ottawa: Health Canada.

Anxiety Review Panel. Evans, M., Bradwejn, J., & Dunn, L. (Eds.). (2000). *Guidelines for the treatment of anxiety disorders in primary care.* Toronto: Queen's Printer of Ontario.

Aos, S., Lieb, R., Mayfiel, J., Miller, M., & Pennucci, A. (2004). *Benefits and costs of prevention and early intervention programs for youth.* (No. 04-07-3901). Olympia, WA: Washington State Institute for Public Policy.

APA. *See* American Psychiatric Association.

Arboleda-Florez, J., & Holley, H. L. (1991). Antisocial burnout: An exploratory study. *Bulletin of the American Academy of Psychiatry and Law, 19,* 173–183.

Arch, J., & Craske, M. G. (2008). Panic disorder. In W. E. Craighead, D. J. Miklowitz, & L. W. Craighead (Eds.), *Psychopathology: History, diagnosis, and empirical foundations* (pp. 115–158). Hoboken, NJ: Wiley.

Archer, J. (1991). The influence of testosterone on human aggression. *The British Journal of Psychology, 82,* 1–28.

Archer, R. P., Krishnamurthy, R., & Stredny, R. V. (2007). The Minnesota Multiphasic Personality Inventory–Adolescent. In S. R. Smith & L. Handler (Eds.), *The clinical assessment of children and adolescents: A practitioner's handbook* (pp. 237–266). Mahwah, NJ: Erlbaum.

Arieti, S. (1963). Psychopathic personality: Some views on its psychopathology and psychodynamics. *Comprehensive Psychiatry, 4,* 301–312.

Arkowitz, H., Westra, H. A., Miller, W. R., & Rollnick, S. (Eds.). (2008). *Motivational interviewing in the treatment of psychological problems.* New York: Guilford Press.

Arseneault, L., Cannon, M., Poulton, R., Murray, R., Caspi, A., & Moffitt, T. E. (2002). Cannabis use in adolescence and risk for adult psychosis: Longitudinal prospective study. *British Medical Journal, 325,* 1212–1213.

Arterbutrn, D. E., Crane, P. K., & Sullivan, S. D. (2006). The coming epidemic of obesity in elderly Americans. *Journal of the American Geriatrics Society, 52,* 1907–1912.

Åsberg, M. (1976). Treatment of depression with tricyclic drugs—Pharmacokinetic and pharmacodynamic aspects. *Pharmacopsychiatry and Neuropsychopharmacology, 9,* 18–26.

Ashcroft, M. H., Krause, J. A., & Hopko, D. R. (2007). Is math anxiety a mathematical learning disability? In D. B. Berch & M. Mazzacco (Eds.), *Why is math so hard for some children? The nature and origins of mathematical learning difficulties and disabilities* (pp. 329–348). Baltimore, MD: Paul H. Brookes.

Ashton, A. K. (2007). The new sexual pharmacology: A guide for clinicians. In S. R. Leiblum (Ed.), *Priniciples and practices of sex therapy* (4th ed., pp. 509–541). New York: Guilford Press.

Ashton, H. (2005). The diagnosis and management of benzodiazepine dependence. *Current Opinion in Psychiatry, 18,* 249–255.

Assembly of First Nations and First Nations Information Governance Committee. (2007). First Nations Regional Longitudinal Health Survey (RHS) 2002/03: Results for adults, youth and children living in First Nations communities. Ottawa: Author.

Astley, S. J., Bailey, D., Talbot, C., & Clarren, S. K. (2000). Fetal alcohol syndrome (FAS) primary prevention through FAS diagnosis: Identification of high-risk birth mothers through the diagnosis of their children. *Alcohol, 35* (5), 499–508.

Atkinson, L., & Feldman, M. (1994). Survey of aberrant behaviour and its treatment in persons with developmental disabilities in Ontario. [Report submitted to Ontario Ministry of Community and Social Services]. Toronto: Ontario Mental Health Foundation.

Avery, D. H. (1993). Electroconvulsive therapy. In D. L. Dunner (Ed.), *Current psychiatric therapy* (pp. 524–528). Philadelphia: W. B. Saunders.

Aybek, S., Kanaan, R. A., & David, A. S. (2008). The neuropsychiatry of conversion disorder. *Current Opinion in Psychiatry, 21,* 275–280.

Ayers, C. R., Sorrell, J. T., Thorp, S. R., & Wetherell, J. L. (2007). Evidence-based psychological treatments for late-life anxiety. *Psychology and Aging, 22,* 8–17.

Azrin, N. H. (1976). Improvements in the community-reinforcement approach to alcoholism. *Behaviour Research and Therapy, 14,* 339–348.

Babiak, P., & Hare, R. D. (2006). *Snakes in suits: When psychopaths go to work.* New York: Regan Books/HarperCollins.

Babor, T., de la Fuente, J. R., Saunders, J., & Grant, M. (1992). *The Alcohol Use Disorders Identification Test: Guidelines for use in primary health care.* Geneva: World Health Organization.

Bach, A. K., Brown, T. A., & Barlow, D. H. (1999). The effects of false negative feedback on efficacy expectancies and sexual arousal in sexually functional males. *Behavior Therapy, 30,* 79–95.

Baer, R. A. (2003). Mindfulness training as a clinical intervention: A conceptual and empirical review. *Clinical Psychology: Science & Practice, 10,* 125–143.

Bagley, C. (1991). Poverty and suicide among native Canadians: A replication. *Psychological Reports, 69,* 149–150.

Bailey, D. B., Jr., Raspa, M., & Olmsted, M. G. (2010). Using a parent survey to advance knowledge about the nature and consequences of Fragile X syndrome. *American Journal on Intellectual and Developmental Disabilities, 115,* 447–460.

Bajbouj, M., & Grimm, S. (2010). Efficacy of vagus nerve stimulation in the treatment of depression. *Expert Review of Neurotherapeutics, 10,* 87.

Baker, S. L., Patterson, M. D., & Barlow, D. H. (2002). Panic disorder and agoraphobia. In M. M. Antony & D. H. Barlow (Eds.), *Handbook of assessment and treatment planning for psychological disorders* (pp. 67–112). New York: Guilford Press.

Baker-Morrissette, S., Bitran, S., & Barlow, D. H. (2010). Panic disorder and agoraphobia. In M. M. Antony & D. H. Barlow (Eds.), *Handbook of assessment and treatment planning for psychological disorders* (2nd ed., pp. 141–185). New York: Guilford Press.

Bakkevig, J. F., & Karterud, S. (2010). Is the *Diagnostic and Statistical Manual of Mental Disorders, Fourth Edition,* histrionic personality disorder category a valid construct? *Comprehensive Psychiatry, 51,* 462–470. doi:10.1016/j.comppsych.2009.11.009

Ballinger, B., & Yalom, I. (1995). Group therapy in practice. In B. Bongar & L. E. Beutler (Eds.), *Comprehensive textbook of psychotherapy: Theory and practice* (pp. 189–204). New York: Oxford University Press.

Baltes, P. B., & Baltes, M. M. (1990). Psychological perspectives on successful aging: The model of selective optimization with compensation. In P. B. Baltes & M. M. Baltes (Eds.), *Successful Aging* (pp. 1–34). Cambridge, UK: Cambridge University Press.

Bancroft, J. (1989). *Human sexuality and its problems* (2nd ed.). New York: Churchill Livingstone.

Bancroft, J. (2000, October). *Sexual wellbeing of women in heterosexual relationships: A national survey.* Paper presented at Female Sexual Function Forum: New perspectives in the management of female sexual dysfunction. Boston.

Bandura, A. (1973). *Aggression: A social learning analysis.* Englewood Cliffs, NJ: Prentice Hall.

Bandura, A. (1976). *Social learning theory.* Englewood Cliffs, NJ: Prentice Hall.

Bandura, A. (1977). Self-efficacy: Toward a unifying theory of behavioral change. *Psychological Review, 84,* 191–215.

Bandura, A. (2000a). Exercise of human agency through collective efficacy. *Current Directions in Psychological Science, 9,* 75–78.

Bandura, A. (2000b). Social cognitive theory: An agentic perspective. *Annual Review of Psychology, 52,* 1–26.

Bandura, A., & Menlove, F. L. (1968). Factors determining vicarious extinction of avoidance behavior through symbolic modelling. *Journal of Personality and Social Psychology, 8,* 99–108.

Bandura, A., Ross, D., & Ross, S. A. (1961). Transmission of aggression through imitation of aggressive models. *Journal of Abnormal and Social Psychology, 63,* 575–582.

Bandura, A., Ross, D., & Ross, S. A. (1963). Imitation of film-mediated aggressive models. *Journal of Abnormal and Social Psychology, 66,* 3–11.

Bandura, A., & Walters, R. H. (1959). *Adolescent aggression.* New York: Ronald Press.

Bandura, A., & Walters, R. H. (1963). *Social learning and personality development.* New York: Holt, Rinehart & Winston.

Banerjee, T. D., Middleton, F., & Faraone, S. V. (2007). Environmental risk factors for attention-deficit hyperactivity disorder. *Acta Paediatrica, 96* (9), 1269–1274.

Banham, K. M. (1951). Senescence and the emotions: A genetic theory. *Journal of Genetic Psychology, 78,* 175–183.

Barasch, A., Frances, A., Hurt, S., Clarkin, J., & Cohen, S. (1985). Stability and distinctness of borderline personality disorder. *American Journal of Psychiatry, 142,* 1484–1486.

Barbaree, H., Seto, M., Serin, R. C., Amos, N., & Preston, D. L. (1994). Comparisons between sexual and non-sexual rapist sub-types. *Criminal Justice & Behavior, 21,* 95–114.

Barbaree, H. E. (1990). Stimulus control of sexual arousal: Its role in sexual assault. In W. L. Marshall, D. R. Laws, & H. E. Barbaree, *Handbook of sexual assault: Issues, theories, and treatment of the offender* (pp. 115–142). New York: Plenum Press.

Barbaree, H. E., & Seto, M. C. (1997). Pedophilia: Assessment and treatment. In D. R. Laws & W. O'Donohue (Eds.), *Sexual deviance: Theory, assessment, and treatment* (pp. 175–193). London: Guilford Press.

Barbui, C., Cipriani, A., Patel, V., Ayuso-Mateos, L., & van Ommeren, M. (2011). Efficacy of antidepressants and benzodiazepines in minor depression: A systematic review and meta-analysis. *British Journal of Psychiatry, 198,* 11–16. doi:10.1192/bjp.109.076448

Barden, N. (2004). Implication of the hypothalamic-pituitary-adrenal axis in the physiopathology of depression. *Journal of Psychiatry & Neuroscience, 29,* 185–193.

Barefoot, J. C. (1992). Developments in the measurement of hostility. In H. S. Friedman (Ed.), *Hostility, coping and health* (pp. 13–31). Washington, DC: American Psychological Association.

Barefoot, J. C., & Schroll, M. (1996). Symptoms of depression, acute myocardial infarction and total mortality in a community sample. *Circulation, 93,* 1976–1980.

Barefoot, J. C., Dodge, K. A., Peterson, B. L., Dahlstrom, W. G., & Williams, R. B. (1989). The Cook-Medley Hostility Scale: Item content and ability to predict survival. *Psychosomatic Medicine, 51,* 46–57.

Bar-Haim, Y., Dan, O., Eshel, Y., & Sagi-Schwartz, A. (2007). Predicting children's anxiety from early attachment relationships. *Journal of Anxiety Disorders, 21,* 1061–1068.

Bar-Haim, Y., Lamy, D., Pergamin, L., Bakermans-Kranenburg, M. J., & van Ijzendoorn, M. H. (2007). Threat-related attentional bias in anxious and nonanxious individuals: A meta-analytic study. *Psychological Bulletin, 133,* 1–24.

Barkley, R. A. (1997). Behavioral inhibition, sustained attention, and executive functions: Constructing a unified theory of ADHD. *Psychological Bulletin, 121* (1), 65–94.

Barkley, R. A., & Benton, C. M. (1998). *Your defiant child: Eight steps to better behavior.* New York: Guilford Press.

Barlow, D. H. (2002). *Anxiety and its disorders* (2nd ed.). New York: Guilford Press.

Barlow, D. H., & Durand, V. M. (1995). Substance-related disorders. In *Abnormal psychology: An integrated approach.* New York: Brooks/Cole.

Barlow, D. H., Gorman, J. M., Shear, M. K., & Woods, S. W. (2000). Cognitive-behavioral therapy, imipramine, or their combination for panic disorder: A randomized controlled trial. *Journal of the American Medical Association, 283,* 2529–2536.

Barlow, M. R., & Freyd, J. J. (2009). Adaptive dissociation: Information processing and response to betrayal. In P. F. Dell & J. A. O'Neil (Eds.), *Dissociation and the dissociative disorders: DSM-V and beyond* (pp. 93–105). New York: Routledge.

Barnes, G. M., Farrell, M. P., & Cairns, A. L. (1986). Parental socialization factors and adolescent drinking behaviors. *Journal of Marriage and the Family, 48,* 27–36.

Barnes, T. E., & the Schizophrenia Consensus Group of the British Association for Psychopharmacology. (2011). Evidence-based guidelines for the pharmacological treatment of schizophrenia: Recommendations from the British Association for Psychopharmacology. *Journal of Psychopharmacology, 25,* 567–620. doi:10.1177/0269881110391123jop.sagepub.com

Barnett, P. A., Spence, J. D., Manuck, S. B., & Jennings, J. R. (1997). Psychological stress and the progression of carotid artery disease. *Journal of Hypertension, 15,* 49–55.

Barnett, W. S. (2011). Effectiveness of early education. *Science, 333,* 975–978.

Baroff, G. S. (1986). *Mental retardation: Nature, cause and management* (2nd ed.). Washington, DC: Hemisphere.

Baron, M., Risch, N., Levitt, M., & Gruen, R. (1985). Familial transmission of schizotypal and borderline personality disorders. *American Journal of Psychiatry, 142,* 927–934.

Baron, R. A., & Byrne, D. (1977). *Social psychology: Understanding human interaction* (2nd ed.). Boston: Allyn and Bacon.

Barrett, F. M. (1980). Sexual experience, birth control usage, and sex education of unmarried Canadian university students: Changes between 1968 and 1978. *Archives of Sexual Behavior, 9,* 367–390.

Barrett, P. M., Farrell, L., Pina, A. A., Persis, T. S., & Piacentini, J. (2008). Evidence-based psychosocial treatments for child and adolescent obsessive-compulsive disorder. *Journal of Clinical Child and Adolescent Psychology, 37,* 131–155.

Barsky, A. J., & Klerman, G. L. (1983). Overview: Hypochondriasis, bodily complaints, and somatic styles. *American Journal of Psychiatry, 140,* 273–283.

Bartels, S. J., Dums, A. R., Oxman, T. E., Schneider, L., Areán, P., Alexopoulos, G., et al. (2003). Evidence-based practices in geriatric mental health care: An overview of systematic reviews and meta-analyses. *Psychiatric Clinics of North America, 26,* 971–990.

Bartels, S. J., Forester, B., Mueser, K. T., Miles, K. M., Dums, A. R., Pratt, S. I., et al. (2004). Enhanced skills training and health care management for older persons with severe mental illness. *Community Mental Health Journal, 40* (1), 75–90.

Barth, J., Schumacher, M., & Herrmann-Lingen, C. (2004). Depression as a risk factor for mortality in patients with coronary heart disease: A meta-analysis. *Psychosomatic Medicine, 66,* 812–813.

Bartholomew, A. A., Badger, P., & Milte, K. L. (1977). The psychologist as an expert witness in the criminal courts. *Australian Psychologist, 12,* 133–150.

Bartholomew, K. (1989). Attachment styles in young adults: Implications for self-control and interpersonal functioning. Unpublished doctoral dissertation, Stanford University.

Bartholomew, K. (1990). Avoidance of intimacy: An attachment perspective. *Journal of Personal and Social Relationships, 7,* 147–178.

Bartlett, C. P., Vowels, C. L., & Saucier, D. A. (2008). Meta-analyses of the effects of media images on men's body-image concerns. *Journal of Social and Clinical Psychology, 27,* 279–310.

Bartlett, P. (2000). Structures of confinement in 19th-century asylums: A comparative study using England and Ontario. *International Journal of Law and Psychiatry, 23,* 1–13.

Bates, M. E., Bowden, S. C., & Barry, D. (2002). Neurocognitive impairment associated with alcohol use disorders: Implications for treatment. *Experimental and Clinical Psychopharmacology, 10,* 193–212.

Bathje, G. J., & Pryor, J. B. (2011). The relationships of public and self-stigma to seeking mental health services. *Journal of Mental Health Counseling, 33,* 161–177.

Batshaw, M. L., & Perret, Y. M. (1986). *Children with handicaps: A medical primer.* Baltimore, MD: Paul Brookes.

Battle, C., Shea, M., Johnson, D., Yen, S., Zlotnick, C., Zanarini, M., et al. (2004). Childhood maltreatment associated with adult personality disorders: Findings from the Collaborative Longitudinal Personality Disorders Study. *Journal of Personality Disorders, 18* (2), 193–211.

Bauer, N. S., & Webster-Stratton, C. (2007). Prevention of behavioral disorders in primary care. *Current Opinions in Pediatrics, 18,* 654–660.

Baumbach, J., & Turner, L. A. (1992). Female gender disorder: A new model and clinical applications. *Journal of Psychology and Human Sexuality, 5,* 107–129.

Baumeister, E. A., Storch, E., & Geffken, G. (2008). Peer victimization in children with learning disabilities. *Child and Adolescent Social Work Journal, 25,* 11–23.

Bauminger, N., Edelsztein, H. S., & Morash, J. (2005). Social information processing and emotional understanding in children with LD. *Journal of Learning Disabilities, 38,* 45–61.

Baxter, C. (1989). Parent-perceived attitudes of professionals: Implications for service providers. *Disability, Handicap & Society, 4,* 259–269.

Baxter, L. R., Phelps, M. E., Mazziotta, J. C., Guze, B. H., Schwartz, J. M., & Selin, C. E. (1987). Local cerebral glucose metabolic rates in obsessive-compulsive disorder. *Archives of General Psychiatry, 44,* 211–218.

Baydala, L., Dasmussen, C., Birch, J., Sherman, J., Wikman, E., Charchun, J., Kennedy, M., & Bisanz, J. (2009). Self-beliefs and behavioural development as related to academic achievement in Canadian Aboriginal children. *Canadian Journal of School Psychology, 24,* 19–33.

Baym, C. L., & Gonsalves, B. D. (2010). Comparison of neural activity that leads to true memories, false memories, and forgetting: An fMRI study of the misinformation effect. *Cognitive, Affective, and Behavioral Neuroscience, 10,* 339–348.

Bazzo, G., Nota, L., Soresi, S., Ferrari, L., & Minnes, P. (2007). Attitudes of social service providers towards the sexuality of individuals with intellectual disability. *Journal of Applied Research in Intellectual Disabilities, 20,* 110–115.

Beach, S. R. H., & O'Leary, K. D. (1992). Treating depression in the context of marital discord: Outcome and predictors of response of marital therapy versus cognitive therapy. *Behavior Therapy, 23,* 507–528.

Beardslee, W. R., Wright, E. J., Gladstone, T. R. G., & Forbes, P. (2007). Long-term effects from a randomized trial of two public health preventive interventions for parental depression. *Journal of Family Psychology, 21,* 703–713.

Beatty, M. J., Heisel, A. D., Hall, A. E., Levine, T. R., & La France, B. H. (2002). What can we learn from the study of twins about genetic and environmental influences on interpersonal affiliation, aggressiveness, and social anxiety? A meta-analytic study. *Communication Monographs, 69,* 1–18.

Bebko, J. M., Perry, A., & Bryson, S. E. (1996). Multiple method validation study of Facilitated Communication: II. Individual differences and subgroup results. *Journal of Autism and Developmental Disorders, 26,* 19–42.

Beblo, T., Driessen, M., Mertens, M., Wingenfeld, K., Piefke, M., Rullkoetter, N., et al. (2006). Functional MRI correlates of the recall of unresolved life events in borderline personality disorder. *Psychological Medicine, 36,* 845–856.

Bech, P., Cialdella, P., Haugh, M. C., Birkett, M. A., Hours, A., Boissel, J. P., & Tollefson, G. D. (2000). Meta-analysis of randomised controlled trials of fluoxetine v. placebo and tricyclic antidepressants in the short-term treatment of major depression. *British Journal of Psychiatry, 176,* 421–428.

Beck, A. T. (1963). Thinking and depression: I. Idiosyncratic content and cognitive distortions. *Archives of General Psychiatry, 9,* 36–46.

Beck, A. T. (1967). *Depression: Causes and treatment.* Philadelphia: University of Pennsylvania Press.

Beck, A. T. (1976). *Cognitive therapy and the emotional disorders.* New York: International Universities Press.

Beck, A. T. (1983). Cognitive therapy of depression: New perspectives. In P. J. Clayton & J. E. Barrett (Eds.), *Treatment of depression: Old controversies and new approaches* (pp. 265–290). New York: Raven.

Beck, A. T., & Dozois, D. J. A. (2011). Cognitive therapy: Current status and future directions. *Annual Review of Medicine, 62,* 397–409. doi:10.1146/annurev-med-052209-100032

Beck, A. T., & Dozois, D. J. A. (in press). Cognitive theory and therapy: Past, present and future. In S. Bloch, S. A. Green, & J. Holmes (Eds.), *Psychiatry: Past, present and prospect.* Oxford, UK: Oxford University Press.

Beck, A. T., & Emery, G. (1985). *Anxiety disorders and phobias: A cognitive perspective.* New York: Basic Books.

Beck, A. T., Freeman, A., & Davis, D. D. (2004). *Cognitive therapy of personality disorders* (2nd ed.). New York: Guilford Press.

Beck, A. T., Freeman, A., Pretzer, J., Davis, D. D., Fleming, B., Ottaviani, R., et al. (1990). *Cognitive therapy of personality disorders.* New York: Guilford Press.

Beck, A. T., & Rector, N.A. (2000). Cognitive therapy of schizophrenia: A new therapy for the new millennium. *American Journal of Psychotherapy, 54,* 291–300.

Beck, A. T., Rector, N. A., Stolar, N., & Grant, P. (2009). *Schizophrenia: Cognitive theory, research, and therapy.* New York: Guilford Press.

Beck, A. T., Rush, P. J., Shaw, B. F., & Emery, G. (1979). *Cognitive therapy of depression.* New York: Guilford Press.

Beck, A. T., Ward, C. H., Mendelson, M., Mock, J. E., & Erbaugh, J. K. (1962). Reliability of psychiatric diagnosis: II. A study of consistency of clinical judgements and ratings. *American Journal of Psychiatry, 119,* 351–357.

Beck, J. C. (1978). Social influences on the prognosis of schizophrenia. *Schizophrenia Bulletin, 4* (1), 86–90.

Beck, J. G. (1993). Vaginismus. In W. O'Donohue & J. G. Greer (Eds.), *Handbook of sexual dysfunctions: Assessment and treatment* (pp. 381–397). Boston: Allyn and Bacon.

Becker, E. S., Rinck, M., Turke, V., Kause, P., Goodwin, R., Neumer, S., & Margraf, J. (2007). Epidemiology of specific phobia subtypes: Findings from the Dresden Mental Health Study. *European Psychiatry, 22,* 69–74.

Becker, J. B., Breedlove, S. M., Crews, D., & McCarthy, M. M. (Eds.). (2002). *Behavioral endocrinology.* Cambridge, MA: MIT Press.

Becker, K., El-Faddagh, M., Schmidt, M. H., Esser, G., & Laucht, M. (2008). Interaction of dopamine transporter genotype with prenatal smoke exposure on ADHD symptoms. *The Journal of Pediatrics, 152,* 263–269. doi:10.1016/j.jpeds.2007.07.004

Becker, K. A. (2003). *History of the Stanford-Binet Intelligence Scales: Content and psychometrics.* (Stanford-Binet Intelligence Scales, Fifth Edition Assessment Service Bulletin No. 1). Itasca, IL: Riverside.

Becker-Blease, K. A., Deater-Deckard, K., Eley, T., Freyd, J. J., Stevenson, J., & Plomin, R. (2004). A genetic analysis of individual differences in dissociative behaviors in childhood and adolescence. *Journal of Child Psychology and Psychiatry, 45,* 522–532.

Beckwith, B. E. (2001). Thyroid disorders. In R. E. Tarter, M. Butters, & S. R. Beers (Eds.), *Medical neuropsychology* (2nd ed., pp. 163–180). New York: Kluwer Academic/Plenum.

Beirness, D. J., Beasley, E., & LeCavalier, J. (2009). The accuracy of evaluations by Drug Recognition Experts in Canada. *Canadian Society of Forensic Sciences Journal, 42,* 75–79.

Beirness, D. J., LeCavalier, J., & Singhal, D. (2007). Evaluation of the Drug Evaluation and Classification program: A critical review of the evidence. *Traffic Injury Prevention, 8,* 368–376.

Belanger, A., Martel, L., & Caron-Malenfant, E. (2005). *Population projections for Canada, provinces and territories: 2005–2031.* Statistics Canada Demography Division. Catalogue no. 91-520-XIE.

Bellani, M., Marzi, C. A., Savazzi, S., Perlini, C., Cerruti, S., Ferro, A., et al. (2010). Laterality effects in schizophrenia and bipolar disorder. *Experimental Brain Research, 201* (2), 339–344. doi:10.1007/s00221-009-2021-0

Bemporad, J. R. (1992). *Psychoanalytically orientated psychotherapy.* New York: Guilford Press.

Bemporad, J. R. (1997). Cultural and historical aspects of eating disorders. *Theoretical Medicine, 18,* 401–420.

Benazzi, F. (2000). Late-life chronic depression: A 399-case study in private practice. *International Journal of Geriatric Depression, 15,* 1–6.

Benbadis, S. R., & Allen-Hauser, W. (2000). An estimate of the prevalence of psychogenic non-epileptic seizures. *Seizure, 9,* 280–281.

Bender, L. (1938). The Visual Motor Gestalt Test and its clinical use. *Archives of Neurology and Psychiatry, 30,* 514–537.

Bender, W. N., & Wall, M. E. (1994). Social-emotional development of students with learning disabilities. *Learning Disability Quarterly, 17* (4), 323–341.

Bennett, A. E. (1947). Mad doctors. *Journal of Nervous and Mental Disease, 106,* 11–18.

Benowitz, N. (1990). Clinical pharmacology of caffeine. *Annual Review of Medicine, 41,* 277–288.

Bentall, R. P. (1994). Cognitive biases and abnormal beliefs: Towards a model of persecutory delusions. In A. S. David & J. C. Cutting (Eds.), *The neuropsychology of schizophrenia* (pp. 337–360). Brain damage, behaviour and cognition series. London: Lawrence Erlbaum.

Berard, G. (1993). *Hearing equals behavior.* New Canaan, CT: Keats.

Bergem, A. L., Engedal, K., & Kringlen, E. (1997). The role of heredity in late-onset Alzheimer disease and vascular dementia: A twin study. *Archives of General Psychiatry, 54* (3), 264–270.

Bergeron, S., Brown, C., Lord, M. J., Oala, M., Binik, Y. M., & Khalifé, S. (2002). Physical therapy for vulvar vestibulitis syndrome: A retrospective study. *Journal of Sex and Marital Therapy, 28,* 183–192.

Bergeron, S., Pukall, C. F., & Mailloux, G. (2008). Vulvar pain syndrome: Treatment and quantitative sensory testing. In A. P. Baranowski, P. Abrams, & M. Fall (Eds.), *Urogenital pain in clinical practice* (pp. 295–307). New York: Informa Healthcare.

Bergin, A. E. (1971). The evaluation of therapeutic outcomes. In A. E. Bergin & S. L. Garfield (Eds.), *The evaluation of therapeutic outcomes* (pp. 217–270). New York: Wiley.

Berkman, L. F., & Syme, S. L. (1979). Social networks, host resistance, and mortality: A nine-year follow-up study of Alameda County residents. *American Journal of Epidemiology, 109,* 186–204.

Berman, L. A., Berman, J. R., Chhabra, S., & Goldstein, I. (2001). Novel approaches to female sexual dysfunction. *Expert Opinion on Investigating Drugs, 10,* 85–95.

Berman, W. H., & Sperling, M. B. (1994). The structure and function of adult attachment. In M. B. Sperling & W. H. Berman (Eds.), *Attachment in adults: Clinical and developmental perspectives* (pp. 3–28). New York: Guilford Press.

Berner, W., Berger, P., & Hill, A. (2003). Sexual sadism. *International Journal of Offender Therapy & Comparative Criminology, 47,* 383–395.

Berstein, C. A. (2011). Meta-structure in DSM-5 process. *Psychiatric News, 46* (5), 7–9.

Bernstein, D. P., Cohen, P., Velez, C. N., Schwab-Stone, M., Siever, L. J., & Shinsato, L. (1993). Prevalence and stability of the DSM-III-R personality disorders in a community-based survey of adolescents. *American Journal of Psychiatry, 50,* 1237–1243.

Bernstein, E. M., & Putnam, F. W. (1986). Development, reliability and validity of a dissociation scale. *Journal of Nervous and Mental Disease, 174,* 727–735.

Bernstein, S. M., Steiner, B. W., Glaiser, J. T. D., & Muir, C. F. (1981). Changes in patients with gender identity problems after parental death. *American Journal of Psychiatry, 138,* 41–45.

Berrios, G. (1995). Mental retardation [clinical section II]. In G. Berrios & R. Porter (Eds.), *A history of clinical psychiatry* (pp. 225–238). London: Athlone Press.

Berry-Kravis, E., Raspa, M., Loggin-Hester, L., Bishop, E., Holiday, D., & Bailey, D. B., Jr. (2010). Seizures in Fragile X syndrome: Characteristics and comorbid diagnoses. *American Journal on Intellectual and Developmental Disabilities, 115,* 461–472.

Bertschy, G. (1995). Methadone maintenance treatment: An update. *European Archives of Psychiatry and Clinical Neuroscience, 245* (2), 114–124.

Bethell, L. (1984). *The Cambridge history of Latin America: Vol. I. Colonial Latin America.* New York: Cambridge University Press.

Betz, N. E., Mintz, L., & Speakmon, G. (1994). Gender differences in the accuracy of self-reported weight. *Sex Roles, 30,* 543–551.

Beutler, L. E., Machado, P. P. P., & Neufeldt, S. A. (1994). Therapist variables. In A. E. Bergin & S. L. Garfield (Eds.), *Handbook of psychotherapy and behavior change* (4th ed., pp. 229–269). New York: Wiley.

Bewernick, B. H., Hurlemann, R., Matusch, A., Kayser, S., Grubert, C., Hadrysiewicz, B., et al. (2010). Nucleus accumbens deep brain stimulation decreases ratings of depression and anxiety in treatment-resistant depression. *Biological Psychiatry, 67,* 110–116.

Beynon, S., Soares-Weiser, K., Woolacott, N., Duffy, S., & Geddes, J. R. (2008). Psychosocial interventions for the prevention of relapse in bipolar disorder: Systematic review of controlled trials. *British Journal of Psychiatry, 192,* 5–11.

Bialystok, E., Craik, F. I. M., & Freedman, M. (2007). Bilingualism as a protection against the onset of symptoms of dementia. *Neuropsychologia, 45,* 459–464.

Biedel, D. C., & Turner, S. M. (1988). Comorbidity of test anxiety and other anxiety disorders in children. *Journal for Abnormal Child Psychology, 16,* 275–287.

Biederman, J., Petty, C. R., Dolan, C., Hughes, S., Mick, E., Monuteaux, M. C., & Faraone, S. V. (2008). The long-term longitudinal course of oppositional defiant disorder and conduct disorder in ADHD boys: Findings from a controlled 10-year prospective longitudinal follow-up study. *Psychological Medicine,38,* 1027–1036. doi:10.1017/S0033291707002668

Biederman, J., Petty, C. R., Evans, M., Small, J., & Faraone, S. V. (2010). How persistent is ADHD? A controlled 10-year follow-up study of boys with ADHD. *Psychiatry Research, 177* (3), 299–304. doi:10.1016/j.psychres.2009.12.010

Biederman, T., Spencer, T., & Wilens, T. (1997). Psychopharmacology. In J. M. Wiener (Ed.), *Textbook of child and adolescent psychiatry* (2nd ed., pp. 779–812). Washington, DC: American Academy of Child and Adolescent Psychiatry, American Psychiatric Press.

Bienvenu, O. J., Hettema, J. M., Neale, M. C., Prescott, C. A., & Kendler, K. S. (2007). Low extraversion and high neuroticism as indices of genetic and environmental risk for social phobia, agoraphobia, and animal phobia. *American Journal of Psychiatry, 164,* 1714–1721.

Billings, J. H., Scherwitz, L. W., Sullivan, R., Sparler, S., & Ornish, D. M. (1996). The Lifestyle Heart Trial: Comprehensive treatment and group support therapy. In R. Allen & S. Scheidt (Eds.), *Heart and mind: The practice of cardiac psychology* (pp. 233–253). Washington, DC: American Psychological Association.

Binder, J. L., Strupp, H. S., & Henry, W. P. (1995). Psychodynamic therapies in practice: Time-limited psychodynamic psychotherapy. In B. Bongar & L. E. Beutler (Eds.), *Comprehensive textbook of psychotherapy: Theory and practice* (pp. 48–63). New York: Oxford University Press.

Binik, Y. M. (2010a). The DSM diagnostic criteria for dyspareunia. *Archives of Sexual Behavior, 39,* 292–303.

Binik, Y. M. (2010b). The DSM diagnostic criteria for vaginismus. *Archives of Sexual Behavior, 39,* 278–291.

Binik, Y. M., Bergeron, S., & Khalifé, S. (2007). Dyspareunia and vaginismus: So-called sexual pain. In S. R. Leiblum (Ed.), *Principles and practices of sex therapy* (4th ed., pp. 124–156). New York: Guilford Press.

Birbaumer, N., Wolfgang, G., Diedrich, O., Klose, U., Erb, M., Lotze, M., et al. (1998). fMRI reveals amygdala activation to human faces in social phobics. *Neuroreport, 9,* 1223–1226.

Birchall, H. (1999). Interpersonal psychotherapy in the treatment of eating disorders. *European Eating Disorders Review, 7,* 315–320.

Bird, V., Premkumar, T., Kendall, C., Whittington, C., Mitchell, J., & Kuipers, E. (2010). Early intervention services, cognitive-behavioural therapy and family intervention in early psychosis: Systematic review. *British Journal of Psychiatry, 197,* 350–356.

Birmaher, B., Ryan, N. D., Williamson, D. E., Brent, D. A., Kaufman, J., Dahl, R. E., et al. (1996). Childhood and adolescent depression: A review of the past 10 years: Part 1. *Journal of the Academy of Child and Adolescent Psychiatry, 35,* 1427–1439.

Birnbaum, K. (1914). *Die psychopathischen verbrecker* (2nd ed.). Leipzig: Thième.

Birren, J. E., & Renner, V. J. (1980). Concepts and issues of mental health and aging. In J. E. Birren & R. B. Sloane (Eds.), *Handbook of mental health and aging* (pp. 3–33). Englewood Cliffs, NJ: Prentice-Hall.

Bishop, S., Gahagan, S., & Lord, C. (2007). Re-examining the core features of autism: A comparison of autism spectrum disorder and fetal alcohol spectrum disorder. *Journal of Child Psychology and Psychiatry, 48,* 1111–1121.

Bisson, J. I., Ehlers, A., Matthews, R., Pilling, S., Richards, D., & Turner, S. (2007). Psychological treatments for chronic post-traumatic stress disorder: Systematic review and meta-analysis. *British Journal of Psychiatry, 190,* 97–104.

Bjorntorp, P. (2001). Do stress reactions cause abdominal obesity and comorbidities? *Obesity Reviews, 2,* 73–86.

Black, B., & Uhde, T. W. (1995). Psychiatric characteristics of children with selective mutism: A pilot study. *Journal of the American Academy of Child & Adolescent Psychiatry, 34,* 847–856.

Black, D. N., Seritan, A. L., Taber, K. H., & Hurley, R. A. (2004). Conversion hysteria: Lessons from functional imaging. *Journal of Neuropsychiatry & Clinical Neuroscience, 16,* 245–251.

Black, D. W. (2000). The epidemiology and phenomenology of compulsive sexual behavior. *CNS Spectrums, 5,* 26–72.

Black, D. W., & Andreasen, N. C. (2010). *Introductory text of psychiatry* (5th ed.). Washington, DC: American Psychiatric Press.

Blackburn, R. (1992). Criminal behavior, personality disorder, and mental confusion: The origins of confusion. *Criminal Behavior and Mental Health, 2,* 66–77.

Blair, R. J. R. (2001). Neurocognitive models of aggression, the antisocial personality disorders, and psychopathy. *Journal of Neurology, Neurosurgery, & Psychiatry, 71,* 727–731.

Blair, R. J. R. (2003). Neurobiological basis of psychopathy. *British Journal of Psychiatry, 182,* 5–7.

Blair, R. J. R., Peschardt, K. S., Budhani, S., Mitchell, D. G. V., & Pine, D. S. (2006). The development of psychopathy. *Journal of Child Psychology and Psychiatry, 47,* 262–275.

Blais, M. A., Baity, M. R., & Hopwood, C. J. (Eds.). (2010). *Clinical applications of the Personality Assessment Inventory.* New York: Taylor & Francis.

Blake, D. D., Weathers, F. W., Nagy, L. M., Kaloupek, D. G., Klauminzer, G., Charney, D. S., et al. (1990). A clinician rating scale for assessing current and lifetime PTSD: The CAPS-1. *The Behavior Therapist, 13,* 187–188.

Blanchard, R. (2010a). The DSM criteria for pedophilia. *Archives of Sexual Behavior, 39,* 304–316.

Blanchard, R. (2010b). The DSM criteria for transvestic fetishism. *Archives of Sexual Behavior, 39,* 363–372.

Blanchflower, D. G., & Oswald, A. J. (2008). Is well-being U-shaped over the life cycle? *Social Sciences and Medicine, 66,* 1733–1749.

Bland, R., Newman, S., Dyck, R., & Orn, H. (1990). Prevalence of psychiatric disorders and suicide attempts in a prison population. *Canadian Journal of Psychiatry, 35,* 407–413.

Bland, R. C., Newman, S. C., & Orn, H. (1988). Period prevalence of psychiatric disorders in Edmonton. *Acta Psychiatrica Scandinavica, 77* (Suppl. 338), 33–42.

Bland, R. C., Orn, H., & Newman, S. C. (1988). Lifetime prevalence of psychiatric disorders in Edmonton. *Acta Psychiatrica Scandinavica, 77(Suppl. 338),* 24–32.

Blankstein, K. R., Lumley, C. H., & Crawford, A. (2007). Perfectionism, hopelessness, and suicide ideation: Revisions to diathesis-stress and specific vulnerabiltiy models. *Journal of Rational-Emotive and Cognitive-Behavior Therapy, 25,* 279–319.

Blatt, B., & Kaplan, F. M. (1966). *Christmas in purgatory: A photographic essay on mental retardation.* Boston: Allyn and Bacon.

Blatt, S. J. (2004). *Experiences of depression: Theoretical, clinical, and research perspectives.* Washington, DC: American Psychological Association.

Blatt, S. J., Quinlan, D. M., Chevron, E. S., McDonald, C., & Zuroff, D. (1982). Dependency and self-criticism: Psychological dimensions of depression. *Journal of Consulting and Clinical Psychology, 50,* 113–124.

Blazer, D. (1990). *Emotional problems in later life.* New York: Springer.

Blazer, D. G. (2003). Depression in late life: Review and commentary. *Journal of Gerontology: Medical Sciences, 58A,* 249–265.

Bleuler, E. (1950). *Dementia praecox, or the group of schizophrenias* (J. Zinkin, Trans.). New York: International Universities Press. (Original work published 1911).

Bliwise, D. L. (2004). Sleep disorders in Alzheimer's disease and other dementias. *Clinical Cornerstone, 6* (1), S16–S28.

Bliwise, D. L. (2006). Periodic leg movements in sleep and restless legs syndrome: Considerations in geriatrics. *Sleep Medicine Clinics, 1,* 263–271.

Blonigen, D. M., Carlson, S. R., Krueger, R. F., & Patrick, C. J. (2003). A twin study of self-reported psychopathic personality traits. *Personality and Individual Differences, 35,* 179–197.

Blonigen, D. M., Hicks, B. M., Krueger, R. F., Patrick, C. J., & Iacono, W. G. (2005). Psychopathic personality traits: Heritability and genetic overlap with internalizing and externalizing psychopathology. *Psychological Medicine, 35,* 637–648.

Bloom, B. L. (1984). *Community mental health* (2nd ed.). Monterey, CA: Brooks/Cole.

Blum, H. P. (1991). Sadomasochism in the psychoanalytic process, within and beyond the pleasure principle: Discussion. *Journal of the American Psychoanalytic Association, 39,* 431–450.

Blumenthal, S. (1990, December 26). Youth suicide: The physician's role in suicide prevention. *Journal of the American Medical Association, 264,* 3194–3196.

Bockoven, J. S. (1963). *Moral treatment in American psychiatry.* New York: Springer.

Boelen, P. A., & Reijntjes, A. (2009). Intolerance of uncertainty and social anxiety. *Journal of Anxiety Disorders, 23,* 130–135.

Bögels, S. M., & Mansell, W. (2004). Attention processes in the maintenance and treatment of social phobia: Hypervigilance, avoidance and self-focused attention. *Clinical Psychology Review, 24,* 827–856.

Boggs, C. D., Morey, L. C., Skodol, A. E., Shea, M., Sanislow, C. A., Grilo, C. M., et al. (2005). Differential impairment as an indicator of sex bias in DSM-IV criteria for four personality disorders. *Psychological Assessment,17,* 492–496. doi:10.1037/1040-3590.17.4.492

Bohman, M., Sigvardsson, S., & Cloninger, C. R. (1981). Maternal inheritance of alcohol abuse: Cross-fostering analysis of adopted women. *Archives of General Psychiatry, 38,* 965–969.

Bohne, A., Keuthen, N. J., Wilhelm, S., Deckersbach, T., & Jenike, M. A. (2002). Prevalence of symptoms of body dysmorphic disorder and its correlates: A cross-cultural comparison. *Psychosomatics,43,* 486–490.

Bond, I., & Evans, D. (1967). Avoidance therapy: Its use in two cases of underwear fetishism. *Canadian Medical Association Journal, 96,* 1160–1162.

Bonnie, R., & Monahan, J. (2005). From coercion to contract: Reframing the debate on mandated community treatment for people with mental disorders. *Law & Human Behavior, 29,* 485–503.

Book, A. S., Quinsey, V. L., & Langford, D. (2007). Psychopathy and the perception of affect and vulnerability. *Criminal Justice and Behavior, 34,* 531–544. doi:10.1177/0093854806293554

Booth, T., & Booth, W. (1996). Sounds of silence: Narrative research with inarticulate subjects. *Disability and Society, 11,* 55–69.

Bootzin, R. R., & Perlis, M. L. (1992). Nonpharmacological treatments of insomnia. *Journal of Clinical Psychiatry, 53* (Suppl. 6), 37–41.

Borduin, C. M., Mann, B. J., Cone, L. T., Henggeler, S. W., Fucci, B. R., Blaske, D. M., & Williams, R. A. (1995). Multisystemic treatment of serious juvenile offenders: Long-term prevention of criminality and violence. *Journal of Consulting and Clinical Psychology, 63,* 569–578.

Borkovec, T. D., & Inz, J. (1990). The nature of worry in generalized anxiety disorder: A predominance of thought activity. *Behaviour Research and Therapy, 28,* 153–158.

Borkovec, T. D., & Hu, S. (1990). The effect of worry on cardiovascular response to phobic imagery. *Behaviour Research and Therapy, 28,* 69–73.

Borkovec, T. D., Lyonsfields, J. D., Wiser, S. L., & Deihl, L. (1993). The role of worrisome thinking in the suppression of cardiovascular response to phobic imagery. *Behaviour Research and Therapy, 31,* 321–324.

Borkovec, T. D., Ray, W. J., & Stober, J. (1998). Worry: A cognitive phenomenon intimately linked to affective, physiological, and interpersonal behavioral processes. *Cognitive Therapy and Research, 22,* 561–576.

Borkovec, T. D., & Roemer, L. (1995). Perceived functions of worry among generalized anxiety disorder subjects: Distraction from more emotionally distressing topics? *Journal of Behavior Therapy and Experimental Psychiatry, 26,* 25–30.

Bornovalova, M. A., Hicks, B. M., Iacono, W. G., & McGue, M. (2009). Stability, change, and heritability of borderline personality disorder traits from adolescence to adulthood: A longitudinal twin study. *Development and Psychopathology, 21,* 1335–1353. doi:10.1017/S0954579409990186

Bornstein, R. F. (2011). Toward a multidimensional model of personality disorder diagnosis: Implications for DSM-5. *Journal of Personality Assessment, 93,* 362–369. doi:10.1080/00223891.2011.577474

Bornstein, R. F., Klein, D. N., Mallon, J. C., & Slater, J. F. (1988). Schizotypal personality disorder in an outpatient population: Incidence and clinical characteristics. *Journal of Clinical Psychology, 44,* 322–325.

Borruto, F., Comparetto, C., Acanfora, L., Bertini, G., & Rubaltelli, F. F. (2002). Role of ultrasound evaluation of nuchal translucency in prenatal diagnosis. *Clinical Experimental Obstetrics & Gynecology, 29,* 235–241.

Borthwick-Duffy, S. A. (1994). Epidemiology and prevalence of psychopathology in people with mental retardation. *Journal of Consulting and Clinical Psychology, 62,* 17–27.

Boscarino, J. A. (1997). Diseases among men 20 years after exposure to severe stress: Implications for clinical research and medical care. *Psychosomatic Medicine, 59,* 605–614.

Bosch, J. A., de Geus, E. J. C., Ligtenberg, T. J. M., Nazmi, K., Veerman, E. C. I., Hoogstraten, J., & Amerongen, A. V. N. (2000). Salivary MUC5B-mediated adherence (Ex Vivo) of *Helicobacter pylori* during acute stress. *Psychosomatic Medicine, 62,* 40–49.

Botvin, G. J. (2000). *Life skills training.*Princeton, NJ: Princeton Health Press.

Botvin, G. J., Baker, E., Dusenbury, L., Botvin, E. M., & Diaz, T. (1995). Long-term follow-up results of a randomized drug abuse prevention trial in a white middle-class population. *Journal of the American Medical Association, 273* (14), 1106–1112.

Botvin, G. J., Baker, E., Dusenbury, L., Tortu, S., & Botvin, E. M. (1990). Preventing adolescent drug abuse through a multimodal cognitive-behavioral approach: Results of a three-year study. *Journal of Consulting and Clinical Psychology, 58,* 437–446.

Bouaboula, M., Rinaldi, M., Carayon, P., Carillon, C., Delpech, B., Shire, D., Le-Fur, G., & Casellas, P. (1993). Cannabinoid-receptor expression in human leukocytes. *European Journal of Biochemistry, 214* (1), 173–180.

Bouchard, C. (1994). Discours et parcours de la prévention de la violence: Une réflexion sur les valeurs en jeu. *Canadian Journal of Community Mental Health, 13* (2), 37–46.

Bouton, M. E., Mineka, S., & Barlow, D. H. (2001). A modern learning theory perspective on the etiology of panic disorder. *Psychological Bulletin, 108,* 4–32.

Bowden, S., Saklofske, D. H., & Weiss, L. G. (2011). Augmenting the core battery with supplementary subtests: Wechsler Adult Intelligence Scale-IV measurement invariance across the United States and Canada. *Assessment,18,* 133–140.

Bowen, R. C., Offord, D. R., & Boyle, M. H. (1990). The prevalence of overanxious disorder and separation anxiety disorder: Results from the Ontario Child Health Study. *Journal of the American Academy of Child and Adolescent Psychiatry, 29* (5), 753–758.

Bowlby, J. (1973). *Attachment and loss.* New York: Basic Books.

Bowlby, J. (1977). The making and breaking of affectional bonds: 1. Aetiology and psychopathology in the light of attachment theory. *British Journal of Psychiatry, 30,* 301–210.

Bowlby, J. (1988). *A secure base: Parent-child attachment and healthy human development.* New York: Basic Books.

Boylan, K., Vaillancourt, T., Boyle, M., & Szatmari, P. (2007). Comorbidity of internalizing disorders in children with oppositional defiant disorder. *European Journal of Child and Adolescent Psychiatry, 16* (8), 484–494.

Boyle, M., & Offord, D. (1990). Primary prevention of conduct disorder: Issues and prospects. *Journal of the American Academy of Child and Adolescent Psychiatry, 29,* 227–233.

Boyle, M. H., & Offord, D. R. (1991). Psychiatric disorder and substance use in adolescence. *Canadian Journal of Psychiatry, 36,* 699–705.

Braaten, E. B., Otto, S., & Handelsman, M. M. (1993). What do people want to know about psychotherapy? *Psychotherapy, 30,* 565–570.

Brabban, A., Tai, S., & Turkington, D. (2009). Predictors of outcome in brief cognitive behavior therapy for schizophrenia. *Schizophrenia Research, 35,* 859–864.

Braden, M. L. (1989). *Logo reading system.* Obtainable at 219 East St. Vrain, Colorado Springs, CO.

Bradford, J. M. (2000). The treatment of sexual deviation using a pharmacological approach. *Journal of Sex Research, 37,* 248–257.

Bradford, J. M. (2001). The neurobiology, neuropharmacology, and pharmacological treatment of paraphilias and compulsive sexual behavior. *Canadian Journal of Psychiatry, 46,* 26–34.

Bradley, E. A., Bolton, P. F., & Bryson, S. (2004). Psychiatric co-morbidity in persons with intellectual disabilities with and without autism. *Journal of Intellectual Disability Research, 48,* 296.

Bradley, E. A., & Summers, J. (2003). Developmental disability and behavioral, emotional and psychiatric disturbances. In I. Brown & M. Percy (Eds.), *Developmental disability in Ontario* (2nd ed., pp. 751–774). Toronto: Ontario Association on Developmental Disability.

Bradley, E. A., Summers, J., Brereton, A. V., Einfeld, S. L., Havercamp, S. M., Holt, G., et al. (2007). Intellectual disabilities and behavioural, emotional and psychiatric disturbances. In I. Brown & M. Percy (Eds.), *A comprehensive guide to intellectual and developmental disabilities* (pp. 645–666). London: Paul Brookes.

Bradley, S. J., & Zucker, K. J. (1997). Gender identity disorder: A review of the past 10 years. *Journal of the American Academy of Child and Adolescent Psychiatry, 36,* 872–880.

Braff, D. L., Freedman, R., Schork, N. J., & Gottesman, I. I. (2007). Deconstructing schizophrenia: An overview of the use of endophenotypes in order to understand a complex disorder. *Schizophrenia Bulletin, 33,* 21–32.

Bramon-Bosch, E., Troop, N., & Treasure, J. L. (2000). Eating disorders in males: A comparison with female patients. *European Eating Disorders Review, 8,* 321–328.

Brand, B. L., Classen, C. C., McNary, S. W., & Zaveri, P. (2009). A review of dissociative disorders treatment studies. *Journal of Nervous and Mental Disease, 197,* 646–654.

Braun, D. L., Sunday, S. R., Huang, A., & Halmi, K. A. (1999). More males seek treatment for eating disorders. *International Journal of Eating Disorders, 25,* 415–424.

Bremner, J. D. (1999). Does stress damage the brain? *Biological Psychiatry, 45,* 797–805.

Bremner, J. D. (2001). A biological model for delayed recall of childhood abuse. In J. J. Freyd & A. P. DePrince (Eds.), *Trauma and cognitive science: A meeting of minds, science, and human experience* (pp. 165–183). New York: Haworth Press.

Bremner, J. D., Randall, P., Vermetten, E., Staib, L., Bronen R. A., Mazure C., et al. (1997). Magnetic resonance imaging-based measurement of hippocampal volume in posttraumatic stress disorder related to childhood physical and sexual abuse: A preliminary report. *Biological Psychiatry, 41,* 23–32.

Brendgen, M., Vitaro, F., Boivin, M., Dionne, G., & Perusse, D. (2006). Genetic and environmental effects on reactive versus proactive aggression. *Developmental Psychology, 42,* 1299–1312.

Brent, D., Kales, R., Edelbrock, C., Costello, A. J., Dulcan, M. K., & Conover, N. (1996). Psychopathology and its relation to suicidal ideation in childhood and adolescence. *Journal of the American Academy of Child & Adolescent Psychiatry, 25,* 666–673.

Bresnahan, M., & Susser, E. (2003). Investigating socioenvironmental influences in schizophrenia: Conceptual and design issues. In R. M. Murray, P. B. Jones, E. Susser, J. Van Os, & M. Cannon (Eds.), *The epidemiology of schizophrenia* (pp. 5–17). Cambridge, UK: Cambridge University Press.

Breton, J. J., Bergeron, L., Valla, J. P., Berthiaume, C., Gaudet, N., Lambert, J., et al. (1999). Quebec child mental health survey: Prevalence of DSM-III-R mental health disorders. *Journal of Child Psychology and Psychiatry, 40,* 375–384.

Brewerton, T. D. (1995). Toward a unified theory of serotonin dysregulation in eating and related disorders. *Psychoneuroendocrinology, 20,* 561–590.

Brewerton, T. D. (2007). Eating disorders, trauma, and comorbidity: Focus on PTSD. *Eating Disorders: The Journal of Treatment & Prevention, 15,* 285–304.

Brewin, C. (2011). The nature and significance of memory disturbance in posttraumatic stress disorder. *Annual Review of Clinical Psychology, 7,* 203–227.

Brewin, C. R., Dalgleish, T., & Stephen, J. (1996). A dual representation theory of posttraumatic stress disorder. *Psychological Review, 103,* 670–686.

Brezo, J., Barker, E. D., Paris, J., Hebert, M., Vitaro, F., Tremblay, R. E., & Turecki, G. (2008). Childhood trajectories of anxiousness and disruptiveness as predictors of suicide attempts. *Archives of Pediatrics and Adolescent Medicine, 162* (11), 1015–1021. doi:10.1001/archpedi.162.11.1015

Brickner, R. M. (1934). An interpretation of frontal lobe function based upon the study of a case of partial bilateral frontal lobectomy. *Research and Publications of the Association for the Research of Nervous and Mental Disease, 13,* 259–351.

Brickner, R. M. (1936). *The intellectual functions of the frontal lobes.* New York: Macmillan.

Bridge, J. A., Iyengar, S., Salary, C. B., Barbe, R. P., Birmaher, B., Pincus, H. A., et al. (2007). Clinical response and risk for reported suicidal ideation and suicide attempts in pediatric antidepressant treatment: A meta-analysis of randomized controlled trials. *Journal of the American Medical Association, 297,* 1683–1696.

Briere, J., & Zaidi, L. Y. (1989). Sexual abuse histories and sequelae in female psychiatric emergency room patients. *American Journal of Psychiatry, 146,* 1602–1606.

Briken, P., Nika, E., & Berner, W. (2001). Treatment of paraphilia with luteinizing hormone-releasing hormone agonists. *Journal of Sex & Marital Therapy, 27,* 45–55.

Brink, J., Doherty, D., & Boer, A. (2001). Mental disorder in federal offenders: A Canadian prevalence study. *International Journal of Law and Psychiatry, 24,* 339–356.

Broadway, J., & Mintzer, J. (2007). The many faces of psychosis in the elderly. *Current Opinions in Psychiatry, 20,* 551–558.

Brodie, D. A. (1971). Stress ulcer as an experimental model of peptic ulcer disease. In C. J. Pfeiffer (Ed.), *Peptic ulcer* (pp. 71–83). Philadelphia: Lippincott.

Brody, N. (1992). *Intelligence* (2nd ed.). San Diego, CA: Academic Press.

Broekman, B. F. P., Olff, M., & Boer, F. (2007). The genetic background to PTSD. *Neuroscience & Biobehavioral Reviews, 31,* 348–362.

Bronfenbrenner, U. (1977). Ecology of the family as a context for human development: Research perspectives. *Developmental Psychology, 22,* 723–742.

Brotman, M. A., Schmajuk, M., Rich, B. A., Dickstein, D. P., Guyer, A. E., Costello, E. J., et al. (2006). Prevalence, clinical correlates, and longitudinal course of severe mood dysregulation in children. *Biological Psychiatry, 60,* 991–997. doi:10.1016/j.biopsych.2006.08.042

Brotto, L. A. (2010a). The DSM diagnostic criteria for hypoactive sexual desire disorder. *Archives of Sexual Behavior, 39,* 221–239.

Brotto, L. A. (2010b). The DSM criteria for sexual aversion disorder. *Archives of Sexual Behavior, 39,* 271–277.

Brower, M. C., & Price, B. H. (2001). Neuropsychiatry of frontal lobe dysfunction in violent and criminal behaviour: A critical review. *Journal of Neurology, Neurosurgery, and Psychiatry, 71,* 720–727.

Brown, G. K., Ten Have, T., Henriques, G. R., Xie, S. X., Hollander, J. E., & Beck, A. T. (2005). Cognitive therapy for the prevention of suicide attempts: A randomized controlled trial. *Journal of the American Medical Association, 294,* 563–570.

Brown, G. W., & Harris, T. O. (1989). Depression. In G. W. Brown & T. O. Harris (Eds.), *Life events and illness* (pp. 49–93). New York: Guilford Press.

Brown, G. W., Harris, T. O., & Bifulco, A. (1986). Long-term effects of early loss of parent. In M. Rutter, C. E. Izard, & P. B. Read (Eds.), *Depression in young people: Developmental and clinical perspectives* (pp. 251–298). New York: Guilford Press.

Brown, I., & Radford, J. P. (2007). Historical overview of intellectual and developmental disabilities. In I. Brown & M. Percy (Eds.), *A comprehensive guide to intellectual and developmental disabilities* (pp. 17–34). London: Paul Brookes.

Brown, J. (1985). Historical perspective on child abuse. In A. Downer (Ed.), *Prevention of child sexual abuse: A trainer's manual.* Seattle, WA: Seattle Institute for Child Advocacy Committee for Children.

Brown, R. I. (Ed.). (1997). *Quality of life for people with disabilities: Models, research and practice* (2nd ed.). Cheltenham, UK: Stanley Thornes.

Brown, R. I., & Brown, I. (2004). *Quality of life and disability: An approach for community practitioners.* London: Jessica Kingsley.

Brown, R. J., Cardena, E., Nijenhuis, E., Sar, V., & van der Hart, O. (2007). Should conversion disorder be reclassified as a dissociative disorder in DSM-V? *Psychosomatics, 48,* 369–378.

Brown, T. A., & Barlow, D. H. (2009). A proposal for a dimensional classification system based on shared features of the DSM-IV anxiety and mood disorders: Implications for assessment and treatment. *Psychological Assessment, 21,* 256–271.

Brown, T. A., O'Leary, T. A., & Barlow, D. H. (2001). Generalized anxiety disorder. In D. H. Barlow (Ed.), *Clinical handbook of psychological disorders* (3rd ed., pp. 154–208). New York: Guilford Press.

Browne, E. G. (1921). *Arabian medicine.* New York: Macmillan.

Brownell, K. D., & Fairburn, C. G. (Eds.). (1995). *Eating disorders and obesity: A comprehensive handbook.* New York: Guilford Press.

Brownmiller, S. (1975). *Against our will: Men, women, and rape.* New York: Bantam Books.

Bruce, K., & Steiger, H. (2006). Prognostic implications of personality disorders in eating disorders. In R. A. Sansone & J. L. Levitt (Eds.), *Personality disorders and eating disorders: Exploring the frontier* (pp. 247–262). New York: Routledge.

Bruce, K. R., Steiger, H., Ng Yin Kin, N. M. K., & Israel, M. (2006). Reduced platelet [^{3}H]paroxetine binding in anorexia nervosa: Relationship to eating symptoms and personality pathology. *Psychiatry Research, 142,* 225–232.

Bruce, M. L., Takeuchi, D. T., & Leaf, P. J. (1991). Poverty and psychiatric status: Longitudinal evidence from the New Haven Epidemiologic Catchment Area Study. *Archives of General Psychiatry, 48,* 470–474.

Bruch, H. (1978). *The golden cage.* Cambridge, MA: Harvard University Press.

Bruininks, R. H., Woodcock, R. W., Weatherman, R. F., & Hill, B. K. (1996). *The Scales of Independent Behavior—Revised.* Itasca, IL: Riverside.

Brunner, R., Henze, R., Parzer, P., Kramer, J., Feigl, N., Lutz, K., et al. (2010). Reduced prefrontal and orbitofrontal gray matter in female adolescents with borderline personality disorder: Is it disorder specific? *Neuroimage, 49,* 114–120. doi:10.1016/j.neuroimage.2009.07.070

Bryan, S., & Walsh, P. (2003). Physical activity and obesity in Canadian women. In Canadian Institute for Health Information, *Women's Health Surveillance Report.*

Bryan, T., Burstein, K., & Ergul, C. (2004). The social-emotional side of learning disabilities: A science-based presentation of the state of the art. *Learning Disability Quarterly, 27,* 45–51.

Bryant, R. A., & Das, P. (2011). The neural circuitry of conversion disorder and its recovery. *Journal of Abnormal Psychology.* Advance online publication. doi:10.1037/a0025076

Bryer, J. B., Nelson, B. A., Miller, J. B., & Krol, P. K. (1987). Childhood sexual and physical abuse as factors in adult psychiatric illness. *American Journal of Psychiatry, 144,* 1426–1430.

Bryson, S. E. (1996). Brief report: Epidemiology of autism. *Journal of Autism and Developmental Disorders, 26,* 165–167.

Buchanan, R. W., & Carpenter, W. T. (2000). Schizophrenia: Introduction and overview. In B. J. Sadock & V. A. Sadock (Eds.), *Kaplan and Sadock's comprehensive textbook of psychiatry* (7th ed., Vol. 1, pp. 1096–1110). Philadelphia: Lippincott Williams & Wilkins.

Budney, A. J., Moore, B. A., Vandrey, R. G., & Hughes, J. R. (2003). The time course and significance of cannabis withdrawal. *Journal of Abnormal Psychology, 112,* 393–402.

Buhin, L., & Vera, E. (2009). Preventing racism and promoting social justice: Person-centered and environment-centered interventions. *Journal of Primary Prevention, 30,* 43–59.

Bukatko, D., & Daehler, M. W. (2012). *Child development: A thematic approach* (6th ed.). Belmont, CA: Wadsworth.

Bulik, C. M., Berkman, N. D., Brownley, K. A., Sedway, J. A., & Lohr, K. N. (2007). Anorexia nervosa treatment: A systematic review of randomized controlled trials. *International Journal of Eating Disorders, 40,* 310–320.

Bulik, C. M., & Kendler, K. S. (2000). I am what I (don't) eat: Establishment of an identity independent of an eating disorder. *American Journal of Psychiatry, 157,* 1755–1760.

Bullough, V. L. (1976). *Sexual variance in society and history.* Chicago: University of Chicago Press.

Bulmash, E., Harkness, K. L., Stewart, J. G., & Bagby, R. M. (2009). Personality, stressful life events, and treatment response in major depression. *Journal of Consulting and Clinical Psychology, 77,* 1067–1077.

Burke, J. D., Loeber, R., & Birmaher, B. (2002). Oppositional defiant disorder and conduct disorder: A review of the past 10 years, Part II. *Journal of the Academy of Child and Adolescent Psychiatry, 41* (11), 1275–1293.

Burmeister, M., McInnis, M. G., & Zöllner, S. (2008). Psychiatric genetics: Progress amid controversy. *Nature Reviews Genetics, 9,* 527–540.

Burns, J. F. (2010, May 25). British Medical Council bars doctor who linked vaccine with autism. *The New York Times,* p. A4.

Burns, M. K., Jacob, S., & Wagner, A. R. (2008). Ethical and legal issues associated with using response-to-intervention to assess learning disabilities. *Journal of School Psychology, 46,* 263–279.

Butcher, J. N. (2010). Personality assessment from the nineteenth to the early twenty-first century: Past achievements and contemporary challenges. *Annual Review of Clinical Psychology, 6,* 1–20.

Butcher, J. N., Atlis, M. M., & Hahn, J. (2004). The Minnesota Multiphasic Personality Inventory-2 (MMPI-2). In M. Hersen (Series Ed.), M. J. Hilsenroth & D. L. Segal (Vol. Eds.), *Comprehensive handbook of psychological assessment: Vol. 2. Personality assessment* (pp. 30–38). Hoboken, NJ: Wiley.

Butcher, J. N., Dahlstrom, W. G., Graham, J. R., Tellegen, A., & Kaemmer, B. (1989). *Minnesota Multiphasic Personality Inventory: MMPI-2: Manual for administration and scoring.* Minneapolis: University of Minnesota Press.

Butcher, J. N., Mineka, S., Hooley, J. M., Taylor, S., & Antony, M. M. (2010). *Abnormal Psychology,* Canadian Edition (pp 122–123).

Butcher, J. N., Williams, C. L., Graham, J. R., Archer, R., Tellegen, A., Ben-Porath, Y. S., & Kaemmer, B. (1992). *MMPI-A: Manual for administration, scoring, and interpretation.* Minneapolis: University of Minnesota Press.

Butler, A. C., Chapman, J. E., Forman, E. M., & Beck, A. T. (2006). The empirical status of cognitive-behavioral therapy: A review of meta-analyses. *Clinical Psychology Review, 26,* 17–31.

Butler-Jones, D. (2010). *The Chief Public Health Officer's report on the state of public health in Canada: Growing older—adding life to years.* Retrieved from http://publichealth.gc.ca/CPHOreport

Butt, P., Beirness, D., Cesa, F., Gliksman, L., Paradis, C., & Stockwell, T. (in press). *Alcohol and health in Canada: A summary of evidence and guidelines for low risk drinking.* Ottawa: Canadian Centre on Substance Abuse.

Buttner, G., & Hasselhorn, M. (2011). Learning disabilities: Debates on definitions, causes, subtypes, and responses. *International Journal of Disability, Development and Education, 58* (1), 75–87.

Byer, C., Shainberg, L., & Galliano, G. (2002). *Dimensions of human sexuality.* New York: McGraw-Hill.

Byers, A. L., Yaffe, K., Covinsky, K. E., Friedman, M. B., & Bruce, M. L. (2010). High occurrence of mood and anxiety disorders among older adults: The National Comorbidity Survey Replication. *Archives of General Psychiatry, 67* (5), 489–496.

Byers, E. S., & Grenier, G. (2003). Premature or rapid ejaculation: Heterosexual couples' perceptions of men's ejaculatory behavior. *Archives of Sexual Behavior, 32* (3), 261–270.

Byers, E. S., Henderson, J., & Hobson, K. M. (2009). University students' definitions of sexual abstinence and having sex. *Archives of Sexual Behavior, 38,* 665–674.

Byers, E. S., Price, L., & Dating Violence Research Team. (1997). A multidisciplinary collaborative approach to understanding dating violence. In J. Proulx & W. Josephson (chairs), *Dating violence research in Canada: Problem, projects, prevention.* Symposium presented at the meeting of the Canadian Psychological Association, Toronto. [Abstract published in *Canadian Psychology, 38,* 137–138.]

Byrne, S. M., Fursland, A., Allen, K. L., & Watson, H. (2011). The effectiveness of enhanced cognitive behavioural therapy for eating disorders: An open trial. *Behaviour Research and Therapy, 49,* 219–226.

Cacioppo, J. T., & Berntson, G. G. (1992). Social psychological contributions to the decade of the brain. *American Psychologist, 47,* 1019–1028.

Cairney, J., Corna, L. M., & Streiner, D. L. (2010). Health care use in later life: Results from a national survey of Canadians. *Canadian Journal of Psychiatry, 55* (3), 157–164.

Cairney, J., Corna, L. M., Veldhuizen, S., Herrmann, N., & Streiner, D. L. (2008). Comorbid depression and anxiety in later life: Patterns of association, subjective well-being, and impairment. *American Journal of Geriatric Psychiatry, 16,* 201–208.

Cairney, J., McCabe, L., Veldhuizen, S., Corna, L. M., Streiner, D., & Herrmann, N. (2007). Epidemiology of social phobia in later life. *American Journal of Geriatric Psychiatry, 15,* 224–233.

Cairns, J. C., Styles, L. D., & Leichner, P. (2007). Evaluation of meal support training for parents and caregivers using a video and a manual. *Journal of the Canadian Academy of Child and Adolescent Psychiatry, 16,* 164–166.

Cairns, R. B., Cairns, B. D., Neckerman, H. J., Gest, S. D., & Gariepy, J. L. (1988). Social networks and aggressive behaviour: Peer support or peer rejection? *Developmental Psychology, 24,* 815–823.

Cairo, T. A., Woodward, T. S., & Ngan, E. T. C. (2006). Decreased encoding efficiency in schizophrenia. *Biological Psychiatry, 59,* 740–746.

Caldwell, A. (1978). History of psychopharmacology. In W. G. Clark & J. del Giudice (Eds.), *Principles of psychopharmacology* (2nd ed., pp. 9–40). New York: Academic Press.

Calmes, C. A., & Roberts, J. E. (2007). Repetitive thought and emotional distress: Rumination and worry as prospective predictors of depressive and anxious symptomatology. *Cognitive Therapy and Research, 30,* 343–356.

Camara, W. J., Nathan, J. S., & Puente, A. E. (2000). Psychological test usage: Implications for professional psychology. *Professional Psychology: Research and Practice, 31,* 141–154.

Cambor, R., & Millman, R. B. (1991). Alcohol and drug abuse in adolescence. In M. Lewis (Ed.), *Child and adolescent psychiatry: A comprehensive textbook* (pp. 736–754). Baltimore: Williams & Wilkins.

Camilli, G., Vargas, S., Ryan, S., & Barnett, W. S. (2010). Meta-analysis of the effects of early education interventions on cognitive and social development. *Teachers College Record, 112,* 579–620.

Campbell, E. (1990). The psychopath and the definition of "mental disease of defect" under the Model Penal Code test of insanity: A question of psychology or a question of law? *Nebraska Law Review, 69,* 190–229.

Campbell, M., Adams, P., Small, A. M., Kafantaris, V., Silva, R. R., Shell, J., et al. (1995). Lithium in hospitalized aggressive children with conduct disorder: A double-blind and placebo-controlled study. *Journal of the American Academy of Child and Adolescent Psychiatry, 34,* 397–534.

Campbell, M. A. (2003). The relative contribution of psychopathy and traditional risk factors in predicting young offender recidivism. Unpublished doctoral dissertation. Dalhousie University, Halifax, NS.

Campbell, M. A., Porter, S., & Santor, D. (2004). Psychopathic traits in adolescent offenders: An evaluation of criminal history, clinical, and psychosocial correlates. *Behavioral Sciences and the Law, 22,* 23–47.

Canadian Association for Suicide Prevention. (2004). *Blueprint for a Canadian national suicide prevention strategy.* Edmonton, AB: Author.

Canadian Association for Suicide Prevention. (2009). *The CASP blueprint for a Canadian national suicide prevention strategy* (2nd ed.).Edmonton, AB: Author.

Canadian Centre on Substance Abuse. (2004a). *Canadian Addiction Survey (CAS) highlights.* Ottawa: Canadian Centre on Substance Abuse.

Canadian Centre on Substance Abuse. (2004b). *Needle exchange programs (NEPs): FAQs.* Ottawa: Canadian Centre on Substance Abuse.

Canadian Institute for Health Information. (2008). *Hospital mental health services in Canada, 2005–2006.* Ottawa: Author.

Canadian Institute for Health Information. (2009). *Improving the health of Canadians: Exploring positive mental health.*Ottawa: Author.

Canadian Medical Association. (2008). *8th Annual National Report Card on Health Care.* Ipsos Reid Public Affairs. Retrieved from http://www.cma.ca/multimedia/CMA/Content_Images/Inside_cma/Annual_Meeting/2008/GC_Bulletin/National_Report_Card_EN.pdf

Canadian Psychological Association. (2000). *Canadian code of ethics for psychologists* (3rd ed.). Ottawa: Canadian Psychological Association.

Canadian Psychological Association. (2009, August 4). *Canadian Psychological Association (CPA) position on publication and dissemination of psychological tests.* Retrieved from http://www.cpa.ca/cpasite/userfiles/Documents/Practice_Page/2009_CPAPsychologicaltest_statement.pdf

Canadian Psychological Association Task Force on Prescriptive Authority for Psychologists in Canada. (2010). *Report to the Canadian Psychological Association Board of Directors.* Retrieved from http://www.cpa.ca

Canadian Study of Health and Aging Working Group. (1994). Canadian Study of Health and Aging: Study methods and prevalence of dementia. *Canadian Medical Association Journal, 150,* 899–912.

Cannon, M., Jones, P. B., & Murray, R. M. (2002). Obstetric complications and schizophrenia: Historical and meta-analytic review. *American Journal of Psychiatry, 159,* 1080–1092.

Cannon, W. B. (1942). "Voodoo" death. *American Anthropologist, 44,* 169.

Cantor, J. (2000). Media violence. *Journal of Adolescent Health, 27* (2), 30–34.

Cantor-Graae, E. (2007). The contribution of social factors to the development of schizophrenia: A review of recent findings. *Canadian Journal of Psychiatry, 52,* 277–286.

Cantwell, D. P. (1996). Classification of child and adolescent psychopathology. *Journal of Child Psychology and Psychiatry and Allied Disciplines, 37,* 3–12.

Cantwell, D. P., Baker, L., & Rutter, M. (1978). Family factors in the syndrome of infantile autism. In M. Rutter & E. Schopler (Eds.), *Autism: A reappraisal of concepts and treatment.* New York: Plenum Press.

Caplan, G. (1964). *Principles of preventive psychiatry.* New York: Basic Books.

Carey, G. (1992). Twin imitation for antisocial behaviour: Implications for genetic and family environment research. *Journal of Abnormal Psychology, 101* (1), 18–25.

Carlat, D. J., Camargo, C. A., Jr., & Herzog, D. B. (1997). Eating disorders in males: A report on 135 patients. *American Journal of Psychiatry, 154,* 1127–1132.

Carlson, E. A. (1998). A prospective longitudinal study of attachment disorganization/disorientation. *Child Development, 69,* 1107–1128.

Carlson, E. A., Yates, T. M., & Sroufe, L. A. (2009). Dissociation and development of the self. In P. F. Dell & J. A. O'Neil (Eds.), *Dissociation and the dissociative disorders: DSM-V and beyond* (pp. 39–52). New York: Routledge.

Carlson, E. N., Vazire, S., & Oltmanns, T. F. (2011). You probably think this paper's about you: Narcissists' perceptions of their personality and reputation. *Journal of Personality and Social Psychology, 101,* 185–201. doi:10.1037/a0023781

Carmody, J., Baer, R. A., Lykins, E. L. B., & Olendzki, N. (2009). An empirical study of the mechanisms of mindfulness in a mindfulness-based stress reduction program. *Journal of Clinical Psychology, 65,* 613–626.

Carnes, P. (1983). *Out of the shadows: Understanding sexual addiction.* Minneapolis, MN: Compcare.

Carnes, P. (1989). *Contrary to love: Helping the sex addict.* Minneapolis, MN: Compcare.

Carney, R. M., Freedland, K. E., Rich, M. W., & Jaffe, A. S. (1995). Depression as a risk factor for cardiac events in established coronary heart disease: A review of possible mechanisms. *Annals of Behavioral Medicine, 17,* 142–149.

Carney, S., Cowen, P., Dearness, K., Eastaugh, J., Freemantle, N., Geddes, J., et al. (2003). Efficacy and safety of electroconvulsive therapy in depressive disorders: A review. *The Lancet, 361,* 9360.

Caron, J., & Liu, A. (2010). A descriptive study of the prevalence of psychological distress and mental disorders in the Canadian population: Comparison between low-income and non-low-income populations. *Chronic Diseases in Canada, 30,* 84–94.

Carr, E. G., Horner, R. H., Turnbull, A. P., Marquis, J. G., Magito-McLaughlin, D., McAtee, M. L., et al. (1999). *Positive behavior support for people with developmental disabilities: A research synthesis* [Monograph]. Washington, DC: American Association on Mental Retardation.

Carroll, R. A. (2007). Gender dysphoria and transgender experiences. In S. R. Leiblum (Ed.), *Principles and practices of sex therapy* (4th ed., pp. 477–508). New York: Guilford Press.

Carstensen, L. L. (2006). The influence of a sense of time on human development. *Science, 312,* 1913–1915.

Carstensen, L. L., Isaacowitz, D. M., & Charles, S. T. (1999). Taking time seriously: A theory of socioemotional selectivity. *The American Psychologist, 54,* 165–181.

Carter, A. S., Wagmiller, R. J., Gray, S. A. O., McCarthy, K. J., Horwitz, S. M., & Briggs-Gowan, M. J. (2010). Prevalence of DSM-IV disorder in a representative, healthy birth cohort at school entry: Sociodemographic risks and social adaptation. *Journal of the American Academy of Child & Adolescent Psychiatry,49* (7), 686–698. doi:10.1097/00004583-201007000-00009

Carter, J. C. (2002). Self-help books in the treatment of eating disorders. In C. G. Fairburn & K. D. Brownell (Eds.), *Eating disorders and obesity* (pp. 358–361). New York: Guilford Press.

Carter, J. C., Bewell, C., Blackmore, E., & Woodside, D. B. (2006). The impact of childhood sexual abuse in anorexia nervosa. *Child Abuse & Neglect, 30,* 257–269.

Carter J. C., & Fairburn, C. G. (1998). Cognitive-behavioral self-help for binge eating disorder: A controlled effectiveness study. *Journal of Consulting and Clinical Psychology, 66,* 616–623.

Carter, J. C., Olmsted, M. P., Kaplan, A. S., McCabe, R. E., Mills, J. S., & Aimé, A. (2003). Self-help for bulimia nervosa: A randomized controlled trial. *American Journal of Psychiatry, 160,* 973–978.

Cartwright-Hatton, S., Roberts, C., Chitsabesan, P., Fothergill, C., & Harrington, R. (2004). Systematic review of the efficacy of cognitive behaviour therapies for childhood and adolescent anxiety disorders. *British Journal of Clinical Psychology, 43,* 421–436.

Caruso, S., Intelisano, G., Lupo, L., & Agnello, C. (2001). Premenopausal women affected by sexual arousal disorder treated with sildenafil: A double-blind, cross-over, placebo-controlled study. *British Journal of Gynaecology, 108,* 623–628.

Carver, C. (1998). Premature ejaculation: A common and treatable concern. *Journal of the American Nurses Psychiatric Association, 4* (6), 199–204.

Case, R. B., Moss, A. J., Case, N., McDermott, M., & Eberly, S. (1992). Living alone after myocardial infarction: Impact on prognosis. *Journal of the American Medical Association, 267,* 515–519.

Cash, F., Morrow, J. A., Hrabosky, J. I., & Perry, A. A. (2004). How has body image changed? A cross-sectional investigation of college women and men from 1983 to 2001. *Journal of Consulting and Clinical Psychology, 72,* 1081–1089.

Caspi, A., McClay, J., Moffitt, T. E., Mill, J., Martin, J., Craig, I. W., et al. (2002). Role of genotype in the cycle of violence in maltreated children. *Science, 297,* 851–854.

Caspi, A., Moffitt, T. E., Cannon, M., McClay, J., Murray, R., Harrington, H., et al. (2005). Moderation of the effect of adolescent-onset cannabis use on adult psychosis by a functional polymorphism in the Catechol-O-Methyltransferase gene: Longitudinal evidence of a gene x environment interaction. *Biological Psychiatry, 57,* 1117–1127.

Caspi, A., Moffitt, T. E., Newman, D. L., & Silva, P. A. (1996). Behavioral observations at age 3 predict adult psychiatric disorders: Longitudinal evidence from a birth cohort. *Archives of General Psychiatry, 53,* 1033–1039.

Caspi, A., Sugden, K., Moffitt, T. E., Taylor, A., Craig, I. W., Harrington, H., et al. (2003). Influence of life stress on depression: Moderation by a polymorphism in the 5-HTT gene. *Science, 301,* 386–389.

Cassin, S. E., Singer, A. R., Dobson, K. S., & Altmaier, E. M. (2007). Professional interests and career aspirations of graduate students in professional psychology: An exploratory study. *Training and Education in Professional Psychology, 1,* 26–37.

Cassin, S. E., von Ranson, K. M., Heng, K., Brar, J., & Wojtowicz, A. E. (2008). Adapted motivational interviewing for women with binge eating disorder: A randomized controlled trial. *Psychology of Addictive Behaviors, 22,* 417–435.

Castle, D. J., & Rossell, S. L. (2006). An update on body dysmorphic disorder. *Current Opinion in Psychiatry, 19,* 74–78.

Cawley, R. (1974). Psychotherapy and obsessional disorders. In H. R. Beech (Ed.), *Obsessional states* (pp. 259–290). London: Methuen.

CCSMH. (2006a). Canadian Coalition for Seniors Mental Health national guidelines for seniors' mental health: Assessment of suicide risk and prevention of suicide. Retrieved from http://ccsmh.ca/en/natlguidelines/initiative.cfm

CCSMH. (2006b). Canadian Coalition for Seniors Mental Health national guidelines for seniors' mental health: The assessment and treatment of depression. Retrieved from http://ccsmh.ca/en/natlguidelines/initiative.cfm

CCSMH. (2006c). Canadian Coalition for Seniors Mental Health national guidelines for seniors' mental health: The assessment and treatment of delirium. Retrieved from http://ccsmh.ca/en/natlguidelines/initiative.cfm

Centers for Disease Control. (1992). *Youth suicide prevention program: A resource guide.* Atlanta, GA: Author.

Centers for Disease Control. (2011). Quitting smoking among adults: United States 2001–2010. *Morbidity and Mortality Weekly Report, 60,* 1513–1519.

Chadwick, P., Birchwood, M., & Trower, P. (1996). *Cognitive therapy for delusions, voices, and paranoia.* West Sussex, UK: John Wiley & Sons.

Chamberland, C., Dallaire, N., Lindsay, J., Hébert, J., Fréchette, L., Beaudoin, G., & Cameron, S. (1998). Les conditions de réussite en prévention hr/promotion en enfance-famille-jeunesse: Une question de justification et de faisabilité. *Revue Canadienne de Santé Mentale Communautaire, 17* (1), 37–59.

Chambless, D. L., & Ollendick, T. H. (2001). Empirically supported psychological interventions: Controversies and evidence. *Annual Review of Psychology, 52,* 685–716.

Chambless, D. L., Sanderson, W. C., Shoham, V., Johnson, S. B., Pope, K. S., Crits-Christoph, P., et al. (1996). An update on empirically validated therapies. *The Clinical Psychologist, 49* (2), 5–18.

Champion, H., & Furnham, A. (1999). The effect of the media on body satisfaction in adolescent girls. *European Eating Disorders Review, 7,* 213–228.

Chan, R. C., Xu, T., Heinrichs, R. W., Yu, Y., & Wang, Y. (2010). Neurological soft signs in schizophrenia: A meta-analysis. *Schizophrenia Bulletin, 36,* 1089–1104.

Chandler, J. J., & Lalonde, C. (1998). Cultural continuity as a hedge against suicide in Canada's First Nations. *Transcultural Psychiatry, 35,* 191–219.

Chang, S. M., Hahm, B., Lee, J., Shin, M. S., Jeon, H. J., Hong, J., Lee, H. B., Lee, D., & Cho, M. J. (2008). Cross-national difference in the prevalence of depression caused by the diagnostic threshold. *Journal of Affective Disorders, 106,* 159–167.

Chapman, R. J., & Hesketh, L. (2000). Behavioral phenotype of individuals with Down syndrome. *Mental Retardation and Developmental Disabilities Research Reviews, 6*, 84–95.

Charavustra, A., & Cloitre, M. (2008). Social bonds and posttraumatic stress disorder. *Annual Review of Psychology, 59*, 301–328.

Charles, S. T. (2010). Strength and vulnerability integration: A model of emotional well-being across adulthood. *Psychological Bulletin, 136* (6), 1068–1091.

Charles, S. T., & Piazza, J. R. (2009). Strength and vulnerability across the lifespan: An integration of literature on aging, emotional well-being and emotion regulation. *Social and Personality Psychology Compass, 3* (5),711–724.

Charney, D. S., Barlow, D. H., Botteron, K., Cohen, J. D., Goldman, S., Gur, R. E., et al. (2002). Neuroscience research agenda to guide development of a pathophysiologically based classification system. In D. J Kupfer, M. B. First, & D. A. Regier (Eds.), *A research agenda for DSM-V* (pp. 31–83). Washington, DC: American Psychiatric Association.

Chatfield, J. (2002). AAP guideline on treatment of children with ADHD. *American Family Physician, 65*, 726–728.

Cheetham, T., Gitta, M., & Morrison, B. (2003). Some common syndromes associated with developmental disabilities. In I. Brown & M. Percy (Eds.), *Developmental disabilities in Ontario* (2nd ed., pp. 145–170). Toronto: Ontario Association on Developmental Disabilities.

Chen, Y., Nettles, M. E., & Chen, S. (2009). Rethinking dependent personality disorder: Comparing different human relatedness in cultural contexts. *Journal of Nervous and Mental Disease, 197*, 793–800. doi:10.1097/NMD.0b013e3181be76ae

Cheung, R., & Okazaki, S. (1991). Counseling Americans of Southeast Asian descent: The impact of the refugee experience. In C. C. Lee & B. L. Richardson (Eds.), *Multicultural issues in counseling: New approaches to diversity* (pp. 107–126). Alexandria: American Association for Counseling and Development.

Chida, Y., & Mao, X. (2009). Does psychological stress predict symptomatic herpes simplex virus recurrence? A meta-analytic investigation on prospective studies. *Brain, Behavior and Immunity*, *23*, 917–925.

Chida, Y., & Steptoe, A. (2009). The association of anger and hostility with future coronary heart disease: A meta-analytic review of prospective evidence. *Journal of the American College of Cardiology, 53*, 936–946.

Chien, H., Ku, C., Lu, R., Chu, H., Tao, Y., & Chou, K. (2003). Effects of social skills training on improving social skills of patients with schizophrenia. *Archives of Psychiatric Nursing, 1(5)*, 228–236.

Children's Health Policy Centre. (2010). Preventing substance abuse in children and youth. *Children's Mental Health Research Quarterly, 4* (2), 1–16.

Chiswick, D. (1992). Compulsory treatment of patients with psychopathic disorder: An abnormally aggressive or seriously irresponsible exercise. *Criminal Behavior and Mental Health, 2*, 106–113.

Chivers, M. L., & Bailey, J. M. (2005). A sex difference in features that elicit genital response. *Biological Psychology, 70*, 115–120. doi:10.1016/j.biopsycho.2004.12.002

Chivers, M. L., Reiger, G., Latty, E., & Bailey, J. M. (2004). A sex difference in the specificity of sexual arousal. *Psychological Science, 15*, 736–744.

Chivers, M. L., Seto, M. C., & Blanchard, R. (2007). Gender and sexual orientation differences in sexual response to sexual activities versus gender of actors in sexual films. *Journal of Personality and Social Psychology, 93*, 1108–1121. doi:10.1037/0022-3514.93.6.1108

Chivers, M. L., Seto, M. C., Lalumière, M. L., Laan, E., & Grimbos, T. (2010). Agreement of self-reported and genital measures of sexual arousal in men and women: A meta-analysis. *Archives of Sexual Behavior, 39*, 5–56. doi:10.1007/s10508-009-9556-9

Chodosh, J., Kado, D. M., Seeman, T. E., & Karlamangla, A. S. (2007). Depressive symptoms as a predictor of cognitive decline: MacArthur studies of successful aging. *American Journal of Geriatric Psychiatry, 15*, 406–415.

Chong, S. L., & Siegel, L. S. (2008). Stability of computational deficits in math learning disability from second through fifth grades. *Developmental Neuropsychology. Special Issue: Mathematics ability, performance, and achievement, 33*, 300–317.

Chou, K-L. (2009). Age at onset of generalized anxiety disorder in older adults. *American Journal of Geriatric Psychiatry, 17*, 455–464.

Chou, K-L., Mackenzie, C. S., Liang, K., & Sareen, J. (2011). Three-year incidence and predictors of first onset of DSM-IV mood, anxiety, and substance disorders in older adults: Results from Wave 2 of the National Epidemiologic Survey of Alcohol and Related Conditions. *Journal of Clinical Psychiatry, 72* (2), 144–155.

Choy, Y., Fyer, A. J., & Lipsitz, J. D. (2007). Treatment of specific phobia in adults. *Clinical Psychology Review, 27*, 266–286.

Christianson, S., Forth, A. E., Hare, R. D., Strachan, C., Lidberg, L., & Thorell, L. (1996). Remembering details of emotional events: A comparison between psychopathic and nonpsychopathic offenders. *Personality and Individual Differences, 20*, 437–443.

Chronis-Tuscano, A., Degnan, K. A., Pine, D. S., Perez-Edgar, K., Henderson, H. A., Diaz, Y., et al. (2009). Stable early maternal report of behavioral inhibition predicts lifetime social anxiety disorder in adolescence. *Journal of the American Academy of Child & Adolescent Psychiatry, 48* (9), 928–935. doi:10.1097/CHI.0b013e3181ae09df

Chrousos, G. P., & Kino, T. (2007). Glucocorticoid action networks and complex psychiatric and/or somatic disorders. *Stress: The International Journal on the Biology of Stress, 10*, 213–219.

Chudley, A. E., Conry, J., Cook, J. L., Loock, C., Rosales, T., & LeBlanc, N. (2005). Fetal alcohol spectrum disorder: Canadian guidelines for diagnosis. *Canadian Medical Association Journal, 172* (5, Suppl.), S1–S21.

Chugani, D. C. (2002). Role of altered brain serotonin mechanisms in autism. *Molecular Psychiatry, 7* (Suppl. 2), S16–S17.

Cicchetti, D., & Beeghly, M. (1990). *Children with Down syndrome: A developmental perspective.* New York: Cambridge University Press.

Clark, D. A., & Beck, A. T. (1999). *Scientific foundations of cognitive theory and therapy of depression.* New York: John Wiley & Sons.

Clark, D. A., & Beck, A. T. (2010a). Cognitive theory and therapy of anxiety and depression: Convergence with neurobiological findings. *Trends in Cognitive Sciences, 14*, 418–424.

Clark, D. A., & Beck, A. T. (2010b). *Cognitive therapy of anxiety disorders: Science and practice.* New York: Guilford Press.

Clark, D. A., Beck, A. T., & Alford, B. A. (1999). *Scientific foundations of cognitive theory and therapy of depression.* Philadelphia: Wiley.

Clark, D. A., & Purdon, C. (2009). Mental control of unwanted intrusive thoughts: A phenomenological study of nonclinical individuals. *International Journal of Cognitive Therapy, 2*, 267–281.

Clark, D. B., Birmaher, B., Axelson, D., Monk, K., Kalas, C., Ehmann, M., et al. (2005). Fluoxetine for the treatment of childhood anxiety disorders: Open-label, long-term extension to a controlled trial. *Journal of the American Academy of Child and Adolescent Psychiatry, 44* (12), 1263–1270.

Clark, D. M. (1986). A cognitive approach to panic. *Behaviour Research and Therapy, 24*, 461–470.

Clark, D. M. (1996). Panic disorder and social phobia. In D. M. Clark & C. G. Fairburn (Eds.), *Science and practice of cognitive-behaviour therapy* (pp. 119–154). New York: Oxford University Press.

Clark, E., Lutke, J., Minnes, P., & Ouellette-Kuntz, H. (2004). Secondary disabilities among adults with fetal alcohol spectrum disorder in British Columbia. *Journal of Fetal Alcohol Syndrome International, 2*, 1–12.

Clark, L., & Lewis, D. (1977). *Rape: The price of coercive sexuality.* Toronto: Women's Educational Press.

Clarkin, J. F., & Carpenter, D. (1995). Family therapy in historical perspective. In B. Bongar & L. E. Beutler (Eds.), *Comprehensive textbook of psychotherapy: Theory and practice* (pp. 205–227). New York: Oxford University Press.

Cleckley, H. (1941). *The mask of sanity*. St. Louis, MO: Mosby.

Clement, U. (2002). Sex in long-term relationships: A systemic approach to sexual desire problems. *Archives of Sexual Behavior, 31* (3), 241–246.

Cloitre, M. (2009). Effective psychotherapies for posttraumatic stress disorder: A review and critique. *CNS Spectrums, 14*, 32–43.

Cloninger, C. R., Svrakic, D. M., & Przybeck, T. (1993). Psychobiological model of temperament and character. *Archives of General Psychiatry, 50*, 975–990.

Cobham, V. E., Dadds, M. R., & Spence, S. H. (1998). The role of parental anxiety in the treatment of childhood anxiety. *Journal of Consulting and Clinical Psychology, 66*, 893–905. doi:0022-006X/98

Coccaro, E. F. (1996). Neurotransmitter correlates of impulsive aggression in humans. *Annals of the New York Academy of Sciences, 794*, 82–89.

Cohen, K. R., Hunsley, J., Westmacott, R., & Flear, N. (2008). *Development and implementation of an electronic practice network for mental health surveillance in Canada.* Winnipeg: Public Health Agency of Canada.

Cohen, N. (2009, July 28). A Rorschach cheat sheet on Wikipedia. *The New York Times*, p. A1.

Cohen, P., Cohen, J., & Brook, J. (1993). An epidemiology study of disorder in late childhood and adolescence: II. Persistence of disorder. *Journal of Child Psychology and Psychiatry, 34*, 869–877.

Cohen, P., Crawford, T. N., Johnson, J. G., & Kasen, S. (2005). The children in the community study of developmental course of personality disorder. *Journal of Personality Disorders, 19*, 466–486.

Cohen, S., Frank, E., Doyle, W. J., Skoner, D. P., Rabin, B. S., & Gwaltney, J. M. (1998). Types of stressors that increase susceptibility to the common cold in healthy adults. *Health Psychology, 17,* 214–223.

Cohen, S., & Herbert, T. B. (1996). Health psychology: Psychological factors and physical disease from the perspective of human psychoneuroimmunology. *Annual Review of Psychology, 47,* 113–142.

Cohen, S., Kaplan, J. R., Cunnick, J. E., Manuck, S. B., & Rabin, B. S. (1992). Chronic social stress, affiliation and cellular immune response in non-human primates. *Psychological Science, 3,* 301–304.

Cohen, S., Tyrrell, D. A. J., & Smith, A. P. (1993). Negative life events, perceived stress, negative affect and susceptibility to the common cold. *Journal of Personality and Social Psychology, 64,* 131–140.

Cohen, S., & Wills, T. A. (1985). Stress, social support, and the buffering hypothesis. *Psychological Bulletin, 98,* 310–357.

Cohen-Kettenis, P. T., & Arrindell, W. A. (1990). Perceived parental rearing style, parental divorce and transsexualism: A controlled study. *Psychological Medicine, 20,* 613–620.

Cohen-Kettenis, P. T., & Gooren, L. J. (1999). Transsexualism: A review of etiology, diagnosis, and treatment. *Journal of Psychosomatic Research, 46* (4), 315–333.

Cohen-Kettenis, P. T., Owen, A., Kaijser, V. G., Bradley, S. J., & Zucker, K. J. (2003). Demographic characteristics, social competence, and behavior problems in children with gender identity disorder: A cross-national, cross-clinic comparative analysis. *Journal of Abnormal Child Psychology, 31,* 41–53.

Cohen-Kettenis, P. T., & Pfäfflin, F. (2010). The DSM diagnostic criteria for gender identity in adolescents and adults. *Archives of Sexual Behavior, 39,* 499–513.

Cohen-Mansfield, J. (2001). Nonpharmacologic interventions for inappropriate behaviors in dementia. *American Journal of Geriatric Psychiatry, 9,* 361–381.

Coid, J., & Ullrich, S. (2010). Antisocial personality disorder is on a continuum with psychopathy. *Comprehensive Psychiatry, 51,* 426–433. doi:10.1016/j.comppsych.2009.09.006

Colapinto, J. (2000). *As nature made him: The boy who was raised as a girl.* New York: HarperCollins.

Cole, J. O., Saloman, M., Gunderson, J., Sunderland, P., & Simmonds, P. (1984). Drug therapy for borderline patients. *Comprehensive Psychiatry, 25,* 249–254.

Cole, M. G. (2004). Delirium in elderly patients. *American Journal of Geriatric Psychiatry, 12,* 7–21.

Cole, M. G., Bellavance, F., & Mansour, A. (1999). Prognosis of depression in elderly community and primary care populations: A systematic review and meta-analysis. *American Journal of Psychiatry, 156,* 1182–1187.

Coles, M. E., Radomsky, A. S., & Horng, B. (2006). Exploring the boundaries of memory distrust from repeated checking: Increasing external validity and examining thresholds. *Behaviour Research and Therapy, 44,* 995–1006.

Collimore, K. C., Asmundson, G. J. G., Taylor, S., & Abramowitz, J. S. (2009). Classification of hypochondriasis and other somatoform disorders. In D. McKay, J. S. Abramowitz, S. Taylor, & G. J. G. Asmundson (Eds.), *Current perspectives on the anxiety disorders: Implications for DSM-V and beyond* (pp. 431–451). New York: Springer.

Collins, A. (1988). *In the sleep room: The story of the CIA brainwashing experiments in Canada.* Toronto: Lester & Orpen Dennys.

Collins, K. A., Westra, H. A., Dozois, D. J. A., & Burns, D. D. (2004). Gaps in accessing treatment for anxiety and depression: Challenges for the delivery of care. *Clinical Psychology Review, 24,* 583–616.

Comer, J. S., Kendall, P. C., Franklin, M. E., Hudson, J. L., & Pimental, S. S. (2004). Obsessing/worrying about the overlap between obsessive-compulsive disorder and generalized anxiety disorder in youth. *Clinical Psychology Review, 24,* 663–683.

Comer, R. J. (1997). Substance-related disorders. In *Abnormal Psychology* (3rd ed., pp. 427–457). New York: Freeman.

Compton, W. M., & Cottler, L. B. (2004). The Diagnostic Interview Schedule (DIS). In M. Hersen (Series Ed.), D. L. Segal & M. Hilsenroth (Vol. Eds.), *Comprehensive handbook of psychological assessment: Vol. 2. Personality assessment and psychopathology* (pp. 153–162). New York: Wiley.

Conason, A. H., Klomek, A. B., & Sher, L. (2006). Recognizing alcohol and drug abuse in patients with eating disorders. *Quarterly Journal of Medicine, 99,* 335–339.

Condillac, R. A. (2007). Behavioral intervention and intellectual disabilities. In I. Brown & M. Percy (Eds.), *A comprehensive guide to intellectual and developmental disabilities* (pp. 363–372). London: Paul Brookes.

Confronting Eminem. (2000, October 27). *The Globe and Mail.* Retrieved from http://www.fradical.com/globe_and_mail_ editorial_ confronting_eminem.htm

Connolly, K. M., Olatunji, B. O., & Lohr, J. M. (2008). Evidence for disgust sensitivity mediating the sex differences found in blood-injection-injury phobia and spider phobia. *Personality and Individual Differences, 44,* 898–908.

Connoly, J. A., Boriakchanyavat, S., & Lue, T. F. (1996). Ultrasound evaluation of the penis in the assessment of impotence. *Journal of Clinical Ultrasound, 24,* 481–486.

Connor-Greene, P. A. (1988). Gender differences in body weight perception and weight-loss strategies of college students. *Women and Health, 14,* 27–42.

Connor-Smith, J. K., & Weisz, J. R. (2003). Applying treatment outcome research in clinical practice: Techniques for adapting interventions to the real world. *Child and Adolescent Mental Health, 8,* 3–10.

Constitution Act, Schedule B to the Canada Act, (U. K.) 1982, c. 11.

Cook, A. N., & Roesch, R. (in press). "Tough on crime" reforms: What psychology has to say about the recent and proposed justice policy in Canada. *Canadian Psychology.*

Cook, E. P., Warnke, M., & Dupuy, P. (1993). Gender bias and the DSM-III-R. *Canadian Journal of Psychiatry, 24,* 29–34.

Cook, W., & Medley, D. (1954). Proposed hostility and pharisaic virtue scaled for the MMPI. *Journal of Applied Psychology, 38,* 414–418.

Coolidge, F. L., Thede, L. L., & Jang, K. L. (2001). Heritability of personality disorders in childhood: A preliminary investigation. *Journal of Personality Disorders, 15,* 33–40.

Coolidge, F. L., Thede, L. L., & Young, S. E. (2002). The heritability of gender identity disorder in a child and adolescent twin sample. *Behavior Genetics, 32,* 251–257.

Coons, P. M. (1986). The prevalence of multiple personality disorder. *Newsletter of the International Society for the Study of Multiple Personality and Dissociation, 4,* 6–8.

Coons, P. M. (1994). Confirmation of childhood abuse in child and adolescent cases of multiple personality disorder and dissociative disorder not otherwise specified. *Journal of Nervous and Mental Disease, 182,* 461–464.

Coons, P. M. (1998). The dissociative disorders: Rarely considered and underdiagnosed. *The Psychiatric Clinics of North America, 21,* 637–648.

Coons, P. M. (1999). Psychogenic or dissociative fugue: A clinical investigation of five cases. *Psychological Reports, 84,* 881–886.

Coons, P. M., Bowman, E. S., Pellow, T. A., & Schneider, P. (1989). Post-traumatic aspects of the treatment of victims of sexual abuse and incest. *The Psychiatry Clinics of North America, 12,* 325–335.

Cooper v. R. (1980), 1 S.C.R. 1149.

Cooper, M., Corrado, R., Karlberg, A. M., & Adams, L. P. (1992). Aboriginal suicide in British Columbia: An overview. *Canada's Mental Health, 40,* 19–23.

Cooper, Z., & Fairburn, C. G. (2011). The evolution of "enhanced" cognitive behavior therapy for eating disorders: Learning from treatment nonresponse. *Cognitive and Behavioral Practice, 18,* 394–402.

Corcoran, R., Cahill, C., & Frith, C. D. (1997). The appreciation of visual jokes in people with schizophrenia: A study of "mentalizing" ability. *Schizophrenia Research, 24,* 319–327.

Corcos, M., Nezelof, S., Speranza, M., Topa, S., Girardon, N., Guibaud, O., et al. (2001). Psychoactive substance consumption in eating disorders. *Eating Behaviors, 2,* 27–38.

Corna, L. M., Cairney, J., & Streiner, D. L. (2010). Suicide ideation in older adults: Relationship to mental health problems and service use. *The Gerontologist, 50* (6), 785–797.

Cornell, D. G., Warren, J., Hawk, G., Stafford, E., Oram, G., & Pine, D. (1996). Psychopathy in instrumental and reactive violent offenders. *Journal of Consulting and Clinical Psychology, 64,* 783–790.

Corrado, R. R., Cohen, I., Hart, S. D., & Roesch, R. (2000b). Diagnosing mental disorders in offenders: Conceptual and methodological issues. *Criminal Behaviour and Mental Health, 10,* 29–39.

Corrice, A. M., & Glidden, L. M. (2009). The Down syndrome advantage: Fact or fiction? *American Journal on Intellectual and Developmental Disabilities, 114,* 254–268.

Corrigan, P. (2004). How stigma interferes with mental health care. *American Psychologist, 59,* 614–625.

Corrigan, P. W. (2000). Mental health stigma as social attribution: Implications for research methods and attitude change. *Clinical Psychology: Science and Practice, 7,* 48–67.

Corrigan, P. W. (2004). How stigma interferes with mental health care. *American Psychologist,59,* 614–625.

Cosgrove, L., Krimsky, S., Vijayaraghavan, M., & Schneider, L. (2006). Financial ties between DSM-IV panel members and the pharmaceutical industry. *Psychotherapy and Psychosomatics, 75,* 154–160.

Costello, E. J., Angold, A., Burns, B. J., Stangl, D. K., Tweed, D. L., Erkanli, A., et al. (1996). The Great Smokey Mountains study of youth: Goals, design, methods, and the prevalence of DSM-III-TR disorders. *Archives of General Psychiatry, 53,* 1129–1136.

Costello, E. J., Mustillo, S., Erkanli, A., Keeler, G., & Angold, A. (2003). Prevalence and development of psychiatric disorders in childhood and adolescence. *Archives of General Psychiatry, 60,* 837–844.

Costello, R. M. (1975). Alcoholism treatment and evaluation: In search of methods. *International Journal of the Addictions, 10,* 251–275.

Côté, G., & Hodgins, S. (1990). Co-occurring mental disorders among criminal offenders. *Bulletin of the American Academy of Psychiatry and Law, 18,* 271–281.

Cote, S. M., Vaillancourt, T., Barker, E. D., Nagin, D., & Tremblay, R. E. (2007). The joint development of physical and indirect aggression: Predictors of continuity and change during childhood. *Development and Psychopathology, 19,* 37–55.

Cotugno, A. J. (2009). Social competence and social skills training and intervention for children with autism spectrum disorders. *Journal of Autism and Developmental Disorders, 39,* 1268–1277.

Coupland, C., Dhiman, P., Morriss, R., Arthur, A., Barton, G., & Hippisley-Cox, J. (2011). Antidepressant use and risk of adverse outcomes in older people: Population based cohort study. *British Medical Journal.* doi:10.1136/bmj.d4551

Covin, R., Ouimet, A. J., Seeds, P. M., & Dozois, D. J. A. (2008). A meta-analysis of CBT for pathological worry among clients with GAD. *Journal of Anxiety Disorders, 22,* 108–116.

Cowen, E. L. (1977). Baby-steps toward primary prevention. *American Journal of Community Psychology, 5,* 1 16.

Cowen, E. L. (1980). The wooing of primary prevention. *American Journal of Community Psychology, 8,* 258–284.

Cowen, E. L. (1996). The ontogenesis of primary prevention: Lengthy strides and stubbed toes. *American Journal of Community Psychology, 24,* 235–249.

Cowen, E. L. (2000). Psychological wellness: Some hopes for the future. In D. Cicchetti, J. Rappaport, I. Sandler, & R. P. Weissberg (Eds.), *The promotion of wellness in children and adolescents.* Washington, DC: Child Welfare League of America Press.

Cox, B. J., Pagura, J., Stein, M. B., & Sareen, J. (2009). The relationship between generalized social phobia and avoidant personality disorder in a national mental health survey. *Depression and Anxiety, 26,* 354–362. doi:10.1002/da.20475

Cox, D. J. (1988). Incidence and nature of male genital exposure behavior as reported by college women. *Journal of Sex Research, 24,* 227–234.

Cox, M. L., & Zapf, P. A. (2004). An investigation of discrepancies between mental health professionals and the courts in decisions about competency. *Law and Psychology Review, 28,* 109–132.

Coyne, J. C. (1976). Toward an interactional description of depression. *Psychiatry, 39,* 2840.

CPA. See Canadian Psychological Association.

Craig, W., Pepler, D., & Cummings, J. (Eds.). (2009). *Rise up for respectful relationships: Prevent bullying. PREVNet Series, Vol. 2.* Kingston, ON: PREVNet Inc.

Craighead, W. E., Craighead, L. W., & Ilardi, S. S. (1995). Behavior therapies in historical perspective. In B. Bongar & L. E. Beutler (Eds.), *Comprehensive textbook of psychotherapy: Theory and practice* (pp. 64–83). New York: Oxford University Press.

Craske, M. G., & Barlow, D. H. (2001). Panic disorder and agoraphobia. In D. H. Barlow (Ed.), *Clinical handbook of psychological disorders* (3rd ed., pp. 1–59). New York: Guilford Press.

Craske, M. G., & Barlow, D. H. (2008). Panic disorder and agoraphobia. In D. H. Barlow (Ed.), *Clinical handbook of psychological disorders: A step-by-step treatment manual* (pp. 1–64). New York: Guilford Press.

Crawford, T. N., Cohen, P., Johnson, J. G., Kasen, S., First, M. B., Gordon, K., et al. (2005). Self-reported personality disorder in the children in the community sample: Convergent and prospective validity in late adolescence and adulthood. *Journal of Personality Disorders, 19,* 30–52.

Creed, F., & Barsky, A. (2004). A systematic review of the epidemiology of somatisation disorder and hypochondriasis. *Journal of Psychosomatic Research, 56,* 391–408.

Crick, N., & Dodge, K. (1994). A review and reformulation of social information-processing mechanisms in children's social adjustment. *Psychological Bulletin, 115,* 74–101.

Criminal Code of Canada, R.S.C. 1985, c. C-46.

Crisanti, A. S., & Love E. J. (2001). Characteristics of psychiatric inpatients detained under civil commitment legislation: A Canadian study. *International Journal of Law and Psychiatry, 24,* 399–410.

Crits-Christoph, P., & Barber, J. P. (2007). Psychological treatments for personality disorders. In P. E. Nathan & J. M. Gorman (Eds.), *A guide to treatments that work* (3rd ed., pp. 641–658). New York: Oxford University Press.

Crocker, A. C. (1992). Symposium: Prevention of mental retardation and related disabilities. Introduction: Where is the prevention movement? *Mental Retardation, 30,* iii–v.

Crooks, C. V., Wolfe, D. A., Hughes, H., Jaffe, P. G., & Chiodo, D. (2008). Development, evaluation, and national implementation of a school-based program to reduce violence and related risk behaviours: Lessons from the Fourth R. *Institute for the Prevention of Crime Review, 2,* 109–135.

Crooks, R., and Baur, K. (1996). *Our sexuality.* Pacific Grove, CA: Brooks-Cole.

Crossley, N. A., Constante, M., McGuire, P., & Power, P. (2010). Efficacy of atypical v. typical antipsychotics in the treatment of early psychosis: Meta-analysis. *British Medical Journal, 196,* 434–439.

Crossley, R. (1992). Getting the words out: Case studies in facilitated communication. *Topics in Language Disorders, 12,* 1–4.

Crowley, K. (2011). Sleep and sleep disorders in older adults. *Neuropsychology Review, 21,* 41–53.

Cruise, K. R, Evans, L. J., & Pickens, I. B. (2011). Integrating mental health and special education needs into comprehensive service planning for juvenile offenders in long-term custody settings. *Learning and Individual Differences, 21* (1), 30–40.

Cuijpers, P., Geraedts, A. A., van Oppen, P., Andersson, G., Markowitz, J. C., & van Straten, A. (2011). Interpersonal psychotherapy for depression: A meta-analysis. *American Journal of Psychiatry, 168,* 581–592.

Cuijpers, P., van Straten, A., & Smit, F. (2006). Psychological treatment of late-life depression: A meta-analysis of randomized controlled trials. *International Journal of Geriatric Psychiatry, 21,* 1139–1149.

Cummings, J. L., & Benson, D. F. (1992). *Dementia: A clinical approach* (2nd ed.). Stoneham, MA: Butterworth-Heinemann.

Cummings, J. L., & Mega, M. S. (2003). *Neuropsychiatry and behavioral neuroscience.* London: Oxford University Press.

Cummins, R. A., & Lau, A. L. D. (2003). Community integration or community exposure? A review and discussion in relation to people with an intellectual disability. *Journal of Applied Research in Intellectual Disabilities, 16,* 145–157.

Cunningham, C. (2006). COPE: Large-group, community-based, family-centered parent training. In R. A. Barkley (Ed.), *Attention-deficit hyperactivity disorder: A handbook for diagnosis and treatment* (pp. 480–498). New York: Guilford Press.

Cunningham, C. E. (2007). A family-centered approach to planning and measuring the outcome of interventions for children with attention-deficit/hyperactivity disorder. *Journal of Pediatric Psychology, 32* (6), 676–694.

Cunningham, C. E., Boyle, M., Offord, D., Racine, Y., Hundert, J., Secord, M., et al. (2000). Tri-ministry study: Correlates of school-based parenting course utilization. *Journal of Consulting and Clinical Psychology, 68,* 928–933.

Cunningham, C. E., Bremner, R., & Boyle, M. (1995). Large group community-based parenting programs for families of preschoolers at risk for disruptive behaviour disorders: Utilization, cost effectiveness, and outcome. *Journal of Child Psychology and Psychiatry, and Allied Disciplines, 36* (7), 1141–1159.

Cunningham, C. E., Cunningham, L. J., Martorelli, V., Tran, A., Young, J., & Zacharias, R. (1998). The effects of primary division, student-mediated conflict resolution programs on playground aggression. *Journal of Child Psychology and Psychiatry, 39,* 653–662.

Cunningham, C. E., McHolm, A., Boyle, M., & Patel, S. (2005). Behavioral and emotional adjustment, family functioning, academic performance, and social relationships in children with selective mutism. *Journal of Child Psychology and Psychiatry, 45,* 1363–1372.

Cunningham, J. A., & Breslin, F. C. (2004). Only one in three people with alcohol abuse or dependence ever seek treatment. *Addictive Behaviors, 29,* 221–223.

Cunningham, S. J., McGrath, P. J., Ferguson, H. B., Humphreys, P., D'Astous, J. D., Latter, J., et al. (1987). Personality and behavioural characteristics in pediatric migraine. *Headache, 27,* 16–20.

Currier, D., & Mann, J. J. (2008). Stress, genes and the biology of suicidal behavior. *Psychiatric Clinics of North America, 31,* 247–269.

Currin, L., Schmidt, U., Treasure, J., & Jick, H. (2005). Time trends in eating disorder incidence. *British Journal of Psychiatry, 186,* 132–135.

Cuskelly, M., & Dadds, M. (1992). Behavioural problems in children with Down's syndrome and their siblings. *Journal of Child Psychology and Psychiatry, 33,* 749–761.

Cuskelly, M., & Bryde, R. (2004). Attitudes towards the sexuality of adults with an intellectual disability: Parents, support staff and a community sample. *Journal of Intellectual and Developmental Disability, 29,* 255–264.

Custer, R. L. (1982). An overview of compulsive gambling. In P. A. Carone, S. F. Yolles, S. N. Kieffer, & L. W. Krinsky (Eds.), *Addictive disorders updated* (pp. 107–124). New York: Human Sciences Press.

Cyranowski, J., Frank, E., Cherry, C., Houck, P., and Kupfer, D. (2004). Prospective assessment of sexual function in women treated for recurrent major depression. *Journal of Psychiatric Research, 38,* 267–273.

Dalgleish, T. (2004). Cognitive approaches to posttraumatic stress disorder: The evolution of multirepresentational theorizing. *Psychological Bulletin, 130,* 228–260.

Dalton, A. J., & McLachlan, D. R. (1986). Clinical expression of Alzheimer's disease in Down's syndrome. *Psychiatric Clinics of North America, 9,* 659–670.

Daly, B. P., Creed, T., Xanthopoulos, M., & Brown, R. T. (2007). Psychosocial treatments for children with attention deficit/hyperactivity disorder. *Neuropsychology Review, 17,* 73–89. doi:10.1007/s11065-006-9018-2

Daly, M. (1989). Sleep disorders in the elderly. *Primary Care, 16,* 475–488.

D'Amico, E. J., Miles, J. N. V., Stern, S., & Meredith, L. S. (2008). Brief motivational interviewing for teens at risk of substance abuse consequences: A randomized pilot study in a primary care clinic. *Journal of Substance Abuse Treatment, 35,* 53–61.

Damm, J., Eser, D., Schule, C., Obermeier, M., Moller, H., Rupprecht, R., et al. (2010). Influence of age on effectiveness and tolerability of electroconvulsive therapy. *Journal of ECT, 26* (4), 282–288.

Darke, J. L. (1990). Sexual aggression: Achieving power through humiliation. In W. L. Marshall, D. R. Laws, & H. E. Barbaree (Eds.), *Handbook of sexual assault: Issues, theories, and treatment of the offender* (pp. 55–72). New York: Plenum Press.

Darke, S., Ross, J., & Cohen, J. (1994). The use of benzodiazepines among regular amphetamine users. *Addiction, 89,* 1683–1690.

Das, A. (2007). Masturbation in the United States. *Journal of Sex & Marital Therapy, 33,* 301–317.

Das, P., Lagopoulos, J., Sæther, O., & Malhi, G. S. (2008). Is computed tomography still useful as a neuroimaging tool in psychiatry? *Expert Opinion in Medical Diagnostics, 2,* 1003–1011. doi:10.1517/17530050802369966

Dauphinais, P., & King, J. (1992). Psychological assessment with American Indian children. *Applied and Preventive Psychology, 1,* 97–110.

David-Ferdon, C., & Kaslow, N. J. (2008). Evidence-based psychosocial treatments for child and adolescent depression. *Journal of Clinical Child and Adolescent Psychology, 37,* 62–104.

Davidson, L., & Heinrichs, R. W. (2003). Quantification of brain imaging findings on the frontal and temporal lobes in schizophrenia: A meta-analysis. *Psychiatry Research: Neuroimaging, 122,* 69–87.

Davidson, M. (1982). *Uncommon sense: The life and thought of Ludwig von Bertalanffy (1901–1972), father of general systems theory.* Boston: Houghton Mifflin.

Davidson, M., Reichenberg, A., Rabinowitz, J., Weiser, M., Kaplan, Z., & Mark, M. (1999). Behavioral and intellectual markers for schizophrenia in apparently healthy male adolescents. *American Journal of Psychiatry, 156,* 1328–1335.

Davidson, P., Cain, N., Sloane-Reeves, J., Giesow, V. E., Quijano, L. E., Van Heyningen, J., & Shoham, I. (1995). Crisis intervention for community-based individuals with developmental disabilities and behavioral and psychiatric disorders. *Mental Retardation, 33,* 21–30.

Davidson, P., Cain, N., Sloane-Reeves, J., Van Speybroeck, A., Segel, J., Gutkin, J., et al. (1994). Characteristics of community-based individuals with mental retardation and aggressive behavioral disorders. *American Journal on Mental Retardation, 98,* 704–716.

Davies, D. K., Stock, S. E., Holloway, S., & Wehmeyer, M. L. (2010). Evaluating a GPS-based transportation device to support independent bus travel by people with intellectual disability. *Intellectual and Developmental Disabilities, 48,* 454–463.

Davis, C., Shuster, B., Blackmore, E., & Fox, J. (2004). Looking good—Family focus on appearance and the risk for eating disorders. *International Journal of Eating Disorders, 35,* 136–144.

Davis, K. L., Kahn, R. S., Ko, G., & Davidson, M. (1991). Dopamine in schizophrenia: A review and reconceptualization. *American Journal of Psychiatry, 148,* 1474–1486.

Davis, M. (1989). Gender and sexual development of women with mental retardation. *The Disabilities Studies Quarterly, 9* (3), 19–20.

Dawson, G., & Watling, R. (2000). Interventions to facilitate auditory, visual and motor integration in autism: A review of the evidence. *Journal of Autism and Developmental Disorders, 30,* 423–426.

Day, N. L., Leech, S. L., Richardson, G. A., Cornelius, M. D., Robles, N., & Larkby, C. (2002). Prenatal alcohol exposure predicts continued deficits in offspring size at 14 years of age. *Alcoholism: Clinical and Experimental Research, 26,* 1584–1591.

Dayan, J., & Minnes, P. M. (1995). Ethical issues related to the use of Facilitated Communication techniques with persons with autism. *Canadian Psychology, 36,* 183–189.

Deacon, B., & Abramowitz, J. S. (2008). Is hypochondriasis related to obsessive-compulsive disorder, panic disorder, or both? An empirical evaluation. *Journal of Cognitive Psychotherapy, 22,* 115–127.

Deacon, B. J., & Abramowitz, J. S. (2004). Cognitive and behavioral treatments for anxiety disorders: A review of meta-analytic findings. *Journal of Clinical Psychology, 60,* 429–441.

Dean, R. R., Kelsey, J. E., Heller, M. R., & Ciaranello, R. D. (1993). Structural foundations of illness and treatment: Receptors. In D. L. Dunner (Ed.), *Current psychiatric theory.* Philadelphia: Saunders.

DeBakey, M., & Gotto, A. (1977). *The living heart.* New York: Grosset & Dunlap.

Debeck, K., Wood, E., Montaner, J., & Kerr, T. (2009). Canada's new federal "National Anti-drug Strategy": An informal audit of reported funding allocation. *International Journal of Drug Policy, 20,* 188–191.

Deeley, Q., Surgurladze, S., Tunstall, N., Mezey, G., Beer, D., Ambikapathy, A., et al. (2006). Facial emotion processing in criminal psychopathy. *British Journal of Psychiatry, 189,* 533–539.

DeGroot, J. M., Kennedy, S., Rodin, G., & McVey, G. (1992). Correlates of sexual abuse in women with anorexia nervosa and bulimia nervosa. *Canadian Journal of Psychiatry, 37,* 516–518.

De Jong, P. J., & Merckelbach, H. (1998). Blood-injection-injury and fear of spiders: Domain specific individual differences in disgust sensitivity. *Personality and Individual Differences, 24,* 153–158.

De Leo, D., & Heller, T. S. (2008). Social modelling in the transmission of suicidality. *Crisis, 29,* 11–19.

De Los Reyes, A., & Kazdin, A. E. (2005). Informant discrepancies in the assessment of childhood psychopathology: A critical review, theoretical framework, and recommendations for further study. *Psychological Bulletin, 131,* 483–509. doi:10.1037/0033-2909.131.4.483

de Maat, S. M., Dekker, J., Schoevers, R. A., & de Jonghe, F. (2007). Relative efficacy of psychotherapy and combined therapy in the treatment of depression: A meta-analysis. *European Psychiatry, 22,* 1–8.

Denckla, M. (1996). Brain mechanisms. In M. M. Bristol, D. J. Cohen, E. J. Costello, M. Denckla, T. J. Eckberg, R. Kallen, H. C. Kraemer, et. al., State of the science in autism: Report to the National Institutes of Health. *Journal of Autism and Developmental Disorders, 26,* 134–140.

Dennerstein, L., Dudley, E., Lehert, P., & Burger, H. G. (2000, October). *Sexual functioning during the menopausal transition.* Paper presented at Female Sexual Function Forum: New perspectives in the management of female sexual dysfunction, Boston.

Dennerstein, L., Smith, A. M., Morse, C. A., & Burger, H. G. (1994). Sexuality and the menopause. *Journal of Psychosomatic Obstetrics and Gynecology, 15,* 59–66.

Dennis, C. L., Hodnett, E., Kenton, L., Weston, J., Zupancic, J., Stewart, D. E., & Kiss, A. (2009). Effect of peer support on prevention of postnatal depression among high risk women: Multisite randomised controlled trial. *British Medical Journal, 338.* doi:10.1136/bmj.a3064

Denys, D., Van Nieuwerburgh, F., Deforce, D., & Westenberg, H. G. M. (2007). Prediction of response to paroxetine and venlafaxine by serotonin-related genes in obsessive-compulsive disorder in a randomized, double-blind trial. *The Journal of Clinical Psychiatry, 68,* 747–753.

De Oliveira-Souza, R., Hare, R. D., Bramati, I. E., Garrido, G. J., Ignacio, F. A., Tovar-Moll, F., et al. (2008). Psychopathy as a disorder of the moral brain: Fronto-temporo-limbic grey matter reductions demonstrated by voxel-based morphometry. *Neuroimage, 40,* 1202–1213.

Department of Health. (2001). Treatment choice in psychological therapies and counselling: Evidence based clinical practice guideline. Retrieved from http://www.dh.gov.uk/assetRoot/04/05/82/45/04058245.pdf

Depla, M. F. I. A., ten Have, M. L., van Balkom, A. J. L. M., & de Graaf, R. (2008). Specific fears and phobias in the general population: Results from the Netherlands mental health survey and incidence study (NEMESIS). *Social Psychiatry and Psychiatric Epidemiology, 43,* 200–208.

Depue, R. A. (1999). *Neurobehavioral systems, personality, and psychopathology.* New York: Springer-Verlag.

Depue, R. A., Luciana, M., Arbisi, P., Collins, P., & Leon, A. (1994). Dopamine and the structure of personality: Relation of agonist-induced dopamine activity to positive emotionality. *Journal of Personality and Social Psychology, 67,* 485–498.

DeRubeis, R. J., Hollon, S. D., Amsterdam, J. D., Shelton, R. C., Young, P. R., Salomon, R. M., et al. (2005). Cognitive therapy vs medications in the treatment of moderate to severe depression. *Archives of General Psychiatry, 62,* 409–416.

DeRyck, B., Gekoski, W. L., Knox, V. J., & Zivian, M. T. (1996, October). *Mental disorders in older adults: The beliefs and attitudes of clinical psychology graduate students.* Quebec: Canadian Association on Gerontology.

DeStefano, F., Bhasin, T. K., Thompson, W. W., Yeargin-Allsopp, M., & Boyle, C. (2004). Age at first measles-mumps-rubella vaccination in children with autism and school-matched control subjects: A population-based study in metropolitan Atlanta. *Pediatrics,113* (2), 259–266.

Deutsch, A. (1948). *The shame of the States.* New York: Harcourt Brace.

DeWall, C., Buffardi, L. E., Bonser, I., & Campbell, W. (2011). Narcissism and implicit attention seeking: Evidence from linguistic analyses of social networking and online presentation. *Personality and Individual Differences, 51,* 57–62. doi:10.1016/j.paid.2011.03.011

Diamond, D. B. (1997). The fate of the ego in contemporary psychiatry with particular reference to etiologic theories of schizophrenia. *Psychiatry: Interpersonal and Biological Processes, 60,* 67–88.

Diamond, M. (1982). Sexual identity, monozygotic twins reared in discordant sex roles and a BBC follow-up. *Archives of Sexual Behavior, 11,* 181–186.

Diaz, J. H. (2004). The global epidemiology, syndromic classification, management, and prevention of spider bites. *The American Journal of Tropical Medicine and Hygiene, 71,* 239–250.

Di Castelnuovo, A., Costanzo, S., Bagnardi, V., Donati, M. B., Iacoviello, L., & de Gaetano, G. (2006). Alcohol dosing and total mortality in men and women: An updated meta-analysis of 34 prospective studies. *Archives of Internal Medicine, 166,* 2437–2445.

Dickerson, F. B., & Lehman, A. (2011). Evidence based psychotherapy for schizophrenia: 2011 update. *Journal of Nervous and Mental Disease, 199,* 520–526.

Dickey, R., & Steiner, B. W. (1990). Hormone treatment and surgery. In R. Blanchard & B. W. Steiner (Eds.), *Clinical management of gender identity disorders in children and adults* (pp. 139–158). Washington, DC: American Psychiatric Press.

Dickinson, D., Ramsey, M., & Gold, J. M. (2007). Overlooking the obvious: A meta-analytic comparison of digit symbol coding tasks and other cognitive measures in schizophrenia. *Archives of General Psychiatry, 64,* 532–542.

Dickson, H., Laurens, K. R., Cullen, A. E., & Hodgins, S. (2011). Meta-analyses of cognitive and motor function in youth aged 16 years and younger who subsequently develop schizophrenia. *Psychological Medicine.*

Dickstein, D. P., Towbin, K. E., Van Der Veen, J. W., Rich, B. A., Brotman, M. A., Knopf, L., et al. (2009). Randomized double-blind placebo-controlled trial of lithium in youths with severe mood dysregulation. *Journal of Child and Adolescence Psychopharmacology, 19,* 61–73. doi:10.1089/cap.2008.044

Diener, E., Suh, E. M., Lucas, R. E., & Smith, H. L. (1999). Subjective well-being: Three decades of progress. *Psychological Bulletin, 125,* 276–302.

Dimidjian, S., Barrera, M., Martell, C., Muñoz, R. F., & Lewinsohn, P. M. (2011). The origins and current status of behavioral activation for depression. *Annual Review of Clinical Psychology, 7,* 1–38.

Dimidjian, S., Hollon, S. D., Dobson, K. S., Schmaling, K. B., Kohlenberg, R. J., Addis, M. E., et al. (2006). Randomized trial of behavioral activation, cognitive therapy, and antidepressant medication in the acute treatment of adults with major depression. *Journal of Consulting and Clinical Psychology, 74,* 658–670.

Dimsdale, J. E., & Ziegler, M. G. (1991). What do plasma and urinary measures of catecholamines tell us about human response to stressors? *Circulation, 83* (Suppl. II), II-36–II-42.

DiNardo, P., Brown, T. A., & Barlow, D. H. (1994). *Anxiety disorders interview schedule for DSM-IV.* Albany, NY: Graywind.

Dire Straits' song should be censored, council rules. (2011, January 13). *CTV Television Network.* Retrieved from http://www.ctv.ca

Dishion, T. J., & Patterson, S. G. (1996). *Preventive parenting with love, encouragement, and limits: The preschool years.* Eugene, OR: Castalia.

Distel, M. A., Vink, J. M., Willemsen, G., Middeldorp, C. M., Merckelbach, H. L. G. J., & Boomsma, D. I. (2008). Heritability of self-reported phobic fear. *Behavior Genetics, 38,* 24–33.

Dixon, J. F., & Hokin, L. E. (1998). Lithium acutely inhibits and chronically up regulates and stabilizes glutamate uptake by presynaptic nerve endings in mouse cerebral cortex. *Proceedings of the National Academy of Sciences, 95,* 8363–8368.

Dobson, D. J. G., & Dobson, K. S. (2009). *Evidence-based practice of cognitive behavior therapy.* New York: Guilford Press.

Dobson, J. C., Kushida, E., Williamson, M., & Friedman, E. G. (1976). Intellectual performances of 36 phenylketonuria patients and their nonaffected siblings. *Pediatrics, 58,* 53–58.

Dobson, K. S. (1989). A meta-analysis of the efficacy of cognitive therapy for depression. *Journal of Consulting and Clinical Psychology, 57,* 414–419.

Dobson, K. S., & Dozois, D. J. A. (2010). Historical and philosophical bases of the cognitive-behavioral therapies. In K. S. Dobson (Ed.), *Handbook of cognitive-behavioral therapies* (3rd ed., pp. 3–38). New York: Guilford Press.

Dobson, K. S., Hollon, S. D., Dimidjian, S., Schmaling, K. B., Kohlenberg, R. J., Gallop, R. J., et al. (2008). Randomized trial of behavioral activation, cognitive therapy, and antidepressant medication in the prevention of relapse and recurrence in major depression. *Journal of Consulting and Clinical Psychology, 76,* 468–477.

Docter, R. F., & Prince, V. (1997). Transvestism: A survey of 1032 cross-dressers. *Archives of Sexual Behavior, 26* (6), 589–605.

Dodge, K. A. (1986). A social information processing model of social competence in children. In M. Perlmutter (Ed.), *Minnesota symposium in child psychology* (Vol. 18, pp. 77–125). Hillsdale, NJ: Lawrence Erlbaum Associates.

Dohrenwend, B. P., Levav, I., Shrout, P. E., Schwartz, S., Naveh, G., Link, B. G., et al. (1992). Socioeconomic status and psychiatric disorders: The causation-selection issue. *Science, 255,* 946–952.

Dolan, B. M., Birtchnell, S. A., & Lacey, J. H. (1987). Body image distortion in non-eating disordered women and men. *Journal of Psychosomatic Research, 31,* 513–520.

Dols, M. W. (2006). Historical perspective: Medical madness. *Journal of Muslim Mental Health, 1,* 77–95.

Donahey, K. M., & Carroll, R. A. (1993). Gender differences in factors associated with hypoactive sexual desire. *Journal of Sex & Marital Therapy, 19,* 25–40.

D'Onise, K., Lynch, J. W., Sawyer, M. G., & McDermott, R. A. (2010). Can preschool improve child health outcomes? A systematic review. *Social Science and Medicine, 70,* 1423–1440.

Donnellan, A. M., Mirenda, P. L., Mesaros, R. A., & Fassbender, L. L. (1984). Analyzing the communicative functions of aberrant behavior. *Journal of the Association of Persons with Severe Handicaps, 9,* 201–212.

D'Onofrio, B. M., Slutske, W. S., Turkheimer, E., Emery, R. E., Harden, K. P., Heath, A. C., et al. (2007). Intergenerational transmission of childhood conduct problems: A children of twins study. *Archives of General Psychiatry, 64* (7), 820–829. doi:10.1001/archpsyc.64.7.820

Doren, D. M. (2002). *Evaluating sex offenders: A manual for civil commitment and beyond.* Thousand Oaks, CA: Sage.

Dorey, G., Speakman, M., Feneley, R., Swinkels, A., Dunn, C., & Ewings, P. (2004). Randomised controlled trial of pelvic floor muscle exercises and manometric biofeedback for erectile dysfunction. *British Journal of General Practice, 54,* 819–825.

Douglas, K., & Koch, W. J. (2001). Civil commitment and civil competence: Psychological issues. In R. Schuller & J. R. P. Ogloff (Eds.), *An introduction to law and psychology: Canadian perspectives.* Toronto: University of Toronto Press.

Douglas, K. S., Ogloff, J. R. P., Nicholls, T., & Grant, I. (1999). Assessing risk for violence among psychiatric patients: The HCR-20 Violence Risk Assessment Scheme and the Psychopathy Checklist: Screening Version. *Journal of Consulting and Clinical Psychology, 67,* 917–930.

Douglas, K. S., & Reeves, K. A. (2010). Historical-Clinical-Risk Management-20 (HCR-20) violence risk assessment scheme: Rationale, application, and empirical overview. In R. K. Otto & K. S. Douglas (Eds.), *Handbook of violence risk assessment* (pp. 147–185). New York: Routledge.

Douglas, K. S., Vincent, G. M., & Edens, J. F. (2007). Risk for criminal recidivism: The role of psychopathy. In C. J. Patrick (Ed.), *Handbook of psychopathy* (pp. 533–554). New York: Guilford Press.

Douglas, K. S., Webster, C. D., Hart, S. D., Eaves, D., & Ogloff, J. R. P. (Eds.). (2001). *HCR-20 violence risk management companion guide.* Burnaby, BC: Mental Health, Law, & Policy Institute, Simon Fraser University, and Department of Mental Health Law and Policy, Florida Mental Health Institute, University of South Florida.

Douville, R., & Casanova, J.-D. (1967). *La vie quotidienne des Indiens du Canada à l'époque de la colonisation Francaise.* Paris: Librarie Hachette.

Dozois, D. J. A. (2007). Stability of negative self-structures: A longitudinal comparison of depressed, remitted, and nonpsychiatric controls. *Journal of Clinical Psychology, 63,* 319–338.

Dozois, D. J. A. (2011). Training in professional psychology. The content and process of learning. *Psynopsis.*

Dozois, D. J. A., & Beck, A. T. (2008). Cognitive schemas, beliefs and assumptions. In K. S. Dobson & D. J. A. Dozois (Eds.), *Risk factors in depression* (pp. 123–145). Oxford, UK: Elsevier.

Dozois, D. J. A., & Beck, A. T. (2011). Cognitive therapy. In J. D. Herbert & E. M. Forman (Eds.), *Acceptance and mindfulness in cognitive behavioral therapy: Understanding and applying the new therapies* (pp. 26–56). New York: John Wiley & Sons.

Dozois, D. J. A., Covin, R., & Brinker, J. K. (2003). Normative data on cognitive measures of depression. *Journal of Consulting and Clinical Psychology, 71,* 71–80.

Dozois, D. J. A., & Dobson, K. S. (2001a). Information processing and cognitive organization in unipolar depression: Specificity and comorbidity issues. *Journal of Abnormal Psychology, 110,* 236–246.

Dozois, D. J. A., & Dobson, K. S. (2001b). A longitudinal investigation of information processing and cognitive organization in clinical depression: Stability of schematic interconnectedness. *Journal of Consulting and Clinical Psychology, 69,* 914–925.

Dozois, D. J. A., & Dobson, K. S. (Eds.). (2004). *The prevention of anxiety and depression: Theory, research, and practice.* Washington, DC: American Psychological Association.

Dozois, D. J. A., & Dobson, K. S. (2010). Depression. In M. M. Antony & D. H. Barlow (Eds.), *Handbook of assessment and treatment planning for psychological disorders* (2nd ed., pp. 344–389). New York: Guilford Press.

Dozois, D. J. A., Dobson, K. S., & Westra, H. A. (2004). The comorbidity of anxiety and depression, and the implications of comorbidity for prevention. In D. J. A. Dozois & K. S. Dobson (Eds.), *The prevention of anxiety and depression: Theory, research, and practice* (pp. 261–280). Washington, DC: American Psychological Association.

Dozois, D. J. A., & Frewen, P. A. (2006). Specificity of cognitive structure in depression and social phobia: A comparison of interpersonal and achievement content. *Journal of Affective Disorders, 90,* 101–109.

Dozois, D. J. A., Frewen, P. A., & Covin, R. (2006). In M. Hersen & J. C. Thomas (Series Eds.), J. C. Thomas & D. L. Segal (Vol. Eds.), *Comprehensive handbook of personality and psychopathology: Vol. 1. Personality and everyday functioning.* New York: Wiley.

Dozois, D. J. A., Seeds, P. M., & Collins, K. A. (2009). Transdiagnostic approaches to the prevention of depression and anxiety. *International Journal of Cognitive Psychotherapy: An International Quarterly, 23,* 44–59.

Dozois, D. J. A., & Westra, H. A. (2004). The nature of anxiety and depression: Implications for prevention. In D. J. A. Dozois & K. S. Dobson (Eds.), *The prevention of anxiety and depression: Theory, research, and practice* (pp. 9–41). Washington, DC: American Psychological Association.

Dragt, S., Nieman, D. H., Veltman, D., Becker, H. E., van de Fliert, R., de Haan L., & Linszen, D. H. (2011). Environmental factors and social adjustment as predictors of a first psychosis in subjects at ultra high risk. *Schizophrenia Research, 125,* 69–76.

Drake, R. E., & Vaillant, G. E. (1985). A validity study of axis II of DSM-III. *American Journal of Psychiatry, 142,* 553–558.

Drevets, W. C. (2000). Functional anatomical abnormalities in limbic and prefrontal cortical structures in major depression. *Progress in Brain Research, 126,* 413–431.

Dryden, W., David, D., & Ellis, A. (2010). Rational emotive behavior therapy. In K. S. Dobson (Ed.), *Handbook of cognitive-behavioral therapies* (3rd ed., pp. 226–276). New York: Guilford Press.

Dugas, M. J., Gagnon, F., Ladouceur, R., & Freeston, M. H. (1998). Generalized anxiety disorder: A preliminary test of a conceptual model. *Behaviour Research and Therapy, 36* (2), 215–226.

Dugas, M. J., Hedayati, M., Karavidas, A., Buhr, K., Francis, K., & Phillips, N. A. (2005). Intolerance of uncertainty and information processing: Evidence of biased recall and interpretations. *Cognitive Therapy and Research, 29,* 57–70.

Dugas, M. J., Marchand, A., & Ladouceur, R. (2005). Further validation of a cognitive-behavioural model of generalized anxiety disorder: Diagnostic and symptom specificity. *Journal of Anxiety Disorders, 19,* 329–343.

Dugas, M. J., & Robichaud, M. (2007). *Cognitive-behavioral treatment for generalized anxiety disorder: From science to practice.* New York: Routledge.

Dukes, E., & McGuire, B. E. (2009). Enhancing capacity to make sexuality-related decisions in people with intellectual disability. *Journal of Intellectual Disability Research, 53,* 727–734.

Dunbar, H. F. (1935). *Emotions and bodily changes.* New York: Columbia University Press.

Dunsmoor, J. E., Prince, S. E., Murty, V. P., Kragel, P. A., & LaBar, K. S. (2011). Neurobehavioral mechanisms of human fear generalization. *NeuroImage, 55,* 1878–1888.

Durkheim, E. (1951). *Suicide: A study in sociology* (trans. G. Simpson & J. A. Spaulding). New York: The Free Press.

Durkin, M. (2002). The epidemiology of developmental disabilities in low income countries. *Mental Retardation and Developmental Disabilities Research Reviews, 8,* 206–211.

Durlak, J. A. (Ed.). (1998). Program implementation in preventive trials [special issue]. *Journal of Prevention and Intervention in the Community, 17* (2).

Durlak, J. A., & DuPre, E. P. (2008). Implementation matters: A review of research on the influence of implementation on program outcomes and the factors affecting implementation. *American Journal of Community Psychology, 41,* 327–350.

Durlak, J. A., Taylor, R. D., Kawashima, K., Pachan, M. K., DuPre, E. P., Cello, C. I., et al. (2007). Effects of positive youth development programs on school, family, and community systems. *American Journal of Community Psychology, 39,* 269–286.

Dutton, D. G. (2002). The neurobiology of abandonment homicide. *Aggression and Violent Behavior, 7,* 407–421.

Dutton, D. G., Saunders, K., Starzomski, A., & Batholomew, K. (1994). Intimacy-anger and insecure attachment as precursors of abuse in intimate relationships. *Journal of Applied Social Psychology, 24,* 1367–1386.

Dutton, D. G., & Starzomski, A. J. (1993). Borderline personality in perpetrators of psychological and physical abuse. *Violence and Victims, 8,* 327–337.

Dvorak-Bertsch, J. D., Curtin, J. J., Rubinstein, T. J., & Newman, J. P. (2009). Psychopathic traits moderate the interaction between cognitive and affective processing. *Psychophysiology,46* (5), 913 –921. doi:10.1111/j.1469-8986.2009.00833.x

Dykens, E. M. (2000). Annotation: Psychopathology in children with intellectual disability. *Journal of Child Psychology and Psychiatry, 41,* 407–417.

Dykens, E. M., Hodapp, R. M., & Finucane, B. M. (2000). *Genetics and mental retardation syndromes: A new look at behavioral interventions.* Baltimore, MD: Paul H. Brookes.

Dykens, E. M., Hodapp, R. M., & Leckman, J. F. (1987). Strengths and weaknesses in the intellectual functioning of males with Fragile X syndrome. *American Journal of Mental Deficiency, 92,* 234–236.

Dykens, E. M., Hodapp, R. M., & Leckman, J. F. (1994). *Behavior and development in Fragile X syndrome.* London: Sage.

Dykens, E. M., Leckman, J. F., Paul, R., & Watson, M. (1988). Cognitive, behavioral and adaptive functioning in Fragile X and non-Fragile X retarded men. *Journal of Autism and Developmental Disorders, 18,* 41–52.

Dykman, B. M., Horowitz, L. M., Abramson, L. Y., & Usher, M. (1991). Schematic and situational determinants of depressed and nondepressed students' interpretation of feedback. *Journal of Abnormal Psychology, 100,* 45–55.

Dyson, L. L., Edgar, E., & Crnic, K. (1989). Psychological predictors of adjustment by siblings of developmentally disabled children. *American Journal on Mental Retardation, 94,* 292–302.

D'Zurilla, T. J., & Goldfried, M. R. (1971). Problem solving and behavior modification. *Journal of Abnormal Psychology, 78,* 107–126.

D'Zurilla, T. J., & Nezu, A. M. (2010). Problem-solving therapy. In K. S. Dobson (Ed.), *Handbook of cognitive-behavioral therapies* (3rd ed., pp. 197–225). New York: Guilford Press.

Eagles, J. M., Johnston, M. I., Hunter, D., Lobban, M., & Millar, H. R. (1995). Increasing incidence of anorexia nervosa in the female population of northeast Scotland. *American Journal of Psychiatry, 152,* 1266–1271.

Early Head Start Benefits Children and Families. (2006). Retrieved from http://www.earlychildhoodrc.org/events/presentations/raikes.pdf

Ebly, E. M., Parhad, I. M., Hogan, D. B., & Fung, T. S. (1994). Prevalence and types of dementia in the very old: Results from Canadian Study of Health and Aging. *Neurology, 44,* 1593–1600.

Eccles, W. J. (1959). *Frontenac: The courtier governor.* Toronto: McClelland and Stewart.

Eckenrode, J., Campa, M., Luckey, D. W., Henderson, C. R., Jr., Cole, R., Kitzman, H., Anson, E., Sidora-Arcoleo, K., Powers, J., & Olds, D. (2010). Long-term effects of the prenatal infancy nurse home visitation on the life course of youths: 19-year follow-up of a randomized trial. *Archives of Pediatric and Adolescent Medicine, 164,* 9–15.

Edens, J. F., Marcus, D. K., & Morey, L. C. (2009). Paranoid personality has a dimensional latent structure: Taxometric analyses of community and clinical samples. *Journal of Abnormal Psychology, 118,* 545–553. doi:10.1037/a0016313

Eddy, K. T., Keel, P. K., Dorer, D. J., Delinsky, S. S., Franco, D. L., & Herzog, D. B. (2002). Longitudinal comparison of anorexia nervosa subtypes. *International Journal of Eating Disorders, 31,* 191–201.

Egan, S. K., & Perry, D. G. (1998). Does low self-regard invite victimization? *Developmental Psychology, 34,* 299–309. doi:10.1037/0012-1649.34.2.299

Ehlers, A., & Clark, D. M. (2000). A cognitive model of posttraumatic stress disorder. *Behaviour Research and Therapy, 38,* 319–345.

Ehlers, A., & Clark, D. M. (2003). Early psychological interventions for adult survivors of trauma: A review. *Biological Psychiatry, 53,* 817–826.

Ehlers, C. L., & Schuckit, M. A. (1990). EEG fast frequency activity in sons of alcoholics. *Biological Psychiatry, 27,* 631–641.

Einstein, D. A., & Menzies, R. G. (2004). The presence of magical thinking in obsessive compulsive disorder. *Behaviour Research and Therapy, 42,* 539–549.

El-Badri, S. R., & Robertshaw, B. A. (1998). Sexual fetishism associated with temporal lobe dysrhythmia and learning disability: Two case studies. *British Journal of Learning Disabilities, 26* (3), 110–114.

El-Gabalawy, R., Mackenzie, C. S., Shooshtari, S., & Sareen, J. (in press). Comorbid physical health problems and anxiety disorders: A population-based exploration of prevalence and health outcomes among older Canadian adults. *General Hospital Psychiatry.*

Elias, M. J. (1987). Establishing enduring prevention programs: Advancing the legacy of Swampscott. *American Journal of Community Psychology, 15,* 539–553.

Elkin, I. (1994). The NIMH Treatment of Depression Collaborative Research Program: Where we began and where we are. In A. E. Bergin & S. L. Garfield (Eds.), *Handbook of psychotherapy and behavior change* (4th ed., pp. 114–139). New York: Wiley.

Elkin, I., Shea, M. T., Watkins, J. T., Imber, S. M., Sotsky, S. M., Collins, J. F., et al. (1989). National Institute of Mental Health Treatment of Depression Collaborative Research Program: General effectiveness of treatments. *Archives of General Psychiatry, 46,* 971–982.

Elksnin, L. K., & Elksnin, N. (2004). The social-emotional side of learning disabilities. *Learning Disability Quarterly, 27,* 1–6.

Elliott, R., & Greenberg, L. S. (1995). Experiential therapy in practice: The process-experiential approach. In B. M. Bongar & L. E. Beutler (Eds.), *Comprehensive textbook of psychotherapy: Theory and practice* (pp. 123–139). New York: Oxford University Press.

Elliott, R., Greenberg, L. S., & Lietaer, G. (2004). Research on experiential psychotherapies. In M. J. Lambert (Ed.), *Bergin and Garfield's handbook of psychotherapy and behavior change* (5th ed., pp. 493–539). New York: Wiley.

Ellis, A. (1962). *Reason and emotion in psychotherapy.* New York: Lyle Stuart.

Ellis, A. (1991). *Reason and emotion in psychotherapy.* New York: Citadel.

Ellis, A. (1999). Early theories and practices of rational emotive behavior therapy and how they have been augmented and revised during the last three decades. *Journal of Rational-Emotive and Cognitive Therapy, 17,* 69–93.

Ellis, A. (2004). Why rational emotive behavior therapy is the most comprehensive and effective form of behavior therapy. *Journal of Rational-Emotive and Cognitive-Behavior Therapy, 22,* 85–92.

El-Sakka, A. (2006). Intracavernosal prostaglandin E_1 self vs office injection therapy in patients with erectile dysfunction. *International Journal of Impotence Research, 18,* 180–185.

Emerson, E., & Hatton, C. (2007). Contribution of socioeconomic position to health inequalities of British children and adolescents with intellectual disabilities. *American Journal on Mental Retardation, 112,* 140–150.

Emmelkamp, P. M. (1994). Behavior therapy with adults. In A. E. Bergin & S. L. Garlfield (Eds.), *Handbook of psychotherapy and behavior change* (4th ed., pp. 379–427). New York: Wiley.

Endler, N. S., & Magnusson, D. (1976). *Interactional psychology and personality.* Washington, DC: Hemisphere.

Eng, M. Y., Luczak, S. E., & Wall, T. L. (2007). ALDH2, ADH1B, and ADH1C genotypes in Asians: A literature review. *Alcohol Research & Health, 30,* 22–27.

Engel, G. L. (1977). The need for a new medical model: A challenge for biomedicine. *Science, 196,* 129–136.

Epp, A., & Dobson, K. S. (2010). The evidence base for cognitive-behavioral therapy. In K. S. Dobson (Ed.), *Handbook of cognitive-behavioral therapies* (pp. 39–73). New York: Guilford Press.

Epp, J. (1986). Achieving health for all: A framework for health promotion. *Canadian Journal of Public Health, 77,* 393–407.

Epp, J. (1988). *Mental health for Canadians: Striking a balance.* Ottawa: Minister of Supplies and Services.

Ericson, M., Tuvblad, C., Raine, A., Young-Wolff, K., & Baker, L. A. (2011). Heritability and longitudinal stability of schizotypal traits during adolescence. *Behavior Genetics, 41,* 499–511. doi:10.1007/s10519-010-9401-x

Erickson, J., & Johnson, G. M. (2011). Internet use and psychological wellness during late adulthood. *Canadian Journal on Aging, 30,* 197–209.

Erikson, E. (1950). *Childhood and society.* New York: Norton.

Erlenmeyer-Kimling, L., Rock, D., Roberts, S. A., Janal, M., Kestenbaum, C., Cronblatt, B., et al. (2000). Attention, memory, and motor skills as childhood predictors of schizophrenia-related psychoses: The New York High-Risk Project. *American Journal of Psychiatry, 157,* 1416–1422.

EsbjØrn, B. H., Hoeyer, M., Dyrborg, J., Leth, I., & Kendall, P. C. (2010). Prevalence and co-morbidity among anxiety disorders in a national cohort of psychiatrically referred children and adolescents. *Journal of Anxiety Disorders, 24,* 866–872. doi:10.1016/j.janxdis.2010.06.009

Escamilla, M. A., & Zavala, J. M. (2008). Genetics of bipolar disorder. *Dialogues in Clinical Neuroscience, 10* (2), 141–152.

Esposito, E., Wang, J. L., Adair, C. E., Williams, J. V., Dobson, K., Schopflocher, D., et al. (2007). Frequency and adequacy of depression treatment in a Canadian population sample. *Canadian Journal of Psychiatry, 52,* 780–789.

Essau, C. A., Sasagawa, S., Ishikawa, S. I., Okajima, I., O'Callaghan, J., & Bray, D. (in press). A Japanese form of social anxiety (taijin kyofusho): Frequency and correlates in two generations of the same family. *International Journal of Social Psychiatry.*

Essex, M. J., Klein, M. H., Slattery, M. J., Goldsmith, H. H., & Kalin, N. H. (2010). Early risk factors and developmental pathways to chronic high inhibition and social anxiety disorder in adolescence. *The American Journal of Psychiatry,167* (1), 40–46. doi:10.1176/appi.ajp.2009.07010051

Etkin, A., & Wager, T. D. (2007). Functional neuroimaging of anxiety: A meta-analysis of emotional processing in PTSD, social anxiety disorder, and specific phobia. *American Journal of Psychiatry, 164,* 1476–1488.

Eubig, P. A., Aguiar, A., & Schantz, S. L. (2010). Lead and PCBs as risk factors for attention deficit/hyperactivity disorder. *Environmental Health Perspectives, 118,* 1654–1667. doi:10.1289/ehp.0901852

Evans, G. W. (2003). A multimethodological analysis of cumulative risk and allostatic load among rural children. *Developmental Psychology, 39,* 924–933.

Evans, R. G. (1994). Introduction. In R. G. Evans, M. L. Barer, & T. R. Marmor (Eds.), *Why are some people healthy and others not? The determinants of health of populations.* New York: Aldine de Gruyter.

Everaerd, W. (1993). Male erectile disorder. In W. O'Donohue & J. H. Geer (Eds.), *Handbook of sexual dysfunctions: Assessment and treatment* (pp. 201–224). Needham Heights, MA: Allyn & Bacon.

Everson-Rose, S. A., & Lewis, T. T. (2005). Psychosocial factors and cardiovascular disease. *Annual Review of Public Health, 26,* 469–500.

Evraire, L. E., & Dozois, D. J. A. (2011). An integrative model of excessive reassurance seeking and negative feedback seeking in the development and maintenance of depression. *Clinical Psychology Review, 31,* 1291–1303.

Evraire, L. E., & Dozois, D. J. A. (2012). *If it be love indeed tell me how much: Exploring the origins and dynamics of excessive reassurance seeking.* Manuscript submitted for publication.

Exner, J. E. (1993). *The Rorschach: A comprehensive system, Vol 1. Basic foundations* (3rd ed.). New York: Wiley.

Exner, J. E. (2002). *The Rorschach: A comprehensive system, Vol. 1. Basic foundations and principles of interpretation* (4th ed.). New York: Wiley.

Exner, J. E., & Erdberg, P. (2005). *The Rorschach: A comprehensive system, Vol. 2. Advanced interpretation* (3rd ed.). New York: Wiley.

Eyberg, S. M., Nelson, M. M., & Boggs, S. R. (2008). Evidence-based psychosocial treatments for children and adolescents with disruptive behaviour. *Journal of Clinical Child and Adolescent Psychology, 37,* 215–237.

Eysenck, H. J. (1952). The effects of psychotherapy: An evaluation. *Journal of Consulting Psychology, 16,* 319–324.

Ezpeleta, L., Keeler, G., Erkanli, A., Costello, J., & Angold, A. (2001). Epidemiology of psychiatric disability in childhood and adolesence. *Journal of Child Psychopathology, 42,* 901–914.

Fabrega, H. (2007). How psychiatric conditions were made. *Psychiatry, 70,* 130–153.

Fagan, T. J., Ax, R. K., Liss, M., Resnick, R. J., & Moody, S. (2007). Prescriptive authority and preferences for training. *Professional Psychology: Research and Practice, 38,* 104–111.

Fairburn, C. G. (2008). *Cognitive behavior therapy and eating disorders.* New York: Guilford Press.

Fairburn, C. G. (2002). Cognitive-behavioral therapy for bulimia nervosa. In C. G. Fairburn & K. D. Brownell (Eds.), *Eating disorders and obesity* (pp. 358–361). New York: Guilford Press.

Fairburn, C. G., & Bohn, K. (2005). Eating disorder NOS (EDNOS): An example of the troublesome "not otherwise specified" (NOS) category in DSM-IV. *Behaviour Research and Therapy, 43,* 691–701.

Fairburn, C. G., & Cooper, Z. (1993). The Eating Disorder Examination (12th ed.). In C. G. Fairburn & G. T. Wilson (Eds.), *Binge eating: Nature, assessemnt and treatment,* (pp. 317–355). New York: Guilford Press.

Fairburn, C. G., Cooper, Z., Doll, H. A., Norman, P., & O'Connor, M. (2000). The natural course of bulimia nervosa and binge eating disorder in young women. *Archives of General Psychiatry, 57* (7), 659–665.

Fairburn, C. G., Cooper, Z., Doll, H. A., O'Connor, M. E., Bohn, K., Hawker, D. M., et al. (2009). Transdiagnostic cognitive-behavioural therapy for patients with eating disorders: A two-site trial with 60-week follow-up. *American Journal of Psychiatry, 166,* 311–319.

Fairburn, C. G., Cooper, Z., Doll, H. A., & Welch, S. L. (1999). Risk factors for anorexia nervosa—Three integrated case-control comparisons. *Archives of General Psychiatry, 56,* 468–476.

Fairburn, C. G., Cooper, Z., & Shafran, R. (2003). Cognitive behaviour therapy for eating disorders: A "transdiagnostic" theory and treatment. *Behaviour Research & Therapy, 41,* 509–528.

Fairburn, C. G., Jones, R., Peveler, R. C., Hope, R. A., & O'Connor, M. E. (1993). Psychotherapy and bulimia nervosa: The longer-term effects of interpersonal psychotherapy, behavior therapy, and cognitive therapy. *Archives of General Psychiatry, 48,* 463–469.

Fairburn, C. G., Marcus, M. D., & Wilson, G. T. (1993). Cognitive-behavioral therapy for binge eating and bulimia nervosa: A comprehensive treatment manual. In C. G. Fairburn & G. T. Wilson (Eds.), *Binge eating: Nature, assessment and treatment* (pp. 361–404). New York: Guilford Press.

Fairburn, C. G., Shafran, R., & Cooper, Z. (1998). A cognitive behavioural theory of anorexia. *Behaviour Research and Therapy, 37,* 1–13.

Falconer, D. S. (1960). *Introduction to quantitative genetics.* New York: Ronald Press.

Fallon, B. A. (2004). Pharmacotherapy of somatoform disorders. *Journal of Psychosomatic Research, 56,* 455–460.

Faraone, S. V., & Khan, S. A. (2006). Candidate gene studies of attention-deficit/hyperactivity disorder. *The Journal of Clinical Psychiatry, 67* (Suppl. 8), 13–20.

Faraone, S. V., Spencer, T., Aleardi, M., Pagano, C., & Biederman, J. (2004). Meta-analysis of the efficacy of methylphenidate for treating adult attention-deficit/hyperactivity disorder. *Journal of Clinical Psychopharmacology, 24,* 24–29.

Faris, R. E. L., & Dunham, H. W. (1939). *Mental disorders in urban areas.* Chicago: University of Chicago Press.

Farmer, A. E. (1996). The genetics of affective disorder. *International Review of Psychiatry, 8,* 369–372.

Farrington, D. P., Jolliffe, D., Loeber, R., Stouthamer-Loeber, M., & Kalb, L. M. (2001). The concentration of offenders in families, and family criminality in the prediction of boys' delinquency. *Journal of Adolescence, 24,* 579–596.

Farrington, D. P., Loeber, R., Elliot, D. S., Hawkins, J. D., Kandel, D. B., Klein, M. W., et al. (1990). Advancing knowledge about the onset of delinquency and crime. *Advances in Clinical Child Psychology, 13,* 283–342.

Fava, G. A., Fabbri, S., & Sonino, N. (2002). Residual symptoms in depression: An emerging therapeutic target. *Progress in Neuro-Pyschopharmacology and Biological Psychiatry, 26,* 1019–1027.

Fedoroff, J. P. (1993). Serotonergic drug treatment of deviant sexual interests. *Annals of Sex Research, 6,* 105–121.

Fehr, B., Samson, D., & Paulhus, D. L. (1992). The construct of Machiavellianism: Twenty years later. In C. D. Spielberger & J. N. Butcher (Eds.), *Advances in personality assessment* (Vol. 9., pp. 77–116). Hillsdale, NJ: Erlbaum.

Feinberg, M. E., Greenberg, M. T., & Osgood, D. W. (2004). Readiness, functioning, and perceived effectiveness in community prevention coalitions: A study of communities that care. *American Journal of Community Psychology, 33,* 163–176.

Feinstein, S. B., Fallon, B. A., Petkova, E., & Liebowitz, M. R. (2003). Item-by-item factor analysis of the Yale-Brown Obsessive Compulsive Scale Symptom Checklist. *Journal of Neuropsychiatry and Clinical Neurosciences, 15,* 187–193.

Feldman, M. A., Condillac, R. A., Tough, S. E., Hunt, S., & Griffiths, D. (2002). Effectiveness of community positive behavioral intervention for persons with developmental disabilities and severe behavioral challenges. *Behavior Therapy, 33,* 377–398.

Feldman, M. B., & Meyer, I. H. (2007). Eating disorders in diverse lesbian, gay, and bisexual populations. *International Journal of Eating Disorders, 40,* 218–226.

Fergus, S., & Zimmerman, M. A. (2005). Adolescent resilience: A framework for understanding healthy development in the face of risk. *Annual Review of Public Health, 26,* 399–419.

Fetveit, A. (2009). Late-life insomnia: A review. *Geriatrics and Gerontology International, 9,* 220–234.

Fichter, M., Cebulla, M., Quadflieg, N., & Naab, S. (2008). Guided self-help for binge eating/purging anorexia nervosa before inpatient treatment. *Psychotherapy Research, 18,* 594–603.

Fichter, M. M., & Quadflieg, N. (2007). Long-term stability of eating disorder diagnoses. *International Journal of Eating Disorders. Special Issue on Diagnosis and Classification, 40,* S61–S66.

Fick, D. M., Cooper, J. W., Wade, W. E., Waller, J. L., MacLean, R., & Beers, M. H. (2003). Updating the Beers criteria for potentially inappropriate medication use in older adults. *Archives of Internal Medicine, 163,* 2716–2724.

Filipek, P. A., Steinberg-Epstein, R., & Book, T. M. (2006). Intervention for autistic spectrum disorders. *NeuroRx, 3,* 207–216.

Findling, R. L., McNamara, N. K., Branicky, L. A., Schluchter, M. D., Lemon, E., & Blumer, J. L. (2000). A double-blind pilot study of risperidone in the treatment of conduct disorder. *Journal of the American Academy of Child and Adolescent Psychiatry, 39,* 509–516.

Fink, M., & Taylor, M. A. (2007). Electroconvulsive therapy: Evidence and challenges. *Journal of the American Medical Association, 298,* 330–332.

Finkelhor, D. (Ed.). (1984). *Child sexual abuse: New theory and research.* New York: Free Press.

Finlay, W. M. L., & Lyons, E. (2001). Methodological issues in interviewing and using self-report questionnaires with people with mental retardation. *Psychological Assessment, 13* (3), 319–335.

Finn, P. R., Zeitouni, N. C., & Pihl, R. O. (1990). Effects of alcohol on psychophysiological hyper reactivity to non-aversive and aversive stimuli in men at high risk for alcoholism. *Journal of Abnormal Psychology, 99,* 79–85.

Firestone, P., Bradford, J. M. W., McCoy, M., Greenberg, D. M., Larose, M. R., & Curry, S. (1998). Recidivism factors in convicted rapists. *Journal of American Academy Psychiatry and Law, 26* (2), 185–200.

Firestone, P., Dixon, K. L., Nunes, K. L., & Bradford, J. M. W. (2005). A comparison of incest offenders based on victim age. *Journal of the American Academy of Psychiatry and the Law, 33* (2), 223–232.

Firestone, P., Kingston, D. A., Wexler, A., & Bradford, J. M. (2006). Long-term follow-up of exhibitionists. *Journal of the American Academy of Psychiatry and the Law, 34,* 349–359.

Firestone, P., & Ledingham, J. (2007). Behaviour and emotional disorders of childhood and adolescence. In P. Firestone and D. Dozois (Eds.), *Abnormal psychology: Perspectives* (3rd ed., pp. 365–387). Toronto: Pearson Prentice Hall.

First, M. B., Gibbon, M., Spitzer, R. L., & Williams, J. B. W. (1996). *Structured Clinical Interview for DSM-IV Axis I Disorders—Research Version* (SCID-I, Version 2.0, February, 1996, Final version). New York: Biometrics Research.

First, M. B., Gibbon, M., Spitzer, R. B., & Williams, J. B. W. (1997). *Structured clinical interview for DSM-IV Axis II personality disorders.* Washington, DC: American Psychiatric Press.

First, M. B., Spitzer, R. B., Gibbon, M., & Williams, J. B. W. (1996). *Structured clinical interview for DSM-IV Axis I disorders—Clinician version.* Washington, DC: American Psychiatric Press.

First, M. B., Spitzer, R. B., Gibbon, M., & Williams, J. B. W. (2007). *Structured clinical interview for DSM-IV-TR Axis I disorders—Research version.* New York: Biometrics Research.

First, M. B., Williams, J. B. W., & Spitzer, R. L. (1996). *DTREE: The DSM-IV expert.* Toronto: MHS.

First Nations and Inuit Health Branch. (2004). 2004 baseline study among First Nations on-reserve and Inuit in the North: Final Report. Ottawa: Author.

Fisak, B., & Grills-Taquechel, A. E. (2007). Parental modeling, reinforcement, and information transfer: Risk factors in the development of child anxiety? *Clinical Child and Family Psychology Review, 10* (3), 213–231.

Fischbach, G. D. (1992). Mind and brain. *Scientific American, 267,* 48–57.

Fischer, B., Cruz, M. F., & Rehm, J. (2006). Illicit opioid use and its key characteristics: A select overview and evidence from a Canadian multisite cohort of illicit opioid users (OPICAN). *Canadian Journal of Psychiatry, 51,* 624–634.

Fischtein, D., Herold, E. S., & Desmarais, S. (2007). How much does gender explain in sexual attitudes and behaviors? A survey of Canadian adults. *Archives of Sexual Behavior, 36,* 451–461.

Fish, J. M. (Ed.). (2002). *Race and intelligence: Separating science from myth.* Mahwah, NJ: Erlbaum.

Fiske, A., Wetherell, J. L., & Gatz, M. (2009). Depression in older adults. *Annual Review of Clinical Psychology, 5,* 363–389.

Flamenbaum, R., & Holden, R. R. (2007). Psychache as a mediator in the relationship between perfectionism and suicidality. *Journal of Counseling Psychology, 54,* 51–61.

Flanagan, E. H., Keeley, J., & Blashfield, R. K. (2008). An alternative hierarchical organization of the mental disorders of the DSM-IV. *Journal of Abnormal Psychology, 117,* 693–698.

Flay, B. R., Biglan, A., Boruch, R. F., Gonzalez Castro, R., Gottfredson, D., Kellam, S., et al. (2005). Standards of evidence: Criteria for efficacy, effectiveness and dissemination. *Prevention Science, 6,* 151–175.

Fletcher, J. M., Francis, D. J., Shaywitz, S., Lyon, G. R., Floorman, B. R., Stuebing, K. K., et al. (1999). Intelligence testing and the discrepancy model for children with learning disabilities. *Learning Disabilities Research & Practice, 13,* 186–203.

Flint, A. J. (1994). Epidemiology and comorbidity of anxiety disorders in the elderly. *American Journal of Psychiatry, 151,* 640–649.

Flory, K., Molina, B. S., Pelham, W. E., Jr., Gnagy, E., & Smith, B. (2006). Childhood ADHD predicts risky sexual behavior in young adulthood. *Journal of Clinical Child and Adolescent Psychology, 35* (4), 571–577.

Flynt, S. W., Wood, T. A., & Scott, R. L. (1992). Social support of mothers of children with mental retardation. *American Journal of Mental Retardation, 4,* 233–236.

Foa, E. B., & Kozak, M. J. (1995). DSM-IV field trial: Obsessive-compulsive disorder. *American Journal of Psychiatry, 152,* 90–96.

Foley, D. L., Pickles, A., Maes, H. M., Silberg, J. L., & Eaves, L. J. (2004). Course and short-term outcomes of separation anxiety disorder in a community sample of twins. *Journal of the American Academy of Child and Adolescent Psychiatry, 43* (9), 1107–1114.

Fombonne, E. (1995). Anorexia nervosa: No evidence of an increase. *British Journal of Psychiatry, 166,* 462–471.

Fombonne, E. (1996). Is bulimia nervosa increasing in frequency? *International Journal of Eating Disorders, 19,* 287–296.

Fombonne, E. (2003). Epidemiological surveys of autism and other pervasive developmental disorders: An update. *Journal of Autism and Developmental Disorders, 27,* 641–651.

Fombonne, E. (2008). Thimerosal disappears but autism remains. *Archives of General Psychiatry, 65* (1), 15–16.

Fonseca-Pedrero, E., Lemos-Giráldez, S., Muñiz, J., García-Cueto, E., & Campillo-Álvarez, Á. (2008). Schizotypy in adolescence: The role of gender and age. *Journal of Nervous and Mental Disease, 196,* 161–165. doi:10.1097/NMD.0b013e318162aa79

Foote, B., Smolin, Y., Kaplan, M., Legatt, M. E., & Lipschitz, D. (2006). Prevalence of dissociative disorders in psychiatric outpatients. *American Journal of Psychiatry, 163,* 623–629.

Ford, M. R., & Widiger, T. A. (1989). Sex bias in the diagnosis of histrionic and antisocial personality disorders. *Journal of Consulting and Clinical Psychology, 57,* 301–305.

Fordyce, W. E. (1976). *Behavioural methods for chronic pain and illness.* St. Louis, MO: Mosby.

Forehand, R., Biggar, H., & Kotchick, B. A. (1998). Cumulative risk across family stressors: Short- and long-term effects for adolescents. *Journal of Abnormal Child Psychology, 26,* 119–128.

Forman, M. (Director). (1975). *One flew over the cuckoo's nest* [Motion picture]. USA: Fantasy Films.

Forsyth, J. P., & Chorpita, B. F. (1997). Unearthing the nonassociative origins of fears and phobias: A rejoinder. *Journal of Behaviour Therapy and Experimental Psychiatry, 28,* 297–305.

Forth, A. E., Kosson, D., & Hare, R. D. (2003). Manual for the youth version of the Hare Psychopathy Checklist-Revised (PCL-YV). Toronto: Multihealth Systems.

Foster, J. R., & Martin, C. C. (1990). Dementia. In D. Bienenfeld (Ed.), *Verwoerdt's clinical geropsychiatry* (3rd ed., pp. 66–84). Baltimore, MD: Williams & Wilkins.

Fournier, J. C., DeRubeis, R. J., Hollon, S. D., Dimidjian, S., Amsterdam, J. D., Shelton, R. C., et al. (2010). Antidepressant drug effects and depression severity. *Journal of the American Medical Association, 303,* 47–53.

Fowler, D., Garety, P. A., & Kuipers, E. (1995). *Cognitive behaviour therapy for psychosis: Theory and practice.* Toronto: Wiley.

Fox, D. R., Ireland, D., Lister-Sharp, D. J., & Breen, R. (2003). Longer-term primary prevention for alcohol misuse in young people: A systematic review. *Addiction, 98,* 397–411.

Frances, A. (1985). Validating schizotypal personality disorders: Problems with the schizophrenic connection. *Schizophrenia Bulletin, 11,* 595–597.

Frances, A. (2009). A warning sign on the road to DSM-V: Beware of its unintended consequences. *Psychiatric Times.* Retrieved from http://www.psychiatrictimes.com/display/article/10168/1425378?verify=0A

Frank, E., Kupfer, D. J., Thase, M. E., Mallinger, A. G., Swartz, H. A., Fagiolini, A. M., et al. (2005). Two-year outcomes for interpersonal and social rhythm therapy in individuals with bipolar I disorder. *Archives of General Psychiatry, 62,* 996–1004.

Frank, E., & Spanier, C. (1995). Interpersonal psychotherapy for depression: Overview, clinical efficacy, and future directions. *Clinical Psychology: Science and Practice, 2,* 349–369.

Frank, E., Swartz, H. A., & Kupfer, D. J. (2000). Interpersonal and social rhythm therapy: Managing the chaos of bipolar disorder. *Biological Psychiatry, 48,* 593–604.

Frank, J. D. (1961). *Persuasion and healing.* Baltimore, MD: Johns Hopkins University Press.

Frankel, E. B., & Gold, S. (2007). Principles and practices of early intervention. In I. Brown & M. Percy (Eds.), *A comprehensive guide to intellectual and developmental disabilities* (pp. 451–466). London: Paul Brookes.

Frankl, V. E. (1962). *Man's search for meaning.* Boston: Beacon Press.

Franklin, J. C., Schiele, B. C., Brozek, J., & Keys, A. (1948). Observations of human behavior in experimental semistarvation and rehabilitation. *Journal of Clinical Psychology, 4,* 28–45.

Franklin, M. E., Abramowitz, J. S., Bux, D. A., Zoellner, L. A., & Feeny, N. C. (2002). Cognitive-behavioral therapy with and without medication in the treatment of obsessive-compulsive disorder. *Professional Psychology: Research and Practice, 33,* 162–168.

Franklin, M. E., & Foa, E. B. (2008). Obsessive-compulsive disorder. In D. H. Barlow (Ed.), *Clinical handbook of psychological disorders: A step-by-step treatment manual* (4th ed., pp. 164–215). New York: Guilford Press.

Frasure-Smith, N., Lesperance, F., Juneau, M., Talajic, M., & Bourassa, M. G. (1999). Gender, depression and one-year prognosis after myocardial infarction. *Psychosomatic Medicine, 61,* 26–37.

Frasure-Smith, N., Lesperance, F., & Talajic, M. (1993). Depression following myocardial infarction: Impact on 6-month survival. *Journal of the American Medical Association, 270,* 1819–1825.

Frazier, P., Anders, S., Perera, S., Tomich, P., Tennen, H., Park, C., & Tashiro, T. (2009). Traumatic events among undergraduate students: Prevalence and associated symptoms. *Journal of Counseling Psychology, 56,* 450–460.

Freeman, D., Pugh, K., & Garety, P. (2008). Jumping to conclusions and paranoid ideation in the general population. *Schizophrenia Research, 102,* 254–260.

Freeston, M. H., Rheaume, J., Letarte, H., Dugas, M. J., & Ladouceur, R. (1994). Why do people worry? *Personality and Individual Differences, 17,* 791–802.

Freitas-Ferrari, M. C., Hallak, J. E. C., & Trzesniak, C. (2010). Neuroimaging in social anxiety disorder: A systematic review of the literature. *Progress in Neuro-Psychopharmacology and Biological Psychiatry, 34,* 565–580.

Frenkel-Brunswik, E. (1968). Adjustments and reorientation in the course of the life span. In B. L. Neugarten (Ed.), *Middle age and aging* (pp. 77–84). Chicago: University of Chicago Press.

Freud, S. (1905). Psychical (or mental) treatment. In J. Strachey (Ed.), *The complete psychological works* (Vol. 7). New York: Norton.

Freud, S. (1971). Mourning and melancholia (J. Riviere, Trans.). In M. Khan (Ed.), *Collected papers* (Vol. 4, pp. 152–170). London: Hogarth Press. (Original work published in 1917).

Freund, K. (1981). Assessment of pedophilia. In M. Cook & K. Howells (Eds.), *Adult sexual interest in children* (pp. 139–179). London: Academic Press.

Freund, K. (1990). Courtship disorder. In W. L. Marshall, D. R. Laws, & H. E. Barbaree (Eds.), *Handbook of sexual assault: Issues, theories and treatment of the offender* (pp. 195–207). New York: Plenum Press.

Frewen, P. A., Dozois, D. J. A., & Lanius, R. A. (2008). Neuroimaging studies of psychological interventions for mood and anxiety disorders: Empirical and methodological review. *Clinical Psychology Review, 28,* 228–246.

Frewen, P. A., Lanius, R. A., Dozois, D. J. A., Neufeld, R. W. J., Pain, C., & Densmore, M. (2008). Clinical and neural correlates of alexithymia in PTSD. *Journal of Abnormal Psychology, 117,* 171–181.

Frezza, M., Di Padova, C., Pozzato, G., Terpin, M., Baraona, E., & Lieber, C. S. (1990). High blood alcohol levels in women: The role of decreased gastric alcohol dehydrogenase activity and first-pass metabolism. *New England Journal of Medicine, 322* (2), 95–99.

Frick, P. J. (2002). Juvenile psychopathy from a developmental perspective: Implications for construct development and use in forensic assessments. *Law and Human Behavior, 26,* 247–253.

Frick, P. J. (2006). Developmental pathways to conduct disorder. *Child Psychiatric Clinics of North America, 15,* 311–332.

Frick, P. J., Barry, C. T., & Kamphaus, R. W. (2010). Projective techniques. In P. J. Frick, C. T. Barry, & R. W. Kamphaus (Eds.), *Clinical assessment of child and adolescent personality and behavior* (3rd ed., pp. 225–251). New York: Springer.

Frick, P. J., Bodin, S. D., & Barry, C. T. (2000). Psychopathic traits and conduct problems in community and clinic-referred samples of children: Further development of the Psychopathy Screening Device. *Psychological Assessment, 12,* 382–393.

Frick, P. J., & Ellis, M. (1999). Callous-unemotional traits and subtypes of conduct disorder. *Clinical Child and Family Psychology Review, 2,* 149–168.

Friedman, H. S., & Booth-Kewley, S. (1987). Personality, Type A behavior, and coronary heart disease: The role of emotional expression. *Journal of Personality and Social Psychology, 53,* 783–792.

Friedman, M., & Rosenman, R. H. (1959). Association of specific behavior pattern with blood and cardiovascular findings. *Journal of the American Medical Association, 169,* 1286–1296.

Friedman, M., & Rosenman, R. H. (1974). *Type A behavior and your heart.* New York: Knopf.

Friedman, M., Thoresen, C. E., Gill, J., Ulmer, D., Powell, L. H., Price, B. A., et al. (1986). Alteration of Type A behavior and its effect on cardiac recurrences in postmyocardial infarction patients: Summary results of the Recurrent Coronary Prevention Project. *American Heart Journal, 112,* 653–665.

Friedman, M. J. (2009). PTSD and other posttraumatic syndromes. In D. McKay, J. S. Abramowitz, S. Taylor, & G. J. G. Asmundson (Eds.), *Perspectives on the anxiety disorders: Implications for DSM-V and beyond* (pp. 377–409). New York: Springer.

Froehlich, T. E., Anixt, J. S., Loe, I. M., Chirdkiatgumchai, V., Kuan, L., & Gilman, R. C. (2011). Update on environmental risk factors for attention-deficit/hyperactivity disorder. *Current Psychiatry Reports, 13,* 333–344. doi:10.1007/s11920-011-0221-3

Fromm-Reichmann, F. (1959). *Psychoanalysis and psychotherapy: Selected papers.* Chicago: University of Chicago Press.

Fuchs, D., & Fuchs, L. (2006). Introduction to response to intervention: What, why and how valid is it? *Reading Research Quarterly, 41,* 93–99.

Fuchs, D., Mock, D., Morgan, P. L., & Young, C. (2003). Responsiveness-to-instruction: Definitions, evidence, and implications for the learning disabilities construct. *Learning Disabilities Research and Practice, 18,* 157–171.

Fudge Schormans, A., & Mandamin-Cameron, R. (2007). The intersection of race, disability and child maltreatment: Aboriginal children with developmental disabilities and the child welfare system. *Journal on Developmental Disabilities, 13,* 1–21.

Fulero, S. M. (1995). Review of the Hare Psychopathy Checklist–Revised. In J. C. Conoley & J. C. Impara (Eds.), *Twelfth mental measurements yearbook* (pp. 453–454). Lincoln, NE: Buros Institute.

Funkenstein, D., King, S., & Drolette, M. (1957). *Mastery of stress.* Cambridge, MA: Harvard University Press.

Furby, L., Weinrott, M. R., & Blackshaw, L. (1989). Sex offender recidivism: A review. *Psychological Bulletin, 105,* 3–30.

Furnham, A., & Nordling, R. (1998). Cross-cultural differences in preferences for specific male and female body shapes. *Personality and Individual Differences, 25,* 635–648.

Furukawa, T. A., Watanabe, N., & Churchill, R. (2006). Psychotherapy plus antidepressant for panic disorder with or without agoraphobia: Systematic review. *British Journal of Psychiatry, 188,* 305–312.

Gabbard, G. O., & Coyne, L. (1987). Predictors of response of antisocial patients to hospital treatment. *Hospital and Community Psychiatry, 38,* 1181–1185.

Gabrielli, W. F., Jr., Mednick, S. A., Volavka, J., Pollock, V. E., Schulsinger, F., & Itil, T. M. (1982). Electroencephalograms in children of alcoholic fathers. *Psychophysiology, 19,* 404–407.

Gagliese, L., & Katz, J. (2000). Medically unexplained pain is not caused by psychopathology. *Pain Research and Management, 5,* 251–257.

Gallagher-Thompson, D., & Coon, D. W. (2007). Evidence-based psychological treatments for distress in family caregivers of older adults. *Psychology and Aging, 22,* 37–51.

Galligan, P. T. (1996, March 15). *Report to the Attorney General of Ontario on certain matters relating to Karla Homolka.* Toronto: Government of Ontario.

Garb, H. N. (1997). Race bias, social class bias, and gender bias in clinical judgment. *Clinical Psychology: Science and Practice, 4,* 99–120.

Garety, P. A., & Freeman, D. (1999). Cognitive approaches to delusions: A critical review of theories and evidence. *British Journal of Clinical Psychology, 38,* 113–154.

Garfield, S. L. (1994). Research on client variables in psychotherapy. In A. E. Bergin & S. L. Garfield (Eds.), *Handbook of psychotherapy and behavior change* (4th ed., pp. 190–228). New York: Wiley.

Garfinkel, P. E., Lin, E., Goering, P., Spegg, C., Goldbloom, D. S., Kennedy, S., et al. (1995). Bulimia nervosa in a Canadian community sample: Prevalence and comparison of subgroups. *American Journal of Psychiatry, 152* (7), 1052–1058.

Garner, D. M., Garfinkel, P. E., Schwartz, D. M., & Thompson, M. M. (1980). Cultural expectations of thinness of women. *Psychological Reports, 47,* 483–491.

Garner, D. M., Olmsted, M. P., & Polivy, J. (1983). Development and validation of a multidimensional eating disorder inventory for anorexia and bulimia. *International Journal of Eating Disorders, 2,* 15–34.

Garrick, T., Minor, R. T., Buack, S., et al. (1989). Predictable and unpredictable shock stimulates gastric contractility and causes mucosal injury in rats. *Behavioural Neuroscience, 103,* 124–130.

Garyfallos, G., Katsigiannopoulos, K., Adamopoulou, A., Papazisis, G., Karastergiou, A., & Bozikas, V. P. (2010). Comorbidity of obsessive-compulsive disorder with obsessive-compulsive personality disorder: Does it imply a specific subtype of obsessive-compulsive disorder? *Psychiatry Research, 177,* 156–160. doi:10.1016/j.psychres.2010.01.006

Gater, R., Tansella, M., Korten, A., Tiemens, B. G., Mavreas, V. G., & Olatawura, M. O. (1998). Sex differences in the prevalence and detection of depressive and anxiety disorders in general health care settings. *Archives of General Psychiatry, 55,* 405–413.

Gatz, M., Kasl-Godley, J. E., & Karel, M. J. (1996). Aging and mental disorders. In J. E. Birren & K. W. Schaie (Eds.), *Handbook of the psychology of aging* (pp. 365–382). San Diego, CA: Academic Press.

Gatz, M., Popkin, S. J., Pino, C. P., & Vanden Bos, G. R. (1985). Psychological interventions with older adults. In J. E. Birren & K. W. Schaie (Eds.), *Handbook of the psychology of aging* (2nd ed., pp. 755–785). New York: Van Nostrand Reinhold.

Gawin, F. H., & Kleber, H. D. (1986). Abstinence symptomatology and psychiatric diagnosis in cocaine abusers. *Archives of General Psychiatry, 43,* 107–113.

Geary, D. C. (2011). Consequences, characteristics, and causes of mathematical learning disabilities and persistent low achievement in mathematics. *Journal of Developmental & Behavioral Pediatrics, 32,* 250–263.

Geary, D. C., Hoard, M. K., Nugent, L., & Byrd-Craven, J. (2008). Development of number line representations in children with mathematical learning disability. *Developmental Neuropsychology. Special Issue: Mathematics ability, performance, and achievement, 33,* 277–299.

Geddes, J. R., Burgess, S., Hawton, K., Jamison, K., & Goodwin, G. M. (2004). Long-term lithium therapy for bipolar disorder: Systematic review and meta-analysis of randomized control trials. *American Journal of Psychiatry, 161,* 217–222.

Gedye, A. (1995). *The Dementia Scale for Down Syndrome manual.* Vancouver, BC: Gedye Research and Consulting.

Geer, J. H., Davison, G. C., & Gatchel, R. I. (1970). Reduction of stress in humans through nonveridical perceived control of aversive stimulation. *Journal of Personality and Social Psychology, 16,* 731–738.

Geeraert, L., Van de Noortgate, W., Grietans, H., & Onghenea, P. (2004). The effects of early prevention programs for families with young children at risk for physical child abuse and neglect: A meta-analysis. *Child Maltreatment, 9,* 277–291.

Gelernter, J., and Kranzler, H. R. (2009). Genetics of alcohol dependence. *Human Genetics, 126,* 91–99.

Geller, J., Johnston, C., & Madsen, K. (1997). The role of shape and weight in self-concept: The shape and weight based self-esteem inventory. *Cognitive Therapy and Research, 21,* 5–24.

Geller, J. L., Fisher, W. H., Grudzinskas, A. J., Clayfield, J. C., & Lawlor, T. (2006). Involuntary outpatient treatment as "desintitutionalized coercion": The net-widening concerns. *International Journal of Law and Psychiatry, 29,* 551–562.

Gendall, K. A., Sullivan, P. E., Joyce, P. R., Carter, F. A., & Bulik, C. M. (1997). The nutrient intake of women with bulimia nervosa. *International Journal of Eating Disorders, 21,* 115–127.

Gendreau, P. (1996). The principles of effective intervention with offenders. In A. T. Harland (Ed.), *Choosing correctional options that work: Defining the demand and evaluating the supply* (pp. 117–130). Thousand Oaks, CA: Sage.

Gentes, E. L., & Ruscio, A. M. (2011). A meta-analysis of the relation of intolerance of uncertainty to symptoms of generalized anxiety disorder, major depressive disorder, and obsessive-compulsive disorder. *Clinical Psychology Review, 31,* 923–933.

George, L. K., Blazer, D. G., & Hughes, D. C. (1989). Social support and the outcome of major depression. *British Journal of Psychiatry, 154,* 478–485.

George, M. S., Rush, A. J., Marangell, L. B., Sackeim, H. A., Brannan, S. K., Davis, S. M., et al. (2005). A one-year comparison of vagus nerve stimulation with treatment as usual for treatment-resistant depression. *Biological Psychiatry, 58,* 364–373.

Gerardin, P., Cohen, D., Mazet, P., & Flament, M. F. (2002). Drug treatment of conduct disorder in young people. *European Neuropsychopharmacology, 12,* 361–370.

Gerber, A. J., Kocsis, J. H., Milrod, B. L., Roose, S. P., Barber, J. P., Thase, M. E., et al. (2011). A quality-based review of randomized controlled trials of psychodynamic psychotherapy. *American Journal of Psychiatry, 168,* 19–28.

Germain, A., & Thase, M. E. (2008). Sleep dysregulation and related regulatory models. In K. S. Dobson & D. J. A. Dozois (Eds.), *Risk factors in depression* (pp. 91–117). Oxford, UK: Elsevier/Academic Press.

Gershon, A. A., Dannon, P. N., & Grunhaus, L. (2003). Transcranial magnetic stimulation in the treatment of depression. *American Journal of Psychiatry, 160,* 835–845.

Gershuny, B. S., & Thayer, J. F. (1999). Relations among psychological trauma, dissociative phenomena, and trauma-related distress: A review and integration. *Clinical Psychology Review, 19,* 631–657.

Gersten, R., Clarke, B., & Mazzacco, M. (2007). Historical and contemporary perspectives on mathematical learning disabilities. In D. B. Berch & M. Mazzacco (Eds.), *Why is math so hard for some children? The nature and origins of mathematical learning difficulties and disabilities* (pp. 7–27). Baltimore, MD: Paul H. Brookes.

Gerstley, L. J., McLellan, A. T., Alterman, A. I., Woody, G. E., Luborsky, L., & Prout, M. (1989). Ability to form an alliance with the therapist: A possible marker of prognosis for patients with antisocial personality disorder. *American Journal of Psychiatry, 146,* 508–512.

Ghaziuddin, M. (2008). Defining the behavioral phenotype of Asperger syndrome. *Journal of Autism and Developmental Disorders, 38,* 138–142.

Gibbins, C., & Weiss, M. (2007). Clinical recommendations in current practice guidelines for diagnosis and treatment of ADHD in adults. *Current Psychiatry Reports, 9* (5), 420–426.

Gibbons, M. B. C., Crits-Christoph, P., & Hearon, B. (2008). The empirical status of psychodynamic therapies. *Annual Review of Clinical Psychology, 4,* 93–108.

Giesen-Bloo, J., Van Dyck, R., Spinhoven, P., Van Tilburg, W., Dirksen, C., Van Asselt, T., et al. (2006). Outpatient psychotherapy for borderline personality disorder: Randomized trial of schema-focused therapy vs. transference-focused psychotherapy. *Archives of General Psychiatry, 63,* 649–658.

Gilbert, M. (1996, July 27). The movement to break the gender barrier. *The Globe and Mail,* p. C-7.

Gilbertson, M. W., Shenton, M. E., Ciszewski, A., Kasai, K., Lasko, N. B., Orr, S. P., & Pitman, R. K. (2002). Smaller hippocampal volume predicts pathologic vulnerability to psychological trauma. *Nature Neuroscience, 5,* 1242–1247.

Gillberg, C., & Gillberg, C. (1989). Asperger syndrome—some epidemiological considerations: A research note. *Journal of Child Psychology and Psychiatry 30,* 631–638.

Gilmore, L., & Chambers, B. (2010). Intellectual disability and sexuality: Attitudes of disability support staff and leisure industry employees. *Journal of Intellectual & Developmental Disability, 35,* 22–28.

Gilna, S. (2004). Testosterone and erectile dysfunction. *The Journal of Men's Health and Gender, 1,* 407–412.

Gilpin, N. W., & Koob, G. F. (2008). Overview: Neurobiology of alcohol dependence with a focus on motivational mechanisms. *Alcohol Research & Health, 31,* 185–195.

Giltz, M. (2007, March 27). Second set. *The Advocate.* Retrieved from http://findarticles.com/p/articles/mi_m1589/is_/ai_n19039120

Gitlin, M. J. (1993). Pharmacotherapy of personality disorders: Conceptual framework and clinical strategies. *Journal of Clinical Psychopharmacology, 13,* 343–353.

Gitlin, M. J., Swendsen, J., Heller, T. L., & Hammen, C. L. (1995). Relapse and impairment in bipolar disorder. *American Journal of Psychiatry, 152,* 1635–1640.

Gittelman, R., Abicoff, H., Pollack, E., Klein, D., Katz, S., & Mattes, J. (1980). A controlled trial of behavior modification and methylphenidate in hyperactive children. In C. Whalen & B. Henker (Eds.), *Hyperactive children: The social ecology of identification and treatment* (pp. 221–246). New York: Academic Press.

Gjedde, A., & Wong, D. F. (1987). Positron tomographic quantification of neuroreceptors in human brain in vivo—with special reference to the D_2 dopamine receptors in caudate nucleus. *Neurosurgical Review, 10,* 9–18.

Gladstone, J., Nulman, I., & Koren, G. (1996). Reproductive risks of binge drinking during pregnancy. *Reproductive Toxicology, 10,* 3–13.

Glanze, W. D., Anderson, K. N., & Anderson, L. E. (1985). *The Mosby medical encyclopedia.* New York: American Library.

Glaser, R., Pearl, D. K., Kiecolt-Glaser, J. K., & Malarkey, W. B. (1994). Plasma cortisol levels and reactivation of latent Epstein-Barr virus in response to examination stress. *Psychoneuroendocrinology, 19,* 765–772.

Glatt, A. E., Zinner, S. H., & McCormack, W. M. (1990). The prevalence of dyspareunia. *Obstetrics & Gynecology, 75,* 433–436.

Glausiusz, J. (1997, January). The genes of 1996. *Discover,* p. 36.

Gleaves, D. H. (1996). The sociocognitive model of dissociative identity disorder: A reexamination of the evidence. *Psychological Bulletin, 120,* 42–59.

Glidden, L. M. (1993). What we do not know about families with children who have developmental disabilities: Questionnaire on resources and stress as a case study. *American Journal on Mental Retardation, 1993,* 481–495.

Glidden, L. M. (Ed.). (2001). Autism. *International Review of Research in Mental Retardation* (Vol. 23). San Diego, CA: Academic Press.

Goddard, H. (1912). *The Kallikak family: A study in the heredity of feeblemindedness.* New York: Macmillan.

Goeree, R., Farahati, F., Burke, N., Blackhouse, G., O'Reilly, D., Pyne, J., & Tarride, J. E. (2005). The economic burden of schizophrenia in Canada in 2004. *Current Medical Research and Opinion, 21* (12), 2017–2028.

Goettmann, C., Greaves, G. B., & Coons, P. M. (1994). *Multiple personality and dissociation 1791–1992: A complete bibliography.* Atlanta, GA: Greaves.

Goldapple, K., Segal, Z., Garson, C., Lau, M., Bieling, P., Kennedy, S., & Mayberg, H. (2004). Modulation of cortical-limbic pathways in major depression: Treatment-specific effects of cognitive behavior therapy. *Archives of General Psychiatry, 61,* 34–41.

Goldberg, J. F., & Kocsis, J. H. (1996). Relapse during SSRI treatment for depression. *Medscape Psychiatry & Mental Health eJournal, 1.*

Goldberg, R. L., Mann, L. S., Wise, T. N., & Segall, E. R. (1985). Parental qualities as perceived by borderline personality disorder. *Hillside Journal of Clinical Psychiatry, 7,* 134–140.

Goldberg, S. C., Schulz, S. C., Schulz, P. M., Resnick, R. J., Hamer, R. M., & Friedel, R. O. (1986). Borderline and schizotypal personality disorder treated with low-dose thiothixene versus placebo. *Archives of General Psychiatry, 43,* 680–686.

Golden, C. J. (2004). The adult Luria-Nebraska Neuropsychological Battery. In M. Hersen (Series Ed.), G. Goldstein & S. R. Beers (Vol. Eds.), *Comprehensive handbook of psychological assessment: Vol. 1. Intellectual and neuropsychological assessment* (pp. 133–156). New York: Wiley.

Goldfinger, C., Pukall, C. F., Gentilcore-Saulnier, E., McLean, L., & Chamberlain, S. (2009). A prospective study of pelvic floor physical therapy: Pain and sexual outcomes in provoked vestibulodynia. *The Journal of Sexual Medicine, 6,* 1955–1968.

Goldfried, M. R., & Norcross, J. C. (1995). Integrative and eclectic therapies in historical perspective. In B. Bongar & L. E. Beutler (Eds.), *Comprehensive textbook of psychotherapy: Theory and practice* (pp. 254–273). New York: Oxford University Press.

Goldman, M. S., Del Boca, F. K., & Darkes, J. (1999). Alcohol expectancy theory: The application of cognitive neuroscience. In K. E. Leonard & H. T. Blane (Eds.), *Psychological theories of drinking and alcoholism* (2nd ed., pp. 203–246). New York: Guilford Press.

Goldstein, G. (1990). Neuropsychological heterogeneity in schizophrenia: A consideration of abstraction and problem-solving abilities. *Archives of Clinical Neuropsychology, 5* (3), 251–264.

Goldstein, H., & Wickstrom, S. (1986). Peer intervention effects on communicative interaction among handicapped and nonhandicapped preschoolers. *Journal of Applied Behavior Analysis, 19,* 209–214.

Goldstein, T. F., Lue, T. F., Padma-Nathan, H., Rosen, R. C., Steers, W. D., & Wicker, P. A. (1998, May 14). Oral sildenafil in the treatment of erectile dysfunction. *New England Journal of Medicine, 338,* 1397–1404.

Gonzalez, J. E. J., & Espinel, A. I. G. (1999). Is IQ-achievement discrepancy relevant in the definition of arithmetic learning disabilities? *Learning Disability Quarterly, 22,* 291–301.

González-Maeso, J., Ang, R. L., Yuen, T., Chan, P., Weusstaub, N. V., López-Giménez, J. F., et al. (2008). Identification of a serotonin/glutamate receptor complex implicated in psychosis. *Nature, 452,* 93–97.

Goode, E. (1994, September). Battling deviant behavior. *US News and World Report,* 74–75.

Gordon, B. (2004). The Wechsler Preschool and Primary Scale of Intelligence, Third Edition (WPPSI-III). *Canadian Journal of School Psychology,19,* 205–220.

Gore, S., & Eckenrode, J. (1994). Context and process in research on risk and resilience. In R. J. Haggerty, L. R. Sherrod, N. Garmezy, & M. Rutter (Eds.), *Stress, risk, and resilience in children and adolescents: Processes, mechanisms, and interventions* (pp. 19–63). New York: Cambridge University Press.

Gormley, W. T. (2011). From science to policy in early childhood education. *Science, 333,* 978–981.

Gortner, E. T., Gollan, J. K., Dobson, K. S., & Jacobson, N. S. (1998). Cognitive-behavioral treatment for depression: Relapse prevention. *Journal of Consulting and Clinical Psychology, 66,* 377–384.

Gorton, G., & Akhtar, S. (1990). The literature on personality disorders, 1985–1988: Trends, issues, and controversies. *Hospital and Community Psychiatry, 41,* 39–51.

Gosselin, C., & Wilson, G. (1980). *Sexual variations.* London: Faber & Faber.

Gostin, L. (2005). The future of communicable disease control: Toward a new concept in public health law. *Milbank Quarterly, 83* (4), 1–17.

Gotlib, L. H., & Joormann, J. (2010). Cognition and depression: Current status and future directions. *Annual Review of Clinical Psychology, 6,* 285–312.

Gotowiec, A., & Beiser, M. (1994). Aboriginal children's mental health: Unique challenges. *Canada's Mental Health, 49,* 7–11.

Gottesman, I. I. (1991). *Schizophrenia genesis: The origins of madness.* New York: Freeman.

Gottesman, I. I., McGuffin, P., & Farmer, A. E. (1987). Clinical genetics as clues to the "real" genetics of schizophrenia: A decade of modest gains while playing for time. *Schizophrenia Bulletin, 13,* 23–47.

Gould, R. A., Otto, M. W., & Pollack, M. H. (1995). A meta-analysis of treatment outcome for panic disorder. *Clinical Psychology Review, 15,* 819–844.

Gould, S. J. (1985). *The flamingo's smile: Reflections in natural history.* New York: Norton.

Gourlay, D. L. (2000). Cocaine. In B. Brands (Ed.), *Management of alcohol, tobacco and other drug problems. A physician's manual* (pp. 175–187). Toronto: Centre for Addiction and Mental Health.

Government of Alberta. (1999, November 2). News release. Retrieved from http://www.gov.ab.ca/acn/199911/8353.html

Government of Canada. (2006). *The human face of mental health and mental illness in Canada, 2006.* Ottawa: Minister of Public Works and Government Services Canada.

Grabe, S., Ward, L. M., & Shibley Hyde, J. (2008). The role of the media in body image concerns among women: A meta-analysis of experimental and correlational studies. *Psychological Bulletin, 134,* 460–476.

Grafman, J., Schwab, K., Warden, D., Pridgen, A., Brown, H. R., & Salazar, A. M. (1996). Frontal lobe injuries, violence, and aggression: A report of the Vietnam Head Injury Study. *Neurology, 46,* 1231–1238.

Graham, C. A. (2010a). The DSM diagnostic criteria for female orgasmic disorder. *Archives of Sexual Behavior, 39,* 256–270.

Graham, C. A. (2010b). The DSM diagnostic criteria for female sexual arousal disorder. *Archives of Sexual Behavior, 39,* 240–255.

Graham, D. Y., Lew, G. M., Klein, P. D., et al. (1992). Effect of treatment of *Helicobacter pylori* infection on long-term recurrence of gastric or duodenal ulcer: A randomized, controlled study. *Annals of Internal Medicine, 116,* 705–708.

Graham, P. (1994). Prevention. In M. Rutter, E. Taylor, & L. Hersov (Eds.), *Child and adolescent psychiatry* (3rd ed., pp. 815–828). Oxford, UK: Blackwell Scientific Publications.

Granholm, E., McQuaid, J. R., McClure, F. S., Auslander, L. A., Perivoliotis, D., Pedrelli, P., et al. (2005). A randomized, controlled trial of cognitive behaviors social skills training for middle-aged and older outpatients with chronic schizophrenia. *American Journal of Psychiatry, 162* (3), 520–529.

Grant, B., Stinson, F. S., Dawson, D. A., Chou, P., Dufour, M., Compton, W., et al. (2004). Prevalence and co-occurrence of substance use disorders and independent mood and anxiety disorders: Results from the National Epidemiologic Survey on Alcohol and Related Conditions. *Archives of General Psychiatry, 61* (8), 807–816.

Grant, I. (1997). Canada's new mental disorder disposition provisions: A case study of the British Columbia Criminal Code Review Board. *International Journal of Law and Psychiatry, 20* (4), 419–443.

Grant, I., Ogloff, J. R. P., & Douglas, K. D. (2000). The British Columbia Review Panel: Factors influencing decision-making. *International Journal of Law and Psychiatry, 23,* 173–194.

Grant, P. M., Huh, G. A., Perivoliotis, D., Stolar, N. M., & Beck, A. T. (2011). Randomized trial to evaluate the efficacy of cognitive therapy for low-functioning patients with schizophrenia. *Archives of General Psychiatry.* Advance online publication. doi:10.1001/archgenpsychiatry.2011.129

Gray, J., Clark, A., Higenbottam, J., Ledwidge, B., & Paredes, J. (1985). Review panels for involuntary psychiatric patients: Which patients apply? *Canadian Journal of Psychiatry, 30,* 573–576.

Gray, J. E., & O'Reilly, R. L. (2001). Clinically significant differences among Canadian mental health acts. *Canadian Journal of Psychiatry, 46,* 315–321.

Gray, J. E., & O'Reilly, R. L. (2005). Canadian compulsory community treatment laws: Recent reforms. *International Journal of Law and Psychiatry, 28,* 13–22.

Grant, J. E., & Phillips, K. A. (2004). Is anorexia nervosa a subtype of body dysmorphic disorder? Probably not, but read on. . . *Harvard Review of Psychiatry, 12,* 123–126.

Greaves, G. B. (1980). Multiple personality: 165 years after Mary Reynolds. *The Journal of Nervous and Mental Disease, 168,* 577–596.

Green, G. (1994). The quality of the evidence. In H. C. Shane (Ed.), *Facilitated Communication: The clinical and social phenomenon.* San Diego, CA: Singular.

Green, G. (1996). Early behavioral intervention for autism: What does the research tell us? In C. Maurice, S. Luce, & G. Green (Eds.), *Behavioral intervention for young children with autism* (pp. 29–44). Austin, TX: Pro Ed.

Green, M. F. (2001). *Schizophrenia revealed.* New York: W. W. Norton.

Green, N. S., & Pass, K. A. (2005). Neonatal screening by DNA microarray: Spots and chips. *Nature Reviews: Genetics, 6,* 147–151.

Green, R., & Blanchard, R. (1995). Gender identity disorders. In H. I. Kaplan & B. J. Sadock (Eds.), *Comprehensive textbook of psychiatry* (pp. 1345–1360). Baltimore, MD: Williams & Wilkins.

Green, R., & Fleming, D. T. (1990). Transsexual surgery follow-up: Status in the 1990s. *Annual Review of Sex Research, 1,* 163–174.

Green, R. C., Cupples, L. A., Kurz, A., Auerbach, S., Go, R., Sadovnick, D., et al. (2003). Depression as a risk factor for Alzheimer disease: The mirage study. *Archives of Neurology, 60,* 753–759.

Greenberg, L. (2008). Emotion and cognition in psychotherapy: The transforming power of affect. *Canadian Psychology, 49,* 49–59.

Greenberg, L., Elliot, R., & Lietaer, G. (1994). Research on experiential therapies. In A. E. Bergin, & S. L. Garlfield, (Eds.), *Handbook of psychotherapy and behavior change* (4th ed., pp. 509–539). New York: Wiley.

Greenberg, R. P., Bornstein, R. F., Zborowski, M. J., Fisher, S., & Greenberg, M. D. (1994). A meta-analysis of fluoxetine outcome in the treatment of depression. *Journal of Nervous and Mental Disease, 182,* 547–551.

Greenberger, D., & Padesky, C. A. (1995). *Mind over mood: Change how you feel by changing the way you think.* New York: Guilford Press.

Greene, R. L., & Clopton, J. R. (2004). Minnesota Multiphasic Personality Inventory-2 (MMPI-2). In M. E. Maruish (Ed.), *The use of psychological testing for treatment planning and outcome assessment: Vol. 3. Instruments for adults* (3rd ed., pp. 449–478). Mahwah, NJ: Erlbaum.

Greenfield, T. K., Stoneking, B. C., Humphreys, K., Sundby, E., & Bond, J. (2008). A randomized trial of a mental health consumer-managed alternative to civil commitment for acute psychiatric crisis. *American Journal of Community Psychology, 42,* 135–144.

Greenfield-Spira, E., & Fischel, J. E. (2005). The impact of preschool inattention, hyperactivity, and impulsivity on social and academic development: A review. *Journal of Child Psychology and Psychiatry, 46,* 755–773.

Greisberg, S., & McKay, D. (2003). Neuropsychology of obsessive-compulsive disorder: A review and treatment implications. *Clinical Psychology Review, 23,* 95–117.

Grenier, G., & Byers, E. S. (1995). Rapid ejaculation: A review of conceptual, etiological and treatment issues. *Archives of Sexual Behavior, 24,* 446–472.

Grigorenko, E. L. (2006). Learning disabilities in juvenile offenders. *Child & Adolescent Psychiatric Clinics of North America, 15,* 353–371.

Grilo, C. M., Sanislow, C. A., Shea, M. T., Skodol, A. E., Stout, R. L., Pagano, M. E., et al. (2003). The natural course of bulimia nervosa and eating disorder not otherwise specified is not influenced by personality disorders. *International Journal of Eating Disorders, 34,* 319–330.

Grinker, R. R., Werble, B., & Drye, R. C. (1968). *The borderline syndrome.* New York: Basic Books.

Grisso, T. (1993). The differences between forensic psychiatry and forensic psychology. *Bulletin of the American Academy of Psychiatry and the Law, 21,* 133–145.

Groesz, L. M., Levine, M. P., & Murnen, S. K. (2002). The effect of experimental presentation of thin media images on body satisfaction: A meta-analytic review. *International Journal of Eating Disorders, 31,* 1–16.

Grogan, S. (2008). *Body image: Understanding body dissatisfaction in men, women and children* (2nd ed.). New York: Taylor & Francis.

Gross-Isseroff, R., Blegon, A., Voet, H., & Weizman, A. (2002). The suicide brain: A review of postmortem receptor/transporter binding studies. *Neuroscience and Biobehavioral Reviews, 22,* 653–661.

Grossman, H. J. (Ed.). (1983). *Classification in mental retardation.* Washington, DC: American Association on Mental Deficiency.

Groth-Marnat, G. (2009). *Handbook of psychological assessment* (5th ed.). New York: Wiley.

Grove, W. M., & Lloyd M. (2006). Meehl's contribution to clinical versus statistical prediction. *Journal of Abnormal Psychology, 115,* 192–194. doi:10.1037/0021-843X.115.2.192

Gruenberg, A. M., & Goldstein, R. D. (2003). Multiaxial assessment in the twenty-first century. In K. A. Phillips, M. B. First, & H. A. Pincus (Eds.), *Advancing DSM: Dilemmas in psychiatric diagnosis* (pp. 145–152). Washington, DC: American Psychiatric Association.

Guay, A. (2000, October). *Premenopausal and postmenopausal women with low libido have decreased testosterone and dehydroepiandrosterone-sulphate (DHEA-S) levels.* Paper presented at Female Sexual Function Forum: New Perspectives in the Management of Female Sexual Dysfunction, Boston.

Gunderson, J. G., & Singer, M. T. (1975). Defining borderline patients: An overview. *American Journal of Psychiatry, 132,* 1–10.

Gunzerath, L., Faden, V., Zakhari, S., & Warren, K. (2004). National Institute on Alcohol Abuse and Alcoholism report on moderate drinking. *Alcoholism: Clinical and Experimental Research, 28,* 829–847.

Gutjahr, E., Gmel, G., & Rehm, J. (2001). Relation between average volume of alcohol consumption and disease: An overview. *European Addiction Research, 7,* 117–127.

Guo, G., Jia, K-R, Shi, Y., Liu, X-F, Liu, K-Y, Qi, W., et al. (2009). Psychological stress enhances the colonization of the stomach by *Helicobacter pylori* in the BALB/c mouse. *Stress, 12,* 478–485.

Guralnik, O., Giesbrecht, T., Knutelska, M., Sirroff, B., & Simeon, D. (2007). Cognitive functioning in depersonalization disorder. *Journal of Nervous and Mental Disease, 195* (12), 983–988.

Guyton, A. C. (1991). *Textbook of medical physiology* (8th ed., pp. 365–384). Philadelphia: Saunders.

Hachett, M. L., Yapa, C., Parag, V., & Anderson, C. S. (2005). Frequency of depression after stroke: A systematic review of observational studies. *Stroke, 36,* 1330–1340.

Hadjistavropoulos, H. D., Craig, K. D., & Hadjistavropoulos, T. (1998). Cognitive and behavioural responses to illness information: The role of health anxiety. *Behaviour Research and Therapy, 36* (2), 149–164.

Häfner, H., & an der Heiden, W. (1999). The course of schizophrenia in the light of modern follow-up studies: The ABC and WHO studies. *European Archives of Psychiatry and Clinical Neurosciences, 249* (Suppl. 4), 14–26.

Hagberg, B., Aicardi, J., Dias, K., & Ramos, O. (1983). A progressive syndrome of autism, dementia, ataxia, and loss of purposeful hand use in girls. Rett's syndrome: Report of 35 cases. *Annals of Neurology, 14,* 471–479.

Hagerman, R. (1987). Fragile X syndrome. *Current Problems in Pediatrics, 17,* 621–674.

Hagerman, R. J., Rivera, S. M., & Hagerman, P. J. (2008). The Fragile X family of disorders: A model for autism and targeted treatments. *Current Pediatric Reviews, 4,* 40–52.

Hahlweg, K., & Markman, H. J. (1988). Effectiveness of behavioral marital therapy: Empirical status of behavioral techniques in preventing and alleviating marital distress. *Journal of Consulting and Clinical Psychology, 56,* 440–447.

Häkkänen-Nyholm, H., & Hare, R. D. (2009). Psychopathy, homicide, and the courts: Working the system. *Criminal Justice and Behavior, 36,* 761–777. doi:10.1177/0093854809336946

Haldipur, C. V. (1984). Madness in ancient India; Concept of insanity in Charaka Samhita (1st century A.D.). *Comprehensive Psychiatry, 25,* 335–344.

Hall, G. C. N., & Hirschman, R. (1991). Toward a theory of sexual aggression: A quadripartite model. *Journal of Consulting and Clinical Psychology, 59,* 662–669.

Halperin, J. M., & Schulz, K. P. (2006). Revisiting the role of the prefrontal cortex in pathophysiology of attention-deficit/hyperactivity disorder. *Psychological Bulletin, 132* (4), 560–581.

Hamilton, S., Rothbart, M., & Dawes, R. M. (1986). Sex bias, diagnosis, and DSM-III. *Sex Roles, 15,* 269–274.

Hammen, C. (1991). Generation of stress in the course of unipolar depression. *Journal of Abnormal Psychology, 101,* 45–52.

Hammen, C., & Shih, J. H. (2008). Stress generation and depression. In K. S. Dobson & D. J. A. Dozois (Eds.), *Risk factors in depression* (pp. 409–428). Oxford, UK: Elsevier/Academic Press.

Hancock, J., Woodworth, M. T., & Porter, S. (2011, in press). Hungry like the wolf: A word pattern analysis of the language of psychopaths. *Legal and Criminological Psychology.*

Hans, S. L., Auerbach, J. G., Styr, B., & Marcus, J. (2004). Offspring of parents with schizophrenia: Mental disorders during childhood and adolescence. *Schizophrenia Bulletin, 30,* 303–315.

Hansen, P. E., Ravnkilde, B., Videbech, P., Clemmensen, K., Sturlason, R., Reiner, M., et al. (2011). Low-frequency repetitive transcranial magnetic stimulation inferior to electroconvulsive therapy in treating depression. *Journal of ECT, 27,* 26–32.

Hanson, K. R., & Morton-Bourgon, K. E. (2005). The characteristics of persistent sexual offenders: A meta-analysis of recidivism studies. *Journal of Consulting and Clinical Psychology, 73,* 1154–1163.

Hanson, R. K., Gordon A., Harris, A. J., Marques, J. K., Murphy, W., Quinsey, V. L., & Seto, M. (2002). First report of the collaborative outcome data project on the effectiveness of psychological treatment for sex offenders. *Sexual Abuse: A Journal of Research and Treatment, 14,* 169–194.

Harari, D., Bakermans-Kranenburg, M. J., & van Ijzendoorn, M. J. (2007). Attachment, disorganization, and dissociation. In E. Vermetten, M. J. Dorahy, & D. Spiegel (Eds.), *Traumatic dissociation: Neurobiology and treatment* (pp. 31–54). Washington, DC: American Psychiatric Publishing.

Harburg, E., Davis, D. R., & Caplan, R. (1982). Parent and offspring alcohol use. *Journal of Studies on Alcohol, 43,* 497–516.

Harding, C. M., Brooks, G. W., Ashikaga, T., Strauss, J. S., & Breier, A. (1987). The Vermont longitudinal study of persons with severe mental illness. I. Methodology, study sample, and overall status 32 years later. *American Journal of Psychiatry, 144,* 18–26.

Harding, T. W. (1992). Psychopathic disorder: Time for a decent burial of a bad legal concept? *Criminal Behavior and Mental Health, 2,* vi–ix.

Hardy, J. D., & Smith, T. W. (1988). Cynical hostility and vulnerability to disease: Social support, life stress and physiological response to conflict. *Health Psychology, 7,* 447–459.

Hare, E. (1988). Schizophrenia as a recent disease. *British Journal of Psychiatry, 153,* 521–531.

Hare, R. D. (1970). *Psychopathy: Theory and research.* New York: Wiley.

Hare, R. D. (1980). A research scale for the assessment of psychopathy in criminal populations. *Personality and Individual Differences, 1,* 111–119.

Hare, R. D. (1983). Diagnosis of antisocial personality disorder in two prison populations. *American Journal of Abnormal Psychiatry, 140,* 887–890.

Hare, R. D. (1985). A comparison of procedures for the assessment of psychopathy. *Journal of Consulting and Clinical Psychology, 53,* 7–16.

Hare, R. D. (1991). *The Hare Psychopathy Checklist–Revised.* Toronto: Multihealth Systems.

Hare, R. D. (1993). *Without conscience: The disturbing world of the psychopaths among us.* New York: Simon & Schuster.

Hare, R. D. (1996). Psychopathy: A clinical construct whose time has come. *Criminal Justice and Behavior, 23,* 25–54.

Hare, R. D. (1998). Psychopathy and its nature: Implications for mental health and criminal justice systems. In T. Millon, E. Simonsen, M. Birkert-Smith, & R. D. Davis (Eds.), *Psychopathy: Antisocial criminal and violent behavior* (pp. 188–212). New York: Guilford Press.

Hare, R. D. (2003). *The Hare Psychopathy Checklist–Revised* (2nd ed.). Toronto: Multihealth Systems.

Hare, R. D., & Hare, A. S. (1967). Psychopathic behaviour: A bibliography. *Excerpta Criminologica, 7,* 365–386.

Hare, R. D., Hart, S. D., & Harpur, T. J. (1991). Psychopathy and DSM-IV criteria for antisocial personality disorder. *Journal of Abnormal Psychology, 100,* 391–398.

Hare, R. D., & Neumann, C. S. (2009). Psychopathy: Assessment and forensic implications. *The Canadian Psychiatric Association Journal / La Revue de l'Association des psychiatres du Canada, 54,* 791–802.

Harkness, K. L. (2008). Life events and hassles. In K. S. Dobson & D. J. A. Dozois (Eds.), *Risk factors in depression* (pp. 317–341). Oxford, UK: Elsevier/Academic Press.

Harkness, K. L., Alavi, N., Monroe, S. M., Slavich, G. M., Gotlib, I. H., & Bagby, R. M. (2010). Sex differences in life events prior to onset of major depressive disorder: The moderating effect of age. *Journal of Abnormal Psychology, 119,* 791–803.

Harkness, K. L., & Lumley, M. N. (2007). Child abuse and neglect and the development of depression in children and adolescents. In J. Abela & B. Hankin (Eds.), *Depression in children and adolescents.* New York: Guilford Press.

Harkness, K. L., Stewart, J. G., & Wynne-Edwards, K. E. (2011). Cortisol reactivity to social stress in adolescents: Moderation by depression severity and child maltreatment. *Psychoneuroendocrinology, 36,*173–181.

Harley, M., Kelleher, I., Clarke, M., Lynch, F., Arseneault, L., Connor, D., et al. (2010). Cannabis use and childhood trauma interact additively to increase the risk of psychotic symptoms in adolescence. *Psychological Medicine, 40,* 1627–1631.

Harlow, J. M. (1848). Passage of an iron rod through the head. *Boston Medical and Surgical Journal, 39,* 389–393.

Harlow, J. M. (1868). Recovery from the passage of an iron rod through the head. *Publications of the Massachusetts Medical Society, 2,* 327–347.

Harper, S. (2011). An examination of structural dissociation of the personality and the implications for cognitive behavioural therapy. *The Cognitive Behaviour Therapist, 4,* 53–67.

Harpur, T. J., & Hare, R. D. (1994). The assessment of psychopathy as a function of age. *Journal of Abnormal Psychology, 103,* 604–609.

Harrington, A. (2008). *The cure within: A history of mind-body medicine.* New York: Norton.

Harris, G. T. (1989). The relationship between neuroleptic drug dose and the performance of psychiatric patients in a maximum security token economy program. *Journal of Behavior Therapy and Experimental Psychiatry, 20,* 57–67.

Harris, G. T., Rice, M. E., & Cormier, C. A. (1991). Length of detention in matched groups of insanity acquittees and convicted offenders. *International Journal of Law and Psychiatry, 14,* 223–236.

Harris, G. T., Rice, M. E., & Quinsey, V. L. (1993). Violent recidivism of mentally disordered offenders: The development of a statistical prediction instrument. *Criminal Justice and Behavior, 20,* 315–335.

Harris, G. T., Rice, M. E., Quinsey, V. L., Lalumiere, M. L., Boer, D., & Lang, C. (2003). A multi-site comparison of actuarial risk instruments for sex offenders. *Psychological Assessment, 15,* 413–425.

Harris, J. C. (1995). Schizophrenia: A neurodevelopmental disorder. In J. C. Harris, *Developmental neuropsychiatry. Vol. II: Assessment, diagnosis, and treatment of developmental disorders* (pp. 332–333). Cambridge, UK: Cambridge University Press.

Harrison, P., & Oakland, T. (2003). *Adaptive Behavior Assessment System* (2nd ed.). San Antonio, TX: The Psychological Corporation.

Harrison, P. J. (1999). The neuropathology of schizophrenia: A critical review of the data and their interpretation. *Brain, 122,* 593–624.

Harrow, M., Lanin-Kettering, L., & Miller, J. G. (1989). Impaired perspective and thought pathology in schizophrenic and psychotic disorders. *Schizophrenia Bulletin, 15,* 605–623.

Hart, S. D. (2001a). Assessing and managing violence risk. In K. S. Douglas, C. D. Webster, S. D. Hart, D. Eaves, & J. R. P. Ogloff (Eds.), *HCR-20 violence risk management companion guide* (pp. 13–25). Burnaby, BC: Mental Health, Law, & Policy Institute, Simon Fraser University, and Department of Mental Health Law and Policy, Florida Mental Health Institute, University of South Florida.

Hart, S. D. (2001b). Forensic issues. In J. Livesley (Ed.), *The handbook of personality disorders* (pp. 555–569). New York: Guilford Press.

Hart, S. D., & Hare, R. D. (1989). Discriminant validity of the Psychopathy Checklist in a forensic psychiatric population. *Psychological Assessment: A Journal of Consulting and Clinical Psychology, 1,* 211–218.

Hart, S. D., & Hare, R. D. (1992). Predicting fitness to stand trial: The relative power of demographic, criminal, and clinical variables. *Forensic Reports, 5,* 53–65.

Hart, S. D., & Hare, R. D. (1997). Psychopathy: Assessment and association with criminal behavior. In D. Stoff, J. Breiling, & J. D. Maser (Eds.), *Handbook of antisocial behavior* (pp. 22–35). New York: Wiley.

Hart, S. D., Roesch, R., Corrado, R. R., & Cox, D. N. (1993). The Referral Decision Scale: A validation study. *Law and Human Behavior, 17,* 611–623.

Hartmann, U., Heiser, K., Ruffer-Hesse, C., & Kloth, G. (2002). Female sexual desire disorders: Subtypes, classification, personality factors and new directions for treatment. *World Journal of Urology, 20* (2), 79–88.

Hartung, C. M., & Widiger, T. A. (1998). Gender differences in the diagnosis of mental disorders: Conclusions and controversies of the DSM-IV. *Psychological Bulletin, 123,* 260–278.

Harvey, P. D. (2001). Cognitive and functional impairments in elderly patients with schizophrenia: A review of the recent literature. *Harvard Review of Psychiatry, 9,* 59–68.

Harvey, P. D., & Keefe, R. S. E. (2001). Studies of cognitive change in patients with schizophrenia following novel antipsychotic treatment. *American Journal of Psychiatry, 158,* 176–184.

Harvey, P. D., Koren, D., Reichenberg, A., & Bowie C. R. (2006). Negative symptoms and cognitive deficits: What is the nature of their relationship? *Schizophrenia Bulletin, 32,* 250–258.

Hasher, L., Goldstein, D., & May, C. P. (2005). It's about time: Circadian rhythms, memory, and aging. In C. Izawa & N. Ohta (Eds.), *Human learning and memory: Advances in theory and application: The 4th Tsukuba International Conference on Memory* (pp. 199–217). Mahwah, NJ: Lawrence Erlbaum Associates.

Haslam, J. (1976). *Observations on madness and melancholy.* New York: Arno Press. (Original work published 1809)

Hastings, R. P., & Taunt, H. M. (2002). Positive perceptions in families of children with developmental disabilities. *American Journal on Mental Retardation, 107,* 116–127.

Hatchett, G. T., & Park, H. L. (2003). Comparison of four operational definitions of premature termination. *Psychotherapy, 40,* 226–231.

Hatzimouratidis, K., & Hatzichristou, D. G. (2005). A comparative review of the options for treatment of erectile dysfunction: Which treatment for which patient? *Drugs, 65,* 1621–1650.

Hawgood, J., & De Leo, D. (2008). Anxiety disorders and suicidal behaviour: An update. *Current Opinion in Psychiatry, 21,* 51–64.

Hawe, P., Shiell, A., & Riley, T. (2004). Complex interventions: How "out of control" can a randomized trial be? *British Medical Journal, 328,* 1561–1563.

Haworth-Hoeppner, S. (2000). The critical shapes of body image: The role of culture and family in the production of eating disorders. *Journal of Marriage and the Family, 62,* 212–227.

Hawton, K., Catalan, J., & Fagg, J. (1992). Sex therapy for erectile dysfunction: Characteristics of couples, treatment outcome, and prognostic factors. *Archives of Sexual Behavior, 21,* 161–176.

Hawton, K., & Harriss, L. (2007). Deliberate self-harm in young people: Characteristics and subsequent mortality in a 20-year cohort of patients presenting to hospital. *Journal of Clinical Psychiatry, 68,* 1574–1583.

Hay, P., & Fairburn, C. G. (1998). The validity of the DSM-IV scheme for classifying bulimic eating disorders. *International Journal of Eating Disorders, 23,* 7–15.

Hayden, E. P., Dougherty, L. R., Maloney, B., Durbin, C. E., Olino, T. M., Nurnberger, J. I., Jr., et al. (2008). Temperamental fearfulness in childhood and the serotonin transporter promoter region polymorphism: A multimethod association study. *Psychiatric Genetics, 17,* 135–142.

Hayden, E. P., Dougherty, L. R., Maloney, B., Olino, T. M., Durbin, C. E., Sheihk, H. I., et al. (2008). Early-emerging cognitive vulnerability to depression and the serotonin transporter promoter region polymorphism. *Journal of Affective Disorders, 107,* 227–230.

Hayden, E. P., Klein, D. N., Dougherty, L. R., Olino, T. M., Durbin, C. E., Sheikh, H. I., & Singh, S. (2010a). The dopamine D_2 receptor gene and depressive and anxious symptoms in childhood: Associations and evidence for gene-environment correlation and gene-environment interaction. *Psychiatric Genetics, 20,* 304–310.

Hayden, E. P., Klein, D. N., Dougherty, L. R., Olino, T. M., Durbin, C. E., Sheikh, H. I., & Singh, S. (2010b). The role of BDNF genotype, parental depression, and relationship discord in predicting early-emerging negative emotionality. *Psychological Science, 21,* 1678–1685.

Hayden, E. P., Klein, D. N., Sheikh, H. I., Olino, T. M., Dougherty, L. R., Dyson, M. W., et al. (2010). The serotonin transporter promoter polymorphism and childhood positive and negative emotionality. *Emotion, 10,* 696–702.

Hayes, S. C., Villatte, M., Levin, M., & Hildebrandt, M. (2011). Open, aware, and active: Contextual approaches as an emerging trend in the behavioural and cognitive therapies. *Annual Review of Clinical Psychology, 7,* 141–168.

Health and Welfare Canada. (1988). *The epidemiology of mental retardation.* Report of the Working Group. Ottawa: Ministry of National Health and Welfare.

Health Canada. (1998). HIV and AIDS among women in Canada. *HIV/ AIDS Epi Update.* Ottawa: Author.

Health Canada. (1999). Measuring up: A health surveillance update on Canadian children and youth. Retrieved from http://www.hc-sc.gc.ca/pphb-dgspsp/publicat/meas-haut/mu_y_e.html

Health Canada. (2002). *A report on mental illnesses in Canada.* Ottawa: Health Canada Editorial Board. Retrieved from http://www.phac-aspc.gc.ca/publicat/miic-mmac/index.html

Health Canada. (2003). *Canadian community health survey: Mental health and well-being.* Ottawa: Author.

Health Canada. (2006). New antidepressants linked to serious lung disorders in newborns. Retrieved from http://www.hc-sc.gc.ca/media/advisories-avis/_2006/2006_11-eng.php

Health Canada. (2010a). Canadian Alcohol and Drug Use Monitoring Survey (CADUMS). Retrieved from http://www.hc-sc.gc.ca/hc-ps/drugs-drogues/stat/_2010/summary-sommaire-eng.php

Health Canada. (2010b). Canadian Tobacco Use Monitoring Survey (CTUMS) 2010. Retrieved from http://www.hc-sc.gc.ca/hc-ps/tobac-tabac/research-recherche/stat/ctums-esutc_2010_graph-eng.php

Health Canada. (2010c). Health Canada reminds Canadians to manage caffeine consumption. Retrieved from http://www.hc-sc.gc.ca/ahc-asc/media/advisories-avis/_2010/2010_40-eng.php

Health Canada. (2011). Caffeine in food. Retrieved from http://www.hc-sc.gc.ca/fn-an/securit/addit/caf/food-caf-aliments-eng.php

Health Care Consent Act, S.O. 1996, c. 2, Sch. A, art. 4.

Heatherton, T. F., & Baumeister, R. F. (1991). Binge-eating as escape from self-awareness. *Psychological Bulletin, 110,* 86–108.

Heaton, R. K., Chelune, G. J., Talley, J. L., Kay, G. G., & Curtiss, G. (1993). *Wisconsin Card Sorting Test manual: Revised and expanded.* Odessa, FL: Psychological Assessment Resources.

Hebb, D. O., & Penfield, W. (1940). Human behavior after extensive bilateral removals from the frontal lobes. *Archives of Neurology and Psychiatry, 44,* 421–438.

Heber, R. (1959). A manual on terminology and classification in mental retardation. *American Journal of Mental Deficiency, 56* (Monograph Suppl.).

Hechtman, L. (1996). Families of children with attention deficit hyperactivity disorder: A review. *Canadian Journal of Psychiatry, 41* (6), 350–360.

Hecker, M. H. L., Chesney, M., Black, G. W., & Frautschi, N. (1988). Coronary-prone behaviors in the Western Collaborative Group Study. *Psychosomatic Medicine, 50,* 153–164.

Heim, C., & Nemeroff, C. B. (2001). The role of childhood trauma in the neurobiology of mood and anxiety disorders: Preclinical and clinical studies. *Biological Psychiatry, 49,* 1023–1039.

Heim, N., & Hursch, C. J. (1979). Castration for sex offenders: Treatment or punishment? A review and critique of recent European literature. *Archives of Sexual Behavior, 8,* 281–305.

Heim, C., Newport, D. J., Heit, S., Graham, Y. P., Wilcox, M., Bonsall, R., et al. (2000). Pituitary-adrenal and autonomic responses to stress in women after sexual and physical abuse in childhood. *Journal of the American Medical Association, 284,* 592–597.

Heinberg, L. J., Thompson, J. K., & Stormer, S. (1995). Development and validation of the sociocultural attitudes towards appearance questionnaire. *International Journal of Eating Disorders, 17,* 81–89.

Heinrichs, R. W. (2001). *In search of madness: Schizophrenia and neuroscience.* New York: Oxford University Press.

Heinrichs, R. W. (2004). Meta-analysis and the science of schizophrenia: Variant evidence or evidence of variants? *Neuroscience and Biobehavioral Reviews, 28,* 379–394.

Heinrichs, R. W., & Awad, A. G. (1993). Neurocognitive subtypes of chronic schizophrenia. *Schizophrenia Research, 9* (1), 49–58.

Heinrichs, R. W., Miles, A. A., Smith, D., Zargarian, T., McDermid Vaz, S., Goldberg, J. O., & Ammari, N. (2008). Cognitive, clinical, and functional characteristics of verbally superior schizophrenia patients. *Neuropsychology, 22,* 321–328.

Heinrichs, R. W., & Zakzanis, K. K. (1998). Neurocognitive deficit in schizophrenia: A quantitative review of the evidence. *Neuropsychology, 12,* 426–445.

Heinrichs, W. (2007). Cognitive improvement in response to antipsychotic drugs. *Archives of General Psychiatry, 64,* 631–632.

Heisel, M. J. (2006). Suicide and its prevention among older adults. *Canadian Journal of Psychiatry, 51,* 143–154.

Hellekson, K. L. (2001). NIH consensus statement on phenylketonuria. *American Family Physician, 63,* 1430–1432.

Helms, J. E. (1992). Why is there no study of cultural equivalence of standardized cognitive ability testing? *American Psychologist, 47,* 1083–1101.

Hemphill, J. F., & Hare, R. D. (2004). Some misconceptions about the Hare PCL-R and risk assessment: A reply to Gendreau, Goggin, and Smith. *Criminal Justice and Behavior, 31* (2), 203–243.

Hemphill, J. F., Hare, R. D., & Wong, S. (1998). Psychopathy and recidivism: A review. *Legal and Criminological Psychology, 3,* 139–170.

Henderson, S. (2002). The National Survey of Mental Health and Well-Being in Australia: Impact on policy. *Canadian Journal of Psychiatry, 47,* 819–824.

Hendriks, G. J., Oude Voshaar, R. C., Keijsers, G. P. J., Hoogduin, C. A. L., & van Balkom, A. J. L. M. (2008). Cognitive-behavioural therapy for late-life anxiety disorders: A systematic review and meta-analysis. *Acta Psychiatrica Scandinavica, 117,* 403–411.

Henggeler, S. W., & Schoenwald, S. K. (1993). Multisystemic therapy with juvenile offenders: An effective family-based treatment. *The Family Psychologist, 9,* 24–26.

Henke, P. G. (1988). Recent studies of the central nucleus of the amygdala and stress ulcers. *Neuroscience and Biobehavioral Reviews, 12,* 143–150.

Henke, P. G. (1990). Hippocampal pathway to the amygdala and stress ulcer development. *Brain Research Bulletin, 25,* 691–695.

Henke, P. G. (1992). Stomach pathology and the amygdala. In J. P. Aggleton (Ed.), *The amygdala: Neurobiological aspects of emotion, memory and mental dysfunction* (pp. 323–338). New York: Wiley.

Henriques, G., & Leitenberg, H. (2002). An experimental analysis of cognitive errors in the development of depressed mood following negative social feedback. *Cognitive Therapy and Research, 26,* 245–260.

Henry, W. P., Strupp, H. H., Schacht, T. E., & Gaston, L. (1994). Psychodynamic approaches. In A. E. Bergin & S. L. Garfield (Eds.), *Handbook of psychotherapy and behavior change* (4th ed., pp. 467–508). New York: Wiley.

Herbert, T. B., & Cohen, S. (1993). Stress and immunity in humans: A meta-analytic review. *Psychosomatic Medicine, 55,* 364–379.

Herman, J. P., Prewitt, C. M.-F., & Cullinan, W. E. (1996). Neuronal circuit regulation of the hypothalamo-pituitary-adrenocortical stress axis. *Critical Reviews in Neurobiology, 10,* 371–394.

Herrnstein, R., & Murray, C. (1994). *The bell curve: Intelligence and class structure in American life.* New York: The Free Press.

Hershkowitz, D. (1998). *The madness of epic: Reading insanity from Homer to Statius.* Oxford, UK: Oxford University Press.

Herzog, D. B., Greenwood, D. N., Dorer, D. J., Flores, A. T., Ekeblad, E. R., Richards, A., et al. (2000). Mortality in eating disorders: A descriptive study. *International Journal of Eating Disorders, 28,* 20–26.

Hesse, E., Main, M., Abrams, K. Y., & Rifkin, A. (2003). Unresolved states regarding loss or abuse can have "second-generation" effects: Disorganized, role-inversion and frightening ideation in the offspring of traumatized non-maltreating parents. In D. J. Siegel & M. F. Solomon (Eds.), *Healing trauma: Attachment, mind, body and brain* (pp. 57–106). New York: Norton.

Hetrick, S., Merry, S., McKenzie, J., Sindahl, P., & Proctor, M. (2007). Selective serotonin reuptake inhibitors (SSRIs) for depressive disorders in children and adolescents. *Cochrane Database of Systematic Reviews, 3*: CD004851.

Hettema, J. M., Neale, M. C., & Kendler, K. S. (2001). A review and meta-analysis of the genetic epidemiology of anxiety disorders. *American Journal of Psychiatry, 158,* 1568–1578.

Higgenbottam, J., Ledwidge, B., Paredes, J., Hansen, M., Kogan, C., & Lambert, L. (1985). Variables affecting the decision making of a review panel. *Canadian Journal of Psychiatry, 30,* 577–581.

Higgins, S. T., Budney, A. J., Bickel, W. K., Foerg, F. E., & Badger, G. J. (1994). Alcohol dependence and simultaneous cocaine and alcohol use in cocaine-dependent patients. *Journal of Addictive Diseases, 13* (4), 177–189.

Higgins, S. T., Budney, A. J., Bickel, W. K., Hughes, J., Foerg, F., & Badger, G. (1993). Achieving cocaine abstinence with a behavioral approach. *American Journal of Psychiatry, 150* (5), 763–769.

Hilgard, E. R. (1986). *Divided consciousness: Multiple controls in human thought and action* (expanded. ed.). New York: Wiley.

Hill, A. B. (1965). The environment and disease: Association or causation? *Proceedings of the Royal Society of Medicine, 58,* 295–300.

Hill, S. K., Harris, M. S., Herbener, E. S., Pavuluri, M., & Sweeney, J. A. (2008). Neurocognitive allied phenotypes for schizophrenia and bipolar disorder. *Schizophrenia Bulletin, 34,* 743–759.

Hill, S. Y., & Steinhauer, S. R. (1993). Assessment of prepubertal and postpubertal boys and girls at risk for developing alcoholism with P300 from a visual discrimination task. *Journal of Studies on Alcohol, 54,* 350–358.

Hill, S. Y., Steinhauer, S. R., Lowers, L., & Locke, J. (1995). Eight-year follow-up of P300 and clinical outcome in children from high-risk alcoholism families. *Biological Psychiatry, 37,* 823–827.

Hinshaw, S. P., & Anderson, C. A. (1996). Conduct and oppositional defiant disorders. In E. J. Mash & R. A. Barkley (Eds.), *Child psychopathology* (pp. 113–149). New York: Guilford Press.

Hinshaw, S. P., & Lee, S. S. (2003). Conduct and oppositional defiant disorders. In E. J. Mash & R. A. Barkley (Eds.), *Child psychopathology* (2nd ed., pp. 144–198). New York: Guilford Press.

Hirsch, C. R., & Clark, D. M. (2004). Information-processing bias in social phobia. *Clinical Psychology Review, 24,* 799–825.

Hirschfeld, R. (2001). Comorbidity of major depression and anxiety disorders: Recognition and management in primary care. *Journal of Clinical Psychiatry, 3,* 244–254.

Hisfield-Becker, D. R., Micco, J. A., Simoes, N. A., & Henin, A. (2008). High risk studies and developmental antecedents of anxiety disorder. *American Journal of Medical Genetics Part C (Seminars in Medical Genetics), 148C,* 99–117.

Hoag, H. (2008). Inducing seizures among seniors. *Canadian Medical Association Journal, 178,* 1268–1266.

Hobson, J., Shine, J., & Roberts, R. (2000). How do psychopaths behave in a prison therapeutic community? *Psychology, Crime, and Law, 6,* 139–154.

Hoch, C. C., Reynolds, C. F., III, Jennings, J. R., Monk, T. H., Buysse, D. J., Machem, M. A., & Kupfer, D. J. (1992). Daytime sleepiness and performance among healthy 80 and 20 year olds. *Neurobiology of Aging, 13,* 353–356.

Hodgins, D. C. (2005). Can patients with alcohol use disorders return to social drinking? Yes, so what should we do about it? *Canadian Journal of Psychiatry,50,* 264–265.

Hodgins, D. C., Currie, S. R., Currie, G., & Fick, G. H. (2009). A randomized trial of brief motivational treatments for pathological gamblers: More is not necessarily better. *Journal of Consulting and Clinical Psychology, 77,* 950–960. doi:10.1037/a0016318

Hodgins, D. C., Currie, S. R., & el-Guebaly, N. (2001). Motivational enhancement and self-help treatments for problem gambling. *Journal of Consulting and Clinical Psychology, 69,* 50–57.

Hodgins, D. C., Currie, S. R., el-Guebaly, N., & Peden, N. (2004). Brief motivational treatment for problem gambling: 24 month follow-up. *Psychology of Addictive Behaviors, 18,* 293–296.

Hodgins, D. C., & Diskin, K. M. (2003). Alcohol problems. In M. Hersen & S. M. Turner (Eds.), *Diagnostic Interviewing* (3rd ed.). New York: Kluwer.

Hodgins, D. C., & el-Guebaly, N. (2000). Natural and treatment assisted recovery from gambling problems: Comparison of resolved and active gamblers. *Addiction, 95,* 777–789.

Hodgins, D. C., Leigh, G., Milne, R., & Gerrish, R. (1997). Drinking goal selection in behavioural self-management treatment of chronic alcoholics. *Addictive Behaviors, 22,* 247–255.

Hodgins, S., & Côté, G. (1990, March). Prevalence of mental disorder among penitentiary inmates in Quebec. *Canada's Mental Health,* 1–4.

Hoefnagels, C., Meesters, C., & Simenon, J. (2007). Social support as predictor of psychopathology in the adolescent offspring of psychiatric patients. *Journal of Child and Family Studies, 16,* 91–101.

Hoehn-Saric, R., Ninan, P., Black, D. W., Stahl, S., Greist, J. H., Lydiard, B., et al. (2000). Multicenter double-blind comparison of sertraline and desipramine for concurrent obsessive-compulsive and major depressive disorders. *Archives of General Psychiatry, 57,* 76–82.

Hoek, H. W., & van Hoeken, D. (2003). Review of the prevalence and incidence of eating disorders. *International Journal of Eating Disorders, 34,* 383–396.

Hoffman, E. J., & Mathew, S. J. (2008). Anxiety disorders: A comprehensive review of pharmacotherapies. *Mount Sinai Journal of Medicine: A Journal of Translational and Personalized Medicine, 75,* 248–262.

Hofmann, S. G., & Barlow, D. H. (2002). Social phobia (social anxiety disorder). In D. H. Barlow (Ed.), *Anxiety and its disorders* (2nd ed., pp. 454–476). New York: Guilford Press.

Hofmann, S. G., Lehman, C. L., & Barlow, D. H. (1997). How specific are specific phobias? *Journal of Behavior Therapy and Experimental Psychiatry, 28,* 233–240.

Hofmann, S. G., Pollack, M. H., & Otto, M. W. (2006). Augmentation treatment of psychotherapy for anxiety disorders with D-Cycloserine. *CNS Drug Reviews, 12,* 208–217.

Hofmann, S. G., Sawyer, A. T., Witt, A. A., & Oh, D. (2010). The effect of mindfulness-based therapy on anxiety and depression: A meta-analytic review. *Journal of Consulting and Clinical Psychology, 78,* 169–183.

Hofschire, L. J., & Greenberg, B. S. (2001). Media's impact on adolescents' body dissatisfaction. In J. D. Brown & J. R. Steele (Eds.), *Sexual teens, sexual media: Investigating media's influence on adolescent sexuality* (pp. 125–149). Mahwah, NJ: Lawrence Erlbaum.

Hollinghurst, S., Peters, T. J., Kaur, S., Wiles, N., Lewis, G., & Kessler, D. (2010). Cost-effectiveness of therapist-delivered online cognitive-behavioural therapy for depression: Randomized controlled trial. *British Journal of Psychiatry, 197,* 297–304.

Hollingshead, A. B., & Redlich, F. C. (1958). *Social class and mental illness: A community study.* New York: Wiley.

Hollon, S. D., & Beck, A. T. (1994). Cognitive and cognitive behavioral therapies. In A. E. Bergin & S. L. Garlfield (Eds.), *Handbook of psychotherapy and behavior change* (4th ed., pp. 428–466). New York: Wiley.

Hollon, S. D., DeRubeis, R. J., Shelton, R. C., Amsterdam, J. D., Salomon, R. M., O'Reardon, J. P., et al. (2005). Prevention of relapse following cognitive therapy vs medications in moderate to severe depression. *Archives of General Psychiatry,* 62, 417–422.

Hollon, S. D., Stewart, M. O., & Strunk, D. (2006). Enduring effects of cognitive behavior therapy in the treatment of depression and anxiety. *Annual Review of Psychology, 57,* 285–315.

Hollon, S. D., Thase, M. E., & Markowitz, J. C. (2002). Treatment and prevention of depression. *Psychological Science in the Public Interest, 3,* 39–77.

Holmes, T. H., & Masuda, M. (1974). Life change and illness susceptibility. In B. S. Dohrenwend & B. P. Dohrenwend (Eds.), *Stressful life events: Their nature and effects.* New York: Wiley.

Holmes, T. H., & Rahe, R. H. (1967). The Social Readjustment Rating Scale. *Journal of Psychosomatic Research, 11,* 213–218.

Holoch, K., Stein, Q., Flanagan, J., & Hansen, K. (2008). Premature ovarian failure: A phenotypic expression of Fragile X premutation. *South Dakota Medicine, 61* (1), 13–15.

Holt, C. S., Heimberg, R. G., & Hope, D. A. (1992). Avoidant personality disorder and the generalized subtype of social phobia. *Journal of Abnormal Psychology, 101,* 318–325. doi:10.1037/0021-843X.101.2.318

Holt, S. E., Meloy, J. R., & Stack, S. (1999). Sadism and psychopathy in violent and sexually violent offenders. *Journal of the American Academy of Psychiatry and Law,* 27, 23–32.

Homan, K. (2010). Athletic-ideal and thin-ideal internalization as prospective predictors of body dissatisfaction, dieting, and compulsive exercise. *Body Image, 7,* 240–245.

Hook, E. B., Cross, P. K., & Regal, R. R. (1990). Factual, statistical and logical issues in the search for a paternal age effect for Down syndrome. *Human Genetics, 85,* 387–388.

Hooley, J. M. (2007). Expressed emotion and relapse of psychopathology. *Annual Review of Clinical Psychology, 3,* 329–352.

Hoon, E. F., Hoon, P. W., Rand, K. H., Johnson, J., Hall, N. R., & Edwards, N. B. (1991). A psycho-behavioral model of genital herpes recurrence. *Journal of Psychosomatic Research, 35,* 25–36.

Hopcroft, R. L., & Bradley, D. B. (2007). The sex difference in depression across 29 countries. *Social Forces, 85,* 1111–1136.

Horen, S. A., Leichner, P. P., & Lawson, J. S. (1995). Prevalence of dissociative symptoms and disorders in an adult psychiatric inpatient population in Canada. *Canadian Journal of Psychiatry, 40,* 185–191.

Horner, R. H., Carr, E. G., Strain, P. S., Todd, A. W., & Reed, H. K. (2002). Problem behavior interventions for young children with autism: A research synthesis. *Journal of Autism and Developmental Disorders, 32,* 423–446.

Horney, K. (1945). *Our inner conflicts: A constructive theory of neurosis.* New York: Norton.

Horowitz, A. V., & Wakefield, J. C. (2007). *The loss of sadness: How psychiatry transformed normal sorrow into depressive disorder.* New York: Oxford University Press.

Hospers, H. J., & Jansen, A. (2005). Why homosexuality is a risk factor for eating disorders in males. *Journal of Social and Clinical Psychology, 24,* 1188–1201.

House, J. S., Landis, K. R., & Umberson, D. (1988). Social relationships and health. *Science, 241,* 540–545.

Houts, A. C. (2001a). The diagnostic and statistical manual's new white coat and circularity of plausible dysfunctions: Response to Wakefield, Part 1. *Behavior Research and Therapy, 39,* 315–345.

Houts, A. C. (2001b). Harmful dysfunction and the search for value neutrality in the definition of mental disorder: Response to Wakefield, Part 2. *Behavior Research and Therapy, 39,* 1099–1132.

Howard, J. S., Sparkman, C. R., Cohen, H. G., Green, G., & Stanislaw, H. A. (2005). Comparison of intensive behavior analytic and eclectic treatments for young children with autism. *Research in Developmental Disabilities, 26,* 359–383.

Howard, R., Castle, D., Wessely, S., & Murray, R. (1993). A comparative study of 470 cases of early-onset and late-onset schizophrenia. *British Journal of Psychiatry, 163,* 352–357.

Howes, O. D., & Kapur, S. (2009). The dopamine hypothesis of schizophrenia: Version III—the final common pathway. *Schizophrenia Bulletin, 35,* 549–562.

Howlin, P., Gordon, K., Pasco, G., Wade, A., & Charman, T. (2007). A group randomised, controlled trial of the Picture Exchange Communication System for children with autism. *Journal of Child Psychology and Psychiatry, 48,* 473–481.

Howlin, P., Magiati, I., & Charman, T. (2009). Systematic review of early intensive behavioral interventions for children with autism. *American Journal on Intellectual and Developmental Disabilities, 114,* 23–41.

Huang, Y., Kotov, R., de Girolamo, G., Preti, A., Angermeyer, M., Benjet, C., et al. (2009). DSM-IV personality disorders in the WHO World Mental Health Surveys. *British Journal of Psychiatry, 195* (1), 46–53. doi:10.1192/bjp.bp.108.058552

Huettell, S., Song, A. W., & McCarthy, G. (2008). *Functional magnetic resonance imaging* (2nd ed.). Sunderland, MS: Sinauer Associates.

Hughes, M. W., Schuster, J. W., & Nelson, C. M. (1993). The acquisition of independent dressing skills by students with multiple disabilities. *Journal of Developmental and Physical Disabilities, 5,* 233–252.

Humphreys, K. (2003). A research-based analysis of the Moderation Management controversy. *Psychiatric Services, 54,* 621–622.

Hunsley, J., & Bailey, J. M. (1999). The clinical utility of the Rorschach: Unfulfilled promise and an uncertain future. *Psychological Assessment, 11,* 266–277.

Hunsley, J., & Bailey, J. M. (2001). Whither the Rorschach? An analysis of the evidence. *Psychological Assessment, 13,* 472–485.

Hunsley, J., & Di Giulio, G. (2002). Dodo bird, phoenix, or urban legend? The question of psychotherapy equivalence. *Scientific Review of Mental Health Practice, 1,* 11–22.

Hunsley, J., Dobson, K., Johnston, C., & Mikail, S. (1999). Empirically supported treatments in psychology: Implications for Canadian professional psychology. *Canadian Psychology, 40,* 289–301.

Hunsley, J., & Lee, C. M. (1995). The marital effects of individually oriented psychotherapy: Is there evidence for the deterioration hypothesis? *Clinical Psychology Review, 15,* 1–22.

Hunsley, J., & Lee, C. M. (2007). Research-informed benchmarks for psychological treatments: Efficacy studies, effectiveness studies, and beyond. *Professional Psychology: Research and Practice, 38,* 21–33.

Hunsley, J., & Lee, C. M. (2010). *Introduction to clinical psychology: An evidence-based approach.* Mississauga, ON: John Wiley and Sons.

Hunsley, J., Lee, C. M., & Aubry, T. D. (1999). Who uses psychological services in Canada? *Canadian Psychology, 40,* 232–240.

Hunsley, J., Lee, C. M., & Wood, J. M. (2003). Controversial and questionable assessment techniques. In S. O. Lilienfeld, S. J. Lynn, & J. M. Lohr (Eds.), *Science and pseudoscience in clinical psychology* (pp. 39–76). New York: Guilford Press.

Hunter, J. M., Shannon, G. W., & Sambrook, S. L. (1986). Rings of madness: Service areas of 19th century asylums in North America. *Social Science and Medicine, 23,* 1033–1050.

Hurd, H. M., Drewry, W. F., Dewey, R., Pilgrim, C. W., Blumer, G. A., & Burgess, T. J. W. (1916). *The institutional care of the insane in the United States and Canada.* Baltimore, MD: Johns Hopkins Hospital Press.

Hurley, S. F. (1997). The effectiveness of needle-exchange programs for the prevention of HIV infection. *The Lancet, 349,* 1797–1800.

Hylton, J. H. (1995). Care or control: Health or criminal justice options for the long-term seriously mentally ill in a Canadian province. *International Journal of Law and Psychiatry, 18,* 45–59.

Hyman, S. E. (2010). The diagnosis of mental disorders: The problem of reification. *The Annual Review of Clinical Psychology, 6,* 155–179.

Hymel, S., Schonert-Reichl, K. A., Bonanno, R. A., Vaillancourt, T., & Rocke-Henderson, N. (2009). Bullying and morality: Understanding how good kids can behave badly. In S. R. Jimerson, S. M. Swearer, & D. L. Espelage (Eds.), *The international handbook of school bullying.* Mahwah, NJ: Lawrence Erlbaum Associates.

Ihl, R., Frolich, L., Winblad, B., Schneider, L., Burns, A., Moller, H-J., et al. (2011). World Federation of Societies of Biological Psychiatry (WFSBP) guidelines for the biological treatment of Alzheimer's disease and other dementias. *The World Journal of Biological Psychiatry, 12,* 2–32. doi:10.3109/15622975.2010.538083

Imbierowicz, K., & Egle, U. T. (2003). Childhood adversities in patients with fibromyalgia and somatoform pain disorder. *European Journal of Pain, 7,* 113–119.

IMS Brogan. (2011). Top 10 dispensed therapeutic classes in Canada, 2010. Retrieved from http://www.imsbrogran.com

Ingram, R. E., Miranda, J., & Segal, Z. V. (1998). *Cognitive vulnerability to depression.* New York: Guilford Press.

Ingram, R. E., Nelson, T., Steidtmann, D. K., & Bistricky, S. L. (2007). Comparative data on child and adolescent cognitive measures associated with depression. *Journal of Consulting and Clinical Psychology, 75,* 390–403.

Ingram, R. E. & Price, J. M. (Eds.). (2001). *Vulnerability to psychopathology: Risk across the lifespan*. New York: Guilford Press.

Ingram, R. E., & Price, J. M. (Eds.). (2010). *Vulnerability to psychopathology: Risk across the lifespan* (2nd ed.). New York: Guilford Press.

Innes, K. E., Selfe, T. K., & Agarwal, P. (2011). Prevalence of restless legs syndrome in North American and Western European populations: A systematic review. *Sleep Medicine, 12* (7), 623–634.

Institute of Medicine. (1994). *Reducing risks for mental disorders: Frontiers for preventive intervention research.* Washington, DC: National Academy Press.

Iacono, W. G., Bassett, A. S., & Jones, B. D. (1988). Eye tracking dysfunction is associated with parital trisomy of chromosome 5 and schizophrenia. *Archives of General Psychiatry, 45,* 1140–1141.

Ironson, G., Taylor, C. B., Boltwood, M., Bartzokis, T., Dennis, C., Chesney, M., et al. (1992). Effects of anger on left ventricular ejection fraction in coronary artery disease. *American Journal of Cardiology, 70,* 281–285.

Irvine, J., Baker, B., Smith, J., Jandciu, S., Paquette, M., Cairns, J., et al. (1999). Poor adherence to placebo or amiodarone therapy predicts mortality: Results from the CAMIAT study. *Psychosomatic Medicine, 61,* 566–575.

Irvine, J., & Logan, A. G. (1991). Relaxation behavior therapy as sole treatment for mild hypertension. *Psychosomatic Medicine, 53,* 587–597.

Irvine, J., & Ritvo, P. G. (1998). Health risk behavior change and adaptation in cardiac patients, *Clinical Psychology and Psychotherapy, 5,* 86–101.

Isaacowitz, D. M. (2005). Correlates of well-being in adulthood and old age: A tale of two optimisms. *Journal of Research in Personality, 39* (2), 224–244.

Jackson, A., Cavanagh, J., & Scott, J. (2003). A systematic review of manic and depressive prodromes. *Journal of Affective Disorders, 74,* 209–217.

Jackson, D. N., & Messick, S. (1961). Acquiescence and desirability as response determinants on the MMPI. *Education and Psychological Measurement, 21,* 771–790.

Jackson, S. W. (1986). *Melancholia and depression: From Hippocratic times to modern times.* New Haven, CT: Yale University Press.

Jacobs, G. D., Pace-Shott, E. F., Stickgold, R., & Otto, M. W. (2004). Cognitive behavior therapy and pharmacotherapy for insomnia. *Archives of Internal Medicine, 164,* 1888–1896.

Jacobson, J. W., Mulick, J. A., & Schwartz, A. A. (1995). A history of facilitated communication: Science, pseudoscience and antiscience. *American Psychologist, 50,* 750–765.

Jacobson, N. S., & Addis, M. E. (1993). Research on couples and couple therapy: What do we know? Where are we going? *Journal of Consulting and Clinical Psychology, 61,* 85–93.

Jacobson, N. S., Dobson, K. S., Truax, P. A., Addis, M. E., Koerner, K., Gollan, J. K., et al. (1996). A component analysis of cognitive-behavioral treatment for depression. *Journal of Consulting and Clinical Psychology, 64,* 295–304.

Jacobson, N. S., & Margolin, G. (1979). *Marital therapy: Strategies based on social learning and behavior exchange principles.* New York: Brunner/Mazel.

Jaffe, J. H. (1995). Drug addiction and drug abuse. In L. S. Goodman & A. Gilman (Eds.), *The pharmacological basis of therapeutic behaviour.* New York: Macmillan.

Jaffee, S. R., Caspi, A., Moffitt, T. E., Dodge, K. A., Rutter, M., Taylor, A., et al. (2005). Nature x nurture: Genetic vulnerabilities interact with physical maltreatment to promote conduct problems. *Development and Psychopathology, 17,* 67–84.

Jamison, K. R. (1995). *An unquiet mind.* New York: Vintage.

Jang, K. L., Paris, J., Zweig-Frank, H., & Livesley, W. J. (1998). Twin study of dissociative experience. *Journal of Nervous and Mental Disease, 186,* 345–351.

Jannini, E. A., Lombardo, F., & Lenzi, A. (2005). Correlation between ejaculatory and erectile dysfunction. *International Journal of Andrology, 28,* 40–45.

Janus, S. S., & Janus, C. (1993). *The Janus report on sexual behavior.* New York: Wiley.

Jenike, M. A. (1998). Theories of etiology. In M. A. Jenike, L. Baer, & W. E. Minichiello (Eds.), *Obsessive-compulsive disorders: Practical management* (3rd ed., pp. 203–221). St. Louis, MO: Mosby.

Jenkins, M. R., & Culbertson, J. L. (1996). Prenatal exposure to alcohol. In R. L. Adams, O. A. Pausons, & J. L. Culbertson (Eds.), *Neuropychology for clinical practices: Etiology, assessment, and treatment of common neurological disorders* (pp. 409–452). Washington, DC: American Pychological Association.

Jensen, A. R. (1997). Psychometric *g* and the race question. In J. Kingma & W. Tomic (Eds.), *Advances in cognition and educational practices: Reflections on the concept of intelligence* (Vol. 4). London: Reed Elsevier.

Jensen, P. S. (2003). Comorbidity and child psychopathology: Recommendations for the next decade. *Journal of Abnormal Child Psychology, 31,* 293–300.

Jensen Doss, A., & Weisz, J. R. (2006). Syndrome co-occurrence and treatment outcomes in youth mental health clinics. *Journal of Consulting and Clinical Psychology, 74,* 416–425.

Jeste, D. V., del Carmen, R., Lohr, J. B., & Wyatt, R. J. (1985). Did schizophrenia exist before the eighteenth century? *Comprehensive Psychiatry, 26,* 493–503.

Jeste, D. V., Harris, M. J., Pearlson, G. D., Rabins, P., Lesser, I., Miller, B., et al. (1988). Late-onset schizophrenia: Studying clinical validity. *Psychiatric Annals of North America, 11,* 1–13.

Jeste, D. V., Manley, M., & Harris, M. J., (1991). Psychoses. In J. S. Sadavoy, L. W. Lazarus, & L. F. Jarvik (Eds.), *Comprehensive review of geriatric psychiatry* (pp. 353–368). Washington, DC: American Psychiatric Press, Inc.

Joe, G. W., Dansereau, D. F., & Simpson, D. D. (1994). Node-link mapping for counselling cocaine users in methadone treatment. *Journal of Substance Abuse, 6* (4), 393–406.

Joffe, J. M., & Albee, G. W. (Eds.). (1981). *Prevention through political action and social change.* Hanover, NH: University Press of New England.

Joffe, R. T., Swinson, R. P., & Regan, J. J. (1988). Personality features of obsessive-compulsive disorder. *American Journal of Psychiatry, 145,* 1127–1129.

Johnson, C., & Connors, M. E. (1987). *The etiology and treatment of bulimia nervosa.* New York: Basic Books.

Johnson, C. P., Myers, S. M., & the Council of Children with Disabilities. (2007). American Academy of Pediatrics: Identification and evaluation of children with autism spectrum disorders. *Pediatrics, 120,* 1183–1215.

Johnson, D. J., & Myklebust, H. R. (1971). *Learning disabilities.* New York: Grune & Stratton.

Johnson, J., Weissman, M. M., & Klerman, G. L. (1990). Panic disorder and suicide attempts. *Archives of General Psychiatry, 47,* 805–808.

Johnson, J. G., Cohen, P., Dohrenwend, B. P., Link, B. G., & Brook, J. S. (1999). A longitudinal investigation of social causation and social selection processes involved in the association between socioeconomic status and psychiatric disorders. *Journal of Abnormal Psychology, 108,* 490–499.

Johnson, J. G., Cohen, P., Kasen, S., & Brook, J. S. (2006). Dissociative disorders among adults in the community, impaired functioning, and Axis I and II comorbidity. *Journal of Psychiatric Research, 40,* 131–140.

Johnson, S. M., Hunsley, J., Greenberg, L., & Schindler, D. (1999). Emotionally focused couples therapy: Status and challenges. *Clinical Psychology: Science and Practice, 6,* 67–79.

Johnstone, E. C., Crow, T. J., Frith, C. D., Husband, J., & Kreel, L. (1976). Cerebral ventricular size and cognitive impairment in chronic schizophrenia. *Lancet, 2,* 924–926.

Joiner, T. E., Jr., Katz, J., & Lew, A. (1997). Self-verification and depression among youth psychiatric inpatients. *Journal of Abnormal Psychology, 106,* 608–618.

Jones, D. J., Forehand, R., McKee, L. G., Cuellar, J., & Kincaid, C. (2010). Behavioral parent training: Is there an "App" for that? *The Behavior Therapist, 3,* 72–77.

Jones, K. L., & Smith, D. W. (1973). Recognition of the Fetal Alcohol Syndrome in early infancy. *The Lancet, 2,* 999–1001.

Jones, W. R., & Morgan, J. F. (2010). Eating disorders in men: A review of the literature. *Journal of Public Mental Health, 9,* 23–31.

Jorge, R. E., Moser, D. J., Acion, L., & Robinson, R. G. (2008). Treatment of vascular depression using repetitive transcranial magnetic stimulation. *Archives of General Psychiatry, 65,* 268–276.

Joshi, R., Herman, C. P., & Polivy, J. (2004). Self-enhancing effects of exposure to thin-body images. *International Journal of Eating Disorders, 35,* 333–341.

Joshi, I., Percy, M., & Brown, I. (2002). Advances in understanding causes of autism and effective interventions. *Journal on Developmental Disabilities, 9,* 1–28.

Joyce, T., Globe, A., & Moody, C. (2006). Assessment of the component skills for cognitive therapy in adults with intellectual disability. *Journal of Applied Research in Intellectual Disability, 19,* 17–23.

Julien, R. M. (2007). *A primer of drug action: A concise, non-technical guide to the actions, uses and side effects of psychoactive drugs.* New York: Worth.

Jung, C. G. (1956). Recent thoughts on schizophrenia. In H. Read, M. Fordham, G. Adler, & W. McGuire (Eds.), *The collected works of C. G. Jung* (R. F. C. Hull, Trans., pp. 250–255). Princeton, NJ: Princeton University Press.

Juodis, M., Starzomski, A., Porter, S., & Woodworth, M. (2012). A comparison of domestic and non-domestic homicides: Further evidence for distinct dynamics and heterogeneity of domestic homicide perpetrators. Manuscript under review.

Kabat-Zinn, J. (1994). *Wherever you go there you are: Mindfulness meditation in everyday life.* New York: Hyperion.

Kabat-Zinn, J. (2003). Mindfulness-based interventions in context: Past, present, and future. *Clinical Psychology: Science & Practice, 10,* 144–156.

Kafka, M. P. (1997). Hypersexual desire disorder in males: An operational definition and clinical implications for males with paraphilias and paraphilia-related disorders. *Archives of Sexual Behavior, 26,* 505–526.

Kafka, M. P. (2007). Paraphilia-related disorders: The evaluation and treatment of nonparaphilic hypersexuality. In S. R. Leiblum (Ed.), *Principles and practices of sex therapy* (4th ed., pp. 442–476). New York: Guilford Press.

Kafka, M. P. (2010a). The DSM criteria for fetishism. *Archives of Sexual Behavior, 39,* 357–362.

Kafka, M. P. (2010b). Hypersexual disorder: A proposed diagnosis for DSM-V. *Archives of Sexual Behavior, 39,* 377–400.

Kagan, J. (1995). *Galen's prophecy.* New York: Basic Books.

Kagan, J., Reznick, J. S., Clarke, C., Snidman, N., & Garcia-Coll, C. (1984). Behavioural inhibition to the unfamiliar. *Child Development, 51,* 2212–2225.

Kahana, S., Drotar, D., & Frazier, T. (2008). Meta-analysis of psychological interventions to promote adherence to treatment in pediatric chronic health conditions. *Journal of Pediatric Psychology, 33,* 590–611.

Kalberg, W. O., & Buckley, D. (2007). FASD: What types of intervention and rehabilitation are useful? *Neuroscience and Biobehavioral Reviews, 31,* 278–285.

Kamphaus, R. W., & Kroncke, A. P. (2004). "Back to the future" of the Stanford-Binet intelligence scales. In M. Hersen (Series Ed.), G. Goldstein & S. R. Beers (Vol. Eds.), *Comprehensive handbook of psychological assessment: Vol. 1. Intellectual and neuropsychological assessment* (pp. 50–69). New York: Wiley.

Kane, J. M. (1989). The current status of neuroleptic therapy. *Journal of Clinical Psychiatry, 50,* 322–328.

Kanfer, F. H., & Phillips, J. S. (1970). *Learning foundations of behavior therapy.* New York: Wiley.

Kanner, A. D., Coyne, J. C., Schaefer, C., & Lazarus, R. S. (1981). Comparisons of two modes of stress measurement: Daily hassles and uplifts versus major life events. *Journal of Behavioral Medicine, 4,* 1–39.

Kanner, L. (1935). *Child psychiatry.* Springfield, IL: Charles C. Thomas.

Kanner, L. (1943). Autistic disturbances of affective contact. *Nervous Child, 2,* 217–250.

Kaplan, H. I., & Sadock, B. J. (1998). *Synopsis of psychiatry* (8th ed.). Baltimore, MD: Williams & Wilkins.

Kaplan, H. S. (1974). *The new sex therapy: Active treatment of sexual dysfunctions.* New York: Brunner/Mazel.

Kaplan, H. S. (1979). *Disorders of sexual desire and other new concepts and techniques in sex therapy.* New York: Brunner/Mazel.

Kaplan, J. R., Manuck, S. B., Clarkson, T. B., Lusso, F. M., Taub, D. M., & Miller, E. W. (1983). Social stress and atherosclerosis in normocholesterolemic monkeys. *Science, 220,* 733–735.

Kaplan, M. (1983a). The issue of sex bias in DSM-III: Comments on the articles by Spitzer, Williams, and Kass. *American Psychologist, 38,* 802–803.

Kaplan, M. (1983b). A woman's view of the DSM-III. *American Psychologist, 38,* 786–792.

Kar, N. (2011). Cognitive behavioral therapy for the treatment of post-traumatic stress disorder: A review. *Neuropsychiatric Disease and Treatment, 7,* 167–181.

Karasek, R. A., Baker, D., Marxer, F., Ahlborn, A., & Theorell, T. (1981). Job decision latitude, job demands and cardiovascular disease: A prospective study of Swedish men. *American Journal of Public Health, 71,* 694–705.

Karasek, R. A., Theorell, T. G., Schwartz, J., Pieper, C., & Alfredsson, L. (1982). Job, psychological factors and coronary heart disease: Swedish prospective findings and U. S. prevalence findings using a new occupational inference method. *Advances in Cardiology, 29,* 62–67.

Karg, K., Burmeister, M., Shedden, K., & Sen, S. (2011). The serotonin transporter promoter variant (5-HTTLPR), stress, and depression meta-analysis revisited: Evidence for genetic moderation. *Archives of General Psychiatry, 68,* 444–454.

Karl, A., Schaefer, M., Malta, L. S., Dörfel, D., Rohleder, N., & Werner, A. (2006). A meta-analysis of structural brain abnormalities in PTSD. *Neuroscience & Biobehavioral Reviews, 30,* 1004–1031.

Karlin, B. E., & Duffy, M. (2004). Geriatric mental health policy: Impact on service delivery and directions for effecting change. *Professional Psychology: Research and Practice, 35* (5), 509–519.

Karlsgodt, K. H., Sun, D., & Cannon, T. D. (2010). Structural and functional brain abnormalities in schizophrenia. *Current Directions in Psychological Science, 19* (4), 226–231.

Karnesh, L. J., & Zucker, E. M. (1945). *Handbook of psychiatry.* St. Louis, MO: Mosby.

Karon, B. P., & VandenBos, G. R. (1981). *Psychotherapy of schizophrenia: The treatment of choice.* New York: Aronson.

Kasai, K., Iwanami, A., Yamasue, H., Kuroki, N., Nakagome, K., & Fukuda, M. (2002). Neuroanatomy and neurophysiology in schizophrenia. *Neuroscience Research, 2,* 93–110.

Kasari, C., Freeman, S., & Paparella, T. (2006). Joint attention and symbolic play in young children with autism: A randomized controlled intervention study. *Journal of Child Psychology and Psychiatry, 47,* 611–620.

Kaschak, E. (1992). *Engendered lives.* New York: Basic Books.

Kashdan, T. B. (2007). Social anxiety spectrum and diminished positive experiences: Theoretical synthesis and meta-analysis. *Clinical Psychology Review, 27,* 348–365.

Katz, L. Y., & Cox, B. J. (2002). Dialectical behavior therapy for suicidal adolescent inpatients: A case study. *Clinical Case Studies, 1,* 81–92.

Katz, L. Y., Kozyrskyj, A. L., Prior, H. J., Enns, M. W., Cox, B. J., & Sareen, J. (2008). Effect of regulatory warnings on antidepressant prescription rates, use of health services and outcomes among children, adolescents and young adults. *Canadian Medical Association Journal, 178,* 1005–1011.

Katzir, R., Youngsuk, K., Wolf, M., O'Brien, B., & Kennedy, B. (2006). Reading fluency: The whole is more than the parts. *Annuals of Dyslexia, 56,* 51–82.

Kavale, K. A., & Forness, S. R. (1996). Social skill deficits and learning disabilities: A meta-analysis. *Journal of Learning Disabilities, 29,* 226–237.

Kaweionnehta Human Resource Group (October, 1993). *First Nations and Inuit community youth solvent abuse survey and study.* Unpublished document, Addiction and Community Funded Programs.

Kaye, W. (2008). Neurobiology of anorexia and bulimia nervosa. *Physiology & Behavior, 94,* 121–135.

Kaye, W. H., Gendall, K., & Strober, M. (1998). Serotonin neuronal function and selective serotonin reuptake inhibitor treatment in anorexia and bulimia nervosa. *Biological Psychiatry, 44,* 825–838.

Kazarian, S. S., & Malla, A. K. (1992). Working with the families of long-term patients: An expressed emotion perspective. In E. Persad, S. S. Kazarian, & L. W. Joseph (Eds.), *The mental hospital in the 21st century* (pp. 91–106). Toronto: Wall & Emerson.

Kazdin, A. E. (1992). *Methodological issues and strategies in clinical research.* Washington, DC: American Psychological Association.

Kazdin, A. E. (1993). Adolescent mental health: Prevention and treatment programs. *American Psychologist, 48,* 127–141.

Kazdin, A. E. (1997). Parent management training: Evidence, outcomes, and issues. *Journal of the American Academy of Child and Adolescent Psychiatry, 36,* 1349–1356.

Kazdin, A. E. (2003a). Clinical significance: Measuring whether interventions make a difference. In A. E. Kazdin (Ed.), *Methodological issues and strategies in clinical research* (3rd ed., pp. 691–710). Washington, DC: American Psychological Association.

Kazdin, A. E. (2003b). *Research design in clinical psychology* (4th ed.). Needham Heights, MA: Allyn & Bacon.

Kazdin, A. E., & Bass, D. (1989). Power to detect differences between alternative treatments in comparative psychotherapy outcome research. *Journal of Consulting and Clinical Psychology, 57,* 138–147.

Kazdin, A. E., Esveldt-Dawson, K., French, N. H., & Unis, A. S. (1987a). Effects of parent management training and problem solving skills training combined in the treatment of antisocial child behavior. *Journal of the American Academy of Child and Adolescent Psychiatry, 26* (3), 416–424.

Kazdin, A. E., Esveldt-Dawson, K., French, N. H., & Unis, A. S. (1987b). Problem solving skills training and relationship therapy in the treatment of antisocial child behavior. *Journal of Consulting and Clinical Psychology, 55* (1), 76–85.

Kazdin, A. E., Mazurick, J. L., & Siegel, T. C. (1994). Treatment outcome among children with externalizing disorder who terminate prematurely versus those who complete psychotherapy. *Journal of the American Academy of Child and Adolescent Psychiatry, 33,* 549–557.

Kazdin, A. E., Siegel, T. C., & Bass, D. (1990). Drawing upon clinical practice to inform research on child and adolescent psychotherapy: A survey of practitioners. *Professional Psychology: Research and Practice, 21,* 189–198.

Kazdin, A. E., & Whitley, M. K. (2006). Comorbidity, case complexity, and effects of evidence-based treatment for children referred for disruptive behavior. *Journal of Consulting and Clinical Psychology, 74,* 455–467.

Keck, P. E., Jr., & McElroy, S. L. (1997). The new antipsychotics and their therapeutic potential. *Psychiatric Annals, 27,* 320–331.

Keefe, R. S. E., Bilder, R. M., Davis, S. M., Harvey, P. D., Palmer, B. W., Gold, J. M., et al. (2007). Neurocognitive effects of antipsychotic medication in patients with chronic schizophrenia in the CATIE trial. *Archives of General Psychiatry, 64,* 633–647.

Keel, P. K., Dorer, D. J., Franko, D. L., Jackson, S. C., & Herzog, D. B. (2005). Postremission predictors of relapse in women with eating disorders. *American Journal of Psychiatry, 162,* 2263–2268.

Keel, P. K., & Striegel-Moore, R. H. (2009). The validity and clinical utility of purging disorder. *International Journal of Eating Disorders, 42,* 706–719.

Keller, M. B., McCullough, J. P., Jr., Klein, D. N., Arnow, B. A., Dunner, D. L., Gelenberg, A. J., et al. (2000). A comparison of nefazodone, the cognitive behavioral analysis system of psychotherapy, and their combination for the treatment of chronic depression. *New England Journal of Medicine, 342,* 1462–1470.

Kelly, T., Soloff, P. H., Cornelius, J., George, A., Lis, J. A., & Ulrich, R. (1992). Can we study (treat) borderline patients? Attrition from research and open treatment. *Journal of Personality Disorders, 6,* 417–433.

Kelsoe, J. R. (1997). The genetics of bipolar disorser. *Psychiatric Annals, 27,* 285–292.

Kendall, P. C., & Hedtke, K. (2006). *The Coping CAT workbook* (2nd ed.). Ardmore, PA: Workbook Publishing.

Kendall, P. C., Marrs-Garcia, A., Nath, S. R., & Sheldrick, R. C. (1999). Normative comparisons for the evaluation of clinical significance. *Journal of Consulting and Clinical Psychology, 67,* 285–299.

Kendall-Tackett, M. (2010). *The psychoneuroimmunology of chronic disease: Exploring the links between inflammation, stress and illness.* Washington, DC: American Psychological Association.

Kendler, K. (1998). Boundaries of major depression: An evaluation of DSM-IV criteria. *American Journal of Psychiatry, 155,* 172–177.

Kendler, K. S. (1985). Diagnostic approaches to schizotypal personality disorder: A historical perspective. *Schizophrenia Bulletin, 11,* 538–553.

Kendler, K. S. (2000). Schizophrenia: Genetics. In B. J. Sadock & V. A. Sadock (Eds.), *Kaplan and Sadock's comprehensive textbook of psychiatry* (7th ed., Vol. 1, pp. 1147–1159). Philadelphia: Lippincott Williams & Wilkins.

Kendler, K. S., Eaves, L. J., Loken, E. K., Pedersen, N. L., Middeldorp, C. M., Reynolds, C., et al. (2011). The impact of environmental experiences on symptoms of anxiety and depression across the life span. *Psychological Science, 22* (10), 1343–1352. doi:10.1177/0956797611417255

Kendler, K. S., Gallagher, T. J., Abelson, J. M., & Kessler, R. C. (1996). Lifetime prevalence, demographic risk factors, and diagnostic validity of nonaffective psychosis as assessed in a U.S. community sample: The National Comorbidity Survey. *Archives of General Psychiatry, 53,* 1022–1031.

Kendler, K. S., Gardner, C. O., Annas, P., & Lichtenstein, P. (2008). The development of fears from early adolescence to young adulthood: A multivariate study. *Psychological Medicine, 38,* 1–11.

Kendler, K. S., Heath, A. C., Martin, N. G., & Eaves, L. J. (1986). Symptoms of anxiety and depression in a volunteer twin population: The etiologic role of genetic and environmental factors. *Archives of General Psychiatry, 43,* 213–221.

Kendler, K. S., Kessler, R. C., Walters, E. E., MacLean, C., Neale, M. C., Heath, A. C., et al. (1995). Stressful life events, genetic liability, and onset of an episode of major depression in women. *American Journal of Psychiatry, 152,* 833–842.

Kendler, K. S., Masterson, C. C., & Davis, K. L. (1985). Psychiatric illness in first degree relatives of patients with paranoid psychosis, schizophrenia and medical controls. *British Journal of Psychiatry, 147,* 524–531.

Kendler, K. S., Neale, M. C., Kessler, R. C., Heath, A. C., & Eaves, L. J. (1992). Major depression and generalized anxiety disorder: Same genes, (partly) different environments? *Archives of General Psychiatry, 49,* 716–722.

Kendler, K. S., & Prescott, C. A. (2006). *Genes, environment, and psychopathology: Understanding the causes of psychiatric and substance use disorders.* New York: Guilford Press.

Keng, S. L., Smoski, M. J., & Robins, C. J. (2011). Effects of mindfulness on psychological health: A review of empirical studies. *Clinical Psychology Review, 31,* 1041–1056.

Kennedy, B. D., Silva, S. G., Tonev, S., Rohde, P., Hughes, J. L., Vitiello, B., et al. (2009). Remission and recovery in the Treatment for Adolescents with Depression Study (TADS): Acute and long-term outcomes. *Journal of the American Academy of Child and Adolescent Psychiatry, 48,* 186–195. doi:10.1097/CHI.0b013e31819176f9

Kennedy, P. J., Hicks, B. M., & Patrick, C. J. (2007). Validity of factors of the Psychopathy Checklist–Revised in female prisoners: Discriminant relations with antisocial behavior, substance abuse, and personality. *Assessment, 14,* 323–340.

Kennedy, S. H., & Giacobbe, P. (2007). Treatment resistant depression—Advances in somatic therapies. *Annals of Clinical Psychiatry, 19,* 279–287.

Kennedy, S. H., Giacobbe, P., Rizvi, S. J., Placenza, F. M., Nishikiwa, Y., Mayberg, H. S., & Lozano, A. M. (2011). Deep brain stimulation for treatment-resistant depression: Follow-up after 3 to 6 years. *American Journal of Psychiatry, 168,* 455–456.

Kenny, M. E., & Hage, S. M. (2009). The next frontier: Prevention as an instrument of social justice. *Journal of Primary Prevention, 30,* 1–10.

Kermis, M. D. (1984). *The psychology of human aging.* Boston: Allyn & Bacon.

Kernberg, O. F. (1967). Borderline personality organization. *Journal of the American Psychoanalytic Association, 15,* 641–685.

Kernberg, O. F. (1975). *Borderline conditions and pathological narcissism.* New York: Jason Aronson.

Kessel, B. (2001). Sexuality in the older person. *Age and Ageing, 30* (2), 121–124.

Kessler, R. C., Aguilar-Gaxiola, S., Alonso, J., Chatterji, S., Lee, S., & Üstün, T. B. (2009). The WHO world mental health (WMH) surveys. *Psychiatrie, 6,* 5–9.

Kessler, R. C., Berglund, P., Demler, O., Jin, R., Merikangas, K. R., & Walters, E. E. (2005). Lifetime prevalence and age-of-onset distributions of DSM-IV disorders in the National Comorbidity Survey Replication. *Archives of General Psychiatry, 62,* 593–602.

Kessler, R. C., Chiu, W. T., Demler, O., & Walters, E. E. (2005). Prevalence, severity, and comorbidity of 12-month DSM-IV disorders in the National Comorbidity Survey Replication. *Archives of General Psychiatry, 62,* 617–627.

Kessler, R. C., McGonagle, K. A., Swartz, M., Blazer, D. G., & Nelson, C. B. (1993). Sex and depression in the National Comorbidity Survey I: Lifetime prevalence, chronicity and recurrence. *Journal of Affective Disorders, 29,* 85–96.

Kessler, R. C., Rubinow, D. R., Holmes, C., Abelson, J. M., & Zhao, S. (1997). The epidemiology of DSM-III-R bipolar I disorder in a general population survey. *Psychological Medicine, 27,* 1079–1089.

Kessler, R. C., Sonnega, A., Bromet, E., Hughes, M., & Nelson, C. B. (1995). Posttraumatic stress disorder in the National Comorbidity Survey. *Archives of General Psychiatry, 52,* 1048–1060.

Kessler, R. C., Zhao, S., Katz, S. J., Kouzis, A. C., Frank, R. G., Edlund, M., & Leaf, P. (1999). Past-year use of outpatient services for psychiatric problems in the National Comorbidity Survey. *American Journal of Psychiatry, 156,* 115–123.

Keyes, C. L. M. (2010). The next steps in the promotion and protection of positive mental health. *Canadian Journal of Nursing Research, 42,* 17–28.

Khan, R. S., Khroury, J., Nichols, W. C., & Lanphear, B. P. (2003). Role of dopamine transporter genotype and maternal prenatal smoking in childhood hyperactive-impulsive, inattentive, and oppositional behaviors. *The Journal of Pediatrics, 143,* 104–110.

Khanna, M. S., & Kendall, P. C. (2010). Computer-assisted cognitive-behavioral therapy for child anxiety: Results of a randomized clinical trial. *Journal of Consulting and Clinical Psychology, 78,* 737–745.

Khaykin, Y., Dorian, P., Baker, B., Shapiro, C., Sandor, P., Mironov, D., et al. (1998). Autonomic correlates of antidepressant treatment using heart-rate variability analysis. *Canadian Journal of Psychiatry, 43,* 183–186.

Kho, K. H., van Vreeswijk, M. F., Simpson, S., & Zwinderman, A. H. (2003). A meta-analysis of electroconvulsive therapy efficacy in depression. *The Journal of ECT, 19,* 139–147.

Kidd, P. M. (2002). Autism, an extreme challenge to integrative medicine. Part 2: Medical management. *Alternative Medicine Reviews, 7* (6), 472–499.

Kiecolt-Glaser, J. K., Loving, T. J., Stowell, J. R., Malarkey, W. B., Lemeshow, S., Dickinson, S. L., & Glaser, R. (2005). Hostile marital interactions, proinflammatory cytokine production, and wound healing. *Archives of General Psychiatry, 62,* 1377–1384.

Kiehl, K. A., Smith, A. M., Mendrek, A., Forster, B. B., Hare, R. D., & Liddle, P. (2004). Temporal lobe abnormalities in semantic processing by criminal psychopaths as revealed by functional magnetic resonance imaging. *Psychiatry Research: Neuroimaging, 130,* 297–312.

Kihlstrom, J. F. (2005). Dissociative disorders. *Annual Review of Clinical Psychology, 1,* 227–253.

Killeen, T. K., Brady, K. T., Gold, P. B., Simpson, K. N., Faldowski, R. A., Tyson, C., et al. (2004). Effectiveness of naltrexone in a community treatment program. *Alcoholism: Clinical and Experimental Research, 28,* 1710–1717.

Kim, M. J., Loucks, R. A., Palmer, A. L., Brown, A. C., Solomon, K. M., Marchante, A. N., & Whalen, P. J. (2011). The structural and functional connectivity of the amygdala: From normal emotion to pathological anxiety. *Behavioural Brain Research, 223,* 403–410.

Kim-Cohen, J., Arseneault, L., Caspi, A., Tomas, M. P., Taylor, A., & Moffitt, T. E. (2005). Validity of DSM-IV conduct disorder in 41/2–5-year-old children: A longitudinal epidemiological study. *American Journal of Psychiatry, 162,* 1108–1117.

King, D. W., Leskin, G. A., King, L. A., & Weathers, F. W. (1998). Confirmatory factor analysis of the Clinician-Administered PTSD Scale: Evidence for the dimensionality of posttraumatic stress disorder. *Psychological Assessment, 10,* 90–96.

Kingdon, D. G., & Turkington, D. (2005). *Cognitive therapy of schizophrenia.* New York: Guilford Press.

Kingston, D. A., Firestone, P., Moulden, H. M., & Bradford, J. M. (2007). The utility of the diagnosis of pedophilia: A comparison of various classification procedures. *Archives of Sexual Behavior, 36,* 423–436.

Kingston, D. A., & Yates, P. M. (2008). Sexual sadism: Assessment and treatment. In D. R. Laws & W. O'Donohue (Eds.), *Sexual deviance: Theory, assessment, and treatment* (2nd ed., pp. 231–249). New York: Guilford Press.

Kinsella, K., & He, W. (2009). *An aging world: 2008.* Washington, DC: U.S. Government Printing Office.

Kinsey, A. C., Pomeroy, W. B., & Martin, C. E. (1948). *Sexual behavior in the human male.* Philadelphia: Saunders.

Kinsey, A. C., Pomeroy, W. B., Martin, C. E., & Gebhard, P. H. (1953). *Sexual behavior in the human female.* Philadelphia: Saunders.

Kinston, W. (1980). A theoretical and technical approach to narcissistic disturbance. *International Journal of Psychoanalysis, 61,* 383–393.

Kirby, M. (Chair). (2008, April 28). Homeless and mental illness: Solving the challenge. Mental Health Commission of Canada Collaboration for Change Forum, Playhouse Theatre, Vancouver, BC. Retrieved from http://www.mentalhealthcommission.ca/SiteCollectionDocuments/Homelessness/Speech_kirbyVan_Apr2808_ENG.pdf

Kirby, M. J. L., & Leon, W. J. (2006). Out of the shadows at last: Transforming mental health, mental illness and addiction services in Canada. The Standing Senate Committee on Social Affairs, Science and Technology. Retrieved from http://www.parl.gc.ca/39/1/parlbus/commbus/senate/com-e/soci-e/rep-e/rep02may06-e.htm

Kirmayer, L. J. (1994). Suicide among Canadian Aboriginal peoples. *Transcultural Psychiatric Research Review, 31,* 3–58.

Kirmayer, L. J. (2001). Cultural variations in the clinical presentation of depression and anxiety: Implications for diagnosis and treatment. *Journal of Clinical Psychiatry, 62* (Suppl. 13), 22–28.

Kirmayer, L. J., & Looper, K. J. (2007). Somatoform disorders. In M. Hersen, S. M. Turner, & D. C. Beidel (Eds.), *Adult psychopathology and diagnosis* (5th ed., pp. 410–472). Hoboken, NJ: John Wiley & Sons.

Kirmayer, L. J., Robbins, J. M., & Paris, J. (1994). Somatoform disorders: Personality and social matrix of somatic distress. *Journal of Abnormal Psychology, 103,* 125–136.

Kirmayer, L. J., & Sartorius, N. (2007). Cultural models and somatic syndromes. *Psychosomatic Medicine, 69,* 832–840.

Kirsh, I., Deacon, B. J., Huedo-Medina, T. B., Scoboria, A., Moore, T. J., & Johnson, B. T. (2008). Initial severity and antidepressant benefits: A meta-analysis of data submitted to the Food and Drug Administration. *PLoS Medicine, 5,* 260–268.

Kisely, S., Campbell, L. A., Scott, A., Preston, N., & Xiao, J. (2006). Randomized and non-randomized evidence for the effect of compulsory community and involuntary out-patient treatment on health service use: Systematic review and meta-analysis. *Psychological Medicine, 37,* 3–14.

Kitzman, H., Olds, D. L., Henderson, C. R., Hanks, C., Cole, R., Tatlebaum, R., et al. (1997). Effect of prenatal and infancy home visitation by nurses on pregnancy outcomes, childhood injuries, and repeated childbearing: A randomized controlled trial. *Journal of the American Medical Association, 278,* 644–652.

Kitzman, H., Olds, D. L., Sidora, K., Henderson, C. R., Hanks, C., Cole, R., et al. (2000). Enduring effects of nurse home visitation on maternal life course: A 3-year follow-up of a randomized trial. *Journal of the American Medical Association, 283,* 1983–1989.

Kivimaki, M., Head, J., Ferrie, J. E., Brunner, E., Marmot, M. G., Vahterra, J., & Shipley, M. J. (2006). Why is evidence on job strain and coronary heart disease mixed? An illustration of measurement challenges in the Whitehall II study. *Psychosomatic Medicine, 68,* 398–401.

Kivnick, H., & Lymburner, A. (2009). CitySongs: Primary prevention in the field. *Journal of Primary Prevention, 30,* 61–73.

Kjeldsen v. R. (1981), 2 S.C.R. 617.

Klein, D. A., & Walsh, B. T. (2004). Eating disorders: Clinical features and pathophysiology. *Physiology & Behavior, 81,* 359–374.

Klein, D. N. (2003). Patients' versus informants' reports of personality disorders in predicting 71/2-year outcome in outpatients with depressive disorders. *Psychological Assessment, 15,* 216–222.

Klein, D. N. (2008). Classification of depressive disorders in the DSM-V: Proposal for a two-dimension system. *Journal of Abnormal Psychology, 117,* 552–560.

Klein, D. N., Taylor, E. B., Dickstein, S., & Harding, K. (1988). Primary early-onset dysthymia: Comparison with primary nonbipolar nonchronic major depression on demographic, clinical, familial, personality, and socioenvironmental characteristics and short-term outcome. *Journal of Abnormal Psychology, 97,* 387–398.

Klein, D. N., Taylor, E. B., Harding, K., & Dickstein, S. (1988). Double depression and episodic major depression: Demographic, clinical, familial, personality, and socioenvironmental characteristics and short-term outcome. *American Journal of Psychiatry, 145,* 1226–1231.

Klein, R. G., Abikoff, H., Klass, E., Ganeles, D., Seese, L. M., & Pollack, S. (1997). Clinical efficacy of methylphenidate in conduct disorder with and without attention deficit hyperactivity disorder. *Archives of General Psychiatry, 54,* 1073–1080.

Klerman, G. L., Weissman, M. M., Rousanville, B. J., & Chevron, E. S. (1984). *Interpersonal psychotherapy of depression.* New York: Basic Books.

Kluft, R. (1999). An overview of the psychotherapy of dissociative identity disorder. *American Journal of Psychotherapy, 53,* 289–319.

Klump, K. L., & Gobrogge, K. L. (2005). A review and primer of molecular genetic studies of anorexia nervosa. *International Journal of Eating Disorders, 37,* S43–S48.

Klump, K. L., Gobrogge, K. L., Perkins, P. S., Thorne, D., Sisk, C. L., & Breedlove, S. M. (2006). Preliminary evidence that gonadal hormones organize and activate disordered eating. *Psychological Medicine, 36,* 539–546.

Klump, K. L., Kaye, W. H., & Strober, M. (2001). The evolving genetic foundations of eating disorders. *Psychiatric Clinics of North America, 24* (2), 215–225.

Knight, B. G., Karel, M. J., Hinrichsen, G. A., Qualls, S. H., & Duffy, M. (2009). Pikes Peak model for training in professional geropsychology. *American Psychologist, 64* (3), 205–214.

Knight, R. (1953). Borderline states. *Bulletin of the Menninger Clinic, 17,* 1–12.

Knopman, D. S., Boeve, B. F., & Petersen, R. C. (2003). Essentials of the proper diagnosis of mild cognitive impairment, dementia, and major subtypes of dementia. *Mayo Clinic Proceedings, 78,* 1290–1308.

Knowles, J. B., Southmayd, S. E., Delva, N., MacLean, A. W., Cairns, J., & Letemendia, F. J. (1979). Five variations of sleep deprivation in a depressed woman. *British Journal of Psychiatry, 135,* 403–410.

Koch, R., Azen, C., Friedman, E. G., Fishler, K., Baumann-Frischling, C., & Lin, T. (1996). Care of the adult with phenylketonuria. *European Journal of Pediatrics, 155* (Suppl.), S90–S92.

Koegel, L. (2000). Interventions to facilitate communication in autism. *Journal of Autism and Developmental Disorders, 30* (5), 383–391.

Koegel, L. K. (1995). Communication and language intervention. In R. L. Koegel & L. K. Koegel (Eds.), *Teaching children with autism: Strategies for initiating positive interactions and improving learning opportunities* (pp. 17–32). Baltimore: Paul H. Brookes.

Koerner, N., Dugas, M. J., Savard, P., Guadet, A., Turcotte, J., & Marchand, A. (2004). The economic burden of anxiety disorders in Canada. *Canadian Psychology, 45,* 191–201.

Kogan, C. S., Turk, J., Hagerman, R. J., & Kornish, K. M. (2008, September 5). Impact of the Fragile X mental retardation 1 (FMR1) gene premutation on neuropsychiatric functioning in adult males without fragile X-associated Tremor/Ataxia syndrome: A controlled study. *American Journal of Medical Genetics Part B Neuropsychiatric Genetics, 147B* (6), 859–872.

Kohut, H. (1977). *The restoration of the self.* New York: International Universities Press.

Kolb, B., Gibb, R., & Robinson, T. E. (2003). Brain plasticity and behavior. *Current Directions in Psychological Science, 12,* 1–5.

Kolb, B., & Teskey, G. C. (2011). Paradoxical phenomena in brain plasticity. In N. Kapur (Ed.), *The paradoxical brain* (pp. 350–364). New York: Cambridge University Press.

Komer, W. J., O'Reilly, R. L., Cernovsky, Z., & Dunbar, S. (1999). Review board outcomes for involuntary patients in provincial psychiatric hospitals. *Canadian Journal of Psychiatry, 44,* 495–498.

Komiya, N., Good, G. E., & Sherrod, N. B. (2000). Emotional openness as a predictor of college students' attitudes toward seeking psychological help. *Journal of Counseling Psychology, 47,* 138–143.

Konnert, C., Dobson, K., & Watt, A. (2009). Geropsychology training in Canada: A survey of doctoral and internship programs. *Canadian Psychology, 50,* 255–260.

Konnopka, A., Leichsenring, F., Leibing, E., & König, H. H. (2009). Cost-of-illness studies and cost-effectiveness analyses in anxiety disorders: A systematic review. *Journal of Affective Disorders, 114,* 14–31.

Konopasky, R. J., & Konopasky, A. W. B. (2000). Remaking penile plethysmography. In D. R. Laws, S. M. Hudson, & T. Ward (Eds.), *Remaking relapse prevention with sex offenders* (pp. 257–284). London: Sage.

Kop, W., & Plumhoff, J. E. (2011). Depression and coronary heart disease: Diagnosis, predictive value, biobehavioral mechanisms and intervention. In R. Allan & J. Fisher (Eds.), *Heart and mind: The practice of cardiac psychology* (2nd ed., pp. 143–168). Washington, DC: American Psychological Association.

Korenman, S. G. (1998). New insights into erectile dysfunction: A practical approach. *American Journal of Medicine, 105,* 135–144.

Koss, M. P. (1988). Stranger and acquaintance rape: Are there differences in the victim's experience? *Psychology of Women Quarterly, 12,* 1–24.

Koss, M. P. (1992). The underdetection of rape: Methodological choices influence incidence estimates. *Journal of Social Issues, 48,* 61–75.

Kovacs, M., & Devlin, B. (1998). Internalizing disorders in childhood. *The Journal of Child Psychology and Psychiatry, 39,* 47–63.

Kraepelin, E. (1896). *Psychiatrie: Ein Lehrbuch für Studierende und Aerzte* (5th ed). Leipzig, Germany: Barth.

Kraepelin, E. (1913). *Psychiatry: A textbook.* Leipzig: Barth.

Kraepelin, E. (1915). *Psychiatrie.* Leipzig: Barth.

Kraepelin, E. (1919). *Dementia praecoxand paraphrenia* (R. M. Barclay, Trans.; G. M. Robertson, Ed.). Edinburgh: E. & S. Livingstone.

Krafft-Ebing, R. V. (1939). *Psychopathia sexualis* (12th ed., V. Robinson, Trans.). New York: Pioneer. (Original work published in 1886)

Krafft-Ebing, R. V. (1901). *Psychopathia sexualia.* Stuttgart: Ferdinand Enke.

Kral, M. (2003). Unikkaartuit: Meanings of well-being, sadness, suicide, and change in two Inuit communities. Final Report to the National Health Research and Development Programs.

Krantz, D. S., & Manuck, S. B. (1984). Acute psychophysiologic reactivity and risk of cardiovascular disease: A review and methodologic critique. *Psychological Bulletin, 96,* 435–464.

Krantz, D. S., et al. (1988). Environmental stress and biobehavioral antecedents of coronary heart disease. *Journal of Consulting and Clinical Psychology, 56,* 333–341.

Kratochwill, T. R., Sheridan, S. M., Carlson, J., & Lasecki, K. L. (1999). Advances in behavioral assessment. In C. R. Reynolds & T. B. Gutkin (Eds.), *The handbook of school psychology* (3rd ed., pp. 350–382). New York: Wiley.

Kreher, D. A., Holcomb, P. J., Goff, D., & Kuperberg, G. R. (2008). Neural evidence for faster and further automatic spreading activation in schizophrenia thought disorder. *Schizophrenia Bulletin, 34,* 473–482.

Kreitman, N. (1976). The coal gas story—United Kingdom suicide rates, 1960–1971. *British Journal of Preventive Social Medicine, 30,* 86–93.

Kresin, D. (1993). Medical aspects of inhibited sexual desire disorder. In W. O'Donohue & J. H. Greer (Eds.), *Handbook of sexual dysfunctions: Assessment and treatment* (pp. 15–52). Boston: Allyn & Bacon.

Krittayaphong, R., Cascio, W. E., Light, K. C., Sheffield, D., Golden, R. N., Finkel, J. B., et al. (1997). Heart rate variability in patients with coronary artery disease: Differences in patients with higher and lower depression scores. *Psychosomatic Medicine, 59,* 231–235.

Kroenke, K., & Swindle, R. (2000). Cognitive-behavioral therapy for somatization and symptom syndromes: A critical review of controlled clinical trials. *Psychotherapy and Psychosomatics, 69,* 205–215.

Kroll, J., & Bachrach, B. (1984). Sin and mental illness in the Middle Ages. *Psychological Medicine, 14,* 507–514.

Kreuger, R. B. (2010a). The DSM diagnostic criteria for sexual masochism. *Archives of Sexual Behavior, 39,* 346–356.

Kreuger, R. B. (2010b). The DSM diagnostic criteria for sexual sadism. *Archives of Sexual Behavior, 39,* 325–345.

Krueger, R. F. (2005). Continuity of Axis I and Axis II: Toward a unified model of personality, personality disorders, and clinical disorders. *Journal of Personality Disorders, 19,* 233–261.

Kuehn, B. M. (2007). CDC: Autism spectrum disorders common. *Journal of the American Medical Association, 297,* 940.

Kuhn, C. M. (1989). Adrenocortical and gonadal steroids in behavioral cardiovascular medicine. In N. Schneiderman, S. M. Weiss, & P. G. Kaufmann (Eds.), *Handbook of research methods in cardiovascular behavioral medicine.* New York: Plenum.

Kukkonen, T. M., Binik, Y. M., Amsel, R., & Carrier, S. (2007). Thermography as a physiological measure of sexual arousal in both men and women. *Journal of Sexual Medicine, 4,* 93–105.

Kukkonen, T. M., Binik, Y. M., Amsel, R., & Carrier, S. (2009). Hot or not? Examining age related differences in genital temperature during sexual arousal via thermography. *Journal of Sexual Medicine, 6* (s4), 378.

Kukkonen, T. M., Binik, Y. M., Amsel, R., & Carrier, S. (2010a). An evaluation of the validity of thermography as a physiological measure of sexual arousal in a non-university adult sample. *Archives of Sexual Behavior, 39,* 861–873.

Kukkonen, T. M., Binik, Y. M., Amsel, R., & Carrier, S. (2010b). The heat is on: Examining the reliability of genital temperature measurement in men and women. *Journal of Sexual Medicine, 7* (s3), 119–120.

Kukull, W. A., & Bowen, J. D. (2002). Dementia epidemiology. *Medical Clinics of North America, 86,* 573–590.

Kuper, H., & Marmot, M. (2003). Job strain, job demands, decision latitude and risk of coronary heart disease within the Whitehall II study. *Journal of Epidemiology and Community Health, 57,* 147–153.

Kuperberg, G. R., Lakshmanan, B. M., Greve, D. N., & West, W. C. (2008). Task and semantic relationship influence both the polarity and localization of hemodynamic modulation during lexico-semantic processing. *Human Brain Mapping, 29,* 544–561.

Kuperberg, G. R., McGuire, P. K., & David, A. S. (1998). Reduced sensitivity to linguistic context in schizophrenic thought disorder: Evidence from on-line monitoring from words in linguistically anomalous sentences. *Journal of Abnormal Psychology, 107,* 423–434.

Kupfer, D. J., & Ehlers, C. L. (1989). Two roads to REM latency. *Archives of General Psychiatry, 46,* 945–948.

Kurtz, J. E., & Blais, M. A. (2007). Introduction to the special issue on the Personality Assessment Inventory. *Journal of Personality Assessment, 88,* 1–4.

Kurtz, M. M., & Mueser, K. T. (2008). A meta-analysis of controlled research on social skills training for schizophrenia. *Journal of Consulting and Clinical Psychology, 76,* 491–504.

Kutcher, M. J., Hampton, S., & Wilson, J. (2010). Child and adolescent mental health policy and plans in Canada: An analytical review. *Canadian Journal of Psychiatry, 55,* 100–107.

Kutchins, H., & Kirk, S. A. (1997). *Making us crazy: DSM: The psychiatric bible and the creation of mental disorders.* New York: Free Press.

Kuyken, W., Byford, S., Taylor, R. S., Watkins, E., Holden, E., White, K., et al. (2008). Mindfulness-based cognitive therapy to prevent relapse in recurrent depression. *Journal of Consulting & Clinical Psychology, 76,* 966–978.

Kyriakopoulos, M., Bargiotas, T., Barker, G. J., & Frangou, S. (2008). Diffusion tensor imaging in schizophrenia. *European Psychiatry, 23,* 255–273.

Laborit, H. (1950). *Physiologie et biologie du système nerveux végétif au service de la chirurgie.* Paris: G. Doin.

LaCroix, A. Z., & Haynes, S. G. (1987). Gender differences in the stressfulness of workplace roles: A focus on work and health. In R. Barnett, G. Baruch, & L. Biener (Eds.), *Gender and stress* (pp. 96–121). New York: Free Press.

Lahey, B. B., Pelham, W. E., Loney, J., Lee, S. S., & Willcutt, E. (2005). Instability of the DSM-IV subtypes of ADHD from preschool through elementary school. *Archives of General Psychiatry, 62,* 896–902.

Lalonde, J. K., Hudson, J. I., Gigante, R. A., & Pope, H. G., Jr. (2001). Canadian and American psychiatrists' attitudes toward dissociative disorders diagnoses. *Canadian Journal of Psychiatry, 46,* 407–412.

Lalumière, M. L., Harris, G. T., & Rice, M. E. (2001). Psychopathy and developmental instability. *Evolution & Human Behavior, 22,* 75–92.

Lalumière, M. L., Quinsey, V. L., Harris, G. T., Rice, M. E., & Trautrimas, C. (2003). Are rapists differentially aroused by coercive sex in phallometric assessments? In R. A. Prentky, E. S. Janus, & M. C. Seto (Eds.), *Sexually coercive behavior: Understanding and management* (pp. 211–224). New York: The New York Academy of Sciences.

Lam, D. H., Watkins, E. R., Hayward, P., Bright, J., Wright, K., Kerr, N., et al. (2003). A randomized controlled study of cognitive therapy for relapse prevention for bipolar affective disorder outcome of the first year. *Archives of General Psychiatry, 60,* 145–152.

Lam, R., & Levitan, R. (2000). Pathophysiology of seasonal affective disorder: A review. *Journal of Psychiatry & Neuroscience, 25,* 469–480.

Lam, R., & Levitt, A. (1999). *Canadian consensus guidelines for the treatment of seasonal affective disorder.* Vancouver: Clinical and Academic Publishing.

Lam, R. W., Kennedy, S. H., Grigoriadis, S., McIntyre, R. S., Milev, R., Ramasubbu, R., Parikh, S. V., Patten, S. B., & Ravindran, A. V. (2009). Canadian Network for Mood and Anxiety Treatments (CANMAT) clinical guidelines for the management of major depressive disorder in adults. III. Pharmacotherapy. *Journal of Affective Disorders, 117,* S26–S43.

Lambert, M. T., & Silva, P. S. (1998). An update on the impact of gun control legislation on suicide. *Psychiatric Quarterly, 69,* 127–134.

Lamont, J. A. (1978). Vaginismus. *American Journal of Obstetrics and Gynecology, 131,* 632–636.

Lanctot, K. L., Herrmann, N., Yau, K. K., Khan, L. R., Liu, B. A., LouLou, M. M., & Einarson, T. R. (2003). Efficacy and safety of cholinesterase inhibitors in Alzheimer's disease: A meta-analysis. *Canadian Medical Association Journal, 16,* 557–564.

Landreville, P., Landry, J., Baillargeon, L., Guerette, A., & Matteau, E. (2001). Older adults' acceptance of psychological and pharmacological treatments for depression. *The Journals of Gerontology Series B: Psychological Sciences and Social Sciences, 56,* P285–P291.

Lang, A. R., Goeckner, D. J., Adessor, V. J., & Marlatt, G. A. (1975). Effects of alcohol on aggression in male social drinkers. *Journal of Abnormal Psychology, 84,* 508–518.

Lang, R., Pugh, G., & Langevin, R. (1988). Treatment of incest and pedophilic offenders: A pilot study. *Behavioral Science and the Law, 6,* 239–255.

Langevin, R. (1983). *Sexual strands: Understanding and treating sexual anomalies in men.* Hillsdale, NJ: Erlbaum.

Langley, R. L. (2005). Animal-related fatalities in the United States: An update. *Wilderness & Environmental Medicine, 16,* 67–74.

Långström, N. (2010). The DSM criteria for exhibitionism, voyeurism, and frotteurism. *Archives of Sexual Behavior, 39,* 317–324.

Långström, N., & Zucker, K. J. (2005). Transvestic fetishism in the general population: Prevalance and correlates. *Journal of Sex and Marital Therapy, 31,* 87–95.

Lanius, R. A., Vermetten, E., Loewenstein, R. J., Brand, B., Schmahl, C., Bremner, J. D., & Spiegel, D. (2010). Emotion modulation in PTSD: Clinical and neurobiological evidence for a dissociative subtype. *American Journal of Psychiatry, 167,* 640–647.

Laroi, F., & Woodward, T. S. (2007). Hallucinations from a cognitive perspective. *Harvard Review of Psychiatry, 15,* 109–117.

Last, C. G., Strauss, C. C., & Francis, G. (1987). Comorbidity among childhood anxiety disorders. *Journal of Nervous and Mental Disease, 175,* 726–730.

Laumann, E. O., Gagnon, J. H., Michael, R. T., & Michaels, S. (1994). *The social organization of sexuality: Sexual practices in the United States.* Chicago: University of Chicago Press.

Laumann, E. O., Paik, A., & Rosen, R. C. (1999). Sexual dysfunction in the United States: Prevalence and predictors. *Journal of the American Medical Association, 281,* 537–544.

Laurendeau, M.-C., & Perreault, R. (1997). L'amorce du virage préventif en santé mentale au Québec: Enquête sur les politiques, les structures et les programmes de prévention en santé mentale. *Psychologie Canadienne, 38,* 13–24.

Lavigne, J. V., Gibbons, R. D., Christoffel, K. K., Arend, R., Rosenbaum, D., Binns, H., et al. (1996). Prevalence rates and correlates of psychiatric disorders among preschool children. *Journal of the American Academy of Child and Adolescent Psychiatry, 35,* 203–214.

Lawler, M., & Nixon, E. (2011). Body dissatisfaction among adolescent boys and girls: The effects of body mass, peer appearance culture and internalization of appearance ideals. *Journal of Youth and Adolescence, 40,* 59–71.

Lawrence, A. (2003). Factors associated with satisfaction or regret following male-to-female sex reassignment surgery. *Archives of Sexual Behavior, 32* (4), 299–315.

Lawrence, P. J., & Williams, T. I. (2011). Pathways to inflated responsibility beliefs in adolescent obsessive-compulsive disorder: A preliminary investigation. *Behavioural and Cognitive Psychotherapy, 39,* 229–234.

Lawson, G., Peterson, J. S., & Lawson, A. (1983). *Alcoholism and the family: A guide to treatment and prevention.* Rockville, MD: Aspen.

Lazarus, R. S., & Folkman, S. (1984). *Stress, appraisal and coping.* New York: Guilford Press.

Learning Disabilities Association of Canada. (2007). Putting a Canadian face on learning disabilities. Retrieved from http://www.pacfold.ca

LeBeau, R. T., Glenn, D., Liao, B., Wittchen, H. U., Beesdo-Baum, K., Ollendick, T., & Craske, M. G. (2010). Specific phobia: A review of DSM-IV specific phobia and preliminary recommendations for DSM-V. *Depression and Anxiety, 27,* 148–167.

Ledley, D. R., & Heimberg, R. G. (2005). Social anxiety disorder. In M. M. Antony, D. R. Ledley, & R. G. Heimberg (Eds.), *Improving outcomes and preventing relapse in cognitive-behavioral therapy* (pp. 38–76). New York: Guilford Press.

LeDoux, J. E. (2000). Emotion circuits in the brain. *Annual Review of Neuroscience, 23,* 155–184.

LeDoux, J. E. (2003). *Synaptic self: How our brains become who we are.* New York: Penguin Books.

Ledwidge, B., Glackman, W., Paredes, J., Chen, R., Dhami, S., Hansen, M., & Higenbottam, J. (1987). Controlled follow-up of patients released by a review panel at one and two years after separation. *Canadian Journal of Psychiatry, 32,* 448–453.

Lee, B. A., MacKenzie, J. J., & Holden, J. J. A. (2003). The nature of Fragile X syndrome. In I. Brown & M. Percy (Eds.), *Developmental disabilities in Ontario* (pp. 229–244). Toronto: Ontario Association on Developmental Disabilities.

Lee, T., & Seeman, P. (1980). Elevation of brain neuroleptic/dopamine receptors in schizophrenia. *American Journal of Psychiatry, 137,* 191–197.

Lee, Z., Klaver, J. R., Hart, S. D., Moretti, M. M., & Douglas, K. S. (2009). Short-term stability of psychopathic traits in adolescent offenders. *Journal of Clinical Child and Adolescent Psychology, 38,* 595–605. doi:10.1080/15374410903103536

Legault, S. E., Langer, A., Armstrong, P. W., & Freeman, M. R. (1995). Usefulness of ischemic response to mental stress in predicting silent myocardial ischemia during ambulatory monitoring. *American Journal of Cardiology, 75,* 1007–1011.

Le Grange, D., Crosby, R. D., Rathouz, P. J., & Leventhal, B. L. (2007). A randomized controlled comparison of family-based treatment and supportive psychotherapy for adolescent bulimia nervosa. *Archives of General Psychiatry, 64,* 1049–1056.

Lehmann, H. E., & Hanrahan, G. E. (1954). Chlorpromazine: New inhibiting agent for psychomotor excitement and manic states. *Archives of Neurology and Psychiatry, 71,* 227–237.

Leibenluft, E., Blair, R. J., Charney, D. S., & Pine, D. S. (2003). Irritability in pediatric mania and other childhood psychopathology. *Annals of the New York Academy of Sciences, 1008,* 201–218. doi:10.1196/annals.1301.022

Leichner, P., Hall, D., & Calderon, R. (2005). Meal support training for friends and families of patients with eating disorders. *Eating Disorders, 13,* 407–411.

Leichsenring, F., & Rabung, S. (2008). Effectiveness of long-term psychodynamic psychotherapy: A meta-analysis. *Journal of the American Medical Association, 300,* 1551–1565.

Leichsenring, F., Salzer, S., Jaeger, U., Kächele, H., Kriesche, R., et al. (2009). Short-term psychodynamic psychotherapy and cognitive-behavioral therapy in generalized anxiety disorder: A randomized controlled trial. *American Journal of Psychiatry, 166,* 875–881.

Lentz, V., Robinson, J., & Bolton, J. M. (2010). Childhood adversity, mental disorder comorbidity, and suicidal behavior in schizotypal personality disorder. *Journal of Nervous and Mental Disease, 198,* 795–801. doi:10.1097/NMD.0b013e3181f9804c

Lenze, E. J., & Wetherell, J. L. (2011). Anxiety disorders: New developments in old age. *American Journal of Geriatric Psychiatry, 19* (4), 301–304.

Lenzenweger, M. F., Lane, M. C., Loranger, A. W., & Kessler, R. C. (2007). DSM-IV personality disorders in the national comorbidity survey replication, *Biological Psychiatry, 62,* 553–564.

Leon, J., Cheung, C. K., & Neumann, P. J. (1998). Alzheimer's disease care: Costs and potential savings. *Health Affairs, 17,* 44–54.

Leonard, H., & Wen, X. (2002). The epidemiology of mental retardation: Challenges and opportunities in the new millennium. *Mental Retardation and Developmental Disabilities Research Reviews, 8,* 117–134.

Leonardo, E. D., & Hen, R. (2006). Genetics of affective and anxiety disorders. *Annual Review of Psychology, 57,* 117–137.

Lépine, J. (2001). Epidemiology, burden, and disability in depression and anxiety. *Journal of Clinical Psychiatry, 62(Suppl. 13),* 4–10.

Lerner, J. W. (1989). Educational interventions in learning disabilities. *Journal of the American Academy of Child and Adolescent Psychiatry, 28,* 326–331.

Lerner, J. W., & Lerner, S. R. (1991). Attention deficit disorder: Issues and questions. *Focus on Exceptional Children, 24,* 1–17.

Lesch, K. P. (2004). Gene-environment interaction and the genetics of depression. *Journal of Psychiatry and Neuroscience, 29,* 174–184.

Levenson, J. S. (2004). Reliability of sexually violent predator civil commitment criteria. *Law and Human Behavior, 28,* 357–368.

Levenstein, S. (2000). The very model of a modern etiology: A biopsychosocial view of peptic ulcer. *Psychosomatic Medicine, 62,* 176–185.

Levenstein, S., Kaplan, G. A., & Smith, M. (1995). Sociodemographic characteristics, life stressors and peptic ulcer: A prospective study. *Journal of Clinical Gastroenterology, 21,* 185–192.

Levine, E. S., & Padilla, A. M. (1980). *Crossing cultures in therapy: Counseling for the Hispanic.* Monterey, CA: Brooks/Cole.

Levine, S. B. (1989). Comprehensive and sexual health centers: Is it time? *Journal of Sex and Marital Therapy, 15,* 215–224.

Levitan, R. D., Kaplan, A. S., Masellis, M., Basile, V. S., Walker, M. L., Lipson, N., et al. (2001). Polymorphism of the serotonin 5-HT1B receptor gene (HTR1B) associated with minimum lifetime body mass index in women with bulimia nervosa. *Biological Psychiatry, 50,* 640–643.

Levitt, A., Boyle, M., Joffe, R., & Baumal, Z. (2000). Estimated prevalence of the seasonal subtype of major depression in a Canadian community sample. *Canadian Journal of Psychiatry, 45,* 650–654.

Levy, D. L., Holzman, P. S., Matthysse, S., & Mendell, N. R. (1993). Eye tracking dysfunction and schizophrenia: A critical perspective. *Schizophrenia Bulletin, 19,* 461–536.

Levy, T. M. (2000). *Handbook of attachment interventions.* San Diego, CA: Academic Press.

Lewinsohn, P. M., Mischel, W., Chaplin, W., & Barton, R. (1980). Social competence and depression: The role of illusory self-perceptions. *Journal of Abnormal Psychology, 90,* 213–219.

Lewontin, R. C., Rose, S., & Kamin, L. J. (1984). *Not in our genes: Biology, ideology, and human nature.* New York: Pantheon Books.

Lezak, M. D. (1995). *Neuropsychological assessment* (3rd ed.). New York: Oxford University Press.

Libby, A. M., Brent, D. A., Morrato, E. H., Orton, H. D., Allen, R., & Valuck, R. J. (2007). Decline in treatment of pediatric depression after FDA advisory on risk of suicidality with SSRIs. *American Journal of Psychiatry, 164,* 884–891.

Libby, P. (2002). Atherosclerosis: The new view. *Scientific American, May,* 46–55.

Lichtenstein, P., & Annas, P. (2000). Heritability and prevalence of specific fears and phobias in childhood. *Journal of Child Psychology and Psychiatry, 4,* 927–937.

Lieberman, A. (2006). Depression in Parkinson's disease: A review. *Acta Neurologica Scandinavica, 113,* 1–8.

Lieberman, A. F., Chu, A., van Horn, P., & Harris, W. W. (2011). Trauma in early childhood: Empirical evidence and clinical implications. *Development and Psychopathology, 23,* 397–410.

Lilenfeld, L. R., Stein, D., Bulik, C. M., Strober, M., Plotnicov, K., Pollice, C., et al. (2000). Personality traits among currently eating disordered, recovered and never ill first-degree female relatives of bulimic and control women. *Psychological Medicine, 30,* 1399–1410.

Lilenfeld, L. R. R., Wonderlich, S., Riso, L. P., Crosby, R., & Mitchell, J. (2006). Eating disorders and personality: A methodological and empirical review. *Clinical Psychology Review, 26,* 299–320.

Lilienfeld, S. O., & Landfield, K. (2008). Issues in diagnosis: Categorical vs. dimensional. In W. E. Craighead, D. J. Miklowitz, & L. W. Craighead (Eds.), *Psychopathology: History, diagnosis, and empirical foundations* (pp. 1–33). Hoboken, NJ: Wiley.

Lilienfeld, S. O., & Marino, L. (1995). Mental disorder as a Roschian concept: A critique of Wakefield's "harmful dysfunction" analysis. *Journal of Abnormal Psychology, 104,* 411–420.

Limosin, F., Rouillon, F., Payan, C., Cohen, J. M., & Strub, N. (2003). Prenatal exposure to influenza as a risk factor for adult schizophrenia. *Acta Psychiatrica Scandinavica, 107,* 331–335.

Linden, W., & Chambers, L. (1994). Clinical effectiveness of non-drug treatment of hypertension: A meta-analysis. *Annals of Behavioral Medicine, 16,* 35–45.

Linden, W., & Moseley, J. V. (2006). The efficacy of behavioral treatments for hypertension. *Applied Psychophysiology and Biofeedback, 31,* 51–63.

Lindsley, O. R., Skinner, B. F., & Solomon, R. L. (1954). A method for the experimental analysis of the behavior of psychotic patients. *American Psychologist, 9,* 419–420.

Linehan, M. M. (1987). Dialectical behavior therapy for borderline personality disorder. *Bulletin of the Menninger Clinic, 41,* 261–276.

Linehan, M. M. (1993). *Cognitive-behavioral treatment of borderline personality disorder.* New York: Guilford Press.

Linehan, M. M., Armstrong, H. E., Suarez, A., Allmon, D., & Heard, H. L. (1991). Cognitive-behavioral treatment of chronically parasuicidal borderline patients. *Archives of General Psychiatry, 48,* 1060–1064.

Linehan, M. M., Comtois, K. A., Murray, A. M., Brown, M. Z., Gallop, R. J., Heard, H. L., et al. (2006). Two-year randomized controlled trial and follow-up of dialectical behavior therapy vs therapy by experts for suicidal behaviors and borderline personality disorder. *Archives of General Psychiatry, 63,* 757–766.

Linehan, M. M., & Heard, H. L. (1992). Dialectical behavior therapy for borderline personality disorder. In J. F. Clarkin, E. Marziali, & H. Munroe-Blum (Eds.), *Borderline personality disorder: Clinical and empirical perspectives* (pp. 248–267). New York: Guilford Press.

Link, B. G., Struening, E. L., Neese-Todd, S., Asmussen, S., & Phelan, J. C. (2001). The consequences of stigma for the self-esteem of people with mental illness. *Psychiatric Services, 52,* 1621–1626.

Links, P. S. (1992). Family environment and family psychopathology in the etiology of borderline personality disorder. In J. F. Clarkin, E. Marziali, & H. Munroe-Blum (Eds.), *Borderline personality disorder: Clinical and empirical perspectives* (pp. 45–66). New York: Guilford Press.

Liotti, G. (2009). Attachment and dissociation. In P. F. Dell & J. A. O'Neil (Eds.), *Dissociation and the dissociative disorders: DSM-V and beyond* (pp. 53–65). New York: Routledge.

Lippens, T., & Mackenzie, C. S. (2011). Treatment satisfaction, perceived treatment effectiveness, and dropout among older users of mental health services. *Journal of Clinical Psychology, 67,* 1197–1209.

Lipsitz, J. D., Markowitz, J. C., Cherry, S., & Fyer, A. J. (1999). Open trial of interpersonal psychotherapy for the treatment of social phobia. *American Journal of Psychiatry, 156,* 1814–1816.

Livesley, W. J. (1986). Trait and behavioral prototypes for personality disorder. *American Journal of Psychiatry, 143,* 728–732.

Livesley, W. J., Jang, K. L., & Vernon, P. A. (2003). Genetic basis of personality structure. In Theodore Millon (Ed.), *Handbook of psychology: Personality and social psychology* (Vol. 5). New York: Wiley.

Livesley, W. J., Schroeder, M. L., Jackson, D. N., & Jang, K. L. (1994). Categorical distinctions in the study of personality disorder: Implications for classification. *Journal of Abnormal Psychology, 103,* 6–17.

Livesley, W. J., & West, M. (1986). The DSM-III distinction between schizoid and avoidant personalities. *Canadian Journal of Psychiatry, 31,* 59–62.

Lochner, C., du Toit, P. L., Zungu-Dirwayi, N., Marais, A., van Kradenburg, J., Seedat, S., et al. (2002). Childhood trauma in obsessive-compulsive disorder, trichotillomania, and controls. *Depression and Anxiety, 15,* 66–68.

Lochner, C., Serebro, P., van der Merwe, L., Hemmings, S., Kinnear, C., Seedat, S., & Stein, D. J. (2011). Comorbid obsessive–compulsive personality disorder in obsessive–compulsive disorder (OCD): A marker of severity. *Progress in Neuro-Psychopharmacology & Biological Psychiatry, 35,* 1087–1092. doi:10.1016/j.pnpbp.2011.03.006

Lock, J., & le Grange, D. (2005). Family-based treatment of eating disorders. *International Journal of Eating Disorders. Special Issue: Anorexia Nervosa, 37,* S64–S67.

Loeb, K. L., Walsh, B. T., Lock, J., le Grange, D., Jones, J., Marcus, S., et al. (2007). Open trial of family-based treatment for full and partial anorexia nervosa in adolescence: Evidence of successful dissemination. *Journal of the American Academy of Child & Adolescent Psychiatry, 46,* 792–800.

Loeber, R. (1990). Development and risk factors of juvenile antisocial behavior and delinquency. *Clinical Psychology Review, 10,* 1–42.

Loeber, R., Burke, J. D., Lahey, B. B., Winters, A., & Zera, M. (2000). Oppositional defiant and conduct disorder: A review of the past 10 years, Part I. *Journal of the Academy of Child and Adolescent Psychiatry, 39* (12), 1468–1484.

Loeber, R., Keenan, K., Lahey, B. B., Green, S. M., & Thomas, C. (1993). Evidence for developmentally based diagnoses of oppositional defiant disorder and conduct disorder. *Journal of Abnormal Child Psychology, 21,* 377–410.

Loftus, E. F. (1993). When a lie becomes memory's truth: Memory distortion after exposure to misinformation. *Current Directions in Psychological Science, 1,* 121–123.

Loftus, E. F. (2003). Make-believe memories. *American Psychologist, 58,* 867–873.

Loftus, E. F., & Davis, D. (2006). Recovered memories. *Annual Review of Clinical Psychology, 2,* 469–498.

Loftus, E. F., & Pickrell, J. E. (1995). The formation of false memories. *Psychiatric Annals, 25,* 720–725.

Logsdon, R. G., McCurry, S. M., & Teri, L. (2007). Evidence-based psychological treatments for disruptive behaviors in individuals with dementia. *Psychology and Aging, 22,* 28–36.

Longnecker, M. P. (1994). Alcohol consumption and the risk of cancer in humans: An overview. *Alcohol, 12,* 87–96.

Lonigan, C. J. (2006). Development, assessment, and promotion of preliteracy skills. *Early Education and Development, 17,* 91–114.

Lopez, S. R. (1989). Patient variable biases in clinical judgment: Conceptual overview and methodological considerations. *Psychological Bulletin, 106,* 184–203.

Lopez, S. R., & Hernandez, P. (1986). How culture is considered in evaluations of psychopathology. *Journal of Nervous and Mental Disease, 176,* 598–606.

LoPiccolo, J. (1990). Sexual dysfunction. In A. S. Bellack, M. Hersen, & A. Kazdin (Eds.), *International handbook of behavior therapy and modification* (2nd ed., pp. 547–564). New York: Plenum.

Lord, C. (1993). The complexity of social behavior in autism. In S. Baron-Cohen, H. Tager-Flusberg, & D. Cohen (Eds.), *Understanding other minds: Perspectives from autism* (pp. 292–316). Oxford: Oxford University Press.

Lord, C., & Paul, R. (1997). Language and communication in autism. In D. J. Cohen & F. R. Volkmar (Eds.), *Handbook of autism and pervasive developmental disorders* (pp. 195–225). New York: Wiley.

Lord, C., Risi, S., Lambrecht, L., Cook, E. H., Leventhal, B. L., DiLavore, P. C., et al. (2000). The Autism Diagnostic Observation Schedule-Generic: A standard measure of social and communication deficits associated with the spectrum of autism. *Journal of Autism and Developmental Disorders, 30,* 205–233.

Lord, C., Rutter, M., & Le Couteur, A. (1994). Autism Diagnostic Interview–Revised: A revised version of a diagnostic interview for caregivers of individuals with possible pervasive developmental disorders. *Journal of Autism and Developmental Disorders, 24,* 659–685.

Lord, C., & Schopler, E. (1987). Neurobiological implications of sex differences in autism. In E. Schopler & G. B. Mesibov (Eds.), *Neurobiological issues in autism* (pp. 192–211). New York: Plenum.

Lösel, F. (1998). Treatment and management of psychopaths. In D. Cooke, A. E. Forth, & R. D. Hare (Eds.), *Psychopathy: Theory, research and implications for society.* Dordrecht: The Netherlands: Kluwer.

Lösel, F., & Schmucker, M. (2005). The effectiveness of treatment for sexual offenders: A comprehensive meta-analysis. *Journal of Experimental Criminology, 1,* 117–146.

Loukas, A., Fitzgerald, H. E., Zucker, R. A., & von Eye, A. (2001). Parental alcoholism and co-occurring antisocial behavior: Prospective relationships to externalizing behavior problems in their young sons. *Journal of Abnormal Child Psychology, 29,* 91–106.

Lovaas, O. I. (1977). *The autistic child: Language development through behavior modification.* New York: Irvington.

Lovaas, O. I., Koegel, R. L., Simmons, J. Q., & Long, J. S. (1973). Some generalization and follow-up measures on autistic children in behavior therapy. *Journal of Applied Behavior Analysis, 6,* 131–166.

Lovaas, O. I., & Smith, T. (1988). Intensive behavioral treatment with young autistic children. In B. B. Lahey & A. E. Kazdin (Eds.), *Advances in clinical child psychology* (Vol. 11, pp. 285–324). New York: Plenum Press.

Love, J. M., Kisker, E. E., Ross, C., Raikes, H., Constantine, J., Boller, K., et al. (2005). The effectiveness of Early Head Start for 3-year old children and their parents: Lessons for policy and programs. *Developmental Psychology, 41,* 885–901.

Lovering, J. S. (2003). Down syndrome: Characteristics and health issues. In I. Brown & M. Percy (Eds.), *Developmental disabilities in Ontario* (2nd ed., pp. 171–193). Toronto: Association on Developmental Disabilities.

Lovering, J. S., & Percy, M. (2007). Down syndrome. In I. Brown & M. Percy (Eds.), *A comprehensive guide to intellectual and developmental disabilities* (pp. 149–172). London: Paul Brookes.

Lovett, B. J., & Sheffield, R. A. (2007). Affective empathy deficits in aggressive children and adolescents: A critical review. *Clinical Psychology Review, 27,* 1–13.

Lowenstein, L. (2002). Fetishes and their associated behavior. *Sexuality and Disability, 20* (2), 135–147.

Lu, B. Y., & Ahmed, I. (2010). The mind-body conundrum: The somatopsychic perspective in geriatric depression. *American Journal of Geriatric Psychiatry, 18* (5), 378–381.

Luborsky, L. (1954). A note on Eysenck's article "The effects of psychotherapy: An evaluation." *British Journal of Psychology, 45,* 129–131.

Luborsky, L., Singer, B., & Luborsky, L. (1975). Comparative studies of psychotherapies: Is it true that "everybody has won and all must have prizes?" *Archives of General Psychiatry, 32,* 995–1008.

Lubs, H. A. (1969). A marker X chromosome. *American Journal of Human Genetics, 21,* 231–244.

Lucas, A. R., Beard, C. M., O'Fallon, W. M., & Kurland, L. T. (1991). 50-year trends in the incidence of anorexia nervosa in Rochester, Minn.: A population-based study. *American Journal of Psychiatry, 148* (7), 917–922.

Luckasson, R., Coulter, D. L., Polloway, E. A., Reiss, S., Schalock, R. L., Snell, M. E., et al. (2002). *Mental retardation: Definition, classification and systems of supports* (9th ed.). Washington, DC: American Association on Mental Retardation.

Lumley, M. N., & Harkness, K. L. (2007). Specificity in the relations among childhood adversity, early maladaptive schemas, and symptom profiles in adolescent depression. *Cognitive Therapy and Research, 31,* 639–657.

Lumley, M. N., & Harkness, K. L. (2009). Childhood maltreatment and depressotypic cognitive organization. *Cognitive Therapy and Research, 33,* 511–522.

Lunsky, Y., Tint, A., Robinson, S., Khodaverdian, A., & Jaskulski, C. (2011). Emergency psychiatric service use by individuals with intellectual disabilities living with family. *Journal of Mental Health Research in Intellectual Disabilities, 4,* 172–185.

Luthar, S. S., Cicchetti, D., & Becker, B. (2000). The construct of resilience: A critical evaluation and guidelines for future work. *Child Development, 71,* 543–563.

Lykken, D. T. (1957). A study of anxiety in the sociopathic personality. *Journal of Abnormal and Social Psychology, 55,* 6–10.

Lykken, D. T. (1995). *The antisocial personalities.* Hillsdale, NJ: Erlbaum.

Lynam, D. R. (1996). Early identification of chronic offenders: Who is the fledgling psychopath? *Psychological Bulletin, 120* (2), 209–234.

Lynam, D. R. (2002). Fledgling psychopathy: A view from personality theory. *Law and Human Behavior, 26,* 255–259.

Lynch, C. (2004). Psychotherapy for persons with mental retardation. *Mental Retardation, 42,* 399–405.

Lynch, R. G. (2004). *Exceptional returns: Economic, fiscal, and social benefits of investment in early childhood development.* Washington, DC: Economic Policy Institute.

Lyon, D. R. & Ogloff, J. R. P. (2000). Legal and ethical issues in psychopathy assessment. In C. Gacono (Ed.), *The clinical and forensic assessment of psychopathy: A practitioner's guide* (pp. 139–173). Hillsdale, NJ: Erlbaum.

Machado, P. P. P., Machado, B. C., Gonçalves, S., & Hoek, H. W. (2007). The prevalence of Eating Disorders Not Otherwise Specified. *International Journal of Eating Disorders, 40,* 212–217.

Machalek, K., Brown, I., Birkan, R., Fung, M., & Percy, M. (2003). Prenatal and early life. In I. Brown & M. Percy (Eds.), *Developmental Disabilities in Ontario* (2nd ed.) Toronto: Ontario Association on Developmental Disabilities.

Mackenzie, C., & Peragine, G. (2003). Measuring and enhancing self-efficacy among professional caregivers of individuals with dementia. *American Journal of Alzheimer's Disease and Other Dementias, 18,* 291–299.

Mackenzie, C., Poulin, P., & Seidman-Carlson, R. (2006). A brief mindfulness-based stress reduction intervention for nurses and nurse aides. *Applied Nursing Research, 19,* 105–109.

Mackenzie, C. S., Gekoski, W. L., & Knox, V. J. (1999). Family physicians' beliefs and treatment intentions regarding mental disorders in older adults. *Family Physician, 45,* 1219–1224.

Mackenzie, C. S., Knox, V. J., Smoley, J., & Gekoski, W. L. (2004). The influence of age and gender on advice given to depressed people. *Journal of Mental Health and Aging, 10,* 311–324.

Mackenzie, C. S., Pagura, J., & Sareen, J. (2010). Correlates of help-seeking and perceived need for mental health services among older adults in the Collaborative Psychiatric Epidemiology Surveys. *American Journal of Geriatric Psychiatry, 18,* 1103–1115.

Mackenzie, C. S., Reynolds, K., Cairney, J., Streiner, D. L., & Sareen, J. (in press). Disorder-specific mental health service use for mood and anxiety disorders: Associations with age, sex, and psychiatric comorbidity. *Depression and Anxiety.*

Mackenzie, C. S., Reynolds, K., Chou, K-L., Pagura, J., & Sareen, J. (2011). Prevalence and correlates of generalized anxiety disorder in a national sample of older adults. *American Journal of Geriatric Psychiatry, 19* (4), 305–315.

Mackenzie, C. S., Rosenberg, M., & Major, M. (2006). Evaluation of a psychiatric day hospital program for elderly patients with mood disorders. *International Psychogeriatrics, 18,* 631–641.

Mackenzie, C. S., Scott, T., Mather, A., & Sareen, J. (2008). Older adults' help-seeking attitudes and treatment beliefs concerning mental health problems. *American Journal of Geriatric Psychiatry, 16,* 1010–1019.

Mackenzie, C. S., Wiprzycka, U., Hasher, L., & Goldstein, D. (2007). Does expressive writing reduce stress and improve health for family caregivers of older adults? *The Gerontologist, 47,* 296–306.

Mackenzie, C. S., Wiprzycka, U., Hasher, L., & Goldstein, D. (2008). Seeing the glass half full: Optimistic expressive writing improves mental health among chronically stressed caregivers. *British Journal of Health Psychology, 13,* 73–76.

Mackenzie, C. S., Wiprzycka, U., Hasher, L., & Goldstein, D. (2009). Associations between psychological distress, learning and memory among spouse caregivers of older adults with dementia. *Journal of Gerontology: Psychological Sciences, 64B,* 742–746.

MacLeod, J., & Nelson, G. (2000). Programs for the promotion of family wellness and the prevention of child maltreatment: A meta-analytic review. *Child Abuse and Neglect, 24,* 1127–1149.

Maehler, C., & Schuchardt, K. (2011). Working memory in children with learning disabilities: Rethinking the criterion of discrepancy. *International Journal of Disability, Development and Education, 58* (1), 5–17.

Maffei, C., Fossati, A., Agostoni, I., Barraco, A., Bagnato, M., Deborah, D., et al. (1997). Interrater reliability and internal consistency for the Structured Clinical Interview of DSM-IV Axis II Personality Disorders (SCID-II), version 2.0. *Journal of Personality Disorders, 11,* 279–284.

Magnusson, D. (1988). *Individual development from an interactional perspective: A longitudinal study.* Hillsdale, NJ: Erlbaum.

Magnusson, D., & Bergman, L. R. (1990). A pattern approach to the study of pathways from childhood to adulthood. In L. N. Robins & M. Rutter (Eds.), *Straight and devious pathways from childhood to adulthood* (pp. 101–115). Cambridge, UK: Cambridge University Press.

Maher, W. B., & Maher, B. A. (1985). Psychopathology. 1. From ancient times to the eighteenth century. In G. A. Kimble & K. Schlesinger (Eds.), *Topics in the history of psychology* (Vol. 2). Hillsdale, NJ: Erlbaum.

Mahler, M. S., Pine, F., & Bergman, A. (1975). *The psychological birth of the human infant.* New York: Basic Books.

Maier, W., Lichtermann, D., Klingler, T., Heun, R., & Hallmayer, J. (1992). Prevalence of personality disorders (DSM-III-R) in the community. *Journal of Personality Disorders, 6,* 187–196.

Main, M., & Morgan, H. (1996). Disorganization and disorientation in infant strange situation behaviour: Phenotypic resemblance to dissociative states? In L. L. Michelson & W. J. Ray (Eds.), *Handbook of dissociation.* New York: Plenum.

Malamuth, N. M. (1986). Predictors of naturalistic sexual aggression. *Journal of Personality and Social Psychology, 50,* 953–962.

Malamuth, N. M., Heavey, C. L., & Linz, D. (1993). Predicting men's antisocial behavior against women: The interactional model of sexual aggression. In G. C. N. Hall, R. Hirschman, J. R. Graham, & M. S. Zaragonzee (Eds.), *Sexual aggression: Issues in etiology, assessment and treatment* (pp. 63–99). Bristol, PA: Taylor & Francis.

Malarkey, W. B., Kiecolt-Glaser, J. K., Pearl, D., & Glaser, R. (1994). Hostile behavior during marital conflict alters pituitary and adrenal hormones. *Psychosomatic Medicine, 56,* 41–51.

Malian, I., & Nevin, A. (2002). A review of self-determination literature: Implications for practitioners. *Remedial and Special Education, 2,* 68–74.

Malik, N., Kingdon, D., Pelton, J., Mehta, R., & Turkington, D. (2009). Effectiveness of brief cognitive-behavioral therapy for schizophrenia delivered by mental health nurses: Relapse and recovery at 24 months. *Journal of Clinical Psychiatry, 70,* 201–207.

Malkoff-Schwartz, S., Frank, E., Anderson, B., Sherrill, J. T., Siegel, L., Patterson, D., et al. (1998). Stressful life events and social rhythm disruption in the onset of manic and depressive bipolar episodes: A preliminary investigation. *Archives of General Psychiatry, 55,* 702–707.

Malkoff-Schwartz, S., Frank, E., Anderson, B. P., Hlastala, S. A., Luther, J. F., Sherrill, J. T., et al. (2000). Social rhythm disruption and stressful life events in the onset of bipolar and unipolar episodes. *Psychological Medicine, 30,* 1005–1016.

Malla, A., Norman, R. M. G., & Helmes, E. (1987). Factors associated with involuntary admission to psychiatric facilities in Newfoundland. *Canadian Medical Association Journal, 136,* 1166–1171.

Malone, R. P., Delaney, M. A., Luebbert, J. F., Cater, J., & Campbell, M. (2000). A double-blind placebo-controlled study of lithium in hospitalized aggressive children and adolescents with conduct disorder. *Archives of General Psychiatry, 57,* 649–654.

Mammarella, I. C., Cornoldi, C., Pazzaglia, F., Toso, C., Grimoldi, M., & Vio, C. (2006). Evidence for a double dissociation between spatial-simultaneous and spatial-sequential working memory in visuospatial (nonverbal) learning disabled children. *Brain and Cognition, 62,* 58–67.

Manassis, K., & Monga, S. (2001). A therapeutic approach to children and adolescents with anxiety disorders and associated comorbid conditions. *Journal of the American Academy of Child & Adolescent Psychiatry,* 11–17.

Mangweth, B., Pope, H. G., Jr., Hudson, J. I., Olivardia, R., Kinzl, J., & Biebl, W. (1997). Eating disorders in Austrian men: An intracultural and crosscultural comparison study. *Psychotherapy and Psychosomatics, 66,* 214–221.

Mann, J. J., Huang, Y.-Y., Underwood, M. D., Kassir, S. A., Oppenheim, S., Kelly, T. M., et al. (2000). A serotonin transporter gene promoter polymorphism (5-HTTLPR) and prefrontal cortical binding in major depression and suicide. *Archives of General Psychiatry, 57,* 729–738.

Manning, M., Homel, R., & Smith, C. (2010). A meta-analysis of the effects of early developmental prevention programs in at-risk populations on non-health outcomes in adolescence. *Children and Youth Services Review, 32,* 506–519.

Mansell, S., Sobsey, D., & Calder, P. (1992). Sexual abuse treatment for persons with developmental disabilities. *Professional Psychology: Research and Practice, 23,* 404–409.

Manuck, S. B., Kaplan, J. R., Adams, M. R., & Clarkson, T. B. (1989). Behaviorally elicited heart rate reactivity and atherosclerosis in female cynomolgus monkeys (*Macaca fascicularis*). *Psychosomatic Medicine, 51,* 306–318.

Manuck, S. B., Kaplan, J. R., & Clarkson, T. B. (1983). Behaviorally induced heart rate reactivity and atherosclerosis in cynomolgus monkeys. *Psychosomatic Medicine, 45,* 95–108.

Marchetti, R. L., Kurcgant, D., Neto, J. G., Von Bismark, M. A., & Fiore, L. A. (2009). Evaluating patients with suspected nonepileptic psychogenic seizures. *Journal of Neuropsychiatry and Clinical Neurosciences, 21,* 292–298.

Marcus, S. C., & Olfson, M. (2010). National trends in the treatment for depression from 1998 to 2007. *Archives of General Psychiatry, 67,* 1265–1273.

Markovitz, P. J., Calabrese, J. R., Schulz, C. S., & Meltzer, H. Y. (1991). Fluoxetine in the treatment of borderline and schizotypal personality disorders. *American Journal of Psychiatry, 148,* 1067–1076.

Marlatt, G. A., Demming, B., & Reid, J. B. (1973). Loss of control drinking in alcoholics: An experimental analogue. *Journal of Abnormal Psychology, 81,* 233–241.

Marlatt, G. A., & Gordon, J. R. (Eds.). (1985). *Relapse prevention maintenance strategies in the treatment of addictive behaviors.* New York: Guilford Press.

Marmot, M. G. (1986). Social inequalities in mortality: The social environment. In R. G. Wilkinson (Ed.), *Class and health: Research and longitudinal data.* London: Tavistock.

Marmot, M. G., Kogevinas, M., & Elston, M. A. (1987). Social/economic status and disease. *Annual Review of Public Health, 8,* 111–135.

Marmot, M. G., & Mustard, J. F. (1994). Coronary heart disease from a population perspective. In R. G. Evans, M. L. Barer, & T. R. Marmor (Eds.), *Why are some people healthy and others not?* (pp. 189–216). New York: Aldine de Gruyter.

Marmot, M. G., Siegrist, J., Theorell, T. G., & Feeney, A. (1999). Health and the psychosocial environment at work. In M. G. Marmot & R. B. Wilkinson (Eds.), *Social determinants of health* (pp. 105–131). New York: Oxford University Press.

Marmot, M. G., & Theorell, T. G. (1988). Social class and cardiovascular disease: The contribution of work. *International Journal of Health Services, 18,* 659–674.

Marshall, K., & Wynne, H. (2003). Fighting the odds. *Perspectives on Labour and Income, 4* (12). Ottawa: Statistics Canada.

Marshall, L. A., & Cooke, D. J. (1995). The role of childhood experiences in the aetiology of psychopathy. *Issues in Criminological and Legal Psychology, 24,* 107–108.

Marshall, L. A., & Cooke, D. J. (1999). The childhood experiences of psychopaths: A retrospective study of familial and societal factors. *Journal of Personality Disorders, 13* (3), 211–225.

Marshall, W. L. (1982). A model of dysfunctional behavior. In A. S. Bellack, M. Hersen, & A. E. Kazdin (Eds.), *International handbook of behavior modification and therapy* (pp. 57–78). New York: Plenum.

Marshall, W. L. (1992). The social value of treatment for sexual offenders. *Canadian Journal of Human Sexuality, 1,* 109–114.

Marshall, W. L. (1997). Pedophilia: Psychopathology and treatment. In D. R. Laws & W. O'Donohue (Eds.), *Sexual deviance: Theory, assessment, and treatment* (pp. 152–174). New York: Guilford Press.

Marshall, W. L. (2007). Diagnostic issues, multiple paraphilias, and comorbid disorders in sexual offenders: Their incidence and treatment. *Aggression and Violent Behavior, 12,* 16–35.

Marshall, W. L., Anderson, D., & Champagne, F. (1997). Self-esteem and its relationship to sexual offending. *Psychology, Crime, and Law, 3,* 81–106.

Marshall, W. L., & Barbaree, H. E. (1984). Disorders of personality, impulse and adjustment. In S. M. Turner & M. Hersen (Eds.), *Adult psychopathology: A behavioral perspective* (pp. 406–449). New York: Wiley.

Marshall, W. L., & Barbaree, H. E. (1988). The long-term evaluation of a behavioral treatment program for child molesters. *Behaviour Research and Therapy, 26,* 499–511.

Marshall, W. L., & Barbaree, H. E. (1990). An integrated theory of sexual offending. In W. L. Marshall, D. R. Laws, & H. E. Barbaree (Eds.), *Handbook of sexual assault: Issues, theories, and treatment of the offender* (pp. 257–275). New York: Plenum.

Marshall, W. L., & Barrett, S. (1990). *Criminal neglect: Why sex offenders go free.* Toronto: Doubleday. (Also reprinted in paperback by Seal/Bantam Books, 1992)

Marshall, W. L., Earls, C. M., Segal, Z. V., & Darke, J. L. (1983). A behavioral program for the assessment and treatment of sexual aggressors. In K. Craig & R. McMahon (Eds.), *Advances in clinical behavior therapy* (pp. 148–174). New York: Brunner/Mazel.

Marshall, W. L., & Eccles, A. (1993). Pavlovian conditioning processes in adolescent sex offenders. In H. E. Barbaree, W. L. Marshall, & S. M. Hudson (Eds.), *The juvenile sex offender* (pp. 118–142). New York: Guilford Press.

Marshall, W. L., Eccles, A., & Barbaree, H. E. (1991). Treatment of exhibitionists: A focus on sexual deviance versus cognitive and relationship features. *Behaviour Research and Therapy, 29,* 129–135.

Marshall, W. L., Hudson, S. M., & Hodkinson, S. (1993). The importance of attachment bonds in the development of juvenile sex offending. In H. E. Barbaree, W. L. Marshall, & S. M. Hudson (Eds.), *The juvenile sex offender* (pp. 164–181). New York: Guilford Press.

Marshall, W. L., Hudson, S. M., Jones, R., & Fernandez, Y. M. (1995). Empathy in sex offenders. *Clinical Psychology Review, 15,* 99–113.

Marshall, W. L., & Kennedy, P. (2001). Sexual sadism in sexual offenders: An elusive diagnosis. *Aggression and Violent Behavior: A Review Journal, 7,* 1–22.

Marshall, W. L., Kennedy, P., & Yates, P. (2002). Issues concerning the reliability and validity of the diagnosis of sexual sadism applied in prison settings. *Sexual Abuse: A Journal of Research and Treatment, 14,* 301–311.

Marshall, W. L., Kennedy, P., Yates, P., & Serran, G. (2002). Diagnosing sexual sadism in sexual offenders: Reliability across diagnosticians. *International Journal of Offender Therapy and Comparative Criminology, 46,* 668–676.

Marshall, W. L., & Marshall, L. E. (2000). The origins of sexual offending. *Trauma, Violence & Abuse: A Review Journal, 1,* 250–263.

Marshall, W. L., Marshall, L. E., Serran, G. A., & Fernandez, Y. M. (2006). *Treating sexual offenders: An integrative approach.* New York: Brunner-Routledge.

Martel, M. M., Nikolas, M., Jernigan, K., Friderici, K., Waldman, I., & Nigg, J. T. (2011). The dopamine receptor D4 gene (DRD4) moderates family environmental effects on ADHD. *Journal of Abnormal Child Psychology, 39,* 1–10. doi:10.1007/s10802-010-9439-5

Martin, J. P., & Bell, J. (1943). A pedigree of mental defect showing sex-linkage. *Journal of Neurological Psychiatry, 6,* 154–157.

Martin, S. L., Ramey, C. T., & Ramey, S. L. (1990). The prevention of intellectual impairment in children of impoverished families: Findings of a randomized trial of educational daycare. *American Journal of Public Health, 80,* 844–847.

Martinot, J. L., Peron-Magnan, P., Huret, J. D., Mazoyer, B., Baron, J. C., Boulenger, J. P., et al. (1990). Striatal D_2 dopaminergic receptors assessed with positron emission tomography and [76Br] bromospiperone in untreated schizophrenic patients. *American Journal of Psychiatry, 147,* 44–50.

Martinot, M.-L. P., Bragulat, V., Artiges, E., Dollé, F., Hinnen, F., Jouvent, R., et al. (2001). Decreased presynaptic dopamine function in the left caudate of depressed patients with affective flattening and psychomotor retardation. *American Journal of Psychiatry, 158,* 314–316.

Marziali, E. (1992). The etiology of borderline personality disorder: Developmental factors. In J. F. Clarkin, E. Marziali, & H. Munroe-Blum (Eds.), *Borderline personality disorder: Clinical and empirical perspectives* (pp. 27–44). New York: Guilford Press.

Marziali, E., & Garcia, L. J. (2011). Dementia caregivers' responses to 2 internet-based intervention programs. *American Journal of Alzheimer's Disease & Other Dementias, 26* (1), 36–43.

Mash, E. J., & Barkley, R. A. (Eds.). (2007). *Assessment of childhood disorders* (4th ed.). New York: Guilford Press.

Mash, E. J., & Dozois, D. J. A. (2003). Child psychopathology: A developmental-systems perspective. In E. J. Mash & R. A. Barkley (Eds.), *Child psychopathology* (2nd ed., pp. 3–71). New York: Guilford Press.

Maslow, A. H. (1954). *Motivation and personality.* New York: Harper & Row.

Massie, H., & Szajnberg, N. (1997). The ontogeny of a sexual fetish from birth to age 30 and memory processes: A research case report from a prospective longitudinal study. *International Journal of Psychoanalysis, 78* (4), 755–771.

Masterpasqua, F. (2009). Psychology and epigenetics. *Review of General Psychology, 13,* 194–201. doi:10.1037/a0016301

Masters, W. H., & Johnson, V. E. (1966). *Human sexual response.* Boston: Little, Brown.

Masters, W. H., & Johnson, V. E. (1970). *Human sexual inadequacy.* Boston: Little, Brown.

Mather, N., & Goldstein, S. (2001). *Learning disabilities and challenging behaviors: A guide to intervention and classroom management.* Baltimore, MD: Paul H. Brookes.

Maticka-Tyndale, E. (2001). Sexual health and Canadian youth: How do we measure up? *The Canadian Journal of Human Sexuality, 10,* 1–17.

Matson, J. L., Benavidez, D. A., Compton, L. S., Paclawskyj, T., & Baglio, C. (1996). Behavioral treatment of autistic persons: A review of research from 1980 to the present. *Research in Developmental Disabilities, 17,* 433–465.

Matsunaga, H., Kaye, W. H., McConaa, C., Plotnicov, K., Pollice, C., & Rao, R. (2000). Personality disorders among subjects recovered from eating disorders. *International Journal of Eating Disorders, 27,* 353–357.

Matthews, C., & Adams, E. (2009). Using a social justice approach to prevent the mental health consequences of heterosexism. *Journal of Primary Prevention, 30,* 11–26.

Matusiewicz, A. K., Hopwood, C. J., Banducci, A. N., & Lejuez, C. W. (2010). The effectiveness of cognitive behavioral therapy for personality disorders. *Psychiatric Clinics of North America, 33,* 657–685. doi:10.1016/j.psc.2010.04.007

Maulik, P. K., Eaton, W. W., & Bradshaw, C. P. (2010). The effect of social networks and social support on common mental disorders following specific life events. *Acta Psychiatrica Scandinavica, 122,* 118–128.

May, R. (Ed.) (1961). *Existential psychology.* New York: Random House.

Mayberg, H. S., Brannan, S. K., Mahurin, R. K., McGinnin, S., Silva, J. A., Tekell, J. L., et al. (2000). Regional metabolic effects of fluoxetine in major depression: Serial changes and relationship to clinical response. *Biological Psychiatry, 48,* 830–848.

Mayberg, H. S., Lozano, A. M., Voon, V., McNeely, H. E., Seminowicz, D., Hamani, C., et al. (2005). Deep brain stimulation for treatment-resistant depression. *Neuron, 45,* 651–660.

Mayes, S. D., & Calhoun, S. L. (2005). Test of the definition of learning disability based on the difference between IQ and achievement. *Psychological Reports, 97* (1), 109–116.

Mayes, S. D., & Calhoun, S. (2007). Challenging the assumptions about the frequency and coexistence of learning disability types. *School Psychology International, 28* (4), 437–448.

Mayes, S. D., Calhoun, S. L., & Lane, S. E. (2005). Diagnosing children's written disabilities: Different tests give different results. *Perceptual and Motor Skills, 10,* 72–78.

Mayou, R., Kirmayer, L. J., Simon, G., Kroenke, K., & Sharpe, M. (2005). Somatoform disorders: Time for a new approach in DSM-V. *American Journal of Psychiatry, 162,* 847–855.

Mazur, E. (2006). Biased appraisals of parenting daily hassles among mothers of young children: Predictors of parenting adjustment. *Cognitive Therapy and Research, 30,* 161–175.

Mazzocco, M. M. M., & Holden, J. J. A. (2007). Fragile X syndrome. In I. Brown & M. Percy (Eds.), *A comprehensive guide to intellectual and developmental disabilities* (pp. 173–187). London: Paul Brookes.

McBride, W. G. (1961). Thalidomide and congenital abnormalities. *The Lancet, 2,* 1358.

McBurnett, K., Lahey, B. B., Rathouz, P. J., & Loeber, R. (2000). Low salivary cortisol and persistent aggression in boys referred for disruptive behavior. *Archives of General Psychiatry, 57,* 38–43.

McCabe, R. E., Antony, M. M., Summerfeldt, L. J., Liss, A., & Swinson, R. P. (2003). Preliminary examination of the relationship between anxiety disorders in adults and self-reported history of teasing or bullying experiences. *Cognitive Behaviour Therapy, 32,* 187–193.

McCain, M. N., & Mustard, J. F. (1999). *Reversing the real brain drain: Early years study—Final report.* Toronto: Publications Ontario.

McCain, M. N., Mustard, J. F., & Shanker, S. (2007). *Early years study 2: Putting science into action.* Toronto: Council for Early Child Development.

McCarthy, M., & Thompson, D. (1997). A prevalence study of sexual abuse of adults with intellectual disabilities referred for sex education. *Journal of Applied Research in Intellectual Disabilities, 10,* 105–124.

McClellan, A. T., Arndt, I. O., Metzger, D. S., Woody, G. E., & O'Brien, C. P. (1993). The effects of psychosocial services in substance abuse treatment. *Journal of the American Medical Association,269,* 1953–1959.

McConnell, S. R. (2002). Children with autism: Review of available research and recommendations for educational intervention and future research. *Journal of Autism and Developmental Disorders, 32,* 399–409.

McCord, W., & McCord, J. (1964). *The psychopath: An essay on the criminal mind.* New York: Van Nostrand.

McCrady, B. S., Horvath, A. T., & Delaney, S. I. (2003). Self-help groups. In R. K. Hester & W. R. Miller (Eds.), *Handbook of alcoholism treatment approaches effective alternatives* (3rd ed., pp. 165–187). Boston: Allyn and Bacon.

McCullough, J. P. (2005). Cognitive behavioral analysis system of psychotherapy: Treatment for chronic depression. In J. C. Norcross & M. R. Goldfried (Eds.), *Handbook of psychotherapy integration* (2nd ed., pp. 281–298). London: Oxford University Press.

McCurry, S. M., Logsdon, R. G., Teri, L., & Vitiello, M. V. (2007). Evidence-based psychological treatments for insomnia in older adults. *Psychology and Aging, 22,* 18–27.

McDermid Vaz, S., & Heinrichs, R. W. (2006). Stability and validity of memory-based subtypes of schizophrenia. *Journal of the International Neuropsychological Society, 12,* 782–791.

McDougall, P., Hymel, S., Vaillancourt, T., & Mercer, L. (2001). The consequences of childhood peer rejection. In M. Leary (Ed.), *Interpersonal rejection* (pp. 213–247). New York: Oxford University Press.

McDougle, C. J., Price, L. H., & Volkmar, F. R. (1994). Recent advances in the pharmacotherapy of autism and related conditions. *Child and Adolescent Psychiatric Clinics of North America, 3,* 71–89.

McDowell, I. (2006). *Measuring health: A guide to rating scales and questionnaires, 3rd ed.* New York: Oxford.

McElroy, S. L., Casuto, L. S., Nelson, E. B., Lake, K. A., Soutullo, C. A., Keck, P. E., & Hudson, J. I. (2000). Placebo-controlled trial of sertraline in the treatment of binge eating disorder. *American Journal of Psychiatry, 157,* 1004–1006.

McFarlane, A. H., Bellissimo, A., Norman, G. R., & Lange, P. (2005). Adolescent depression in a school-based community sample: Preliminary findings on contributing social factors. *Journal of Youth and Adolescence, 23,* 601–620.

McFarlane, W. R., Dixon, L., Lukens, E., & Lucksted, A. (2003). Family psychoeducation and schizophrenia: A review of the literature. *Journal of Marital & Family Therapy, 29* (2), 223–245.

McFarlane, T., Olmsted, M. P., & Trottier, K. (2008). Timing and prediction of relapse in a transdiagnostic eating disorder sample. *International Journal of Eating Disorders, 41,* 587–593.

McGee, G. G., Morrier, M. J., & Daly, T. (1999). An incidental teaching approach to early intervention for toddlers with autism. *Journal of the Association for Persons with Severe Handicaps, 24,* 133–146.

McGee, R., Feehan, M., Williams, S., & Anderson, J. (1992). DSM–III disorders from age 11 to age 15 years. *Journal of the American Academy of Child and Adolescent Psychiatry, 31,* 50–59.

McGlashan, T. H. (1994). What has become of the psychotherapy of schizophrenia? *Acta Psychiatrica Scandinavica, 90(Suppl.* 384), 147–152.

McGlashan, T. M. (1987). I. Testing DSM-III symptom criteria for schizotypal and borderline personality disorders. *Archives of General Psychiatry, 44,* 143–148.

McGrath, P. J., Stewart, J. W., Janal, M. N., Petkova, E., Quitkin, F. M., & Klein, D. F. (2000). A placebo-controlled study of fluoxetine versus imipramine in the acute treatment of atypical depression. *American Journal of Psychiatry, 157,* 344–350.

McGue, M. (1999). Behavioral genetic models. In K. E. Leonard & H.T. Blane (Eds.), *Psychological theories of drinking and alcoholism* (2nd ed., pp. 372–421). New York: Guilford Press.

McGue, M., & Gottesman, I. I. (1989). A single dominant gene still cannot account for the transmission of schizophrenia. *Archives of General Psychiatry, 46,* 478–479.

McGuffin, P., Katz, R., & Rutherford, J. (1991). Nature, nurture and depression: A twin study. *Psychological Medicine, 21,* 329–335.

McGuffin, P., Katz, R., Watkins, S., & Rutherford, J. (1996). A hospital-based twin register of the heritability of DSM-IV unipolar depression. *Archives of General Psychiatry, 53,* 129–136.

McGuffin, P., Owen, M. J., O'Donovan, M. C., Thapar A., & Gottesman, I. I. (1994). *Seminars in psychiatric genetics.* London: Gaskell.

McGuire, R. J., Carlisle, J. M., & Young, B. G. (1965). Sexual deviations as conditioned behaviour: A hypothesis. *Behaviour Research and Therapy, 2,* 185–190.

McGurk, S. R., Twamley, E. W., Sitzer, D. I., McHugo, G. J., & Mueser, K. T. (2007). A meta-analysis of cognitive remediation in schizophrenia. *American Journal of Psychiatry, 164,* 1791–1802.

McHolm, A. E., Cunningham, C. E., & Vanier, M. K. (2005). *Helping your child to overcome selective mutism: A guide for parents.* Oakland, CA: New Harbinger Press.

McIntosh, J. L., Santos, J. F., Hubbard, R. W., & Overholser, J. C. (1994). *Elder suicide: Research, theory and treatment.* Washington, DC: American Psychological Association.

McIntosh, V. V., Jordan, J., Carter, F. A., Luty, S. E., McKenzie, J. M., Bulik, C. M., Framptom, C. M., & Joyce, P. R. (2005). Three psychotherapies for anorexia nervosa: A randomized, controlled trial. *American Journal of Psychiatry, 162,* 741–747.

McKay, D., Abramowitz, J. S., Calamari, J. E., Kyrios, M., Radomsky, A., Sookman, D., Taylor, S., & Wilhelm, S. (2004). A critical evaluation of obsessive-compulsive disorder subtypes: Symptoms versus mechanisms. *Clinical Psychology Review, 24,* 283–313.

McKay, D., Abramowitz, J. S., Taylor, S., & Asmundson, G. J. G. (Eds.). (2009). *Perspectives on the anxiety disorders: Implications for DSM-V and beyond.* New York: Springer.

McKnight, J. (1995). *The careless society: Community and its counterfeits.* New York: Basic Books.

McLaughlin, A. E., Campbell, F. A., Pungello, E. P., & Skinner, M. (2007). Depressive symptoms in young adults: The influences of the early home environment and early educational child care. *Developmental Psychology, 78,* 746–756.

McLachlin, B. (2005, February). *Medicine and the law: The challenges of mental illness.* Remarks at the Honourable Mr. Justice Michael O'Byrne/AHFMR Lecture on Law, Medicine and Ethics, sponsored by University of Alberta and University of Calgary, Alberta. Retrieved from http://www.scc-csc.gc.ca/court-cour/ju/spe-dis/bm05-02-17-eng.asp#note31

McLaughlin, K. A., Breslau, J., Green, J. G., Lakoma, M. D., Sampson, N. A., Zaslavsky, A. M., & Kessler, R. C. (2011). Childhood socio-economic status and the onset, persistence, and severity of DSM-IV mental disorders in a US national sample. *Social Science and Medicine, 73,* 1088–1096. doi:10.1016.j.socscimed.2011.06.011

McMain, S. F., Links, P. S., Gnam, W. H., Guimond, T., Cardish, R. J., Korman, L., & Streiner, D. L. (2009). A randomized trial of dialectical behavior therapy versus general psychiatric management for borderline personality disorder. *The American Journal of Psychiatry, 166,* 1365–1374. doi:10.1176/appi.ajp.2009.09010039

McNally, R. J. (1994). *Panic disorder. A critical analysis.* New York: Guilford Press.

McNally, R. J. (2002). Anxiety sensitivity and panic disorder. *Biological Psychiatry, 52,* 938–946.

McQueen, P. C., Spence, M. W., Garner, J. B., Pereira, L. H., & Winsor, E. J. T. (1987). Prevalence of major mental retardation and associated disabilities in the Canadian Maritime provinces. *American Journal of Mental Deficiency, 91,* 460–466.

McVey, G., Tweed, S., & Blackmore, E. (2007). Healthy Schools–Healthy Kids: A controlled evaluation of a comprehensive universal eating disorder prevention program. *Body Image, 4,* 115–136.

McVilly, K. R., & Rawlinson, R. B. (1998). Quality of life issues in the development and evaluation of services for people with intellectual disability. *Journal of Intellectual and Developmental Disability, 23,* 199–218.

Mealey, L. (1995). The sociobiology of sociopathy: An integrated evolutionary model. *Behavioral and Brain Sciences, 18,* 523–599.

Meana, M., Binik, Y. M., Khalife, S., & Cohen, D. R. (1997). Biopsychosocial profile of women with dyspareunia. *Obstetrics & Gynecology, 90,* 583–589.

Meehl, P. E. (1954). *Clinical versus statistical prediction: A theoretical analysis and review of the evidence.* Minneapolis: University of Minnesota Press.

Meehl, P. E. (1959). Some ruminations on the validation of clinical procedures. *Canadian Journal of Psychology, 13,* 102–128.

Meehl, P. E. (1962). Schizotaxia, schizotypy, schizophrenia. *American Psychologist, 17,* 827–838.

Meehl, P. E. (1990). Toward an integrated theory of schizotaxia, schizotypy, schizophrenia. *Journal of Personality Disorders, 4,* 1–99.

Meesters, Y., Dekker, V., Schlangen, L. J., Bos, E. H., & Ruiter, M. J. (2011, January 28). Low intensity blue-enriched white light (750 lux) and standard bright light (10,000 lux) are equally effective in treating SAD: A randomized controlled study. *BMC Psychiatry, 11,* 17.

Mehdizadeh, S. (2010). Self-presentation 2.0: Narcissism and self-esteem on Facebook. *Cyberpsychology, Behavior, and Social Networking, 13,* 357–364. doi:10.1089/cyber.2009.0257

Meichenbaum, D. (1974). *Cognitive behavior modification.* New York: General Learning Corporation.

Meichenbaum, D. (1985). *Stress inoculation training.* New York: Pergamon Press.

Meichenbaum, D. (1995). Cognitive behavioral therapy in historical perspective. In B. Bongar & L. E. Beutler (Eds.), *Comprehensive textbook of psychotherapy: Theory and practice* (pp. 140–158). New York: Oxford University Press.

Meichenbaum, D. (1997). *Treating post-traumatic stress disorder.* Chichester, UK: Wiley.

Meichenbaum, D. (2002). *Treating individuals with anger control problems and aggressive behavior.* Waterloo, ON: Institute Press.

Meichenbaum, D. (2003). Cognitive-behavior therapy: Folktales and the unexpurgated history. *Cognitive Therapy & Research, 27,* 125–129.

Meichenbaum, D. (2007). Stress inoculation training: A preventative and treatment approach. In P. M. Lehrer, R. L. Woolfolk, & W. E. Sime (Eds.), *Principles and practice of stress management* (3rd ed., pp. 497–516). New York: Guilford Press.

Meichenbaum, D., & Goodman J. (1971). Training impulsive children to talk to themselves: A means of developing self-control. *Journal of Abnormal Psychology, 77,* 115–126.

Meichenbaum, D., & Turk, D. (1976). The cognitive behavioral management of anxiety, anger, and pain. In P. O. Davidson (Ed.), *The behavioral management of anxiety, depression, and pain.* New York: Brunner/Mazel.

Melhuish, E. C. (2011). Preschool matters. *Science, 333,* 299–300.

Melton, G. B. (Ed.). (1985). *Nebraska symposium on motivation: Vol. 33. The law as a behavioral instrument.* Lincoln: University of Nebraska Press.

Melton, G. B., Petrila, J., Poythress, N. G., & Slobogin, C. (2007). *Psychological evaluations for the courts: A handbook for mental health professionals and lawyers* (3rd ed.). New York: Guilford Press.

Meltzer, H., Gatward, R., Goodman, R., & Ford, T. (2000). *Mental health of children and adolescents in Great Britain.* London: Stationery Office.

Meltzer, H. Y. (1993). New drugs for the treatment of schizophrenia. *Psychiatric Clinics of North America, 16,* 365–385.

Melzack, R., & Wall, P. D. (1982). *The challenge of pain.* New York: Basic Books.

Mendlewicz, J., & Rainer, J. D. (1977). Adoption study supporting genetic transmission in manic depresssive illness. *Nature, 268,* 327–329.

Mendrek, A., Jiménez, J. A., Mancini-Marïe, A., Fahim, C., & Stip, E. (2011). Correlations between sadness-induced cerebral activations and schizophrenia symptoms: An fMRI study of sex differences. *European Psychiatry, 26,* 320–326. doi:10.1016/j.eurpsy.2010.04.007

Mental Health Commission of Canada. (2009). *Toward recovery and well-being: A framework for a mental health strategy for Canada.* Ottawa: National Library of Canada.

Mental Health Commission of Canada. (2011, April 29). *Formative evaluation: Final technical report.* Retrieved from http://www.mentalhealthcommission.ca/SiteCollectionDocuments/Evaluation/MHCC_Technical_Report_FINAL_ENG.pdf

Menzies, R. G., & Clarke, J. C. (1995). The etiology of phobias: A nonassociative account. *Clinical Psychology Review, 15,* 23–48.

Merikangas, K. R., He, J., Burstein, M., Swanson, S. A., Avenevoli, S., Cui, L., et al. (2010). Lifetime prevalence of mental disorders in U.S. adolescents: Results from the National Comorbidity Survey Replication-Adolescent Supplement (NCS-A). *Journal of the American Academy of Child & Adolescent Psychiatry, 49* (10), 980–989. doi:10.1016/j.jaac.2010.05.017

Merikangas, K. R., & Weissman, M. M. (1986). Epidemiology of DSM-III Axis II personality disorders. In A. J. Frances & R. E. Hales (Eds.), *The American Psychiatric Association Annual Review* (pp. 49–74). Washington, DC: American Psychiatric Press.

Merrick, J., Aspler, S., & Schwartz, G. (2001). Should adults with phenylketonuria have diet treatment? *Mental Retardation, 39,* 215–217.

Merskey, H. (1992). The manufacture of personalities: The production of multiple personality disorder. *British Journal of Psychiatry, 160,* 327–340.

Merskey, H. (1995). *The analysis of hysteria: Understanding conversion and dissociation* (2nd ed.). London: Gaskell.

Messenger, J. C. (1993). Sex and repression in an Irish folk community. In D. N. Suggs & A. W. Miracle (Eds.), *Culture and human sexuality.* Pacific Grove, CA: Brooks/Cole.

Metz, M. E., Pryor, J. L., & Nesvacil, L. J. (1997). Premature ejaculation: A psychophysiological review. *Journal of Sex and Marital Therapy, 23,* 3–24.

Metzger, L. J., Carson, M. A., Lasko, N. B., Paulus, L. A., Orr, S. P., Pitman, R. K., & Yehuda, R. (2008). Basal and suppressed salivary cortisol in female Vietnam nurse veterans with and without PTSD. *Psychiatry Research, 161,* 330–335.

Meyer, G. J., Finn, S. E., Eyde, L. D., Kay, G. G., Moreland, K. L., Dies, R. R., et al. (2001). Psychological testing and psychological assessment: A review of evidence and issues. *American Psychologist, 56,* 128–165.

Meyers, B. S., & Jeste, D. V. (2010). Geriatric psychopharmacology: Evolution of a discipline. *Journal of Clinical Psychiatry, 71,* 1416–1424.

Meyers, W. S., & Keith, C. R. (1991). Homosexual and preoedipal issues in the psychoanalytic psychotherapy of a female-to-male transsexual. In C. W. Socarides & V. D. Volkan (Eds.), *The homosexualities and the therapeutic process* (pp. 75–96). Adison, CT: International Universities Press.

Mezzich, J. E., Good, B. J., Lewis-Frenandez, R., Guarnaccia, P., Lin, K. M., Parron, D., et al. (1993). *Cultural formulation guidelines. Revised cultural proposals for DSM-IV.* Submitted to the DSM-IV Task Force by the Steering Committee, NIMH-Sponsored Group on Culture and Diagnosis.

Miklowitz, D. J. (2008). Adjunctive psychotherapy for bipolar disorder: State of the evidence. *American Journal of Psychiatry, 165,* 1408–1419.

Miklowitz, D. J., George, E. L., Richards, J. A., Simoneau, T. L., & Suddath, R. L. (2003). A randomized study of family-focused psychoeducation and pharmacotherapy in the outpatient management of bipolar disorder. *Archives of General Psychiatry, 60,* 904–912.

Miklowitz, D. J., Otto, M. W., Frank, E., Reilly-Harrington, N. A., Wisniewski, S. R., Kogan, J. N., et al. (2007). Psychosocial treatments for bipolar depression: A 1-year randomized trial from the Systematic Treatment Enhancement Program. *Archives of General Psychiatry, 64,* 419–426.

Miles, C. (1977). Conditions predisposing to suicide: A review. *Journal of Nervous and Mental Disease, 164,* 231–246.

Miles, D. R., & Carey, G. (1997). Genetic and environmental architecture of human aggression. *Journal of Personality and Social Psychology, 72,* 207–217.

Milich, R., Balentine, A. C., & Lynam, D. R. (2001). ADHD combined type and ADHD predominantly inattentive type are distinct and unrelated disorders. *Clinical Psychology, 8,* 463–488.

Millar, J. (1998). *Hepatitis and injection drug use in British Columbia—Pay now or pay later.* Vancouver: Ministry of Health.

Miller, G. E., Chen, E., & Zhou, E. S. (2007). If it goes up, must it come down? Chronic stress and the hypothalamic-pituitary-adrenocortical axis in humans. *Psychological Bulletin, 133,* 25–45.

Miller, G. E., Dopp, J. M., Myers, H. F., Stevens, S. Y., & Fahey, J. L. (1999). Psychosocial predictors of natural killer cell mobilization during marital conflict. *Health Psychology, 18,* 262–271.

Miller, G. E., Rohleder, N., Stetler, C., & Kirschbaum, C. (2005). Clinical depression and regulation of the inflammatory response during acute stress. *Psychosomatic Medicine, 67,* 679–687.

Miller, G. E., Stetler, C. A., Carney, R. M., Freedland, K. E., & Banks, W. A. (2002). Clinical depression and inflammatory risk markers for coronary heart disease. *American Journal of Cardiology, 90,* 1279–1283.

Miller, M. N., & Pumariega, A. J. (2001). Culture and eating disorders: A historical and cross-cultural review. *Psychiatry—Interpersonal and Biological Processes, 64,* 93–110.

Miller, T. Q., Smith, T. W., Turner, C. W., Guijarro, M. L., & Hallet, A. J. (1996). A meta-analytic review of research on hostility and physical health. *Psychological Bulletin, 119,* 322–348.

Miller, W. R., & Rollnick, S. (1991). *Motivational Interviewing.* New York: Guilford Press.

Miller, W. R., & Rollnick, S. (2003). *Motivational interviewing. Preparing people to change addictive behavior* (2nd ed.). New York: Guilford Press.

Miller, W. R., Wilbourne, P. L., & Hettema, J. E. (2003). What works? A summary of alcohol treatment outcome research. In R. K. Hester & W. R. Miller (Eds.), *Handbook of alcoholism treatment approaches effective alternatives* (3rd ed., pp. 13–63). Boston: Allyn and Bacon.

Millon, T. (1969). *Modern psychopathology: A biosocial approach to maladaptive learning and functioning.* Philadelphia: Saunders.

Millon, T. (1981). *Disorders of personality: DSM-III: Axis II.* New York: Wiley.

Millon, T. (1992). The borderline construct: Introductory notes on its history, theory, and empirical grounding. In J. F. Clarkin, E. Marziali, & H. Munroe-Blum (Eds.), *Borderline personality disorder: Clinical and empirical perspectives* (pp. 3–23). New York: Guilford Press.

Millon, T. (1994). *Manual for the MCMI-III.* Mineapolis, MN: National Computer Systems.

Millon, T. (1996). *Disorders of personality: DSM-IV and beyond* (2nd ed.). New York: Wiley.

Millon, T., & Davis, R., with Millon, C., Escovar, L., & Meagher, S. (2000). *Personality disorders in modern life.* New York: Wiley.

Millon, T., Krueger, R. F., & Simonsen, E. (2010). *Contemporary directions in psychopathology: Scientific foundations of the DSM-V and ICD-11.* New York: Guilford Press.

Millon, T., & Meagher, S. E. (2004). The Millon Clinical Multiaxial Inventory-III (MCMI-III). In M. Hersen (Series Ed.), M. J. Hilsenroth & D. L. Segal (Vol. Eds.), *Comprehensive handbook of psychological assessment: Vol. 2. Personality assessment* (pp. 108–121). Hoboken, NJ: Wiley.

Millon, T., Simonsen, R., & Birket-Smith, M. (1998). Historical conceptions of psychopathy in the United States and Europe. In T. Millon, E. Simonsen, M. Birket-Smith, & R. D. Davis (Eds.), *Psychopathy: Antisocial, criminal, and violent behavior* (pp. 3–31). New York: Guilford Press.

Mills, D. E., & Prkachin, K. M. (1993). Psychological stress reverses antiaggregatory effects of dietary fish oil. *Journal of Behavioral Medicine, 16,* 403–412.

Mills, J., Polivy, J., Herman, C. P., & Tiggemann, M. (2002). Effects of exposure to thin media images: Evidence of self-enhancement among restrained eaters. *Personality and Social Psychology Bulletin, 28,* 1687–1699.

Milner, B. (1963). Effects of different brain lesions on card sorting. *Archives of Neurology, 9,* 90–100.

Milner, B. (1964). Some effects of frontal lobectomy in man. In J. M. Warren & K. Akert (Eds.), *The frontal granular cortex and behavior* (pp. 313–331). New York: McGraw-Hill.

Miner, J. (2009, October 8). Psychiatric pioneer, 86, slams too much reliance on drugs. *London Free Press.* Retrieved from http://www.lfpress.com

Minnes, P., & Woodford, L. (2004). Well-being in aging parents caring for an adult with a developmental disability. *Journal on Developmental Disabilities, 11,* 47–66.

Minnes, P. M. (1992). Facilitated Communication: An overview and directions for research. *Journal of Developmental Disabilities, 1,* 57–67.

Minnes, P. M. (1998). Mental retardation: The impact upon the family. In J. A. Burack, R. M. Hodapp, & E. Zigler (Eds.), *Handbook of mental retardation and development* (pp. 693–712). Cambridge: Cambridge University Press.

Mirenda, P. L., & Schuler, A. (1988). Augmenting communication for persons with autism: Issues and strategies. *Topics in Language Disorders, 9,* 24–43.

Mischel, W. (1968). *Personality and assessment.* New York: Wiley.

Mishna, F. (2003). Learning disabilities and bullying: Double jeopardy. *Journal of Learning Disabilities, 36,* 336–347.

Mishna, F., Muskat, B., & Wiener, J. (2010). "I'm not lazy; it's just that I learn differently": Development and implementation of a manualized school-based group for students with learning disabilities. *Social Work with Groups, 33,* 139–159.

Mitchell, A. J. (2011). Why do physicians have difficulty diagnosing depression in the elderly? *Aging Health, 7* (1), 99–101.

Mitchell, D. G. V., Colledge, E., Leonard, A., & Blair, R. J. R. (2002). Risky decisions and response reversal: Is there evidence of orbitofrontal cortex dysfunction in psychopathic individuals? *Neuropsychologia, 40,* 2013–2033.

Mitka, M. (1998). Viagra leads as rivals are moving up. *Journal of the American Medical Association, 280,* 119–120.

Mody, M. (2003). Phonological basis in reading disability: A review and analysis of the evidence. *Reading and Writing, 16,* 21–39.

Moehle, K. A., & Levitt, E. E. (1991). The history of the concepts of fear and anxiety. In C. E. Walker (Ed.), *Clinical psychology: Historical and research foundations* (pp. 159–182). New York: Plenum Press.

Moffitt, T. E. (1990a). Juvenile delinquency and attention deficit disorder: Boys' developmental trajectories from age 3 to age 15. *Child Development, 6,* 893–910.

Moffitt, T. E. (1990b). The neuropsychology of delinquency: A critical review. In M. Tonry & N. Morris (Eds.), *Crime and justice: A review of research* (pp. 99–169). Chicago: University of Chicago Press.

Moffit, T. E. (1993). Adolescence-limited and life-course-persistent antisocial behavior: A developmental taxonomy. *Psychological Review, 100,* 674–701.

Mohlman, J., Gorenstein, E. E., Kleber, M., de Jesus, M., Gorman, J. M., & Papp, L. A. (2003). Standard and enhanced cognitive-behavior therapy for late-life generalized anxiety disorder: Two pilot investigations. *American Journal of Geriatric Psychiatry, 11,* 24–32.

Mohr, D. C., & Beutler, L. E. (1990). Erectile dysfunction: A review of diagnostic and treatment procedures. *Clinical Psychology Review, 10,* 123–150.

Mojtabai, R., & Olfson, M. (2010). National trends in psychotropic medication polypharmacy in office-based psychiatry. *Archives of General Psychiatry, 67,* 26–36.

Molina, B., Flory, K., Hinshaw, S., Greiner, A. R., Arnold, L. E., Swanson, J. M., et al. (2007). Delinquent behavior and emerging substance use in the MTA at 36 months: Prevalence, course, and treatment effects. *Journal of the American Academy of Child and Adolescent Psychiatry, 46,* 1028–1040.

Möller, H. J., & Von Zerssen, D. (1995). Course and outcome of schizophrenia. In S. R. Hirsch & D. R. Weinberger (Eds.), *Schizophrenia* (pp. 106–127). Oxford, UK: Blackwell Science.

Monahan, J. (1981/1995). *The clinical prediction of violent behavior*. Northvale, NJ: Jason Aronson.

Mond, J. M., Hay, P. J., Rodgers, B., & Owen, C. (2007). Health service utilization for eating disorders: Findings from a community-based study. *International Journal of Eating Disorders, 40,* 399–408.

Money, J. (1984). Paraphilias: Phenomenology and classification. *American Journal of Psychotherapy, 38,* 164–179.

Money, J. (1987). Sin, sickness, or status: Homosexual gender identity and psychoneuroednocrinology. *American Psychologist, 42,* 384–399.

Monroe, S. M., & Harkness, K. L. (2005). Life stress, the "kindling" hypothesis, and the recurrence of depression: Considerations from a life stress perspective. *Psychological Review, 112,* 417–445.

Monroe, S. M., Kupfer, D. J., & Frank, E. (1992). Life stress and treatment course of recurrent depression. I. Response during index episode. *Journal of Consulting and Clinical Psychology, 60,* 718–724.

Monroe, S. M., & Simons, A. D. (1991). Diathesis-stress theories in the context of life stress research: Implications for the depressive disorders. *Psychological Bulletin, 110,* 406–425.

Moos, R. H. (1996). Understanding environments: The key to improving social processes and program outcomes. *American Journal of Community Psychology, 24,* 193–201.

Moran, M. G., Thompson, T. L., & Nies, A. S. (1988). Sleep disorders in the elderly. *American Journal of Psychiatry, 145,* 1369–1377.

Moreno, C., Laje, G., Blanco, C., Jiang, H., Schmidt, A. B., & Olfson, M. (2007). National trends in the outpatient diagnosis and treatment of bipolar disorder in youth. *Archives of General Psychiatry, 64,* 1032–1039.

Morey, L. C. (1988). Personality disorders in DSM-III and DSM-III-R: Convergence, coverage, and internal consistency. *American Journal of Psychiatry, 145,* 573–577.

Morey, L. C. (1991). *The Personality Assessment Inventory professional manual.* Odessa, FL: Psychological Assessment Resources.

Morgan, A. H. (1973). The heritability of hypnotic susceptibility in twins. *Journal of Abnormal Psychology, 82,* 55–61.

Morin, C. M. (2006). Cognitive behavioral therapy of insomnia. *Sleep Medicine Clinics, 1,* 375–386.

Morin, C. M., Mimeault, V., & Gagne, A. (1999). Nonpharmacological treatment of late-life insomnia. *Journal of Psychosomatic Research, 46,* 103–116.

Morissette, S. B., Spiegel, D. A., & Barlow, D. H. (2008). Combining exposure and pharmacotherapy in the treatment of social anxiety disorder: A preliminary study of state dependent learning. *Journal of Psychopathology and Behavioral Assessment, 30,* 211–219.

Morison, S. (1997). Resiliency in the aftermath of deprivation: A second look at the development of Romanian orphanage children. Manuscript submitted to *Merrill-Palmer Quarterly.*

Morse, S. J. (2002). Uncontrollable urges and irrational people. *Virginia Law Review, 88,* 1025–1078.

Morse, S. J. (2004). Preventive confinement of dangerous offenders. *Journal of Law, Medicine, and Ethics, 32,* 56–72.

Mosher, L. R., & Keith, S. J. (1980). Psychosocial treatment: Individual, group, family, and community support approaches. *Schizophrenia Bulletin, 6,* 10–41.

Moulden, H. M., Firestone, P., Kingston, D. A., & Bradford, J. M. (2007). Recidivism in pedophiles: An investigation using different methods of defining pedophilia. Manuscript in preparation.

Mowrer, O. H. (1947). On the dual nature of learning—A reinterpretation of "conditioning" and "problem-solving." *Harvard Educational Review, 17,* 102–148.

MP wants rapper 50 Cent banned from Canada. (2005, November 23). *CTV Television Network.* Retrieved from http://www.ctv.ca

Mudford, O. C., Cross, B. A., Breen, S., Cullen, C., Reeves, D., Gould, J., & Douglas, J. (2000). Auditory integration training for children with autism: No behavioral benefits detected. *American Journal on Mental Retardation, 105,* 118–129.

Mueser, K. T., & McGurk, S. R. (2004). Schizophrenia. *The Lancet, 363,* 2063–2072.

Mufson, L., Weissman, M. M., Moreau, D., & Garfinkel, R. (1999). Efficacy of interpersonal psychotherapy for depressed adolescents. *Archives of General Psychiatry, 56,* 573–579.

Muhle, R., Trentacosta, S. V., & Rapin, I. (2004). The genetics of autism. *Pediatrics, 113,* e472–486.

Müijen, M., & Hadley, T. R. (1995). Community care: Parts and systems. In S. R. Hirsch & D. R. Weinberger (Eds.), *Schizophrenia* (pp. 649–663). Oxford, UK: Blackwell Science.

Mulkens, S. A. N., de Jong, P. J., & Merckelbach, H. (1996). Disgust and spider phobia. *Journal of Abnormal Psychology, 105,* 464–468.

Mummery, W. K., & Hagen, L. C., (1996). Tobacco pricing, taxation, consumption, and revenue: Alberta 1985–1995. *Canadian Journal of Public Health, 87* (5), 314–316.

Mundy, P., Sigman, M., & Kasari, C. (1990). Joint attention, developmental level and symptom presentation in autism. *Development and Psychopathology, 6,* 389–401.

Munoz, L. C., & Frick, P. J. (2007). The reliability, stability, and predictive utility of the self-report version of the Antisocial Process Screening Device. *Scandinavian Journal of Psychology, 48,* 292–312.

Muñoz, R., Cuijpers, P., Smit, F., Barrera, A. Z., & Leykin, Y. (2010). Prevention of major depression. *Annual Review of Clinical Psychology, 6,* 181–212.

Munro, J. D. (1986). Epidemiology and the extent of mental retardation. *Psychiatric Perspectives on Mental Retardation, 9,* 591–624.

Munroe, S. (2002). Medical marijuana regulations issued. Retrieved from http://www.canadaonline.about.com/library/weekly/aa070601a.htm

Murphy, D. (2005). Can evolution explain insanity? *Biology and Philosophy, 20,* 745–766.

Murray, C. J. L., & Lopez, A. D. (1996). *The global burden of disease.* Geneva: World Health Organization, Harvard School of Public Health, & World Bank.

Murray, J. L., & Minnes, P. M. (1994a). Staff attitudes towards the sexuality of persons with intellectual disability. *Australia and New Zealand Journal of Developmental Disabilities, 19,* 45–52.

Murray, J. L., & Minnes, P. M. (1994b). Persons with developmental disabilities who have AIDS: What are the attitudes of those employed in the field? *Journal of Developmental Disabilities, 3,* 734–784.

Murray, M. E. (1979). Minimal brain dysfunction and borderline personality adjustment. *American Journal of Psychotherapy, 33,* 391–403.

Murrie, D. C., & Cornell, D. G. (2000). The Millon Adolescent Clinical Inventory and psychopathy. *Journal of Personality Assessment, 75,* 110–125.

Musto, D. F. (1992). Cocaine's history, especially the American experience. In *Cocaine: Scientific and social dimensions.* Chichester, UK: Wiley.

Musty, R. E., & Kabak, L. (1995). Relationships between motivation and depression in chronic marijuana users. *Life Sciences, 56,* 2151–2155.

Myrtek, M. (2007). Type A behavior and hostility as independent risk factors for coronary heart disease. In J. Jordan, B. Bardé, & A. M. Zeiher (Eds.), *Contributions toward evidence-based psychocardiology: A systematic review of the literature* (pp. 159–183). Washington, DC: American Psychological Association.

Nachshen, J., Garcin, N., & Minnes, P. (2005). Problem behaviour in children with intellectual disabilities: Parenting stress, empowerment, and school services. *Mental Health Aspects of Developmental Disabilities, 8,* 105–114.

Nachshen, J., Woodford, L., & Minnes, P. M. (2001). The Family Stress and Coping Interview: Interview for families of children with developmental disabilities: A lifespan perspective on family adjustments. Submitted to *Journal of Intellectual Disability Research.*

Nachshen, J. S., & Minnes, P. (2005). Empowerment in parents of school-aged children with and without developmental disabilities. *Journal of Intellectual Disability Research, 49,* 889–904.

Nagel, B., & Leiper, R. (1999). A national survey of psychotherapy with people with learning disabilities. *Clinical Psychology Forum, 129,* 14–18.

Nakdimen, K. A. (1986). A new formulation for borderline personality disorder? *American Journal of Psychiatry, 143,* 1069.

Narash-Eisikovits, O., Dierberger, A., & Westen, D. (2002). A multidimensional meta-analysis of pharmacotherapy for bulimia nervosa: Summarizing the range of outcomes in controlled clinical trials. *Harvard Review of Psychiatry, 10,* 193–211.

Nathan, P. E., & Gorman, J. M. (Eds.). (2007). *A guide to treatments that work* (3rd ed.). New York: Oxford University Press.

Nation, M., Crusto, C., Wandersman, A., Kumpfer, K. L., Seybolt, D., Morrissey-Kane, E., & Davino, K. (2003). What works in prevention: Principles of effective prevention programs. *American Psychologist, 58,* 449–456.

National Commission on Testing and Public Policy. (1990). *From gatekeeper to gateway: Transforming testing in America.* Chestnut Hill, MA: Boston College.

National Institute for Clinical Excellence. (2004). *Anxiety: Management of anxiety (panic disorder, with or without agoraphobia, and generalized anxiety disorder) in adults in primary, secondary and community care.* Retrieved from http://www.nice.org.uk/CG022quickrefguide

National Institute for Health and Clinical Excellence. (2008, September). *Attention deficit hyperactivity disorder: Diagnosis and management of ADHD in children, young people, and adults.* Retrieved from http://www.nice.org.uk

National Institute for Health and Clinical Excellence. (2009, October). *Depression: The treatment and management of depression in adults. Clinical guideline 90.* Retrieved from http://www.nice.org.uk

National Institute for Health and Clinical Excellence. (2010, May). *Guidance on the use of electroconvulsive therapy. Technology appraisal 59.* Retrieved from http://www.nice.org.uk

National Institute for Health and Clinical Excellence. (2011, January). *Generalised anxiety disorder and panic disorder (with or without agoraphobia) in adults. Clinical guideline 113.* Retrieved from http://www.nice.org.uk

National Institute of Mental Health Psychopharmacology Service Center Collaborative Study Group. (1964). Phenothiazine treatment in acute schizophrenia: Effectiveness. *Archives of General Psychiatry, 10,* 246–261.

National Institute on Drug Abuse. (1992). *Alcohol Alert 15: Alcohol and AIDA.* Washington, DC: U.S. Government Printing Office.

Neeleman, J. (1996). Suicide as a crime in the UK: Legal history, international comparisons and present implications. *Acta Psychiatrica Scandinavica, 94,* 252–257.

Nelson, G., & Prilleltensky, I. (2010). *Community psychology: In pursuit of liberation and well-being* (2nd ed.). New York: Palgrave.

Nelson, G., Prilleltensky, I., Laurendeau, M.-C., & Powell, B. (1996). The prevention of mental health problems in Canada: A survey of provincial policies, structures, and programs. *Canadian Psychology, 37,* 161–172.

Nelson, H. (1997). *Cognitive behavioural therapy with schizophrenia: A practice manual.* Cheltenham, UK: Stanley Thornes.

Nestadt, G., Romanoski, A. J., Chahal, R., Merchant, A., Folstein, J. F., Gruenberg, E. M., & McHugh, P. R. (1990). An epidemiological study of histrionic personality disorder. *Psychological Medicine, 20,* 413–422.

Neuman, R. J., Lobos, E., Reich, W., Henderson, C. A., Sun, L. W., & Todd, R. D. (2007). Prenatal smoking exposure and dopaminergic genotypes interact to cause a severe ADHD subtype. *Biological Psychiatry, 61,* 1320–1328.

Neumärker, K. (2000). Mortality rates and causes of death. *European Eating Disorders Review, 8,* 181–187.

Neumeister, A., Hu, X., Luckenbaugh, D. A., Schwarz, M., Nugent, A. C., Bonne, O., et al. (2006). Differential effects of 5-HTTLPR genotypes on the behavioral and neural responses to tryptophan depletion in patients with major depression and controls. *Archives of General Psychiatry, 63,* 978–986.

Neve, M., & Turner, T. (2001). A history of child and adolescent psychiatry. In M. Rutter & E. Taylor (Eds.), *Child and adolescent psychiatry* (4th ed., pp. 382–396). New York: Blackwell Scientific.

Newcomb, M. D. (1994). Predictors of drug use and implications for the workplace. In S. MacDonald & D. Roman (Eds.), *Research advances in alcohol and drug problems: Vol. II. Drug testing in the workplace.* New York: Plenum.

Newth, S., & Rachman, S. (2001). The concealment of obsessions. *Behaviour Research and Therapy, 39,* 457–464.

Nezu, A. M., Ronan, G. F., Meadows, E. A., & McClure, K. S. (2000). *Practitioner's guide to empirically based measures of depression.* New York: Kluwer Academic/Plenum.

Nietzel, M. T., Winett, R. A., Macdonald, M. L., & Davidson, W. S. (1977). *Behavioral approaches to community psychology.* New York: Pergamon Press.

Nijenhuis, E. R. S., & den Boer, J. A. (2009). Psychobiology of traumatization and trauma-related structural dissociation of the personality. In P. F. Dell & J. A. O'Neil (Eds.), *Dissociation and the dissociative disorders: DSM-V and beyond* (pp. 337–365). New York: Routledge.

Nijmeijer, J. S., Minderaa, R. B., Buitelaar, J. K., Mulligan, A., Hartman, C. A., & Hoekstra, P. J. (2008). Attention-deficit/hyperactivity disorder and social dysfunctioning. *Clinical Psychology Review, 28,* 692–708. doi:10.1016/j.cpr.2007.10.003

Nirje, B. (1969). The normalization principle and its human management implications. In R. Kugel & W. Wolfensberger (Eds.), *Changing patterns in residential services for the mentally retarded.* Washington, DC: Government Printing Office.

Niznikiewicz, M. A., Kubicki, M., & Shenton, M. E. (2003). Recent structural and functional imaging findings in schizophrenia. *Current Opinion in Psychiatry, 16,* 123–147.

Nock, M. K., Kazdin, A. E., Hiripi, E., & Kessler, R. C. (2007). Lifetime prevalence, correlates, and persistence of oppositional defiant disorder: Results from the National Comorbidity Survey Replication. *Journal of Child Psychology and Psychiatry, 48* (7), 703–713. doi:10.1111/j.1469-7610.2007.01733.x

Noland, J. S., Singer, L. T., Arendt, R. E., Minnes, S., Short, E. J., & Bearer, C. F. (2003). Executive functioning in preschool-age children prenatally exposed to alcohol, cocain and marijuana. *Alcoholism: Clinical and Experimental Research, 27,* 647–656.

Norasakkunkit, V., & Kalick, S. M. (2009). Experimentally detecting how cultural differences on social anxiety measures misrepresent cultural differences in emotional well-being. *Journal of Happiness Studies, 10,* 313–327.

Norberg, M. M., Diefenbach, G. J., & Tolin, D. F. (2008). Quality of life and anxiety and depressive disorder comorbidity. *Journal of Anxiety Disorders, 22,* 1516–1522.

Norcross, J. C. (Ed.). (2002). *Psychotherapy relationships that work.* New York: Oxford University Press.

Norcross, J. C. (Ed.). (2011). *Psychotherapy relationships that work* (2nd ed.). New York: Oxford University Press.

Norcross, J. C., Karpiak, C. P., & Santoro, S. O. (2005). Clinical psychologists across the years: The Division of Clinical Psychology from 1960–2003. *Journal of Clinical Psychology, 61,* 1467–1483.

Nordhus, I. H., & Pallesen, S. (2003). Psychological treatment of late-life anxiety: An empirical review. *Journal of Consulting and Clinical Psychology, 71,* 643–651.

Norquist, G. S., & Narrow, W. E. (2000). Schizophrenia: Epidemiology. In B. J. Sadock & V. A. Sadock (Eds.), *Kaplan and Sadock's comprehensive textbook of psychiatry* (7th ed., Vol. 1, pp. 1110–1117). Philadelphia: Lippincott Williams & Wilkins.

Norton, P. J., & Price, E. C. (2007). A meta-analytic review of adult cognitive-behavioral treatment outcome across the anxiety disorders. *The Journal of Nervous and Mental Disease, 195,* 521–531.

Noyes, R., Jr., Langbehn, D. R., Happel, R. L., Stout, L. R., Muller, B. A., & Longley, S. L. (2001). Personality dysfunction among somatizing patients. *Psychosomatics, 42,* 320–309.

Nulman, I., Ickeowicz, I., Koren, G., & Knittel-Keren, D. (2007). Fetal alcohol spectrum disorder. In I. Brown & M. Percy (Eds.), *A comprehensive guide to intellectual and developmental disabilities* (pp. 213–228). London: Paul Brookes.

Nussbaum, N. L., & Bunner, M. R. (2009). Halstead-Reitan neuropsychological test batteries for children. In C. R. Reynolds & E. Fletcher-Janzen (Eds.), *Handbook of clinical child neuropsychology: Critical issues in neuropsychology* (3rd ed., pp. 247–266). New York: Springer.

Oberle, I., Rousseau, F., Heitz, D., Kretz, C., Devys, D., Hanauer, A., et al. (1991). Instability of a 550-base pair DNA segment and abnormal methylation in Fragile X syndrome. *Science, 252,* 1097–1102.

O'Connell, M. E., Boat, T., & Warner, K. E. (Eds.). (2009). *Preventing mental, emotional, and behavioural disorders among young people: Progress and possibilities.* Washington, DC: National Academies Press.

Odom, S. L., Teferra, T., & Kaul, S. S. (2004). An overview of international approaches to early intervention for young children with special needs and their families. *Young Children, 59,* 38–43.

O'Donohue, W., Regev, L. G., & Hagstrom, A. (2000). Problems with the DSM-IV diagnosis of pedophilia. *Sexual Abuse: A Journal of Research and Treatment, 12,* 95–105.

O'Donovan, M. C., & Owen, M. J. (1992). Advances and retreats in the molecular genetics of major mental illness. *Annals of Medicine, 24,* 171–177.

O'Donovan, M. C., & Owen, M. J. (1996). The molecular genetics of schizophrenia. *Annals of Medicine, 28,* 541–546.

Oertel-Knöchel, V., Bittner, R. A., Knöchel, C., Prvulovic, D., & Hampel, H. (2011). Discovery and development of integrative biological markers for schizophrenia. *Progress in Neurobiology.* Advance online publication. http://www.elsevier.com/wps/find/journaldescription.cws_home/412/description#description

Offord, D. R., Alder, R. J., & Boyle, M. H. (1986). Prevalence and sociodemographic correlates of conduct disorder. *American Journal of Social Psychiatry, 6,* 272–278.

Offord, D. R., & Bennett, K. J. (1994). Conduct disorder: Long-term outcomes and intervention effectiveness. *Journal of the American Academy of Child and Adolescent Psychiatry, 33,* 1069–1078.

Offord, D. R., Boyle, M. H., Campbell, D., Cochrane, J., Goering, P., Lin, E., et al. (1994). *Mental health in Ontario: Selected findings from the Mental Health Supplement to the Ontario Health Survey.* Toronto: Ontario Ministry of Health.

Offord, D. R., Boyle, M. H., Racine, Y., Szatmari, P., Fleming, J. E., Sanford, M., et al. (1996). Integrating assessment data from multiple informants. *Journal of the American Academy of Child and Adolescent Psychiatry, 35* (8), 1078–1085.

Offord, D. R., Boyle, M. H., Racine, Y. A., Fleming, J. E., Cadman, D. T., Blum, H. M., et al. (1992). Outcome, prognosis, and risk in a longitudinal follow-up study. *Journal of the American Academy of Child and Adolescent Psychiatry, 31,* 916–923.

Offord, D. R., Boyle, M. H., Szatmari, P., Rae-Grant, N. I., Links, P. S., Cadman, D. T., et al. (1987). Ontario Child Health Study: II. Six-month prevalence of disorder and rates of service utilization. *Archives of General Psychiatry, 44,* 832–836.

O'Hara, M., Stuart, S., Gorman, L. L., & Wenzel, A. (2000). Efficacy of interpersonal psychotherapy for postpartum depression. *Archives of General Psychiatry, 57,* 1039–1045.

O'Hara, M. W. (1995). Postpartum depression. In L. B. Alloy (Ed.), *Series in psychopathology* (pp. 1–27). New York: Springer-Verlag.

O'Hara, M. W., Neunaber, D. J., & Zekoski, E. M. (1984). A prospective study of postpartum depression: Prevalence, course, and predictive factors. *Journal of Abnormal Psychology, 91,* 158–171.

Ohayon, M. M., Shapiro, C. M., & Kennedy, S. H. (2000). Differentiating DSM-IV anxiety and depressive disorders in the general population: Comorbidity and treatment consequences. *Canadian Journal of Psychiatry, 45,* 166–172.

Ohayon, M. M., & Schatzberg, A. F. (2010). Social phobia and depression: Prevalence and comorbidity. *Journal of Psychosomatic Research, 68,* 235–243.

Olds, D., Henderson, C., Cole, R., Eckenrode, J., Kitzman, H., Luckey, D., et al. (1998). Long-term effects of nurse home visitation on children's criminal and antisocial behavior. *Journal of the American Medical Association, 260,* 1238–1244.

Olds, D. L. (1988). The Prenatal/Early Infancy Project. In R. H. Price, E. L. Cowen, R. P. Lorion, & J. Ramos-McKay (Eds.), *Fourteen ounces of prevention: A casebook for practitioners* (pp. 9–23). Washington, DC: American Psychological Association.

Olds, D. L. (1997). The Prenatal Early Infancy Project: Preventing child abuse and neglect in the context of promoting maternal and child health. In D. A. Wolfe, R. J. McMahon, & R. DeV. Peters (Eds.), *Child abuse: New directions in prevention and treatment across the lifespan.* Thousand Oaks, CA: Sage.

Olds, D. L., Eckenrode, J., Henderson, C. R., Kitzman, H., Powers, J., Cole, R., et al. (1997). Long-term effects of home visitation on maternal life course and child abuse and neglect: Fifteen-year follow-up of a randomized trial. *Journal of the American Medical Association, 278,* 637–643.

Olds, D. L., Kitzman, H., Hanks, C., Cole, R., Anson, E., Sidora-Arcoleo, K., et al. (2007). Effects of nurse home visiting on maternal and child functioning: Age 9 follow-up of a randomized trial. *Pediatrics, 120,* 832–845.

Olds, D. L., Kitzman, H., Cole, R., Robinson, J., Sidora, K., Luckey, D. W., et al. (2004). Effects of nurse home-visiting on maternal life course and child development: Age 6 follow-up results of a randomized trial. *Pediatrics, 114,* 1550–1559.

Olds, D. L., Robinson, J., O'Brien, R., Lucky, D. W., Pettitt, L. M., Henderson, C. R., et al. (2002). Home visiting by paraprofessionals and nurses: A randomized, controlled trial. *Pediatrics, 110,* 486–496.

Olds, D. L., Robinson, J., Pettitt, L., Luckey, D. W., Holmberg, J., Ng, R. K., et al. (2004). Effects of home visits by paraprofessionals and by nurses: Age 4 follow-up results of a randomized trial. *Pediatrics, 114,* 1560–1568.

Olff, M., Langeland, W., Draijer, N., & Gersons, B. P. R. (2007). Gender differences in posttraumatic stress disorder. *Psychological bulletin, 133,* 183.

Olfson, M., & Marcus, S. C. (2009). National patterns in antidepressant medication treatment. *Archives of General Psychiatry, 66,* 848–856.

Olfson, M., & Marcus, S. C (2010). National trends in outpatient psychotherapy. *American Journal of Psychiatry, 167,* 1456–1463.

Olfson, M., Marcus, S. C., Tedeschi, M., & Wan, G. J. (2006). Continuity of antidepressant treatment for adults with depression in the United States. *American Journal of Psychiatry, 163,* 101–108.

Olivardia, R., Pope, H. G., Jr., Mangweth, B., & Hudson, J. I. (1995). Eating disorders in college men. *American Journal of Psychiatry, 152,* 1279–1285.

Olsen, J., Pereira, A., & Olsen, S. F. (1991). Does maternal tobacco smoking modify the effect of alcohol on fetal growth? *American Journal of Public Health, 81,* 69–73.

Olshansky, S. (1966). Parent responses to a mentally defective child. *Mental Retardation, 4,* 21–23.

Olson, R., & Byrne, B. (2005). Genetic and environmental influences on reading and language ability and disability. In H. W. Catts & A. G. Kamhi (Eds.), *The connections between language and reading disabilities* (pp. 173–200). Mahwah, NJ: Erlbaum.

O'Neill, J., & Fischer, D. (2005, June 11). Fighting for the right to refuse treatment. *The Ottawa Citizen,* p. E1.

O'Nise, K., Lynch, J. W., Sawyer, M. G., & McDermott, R. A. (2010). Can preschool improve child health outcomes? A systematic review. *Social Science & Medicine, 70,* 1423–1440.

O'Reardon, J. P., Solvason, H. B., Janicak, P. G., Sampson, S., Isenberg, K. E., Nahas, Z., et al. (2007). Efficacy and safety of transcranial magnetic stimulation in the acute treatment of major depression: A multisite randomized controlled trial. *Biological Psychiatry, 62,* 1208–1216.

Orford, J. (2001). *Excessive appetites: A psychological view of addictions* (2nd ed.). New York: John Wiley & Sons.

Orsillo, S. M., Theodore-Oklota, C., Luterek, J. A., & Plumb, J. (2007). The development and psychometric evaluation of the emotional reactivity and numbing scale. *Journal of Nervous & Mental Disease, 195,* 830–836.

Orsmond, G. I., & Seltzer, M. M. (2000). Brothers and sisters of adults with mental retardation: Gendered nature of the sibling relationship. *American Journal on Mental Retardation, 105,* 486–508.

Osler, W. (1910). The Lumleian Lectures in angina pectoris. *The Lancet,* 839–844.

Oswald, D. P., & Sonenklar, N. A. (2007). Medication use among children with autism-spectrum disorders. *Journal of Child and Adolescent Psychopharmacology, 17,* 348–355.

Ouellette-Kuntz, H., Shooshtari, S., Temple, B., Brownell, M., Burchill, C., Yu, C. T., Holden, J. J. A., & Hennen, B. (2009). Estimating administrative prevalence of intellectual disabilities in Manitoba. *Journal on Developmental Disabilities, 15* (3), 69–80.

Ouimet, A. J., Covin, R., & Dozois, D. J. A. (in press). Generalized anxiety disorder. In P. Sturmey & M. Hersen (Eds.), *Handbook of evidence-based practice in clinical psychology. Volume II: Adult disorders.* New York: Wiley.

Ounce of Prevention Fund (1994). *A head start on Head Start: Effective birth-to-three strategies.* Chicago: Ounce of Prevention Fund.

Ouwehand, C., de Ridder, D. T. D., & Bensing, J. M. (2007). A review of successful aging models: Proposing proactive coping as an important additional strategy. *Clinical Psychology Review, 27,* 873–884.

Ozonoff, S., Pennington, B. F., & Rogers, S. (1991). Executive function deficits in high-functioning autistic individuals: Relationship to theory of mind. *Journal of Child Psychology and Psychiatry, 32,* 1081–1105.

Pachana, N. A., Emery, E., Konnert, C. A., Woodhead, E., & Edelstein, B. A. (2010). Geropsychology content in clinical training programs: A comparison of Australian, Canadian, and U.S. data. *International Psychogeriatrics, 22* (6), 909–918.

Padilla, C., & Isaacson, R. S. (2011). Genetics of dementia. *CONTINUUM Lifelong Learning in Neurology, 17* (2), 326–342.

Paglia-Boak, A., Adlaf, E. M., & Mann, R. E. (2011). *Drug use among Ontario students, 1977–2011: Detailed OSDUHS findings.* CAMH Research Document Series No. 32. Toronto, ON: Centre for Addiction and Mental Health.

Paglia-Boak, A., Mann, R. E., Adlaf, E. M., & Rehm, J. (2009). *Drug use among Ontario students, 1977–2009: Detailed OSDUHS findings* (CAMH Research Document Series No. 27). Toronto: Centre for Addiction and Mental Health.

Paíno-Piñeiro, M., Fonseca-Pedrero, E., Lemos-Giráldez, S., & Muñiz, J. (2008). Dimensionality of schizotypy in young people according to sex and age. *Personality and Individual Differences, 45,* 132–138. doi:10.1016/j.paid.2008.03.011

Palacios, S., Menendez, C., Jurado, A. R., Castano, R., & Vargas, J. C. (1995). Changes in sex behaviour after menopause: Effects of tibolone. *Maturitas, 22* (2), 155–161.

Palombo, J. (2006). *Nonverbal learning disabilities: A clinical perspective.* New York: W. W. Norton.

Pampallona, S., Bollini, P., Tibaldi, G., Kupelnick, B., & Munizza, C. (2004). Combined pharmacotherapy and psychological treatment for depression. *Archives of General Psychiatry, 61,* 714–719.

Panskepp, J. (1998). The sources of fear and anxiety in the brain. In J. Panskepp, *Affective neuroscience: The foundations of human and animal emotions* (pp. 206–224). New York: Oxford University Press.

Pantony, K., & Caplan, P. J. (1991). Delusional dominating personality disorder: A modest proposal for identifying some consequences of rigid masculine socialization. *Canadian Psychology, 32,* 120–135.

Paris, J. (1996). A critical review or recovered memories in psychotherapy. Part I. Trauma and memory. *Canadian Journal of Psychiatry, 41,* 201–205.

Paris, J. (2009). The treatment of borderline personality disorder: Implications of research on diagnosis, etiology, and outcome. *Annual Review of Clinical Psychology, 5,* 277–290. doi:10.1146/annurev.clinpsy.032408.153457

Paris, J., & Frank, H. (1989). Perceptions of parental bonding in borderline patients. *American Journal of Psychiatry, 146,* 1498–1499.

Park, D. C., & Radford, J. P. (1998). From the case files: Reconstructing a history of involuntary sterilisation. *Disability and Society, 13,* 317–342.

Parsons, T. D., & Rizzo, A. A. (2008). Affective outcomes of virtual reality exposure therapy for anxiety and specific phobias: A meta-analysis. *Journal of Behavior Therapy and Experimental Psychiatry, 39,* 250–261.

Partridge, G. E. (1928). Psychopathic personalities among boys in a training school for delinquents. *American Journal of Psychiatry, 8,* 159–186.

Partridge, G. E. (1929). Psychopathic personality and personality investigation. *American Journal of Psychiatry, 8,* 1053–1055.

Partridge, G. E. (1930). Current conceptions of psychopathic personality. *American Journal of Psychiatry, 10,* 53–99.

Patrick, M., Hobson, R. P., Castle, D., & Howard, R. (1994). Personality disorder and the mental representation of early social experiences. *Development and Psychopathology, 6,* 375–388.

Patten, S. B., & Juby, H. (2008). *A profile of clinical depression in Canada.* Research Data Centres Synthesis Series #1. Retrieved from http://hdl.handle.net/1880/46327

Patten, S. B., Wang, J. L., Williams, J. V. A., Currie, S., Beck, C. A., Maxwell, C. J., & el-Guebaly, N. (2006). Descriptive epidemiology of major depression in Canada. *Canadian Journal of Psychiatry, 51,* 84–90.

Patterson, G. (1986). Performance models for antisocial boys. *American Psychologist, 44,* 432–444.

Patterson, G. R. (1982). *Coercive family process.* Eugene, OR: Castalia.

Patterson, C., Feightner, J., Garcia, A., & MacKnight, C. (2007). General risk factors for dementia: A systematic evidence review. *Alzheimer's & Dementia, 3,* 341–347.

Pattison, E. M., Sobell, M. B., & Sobell, L. C. (1977). *Emerging concepts of alcohol dependence.* New York: Springer.

Patton, J. R., Payne, J. S., & Beirne Smith, M. (1986). *Mental retardation* (2nd ed.). Toronto: Merrill.

Paulhus, D. L., & Williams, K. M. (2002). The Dark Triad of personality: Narcissism, Machiavellianism and psychopathy. *Journal of Research in Personality, 36,* 556–563. doi:10.1016/S0092-6566(02)00505-6

Paulsen, J. S., Heaton, R. K., Sadek, J. R., Perry, W., Delis, D. C., Braff, D., et al. (1995). The nature of learning and memory impairments in schizophrenia. *Journal of the International Neuropsychological Society, 1,* 88–99.

Pawluck, D. E., & Gorey, K. M. (1998). Secular trends in the incidence of anorexia nervosa: Integrative review of population-based studies. *International Journal of Eating Disorders, 23,* 347–352.

Pearl, R., & Bay, M. (1999). Psychosocial correlates of learning disabilities. In V. L. Schwean & D. H. Saklofske (Eds.), *Handbook of psychosocial characteristics of exceptional children* (pp. 443–470). New York: Kluwer/Plenum.

Pearlson, G. D., Kreger, L., Rabins, P. V., Chase, G. A., Cohen, B., Wirth, J. B., et al. (1989). A chart review study of late-onset and early-onset schizophrenia. *American Journal of Psychiatry, 146,* 1568–1574.

Peindl, K. S., Zolnik, E. J., Wisner, K. L., & Hanusa, B. H. (1995). Effects of postpartum psychiatric illnesses on family planning. *International Journal of Psychiatry Medicine, 25,* 291–300.

Peirson, L., & Prilleltensky, I. (1994). Understanding school change to facilitate prevention: A study of change in a secondary school. *Canadian Journal of Community Mental Health, 13* (2), 127–144.

Pelham, W. E., & Fabiano, G. A. (2008). Evidence-based psychosocial treatments for attention-deficit/hyperactivity disorder. *Journal of Clinical Child and Adolescent Psychology, 37,* 184–214. doi:10.1080/15374410701818681

Pendery, M. L., Maltzman, I. M., & West, L. J. (1982). Controlled drinking by alcoholics? New findings and reevaluation of a major affirmative study. *Science, 217,* 169–174.

Penn, D. L., & Martin, J. (1998). The stigma of severe mental illness: Some potential solutions for a recalcitrant problem. *Psychiatric Quarterly, 69,* 235–247.

Pennebaker, J. W. (1995). *Emotion, disclosure, and health.* Washington, DC: American Psychological Association.

Percy, M., Lewkis, S., & Brown, I. (2003). An introduction to genetics and development. In I. Brown & M. Percy (Eds.), *Developmental disabilities in Ontario* (2nd ed., pp. 89–116). Toronto: Association on Developmental Disabilities.

Percy, M., Lewkis, S. Z., & Brown, I. (2007). Introduction to genetics and development. In I. Brown & M. Percy (Eds.), *A comprehensive guide to intellectual and developmental disabilities* (pp. 87–108). London: Paul Brookes.

Perfetti, C. A., & Bell, L. (1991). Phonemic activation during the first 40 ms of word identification: Evidence from backward masking and priming. *Journal of Memory & Language, 30,* 473–485.

Perry, A. (1991). Rett syndrome: A comprehensive review of the literature. *American Journal on Mental Retardation, 96,* 275–290.

Perry, A., Bryson, S. E., & Bebko, J. M. (1993). Multiple method validation study of facilitated communication: Preliminary group results. *Journal of Developmental Disabilities, 2,* 1–19.

Perry, A., Condillac, R. A., & Freeman, N. L. (2002). Best practices and practical strategies for assessment and diagnosis of autism. *Journal on Developmental Disabilities, 9,* 61–75.

Perry, A., Cummings, A., Dunn Geier, J., Freeman, N., Hughes, S., LaRose, L., Managhan, T., Reitzel, J., & Williams, J. (2008). Effectiveness of Intensive Behavioral Intervention in a large, community-based program. *Research in Autism Spectrum Disorders, 2,* 621–642.

Perry, A., Harris, K., & Minnes, P. (2004). Family environments and family harmony: An exploration across severity, age, and type of developmental disability. *Journal on Developmental Disability, 11,* 15–24.

Perry, J. C., & Klerman, G. L. (1978). The borderline patient: A comparative analysis of four sets of diagnostic criteria. *Archives of General Psychiatry, 35,* 141–150.

Pert, L., Ferriter, M., & Saul, C. (2004). Parental loss before the age of 16 years: A comparative study of patients with personality disorder and patients with schizophrenia in a high secure hospital's population. *Psychology and Psychotherapy: Theory, Research, and Practice, 77,* 403–407.

Peters, R. DeV. (1988). Mental health promotion in children and adolescents: An emerging role for psychology. *Canadian Journal of Behavioural Science, 20,* 389–401.

Peters, R. DeV., Bradshaw, A. J., Petrunka, K., Nelson, G., Herry, Y., Craig, W., et al. (2010). The Better Beginnings, Better Futures Project: An ecological, community-based prevention approach—findings from Grade 3 to Grade 9. *Monographs of the Society for Research in Child Development, 75* (3), 1–176.

Peters, R. DeV., Nelson, G., Petrunka, K., Pancer, S. M., Loomis, C., Hasford, J., et al. (2010). *Investing in our future: Highlights of Better Beginnings, Better Futures research findings at grade 12.* Kingston, ON: Better Beginnings, Better Futures Research Coordination Unit, Queen's University.

Peters, R. Dev., Peters, J. E., Laurendeau, M.-C., Chamberland, C., & Peirson, L. (2001). Social policies for promoting the well-being of Canadian children and families. In I. Prilleltensky, G. Nelson, & L. Peirson (Eds.), *Promoting family wellness and preventing child maltreatment: Fundamentals for thinking and action.* Toronto: University of Toronto Press.

Petersen, J. L., & Hyde, J. S. (2010). A meta-analytic review of research in gender differences in sexuality, 1993–2007. *Psychological Bulletin, 136* (1), 21–38.

Petersen, R. C., Doody, R., Kurz, A., Mohs, R. C., Morris, J. C., Rabins, P. V., et al. (2001). Current concepts in mild cognitive impairment. *Archives of Neurology, 58,* 1985–1992.

Petersen, R. C., & O'Brien, J. (2006). Mild cognitive impairment should be considered for DSM-V. *Journal of Geriatric Psychiatry and Neurology, 19,* 147–154.

Petersen, T., Papakostas, G. I., Mahal, Y., Guyker, W. M., Beaumont, E. C., Alpert, J. E., Fava, M., & Nierenberg, A. A. (2004). Psychosocial functioning in patients with treatment resistant depression. *European Psychiatry, 19,* 196–201.

Peterson, R. A., & Reiss, S. (1993). *Anxiety Sensitivity Index Revised test manual.* Worthington, OH: IDS Publishing Corporation.

Petronis, A. (2004). The origin of schizophrenia: Genetic thesis, epigenetic antithesis, and resolving synthesis. *Biological Psychiatry, 55,* 965–970.

Petronis, A. (2010). Epigenetics as a unifying principle in the aetiology of complex traits and diseases. *Nature, 465,* 721–727.

Pezawas, L., Meyere-Lindenberg, A., Drabant, E. M., Verchinski, B. A., Munoz, K. E., Kolachana, B. S., et al. (2005). 5-HTTLPR polymorphism impacts human cingulate-amygdala interactions: A genetic susceptibility mechanism for depression. *Nature Neuroscience, 8,* 828–834.

Pfammatter, M., Junghan, U. M., & Brenner, H. D. (2006). Efficacy of psychological therapy in schizophrenia: Conclusions from meta-analyses. *Schizophrenia Bulletin, 32* (Suppl. 1), S64–S80.

Pfohl, B., Coryell, W., Zimmerman, M., & Stangl, D. (1986). DSM-III personality disorders: Diagnostic overlap and internal consistency of individual DSM-III criteria. *Comprehensive Psychiatry, 27,* 21–34.

Phillips, E. L. (1991). George Washington University's international data on psychotherapy delivery systems: Modeling new approaches to the study of therapy. In L. E. Beutler & M. Crago (Eds.), *Psychotherapy research: An international review of programmatic studies* (pp. 263–273). Washington, DC: American Psychological Association.

Phillips, K. A., & Diaz, S. F. (1997). Gender differences in body dysmorphic disorder. *Journal of Nervous and Mental Disease, 185,* 570–577.

Phillips, K. A., Pinto, A., Menard, W., Eisen, J. L., Mancebo, M., & Rasmussen, S. A. (2007). Obsessive-compulsive disorder versus body dysmorphic disorder: A comparison study of two possibly related disorders. *Depression and Anxiety, 24,* 399–409.

Phillips, L. H., Henry, J. D., Hosie, J. A., & Milne, A. B. (2006). Age, anger regulation and well-being. *Aging and Mental Health, 10* (3), 250–256.

Piasecki, T. M., Richardson, A. E., & Smith, S. M. (2007). Self-monitored motives for smoking among college students. *Psychology of Addictive Behaviors, 21,* 328–337.

Piccinelli, M., & Wilkinson, G. (2000). Gender differences in depression: Critical review. *British Journal of Psychiatry, 177,* 486–492.

Piek, J., Lidke, G., & Terberger, T. (2008). Ancient trephinations in Neolithic people: Evidence for Stone Age neurosurgery? Available from Nature Precedings at http://hdl.handle.net/10101/npre.2008.1615.1

Piersma, H. L. (1987a). The MCMI as a measure of DSM-III Axis II diagnoses: An empirical comparison. *Journal of Clinical Psychology, 43,* 478–483.

Piersma, H. L. (1987b). Millon Clinical Multiaxial Inventory (MCMI) computer-generated diagnoses: How do they compare to clinician judgment? *Journal of Psychopathology and Behavioral Assessment, 9,* 305–312.

Pihl, R. O., & Peterson, J. B. (1991). Attention-deficit hyperactivity disorders, childhood conduct disorder and alcoholism: Is there an association? *Alcohol Health Research World, 15,* 25–31.

Pine, D. S. (2007). Research review: A neuroscience framework for pediatric anxiety disorders. *Journal of Child Psychology and Psychiatry, and Allied Disciplines, 48* (7), 631–648.

Pinel, J. P. J. (1997). *Biopsychology* (3rd ed.). Needham Heights, MA: Allyn and Bacon.

Pinel, P. (1809). *Traite medico-phiosophique sur l'alienation mentale* (2nd ed.). Paris: Chez J. Ant Brosson.

Pinquart, M., Duberstein, P. R., & Lyness, J. M. (2006). Treatments for later-life depressive conditions: A meta-analytic comparison of pharmacotherapy and psychotherapy. *American Journal of Psychiatry, 163,* 1493–1501.

Piper, A., & Merskey, H. (2004a). The persistence of folly: A critical examination of dissociative identity disorder. Part I. The excesses of an improbable concept. *Canadian Journal of Psychiatry, 49,* 592–600.

Piper, A., & Merskey, H. (2004b). The persistence of folly: Critical examination of dissociative identity disorder. Part II. The defence and decline of multiple personality or dissociative identity disorder. *Canadian Journal of Psychiatry, 49,* 678–683.

Pistrang, N., Barker, C., & Humphreys, K. (2010). The contributions of mutual help groups for mental health problems to psychological well-being: A systematic review. In L. D. Brown & S. Wituk (Eds.), *Mental health self-help: Consumer and family initiatives* (pp. 61–85). New York: Springer.

Pithers, W. D., Beal, L. S., Armstrong, J., & Petty, J. (1989). Identification of risk factors through clinical interviews and analysis of records. In D. R. Laws (Ed.), *Relapse prevention with sex offenders* (pp. 77–87). New York: Guilford Press.

Pizzagalli, D. A., Iosifescu, D., Hallett, L. A., Ratner, K. G., & Fava, M. (2009). Reduced hedonic capacity in Major Depressive Disorder: Evidence from a probabilistic reward task. *Journal of Psychiatric Research, 43,* 76–87.

Plomin, R. (1990). The role of inheritance in behaviour. *Science, 248,* 183–188.

Plomin, R., & Neiderhiser J. M. (1992). Genetics and experience. *Current Directions in Psychological Science, 1,* 160–163.

Pogue-Geile, M. F., & Gottesman, I. (1999). Schizophrenia: Study of a genetically complex phenotype. In B. C. Jones & P. Mormede (Eds.), *Neurobehavioral genetics: Methods and applications* (pp. 247–264). Boca Raton, FL: CRC Press.

Polan, M., Desmond, J., Banner, L., Pryor, M., McCallum, S., Atlas, S., et al. (2003). Female sexual arousal: A behavioural analysis. *Fertility and Sterility, 8* (6), 1480–1487.

Polanczyk, G., de Lima, M. S., Horta, B. L., Biederman, J., & Rohde, L. A. (2007). The worldwide prevalence of ADHD: A systematic review and metaregression analysis. *The American Journal of Psychiatry, 164* (6), 942–948.

Polanczyk, G., & Rohde, L. A. (2007). Epidemiology of attention-deficit/hyperactivity disorder across the lifespan. *Current Opinion in Psychiatry, 20* (4), 386–392.

Pole, N. (2007). The psychophysiology of posttraumatic stress disorder: A meta-analysis. *Psychological Bulletin, 133,* 725–746.

Polich, J. M., Armor, D. J., & Braiker, H. B. (1981). *The course of alcoholism: Four years after treatment.* New York: Wiley.

Polivy, J., & Herman, C. P. (1987). The diagnosis and treatment of normal eating. *Journal of Consulting and Clinical Psychology, 55,* 635–644.

Polivy, J., & Herman, C. P. (2002). Causes of eating disorders. *Annual Review of Psychology, 53,* 187–213.

Polivy, J., & Herman, C. P. (2004). Sociocultural idealization of thin female body shapes: An introduction to the special issue on body image and eating disorders. *Journal of Social & Clinical Psychology. Special Issue: Body Image and Eating Disorders, 23,* 1–6.

Polivy, J., Herman, C. P., Mills, J., & Wheeler, H. B. (2003). Eating disorders in adolescence. In G. Adams & M. Berzonsky (Eds.), *The Blackwell handbook of adolescence* (pp. 523–549). Oxford, UK: Blackwell.

Pollack, A. L., & Webster, C. D. (1993). Psychology and the law: The emerging role of forensic psychology. In K. S. Dobson & D. J. G. Dobson (Eds.), *Professional psychology in Canada* (pp. 391–412). Toronto: Hogrefe & Huber.

Polvan, N. (1969). Historical aspects of mental ills in Middle East discussed. *Roche Reports, 6,* 3.

Pomarol-Clotet, E., Salvador, R., Sarró, S., Gomar, J., Vila, F., Martinez, A., et al. (2008). Failure to deactivate in the prefrontal cortex in schizophrenia: Dysfunction of the default mode network? *Psychological Medicine, 38,* 1185–1193.

Pomerleau, O. F., Colins, A. L., Shiffman, S., & Sanderson, C. S. (1993). Why some people smoke and others do not: New perspectives. *Journal of Consulting and Clinical Psychology, 61,* 723–731.

Pope, H. G., Barry, S., Bodkin, A., & Hudson, J. I. (2006). Tracking scientific interest in the dissociative disorders: A study of scientific publication output 1984–2003. *Psychotherapy and Psychosomatics, 75,* 19–24.

Pope, H. G., Jr., Oliva, P., Hudson, J. I., Bodkin, J., & Gruber, A. (1999). Attitudes toward DSM-IV dissociative disorders diagnoses among board certified American psychiatrists. *American Journal of Psychiatry, 156,* 321–323.

Popeo, D. M. (2011). Delirium in older adults. *Mount Sinai Journal of Medicine, 78,* 571–582.

Porjesz, B., & Begleiter, H. (1997). Event-related potentials in COAs (children of alcoholics) (includes related article on COAs at risk of developing alcoholism). *Alcohol Health & Research World, 21* (3), 236–250.

Porporino, F. J., & Motiuk, L. L. (1995). The prison careers of mentally disordered offenders. *International Journal of Law and Psychiatry, 18,* 29–44.

Porter, R. (1995). Mood disorders [social section]. In G. Berrios & R. Porter (Eds.), *A history of clinical psychiatry* (pp. 409–420). London: Athlone Press.

Porter, R., & Wright, D. (Eds.). (2003). *The confinement of the insane: International perspectives, 1800–1965.* Cambridge, UK: Cambridge University Press.

Porter, S. (1996). Without conscience or without active conscience? The etiology of psychopathy revisited. *Aggression and Violent Behavior, 1,* 179–189.

Porter, S., Birt, A. R., & Boer, D. P. (2001). Investigation of the criminal and conditional release histories of Canadian federal offenders as a function of psychopathy and age. *Law and Human Behavior, 25,* 647–661.

Porter, S., Fairweather, D., Drugge, J., Hervé, H., Birt, A. R., & Boer, D. P. (2000). Profiles of psychopathy in incarcerated sexual offenders. *Criminal Justice & Behavior, 27,* 216–233.

Porter, S., & Porter, S. (2007). Psychopathy and violent crime. In H. Hervé & J. C. Yuille (Eds.), *The psychopath: Theory, research, and practice* (pp. 287–300). Mahwah, NJ: Erlbaum.

Porter, S., ten Brinke, L., & Wilson, K. (2009). Crime profiles and conditional release performance of psychopathic and non-psychopathic sexual offenders. *Legal and Criminological Psychology, 14,* 109–118. doi:10.1348/135532508X284310

Porter, S., & Woodworth, M. (2007). I'm sorry I did it... but he started it: A comparison of the official and self-reported homicide descriptions of psychopaths and non-psychopaths. *Law and Human Behavior, 31,* 91–107.

Porter, S., Woodworth, M., Earle, J., Drugge, J., & Boer, D. P. (2003). Characteristics of violent behavior exhibited during sexual homicides by psychopathic and non-psychopathic murderers. *Law and Human Behavior, 27,* 459–470.

Porter, S., Yuille, J. C., & Lehman, D. (1999). The nature of real, implanted, and fabricated memories for emotional childhood events: Implications for the recovered memory debate. *Law and Human Behavior, 23,* 517–538.

Posey, D. J., & McDougall, C. J. (2001). Pharmacotherapeutic management of autism. *Expert Opinion in Pharmacotherapy, 2,* 587–600.

Potthoff, J. G., Holahan, C. J., & Joiner, T. E., Jr. (1995). Reassurance seeking, stress generation and depressive symptoms: An integrative model. *Journal of Personality and Social Psychology, 68,* 664–670.

Pötzl-Malikova, M. (1982). *Franz Xaver Messerschmidt.* Vienna: Jugend und Volk.

Pötzl-Malikova, M. (1987). Zur Beziehung Franz Anton Mesmer—Franz Xaver Messerschmidt. *Wiener Jahrbuch für Kunstgeschichte, Band XL,* 257–267.

Poulin, F., Dishion, T. J., & Haas, E. (1999). The peer influence paradox: Relationship quality and deviancy training within male adolescent friendships. *Merrill–Palmer Quarterly, 45,* 42–61.

Poulton, R., & Menzies, R. G. (2002). Fear born and bred: Toward a more inclusive theory of fear acquisition. *Behaviour Research and Therapy, 40,* 197–208.

Poythress, N. G., Skeem, J. L., & Lilienfeld, S. O. (2006). Associations among early abuse, dissociation, and psychopathy in an offender sample. *Journal of Abnormal Psychology, 115,* 288–297.

Prause, N., & Janssen, E. (2006). Blood flow: Vaginal photoplethysmography. In I. Goldstein et al. (Eds.), *Women's sexual function and dysfunction: Study, diagnosis and treatment* (pp. 359–367). New York: Taylor and Francis.

Preston, D., & Carter, M. (2009). A review of the efficacy of the picture exchange communication system intervention. *Journal of Autism and Developmental Disorders, 39,* 1471–1486.

Price, E. L., McLeod, P. J., Gleich, S. S., & Hand, D. (2006). One-year prevalence rates of major depressive disorder in first-year university students. *Canadian Journal of Counselling, 40,* 68–81.

Price, R. H., Cowen, E. L., Lorion, R. P., & Ramos-McKay, J. (Eds.). (1988). *Fourteen ounces of prevention: A casebook for practitioners.* Washington, DC: American Psychological Association.

Price, R. H., Cowen, E. L., Lorion, R. P., & Ramos-McKay, J. (1989). The search for effective prevention programs: What we learned along the way. *American Journal of Orthopsychiatry, 59,* 49–58.

Prilleltensky, I. (1994a). Empowerment in mainstream psychology: Legitimacy, obstacles, and possibilities. *Canadian Psychology, 35,* 358–374.

Prilleltensky, I. (1994b). *The morals and politics of psychology: Psychological discourse and the status quo.* Albany: State University of New York Press.

Prilleltensky, I. (2005). Promoting well-being: Time for a paradigm shift in health and human services. *Scandinavian Journal of Public Health, 33,* 53–60.

Prilleltensky, I., & Nelson, G. (in press). Critical psychology, prevention, and social justice. In E. Vera (Ed.), *The Oxford handbook of prevention in counseling psychology.* New York: Oxford University Press.

Prilleltensky, I., & Prilleltensky, O. (2006). *Promoting well-being: Linking personal, organizational, and community change.* Hoboken, NJ: John Wiley and Sons.

Prince, J. B. (2006). Pharmacotherapy of attention-deficit hyperactivity disorder in children and adolescents: Update on new stimulant preparations, atomoxetine, and novel treatments. *Child and Adolescent Psychiatric Clinics of North America, 15* (1), 13–50.

Prinz, R. J., Sanders, M. R., Shapiro, C. J., Whitaker, D. J., & Lutzker, J. R. (2009). Population-based prevention of child maltreatment: The U.S. Triple P system population trial. *Prevention Science, 10,* 1–12.

Prior, M., & Cummins, R. A. (1992). Questions about facilitated communication and autism. *Journal of Autism and Developmental Disorders, 22,* 331–338.

Pritchard, J. C. (1835). *A treatise on insanity and other disorders affecting the mind.* London: Sherwood, Gilbert & Piper.

Prkachin, K. M., Mills, D. E., Kaufman, F. L., & Carew, W. L. C. (1991). Cynical hostility, the perception of contingency and cardiovascular activity. *Canadian Journal of Behavioural Science, 23,* 455–468.

Prkachin, K. M., Mills, D. E., Zwaal, C. & Husted, J. (2001). Comparison of hemodynamic responses to social and nonsocial stress: Evaluation of an anger interview. *Psychophysiology, 38,* 879–885.

Prkachin, K. M., & Silverman, B. (2002). Hostility and facial expression: Is social regulation more important than negative affect? *Health Psychology, 21,* 33–39.

Public Health Agency of Canada. (2002). *A report on mental illnesses in Canada.* Retrieved from http://www.phac-aspc.gc.ca/publicat/miic-mmac

Pueschel, S. M. (Ed.). (2006). *Adults with Down syndrome.* Baltimore, MD: Paul H. Brookes.

Pujol, J., Soriano-Mas, C., Alonso, P., Cardoner, N., Menchon, J., Deus, J., & Vellejo, J. (2004). Mapping structural brain alterations in obsessive-compulsive disorder. *Archives of General Psychiatry, 61,* 720–730.

Pukall, C. F., & Binik, Y. M. (2009). Vulvodynia. In E. A. Mayer & M. C. Bushnell (Eds.), *Functional pain syndromes: Presentation and pathophysiology* (pp. 71–84). Seattle, WA: IASP Press.

Pukall, C. F., Payne, K. A., Binik, Y. M., & Khalifé, S. (2003). Pain measurement in vulvodynia. *Journal of Sex and Marital Therapy, 29* (supp), 111–120.

Pukall, C. F., Smith, K. B., & Chamberlain, S. M. (2007). Provoked vestibulodynia. *Women's Health, 3,* 583–592.

Qiu, C., de Ronchi, D., & Fratiglioni, L. (2007). The epidemiology of the dementias: An update. *Current Opinions in Psychiatry, 20,* 380–385.

The quiet epidemic: A nine-part series. (2003, October). *Ottawa Citizen.*

Quinsey, V. L. (1995). The prediction and explanation of criminal violence. *International Journal of Law and Psychiatry, 18,* 117–127.

Quinsey, V. L. (2010). Coercive paraphilic disorder. *Archives of Sexual Behavior, 39,* 405–410.

Quinsey, V. L., Harris, G. T., Rice, M. E., & Cormier, C. A. (2006). *Violent offenders: Appraising and managing risk* (2nd ed.). Washington, DC: American Psychological Association.

Quinsey, V. L., Harris, G. T., Rice, M. E., & Lalumière, M. L. (1993). Assessing treatment efficacy in outcome studies of sex offenders. *Journal of Interpersonal Violence, 8,* 512–523.

R.v. Abbey (1982), 2 S.C.R. 24.

R.v. Chaulk (1990), 3 S.C.R. 1303.

R.v. F. D. M. (1987), 33 C.C.C. (3d) 116 (Man. C. A.).

R.v. Hadfield (1800), 27 St. Tr. 1281, 1312.

R.v. J. A. P. (2000), 192 Sask. R. 80 (Prov. Ct.).

R.v. M'Naghten (1843), 10 Cl. & F. 200, 8 E.R. 718.

R.v. Pritchard (1836), 7 Car. & P. 304.

R.v. Rabey (1980), 2 S.C.R. 513.

R.v. Swain [1991], 1 S.C.R. 933.

R.*v. Taylor* (1992), 77 C.C.C. (3d) 551 (Ont. C.A.).

R.v. Whittle (1994), 2 S.C.R. 914.

Rabin, L. A., Barr, W. B., & Burton, L. A. (2005). Assessment practices of clinical neuropsychologists in the United States and Canada: A survey of INS, NAN, and APA Division 40 members. *Archives of Clinical Neuropsychology, 20,* 33–65.

Rabinowitz Greenberg, S. R., Firestone, P., Bradford, J. M., & Greenberg, D. M. (2002). Prediction of recidivism in exhibitionists: Psychological, phallometric, and offence factors. *Sexual Abuse: A Journal of Research and Treatment, 14* (4), 329–347.

Rabins, P. V. (1992). Schizophrenia and other psychoses. In J. E. Birren, R. B. Sloane, & G. D. Cohen (Eds.), *Handbook of mental health and aging* (2nd ed.) (pp. 464–475). San Diego, CA: Academic Press.

Rachman, S. (1971). *The effects of psychotherapy.* Oxford, UK: Pergamon Press.

Rachman, S. (1977). The conditioning theory of fear-acquisition: A critical examination. *Behaviour Research and Therapy, 15,* 375–387.

Rachman, S. (1993). Obsessions, responsibility and guilt. *Behaviour Research and Therapy, 31,* 149–154.

Rachman, S. (1997). A cognitive theory of obsessions. *Behaviour Research and Therapy, 35,* 793–802.

Rachman, S. (1998). A cognitive theory of obsessions: Elaborations. *Behaviour Research and Therapy, 36,* 385–401.

Rachman, S., Radomsky, A. S., & Shafran, R. (2008). Safety behavior: A reconsideration. *Behaviour Research and Therapy, 46,* 163–173.

Rachman, S., Shafran, R., Mitchell, D., Trant, J., & Teachman, B. A. (1996). How to remain neutral: An experimental analysis of neutralization. *Behaviour Research and Therapy, 34,* 889–898.

Rachmann, S. (1977). The conditioning theory of fear-acquisition: A critical examination. *Behaviour Research and Therapy, 31,* 375–387.

Radden, J. (2004). Melancholia in the writing of a sixteenth-century Spanish nun. *Harvard Review of Psychiatry, 12,* 293–297.

Radomsky, A. S., & Alcolado, G. M. (2010). Don't even think about checking: Mental checking causes memory distrust. *Journal of Behavior Therapy and Experimental Psychiatry, 41,* 345–351.

Radomsky, A. S., Gilchrist, P. T., & Dussault, D. (2006). Repeated checking really does cause memory distrust. *Behaviour Research and Therapy, 44,* 305–316.

Radomsky, A. S., & Rachman, S. (2004). The importance of importance in OCD memory research. *Journal of Behavior Therapy and Experimental Psychiatry, 35,* 137–151.

Raine, A. (1993). *The psychopathology of crime: Criminal behavior as a clinical disorder.* San Diego, CA: Academic Press.

Raine, A., Lencz, T., Bihrle, S., LaCasse, L., & Colletti, P. (2000). Reduced prefrontal gray matter volume and reduced autonomic activity in antisocial personality disorder. *Archives of General Psychiatry, 57,* 119–127.

Raine, A., Lencz, T., Yaralian, P., Bihrle, S., LaCasse, L., Ventura, J., & Colletti, P. (2002). Prefrontal structural and functional deficits in schizotypal personality disorder. *Schizophrenia Bulletin, 28* (3), 501–513.

Raine, A., Venables, P. H., & Mednick, S. A. (1997). Low resting heart rate at age 3 years predisposes to aggression at age 11 years: Evidence from the Mauritius Child Health Project. *Journal of the American Academy of Child and Adolescent Psychiatry, 36,* 1457–1464.

Ramage-Morin, P. (2004). Panic disorder and coping. *Health Reports, 15* (Suppl.), 33–63 (Statistics Canada cat. no. 82-003). Retrieved from http://www.statcan.ca/english/freepub/82-003-SIE/2004000/panic.htm

Ramey, C. T., & Ramey, S. L. (1992). Effective early intervention. *Mental Retardation, 30,* 337–345.

Ranney, L., Melvin, C., Lux, L., McClain, E., Morgan, L., & Lohr, K. (2006). *Tobacco use: Prevention, cessation, and control* (Evidence Report/ Technology Assessment No. 140). Rockville, MD: Agency for Healthcare Research and Quality.

Rapanaro, C., Bartu, A., & Lee, A. H. (2008). Perceived benefits and negative impact of challenges encountered in caring for young adults with intellectual disabilities in the transition to adulthood. *Journal of Applied Research in Intellectual Disabilities, 21,* 34–47.

Rapaport, M. H., Clary, C., Fayyad, R., & Endicott, J. (2005). Quality-of-life impairment in depressive and anxiety disorders. *American Journal of Psychiatry, 162,* 1171–1178.

Rapee, R. M., & Spence, S. H. (2004). The etiology of social phobia: Empirical evidence and an initial model. *Clinical Psychology Review, 24,* 737–767.

Rappaport, J. (1987). Terms of empowerment/exemplars of prevention: Toward a theory for community psychology. *American Journal of Community Psychology, 15,* 121–148.

Raskind, M. A., & Peskind, E. R. (1992). Alzheimer's disease and other dementing disorders. In J. E. Birren, R. B. Sloane, & G. D. Cohen (Eds.), *Handbook of mental health and aging* (2nd ed., pp. 478–513). San Diego, CA: Academic Press.

Rasmussen, K., Almvik, R., & Levander, S. (2001). Attention deficit hyperactivity disorder, reading disability, and personality disorders in a prison population. *Journal of the American Academy of Psychiatry and the Law, 29,* 186–193.

Raspa, M., Bailey, D. B., Jr., & Bishop, E. (2010). Obesity, food selectivity and physical activity in individuals with Fragile X syndrome. *American Journal on Intellectual and Developmental Disabilities, 115,* 482–495.

Rassin, E., Merckelbach, H., Muris, P., & Schmidt, H. (2001). The thought-action fusion scale: Further evidence for its reliability and validity. *Behaviour Research and Therapy, 39,* 537544.

Rassin, E., & Koster, E. (2003). The correlation between thought-action fusion and religiosity in a normal sample. *Behaviour Research and Therapy, 41,* 361–368.

Ratcliffe, G. E., Enns, M. W., Belik, S., & Sareen, J. (2008). Chronic pain conditions and suicidal ideation and suicide attempts: An epidemiologic perspective. *Clinical Journal of Pain, 24* (3), 204–210.

Rathbone, B. J., & Healey, V. (Eds.). (1989). *Campylobacter pylori and gastroduodenal disease.* Oxford, UK: Blackwell.

Rauch, S. L., Whalen, P. J., Dougherty, D., & Jenike, M. A. (1998). Neurobiological models of obsessive-compulsive disorder. In M. A. Jenike, L. Baer, & W. E. Minichiello (Eds.), *Obsessive-compulsive disorders: Practical management* (3rd ed., pp. 222–253). St. Louis, MO: Mosby.

Rauschenberger, S. L., & Lynn, S. J. (1995). Fantasy proneness, DSM-III-R Axis I psychopathology, and dissociation. *Journal of Abnormal Psychology, 104,* 373–380.

Ray, O., & Ksir, C. (1990). *Drugs, society, & human behaviour.* St. Louis, MO: Times Mirror/Mosby College Publishing.

Read, S. (1996). The dementias. In J. S. Sadavoy, L. W. Lazarus, & L. F. Jarvik (Eds.), *Comprehensive review of geriatric psychiatry* (pp. 287–310). Washington, DC: American Psychiatric Press.

Reaves, J. (2001, February 7). Will Robert Downey Jr.'s case spark a change in drug sentencing? *Time.* Retrieved from http://www.time.com/time/nation/article/0,8599,98373,00.html

Rector, N. A., Seeman, M. V., & Segal, Z. V. (2003). Cognitive therapy for schizophrenia: A preliminary randomized controlled trial. *Schizophrenia Research, 63,* 1–11.

Reger, M. A., & Gahm, G. A. (2009). A meta-analysis of the effects of Internet and computer-based cognitive-behavioral treatments for anxiety. *Journal of Clinical Psychology, 65,* 53–75.

Rehm, J., Baliunas, S., Brochu, B., Sarnocinska-Hart, A., & Taylor, B. (2006). *The costs of substance abuse in Canada 2002: Highlights.* Ottawa: Canadian Centre on Substance Abuse.

Reich, D., Zanarini, M. C., & Bieri, K. A. (2009). A preliminary study of lamotrigine in the treatment of affective instability in borderline personality disorder. *International Clinical Psychopharmacology, 24,* 270–275. doi:10.1097/YIC.0b013e32832d6c2f

Reich, J. (1987). Sex distribution of DSM-III personality disorders in psychiatric outpatients. *American Journal of Psychiatry, 144,* 485–488.

Reich, J. (1990). Comparison of males and females with DSM-III dependent personality disorder. *Psychiatry Research, 33,* 207–214.

Reich, J., & Green, A. I. (1991). Effect of personality disorders on outcome of treatment. *Journal of Nervous and Mental Disease, 179,* 74–82.

Reich, S., Riemer, M., Prilleltensky, I., & Montero, M. (Eds.). (2007). *International community psychology: History and theories.* New York: Springer.

Reichard, S., & Tillman, C. (1950). Patterns of parent-child relationships in schizophrenia. *Psychiatry, 13,* 247–257.

Reid, D. H., Wilson, P. G., & Faw, G. D. (1983). Teaching self-help skills. In J. L. Matson & J. A. Mulick (Eds.), *Handbook of mental retardation.* New York: Pergamon Press.

Reid, W. H., & Gacono, C. (2000). Treatment of antisocial personality, psychopathy, and other characterologic antisocial syndromes. *Behavioral Sciences & the Law, 18,* 647–662.

Reilly, D., Huws, J., Hastings, R., & Vaughan, F. (2010). Life and death of a child with Down syndrome and a congenital heart condition: Experiences of six couples. *Intellectual and Developmental Disabilities, 48,* 403–416.

Reinders, H. S. (2008). Persons with disabilities as parents: What is the problem? *Journal of Applied Research in Intellectual Disabilities, 21,* 308–314.

Reinisch, J. M., & Beasley, R. (1990). *Kinsey Institute new report on sex* (pp. 162–163). Bloomington, IN: Martin.

Reiss, D., & Price, R. H. (1996). National research agenda for prevention research: The National Institute of Mental Health Report. *American Psychologist, 51,* 1109–1115.

Reiss, S. (1990). Prevalence of dual diagnosis in community-based day programs in the Chicago metropolitan area. *American Journal on Mental Retardation, 94,* 578–585.

Reissing, E. D., Binik, Y. M., & Khalifé, S. (1999). Does vaginismus exist? A critical review of the literature. *Journal of Nervous and Mental Disease, 187,* 261–274.

Reissing, E. K., Binik, Y. M., Khalifé, S., Cohen, D., & Amsel, R. (2004). Vaginal spasm, pain, and behavior: An empirical investigation of the diagnosis of vaginismus. *Archives of Sexual Behavior, 33,* 5–17.

Reitan, R., & Wolfson, D. (2004). Theoretical, methodological, and validational bases of the Halstead-Reitan Neuropsychological Test Battery. In M. Hersen (Series Ed.), G. Goldstein & S. R. Beers (Vol. Eds.), *Comprehensive handbook of psychological assessment: Vol. 1. Intellectual and neuropsychological assessment* (pp. 105–131). New York: Wiley.

Renaud, C. A., & Byers, E. S. (1999). Exploring the frequency, diversity and content of university students' positive and negative sexual cognitions. *Canadian Journal of Human Sexuality, 8* (1), 17–30.

Renshaw, D. (1998). When the patient's chief complaint is sexual disinterest. *Medical Update for Psychiatrists, 3* (5), 159–164.

Renwick, R., Brown, I., & Raphael, D. (1994). Quality of life: Linking a conceptual approach to service delivery. *Journal of Developmental Disabilities, 3,* 32–44.

Renwick, R., Goldie, R. S., & King, S. (1999). Children who have HIV. In I. Brown & M. Percy (Eds.), *Developmental disabilities in Ontario* (pp. 323–335). Toronto: Front Porch.

Reschly, D. J. (2005). Learning disabilities identification: Primary intervention, secondary intervention, and then what? *Journal of Learning Disabilities, 38,* 510–515.

Resick, P. A., & Schnicke, M. K. (1993). *Cognitive processing therapy for rape victims: A treatment manual.* Thousand Oaks, CA: Sage.

Reutens, S., Nielsen, O., & Sachdev, P. (2010). Depersonalization disorder. *Current Opinion in Psychiatry, 23,* 278–283.

Rhee, S. H., & Waldman, I. D. (2002). Genetic and environmental influences on antisocial behavior: A meta-analysis of twin and adoption studies. *Psychological Bulletin, 128,* 490–529.

Rice, M. E. (1997). Violent offender research and implications for the criminal justice system. *American Psychologist, 52,* 414–423.

Rice, M. E., & Harris, G. T. (1993). Treatment for prisoners with mental disorder. In J. H. Steadman & J. J. Cocozza (Eds.), *Mental illness in America's prisons* (pp. 91–130). Seattle, WA: National Coalition for the Mentally Ill in the Criminal Justice System.

Rice, M. E. & Harris, G. T. (1997b). The treatment of adult offenders. In D. M. Stoff, J. Breiling, & J. D. Maser (Eds.), *Handbook of antisocial behavior* (pp. 425–435). New York: Wiley.

Rice, M. E., & Harris, G. T. (1997a). Cross-validation and extension of the Violence Risk Appraisal Guide for child molesters and rapists. *Law and Human Behavior, 21,* 231–241.

Rice, M. E., Harris, G. T., & Cormier, C. A. (1992). An evaluation of a maximum security therapeutic community for psychopaths and other mentally disordered offenders. *Law and Human Behavior, 16,* 399–412.

Rice, M. E., Harris, G. T., & Quinsey, V. L. (1996). Treatment of forensic patients. In B. Sales & S. Shah (Eds.), *Mental health and the law: Research, policy, and practice* (pp. 141–190). New York: Carolina Academic Press.

Rice, M. E., Quinsey, V. L., & Harris, G. T. (1991). Predicting sexual recidivism among treated and untreated extrafamilial child molesters from a maximum security psychiatric institution. *Journal of Consulting and Clinical Psychology, 59,* 381–386.

Rich, C. L., Young, D., & Fowler, R. C. (1986). San Diego suicide study: Young vs old subjects. *Archives of General Psychiatry, 43,* 577–582.

Richards, H. J., Casey, J. O., & Lucente, S. W. (2003). Psychopathy and treatment response in incarcerated female substance abusers. *Criminal Justice and Behavior, 30,* 251–276.

Richters, J. E., Arnold, L. E., Jensen, P. S., Abikoff, H., Conners, C. K., Greenhill, L. L., et al. (1995). NIMH collaborative multisite multimodal treatment study of children with ADHD: I. background and rationale. *Journal of the American Academy of Child and Adolescent Psychiatry, 34* (8), 987–1000.

Rief, W., Hiller, W., & Margraf, J. (1998). Cognitive aspects of hypochondriasis and the somatization syndrome. *Journal of Abnormal Psychology, 107,* 587–595.

Riley, D. (1994). The harm reduction model: Pragmatic approaches to drug use form the area between intolerance and neglect. Ottawa: Canadian Centre on Substance Abuse.

Riley, R., & Richman, A. (1983). Involuntary hospitalization in Canadian psychiatric inpatient facilities, 1970–1978. *Canadian Journal of Psychiatry, 28,* 536–541.

Rimland, B. (1991). Facilitated communication: Problems, puzzles and paradoxes: Six challenges for researchers. *Autism Research Review International, 5,* 3.

Rimland, B. (1993). Controlled evaluations of facilitated communication. *Autism Research Review International, 7,* 7.

Rimland, B., & Baker, S. M. (1996). Brief report: Alternative approaches to the development of effective treatments for autism. *Journal of Autism and Developmental Disorders, 26,* 237–241.

Risbrough, V. B., & Stein, M. B. (2006). Role of corticotrophin releasing factor in anxiety disorders: A translational research perspective. *Hormones and Behavior, 50,* 550–561.

Ritterband, L. M., Thorndike, F. P., Gonder-Frederick, L. A., Mager, J. C., Bailey, E. T., Saylor, D. K., & Morin, C. M. (2009). Efficacy of Internet-based behavioral intervention with insomnia. *Archives of General Psychiatry, 66,* 692–698.

Rivers, P. C. (1994). *Alcohol and human behavior: Theory, research, and practice.* Englewood Cliffs, NJ: Prentice-Hall.

Rizvi, S. L., Dimeff, L. A., Skutch, J., Carroll, D., & Linehan, M. (2011). A pilot study of the DBT coach: An interactive mobile phone application for individuals with borderline personality disorder and substance abuse disorder. *Behavior Therapy, 42,* 589–600.

Roberts, A. H., Kewman, D. G., Mercier, L., & Hovell, M. (1993). The power of nonspecific effects in healing: Implications for psychosocial and biological treatments. *Clinical Psychology Review, 13,* 375–391.

Roberts, B. W., Walton, K. E., & Viechtbauer, W. (2006). Patterns of mean-level change in personality traits across the life course: A meta-analysis of longitudinal studies. *Psychological Bulletin, 132,* 1–25.

Robins, C. J., & Chapman, A. L. (2004). Dialectical behaviour therapy: Current status, recent developments, and future directions. *Journal of Personality Disorders, 18,* 73–89.

Robins, L. N. (1966). *Deviant children grow up: A sociological and psychiatric study of sociopathic personality.* Baltimore, MD: Williams & Wilkins.

Robins, L. N., Cottler, L. B., Bucholz, K. K., Compton, W. M., North, C. S., & Rourke, K. M. (2000). *Diagnostic Interview Schedule for the DSM-IV (DIS-IV).* St. Louis, MO: Washington University Medical School.

Robins, L. N., & Helzer, J. E. (1985). *Diagnostic Interview Schedule, Version III-A.* St. Louis, MO: Department of Psychiatry, Washington University School of Medicine.

Robins, L. N., Helzer, J. E., Croughan, J., & Ratcliff, K. S. (1981). National Institute of Mental Health Diagnostic Interview Schedule: Its history, characteristics, and validity. *Archives of General Psychiatry, 38,* 381–389.

Robins, L. N., & Regier, D. A. (1991). *Psychiatric disorders in America: The Epidemiological Catchment Area Study.* New York: Free Press.

Robinson, M., Oddy, W. H., Li, J., Kendall, G. E., Klerk, N. H., Silburn, S. R., et al. (2008). Pre- and postnatal influences on preschool mental health: A large-scale cohort study. *Journal of Child Psychology and Psychiatry, 49,* 1118–1128.

Rockert, W., Kaplan, A. S., & Olmsted, M. P. (2007). Eating disorder not otherwise specified: The view from a tertiary care treatment center. *International Journal of Eating Disorders. Special Issue on Diagnosis and Classification, 40,* S99–S103.

Roder, V., Mueller, D. R., Mueser, K. T., & Brenner, H. D. (2006). Integrated Psychological Therapy (IPT) for schizophrenia: Is it effective? *Schizophrenia Bulletin, 32* (Suppl. 1), S81–S93.

Rodewald, F., Wilhelm-Gossling, C., Emrich, H. M., Reddemann, L., & Gast, U. (2011). Axis-I comorbidity in female patients with dissociative identity disorder and dissociative identity disorder not otherwise specified. *Journal of Nervous and Mental Disease, 199,* 122–131.

Roeleveld, N., Zielhuis, G. A., & Gabreels, F. (1997). The prevalence of mental retardation: A critical review of recent literature. *Developmental Medicine and Child Neurology, 39,* 125–132.

Roelofs, K., Hoogduin, K. A., Keijsers, G. P., Naring, G. W., Moene, F. C., & Sandijck, P. (2002). Hypnotic susceptibility in patients with conversion disorder. *Journal of Abnormal Psychology, 111,* 390–395.

Roemer, L., Orsillo, S. M., & Barlow, D. H. (2002). Generalized anxiety disorder. In D. H. Barlow (Ed.), *Anxiety and its disorders* (2nd ed., pp. 477–515). New York: Guilford Press.

Roesch, R. (1995). Mental health intervention in jails. In G. Davies, S. Lloyd-Bostock, M. McMurran, & C. Wilson (Eds.), *Psychology, law, and criminal justice* (pp. 520–531). New York: Walter de Gruyter.

Roesch, R., & Golding, S. L. (1980). *Competency to stand trial.* Urbana: University of Illinois Press.

Roesch, R., Ogloff, J. R. P., Hart, S. D., Dempster, R. J., Zapf, P. A., & Whittemore, K. E. (1997). The impact of Canadian Criminal Code changes on remands and assessments of fitness to stand trial and criminal responsibility in British Columbia. *Canadian Journal of Psychiatry, 42,* 509–514.

Roesch, R., Zapf, P. A., Webster, C. D., & Eaves, D. (1998). *The Fitness Interview Test.* Burnaby, BC: Mental Health, Law, & Policy Institute, Simon Fraser University.

Rogaeva, E., Kawarai, T., & St. George-Hyslop, P. (2006). Genetic complexity of Alzheimer's disease: Successes and challenges. *Journal of Alzheimer's Disease, 9,* 381–387.

Rogeness, G. A., Cepeda, C., Macedo, C. A., Fischer, C., & Harris, W. R. (1990). Differences in heart rate and blood pressure in children with conduct disorder, major depression, and separation anxiety. *Psychiatry Research, 33,* 199–206.

Rogers, C. R. (1961). *On becoming a person.* Boston: Houghton Mifflin.

Rogers, J., Shelton, S., Shelledy, W., Garcia, R., & Kalin, N. (2008). Genetic influences on behavioral inhibition and anxiety in juvenile rhesus macaques. *Genes, Brain and Behavior, 7,* 463–469.

Rogers, R., Dion, K. L., & Lynett, E. (1992). Diagnostic validity of antisocial personality disorder. *Law and Human Behavior, 16,* 677–689.

Rogers, R., Duncan, J. C., Lynett, E., & Sewell, K. W. (1994). Prototypical analysis of antisocial personality disorder: DSM-IV and beyond. *Law and Human Behavior, 18,* 471–484.

Rogers, S. (2002). Interventions that facilitate socialization in children with autism. *Journal of Autism and Developmental Disorders, 30,* 351–372.

Rogers, S. J., & Vismara, L. A. (2008). Evidence-based comprehensive treatments for early autism. *Journal of Clinical Child and Adolescent Psychology, 37,* 8–38.

Rogler, L. H., & Hollingshead, A. B. (1985). *Trapped: Families and schizophrenia* (3rd ed.). Maplewood: Waterfront Press.

Rohrbaugh, M., Shoham, V., Spungen, C., & Steinglass, P. (1995). Family systems therapy in practice. In B. Bongar & L. E. Beutler (Eds.), *Comprehensive textbook of psychotherapy: Theory and practice* (pp. 228–253). New York: Oxford University Press.

Roid, G. H. (2003). *Stanford-Binet Intelligence Scales* (5th ed.). Itasca, IL: Riverside.

Romanow, R. J., & Marchildon, G. P. (2003). Psychological services and the future of health care in Canada. *Canadian Psychology, 44,* 283–295.

Romberger, D. J., & Grant, K. (2004). Alcohol consumption and smoking status: The role of smoking cessation. *Biomedical Pharmacotherapy, 58,* 77–83.

Ronningstam, E., & Gunderson, J. G. (1990). Identifying criteria for narcissistic personality disorder. *American Journal of Psychiatry, 147,* 918–922.

Rosen, R. C., & Leiblum, S. R. (1995). Treatment of sexual disorders in the 1990s: An integrated approach. *Journal of Consulting and Clinical Psychology, 63,* 877–890.

Rosenbach, A., & Hunot, V. (1995). The introduction of a methadone prescribing programme to a drug-free treatment service: Implications for harm reduction. *Addiction, 90,* 815–821.

Rosenbaum, M., & Patterson, K. M. (1995). Group psychotherapy in historical perspective. In B. Bongar & L. E. Beutler (Eds.), *Comprehensive textbook of psychotherapy: Theory and practice* (pp. 173–188). New York: Oxford University Press.

Rosenberg, D. R., & Keshavan, M. S. (1998). Toward a neurodevelopmental model of obsessive-compulsive disorder. *Biological Psychiatry, 43,* 623–640.

Rosenberger, P. H., & Miller, G. A. (1989). Comparing borderline definitions: DSM-III borderline and schizotypal disorders. *Journal of Abnormal Psychology, 92,* 161–169.

Rosenhan, D. L. (1973). On being sane in insane places. *Science, 179,* 250–258.

Rosenman, R. H., Brand, R. J., Jenkins, C. D., Friedman, M., Straus, R., & Wurm, M. (1975). Coronary heart disease in the Western Collaborative Group Study: Final follow-up experience of 81/2 years. *Journal of the American Medical Association, 233,* 872–877.

Rösler, A., & Witztum, E. (1998). Treatment of men with paraphilia with a long-acting analogue of gonadotropin-releasing hormone. *New England Journal of Medicine, 338.*

Rösler, A., & Witztum, E. (2000). Pharmacotherapy of paraphilias in the next millennium. *Behavioral Sciences and the Law, 18,* 43–56.

Ross, C. A. (1989). *Multiple personality disorder: Diagnosis, clinical features and treatment.* New York: Wiley.

Ross, C. A. (1996). History, phenomenology, and epidemiology of dissociation. In L. K. Michelson & W. J. Ray (Eds.), *Handbook of dissociation* (pp. 3–24). New York: Plenum.

Ross, C. A. (1997). Dissociative identity disorder: Diagnosis, clinical features, and treatment of multiple personality (2nd ed.). New York: Wiley.

Ross, C. A. (2009). Dissociative amnesia and dissociative fugue. In P. F. Dell & J. A. O'Neil (Eds.), *Dissociation and the dissociative disorders: DSM-V and beyond* (pp. 429–434). New York: Routledge.

Ross, C. A., Anderson, G., Fleisher, W. P., & Norton, G. R. (1991). The frequency of multiple personality disorder among psychiatric inpatients. *American Journal of Psychiatry, 148,* 1717–1720.

Ross, C. A., Heber, S., Norton, G. R., Anderson, G., Anderson, D., & Barchet, P. (1989). The dissociative disorders interview schedule: A structured interview. *Dissociation, 2,* 169–189.

Ross, G. W., & Bowen, J. D. (2002). The diagnosis and differential diagnosis of dementia. *Medical Clinics of North America, 86,* 455–476.

Roth, A., & Fonagy, P. (1996). *What works for whom? A critical review of psychotherapy research.* New York: Guilford Press.

Rourke, B. P. (1989). *Nonverbal learning disabilities: The syndrome and the model.* New York: Guilford Press.

Rourke, B. P., Ahmad, S. A., Hayman-Abello, S. E., & Warriner, E. M. (2002). Child clinical/pediatric neuropsychology: Some recent advances. *Annual Review of Psychology, 53,* 309–339.

Rourke, B. P., & Finlayson, M. A. (1978). Neuropsychological significance of variations in patterns of academic performance: Verbal and visual-spatial abilities. *Journal of Abnormal Child Psychology, 6,* 121–133.

Rowe, R., Costello, E. J., Angold, A., Copeland, W. E., & Maughan, B. (2010). Developmental pathways in oppositional defiant disorder and conduct disorder. *Journal of Abnormal Psychology, 119* (4), 726–738. doi:10.1037/a0020798

Roy, A., Nielsen, D., Rylander, G., Sarchiapone, M., & Segal, N. (1999). Genetics of suicide in depression. *Journal of Clinical Psychiatry* (Suppl. 2), 12–17.

Royal Canadian Mounted Police. (2000). *Designer drugs and raves.* Vancouver: RCMP E Division.

Royer, J. M., & Walles, R. (2007). Influences of gender, ethnicity, and motivation on mathematical performance. In D. B. Berch & M. Mazzacco (Eds.), *Why is math so hard for some children? The nature and origins of mathematical learning difficulties and disabilities* (pp. 349–367). Baltimore, MD: Paul H. Brookes.

Rozanski, A., Bairey, C. N., Krantz, D. S., Friedman, J., Resser, K. J., Morell, M., et al. (1988). Mental stress and the induction of silent myocardial ischemia in patients with coronary artery disease. *New England Journal of Medicine, 318,* 1005–1012.

Rugulies, R. (2002). Depression as a predictor for coronary heart disease: a review and meta-analysis. *American Journal of Preventive Medicine, 23,* 51–61.

Ruscio, A., Brown, T., Chiu, W., Sareen, J., Stein, M., & Kessler, R. (2008). Social fears and social phobia in the USA: Results from the national comorbidity survey replication. *Psychological Medicine, 38,* 15–28.

Rush, A. J., Marangell, L. B., Sackeim, H. A., George, M. S., Brannan, S. K., Davis, S. M. et al. (2005). Vagus nerve stimulation for treatment-resistant depression: A randomized, controlled acute phase trial. *Biological Psychiatry, 58,* 347–354.

Rushton, J. P. (2002). Race, brain size, and IQ. *The General Psychologist, 37* (2), 28–33.

Ruskin, P. E. (1990). Schizophrenia and delusional disorders. In D. Bienenfeld (Ed.), *Verwoerdt's clinical geropsychiatry* (3rd ed., pp. 125–136). Baltimore, MD: Williams & Wilkins.

Russ, E., Heim, A., & Westen, D. (2003). Parental bonding and personality pathology assessed by clinician report. *Journal of Personality Disorders, 17,* 522–536.

Russek, L. G., & Schwartz, G. E. (1997). Perceptions of parental caring predict health status in midlife: A 35-year follow-up of the Harvard Mastery of Stress study. *Psychosomatic Medicine, 59,* 144–149.

Russell, S., & Nehra, A. (2003). The physiology of erectile dysfunction. *Herz, 28* (4), 277–283.

Rutherford, M. J., Cacciola, J. S., & Alterman, A. I. (1999). Antisocial personality disorder and psychopathy in cocaine-dependent women. *American Journal of Psychiatry, 156,* 849–856.

Rutter, M. (1987). Psychosocial resilience and protective mechanisms. *American Journal of Orthopsychiatry, 57* (3), 316–331.

Rutter, M., Bailey, A., Simonoff, E., & Pickles, A. (1997). Genetic influences and autism. In D. J. Cohen & F. R. Volkmar (Eds.), *Handbook of autism and pervasive developmental disorders* (pp. 370–387). New York: Wiley.

Rutter, M., Tizard, J., Yule, W., Graham, P., & Whitmore, K. (1976). Research report: Isle of Wight Studies, 1964–1974. *Psychological Medicine, 6,* 313–332.

Ryan, M. L., Shochet, I. M., & Stallman, H. M. (2010). Online resilience interventions might engage psychologically distressed university students who are unlikely to seek formal help. *Advances in Mental Health, 9,* 73–83.

Rynn, M. A., Siqueland, L., & Rickels, K. (2001). Placebo-controlled trial of sertraline in the treatment of children with generalized anxiety disorder. *The American Journal of Psychiatry, 158* (12), 2008–2014.

Sachs, G. S., & Gardner-Schuster, E. E. (2007). Adjunctive treatment of acute mania: A clinical overview. *Acta Psychiatrica Scandinavica, 116,* 27–34.

Sacker, A., Done, D. J., Crow, T. J., & Goldberg, J. (1995). Antecedents of schizophrenia and affective illness: Obstetric complications. *British Journal of Psychiatry, 166,* 734–741.

Sackett, D. L., Straus, S. E., Richardson, W. S., Rosenberg, W., & Haynes, R. B. (2000). *Evidence-based medicine: How to practice and teach EBM* (2nd ed.). New York: Churchill Livingstone.

Sackheim, H. A., Prudic, J., Devanand, D. P., Nobler, M. S., Lisanby, S. H., Peyser, S., et al. (2000). A prospective, randomized, double-blind comparison of bilateral and right unilateral electroconvulsive therapy at different stimulus intensities. *Archives of General Psychiatry, 57,* 425–434.

St. George-Hyslop, P. (2006). Genetics of dementia. *CONTINUUM Lifelong Learning in Neurology, 14* (2), 29–48.

St. Pierre, E. S., & Melnyk, W. T. (2004). The prescription privilege debate in Canada: The voice of today's and tomorrow's psychologists. *Canadian Psychology, 45,* 284–292.

Sala, M. M., Caverzasi, E. E., Lazzaretti, M. M., Morandotti, N. N., De Vidovich, G. G., Marraffini, E. E., et al. (2011). Dorsolateral prefrontal cortex and hippocampus sustain impulsivity and aggressiveness in borderline personality disorder. *Journal of Affective Disorders, 131,* 417–421. doi:10.1016/j.jad.2010.11.036

Saladin, M. E., & Santa Ana, E. J. (2004). Controlled drinking: More than just a controversy. *Current Opinion in Psychiatry, 17,* 175–187.

Salekin, R. T., & Frick, P. J. (2005). Psychopathy in children and adolescents: A developmental psychopathology perspective. *Journal of Abnormal Child Psychology, 33,* 403–409.

Salekin, R. T., Rogers, R., & Sewell, K. W. (1996). A review and meta-analysis of the Psychopathy Checklist and Psychopathy Checklist–Revised: Predictive validity of dangerousness. *Clinical Psychology: Science and Practice, 3,* 203–215.

Salkovskis, P. M. (1985). Obsessional-compulsive problems: A cognitive-behavioural analysis. *Behaviour Research and Therapy, 23,* 571–583.

Salkovskis, P. M. (1996). The cognitive approach to anxiety: Threat beliefs, safety-seeking behavior, and the special case of health anxiety and obsessions. In P. M. Salkovskis (Ed.), *Frontiers of cognitive therapy* (pp. 48–74). New York: Guilford Press.

Salkovskis, P. M., & Warwick, H. M. C. (1986). Morbid preoccupations, health anxiety and reassurance: A cognitive-behavioural approach to hypochondriasis. *Behaviour Research and Therapy, 24,* 597–602.

Sallows, G. O., & Graupner, T. D. (2005). Intensive behavioral treatment for children with autism: Four-year outcome and predictors. *American Journal of Mental Retardation, 110,* 417–438.

Salmon, P., & Calderbank, S. (1996). The relationship of childhood physical and sexual abuse to adult illness behaviour. *Journal of Psychosomatic Research, 40,* 329–336.

Samaan, R. A. (2000). The influences of race, ethnicity, and poverty on the mental health of children. *Journal of Health Care for the Poor and Underserved, 11,* 100–110.

Sampson, P. D., Streissguth, A. P., Bookstein, F. L., Little, R. E., Clarren, S. K., Dehaene, P., et al. (1997). Incidence of fetal alcohol syndrome and prevalence of alcohol-related neurodevelopmental disorder. *Teratology, 56,* 317–326.

Samuel, D. B., Lynam, D. R., Widiger, T. A., & Ball, S. A. (2011). An expert consensus approach to relating the proposed DSM-5 types and traits. *Personality Disorders: Theory, Research, and Treatment, 3.* doi:10.1037/a0023787

Samuel, D. B., & Widiger, T. A. (2009). Comparative gender biases in models of personality disorder. *Personality and Mental Health, 3,* 12–25. doi:10.1002/pmh.61

Samuels, J., Eaton, W., Bienvenu, O., Brown, C., Costa, P., & Nestadt, G. (2002). Prevalence and correlates of personality disorders in a community sample. *British Journal of Psychiatry, 180(6),* 536–542.

Samuels, J., Shugart, Y., Grados, M., Willour, V., Bienvenu, O., Greenberg, B., Murphy, D., et al. (2007). Significant linkage to compulsive hoarding on chromosome 14 in families with obsessive-compulsive disorder: Results from the OCD Collaborative Genetics Study. *American Journal of Psychiatry, 164,* 493–499.

Sánchez-Meca, J., Rosa-Alcázar, A. I., Marín-Martínez, F., & Gómez-Conesa, A. (2010). Psychological treatment of panic disorder with or without agoraphobia: A meta-analysis. *Clinical Psychology Review, 30,* 37–50.

Sandak, R., Mencl, W. E., Frost, S. J., & Pugh, K. R. (2004). The neurobiological basis of skilled and impaired reading: Recent findings and new directions. *Scientifica Studies of Reading, 8* (3), 273–292.

Sanday, P. R. (1981). The socio-cultural context of rape: A cross-cultural study. *Journal of Social Issues, 37,* 5–27.

Sanders, M. R. (2010). Adopting a public health approach to the delivery of evidence-based parenting interventions. *Canadian Psychology, 51,* 17–23.

Sandler, I. (2001). Quality and ecology of adversity as common mechanisms of risk and resilience. *American Journal of Community Psychology, 29,* 19–61.

Sandnabba, N. K., Santtila, P., Alison, L., & Nordling, N. (2002). Demographics, sexual behavior, family background, and abuse experiences of practitioners of sadomasochistic sex: A review of recent research. *Sexual and Relationship Therapy, 17,* 39–55.

Santtila, P., Sandnabba, N. K., Alison, L., & Nordling, N. (2002). Investigating the underlying structure in sadomasochistically oriented behavior. *Archives of Sexual Behavior, 31* (2), 185–196.

Sapers, H. (2010). *Annual report of the office of the correctional investigator 2009–2010.* Retrieved from the Office of the Correctional Officers website: http://www.oci-bec.gc.ca

Sapolsky, R., & Plotsky, P. M. (1990). Hypercortisolism and its possible neural basis. *Biological Psychiatry, 27,* 937–952.

Sapolsky, R. M. (1989). Hypercortisolism among socially subordinate wild baboons originates at the CNS level. *Archives of General Psychiatry, 46,* 1047–1051.

Sapolsky, R. M. (1990). Stress in the wild. *Scientific American, 262,* 116–123.

Sapolsky, R. M. (1994). *Why zebras don't get ulcers: A guide to stress, stress-related diseases, and coping.* New York: Freeman.

Sapolsky, R. M. (1995). Social subordinance as a marker of hypercortisolism. Some unexpected subtleties. *Annals of the New York Academy of Sciences,* 626–639.

Sapolsky, R. M. (2000). Glucocorticoids and hippocampal atrophy in neuropsychiatric disorders. *Archives of General Psychiatry, 57,* 925–935.

Sarafino, E. P. (1997.) *Health psychology: Biopsychosocial interactions.* New York: Wiley.

Sareen, J., Campbell, D. W., Leslie, W. D., Malisza, K. L., Stein, M. B., Paulus, M. P., et al. (2007). Striatal function in generalized social phobia: A functional magnetic resonance imaging study. *Biological Psychiatry, 61,* 396–404.

Sareen, J., Cox, B. J., Afifi, T. O., Clara, I., & Yu, B. N. (2005). Perceived need for mental health treatment in a nationally representative Canadian survey. *Canadian Journal of Psychiatry, 50,* 643–651.

Sareen, J., Cox, B. J., Afifi, T. O., Yu, B. N., & Stein, M. B. (2005). Mental health service use in a nationally representative Canadian survey. *Canadian Journal of Psychiatry, 50,* 753–761.

Sattler, J. M. (2008). *Assessment of children: Cognitive applications* (5th ed.). La Mesa, CA: Author.

Savage, C. R. (1998). Neuropsychology of obsessive-compulsive disorder: Research findings and treatment implications. In M. A. Jenike, L. Baer, & W. E. Minichiello (Eds.), *Obsessive-compulsive disorders: Practical management* (3rd ed., pp. 254–275). St. Louis, MO: Mosby.

Savage, C. R., Baer, L., Keuthen, N. J., Brown, H. D., Rauch, S. L., & Jenike, M. A. (1999). Organizational strategies mediate nonverbal memory impairment in obsessive-compulsive disorder. *Biological Psychiatry, 45,* 905–916.

Sawchuk, C. N., Lohr, J. M., Tolin, D. F., Lee, T. C., & Kleinknecht, R. A. (2000). Disgust sensitivity and contamination fears in spider and blood-injection-injury phobias. *Behaviour Research and Therapy, 38,* 753–762.

Scarr, S., & McCartney, K. (1983). How people make their own environments: Environmental effects. *Child Development, 54,* 424–435.

Schachar, R., Jadad, A. R., Gauld, M., Boyle, M., Booker, L., Snider, A., et al. (2002). Attention-deficit hyperactivity disorder: Critical appraisal of extended treatment studies. *Canadian Journal of Psychiatry, 47,* 337–348.

Schachter, S., & Latane, B. (1964). Crime, cognition, and the autonomic nervous system. In D. Levine (Ed.), *Nebraska Symposium on Motivation* (Vol. 12). Lincoln, NB: University of Nebraska Press.

Schaffer, A., Cairney, J., Cheung, A., Veldhuizen, S., & Levitt, A. (2006). Community survey of bipolar disorder in Canada: Lifetime prevalence and illness characteristics. *The Canadian Journal of Psychiatry, 51,* 9–16.

Schaler, J. A. (2004). *Szasz under fire: The psychiatric abolitionist faces his critics.* Chicago: Open Court.

Schalock, R. L. (Ed.). (1996). *Quality of life. Vol. I: Conceptualization and measurement.* Washington, DC: American Association on Mental Retardation.

Schalock, R. L. (Ed.). (1997). *Quality of life. Vol. II: Application to persons with disabilities.* Washington, DC: American Association on Mental Retardation.

Schalock, R. L. (2002). What's in a name? *Mental Retardation, 40,* 57–59.

Schalock, R. L., Stark, J. A., Snell, M. E., Coulter, D. L., Polloway, E. A., Luckasson, R., et al. (1994). The changing conception of mental retardation: Implications for the field. *Mental Retardation, 32,* 181–193.

Scherk, H., Pajonk, F. G., & Leucht, S. (2007). Second-generation antipsychotic agents in the treatment of acute mania: A systematic review and meta-analysis of randomized controlled trials. *Archives of General Psychiatry, 64,* 442–455.

Schildkraut, J. J. (1965). The catecholamine hypothesis of affective disorders: A review of supporting evidence. *American Journal of Psychiatry, 122,* 609–622.

Schmauk, F. J. (1970). Punishment, arousal, and avoidance learning in sociopaths. *Journal of Abnormal Psychology, 76,* 325–335.

Schnell, K., Dietrich, T., Schnitker, R., Daumann, J., & Herpertz, S. C. (2007). Processing of autobiographical memory retrieval cues in borderline personality disorder. *Journal of Affective Disorders, 97,* 253–259.

Schneier, F. R. (2011). Pharmacotherapy of social anxiety disorder. *Expert Opinion on Pharmacotherapy, 12,* 1–11.

Schnell, K., & Herpertz, S. C. (2007). Effects of dialectic-behavioral-therapy on the neural correlates of affective hyperarousal in borderline personality disorder. *Journal of Psychiatric Research, 41,* 837–847.

Schoenman, T. J. (1984). The mentally ill witch in textbooks of abnormal psychology: Current status and implications of a fallacy. *Professional Psychology, 15,* 299–314.

Schopp, R. F. (2001). *Competence, condemnation, and commitment: An integrated theory of mental health law.* Washington, DC: American Psychological Association.

Schreibman, L. (2000). Intensive behavioral/psychoeducational treatments for autism: Research needs and future directions. *Journal of Autism and Developmental Disorders, 30,* 373–376.

Schuck, P. (1999, April 20). London psychiatric pioneer gets recognition at long last. *The London Free Press.* Retrieved from http://www.physicianscanada.net/article1.htm

Schulsinger, F., Kety, S. S., Rosenthal, D., & Wender, P. H. (1979). A family study of suicide. In M. Schou & E. Stromgren (Eds.), *Origin, prevention and treatment of affective disorders* (pp. 277–287). New York: Academic Press.

Schulz, R., & Beach, S. R. H. (1999). Caregiving as a risk factor for mortality: Caregiver Health Effects Study. *Journal of the American Medical Association, 282,* 2215–2219.

Schulz, R., & Martire, L. M. (2004). Family caregiving of persons with dementia: Prevalence, health effects, and support strategies. *American Journal of Geriatric Psychiatry, 12,* 240–249.

Schwartz, C. E., Sidman, N., & Kagan, J. (1999). Adolescent social anxiety as an outcome of inhibited temperament in childhood. *Journal of the American Academy of Child & Adolescent Psychiatry, 38,* 1008–1015.

Schwartz, J. B., & Nye, C. (2006). A systematic review, synthesis, and evaluation of the evidence for teaching sign language to children with autism. *Evidence Based Practice Briefs, 1,* 1–17.

Schwarz, E., & Bahn, S. (2008). The utility of biomarker discovery approaches for the detection of disease mechanisms in psychiatric disorders. *British Journal of Pharmacology, 153* (Suppl. 1), 133–136.

Schweinhart, L. J., Montie, J., Xiang, Z., Barnett, W. S., Belfield, C. R., & Nores, M. (2005). *Lifetime effects: The High/Scope Perry Preschool study through age 40.* (Monographs of the High/Scope Educational Research Foundation, 14). Ypsilanti, MI: High/Scope Press.

Schweinhart, L. J., & Weikart, D. P. (1988). The High/Scope Perry Preschool Program. In R. H. Price, E. L. Cowen, R. P. Lorion, & J. Ramos-McKay (Eds.), *Fourteen ounces of prevention: A casebook for practitioners* (pp. 53–65). Washington, DC: American Psychological Association.

Scogin, F., Welsh, D., Hanson, A., Stump, J., & Coates, A. (2005). Evidence-based psychotherapies for depression in older adults. *Clinical Psychology: Science and Practice, 12,* 222–237.

Scorgie, K., & Sobsey, D. (2000). Transformational outcomes associated with parenting children who have disabilities. *Mental Retardation, 38,* 195–206.

Scorsese, M. (Director). (2010). *Shutter Island* [Motion Picture]. USA: Paramount Pictures.

Scott, A. I. F. (2010). Electroconvulsive therapy, practice and evidence. *British Journal of Psychiatry, 196,* 171–172.

Scott, K. (1994). Substance use among indigenous Canadians. In D. McKenzie (Ed.), *Research issues: Substance abuse among indigenous Canadians.* Ottawa: Canadian Centre on Substance Abuse.

Scott, T., Mackenzie, C. S., Chipperfield, J., & Sareen, J. (2010). Mental health service use among Canadian older adults with anxiety disorders and high levels of anxiety symptoms. *Aging and Mental Health, 14,* 790–800.

Seaburn, D., Landau-Stanton, J., & Horwitz, S. (1995). Core techniques in family therapy. In R. H. Mikesell, D. Lusterman, & S. H. McDaniel (Eds.), *Integrating family therapy: Handbook of family psychology and systems theory* (pp. 5–26). Washington, DC: American Psychological Association.

Sealy, P., & Whitehead, P. C. (2004). Forty years of deinstitutionalization of psychiatric services in Canada: An empirical assessment. *Canadian Journal of Psychiatry, 49,* 249–257.

Sebat, S., Lakshmi, B., Malhotra, D., Troge, J., Lese-Martin, C., Walsh, T., Yamrom, B., et al. (2007). Strong associations of de novo copy number mutations with autism. *Science, 316,* 445–449.

Sedvall, G. (1992). The current status of PET scanning with respect to schizophrenia. *Neuropsychopharmacology, 7,* 41–54.

Seeds, P. M., & Dozois, D. J. A. (2010). Prospective evaluation of a cognitive vulnerability-stress model for depression: The interaction of schema self-structure and negative life events. *Journal of Clinical Psychology, 66,* 1307–1323.

Seehusen, D. A., Baldwin, L.-M., Runkle, G. P., & Clark, G. (2005). Are family physicians appropriately screening for postpartum depression? *Obstetrics Obstetrical & Gynecological Survey, 60,* 630–631.

Seeman, P., Chau-Wong, M., Tedesco, J., & Wong, K. (1976). Dopamine receptors in human and calf brains, using [^{3}H] apomorphine and an antipsychotic drug. *Proceedings of the National Academy of Science USA, 73,* 4353–4358.

Seeman, P., & Lee, T. (1975). Antipsychotic drugs: Direct correlation between clinical potency and presynaptic action on dopamine neurons. *Science, 188,* 1217–1219.

Segal, Z. V., Bieling, P., Young, T., MacQueen, G., Cooke, R., Martin, L., et al. (2010). Antidepressant monotherapy vs sequential pharmacotherapy and mindfulness-based cognitive therapy, or placebo, for relapse prophylaxis in recurrent depression. *Archives of General Psychiatry, 67,* 1256–1264.

Segal, Z. V., Kennedy, S. H., & Cohen, N. L. (2001). Clinical guidelines for the treatment of depressive disorders. V. Combining psychotherapy and pharmacotherapy. *Canadian Journal of Psychiatry, 46* (Suppl. 91), 59–62.

Segal, Z. V., Kennedy, S., Gemar, M., Hood, K., Pedersen, R., & Buis, T. (2006). Cognitive reactivity to sad mood provocation and the prediction of depressive relapse. *Archives of General Psychiatry, 63,* 749–755.

Segal, Z. V., & Shaw, B. F. (1996). Cognitive therapy. In L. J. Dickstein, J. M. Oldham, & M. B. Riba, *Annual Review of Psychiatry* (Vol. 15, pp. 69–90). Washington, DC: American Psychiatric Press.

Segal, Z. V., Williams, J. M. G., & Teasdale, J. D. (2002). *Mindfulness-based cognitive therapy for depression: A new approach to preventing relapse.* New York: Guilford Press.

Séguin, M., Lesage, A., Chawky, N., Guy, A., Daigle, F., Girard, G., et al. (2006). Suicide cases in New Brunswick from April 2002 to May 2003: The importance of better recognizing substance and mood disorder comorbidity. *The Canadian Journal of Psychiatry, 51,* 581–586.

Seibyl, J. P., Scanley, E., Krystal, J. H., & Innis, R. B. (2004). Neuroimaging methodologies: Utilizing radiotracers or nuclear magnetic resonance. In D. S. Charney & E. J. Nester (Eds.), *Neurobiology of mental illness* (2nd ed., pp. 190–209). Oxford, UK: Oxford University Press.

Seidman, B. T., Marshall, W. L., Hudson, S. M., & Robertson, P. J. (1994). An examination of intimacy and loneliness in sex offenders. *Journal of Interpersonal Violence, 9,* 518–534.

Seidman, L. J. (2006). Neuropsychological functioning in people with ADHD across the lifespan. *Clinical Psychology Review, 26* (4), 466–485.

Seidman, S. N., & Roose, S. P. (2000). The relationship between depression and erectile dysfunction. *Current Psychiatric Reports, 2.*

Seligman, M. E. P. (1971). Phobia and preparedness. *Behavior Therapy, 2,* 307–320.

Seligman, M. E. P. (1975). *Helplessness: On depression, development and death.* San Francisco: Freeman.

Selye, H. (1956). *The stress of life.* New York: McGraw-Hill.

Semrud-Clikeman, M., & Fine, J. (2011). Presence of cysts on magnetic resonance images (MRIs) in children with Asperger disorder and nonverbal learning disabilities. *Journal of Child Neurology, 26* (4), 417–475.

Semrud-Clikeman, M., & Hynd, G. W. (1990). Right hemispheric dysfunction in nonverbal learning disabilities: Social, academic, and adaptive functioning in adults and children. *Psychological Bulletin, 107* (2), 196–209.

Serban, G., Conte, H. R., & Plutchik, R. (1987). Borderline and schizotypal personality disorders: Mutually exclusive or overlapping? *Journal of Personality Assessment, 5,* 15–22.

Serin, R. C., & Amos, N. L. (1995). The role of psychopathy in the assessment of dangerousness. *International Journal of Law and Psychiatry, 18,* 231–238.

Serin, R. C., & Brown, S. L. (2000). The clinical use of the Hare Psychopathy Checklist–Revised in contemporary risk assessment. In C. Gacono (Ed.), *The clinical and forensic assessment of psychopathy: A practitioner's guide* (pp. 251–268). Hillsdale, NJ: Erlbaum.

Serin, R. C., & Kuriychuk, M. (1994). Social and cognitive processing deficits in violent offenders: Implications for treatment. *International Journal of Law and Psychiatry, 17,* 431–441.

Serin, R. C., & Preston, D. L. (2001). Managing and treating violent offenders. In J. B. Ashford, B. D. Sales, & W. Reid (Eds.), *Treating adult and juvenile offenders with special needs* (pp. 249–272). Washington, DC: American Psychological Association.

Seto, M. C., & Kuban, M. (1996). Criterion-related validity of a phallometric test for paraphilic rape and sadism. *Behaviour Research and Therapy, 34,* 175–183.

Seymour, A. (2006, August 17). Man who fought treatment ready to "get on with his life": Starson well enough to join community, psychiatrist tells panel. *The Ottawa Citizen,* p. B1.

Shadish, W. R., & Baldwin, S. A. (2005). Effects of behavioral marital therapy: A meta-analysis of randomized controlled trials. *Journal of Consulting and Clinical Psychology, 73,* 6–14.

Shadish, W. R., Matt, G. E., Navarro, A. M., Siegle, G., Crits-Christoph, P., Hazelrigg, M. D., et al. (1997). Evidence that therapy works in clinically representative conditions. *Journal of Consulting and Clinical Psychology, 65,* 355–365.

Shaffer, D., & Craft, L. (1999). Methods of adolescent suicide prevention. *Journal of Clinical Psychiatry, 60* (Suppl. 2), 70–74.

Shaffer, D., Fisher, P., Dulcan, M., Davies, M., Piacentini, J., Schwab-Stone, M. E., et al. (1996). The NIMH Diagnostic Interview Schedule for Children Version 2.3 (DISC–2.3): Description, acceptability, prevalence rates, and performance in the MECA study. *Journal of the American Academy of Child and Adolescent Psychiatry, 35,* 865–877.

Shaffer, D., Garland, A., Gould, M., Fisher, P., & Trautman, P. (1988). Preventing teenage suicide: A critical review. *Journal of the American Academy of Child & Adolescent Psychiatry, 27,* 675–686.

Shafran, R., & Rachman, S. (2004). Thought-action fusion: A review. *Journal of Behavior Therapy and Experimental Psychiatry, 35,* 87–107.

Shamblen, S. R., & Derzon, J. H. (2009). A preliminary study of the population-adjusted effectiveness of substance abuse prevention programming: Towards making IOM program types comparable. *Journal of Primary Prevention, 30,* 89–107.

Shapiro, D. (1981). *Autonomy and rigid character.* New York: Basic Books.

Shapiro, F. (2001). *Eye movement desensitization and reprocessing: Basic principles, protocols, and procedures* (2nd ed.). New York: Guilford Press.

Shapiro, S. L., Carlson, L. E., Astin, J. A., & Freedman, B. (2006). Mechanisms of mindfulness. *Journal of Clinical Psychology, 62,* 373–386.

Shaw, J., & Porter, S. (2012, in press). Psychopathy and the criminal career trajectory. In H. Hakkanen-Nyholm & Nyholm, J. (Eds.), *Psychopathy and law.* West Sussex, UK: Wiley.

Shaw, P., Eckstrand, K., Sharp, W., Blumenthal, J., Lerch, J. P., Greenstein, D., et al. (2007). Attention-deficit/hyperactivity disorder is characterized by a delay in cortical maturation. *Proceedings of the National Academy of Sciences of the United States of America, 104,* 19649–19654. doi:10.1073/pnas.0707741104

Shaywitz, S. (2008). Why some smart people can't read. In M. H. Immordino-Yang (Ed.), *The Jossey-Bass reader on the brain and learning* (pp. 242–250). San Francisco: Jossey-Bass.

Shaywitz, S. E., Morris, R., & Shaywitz, B.A. (2008). The education of dyslexic children from childhood to young adulthood. *Annual Review of Psychology, 59,* 451–475.

Shaywitz, S. E., Shaywitz, B. A., Fletcher, J., & Escobar, M. (1990). Prevalence of reading disability in boys and girls: Results of the Connecticut Longitudinal Study. *Journal of the American Medical Association, 254,* 998–1002.

Sheikh, J. I., & Cassidy, E. L. (2000). Treatment of anxiety disorders in the elderly: Issues and strategies. *Journal of Anxiety Disorders, 14,* 173–190.

Sheline, Y. I., Sanghavi, M., Mintun, M. A., & Gado, M. H. (1999). Depression duration but not age predicts hippocampal volume loss in medically healthy women with recurrent major depression. *Journal of Neuroscience, 19,* 5034–5043.

Shelton, D. (2006). A study of young offenders with learning disabilities. *Journal of Correctional Health Care, 12* (1), 36–44.

Shenton, M. E., Dickey, C. C., Frumin, M., & McCarley, R. W. (2001). A review of MRI findings in schizophrenia. *Schizophrenia Research, 49,* 1–52.

Sher, K. J., Trull, T. J., Bartholow, B. D., & Vieth, A. (1999). Personality and alcoholism: Issues, methods, and etiological processes. In K. E. Leonard & H. T. Blane (Eds.), *Psychological theories of drinking and alcoholism* (2nd ed., pp. 54–105). New York: Guilford Press.

Shields, S. (2000). Enhanced surveillance of Canadian street youth—Phase II: Self-identified Aboriginal youth. Ottawa: Bureau of HIV/AIDS, STD and TB.

Shinn, M., & Toohey, S. (2003). Community contexts of human welfare. *Annual Review of Psychology, 54,* 427–459.

Shogren, K. A., & Broussard, R. (2011). Exploring the perceptions of self-determination of individuals with intellectual disability. *Intellectual and Developmental Disabilities, 49,* 86–102.

Shorter, E. (1997). *A history of psychiatry: From the era of the asylum to the age of Prozac.* New York: Wiley.

Shrivastava, A., Johnston, M., Shah, N., & Burueau, Y. (2010). Redefining outcome measures in schizophrenia: Integrating social and clinical parameters. *Current Opinion in Psychiatry, 23,* 120–126.

Siegel, L. S. (1999). Issues in the definition and diagnosis of learning disabilities: A perspective on *Guckenberger v. Boston University. Journal of Learning Disabilities, 32,* 304–319.

Siegel, S. (1983). Classical conditioning, drug tolerance and drug dependence. In Y. Israel, F. B. Glaser, R. R. Kalant, W. Popham, W. Schmidt, & R. G. Smart (Eds.), *Research advances in alcohol and drug problems* (Vol. 7, pp. 207–246). New York: Plenum.

Siegle, G. J., Steinhauer, S. R., Thase, M. E., Stenger, V. A., & Carter, C. S. (2002). Can't shake that feeling: fMRI assessment of sustained amygdala activity in response to emotional information in depressed individuals. *Biological Psychiatry, 51,* 693–707.

Sierra, M., Senior, C., Dalton, J., McDonough, M., Bond, A., Phillips, M. L., et al. (2002). Autonomic response in depersonalization disorder. *Archives of General Psychiatry, 59,* 833–838.

Siever, L. J. (1985). Biological markers in schizotypal personality disorders. *Schizophrenia Bulletin, 11,* 564–575.

Siever, L. J., & Davis, K. L. (1991). A psychobiological perspective on the personality disorders. *American Journal of Psychiatry, 148,* 1647–1658.

Sigelman, C. K., Schoenrock, C. J., Winer, J. L., Spanhel, C. L., Hromas, S. G., Martin, P. W., et al. (1981). Issues in interviewing mentally retarded persons: An empirical study. In R. H. Bruininks, C. E. Meyers, B. B. Sigford, & K. C. Lakin (Eds.), *Deinstitutionalization and community adjustment of mentally retarded people. Monograph of the American Association on Mental Deficiency,* No. 4 (pp. 114–132).

Sigman, M., & Mundy, P. (1989). Social attachments in autistic children. *Journal of Child Psychiatry, 28,* 74–81.

Silberg, J. L., Maes, H., & Eaves, L. J. (2010). Genetic and environmental influences on the transmission of parental depression to children's depression and conduct disturbance: An extended children of twins study. *Journal of Child Psychology and Psychiatry, 51* (6), 734–744. doi:10.1111/j.1469-7610.2010.02205.x

Silbersweig, D., Clarkin, J. F., Goldstein, M., Kernberg, O. F., Tuescher, O., Levy, K. N., et al. (2007). Failure of frontolimbic inhibitory function in the context of negative emotion in borderline personality disorder. *American Journal of Psychiatry, 164,* 1832–1841.

Silver, C. H., Ruff, R. M., Iverson, G. L., Barth, J. T., Broshek, D. K., Bush, S.S., et al. (2008). Learning disabilities: The need for neuropsychological evaluation. *Archives of Clinical Neuropsychology, 23,* 217–219.

Silverman, K., Evans, S. M., Strain, E. C., & Griffiths, R. R. (1992). Withdrawal syndrome after the double-blind cessation of caffeine consumption. *New England Journal of Medicine, 327* (16), 1109–1114.

Silverman, W. K., & Hinshaw, S. P. (2008). The second special issue on evidence-based psychosocial treatments for children and adolescents: A 10-year update. *Journal of Clinical Child and Adolescent Psychology, 37,* 1–7.

Silverman, K. W., Ortiz, C. D., Viswesvaran, C., Burns, B. J., Kolko, D. J., Putnam, F. W., et al. (2008). Evidence-based psychosocial treatments for children and adolescents exposed to traumatic events. *Journal of Clinical Child and Adolescent Psychology, 37,* 156–183.

Silverman, W. K., Pina, A. A., & Viswesvaran, C. (2008). Evidence-based psychosocial treatments for phobic and anxiety disorders in children and adolescents. *Journal of Clinical Child and Adolescent Psychology, 37,* 105–130.

Sivertsen, B. (2007). Chronic primary insomnia among older individuals. *Geriatrics and Aging, 10* (6), 385–388.

Simeon, D. (2009). Depersonalization disorder. In P. F. Dell & J. A. O'Neil (Eds.), *Dissociation and the dissociative disorders: DSM-V and beyond* (pp. 435–444). New York: Routledge.

Simeon, D., Gross, S., Orna, G., Stein, D., Schmeidler, J., & Hollander, E. (1997). Feeling unreal: 30 cases of DSM-III-R depersonalization disorder. *American Journal of Psychiatry, 154,* 1107–1113.

Simeon, D., Guralnik, O., Hazlett, E. A., Spiegel-Cohen, J., Hollander, E., & Buchsbaum, M. S. (2000). Feeling unreal: A PET study of depersonalization disorder. *American Journal of Psychiatry, 157,* 1782–1788.

Simeon, D., Knutelska, M., Nelson, D., & Guralnik, O. (2003). Feeling unreal: A depersonalization disorder update of 117 cases. *Journal of Clinical Psychiatry, 64* (9), 990–997.

Simeon, D., Guralnik, O., Knutelska, M., Yehuda, R., & Schmeidler, J. (2003). Basal norepinephrine in depersonalization disorder. *Psychiatry Research, 121,* 93–97.

Simeon, D., Guralnik, O., Knutelska, M., & Schmeidler, J. (2001).The role of childhood interpersonal trauma in depersonalization disorder. *American Journal of Psychiatry, 158,* 1027–1033.

Simmons, H. G. (1987). Psychosurgery and the abuse of psychiatric authority in Ontario. *Journal of Health Politics, Policy and Law, 12,* 537–550.

Simon, G. E. (2002). Management of somatoform and factitious disorders. In P. Nathan, & J. M. Gorman (Eds.), *A guide to treatments that work* (2nd ed., pp. 408–422). London: Oxford University Press.

Simon, G. E., & Perlis, R. H. (2010). Personalized medicine for depression: Can we match patients with treatments? *American Journal of Psychiatry, 167,* 1445–1455. doi:10.1176/appi.ajp.2010.0911680

Simon, T. J., & Rivera, S. M. (2007). Neuroanatomical approaches to the study of mathematical ability and disability. In D. B. Berch & M. Mazzacco (Eds.), *Why is math so hard for some children? The nature and origins of mathematical learning difficulties and disabilities* (pp. 283–305). Baltimore, MD: Paul H. Brookes.

Simonoff, E., Pickles, A., Meyer, J. M., Silberg, J. L., Maes, H. H., Loeber, R., et al. (1997). The Virginia Study of Adolescent Behavioral Development: Influences of age, sex, and impairment on rates of disorder. *Archives of General Psychiatry, 54,* 801–808.

Simons, J. S., & Carey, M. P. (2001). Prevalence of sexual dysfunctions: Results from a decade of research. *Archives of Sexual Behavior, 30,* 177–219.

Simpson, T. L., Kivlahan, D. R., Bush, K. R., & McFall, M. E. (2005). Telephone self-monitoring among alcohol use disorder patients in early recovery: A randomized study of feasibility and measurement reactivity. *Drug and Alcohol Dependence, 79,* 241–250.

Single, E., MacLennan, A., & MacNeil, P. (1994). *Horizons, 1994.* Ottawa: Canadian Centre on Substance Abuse.

Skeem, J., Johansson, P., Andershed, H., Kerr, M, & Louden, J. E. (2007). Two subtypes of psychopathic violent offenders that parallel primary and secondary variants. *Journal of Abnormal Psychology, 116,* 395–409.

Skeem, J. L., Monahan, J., & Mulvey, E. P. (2002). Psychopathy, treatment involvement, and subsequent violence among civil psychiatric patients. *Law and Human Behavior, 26,* 577–603.

Skeem, J. L., & Mulvey, E. P. (2001). Psychopathy and community violence among civil psychiatric patients: Results from the MacArthur Violence Risk Assessment Study. *Journal of Consulting and Clinical Psychology, 69,* 358–374.

Skinner, B. F. (1953). *Science and human behavior.* New York: Macmillan.

Skinner, C. H., Freeland, J. T., & Shapiro, E. S. (2003). Procedural issues associated with the behavioral assessment of children. In C. R. Reynolds & R. W. Kamphaus (Eds.), *Handbook of psychological and educational assessment of children: Personality, behavior and context* (2nd ed., pp. 30–47). New York: Guilford Press.

Skinner, M. E., & Lindstrom, B. D. (2003). Bridging the gap between high school and college: Strategies for the successful transition of students with learning disabilities. *Preventing School Failure, 47,* 132–137.

Sklar, L. S., & Anisman, H. (1979). Stress and coping factors influence tumor growth. *Science, 205,* 513–515.

Skodol, A. E., Bender, D. S., Morey, L. C., Clark, L., Oldham, J. M., Alarcon, R. D., et al. (2011). Personality disorder types proposed for DSM-5. *Journal of Personality Disorders, 25,* 136–169. doi:10.1521/pedi.2011.25.2.136

Skodol, A. E., Gunderson, J. G., Shea, M. T., McGlashan, T. H., Morey, L. C., Sanislow, C. A., et al. (2005). The collaborative longitudinal personality disorders study (CLPS): Overview and implications. *Journal of Personality Disorders, 19,* 487–504.

Skrtic, T. M., Summers, J. A., Brotherson, M. J., & Turnbull, A. P. (1984). Severely handicapped children and their brothers and sisters. In J. Blacher (Ed.), *Severely handicapped young children and their families: Research in review* (pp. 215–246). New York: Academic Press.

Skuse, D., Bruce, H., Dowdney, L., & Mrazek, D. (2011). *Child psychology and psychiatry: Frameworks for practice.* Oxford: Wiley.

Slade, P. D. (1974). Psychometric studies of obsessional illness and obsessional personality. In H. R. Beech (Ed.), *Obsessional states* (pp. 95–112). London: Methuen.

Slater, E., & Glithero, E. (1965). A follow-up of patients diagnosed as suffering from hysteria. *Journal of Psychosomatic Research, 9,* 9–13.

Slovenko, R. (2001). Aphrodisiacs—then and now. *Journal of Psychiatry and Law, 29* (1), 103–116.

Slutske, W., Heath, A. C., Dunne, M. P., Statham, D. J., Dinwiddie, S. H., Madden, P. A. F., et al. (1997). Modeling genetic and environmental influences on the etiology of conduct disorder: A study of 2,682 adult twin pairs. *Journal of Abnormal Psychology, 106* (2), 266–279.

Smalley, S. L., & Collins, F. (1996). In M. M. Bristol, D. J. Cohen, E. J. Costello, M. Denckla, T. J. Eckberg, R. Kallen, et al., State of the science in autism: Report to the National Institutes of Health. *Journal of Autism and Developmental Disorders, 26,* 195–198.

Smith, A., Stewart, D., Peled, M., Poon, C., Saewyc, E., & McCreary Centre Society. (2009). *A picture of health: Highlights from the 2008 British Columbia Adolescent Health Survey.* Vancouver, BC: McCreary Centre Society.

Smith, A. M., Gacono, C. B., & Kaufman, L. (1997). A Rorschach comparison of psychopathic and nonpsychopathic conduct disordered adolescents. *Journal of Clinical Psychology, 53,* 289–300.

Smith, G. T., Goldman, M., Greenbaum, P. E., & Christiansen, B. A. (1995). Expectancy for social facilitation from drinking: The divergent paths of high-expectancy and low-expectancy adolescents. *Journal of Abnormal Psychology, 104,* 32–40.

Smith, G. T., & Oltmanns, T. F. (2009). Scientific advances in the diagnosis of psychopathology: Introduction to the special section. *Psychological Assessment, 21,* 241–242.

Smith, J. D. (2002). The myth of mental retardation: Paradigm shifts, disaggregation and developmental disabilities. *Mental Retardation, 40,* 62–64.

Smith, M. L., Glass, G. V., & Miller, T. I. (1980). *The benefits of psychotherapy.* Baltimore, MD: Johns Hopkins University Press.

Smith, P. (2007). Have we made any progress? Including students with intellectual disabilities in regular education classrooms. *Intellectual and Developmental Disabilities, 45,* 297–309.

Smith, T., Groen, A. D., & Wynn, J. W. (2000). Randomized trial of intensive early intervention for children with pervasive developmental disorder. *American Journal on Mental Retardation, 105* (4), 269–285.

Smith, T. W. (1992). Hostility and health: Current status of a psychosomatic hypothesis. *Health Psychology, 11,* 139–150.

Smith, T. W., & Frohm, K. D. (1985). What's so unhealthy about hostility? Construct validity and psychosocial correlates of the Cook and Medley Ho scale. *Health Psychology, 4,* 503–520.

Smith, T. W., Uchino, B. N., Berg, C. A., Florsheim, P., Pearce, G., Hawkins, M., et al. (2008). Associations of self-reports versus spouse ratings of negative affectivity, dominance, and affiliation with coronary artery disease: Where should we look and who should we ask when studying personality and health? *Health Psychology, 27,* 676–684.

Smolak, L., & Levine, M. P. (1996). Adolescent transitions and the development of eating problems. In L. Smolak, M. P. Levine, & R. Streigel-Moore (Eds.), *The developmental psychopathology of eating disorders: Implications for research, prevention, and treatment* (pp. 207–233). Hillsdale, NJ: Lawrence Erlbaum Associates.

Smolak, L., Levine, M. P., & Schermer, F. (1999). Parental input and weight concerns among elementary school children. *International Journal of Eating Disorders, 25,* 263–271.

Smyer, M. A. (1995). Prevention and early intervention for mental disorders of the elderly. In M. Gatz (Ed.), *Emerging issues in mental health and aging* (pp. 163–182). Washington DC: American Psychological Association.

Snowling, M. J. (1996). Contemporary approaches to the teaching of reading. *Journal of Child Psychology and Psychiatry, 37,* 139–148.

Snyder, J. J. (1977). Reinforcement and analysis of interaction in problem and nonproblem families. *Journal of Abnormal Psychology, 86,* 528–535.

Snyder, S. M., Hall, J. R., Cornwell, S. L., & Quintana, H. (2006). Review of clinical validation of ADHD behavior rating scales. *Psychological Reports, 99* (2), 363–378.

Sobell, L. C., Toneatto, A., & Sobell, M. B. (1990). Behavior therapy. In A. S. Bellack & M. Hersen (Eds.), *Handbook of comparative treatments for adult disorders* (pp. 479–505). New York: Brunner/Mazel.

Sobell, M. B., & Sobell, L. C. (1973). Alcoholics treated by individualized behavior therapy: One year treatment outcome. *Behaviour Research and Therapy, 11,* 599–618.

Sobell, M. B., & Sobell, L. C. (1976). Second year treatment outcome of alcoholics treated by individualized behavior therapy: Results. *Behaviour Research and Therapy, 14,* 195–215.

Sobsey, D., Gray, S., Wells, D., Pyper D., & Reimer-Heck, B. (1991). *Disability, sexuality and abuse: An annotated bibliography.* Baltimore, MD: Paul H. Brookes.

Soderstrom, H., Blennow, K., Manhem, A., & Forsman, A. (2001). CSF studies in violent offenders: I. 5-HIAA as a negative and HVA as a positive predictor of psychopathy. *Journal of Neural Transmission, 108,* 869–878.

Softley, I. (Director). (2001). *K-Pax* [Motion Picture]. USA: Intermedia Films.

Solomon, D. A., Keller, M. B., Leon, A. C., Mueller, T. I., Lavori, P. W., Shea, M. T., et al. (2000). Multiple recurrences of major depressive disorder. *American Journal of Psychiatry, 157,* 229–233.

Spacarelli, S., Colter, S., & Penman, D. (1992). Problem solving skills training as a supplement to behavioural parent education. *Cognitive Therapy Research, 16,* 1–18.

Spanos, N. (1996). *Multiple identities and false memories: A sociocognitive perspective.* Washington, DC: American Psychiatric Press.

Sparrow, S. S., Cicchetti, D. V., & Balla, D. A. (2006). *Vineland Adaptive Behavior Scales (Second Edition) Vineland II.* Toronto: Pearson Education.

Spector, I. P., & Carey, M. P. (1990). Incidence and prevalence of the sexual dysfunctions: A critical review of the literature. *Archives of Sexual Behavior, 19,* 389–408.

Speisman, J., Lazarus, R. S., Mordkoff, A., & Davidson, L. (1964). Experimental reduction of stress based on ego defense theory. *Journal of Abnormal and Social Psychology, 68,* 367–380.

Spence, S. H., Donovan, C. L., March, S., Gamble, A., Anderson, R. E., Prosser, S., & Kenardy, J. (2011). A randomized controlled trial of online versus clinic-based CBT for adolescent anxiety. *Journal of Consulting and Clinical Psychology, 79,* 629–642.

Spencer, T., Biederman, J., Wilens, T., Harding, M., O'Donnell, D., & Griffin, S. (1996). Pharmacotherapy of attention-deficit hyperactivity disorder across the lifecycle: A literature review. *Journal of the American Academy of Child and Adolescent Psychiatry, 35,* 409–432.

Spencer, T. J., Biederman, J., & Mick, E. (2007). Attention-deficit/hyperactivity disorder: Diagnosis, lifespan, comorbidities, and neurobiology. *Journal of Pediatric Psychology, 32* (6), 631–642.

Sperry, L. (2003). *Handbook of diagnosis and treatment of DSM-IV-TR personality disorders.* New York: Brunner-Routledge.

Spicer, C. C., Stewart, D. N., & Winser, D. M. R. (1944). Perforated peptic ulcer during the period of heavy air raids. *The Lancet,* January 1, 14.

Spittal, P. M., Tyndall, M., Li, K., Laliberta, N., Wood, E., Craib, K., O'Shaughnessy, M. V., et al. (1998). *Vancouver injection drug study.* Vancouver: British Columbia Centre for Excellence in HIV/AIDS.

Spitzer, R. L., Endicott, J., & Gibbon, M. (1979). Crossing the border into borderline personality and borderline schizophrenia. *Archives of General Psychiatry, 36,* 17–24.

Spitzer, B. L., Henderson, K. A., & Zivian, M. T. (1999). Gender differences in population versus media body sizes: A comparison over four decades. *Sex Roles, 40,* 545–565.

Spoth, R. L., Redmond, C., Trudeau, L., & Shin, C. (2002). Longitudinal substance initiation outcomes for a universal preventive intervention combining family and school programs. *Psychology of Addictive Behaviors, 16* (2), 129–134.

Sprock, J., Blashfield, R. K., & Smith, B. (1990). Gender weighting of DSM-III-R personality disorder criteria. *American Journal of Psychiatry, 147,* 586–590.

Stallard, P., Richardson, T., Velleman, S., & Attwood, M. (2011). Computerized CBT (Think, Feel, Do) for depression and anxiety in children and adolescents: Outcomes and feedback from a pilot randomized controlled trial. *Behavioural and Cognitive Psychotherapy, 39,* 273–284.

Stanford, M. S., Ebner, D., Patton, J. H., & Williams, J. (1994). Multi-impulsivity within an adolescent psychiatric population. *Personality and Individual Differences, 16,* 395–402.

Stanley, M. A., & Beck, J. G. (2000). Anxiety disorders. *Clinical Psychology Review, 20,* 731–754.

Starson v. Swayze (2003), 1 S.C.R. 722.

Statistics Canada. (1999). *Statistical report on the health of Canadians.* Retrieved from http://www.statcan.ca:8096/bsolc/english/bsolc?catno=82-570-XWE

Statistics Canada. (2003a, September 3). Canadian Community Health Survey: Mental health and well-being. *The Daily.* Retrieved from http://www.statcan.ca/Daily/English/030903/d030903a.htm

Statistics Canada. (2003b). *Canadian tobacco use monitoring survey.* Ottawa: Statistics Canada.

Statistics Canada. (2004). *Mortality: Summary list of causes, 2004.* Catalogue no. 84F0209XIE. Ottawa: Author.

Statistics Canada. (2006, October). Canada's population by age and sex. *The Daily.*

Statistics Canada. (2007). *Mortality: Summary list of causes, 2000, 2001, 2002, 2003.* Ottawa: Author.

Stefan, S. (2006). *Emergency department treatment of the psychiatric patient: Policy issues and legal requirements.* New York: Oxford University Press.

Steffy, R. A., Asarnow, R. F., Asarnow, J. R., MacCrimmon, D. J., & Cleghorn, J. M. (1984). The McMaster-Waterloo High-Risk Project: Multifaceted strategy for high-risk research. In N. F. Watt, E. J. Anthony, L. C. Wynne, & J. E. Rolf (Eds.), *Children at risk for schizophrenia: A longitudinal perspective* (pp. 401–413). Cambridge UK: Cambridge University Press.

Steffy, R. A., & Waldman, I. (1993). Schizophrenics' reaction time: North star or shooting star? In R. L. Cromwell & C. R. Snyder (Eds.), *Schizophrenia: Origins, processes, treatment, and outcome* (pp. 111–134). New York: Oxford University Press.

Steiger, H., Bruce, K., Gauvin, L., Groleau, P., Joober, R., Israel, M., Richardson, J., & Ng Yin Kin, F. (2011). Contributions of the glucocorticoid receptor polymorphism (Bcl1) and childhood abuse to risk of bulimia nervosa. *Psychiatry Research, 187,* 193–197.

Steiger, H., & Israel, M. (2009). Treatment of psychiatric comorbidities. In C. M. Grilo & J. E. Mitchell (Eds.), *Treatment of eating disorders* (pp. 447–457). New York: Guilford Press.

Steiger, H., Richardson, J., Israel, M., Ng Ying Kin, N. M. K., Bruce, K., Mansour, S., & Parent, A. M. (2005). Reduced density of platelet-binding sites for [^{3}H] paroxetine in remitted bulimic women. *Neuropsychopharmacology, 30,* 1028–1032.

Steiger, H., Young, S. N., Kin, N. M. K., Koerner, N., Israel, M., Lageix, P., et al. (2001). Implications of impulsive and affective symptoms for serotonin function in bulimia nervosa. *Psychological Medicine, 31,* 85–95.

Stein, A., Woolley, H., Cooper, S., Winterbottom, J., Fairburn, C. G., & Cortina-Borja, M. (2006). Eating habits and attitudes among 10-year-old children of mothers with eating disorders: Longitudinal study. *British Journal of Psychiatry, 189,* 324–329.

Stein, K. F., & Corte, C. (2007). Identity impairment and the eating disorders: Content and organization of the self-concept in women with anorexia nervosa and bulimia nervosa. *European Eating Disorders Review, 15,* 58–69.

Stein, M. B., Goldin, P. R., Sareen, J., Zorrila, L. T. E., & Brown, G. G. (2002). Increased amygdala activation to angry and contemptuous faces in generalized social phobia. *Archives of General Psychiatry, 59,* 1027–1034.

Stein, M. T., Klin, A., & Miller, K. (2004). When Asperger's syndrome and a nonverbal learning disability look alike. *Pediatrics, 114,* 1458–1463.

Stein, R. M., & Ellinwood, E. H. (1993). Stimulant use: Cocaine and amphetamine. In D. L. Dunner (Ed.), *Current psychiatric therapy* (pp. 98–105). Philadelphia: Saunders.

Steiner, M., Lepage, P., & Dunn, E. J. (1997). Serotonin and gender-specific psychiatric disorders. *International Journal of Psychiatry in Clinical Practice, 1,* 3–13.

Steinhauer, S. R., & Hill, S. Y. (1993). Auditory event-related potentials in children at high risk for alcoholism. *Journal of Studies on Alcohol, 54,* 408–421.

Steinhausen, C. H., Rauss-Mason, C., & Seidel, R. (1991). Follow-up studies of anorexia nervosa: A review of four decades of outcome research. *Psychological Medicine, 21,* 447–451.

Steinhausen, H. C., Seidel, R., & Metzke, C. W. (2000). Evaluation of treatment and intermediate and long-term outcome of adolescent eating disorders. *Psychological Medicine, 30,* 1089–1098.

Stepanski, E., Rybarczyk, B., Lopez, M., & Stevens, S. (2003). Assessment and treatment of sleep disorders in older adults: A review for rehabilitation psychologists. *Rehabilitation Psychology, 48,* 23–36.

Stephens, R. S., Roffman, R. A., & Curtin, L. (2000). Comparison of extended versus brief treatment for marijuana use. *Journal of Consulting and Clinical Psychology, 61,* 1100–1104.

Stepp, S. D., Hallquist, M. N., Morse, J. Q., & Pilkonis, P. A. (2011). Multimethod investigation of interpersonal functioning in borderline personality disorder. *Personality Disorders: Theory, Research, and Treatment, 2,* 175–192. doi:10.1037/a0020572

Stevens, D., Charman, R., & Blair, R. J. R. (2001). Recognition of emotion in facial expressions and vocal tones in children with psychopathic tendencies. *Journal of Genetic Psychology, 162,* 201–211.

Stevenson, J., & Meares, R. (1992). An outcome study of psychotherapy for patients with borderline personality disorder. *American Journal of Psychiatry, 149,* 358–362.

Stewart, R., Besset, A., Bebbington, P., Brugha, T., Lindesay, J., Jenkins, R., Singleton, N., & Meltzer, H. (2006). Insomnia comorbidity and impact and hypnotic use by age group in a national survey population aged 16 to 74 years. *Sleep, 29* (11), 1391–1397.

Stewart, R. E., & Chambless, D. L. (2009). Cognitive-behavioral therapy for adult anxiety disorders in clinical practice: A meta-analysis of effectiveness studies. *Journal of Consulting and Clinical Psychology, 77,* 595–606.

Stewart, S. E., & Pauls, D. L. (2010). The genetics of obsessive-compulsive disorder. *Focus, 8,* 350.

Stewart, S. H., Westra, H. A., Thompson, C. E., & Conrad, B. E. (2000). Effects of naturalistic benzodiazepine use on selective attention to threat cues among anxiety disorder patients. *Cognitive Therapy & Research, 24,* 67–85.

Stice, E., Schupak-Neuberg, E., Shaw, H. E., & Stein, R. I. (1994). Relation of media exposure to eating disorder symptomatology: An examination of mediating mechanisms. *Journal of Abnormal Psychology, 103,* 836–840.

Stice, E., & Shaw, H. (2004). Eating disorder prevention programs: A meta-analytic review. *Psychological Bulletin, 130,* 206–227.

Stichter, J. P., Herzog, M. J., Visovsky, K., Schmidt, C., Randolph, J., Schultz, T., & Gage, N. (2010). Social competence intervention for youth with Asperger syndrome and high-functioning autism: An initial investigation. *Journal of Autism and Developmental Disorders, 40,* 1067–1079.

Still, B. (1932). *The history of pediatrics: The progress of the study of diseases of children up to the end of the eighteenth century.* London: Oxford University Press.

Stone, A. A., Schwartz, J. E., Broderick, J. E., & Deaton, A. (2010). A snapshot of the age distribution of psychological well-being in the United States. *Proceedings of the National Academy of Sciences, 107,* 9985–9990.

Stone, G. L. (1995). Review of the Hare Psychopathy Checklist—Revised. In J. C. Conoley & J. C. Impara (Eds.), *Twelfth mental measurements yearbook* (pp. 454–455). Lincoln, NE: Buros Institute.

Stone, J., Smyth, R., Carson, A., Lewis, S., Prescott, R., Warlow, C., & Sharpe, M. (2005). Systematic review of misdiagnosis of conversion symptoms and "hysteria." *British Medical Journal, 331,* 989.

Stone, J., Smyth, R., Carson, A., Warlow, C., & Sharpe, M. (2006). *La belle indifférence* in conversion symptoms and hysteria: Systematic review. *British Journal of Psychiatry, 188,* 204–209.

Stone, J., Warlow, C., & Sharpe, M. (2010). The symptom of functional weakness: A controlled study of 107 patients. *Brain, 133,* 1537–1551.

Stone, M. (1993). Long-term outcome in personality disorders. *British Journal of Psychiatry, 162,* 299–313.

Stone, W. L., Lemanek, K. L., Fishel, P. T., Fernandez, M. C., & Altemeier, W. A. (1990). Play and imitation skills in the diagnosis of autism in young children. *Pediatrics, 86,* 267–272.

Stravynski, A., Lesage, A., Marcouiller, M., & Elie, R. (1989). A test of the therapeutic mechanism in social skills training with avoidant personality disorder. *Journal of Nervous and Mental Disease, 177,* 739–744.

Streiner, D. L., Cairney, J., & Veldhuizen, S. (2006). The epidemiology of psychological problems in the elderly. *Canadian Journal of Psychiatry, 51* (3), 185–191.

Streissguth, A. P., & O'Malley, K. (2000). Neuropsychiatric implications and long-term consequences of fetal alcohol spectrum disorders. *Seminars in Clinical Neuropsychiatry* 5, 177–190.

Streissguth, A. P., Barr, H. M., & Sampson, P. D. (1990). Moderate prenatal alcohol exposure: Effects on child IQ and learning problems at age 71/2 years. *Alcoholism: Clinical and Experimental Research, 14,* 662–669.

Streissguth, A. P., Bookstein, F. L., & Barr, H. M. (1996). A dose-response study of the enduring effects of prenatal alcohol exposure: Birth to 14 years. In H. Spohn & H. Steinhausen (Eds.), *Alcohol, pregnancy and the developing child* (pp. 141–168). Cambridge, UK: Cambridge University Press.

Striegel-Moore, R. H. (1993). Etiology of binge eating: A developmental perspective. In C. G. Fairburn & G. T. Wilson (Eds.), *Binge eating: Nature, assessment and treatment* (pp. 144–172). New York: Guilford Press.

Striegel-Moore, R. H. (1997). Risk factors for eating disorders. *Annals of the New York Academy of Sciences: Adolescent nutritional disorders: Prevention and treatment, 817,* 98–109.

Striegel-Moore, R. H., Franko, D. L., & Garcia, J. (2009). The validity and clinical utility of night eating syndrome. *International Journal of Eating Disorders, 42,* 720–738.

Stringaris, A., & Goodman, R. (2009). Longitudinal outcome of youth oppositionality: Irritable, headstrong, and hurtful behaviors have distinctive predictions. *Journal of the American Academy of Child and Adolescent Psychiatry, 48,* 404–412. doi:10.1097/CHI.0b013e3181984f30

Strober, M., Freeman, R., Lampert, C., Diamond, J., & Kaye, W. (2000). Controlled family study of anorexia nervosa and bulimia nervosa: Evidence of shared liability and transmission of partial syndromes. *American Journal of Psychiatry, 157,* 393–401.

Strober, M., Morrell, W., Burroughs, J., Lampert, C., Danforth, H., & Freeman, R. (1988). A family study of bipolar I disorder in adolescence: Early onset of symptoms linked to increased familial loading and lithium resistance. *Journal of Affective Disorders, 15,* 255–268.

Strong, S. M., Williamson, D. A, Netemeyer, R. G., & Geer, J. H. (2000). Eating disorder symptoms and concerns about body differ as a function of gender and sexual orientation. *Journal of Social and Clinical Psychology, 19,* 240–255.

Stuart, H., Arboleda-Florez, J., & Crisanti, A. S. (2001). Impact of legal reforms on length of forensic assessments in Alberta, Canada. *International Journal of Law and Psychiatry, 24,* 527–538.

Suarez, E., & Williams, R. B. (1989). Situational determinants of cardiovascular and emotional reactivity in high and low hostile men. *Psychosomatic Medicine, 51,* 404–418.

Suárez, L., Bennett, S., Goldstein, C., & Barlow, D. H. (2009). Understanding anxiety disorders from a "triple vulnerabilities" framework. In M.M. Antony & M.B. Stein (Eds.), *Oxford handbook of anxiety and related disorders* (pp. 153–172). New York: Oxford.

Suedfeld, P., & Landon, P. B. (1978). Approaches to treatment. In R. D. Hare & D. Schalling (Eds.), *Psychopathic behavior: Approaches to research* (pp. 347–376). Chichester, UK: Wiley.

Suicide rates on the rise in China. (2004, March 31). *China Daily.*

Sullivan, P. F. (2008). Schizophrenia genetics: The search for a hard lead. *Current Opinion in Psychiatry, 21,* 157–160.

Sullivan, P. F., Neale, M. C., & Kendler, K. S. (2000). Genetic epidemiology of major depression: Review and meta-analysis. *American Journal of Psychiatry, 157,* 1552–1562.

Summerfeldt, L. J., Kloosterman, P. H., & Antony, M. M. (2010). Structured and semistructured diagnostic interviews. In M. M. Antony & D. H. Barlow (Eds.), *Handbook of assessment and treatment planning for psychological disorders* (2nd ed., pp. 95–137). New York: Guilford Press.

Suppes, T., Webb, A., Paul, B., Carmody, T., Kraemer, H., & Rush, A. J. (1999). Clinical outcome in a randomized 1-year trial of clozapine versus treatment as usual for patients with treatment-resistant illness and a history of mania. *American Journal of Psychiatry, 156,* 1164–1169.

Suzuki, K., Takei, N., Kawai, M., Minabe, Y., & Mori, N. (2003). Is Taijin Kyofusho a culture-bound syndrome? *American Journal of Psychiatry, 160,* 1358.

Svartberg, M., & Stiles, T. C. (1991). Comparative effects of short-term psychodynamic psychotherapy: A meta-analysis. *Journal of Consulting and Clinical Psychology, 59,* 704–714.

Swann, W. B., Jr. (1990). To be adored or to be known: The interplay of self-enhancement and self-verification. In R. M. Sorrentino & E. T. Higgins (Eds.), *Foundations of social behavior* (Vol. 2, pp. 408–448). New York: Guilford Press.

Swann, W. B., Jr., Wenzlaff, R. M., Krull, D. S., & Pelham, B. W. (1992). The allure of negative feedback: Self-verification strivings among depressed persons. *Journal of Abnormal Psychology, 101,* 293–306.

Swann, W. B., Jr., Wenzlaff, R. M., & Tafarodi, R. W. (1992). Depression and the search for negative evaluations: More evidence of the role of self-verification strivings. *Journal of Abnormal Psychology, 101,* 314–317.

Swanson, H. L. (2007). Cognitive aspects of math disabilities. In D.B. Berch & M. Mazzacco (Eds.), *Why is math so hard for some children? The nature and origins of mathematical learning difficulties and disabilities* (pp. 133–144). Baltimore, MD: Paul H. Brookes Publishing.

Swanson, J. M., Elliott, G. R., Greenhill, L. L., Wigal, T., Arnold, L. E., Vitiello, B., et al. (2007). Effects of stimulant medication on growth rates across 3 years in the MTA follow-up. *Journal of the American Academy of Child and Adolescent Psychiatry, 46* (8), 1015–1027.

Swartz, M. S., & Swanson, J. W. (2004). Involuntary outpatient commitment, community treatment orders, and assisted outpatient treatment: What's in the data? *Canadian Journal of Psychiatry, 49,* 585–591.

Swazey, J. P. (1974). *Chlorpromazine in psychiatry: A study of therapeutic innovation.* Cambridge, MA: MIT Press.

Sweet, M. A., & Applebaum, M. I. (2004). Is home visiting an effective strategy? A meta-analytic review of home visiting programs for families with young children. *Child Development, 75,* 1435–1456.

Swift, R. M. (2003). Medications. In R. K. Hester & W. R. Miller (Eds.), *Handbook of alcoholism treatment approaches: Effective alternatives* (3rd ed., pp. 259–281). Boston: Allyn and Bacon.

Symons, F. J., Byiers, B. J., Raspa, M., Bishop, E., & Bailey, D. B., Jr. (2010). Self-injurious behaviour and Fragile X syndrome: Findings from the National Fragile X survey. *American Journal on Intellectual and Developmental Disabilities, 115,* 473–481.

Sypeck, M. F., Gray, J. J., Etu, S. F., Ahrens, A. H., Mosimann, J. E., & Wiseman, C. V. (2006). Cultural representations of thinness in women, redux: Playboy magazine's depiction of beauty from 1979 to 1999. *Body Image 3,* 229–235.

Szabo, G., Tabakoff, B., & Hoffman, P. L. (1994). The NDMA receptor antagonist dizocilpine differentially affects environment-dependent and environment-independent ethanol tolerance. *Psychopharmacology, 113* (3–4), 511–517.

Szasz, T. S. (1961). *The myth of mental illness.* New York: Harper & Row.

Szasz, T. S. (1970). *The manufacture of madness.* New York: Harper & Row.

Szatmari, P., Boyle., M., & Offord, D. R. (1989). ADDH and conduct disorder: Degree of diagnostic overlap and differences among correlates. *Journal of the American Academy of Child and Adolescent Psychiatry, 28,* 865–872.

Tabakoff, B., & Hoffman, P. L. (1991). Neurochemical effects of alcohol. In R. J. Frances & S. I. Muller (Eds.), *Clinical textbook of addictive disorders* (pp. 501–525). New York: Guilford Press.

Tai, S., & Turkington, D. (2009). The evolution of cognitive behavior therapy for schizophrenia: Current practice and recent developments. *Schizophrenia Bulletin, 35* (5), 865–873.

Takayanagi, Y., Takahashi, T., Orikabe, L., Mozue, Y., Kawasaki, Y., Nakamura, K., . . . Suzuki, M. (2011). Classification of first-episode schizophrenia patients and healthy subjects by automated MRI measures of regional brain volume and cortical thickness. *PLoS ONE, 6*: e21047. doi:10.1371/journal.pone.0021047

Talge, N. M., Neal, C., Glover, V., & Early Stress, Translational Research and Prevention Science Network: Fetal and Neonatal Experience on Child and Adolescent Mental Health. (2007). Antenatal maternal stress and long-term effects on child neurodevelopment: How and why? *Journal of Child Psychology and Psychiatry, and Allied Disciplines, 48* (3–4), 245–261.

Tambs, K., Czajkowsky, N., Røysamb, E., Neale, M. C., Reichboirn-Kjennerud, T., Aggen, S. H. . . . Kendler, K. S. (2009). Structure of genetic and environmental risk factors for dimensional representations of DSM-IV anxiety disorders. *British Journal of Psychiatry, 195,* 30–307.

Tandon, R., Keshavan, M., & Nasrallah, H. A. (2008). Schizophrenia, "just the facts": What we know in 2008. Part 2: Epidemiology and etiology. *Schizophrenia Research, 102,* 1–18.

Tandon, R., Nasrallah, H. A., & Keshavan, M. S. (2010). Schizophrenia, "just the facts" 5: Treatment and prevention past, present, and future. *Schizophrenia Research, 122,* 1–23.

Tausig, H. B. (1962). Thalidomide: A lesson in remote effects of drugs. *American Journal of Diseases of Children, 104,* 111–113.

Tausk, V. (1948). On the origin of the "influencing machine" in schizophrenia. In R. Fleiss (Ed.), *The psychoanalytic reader* (pp. 31–64). New York: International Universities Press.

Tavris, C. (1992). *The mismeasure of women.* New York: Simon and Schuster.

Taylor, C. B., Bryson, S., Luce, K. H., Cunning, D., Doyle, A. C., Abascal, L. B., . . . Wilfley, D. E. (2006). Prevention of eating disorders in at-risk college-age women. *Archives of General Psychiatry, 63,* 881–888.

Taylor, S., Afifi, T. O., Stein, M. B., Asmundson, G. J. G., & Jang, K. L. (2010). Etiology of obsessive beliefs: A behavioral-genetic analysis. *Journal of Cognitive Psychotherapy, 24,* 177–186.

Taylor, S., & Cox, B. J. (1998). An expanded Anxiety Sensitivity Index: Evidence for a hierarchic structure in a clinical sample. *Journal of Anxiety Disorders, 12,* 463–483.

Taylor, S., Zvolensky, M. J., Cox, B. J., Deacon, B., Heimberg, R. G., Ledley, D. R., et al. (2007). Robust dimensions of anxiety sensitivity: Development and initial validation of the Anxiety Sensitivity Index-3. *Psychological Assessment, 19,* 176–188.

Taylor, T.K., Schmidt, F., Pepler, D., & Hodgins, C. (1998). A comparison of eclectic treatment with Webster-Stratton's parents and children series in a children's mental health setting: A randomized controlled trial. *Behavior Therapy, 29,* 221–240.

Teasdale, J. D., Segal, Z. V., Williams, J. M., Ridgeway, V. A., Soulsby, J. M., & Lau, M. A. (2000). Prevention of relapse/recurrence in major depression by mindfulness-based cognitive therapy. *Journal of Consulting & Clinical Psychology, 68,* 615–623.

Tellegen, A., Lykken, D. T., Bouchard, T. J., Wilcox, K. J., Segal, N. L., & Rich, S. (1988). Personality similarity in twins reared apart and together. *Journal of Personality and Social Psychology, 54,* 1031–1039.

Temple, E., Deutsch, G., Poldrack, R., Miller, S., & Tallal, P. (2003). Neural deficits in children with dyslexia ameliorated by behavioral remediation: Evidence from fMRI. *Proceedings of the National Academy of Sciences, 100,* 2860–2865.

Tennent, G., Tennent, D., Prins, H., & Bedford, A. (1993). Is psychopathic disorder a treatable condition? *Medicine, Science, and the Law, 33,* 63–66.

Teodorescu, M. C., & Husain, N. F. (2010). Nonpharmacologic approaches to insomnia in older adults. *Annals of Long Term Care, 18* (8), 36–42.

Terman, M., Terman, J. S., Quitkin, F. M., McGrath, P. J., Stewart, J. W., & Rafferty, B. (1989). Light therapy for seasonal affective disorder: A review of efficacy. *Neuropsychopharmacology, 2,* 1–22.

Test, D. W., Fowler, C. H., Wood, W. M., Brewer, M., & Eddy, S. (2005). A conceptual framework of self-advocacy for students with disabilities. *Remedial and Special Education, 26,* 43–54.

Thaper, A., & McGuffin, P. (1995). Are anxiety symptoms in childhood heritable? *Journal of Child Psychology and Psychiatry, 36,* 439–447.

Thase, M. E., Greenhouse, J. B., Frank, E., Reynolds III, C. F., Pilkonis, P. A., Hurley, K., et al. (1997). Treatment of major depression with psychotherapy or psychotherapy-pharmacotherapy combinations. *Archives of General Psychiatry, 54,* 1009–1015.

Thase, M. E., & Howland, R. H. (1995). Biological processes in depression: An updated review and integration. In E. E. Beckham & W. R. Leber (Eds.), *Handbook of depression* (2nd ed.). New York: Guilford Press.

Thase, M. E., Jindal, R., & Howland, R. H. (2002). Biological aspects of depression. In I. H. Gotlib & C. L. Hammen (Eds.), *Handbook of depression* (3rd ed., pp. 192–218). New York: Guilford Press.

Thase, M. E., & Rush, A. J. (1997). When at first you don't succeed: Sequential strategies for antidepressant nonresponders. *Journal of Clinical Psychiatry, 58,* 23–29.

Thayer, J. F., & Friedman, B. H. (2002). Stop that! Inhibition, sensitization and their neurovisceral concomitants. *Scandinavian Journal of Psychology, 43,* 123–130.

Thayer, J. F., Friedman, B. H., & Borkovec, T. D. (1996). Autonomic characteristics of generalized anxiety disorder and worry. *Biological Psychiatry, 39,* 255–266.

Thigpen, C. H., & Cleckley, H. M. (1957). *The three faces of Eve.* New York: McGraw Hill.

Thomas, A. M., & LoPiccolo, J. (1994). Sexual functioning in persons with diabetes: Issues in research, treatment, and education. *Clinical Psychology Review, 14,* 61–86.

Thombs, D. L. (1993). The differentially discriminating properties of alcohol expectancies for female and male drinkers. *Journal of Counseling and Development, 71,* 321–325.

Thompson, J. K., & Stice, E. (2001). Thin-ideal internalization: Mounting evidence for a new risk factor for body-image disturbance and eating pathology. *Current Directions in Psychological Science, 10,* 181–183.

Thompson, J. R., Bradley, V. J., Buntinx, W. H. E., Schalock, R. L., Shogren, K. A., Snell, M. E., et al. (2009). Conceptualizing supports and the support needs of people with intellectual disabilities. *Intellectual Disability, 47,* 135–146.

Thompson, R. A. (2008). Early attachment and later development: Familiar questions, new answers. New York: Guilford Press.

Thompson-Pope, S. K., & Turkat, I. D. (1988). Reactions to ambiguous stimuli among paranoid personalities. *Journal of Psychopathology and Behavioral Assessment, 10,* 21–32.

Thornton, D. (2010). Evidence regarding the need for a diagnostic category for a coercive paraphilia. *Archives of Sexual Behavior, 39,* 411–418.

Tiggemann, M., & Pickering, A. S. (1996). Role of television in adolescent women's body dissatisfaction and drive for thinness. *International Journal of Eating Disorders, 20,* 199–203.

Tiggemann, M., & Polivy, J. (2010). Upward and downward: Social comparison processing of thin idealized media images. *Psychology of Women Quarterly, 34,* 356–364.

Tiihonen, J., Haukka, J., Taylor, M., Haddad, P. M., Patel, M. X., & Korhonen, P. (2011). A nationwide cohort study of oral and depot antipsychotics after first hospitalization for schizophrenia. *American Journal of Psychiatry, 168,* 603–609.

Tillich, P. (1952). *The courage to be.* New Haven, CT: Yale University Press.

Timmons, K. A., & Joiner, T. E. (2008). Reassurance seeking and negative feedback seeking. In K. S. Dobson & D. J. A. Dozois (Eds.), *Risk factors in depression* (pp. 429–446). Oxford, UK: Elsevier/Academic Press.

Titov, N., Dear, B. F., Schwenke, G., Andrews, G., Johnston, L., Craske, M., & McEvoy, P. (2011). Transdiagnostic internet treatment for anxiety and depression: A randomized controlled trial. *Behaviour Research and Therapy, 49,* 441–452.

Tiwari, A. K., Zai, C. C., Müller, D. J., & Kennedy, J. L. (2010). Genetics in schizophrenia: Where are we and what next? *Dialogues in Clinical Neuroscience, 12,* 289–303.

Tobler, N. S. (2000). Lessons learned. *Journal of Primary Prevention, 20,* 261–274.

Tobler, N. S., Roona, M. R., Ochshorn, P., Marshall, D. G., Streke, A. V., & Stackpole, K. M. (2000). School-based adolescent drug prevention programs: 1998 meta-analysis. *Journal of Primary Prevention, 20,* 275–336.

Toch, H. (1971). *The social psychology of social movements.* London: Methuen.

Tohen, M., Jacobs, T. G., Grundy, S. L., McElroy, S., Banov, M. C., Janicak, P. G., et al. (2000). Efficacy of olanzapine in acute bipolar mania: A double-blind, placebo-controlled study. *Archives of General Psychiatry, 57,* 841–849.

Tolin, D. F., & Foa, E. B. (2006). Sex differences in trauma and posttraumatic stress disorder: A quantitative review of 25 years of research. *Psychological Bulletin, 132,* 959–992.

Tomasulo, D. (1994). Action techniques in group counseling: The double. *Habilitative Mental Healthcare Newsletter, 13,* 41–45.

Tomasulo, D., Keller, E., & Pfadt, A. (1995). The healing crowd: Process, content and technique issues in group counseling for people with mental retardation. *Habilitative Mental Healthcare Newsletter, 14,* 43–49.

Torgersen, S. (1984). Genetic and nosological aspects of schizotypal and borderline personality disorders. *Archives of General Psychiatry, 41,* 546–554.

Torgersen, S., & Alnaes, R. (1992). Differential perception of parental bonding in schizotypal and borderline personality disorder patients. *Comprehensive Psychiatry, 33,* 34–88.

Torrey, E. F. (1995). *Surviving schizophrenia: A family manual.* (3rd ed.) New York: Harper & Row.

Torrey, E. F., & Miller, J. (2001). *The invisible plague: the rise of mental illness from 1750 to the present.* New Jersey: Rutgers University Press.

Tougas, G., Chen, Y., Hwang, P., Liu, M. M., & Eggleston, A. (1999). Prevalence and impact of upper gastrointestinal symptoms in the Canadian population: Findings from the DIGEST study. Domestic/International Gastroenterology Surveillance Study. *American Journal of Gastroenterology, 94,* 2845–2854.

Tough, S. C., Clarke, M., Hicks, M., & Clarren, S. (2004). Clinical practice characteristics and preconception counselling strategies of health care providers who recommend alcohol abstinence during pregnancy. *Alcoholism. Clinical and Experimental Research, 28,* 1724–1731.

Tourigny-Rivard, M. (1997). Pharmacotherapy of affective disorders in old age. *Canadian Journal of Psychiatry, 42,* 10S–18S.

Traffic Injury Research Foundation. (2001). *The road safety monitor. Drinking and driving.* Ottawa: Traffic Injury Research Foundation.

Tran, L., Sanchez, T., Arellano, B., & Swanson, H. L. (2011). A meta-analysis of the RTI literature for children at risk for reading disabilities. *Journal of Learning Disabilities, 44* (3), 283–295.

Treatment for Adolescent Depression Study Team. (2004). Fluoxetine, cognitive-behavioral therapy, and their combination for adolescents with depression. *Journal of the American Medical Association, 292,* 807–820.

Treatment for Adolescents with Depression Study (TADS) Team. (2003). Treatment for adolescents with depression study (TADS): Rationale, design, and methods. *Journal of the American Academy of Child & Adolescent Psychiatry, 42,* 531–542.

Tremblay, P., King, P., & Baines, G. (1994). Clinical and demographic characteristics of voluntary and involuntary psychiatric inpatients. *Canadian Journal of Psychiatry, 39,* 297–299.

Trestrail, J. H. (1991). Mushroom poisoning in the United States—An analysis of 1989 United States poison center data. *Clinical Toxicology, 29,* 459–465.

Trottier, K., McFarlane, T., Olmsted, M. P., & McCabe, R. (under review). The Weight Influenced Self-Esteem Questionnaire (WISE-Q): Factor structure and psychometric properties.

Troyb, E., Knoch, K., & Barton, M. (2011). Phenomenology of ASD: Definition, syndromes and major features. In D. A. Fein (Ed.), *The neuropsychology of autism* (p. 17). New York: Oxford University Press.

Trull, T. J., Widiger, T. A., & Frances, A. (1987). Covariation of criteria for avoidant, schizoid, and dependent personality disorders. *American Journal of Psychiatry, 144,* 767–771.

Truscott, D., & Crook, K. H. (2004). *Ethics for the practice of psychology in Canada.* Edmonton: University of Alberta Press.

Trzaskowski, M., Zavos, H. M. S., Haworth, C. M. A., Plomin, R., & Eley, T. C. (2011). Stable genetic influence on anxiety-related behaviours across middle childhood. *Journal of Abnormal Child Psychology.* Advance online publication. doi:10.1007/s10802-011-9545-z

Tsoi, W. F. (1990). Developmental profile of 200 male and 100 female transsexuals in Singapore. *Archives of Sexual Behavior, 19,* 595–605.

Tsuang, D. W., & Bird, T. D., (2002). Genetics of dementia. *Medical Clinics of North America, 86,* 591–614.

Tsuchiya, M., Kawakami, N., Ono, Y., Nakane, Y., Nakamura, Y., Tachimori, H., . . . Watanabe, M. (2009). Lifetime comorbidities between phobic disorders and major depression in Japan: Results from the world mental health Japan 2002–2004 survey. *Depression and Anxiety, 26,* 949–955.

Tuma, T. A. (2000). Outcome of hospital-treated depression at 4.5 years: An elderly and a younger adult cohort compared. *British Journal of Psychiatry, 176,* 224–228.

Turetsky, B. I., Moberg, P. J., & Mozley, L. H. (2002). Memory-delineated subtypes of schizophrenia: Relationship to clinical, neuroanatomical and neurophysiological measures. *Neuropsychology, 16,* 481–490.

Turk, C. L., Heimberg, R. G., & Magee, L. (2008). Social anxiety disorder. In D. H. Barlow (Ed.), *Clinical handbook of psychological disorders: A step-by-step treatment manual* (pp. 123–163). New York: Guilford Press.

Turkat, I. D., & Banks, D. (1987). Paranoid personality and its disorder. *Journal of Psychopathology and Behavioral Assessment, 9,* 295–304.

Turkat, I. D., Keane, S. P., & Thompson-Pope, S. K. (1990). Social processing in paranoid personalities. *Journal of Psychopathology and Behavioral Assessment, 12,* 263–269.

Turkat, I. D., & Levin, R. A. (1984). Formulation of personality disorders. In H. E. Adams & P. B. Sutker (Eds.), *Comprehensive handbook of psychotherapy* (pp. 495–522). New York: Plenum.

Turkington, D., Dudley, R., Warman, D. M., & Beck, A. T. (2004). Cognitive-behavioral therapy for schizophrenia: A review. *Journal of Psychiatric Practice, 10,* 5–16.

Turkington, D., & Morrison, A. P. (in press). Cognitive therapy for negative symptoms of schizophrenia. *Archives of General Psychiatry.*

Turnbull, A. P., Brown, I., & Turnbull, H. R., III. (Eds.). (2003). *Family quality of life: An introduction to conceptualization, measurement and application.* Washington, DC: American Association on Mental Retardation.

Turnbull, A. P., Summers, J. A., & Brotherson, M. J. (1986). Family life cycle: Theoretical and empirical implications and future directions for families with mentally retarded members. In J. J. Gallagher, & P. M. Vietze (Eds.), *Families of handicapped persons: Research, programs and policy issues* (pp. 45–65). Baltimore, MD: Brookes.

Turnbull, R., Turnbull, A., Warren, S., Eidelman, S., & Marchand, P. (2002). Shakespeare redux or Romeo and Juliet revisited: Embedding a terminology and name change in a new agenda for the field of mental retardation. *Mental Retardation, 40,* 65–70.

Turnbull, S., Ward, A., Treasure, J., & Jick, H. (1996). The demand for eating disorder care: An epidemiological study using the general practice research database. *British Journal of Psychiatry, 169,* 705–712.

Turner, J. R. (1994). *Cardiovascular reactivity and stress: Patterns of physiological response.* New York: Plenum.

Turner, S. M., Beidel, D. C., & Costello, A. (1987). Psychopathology in the offspring of anxiety disorders patients. *Journal of Consulting and Clinical Psychology, 55,* 229–235.

Turner, S. M., Beidel, D. C., Dancu, C. V., & Keys, D. J. (1991). Social Phobia: Axis I and II correlates. *Journal of Abnormal Psychology, 100,* 102–106.

Turner, T. H. (1992). Schizophrenia as a permanent problem: Some aspects of historical evidence in the recency (new disease) hypothesis. *History of Psychiatry, 3,* 413–429.

Udry, J. R. (1993). The politics of sex research. *Journal of Sex Research, 30,* 103–110.

UK ECT Review Group. (2003). Efficacy and safety of electroconvulsive therapy in depressive disorders: A systematic review and meta-analysis. *The Lancet, 361,* 799–808.

United States Department of Health and Human Services. (2000). *Evidence-based findings on the efficacy of syringe exchange programs: An analysis prepared for the Assistant Secretary for Health and Surgeon General.* Washington, DC: US Department of Health and Human Services.

Unützer, J. (2007). Late-life depression. *New England Journal of Medicine, 357,* 2269–2276.

Vaillancourt, T., Clinton, J., McDougall, P., Schmidt, L., & Hymel, S. (2009). The neurobiology of peer victimization and rejection. In S. R. Jimerson, S. M. Swearer, & D. L. Espelage (Eds.), *The international handbook of school bullying.* Mahwah, NJ: Lawrence Erlbaum Associates, Inc.

Vaillancourt, T., Duku, E., Becker, S., Schmidt, L., Nicol, J., Muir, C., & MacMillian, H. (2011). Peer victimization, depressive symptoms, and high salivary cortisol predict poor memory in children. *Brain and Cognition, 77,* 191–199. doi:10.1016/j.bandc.2011.06.012

Valas, H. (1999). Low achieving students: Peer acceptance, loneliness, self-esteem and depression. *Social Psychology of Education, 3,* 173–192.

Valenstein, E. S. (1986). Great and desperate cures: The rise and decline of psychosurgery and other radical treatments for mental illness. New York: Basic Books.

Vancouver Coastal Health (2003). *Injection drug use in Downtown Eastside.* Vancouver: Vancouver Coastal Health.

Van der Ham, T., Meulman, J. J., Van Strien, D. C., & Van Engeland, H. (1997). Empirically based subgrouping of eating disorders in adolescents: A longitudinal perspective. *British Journal of Psychiatry, 170,* 363–368.

Van der Kolk, B. A., & Van der Hart, O. (1989). Pierre Janet and the breakdown of adaptation in psychological trauma. *American Journal of Psychiatry, 146,* 1530–1540.

van der meer, L. A., & Rispoli, M. (2010). Communication interventions involving speech-generating devices for children with autism: A review of the literature. *Developmental Neurorehabilitation, 13* (4), 294–306.

van Elst, L. T., Woermann, F. G., Lemieux, L., Thompson, P. J., & Trimble, M. R. (2000). Affective aggression in patients with temporal lobe epilepsy: A quantitative MRI study of the amygdala. *Brain, 123,* 234–243.

Vanfurth, E. F., Vanstrien, D. C., Martina, L. M. L., Vanson, M. J. M., Hendrickx, J. J. P., & Vanengeland, H. (1996). Expressed emotion and the prediction of outcome in adolescent eating disorders. *International Journal of Eating Disorders, 20,* 19–31.

van Goozen, S. H. M., Matthys, W., Cohen-Kettenis, P. T., Gispen-de Wied, C., Wiegant, V. M., & Engeland, H. V. (1998). Salivary cortisol and cardiovascular activity during stress in oppositional-defiant disorder boys and normal controls. *Biological Psychiatry, 43,* 531–539.

Van Grootheest, D. S., Bartels, M., Van Beijsterveldt, C. E. M., Cath, D. C., Beekman, A. T., Hudziak, J. J., & Boomsma, D. I. (2008). Genetic and environmental contributions to self-report obsessive-compulsive symptoms in Dutch adolescents at ages 12, 14, and 16. *Journal of the American Academy of Child & Adolescent Psychiatry, 47,* 1182–1188.

van't Veer-Tazelaar, P. J., van Marwijk, H. W., van Oppen, P., van Hout, H. P., van der Horst, H. E., Cuijpers, P., . . . Beekman, A. T. (2009). Stepped-care prevention of anxiety and depression in late life: A randomized controlled trial. *Archives of General Psychiatry, 66,* 297–304.

Vasiliadis, H. M., Tempier, R., Lesage, A., & Kates, N. (2009). General practice and mental health care: Determinants of outpatient service use. *Canadian Journal of Psychiatry, 54,* 468–476.

Vaz, F. J., Guisado, J. A. & Peñas-Lledó, E. M. (2003). History of anorexia nervosa in bulimic patients: Its influence on body composition. *International Journal of Eating Disorders, 34,* 148–155.

Vellutino, F. R., Fletcher, J. M., Snowling, M. J., & Scanlon, D.M. (2004). Specific reading disability (dyslexia): What have we learned in the past four decades? *Journal of Child Psychology and Psychiatry, 45* (1), 2–40.

Venter, A., Lord, C., & Schopler, E. (1992). A follow-up study of high-functioning autistic children. *Journal of Child Psychology and Psychiatry, 33,* 489–507.

Verdoux, H., & Bégaud, B. (2004). Pharmaco-epidemiology: What do (and don't) we know about utilization and impact of psychotropic medications in real-life conditions? *British Journal of Psychiatry, 185,* 93–94.

Verhoeff, N. P. L.G., Wilson, A. A., Takeshita, S., Trop, L., Hussey, D., Singh, et al. (2004). In-vivo imaging of Alzheimer disease beta-amyloid with [^{11}C]SB-13 PET. *American Journal of Geriatric Psychiatry, 12,* 584–595.

Vernick, J. S., Burris, S., & Strathdee, S. A. (2003). Public opinion about syringe exchange programmes in the USA: An analysis of national surveys. *International Journal of Drug Policy, 14,* 431–435.

Vessey, J. T., & Howard, K. I. (1993). Who seeks psychotherapy? *Psychotherapy, 30,* 546–553.

Videnieks, M. (2003). Heroin deal ends health service for drug users. *The HEP C Review, 42,* 7.

Viding, E., Blair, R. J. R., Moffitt, T. E., & Plomin, R. (2005). Evidence for substantial genetic risk for psychopathy in 7-year-olds. *Journal of Child Psychology and Psychiatry, 46,* 592–597.

Viljoen, J. L., & Roesch, R. (2007). Assessing adolescents' adjudicative competence. In R. Jackson (Ed.), *Learning forensic assessment* (pp. 291–312). New York: Taylor & Francis.

Viljoen, J. L., Roesch, R., Ogloff, J. R. P., & Zapf, P. A. (2003). The role of Canadian psychologists in conducting fitness and criminal responsibility evaluations. *Canadian Psychology, 44,* 369–381.

Viljoen, J. L., & Zapf, P. A. (2002). Fitness to stand trial evaluations: A comparison of referred and non-referred defendants. *International Journal of Forensic Mental Health, 1,* 127–138.

Vincent, K. R., & Harman, M. J. (1991). The Exner Rorschach: An analysis of its clinical validity. *Journal of Clinical Psychology, 47* (4), 596–599.

Vitacco, M. J., Rogers, R., Neumann, C. S., Durrant, S., & Collins, M. (2000, March). *Adolescent psychopathy: Contributions of sensation seeking, impulsivity, and externalizing disorders.* Paper presented at the biennial conference of the American Psychology and Law Society, New Orleans, United States.

Vitale, J. E., Smith, S. S., Brinkley, C. A., & Newman, J. P. (2002). The reliability and validity of the Psychopathy Checklist-Revised in a sample of female offenders. *Criminal Justice and Behavior, 29* (2), 202–231.

Vitaliano, P. P., Zhang, J., & Scanlan, J. M. (2003). Is caregiving hazardous to one's physical health? A meta-analysis. *Psychological Bulletin, 129,* 946–972.

Vitaro, F., Trembay, R. E., Kerr, M., Pagani, L., & Bukowski, W. M. (2007). Disruptiveness, friends' characteristics, and delinquency in early adolescence: A test of two competing models of development. *Child Development, 68* (4), 676–689.

Vitiello, M. V., & Prinz, P. N. (1994). Sleep disturbances in the elderly. In M. L. Albert, & J. E. Knoefel (Eds.), *Clinical neurology of aging,* New York: Oxford University Press.

Vittengl, J. R., Clark, L. A., Dunn, T. W., & Jarrett, R. B. (2007). Reducing relapse and recurrence in unipolar depression: A comparative meta-analysis of cognitive-behavioral therapy's effects. *Journal of Consulting and Clinical Psychology, 75,* 475–488.

Vogel, D. L., Wade, N. G., & Haake, S. (2006). Measuring the self-stigma associated with seeking psychological help. *Journal of Counseling Psychology, 53,* 325–337.

Volkmar, F. R., Carter, A., Grossman, J., & Klin, A. (1997). Social development in autism. In D. J. Cohen & F. R. Volkmar (Eds.), *Handbook of autism and pervasive developmental disorders* (pp. 173–194). New York: Wiley.

Volkmar, F. R., Klin, A., Marance, W., & Cohen, D. J. (1997). Childhood disintegrative disorder. In D. J. Cohen & F. R. Volkmar (Eds.), *Handbook of autism and pervasive developmental disorders* (2nd ed., pp. 47–59). New York: Wiley.

Volkmar, F. R., & Schwab-Stone, M. (1996). Childhood disorders in DSM-IV. *Journal of Child Psychology and Psychiatry, 37,* 779–784.

Volpicelli, J. R., Alterman, A. I., Hayashida., M., & O'Brien, C. P. (1992). Naltrexone in the treatment of alcohol dependence. *Archives of General Psychiatry, 49,* 876–880.

Von Korff, M., Dworkin, S. F., & LeResche, L. (1990). Graded chronic pain status: An epidemiologic evaluation. *Pain, 40,* 279–291.

Waddell, C., Hua, J. M., Garland, O.M., Peters, R. DeV., & McEwan, K. (2007). Preventing mental disorder in children: A systematic review to inform policy-making. *Canadian Journal of Public Health, 98,* 174–178.

Waddell, C., McEwan, K., Peters, R. DeV., Hua, J. M., & Garland, O. (2007). Preventing mental disorders in children: A public health priority. *Canadian Journal of Public Health, 98,* 174–178.

Waddell, C., McEwan, K., Shepherd, C., Offord, D. R., & Hua, J. M. (2005). A public health strategy to improve the mental health of Canadian children. *Canadian Journal of Psychiatry, 50,* 226–233.

Waddell, C., Offord, D. R., Shepherd, C., Hua, J. M., & McEwan, K. (2002). Child psychiatric epidemiology and Canadian public policy-making: The state of the science and the art of the possible. *Canadian Journal of Psychiatry, 47,* 825–832.

Wade, C., Llewellyn, G., & Matthews, J. (2008). Review of parent training interventions for parents with intellectual disability. *Journal of Applied Research in Intellectual Disabilities, 21,* 351–366.

Wagner, K. D., Berard, R., Stein, M. B., Wetherhold, E., Carpenter, D. J., Perera, P., et al. (2004). A multicenter, randomized, double-blind, placebo-controlled trial of paroxetine in children and adolescents with social anxiety disorder. *Archives of General Psychiatry, 61* (11), 1153–1162.

Wahlbeck, K., Cheine, M., Essali, A., & Adams, C. (1999). Evidence of clozapine's effectiveness in schizophrenia: A systematic review and meta-analysis of randomized trials. *American Journal of Psychiatry, 156,* 990–999.

Wakefield, A. J., Murch, S. H., Anthony, A., Linnell, J., Casson, D. M., Malik, M., Berelowitz, M., Dhillon, A. P., Thomson, M. A., Harvey, P., Valentine, A., Davies, S. E., & Walker-Smith, J. A. (1998). Ileal-lymphoid-nodular hyperplasia, non-specific colitis, and pervasive developmental disorder in children. *The Lancet, 351,* 9103, 637–641.

Wakefield, J. (1992). Disorder as dysfunction: A conceptual critique of DSM-III-R's definition of mental disorder. *Psychological Review, 99,* 232–247.

Wakefield, J. C. (1993). Limits of operationalization: A critique of Spitzer and Endicott's (1978) proposed operational criteria for mental disorder. *Journal of Abnormal Psychology, 102,* 160–172.

Wakefield, J. C. (1997). Diagnosing DSM-IV—Part 1: DSM-IV and the concept of disorder. *Behaviour Research and Therapy, 35,* 633–649.

Wakefield, J. C. (1999). Evolutionary versus prototype analyses of the concept of disorder. *Journal of Abnormal Psychology, 108,* 374–399.

Wakeling, A. (1996). Epidemiology of anorexia nervosa. *Psychiatry Research, 62,* 3–9.

Wakely, M., Hooper, S., de Kruif, R., & Swartz, C. (2006). Subtypes of written expression in elementary school children: A linguistic-based model. *Developmental Neuropsychology, 29* (1), 125–159.

Wakschlag, L. S., Lahey, B. B., Loeber, R., Green, S. M., Gordon, R. A., & Leventhal, B. L. (1997). Maternal smoking during pregnancy and the risk of conduct disorder in boys. *Archives of General Psychiatry, 54,* 670–676.

Walcott, D. D., Pratt, H. D., & Patel, D. R. (2003). Adolescents and eating disorders: Gender, racial, ethnic, sociocultural, and socioeconomic issues. *Journal of Adolescent Research, 18,* 223–243.

Wald, N. J., Kennard, A., Densem, J. W., Cuckle, H. S., Chard, T., & Butler, L. (1992). Antenatal maternal serum screening for Down's syndrome: Results of a demonstration project. *British Medical Journal, 305,* 391–394.

Waldinger, M. D. (2005). Relevance of an evidence-based ejaculation time cutoff point for neurobiological research of premature ejaculation. *The Journal of Comparative Neurology, 493,* 46–50.

Waldinger, M. D., Hengeveld, M. W., Zwinderman, A. H., & Olivier, B. (1998). An empirical operationalization study of DSM-IV diagnostic criteria for premature ejaculation. *International Journal of Psychiatry and Clinical Practice, 2,* 278–293.

Waldron, H. B., & Turner, C. W. (2008). Evidence-based psychosocial treatments for adolescent substance abuse. *Journal of Clinical Child and Adolescent Psychology, 37,* 238–261.

Walen, S. R., DiGiuseppe, R., & Dryden, W. (1992). *A practitioner's guide to rational-emotive therapy* (2nd ed.). London: Oxford University Press.

Walker, E. F., & Diforio, D. (1997). Schizophrenia: A neural diathesis-stress model. *Psychological Review, 104,* 667–685.

Walker, E. F., Mittal, V., & Tessner, K. (2008). Stress and the hypothalamic pituitary adrenal axis in the developmental course of schizophrenia. *Annual Review of Clinical Psychology, 4,* 189–216.

Walker, E. F., Savoie, T., & Davis, D. (1994). Neuromotor precursors of schizophrenia. *Schizophrenia Bulletin, 20,* 441–451.

Walkup, J., Labellarte, M., Riddle, M. A., Pine, D. S., Greenhill, L., Fairbanks, J., et al. (2002). Treatment of pediatric anxiety disorders: An open label extension of the research units on pediatric psychopharmacology anxiety study. *Journal of Child and Adolescent Psychopharmacology, 12* (3), 175–188.

Walkup, J. T., Albano, A. M., Piacentini, J., Birmaher, B., Compton, S. N., Sherrill, J. T., et al. (2008). Cognitive behavioral therapy, sertraline, or a combination in childhood anxiety. *The New England Journal of Medicine,* doi:10.1056/NEJMoa0804633.

Wall, P. D., & Melzack, R. (1999). *Textbook of pain* (4th ed.). Edinburgh: Churchill Livingstone.

Wallace, J., & Pfohl, B. (1995). Age-related differences in the symptomatic expression of major depression. *Journal of Nervous and Mental Disease, 183,* 99–102.

Wallace, J., Schneider, T., & McGuffin, P. (2002). Genetics of depression. In I. H. Gotlib & C. L. Hammen (Eds.), *Handbook of depression* (pp. 169–191). New York: Guilford Press.

Wallace, J. F., Schmitt, W. A., Vitale, J. E., & Newman, J. P. (2000). Experimental investigations of information-processing deficiencies in psychopaths: Implications for diagnosis and treatment. In C. Gacono (Ed.), *The clinical and forensic assessment of psychopathy: A practitioner's guide* (pp. 87–109). Hillsdale, NJ: Erlbaum.

Wallach, H. S., Safir, M. P., & Bar-Zvi, M. (2009). Virtual reality cognitive behavior therapy for public speaking anxiety. *Behavior Modification, 33,* 314–338.

Waller, G. (1991). Sexual abuse as a factor in eating disorders. *British Journal of Psychiatry, 159,* 664–671.

Waller, N. G., Putnam, F. W., & Carlson, E. B. (1996). Types of dissociation and dissociative types: A taxometric analysis of dissociative experiences. *Psychological Methods, 1,* 300–321.

Waller, N. G., & Ross, C. A. (1997). The prevalence and biometric structure of pathological dissociation in the general population: Taxometric and behaviour genetic findings. *Journal of Abnormal Psychology, 106,* 499–510.

Wallgren, H., & Barry, H. (1971). *Actions of alcohol.* Amsterdam: Elsevier.

Walsh, A. E. S., Oldman, A. D., Franklin, M., Fairburn, C. G., & Cowen, P. J. (1995). Dieting decreases plasma tryptophan and increases the prolactin response to *d*-fenfluramine in women but not men. *Journal of Affective Disorders, 33,* 89–97.

Walsh, B. T., Agras, W. S., Devlin, M. J., Fairburn, C. G., Wilson, G. T., Kahn, C., & Chally, M. K. (2000). Fluoxetine for bulimia nervosa following poor response to psychotherapy. *American Journal of Psychiatry, 157,* 1332–1334.

Walsh, B. T., Seidman, S. N., Sysko, R., & Gould, M. (2002). Placebo response in studies of major depression. *Journal of the American Medical Association, 287,* 1840–1847.

Walsh, J. (1990). Assessment and treatment of the schizotypal personality disorder. *Journal of Independent Social Work, 4,* 41–59.

Walsh, K. (2002). Thoughts on changing the term *mental retardation. Mental Retardation, 40,* 70–75.

Walters, G. D. (1999). *The addiction concept: Working hypothesis or self-fulfilling prophesy?* Boston: Allyn & Bacon.

Wampold, B. E., Mondin, G. W., Moody, M., Stich, F., Benson, K., & Ahn, H. (1997). A meta-analysis of outcome studies comparing bona fide psychotherapies: Empirically, "All must have prizes." *Psychological Bulletin, 122,* 203–215.

Wandersman, A., Duffy, J., Flaspohler, P., Noonan, R., Lubell, K., Stillman, L., et al. (2008). Bridging the gap between prevention research and practice: The interactive systems framework for dissemination and implementation. *American Journal of Community Psychology, 41,* 171–181.

Wang, J. L., Schmitz, N., & Dewa, C. S. (2010). Socioeconomic status and the risk of major depression: The Canadian National Population Health Survey. *Journal of Epidemiology and Community Health, 64,* 447–452.

Wang, W., Kumar, P., Minhas, S., & Ralph, D. (2005). Proposals or findings for a new approach about how to define and diagnose premature ejaculation. *European Urology, 48,* 418–423.

Ward, T., & Beech, A. (2006). An integrated theory of sexual offending. *Aggression and Violent Behavior, 11,* 44–63.

Ward, T., Hudson, S. M., Marshall, W. L., & Siegert, R. (1995). Attachment style and intimacy deficits in sex offenders: A theoretical framework. *Sexual Abuse: A Journal of Research and Treatment, 7,* 317–335.

Ward, T., Polaschek, D. L. L., & Beech, A. (2006). *Theories of sexual offending.* West Sussex, UK: John Wiley and Sons.

Warne, J. P., & Dallman, M. F. (2007). Stress, diet and abdominal obesity: Y? *Nature Medicine, 13,* 781–783.

Warner, R. (1978). The diagnosis of antisocial and hysterical personality disorders: An example of sex bias. *Journal of Nervous and Mental Disease, 166,* 839–845.

Warren, J. I., Burnette, M. L., South, S. C., Chauhan, P., Bale, R., Friend, R., et al. (2003). Psychopathy in women: Structural modeling and comorbidity. *International Journal of Law and Psychiatry, 26,* 233–242.

Warren, S. L., Huston, L., Egeland, B., & Sroufe, L. A. (1997). Child and adolescent anxiety disorders and early attachment. *Journal of the American of Child and Adolescent Psychiatry, 36,* 637–644.

Wartenberg, A. A., Nirenberg, T. D., Liepman, M. R., Silvia, L. Y., Begin, A. M., & Monti, P. M. (1990). Detoxification of alcoholics: Improving care by symptom-triggered sedation. *Alcoholism in Clinical and Experimental Research, 14,* 71–75.

Wasik, B. H., Ramey, C. T., Bryant, D. M., & Sparling, J. J. (1990). A longitudinal study of two early intervention strategies: Project CARE. *Child Development, 61,* 1682–1692.

Wass, R. S. (2008). Neuroanatomical and neurobehavioral effects of heavy prenatal alcohol exposure. In J. Brick (Ed.), *Handbook of the medical consequences of alcohol and drug abuse* (2nd ed., pp. 177–217). New York: Haworth Press.

Waterhouse, L., Morris, R., Allen, D., Dunn, M., Fein, D., Feinstein, C., et al. (1996). Diagnosis and classification in autism. *Journal of Autism and Developmental Disorders, 26,* 59–86.

Waters, A. M., & Craske, M. G. (2005). Generalized anxiety disorder. In M. M. Antony, D. R., Ledley, & R. G. Heimberg (Eds.), *Improving outcomes and preventing relapse in cognitive-behavioral therapy* (pp. 77–127). New York: Guilford Press.

Waters, E. (1995). Let's not wait till it's broke: Interventions to maintain and enhance mental health in late life. In M. Gatz (Ed.), *Emerging issues in mental health and aging* (pp. 183–209). Washington DC: American Psychological Association.

Watson, D. (2005). Rethinking the mood and anxiety disorders: A quantitative hierarchical model for DSM-V. *Journal of Abnormal Psychology, 114,* 522–536.

Watson, D., Wakiza, G., & Simms, L. J. (2005). Basic dimensions of temperament and their relation to anxiety and depression: A symptom-based perspective. *Journal of Research in Personality, 39,* 46–66.

Watson, J. B. (1913). Psychology as the behaviorist views it. *Psychological Review, 20,* 158–177.

Watson, J. B., & Rayner, R. (1920). Conditioned emotional reactions. *Journal of Experimental Psychology, 3,* 1–14.

Watson, T. L., & Andersen, A. E. (2003). A critical examination of the amenorrhea and weight criteria for diagnosing anorexia nervosa. *Acta Psychiatrica Scandinavica, 108,* 175–182.

Webster, C. D., Douglas, K. S., Eaves, D., & Hart, S. D. (1997). *HCR-20: Assessing risk for violence, version 2.* Burnaby, BC: Mental Health, Law, & Policy Institute, Simon Fraser University.

Webster-Stratton, C., & Reid, J. M. (2008). Preventing and treating conduct disorders. In A. E. Kazdin & J. R. Weisz (Eds.), *The incredible years parents, teachers, and children training series: A multifaceted treatment approach for young children with conduct problems* (pp. 224–240). New York: Guilford Press.

Webster-Stratton, C. H. (1996). *The incredible years: A guide for parents of children aged 2–8 years.* London: Lavis.

Weddington, W. W., Brown, B. S., Haertzen, M. H., Cone, E. J., Dax, E. M., Herning, R. I., & Michaelson, B. S. (1990). Changes in mood, craving, and sleep during short-term abstinence reported by male cocaine addicts. *Archives of General Psychiatry, 47,* 861–868.

Weems, C. F., Costa, N. M., Watts, S. E., Taylor, L. K., & Cannon, M. F. (2007). Cognitive errors, anxiety sensitivity, and anxiety control beliefs: Their unique and specific associations with childhood anxiety symptoms. *Behavior Modification, 31,* 174–201.

Weems, C. F., Silverman, W. K., & LaGreca, A. M. (2000). What do youth referred for anxiety problems worry about? Worry and its relation to anxiety and anxiety disorders in children and adolescents. *Journal of Abnormal Child Psychology, 28* (1), 63–72.

Wehmeyer, M. L., Palmer, S., Smith, S., Parent, W., Davies, D. K., & Stock, S. E. (2006). Technology use by people with intellectual and developmental disabilities to support employment activities: A single-subject design meta-analysis. *Journal of Vocational Rehabilitation, 24,* 81–86.

Weiler, B. L., & Widom, C. S. (1996). Psychopathy and violent behavior in abused and neglected young adults. *Criminal Behaviour and Mental Health, 6,* 253–271.

Weinberger, D. R. (1995). Schizophrenia as a neurodevelopment disorder: A review of the concept. In S. R. Hirsch & D. R. Weinberger (Eds.), *Schizophrenia* (pp. 293–323). London: Blackwood.

Weinberger, M., Hiner, S. L., & Tierney, W. M. (1987). In support of hassles as a measure of stress in predicting health outcomes. *Journal of Behavioral Medicine, 10,* 19–31.

Weiner, D. B. (1979). The apprenticeship of Philippe Pinel: A new document, "Observations of Citizen Pussin on the insane." *American Journal of Psychiatry, 136,* 1128–1134.

Weiner, H. (1996). Use of animal models in peptic ulcer disease. *Psychosomatic Medicine, 58,* 524–545.

Weisberg, R. B., Brown, T. A., Wincze, J. P., & Barlow, D. H. (2001). Causal attributions and male sexual arousal. *Journal of Abnormal Psychology, 110,* 324–334.

Weiss, B., & Weisz, J. R. (1995). Relative effectiveness of behavioral and nonbehavioral child psychotherapy. *Journal of Consulting and Clinical Psychology, 63,* 317–320.

Weiss, L. G., Saklofske, D. H., Coalson, D., & Raiford, S. E. (Eds.). (2010). *WAIS-IV: Clinical use and interpretation.* San Diego, CA: Academic Press.

Weiss, J. (1972). Psychological factors in stress and disease. *Scientific American, 226,* 104–113.

Weiss, J. M. (1970). Somatic effects of predictable and unpredictable shock. *Psychosomatic Medicine, 32,* 397–408.

Weiss, J. M. (1971). Effects of coping behavior with and without a feedback signal on stress pathology in rats. *Journal of Comparative and Physiological Psychology, 77,* 22–30.

Weissberg, R. P., & Greenberg, M. T. (1998). School and community competence-enhancement and prevention programs. In W. Damon (Series Ed.), I. E. Siegel & K. A. Renninger (Vol. Eds.), *Handbook of child psychology: Vol. 4. Child psychology in practice* (5th ed., pp. 877–954). New York: Wiley.

Weissberg, R. P., Kumpfer, K., & Seligman, M. E. P. (Eds.). (2003). Prevention that works for children and youth: An introduction. *American Psychologist, 58,* 425–432.

Weissman, M. M., Bland, R. C., Canino, G. J., Faravelli, C., Greenwald, S., Hwu, H. G., et al. (1997). The cross-national epidemiology of panic disorder. *Archives of General Psychiatry, 54,* 305–309.

Weissman, M. M., Leaf, P. J., Bruce, M. L., & Florio, L. (1988). The epidemiology of dysthymia in five communities: Rates, risks, comorbidity, and treatment. *American Journal of Psychiatry, 145,* 815–819.

Weissman, M. M., Myers, J. K., & Harding, P. S. (1978). Psychiatric disorders in a U.S. urban community: 1975–1976. *American Journal of Psychiatry, 135,* 459–462.

Weissman, M. M., Prusoff, B. A., DiMascio, A., Neu, Goklaney, & Klerman, G. (1979). The efficacy of drugs and psychotherapy in the treatment of acute depressive episodes. *American Journal of Psychiatry, 136* (4B), 555–558.

Weisz, J. R., Jensen-Doss, A., & Hawley, K. M. (2006). Evidence-based youth psychotherapies versus usual clinical care. *American Psychologist, 61,* 671–689.

Wells, A., & Papageorgiou, C. (1995). Worry and the incubation of intrusive images following stress. *Behaviour Research and Therapy, 33,* 579–583.

Wenzlaff, R. M., & Wegner, D. M. (2000). Thought suppression. *Annual Review of Psychology, 51,* 59–91.

Wertheim, E. H., Paxton, S. J., Schutx, H. K., & Muir, S. L. (1997). Why do adolescent girls watch their weight? An interview study examining sociocultural pressures to be thin. *Journal of Psychosomatic Research, 42,* 345–355.

West, M., Adam, K., Spreng, S., & Rose, S. (2001). Attachment disorganization and dissociative symptoms in clinically treated adolescents. *Canadian Journal of Psychiatry, 46,* 627–631.

West, M., Keller, A., Links, P. S., & Patrick, J. (1993). Borderline disorder and attachment pathology. *Canadian Journal of Psychiatry, 38,* 16–22.

West, R. (2006). *Theory of addiction.* Oxford, UK: Blackwell.

West, S. L., & O'Neal, K. K. (2004). Project D.A.R.E. outcome effectiveness revisited. *American Journal of Public Health, 94,* 1027–1029.

Westen, D., & Morrison, K. (2001). A multidimensional meta-analysis of treatments for depression, panic, and generalized anxiety disorder: An empirical examination of the status of empirically supported therapies. *Journal of Consulting and Clinical Psychology, 69,* 875–899.

Westra, H. A., & Stewart, S. H. (1998). Cognitive behavioural therapy and pharmacotherapy: Complementary or contradictory approaches to the treatment of anxiety? *Clinical Psychology Review, 18,* 307–340.

Westra, H. A., Stewart, S. H., Teehan, M., Johl, K., Dozois, D. J. A., & Hill, T. (2004). Benzodiazepine use associated with decreased memory for psychoeducation material in cognitive behavioral therapy for panic disorder. *Cognitive Therapy & Research, 28,* 193–208.

Wetherell, J. L., Afari, N., Ayers, C. R., Stoddard, J. A., Ruberg, J., Sorrell, J. T., et al. (2011). Acceptance and commitment therapy for generalized anxiety disorder in older adults: A preliminary report. *Behavior Therapy, 42,* 127–134.

Wharf, B. (1989). Implementing "Achieving health for all." *Canadian Review of Social Policy, 24,* 42–48.

Wheeler, D. L., Jacobson, J. W., Paglieri, R. A., & Schwartz, A. A. (1993). An experimental assessment of facilitated communication. *Mental Retardation, 31,* 49–60.

Wheeler, S., Book, A., & Costello, K. (2009). Psychopathic traits and perceptions of victim vulnerability. *Criminal Justice and Behavior, 36,* 635–648. doi:10.1177/0093854809333958

White, A. M., Jamieson-Drake, D. W., & Swartzwelder, H. S. (2002). Prevalence and correlates of alcohol-induced blackouts among college students: Results of an e-mail survey. *Journal of American College Health, 51,* 117–132.

White, C., Holland, E., Marsland, D., & Oakes, P. (2003). The identification of environments and cultures that promote the abuse of people with intellectual disabilities: A review of the literature. *Journal of Applied Research in Intellectual Disabilities, 16,* 1–9.

White, K. S., & Barlow, D. H. (2002). Specific phobias. In D. H. Barlow (Ed.), *Anxiety and its disorders* (2nd ed., pp. 328–379). New York: Guilford Press.

White, P. (2009, July 31). Rorschach and Wikipedia: The battle of the inkblots. *The Globe and Mail.* Retrieved from http://www.theglobeandmail.com

Whitman, B. Y. (2008). Human behavior genetics: Implications for neurodevelopmental disorders. In P. J. Accardo (Ed.), *Capute and Accardo's neurodevelopmental disabilities in infancy and childhood: Vol 1: Neurodevelopmental diagnosis and treatment* (3rd ed., pp. 175–197). Baltimore, MD: Paul H. Brookes.

Whittal, M. L., Agras, W. S., & Gould, R. A. (1999). Bulimia nervosa: A meta-analysis of psychosocial and pharmacological treatments. *Behavior Therapy, 30,* 117–135.

Whittal, M. L., Thordarson, D. S., & McLean, P. D. (2005). Treatment of obsessive-compulsive disorder: Cognitive behavior therapy vs. exposure and response prevention. *Behaviour Research and Therapy, 43,* 1559–1576.

Widiger, T. A., & Boyd, S. E. (2009). Personality disorders: Assessment instruments. In J. N. Butcher (Ed.), *Oxford handbook of personality assessment* (pp. 336–363). New York: Oxford University Press.

Widiger, T. A., & Clark, L. A. (2000). Toward DSM-V and the classification of psychopathology. *Psychological Bulletin, 126,* 946–963.

Widiger, T. A., & Frances, A. J. (1989). Epidemiology, diagnosis, and comorbidity of borderline personality disorder. In A. Tasman, R. E. Hales, & A. J. Frances (Eds.), *Review of Psychiatry* (Vol. 8, pp. 8–24). Washington, DC: American Psychiatric Press.

Widiger, T. A., Frances, A. J., & Trull, T. J. (1987). A psychometric analysis of the social-interpersonal and cognitive-perceptual items for the schizotypal personality disorder. *Archives of General Psychiatry, 44,* 741–745.

Widiger, T. A. & Lowe, J. R. (2010). Personality disorders. In M. M. Antony & D. H. Barlow (Eds.), *Handbook of assessment and treatment planning for psychological disorders* (2nd ed., pp. 571–605). New York: Guilford Press.

Widiger, T. A., Miele, G. M., & Tilly, S. M. (1992). Alternative perspectives on the diagnosis of borderline personality disorder. In J. F. Carkin, E. Marziali, & H. Munroe-Blum (Eds.), *Borderline personality disorder: Clinical and empirical perspectives* (pp. 89–115). New York: Guilford Press.

Widiger, T. A., & Rogers, J. H. (1989). Prevalence and comorbidity of personality disorders. *Psychiatric Annals, 19,* 132–136.

Widiger, T. A., & Spitzer, R. L. (1991). Sex bias in the diagnosis of personality disorders: Conceptual and methodological issues. *Clinical Psychology Review, 11,* 1–22.

Widiger, T. A., & Trull, T. J. (1991). Diagnosis and clinical assessment. *Annual Review of Psychology, 41,* 109–135.

Widiger, T. A., & Trull, T. J. (1992). Personality and psychopathology: An application of the five-factor model. *Journal of Personality, 60,* 363–393.

Widiger, T. A., & Trull, T. J. (1993). Borderline and narcissistic personality disorders. In P. B. Sutker & H. E. Adams (Eds.), *Comprehensive handbook of psychopathology* (2nd ed., pp. 371–397). New York: Plenum Press.

Widmer, E. D., Tread, J., & Newcomb, R. (1998). Attitudes toward nonmarital sex in 24 countries. *Journal of Sex Research, 35,* 349–358.

Wiederhold, B. K., & Wiederhold, M. D. (2004). *Virtual reality therapy for anxiety disorders: Advances in evaluation and treatment.* Washington, DC: American Psychological Association.

Wierzbicki, M., & Pekarik, G. (1993). A meta-analysis of psychotherapy dropout. *Professional Psychology: Research and Practice, 24,* 190–195.

Wikler, L., M., Wasow, M., & Hatfield, E. (1981). Chronic sorrow revisited: Parents vs. professional depiction of the adjustment of parents of mentally retarded children. *American Journal of Orthopsychiatry, 51,* 63–70.

Wilde, J. (2003, November 8). More than skin deep. *The Guardian.* Retrieved from http://www.guardian.co.uk/film/2003/nov/08/features

Wilens, T., McBurnett, K., Stein, M., Lerner, M., Spencer, T., & Wolraich, M. (2005). ADHD treatment with once-daily OROS methylphenidate: Final results from a long-term open-label study. *Journal of the American Academy of Child and Adolescent Psychiatry, 44,* 1015–1023.

Wilhelm, S., & Steketee, G. S. (2006). *Cognitive therapy for obsessive-compulsive disorder: A guide for professionals.* New York: New Harbinger.

Williams, J. H. G., & Ross, L. (2007). Consequences of prenatal toxin exposure for mental health in children and adolescents: A systematic review. *European Child and Adolescent Psychiatry, 16,* 243–253.

Williams, J. M., Mathews, A., & MacLeod, C. (1996). The emotional Stroop task and psychopathology. *Psychological Bulletin, 120,* 3–24.

Williams, J. M. G. (1997). *Cry of pain*. London: Penguin.

Williams, J. M. G. (2008). Mindfulness, depression and modes of mind. *Cognitive Therapy and Research, 32,* 721–733.

Williams, M., Teasdale, J., Segal, Z., & Kabat-Zinn, J. (2007). *The mindful way through depression: Freeing yourself from chronic unhappiness*. New York: Guilford Press.

Williams, R. B., Barefoot, J. C., Califf, R. M., Haney, T. L., Saunders, W. B., Pryor, D. B., et al. (1992). Prognostic importance of social and economic resources among medically treated patients with angiographically documented coronary artery disease. *Journal of the American Medical Association, 267,* 520–524.

Williamson, S., Hare, R. D., & Wong, S. (1987). Violence: Criminal psychopaths and their victims. *Canadian Journal of Behavioral Science, 19,* 454–462.

Williamson, S., Harpur, T. J., & Hare, R. D. (1991). Abnormal processing of affective words by psychopaths. *Psychophysiology, 28,* 260–273.

Willoughby, M. T. (2003). Developmental course of ADHD symptomatology during the transition from childhood to adolescence: A review with recommendations. *Journal of Child Psychology and Psychiatry, and Allied Disciplines, 44* (1), 88–106.

Wilson, D., Peters, R., Ritchie, K., & Ritchie, C. W. (2011). Latest advances on interventions that may prevent, delay or ameliorate dementia. *Therapeutic Advances in Chronic Disease, 2* (3), 161–173.

Wilson, D. S., Near, D., & Miller, R. R. (1996). Machiavellianism: A synthesis of the evolutionary and psychological literatures. *Psychological Bulletin, 119,* 285–299.

Wilson, G. T. (1999). Treatment of bulimia nervosa: The next decade. *European Eating Disorders Review, 7,* 77–83.

Wilson, G. T., & Lawson, D. M. (1976). Effects of alcohol on sexual arousal in women. *Journal of Abnormal Psychology, 85,* 489–497.

Wilson, K., Demetrioff, S., & Porter, S. (2008). A pawn by any other name? Social information processing as a function of psychopathic traits. *Journal of Research in Personality, 42,* 1651–1656. doi:10.1016/j.jrp.2008.07.006

Wilson, M., Joffe, R. T., & Wilkerson, B. (2000). The unheralded business crisis in Canada: Depression at work. Business and Economic Roundtable on Mental Health. Retrieved from http://www.mentalhealthroundtable.ca/aug_round_pdfs/Roundtable%20report_Jul20.pdf

Wilson, R. J., Abracen, J., Picheca, J. E., Malcolm, P. B., & Prinzo, M. (2003, October). Pedophilia: An evaluation of diagnostic and risk management methods. Paper presented at the 22nd Annual Research and Treatment Conference of the Association for the Treatment of Sexual Abusers, St Louis, MO.

Wilson, T. G. (1993). Psychological and pharmacological treatments of bulimia nervosa: A research update. *Applied and Preventative Psychology, 2,* 35–42.

Wilson, W. H., Ellinwood, E. H., Mathew, R. J., & Johnson, K. (1994). Effects of marijuana on performance of a computerized cognitive-neurological test battery. *Psychiatry Research, 51,* 115–125.

Wilson-Bates, F. (2008). *Lost in transition: How a lack of capacity in the mental health system is failing Vancouver's mentally ill and draining police resources.* Vancouver: Vancouver Police Department.

Wincze, J. P., Bach, A. K., & Barlow, D. H. (2008). Sexual dysfunction. In D. H. Barlow (Ed.), *Clinical handbook of psychological disorders: A step-by-step treatment manual* (pp. 615–661). New York: Guilford Press.

Wincze, J. P., & Carey, M. P. (2001). *Sexual dysfunction: A guide for assessment and treatment* (2nd ed.). New York: Guilford Press.

Wing, L., & Potter, D. (2002). The epidemiology of autistic spectrum disorders: Is the prevalence rising? *Mental Retardation and Developmental Disabilities Research Reviews, 8,* 151–161.

Wing, L., & Potter, D. (2009). The epidemiology of autism spectrum disorders: Is the prevalence rising? In S. Goldstein, J. Naglieri, & S. Ozonoff (Eds.), *Assessment of autism spectrum disorders* (pp. 18–54). New York: Guilford Press.

Winick, B. J. (2008). Civil commitment. In B. Cutler (Ed.), *Encyclopedia of psychology and law* (pp. 89–92). Thousand Oaks, CA: Sage.

Winzer-Serhan, U. H. (2008). Long term consequences of maternal smoking and developmental chronic nicotine exposure. *Frontiers in Bioscience, 13,* 636–649.

Wise, R. A., & Bozarth, M. A. (1987). A psychomotor stimulant theory of addiction. *Psychological Review, 94,* 469–492.

Wise, T. N., & Birket-Smith, M. (2002). The somatoform disorders for DSM-V: The need for changes in process and content. *Psychosomatics, 43,* 437–440.

Wiseman, C. V., Gray, J. J., Mosimann, J. E., & Ahrens, A. H. (1992). Cultural expectations of thinness in women: An update. *International Journal of Eating Disorders, 11,* 85–89.

Witkiewitz, K. &., & Marlatt, G. A. (2004). Relapse prevention for alcohol and drug problems. *American Psychologist, 59,* 224–235.

Wolery, M., & Bailey, D. B. (2002). Early childhood special education research. *Journal of Early Intervention, 25,* 88–99.

Wolfe, B. E., Metzger, E. D., & Jimerson, D. C. (1997). Research update on serotonin function in bulimia nervosa and anorexia nervosa. *Psychopharmacology Bulletin, 33,* 345–354.

Wolfensberger, W. (1972). *The principle of normalization in human services.* Toronto: Leonard Crainford.

Wolfensberger, W. (1975). *The origin and nature of our institutional models.* Syracuse, NY: Human Policy Press.

Wolfensberger, W. (2002). Needed or at least wanted: Sanity in the language wars. *Mental Retardation, 40,* 75–80.

Wolitzky-Taylor, K. B., Castriotta, N., Lenze, E. J., Stanley, M. A., & Craske, M. G. (2010). Anxiety disorders in older adults: A comprehensive review. *Depression and Anxiety, 27,* 190–211.

Wolpe, J. (1958). *Psychotherapy by reciprocal inhibition.* Stanford, CA: Stanford University Press.

Wolpe, J., & Rachman, S. (1960). Psychoanalytic evidence: A critique based on Freud's case of Little Hans. *Journal of Nervous and Mental Disease, 131,* 135–145.

Wong, D. F., Wagner, H. N., Jr., Tune, L. E., Dannals, R. F., Pearlson, G. D., Links, J. M., et al. (1986). Positron emission tomography reveals elevated D_2 dopamine receptors in drug-naive schizophrenics. *Science, 234,* 1558–1562.

Wong, S. (1984). *The criminal and institutional behaviors of psychopaths.* Programs Branch Users Report. Ottawa: Ministry of the Solicitor General of Canada.

Wong, S., & Hare, R. D. (2005). *Guidelines for a psychopathy treatment program.* Toronto: Multi-Health Systems.

Wood, J. M., & Lilienfeld, S. O. (1999). The Rorschach inkblot test: A case of overstatement? *Assessment, 6,* 341–351. doi:10.1177/107319119900600405

Woodhouse, K. W. (1993). Sleep disorders in the elderly. In R. Levy, R. Howard, & A. Burns (Eds.), *Treatment and care in old age psychiatry.* Petersfield, UK: Wrightson Biomedical Publishing.

Woodside, D. B., & Kaplan, A. S. (1994). Day hospital treatment in males with eating disorders—Response and comparison to females. *Journal of Psychosomatic Research, 38,* 471–475.

Woodworth, M., & Porter, S. (2002). In cold blood: Characteristics of criminal homicides as a function of psychopathy. *Journal of Abnormal Psychology, 111,* 436–445.

Woody, S. R., & Tolin, D. F. (2002). The relationship between disgust sensitivity and avoidant behaviour: Studies of clinical and nonclinical samples. *Anxiety Disorders, 16,* 543–559.

Woolfolk, R. L., & Allen, L. A. (2007). *Treating somatization: A cognitive-behavioral approach.* New York: Guilford Press.

Woolfolk, R. L., & Allen, L. A. (2010). Affective-cognitive behavioral therapy for somatization disorder. *Journal of Cognitive Psychotherapy, 24,* 116–131.

World Health Organization (1992). *International classification of diseases and related health problems* (10th rev.). Geneva: WHO.

World Health Organization. (2000). Cross-national comparisons of the prevalences and correlates of mental disorders. WHO International Consortium in Psychiatric Epidemiology. *Bulletin of the World Health Organization, 78* (4), 413–426.

World Health Organization. (2008). *Depression.* Retrieved from http://www.who.int/mental_health/management/depression/definition/en

Wright, D., Moran, J., & Gouglas, S. (2003). The confinement of the insane in Victorian Canada: The Hamilton and Toronto asylums. In R. Porter & D. Wright (Eds.). *The confinement of the insane: International perspectives, 1800–1965* (pp. 100–128). New York: Cambridge University Press.

Wrightsman, L. S., & Porter, S. (2005). *Forensic psychology* (1st Canadian ed.). Toronto: Thomson Nelson.

Wu, J. C., & Bunney, W. E. (1990). Sleep deprivation and relapse. *American Journal of Psychiatry, 147,* 14–21.

Wu, K. D., & Watson, D. (2005). Hoarding and its relation to obsessive-compulsive disorder. *Behaviour research and therapy, 43,* 897–921.

Wulsin, L. R., & Singal, B. M. (2003). Do depressive symptoms increase the risk for the onset of coronary disease? A systematic, quantitative review. *Psychosomatic Medicine, 65,* 201–210.

Wyatt Kaminski, J., Valle, L. A., Filene, J. H., & Boyle, C. L. (2008). A meta-analytic review of componenets associated with parent training program effectiveness. *Journal of Abnormal Child Psychology, 36,* 567–589. doi:10.1007/s10802-007-9201-9

Wykes, T., Huddy, V., Cellard, C., McGurk, S. R., & Czobor, P. (2011). A meta-analysis of cognitive remediation for schizophrenia: Methodology and effect sizes. *American Journal of Psychiatry, 168,* 472–485.

Wyngaarden, M. (1981). Interviewing mentally retarded persons: Issues and strategies. In R. Bruininks, C. E. Meyers, B. B. Sigford, & K. C. Lakin (Eds.), *Deinstitutionalization and community adjustment of mentally retarded people.* Monograph No. 4 (pp. 107–113). Washington, DC: American Association on Mental Deficiency.

Yang, M., Wong, S. C., & Coid, J. (2010). The efficacy of violence prediction: A meta-analytic comparison of nine risk assessment tools. *Psychological Bulletin, 136,* 740–767.

Yang, Y., Raine, A., Lencz, T., Bihrle, S., LaCasse, L., & Colletti, P. (2005). Volume reduction in prefrontal gray matter in unsuccessful criminal psychopaths. *Biological Psychiatry, 57,* 1103–1108.

Yassa, R., Dastoor, D., Nastase, C., Camille, Y., & Belzile, L. (1993). The prevalence of late-onset schizophrenia in a psychogeriatric population. *Journal of Geriatric Psychiatry and Neurology, 6,* 120–125.

Yates, P. M., Goguen, B. C., Nicholaichuk, T. P., Williams, S. M., Long, C. A., Jeglic, E., et al. (2000). *National sex offender programs (moderate, low, and maintenance intensity levels).* Ottawa: Correctional Service of Canada.

Yehuda, R., Golier, J. A., Halligan, S. L., Meaney, M., & Bierer, L. M. (2004). The ACTH response to dexamethasone in PTSD. *American Journal of Psychiatry, 161,* 1397–1403.

Yehuda, R., Halligan, S. L., Golier, J. A., Grossman, R., & Bierer, L. M. (2004). Effects of trauma exposure on the cortisol response to dexamethazone administration in PTSD and major depressive disorder. *Psychoneuroendocrinology, 29,* 389–404.

Yin, L., Wang, J., Klein, P. S., & Lazar, M. A. (2006). Nuclear receptor Rev-ErbA alpha is a critical lithium-sensitive component of the circadian clock. *Science, 311,* 1002–1005.

Young, A. H., & Hammond, J. M. (2007). Lithium in mood disorders: Increasing evidence base, declining use? *British Journal of Psychiatry, 191,* 474–476.

Young, J. E. (1994). *Cognitive therapy for personality disorders: A schema-focused approach* (rev. ed.). Sarasota, FL: Professional Resource Press.

Young, J. E. (1999). *Cognitive therapy for personality disorders: A schema-focused approach* (3rd ed.). Sarasota, FL: Professional Resource Press.

Young, J. E., Klosko, J. S., & Weishaar, M. E. (2003). *Schema therapy: A practitioner's guide.* New York: Guilford Press.

Young, T., Shahar, E., Nieto, F. J., Redline, S., Newman, A. B., Gottlieb, D. J., et al. (2002). Predictors of sleep-disordered breathing in community-dwelling adults. *Archives of Internal Medicine, 162,* 893–900.

Young, T. K. (1998). *Population health.* New York: Oxford University Press.

Youngren, M. A., & Lewinsohn, P. M. (1980). The functional relationship between depressed and problematic interpersonal behavior. *Journal of Abnormal Psychology, 89,* 333.

Youth Criminal Justice Act, R.S.C. 2002, c. 1.

Yu, S., Pritchard, M. D., Kremer, E., Lynch, M., Nancarrow, J., Baker, E., et al. (1991). Fragile X genotype characterized by an unstable region of DNA. *Science, 252,* 1179–1181.

Yusuf, S., Hawken, S., Ounpuu, S., Dans, T., Avezum, A., Lanas, F., McQueen, M., Budaj, A., Pais, P., Varigos, J., Lisheng, L., & the INTERHEART Study Investigators (2004). Effect of potentially modifiable risk factors associated with myocardial infarction in 52 countries (the INTERHEART study): Case-control study. *The Lancet, 364,* 937–952.

Zakowski, S. G., McAllister, C. G., Deal, M., & Baum, A. (1992). Stress, reactivity, and immune function in healthy men. *Health Psychology, 11,* 223–232.

Zammit, S., & Owen, M. J. (2006). Stressful live events, 5-HTT genotype and risk of depression. *British Journal of Psychiatry, 188,* 199–201.

Zanarini, M., Skodol, A., Bender, D., Dolan, R., Sanislow, C., Schaefer, E., et al. (2000). The Collaborative Longitudinal Personality Disorders Study: Reliability of Axis I and II diagnoses. *Journal of Personality Disorders, 14* (4), 291–299.

Zanarini, M. C., Frankenburg, F. R., Hennen, J., Reich, B., & Silk, K. R. (2005). The McLean study of adult development (MSAD): Overview and implications of the first six years of prospective follow-up. *Journal of Personality Disorders, 19,* 505–523.

Zapf, P. A., Golding, S. L., & Roesch, R. (2005). Criminal responsibility and the insanity defense. In I. B. Weiner & A. K. Hess (Eds.), *Handbook of forensic psychology* (3rd ed., pp. 332–363). New York: Wiley.

Zapf, P. A., & Roesch, R. (1997). Assessing fitness to stand trial: A comparison of institution-based evaluations and a brief screening interview. *Canadian Journal of Community Mental Health, 16,* 53–66.

Zapf, P. A., & Roesch, R. (1998). Fitness to stand trial: Characteristics of remands since the 1992 criminal code amendments. *Canadian Journal of Psychiatry, 43,* 287–293.

Zapf, P. A., & Roesch, R. (2009). *Best practices in forensic mental health assessments: Evaluation of competence to stand trial.* New York: Oxford University Press.

Zapf, P. A., Roesch, R., & Viljoen, J. L. (2001). Assessing fitness to stand trial: The utility of the Fitness Interview Test (revised edition). *Canadian Journal of Psychiatry, 46,* 426–432e.

Zarit, S. H., & Zarit, J. M. (1998). *Mental disorders in older adults: Fundamentals of assessment and treatment.* New York: Guilford Press.

Zemishlany, Z., Siever, L. J., & Coccaro, E. F. (1988). Biological factors in personality disorders. *Israel Journal of Psychiatry and Related Sciences, 25,* 12–23.

Zigler, E. (1967). Familial mental retardation: A continuing dilemma. *Science, 155,* 292–298.

Zigler, E., & Hodapp, R. M. (1991). *Understanding mental retardation.* Cambridge, UK: Cambridge University Press.

Zigler, E., Hodapp, R. M., & Edison, M. (1990). From theory to practice in the care and education of mentally retarded individuals. *American Journal on Mental Retardation, 95,* 1–12.

Zigman, W. B., Schupf, N., Lubin, R. A., & Silverman, W. P. (1987). Premature regression of adults with Down syndrome. *American Journal of Mental Deficiency, 92,* 161–168.

Zilboorg, G., & Henry, G. W. (1941). *A history of medical psychology.* New York: Norton.

Zimmerman, M. (1994). Diagnosing personality disorders: A review of issues and research methods. *Archives of General Psychiatry, 51,* 225–245.

Zimmerman, M., & Coryell, W. H. (1990). Diagnosing personality disorders in the community: A comparison of self-report and interview measures. *Archives of General Psychiatry, 47,* 527–531.

Zimmerman, M., Mattia, J. I., & Posternak, M. A. (2002). Are subjects in pharmacological treatment trials of depression representative of patients in routine clinical practice? *American Journal of Psychiatry, 159,* 469–473.

Zisook, S., & Kendler, K. S. (2007). Is bereavement-related depression different than non-bereavement-related depression? *Psychological Medicine, 37,* 779–794.

Zivian, M. T., Larsen, W., Knox, V. J., Gekoski, W. L., & Hatchette, V. (1992). Psychotherapy for the elderly: Psychotherapists' preferences. *Psychotherapy, 29,* 668–674.

Zlotnick, C. (1999). Antisocial personality disorder, affect dysregulation and childhood abuse among incarcerated women. *Journal of Personality Disorders, 13,* 90–95.

Zoccolillo, M., & Rogers, K. (1991). Characteristics and outcome of hospitalized adolescent girls with conduct disorder. *Journal of the American Academy of Child & Adolescent Psychiatry, 30* (6), 973–981.

Zoccolillo, M. (1993). Gender and the development of conduct disorder. *Development and Psychopathology, 5,* 65–78.

Zucker, K. J. (1990). Gender identity disorders in children. In R. Blanchard & B. W. Steiner (Eds.), *Clinical management of gender identity disorders in children and adults* (pp. 27–45). Washington, DC: American Psychiatry Press.

Zucker, K. J. (2005). Gender identity disorder in children and adolescence. *Annual Review of Clinical Psychology, 1,* 467–492.

Zucker, K. J. (2010a). The DSM diagnostic criteria for gender identity disorder in children. *Archives of Sexual Behavior, 39,* 477–498.

Zucker, K. J. (2010b). Reports from the DSM-V Work Group on Sexual and Gender Identity Disorders. *Archives of Sexual Behavior, 39,* 217–220.

Zucker, K. J., Beaulieu, N., Bradley, S. J., Grimshaw, G. M., & Wilcox, A. (2001). Handedness in boys with gender identity disorder. *Journal of Child Psychology and Psychiatry, 42,* 767–776.

Zucker, K. J., & Bradley, S. J. (1995). *Gender identity disorder and psychosexual problems in children and adolescents.* New York: Guilford Press.

Name Index

A

Abbott, A., 313
Abel, G., 348
Abel, G.G., 348, 354
Abelson, J.M., 180, 208
Abracen, J., 349
Abramowitz, J.S., 90, 112, 119, 125, 141, 142, 458
Abrams, K.Y., 135
Abramson, E.E., 246
Abramson, L.Y., 184
Acanfora, L., 366
Achenbach, T.M., 82, 343
Acion, L., 444
Ackerknect, E.H., 7, 17
Ackerly, S.S., 222
Adalf, E.M., 263–264
Adams, C., 445
Adams, E., 484
Adams, L.P., 198
Adams, M.R., 166
Adamson, S.J., 274
Addington, J., 230
Addis, M.E., 460
Ader, R., 153
Adessor, V.J., 268
Adlaf, E., 284
Adlaf, E.M., 287, 288
Adler, D.A., 61
Adler N.E., 45
Afifi, T.O., 111
Afifi, T.O., 492
Agarwal, P., 430
Agnello, C., 339
Agras, S., 237, 248
Agras, W.S., 243, 252, 253
Agrawal, A., 270
Aguiar, A., 398
Ahlborn, A., 158
Ahmad, S.A., 387
Ahmed, I., 422, 425–426
Ahrens, A.H., 245–246, 247
Aicardi, J., 380
Ainscow, M., 374
Akhtar, S., 320
Alavi, N., 189
Albee, G.W., 468, 470, 471, 473, 482, 484
Alcolado, G.M., 112
Alda, M., 186
Alden, L.E., 107, 108, 109
Alder, R.J., 403
Aleardi, M., 448
Alexander, F., 161, 450
Alexander, M.G., 328
Alexopoulous, G.S., 426
Alford, B.A., 39
Alford, B.A., 41
Alfredsson, L., 157
Alison, L., 347
Allardyce, J., 214
Allebeck, P., 432
Allen-Hauser, W., 138
Allen, K.L., 252
Allen, L.A., 140, 143–144
Alloy, L.B., 184
Almvik, R., 388
Alnaes, R., 303
Alonso, J., 419
Altemeier, W.A., 379
Alterman, A.I., 275, 300, 310
Althof, S., 334
Althof, S.E., 337, 339
Altmaier, E.M., 453
Aman, M.G., 382
Ambrogne, J.A., 274
Ames, E., 368
Amir, N., 40
Ammari, N., 216
Amminger, G.P., 382
Amos, N., 313
Amos, N.L., 312
Amsel, R., 329, 335
Amstadter, A.B., 461
an der Heiden, W., 208
Ancoli-Israel, S., 427, 429, 430
Andersen, A.E., 250
Andershed, H., 314
Anderson, A.E., 243
Anderson, B.J., 340
Anderson, C.A., 401
Anderson, C.S., 426
Anderson, D., 352
Anderson, G., 132
Anderson, J., 410
Anderson, J.C., 409
Anderson, K.N., 49
Anderson, L.E., 49
Anderson, S.W., 223, 405
Andreasen, N.C., 70
Andreasen, N.C., 208, 211–212
Andrés, S., 83–84
Andrews, G., 52, 117, 176
Angold, A., 58, 394, 403, 404, 409
Angus, L.E., 316
Anisman, H., 162
Annas, P., 410
Anstendig, K.D., 413
Antony, M.M., 74, 82, 102, 108, 122, 124, 452
Aos, S., 480
Applebaum, M.I., 478
Arbisi, P., 304
Arboleda-Florez, J., 310
Arboleda-Florez, J., 503
Arch, J., 90, 101, 102
Archer, J., 405
Archer, R., 79
Archer, R.P., 80
Arellano, B., 388
Arieti, S., 303
Arkowitz, H., 453
Armor, D.J., 274
Armstrong, J., 352
Armstrong, P.W., 166
Arndt, I.O., 283
Arrindell, W.A., 343
Arseneault, L., 405
Arterbutrn, D.E., 430
Asarnow, J.R., 221
Asarnow, R.F., 221
Åsberg, M., 200
Ashcroft, M.H., 386
Ashikaga, T., 432
Ashton, A.K., 339
Ashton, H., 126
Asmundson, G.J.G., 111, 119, 142
Asmussen, S., 43
Aspler, S., 366
Astin, J.A., 43
Astley, S.J., 270
Atkinson, L., 376
Atlis, M.M., 80
Attwood, M., 461
Aubry, T.D., 455
Auerbach, J.G., 304
Avery, D.H., 444
Awad, A.G., 216
Ax, R.K., 449
Aybek, S., 139
Ayers, C.R., 431–432
Ayuso-Mateos, L., 447

B

Babiak, P., 312
Babor, T., 268
Bach, A.K., 336
Bachrach, B., 11
Badger, G.J., 263
Badger, P., 505
Baer, R.A., 90
Baer, R.A., 43
Bagby, R.M., 183
Bagley, C., 198
Baglio, C., 382
Bahn, S., 215
Bailey, D., 270
Bailey, D.B., 369
Bailey, D.B., Jr., 372
Bailey, J.M., 330
Baillargeon, L., 427
Baines, G., 495
Baity, M.R., 80
Bajbouj, M., 197
Baker, D., 158
Baker, E., 480
Baker, L., 381
Baker, L.A., 301
Baker-Morrissette, S., 102
Baker, S.L., 102
Baker, S.M., 382
Bakermans-Kranenburg, M.J., 108, 135
Bakermans-Kranenburg, M.J., 40
Bakkevig, J.F., 302
Baldwin, L.-M., 182
Baldwin, S.A., 454
Balentine, A.C., 396
Baliunas, S., 270
Ball, S.A., 296
Balla, D.A., 362
Ballinger, B., 454
Baltes, M.M., 419, 423
Baltes, P.B., 419, 423
Bancroft, J., 332, 342
Banducci, A.N., 320
Bandura, A., 20, 39, 304
Banerjee, T.D., 398, 399
Banham, K.M., 420
Banks, D., 305
Banks, W.A., 169
Bar-Haim, Y., 40, 100, 108
Barasch, A., 315
Barbaree, H., 313
Barbaree, H.E., 299, 303, 348, 349, 350, 352, 354
Barber, J.P., 460
Barbui, C., 447
Barden, N., 32
Barefoot, J.C., 167, 169
Bargiotas, T., 225
Barker, C., 469
Barker, E.D., 404
Barker, G.J., 225
Barkley, R.A., 74, 396, 398, 401
Barlow, D.H., 100
Barlow, D.H., 30–31, 58, 84, 90, 97, 100, 101, 102, 103, 104, 117, 122, 124–125, 126, 176, 336, 337, 342, 452
Barlow, M.R., 131
Barnes, G.M., 273
Barnes, T.E., 445
Barnett, P.A., 167
Barnett, W.S., 471, 477
Baroff, G.S., 366
Baron, M., 316
Baron, R.A., 346
Barr, H.M., 367, 368
Barr, W.B., 71
Barrera, A.Z., 481
Barrera, M., 452
Barrett, F.M., 328
Barrett, P.M., 459, 460
Barrett, S., 350
Barry, C.T., 77, 314
Barry, D., 269
Barry, H., 268
Barry, S., 131
Barsky, A., 138
Barsky, A.J., 143
Bartels, S.J., 420, 433
Barth, J., 168
Bartholomew, A.A., 505
Bartholomew, K., 303, 316
Bartholow, B.D., 272
Bartlett, C.P., 248
Bartlett, P., 19
Barton, M., 377
Barton, R., 184
Bartu, A., 373
Bass, D., 458
Bass, D., 407
Bates, M.E., 269
Bathje, G.J., 43
Batshaw, M.L., 368
Battle, C., 304
Bauer, N.S., 304
Baum.A., 153
Baumal, Z., 182
Baumbach, J., 344
Baumeister, E.A., 388
Baumeister, R.F., 236
Bauminger, N., 387
Baur, K., 337
Baxter, L.R., 112, 372
Bay, M., 388
Baydala L., 61
Baym, C.L., 132
Bazzo, G., 375
Beach, S.R.H., 440
Beach, S.R.H., 461
Beal, L.S., 352
Beard, C., 40
Beardslee, W.R., 481
Beasley, E., 287
Beasley, R., 347
Beatty, M.J., 108
Beaulieu, N., 342
Bebko, J.M., 384
Beblo, T., 305
Bech, P., 447
Bechara, A., 405
Beck, A., 39
Beck, A.T., 26, 27, 39, 40, 41, 83, 97, 99, 121, 183, 184, 190, 191, 201, 228, 304, 320, 338, 452
Beck, A.T., 27, 39
Beck, J.G., 339, 431
Becker, B., 471
Becker-Blease, K.A., 135
Becker, E.S., 104
Becker, J.B., 151
Becker, J.V., 354
Becker, K., 399
Becker, K.A., 75
Beckwith, B.E., 32
Bedford, A., 310
Beech, A., 353
Beeghly, M., 370

Bégaud, B., 445
Begleiter, H., 272
Beidel, D.C., 319, 411
Beirness, D.J., 287
Beiser, M., 198
Belanger, A., 417
Belik, S., 425
Bell, J., 371
Bell, L., 386
Bellani, M., 316
Bellavance, F., 425
Bellissimo, A., 32
Belzile, L., 432
Bemporad, J.R., 234
Ben-Porath, Y.S., 79
Benavidez, D.A., 382
Benazzi, F., 425
Benbadis, S.R., 138
Bender, L., 71
Bender, W.N., 388
Bennett, A.E., 13
Bennett, K.J., 405, 407
Bennett, S., 100
Benowitz, N., 279
Bensing, J.M., 423
Benson, D.F., 435
Bentall, R.P., 211
Benton, A.L., 222
Berard, G., 384
Bergem, A.L., 437
Berger, P., 347
Bergeron, S., 335, 340
Bergin, A.E., 456
Berglund, P., 6, 101, 103–104, 108, 110
Bergman, A., 303
Bergman, L.R., 403
Berkman, L.F., 158
Berkman, N.D., 252
Berman, J.R., 336
Berman, L.A., 336
Berman, W.H., 316
Berner, W., 347, 353
Bernstein, C.P., 306
Bernstein, E.M., 131
Bernstein, S.M., 343
Berntson, G.G., 46
Berrios, G., 210
Berry-Kravis, E., 372
Berstein, C.A., 52
Bertini, G., 366
Bertschy, G., 286
Bethell, L., 261
Betz, N.E., 251
Beutler, L.E., 339, 340
Beutler, L.E., 455
Bewell, C., 250
Bewernick, B.H., 197
Beynon, S., 460
Bhasin, T.K., 381
Bialystok, E., 440
Bickel, W.K., 263
Biedel, D.C., 409
Biederman, J., 396–397, 404, 448
Biederman, T., 448
Bienvenu, O.J., 98
Bierer, L.M., 116
Bieri, K.A., 322
Bifulco, A., 472
Biggar, H., 473
Bihrle, S., 313
Billings, J.H., 170–171
Binder, J.L., 450
Binik, Y.M., 329, 335, 336, 338
Birbaumer, N., 108, 177
Birchall, H., 252
Birchwood, M., 229
Bird, T.D., 438
Bird, V., 460
Birkan, R., 366
Birket-Smith, M., 142, 302
Birmaher, B., 180, 403
Birnbaum, K., 302
Birren, J.E., 420
Birt, A.R., 307, 312
Birtchnell, S.A., 250
Bishop, E., 372
Bishop, S., 368
Bisson, J.I., 459
Bistricky, S.L., 94
Bitran, S., 102
Bittner, R.A., 215
Bjorntorp, P., 151
Black, B., 413
Black, D.N., 139
Black, D.W., 70, 336
Black, G.W., 167
Blackburn, R., 307
Blackmore, E., 248, 250, 255
Blackshaw, L., 353
Blair, R.J., 404
Blair, R.J.R., 309, 313, 403, 405
Blais, M.A., 80
Blake, D.D., 115
Blanchard, E.B., 354
Blanchard, R., 330, 342, 349
Blanchflower, D.G., 419
Bland, R., 498
Bland, R.R., 298
Blankstein, K.R., 200
Blashfield, R.K., 57, 300
Blatt, B., 360
Blatt, S.J., 183
Blazer, D., 434
Blazer, D.G., 178, 425, 426
Blegon, A., 200
Blennow, K., 313
Bleuler, E., 210, 211, 212, 216, 219
Bliwise, D.L., 429, 430
Blonigen, D.M., 313
Bloom, B.L., 471
Blum, H.P., 347
Blumenthal, S., 198
Boat, T., 468
Bockoven, J.S., 15
Bodin, S.D., 314
Bodkin, A., 131
Bodkin, J., 136
Boelen, P.A., 108
Boer, A., 498
Boer, D.P., 307, 312, 313
Boer, F., 116
Boeve, B.F., 435
Bögels, S.M., 108–109
Boggs, C.D., 300
Bohman, M., 91
Bohn, K., 240
Bohne, A., 138
Boivin, M., 405
Bollini, P., 459
Bolton, J.M., 302
Bolton, P.F., 376
Bonanno, R.A., 395
Bond, I., 353
Bond, J., 495
Bonnie, R., 494
Bonser, I., 318
Book, A., 312
Book, A.S., 312
Book, T.M., 382
Bookstein, F.L., 368
Booth-Kewley, S., 30
Booth, T., 363
Booth, W., 363
Bootzin, R.R., 429
Borduin, [illegible], 309
Borduin, C.M., 309
Boriakchanyavat, S., 329
Borkovec, T.D., 31, 117, 118, 119
Bornovalova, M.A., 301
Bornstein, R.F., 192, 295, 299
Borruto, F., 366
Borthwick-Duffy, S.A., 376
Bos, E.H., 444
Boscarino, J.A., 156
Bosch, J.A., 163
Botvin, E.M., 480
Botvin, E.M., 480
Botvin, G.J., 480
Botvin, G.J., 480
Bouaboula, M., 287
Bouchard, C., 484
Bouton, M.E., 103
Bowden, S., 76
Bowden, S.C., 269
Bowen, J.D., 435, 438
Bowen, R.C., 409
Bower, E., 40
Bowie, C.R., 211
Bowlby, J., 100, 303, 316
Bowman, E.S., 136
Boylan, K., 403
Boyle, C., 381
Boyle, C.L., 401
Boyle, M., 182, 400, 403, 407, 413
Boyle, M.H., 403, 409
Bozarth, M.A., 272
Braaten, E.B., 455
Brabban, A., 229
Braden, M.L., 372
Bradford, J.M., 348, 349, 353
Bradford, J.M.W., 328
Bradley, D.B., 189
Bradley, E.A., 376
Bradley, S.J., 342, 343
Bradshaw, A.J., 470, 480
Bradshaw, C.P., 44
Braff, D., 215
Braiker, H.B., 274
Bramon-Bosch, E., 250
Brand, B.L., 137
Brar, J., 453
Braun, D.L., 250
Breedlove, S.M., 151
Breen, R., 480
Breier, A., 432
Bremner, J.D., 132, 188
Bremner, R., 400
Brendgen, M., 405
Brenner, H.D., 229, 460
Brent, D., 410
Breslin, F.C., 290
Bresnahan, M., 208
Breton, J.J., 394
Brewer, M., 388
Brewerton, T.D., 244, 250
Brewin, C., 115, 116
Brezo, J., 411
Brickner, R.M., 222
Bridge, J.A., 447
Briere, J., 316
Briken, P., 353
Brink, J., 498
Brinker, J.K., 83
Brinkley, C.A., 313
Broadway, J., 432, 434, 437
Brochu, B., 270
Broderick, J.E., 419
Brodie, D.A., 161
Brody, N., 75
Broekman, B.F.P., 116
Broman-Fulks, J., 461
Bronfenbrenner, U., 474
Brook, J., 404
Brook, J.S., 208
Brooks, G.W., 432
Brotherson, M.J., 372, 373
Brotman, M.A., 404
Brotto, L.A., 333
Broussard, R., 360
Brower, M.C., 313
Brown, G.K., 201, 410
Brown, G.W., 185
Brown, G.W., 472, 473
Brown, I., 360, 363, 366, 374
Brown, J., 326
Brown, R.I., 374
Brown, R.J., 139
Brown, R.T., 401
Brown, S.L., 312
Brown, T.A., 102, 117, 176, 336, 337
Brown, T.A., 58
Browne, E.G., 11
Brownell, K.D., 45
Brownley, K.A., 252
Brownmiller, S., 351
Brozek, J., 244
Bruce, H., 105
Bruce, K., 256
Bruce, K.R., 245
Bruce, M.L., 178, 431
Bruce, M.L., 45
Bruch, H., 234, 249
Bruininks, R.H., 363
Brunner, R., 316
Bryan, S., 247
Bryan, T., 388
Bryant, D.M., 369
Bryant, R.A., 139
Bryde, R., 375
Bryer, J.B., 316
Bryson, S., 376
Bryson, S.E., 378, 384
Buchanan, R.W., 207
Buckley, D., 368
Budhani, S., 309, 403
Budney, A.J., 263, 288
Buffardi, L.E., 318
Buhin, L., 484
Bukatko, D., 75
Bukowski, W.M., 405
Bulik, C.M., 236, 249, 252
Bullough, V.L., 325
Bulmash, E., 183, 188
Bunner, M.R., 72
Bunney, W.E., 188
Burger, H.G., 330–331
Burgess, S., 447
Burke, J.D., 395, 403, 405
Burmeister, M., 187, 220
Burns, D.D., 126
Burns, J.F., 381
Burns, M.K., 385
Burris, S., 285
Burstein, K., 388
Burton, L.A., 71
Burueau, Y., 208
Bush, K.R., 84
Butcher, J.N., 79, 80
Butler, A.C., 191
Butler-Jones, D., 419
Buttner, G., 385, 386, 388
Bux, D.A., 125
Byer, C., 337
Byers, A.L., 431
Byers, E.S., 326, 328, 337, 347, 348
Byiers, B.J., 372
Byrd-Craven, J., 386
Byrne, B., 387
Byrne, D., 346
Byrne, S.M., 252

C

Cacciola, J.S., 300, 310
Cacioppo, J.T., 46
Cahill, C., 211
Cairney, J., 90, 419, 421, 425, 431
Cairns, A.L., 273
Cairns, B.D., 403
Cairns, J.C., 254

Cairns, R.B., 403
Cairo, T.A., 224
Calabrese, J.R., 306
Calamari, J.E., 112
Calder, P., 375
Calderbank, S., 143
Calderon, R., 254
Caldwell, A., 18
Calhoun, S., 387
Calhoun, S.L., 386
Calmes, C.A., 31
Camara, W.J., 71, 72, 77
Cambor, R., 278, 285, 287
Camille, Y., 432
Camilli, G., 471, 477
Campbell, E., 310
Campbell, F.A., 477
Campbell, L.A., 495
Campbell, M., 406
Campbell, M.A., 302, 313, 314
Campbell, W., 318
Campillo-Álvarez, Á., 306
Cannon, M., 221
Cannon, M.F., 40
Cannon, T.D., 223
Cantor-Graae, E., 217
Cantor, J., 352
Cantwell, D.P., 52, 381
Caplan, P.J., 44, 300
Caplan, R., 273
Cardena, E., 139
Carew, W.L.C., 168
Carey, G., 91, 309
Carey, M.P., 332, 333, 334, 335
Carlat, D.J., 251
Carlisle, J.M., 351
Carlson, E.A., 131, 135
Carlson, E.B., 131
Carlson, E.N., 318
Carlson, J., 84
Carlson, L.E., 43
Carlson, S.R., 313
Carmody, J., 43
Carnes, P., 335
Carney, R.M., 169
Carney, S., 196
Caron-Malenfant, E., 417
Carpenter, D., 426, 454
Carpenter, W.T., 207
Carr, E.G., 382
Carrier, S., 329
Carroll, D., 461
Carroll, R.A., 333, 344
Carson, A., 139
Carstensen, L.L., 423
Carter, A., 377, 378, 380
Carter, F.A., 236
Carter, J.C., 250, 255
Carter, M., 383
Cartwright-Hatton, S., 412
Caruso, S., 339
Carver, C., 337
Casanova, J.-D., 261
Case, R.B., 158
Cash, F., 248
Caspi, A., 32, 93, 272, 405–406
Caspi, A., 33
Cassidy, E.L., 431–432
Cassin, S.E., 453
Cassin, S.E., 453
Castano, R., 330
Castle, D., 432
Castle, D., 303
Castle, D.J., 142
Castriotta, N., 421
Catalan, J., 339
Cater, J., 406
Cavanagh, J., 188
Cawley, R., 319
Cebulla, M., 255
Cellard, C., 460
Cepeda, C., 405
Cercone, J., 461
Cernovsky, Z., 496
Chadwick, P., 229
Chamberlain, S., 340
Chamberlain, S.M., 335
Chamberland, C., 481
Chamberland, C., 482
Chambers, B., 375
Chambers, L., 170
Chambless, D.L., 462
Chambless, D.L., 462
Champagne, F., 352
Champion, H., 246
Chandler, J.J., 198
Chang, S.M., 6
Chaplin, W., 184
Chapman, A.L., 321, 322
Chapman, J.E., 191
Chapman, R.J., 370
Charavustra, A., 43
Charles, S.T., 423, 424, 426
Charman, R., 313
Charman, T., 383
Charney, D.S., 33, 70, 71, 90, 404
Chatfield, J., 400
Chau-Wong, M., 226
Cheetham, T., 366
Cheine, M., 445
Chelune, G.J., 222
Chen, E., 151
Chen, Y., 161
Cherry, C., 336
Cherry, S., 458
Chesney, M., 167
Cheung, A., 90
Cheung, C.K., 440
Cheung, R., 61
Chevron, E.S., 183, 191
Chhabra, S., 336
Chida, Y., 148, 160
Chien, H., 229
Chiodo, D., 481
Chipperfield, J., 432
Chiswick, D., 309
Chitsabesan, P., 412
Chiu, W.T., 100, 104, 110, 117
Chivers, M.L., 330
Chodosh, J., 426
Chong, S.l., 386
Chorpita, B.F., 104
Chou, K-L., 425
Chou, K-L., 432
Choy, Y., 124
Christiansen, B.A., 272
Christianson, S., 313
Chronis-Tuscano, A., 411
Chrousos, G.P., 151
Chu, A., 135
Chudley, A.E., 367
Churchill, R., 459
Ciaranello, R.D., 29
Cicchetti, D., 370
Cicchetti, D., 471
Cicchetti, D.V., 362
Cipriani, A., 447
Clara, I., 492
Clark, A., 496
Clark, D.A., 97, 99, 110, 121, 184
Clark, D.A., 26, 39, 40
Clark, D.B., 413
Clark, D.M., 103, 117, 125, 126
Clark, G., 182
Clark, L., 351
Clark, L.A., 50
Clark, L.A., 459
Clarke, B., 386
Clarke, C., 411
Clarke, D.M., 107, 108
Clarke, E., 367
Clarke, J.C., 104, 105
Clarke, M., 270
Clarkin, J., 315
Clarkin, J.F., 454
Clarkson, T.B., 166
Clarren, S., 270
Clarren, S.K., 270
Clary, C., 100
Classen, C.C., 137
Clayfield, J.C., 495
Cleghorn, J.M., 221
Clement, U., 333
Clinton, J., 395
Cloitre, M., 43, 90
Cloninger, C.R., 91, 304
Clopton, J.R., 80
Coalson, D., 76
Cobham, V.E., 412
Coccaro, E.F., 305, 405
Cohen, D., 335
Cohen, D.J., 380
Cohen, D.R., 335
Cohen, H.G., 382
Cohen, I., 498
Cohen, J., 263, 404
Cohen, J.M., 220
Cohen-Kettenis, P.T., 342, 343
Cohen-Kettenis, P.T., 342
Cohen, K.R., 448
Cohen, K.R., 455
Cohen-Mansfield, J., 438
Cohen, N., 77, 153
Cohen, N.L., 194
Cohen, P., 208, 295, 301, 303, 305, 306, 404
Cohen, S., 153, 160, 315, 410
Cohen, S., 43
Coid, J., 302, 307, 497
Colapinto, J., 342
Cole, J.O., 322
Cole, M.G., 425, 433, 434
Coles, M.E., 112
Colins, A.L., 280
Colledge, E., 313
Colletti, P., 313
Collier-Crespin, A., 382
Collimore, K.C., 142
Collins, A., 14
Collins, F., 381
Collins, K.A., 121, 126
Collins, M., 314
Collins, P., 304
Colter, S., 406–407
Comer, J.S., 111
Comparetto, C., 366
Compton, L.S., 382
Compton, W.M., 73
Conason, A.H., 244
Condillac, R.A., 376, 381
Connoly, J.A., 329
Connor-Greene, P.A., 251
Connor-Smith, J.K., 460
Connors, M.E., 250
Conrad, B.E., 120
Constante, M., 445
Cook, A.N., 498
Cook, E.P., 60
Cook, W., 167
Cooke, D.J., 313
Coolidge, F.L., 305, 342
Coon, D.W., 440
Coons, P.M., 102, 103, 131, 133, 135, 136, 303
Cooper, M., 198
Cooper, Z., 237, 243, 248, 252
Copeland, W.E., 404
Corcoran, R., 211
Corcos, M., 244
Cormier, C.A., 311, 314, 502
Corna, L.M., 421, 425, 431
Cornell, D.G., 312, 314
Cornwell, S.L., 399
Corrado, R., 198
Corrado, R.R., 498
Corrado, R.R., 498
Corrice, A.M., 372
Corrigan, P., 43, 208
Corrigan, P.W., 43
Corte, C., 249
Coryell, W., 301
Coryell, W.H., 317
Cosgrove, L., 62
Costa, N.M., 40
Costello, A., 411
Costello, E.J., 394, 404, 410
Costello, J., 403
Costello, J., 58
Costello, K., 312
Costello, R.M., 276
Côté, G., 309, 498
Cote, S.M., 404
Cottler, L.B., 73
Cotugno, A.J., 383
Covin, R., 39
Covin, R., 83, 126
Covinsky, K.E., 431
Cowen, E.L., 470, 481
Cowen, E.L., 477
Cowen, P.J., 245
Cox, B., 102
Cox, B.J., 314, 319
Cox, B.J., 492
Cox, D.J., 348
Cox, D.N., 498
Cox, M.L., 501
Coyne, J.C., 155, 184, 185
Coyne, L., 311
Craft, L., 200
Craig, K.D., 143
Craig, W., 481
Craighead, L.W., 451
Craighead, W.E., 451
Craik, F.I.M., 440
Crane, P.K., 430
Craske, M.G., 84, 90, 101, 102–103, 122, 421
Crawford, A., 200
Crawford, T.N., 295, 298
Creed, R., 138
Creed, T., 401
Crews, D., 151
Crick, N., 406
Crisanti, A.S., 503
Crisanti, A.S., 495
Crits-Christoph, P., 458, 460
Crnic, K., 373
Crocker, A.C., 369
Crook, K.H., 503, 504
Crooks, C.V., 481
Crooks, R., 337
Crosby, R., 249
Crosby, R.D., 254
Cross, P.K., 365
Crossley, N.A., 445
Crossley, R., 384
Croughan, J., 309
Crow, T.J., 220, 223
Crowley, K., 427, 429
Cruise, K.R., 388
Cruz, M.F., 263
Cuellar, J., 461
Cuijpers, P., 426
Cuijpers, P., 458, 481
Culbertson, J.L., 368
Cullen, A.E., 221
Cullinan, W.E., 151
Cummings, J., 481
Cummings, J.L., 435
Cummings, J.L., 30

Cummins, R.A., 373, 384
Cunningham, C.E., 400–401, 407, 413
Cunningham, J.A., 290
Cunningham, S.J., 86
Currie, G., 290
Currie, S.R., 290
Currier, D., 199
Currin, L., 237
Curtin, J.J., 309
Curtin, L., 288
Curtiss, G., 222
Cuskelly, M., 373, 375
Custer, R.L., 289
Cyranowski, J., 336
Czobor, P., 460

D

Dadds, M., 373
Dadds, M.R., 412
Daehler, M.W., 75
Dahlstrom, W.G., 79
Dalgleish, T., 116
Dallman, M.F., 151
Dalton, A.J., 370
Daly, B.P., 401
Daly, M., 428, 429
Daly, T., 382
Damasio, A., 405
Damasio, H., 223, 405
D'Amico, E.J., 453
Damm, J., 427
Dan, O., 100
Dancu, C.V., 319
Dannon, P.N., 197
Dansereau, D.F., 283
Darke, J.L., 351
Darke, S., 263
Darkes, J., 272
Das, A., 327
Das, P., 69, 139
Dastoor, D., 432
Daumann, J., 305
Dauphinais, P., 61
David, A.S., 139
David, D., 39
David-Ferdon, C., 460
Davidson, L., 156, 224
Davidson, M., 45, 221, 226
Davidson, P., 376, 377
Davidson, W.S., 276
Davies, D.K., 374
Davis, C., 248
Davis, D., 132, 221
Davis, D.D., 304
Davis, D.R., 273
Davis, K.L., 226, 304, 305
Davis, M., 375
Davis, R., 25
Davison, G.C., 157
Dawes, R.M., 61
Dawson, G., 384
Day, N.L., 270
Dayan, J., 384
de Graaf, R., 104
de Jong, P.J., 105
de Jonghe, F., 459
de Kruif, R., 386
de la Fuente, J.R., 268
De Leo, D., 410, 431
de Lima, M.S., 396
De Los Reyes, A., 393
de Maat, S.M., 459
De Oliveira-Souza, R., 313
de Ridder, D.T.D., 423
Deacon, B., 141
Deacon, B.J., 90, 458
Deal, M., 153
Dean, R.R., 29
Deaton, A., 419
Debeck, K., 480
Deckersbach, T., 138
Deeley, Q., 313
Deforce, D., 112
DeGroot, J.M., 249
Deihl, L., 118
Dekker, J., 459
Dekker, V., 444
Del Boca, F.K., 272
del Carmen, R., 208
Delaney, M.A., 406
Delaney, S.I., 276
Demetrioff, S., 312
Demler, O., 100
Demming, B., 272
den Boer, J.A., 134
Dennerstein, L., 330–331
Dennis, C.L., 468
Denys, D., 112
Depla, M.F.I.A., 104
Depue, R.A., 28, 304
DeRubeis, R.J., 191
DeRyck, B., 421
Derzon, J.H., 480
Desmarais, S., 327
DeStefano, F., 381
Deutsch, G., 387
Devlin, B., 409, 411
Dewa, C.S., 45
DeWall, C., 318
Di Giulio, G., 458
Diamond, D.B., 216
Diamond, J., 244
Diamond, M., 342
Dias, K., 380
Diaz, J.H., 105
Diaz, S.F., 142
Diaz, T., 480
Dickerson, F.B., 229
Dickey, C.C., 223
Dickey, R., 344
Dickson, H., 221
Dickstein, D.P., 404
Dickstein, S., 178
DiDomenico, L., 250
Diedrich, O., 109
Diefenbach, G.J., 100
Diener, E., 418
Dierberger, A., 252
Dietrich, T., 305
Diforio, D., 219
DiGiuseppe, R., 39
Dimeff, L.A., 461
Dimidjian, S., 191, 452
Dimsdale, J.E., 166
DiNardo, P., 102
Dion, K.L., 301
Dionne, G., 405
Dishion, T.J., 405, 406
Distel, M.A., 105
Dixon, J.F., 193
Dixon, K.L., 328
Dixon, L., 229
Dobson, D.J.G., 190, 452
Dobson, J.C., 366
Dobson, K., 190, 421
Dobson, K.S., 459
Dobson, K.S., 25, 39, 74, 82, 83, 90, 184, 190, 191, 452, 453
Dobson, K.S., 45, 459
Dobson, K.S.Muñoz, R., 481
Docherty, J.P., 426
Docter, R.F., 346
Dodge, K., 406
Dodge, K.A., 406
Doherty, D., 498
Dohrenwend, B.P., 200
Dohrenwend, B.P., 45
Dolan, B.M., 251
Dolan, C., 396–397
Doll, H.A., 237, 248
Donahey, K.M., 333
Done, D.J., 220
D'Onise, K., 477
Donnellan, A.M., 383
D'Onofrio, B.M., 405
Doren, D.M., 350
Dorer, D.J., 237
Dorey, G., 340
Dougherty, D., 112
Dougherty, L.R., 187
Douglas, K., 492
Douglas, K.D., 495
Douglas, K.S., 312, 314
Douglas, K.S., 496, 497
Douville, R., 261
Dowdney, L., 105
Dozois, D.J.A., 6, 8, 25, 26, 46, 50
Dozois, D.J.A., 21, 25, 26–27, 39, 40, 41, 45, 71, 74, 82, 83, 94, 99, 100, 108, 121, 126, 184, 185, 191, 452, 481
Dragt, S., 217
Draijer, N., 116
Drake, J., 352
Drake, J.L., 354
Drake, R.E., 299
Drake, R.E., 61
Drevets, W.C., 188
Drolette, M., 162
Drotar, D., 460
Drugge, J., 313
Dryden, W., 39
Dryden, W., 39
Drye, R.C., 315
Duberstein, P.R., 427
Dudley, E., 331
Duffy, M., 421
Duffy, S., 460
Dugas, M.J., 119, 126
Dukes, E., 375
Dunbar, S., 496
Duncan, J.C., 299
Dunham, H.W., 216
Dunn, E.J., 245
Dunn, T.W., 459
Dunsmoor, J.E., 98
DuPre, E.P., 483
Dupuy, P., 60
Durand, V.M., 342
Durkheim, E., 199
Durkin, M., 367
Durlak, J.A., 479, 483, 484
Durrant, S., 314
Dusenbury, L., 480
Dussault, D., 112
Dutton, D.G., 300, 303
Dvorak-Bertsch, J.D., 309
Dworkin, S.F., 140
Dyck, R., 498
Dykens, E.M., 364, 371, 372, 376
Dykman, B.M., 184
Dyrborg, J., 410
Dyson, L.L., 373
D'Zurilla, T.J., 453

E

Eagles, J.M., 237
Earle, J., 313
Earls, C.M., 354
Eaton, W.W., 44
Eaves, D., 497
Eaves, D., 501
Eaves, L.J., 405, 409, 411
Ebner, D., 314
Eccles, A., 348, 351
Eccles, W.J., 261
Eckenrode, J., 472, 473
Eckenrode, J., 478
Eddy, K.T., 242
Eddy, S., 388
Edelbrock, C., 343
Edelstein, B.A., 421
Edelsztein, H.S., 388
Edens, J.F., 306, 312
Edgar, E., 373
Edison, M., 362, 373
Egan, S.K., 312
Egeland, B., 100
Eggleston, A., 161
Egle, U.T., 143
Ehlers, A., 116, 125, 126
Ehlers, C.L., 188, 272
Eidelman, S., 361
Einstein, D.A., 111
El-Badri, S.R., 346
El-Gabalawy, R., 422
el-Guebaly, N., 290
El-Sakka, A., 339
Elias, M.J., 473
Elie, R., 322
Elkin, I., 459
Elksnin, L.K., 388
Elksnin, N., 387–388
Ellinwood, E.H., 287
Elliot, R., 450
Elliott, R., 451
Elliott, R., 458
Ellis, A., 39
Ellis, A., 39
Ellis, M., 314
Elston, M.A., 156
Emerson, E., 368, 376
Emery, E., 421
Emery, G., 39, 99, 121
Emrich, H.M., 135
Endicott, J., 100, 315
Endler, N.S., 82
Eng, M.U., 271
Engedal, K., 437
Engel, G.L., 148
Enns, M.W., 425
Epp, A., 90
Epp, J., 469
Erb, M., 108–109
Erdberg, P., 77
Ergul, C., 388
Ericson, M., 301
Erikson, E., 423
Erkani, A., 394
Erkanli, A., 58
Erlenmeyer-Kimling, L., 221
Erwin Ackerknecht, 7
EsbjØrn, B.H., 409–410
Escamilla, M.A., 425
Escobar, M., 387
Eshel, Y., 100
Espinel, A.I.G., 385
Esposito, E., 455
Essali, A., 445
Essex, M.J., 411
Esveldt-Dawson, K., 406
Etkin, A., 98
Eubig, P.A., 398
Evans, D., 353
Evans, G.W., 473
Evans, L.J., 388
Evans, R.G., 156, 157
Evans, S.M., 284
Everaerd, W., 337
Everson-Rose, S.A., 169
Evraire, L.E., 25, 26, 185
Exner, J.E., 77
Eyberg, S.M., 460
Ezpeleta, L., 58

F

Fabbri, S., 194
Fabiano, G.A., 460
Fabrega, H., 5
Faden, V., 269
Fagan, T.J., 449
Fagg, J., 339
Fahim, C., 70

Fairburn, C.G., 45, 237, 240–241, 242, 243, 245, 248, 252, 253, 255
Fallon, B.A., 112
Faraone, S.V., 397, 398, 448
Faris, R.E.L., 216
Farmer, A.E., 186
Farrell, L., 459
Farrell, M.P., 273
Farrington, D.P., 403
Fassbender, L.L., 383
Fava, G.A., 194
Fava, M., 190
Faw, G.D., 374
Fayyad, R., 100
Fedoroff, J.P., 353
Feehan, M., 410
Feeney, A., 158
Feeny, N.C., 125
Fehr, B., 302
Feightner, J., 438
Feinberg, M.E., 484
Feinstein, S.B., 112
Feldman, M., 376
Feldman, M.A., 376
Feldman, M.B., 251
Felten, D.L., 153
Fergus, S., 472
Fernandez, M.C., 379
Fernandez, Y.M., 349, 352, 354
Ferrari, L., 375
Ferriter, M., 303
Fetveit, A., 428, 429
Fichter, M., 255
Fichter, M.M., 242
Fick, D.M., 445
Fick, G.H., 290
Filene, J.H., 401
Filipek, P.A., 382
Findling, R.L., 406
Fine, J., 387
Fink, M., 444
Finkelhor, D., 353
Finlay, W.M.L., 363
Finlayson, M.A., 387
Finn, P.R., 272
Finucane, B.M., 364
Fiore, L.A., 139
Firestone, P., 328, 348, 349, 350, 406, 407
First, M.B., 74, 102
Fisak, B., 411
Fischbach, G.D., 71
Fischel, J.E., 396
Fischer, B., 263
Fischer, C., 405
Fischer, D., 488
Fischtein, D., 327
Fish, J.M., 32
Fishel, P.T., 379
Fisher, P., 200
Fisher, S., 192
Fisher, T.D., 328
Fisher, W.H., 495
Fiske, A., 425
Fitzgerald, H.E., 405
Flamenbaum, R., 200
Flanagan, E.H., 57
Flaum, M., 208–209, 211
Flay, B.R., 483
Flear, N., 448
Fleisher, W.P., 132
Fleming, D.T., 344
Fletcher, J., 387
Fletcher, J.M., 385, 387
Florio, L., 178
Flory, K., 398
Flynt, S.W., 372
Foa, E.B., 90, 110, 111, 116
Foerg, F.E., 263
Foley, D.L., 409, 410
Folkman, S., 155
Fombonne, E., 237, 377, 382
Fonagy, P., 462
Fonseca-Pedrero, E., 306
Foote, B., 132
Forbes, P., 481
Ford, M.R., 299, 300
Ford, T., 394
Fordyce, W.E., 148
Forehand, R., 461, 473
Forman, E.M., 191
Forman, M., 14
Forness, S.R., 388
Forsman, A., 313
Forsyth, J.P., 104
Forth, A.E., 314
Foster, J.R., 435, 436, 437, 439
Fothergill, C., 412
Fournier, J.C., 191, 193, 447
Fowler, C.H., 388
Fowler, D., 228
Fowler, R.C., 199
Fox, D.R., 480
Fox, J., 248
Frances, A., 59, 296, 315, 319
Frances, A.J., 299, 301
Francis, G., 409
Frangou, S., 225
Frank, E., 188, 192, 195, 336
Frank, E., 459
Frank, H., 316
Frankel, E.B., 369
Frankenberg, F.R., 295
Frankl, V., 42
Franklin, J.C., 244
Franklin, M., 245
Franklin, M.E., 90, 111, 125
Franko, D.L., 237, 242
Frasure-Smith, N., 168, 169
Fratiglioni, L., 435
Frautschi, N., 167
Frazier, P., 116
Frazier, T., 460
Freedland, K.E., 169
Freedman, B., 43
Freedman, M., 440
Freedman, M., 440
Freedman, R., 215
Freeland, J.T., 84
Freeman, A., 304
Freeman, D., 211
Freeman, M.R., 166
Freeman, N.L., 381
Freeman, R., 244
Freeman, S., 383
Freeston, M.H., 119
Freitas-Ferrari, M.C., 108
French, N.H., 406
French, T.M., 450
Frenkel-Brunswik, E., 420
Freud, Sigmund, 25
Freund, K., 348, 349, 351
Frewen, P.A., 27, 71, 108, 115
Frewen, P.A., 39
Freyd, J.J., 131
Frezza, M., 268
Frick, P.J., 77, 314
Friedman, B.H., 30–31, 118
Friedman, E.G., 366
Friedman, H.S., 30
Friedman, M., 170
Friedman, M.B., 431
Friedman, M.J., 113, 167
Frith, C.D., 211, 223
Froehlich, T.E., 398–399
Frohm, K.D., 168
Fromm-Reichmann, F., 216
Frost, S.J., 386
Frumin, M., 223
Fryer, A.J., 124
Fuchs, D., 386, 387
Fuchs, L., 387
Fudge Schormans, A., 368
Fulero, S.M., 312
Fung, M., 366
Funkenstein, D., 162
Furby, L., 353
Furnham, A., 246, 251
Fursland, A., 252
Furukawa, T.A., 459
Fyer, A.J., 458

G

Gabbard, G.O., 311
Gabreels, F., 361
Gabrielli, W.F., 272
Gacono, C., 310
Gacono, C.B., 314
Gado, M.H., 188
Gaebel, W., 214
Gagliese, L., 141
Gagne, A., 429
Gagnon, F., 119
Gagnon, J.H., 327
Gahagan, S., 368
Gahm, G.A., 461
Gallagher-Thompson, D., 440
Gallagher, T.J., 208
Galliano, G., 337
Galligan, P.T., 308
Garb, H.N., 62
Garcia, A., 438
Garcia-Coll, C., 411
García-Cueto, E., 306
Garcia, J., 242
Garcia, L.J., 440
Garcia, R., 98
Garcin, N., 372
Gardner-Schuster, E.E., 182
Garety, P., 211
Garety, P.A., 211, 228
Garfield, S.L., 456
Garfinkel, P.E., 237, 245
Garfinkel, R., 458
Gariepy, J.L., 403
Garland, A., 200
Garland, O.M., 468, 481
Garner, D.M., 243, 245, 250
Garner, J.B., 361
Garrick, T., 161
Garyfallos, G., 319
Gast, U., 134–135
Gaston, L., 450
Gatchel, R.I., 157
Gater, R., 189
Gatward, R., 394
Gatz, M., 418, 421, 425
Gawin, F.H., 283
Geary, D.C., 386, 387, 388
Gebhard, P.H., 326
Geddes, J.R., 447, 460
Gedye, A., 370
Geer, J.H., 157, 251
Geeraert, L., 478
Geffken, G., 388
Gekoski, W.L., 421
Gelernter, J., 270
Geller, J., 239
Geller, J.L., 495
Gendall, K., 244
Gendall, K.A., 236
Gendreau, P., 310, 311
Gentes, E.L., 119
Gentilcore-Saulnier, E., 340
George, E.I., 195
George, L.K., 425
George, M.S., 197
Gerardin, P., 406
Gerber, A.J., 458
Germain, A., 188
Gerrish, R., 274
Gershon, A.A., 197
Gershuny, B.S., 131
Gersons, B.P.R., 116
Gerstein, R.K., 184
Gersten, R., 386
Gerstley, L.J., 310
Gest, S.D., 403
Ghaziuddin, M., 387
Giacobbe, P., 444
Gibb, R., 28, 30
Gibbins, C., 397
Gibbon, M., 74, 102, 315
Gibbons, M.B.C., 458
Giesbrecht, T., 134
Giesen-Bloo, J., 321
Gigante, R.A., 136
Gilbertson, M.W., 116
Gilchrist, P.T., 112
Gillberg, C., 380
Gilmore, L., 375
Gilna, S., 337
Gilpin, N.W., 270
Giltz, M., 343
Gitlin, M.J., 193, 306–307, 322
Gitta, M., 366
Gittelman, R., 409
Gjedde, A., 226
Gladstone, J., 367
Gladstone, T.R.G., 481
Glaiser, J.T.D., 343
Glanze, W.D., 49
Glaser, R., 154, 160
Glass, G.V., 457
Glatt, A.E., 335
Glausiusz, J., 33
Gleaves, D.H., 132
Gleich, S.S., 4
Glidden, L.M., 372, 373, 381
Glithero, E., 137
Globe, A., 376
Glover, V., 411
Gmel, G., 269
Gnagy, E., 398
Gobrogge, K.L., 244
Goddard, H., 360
Goeckner, D.J., 268
Goeree, R., 208
Goettmann, C., 131
Goff, D., 211
Gold, S., 369
Goldapple, K., 71
Goldberg, J., 220
Goldberg, J.F., 193
Goldberg, R.L., 303
Goldberg, S.C., 306, 322
Golden, C.J., 72
Goldfinger, C., 340
Goldfried, M.R., 453
Goldie, R.S., 367
Golding, S.L., 501
Golding, S.L., 499
Goldman, M., 272
Goldman, M.S., 272
Goldsmith, H.H., 411
Goldstein, C., 100
Goldstein, D., 428, 440
Goldstein, G., 216
Goldstein, H., 383
Goldstein, I., 336
Goldstein, S., 388
Goldstein, T.F., 329, 339
Golier, J.A., 116
Gollan, J.K., 459
Gómez-Conesa, A., 90
Gonçalves, S., 237
Gonsalves, B.D., 132
Gonzalez, J.E.J., 385
Good, G.E., 43
Goodman J., 20
Goodman, R., 394, 403
Goodwin, G.M., 447
Gooren, L.J., 343
Gordon, B., 75

Gordon, K., 383
Gore, S., 472, 473
Gorery, K.M., 237
Gorman, J.M., 90, 458, 463
Gorman, L.L., 458
Gormley, W.T., 471, 483
Gortner, E.T., 459
Gorton, G., 320
Gosselin, C., 345
Gostin, L., 492
Gotlib, L.H., 27
Gotowiec, A., 198
Gottesman, I., 220
Gottesman, I.I., 215, 216, 219, 220
Gouglas, S., 19
Gould, M., 193, 200
Gould, R.A., 90, 252
Gould, S.J., 7
Gourlay, D.L., 282, 283
Grabe, S., 246
Grafman, J., 405
Graham, C.A., 329, 333, 334
Graham, D.Y., 163
Graham, J.R., 79
Graham, P., 393
Granholm, E., 433
Grant, B., 298
Grant, I., 312, 495, 496, 502, 503
Grant, J.E., 142
Grant, K., 263
Grant, M., 268
Grant, P., 27, 228
Grant, P.M., 229
Grant, P.M., 27
Graupner, T.D., 382
Gray, J., 496
Gray, J.E., 492, 494
Gray, J.J., 245–246, 247
Gray, S., 375
Greaves, G.B., 131, 135
Green, A.I., 320
Green, G., 382, 384
Green, M.F., 211
Green, N.S., 366
Green, R., 342, 344
Green, R.C., 426
Green, S.M., 401
Greenbaum, P.E., 272
Greenberg, B.S., 246
Greenberg, L., 448, 450, 451
Greenberg, L., 454
Greenberg, L.S., 451
Greenberg, L.S., 458
Greenberg, M.D., 192
Greenberg, M.T., 470
Greenberg, M.T., 484
Greenberg, R.P., 192
Greenberger, D., 122
Greene, R.L., 80
Greenfield-Spira, E., 396
Greenfield, T.K., 495
Greisberg, S., 112
Grenier, G., 326, 337
Greve, D.N., 225
Griesz, L.m., 246
Grietans, H., 478
Griffiths, D., 376
Griffiths, R.R., 284
Grigorenko, E.L., 388
Grills-Taquechel, A.E., 411
Grilo, C.M., 301
Grimbos, T., 330
Grimm, S., 197
Grimshaw, G.M., 342
Grinker, R.R., 315
Grisso, T., 505
Groen, A.D., 382
Grogan, S., 246
Gross-Isseroff, R., 200
Grossman, H.J., 361
Grossman, J., 377
Groth-Marnat, G., 71, 75, 76, 78
Grove, W.M., 68
Gruber, A., 136
Grudzinskas, A.J., 495
Gruen, R., 316
Grunhaus, L., 197
Guay, A., 336
Guerette, A., 427
Guijarro, J.L., 167
Guisado, J.A., 243
Gunderson, J.G., 315, 317
Gunter, T.D., 93
Gunzerath, L., 269, 270
Guo, G., 164
Guralnik, O., 134
Gutjahr, E., 269
Guyton, A.C., 152, 153

H

Haake, S., 43
Haas, E., 405
Hachett, M.L., 426
Hadjistavropoulos, H.D., 143
Hadjistavropoulos, T., 143
Hadley, T.R., 208
Häfner, H., 208
Hagberg, B., 380
Hage, S.M., 484
Hagen, L.C., 279
Hagerman, P.J., 364
Hagerman, R.J., 364, 372
Hagstrom, A., 349
Hahlweg, K., 460
Hahn, J., 80
Häkkänen-Nyholm, H., 311
Haldipur, C.V., 208
Hall, A.E., 108
Hall, D., 253–254
Hall, G.C.N., 353
Hall, J.R., 399
Hallak, J.E.C., 108
Hallet, J., 167
Hallett, L.A., 190
Halligan, S.L., 116
Hallmayer, J., 298
Hallquist, M.N., 315
Halmi, K.A., 250
Halperin, J.M., 396, 398
Hamilton, S., 61
Hammen, C., 185
Hammen, C.L., 193
Hammer, L., 248
Hammond, J.M., 447
Hampel, H., 215
Hampton, S., 482
Hancock, J., 313
Hand, D., 4
Handelsman, M.M., 455
Hanrahan, G.E., 227
Hans, A.L., 304
Hansen, P.E., 197
Hanson, A., 459
Hanson, K.R., 311
Hanson, R.K., 354
Hanusa, B.H., 182
Harari, D., 135
Harburg, E., 273
Harding, C.M., 432
Harding, K., 178
Harding, P.S., 138
Harding, T.W., 312
Hardy, J.D., 168
Hare, A.S., 303
Hare, E., 209
Hare, R.D., 301, 302, 307, 308, 309, 311, 312, 313, 314, 315, 501
Harkness, K.L., 183, 185–186, 188, 189
Harley, M., 221
Harlow, J.M., 222
Harper, S., 136
Harpur, T.J., 307, 313
Harrington, R., 147, 412
Harris, G.T., 311, 312, 313, 314, 350, 351, 353, 354
Harris, G.T., 502
Harris, J.C., 366
Harris, K., 373
Harris, M.J., 432
Harris, M.S., 215
Harris, T.O., 185
Harris, T.O., 472
Harris, W.R., 405
Harris, W.W., 135
Harrison, P., 362–363
Harrison, P.J., 225
Harriss, L., 410
Harrow, M., 211
Hart, S.D., 497
Hart, S.D., 307, 309, 311–312, 314, 490, 497
Hart, S.D., 498, 501
Hartmann, U., 336
Hartung, C.M., 60
Harvey, P.D., 211, 228, 432
Hasher, L., 428, 440
Haslam, J., 209
Hasselhorn, M., 385, 386, 388
Hastings, R., 370
Hastings, R.P., 372, 373
Hatchett, G.T., 456
Hatchette, V., 421
Hatfield, E., 373
Hatton, C., 368, 376
Hatzichristou, D.G., 339
Hatzimouratidis, K., 339
Hawe, P., 483
Hawgood, J., 431
Haworth-Hoeppner, S., 248
Hawton, K., 339, 410, 447
Hay, P., 241, 242
Hay, P.J., 254
Hayashida, M., 275
Hayden, E., 46
Hayden, E.P., 187
Hayes, S.C., 452
Hayman-Abello, S.E., 387
Haynes, R.B., 443
Haynes, S.G., 158
He, W., 417
Healey, V., 163
Heard, H.L., 321
Hearon, B., 458
Heath, A.C., 411
Heatherton, T.F., 236
Heaton, R.K., 223
Heavey, C.L., 352
Hebb, D.O., 221
Heber, R., 362
Hechtman, L., 399
Hecker, M.H.L., 167
Hedtke, K., 412
Heim, A., 303
Heim, C., 32
Heim, C., 188
Heimberg, R.G., 124, 319
Heinberg, L.J., 246
Heinrichs, R.W., 206, 210, 215, 216, 217, 218, 221, 222, 223, 224, 226
Heinrichs, W., 228
Heisel, A.D., 108
Heisel, M.J., 425
Heiser, K., 330
Hellekson, K.L., 26
Heller, M.R., 29
Heller, T.L., 193
Heller, T.S., 410
Helmes, E., 495
Helms, J.E., 61
Helzer, J.E., 309, 498
Hemnann, N., 431
Hemphill, J.F., 312
Hen, R., 98
Henderson, J., 328
Henderson, K.A., 247
Henderson, S., 419
Hendriks, G.J., 432
Heng, K., 453
Hengeveld, M.W., 334
Henggeler, S.W., 309
Henin, A., 411
Henke, P.G., 161
Hennen, J., 295
Henriques, G., 40
Henry, G.W., 11
Henry, J.D., 419
Henry, W.P., 450
Henry, W.P., 458
Herbener, E.S., 215
Herbert, T.B., 153, 160
Herman, C.P., 246, 248, 249
Herman, J.P., 151
Hernandez, P., 62
Herold, D.S., 327
Herpertz, S.C., 305
Herrmann-Lingen, C., 168
Herrnstein, R., 32
Hershkowitz, D., 208
Herzog, D.B., 237
Hesketh, L., 370
Hesse, E., 135
Hetrick, S., 413
Hettema, J.E., 277
Hettema, J.M., 98, 102
Heun, R., 298
Hicks, B.M., 301, 313
Hicks, M., 270
Hiem, C., 353
Higenbottam, J., 496
Higgenbottam, J., 496
Higgins, S.T., 263, 283
Hildebrandt, M., 452
Hilgard, E.R., 131
Hill, A., 347
Hill, A.B., 162
Hill, B.K., 363
Hill, S.K., 215
Hill, S.Y., 272
Hiller, W., 140
Hiner, S.L., 155
Hinrichsen, G.A., 421
Hinshaw, S.P., 45, 401, 403, 404, 405, 463
Hiripi, E., 403
Hirsch, C.R., 107, 108
Hirschfeld, R., 178
Hirschman, R., 353
Hisfield-Becker, D.R., 411
Hoag, H., 444
Hoard, M.K., 386
Hobson, J., 314
Hobson, K.M., 328
Hobson, R.P., 303
Hoch, C.C., 430
Hodapp, R.M., 362, 364, 371–372, 373
Hodgins, C., 406
Hodgins, D.C., 274, 290
Hodgins, S., 221, 309
Hodgins, S., 498
Hodkinson, S., 303, 352
Hoefnagels, C., 44
Hoehn-Saric, R., 447
Hock, H.W., 237
Hoeyer, M., 410
Hoffman, E.J., 120
Hoffman, P.L., 272

Hoffmann, P.L., 285
Hofmann, S.G., 90, 104, 124
Hofschire, L.J., 246
Hogan, M.E., 184
Hokin, L.E., 193
Holahan, C.J., 185
Holcomb, P.J., 211
Holden, J.J.A., 371, 372
Holden, R.R., 200
Holland, E., 375
Holley, H.L., 310
Hollinghurst, S., 461
Hollingshead, A.B., 61
Hollon, S.D., 191
Hollon, S.D., 452, 459
Holloway, S., 374
Holmes, C., 180
Holmes, T.H., 155
Holt, C.S., 319
Holt, S.E., 313
Holzman, P.S., 215
Homan, K., 246
Homel, R., 471
Hoogduin, C.A.L., 432
Hook, E.B., 365
Hooley, J.M., 221
Hoon, E.F., 160
Hooper, S., 386
Hopcroft, R.L., 189
Hope, D.A., 319
Hope, R.A., 253
Hopko, D.R., 386
Hopwood, C.J., 80, 320
Horen, S.A., 132
Horner, R.H., 382
Horney, K., 318
Horng, B., 112
Horowitz, A.V., 177
Horowitz, L.M., 184
Horta, B.L., 396
Horvath, A.T., 276
Horwitz, S., 454
Hosie, J.A., 419
Hospers, H.J., 251
Houck, P., 336
House, J.S., 158
Houts, A.C., 5
Hovell, M., 453
Howard, J.S., 382
Howard, K.I., 455
Howard, R., 303, 432
Howes, O.D., 226
Howland, R.H., 187, 188
Howlin, P., 383
Hrabosky, J.I., 248
Hu, S., 118
Hua, J.M., 394
Hua, J.M., 468, 481
Huang, A., 250
Huang, Y., 302
Hubbard, R.W., 425
Huddy, V., 460
Hudson, J.I., 136, 251
Hudson, J.L., 111, 131
Hudson, S.M., 303, 352
Huettell, S., 223
Hughes, D.C., 425
Hughes, H., 481
Hughes, J.R., 288
Hughes, M.W., 374
Hughes, S., 396–397
Huh, G.A., 27
Humphreys, K., 274, 469
Humphreys, K., 495
Hunot, V., 286
Hunsley, J., 56, 78, 190, 448, 454, 455
Hunsley, J., 454, 458, 462
Hunt, S., 376
Hunter, D., 237
Hunter, J.M., 15
Hurd, H.M., 19
Hurley, R.A., 139
Hurley, S.F., 285
Hursch, C.J., 353
Hurt, S., 315
Husain, N.F., 430
Husband, J., 223
Husted, J., 166
Huston, L., 100
Huta, V., 108
Huws, J., 370
Hwang, P., 161
Hyde, J.S., 328
Hylton, J.H., 502
Hymel, S., 395, 405

I

Iacono, W.G., 301, 313
Ickeowicz, I., 367
Ihl, R., 438
Ijzendoorn, M.J., 40
Ilardi, S.S., 451
Imbierowicz, K., 143
Ingram, R.E., 40, 44, 46, 94
Innes, K.E., 430
Innis, R.B., 70
Intelisano, G., 339
Inz, J., 118
Iosifescu, D., 190
Ireland, D., 480
Ironson, G., 166, 168
Irvine, J., 169, 171
Isaacowitz, D.M., 419, 423
Isaacson, R.S., 437–438
Israel, M., 245, 256
Ivis, F.J., 284

J

Jackson, A., 80, 188
Jackson, D.N., 299
Jackson, S.C., 237
Jackson, S.W., 175
Jacob, S., 385
Jacobs, G.D., 460
Jacobson, J.W., 384
Jacobson, N.S., 191, 459
Jacobson, N.S., 459, 460
Jaffe, A.S., 168
Jaffe, J.H., 279
Jaffe, P.G., 481
Jaffee, S.R., 406
Jamieson-Drake, D.W., 269
Jamison, K., 447
Jamison, K.R., 180
Jang, K.L., 111, 135, 299, 303, 305
Jannini, E.A., 334
Jansen, A., 251
Janssen, E., 329
Janus, C., 336
Janus, S.S., 336
Jarrett, R.B., 459
Jaskulski, C., 377
Jenike, M.A., 111, 112, 138
Jenkins, M.R., 368
Jennings, J.R., 167
Jensen, A.R., 32
Jensen-Doss, A., 461
Jensen, P.S., 393
Jeste, D.V., 208, 421, 432
Jick, H., 237
Jiménez, J.A., 70
Jimerson, D.C., 245
Jindal, R., 187
Joe, G.W., 283
Joffe, J.M., 470, 484
Joffe, R., 182
Joffe, R.T., 176, 319
Johansson, P., 314
Johnson, C., 250
Johnson, C.P., 379
Johnson, D.J., 387
Johnson, J., 319
Johnson, J.G., 132, 208, 295
Johnson, J.G., 461
Johnson, K., 287
Johnson, S.M., 454
Johnson, V.E., 326, 328, 331–332, 337, 338
Johnston, C., 190, 239
Johnston, M., 208
Johnston, M.I., 237
Johnstone, E.C., 223
Joiner, T.E., 185
Joiner, T.E., Jr., 185
Jolliffe, D., 403
Jones, D.J., 461
Jones, P.B., 221
Jones, R., 253, 352
Jones, R.D., 223
Jones, W.R., 250
Joormann, J., 27
Jorge, R.E., 444
Joshi, I., 382
Joshi, R., 246
Joyce, P.R., 236
Joyce, T., 376
Juby, H., 4
Julien, R.M., 226, 227
Jung, C.G., 216
Junghan, U.M., 460
Juodis, M., 312
Jurado, A.R., 330

K

Kabak, L., 287
Kabat-Zinn, J., 20, 43, 90, 191
Kado, D.M., 426
Kaemmer, B., 79
Kafka, M.P., 336, 345
Kagan, J., 108, 411
Kahana, S., 460
Kahn, R.S., 226
Kaijser, V.G., 343
Kalb, L.M., 403
Kalberg, W.O., 368
Kalick.S.M., 106
Kalin, N., 98
Kalin, N.H., 411
Kamin, L.J., 91
Kamphaus, R.W., 75, 77
Kanaan, R.A., 139
Kane, J.M., 227
Kanfer, F.H., 83
Kanner, A.D., 155
Kanner, L., 381, 393
Kaplan, A.S., 240, 250
Kaplan, F.M., 360
Kaplan, G.A., 161
Kaplan, H.I., 30
Kaplan, H.S., 330, 332, 336
Kaplan, J.R., 166
Kaplan, M., 132, 299
Kapur, S., 226
Kar, N., 90
Karasek, R.A., 158
Karel, M.J., 418, 421
Karg, K., 187
Karl, A., 116
Karlamangla, A.S., 426
Karlberg, A.M., 198
Karlin, B.E., 421
Karlsgodt, K.H., 223
Karnesh, L.J., 13
Karon, B.P., 228
Karterud, S., 302
Kasai, K., 223
Kasari, C., 379, 383
Kaschak, E., 60
Kasen, S., 295
Kashdan, T.B., 109
Kasl-Godley, J.E., 418
Kaslow, N.J., 460
Kates, N., 455
Katz, I.R., 426
Katz, J., 141, 185
Katz, L.Y., 314, 447
Katz, R., 186
Katzir, R., 386
Kaufman, F.L., 168
Kaufman, L., 314
Kaul, S.S., 369
Kavale, K.A., 388
Kawai, M., 61
Kawarai, T., 437
Kay, G.G., 222
Kaye, W., 244
Kaye, W.H., 244, 249
Kazarian, S.S., 229
Kazdin, A.E., 93, 458
Kazdin, A.E., 86, 393, 403, 406, 407
Kazdin, A.E., 461
Keane, S.P., 305
Keck, P.E., Jr., 445
Keefe, R.S.E., 228
Keel, P.K., 237, 242
Keeler, G., 58
Keeley, J., 57
Keenan, K., 401
Keijsers, G.P.J., 432
Keith, C.R., 342
Keith, S.J., 228
Keller, A., 303
Keller, E., 375
Keller, M.B., 194
Kelly, T., 299
Kelsey, J.E., 29
Kelsoe, J.R., 186
Kendall, C., 460
Kendall, P.C., 111
Kendall, P.C., 410, 412, 461
Kendall-Tackett, M., 153
Kendler, K.S., 32, 98, 176, 177, 186, 208, 220, 249, 305, 306, 411, 412
Keng, S.L., 43
Kennedy, B., 386
Kennedy, B.D., 85
Kennedy, J.L., 220
Kennedy, P., 351
Kennedy, P.J., 313
Kennedy, S., 249
Kennedy, S.H., 126, 194, 444
Kenny, M.E., 484
Kermis, M.D., 420
Kernberg, O.F., 315, 320
Kerr, M., 314
Kerr, T., 480
Keshavan, M., 220
Keshavan, M.S., 112, 208
Kessel, B., 330
Kessler, R.C., 6, 100, 101, 104, 108, 110, 116, 117, 177–178, 180, 208, 298, 403, 411, 419, 455
Kety, S.S., 199
Keuthen, N.J., 138
Kewman, D.G., 453
Keyes, C.L.M., 470
Keys, A., 244
Keys, D.J., 319
Keyser, J., 184
Khalifé, S., 335, 336
Khan, R.S., 399
Khan, S.A., 398
Khanna, M.S., 461
Khaykin, Y., 169
Kho, K.H., 196
Khodaverdian, A., 377

Kidd, P.M., 382
Kiecolt-Glaser, J.K., 154
Kiehl, K.A., 313
Kihlstrom, J.F., 129, 132, 136
Killeen, T.K., 275
Kim-Cohen, J., 403
Kim, M.J., 98
Kincaid, C., 461
King, D.W., 115
King, J., 61
King, L.A., 115
King, P., 495
King, S., 162, 367
Kingdon, D.G., 228, 229
Kingston, D.A., 347, 348, 349, 350
Kino, T., 151
Kinsella, K., 417
Kinsey, A.C., 326, 332, 334, 336
Kinston, W., 320
Kirby, M.J.L., 20, 482
Kirk, S.A., 62
Kirmayer, L.J., 106, 135, 138, 140, 142, 143, 198
Kirschbaum, C., 169
Kisely, S., 495
Kitzman, H., 478
Kivimaki, M., 158
Kivlahan, D.R., 84
Kivnick, H., 484
Klaver, J.R., 314
Kleber, H.D., 283
Klein, D.A., 245
Klein, D.N., 56, 178, 187, 297, 299
Klein, M.H., 411
Klein, P.S., 193
Klein, R.G., 406
Kleinknecht, R.A., 105
Klerman, G.L., 143, 191, 315, 319
Klin, A., 377, 380, 387
Klingler, T., 298
Klomek, A.B., 244
Kloosterman, P.H., 74
Klose, U., 108–109
Klosko, J.S., 40, 304
Klosko, J.S., 39, 40
Kloth, G., 336
Kluft, R., 132, 135, 136
Klump, K.L., 244, 245
Knight, B.G., 421
Knight, R., 315
Knittel-Keren, D., 367
Knöchel, C., 215
Knock, K., 377
Knopman, D.S., 435, 436, 437, 439
Knowles, J.B., 188
Knox, V.J., 421
Knutelska, M., 134
Ko, G., 226
Koch, R., 366
Koch, W.J., 492
Kocsis, J.H., 193
Koegel, L., 383
Koegel, L.K., 383
Koegel, R.L., 382
Koerner, N., 100
Kogan, C.S., 372
Kogevinas, M., 156
Kohut, H., 320
Kolb, B., 28, 30
Komer, W.J., 496
Komiya, N., 43
König, H.H., 100
Konnert, C., 421
Konnert, C.A., 421
Konnopka, A., 100
Konopasky, A.W.R., 349
Konopasky, R.J., 349
Koob, G.F., 270
Kop, W., 168
Koren, D., 211
Koren, G., 367
Korenman, S.G., 336
Kornish, K.M., 372
Korten, A., 189
Koss, M.P., 350
Kosson, D., 314
Koster, E., 111
Kotchick, B.A., 473
Kovacs, M., 409, 411
Kozak, M.J., 110, 111
Kraemer, H.C., 253
Kraepelin, E., 210, 211, 212, 216, 219, 221–222, 224, 227
Krafft-Ebing, R.V., 303, 326, 335
Kragel, P.A., 98
Kral, M., 198
Krantz, D.S., 166
Kranzler, H.R., 270
Kratochwill, T.R., 84
Krause, J.A., 386
Kreel, L., 223
Kreher, D.A., 211
Kreitman, N., 200
Kresin, D., 337
Krimsky, S., 62
Kringlen, E., 437
Krishnamurthy, R., 80
Krittayaphong, R., 169
Kroenke, K., 142, 143
Krol, P.K., 316
Kroll, J., 11
Kroncke, A.P., 75
Krueger, R.B., 346
Krueger, R.F., 57, 313
Krueger, R.F., 52
Krull, D.S., 185
Krystal, J.H., 70
Ksir, C., 265
Kuban, M., 351
Kubicki, M., 223
Kuehn, B.M., 377
Kuipers, E., 228, 460
Kukkonen, T.M., 329
Kukull, W.A., 435, 438
Kumar, P., 334
Kumpfer, K., 476
Kupelnick, B., 459
Kuper, H., 158
Kuperberg, G.R., 211, 225
Kupfer, D., 336
Kupfer, D.J., 188
Kurcgant, D., 139
Kuriychuk, M., 311
Kurtz, J.E., 80
Kurtz, M.M., 229
Kushida, E., 366
Kutcher, M.J., 482
Kutchins, H., 62
Kuyken, W., 191
Kyriakopoulos, M., 225
Kyrios, M., 112

L

Laan, E., 330
LaBar, K., 98
LaCasse, L., 313
Lacey, J.H., 250
LaCroix, A.Z., 158
Ladouceur, R., 119
LaFrance, B.H., 108
Lagopoulos, J., 69
LaGreca, A.M., 409
Lahey, B.B., 395, 396, 401, 405
Lakshmanan, B.M., 225
Lalonde, C., 198
Lalonde, J.K., 106
Lalumiere, M.L., 313, 330, 351, 354
Lam, D.H., 195
Lam, K.S.L., 382
Lam, R., 182, 196
Lam, R.W., 193
Lambert, M.T., 200
Lamont, J.A., 335
Lampert, C., 244
Lamy, D., 40
Lamy, D., 108
Lanctot, K.L., 438
Landau-Stanton, J., 454
Landfield, K., 4
Landfield, K., 5, 7, 53
Landis, K.R., 158
Landon, P.B., 310
Landreville, P., 427
Landry, J., 427
Lane, M.C., 298
Lane, S.E., 386
Lang, A.R., 268
Lang, R., 354
Lange, P., 32
Langeland, W., 116
Langer, A., 166
Langevin, R., 349, 354
Langford, D., 312
Langley, R.L., 105
Långström, N., 346, 348
Lanin-Kettering, L., 211
Lanius, R.A., 27, 71, 115
Laroi, F., 210
Larsen, W., 421
Lasecki, K.L., 84
Last, C.G., 409
Latane, B., 303
Latty, E., 330
Lau, A.L.D., 373
Laumann, E.O., 327, 332, 333, 336
Laurendeau, M.-C., 482
Laurens, K.R., 221
Lavigne, J.V., 396
Lawler, M., 248
Lawlor, T., 495
Lawrence, A., 344
Lawrence, P.J., 110
Lawson, A., 273
Lawson, D.M., 268
Lawson, G., 273
Lawson, J.S., 132
Lazar, M.A., 193
Lazarus, R.S., 155, 156
Le Couteur, A., 381
le Grange, D., 254
Leaf, P.J., 45
Leaf, P.J., 178
LeBeau, R.T., 104
LeCavalier, J., 287
Leckman, J.F., 371–372
Ledingham, J., 406, 407
Ledley, D.R., 124
LeDoux, J.E., 30, 98, 161
Ledwidge, B., 496
Lee, A.H., 373
Lee, B.A., 371
Lee, C.M., 462
Lee, C.M., 56, 454
Lee, C.M., 455
Lee, S.S., 45, 396, 403, 404, 405
Lee, T., 225, 226
Lee, T.C., 105
Lee, Z., 314
Leeuw, I., 124
Legatt, M.E., 132
Legault, S.E., 166
Lehert, P., 331
Lehman, A., 229
Lehman, C.L., 104
Lehman, D., 316
Lehmann, H.E., 227
Leibenluft, E., 404
Leibing, E., 100
Leiblum, S.R., 337
Leichner, P., 254
Leichner, P.P., 132
Leichsenring, F., 100
Leichsenring, F., 458, 460
Leigh, G., 274
Leiper, R., 376
Leitenberg, H., 40
Lejuez, C.W., 320–321
Lemanek, K.L., 379
Lemieux, L., 405
Lemos-Giráldez, S., 306
Lencz, T., 313
Lentz, V., 302
Lenze, E.J., 421, 431
Lenzenweger, M.F., 298, 299, 309
Lenzi, A., 334
Leon, A., 304
Leon, J., 440
Leon, W.J., 20, 482
Leonard, A., 313
Leonard, H., 361
Leonardo, E.D., 98
Lepage, P., 245
Lepine, J., 419
Lépine, J., 106
LeResche, L., 140
Lerner, J.W., 387
Lerner, S.R., 387
Lesage, A., 322
Lesage, A., 455
Lesch, K.P., 32
Leskin, G.A., 115
Lesperance, F., 168
Letarte, H., 118–119
Leth, I., 409–410
Leucht, S., 447
Levander, S., 388
Levenson, J.S., 349
Levenstein, S., 161, 163, 164
Leventhal, B.L., 254
Levin, M., 452
Levin, R.A., 303, 319
Levine, E.S., 62
Levine, M.P., 246, 248, 250
Levine, S.B., 332
Levine, T.R., 108
Levitan, R., 182
Levitan, R.D., 245
Levitt, A., 90, 182, 196
Levitt, E.E., 97
Levitt, M., 316
Levy, D.L., 215
Levy, T.M., 303
Lew, A., 185
Lewinsohn, P.M., 184, 452
Lewis, D., 351–352
Lewis, T.T., 169
Lewkis, S., 363
Lewontin, R.C., 91
Leykin, Y., 481
Lezak, M.D., 222
Liang, K., 425
Libby, A.M., 447
Libby, P., 169
Lichtenstein, P., 410
Lichtermann, D., 298
Lidke, G., 8
Lieb, R., 480
Lieberman, A., 426
Lieberman, A.F., 135
Liebowitz, M.R., 112
Lietaer, G., 450, 458
Lilenfeld, L.R., 249
Lilenfeld, L.R.R., 249
Lilienfeld, S.O., 4, 5, 314
Lilienfeld, S.O., 5, 7, 53
Limosin, F., 220
Linden, W., 170
Lindsley, O.R., 451
Lindstrom, B.D., 388
Linehan, M., 461
Linehan, M.M., 304, 316, 321, 460
Link, B.G., 208

Link, B.G., 43
Links, P.S., 303, 316
Linz, D., 352
Liotti, G., 135
Lippens, T., 421
Lipschitz, D., 132
Lipsitz, J.D., 124
Lipsitz, J.D., 458
Liss, A., 108
Liss, M., 449
Lister-Sharp, D.J., 480
Liu, M.M., 161
Livesley, W.J., 135, 299, 303, 306
Llewellyn, G., 375
Lloyd M., 68
Lobban, M., 237
Lochner, C., 250, 319
Lock, J., 254
Locke, J., 272
Loeb, K.L., 254
Loeber, R., 352, 395, 401, 403, 404, 405
Loftus, E.F., 132, 316
Logan, A.G., 171
Logsdon, R.G., 427, 438
Lohr, J.B., 208
Lohr, J.M., 105
Lohr, K., 280
Lohr, K.N., 252
Lombardo, F., 334
Loney, J., 396
Long, J.S., 382
Lonigan, C.J., 385, 386
Looper, K.J., 138, 143
Lopez, A.D., 177
Lopez, M., 427
Lopez, S.R., 62
LoPiccolo, J., 339, 340
Loranger, A.W., 298
Lord, C., 368, 378, 379, 381
Lorion, R.P., 477
Lösel, F., 354
Lösel, F., 314
Lotze, M., 108–109
Louden, J.E., 314
Loukas, A., 405
Lovaas, O.I., 382, 383
Love E.J., 495
Love, J.M., 481
Lovering, J.S., 370
Lovett, B.J., 405
Lowe, J.R., 74
Lowenstein, L., 345, 346
Lowers, L., 272
Lu, B.Y., 422, 425–426
Lubin, R.A., 370
Luborsky, L., 456, 458
Luborsky, L., 458
Lubs, H.A., 371
Lucas, R.E., 419
Luciana, M., 304
Luckasson, R., 362
Lucksted, A., 229
Luczak, S.E., 271
Lue, T.F., 329
Luebbert, J.F., 406
Lukens, E., 229
Lumley, C.H., 200
Lumley, M.N., 183, 186
Lunsky, Y., 377
Lupo, L., 339
Luterek, J.A., 115
Luthar, S.S., 471, 472
Lutke, J., 367
Lutzker, J., 483
Lux, L., 280
Lykins, E.L.B., 43
Lykken, D.T., 307, 309
Lymburner, A., 484
Lynam, D.R., 296, 314, 396, 403
Lynch, C., 375, 483
Lynch, J.W., 471, 477
Lyness, J.M., 427
Lynett, E., 299, 301
Lynn, S.J., 135
Lynskey, M.T., 270
Lyon, D.R., 312
Lyons, E., 363
Lyonsfields, J.D., 118

M

MacCrimmon, D.J., 221
Macdonald, M.L., 276
Macedo, C.A., 405
Machado, B.C., 237
Machado, P.P.P., 237
Machado, P.P.P., 455
Machalek, K., 366
Mackenzie, C., 440
Mackenzie, C.S., 419, 421, 422, 425, 426, 431, 432, 440
MacKenzie, J.J., 371
MacKnight, C., 438
MacLennan, A., 284
MacLeod, C., 99
MacLeod, J., 478
MacNeil, P., 284
Madsen, K., 239
Maehler, C., 386
Maes, H., 405
Maes, H.M., 409
Maffei, C., 299
Magee, L., 124
Magiati, I., 383
Magnusson, D., 82, 403
Maher, B.A., 8
Maher, W.B., 8
Mahler, M.S., 303
Maier, W., 298
Mailloux, G., 340
Main, M., 135
Major, M., 427
Malamuth, N.M., 352
Malarkey, W.B., 154
Malcolm, P.B., 349
Malhi, G.S., 69
Malian, I., 388
Malik, N., 229
Malkoff-Schwartz, S., 188
Malla, A., 495
Malla, A.K., 229
Mallon, J.C., 299
Malone, R.P., 406
Maloney, B., 187
Maltzman, I.M., 274
Mammarella, I.C., 385
Manassis, K., 410
Mancini-Marïe, A., 70
Mandamin-Cameron, R., 368
Mangweth, B., 251
Manhem, A., 313
Manley, M., 432
Mann, J.J., 199, 200
Mann, L.S., 303
Mann, R.E., 263
Manning, M., 471, 477
Mansell, S., 375
Mansell, W., 108–109
Mansour, A., 425
Manuck, S.B., 166, 167
Mao, X., 160
Marance, W., 380
Marchand, A., 119
Marchand, P., 361
Marchetti, R.L., 139
Marchildon, G.P., 449
Marcouiller, M., 322
Marcus, D.K., 306
Marcus, J., 304
Marcus, M.D., 252
Marcus, S.C., 427, 447, 455
Margolin, G., 460
Margraf, J., 140
Marín-Martínez, F., 90
Marino, L., 5
Markman, H.J., 460
Markovitz, P.J., 322
Markovitz, P.M., 306
Markowitz, J.C., 191
Markowitz, J.C., 458
Marlatt, G.A., 268, 272, 277
Marmot, M., 158
Marmot, M.G., 156, 157, 158
Marshall, K., 289
Marshall, L.A., 313
Marshall, L.E., 349, 352, 354
Marshall, W.L., 25, 299, 303, 348, 349, 350, 351, 352, 354
Marsland, D., 375
Martel, L., 417
Martel, M.M., 399
Martell, C., 452
Martin, C.C., 435, 436, 437, 439
Martin, C.E., 326
Martin, J., 43
Martin, J.P., 371
Martin, N.G., 411
Martin, S.L., 369
Martinot, J.L., 226
Martinot, M.-L.P., 187
Martire, L.M., 440
Marxer, F., 158
Marziali, E., 316, 440
Mash, E.J., 74
Mash, E.J., 6, 8, 25, 46, 50
Maslow, A., 42
Maslow, Abraham, 25
Massie, H., 345
Masters, W.H., 326, 328, 331, 332, 337, 338
Masterson, C.C., 305
Masuda, M., 155
Mather, A., 421
Mather, N., 388
Mathew, R.J., 287
Mathew, S.J., 120
Mathews, A., 99
Maticka-Tyndale, E., 328
Matson, J.L., 382, 383
Matsunaga, H., 244
Matteau, E., 427
Matthews, C., 484
Matthews, J., 375
Matthysse, S., 215
Mattia, J.I., 445
Matusiewicz, A.K., 320
Maughan, B., 404
Maulik, P.K., 44
Mavreas, V.G., 189
May, C.P., 428
May, R., 42
Mayberg, H.S., 188, 197
Mayes, S.D., 386, 387
Mayfiel, J., 480
Mayou.R., 142
Mazur, E., 40
Mazurick, J.L., 406
Mazzacco, M., 386
Mazzocco, M.M.M., 372
McAllister, C.G., 153
McBride, W.G., 368
McBurnett, K., 405
McCabe, R., 239
McCabe, R.E., 108, 124
McCain, M.N., 482
McCarley, R.W., 223
McCarthy, G., 223
McCarthy, M., 375
McCarthy, M.M., 151
McClain, E., 280
McClellan, A.T., 283
McClure, K.S., 82
McConnell, S.R., 384
McCord, J., 303, 313
McCord, W., 303, 313
McCormack, W.M., 335
McCrady, B.S., 276
McCullough, J.P., 178
McCurry, S.M., 427, 430, 438
McDermid Vaz, S., 216
McDermott, R.A., 471, 477
McDonald, C., 183
McDougall, C.J., 382
McDougall, P., 395, 405
McDougle, C.J., 382
McElroy, S.L., 445, 447
McEwan, K., 481
McEwan, K., 394, 468, 481
McEwan, K., 482
McFall, M.E., 84
McFarlane, A.H., 32
McFarlane, T., 239
McFarlane, W.R., 229
McGee, G.G., 382
McGee, R., 409, 410
McGlashan, T.H., 306
McGlashan, T.M., 315
McGonagle, K.A., 178
McGrath, P.J., 447
McGue, M., 270, 272, 301
McGuffin, P., 32, 186, 219, 411
McGuire, B.E., 375
McGuire, P., 445
McGuire, R.J., 351
McGurk, S.R., 208, 229
McGurk, S.R., 460
McHolm, A., 413
McHolm, A.E., 413
McHugo, G.J., 229
McInnis, M.G., 220
McIntosh, J.L., 425
McIntosh, V.V., 252
McKay, D., 111, 112, 119
McKee, L.G., 461
McKenzie, J., 413
McKnight, J., 475
McLachlan, D.R., 370
McLachlin, B., 488
McLaughlin, A.E., 477
McLaughlin, K.A., 412
McLean, L., 340
McLean, P.D., 124
McLeod, P.J., 4
McMain, S.F., 321
McNally, R.J., 25, 103
McNary, S.W., 137
McNicholas, F., 248
McQueen, P.C., 361
McVey, G., 249, 255
McVilly, K.R., 374
Meadows, E.A., 82
Meagher, S.E., 80
Mealey, L., 309, 313
Meana, M., 335
Meaney, M., 116
Meares, R., 320
Medley, D., 167
Mednick, S.A., 405
Meehl, P.E., 68, 221
Meesters, C., 44
Meesters, Y., 444
Mega, M.S., 30
Mehdizadeh, S., 318
Mehta, R., 229
Meichenbaum, D., 451
Meichenbaum, D., 20
Melhuish, E.C., 471, 477
Melnyk, W.T., 449
Meloy, J.R., 313
Melton, G.B., 490
Melton, G.B., 492, 503
Mcltzer, H., 394
Meltzer, H.Y., 227, 306
Melvin, C., 280

Melzack, R., 140, 148
Mencl, W.E., 386
Mendell, N.R., 215
Mendlewicz, J., 186
Mendrek, A., 70
Menendez, C., 330
Menlove, F.L., 39
Menzies, R.G., 104, 105, 111
Mercer, L., 405
Mercier, L., 453
Merckelbach, H., 105, 111
Meredith, L.S., 453
Merikangas, K.R., 298, 394, 395
Merrick, J., 366
Merry, S., 413
Merskey, H., 130, 136
Mesaros, R.A., 383
Messenger, J.C., 328
Messick, S., 80
Metz, M.E., 337
Metzger, D.S., 283
Metzger, E.D., 245
Metzger, L.J., 116
Metzke, C.W., 237
Meulman, J.J., 242
Meyer, G.J., 67, 85, 344
Meyer, I.H., 251
Meyers, B.S., 421
Meyers, W.S., 342
Mezzich, J.E., 61
Micco, J.A., 411
Michael, R.T., 327
Michaels, S., 327
Mick, E., 396
Middleton, F., 398
Miele, G.M., 315
Mikail, S., 190
Miklowitz, D.J., 195, 460
Miles, A.A., 216
Miles, C., 199
Miles, D.R., 309
Miles, J.N.V., 453
Milich, R., 396
Millar, J., 285
Miller, G.A., 315
Miller, G.E., 151, 169
Miller, H.R., 237
Miller, J., 209
Miller, J.B., 316
Miller, J.G., 211
Miller, K., 387
Miller, M., 480
Miller, M.N., 234
Miller, R.R., 302
Miller, S., 387
Miller, T.I., 457
Miller, T.Q., 167
Miller, W.R., 277, 290
Miller, W.R., 453
Millman, R.B., 278, 285, 287
Millon, T., 25, 52, 80, 299, 301, 302, 315, 318–319
Mills, D.E., 166, 168
Mills, J., 246, 248
Milne, A.B., 419
Milne, R., 274
Milner, B., 223
Milte, K., 505
Mimeault, V., 429
Minabe, Y., 61
Mineka, S., 103
Miner, J., 20
Minhas, S., 334
Minnes, P., 367, 372, 373, 375
Minnes, P.M., 372, 373, 375, 384
Mintun, M.A., 188
Mintz, L., 251
Mintzer, J., 432, 434, 437
Miranda, J., 40
Mirenda, P.L., 383
Mischel, W., 82, 184
Mishna, F., 388
Mitchell, A.J., 426
Mitchell, D., 110
Mitchell, D.G.V., 309, 313, 403
Mitchell, J., 249
Mitchell, J., 460
Mitka, M., 339
Mittal, V., 219
Moberg, P.J., 216
Mock, D., 386
Mody, M., 385, 386
Moehle, K.A., 97
Moffitt, T.E., 272, 309, 313, 403, 405
Mohlman, J., 431
Mohr, D.C., 339, 340
Mojtabai, R., 444
Molina, B., 398
Möller, H.J., 207–208
Monahan, J., 497
Monahan, J., 315, 494–495
Mond, J.M., 254
Money, J., 341, 347, 349
Monga, S., 410
Monroe, S.M., 185, 188, 399
Montaner, J., 480
Montero, M., 469
Monuteaux, M.C., 396–397
Moody, C., 376
Moody, S., 449
Moore, B.A., 288
Moos, R.H., 470
Moran, J., 19
Moran, M.G., 427
Morash, J., 388
Mordkoff, A., 156
Moreau, D., 458
Moreno, C., 181
Moretti, M.M., 314
Morey, L.C., 80, 301, 305, 306, 317, 319
Morgan, A.H., 135
Morgan, J.F., 250
Morgan, L., 280
Morgan, P.L., 386
Morgan, H., 135
Mori, N., 61
Morin, C.M., 429, 460
Morison, S., 368
Morissette, S.B., 124
Morrier, M.J., 382
Morris, R., 385, 386
Morrison, A.P., 27
Morrison, B., 366
Morrison, K., 458
Morrow, J.A., 248
Morse, C.A., 330
Morse, J.Q., 315
Morse, S.J., 492
Morton-Bourgon, K.E., 311
Moseley, J.V., 170
Moser, D.J., 444
Mosher, L.R., 228
Mosimann, J.E., 245, 247
Motiuk, L.L., 310, 498
Moulden, H.M., 349
Mowrer, O.H., 38, 99
Mozley, L.H., 216
Mrazek, D., 105
Mudford, O.C., 384
Mueller, D.R., 229
Mueser, K.T., 208, 229
Mufson, L., 458
Muhle, R., 381
Müijen, M., 208
Muir, C.R., 210
Muir, S.L., 246
Mulick, J.A., 384
Mulkens, S.A.N., 105
Müller, D.J., 220
Mulvey, E.P., 312, 315
Mummery, W.K., 279
Mundy, P., 378, 379
Muñiz, J., 306
Munizza, C., 459
Munoz, L.C., 314
Muñoz, R.F., 452
Munro, J.D., 361
Munroe, S., 288
Muris, P., 111
Murnen, S.K., 246
Murphy, D., 5
Murray, C., 32
Murray, C.J.L., 177
Murray, J.L., 375
Murray, M.E., 316
Murray, R., 432
Murray, R.M., 221
Murrie, D.C., 314
Murty, V.P., 98
Muskat, B., 388
Mustard, J.F., 482
Musto, D.F., 282
Musty, R.E., 287
Myers, J.K., 138
Myers, S., 379
Myklebust, H.R., 387
Myrtek, M., 148

N

Naab, S., 255
Nachshen, J., 372, 373
Nagel, B., 376
Nagin, D., 404
Nakdimen, K.A., 299, 302
Narash-Eisikovits, O., 252
Narrow, W.E., 208
Nasrallah, H.A., 208, 220
Nastase, C., 432
Nathan, J.S., 71
Nathan, P.E., 458, 463
Nation, M., 481
Neal, C., 411
Neale, M.C., 98, 186, 411
Near, D., 302
Neckerman, H.J., 403
Neese-Todd, S., 43
Nehra, A., 337
Neiderhiser J.M., 46
Nelson, B.A., 316
Nelson, C.B., 178
Nelson, C.M., 374
Nelson, D., 134
Nelson, G., 478, 484
Nelson, G., 468, 469, 480, 482
Nelson, H., 228
Nelson, M.M., 460
Nelson, T., 94
Nemeroff, C.B., 32
Nestadt, G., 300
Nesvacil, L.J., 337
Netemeyer, R.G., 251
Neto, J.G., 139
Neufeldt, S.A., 455
Neuman, R.J., 399
Neumann, C.S., 314
Neumann, P.J., 440
Neumärker, K., 237
Neumeister, A., 272
Neunaber, D.J., 182
Neve, M., 392
Nevin, A., 388
Newcomb, M.D., 263
Newcomb, R., 328
Newman, D.L., 272
Newman, J.P., 309, 310, 313
Newman, S., 498
Newman, S.C., 298
Newth, S., 110
Nezu, A.M., 82, 453
Ng Yin Kin, N.M.K., 245
Ngan, E.T.C., 224
Nicholls, T., 312
Nicholls, T., 496
Nielsen, D., 199
Nielsen, O., 133
Nies, A.S., 427
Nietzel, M.T., 276
Nijenhuis, E., 139
Nijenhuis, E.R.S., 134
Nijmeijer, J.S., 396
Nika, E., 353
Nirje, B., 373
Nixon, E., 248
Niznikiewicz, M.A., 223
Nock, M.K., 403
Noland, J.S., 368
Norasakkunkit, V., 106
Norberg, M.M., 100
Norcross, J.C., 453, 463–464
Nordhus, I.H., 431
Nordling, N., 347
Nordling, R., 251
Norman, G.R., 32
Norman, P., 237
Norman, R.M.G., 495
Norquist, G.S., 208
Norton, G.R., 132
Norton, P.J., 120, 458
Nota, L., 375
Noyes, R., Jr., 140
Nugent, L., 386
Nulman, I., 367
Nunes, K.L., 328
Nussbaum, L.N., 72
Nye, C., 383

O

Oakes, P., 375
Oakland, T., 362
O'Brien, B., 386
O'Brien, C.P., 275, 283
O'Brien, J., 55
O'Connell, M.E., 468, 481
O'Connor, M., 237, 253
Odom, S.L., 369
O'Donohue, W., 349
O'Donovan, M.C., 219
Oertel-Knöchel, V., 215
Offord, D.R., 297, 393, 394, 403, 404, 405, 407, 409, 468
Ogloff, J.R.P., 312, 497
Ogloff, J.R.P., 495, 496, 505
Oh, D., 90
O'Hara, M., 458
O'Hara, M.W., 182
Ohayon, M.M., 107, 126
Okazaki, S., 61
Olatawura, M.O., 189
Oldman, A.D., 245
Olds, D., 478
Olds, D.L., 478
Olds, D.L., 477, 478
O'Leary, K.D., 460–461
O'Leary, T.A., 117
Olendzki, N., 43
Olff, M., 116
Olfson, M., 427, 444, 447
Olfson, M., 455
Olino, T.M., 187
Oliva, P., 136
Olivardia, R., 251
Olivier, B., 334
Ollendick, T.H., 463
Olmstead, M.G., 372
Olmstead, M.P., 240, 243
Olmsted, M.P., 239
Olsen, J., 368
Olsen, S.F., 368
Olshansky, S., 373
Olson, R., 387
Oltmanns, T.F., 318
O'Malley, K., 367

O'Neal, K.K., 480
O'Neill, J., 488
Onghenea, P., 478
O'Nise, K., 471
O'Reardon, J.P., 197
O'Reilly, R.L., 492, 494
O'Reilly, R.L., 496
Orford, J., 335
Orn, H., 298, 498
Ornish, D.M., 170
Orsillo, S.M., 82, 115, 126
Orsmond, G.I., 373
Osgood, D.W., 484
Osler, W., 167
Oswald, A.J., 419
Oswald, D.P., 382
Otto, M.W., 90, 124, 460
Otto, S., 455
Oude Voshaar, R.C., 432
Ouellette-Kuntz, H., 361
Ouellette-Kuntz, H., 367
Ouimet, A.J., 126
Ouwehand, C., 423
Overholser, J.C., 425
Owen, A., 343
Owen, C., 254
Owen, M.J., 33, 219

P

Pace-Shott, E.F., 460
Pachana, N.A., 421
Paclawskyj, T., 382
Padesky, C.A., 122
Padilla, A.M., 62
Padilla, C., 437–438
Pagani, L., 405
Pagano, C., 448
Paglia-Boak, A., 263, 268, 270, 278, 279, 283, 284, 287, 288
Paglieri, R.A., 384
Pagura, J., 319, 419, 431, 432
Paik, A., 332
Paíno-Piñeiro, M., 306
Pajonk, F.G., 447
Palacios, S., 330
Pallesen, S., 431
Palombo, J., 387
Pampallona, S., 459
Panskepp, J., 98
Pantony, K., 44, 300
Panzarella, C., 184
Papageorgiou, C., 119
Paparella, T., 383
Parag, V., 426
Paredes, J., 496
Paris, J., 135, 316–317
Park, D.C., 8
Park, H.L., 456
Parsons, T.D., 124
Partridge, G.E., 302, 303
Pasco, G., 383
Pass, K.A., 366
Patel, D.R., 44
Patel, S., 413
Patel, V., 447
Patrick, C.J., 313
Patrick, J., 303
Patrick, M., 303
Patten, S.B., 4
Patterson, C., 438
Patterson, G., 406
Patterson, G.R., 406
Patterson, K.M., 454
Patterson, M.D., 102
Patterson, S.G., 406
Pattison, E.M., 274
Patton, J.H., 314
Patton, J.R., 365
Paul, R., 379
Paulhus, D.L., 302
Pauls, D.L., 111
Paulsen, J.S., 216
Pavuluri, M., 215
Pawluck, D.E., 237
Paxton, S.J., 246
Payan, C., 220
Payne, K.A., 335
Pearl, D., 154
Pearl, R., 388
Peden, N., 290
Peindl, K.S., 182
Peirson, L., 481
Peirson, L., 475
Pekarik, G., 456
Pelham, B.W., 185
Pelham, W.E., 396
Pelham, W.E., 460
Pelham, W.E., Jr., 398
Pellow, T.A., 136
Pelton, J., 229
Peñas-Lledó, E.M., 243
Pendery, M.L., 274
Penfield, W., 222
Penman, D., 406–407
Penn, D.L., 43
Pennebaker, J.W., 116
Pennucci, A., 480
Pepler, D., 406–407
Pepler, D., 481
Peragine, G., 440
Percy, M., 363–364, 365, 366, 370
Pereira, A., 368
Pereira, L.H., 361
Perfetti, C.A., 386
Pergamin, L., 108
Pergamin, L., 40
Perivoliotis, D., 27
Perlis, M.L., 429
Perlis, R.H., 448
Perreault, R., 482
Perret, Y.M., 368
Perry, A., 373, 380, 381, 383, 384
Perry, A.A., 248
Perry, D.G., 312
Perry, J.C., 315
Persis, T.S., 459
Pert, L., 303
Perusse, D., 405
Peschardt, K.S., 309, 403
Peskind, E.R., 437
Peters, J.E., 481
Peters, R., 436
Peters, R.DeV., 469
Peters, R.DeV., 468, 470, 480, 481
Peters, R.Dev., 481
Petersen, J.L., 328
Petersen, R.C., 435
Petersen, R.C., 55
Peterson, J.B., 272
Peterson, J.S., 273
Peterson, R.A., 102
Peterson, T., 196
Petkova, E., 112
Petrila, J., 492
Petronis, A., 220
Petty, C.R., 397
Petty, J., 352
Peveler, R.C., 253
Pezawas, L., 188
Pfadt, A., 375
Pfäfflin, F., 342
Pfammatter, M., 460
Pfohl, B., 301, 426
Phelan, J.C., 43
Philibert, R.A., 93
Philippe, J.P., 32
Phillips, E.L., 456
Phillips, J.S., 83
Phillips, K.A., 142
Phillips, L.H., 419
Piacentini, J., 459
Piasecki, T.M., 84
Piazza, J.R., 423
Piccinelli, M., 189
Picheca, J.E., 349
Pickens, I.B., 388
Pickering, A.S., 44
Pickles, A., 409
Pickrell, J.E., 132
Piek, J., 8
Pieper, C., 157
Pierre, E.S., 449
Piersma, H.L., 80
Pihl, R.O., 272
Pilkonis, P.A., 315
Pimental, S.S., 111
Pina, A.A., 459
Pina, A.A., 459
Pine, D.S., 309, 403, 404, 411, 412
Pine, F., 303
Pinel, P., 208, 302
Pinquart, M., 427
Piper, A., 136
Pistrang, N., 469
Pithers, W.D., 352
Pizzagalli, D.A., 190
Plomin, R., 46, 92, 313
Plotsky, P.M., 188
Plumb, J., 115
Plumhoff, J.E., 168
Pogue-Geile, M.F., 220
Polan, M., 333
Polanczyk, G., 396
Polaschek, D.L.L., 353
Poldrack, R., 387
Pole, N., 115
Polich, J.M., 274
Polivy, J., 243, 246, 248, 249
Pollack, A.L., 505
Pollack, M.H., 90, 124
Polvan, N., 10
Pomerleau, O.F., 280
Pomeroy, W.B., 326
Pope, H.G., 131, 135
Pope, H.G., Jr., 136, 251
Popeo, D.M., 434
Porjesz, B., 272
Porporino, F.J., 310
Porporino, F.J., 498
Porter, R., 14, 210
Porter, S., 303, 307, 308, 311, 312, 313, 314, 316
Posey, D.J., 382
Posternak, M.A., 445
Potter, D., 377–378
Potthoff, J.G., 185
Pötzl-Malikova, M., 209
Poulin, F., 405
Poulin, P., 440
Poulton, R., 105
Powell, B., 482
Power, P., 445
Poythress, N.G., 314
Poythress, N.G., 492
Pratt, H.D., 44
Prause, N., 329
Premkumar, T., 460
Prescott, C.A., 32, 98
Preston, D., 383
Preston, D.L., 311, 313
Preston, N., 495
Prewitt, C.M.-F., 151
Price, B.H., 313
Price, E.C., 120, 458
Price, E.L., 4
Price, J.M., 44, 46
Price, L.H., 382
Price, R.H., 481
Price, R.H., 477
Prilleltensky, I., 468, 470, 474, 475, 484
Prilleltensky, I., 469, 482
Prilleltensky, O., 468
Prince, J.B., 399–400
Prince, S.E., 98
Prince, V., 346
Prins, H., 310
Prinz, P.N., 427, 428
Prinz, R.J., 483
Prinzo, M., 349
Prior, M., 384
Pritchard, J.C., 302
Prkachin, K.M., 166, 168
Proctor, M., 413
Prvulovic, D., 215
Pryor, J.B., 43
Pryor, J.L., 337
Przybeck, T., 304
Puente, A.E., 71
Pueschel, S.M., 370
Pugh, G., 354
Pugh, K., 211
Pugh, K.R., 386
Pujol, J., 112
Pukall, C.F., 335, 340
Pumariega, A.J., 234
Pungello, E.P., 477
Purdon, C., 110
Purdon, C.L., 108
Putnam, F.W., 131
Pyper, D., 375

Q

Qiu, C., 434–435, 438
Quadflieg, N., 242, 255
Qualls, S.H., 421
Quinlan, D.M., 183
Quinsey, V.L., 311, 312, 313, 315, 350, 351, 353, 354
Quintana, H., 399

R

Rabin, L.A., 71
Rabins, P.V., 432
Rabung, S., 460
Rachman, S., 40, 90, 104, 110, 111, 112, 411, 456
Radden, J., 12
Radford, J.P., 8, 360
Radomsky, A., 112
Radomsky, A.S., 40, 90, 112
Rahe, R.H., 155
Raiford, S.E., 76
Raine, A., 301, 304, 309, 313, 405
Rainer, J.D., 186
Ralph, D., 334
Ramey, C.T., 369
Ramey, S.L., 369
Ramos-McKay, J., 477
Ramos, O., 380
Ranney, L., 280
Rapanaro, C., 373
Rapaport, M.H., 100
Rapee, R.M., 108
Raphael, D., 374
Rapin, I., 381
Rappaport, J., 470
Raskind, M.A., 437
Rasmussen, K., 388
Raspa, M., 372
Rassin, E., 111
Ratcliff, K.S., 309
Ratcliffe, G.E., 425
Rathbone, B.J., 163
Rathouz, P.J., 254, 405
Ratner, K.G., 190
Rauch, S.L., 112
Rauschenberger, S.L., 135
Rauss-Mason, C., 240
Rawlinson, R.B., 374
Ray, O., 265
Ray, W.J., 117
Rayner, R., 37, 99, 104

Read, S., 438
Reaves, J., 273
Rector, N.A., 228
Rector, N.A., 27
Reddemann, L., 135
Redmond, C., 480
Reed, H.K., 382
Reeves, K.A., 497
Regal, R.R., 365
Regan, J.J., 319
Reger, M.A., 461
Regev, L.G., 349
Regier, D.A., 310
Rehm, J., 263, 269, 270
Reich, B., 295
Reich, D., 322
Reich, J., 300, 319, 320
Reich, S., 469
Reichard, S., 216
Reichenberg, A., 211
Reid, D.J., 374
Reid, J.B., 272
Reid, J.M., 407
Reid, W.H., 310
Reiger, G., 330
Reijntjes, A., 108
Reilly, D., 370
Reimer-Heck, B., 375
Reinders, H.S., 375
Reinisch, J.M., 347
Reiss, D., 481
Reiss, S., 376
Reissing, E.D., 335, 336
Reissing, E.K., 338
Reiss.S., 102
Reitan, R., 72
Renaud, C.A., 347
Renner, V.J., 420
Renshaw, D., 336
Renwick, R., 367, 374
Reschly, D.J., 388
Rescorla, L.A., 82
Resick, P.A., 116
Resnick, R.J., 449
Reutens, S., 133
Reynolds, C.F., 426
Reynolds, K., 421, 432
Reznick, J.S., 411
Rheaume, J., 119
Rhee, S.H., 309
Rhee, W.H., 405
Rice, M.E., 311, 312, 313, 314, 351, 353, 354
Rice, M.E., 502
Rich, M.W., 168, 199
Richards, H.J., 314
Richards, J.A., 195
Richardson, A.E., 84
Richardson, T., 461
Richardson, W.S., 443
Richman, A., 495
Richters, J.E., 398
Rickels, K., 413
Rief, W., 140
Riemer, M., 469
Rifkin, A., 135
Riley, D., 285
Riley, R., 495
Riley, T., 483
Rimland, B., 382, 384
Risbrough, V.B., 32
Risch, N., 316
Riso, L.P., 249
Rispoli, M., 383
Ritchie, C.W., 436
Ritchie, K., 436
Ritterband, L.M., 461
Ritvo, P.G., 171
Rivera, S.M., 364, 387
Rivers, P.C., 275
Rizvi, S.L., 461
Rizzo, A.A., 124
Robbins, J.M., 135
Roberts, A.H., 453
Roberts, B.W., 419
Roberts, C., 412
Roberts, J.E., 31
Roberts, R., 314
Robertshaw, B.A., 346
Robichaud, M., 126
Robins, C.J., 43, 321, 322
Robins, L.N., 73, 309, 310
Robins, L.N., 498
Robinson, J., 302
Robinson, J., 478
Robinson, M., 405
Robinson, R.G., 444
Robinson, S., 377
Robinson, T.E., 28, 30
Rocke-Henderson, N., 395
Rockert, W., 240
Roder, V., 229
Rodewald, F., 134–135
Rodgers, B., 254
Rodin, G., 249
Roeleveld, N., 361
Roelofs, K., 139, 143
Roemer, L., 82, 119, 126
Roesch, R., 498
Roesch, R., 498, 499, 500
Roesch, R., 501, 502, 503, 505
Roffman, R.A., 288
Rogaeva, E., 438
Rogeness, G.A., 405
Rogers, C., 41
Rogers, J., 98
Rogers, J.H., 299
Rogers, K., 403
Rogers, R., 299, 301, 307, 312, 314
Rogers, S., 384
Rogers, S.J., 460
Rogler, L.H., 61
Rohde, L.A., 396
Rohleder, N., 169
Rohrbaugh, M., 454
Roid, G.H., 75, 362
Rollnick, S., 290, 453
Romanow, R.J., 449
Romberger, D.J., 263
Ronan, G.F., 82
Ronchi, D., 435
Ronningstam, E., 317
Roose, S.P., 334
Rosa-Alcázar, A.I., 90
Rose, D.T., 184
Rose, S., 91
Rosen, R.C., 332, 337
Rosenbach, A., 286
Rosenbaum, M., 454–455
Rosenberg, D.R., 112
Rosenberg, M., 427
Rosenberg, W., 443
Rosenberger, P.H., 315
Rosenhan, D.L., 43, 60
Rosenman, R.H., 167
Rosenthal, D., 199
Rösler, A., 353
Ross, C.A., 102, 130, 131, 132, 134, 135, 136
Ross, D., 39
Ross, J., 263
Ross, L., 398–399
Ross, S.A., 39
Rossell, S.L., 142
Roth, A., 462
Roth, T., 427
Rothbart, M., 61
Rouillon, F., 220
Rouleau, J.-L., 348
Rourke, B.P., 387
Rousanville, B.J., 191
Rowa, K., 108
Rowe, R., 404
Roy, A., 199
Royer, J.M., 386
Rozanski, A., 166
Rubaltelli, F.F., 366
Rubinow, D.R., 180
Rubinstein, T.J., 309
Ruffer-Hesse, C., 336
Ruggiero, K.J., 461
Rugulies, R., 168
Ruiter, M.J., 444
Runkle, G.P., 182
Ruscio, A., 108
Ruscio, A.M., 119
Rush, A.J., 196, 197
Rush, P.J., 39
Ruskin, P.E., 432
Russ, E., 303
Russek, L.G., 162
Russell, S., 337
Rutherford, J., 186
Rutherford, M.J., 300
Rutter, M., 381, 393, 473
Ryan, M.L., 461
Ryan, S., 471
Rybarczyk, B., 427
Rylander, G., 199
Rynn, M.A., 413

S

Sachdev, P., 133
Sachs, G.S., 182
Sacker, A., 220
Sackett, D.L., 443
Sackheim, H.A., 444
Sadock, B.J., 30
Sæther, O., 69
Sagi-Schwartz, A., 100
Saklofske, D.H., 76
Sala, M.M., 316
Saladin, M.E., 274
Salekin, R.T., 312, 314
Salkovskis, P.M., 110, 112, 143
Sallows, G.O., 382
Salmon, P., 143
Samaan, R.A., 45
Sambrook, S.L., 15
Sampson, P.D., 367
Samson, D., 302
Samuel, D.B., 296, 300
Samuels, J., 109, 298
Sánchez-Meca, J., 90
Sanchez, T., 388
Sandak, R., 386, 387
Sanday, P.R., 352
Sanders, M.R., 483
Sanders, M.R., 483
Sanderson, C.S., 280
Sandler, I., 472
Sandnabba, N.K., 347
Sanghavi, M., 188
Sano, N., 124
Santa Ana, E.J., 274
Santor, D., 313, 314
Santos, J.F., 425
Santtila, P., 347
Sapolsky, R., 155, 188
Sapolsky, R.M., 156, 157, 158, 188
Sar, V., 139
Sarchiapone, M., 199
Sareen, J., 319, 419, 421, 422, 425, 431, 432
Sareen, J., 492
Sarnocinska-Hart, A., 270
Sartorius, N., 110
Sattler, J.M., 75, 83
Saucier, D.A., 248
Saul, C., 303
Saunders, J., 268
Saunders, K., 303
Savage, C.R., 112
Savoie, T., 221
Sawchuk, C.N., 105
Sawyer, A.T., 90
Sawyer, M.G., 471
Sawyer, M.G., 477
Scanlan, J.M., 440
Scanley, E., 70
Scanlon, D.M., 385
Schachar, R., 400
Schacht, T.E., 450
Schachter, S., 303
Schaefer, C., 155
Schaffer, A., 90
Schaler, J.A., 7
Schalock, R.L., 361, 362, 374
Schantz, S.L., 398
Schatzberg, A.F., 107
Scherk, H., 447
Schermer, F., 248
Scherwitz, L.W., 170
Schiele, B.C., 244
Schildkraut, J.J., 187
Schindler, D., 454
Schlangen, L.J., 444
Schmauk, F.J., 310
Schmeidler, J., 134
Schmidt, F., 406
Schmidt, H., 111
Schmidt, L., 395
Schmidt, U., 237
Schmitt, W.A., 310
Schmitz, N., 45
Schneider, L., 62
Schneider, P., 136
Schneider, T., 32
Schneier, F.R., 120
Schnell, K., 305
Schnicke, M.K., 116
Schnitker, R., 305
Schoenman, T.J., 11
Schoenwald, S.K., 309
Schoevers, R.A., 459
Schonert, Reichl, K.A., 395
Schopler, E., 378, 379
Schopp, R.F., 492
Schork, N.J., 215
Schreibman, L., 383
Schroeder, M.L., 299
Schroll, M., 169
Schuchardt, K., 386
Schuck, P., 20
Schuckit, M.A., 272
Schuler, A., 383
Schulsinger, F., 199
Schulz, C.S., 306–307
Schulz, K.P., 396, 398
Schulz, R., 440
Schumacher, M., 168
Schupak-Neuberg, E., 44
Schupf, N., 370
Schuster, J.W., 374
Schutx, H.K., 246
Schwab-Stone, M., 379
Schwartz, A.A., 384
Schwartz, C.E., 108
Schwartz, D.M., 245
Schwartz, G., 366
Schwartz, G.E., 162
Schwartz, J., 157
Schwartz, J.B., 383
Schwartz, J.E., 419
Schwarz, E., 215
Schweinhart, L.J., 476, 477
Scogin, F., 459
Scorgie, K., 373
Scorsese, M., 14
Scott, A., 495
Scott, A.I.F., 444
Scott, J., 188
Scott, K., 264

Scott, R.L., 372
Scott, T., 421, 432
Seaburn, D., 454
Sealy, P., 495
Sebat, S., 381
Sedway, J.A., 252
Seeds, P.M., 121, 126
Seeds, P.M., 25
Seehusen, D.A., 182
Seeman, M.V., 228
Seeman, P., 225, 226
Seeman, T.E., 426
Seftel, A.D., 339
Segal, N., 199
Segal, Z., 20
Segal, Z.V., 20, 40, 43, 191, 194, 202, 228, 354
Segall, E.R., 303
Séguin, M., 298
Seibyl, J.P., 70
Seidel, R., 237, 240
Seidman, B.T., 352
Seidman-Carlson, R., 440
Seidman, L.J., 398
Seidman, S.N., 193, 334
Selfe, T.A., 430
Seligman, M.E.P., 99, 105, 157, 476
Sellman, J.D., 274
Seltzer, M.M., 373
Semrud-Clikeman, M., 387
Sen, S., 187
Serin, R.C., 311, 312–313
Seritan, A.L., 139
Serran, G., 351
Serran, G.A., 349, 354
Seto, M., 313
Seto, M.C., 330, 349, 351
Sewell, K.W., 299, 312
Seymour, A., 488
Shadish, W.R., 454, 461
Shaffer, D., 200, 394
Shafran, R., 90, 110, 111, 252
Shah, N., 208
Shainberg., 337
Shamblen, S.R., 480
Shanker, S., 482
Shannon, G.W., 15
Shapiro, C.J., 483
Shapiro, C.M., 126
Shapiro, D., 304
Shapiro, E.S., 84
Shapiro, F., 90
Shapiro, S.L., 43
Sharpe, M., 139, 142
Shaw, B.F., 191
Shaw, B.F., 39
Shaw, H., 256–257
Shaw, H.E., 44
Shaw, J., 312
Shaw, P., 398
Shaywitz, B.A., 385, 386, 387
Shaywitz, S., 387
Shaywitz, S.E., 385, 386, 387
Shear, M.K., 90
Shedden, K., 187
Sheffield, R.A., 405
Sheikh, H.I., 187
Sheikh, J.I., 431–432
Sheline, Y.I., 188
Shelledy, W., 98
Shelton, D., 388
Shelton, S., 98
Shenton, M.E., 223
Shepherd, C., 394
Sher, K.J., 272
Sher, L., 244
Sheridan, S.M., 84
Sherrod, N.B., 43
Shibley Hyde, J., 246
Shields, S., 264, 285
Shiell, A., 483
Shiffman, S., 280
Shih, J.H., 185
Shin, C., 480
Shine, J., 314
Shinn, M., 472
Shochet, I.M., 461
Shogren, K.A., 360
Shoham, V., 454
Shooshtari, S., 422
Shorter, E., 16–17
Shorter, Edward., 17
Shrivastava, A., 208
Shuster, B., 248
Sidman, N., 108
Siegel, L.S., 385, 386
Siegel, S., 273
Siegel, T.C., 406, 407
Siegert, R., 352
Siegle, G.H., 188
Siegrist, J., 158
Sierra, M., 134
Siever, L.J., 304, 305, 306
Sigelman, C.K., 363
Sigman, J., 378
Sigman, M., 379
Sigvardsson, S., 91
Silberg, J.L., 405, 409
Silbersweig, D., 305
Silk, K.R., 295
Silva, P.A., 272, 409
Silva, P.S., 200
Silver, C.H., 385
Silverman, B., 168
Silverman, K., 284
Silverman, K.W., 460
Silverman, W.K., 409
Silverman, W.K., 459, 463
Silverman, W.P., 370
Simenon, J., 44
Simeon, D., 134, 136
Simmons, H.G., 19
Simmons, J.Q., 382
Simms, L.J., 56
Simoes, N.A., 411
Simon, G., 142
Simon, G.E., 143, 448
Simon, J.T., 387
Simoneau, T.L., 195
Simonoff, E., 394
Simons, A.D., 185, 399
Simons, J.S., 332, 333, 334, 335
Simonsen, E., 52
Simonsen, R., 302
Simpson, D.D., 283
Simpson, S., 196
Simpson, T.L., 84
Sindahl, P., 413
Singal, B.M., 168
Singer, A.R., 453
Singer, B., 458
Singer, M.T., 315
Singhal, D., 287
Single, E., 284
Siqueland, L., 413
Sir Francis Galton., 7
Sirroff, B., 134
Sitzer, D.I., 229
Sivertsen, B., 430
Skeem, J., 314
Skeem, J.L., 312, 315
Skinner, B.F., 24, 451
Skinner, C.H., 84
Skinner, M., 477
Skinner, M.E., 388
Sklar, L.S., 162
Skodol, A.E., 295, 296, 301, 302, 305
Skrtic, T.M., 373
Skuse, D., 105
Skutch, J., 461
Slade, P.D., 319
Slater, E., 137
Slater, J.F., 299
Slattery, M.J., 411
Slobogin, C., 492
Slovenko, R., 339
Slutske, W., 405
Smalley, S.L., 381
Smart, R., 284
Smit, F., 426
Smit, F., 481
Smith, A., 480
Smith, A.M., 314, 330
Smith, A.P., 160
Smith, B., 300, 398
Smith, C., 471
Smith, G.T., 272
Smith, H.L., 419
Smith, J.D., 361
Smith, K.B., 335
Smith, M., 161
Smith, M.L., 457, 458
Smith, P., 374
Smith, S.M., 84
Smith, S.S., 313
Smith, T., 382
Smith, T.W., 148, 167, 168, 327
Smolak, L., 248, 250
Smoley, J., 421
Smolin, Y., 132
Smoski, M.J., 43
Smyer, M.A., 422
Smyth, R., 139
Snidman, N., 411
Snowling, M.J., 385
Snyder, J.J., 304
Snyder, S.M., 399
Soares-Weiser, K., 460
Sobell, L.C., 274, 280
Sobell, M.B., 274, 280
Sobsey, D., 373, 375
Soderstrom, H., 313
Softley, I., 14
Solomon, D.A., 177
Solomon, R.L., 451
Sonenklar, N.A., 382
Song, A.W., 223
Sonino, N., 194
Sookman, D., 112
Soresi, S., 375
Sorrell, J.T., 431
Spacarelli, S., 406
Spanier, C., 459
Spanos, N., 136
Sparkman, C.R., 382
Sparler, S., 170
Sparling, J.J., 369
Sparrow, S.S., 362
Speakmon, G., 251
Spector, I.P., 332, 333, 334, 335
Speisman, J., 156
Spence, J.D., 167
Spence, M.W., 361
Spence, S.H., 108, 412
Spence, S.H., 461
Spencer, T., 396, 448
Spencer, T.J., 396
Sperling, M.B., 316
Sperry, L., 320
Spicer, C.C., 161
Spiegel, D.A., 124
Spitzer, B.L., 247
Spitzer, R.L., 74, 102, 300, 315
Spoth, R.L., 480
Sprock, J., 300
Spungen, C., 454
Sroufe, L.A., 100, 131
Stack, S., 313
Stallard, P., 461
Stallman, H.M., 461
Stanford, M.S., 314
Stangl, D., 301
Stanislaw, H.A., 382
Stanley, M.A., 421, 431, 432
Starzomski, A., 303, 312
Starzomski, A.J., 300
Steffy, R.A., 215, 221
Steidtmann, D.K., 94
Steiger, H., 245, 248–249, 256
Stein, A., 248
Stein, K.F., 249
Stein, M.B., 492
Stein, M.B., 32, 111, 319
Stein, M.T., 387
Stein, R.I., 44
Steinberg-Epstein, R., 382
Steiner, B.W., 343, 344
Steiner, M., 245
Steinglass, P., 454
Steinhauer, S.R., 272
Steinhausen, H.C., 237, 240
Steketee, G.S., 124
Stepanski, E., 427, 430
Stephen, J., 116
Stephens, R.S., 288
Stepp, S.D., 315
Steptoe, A., 148
Stern, S., 453
Stetler, C.A., 169
Stevens, D., 313
Stevens, S., 427
Stevenson, J., 320
Stewart, D.N., 161
Stewart, J.G., 183, 188
Stewart, M.O., 459
Stewart, R., 429
Stewart, R.E., 462
Stewart, S.E., 111
Stewart, S.H., 120
St.George-Hyslop, P., 437–438
Stice, E., 246, 249, 256–257
Stice, E., 44
Stichter, J.P., 383
Stickgold, R., 460
Stiles, T.C., 191
Still, B., 393
Stip, E., 70
Stober, J., 117, 186
Stock, S.E., 374
Stolar, N., 228
Stolar, N., 27
Stolar, N.M., 27
Stone, A.A., 419
Stone, J., 137, 139
Stone, M., 315
Stone, W.L., 379
Stoneking, B.C., 495
Storch, E., 388
Stormer, S., 246
Stouthamer-Loeber, M., 403
Strain, E.C., 284
Strain, P.S., 382
Strathdee, S.A., 285
Straus, S.E., 443
Strauss, C.C., 409
Strauss, J.S., 432
Stravynski, A., 322
Stredny, R.V., 80
Streiner, D.L., 419, 420, 421, 425, 431
Streissguth, A.P., 367, 368
Striegel-Moore, R.H., 234, 242, 249, 250
Stringaris, A., 403
Strober, M., 244, 248
Strong, S.M., 251
Strub, N., 220
Struening, E.L., 43
Strunk, D., 459
Strupp, H.H., 450
Strupp, H.S., 450
Stuart, H., 503
Stuart, S., 458

Styles, L.C., 254
Styr, B., 304
Suarez, E., 168
Suárez, L., 100
Suddath, R.L., 195
Suedfeld, P., 310
Suh, E.M., 418
Sullivan, P.E., 236
Sullivan, P.F., 33, 186
Sullivan, R., 170
Sullivan, S.D., 430
Summerfeldt, L.J., 74, 108
Summers, J., 376
Summers, J.A., 372, 373
Sun, D., 223
Sunday, S.R., 250
Sundby, E., 495
Suppes, T., 445
Susser, E., 208
Suzuki, K., 61
Svartberg, M., 191
Svrakic, D.M., 304
Swallow, S.R., 108
Swann, W.B., Jr., 185
Swanson, H.L., 386, 388
Swanson, J.M., 400
Swartz, C., 386
Swartz, H.A., 188
Swartz, M., 178
Swartzwelder, H.S., 269
Swazey, J.P., 227
Sweeney, J.A., 215
Sweet, M.A., 478
Swendsen, J., 193
Swift, R.M., 275
Swindle, R., 143
Swinson, R.P., 108, 124–125
Sylvia, L.G., 184
Syme, S.L., 158
Symons, F.J., 372
Sypeck, M.F., 246
Sysko, R., 193
Szabo, G., 285
Szajnberg, N., 345–346
Szasz, T.S., 7, 59
Szatmari, P., 403

T
Tabakoff, B., 272, 285–286
Taber, K.H., 139
Tafarodi, R.W., 185
Tai, S., 229
Takei, N., 61
Takeuchi, D.T., 45
Talajic, M., 168
Talbot, C., 270
Talge, N.M., 411
Tallal, P., 387
Talley, J.L., 222
Tambs, K., 98
Tandon, R., 208, 220, 221
Tansella, M., 189
Taunt, H.M., 372, 373
Tausig, H.B., 368
Tausk, V., 216
Taylor, B., 270
Taylor, C.B., 255
Taylor, C.T., 107, 108, 109
Taylor, E.B., 178
Taylor, L.K., 40
Taylor, M.A., 444
Taylor, S., 102, 111, 112, 119, 142
Taylor, T .K., 406
Teachman, B.A., 110
Teague, G.B., 61
Teasdale, J., 20
Teasdale, J.D., 20, 191
Tedeschi, M., 447
Tedesco, J., 226
Teferra, T., 369
Tellegen, A., 79, 135
Tempier, R., 455
Temple, E., 387
ten Brinke, L., 311
ten Have, M.L., 104
Tennent, D., 310
Tennent, G., 310
Teodorescu, M.C., 430
Terberger, T., 8
Teri, L., 427, 438
Terman, M., 196
Teskey, G.C., 30
Tessner, K., 219
Test, D.W., 388
Thapar, A., 219
Thaper, A., 411
Thase, M.E., 187, 188, 191, 194, 196
Thayer, J.F., 31, 118, 131
Thayer, J.F., 31
Thede, L.L., 305, 342
Theodore-Oklota, C., 115
Theorell, T., 158
Theorell, T.G., 156, 157, 158
Thomas, A.M., 340
Thomas, C., 401
Thombs, D.L., 272
Thompson, C.E., 120
Thompson, D., 375
Thompson, J.K., 246, 249
Thompson, J.R., 374
Thompson, M.M., 245
Thompson, P.J., 405
Thompson-Pope, S.K., 305
Thompson, R.A., 100
Thompson, T.L., 427
Thompson, W.W., 381
Thordarson, D.S., 124
Thorp, S.R., 431
Tibaldi, G., 459
Tiemens, B.G., 189
Tierney, W.M., 155
Tiggeman, M., 246
Tiggemann, M., 44
Tiihonen, J., 445
Tillich, P., 42
Tillman, C., 216
Tilly, S.M., 315
Timmons, K.A., 185
Tint, A., 377
Titov, N., 461
Tiwari, A.K., 220
Tizard, J., 393
Tobler, N.S., 480
Todd, A.W., 382
Tohen, M., 445
Tolin, D.F., 100, 105, 116
Tomasulo, D., 375
Toneatto, A., 280
Toohey, S., 472
Torgersen, S., 303, 316
Torrey, E.F., 209
Tortu, S., 480
Tougas, G., 161
Tough, S.C., 270
Tough, S.E., 376
Tran, L., 388
Tranel, D., 223, 405
Trant, J., 110
Trautman, P., 200
Trautrimas, C., 351
Tread, J., 328
Treasure, J., 237
Treasure, J.L., 250
Trembay, R.E., 405
Tremblay, R., 405
Tremblay, R.E., 404
Trentacosta, S.V., 381
Trestrail, J.H., 105
Trimble, M.R., 405
Troop, N., 250
Trottier, K., 239
Trower, P., 229
Troyb, E., 377
Trudeau, L., 480
Trull, T.J., 272, 300, 301, 317, 319
Truscott, D., 503, 504
Trzaskowski, M., 411
Trzesniak, C., 108
Tsoi, W.F., 342
Tsuang, D.W., 438
Tsuchiya, M., 106
Tuma, T.A., 425
Turetsky, B.I., 216
Turk, C.L., 124
Turk, D., 20
Turk, J., 372
Turkat, I.D., 303, 305, 319
Turkington, D., 27, 228, 229
Turnbull, A., 361
Turnbull, A.P., 372, 373, 374
Turnbull, H.R., 374
Turnbull, R., 361
Turnbull, S., 237
Turner, C.W., 167, 460
Turner, J.R., 166
Turner, L.A., 339, 344
Turner, S.M., 319, 409, 411
Turner, T., 392
Turner, T.H., 209
Tuvblad, C., 301
Twamley, E.W., 229
Tweed, S., 255
Tyrrell, D.A.J., 160

U
Udry, J.R., 326
Uhde, T.W., 413
Ullrich, S., 302, 307
Umberson, D., 158
Unis, A.S., 406
Unützer, J., 425, 427
Usher, M., 184

V
Vaillancourt, T., 395, 403, 404, 405
Vaillant, G.E., 299
Valas, H., 388
Valene, P., 246
Valenstein, E.S., 16, 17, 19–227
Valle, L.A., 401
van Balkom, A.J.L.M., 104, 432
Van de Noortgate, W., 478
Van der Ham, T., 242
Van der Hart, O., 130
van der Hart, O., 139
Van der Kolk, B.A., 130
van der Meer, L.A., 383
van Elst, L.T., 405
Van Engeland, H., 242
van Goozen, S.H.M., 405
Van Grootheest, D.S., 111
van Hoeken, D., 237
van Horn, P., 135
van Ijzendoorn, M.H., 40, 108
van Ijzendoorn, M.J., 135
Van Nieuwerburgh, F., 112
van Ommeren, M., 447
Van Os, J., 214
van Straten, A., 426
Van Strien, D.C., 242
van Vreeswijk, M.F., 196
VandenBos, G.R., 228
Vandrey, R.G., 288
Vanfurth, E.F., 248
Vanier, M.K., 413
van't Veer-Tazelaar, P.J., 422
Vargas, J.C., 330
Vargas, S., 471
Vasiliadis, H.M., 455
Vaughan, F., 370
Vaughn, M.G., 93
Vaz, F.J., 243
Vazire, S., 318
Veldhuizen, S., 90, 419, 431
Velleman, S., 461
Vellutino, F.R., 385, 386, 387
Venables, P.H., 405
Venter, A., 379
Vera, E., 484
Verdoux, H., 445
Verhoeff, N.P.L.G., 440
Vernick, J.S., 285
Vernon, P.A., 303
Vessey, J.T., 455
Videnieks, M., 285
Viding, E., 313
Viechtbauer, W., 419
Vieth, A., 272
Vijayaraghavan, M., 62
Viljoen, J.L., 502
Viljoen, J.L., 505, 506
Villatte, M., 452
Vincent, G.M., 312
Vismara, L.A., 460
Viswesvaran, C., 459
Vitacco, M.J., 314
Vitale, J.E., 310, 313
Vitaliano, P.P., 440
Vitaro, F., 405
Vitiello, M.V., 427, 428
Vittengl, J.R., 459
Voet, H., 200
Vogel, D.L., 43
Volkmar, F.R., 377, 378, 379, 380, 382
Volpicelli, J.R., 275
Von Bismark, M.A., 139
von Eye, A., 405
Von Korff, M., 140
von Ranson, K.M., 453
Von Zerssen, D., 207
Vowels, C.L., 248

W
Waddell, C., 394, 395
Waddell, C., 468, 481, 482
Wade, A., 383
Wade, C., 375
Wade, N.G., 43
Wager, T.D., 98
Wagner, A.R., 385
Wagner, K.D., 413
Wahlbeck, K., 445
Wakefield, A.J., 381
Wakefield, J., 59
Wakefield, J.C., 5, 177, 393
Wakeling, A., 237
Wakely, M., 386
Wakiza, G., 56
Wakschlag, L.S., 405
Walcott, D.D., 44
Wald, N.J., 366
Waldinger, M.D., 334
Waldman, I., 215
Waldman, I.D., 309, 405
Waldron, H.B., 460
Walen, S.R., 39
Walker, E.F., 219, 221
Walkup, J.T., 412, 413
Wall, M.E., 388
Wall, P.D., 140, 148
Wall, T.L., 271
Wallace, J., 426
Wallace, J., 32
Wallace, J.F., 310
Waller, G., 249
Waller, N.G., 131, 135
Walles, R., 386
Wallgren, H., 268
Walsh, A.E.S., 245

Walsh, B.T., 193, 245, 447
Walsh, J., 320
Walsh, K., 361
Walsh, P., 247
Walsh, T., 253
Walters, E.E., 100
Walters, G.D., 335
Walters, Richard, 20
Walton, K.E., 419
Wampold, B.E., 458
Wan, G.J., 447
Wandersman, A., 483
Wang, J., 193
Wang, J.L., 45
Wang, W., 334
Ward, A., 237
Ward, L.M., 246
Ward, T., 352, 353
Warlow, C., 139
Warne, J.P., 151
Warner, K.E., 468
Warner, R., 300
Warnke, M., 60
Warren, J.I., 313
Warren, K., 269
Warren, S., 361
Warren, S.L., 100
Warriner, E.M., 387
Wartenberg, A.A., 275
Warwick, H.M.C., 143
Waskik, B.H., 369
Wasow, M., 373
Wass, R.S., 368
Watanabe, N., 459
Waterhouse, L., 379, 380
Waters, A.M., 122
Waters, E., 422
Watkins, S., 186
Watling, T., 384
Watson, D., 56, 109
Watson, D., 56
Watson, H., 252
Watson, J.B., 37, 99, 104
Watson, M., 371
Watson, T.L., 243
Watt, A., 421
Watts, S.E., 40
Weatherman, R.F., 363
Weathers, F.W., 115
Webster, C.D., 505
Webster, C.D., 497, 501
Webster-Stratton, C., 304, 406–407
Webster-Stratton, C.H., 406
Weddington, W.W., 283
Weems, C.F., 409
Weems, C.F., 40
Wegner, D.M., 113
Wehmeyer, M.L., 374
Weikart, D.P., 476
Weiler, B.L., 313
Weinberger, D.R., 217
Weinberger, M., 155
Weiner, D.B., 15
Weiner, H., 161
Weiner, H., 163
Weinrott, M.R., 353
Weisberg, R.B., 337
Weishaar, M.E., 39, 40, 304
Weiss, B., 458
Weiss, J., 163
Weiss, J.M., 162
Weiss, L.G., 76
Weiss, M., 397–398
Weissberg, R.P., 470, 476
Weissman, M.M., 101, 138, 178, 191, 192, 298, 319, 425
Weissman, M.M., 458
Weisz, J.R., 458
Weisz, J.R., 460, 461
Weizman, A., 200
Welch, S.L., 248
Wells, A., 119
Wells, D., 375
Welsh, D., 459
Wen, X., 361
Wender, P.H., 199
Wenzel, A., 458
Wenzlaff, R.M., 113, 185
Werble, B., 315
Wertheim, E.H., 246
Wessely, S., 432
West, L.J., 274
West, M., 136, 303, 306
West, S.L., 480
West, W.C., 225
Westen, D., 252
Westen, D., 458
Westenberg, H.G.M., 112
Westmacott, R., 448
Weston, D., 303
Westra, H.A., 45, 100, 120, 126, 453
Wetherell, J.L., 425, 431
Wexler, A., 348
Whalen, P.J., 112
Wharf, B., 481
Wheelan J., 506
Wheeler, D.L., 384
Wheeler, J.B., 248
Wheeler, S., 312
Whitaker, D.J., 483
White, A.M., 269
White, C., 375
White, K.S., 90
White, P., 77
Whitehead, P.C., 495
Whitehouse, W.G., 184
Whiteside, S.P.H., 90
Whitley, M.K., 461
Whitmore, I., 393
Whittal, M.L., 124, 252
Whittington, C., 460
Wickstrom, S., 383
Widiger, T.A., 60, 61, 74, 296, 299, 300, 301, 316, 317, 319
Widiger, T.A., 50
Widmer, E.D., 328
Widom, C.S., 313
Wiederhold, B.K., 90
Wiederhold, M.D., 90
Wiener, J., 388
Wierzbicki, M., 456
Wikler, L.M., 373
Wilbourne, P.L., 277
Wilcox, A., 342
Wilens, T., 400, 448
Wilhelm-Gossling, C., 135
Wilhelm, S., 112, 124, 138
Wilkerson, B., 176
Wilkinson, G., 189
Willcutt, E., 396
Williams, C.L., 79
Williams, J., 314
Williams, J.B.W., 74, 102
Williams, J.H.G., 398–399
Williams, J.M., 99
Williams, J.M.G., 191, 200
Williams, J.M.G., 20
Williams, K.M., 302
Williams, M., 20
Williams, R.B., 158, 168
Williams, S., 409, 410
Williams, T.I., 110
Williamson, D.A., 251
Williamson, M., 366
Williamson, S., 312, 313
Willoughby, M.T., 396
Wills, T.A., 43
Wilson., 482
Wilson-Bates, F., 498
Wilson, D., 436
Wilson, D.S., 302
Wilson, G., 346
Wilson, G.T., 237, 252, 253, 268
Wilson, K., 312
Wilson, M., 176
Wilson, P.G., 374
Wilson, R.J., 349
Wilson, T.G., 252
Wilson, W.H., 287
Wincze, J.P., 334, 336, 337, 338
Winett, R.A., 276
Wing, L., 377, 378
Winick, B.J., 492, 494
Winser, D.M.R., 161
Winsor, E.J.T., 361
Winters, A., 395
Winzer-Serhan, U.H., 398, 399
Wiprzycka, U., 440
Wise, R.A., 272
Wise, T.N., 142, 303
Wiseman, C.V., 245, 247
Wiser, S.L., 118
Wisner, K.L., 182
Witkiewitz, K., 277
Witt, A.A., 90
Witztum, E., 353
Woermann, F.G., 405
Wojtowicz, A.E., 453
Wold, F.M., 340
Wolery, M., 369
Wolf, M., 386
Wolfe, B.E., 245
Wolfe, D.A., 481
Wolfensberger, W., 359, 360, 361, 373
Wolfgang, G., 108–109
Wolfson, D., 72
Wolitzky-Taylor, K.B., 421, 431
Wolitzky-Taylor, K.B., 431
Wolpe, J., 122
Wonderlich, S., 249
Wong, D.F., 226
Wong, K., 226
Wong, S., 312, 313, 315
Wong, S.C., 497
Wood, E., 480
Wood, T.A., 372
Wood, W.M., 388
Woodcock, R.W., 363
Woodford, L., 373
Woodhead, E., 421
Woods, S.W., 90
Woodside, D.B., 250
Woodward, T.S., 210, 224
Woodworth, M., 312, 313
Woodworth, M.J., 313
Woody, G.E., 283
Woody, S.R., 105
Woolacott, N., 460
Woolfolk, R.L., 140, 143–144
Wright, D., 14
Wright, D., 19
Wright, E.J., 481
Wrightsman, L.S., 308
Wu, J.C., 188
Wu, K.D., 109
Wulsin, L.R., 168
Wyatt Kaminski, J., 401
Wyatt, R.J., 208
Wykes, T., 460
Wyngaarden, M., 363
Wynn, J.W., 382
Wynne-Edwards, K.E., 188
Wynne, H., 289

X
Xanthopoulos, M., 401
Xiao, J., 495

Y
Yaffe, K., 431
Yalom, I., 454
Yang, M., 497
Yang, Y., 313
Yapa, C., 426
Yassa, R., 432
Yates, P., 351
Yates, P.M., 347, 350, 354
Yates, T.M., 131
Yeager, 136
Yeargin-Allsopp, M., 381
Yehuda, R., 116, 134
Yin, L., 193
Young, A.H., 447
Young, B.G., 351
Young, C., 386
Young, D., 199
Young, J.E., 39, 40, 304, 320
Young, J.E., 39, 40
Young, S.E., 342
Young, T., 430
Young, T.K., 162
Young-Wolff, K., 301
Youngren, M.A., 184
Youngsuk, K., 386
Yu, B.N., 492
Yuille, J.C., 316
Yule, W., 393
Yusuf, S., 170

Z
Zai, C.C., 220
Zaidi, L.Y., 316
Zakhari, S., 269
Zakowski, S.G., 153
Zakzanis, K.K., 215, 223
Zammit, S., 33
Zanarini, M., 301
Zanarini, M.C., 295, 301, 305, 322
Zapf, P.A., 505
Zapf, P.A., 501
Zapf, P.A., 499, 500, 501, 502, 503
Zarit, J.M., 435, 436, 439
Zarit, S.H., 435, 436, 439
Zavala, J.M., 425
Zaveri, P., 137
Zborowski, M.J., 192
Zeitouni, N.C., 272
Zekoski, E.M., 182
Zemishlany, Z., 305
Zera, M., 395
Zhang, J., 440
Zhao, S., 180
Zhou, E.S., 151
Ziegler, M.G., 166
Zielasek, J., 214
Zielhuis, G.A., 361
Zigler, E., 362, 368, 373
Zigman, W.B., 370
Zilboorg, G., 11
Zimmerman, M., 299, 301, 317, 445
Zimmerman, M.A., 472
Zinner, S.H., 335
Zinzow, H., 461
Zisook, S., 177
Zivian, M.T., 247, 421
Zlotnick, C., 316
Zoccolillo, M., 403
Zoellner, L.A., 125
Zöllner, S., 220
Zolnik, E.J., 182
Zucker, E.M., 13
Zucker, K.J., 332, 342, 343, 346
Zucker, R.A., 405
Zuroff, D., 183
Zwaal, C., 166
Zweig-Frank, H., 135
Zwinderman, A.H., 196, 334

Subject Index

A

AAMR classification manual, 362
ABAB design, 89
abandonment, 183
ABC model of human disturbance, 39
abdication effect, 384
abdominal obesity, 151, 169
Abecedarian Project, 477
Abilify (aripiprazole), 194
abnormality. *see* psychological abnormality
Aboriginal people
  cultural bias, 61
  and developmental disorders, 368
  and gender identity, 340
  and substance abuse, 264
  and suicide, 198, 199, 264
  and tobacco, 279
abstinence, 275
abstinence syndrome, 278
abuse. *see also* specific types
  and eating disorders, 249–250
  and hypnosis, 137
  and psychotherapy, 136
  and risk for depression, 185–186
academic achievement, 386
academic skill facilitation and remediation, 400
Acamprosate, 275
acetaldehyde, 270
acetaldehyde dehydrogenase, 275
acetylcholine, 17
Achieving Health for All, 481
acid trip, 288
acquired sexual dysfunction, 332
active gene-environment correlation, 93
active placebo, 445
activity scheduling, 190
actus reus, 499
acute stress disorder, 56
Adaptive Behavior Assessment System, 362–363
adaptive behaviour, measurement of, 362–363
addiction. *see also* substance abuse
  defined, 261
  in DSM, 263–264
addictive potential, 280
adenine, 371
ADHD. *see* attention deficit/hyperactivity disorder (ADHD)
adjustment disorders, 57
Adler's individual psychology, 450
adolescents. *see also* childhood disorders
  assessing and treating, 393–394
  bipolar disorders, 180–181
  depression treatment, 194
  evidence-based treatments, 463
  and psychopathy, 314
  risk for depression, 185–186
  suicide, 410
adoption studies, 90–199, 270
adrenal cortex, 32
adrenalin, 151, 281
adrenal medulla, 165
adrenocorticotrophic hormone (ACTH), 151, 187
adjunctive psychotherapy, 194–195
affect, 73
affective disorders, 302
affective features, 167
affective flattening, 211
affirmation field, 475, 476
affirmation quadrants, 475
African-Americans, and cultural bias, 61, 301
aggression
  and childhood disorders, 405, 406
  and psychopathy, 312–313
aging, and mental disorders
  anxiety disorders, 422, 431–432
  case example, 417
  and chronic illnesses, 422
  cohort effect, 420
  comorbidity, 422
  delirium, 433–434
  dementia, 434–440
  demography, changing, 417–418
  depressive disorders, 426–427
  diagnosis, age specific issues, 422
  historical perspective, 420
  misconceptions, 420–421
  mood disorders, 424–425
  normal aging, 420
  older adults by age group, 418
  period effect, 420
  pharmacotherapy, 420–421
  polypharmacy, 422
  prevalence of mental disorders, 419
  prevalence of positive help-seeking attitudes, 422
  prevention, 422
  schizophrenia, 432–433
  sleep disorders, 427–430
  socio-emotional selectivity theory (SST), 424
  strength and vulnerability integration (SAVI), 423–424
  suicide, 425
  systemic barriers, 421
  theoretical frameworks of aging, 422–424
  theoretical progression of cognitive ability, 435
  therapist barriers, 421
  underrepresentation as users of mental health services, 421
  vulnerability versus resilience, 418–419
agonist, 17
agonist drugs, 275
agoraphobia, 49, 101, 119
AIDS, 149, 287–288
Alameda County, California, 158, 159
alarm, 154
alarm theory, 103
alcohol
  addictive potential of, 280
  consumption patterns, 265–268
  as depressant, 278
  effects of, 268–270, 272
  high-risk drinking, 266–268
  history of use, 265
  legal perspective, 489
  long-term effects, 269
  low-risk drinking guidelines, 266
  as risk factor for heart attack, 169
  short-term effects, 268–269
  and sleep, 429
  social costs of, 271
  standard drinks, 265
alcohol abuse and dependence, 278
  abstinence, 275
  and amnestic syndrome, 55
  behavioural treatment, 276–277
  brief interventions, 277–278
  case study, 264
  etiology of, 270–275
  family factors, 273
  family therapy, 277
  fetal alcohol spectrum disorders (FASD), 269
  fetal alcohol syndrome (FAS), 269
  genetic factors, 270–271
  marital therapy, 277
  the Minnesota model, 275
  mutual support groups, 275–276
  neurobiological influences, 271–272
  non-abstinence drinking goals, 275–278
  overlap with other substances, 263
  pharmacotherapy, 275
  psychological factors, 272–273
  psychological treatments, 276–277
  relapse prevention, 277
  residential treatment, 275
  social effects of, 270
  socio-cultural factors, 273–275
  treatment of, 275–278
alcohol dehydrogenase, 268
alcohol expectancy theory, 272
Alcoholics Anonymous, 274, 275, 276
alcohol-related birth defects (ARBD), 367
alcohol-related neurodevelopmental disorder (ARND), 367
Alcohol Use Disorders Identification Test (AUDIT), 266, 267
aldehyde dehydrogenase, 270
Alexander, Franz, 148, 161
Alexander the Great, 10
alleles, 186, 188
Allen Memorial Hospital, 14
all-or-nothing thinking, 40, 184
alogia, 211
alpha-fetoprotein (AFP), 366
Alprostadil, 339
alternate-form reliability, 67
alter personalities, 134
Alzheimer's disease (AD)
  assessment of, 363
  and the brain, 437
  cortical atrophy, 69
  and depression, 436
  described, 436–437
  in *Diagnostic and Statistical Manual of Mental Disorders* (DSM), 436
  diagnostic criteria, 436, 437
  environmental factors, 438
  etiology of, 437–438
  genetics, 219, 437–438
  [illegible], 211
  medical factors, 438
  non-pharmacological interventions, 438
  prevalence of, 435
  treatment, 438
Alzheimer-type dementia, 370
amenorrhea, 239
American Academy of Sleep Medicine, 430
American Association on Intellectual and Developmental Disabilities, 361, 374
American Association on Mental Retardation, 361
American Journal of Mental Retardation, 372
American National Institute of Mental Health (NIMH) funded a large multi-site randomized controlled trial that compared cognitive-behavioural therapy (CBT), 189
American Psychiatric Association, 3, 52, 62
American Psychological Association, 60
American Psychological Association Presidential Task Force on Evidence-Based Practice, 21
amicus curiae, 505
Amin, Idi, 311
Amish, 189
amitriptyline, 322
amnesia, 133
amnestic syndrome, 55
amniocentesis, 366
amotivational syndrome, 287
amphetamines, 280, 281–289, 399
amtriptyline, 192
amygdala
  and aggression, 405
  and anxiety disorders, 412
  and brain functions, 224
  and depression, 188
  dysfunction of, 313
  neural fear circuit, 98
  regulation of emotional states, 161
  and serotonin transporter gene, 189
amyloid, 437
Anafranil (clomipramine), 192
analogue observational setting, 82
analysis of resistance, 449
analysis of transference, 449
Anatomy of Melancholy, 175
Anderson, Hans Christian, 388
androgens, 336
angel dust, 288
anger, 168
angst, 42
anhedonia, 210, 211, 426
animal magnetism, 18
animal phobias, 104
Anna O, 34, 130
anorexia nervosa. *see also* eating disorders
  case example, 238
  characteristics of, 234–235, 236
  cognitive-behaviour therapy (CBT), 252
  defined, 57, 234
  diagnostic criteria, 238, 240, 242–243
  nutritional therapy, 253–254
  as OCD-spectrum disorder, 142
  personality factors, 248–249

physical and psychological complications, 243
prevalence of, 237
relapse rate, 237
schematic representation of core processes, 253
and serotonin, 244–245
anorgasmia, 334, 337
Antabuse, 275
antagonist, 17
antagonist drug, 275
antecedent-behaviour-consequence (ABC) chart, 82, 83
antecedents, 82
anti-androgens, 353
anticonvulsants, 193–194, 322
antidepressants. *see also* specific medications
for Alzheimer's disease (AD), 438
for autism, 382
for bipolar disorder, 194
for cocaine addiction, 283
described, 447
for eating disorders, 251
and generalized anxiety disorder, 126
list of, 446
and metabolic changes, 71
minor tranquilizers, 120
monoamine oxidase inhibitors (MAOIs), 192
and monoamines, 187
for older adults, 427
other classes of, 192–193
for personality disorders, 322
and rapid cycline bipolar disorder, 182
selective serotonin reuptake inhibitor (SSRI), 192
serotonin-norepinephrine reuptake inhibitors (SNRIs), 193
suicidal risk, 447
tricyclic antidepressants, 18, 187, 192–193
for unipolar depression, 192–193
use and effectiveness of, 120
antigens, 152
antihistamines, 18, 429
antioxidants, 438
antipsychotic medications
for Alzheimer's disease, 438
for borderline personality disorder, 322
for conduct disorder, 406
and deinstitutionalization, 18
for delirium, 434
described, 194, 445
extrapyramidal effects, 445
list of, 446
for older adults, 432–433
for schizophrenia, 227–228
second generation, 445
side effects, 445
antisocial behaviour, as criterion for abnormality, 5
antisociality, 351
antisocial personality disorder (APD)
course of, 303
and criminal behaviour, 309
criteria for, 308
defined, 57
described, 295, 307–308
in *Diagnostic and Statistical Manual of Mental Disorders* (DSM), 308
etiology of, 309–310
family factors, 309
fearlessness hypothesis, 309
genetic factors, 309
hospitalization for, 298
and lack of empathy, 301
and pharmacotherapy, 311
prevalence of, 297–298, 299, 309
prognosis, 303
psychological explanations, 302
versus psychopathy, 307, 312
psychopathy. *see* psychopathy
and punishment, 310
summary of, 311
treatment, 310–311
Antisocial Process Screening Device, 321
anxiety, 97
anxiety disorders, 56, 102
agoraphobia, 101
and ANS, 30
behavioural factors, 99
biological factors, 98–99
case example, 49, 97, 431
in children, 395, 396
cognitive factors, 99
and comorbidity, 396
cultural differences, 106
diagnostic issues, 431
discussed, 100
etiology of, 98–100
generalized anxiety disorder, 31–37, 117–119
genetics, 98
historical perspective, 97–98
interpersonal factors, 99–100
obsessive-compulsive disorder. *see* obsessive-compulsive disorder
in older adults, 431–432
panic attacks, 101
panic disorders, 100–101
phobias, 103–104
post-traumatic stress disorder, 113
prevalence among older adults, 431
psychological factors, 99
psychotherapy, effects of, 458–459
and schemas, 40
social anxiety disorder, 106, 107–109
social phobia, 106, 107–109
treatment, 119–123, 251–255
treatment efficacy, 123
treatment in older adults, 431–432
Anxiety Disorders Interview Schedule, 102
anxiety-relief hypothesis, 272
anxiety sensitivity, 103
Anxiety Sensitivity Index, 102
anxiolytics, 322, 445–447
anxious ambivalent, 316
anxious-ambivalent attachments, 100
anxious and fearful disorders, 296, 297
apathy, 211
aphasia, 224
aphrodisiacs, 339
Apolipopritein E (APOE) gene, 438
apolipoprotein A/apolipoprotein B ratio, 169
appearance, 73
apperception, 78
appetite suppressants, 281, 285
appraisals, 155
Aretaeus, 10
Aricept, 438
aripiprazole, 194
Aristotle, 10
arrhythmias, 165, 171
asocial disorders, 306
Asperger disorder, 306, 379–380, 387
Asperger, Hans, 380
asphyxiophilia, 346
assertiveness training, 453
assessment. *see also* specific disorders
actuarial approach, 68
behavioural and cognitive assessment, 82, 85
biological assessment, 68–69
brain imaging techniques, 69–71
case example, 66
clinical approach, 68
cognitive-behavioural assessment, 83
defined, 50
neuropsychological testing, 71–72
observational techniques, 82, 83
psychological assessment. *see* psychological assessment
purposes of, 67
reliability, 67–68
requirements of, 67
self-monitoring, 84–85
tools of, 67
assigned gender, 341
assisted suicide, 198
association, 162
Association for Community Living, 375
associative loosening, 217
associative model, 104, 105
assortative mating, 403
asthma, 281
asylums
in Canada, 19
defined, 10
early establishment of, 12–14, 15
movie depiction, 13–14
ataque de nervios, 106
atherogenesis, 165
atherosclerosis, 165, 166
atherosclerotic plaques, 165, 166
Ativan, 278
atomoxetine, 399
attachment, and anxiety disorders, 99–100
attachment theory
and avoidant personality disorder, 318–319
defined, 303
and dissociative disorders, 135
and personality disorders, 303–304
personality disorders, 316
attention deficit and disruptive behaviour disorders, 54
attention deficit disorder (ADD), 398
attention deficit/hyperactivity disorder (ADHD)
academic skill facilitation and remediation, 400
ADHD combined type (ADHD-HI), 396
ADHD hyperactive-impulsive type (ADHD-H), 396
ADHD inattentive type (ADHD-I), 396
in adults, 398
assessment of, 363, 399
brain structure and function, 398
case example, 88
comorbidity, 396, 403
defined, 54
described, 396
developmental trajectory, 396–398
in *Diagnostic and Statistical Manual of Mental Disorders* (DSM), 397
diagnostic criteria, 397
etiology of, 398–399
gene-environment interactions (G x E), 399
genetics, 398
minimal brain dysfunction, 398
parent training, 401
pharmacotherapy, 399–400
prenatal risk factors, 398–399
prevalence of, 396
psychoeducational interventions, 400
psychosocial factors, 399
side effects of medication, 400
and stimulants, 448
subtypes of, 396
treatment, 281, 399–401, 448
attractiveness, 44
auditory hallucinations, 208, 212
auditory integration training, 384
auditory test, 72
autism
and Asperger disorder, 379–380
assessment of, 363, 381
behavioural interventions, 382–383
behaviour and interests, 379
case example, 377
cerebellum atrophy, 69
child disintegrative disorder (CDD), 380
communication, verbal and nonverbal, 379
defined, 377
described, 54, 378
in *Diagnostic and Statistical Manual of Mental Disorders* (DSM), 378, 379, 381
diagnostic issues, 379
etiology of, 381–382
facilitated communication (FC), 384
and fragile X syndrome, 372
genetics, 219, 381
infantile autism, 393
measles/mumps vaccine (MMR), 381
medications for, 382
nutritional supplements, 382
prevalence of, 377–378
Rett syndrome, 380
and schizophrenia, 377
social interaction, 378
treatment of, 382–384
Autism Diagnostic Interview-Revised (ADI-R), 381
Autism Diagnostic Observation Schedule (ADOS-G), 381
Autism Spectrum Disorder, 379
autistic disorder. *see* autism
autoerotic asphyxia, 346
automatic thought, 41
autonomic, 151
autonomic arousal, 156
autonomic nervous system (ANS), 30, 31, 151, 165
autonomy, principle of, 504
autosomal trait, 26
aversion therapy, 276
aversive drift, 217
aversive stimuli, 412
Avicenna, 10
avoidance
behavioural avoidance, 115
cognitive avoidance, 115
of conflict, 130
covert avoidance, 107, 123
and generalized anxiety disorder, 117–118
in obsessive-compulsive disorder, 112–113

avoidance (*continued*)
overt avoidance, 107
in post-traumatic stress disorder, 115
subtle avoidance, 123
avoidance learning, 309
avoidant personality disorder, 318–319
avoidant/restrictive food intake disorder, 241
avolition, 210, 211
Axis I, 53
Axis II, 53, 80
Axis III, 53
Axis IV, 53
Axis V, 53, 54
axon, 28, 29
azapirones, 120, 126

B

baboons, 156, 157, 159
baby boomers, 417
bacteria, 163–164
Bandura, Albert, 20, 39, 451
barbiturates, 278, 429, 445
basal ganglia, 112, 398
Baycrest Centre for Geriatric Care, 440
A Beautiful Mind, 218
Beck, Aaron T., 26, 39, 40, 183, 451
Beck Anxiety Inventory, 431
becoming, 51
bedlam, 13
behaviour, 73, 149
behavioural activation, 452
behavioural addictions, 262
behavioural and cognitive assessment, 82, 85
behavioural assessment, 102
behavioural avoidance, 115
behavioural avoidance test (BAT), 102
behavioural dimension of hostility, 167
behavioural disinhibition, 272
behavioural experiments, 191
behavioural genetics, 32
behavioural inhibition, 406
behavioural interventions, 382–383
behavioural marital therapy, 460
behavioural medicine, 148
behavioural phenotypes, 364
behavioural theories
behaviourism, 17, 19
versus biological approaches, 24–25
classical conditioning, 36, 37–38
cognitive-behavioural theory, 39
conditioning accounts, 36–38, 39
operant conditioning, 38
social learning theory, 39
two-factor theory, 38
behavioural tolerance, 273
behavioural treatment, 276–277, 353
behaviour rating scales, 82, 84
behaviour therapy, 451
being, 374
Belak, Wade, 199
belief modification, 228
belladonna, 12
belonging, 374
Benadryl, 382
Bender Visual-Motor Gestalt Test, 71, 72
beneficence, principle of, 501
bennies, 281
benzodiazepines
addictive potential of, 280, 447
for alcoholic detoxification, 275
defined, 99
described, 278
for generalized anxiety disorder (GAD), 126
for insomnia, 429
minor tranquilizers, 120
and older adults, 431
benzopyrene, 287
berdache, 340
Berlin, Rudolf, 385
Bernardo, Paul, 309, 312
bestiality, 347
best interests principle, 494
Bethlem Royal Hospital, 13
Better Beginnings, Better Futures, 470, 479–480, 481
biastophilia, 351
bidirectional causation, 45
The Big Bang Theory, 319, 380
Biklen, Douglas, 384
bile, 9
Bill C-30, 500
Binet, Alfred, 75, 130
binge drinking, 367
binge eating, 235, 236, 237, 239
binge eating disorder (BED), 240–241
binge eating/purging type, 239
biofeedback, 170
biological approaches
classification, 16
development of, 15–18
electroconvulsive therapy, 17
versus environmental approaches, 24–25
heredity, 15–16
infection, 16
to personality disorders, 304–305
and psychopathy, 313
psychopharmacology, beginnings of, 17–18
shock therapy, 17
syndromes, 16
biological assessment, 68–69
biological causal factors, 186–189
biologically plausible mechanism, 149
biological models
central nervous system, role of, 28, 30
endocrine system, role of, 31–32
genetics and behaviour, 32–33
peripheral nervous system, role of, 30–31
biological preparedness, 105
biological treatments
193, 203, 233, 251, 283, 427, 444 *see* psychopharmacology
electroconvulsive therapy (ECT). *see* electroconvulsive therapy (ECT)
historical, 444
biomedical model, 148
biopsychosocial model, 46, 148, 376
biosocial theory, 316
biphasic effect, 268
bipolar disorders
adjunctive psychotherapy, 194–195
bipolar I and bipolar II, 180, 181
brain tissue loss, 69–70
in children, 181, 405
and cognitive therapy, 195
cyclothymia, 181
defined, 56
diagnostic criteria, 180
and genetics, 186
hypomania, 178–179
mania, 178–180
medications for, 193–194
and mood stabilizers, 447
and neurotransmitters, 187
prevalence of, 180
rapid cycling bipolar disorder, 181–182
relapse, 194
reliability, 194, 195
and sleep physiology, 188
and suicide, 180
treatment of, 194–195, 460
birth complications, 221–309
bizarre delusions, 213
black bile, 175
blackouts, 269
Blank, Billy, 388
bleeding, 9
blind interpretation, 81
blood alcohol level (BAL), 268
blood flow, 188
bloodletting, 10, 175
blood pressure
explained, 165
as risk factor, 169
and stress, 166, 167
treatment of, 170
variations in, 166
Bloom, Orlando, 388
Blueprint for a Canadian National Suicide Prevention Strategy, 200
blues, 278
blushing, fear of, 61
B-lymphocytes, 153
bodily fluids, 9, 10, 148
body dysmorphic disorder (BBD)
defined, 56, 138
described, 141–142
location of imagined defects, 142
and OCD, 142
prevalence of, 138
treatment of, 143
body image, 235, 236, 245–247, 248, 249, 251
body mass index (BMI), 238, 242–243, 245
body odour, fear of, 61
bonobos, 330
borderline patients, 315
borderline personality disorder (BPD)
attachment theory, 316
biosocial theory, 316
brain dysfunction, 316
criteria for, 317
described, 315–316
diagnosis overlap, 301
in *Diagnostic and Statistical Manual of Mental Disorders* (DSM), 315, 317
diagnostic criteria, 316
etiology of, 316–317
gender differences, 300
prevalence of, 299
borderline personality organization, 315
borderline states, 315
borderline syndrome, 315
Boston Legal, 380
Bowie, Christopher, 230
brain
and Alzheimer's disease (AD), 437
anatomical areas, 28
and attention deficit/hyperactivity disorder (ADHD), 398
and borderline personality disorder, 316
and bullying, 395
and conduct disorder (CD), 405
and dementia, 435
and learning disorders, 387
and oppositional defiant disorder (ODD), 405
and schizophrenia, 221–222, 223
and separation anxiety disorder (SAD), 411
and ulcers, 161–162
brain images, of schizophrenic and normal brains, 71
brain imaging techniques
computed tomography, 69–70
computerized axial tomography (CAT scans), 223
diffusion tensor imaging (DTI), 225
electroencephalogram, 69
event-related potentials (ERPs), 70
functional magnetic resonance imaging, 70
functional techniques, 223
magnetic resonance imaging (MRI), 70, 223, 224
magnetoencephalography, 70
positron emission tomography (PET), 70–71, 223
brain injuries, 364
brain lesion, 438
brain plasticity, 30
brain stem, 98
brainwashing, 14
breathing retraining, 123
breathing techniques, 170
Breuer, Josef, 18, 34, 130
brief interventions, 277–278
brief psychodynamic psychotherapy, 450
broad band instruments, 84
Broca, Paul, 32
bromocriptine, 283
bud, 286–287
Buddhism, 191
bulimia nervosa. *see also* eating disorders
characteristics of, 236
cognitive-behaviour therapy (CBT), 252, 254
defined, 57, 234
diagnostic criteria, 240, 242
family therapy, 254
interpersonal therapy, 252–253, 254
nonpurging type, 240
perpetuating factors, 250
personality factors, 248–249
physical and psychological complications, 243–244
precipitating factors, 250
predisposing factors, 250
prevalence of, 237
prognosis, 237
purging type, 240
and trauma history, 250
treatment of, 251–255
bullycide, 395
bullying, 388, 395
bupropion hydrochloride, 281
buproprion, 193
Burke, Chris, 360, 370
burnout factor, 303
bursa, 153
Burton, Robert, 175

C

Cabanis, 15
Cade, John, 193
caffeine, 280, 283, 284
camphor, 17
Canadian Addiction Survey, 265

Canadian Association for Suicide Prevention (CASP)., 200
Canadian Centre on Substance Abuse national survey, 281
Canadian Coalition for Seniors' Mental Health (CCSMH), 425, 426
Canadian Coalition for Seniors' Mental Health National Guidelines (CCSMH), 433, 434
Canadian Code of Ethics for Psychologists, 384, 503, 504
Canadian Community Health Survey (CCHS), 89–90, 107, 247, 289, 419, 425, 455
Canadian Institutes of Health Research, 256
Canadian legal system, 490–492
Canadian Network for Mood and Anxiety Treatment (CANMAT) guidelines, 193
Canadian Population Health Initiative, 470
Canadian Psychological Association, 21
Canadian Study of Health and Aging, 434
cancer, 287
Candy, John, 164
cannabis
  case example, 286
  dependency, 288
  effects of, psychoactive, 287
  effects of, therapeutic, 287
  prevalence of, 287
  and schizophreniform disorder, 33
  source of, 286
The Canon of Medicine, 10
capability dimension, 475
capable wishes principle, 494
capacity to plan legal strategy, 501
carbamazepine (Tegretol), 193, 322, 382, 447
carbon monoxide, 200
cardiac counselling intervention, 170
cardiac health psychology, 171
cardiac output, 165
cardiovascular disease
  and cardiovascular reactivity, 166
  and depression, 168–169
  dietary factors, 165
  discussed, 164
  and hostility, 154, 167–168
  plumbing analogy, 165
  processes, 164–165
  psychological factors, 167–169
  psychosocial factors, 166–167
  risk factors, 165, 166
  smoking, 165
cardiovascular reactivity, 166
Cardona, 12
card sorting test, 222–223
caregiver stress, 440
Carpenter, Sheena, 251
Casanova, 335
case studies as research method, 88
case study
  Bernardo, Paul, 309
  Burke, Chris, 360
  Carpenter, Sheena, 251
  Charlie Sheen, 181
  Diane, 314
  Downey, Robert Jr., 273
  Helfgott, David, 59
  Hoarders, 109
  Homolka, Karla, 309
  Hughes, Clara, 44
  Ingram, Jeff, 137
  John Candy, 164
  Nash, John, 218
  Raskin, Richard/Renée, 343
castration, 353
castration anxiety, 35
catastrophically misinterpret, 103
catastrophizing, 184
catatonic behaviour, 210, 211–214
catecholamine norepinephrine (NE), 187
catecholamines, 151, 165, 166
categories of disorder
  adjustment disorders, 57
  anxiety disorders, 56
  delirium, dementia, amnesia, and other cognitive disorders, 55
  Diagnostic and Statistical Manual of Mental Disorders (DSM), 53–55, 56, 59
  disorders usually first diagnosed in infancy, childhood, or adolescence, 54–55
  dissociative disorders, 56–57
  eating disorders, 57
  factitious disorders, 56
  impulse control disorders, 57
  mood disorders, 55–56
  other conditions that may be focus of clinical attention, 57
  personality disorders, 57
  schizophrenia and other psychotic disorders, 55
  sexual and gender identity disorders, 57
  sleep disorders, 57
  somatoform disorders, 56
  substance-related disorders, 55
category test, 72
cathartic method, 18, 34
Caucasians, and cultural bias, 301
causality
  bidirectional causation, 45
  biological causal factors, 186–189
  cognitive theories, 183–184
  and health psychology, 162
  interpersonal models, 184–185
  life stress perspective, 185–186
  neurotransmitters, 187
  psychodynamic theories, 183
  psychological and environmental causal factors, 183–186
  sleep neurophysiology, 188
  unidirectional causation, 45
Celexa (citalopram), 192
cellular immunity, 152
Central Intelligence Agency, 14
central nervous system
  and endocrine system, 31–32
  role of, 28, 30
Centre for Addiction and Mental Health, 20, 71
cerebellum, 398
cerebral cortex, 188, 435
cerebrospinal fluid (CSF), 226
cerebrovascular damage, 438
Cerletti, Ugo, 17
Champix, 281
Chantix, 281
Charcot, Jean, 18, 130
Charter of Rights and Freedoms, 490, 500
checking, as OCD, 112
chemical castration, 353
chemically induced sleep, 14
Cher, 388
Child Behaviour Checklist, 343
child brides, 5
child disintegrative disorder (CDD), 380
childhood abuse
  and borderline personality disorder, 316
  and conversion disorder, 139
  and cortisol, 188
  and depression, 188
  and dissociative disorders, 133, 135, 136
  and eating disorders, 249–250
  and personality disorders, 304
  and post-traumatic stress disorder, 116
  and psychological diatheses, 45
  and psychopathy, 313–314
  and risk for depression, 185–186
  and somatoform disorders, 143
childhood anxiety disorders
  brain structure and function, 441
  case example, 407–408
  cognitive-behavioural therapy (CBT), 412
  in *Diagnostic and Statistical Manual of Mental Disorders* (DSM), 408
  fear conditioning, 412
  gene-environment interactions, 412
  genetics, 441
  pharmacotherapy, 412–413
  prenatal risk factors, 411
  psychosocial risk factors, 411–412
  separation anxiety disorder (SAD). *see* separation anxiety disorder (SAD)
  temperament, 411
  treatment, 412–413, 459
childhood development programs, 471
childhood disorders
  anxiety disorders. *see* childhood anxiety disorders
  assessment issues, 393–394
  attention deficit/hyperactivity disorder (ADHD). *see* attention deficit/hyperactivity disorder (ADHD)
  and bullying, 394
  case example, 392
  conduct disorder. *see* conduct disorder (CD)
  disorders usually first diagnosed in infancy, childhood, or adolescence, 54–55, 394
  evidence-based treatments, 463
  historical perspective, 392–393
  oppositional behaviour. *see* oppositional defiant disorder (ODD)
  prevalence of, 394, 468
  psychotherapy, effects of, 460
child molester, 349
children. *see also* childhood disorders
  and bipolar disorders, 180–181
  and risk for depression, 185–186
  and schizophrenia, 221
Children in the Community Study of Developmental Course of Personality Disorder, 295, 301, 303, 306
Children's Apperception Test, 66
chimpanzees, 330
China, 199
Chinese culture, 61
Chivers, Mererdith, 330
chlorpromazine, 18, 20, 227
chocolate, 280
cholera, 89
cholesterol, 157, 165, 166, 269
cholinesterase inhibitors (ChEIs), 438, 439
chorionic villus sampling (CVS), 366
Christianity, 130, 326
Christmas in Purgatory, 360
chromosomal abnormalities
  Fragile X syndrome, 370–372
  and intellectual disabilities, 363, 364, 450
chromosomal gender, 341
chromosomes, 186, 219–220, 365, 437
chronic sorrow, 373
Cialis, 339
Cicero, 175
cingulate cortex, 188, 189
circadian patterns, 428, 429
circulatory shock, 227
circumcision, botched, 342
citalopram, 192
citrated calcium carbamate (CCC), 275
civil code, 492
civil commitment, 492–494
civil mental health law. *see also* law
  best interests principle, 494
  capable wishes principle, 494
  compulsory treatment orders, 494–495
  criminal commitment, 492
  described, 491
  involuntary hospitalization, 492–494, 495–496
  involuntary treatment, 494–495
  research on, 495–497
  reviews and appeals, 495, 496
classical conditioning, 36, 37–38, 99, 104
classic psychosomatic disorders, 148
classification. *see also* categories of disorder; diagnosis
  beginning of, 16
  categorical approach, 58
  dimensional approach, 58
  functions of, 51
  history of abnormality concepts, 51–52
  issues in diagnosis and classification, 59, 60
  medical model, 59
  multiaxial approach, 53
  need for, 50
  objections to, 59, 60
  phenomenological approach, 56
Cleckley, Hervey, 302
client-centred therapy, 450
clienthood, 475
clinical control group, 87
clinical depression. *see also* depression
  in caregivers, 440
  statistical frequency, 2–4
  treatment of, 459
clinical disorders, 299
clinical practice guidelines, 464
Clinical Psychiatry, 16
clinical psychologist, 6
clinical psychology, 468–469
clinical scales, 79, 80
clinical significance, 93–94
clinical utility, 59
Clinician Administered PTSD Scale, 115
clitoris, 329
clomipramine, 120, 124, 192, 382
clonidine, 382
clozapine, 194
Clozaril (clozapine), 194

Cluster A: odd and eccentric disorders
causes of, 305
characteristics of, 297
paranoid personality disorder, 305–306
prevalence of, 298–299
schizoid personality disorder, 306
schizotypal personality disorder, 301, 304, 306–307, 316
treatment sought, 299
Cluster B: dramatic, emotional, or erratic disorders
antisocial personality disorder (APD). *see* antisocial personality disorder (APD)
borderline personality disorder (BPD). *see* borderline personality disorder (BPD)
causes of, 305
characteristics of, 297
histrionic personality disorder (HPD), 300, 301–302, 317
narcissistic personality disorder (NPD), 301, 317–318
prevalence of, 298–299
treatment sought, 299
Cluster C: anxious and fearful disorders
avoidant personality disorder, 318–319
causes of, 305
characteristics of, 297
dependent personality disorder, 319
obsessive-compulsive personality disorder (OCPD), 319–320
prevalence of, 298–299
treatment sought, 299
clusters, 296
CNS depressants, 284
cocaine, 280
biological treatments, 283
dependency, 283
effects of, 283
prevalence, 283
psychological treatments, 283
and schizophrenia, 226
source of, 282
symptoms of use, 283
treatment for, 283
Cocaine Anonymous, 283
cocaine use disorders, 55
codeine, 284
codependents, 277
coefficient alpha, 68
the coercive process, 406
cognitive ability, theoretical progression of, 435
cognitive/attitudinal dimension, 167
cognitive avoidance, 115
cognitive-behavioural assessment, 83
cognitive-behavioural group therapy (CBGT), 124
cognitive-behavioural models, of obsessive-compulsive disorder, 112–113
cognitive-behavioural perspective, 24
cognitive-behavioural theory, 39, 143
cognitive-behavioural therapy (CBT)
activity scheduling, 190
for anxiety disorders, 126, 412
assertiveness training, 453
beginning of, 20
behavioural activation, 452
behavioural experiments, 191
for childhood anxiety disorders, 412
for cocaine abuse, 283
cognitive restructuring, 453
compared to interpersonal psychotherapy, 189
compared to serotonin-based antidepressant (paroxetine), 71
for depression, 459
described, 190, 451–452
for developmental disorders, 376
for eating disorders, 252
exposure therapy, 452
interpersonal psychotherapy (IPT), 191–192
and measurement of cognition, 83
meta-analytic evidence, 458
mindfulness-based strategies, 191, 453
for older adults, 431, 433
for panic disorders, 124, 458–459
for personality disorders, 304, 320–322
problem-solving approach, 453
for psychophysiological disorders, 170
reinforcement, 452
relaxation training, 452
response shaping, 452
for schizophrenia, 228–229
for self-harming youth, 410
for separation anxiety disorder (SAD), 412
and sexual offenders, 353, 354
for sleep disorders, 429
for somatoform disorders, 143–144
for suicidal youth, 410
as suicide prevention, 200
thought records, 190–191
for unipolar depression, 190–192
cognitive distortions, 184
cognitive errors, 40
cognitive markers, 215
cognitive model of panic, 103
cognitive remediation, 229, 230
cognitive restructuring, 120–122, 320, 453
cognitive slippage, 217
cognitive theories
and anxiety disorders, 99
cognitive theory and therapy, 39–41
and mood disorders, 183–184
principles of, 39
and PTSD, 116
rational-emotive behaviour therapy, 39
cognitive therapy (CT)
for bipolar disorder, 195
and neurobiology, 26
and perception, 451–452
cognitive triad, 184
cohesion in group therapy, 464
cohort effect, 420
cold sores, 160
Collaborative Longitudinal Personality Disorders Study, 295
collective unconscious, 216
colour, 167
combat, 156
of commission, 115
common cold, 160
common law, 490, 491–492
communication and exploration, and sexual dysfunctions, 338
communication disorders, 54
Community Education Training Program (COPE), 407
community integration, 373–374
community-level strategies, 470
Community Living for the Mentally Retarded in Ontario: A New Policy Focus, 373
Community Parent Education Program (COPE), 401
community psychology, 468–469
Community Reinforcement Approach (CRA), 276
comorbid anxiety disorder, 141
comorbidity
in childhood disorders, 396
in children and adolescents, 394, 403, 409–410
and classification of disorders, 56
and conduct disorder (CD), 403
defined, 301
and diagnostic overlap, 301–302
and generalized anxiety disorder (GAD), 409–410
heterotypic comorbidity, 410
homotypic comorbidity, 410
and major depressive disorder (MDD), 178
and oppositional defiant disorder (ODD), 403
and post-traumatic stress disorder, 115
and separation anxiety disorder (SAD), 409
competence
for decision making, 487–488, 494
of forensic practitioners, 504
completed suicide, 198
complex PTSD, 115–116
complex somatic symptom disorder, 141
comprehensive programs, 354
comprehensive theories, 352–353
compulsions, 56, 110
compulsive gambling, 289
compulsory treatment orders, 494–495
computed tomography (CT), 69–70
computer games, 280
computerized axial tomography (CAT scans), 28, 223
conclusions, jumping to, 184
concordance, 33, 90
concurrent validity, 51
conditioned stimulus (CS), 36, 99, 125
conditioning accounts, 36–38, 39
conditioning model, 104
conditioning theories, 351
conduct disorder (CD)
comorbidity, 396, 403
defined, 54
described, 401–403
developmental trajectory, 404
in *Diagnostic and Statistical Manual of Mental Disorders* (DSM), 401–403
diagnostic criteria, 401–403
etiology of, 405–406
gender differences, 403
gene-environment interactions, 405–406
genetics, 405
MAOA activity level, 406
neurobiology, 405
neurological factors, 434
parent training, 406–407
pharmacotherapy, 406
prenatal risk factors, 309
prevalence of, 395, 403–404
problem solving, 406
psychosocial risk factors, 405
school- and community-based treatment, 407
subtypes of, 403
treatment, 406–407
conflict, marital, 154
confound, 87
congenital limb deficiency, 368
congenital wordblindness, 385
conscious, 34
consent, competence for, 493
consequences, 82, 83
consistency, 162
constitutional law, 490–491
constitutional vulnerability, 168
construct validity, 68
contamination, as OCD, 112, 113
content-specificity, 40
content validity, 68
contextual field, 474–475
contextual quadrants, 475
contingency management, 276
continuous amnesia, 133
Continuous Performance Test (CPT), 215
continuous positive airway pressure (CPAP), 430
contrasted-groups method, 80
control group, 85
controllability, 157–158, 163
controllable risk factors, 165
controllable, 165
conversion disorder, 9, 56, 130, 138, 139
Cook-Medley hostility scale, 167
Cooper v. R, 500
coping strategy enhancement, 228
coprophilia, 347
core syndrome, 379
coronary heart disease, 158
Correctional Investigator of Canada, 498
correlational research method, 87–88
correlation coefficients, 87
cortical atrophy, 69
cortical dementias, 435
corticotrophin releasing hormone (CRH), 187
corticotropin, 108
cortisol
and the cardiovascular system, 166
and childhood abuse, 188
and conduct disorders, 405
effects of, 32, 143, 151
and military combat, 188
and seasonal affective disorder, 182
counter-transference, 449
couples therapy, 454, 460
courtship disorder theory, 351
covert avoidance, 107, 123
cow, prince's delusion, 11
crack, 282
crank, 281
C-reactive protein, 169
cretinism, 32
Creutzfeldt-Jakob disease, 439
criminal behaviour. *see also* mental health law; mentally disordered offenders
antisocial personality disorder (APD) and, 309
HCR-20 risk factors, 497
and legal insanity, 327
and psychopathy, 311, 312–314
sexual offenders, 327
sexual offending, 351–353

Criminal Code
  amendments to, 500, 503
  criminal responsibility, 499, 500
  described, 491
  fitness to stand trial, 500
  psychology, status of, 505
criminal commitment, 492
criminal law, 491, 499
Criminal Lunatics Acts of 1800, 499
criminal responsibility. *see also* law
  Cooper v. R, 500
  fitness evaluations, 501–503
  Kjeldsen v. R., 500
  mental state at time of offence, 499, 500
  not criminally responsible on account of mental disorder, 499
  Plato, 9
  R. v. Abbey, 500
  R. v. Chaulk, 500
  R. v. Rabey, 500
  R. v. Swain, 500
  Winko v. B.C., 500
criterion validity, 68
Crosby, Sidney, 4
cross-fostering, 91
Cruise, Tom, 388
crystal, 281
cultural bias
  and Aboriginal people, 61
  and African-Americans, 61, 301
  and Caucasians, 301
  in *Diagnostic and Statistical Manual of Mental Disorders* (DSM), 61–62
  and hallucinations, 61
  and Hispanics, 45–46, 61, 301
  and syndromes, 61
cultural/ethnic differences
  anxiety disorders, 106
  and dependent personality disorder, 319
  and sexuality, 328
  in somatization disorder, 140
culturally relative, 6
cumulative liability, 221
cumulative risk, 472–473
curare, 17
current and generalized threat, 116
cyberbullying, 395
cyclothymia, 56, 181
Cynomolgus (macaque) monkeys, 153, 166
Cyproterone Acetate (CPA), 353
cytosine, 371

D
Dallaire, Roméo, 115
Dark Triad, 302
Darwin, Charles, 7, 15
DBT Coach, 461
D-Cycloserine, 124
Dead Man Walking, 308
decision making, competence for, 487–488, 494, 500–501
deep brain stimulation, 197
defecation, 347
defence mechanisms, 35–36
deformity, fear of, 61
dehydration, 269
deinstitutionalization, 18, 495
deliberate self-harm (DSH), 410
delirium
  case example, 433
  defined, 55
  described, 433
  diagnostic issues, 433
  etiology of, 433
  treatment, 434
Della Porta, 12
delta-9.tetrahydrocannabinol (THC), 287
delusional thinking, 209
delusions
  bizarre delusions, 213
  defined, 210
  delusions of grandeur, 211
  historic view of, 12
  mood congruent delusions, 213
  in older adults, 432
  persecutory delusions, 210
  psychotic, 305
  in schizophrenia, 210
  types of, 210
demand characteristics, 82
dementia
  Alzheimer's disease (AD). *see* Alzheimer's disease (AD)
  caregiver stress, 440
  case example, 434
  classification, 435
  cortical dementias, 435
  defined, 16, 28, 55
  dementia with Lewy bodies, 435
  described, 434
  and Down syndrome, 370
  and Fragile X syndrome, 372
  frontotemporal dementia (FTD), 435, 439–440
  Lewy body dementia, 439–440
  mild cognitive impairment (MCI), 435–436
  mixed dementia, 437
  other forms of, 439–440
  prevalence of, 434, 435
  pseudo-dementia, 435
  subcortical dementias, 435
  vascular dementia, 438–439
dementia praecox, 216
Dementia Scale for Down Syndrome (DSDS), 370
Demerol, 284
demonic possession, 9, 11, 61, 130, 175
demons, 209
dendrite, 28, 29
Depakote (valproate), 193
dependence, 262
dependency, 183, 185
dependent personality disorder, 57, 319
dependent variables, 85
depersonalization, 133
depersonalization disorder, 57, 133–134
depressants, 284
depression. *see also* clinical depression; major depressive disorder (MDD); mood disorders; unipolar mood disorders
  and Alzheimer's disease (AD), 436
  and cardiovascular disease, 168–169
  chronic, types of, 179
  and cognitive-behaviour therapy (CBT), 190
  and cognitive therapy, 26
  combinations of psychotherapy and medication, 194–195
  and comorbidity, 396
  continuum, 176
  diagnostic issues in older adults, 426
  and diathesis-stress perspective, 45
  duration, 176
  dysthymic disorder, 426
  etiology of, 425
  gender differences, 189
  and glucose metabolism, 188
  historical perspective, 175
  Hughes, Clara, 44
  interpersonal model, 185
  and neural circuits, 188–189
  and neurotransmitters, 187
  in older adults, 425–427
  postpartum depression. *see* postpartum depression
  prevalence of, 6
  relapse, 191, 192, 193, 201–202
  reliability, 194
  and schemas, 40
  severity, 176
  and stress, 188
  and stressful life events, 32
  treatment of, 17, 191, 426–427, 459, 464
derealization, 133
Derevensky, Jeffery, 290
description, defined, 85
De Seingalt, Giovanni Jacopo Casanova, 335
designer drugs, 281
desipramine, 192
Desyrel (trazodone), 193
developmental disability. *see* intellectual disability
developmental disorders
  adaptive behaviour, 362–363
  autism. *see* autism
  behavioural approach, 376
  biopsychosocial approach, 376
  birth-related causes, 368
  case example, 359, 369, 370, 371, 375
  challenging behaviours, 375–376
  chromosomal abnormalities, 363, 364, 450
  community integration, 373–374
  crisis intervention, 377
  deinstitutionalization, 373–375
  diagnostic issues, 361–363
  Down syndrome, 365, 369–370
  drugs, 368
  dual diagnosis, 376
  early intervention, 369
  effects on family, 372–373
  environmental causes, 367–368
  etiology of, 363–364
  Fragile X syndrome, 370–372
  genetic causes, 363–366
  genetic versus environmental factors, 368–369
  historical perspective, 359–360
  inclusion, 374
  intellectual disability, 361
  interviewing strategies, 363
  IQ scores, distribution of, 362
  mainstreaming, 374
  metabolic disorders, 366
  postnatal environmental factors, 368–369
  prenatal environment, 367–368
  prenatal screening, 366
  prevention, 369
  quality of life, 374
  and sex education, 375
  terminology, 360–361
  treatment of, 376–377
developmental model, 360
Dexedrine, 281
dextroamphetamine, 281, 399
dhat, 106
dhat syndrome, 140
diabetes, 169
diagnosis. *see also* classification; specific disorders
  defined, 49
  by expert, 6–7
Diagnostic and Statistical Manual of Mental Disorders (DSM)
  addiction, 263–264
  Alzheimer's disease (AD), 436, 437
  amenorrhea, 239
  amnestic syndrome, 433
  anorexia nervosa, 238, 239
  antisocial personality disorder (APD), 308–309
  anxiolytic intoxication, 278
  attention deficit/hyperactivity disorder (ADHD), 396, 397
  as authority on abnormality, 2–3, 7
  Autism Spectrum Disorder, 379
  autistic disorder, 378, 379, 381
  avoidance, 115
  avoidant personality disorder, 319
  binge eating disorder (BED), 240, 241
  bipolar disorders, 180
  body dysmorphic disorder, 142
  borderline personality disorder (BPD), 315, 317
  bulimia nervosa, 240
  caffeine-related disorders, 283–284
  categorical approach, 58
  categories of disorder, 53–55, 56, 59
  changes in, 119, 125, 214, 241–363, 386
  child psychiatric disorders, 393
  comorbidity, 56
  complex somatic symptom disorder, 141
  conduct disorder (CD), 401, 402
  conversion disorders, 139
  criticism of, 51, 58, 60–62, 214, 299
  culture bias, 61–62
  culture-bound syndromes, 106
  delirium, 433
  dementia, 434, 435
  dependent personality disorder, 319
  depersonalization disorder, 133
  developmental disorders, 361, 363
  diagnosis of Cindy, 149
  dimensional approach, 58
  disorders usually first diagnosed in infancy, childhood, or adolescence, 394
  disruptive mood dysregulation disorder, 404–405
  dissociative disorders, 130, 131
  dissociative fugue, 133
  dissociative identity disorder, 134
DSM-5, 58–59
  dyspareunia, 334–335
  dysthymic disorder, 178, 179
  eating disorder not otherwise specified (EDNOS), 240–241
  eating disorders, 242, 250
  erectile disorder, 333
  exhibitionism, 348
  female orgasmic disorder, 334
  fetishism, 345
  frotteurism, 348
  functional neurological disorder, 139
  gender bias, 60–61
  gender identity disorder (GID), 341, 342
  generalized anxiety disorder, 117, 118
  genito-pelvic pain/penetration disorder, 335

diagnosis. *see also* classification; specific disorders (*continued*)
- geriatric cognitive disorders, 433
- hallucinogen persisting perception disorder, 290
- histrionic personality disorder, 317
- hypersexuality, 336
- hypnotic intoxication, 278
- hypochondriasis, 141
- intellectual developmental disorder, 361, 363
- and Kraepelin's classification, 16
- learning disabilities, 385
- learning disorders, 385, 386
- legal insanity, 327
- major depressive disorder, 176, 177
- male orgasmic disorder, 334
- mania and hypomania, 178
- mathematic disorder, 385
- mental retardation, 361
- mood disorders, 176
- multiaxial approach, 52–64, 148
- and multiple diagnoses, 302
- narcissistic personality disorder (NPD), 318
- neurocognitive disorders, 433–434
- neurodevelopmental disorders, 361, 386
- objective binge, 235
- obsessive-compulsive and related disorders, 109
- obsessive-compulsive personality disorder (OCPD), 319
- oppositional defiant disorder (ODD), 402
- pain disorder, 140, 141
- panic disorders, 101
- paraphilias, 327, 345
- paraphilias not otherwise specified, 347
- pathological gambling, 289
- pedophilia, 5, 349
- personality disorders, 295, 296, 297, 299
- and politics, 62
- post-traumatic stress disorder (PTSD), 113–115
- premature ejaculation, 334
- primary insomnia, 428, 429
- psychopathy, 311
- psychophysiological disorders, 147
- publication of, 52
- rape, 350
- rapid cycling bipolar disorder, 181–182
- schizophrenia, 212
- schizotypal personality disorder, 307
- sedative intoxication, 278
- separation anxiety disorder (SAD), 408, 409
- sexual aversion disorder, 333
- sexual desire disorders, 333
- sexual dysfunction, 326, 332
- sexual sadism, 327
- sleep disorders, 428
- social phobia, 107
- sociopathic personality disturbance, antisocial reaction, 302
- somatic symptom disorders, 137
- somatoform disorders, 130, 142
- substance abuse, 261
- substance abuse disorders, 280
- substance dependence, 262, 289
- transvestic fetishism, 346

Diagnostic Interview Schedule, 73, 309
diagnostic overshadowing, 376
diagnostic system. *see also* classification
- characteristics of, 51
- clinical utility, 59
- defined, 49
- inter-rater reliability, 51
- perfect diagnostic system, 50
- reliability, 51
- validity, 51

dialectical behaviour therapy (DBT), 321–322
diastole, 165
diastolic blood pressure, 165
diatheses, 184, 185, 217
diathesis-stress formulation, 135
diathesis-stress model, 163, 184
diathesis-stress perspective, 45–46, 399
dietary factors, 165, 169, 170, 475
dieting, 249, 250
differential diagnosis, 102, 242
diffusion tensor imaging (DTI), 225
digestive acid, 161
Dilantin (phenytoin), 193, 368, 382
dimensional approach, 58, 304
dimensions, 304
diphenhydramine (Benadryl), 382
discretionary risk assessment, 497
disease, defined, 149
disease markers, 214–215
disease states and psychosocial factors. *see* psychosocial factors and disease states
disgust sensitivity, 105
disorder of written expression, 386
disorders of overcontrolled behaviour, 394
disorders of undercontrolled behaviour, 394
disorders usually first diagnosed in infancy, childhood, or adolescence, 54–55, 394
disorganized pattern, 135
disorganized speech and thought disorder, 211
disruptive mood dysregulation disorder, 404–405
dissemination, 483–484
dissociation, 115
dissociative amnesia, 56, 133
dissociative disorders
- and attachment theory, 135
- case example, 129
- characteristics of, 131
- depersonalization disorder, 133–134
- described, 131
- dissociative amnesia, 133
- dissociative fugue, 133, 137
- dissociative identity disorder. *see* dissociative identity disorder
- etiology of, 135–136
- and hypnosis, 137
- medication for, 137
- prevalence, 132
- psychotherapy for, 136–137
- repressed memory, 132
- socio-cognitive model, 136
- somatoform disorders. *see* somatoform disorders
- trauma model, 135
- treatment of, 136–137
- types of, 131

dissociative fugue, 57, 133, 137
dissociative identity disorder (DID), 56–57
- defined, 129
- described, 134, 135
- diagnostic criteria, 134
- and diathesis-stress perspective, 45
- historical perspective, 130–131
- prevalence, 135

distress, as criterion for abnormality, 4–5
disulfiram, 275
divalproex, 447
diving, 280
divorce, 472
Dix, Dorothea, 14
dizygotic (DZ) twins, 91, 186
DNA, 371
Dobson, Keith, 459, 464
dominant inheritance, 450
donepezil, 438
dopamine
- and attention deficit/hyperactivity disorder (ADHD), 398
- and autism, 382
- and childhood disorders, 406
- and depression, 187
- and schizophrenia, 29, 225–227
- and social phobia, 108

dopamine beta-hydroxylase (DBH), 398
dopamine-blocking drugs, 226
dopamine-enhancing drugs, 283
dope, 286–287
dorsal tempoparietal subsystem, 387
double-blind trial, 86, 445
double depression, 178
Douglas Mental Health University Institute, 256
downers, 278
Downey, Robert Jr., 273
downregulation, 154
Down syndrome
- and Alzheimer's disease (AD), 437
- chromosomal abnormalities, 365
- described, 369–370
- selective mutism, 413
- types of, 365–366

Down syndrome advantage, 372
doxepin, 192
drag queens, 346
dramatic, emotional, or erratic disorders, 296, 297
dreams, 9, 449
Drew, Lori, 395
Drinker's Check-up, 277
driving fast, 280
Drug Abuse Resistance Education, 480
Drug Evaluation and Classification (DEC), 287
drug interactions, 427
Drug Recognition Experts (DREs), 287
drugs, illegal, 271
DSM-5, publishing date, 2
DTREE software, 74
dual diagnosis, 376
dualistic view, 147
Dual Representation Theory, 116
duration, 176
dyscalculia, 386
dysfunction, as criterion for abnormality, 5
dyslexia, 58, 385, 386, 387
dysmorphophobia, 138
dyspareunia, 330–333, 340
dysphoria, 426
dyssocial personalities, 307
dyssomnia, 57
dysthymia, 56
dysthymic disorder, 178, 179, 426

E

Early Assessment Risk Lists (EARLs), 506
early childhood development, 471, 483
Early Head Start Project, 481
early intensive behavioural intervention (EIBI), 382–383
early intervention, for schizophrenia, 229–230
Early Maladaptive Schemas (EMS), 39
Early Years Centres, 482
Eating Disorder Examination (EDE), 243
eating disorder not otherwise specified (EDNOS), 240
eating disorders
- adverse events, 249–250
- anorexia nervosa. *see* anorexia nervosa
- assessment, 243
- binge eating disorder (BED), 240–241
- biological treatments, 251–252
- biopsychosocial model, 250
- bulimia nervosa. *see* bulimia nervosa
- case example, 234
- causes versus consequences, 244
- characteristics of, 234–236
- classification, validity of, 242–243
- cognitive-behaviour therapy (CBT), 252
- diagnostic criteria, 238, 240, 242, 243
- diagnostic issues, 242–243
- and diathesis-stress perspective, 45
- differential diagnosis, 242
- eating disorder not otherwise specified (EDNOS), 240
- etiology of, 244–247, 248, 250
- family factors, 248
- family therapy, 254
- genetic and biological theories, 244–245
- historical perspective, 234
- individual factors, 248–249
- integrative models, 250
- interpersonal therapy, 252–253
- introduction to, 234
- in males, 250, 251
- maturational issues, 249
- meal support, 253–254
- nutritional therapy, 253–254
- personality factors, 248–249
- physical and psychological complications, 238–244
- Pica's disorder, 54–55
- prevalence of, 237
- prevention, 255–257
- prognosis, 237
- psychological theories, 245–247, 248, 250
- psychological treatments, 252–255
- self-help, 254–255
- socio-cultural factors, 245–247
- transdiagnostic theory, 252
- treatment of, 251–255
- women, 44

Eating Disorders Inventory, 243
Eating Disorders Program (EDP), 256
eccentricities, 306, 420
echolalia, 379
ecological dimension, 474, 479
ecological perspective, 470, 474

Ecstasy, 280, 281, 288
Edison, Thomas, 388
Education Act, 385
educational approach, 471
effect size, 222, 457
effects of psychotherapy, evaluating, 456–458
effects of psychotherapy, for specific disorders
anxiety disorders, 458–459
Axis II disorders, 460
childhood disorders, 460
in clinical settings, 461–462
couple distress, 460–461
mood disorders, 459
serious mental illness, 460
sleep disorders, 460
Effexor (venlafaxine), 193
ego, 34–36
ego analysis, 450
egodystonic, 299
egodystonic homosexuality, 327
egosyntonic, 299, 318
Egyptians, 8, 10
Einstein, Albert, 380
ejaculation, 330, 332, 334, 337, 339
Elavil (amtriptyline), 192
Electra complex, 35
electroconvulsive therapy (ECT)
defined, 17
for depression, 444
described, 196–197, 444
and Ewen Cameron, 14
for older adults, 427
for schizophrenia, 444
side effects, 444
electroencephalogram (EEG)
and alcohol abuse and dependence, 272
described, 69
and sleep patterns, 428
elimination disorders, 55
Ellis, Albert, 39, 451
Elmira, New York, 477–478, 480
emotion, 97, 221
emotional abuse, 134, 135, 186
emotionally focused couples therapy, 454
emotional numbing, 115
emotional responsiveness, 306
emotional symptoms, 211
emotion-focused coping, 155
emotion-focused therapy, 451
emotion processing task, 188–189
emotion regulation system, 316
Empedocles, 175
empirically supported therapy, 462
empirically supported therapy relationships (ESR), 463
empowerment, 470
empty chair technique, 451
encopresis, 376
endocarditis, 286
endocrine system, 31–32, 150
endogenous opiates, 285
endophenotypes, 215
enemas, 347
eneuresis, 368
Enlightenment, 7, 13
enuresis, 376
environmental approaches. *see* psychological approaches
environmental deprivation, 364
environmental factors
Alzheimer's disease (AD), 438
causality, 183–186
and developmental disorders, 364
developmental disorders, 367–368
and developmental disorders, 367–368
developmental disorders, 368–369
mood disorders, 183–186
and psychopathy, 313–314
separation anxiety disorder (SAD), 411
and separation anxiety disorder (SAD), 411
enzyme replacement, 366
epidemiological research, 89, 90
epidemiology, 89
epigenetic mechanisms, 220
epigenetics, 93
epilepsy, 17, 193, 219, 378, 444
epinephrine, 151, 165, 166
Epstein-Barr virus, 160
equipotentiality premise, 104
erectile disorder, 332, 333–334
Erikson, Erik, 450
erogenous zones, 35
estrogen, 337
ethical codes, 503
ethnic/cultural differences, 6, 45
ethyl alcohol, 268
etiology
of alcohol abuse and dependence, 270–275
of Alzheimer's disease (AD), 437–438
of antisocial personality disorder (APD), 309–310
of anxiety disorders, 98–100
of attention deficit/hyperactivity disorder (ADHD), 398–399
of autism, 381–382
of borderline personality disorder (BPD), 316–317
of conduct disorder (CD), 405–406
defined, 26, 50
of delirium, 433
of depression, 425–426
of developmental disorders, 363–364
of dissociative disorders, 135–136
of eating disorders, 244–247, 248, 250
of gender identity disorders (GID), 342–343
of generalized anxiety disorder, 411–412
of generalized anxiety disorder (GAD), 117–119
history of, 9, 10, 11–12
of infection, 16
of learning disorders, 387
of mood disorders, 183, 425–426
of obsessive-compulsive disorder, 111–112, 113
of oppositional defiant disorder (ODD), 405–406
of post-traumatic stress disorder (PTSD), 116
of panic disorders, 102–103
of personality disorders, 303–305
of phobias, 104–105
of primary insomnia, 429
of psychopathy, 313–314
of schizophrenia, 216–217
search for, 26
of separation anxiety disorder (SAD), 411, 412
of sexual arousal disorders, 336–337
of sexual desire disorders, 336
of sexual dysfunctions, 336–338
of sexual offending, 351–353
of social phobia, 108–109
of somatoform disorders, 142–143
eugenics, 7, 360
European Study of the Epidemiology of Mental Disorders, 419
evaluation of psychotherapy. *see* effects of psychotherapy, evaluating
Evans, Josh, 395
event-related potentials (ERPs), 70
evidence-based practice (EBP), 21, 58, 462–464
Evidence-Based Practice of Cognitive-Behavioural Therapy, 465
evidence-based reading interventions, 388
evidence-based treatment, shortage of, 461
evocative (reactive) gene-environment correlation, 93
evolutionary biology, 7
evolutionary psychology, 5
exaltation, 175
excessive dependency, 40
excessive reassurance seeking, 185
excitement stage, 328
exercise, 165, 170, 280
exhaustion, 154
exhibitionism, 345, 348
existential therapy, 450–451
existential views, 41, 42–43
exogenous opiates, 285
exorcism, 11, 130
expectancy theory, 272
experimental effect, 85
experimental group, 85
experimental research methods, 85–87
experiments, defined, 85
exposure and ritual prevention (ERP), 124
exposure therapy, 122, 452
expressed emotion, 221
externalizing problems, 394
external locus of control, 157
external validity, 86
extrapyramidal effects, 445
eye-hand coordination, 268
Eye Movement Desensitization and Reprocessing (EMDR), 123, 459
eye-to-eye contact, fear of, 61
eye tracking, 215
Eysenck, Hans, 456

F

face validity, 68
facilitated communication (FC), 384
factitious disorders, 56, 138
false memory syndrome, 132
familiality effect, 219
family factors
and alcohol abuse and dependence, 273
and antiosocial personality disorder (APD), 309
and eating disorders, 248
parenting style, 472
and personality disorders, 303
family-focused therapy (FFT), 195
family studies, 90, 98, 398
family therapy
and alcohol abuse and dependence, 277
described, 454
and eating disorders, 254
and schizophrenia, 229
fantasies, 12
fast driving, 280
FAS technique, 222
Fatal Attraction, 315
fear conditioning, 412
fear, defined, 97
fear hierarchy, 122
fearlessness hypothesis, 309
fear response, 309
federal role in prevention, 481–482
feeding disorders, 54
Feinberg, Leslie, 340–341
Felbatol (felbamate), 193
female orgasmic disorder, 334
females. *see* women
female sexual arousal disorder, 357
feminist theories, 351–352
fetal alcohol effects, 367–368
fetal alcohol spectrum disorders (FASD), 264, 269–270, 367–368
fetal alcohol syndrome (FAS), 269, 367
fetishism, 326, 345, 346
fidelity, principle of, 504
fight or flight, 30, 97, 188, 406
Fiorinal, 278
First Nations, 198, 199
First Nations and Inuit Community and Youth Solvent Abuse Survey, 264
Fitness Interview Test (FIT-R), 501, 502
fitness to stand trial, 500–501, 503
5-HT, 406
5-HTT, 187, 199
5-hydroxytryptamine (5-HT), 187, 382
flashbacks, 114, 290
flooding, 122
fluid reasoning, 75
fluoxetine, 85–86, 124, 192, 412–413
fluvoxamine, 124, 413
FMR-1 gene, 371, 372
follow-back approach, 221
forebrain, 28, 31
forensic psychology, 503, 504–505
480.bp DAT 1 risk allele, 399
fractional anisotropy (FA), 225
Fragile X syndrome, 365, 450
Frank, Jerome, 453
Franklin, Benjamin, 18
Frankl, Viktor, 42
free association, 448–449
freebasing, 282
Freud, Anna, 450
Freud, Sigmund
on depression and grief, 175
on dissociative disorders, 130
on grief, 175
and hysteria, 18, 130
on older adults, 420
psychoanalysis therapies, 448
psychodynamics theory, 33, 34–36
on schizophrenia, 228
on somatoform disorders, 130
theories of anxiety, 97
Freund, Anna, 393
frontal brain deficiency, 223
frontal cortex, 112
frontal lobe, 221
frontal lobotomies, 227
fronto-limbic dysfunction, 305

frontotemporal dementia
 (FTD), 435, 439–440
frotteurism, 345, 348–349
full mutation, 371
functional magnetic resonance
 imaging (fMRI), 70
functional neurological disorder, 139

G

gabapentin, 193
Gabitril (tiagabine), 193
galactosemia, 450
galantamine, 438
Galen, 10, 11
Galton, Francis, 75
Gamblers Anonymous, 289
gambling
 addictive potential of, 280, 289–290
 gambling disorder, 262
 pathological gambling, 57
 prevalence of, 289
 treatment for, 290
gamma-aminobutyric acid
 (GABA), 28, 98, 108, 120, 193, 227
Gammahydroxybutyrate (GHB)
Gaucher's disease, 366
gender, 44–45
gender-bending, 340
gender bias
 in DSM, 60–61
 and personality disorders, 300–301
 and psychopathy, 300
gender differences
 and antisocial personality disorder (APD), 298
 and attention deficit/hyperactivity disorder (ADHD), 396
 and autism, 377–378
 and body image, 247–248
 and bulimia nervosa, 237
 in childhood disorders, 396
 and conduct disorder (CD), 403
 and dementia, 434–435
 and depression, 189
 and divorce effects, 472
 and dysthymic disorder, 426
 and eating disorders, 245, 250–251
 in math performance, 386
 and oppositional defiant disorder (ODD), 403
 and phobias, 104, 105
 in prevalence of mental health problems, 419
 and PTSD, 116
 and schizophrenia, 208
 and sexuality, 297, 327, 328
 and suicide, 198
gender dysphoria, 341, 342
gender identity, 340–341
gender identity disorders
 (GID), 57, 341
 diagnostic criteria, 341
 etiology of, 342–343
 gender reassignment, 342, 344
 treatment of, 343–344
gender reassignment, 342, 344
gender role, 334
gene-environment interactions
 (G x E)
 and attention deficit/hyperactivity disorder (ADHD), 399
 inheritance studies, 92–93
 and oppositional defiant disorder (ODD), 405–406
 and separation anxiety disorder (SAD), 412
general adaptation syndrome
 (GAS), 154
general belief systems, 99–100
generalized amnesia, 133
generalized anxiety disorder (GAD)
 case example, 64
 comorbidity, 410
 description, 64
 developmental trajectory, 410–411
 diagnosis and assessment, 117, 118
 etiology of, 117–119, 411, 412
 and nervous system, 30–37
 in older adults, 432
 prevalence of, 410
 and separation anxiety disorder (SAD), 409, 410–411
 treatment of, 126, 459
generalized sexual
 dysfunctions, 332
generalized social phobia, 106
general paresis of the insane
 (GPI), 16
genetic contribution, 219
genetic linkage studies, 33
genetic markers, 215
genetics. *see also* heredity
 and Alzheimer's disease (AD), 437–438
 and antisocial personality disorder (APD), 309
 and anxiety disorders, 98
 and attention deficit/hyperactivity disorder (ADHD), 398
 and autism, 381
 and behaviour, 32–33
 behavioural genetics, 32
 and borderline personality disorder, 316
 of conduct disorder (CD), 405
 and developmental disorders, 363–366
 disorders influenced by, 219
 and dissociative disorders, 135
 and eating disorders, 244–245
 and family relationships, 90
 genetic markers, 215
 and learning disorders, 387
 and mood disorders, 186–187
 and obsessive-compulsive disorder, 111
 and oppositional defiant disorder (ODD), 405
 overview of, 365
 and panic disorders, 102
 and personality disorders, 305
 and phenylketonuria (PKU), 26
 and phobias, 105
 and psychopathy, 313
 and schizophrenia, 217, 219, 220, 305
 and separation anxiety disorder (SAD), 411
 and social phobia, 108
 and substance-related disorders, 270–271
 and suicide, 199
 and twins, 186
genital vasocongestion, 330, 357
genotype-environment
 interaction, 32
Geodon (ziprasidone), 194
German measles, 367
gerontologists, 420
geropsychology, 121
Gestalt therapy, 320, 451
Gheel, 13
Ginkgo biloba, 339
Girl, Interrupted, 315
glass, 281
glaucoma, 287
Global Assessment of Functioning
 Scale (GAF Scale), 54
glove anaesthesia, 139
glucocorticoid, 151
glucose, 70, 405
glucose metabolism, 188
glutamate, 193
glutamatergic receptors, 124
Goldberg, Whoopi, 388
gonadal gender, 341
Gould, Glenn, 380
Government of Alberta, 1999, 8
gradient, 156–157
Graham, Sylvester, 326
grandiose delusions, 210
granulocytes, 152
grass. *see* cannabis; marijuana
Great Smokey Mountains
 Study, 410
Greek and Roman thought, 9–10
Greenberg, Les, 451, 454
grip strength test, 72
grossly disorganized behaviour, 211
group therapy, 454
guanine, 371
guided imagery, 123, 170
guilt, 110
gun control legislation, 200

H

habituation, 262
Hadfield, James, 499
Haldol, 382
hallucinations
 auditory hallucinations, 208, 212
 and cannabis, 287
 and cultural bias, 61
 explained, 210
 historic view of, 12
 in older adults, 432
 in schizophrenia, 210
hallucinogen persisting perception
 disorder, 290
hallucinogens, 288–290
hallucinogen use disorders, 55
haloperidol (Haldol), 372, 382
Halstead-Reitan test, 72
Handbook of Cognitive-Behavioral Therapies, 465
hangovers, 269
Hare, Robert, 303, 321
harmful dysfunction, 5
harm reduction approaches, 285
Hartmann, Heinz, 450
Harvard Mastery of Stress
 Study, 162
hashish, 286
Hazelden treatment program, 275
HBIGDA Standards of Care, 344
HCR-20, 497–498
head or brain injuries, 364
Head Start program, 369, 477
health behaviour model, 168
Health Care Consent Act, 487
health psychology, 148, 162
Healthy Schools-Healthy
 Kids, 255
Helfgott, David, 59
Helicobacter pylori, 163
helper T-cells, 153
hemorrhoids, 10
hemp, 280
hepatitis C, 285
hereditary taint, 303
heredity. *see also* genetics; studies of inheritance
 and attention deficit/hyperactivity disorder (ADHD), 398
 biological approach to abnormality, 15–16
 and borderline personality disorder, 316
 and conduct disorder (CD), 405
 and dissociative disorders, 135
 and gender identity disorders (GID), 342
 and intelligence, 75
 and mood disorders, 186
 and obsessive-compulsive disorder, 111
 and oppositional defiant disorder (ODD), 405
 and personality disorders, 304, 305
 and phenylketonuria (PKU), 26
 and phobias, 105
 and schizophrenia, 216, 304
 and social phobia, 108
hermaphroditism, 341
heroin, 280, 285
herpes, 160
heterogeneity, 207
heterotypic comorbidity, 410
heterotypic continuity, 394
heterozygous, 186
Hewlett, William, 388
hierarchy of needs, 42
high-risk children, 221
high-risk drinking, 266–268
high-risk method, 87
high-risk programs, 477–478
high-strain occupations, 158
hindbrain, 28
hippocampus, 116, 188, 224
Hippocrates, 9, 97, 175
Hispanics, 45–46, 61, 301
history of abnormality concepts
 anxiety disorders, 97–98
 in Arab world, 10–11
 causes of disorders, 9, 10, 11–12
 criminal responsibility, 10
 in Europe, 10–12
 evidence from prehistory, 8–9
 evolution of definitions, 7–8
 Greek and Roman thought, 9–10
 Methodism, 10
 Middle Ages, 10–12
 scientific approach, 12–13, 15
 treatment, 10, 11
histrionic personality disorder
 (HPD), 300, 301–302, 317
Hitler, Adolf, 217
HIV, 149, 285, 286, 367
Hoarders, 109
hoarding, 112, 119
Hobbes, Thomas, 32
Homeshare, 359
Homolka, Karla, 309
homosexuality
 and changing norms, 6
 in *Diagnostic and Statistical Manual of Mental Disorders* (DSM), 327
 as a disorder, 327
 in the DSM, 62
 and eating disorders, 251
homotypic comorbidity, 410
homotypic continuity, 394
homozygous, 186
hope, 304, 433
hormones, 151
 and gender identity disorders (GID), 342
 role of, 31–32
 and sexual dysfunctions, 336

hormone therapy, 344, 368
Horney, Karen, 450
hospitalization
for criminal offence, 502
involuntary, 492–494, 495–496, 502
hostility, 154, 167–168
host personalities, 134
hot cognitions, 122
Hôtel Dieu, 19
Howell, Christopher, 395
Hubley, Jamie, 395
Hughes, Clara, 44
human genome, 186
humanistic-experiential approaches, 450–451
humanistic theories, 41–42, 43
humoral immunity, 153
humours, 9, 11, 15, 175
Huntington's disease, 219
Hurler's syndrome, 366
Husserl, Edmund, 41
hyperactivity, 382, 397
hyperaesthesia, 335
hyperammonemia, 366
hypersecretion, 161
hypersexuality, 335–336
hypertension, 166, 170
hyperthyroidism, 102
hypervigilance, 115
hypnosis, 18–19, 132, 136, 137, 143
hypoactive sexual desire disorder, 333
hypochondriasis, 56, 129, 138, 141, 143
hypoglycemia, 32, 102
hypokrisia, 217
hypomania, 178–179, 180
hypothalamic-pituitary-adrenal (HPA) axis, 32, 116, 143, 151, 187, 188, 189, 395
hypothalamus, 32, 98
hypothyroidism, 366
hypoxemia, 430
hypoxyphilia, 346
hysteria, 9, 12, 18, 130
hysterical personality, 300

I

iatrogenic, 136
ice, 281
id, 34
idiographic approach, 95
if-then statements, 40
illness, defined, 149
illness phobias, 104
imaginal exposure, 125
imagined loss, 175
imipramine, 190, 192
immune system, 152–153
immunoglobulins, 153
impairment of control, 263
implantable cardioverter defibrillator, 171
implementation, 483
impotence, 333
impulse control disorders, 57, 262
impulsivity, 397
inattention, 397
incest, 328
incidence, defined, 89
inclusion, 374
The Incredible Years, 401
Incredible Years Parent Program, 406
independent variables, 85
indicated prevention, 469
individual-level strategies, 470
individual therapy, 454
indoleamine serotonin, 187
industrialization, 209
infantile autism, 393
infection, 16
infectious disease, 159, 364
inferior frontal gyrus, 387
inferior longitudinal fasciculus (ILF), 225
inflexibility, 31
information, loss of, 60
information processing biases, 40
Ingram, Jeff, 137
inhalants, 280
Inhibitions, Symptoms and Anxiety, 98
Inis Beag, 328
inkblot test, 77–78
Inquisition, 12
insanity defence. *see* criminal responsibility
insanity, legal, 10, 327
insight, in assessment, 73
instability, 315
insular cortex, 98
insulin, 17
insulin coma, 227
integrative models, 250
integrative theories, 45–46
intellectual developmental disorder, 54, 361
intellectual disability, 361, 362, 364
intelligence
assessment of, 73, 362
correlations of, 77
and learning disorders, 386
sensory intelligence, 75
testing, 61, 75, 76
intelligence quotient (IQ)
and autism, 377–378
controversy over, 362
described, 75
and developmental disorders, 361, 362
distribution of IQ scores, 362
stability of, 75–76
intense exposure, 122
interactionist explanations, 25
interactive-behavioural group therapy, 375
interferon, 153
INTERHEART study, 169
interleukins, 153, 169
intermediate beliefs, 40
intermittent explosive disorder, 57
internal accessory organs, 341
internal consistency, 67
internalizing problems, 394
internal locus of control, 157
internal validity, 86
internal working models, 99
International Classification of Diseases (ICD), 52, 148
International Classification of Mental and Behavioral Disorders (ICD-10), 3, 7, 16
International Congress on Schizophrenia Research, 208
International Personality Disorder Examination, 299
International Statistical Classification of Diseases, Injuries, and Causes of Death (ICD), 52
Internet
addiction, 262
interventions, 461
and older adults, 440
interoceptive exposure, 122
interpersonal and social rhythm therapy (IPSRT), 188, 195
interpersonal dependency, 185
interpersonal disorder, 109
interpersonal factors, 99–100
interpersonal models, 184–185
interpersonal psychodynamic psychotherapy, 450
interpersonal psychotherapy (IPT), 189, 191–192, 459
interpersonal scales, in PAI, 80
interpersonal therapy (IPT), 252–253
interpersonal traumas, 116
interpretation, as psychoanalysis technique, 449
inter-rater reliability, 51, 299, 301
interviews
clinical interviews, 72–73
Clinician Administered PTSD Scale, 115
for developmental disorders, 363
mental status examination, 73
motivational interviewing, 277–278, 453
for personality disorders, 298
and reliability, 301
semi-structured interviews, 73–74, 102
structured interviews, 73, 102
unstructured interviews, 73
intolerance of uncertainty (IU), 119, 126
intracavernous treatment, 339
intrauterine disorders, 364
intravaginal ejaculatory latency time (IELT), 334
Inuit, 198
involuntary hospitalization, 492–494, 495–496
IQ. *see* intelligence quotient (IQ)
Ireland, 328
ischemic heart disease, 164
Isle of Wight Study, 393
isocarboxazid, 192

J

Janet, Pierre, 18, 130
Japan, 61, 106, 198
Jenner, Bruce, 388
Jews, Orthodox, 189
jikoshisen-kyofu, 61
jikoshu-kyofu, 61
job strain, 158
Johnson, Magic, 388
joint, 286
Journal of Applied Research in Intellectual Disability, 372
Journal of Autism and Developmental Disorders, 383
Journal of Clinical Child and Adolescent Psychology, 460
Judeo-Christian tradition, 326
judgment, in assessment, 73
jumping to conclusions, 184
Jung, Carl, 36, 130, 216
justice, principle of, 504

K

Kajander, Ruth, 20
Kanner, Leo, 377, 393
Kellogg, John Harvey, 326
Kennedy, John F., 360
Keppra (levatiracetam), 193
Ketamine (K), 288
Kierkegaard, Søren, 450
killer (K) T-cells, 153
Kirby, Michael, 20
Kirk, Samuel, 385
Kirmayer, Laurence J., 144
kissing, 328
Kjeldsen v. R., 500
Klarman Family Foundation Grants Program in Eating Disorders, 256
Kleine-Levin syndrome, 242
Klein, Melanie, 36, 393
klismaphilia, 347
knowledge, testing, 75
koro, 106
Korsakoff's psychosis, 269
K-Pax, 14
Kraepelin, Emil, 16, 175
Kunin-Lunenfeld Applied Research Unit (KLARU), 440

L

la belle indifférence, 139
labelling theory, 43
La Bicêtre, 13–15
Laborit, Henri, 17, 20, 227
Lamictal (lamotrigine), 193, 322, 447
lanugo, 243
L'Arche, 389
law
civil code, 492
civil mental health law. *see* civil mental health law
common law, 490, 491–492
competency to stand trial, 500–501
constitutional law, 490–491
Criminal Code, 491, 499
criminal law, 491
criminal responsibility, 499–500
defined, 490
mental health acts, compared, 493
psychology in, 503
statutory law, 490, 491
laxative abuse, 236
learning disabilities, 361, 385–386
Learning Disabilities Association of Ontario (LDAO), 385
learning disorders
and comorbidity, 396
defined, 54
disorder of written expression, 386
etiology of, 387
famous people with, 388
intervention, 388
mathematic disorder, 386
nonverbal learning disabilities (NLD), 387
prevalence of, 387
reading disorder, 58, 385, 386
social and emotional well-being, 387–388
youth at risk, 388
learning disorders (LD)
case example, 384–385
controversy in diagnosis, 386
in *Diagnostic and Statistical Manual of Mental Disorders* (DSM), 385
historical perspective, 385
Leary, Timothy, 288
left-handedness, 342
left hemisphere, 387
left hypofrontality, 197
left temporal lobe, 224
left ventricular ejection fraction (LVEF), 168
legal insanity, 10, 327
Lehman, J.F., 19
Leiter International Intelligence Scale, 362
Leno, Jay, 388
Lesch-Nyhan syndrome, 450
lesions, 149

leukotomies, 227
levatiracetam, 193
levels of consciousness, 34, 35
Levitra, 339
Lewy body dementia, 435, 439–440
libido, 35, 36
Librium, 278
life expectancies, 418
Life Goes On, 360, 370
lifelong sexual dysfunction, 332
Life Skills Training, 480
life stress perspective, 185–186
lifestyle modification, 171
ligands, 70, 226
Likelihood-Self, 110
Likelihood TAF, 110
lipoprotein cholesterol, 157
Litchfield, Dr. J. P., 19
lithium, 182, 193, 406, 447
Little Albert, 37, 99
liver cirrhosis, 270
Living with Others, 359
lobotomy, 19
localized amnesia, 133
Locke, John, 24
Lombroso, Cesare, 16, 32
longitudinal studies, 87, 162
loosening of associations, 211
Louis XIV, 198
low-risk drinking guidelines, 266
low-strain occupations, 158
LSD, 14
lumen, 164
lunacy, 208
lunatic, 12
Luria-Nebraska test, 72
luteinizing hormone-releasing hormone agonists (LHRH agonists), 353
Luther, Martin, 11
Lykken's Lever Apparatus, 309
lymphocytes, 153
lymphokines, 153
Lyrica (pregabalin), 193
lysergic acid diethylamide (LSD), 288

M

macaque monkeys, 153, 166
MacArthur Violence Risk Assessment project, 312
machiavellianism, 302
macrosystem, 472
madness, 208
magic mushrooms, 288
magnetic fluid, 18
magnetic resonance imaging (MRI)
  and attention deficit/hyperactivity disorder (ADHD), 398
  and borderline personality disorder, 304–305
  and conversion disorders, 139
  and depression, 188
  explained, 70, 223
  and recovered memory, 132
  and schizophrenia, 223–224
  and short-term memory, 224
magnetoencephalography (MEG), 70
magnification, 184
mainlining, 284
mainstreaming, 374
major depressive disorder
  comorbidity, 178
  course of, 177
  criteria for, 177
  defined, 55–56, 176
  duration, 176
  economic costs, 176
  heritability, 186
  in older adults, 426
  prevalence of, 177, 178
  severity, 176
male erectile disorder, 332, 333–334, 339
male orgasmic disorder, 334
malingering, 138
malnutrition, 364
mania, 10, 56, 178, 180
manic-depression, 175
manic episode, 180
manie sans délire, 302
manual sign language, 383
marijuana. *see also* cannabis
  addictive potential of, 280
  dependency, 288
  effects of, 286–287
  prevalence of, 287
  and psychotic experiences, 221
  therapeutic effects of, 288
marital therapy, 277
Marplan (isocarboxazid), 192
marriage, 154–155
The Mask of Sanity, 302
Maslow, Abraham, 25, 41
mass hysteria, 12
master and slave game, 347
masturbation, 6, 326, 327–328
maternal infections, 367
maternal serum screening (MSS), 366
maternal stress, 309
mathematic disorder, 385, 386
Maudsley approach, 254
May, Rollo, 42
McLachlin, Beverley, 488
McLean Study of Adult Development, 295, 301
meal support, 253–254
measles/mumps vaccine (MMR), 381
mechanism, defined, 149
media influence, 245–247, 250
medical interventions, 353
medical model of classification, 59, 360
medical practitioners, 505
meditation, 170, 191, 453
Medroxyprogesterone Acetate (MPA), 353
Meduna, Ladislas von, 17
Meehl's theory of schizotaxia, schizotypy, and schizophrenia, 217, 219
Meier, Megan, 395
melancholia, 175
melatonin, 182
Mellaril, 382
memory
  as assessment, 73, 75
  and OCD, 112
memory B-cells, 153
memory T-cells, 153
men
  and body image, 247–248
  and borderline personality disorder, 300
  and eating disorders, 250–251
menopause, 330
mens rea, 499
menstruation, 10
mental disorders. *see* law. *see also* psychological disorder; specific disorders
  legal definition, 189
  pedophilia, 5–6
  prevalence among prison inmates, 498
  prevalence of, 62, 468, 492
  and suicide, 199
mental health acts, 493
Mental Health Commission of Canada, 482
mental health, defined, 469–470
Mental Health for Canadians: Striking a Balance, 18, 469, 481
mental health law
  Canadian legal system, 490–492
  case example, 487–488
  criminal law, 499
  mental disorders in Canadian law, 488–490
  mentally disordered offenders, 498–503
mental health promotion. *see also* prevention
  in Canada, 481–483
  defined, 469
  described, 470
  ecological approach, 470
  research and practice, 475–481
  strategies for, 470
mental health services. *see also* mental health promotion
  in Canada, 19–21
  community psychology, 468–469
  recent developments, 20–21
mental hygiene movement, 15
mental illness
  defined, 4
  versus personality disorders, 299
mental institutions, 12
mentally disordered offenders. *see also* criminal responsibility
  fitness evaluations, 501–503
  prevalence of, 498
  research on, 501–503
mental retardation, 54, 361, 362
mental status examination, 73
Merleau-Ponty, Maurice, 41
mescaline, 288
Mesmer, Anton, 18
Mesmer, Franz, 209
Messerschmidt, Franz, 209
meta-analysis, 167, 222, 457
meta-analytic evidence, of effects of psychotherapy, 457–458, 461–462
metabolic activity, 71
metabolic disorders, 364, 366
metabolite, 182
methadone, 280, 286
methamphetamine, 281
Methodism, 10
methylene-dioxyamphetamine (MDA), 281
methylene-dioxymethamphetamine (MDMA), 281, 288
methylphenidate (Ritalin), 279, 281, 382, 399, 406, 448
Metrazol, 17
miasmas, 471
microchip assays, 366
microsystem, 472
midbrain, 28, 98
Middle Ages, 10–12
migraines, 86–87
mild cognitive impairment (MCI), 435–436
military combat, 188
Millon Clinical Multiaxial Inventory (MCMI), 80
mindfulness, 43
Mindfulness Based Cognitive Therapy (MBCT), 191
mindfulness-based strategies, 123, 191, 453
minimal brain dysfunction, 398
Minnesota model, 275
Minnesota Multiphasic Personality Inventory (MMPI), 61, 79–80, 81, 167
minor tranquilizers, 120
Mirapex (pramipexole), 193
mirtazapine, 193
Mithraism, 216
mixed dementia, 437
mixed state, 179
M'Naghten standard, 499
Moderation Management, 274, 276
modern views of psychological abnormality, 15–18, 19
molecular biology, 33
molecular genetics, 220
mondafinil, 193
monitoring of client treatment progress, 464
monkey glove, 166
monoamine oxidase A (MAOA), 405
monoamine oxidase inhibitors (MAOIs), 120, 187, 192, 447
monocytes, 152
mononucleosis, 160
monozygotic (MZ) twins, 91, 186
mood congruent delusions, 213
mood disorders
  biological causal factors, 186–189
  bipolar disorders, 176, 178–182
  case example, 173–175, 424–431
  in children, 395–396
  cognitive theories, 183–184
  defined, 55–56
  depressive disorders, 426–427
  diagnostic issues, 176
  dysthymic disorder, 178, 179
  etiology of, 183, 425
  and genetics, 186–187
  historical perspective, 175
  and hypothalamic-pituitary-adrenal (HPA) axis, 187–188
  interpersonal models, 184–185
  life stress perspective, 185–186
  major depressive disorder. *see* major depressive disorder (MDD)
  neuroimaging, 188–189
  neurostimulation and neurosurgical treatments, 196–197
  and neurotransmitters, 187
  in older adults, 424–425
  and personality disorders, 302
  phototherapy, 195–196
  postpartum onset, 182
  psychodynamic theories, 183
  psychological and environmental causal factors, 183–186
  psychotherapy, effects of, 459
  seasonal pattern, 182
  sleep neurophysiology, 188
  and stress, 187–188
  treatment of, 189–197
  unipolar mood disorders, 176
mood stabilizers, 182, 322, 406, 446, 447
moon, 12
Moors, 12
Moose Factory, 198
moral insanity, 302
moral principle, 35
Moral TAF, 110
moral therapy, 15
Morel, Benedict Augustin, 15
Morgan, W. Pringle, 385
moron, 8
morphine, 284

morphine addiction, 17
mortality
and cardiovascular disease, 164
and eating disorders, 237
and Type A/Type B behaviour, 167
in Whitehall study, 157
mosaicism, 365
motivational interviewing, 277–278
motor skills or communication disorders, 54
motor symptoms, 211
multiaxial system of classification, 53, 54, 148
Multimodal Treatment Study of ADHD, 398
multiple personality disorder. *see* dissociative identity disorder
Munchausen syndrome, 138
Munch, Edvard, 131
myocardial infarction, 164, 165
The Myth of Mental Illness, 7

N

naltrexone, 275, 382
Napoleonic code, 492
narcissistic personality disorder (NPD), 301, 317–318
narcolepsy, 281
Narcotics Anonymous, 278, 283
Nardil (phenelzine), 192
narrow band instruments, 84
Nash, John, 218
National Association of Retarded Citizens in the United States, 360
National Comorbidity Survey, 108
National Comorbidity Survey Replication-Adolescent Supplement (NCS-A), 394
National Comorbidity Survey Replication study, 299, 309, 412
National Institute for Health and Clinical Excellence, 464
National Institute of Mental Health, 326
National Institute of Mental Health Treatment of Depression Collaborative Research Program, 459
National Longitudinal Survey of Children and Youth (NLSCY), 90
National Population Health Survey-Household Component-Longitudinal (NPHS), 90
National Population Health Survey (NPHS), 278, 455
national suicide prevention strategy, 200
Native cultures. *see* Aboriginal people
natural causes, 8, 9
natural environment phobias, 104
natural selection, 7
Nazis, 6, 8
necrophilia, 347
needle exchange programs, 285
negative emotionality, 272
negative feedback seeking, 185
negative punishment, 38
negative reinforcement, 38
negative symptoms, 210, 211
Nembutal, 278
neonatal disorders, 364
Neo-Synalar, 382
nervous system
autonomic nervous system (ANS), 30, 31
central nervous system, 28, 30
parasympathetic nervous system, 30, 31
peripheral nervous system, 30–31
somatic nervous system, 30
sympathetic nervous system, 31
neural fear circuit, 98
neural tube defects, 364
neurasthenia, 6
neuroanatomy, 98–99
neurobiological influences, 271–272
neurobiology, 405
neurochemical imbalance, 225–227
neurochemical theories, 112
neurocognitive disorders, 55, 433–434
neurodevelopmental diathesis-stress theories, 218
neurodevelopmental disorders, 361
neuroendocrine system, 165
neurofibrillary tangles, 437
neurofibromatosis, 450
neuroimaging, 188–189, 313, 438
neuroleptics, 322, 406, 432, 438
neurons, 28, 29, 188
Neurontin (gabapentin), 193
neuropsychological testing, 71–72, 221–222, 223
neuropsychology models, 112
neurosis, 97
neurostimulation and neurosurgical treatments, 196–197
neurosyphilis, 16
neuroticism, 272
neurotoxic ammonia, 366
neurotransmitters
and abnormal behaviour, 29–30
and alcohol abuse and dependence, 271, 275
and anxiety disorders, 98–99
and attention deficit/hyperactivity disorder (ADHD), 398
and autism, 382
and conduct disorder (CD), 405–406
defined, 28, 187
discovery of, 17
disturbances of, 29
and eating disorders, 244–245
functions of, 28–29
gamma-aminobutyric acid (GABA), 120
and mood disorders, 187
and oppositional defiant disorder (ODD), 405–406
and personality disorders, 304
and psychopathy, 313
and scans, 70
and schizophrenia, 225–227
neutralizations, 110
A New Perspective on the Health of Canadians, 481
Nicolai, Friedrich, 209
nicotine. *see also* tobacco
addictive potential of, 280
dependency, 279–280
effects of, 269, 279
replacements, 281
source of, 279
as stimulant, 279
Nicotiniana tabacum, 279
night eating syndrome, 242
nocturnal panic, 103
nomothetic approach, 95
nonassociative model, 104, 105
nondiscretionary risk assessment, 497
non-emotion processing task, 188–189
non-experimental research methods
case studies, 88
correlational method, 87–88
epidemiological research, 89, 90
inheritance studies. *see* studies of inheritance
single-subject research, 88–89
non-generalized social phobia, 106
non-interpersonal traumas, 116
nonmaleficence, principle of, 504
nonpurging type, 240
non-rapid eye movement (NREM) sleep, 188, 428
nonspecific immune responses, 152
nonverbal communication, 379
nonverbal learning disabilities (NLD), 387
noradrenalin, 151
norepinephrine, 165, 166, 187, 405–406
normal aging, 420, 422
normalization, 228, 360
normalization principle, 373
normative comparison, 94
norms, 6, 7
Norpramin (desipramine), 192
North American Aboriginal culture, 61
nortriptyline, 192
nuchal translucency (NT), 366
null hypothesis, 25–28
Nupercainal, 382
nutritional therapy, 253–254
nymphomania, 335

O

obesity, 151, 247, 281, 430
objective binge, 235
object-relations therapy, 320
observational techniques, 82, 83
observer drift, 83
obsessional cluster somatoform disorders, 143
"Obsessions and Phobias," 97, 98
obsessions, defined, 56, 110
obsessive-compulsive disorder (OCD)
and body dysmorphic disorder, 142
case example, 2, 3, 109–110
in children and adolescents, 459
cognitive-behavioural models, 112–113
description, 110–111
diagnosis and assessment, 111
etiology of, 111–112, 113
genetics, 111
hoarding, 109
neurochemical theories, 112
neuropsychology models, 112
and obsessive-compulsive personality disorder (OCPD), 319
ritual prevention, 122
subtypes of, 112
treatment of, 120, 124–459
obsessive-compulsive personality disorder (OCPD), 319
occupational therapist, 7
odd and eccentric disorders, 296, 297
Oedipus complex, 33, 35
olanzapine, 194, 228, 322
Old Order Amish, 189
Olson, Clifford, 312
omega-3 fatty acid supplements, 382
One Flew over the Cuckoo's Nest, 14, 196
Ontario Child Health Study, 393, 407
operant conditioning, 38, 99, 374, 383
opiate antagonists, 322
opioids, 263
defined, 284
dependency, 286
effects of, 285–286
needle exchange programs, 285
prevalence of, 284–285
treatment, 286
opioid use disorders, 55
oppositional behaviour, 310
oppositional defiant disorder (ODD)
comorbidity, 396, 403
defined, 54
described, 401–403
developmental trajectory, 404
in *Diagnostic and Statistical Manual of Mental Disorders* (DSM), 402
diagnostic criteria, 401–403
etiology of, 405–406
gender differences, 403
gene-environment interactions, 405–406
genetics, 405
neurobiology, 405, 434
parent training, 406–407
pharmacotherapy, 406
prenatal risk factors, 309
prevalence of, 403–404
problem solving, 406
psychosocial risk factors, 405
school- and community-based treatment, 407
treatment, 406–407
oral stage, 35
ordering/symmetry, 112
organismic, 83
orgasm, 329
orgasmic disorders, 332, 334, 337
orientation, 73
The Origin of Species, 15
Orthodox Jews, 189
ouija board effect, 384
Out of the Shadows at Last, 20
ovaries, 32
overanxious disorder of childhood, 409
overgeneralization, 184
overlap, 301
overt avoidance, 107
oxcarbazepine, 193
Oxford Movement, 275

P

pain disorder, 56, 138, 140–141
Pamelor (nortriptyline), 192
panic attacks, 101
panic, defined, 97
panic disorders
and agoraphobia, 100–101
case example, 49, 102
cognitive model, 103
defined, 56
diagnosis and assessment, 102
Diagnostic and Statistical Manual of Mental Disorders (DSM), 101
etiology of, 102–103
panic attack record, 84
and personality disorders, 319
specific phobia, 103–105
treatment of, 124, 458–459
Papaverine, 339
Pappenheim, Bertha, 34
Paracelsus, 11, 12
paradox of aging, 419
para-methoxyamphetamine (PMA), 281

paranoia, 40
paranoid delusions, 210
paranoid personality disorder, 305
paraphilias
  biastophilia, 351
  case example, 2, 3, 344–345
  and consenting adults, 345–347
  defined, 57, 345
  diagnosis, 326–327, 345
  Diagnostic and Statistical Manual of Mental Disorders (DSM), 347–348
  exhibitionism, 345, 348
  fetishism, 326, 345, 346
  frotteurism, 345, 348–349
  and nonconsenting persons, 347–351
  pedophilia, 5–6, 345, 348, 349
  rape, 350
  sexual masochism, 345, 346–347
  sexual sadism, 345, 346–347, 350–351
  transvestic fetishism, 345, 346
  unusual sexual variants, 347
  voyeurism, 345, 348
parasomnia, 57
parasuicide, 198
parasympathetic nervous system, 30, 31, 151, 165, 337
parens patriae, 491, 492
parent-child relationship. *see also* family factors
  attachment theory, 303–304
  and avoidant personality disorder, 318–319
  and gender identity disorders (GID), 342–343
  and personality disorders, 303, 304, 316
parent, loss of, 472, 473
parent training, 401–407
Parkinson's, 28, 426, 439
Parnate (tranylcypromine), 192
paroxetine, 71, 192, 413
partialism, 345
participation dimension, 475
passive gene-environment correlation, 93
Pasteur, Louis, 16
pathological gambling, 57, 262, 289
pathological OCD belief, 111
pathological worry, 117, 126
patienthood, 475
patient-therapist goal consensus and collaboration, 464
patriarchal societies, 352
Pavlov, Ivan, 19, 36, 37
Paxil (paroxetine), 192
pedohebephilic disorder, 5
pedophile, 349
pedophilia, 5–6, 345, 348, 349
Peel, Robert, 499
Peeping Toms, 348
peer mediation, 407
peer victimization, 388, 395
pelvic floor physiotherapy, 340
penetrance, 219
penile implants, 340
penis, 329
People First, 360
pep pills, 281
peptic ulcer, 219
perceptual reasoning tests, 75
performance anxiety, 337
Pericles, 9
period effect, 420
periodic leg movements in sleep (PLMS), 430
peripheral nervous system, 30–31
Perls, Frederich (Fritz), 451
perpetuating factors, 250
Perry Preschool Project, 476–477, 480
persecutory delusions, 210
perseverate, 223
personal distress, 4–5
personal dysfunction, 5
personal electronic devices, 84
personality assessment
  personality inventories, 79–80, 82
  projective test, 77
  Rorschach inkblot test, 77–78
Personality Assessment Inventory (PAI), 80
Personality Checklist, 309
personality disorder not otherwise specified, 296, 297
personality disorders. *see also* specific disorders
  attachment theory, 303–304
  biological factors, 304–305
  borderline personality disorder, 299, 300, 315–317
  case examples, 294
  characteristics of, 297
  clusters, 296
  cognitive-behavioural therapy (CBT), 304
  comorbidity and diagnostic overlap, 301–302
  concept of, 294–299
  criteria for, 296
  described, 57
  in *Diagnostic and Statistical Manual of Mental Disorders* (DSM), 295–296, 297
  diagnostic issues, 299–302
  etiology of, 303–305
  functioning ability, 299
  gender and cultural issues, 298, 299, 300–301
  heritability, 304, 305
  historical perspective, 302–303
  histrionic personality disorder, 317
  inpatient versus outpatient prevalence, 299
  and insurance, 299
  multi-method assessment, 297
  narcissistic personality disorder (NPD), 317–318
  paranoid personality disorder, 305–306
  prevalence of, 297–299
  psychodynamic views, 303
  reliability of diagnosis, 301
  schizoid personality disorder, 306
  schizotypal personality disorder, 306–307
  treatment of, 320–322
  treatment sought, 299
Personality Disorder Trait Specified (PDTS), 295, 296
personality inventories
  Millon Clinical Multiaxial Inventory (MCMI), 80
  Minnesota Multiphasic Personality Inventory, 79–80, 81
  Personality Assessment Inventory (PAI), 80
personal responsibility, 110
person by situation interaction, 87
person-centred theory of personality, 41
Persuasion and Healing, 453
pervasive developmental disorders, 377
phagocytic cells, 153
phagocytosis, 152
phallic stage, 35
phallometric assessment, 351
pharmaceutical industry, 62
pharmacotherapy. *see also* specific medications
  and alcohol abuse and dependence, 275
  anticonvulsants, 193–194
  antidepressants, 192–193, 194
  antipsychotics, 194
  and antisocial personality disorder (APD), 311
  and anxiety disorders, 120
  for attention deficit/hyperactivity disorder (ADHD), 399–400
  for bipolar disorder, 193–194
  for childhood anxiety disorders, 412–413
  and conduct disorder (CD), 406
  efficacy of, 124
  monoamine oxidase inhibitors (MAOIs), 192
  and older adults, 420–421
  and oppositional defiant disorder (ODD), 406
  for personality disorders, 322
  selective serotonin reuptake inhibitor (SSRI), 192
  for separation anxiety disorder (SAD), 412–413
  for specific phobias, 124
  for tobacco addiction, 281
  tricyclic antidepressants, 18, 187, 192
  for unipolar depression, 192–193
phase advancement, 182
phase-delayed circadian rhythm, 182
Phencyclidine (PCP), 288
phenelzine, 192
phenomenological approach, 56
phenomenology, 41
phenothiazine, 18
phenotype, 93
Phentolamine, 339
phenylalanine, 26
phenylketonuria, 26, 366, 450, 476
phenytoin (Dilantin), 193, 382
phobias
  and ANS, 30
  case example, 105
  and classical conditioning, 37–38
  defined, 56
  description, 103–104
  diagnosis and assessment, 104
  etiology of, 104–105
  and panic disorders, 103–105
  prevalence, 104
  social phobia, 106, 107–109, 124
  treatment of, 124, 458
  types of, 104
phonological processing, 385, 386
phosphodiesterase inhibitors (PDE5 inhibitors), 339
phototherapy, 182, 195–196
phrenology, 16
physical activity, 169
physical punishers, 310
physiological dependence, 261
physiological hyperarousal, 411
pica, 241, 376
Pica's disorder, 54–55
Pick's disease, 439
picture exchange communication systems (PECS), 383
Pinel, Philippe, 15
pituitary gland, 32
placebo, 445
placebo effect, 86, 190, 192–193
placebo washout, 445
plaques, 165, 437
plasma cells, 153
plateau stage, 329
Plato, 9, 130
Playboy, 245–246, 247
pleasure principle, 34
politics, and the DSM, 62
polygenic characteristics, 217
polypharmacy, 422, 427
polysubstance abuse, 263–264
polythetic approach, 308
positive correlation, 87
positive punishment, 38
positive reinforcement, 38
positive symptoms, 210
positivity effect, 423
positron emission tomography (PET), 28, 70–71, 188, 223, 224, 226
posterior parietal areas, 387
postnatal environmental factors, 368–369
postpartum depression, 23–24, 25, 182, 468
post test, 86
post-traumatic stress disorder (PTSD)
  case example, 113
  cognitive theories, 116
  description, 113–115
  diagnosis and assessment, 114, 115
  in the DSM, 62
  etiology of, 116
  risk factors, 116
  and social support, 43–44
  treatment of, 125–126, 459
  Vietnam veterans, 62, 156
pot. *see* cannabis; marijuana
potential years of life lost (PYLL), 164
poverty, 45, 216, 368, 405, 476, 484
practice separations, 473
pramipexole, 193
precedence, 162
precipitating factors, 250
preconscious, 34
predictive validity, 51
predisposing factors, 250
prefrontal cortex, 398, 399, 405, 412
pregabalin, 193
pre-germ theory era, 471
pregnancy. *see also* prenatal environment
  and alcohol, 266, 270
  and anticonvulsants, 194
  and schizophrenia, 220
  and serotonin reuptake inhibitors (SSRIs), 447
  and smoking, 279, 309
  teenage, 403
prehistory, 8–9
premature ejaculation, 334, 337, 339
premutation, 371
Prenatal Early Infancy Project, 477–478
prenatal environment, 309, 367–368, 398–399, 411
prenatal hormonal gender, 341
prenatal risk factors
  attention deficit/hyperactivity disorder (ADHD), 398
  childhood anxiety disorders, 411
  conduct disorder (CD), 309
prenatal screening, 366

prenatal toxin exposure, 398
prescription privileges, 449
presenting symptoms, 50
pretest, 86
prevalence. *see* specific disorders
prevalence, defined, 89
prevention. *see also* mental health promotion
in Canada, 481–483
case example, 476–477
conceptual framework, 474–475
cumulative risk, 472–473
defined, 469
dissemination, 483–484
early childhood development, 471, 483
ecological dimension, 474
educational approach, 471
high-risk programs, 477–478
historical perspective, 471
implementation, 483
implications of resilience, risk, and protection, 473
indicated prevention, 469
levels of, 469
mechanisms of risk and protection, 473
protective factors, 472, 473
public health approach, 471
research and practice, 475–481
resilience approach, 472
return on investment, 482
risk factors, 472
selective prevention, 469
social justice, 484
of substance abuse, 480
temporal dimension, 474
universal, 469
universal programs, 478–481
The Prevention of Anxiety and Depression, 465
priapism, 339
primary appraisal, 155
primary gain, 130
primary insomnia
causes of, 429
described, 429
in *Diagnostic and Statistical Manual of Mental Disorders* (DSM), 428, 429
diagnostic criteria, 428
etiology of, 429
treatment, 429–430
primary prevention, 469
The Prince, 302
principle of autonomy, 504
principle of beneficence, 504
principle of fidelity, 504
principle of justice, 504
principle of nonmaleficence, 504
proband, 90
problem-focused coping, 155
problem solving, 123, 406, 453
processing speed tests, 75
prodrome, 230
professional standards, 503
progesterone, 182
prognosis, defined, 50
progressive muscle relaxation, 123
Prohibition, 265
projective test, 77
prolactin, 337
promethazine, 227
pronoun reversal, 379
protective factors, 165, 472, 473
Provigil (mondafinil), 193
provincial role in prevention, 482
provoked vestibulodynia, 335
Prozac (fluoxetine), 86, 186, 192
P-Scan, 321
pseudo-dementia, 435
Psilocybe mexicana, 288
psilocybin, 288
psychache, 200
psychedelics, 288
psychiatric nurse, 6
psychiatric social workers, 7
psychiatrist, 6
psychoactive agents, 444
psychoactive medication. *see* psychopharmacology
psychoanalysis, 18–19, 34
psychoanalytically oriented therapy, 450
psychoanalytic psychotherapy, 450
psychoanalytic theory, 342
psychodynamic theories
defence mechanisms, 35–36
explained, 34
Freud, influence of, 36
levels of consciousness, 34, 35
and mood disorders, 183
of personality disorders, 303
psychosexual stages of development, 35
structures of personality, 34–35
psychodynamic therapies
Adler's individual psychology, 450
brief psychodynamic psychotherapy, 450
ego analysis, 450
examples of, 450
interpersonal psychodynamic psychotherapy, 450
techniques of, 448–449
time-limited dynamic psychotherapy (TLDP), 450
psychodynamic treatment techniques, 320
psychoeducation, 124, 228, 229, 400
psychological abnormality
defined, 4, 7
diagnosis by expert, 6–7
heredity, 15–16
historical concepts of. *see* history of abnormality concepts
infection as cause, 16
modern views, 15–19
natural causes, 8, 9
personal distress, 4–5
personal dysfunction, 5
problems with defining, 3
and social norms, 7
statistical concept, 4
summary of definitions, 15
supernatural causes, 8–9
theoretical perspectives on, 23–47
violation of norms, 6
psychological approaches
behaviourism, 19
versus biological approaches, 24–25
cognitive-behaviour therapy (CBT), 20
development of, 18–19
hypnotism, 18
psychoanalysis, 18–19
psychological assessment. *see* assessment
clinical interviews, 72–73
defined, 67
intelligence assessment, 75–76
mental status examination, 73
personality assessment, 76–77, 78, 80, 82
personality inventories, 79–80, 82
semi-structured interviews, 73–74
structured interviews, 73
thematic apperception test, 78
unstructured interviews, 73
psychological autopsies, 298
psychological debriefing, 126
psychological dependence, 262–263
psychological disorders, 4, 6
psychological ethics, 503–504, 505
psychological factors affecting physical condition, 57
psychological process, 150
psychologists, 449, 455
psychology in the legal system, 503, 505–506
psychology of stress, 153–156
psychoneuroimmunology, 153
Psychopathia Sexualis, 326, 335
psychopathic inferiority, 302
psychopathology, 4, 6, 32
psychopaths, 302, 307, 310
psychopathy
and aggression, 312–313
versus antisocial personality disorder (APD), 307, 312
behaviour in, 311–312
as biological abnormality, 302
and conduct disorder (CD), 403
course of, 314
and criminal behaviour, 311, 312–313
described, 311–312
in *Diagnostic and Statistical Manual of Mental Disorders* (DSM), 311
diagnostic strategies, 312
environmental factors, 313–314
etiology of, 313–314
fundamental psychopathy, 314
and gender bias, 300
and genetics, 313
and predicting behaviour, 295
prevalence of, 313
prognosis, 314
secondary psychopathy, 314
treatment of, 314–315
Psychopathy Checklist, 303, 307, 312, 313, 321
psychopharmacology
antidepressants. *see* antidepressants
antipsychotics. *see* antipsychotic medications
anxiolytics, 445–447
beginnings of, 17–18
classification of drugs, 445
commonly prescribed psychotropic medications, 445–446
described, 444–445
efficacy, limitations on, 448
medication trials, 445
mood stabilizers, 447
prescription privileges, 449
stimulants, 448
psychophysiological assessment, 102
psychophysiological disorders
case example, 147
diagnostic issues, 148, 149
disease states and psychosocial factors, 159–169
historical perspective, 147–148
psychological factors affecting physical condition, 57
psychology of stress, 153–156
psychosocial factors that influence disease, 156–157, 158, 159
psychosocial mechanisms of disease, 149–153
and stress physiology, 30
treatment of, 170–171
psychophysiological reactivity model, 167
psychosexual stages of development, 35
psychosis, 55, 210
psychosocial disadvantage, 368–369
psychosocial factors
and attention deficit/hyperactivity disorder (ADHD), 399
and cardiovascular disease, 166–167
and conduct disorder (CD), 405
controllability, 157–158
discussed, 156
and infections disease, 159–160
and oppositional defiant disorder (ODD), 405
and separation anxiety disorder (SAD), 411–412
social status, 156–157
social support, 158, 159
and ulcer, 160–161, 163–164
psychosocial mechanisms of disease
autonomic nervous system, 151
described, 149–150
endocrine system, 150
immune system, 152–153
psychosocial risk factors
childhood anxiety disorders, 411–412
for conduct disorder (CD), 309
conduct disorder (CD), 405
for conduct disorder (CD), 405
psychosocial theories, 33–36
psychosocial variables, 150
psychosocial vulnerability model, 167
psychosomatic disorders, 57, 147
psychosurgery, 19, 227
psychotherapist, 448
psychotherapy
Adler's individual psychology, 450
brief psychodynamic psychotherapy, 450
client-centred therapy, 450
cognitive-behavioural therapy (CBT). *see* cognitive-behavioural therapy (CBT)
context of, 455–456
couples therapy, 454
criticism of, 456–457
defined, 448
for developmental disorders, 376
for dissociative disorders, 136–137
duration of treatment, 456
eclectic and integrative approaches, 453
effects of, 456–462
ego analysis, 450
emotion-focused therapy, 451, 454
evidence-based practice (EBP), 462–464
existential therapy, 450–451
family therapy, 454
Gestalt therapy, 451
group therapy, 454
humanistic-experiential approaches, 450–451
individual therapy, 454
interpersonal psychodynamic psychotherapy, 450
psychodynamic approaches. *see* psychodynamic therapies
rejection of, 17
for schizophrenia, 228–229

psychotherapy (*continued*)
  theoretical orientations, 448–453
  time-limited dynamic psychotherapy (TLDP), 450
  treatment modalities, 454–455
  users of, 455, 456
Psychotherapy Act, 448
psychotropic medications, 434
puberty, and eating disorders, 245, 249
public health approach, 471
public self-consciousness, 109
public stigma, 43
public trustee, 494
punishment, 38, 310
purging, 235, 236, 237
purging disorder, 242
purging type, 240

Q

quality of life, 374
quantitative reasoning, 75
quasi-experimental study, 86–87
Quebec Longitudinal Twin Study, 405
quetiapine, 194
Quran, 10

R

race, 32–38, 45, 75
radioactive binding assay, 226
radioisotopes, 70, 226
radionuclide ventriculography, 168
Rae, Bob, 200
Rain Man, 379
random assignment, 85
randomized controlled trial, 445
Rand report, 274
rape, 350
rapid cycling bipolar disorder, 181–182
rapid eye movement (REM) sleep, 188, 269, 428
rapport, 73
Raskin, Richard, 343
Raslom, Renée, 343
rating scales. *see* scales
rational-emotive therapy, 39, 451
reactivity, 82
reading disorder, 58, 385, 386
Reagan, Ronald, 439
reality principle, 35
reassurance, 185
rebound effect, 113
receptors, 225
recessive autosomal trait, 26
recessive inheritance, 450
recidivism, 354, 355
recovered memory therapy, 132
Recurrent Coronary Prevention Project, 170
red birds, 278
reductionism, 45
reefer, 286–287
re-experiencing, 114–115
referential delusions, 210
refractory period, 330
reframing, 454
reinforcement, 38, 452
Reissing, Elke, 355
relapse, 277
relaxation, 122, 123, 170, 429–430, 452
reliability
  alternate-form reliability, 67
  coefficient alpha, 68
  internal consistency, 67
  inter-rater reliability, 299, 301
  necessity for, 51
  in personality disorder diagnosis, 301, 316
  split-half reliability, 67
  test-retest reliability, 67, 299, 301
religious delusions, 210, 211
reliving, 114
Remeron (mirtazapine), 193
Renaissance, 7, 11, 12
A Report on Mental Illnesses in Canada, 62
repressed experiences, 34
repressed memory, 132
research methods
  controlled experimental research, 85–86
  experimental methods, 85–87
  non-experimental methods. *see* non-experimental research methods
  pros and cons of different designs, 92
  quasi-experimental methods, 86–87
  statistical versus clinical significance, 93–94
residential treatment, 275
resilience, 472
resistance, analysis of, 154, 449
resolution stage, 330
response prevention, 122
response sets, 80
response shaping, 452
responses, overt, 83
response-to-intervention (RTI), 387, 388
responsivity factor, 311
restless leg syndrome (RLS), 430
restringing type, 239
Rett syndrome, 380
return on investment, 482
reversal design, 89
Reversing the Real Brain Drain: Early Years Study-Final Report, 482
reviews and appeals, 496
rheumatoid arthritis, 219
rhinovirus, 160
rhythmic contractions, 161
rhythm test, 72
ripple effect, 459
risk factors
  alcohol as, 169
  blood pressure as, 169
  for cardiovascular disease, 165, 166
  for childhood anxiety disorders, 411–412
  for criminal behaviour, 497
  cumulative risk, 472–473
  HCR-20, 497
  for heart attack, 169
  mechanisms of, 473
  for oppositional defiant disorder (ODD), 309, 405
  for post-traumatic stress disorder (PTSD), 116
  prenatal, 309
  and prevention, 472
  psychosocial, 405
risk for harm to self, 493
Risperdal (risperidone), 194, 228, 382, 406
Ritalin, 279, 281, 382, 399, 448
ritual prevention, 122
rivastigmine, 438
Riverview Hospital, 495
rock, 282
Rogers, Carl, 41
Romanian orphanages, 368–369
Rorschach, Hermann, 77
Rorschach inkblot test, 77–78
Rotman Research Institute, 71, 440
rubella, 367
rumination disorder, 241
Rush, Benjamin, 15
Russell's sign, 244
R. v. Abbey, 500
R. v. Chaulk, 500
R. v. F. D. M., 505
R. v. J. A. P, 506
R. v. Pritchard, 500
R. v. Rabey, 500
R. v. Swain, 500
R. v. Swain, 501
R. v. Taylor, 500
R. v. Whittle, 500
Rypien, Rick, 199

S

sadism, 312–313, 351
safety behaviours, 123
Saltpêtrière, 13
salvia, 288
Sargent, William, 17
Sartre, Jean-Paul, 450
satyriasis, 335
savants, 379
scales
  behaviour rating scales, 82, 84
  clinical scales, 80
  clinical scales in MMPI, 79
  interpersonal scales in PAI, 80
  special scales in MMPI, 79
  Stanford-Binet Intelligence Scales, 75
  treatment consideration scales in PAI, 80
Scales of Independent Behavior-Revised, 363
scatologia, 347
schema-focused therapy (SFT), 320
schemas
  described, 39, 184
  early maladaptive schemas, 40
  and eating disorders, 249
  and personality disorders, 304
schizogenes, 217, 219–220
schizoid personality disorder, 306
schizophrenia
  antipsychotics, 227–228
  biological factors, 219, 222, 223–224, 225–227
  biological versus cognitive approach, 27
  and birth-related complications, 220–221
  bizarre delusions, 213
  and the brain, 221–222, 223
  and brain imaging, 71, 223
  case examples, 2, 3, 206–207, 213
  catatonic behaviour, 211
  catatonic type, 214
  characteristics of, 210–212
  in children, 221
  and cognitive-behaviour therapy (CBT), 228–229
  cognitive remediation, 229
  cognitive subtypes, 215–216
  cortical atrophy, 69
  critique of DSM and symptom-based diagnosis, 214
  defined, 55
  delusions, 210–211, 213
  demographic and socio-economic features, 208
  diagnosis and assessment, 212–216
  in *Diagnostic and Statistical Manual of Mental Disorders* (DSM), 212, 214
  diagnostic criteria, 212
  diagnostic issues, 432
  disorganized speech and thought disorder, 211
  disorganized type, 214
  dopamine hypothesis, 225–226
  duration, 212
  early intervention, 229–230
  early onset, 432
  emotional symptoms, 211
  endophenotypes, 215
  etiology of, 216–217
  exclusionary criteria, 213
  extrapyramidal effects, 445
  family therapy, 229
  and genetics, 217, 219, 220, 305
  grossly disorganized behaviour, 211
  hallucinations, 210
  healthy people, compared to, 222
  Helfgott, David, 59
  and heredity, 304
  historical perspective, 208–210
  and industrialization, 209
  introduction to, 207–208
  late onset, 432
  markers, 214–215
  Meehl's theory, 217
  and Metrazol, 17
  motor symptoms, 211
  negative symptoms of, 70, 210, 211
  neurochemical imbalance, 225–227
  neurodevelopmental diathesis-stress theories, 217–219
  neuropsychological tests, 221–222, 223
  and neurotransmitters, 29, 30
  in older adults, 432–433
  paranoid personality disorder, 305
  paranoid type, 213
  and personality disorders, 304–305
  positive symptoms, 210
  and pregnancy complications, 220
  prevalence of, 208, 216, 220
  psychotherapy, 228–229
  psychotic symptoms of, 210
  residual type, 214
  and schizotypal personality disorder, 306
  and social class, 216
  social/occupational dysfunction, 212
  social skills training, 229
  symptom-based subtypes, 213–214
  theories of anxiety, 217, 219
  treatment of, 17, 227–230, 432–445, 460
  undifferentiated type, 214
  voices commenting on behaviour, 212
schizophreniform disorder, 33
schizophrenogenic, 216
schizotypal personality disorder, 301, 304, 306–307, 316
schizotype, 217
school- and community-based treatment, 407
school failure hypothesis, 388
Schwab, Charles, 300
science, defined, 85
scientific approach, 12–13, 15
The Scream, 131
seasonal affective disorder (SAD), 182, 195–196

Seconal, 278
secondary appraisals, 155
secondary gain, 130
secondary prevention, 469
second biological psychiatry, 17
secure hospital, 502
seizure disorders, 364
sekimen-kyofu, 61
selective amnesia, 133
selective dissociative amnesia, 132
selective mutism, 413
Selective Mutism Service, 413
selective optimization with compensation (SOC), 423
selective prevention, 469
selective serotonin reuptake inhibitors (SSRI), 192, 413
self-actualization, 42
self-criticism, 183
self-efficacy, 473
self-esteem
  assessment of, 68
  and eating disorders, 235, 236, 249
self-harm behaviours, 198, 280, 410
self-help, for eating disorders, 254–255
self-monitoring, 84–85
self-perpetuating interpersonal cycles, 109
self-recovery, 290
self-report questionnaires, 102
self-stigma, 43
senile dementia, 434
senility, 434
sensate focus, 338
sensitivity, of marker, 215
sensorium, 73
sensory deprivation, 14
sensory intelligence, 75
separation anxiety disorder, 54
separation anxiety disorder (SAD), 408
  brain structure and function, 411
  comorbidity, 409–410
  described, 408–409
  developmental trajectory, 410–411
  in *Diagnostic and Statistical Manual of Mental Disorders* (DSM), 409
  environmental factors, 411
  etiology of, 411, 412
  gene-environment interactions, 412
  and generalized anxiety disorder (GAD), 409, 410–411
  genetics, 411
  pharmacotherapy, 412–413
  prenatal risk factors, 411
  prevalence of, 410
  psychosocial risk factors, 411–412
  temperament, 406–407
  treatment, 412–413
seppuku, 198
Serenac, 59
serious mental illness, 460
Seroquel (quetiapine), 194
serotonin
  and alcohol abuse and dependence, 271
  and antidepressants, 120
  and antipsychotic drugs, 226–227
  and conduct disorder (CD), 405
  and depression, 186
  and eating disorders, 244–245
  and hallucinogens, 289
  indoleamine serotonin, 187
  and obsessive-compulsive disorder (OCD), 112
  and oppositional defiant disorder (ODD), 405
  serotonin hypothesis, 112
  and social phobia, 108
  subtypes of, 30
  and suicide, 200
serotonin-based medications, 71, 120, 124
serotonin-norepinephrine reuptake inhibitors (SNRIs), 193, 447
serotonin receptor 1B (HTR1B), 398
serotonin reuptake inhibitors (SSRIs)
  and antidepressants, 120
  for autism, 382
  for bulimia, 252
  for childhood anxiety disorders, 413
  for older adults, 431
  and pregnant women, 447
  for sexual offenders, 353
  side effects, 413, 447
serotonin transporter gene (5-HTT), 199
serotonin transporter gene (HTT), 186, 189
sertraline, 192
severe life events, 185, 188
severe mood dysregulation(SMD), 404
severity, 176
sex education, 338, 375
sex hormones, 31
sex-linked inheritance, 450
sex steroids, 31
sexual abuse
  and eating disorders, 249–250
  and example of dissociative disorder, 129
  and post-traumatic stress disorder, 116
  and repressed/false memory, 131, 132
  and risk for depression, 45, 185–186
  and somatoform disorders, 57, 130, 143
sexual arousal disorders, 332, 333–334, 336–337
sexual assault, 350
sexual aversion disorder, 333
sexual behaviour, 280
sexual concordance, 330
sexual desire disorders, 332, 333, 336
sexual deviancy, 313
sexual disorders. *see* sexual dysfunctions
sexual dysfunctions
  case example, 325, 331
  defined, 57, 332
  in *Diagnostic and Statistical Manual of Mental Disorders* (DSM), 332
  diagnostic criteria, 332
  diagnostic issues, 326–327
  dyspareunia, 334–337
  etiology of, 336–338
  historical perspective, 294–295
  hypersexual disorder, 335–336
  male erectile disorder, 332, 333–334, 339
  orgasmic disorders, 332, 334, 337
  paraphilias, 326–327
  pedophilia, 327
  physical treatments, 339–340
  premature ejaculation, 337, 339
  prevalence of, 332
  psychological interventions, 338
  psychological interventions, evaluation of, 338–339
  sexual arousal disorders, 332, 333–334, 336–337
  sexual desire disorders, 332, 333
  sexual pain disorders, 332, 334–335
  sexual response, 327–330
  subtypes of, 332
  treatment of, 338
  vaginismus, 335, 336, 338, 339
sexual fantasies, 327
sexuality. *see also* sexual disorders
  and age, 330
  arousal, 297–298, 330, 331
  cultural/ethnic differences, 328
  gender differences, 297, 327, 328, 330
  norms, changing, 328
  sexual response, 297–298, 327–330
  thinking about sex, 327
  in women, 330
sexual masochism, 345, 346–347
sexual offenders
  behaviour therapy, 353
  benefits of treatment, 354
  comprehensive programs, 354
  cost-benefit analysis of treatment, 355
  medical interventions, 353
  and recidivism, 354, 355
sexual offending. *see also* specific paraphilias
  comprehensive theories, 352–353
  conditioning theories, 351
  feminist theories, 351–352
sexual orientation, and eating disorders, 251
sexual pain disorders, 332, 334–335
sexual response cycle, 297–298, 331
sexual sadism, 345, 346–347, 350–351
Sexual Sterilization Act, 8
sexual variants, unusual, 347
shamans, 340
The Shame of the States, 14
Shape and Weight-Based Self-Esteem Inventory (SAWBS), 239
shear stress, 166
Sheen, Charlie, 181
shen-k'uei, 106
shenkui, 106
Shields, Brooke, 182
Shine, 59
shock, circulatory, 227
shock therapy, 17
shopping, 280
shubo-kyofu, 61
Shutter Island, 14
siblings of children with disabilities, 373
Siegel, Shep, 272–273
signs, defined, 149
Sildenafil, 339
sin, 11
Sinequan (doxepin), 192
single-blind trial, 445
single-factor explanation, 25
single-subject research, 88–89
situational phobias, 104
situational sexual dysfunctions, 332
Skinner, Burrhus F., 38
skull, 16
sleep apnea, 430
sleep deprivation, 188
sleep disorders
  case example, 427
  described, 57
  in *Diagnostic and Statistical Manual of Mental Disorders* (DSM), 428
  diagnostic issues, 427–428
  in older adults, 427
  periodic leg movements in sleep (PLMS), 430
  primary insomnia, 428, 429–430
  restless leg syndrome (RLS), 430
  sleep apnea, 430
  sleep patterns, normal changes in, 428–429
  treatment of, 460
sleeper effects, 472
sleep hygiene, 428
sleep neurophysiology, 188
sleep restriction, 429
sleep, stages of, 428
sleep terror disorder, 57
sleepwalking disorder, 57
slow-wave sleep, 188
smartphone technology, 461
SMART Recovery (Self-Management and Recovery Training), 276
smoking, 165, 169, 309, 399
social anxiety disorder. *see* social phobia
social competence, 383
social contextual factors, 199, 472
social desirability, 80–82
social drift, 216
social justice, 484
social learning causal model, 406
social learning theory, 20, 39, 143
social perception disability, 387
social phobia
  case example, 106
  cognitive factors, 108
  defined, 56
  description, 106–108
  diagnosis and assessment, 108
  DSM criteria, 107
  etiology of, 108–109
  non-generalized social phobia, 106
  in older adults, 432
  prevalence of, 107–108, 410
  treatment of, 120, 124
social punishers, 310
Social Readjustment Rating Scale, 155
social skills training, 229
social status, 156–157, 216
social stigma. *see* stigma
social support, 43–44, 158, 159
societal-level strategies, 470
socio-cognitive model, 136
socio-cultural influences
  and alcohol abuse and dependence, 273–275
  and developmental disorders, 368
  and eating disorders, 245–247
  gender, 44–45
  Plato, 9
  poverty, 45
  prevention programs, 483
  race, 45
  and separation anxiety disorder (SAD), 411
  social support, 43–44
  stigma, 43
socio-emotional selectivity theory (SST), 423, 424
sociopaths, 302, 307

Socratic approach, 121
sodium amytal, 137
soft sciences, 85
solvent use, 264
somatic amplification, 143
somatic cluster of somatoform disorders, 143
somatic delusions, 210–211
somatic nervous system, 30
somatic symptom disorders, 142
somatization disorder, 56, 138, 140
somatoform disorders
  body dysmorphic disorder, 141–142
  case example, 129
  conversion disorder, 9, 56, 130, 138, 139
  defined, 137
  described, 137, 138
  diagnosis and assessment, 137
  etiology of, 142–143
  historical perspective, 130–131
  hypochondriasis, 56, 138, 141
  obsessional cluster somatoform disorders, 143
  pain disorder, 140–141
  prevalence, 138
  somatic cluster of somatoform disorders, 143
  somatization disorder, 140
  treatment of, 143–144
  types of, 137
somatogenesis, 16
Sophocles, 35
Soranus of Ephesus, 10
SORC, 83
Spain, 12
Spanos, Nick, 136
SPEC, 474–475
Special K, 288
A Special Kind of Hero, 360
Special Olympics, 360
Specialty Guidelines for Forensic Psychology, 504–505
specificity, of marker, 215
specifiers, 182
speech disorder, 210
speed, 281
sphygmomanometer, 165
spinal cord, 98
spiritus vitae, 12
split-half reliability, 67
squeeze technique, 338
Stanford-Binet Intelligence Scales, 75, 362
Starson v. Swayze, 487
statistical concept, 4
statistical significance, 93
statutory law, 490, 491
St. Augustine, 326
stealing, 280
stereotyped behaviours, 382
stereotypy, 360
sterilization, 8, 20
steroids, 280
stigma, 21, 43, 44, 59–60
stimulants
  defined, 279
  described, 448
  list of, 446
  tobacco, 279–281
stimuli, 83, 155
stimulus control, 429
stimulus-stimulus learning, 36–37
Stone Age, 8
Stone, Joss, 388
stop-start technique, 338
Straight Talk, 360
A Streetcar Named Desire, 317
strength and vulnerability integration (SAVI), 423–424
Strengthening Families Program, 480
strength of association, 162
stress
  combat stress, 156
  impact of, 153
  and infectious diseases, 159–160
  job stress, 157
  marriage, physiological changes, and health, 154
  and mood disorders, 187–188
  phases of, 154
  psychology of stress, 155–156
  and schizophrenia, 217
  as stimulus, 155
  stressful life events, 32
  stress hormone, 32
  stress physiology, 30
  and ulcers, 161
stress generation hypothesis, 185
stress management programs, 170
stressor, 155
stress physiology, 30
stress reactivity paradigm, 166
stroke, 164, 165, 426
Stroop colour-word conflict test, 167
structural magnetic resonance imaging (MRI), 223
Structured Clinical Interview (SCID), 74, 102
structures of personality, 34–35
Strychnos toxifera, 17
Student Bodies, 255
Studies in Hysteria, 98, 130
studies of inheritance
  adoption studies, 90–91
  cross-fostering, 91
  family studies, 90
  gene-environment interactions, 93
  genetic relationships, 90
  twin studies, 91–92
St. Vincent de Paul, 12
St. Vitus' dance, 12
subcortical dementias, 435
subincision, 156
subjective units of distress (SUDS), 122
substance abuse. *see also* substance-related disorders
  and Aboriginal Canadians, 264
  and attention deficit/hyperactivity disorder (ADHD), 397–398
  and bipolar disorders, 179
  and body dysmorphic disorder, 142
  defined, 261
  definitions, 261–262
  and dissociative disorders, 133, 134–135
  methods of taking substances, 282
  and panic disorders, 101
  polysubstance abuse, 263–264
  as prenatal risk factor, 309
  prevention, 480
  social costs of, 271
  and somatization disorder, 140
substance dependence, 261
substance intoxication, 261
substance-related disorders. *see also* substance abuse
  addictiveness of commonly used substances and activities, 280
  amphetamines, 281–289
  barbiturates, 278
  benzodiazepine, 278
  caffeine, 283–284
  cannabis, 286–288
  case example, 260
  in children, 395–396
  cocaine, 282–283
  and comorbidity, 396
  described, 55
  diagnosis and assessment, 261–264
  fetal alcohol spectrum disorders (FASD), 269–270
  hallucinogens, 288–290
  harm reduction approaches, 285
  historical perspective, 260–261
  needle exchange programs, 285
  neurobiological influences, 271–272
  opioids, 284–286
  psychological factors, 272–273
  stimulants. *see also* substance abuse
subtle avoidance, 123
succinylcholine, 17
Sudafed, 192
suicidal gestures, 198
suicidal ideation, 198, 201, 281, 410
suicide
  algorithm for evaluation, 201
  among Aboriginal adolescents, 264
  and antidepressants, 447
  assisted suicide, 198
  biological factors, 199–200
  and bipolar disorders, 180
  causes of, 199–200
  and childhood anxiety disorders, 410
  defined, 198
  diathesis-stress model, 200
  and eating disorders, 237
  epidemiology, 198
  historical perspective, 198
  and mental disorders, 199
  multidimensional model, 200
  in older adults, 425
  and postpartum depression, 182
  prevalence of, 198
  prevention, 200
  psychological factors, 200
  rates, 199
  risk factors, 198
  social contextual factors, 199
  treatment, 200–201
  in youth, 410
suicide attempt, 198
superego, 35
supernatural causes, 8–9
Supports Intensity Scale (SIS), 374
suppressor T-cells, 153
surfing, 280
Survey of Youth Canadians (SYC), 90
survivor guilt, 115
susceptibility theory, 388
suspiciousness, 305
switching, 134
Switzerland, 106
Sybil, 136
sympathetic-adrenal medullary (SAM) axis, 151
sympathetic nervous system, 31, 151, 165
symptom induction test, 102
symptoms, defined, 149
synapses, 28, 29, 187
synaptic cleft, 398
synaptosomal associated protein 5 (SNAP 5), 398
syndromes, 16, 61
synesthesia, 289
syphilis spirochete, 16, 69
systematic desensitization, 122, 452
Systematic Treatment Enhancement Program (STEP), 195
systematized amnesia, 133
systems theory, 45
systole, 165
systolic blood pressure, 165

T

tabula rasa, 24
tactual performance test, 72
Tadalafil, 339
taijin kyofusho, 61, 106
the talking cure, 34
talk therapy, 413
tangible punishers, 310
tapping test, 72
Tarantella, 12
tardive dyskinesia, 382
task analysis, 383
Task Force on Promotion and Dissemination of Psychological Procedures, 462
tasty food, 280
taxon, 131
Tay-Sachs disease, 450
technological innovations in treatment, 461
Tegretol (carbamazepine), 193, 194, 382
television, 280
temper dysregulation disorder with dysphoria, 404
temporal dimension, 474–475
temporary substitute decision maker, 494
tension-reduction hypothesis, 272
teratogenic effects, 368
Teresa of Avila, 12
tertiary prevention, 469
testes, 32, 329
testosterone, 337, 405
testosterone gel, 340
test-retest reliability, 67, 299, 301
thalidomide, 368
thematic apperception test (TAT), 78
Theophrastus, 302
theoretical frameworks of aging, 423
theoretical perspectives
  behavioural theories. *see* behavioural theories
  biological models. *see* biological models
  biological versus cognitive approach, 27
  causes, search for, 26
  cognitive theories. *see* cognitive theories
  existential views, 41, 42–43
  general nature of theories, 3
  humanistic theories, 41–42, 43
  integrative theories. *see* integrative theories
  interactionist explanations, 25
  levels of theories, 25
  null hypothesis, 25–28
  peripheral nervous system, 30–31
  psychosocial theories. *see* psychosocial theories
  single-factor explanation, 25
  socio-cultural influences. *see* socio-cultural influences
  testing theories, 25–28
theories. *see* theoretical perspectives
therapeutic alliance, 464
therapies. *see* treatment

therapist barriers, 421
therapist empathy and positive regard, 464
thermographic imaging, 297
thin ideal, 44
thioridazine (Mellaril), 382
thiothixene, 322
thought-action fusion (TAF), 110
thought content, 73
thought disorder, 210
thought process, 73
thought records, 121, 190, 191
threat, 116
The Three Faces of Eve, 136
thymine, 371
thyroid dysregulation, 32, 69
thyroxine, 366
tiagabine, 193
tic disorders, 54–55
time-limited dynamic psychotherapy (TLDP), 450
timeouts, 88, 89
T-lymphocytes, 152, 153
tobacco. *see also* nicotine
  deaths attributable to, 279
  dependency, 279–280
  effects of, 279
  illnesses attributable to, 279
  pharmacological treatments, 281
  prevalence of, 279
  psychological treatments, 280
  second-hand smoke, 279
  social costs of, 271
  treatment for, 280–281
Tofranil (imipramine), 192
token economies, 315
tolerance, 261, 262, 273
tomography, 69–70
Topamax (topiramate), 193
total peripheral resistance, 165
total sexual outlet (TSO), 335
Touched by an Angel, 360
toxic-metabolic poisons, 364
toxic psychosis, 282
traits, 295
transactional model, 155–156, 167, 170
transcranial magnetic stimulation (TMS), 197
transdiagnostic theory, 252
transference, 449
transference-focused therapy (TFT), 320
transgendered, 341
translocation, 365
transsexualism, 341
transudation, 330
transvestic fetishism, 345, 346
transvestite, 346
tranylcypromine, 192
trauma model, 135
trauma-repression hypothesis, 132
trazodone, 193
treatment. *see also* specific therapies
  of alcohol abuse and dependence, 275–278
  of Alzheimer's disease (AD), 438
  of amphetamine abuse, 283
  of antisocial personality disorder (APD), 310–311
  of anxiety disorders, 119–123
  of autism, 382–383
  of barbiturate dependence, 278
  of benzodiazepine dependence, 278
  biological treatments, 444–448
  of bipolar disorders, 193–194, 460
  case example, 443
  chemically induced sleep, 14
  of childhood anxiety disorders, 412–413
  of cocaine abuse, 283
  cognitive-behavioural therapy (CBT), 412
  cognitive restructuring, 120–122
  combinations of psychotherapy and medication, 194–195
  comment on treatments that work, 126
  computerized, 461
  of conduct disorder (CD), 406–407
  of depression, 426–427
  of developmental disorders, 376–377
  dialectical behaviour therapy (DBT), 321–322
  of dissociative disorders, 136–137
  in early asylums, 13–15
  of eating disorders, 251–255
  effectiveness of, 456
  efficacy, 456
  electroconvulsive therapy. *see* electroconvulsive therapy (ECT)
  exposure techniques, 122
  Eye Movement Desensitization and Reprocessing, 123
  of gender identity disorders (GID), 343–344
  of generalized anxiety disorder, 126
  historic, 10, 11
  Internet interventions, 461
  involuntary, 494–495
  LSD, 14
  mindfulness-based strategies, 123
  of mood disorders, 189–197
  movie depiction, 13–14
  neurostimulation and neurosurgical treatments, 196–197
  object-relations therapy, 320
  of obsessive-compulsive disorder (OCD), 124–125
  of oppositional defiant disorder (ODD), 406–407
  other techniques, 123
  for pathological gambling, 290
  of personality disorders, 320–322
  pharmacotherapy. *see* pharmacotherapy
  phototherapy, 195–196
  of post-traumatic stress disorder, 125–126
  of primary insomnia, 429–430
  problem solving, 123
  of psychopathy, 314–315
  psychopharmacology, beginnings of. *see* psychopharmacology
  of psychophysiological disorders, 170–171
  psychotherapy. *see* psychotherapy
  relaxation, 123
  of schizophrenia, 227–230, 460
  school- and community-based treatment, 407
  sensory deprivation, 14
  of separation anxiety disorder (SAD), 412–413
  of sexual dysfunctions, 338
  of sexual offenders, 353–354
  shock therapy. *see* electroconvulsive therapy (ECT)
  of social phobia, 124
  of somatoform disorders, 143–144
  of specific phobias, 124
  for suicide, 200–201
  technological advances in, 461
  of tobacco addiction, 280–281
  of unipolar depression, 192–193
  of vascular dementia, 439
treatment consideration scales, in PAI, 80
treatment effectiveness, 456
treatment efficacy, 456
Treatment for Adolescents with Depression Study (TADS), 85–86
treatment modalities, 454–455
Treatment of Depression Collaborative Research Program (TDCRP), 189
trephination, 8
trichotillomania, 57
tricyclic antidepressants (TCAs)
  for bulimia, 252
  and deinstitutionalization, 18
  described, 192
  introduction of, 192
  mechanisms of, 187
  for obsessive-compulsive disorder (OCD), 120
  side effects, 447
trigeminal neuralgia, 59
Trileptal (oxcarbazepine), 193
Triple P (Positive Parenting Program), 483, 484
triplet repeats, 371
triple vulnerability, 99–100
trisomy 21, 365
truth serum, 137
tuberous sclerosis, 450
Tuinal, 278
Tuke, William, 15
Turner syndrome, 342
12-step programs, 275, 276, 283, 289
Twiggy, 234, 235
Twins Early Development Study, 313
twin studies
  and Alzheimer's disease (AD), 437
  and anxiety disorders, 98
  and attention deficit/hyperactivity disorder (ADHD), 398, 399
  and borderline personality disorder (BPD), 316
  and conduct disorder (CD), 405
  described, 91–92
  and dissociative disorders, 135
  and dyslexia, 387
  and eating disorders, 244
  and mood disorders, 186
  and personality disorders, 305
  and psychopathy, 313
  Quebec Longitudinal Twin Study, 405
  and risk for depression, 185
  and schizotypal personality disorder, 316
  and separation anxiety disorder (SAD), 411
  and specific phobias, 105
  and substance-related disorders, 270
  and suicide, 199
two-factor theory, 38, 99
two-spirit person, 340
Type A behaviour, 167, 170
Type B behaviour, 167

U

ulcers
  in animals, 161
  and brain regions, 161
  case example, 160
  defined, 161
  and *H. pylori*, 163–164
  prevalence of, 161
  and stress, 161, 162–163
ultradian cycling, 182
ultrarapid cycling, 182
uncomplicated PTSD, 116
unconditioned stimulus (UCS), 36, 99
unconscious, 34
unfit to stand trial, 500
unidirectional causation, 45
unipolar mood disorders
  cognitive-behaviour therapy (CBT), 190–192
  combinations of psychotherapy and medication, 194–195
  defined, 176
  and neurotransmitters, 187
  treatment of, 189–192, 193, 194–195
universal approach, 469
Universal Declaration of Human Rights of the United Nations, 490
universality, 454
universal programs, 478–481
Universal Triple P, 483
An Unquiet Mind, 180
unusual sexual variants, 347
uppers, 281
urea, 366
urethral bulb, 329
urination, 347
urophilia, 347
uterus, 9

V

vacuum erection devices, 340
vagina, 329
vaginismus, 335, 336–337, 339, 355
vagus nerve stimulation (VNS), 197
validity
  concurrent validity, 51
  construct validity, 68
  content validity, 68
  criterion validity, 68
  external validity, 86
  face validity, 68
  internal validity, 86
  MMPI scales, 79, 80
  PAI scales, 80
  predictive validity, 51
  and reactivity, 82
Valium, 278
valproate, 193
Vanier, Jean, 389
Vardenafil, 339
varenicline tartrate, 281
vascular dementia, 435, 438–439
vasculature, 164
vasocongestion, 298, 330, 357
venlafaxine, 193
venlafaxine hydrochloride, 120
ventral (occipitotemporal) subsystem, 387
ventricles, 223
verbal communication, 379
verbal comprehension tests, 75
vestibulectomy, 340
vestibulodynia, 340
Viagra, 339
vicarious learning, 99

Vietnam veterans, 62, 156
Vineland Adaptive Behavior Scales Second Edition, 362–363
violation of norms, 6
violence
  and childhood disorders, 405
  and psychopathy, 311–312, 313
  risk assessment, 497
  as socio-cultural influence, 352
virtual reality technology, 123, 124
visual-spatial processing, 75
vitamins, 382, 438
in vivo exposure, 122, 124, 452
in vivo observation, 82
voice and choice, 470
volitional impairment, 489
vomiting, 9
voodoo, 147
voyeurism, 345, 348
vulnerability, 315
vulnerability markers, 215
vulnerability versus resilience, 418–419
vulvar vestibulitis, 335

W

Wagner-Jauregg, Julius von, 16
WAIS-IV, 75
wait-to-fail model, 386
walking, 123
Walters, Richard, 20, 39
wandering uterus, 9
washing/cleaning, as OCD, 112
Watson, John B., 19, 36, 37
waxy flexibility, 211
Wechsler Adult Intelligence Scale, or WAIS, 75, 76
Wechsler Intelligence Scale for Children, 66
Wechsler Intelligence Test for Children (WISC), 75
Wechsler Preschool and Primary Scale of Intelligence (WPPSI), 75
Wechsler Scales, 362
weed. *see* cannabis; marijuana
Weight-Influenced Self-Esteem Questionnaire (WISE-Q), 239
Wellbeing Program, 461
Wellbutrin (buproprion), 193, 281
Western Collaborative Group Study, 167
Weyer, Johannes, 12
Whitehall study, 156, 157
Wilson, Mitchell, 395
Wilson, Woodrow, 388
wine, 438
Winko v. B.C., 500
Wisconsin Card Sorting Test (WCST), 222–223
witchcraft, 11
withdrawal, 261
Without Conscience: The Disturbing World of the Psychopaths Among Us, 321
women
  and Alzheimer's disease (AD), 438
  and anorexia nervosa, 237
  and atherosclerosis, 167
  and attractiveness, 44
  and body image, 245–247, 248
  and dementia, 434–435
  and depression, 189
  with developmental disabilities, assaulted, 375
  and eating disorders, 245–247, 250
  and gender bias, 60–61
  and generalized anxiety disorder, 57
  and lobotomies, 19
  and obesity, 247
  and PDE5 inhibitors, 339
  and personality disorders, 300
  and phobias, 104, 105
  and psychopathy, 313
  and PTSD, 116
  and puberty, 249
  and schizophrenia, 208
  and sexual response, 330
Women for Sobriety, 276
Women's Health Surveillance Report, 247
work, 280
workhouses, 13
working memory, 75
World Health Organization, 3, 52
worry, 117, 118, 126
worry imagery exposure, 122
written expression, disorder of, 386

X

Xanax, 278
X-linked inheritance, 450
X-rays, 69

Y

yellow jackets, 278
Yin and Yang, 148
yoga, 123, 453
Young Autism Project, 382
Your Defiant Child, 401
Your Life Counts, 410
youth at risk, 388
Youth Criminal Justice Act, 491
Ypsilanti, 476

Z

ziprasidone, 194
Zoloft (sertraline), 192
Zonegran (zonisamide), 193
zonisamide, 193
zoophilia, 347
Zyban, 281
Zyprexa (olanzapine), 194

Credits

Randy Plett Photographs/iStockphoto, p. 1; National Museum, Denmark/ Munoz-Yague/Science Photo Library, p. 9 top; National Library of Medicine, p. 9 bottom; Sassetta/Bridgeman Art Library/Getty, p. 11; The Granger Collection, New York. All rights reserved, p. 12; The Granger Collection, New York. All rights reserved, p. 13; Archives du 7e Art/ Photos 12/Alamy, p. 14; Hemera/Thinkstock, p. 23; © Hulton-Deutsch Collection/Corbis, p. 34; AP Photo, p. 38; Courtesy of Dr. Aaron Beck, p. 40; © Bettmann/Corbis, p. 42; Adrian Wyld/CP Images, p. 44; Hemera/Thinkstock, p. 48; Ghislain & Marie David de Lossy/The Image Bank/Getty Images, p. 55 left; Ben Edwards/Stone/Getty Images, p. 55 right; Gary Hershorn/Reuters, p. 59; Anson0618/Shutterstock, p. 65; Sovereign, ISM/Science Photo Library, p. 70; Sovereign, ISM/Science Photo Library, p. 71; © Catchlight Visual Services/Alamy, p. 74; Simon & Schuster/PH College, p. 78 top; Kentoh/Dreamstime/GetStock, p. 96; Photo by Eric Lessing. Copyright ARS, N.Y., p. 100; Dick Hemingway Editorial Photographs, p. 104; Lisa Peardon/Taxi/Getty Images, p. 107; ZUMA Wire Service/Alamy, p. 109; Suzanne Plunkett/AP Photo, p. 113; Scott Gardner/Hamilton Spectator/CP Photo, p. 115; Photo by Paul Eifert. Paul Eifert is an IT Consultant at Concordia University and a freelance photographer in Montreal, Quebec, Canada, p. 125; Olena Vizerskaya/iStockphoto, p. 128; The Granger Collection, New York. All rights reserved, p. 130; Zephyr Picture/Maxx Images, 141; Courtesy of Dr. Laurence J. Kirmayer, p. 144; Ingram Publishing/Thinkstock, p. 146; Andrew Macaskill/Wildlife Pictures Online, p. 157; Alvaro Leiva/Age Fotostock/ Firstlight, p. 159; Theo Westenberger/Paramount/The Kobal Collection, p. 164; Bruce Ayres/Stone/Getty Images, p. 168; Richard Radstone/Taxi/ Getty Images, p. 170; Photo by Mr. Nicholas Geilich. Courtesy of Dr. Jane Irvine, p. 171; Markus Leiminger/iStockphoto, p. 173; ZUMA Wire Service/Alamy, p. 181; Michael Newman / PhotoEdit, p. 195; University of Durham/Simon Fraser/Science Photo Library, p. 196; Photo: Rick Chard. Courtesy of Dr. Zindel V. Segal, p. 202; Julos/ Dreamstime/GetStock, p. 205; AKG-Images, p. 209; Universal Pictures/ Everett Collection/CP Images, p. 218; Courtesy of Dr. Christopher Bowie, p. 230; Elenethewise/iStockphoto, p. 233; Trinity Mirror/Mirrorpix/ Alamy, p. 235; Medical-on-Line/Alamy, p. 239; © National Eating Disorder Information Centre (NEDIC) www.nedic.ca, p. 254; mark wragg/iStockphoto, p. 259; William Hogarth. © Burstein Collection/ Corbis, p. 266; Junji Kurokawa/AP Photo/CP Images, p. 273; Janine Wieder Photolibrary/Alamy, p. 282; © Bettmann/Corbis, p. 288; marekuliasz/Shutterstock, p. 293; Frank Gunn/CP Images, p. 308 left; Phil Snel/CP Images, p. 308 right; Ivy Close Image/Alamy, p. 317; Photo by Scott McCall. Courtesy of Dr. Robert Hare, p. 321; Nixx Photography/ Shutterstock, p. 324; © Bettmann/Corbis, p. 328; Courtesy of Dr. Tuuli Kukkonen, p. 329; AP Photo/CP Images, p. 343 left; Manny Millan/ Sports Illustrated/Getty Images, p. 343 right; Paul Cox/Alamy, p. 346; Photograph by Stéphanie Houle. Copied with permission of the Faculty of Social Sciences, University of Ottawa, p. 355; iStockphoto/Thinkstock, p. 358; Andrew H. Walker/Getty Images, p. 360; Paula Solloway/Alamy, p.371; Chris Polk/FilmMagic/Getty Images, p. 372; David Cooper/ GetStock, p. 389; Milenny Photography/iStockphoto, p. 391; iStockphoto/ Thinkstock, p. 395; Denise Hager/Catchlight Visual Services/Alamy, p. 401; Jennie Hart/Alamy, p. 408; iStockphoto/Thinkstock, p. 416; Denis Balibouse/Reuters, p. 437; Library of Congress Prints and Photographs, LC-USZ62-13040 DLC, p. 439; PaulaConnelly/iStockphoto, p. 442; Woodfin Camp & Associates/James Wilson, p. 444; Bruce Ayres/Stone/ Getty Images, p. 454; Angela Hampton Picture Library/Alamy, p. 459; Courtesy of Deborah Dobson, p. 465; Sergej Khakimullin/Shutterstock, p. 467; Courtesy of the Family Resource Centre, Highfield Community Enrichment Project, p. 479; James Steidl/Shutterstock, p. 486; Courtesy of Dr. Christopher Webster, p. 506.